Frommer's®
Greece

My Greece

by Peter Kerasiotis

I WAS 7 WHEN MY FAMILY MOVED BACK TO GREECE FROM NEW YORK.
It was 3 years after the dictatorship had fallen; 3 years after the country had been stable enough to reclaim its greatest export—democracy; and 4 years from joining what we today call the E.U. Looking back, I realize those were extraordinary years for Greece, but I don't recall those tumultuous events.

What I remember is the first time I saw the Acropolis. My mother took me on top of the ancient hill one day after school. The two of us sat on a bench in front of the Parthenon and stared in silence as the sun set behind the city below us. I also remember the race on summer breaks to see as many islands as we could before I grew up. In fall and winter, we'd take weekend trips to ski in Mount Parnassos or road trips from one end of the country to the other, getting off the highway and taking old dirt roads, stopping at local tavernas forgotten by time. We loved seeing every city, town, and village along the way. Some of my fondest memories are not just of the islands, but also of the Peloponnese, particularly Nafplion.

Like my parents, I left Greece to study in the United States, but Greece is where some of my favorite places and memories lie. Athens isn't just the city I grew up in; it's my home. Welcome; I'll try to show you the best ways to enjoy your time here and create some lifelong memories of your own.

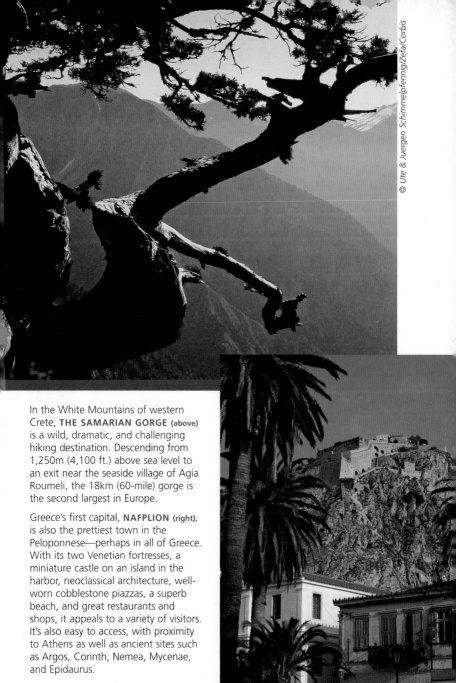

In the White Mountains of western Crete, **THE SAMARIAN GORGE** (above) is a wild, dramatic, and challenging hiking destination. Descending from 1,250m (4,100 ft.) above sea level to an exit near the seaside village of Agia Roumeli, the 18km (60-mile) gorge is the second largest in Europe.

Greece's first capital, **NAFPLION** (right), is also the prettiest town in the Peloponnese—perhaps in all of Greece. With its two Venetian fortresses, a miniature castle on an island in the harbor, neoclassical architecture, well-worn cobblestone piazzas, a superb beach, and great restaurants and shops, it appeals to a variety of visitors. It's also easy to access, with proximity to Athens as well as ancient sites such as Argos, Corinth, Nemea, Mycenae, and Epidaurus.

The cosmopolitan island of **RHODES** has been famous since antiquity for the Colossus of Rhodes—the gigantic statue of the sun god Helios, which stood over the entrance to its harbor. One of the Seven Wonders of the Ancient World, it was destroyed by a massive earthquake in 282 B.C. The harbor remains picturesque, however, especially at dawn, and the island's natural beauty is also undiminished.

© Jon Arnold Images/DanitaDelimont.com

The monastery at Patmos contains a divine array of religious art, such as this exquisite **MOSAIC (left).** In 95 A.D. St John the Theologian (one of Christ's twelve disciples) was exiled on the island of Patmos for 18 months. During that time, he lived in a cave where he was said to have received a series of divine messages that led the biblical chapter of Revelations.

A generally sunny climate and Europe's lowest urban crime rate have fostered a bustling **OUTDOOR CAFE CULTURE (above)** in Athens. Taking coffee and meals on the street is not a luxury but a way of life. Under a floodlit Acropolis, by the sea, in quiet gardens, or on busy intersections, Athenians spend many of their waking hours in the open air.

On the slopes of Mount Parnassos, in a fittingly dramatic natural setting, is Delphi, center of the Ancient World. With extensive ruins—including the ornate **SANCTUARY OF ATHENA** (above), with its three graceful Doric columns—the site continues to dazzle visitors as it did in antiquity, when Greeks and non-Greeks alike came seeking advice from the famed oracle who resided here.

ST. DEMETRIOS (right), depicted in this mosaic, is the patron saint of Thessaloniki, a city of tree-lined boulevards, Byzantine churches, and a bustling waterfront promenade along the Thermaic Gulf. St. Demetrios was born here in 270 A.D. Locals believe his intervention saved the city during many attacks by Slavic nations, the Bulgarians, Arabs, Saracens, and others. Even the liberation of Thessaloniki during the Balkan wars coincided with the feast day of St. Demetrios.

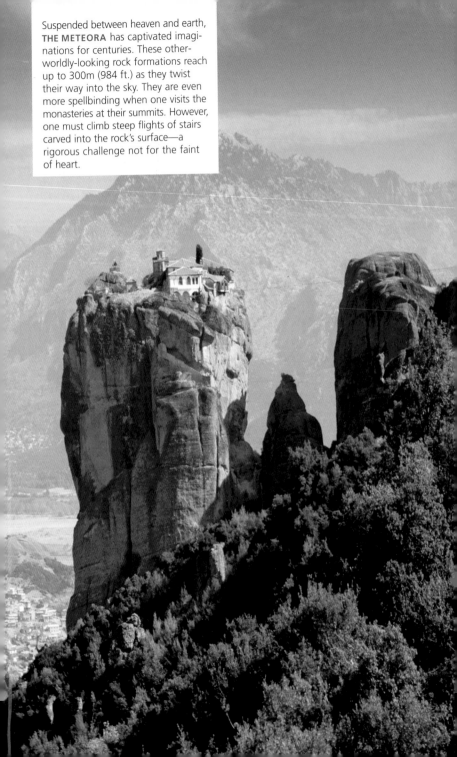

Suspended between heaven and earth, **THE METEORA** has captivated imaginations for centuries. These otherworldly-looking rock formations reach up to 300m (984 ft.) as they twist their way into the sky. They are even more spellbinding when one visits the monasteries at their summits. However, one must climb steep flights of stairs carved into the rock's surface—a rigorous challenge not for the faint of heart.

Greece is a paradise for **SAILING (left),** with its many gulfs and archipelagos, surrounded by the Ionian and the Aegean Sea, as well as 2,000 islands and islets. The water and wind quality vary around each body of water, both of which are full of islands with bays accessible only by boat. There's no better way to see the islands than to rent a yacht and sail from port to port, with no end in sight.

Home of the legendary mountains from which the gods of the ancient world descended, Greece is now becoming legendary for **WINTER SPORTS (below).** With a wide variety of slopes and ski resorts and lower prices than those at better-known wintertime destinations, Greece is attracting an increasing number of visitors for on- and off-piste adventures.

Frommer's®

Greece

6th Edition

by John S. Bowman, Sherry Marker & Peter Kerasiotis

with cruise coverage by Rebecca Tobin

WILEY

Wiley Publishing, Inc.

Published by:

Wiley Publishing, Inc.
111 River St.
Hoboken, NJ 07030-5774

ISBN: 978-0-470-16538-6

Editor: Marc Nadeau
Production Editor: Jana M. Stefanciosa
Cartographer: Andrew Murphy
Photo Editor: Richard Fox
Production by Wiley Indianapolis Composition Services

For information on our other products and services or to obtain technical support, please contact our Customer Care Department within the U.S. at 800/762-2974, outside the U.S. at 317/572-3993 or fax 317/572-4002.

Wiley also publishes its books in a variety of electronic formats. Some content that appears in print may not be available in electronic formats.

Contents

17 The Northeastern Aegean Islands   643

by John S. Bowman

Appendix: The Greek Language   670

Index   677

List of Maps

An Invitation to the Reader

In researching this book, we discovered many wonderful places—hotels, restaurants, shops, and more. We're sure you'll find others. Please tell us about them, so we can share the information with your fellow travelers in upcoming editions. If you were disappointed with a recommendation, we'd love to know that, too. Please write to:

Frommer's Greece, 6th Edition
Wiley Publishing, Inc. • 111 River St. • Hoboken, NJ 07030-5774

An Additional Note

Please be advised that travel information is subject to change at any time—and this is especially true of prices. We therefore suggest that you write or call ahead for confirmation when making your travel plans. The authors, editors, and publisher cannot be held responsible for the experiences of readers while traveling. Your safety is important to us, however, so we encourage you to stay alert and be aware of your surroundings. Keep a close eye on cameras, purses, and wallets, all favorite targets of thieves and pickpockets.

About the Authors

John S. Bowman has been a freelance writer and editor for more than 35 years. He specializes in nonfiction ranging from archaeology to zoology, baseball to biography. He first visited Greece in 1956 and has traveled and lived there over the years. He is the author of numerous guides to various regions in Greece. He currently resides in Northampton, Massachusetts.

Sherry Marker majored in classical Greek at Harvard, studied archaeology at the American School of Classical Studies in Athens, and did graduate work in ancient history at the University of California at Berkeley. The author of a number of guides to Greece, she has also written for the *New York Times, Travel + Leisure,* and *Hampshire Life.* When not in Greece, she lives in Massachusetts.

Peter Kerasiotis, a native Athenian, currently lives in New York City where he works as a web developer and editor. A newcomer to Frommer's, he hopes to continue a career of travel- and screenwriting.

Rebecca Tobin has been covering the travel business for the past seven years as a reporter and editor for industry newspaper *Travel Weekly,* including four years as the paper's cruise editor. She estimates that she's sampled fun, food, and deck chairs on more than 40 cruise ships (and counting). Rebecca is currently *Travel Weekly's* managing editor. She lives in New York.

Other Great Guides for Your Trip:

Frommer's Greek Islands
Frommer's Europe
Frommer's European Cruises & Ports of Call

Frommer's Star Ratings, Icons & Abbreviations

Every hotel, restaurant, and attraction listing in this guide has been ranked for quality, value, service, amenities, and special features using a **star-rating system.** In country, state, and regional guides, we also rate towns and regions to help you narrow down your choices and budget your time accordingly. Hotels and restaurants are rated on a scale of zero (recommended) to three stars (exceptional). Attractions, shopping, nightlife, towns, and regions are rated according to the following scale: zero stars (recommended), one star (highly recommended), two stars (very highly recommended), and three stars (must-see).

In addition to the star-rating system, we also use **seven feature icons** that point you to the great deals, in-the-know advice, and unique experiences that separate travelers from tourists. Throughout the book, look for:

Finds	Special finds—those places only insiders know about
Fun Fact	Fun facts—details that make travelers more informed and their trips more fun
Kids	Best bets for kids and advice for the whole family
Moments	Special moments—those experiences that memories are made of
Overrated	Places or experiences not worth your time or money
Tips	Insider tips—great ways to save time and money
Value	Great values—where to get the best deals

The following **abbreviations** are used for credit cards:

AE	American Express	DISC	Discover	V	Visa
DC	Diners Club	MC	MasterCard		

Frommers.com

Now that you have this guidebook, to help you plan a great trip, visit our website at **www.frommers.com** for additional travel information on more than 3,500 destinations. We update features regularly, to give you instant access to the most current trip-planning information available. At Frommers.com, you'll find scoops on the best airfares, lodging rates, and car rental bargains. You can even book your travel online through our reliable travel booking partners. Other popular features include:

- Online updates of our most popular guidebooks
- Vacation sweepstakes and contest giveaways
- Newsletters highlighting the hottest travel trends
- Online travel message boards with featured travel discussions

What's New in Greece

INTRODUCTION After urging visitors for several years to "Live Your Myth in Greece," in 2007 the Greek National Tourist Office invited travelers to "Explore Your Senses" in Greece. The shift in emphasis suggested that the Greek tourist industry was determined to create an image to supplement the standard travel-poster scenes of temple columns (representing the famous old Greek myths) and island beaches (reminders of the myth of endless sunshine and summer romance). Greece is trying very hard to make travelers aware of a multiplicity of specialized holiday possibilities, ranging from tours to take in the journeys of Saint Paul to watercolor excursions in the Peloponnese. In addition, there's a real effort to let visitors know that they can explore the Greek countryside—even climb a mountain—and then relax in any one of a number of elegant new hotels with their own spas.

If you've found Greek hotels a bit on the boring side on past visits, you'll probably be delighted with the increase in boutique hotels throughout Greece. Before the 2004 Athens Olympics, top-notch hotels were largely confined to Athens and the more fashionable islands such as Hydra, Santorini, and Mykonos. Often, each destination had only one or two really outstanding hotels—and everyone knew what they were. Now, many places in Greece have what almost amounts to an embarrassment of riches as more and more hotels with serious creature comforts open. If you want a hotel with spa facilities, you're in luck. More and more

Greek hotels are joining the international trend of providing spa facilities and services that include a wide range of massage therapies, facials, aromatherapy, hydrotherapy, and thalassotherapy. Many of the hotels that have these facilities are near popular tourist destinations: the Santa Marina Arachova Resort and Spa is a few miles from Delphi, the Olympia Riviera Resort is near ancient Olympia, and the Divani Meteora, near the austere monasteries of the Meteora, now has spa facilities.

Throughout the guide, we single out the best of the new hotels, as well as noting the old standbys that have gone all out to remodel and refresh themselves. Something to keep in mind: These hotels are very popular with weekending Greeks and there is often a 50% weekend price supplement.

When you're planning your trip, remember that Athens and Thessaloniki are not just fair-weather destinations, but very appealing year-round city-break destinations. In fact, much of Greece's cultural life takes place off season—which is just to say that "the season" can be year-round in Greece.

At press time, the Ministry of Culture information site (www.culture.gr) for archaeological sites, monuments, and museums, was being redone. It is to be hoped that it will be up and running again by the time that you read this. It is also to be hoped that the alphabetical system currently employed will be fine-tuned so that Epidaurus will appear under "E" and not under "S" for Sanctuary of Asclepius! Until then, if you cannot find what you are looking for under the first initial of the site, monument, or museum, have a look in broad categories such as "Ancient" and "Acropolis" and "Sanctuary."

PLANNING YOUR TRIP There is no denying that the Olympics of 2004 left Greece with many improvements that benefit tourists. By the same token, the pricing structure of hotels was thrown into turmoil and the normal increases that accompany inflation have yet to take hold as the hotels try to regain their equilibrium. So, more than ever, you must be flexible about prices provided in this guidebook.

GETTING THERE Those who follow the travel industry in the news may be aware that **Olympic Airlines** (www. olympic-airways.gr) continues to operate in bankruptcy and remains up for sale. As we go to press, a new owner has not been announced, but it seems definite that whoever does take over Olympic must maintain the same services.

Moreover, starting in the summer of 2007, two more American airlines joined Olympic and Delta in providing direct flights from the U.S. to Athens. **US Air's** (www.usairways.com) depart from JFK International in New York, while **Continental's** (www.continental.com) depart from Newark, New Jersey. All flights leave daily, at least in the high season.

Also as of 2007, a new airline is promising to provide service to a number of destinations within Greece and eventually Brindisi, Italy: **Airsea Lines**—different from the other two in that it operates only hydroplanes. Its plans call for three principal bases: one at Gouvia, Corfu; one at Lavrion on the coast of Attika to the southeast of Athens; and one at Faliron, the coast just south of Athens. When this edition went to press, only the one service was in operation: Corfu's connections with Ithaka, Lefkada, Kefalonia, Paxoi, and Patras. The planned connections from Attika are to be with Aegean islands: Ioa, Kalymnos, Kos, Mykonos, Paros, Santorini, and Tinos. As this is a new service and much is still being worked out, you are advised to consult their website, **www.airsealines.com**.

It has been called to our attention that at least at some Greek entry points the authorities might stop visitors from bringing in any medications that contain codeine—even the kind of pill that is sold over-the-counter in some countries—unless you are carrying a doctor's prescription. The worst that can happen is that it might be confiscated. In any case it is something to keep in mind.

SETTLING INTO ATHENS

Where to Stay A newcomer in this newly trendy and diverse central neighborhood (right off Omonia Sq. on Patission Ave. right by the National Archaeological Museum) is **Residence Georgio,** an excellent new five-star hotel with a great spa/pool on its roof deck and spacious and very smartly decorated rooms. Nearby is the newly redesigned **Baby Grand,** which has two claims to fame. The first being its "theme rooms" (10 international artists from the fields of urban art, graffiti design, and illustration were handpicked to decorate the 57 "graffiti" rooms with themes ranging from Japanese and Byzantine art to comic book art—check out the Spider-Man, Batman, and Smurfs rooms). Its second claim to fame is its insanely popular **Meat Me** restaurant with its excellent and reasonably priced meat dishes and its glass floor that looks down to the pool. In nearby Psirri, small boutique hotel **Ochre & Brown,** with only 10 rooms and one suite has become the talk of town. That it's home to one of the most popular lounges in the city doesn't hurt its urban-cool reputation, either. Neighboring Plaka finally has a boutique hotel worthy of its charms: the wonderful **Magna Grecia,** housed in an elegant neoclassical mansion built in 1898. In posh Kolonaki, new design hotel **Periscope,** has been stealing the show this year with its smart minimal design and the periscope on its roof deck controlled by loungers in the lobby bar and broadcast over large flatscreen TVs.

Where to Dine Besides the explosion of restaurants in newly hip neighborhoods such as Gazi and Psirri, **Archaion Gefsis (Ancient Flavors)**, has set itself apart from anything in the city with its menu based on ancient Greek recipes. This brilliant concept (to wine and dine like the ancients did, based on recipes recorded by the poet Archestratos) is a hit with locals, tourists, and foodies alike. See chapter 5.

What to See & Do Exploring Athens is easier than ever thanks to the new Metro system—and pleasanter than ever thanks to newly created pedestrian walks linking the major archaeological sites. You can get a map of the system at the main Metro station in Syntagma Square. The **Greek National Tourism Organization (EOT)** at 26 Amalias sometimes has maps of the "Archaeological Park," which stretches from Hadrian's Gate past the Acropolis and Ancient Agora to Kerameikos. As you explore Athens on foot and by Metro, be sure to take in the two new museums at the Acropolis and Syntagma Metro stations, which display antiquities excavated from the Metro sites.

And save time to take in Athens's astonishing variety of small museums: If you have time for only one, go to **Benaki Museum of Islamic Art,** Agio Asomaton and Dipylou, Psirri (© **210/367-1000;** www.benaki.gr.), Greece's first museum of Islamic art. Just a block away, **The Museum of Traditional Pottery,** 4–6 Melidoni, Kerameikos (© **210/331-8491**), has a permanent collection as well as special exhibits of traditional and contemporary Greek pottery.

In nearby Plaka, **Frissiras Museum,** 3–7 Moni Asteriou (© **210/323-4678**), is Athens's first museum to concentrate on 20th-century European art. The new **Pierides Museum of Ancient Cypriot Art,** 34–35 Kastorias, Votanikos (© **210/348-0000;** www.athinais.com.gr), records the art and politics of Cyprus. See chapter 6.

By the time you read this guide, **Piraeus and the Venizelos International Airport will be linked by the Metro** (www.ametro.gr). Trains will run each way once an hour from 5am to 1am, take 50 minutes, and cost 6€ ($7.80).

The well-preserved statue of a *kouros,* found in the Kerameikos in 2000, is now on display in the **Kerameikos Museum,** along with photographs showing its discovery.

Syntagma and certain other areas of central Athens now have **free Wi-Fi** for Internet users.

Athens's **National Gardens,** which had been spruced up and re-planted with thousands of new trees and shrubs before the 2004 Olympics, had a thousand more trees planted.

The **Athens Sightseeing Public Bus,** line 400, is a great way to explore the city's landmarks. Running from June to September, this hop-on/hop-off bus, begins and ends its 90-minute ride in front of the National Archaeological Museum. Tickets are 5€ ($6.50) and valid for 24 hours.

The New Acropolis Museum is set to open gradually, starting in early 2008. The Parthenon Gallery will also feature strikingly empty spots—an eloquent plea to the British Museum for the return of the Parthenon Marbles.

The **National Archaeological Museum** of Athens, regarded by many as one of the 10 finest museums in the world now has two more additions on display: two ancient treasures that have been returned to Greece by the J. Paul Getty Museum in

Los Angeles—a 4th-century-B.C. gold wreath and a 6th-century-B.C. marble statue of a young woman's torso.

The new **National Museum of Contemporary Art** is scheduled to open in winter 2008. It will be housed in yet another brilliantly transformed industrial-to-arts space at the Syngrou-Fix area (at the outskirts of Koukaki) and promises to be exceptional.

French designer Pierre Bideau has radically and brilliantly altered the **lighting of the Acropolis** and many other key monuments across the city. The Acropolis is now also wheelchair accessible—an elevator for travelers with disabilities (also used by the very lazy) has been installed on the north side of the hill. Ask at the ticket desk entrance to be directed to the elevator.

An increasingly popular motive for visiting Greece is to visit the many places associated with the journeys of St. Paul as he moved about organizing the early Christian communities. We have provided an itinerary for those desirous of doing this on their own—what might be called an independent/nondenominational tour. Those who want to go with an organized tour can find many listed on the Internet (simply do an online search for "footsteps of St. Paul tour") but note that many of these are operated out of Turkey and spend a fair amount of time there (fair enough, as Paul came from Turkey). Note, too, that many of these are explicitly organized for Christians—again, understandably.

THE PELOPONNESE In 2007, the **Rio-AntiRio** bridge, which opened in 2004, was formally named the **Harilaos Trikoupis Bridge** after a prominent 19th-century Greek statesman. Most Greeks continue to call the bridge just that: *"e gefyra."* You can learn more about the bridge at www.gefyra.gr.

Where to Stay Two new boutique hotels are making it much more pleasant

to stay in Mistra and in Andritsaina. The seven-unit **Xenonas Pyrgos Mystra,** 3 Manousaki (© 27310/20-970), in Mistra, may be the only place in Greece where you can stay in a handsomely restored traditional mid-19th-century tower house with a view of mountains and medieval ruins—and enjoy flatscreen television, DVD, and Internet in your room. The nine-unit **Avgerinou Syrrakou Inn** in Andritsaina occupies two restored 19th-century stone town houses and has splendid views over the village. See chapter 8.

What to See & Do A branch of Athens's National Museum, the **Alexander Soutzos Museum,** has opened in Nafplion, with a permanent exhibit of paintings and artifacts of the Greek War of Independence and frequently changing special exhibits. **The Peloponnesian Folklore Foundation** in Nafplion has a new permanent exhibition that looks not at rural but at urban Greece in the 19th and 20th centuries. Both these museums are good places to pick up the new brochure **Artspotting Nafplion,** an excellent introduction to the city's galleries and art shops. In Sparta, the **Museum of the Olive and Greek Olive Oil,** in a restored olive warehouse, focuses on the history and cultivation of the olive through the ages in Greece. This is one of several museums responding to recent interest in Greek agriculture and industrial history. Others include the Museum of Hydroelectric Power in Dimitsana, and Arcadia and the Silk Museum, in Serres, Greece.

If you'd like to learn how to cook some of the food you've eaten in Greece, of if you'd like to paint what you see or to write about your experiences, check out the **cooking, painting, and writing courses** offered by the **Hotel Pelops** in Olympia (www.hotelpelops.gr). In your spare time, you can visit the countryside, see ancient Olympia, and eat the delicious food prepared at the Pelops. See chapter 8.

CRETE   In recognition of the growing interest of travelers in more natural destinations, we have added two new major excursions on Crete—one to the **Lasithi Plain** (p. 341) and another to the **Amari Valley** (p. 360). In addition to these, we are recommending two places that offer what are becoming known as "eco-holidays"—**Milia** (p. 344) and **Footscapes** (p. 344). See chapter 9.

Where to Stay   Several new hotels have been added, all relatively upscale in recognition of the many who now travel to Greece and are looking for such accommodations. One of these is the **Megaron** in Iraklion, a grand hotel in a totally renovated early-20th-century building high above the harbor. See chapter 9. Two others are of a different type—renovated centuries-old Venetian mansions in the old quarter of Rethymnon—the **Palazzino di Corina** and the **AVLI Lounge Apartments.** See chapter 9.

What to See & Do   Of interest to many should be the full-scale replica of a Minoan ship that was constructed in one of the old Venetian "arsenali" on the harbor of Chania. A crew of young oarsmen rowed it to the mainland in time for 2004 Olympics, after which it returned to Chania; it is launched into the harbor on only a few special occasions but everyone can appreciate it and its accompanying display in the arsenal. See chapter 9.

THE CYCLADES
Where to Stay   The **Mykonos Grace** won *Odyssey* magazine's "Best New Entry" award for 2007 and was singled out by the *London Sunday Times* as one of the hippest new hotels of 2007 after its complete face-lift that year. Guests can swim in the sea off Ayios Stephanos beach, or in one of several hotel pools, or soak in the spa Jacuzzis or their suite's hot tub. Decor, food, and privacy all get high marks—as do the prices, which are less

extravagant than at some of Mykonos's other boutique hotels. See chapter 10.

What to See & Do   Over the last few years, the **Apollon Theater,** a replica of Milan's La Scala, in Ermoupolis, the capital of Syros, has been completely restored. The **summer music festival,** which started modestly with a few performances in 2004, is now a going concern and a real plus for opera lovers visiting the Cyclades (www.festivaloftheaegean.com). See chapter 10.

CENTRAL GREECE
Where to Stay   In 2007, *Odyssey* magazine promoted the 165-unit **Divani** motel to its prestigious list of the best hotels of the year, because of the Divani's new indoor pool—the Divani already had an outdoor pool—and spa facilities (www.divanis.gr). See chapter 12.

Where to Dine   Litochoro, where most who climb Olympos spend a night, now has an excellent restaurant: you can check out the offerings at the Gastrodromio En Olympo at their website, **www.gastrodromio.gr**. See chapter 12.

What to See & Do   On summer evenings, a new miniature tram service takes passengers on free 30-minute jaunts around the village of Delphi. See chapter 12.

WESTERN GREECE
Ioannina   An old favorite of ours, the **Xenia Hotel** has been demolished and is to be replaced by a grand luxury hotel. Meanwhile, a new find for accommodations in Ioannina is the Hotel Kastro—distinguished both by its location (within the old city walls) and its quiet ambience. See chapter 14.

THE IONIAN ISLANDS
Corfu   Although it has been mentioned as a possibility for some years now, a day excursion to Albania from Corfu has become increasingly attractive. As Albania's economy has begun to improve, so

too have its tourist facilities, and its citizens are extremely pro-American and pro-European. Of particular interest for some can be a visit Butrint, an ancient Greco-Roman city now recognized as a major archaeological site. See chapter 15.

A new find for accommodations on Corfu is the **Fundana Villas** in the countryside at the center of the island. Lovely bungalows and swimming pools in a completely natural setting make it unique on Corfu. See chapter 15.

Kefalonia One of the oldest motifs—and motives—of travel in the Mediterranean has been trying to trace the places associated with Odysseus as described in Homer's epic, in particular, to identify his homeland, Ithaka. We, as do most texts as well as the official Greek version, have gone along with the claim that it is the modern island of Ithaka. It has never been a matter of taking it all that literally—just that this seemed as reasonable a site as anyplace, and after all, what really mattered was paying one's respects to Homer. But in 2005, a team of Englishmen came forward with a strong case for claiming that Odysseus's Ithaka was in fact the Paliki peninsula of present-day Kefalonia. As for the first most obvious objection—that Ithaka was an island and this is a peninsula—they have pretty much established that it has only become joined to the rest of Kefalonia in the centuries since Homer's time. Having made this claim, they have continued their search for actual remains of Odysseus's residence—or at least his culture. Meanwhile, those who remain intrigued by this topic might want to take at least a side trip on Kefalonia to visit the peninsula. But for most people, the present-day island of Ithaka will probably continue to satisfy their imaginations. See chapter 15.

NORTHERN GREECE
What to See & Do More and more waterfront warehouses are being restored in Thessaloniki. The **Photography** and **Contemporary Art** museums occupy two such restored warehouses and have changing exhibits. See chapter 16.

1

The Best of Greece

Greece is, of course, the land of ancient sites and architectural treasures—the Acropolis in Athens, the amphitheater of Epidaurus, and the reconstructed palace at Knossos among the best known. But Greece is much more: It offers age-old spectacular natural sights, for instance—from Santorini's caldera to the gray pinnacles of rock of the Meteora—and modern diversions ranging from elegant museums to luxury resorts. It can be bewildering to plan your trip with so many options vying for your attention. Take us along and we'll do the work for you. We've traveled the country extensively and chosen the very best that Greece has to offer. We've explored the archaeological sites, visited the museums, inspected the hotels, reviewed the tavernas and ouzeries, and scoped out the beaches. Here's what we consider the best of the best.

1 The Best Travel Experiences

- **Making Haste Slowly:** Give yourself time to sit in a seaside taverna and watch the fishing boats come and go. If you visit Greece in the spring, take the time to smell the flowers; the fields are covered with poppies, daisies, and other blooms. Even in Athens, you'll see hardy species growing through the cracks in concrete sidewalks—or better yet, visit Athens's Ancient Agora, which will be carpeted with a dazzling variety of wildflowers. See chapter 6, "Exploring Athens."

- **Island-Hopping in the Cyclades:** Though the Cyclades are bound by unmistakable family resemblance, each island has a unique personality. Distances between islands are small, making travel by ferry pleasant and logistically straightforward (at least in principle). If you are traveling in the off season, when you do not need hotel reservations, don't plan too much in advance and allow yourself to go with the flow—a tactful way of preparing you for the unexpected in island boat schedules! See chapter 10, "The Cyclades."

- **Leaving the Beaten Path:** Persist against your body's and mind's signals that "this may be pushing too far," leave the main routes and major attractions behind, and make your own discoveries of landscape, villages, or activities. For instance, seek out a church or monastery such as Moni Ayios Nikolaos outside Metsovo—you may be rewarded by a moving encounter with the church and its caretaker. When you visit the Cycladic Islands, consider a base on Tinos or Syros. Both are very popular with Greeks but attract hardly any foreigners. See chapter 10, "The Cyclades."

- **Exploring the Naturalists' Greece:** There is a Greece beyond the columns and cafes—a land of rugged terrain and wildflowers and birds and other natural phenomena. Sign up for a special tour (see chapter 2, "Planning Your Trip to Greece"), or go it alone with one of the several beautifully

Greece

MACEDONIA

Serres
Kilkis
MACEDONIA
Giannitsa
Edessa
Pella   Thessaloniki
Kastoria   Vergina
Kozani   Stratoni
Mt. Olympus   Dion
Adriatic Sea
ALBANIA
ZAGORI
Kalpaki
Elassona
Metsovo   Meteora
(Kalambaka)
Ioannina   Larissa
Igoumenitsou   *Lake Pamvotis*
EPIRUS   Trikkala   THESSALY
Corfu   Karditsa   *Pelion Peninsula*
Paxos   Arta   Volos   *Skopelos*
Praveza   *Skiathos*
Karpenissi   Lamia
Ionian Sea   Vonitsa   Loutra
Edipsou
Lefkada   CENTRAL
Agrinio   GREECE   *Mt. Parnassus*
Astakos   Delphi   Livadia
Kefalonia   *Ithaka*   Messolongi
Thebes
Patras
IONIAN ISLANDS   Kyllini   Megara   Athens
Zakinthos   Corinth   Piraeus
PELOPONNESE   SARONIC
GULF
Pirgos   Olympia   Mycenae   ISLANDS
Argos
Tripoli   Nafplion
Andritsena   Epidaurus
Megalopolis
Mistra   Sparta
Kalamata
Pilos
Githio
CRETE   Areopolis   Monemvassia
Kythira

Greece
Aegean Sea
Athens
Mediterranean Sea   CRETE

CRETE
Chania   *Sea of Crete*
Rethymnon   Ayios
Nikolaos
Iraklion
Ayia Galini   Ierapetra

N
0   25 mi
0   25 km

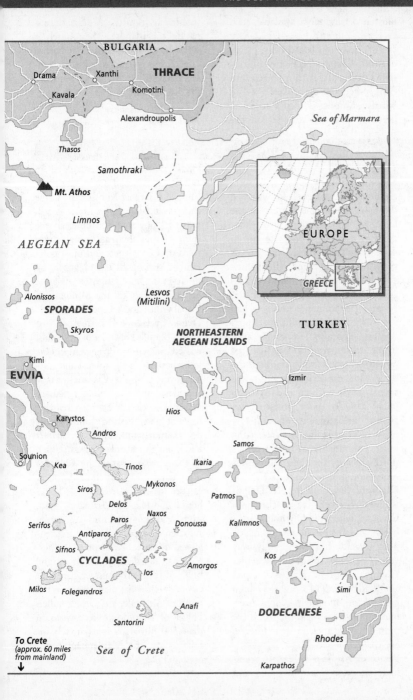

BULGARIA

THRACE

Drama   Xanthi

Kavala   Komotini

Alexandroupolis

Sea of Marmara

Thasos

Samothraki

▲ Mt. Athos

EUROPE

Limnos

AEGEAN SEA

GREECE

Alonissos

SPORADES

Lesvos
(Mitilini)

Skyros

NORTHEASTERN
AEGEAN ISLANDS

TURKEY

Kimi

EVVIA

Izmir

Karystos

Andros

Hios

Sounion

Kea

Tinos

Samos

Siros

Mykonos

Ikaria

Delos

Patmos

Serifos

Paros   Naxos

Donoussa   Kalimnos

Antiparos

Sifnos

CYCLADES

Kos

Ios

Amorgos

Milos   Folegandros

Anafi

Simi

DODECANESE

Santorini

To Crete
(approx. 60 miles
from mainland)
↓

Sea of Crete

Rhodes

Karpathos

illustrated handbooks available, such as Oleg Polunin's *Flowers of Greece and the Balkans* (Oxford Univ. Press); or *Birds of Europe* (McGraw-Hill), by Bertel Bruun and Arthur Singer. And don't forget your binoculars!

- **Sunrise, Sunset:** Get up a little earlier than usual to see the sun rise (preferably from the Aegean, illuminating the islands). Then watch it sink over the mountains (anywhere in Greece, but try not to miss the sunsets that change the Ionian Sea from the deepest blue to a fiery red).

2 The Best of Ancient Greece

- **The Acropolis** (Athens): No matter how many photographs you've seen, nothing can prepare you for watching the light change the marble of the buildings, still standing after thousands of years, from honey to rose to deep red to stark white. If the crowds get you down, think about how crowded the Acropolis was during religious festivals in antiquity. See p. 194.

- **Nemea** (Peloponnese): This gem of a site has it all: a beautifully restored stadium, a handsome museum, even picnic tables with a view of the romantic Doric temple. Look for the three long-standing columns—and several newly restored and reerected ones. If you're lucky, you may see Nemea's archaeologists at work lovingly reconstructing and reerecting more columns from the temple's north facade in their ambitious restoration project. See p. 289.

- **Olympia** (Peloponnese) **& Delphi** (Central Greece): Try to visit both Olympia, where the Olympic Games began, and Delphi, home of the Delphic Oracle. That's the only way you'll be able to decide whether Olympia, with its massive temples and shady groves of trees, or Delphi, perched on mountain slopes overlooking olive trees and the sea, is the most beautiful ancient site in Greece. See chapters 8 and 12.

- **Palace of Knossos** (Crete): A seemingly unending maze of rooms and levels, stairways and corridors, in addition to frescoed walls—this is the Minoan Palace of Knossos. It can be packed at peak hours, but it still exerts its power if you enter in the spirit of the labyrinth. King Minos ruled over the richest and most powerful of Minoan cities and, according to legend, his daughter Ariadne helped Theseus kill the Minotaur in the labyrinth and escape. See p. 332.

- **Delos** (Cyclades): This tiny isle, just 3.2km (2 miles) offshore of Mykonos, was considered by the ancient Greeks to be both the geographical and spiritual center of the Cyclades; many considered this the holiest sanctuary in all of Greece. The extensive remains here testify to the island's former splendor. From Mount Kinthos (really just a hill, but the island's highest point), you can see many of the Cyclades most days; on a very clear day, you can see the entire archipelago. The 3 hours allotted by excursion boats from Mykonos or Tinos are hardly sufficient to explore this vast archaeological treasure. See chapter 10.

- **Vergina** (Northern Greece): In the brilliantly designed museum here, you can peek into what may have been the tomb of Alexander the Great's father, Philip of Macedon. Nearby, more than 300 burial mounds stretch for miles across the Macedonian plain. See p. 635.

3 The Best of Byzantine & Medieval Greece

- **Mistra** (Peloponnese): This Byzantine ghost town has streets lined with the remains of homes both humble and palatial, as well as some of the most beautiful churches in all of Greece. If you have the energy, climb to the top of the defense walls for the superb view over the plain of Sparta. Try to visit in spring, when Mistra is carpeted with wildflowers. See p. 298.

- **Church of Panagia Kera** (Kritsa, Crete): Even if Byzantine art seems a bit stilted and remote, this striking chapel in the foothills of eastern Crete will reward you with its unexpected intimacy. The 14th- and 15th-century frescoes are not only stunning but depict all the familiar biblical stories. See p. 367.

- **The Churches of Thessaloniki** (Northern Greece): Thessaloniki's Byzantine churches are the finest not just in Greece but in the entire world. From tiny Osios David to towering Ayios Dimitrios, these churches boast mosaics and frescoes that give you astonishing glimpses of the artistic grandeur of the mighty Byzantine Empire. See p. 613.

- **Nea Moni** (Hios, Northeastern Aegean): Once home to 1,000 monks, this 12th-century monastery high in the interior mountains of Hios is now quietly inhabited by one elderly but sprightly nun and two friendly monks. Try to catch one of the excellent tours sometimes offered by the monks. The mosaics in the cathedral dome are works of extraordinary power and beauty; even in the half-obscurity of the nave, they radiate a brilliant gold. Check out the small museum, and take some time to explore the extensive monastery grounds. See p. 657.

- **Monemvassia** (Peloponnese): Long called "The Gibraltar of Greece," this rocky promontory crowned by a medieval citadel and church has only one real street (just wide enough for two donkeys to pass each other), no cars, cobbled lanes, beautifully restored stone houses (some of which are now hotels), and views that stretch seemingly forever over the sea. See p. 301.

- **A Clutch of Castles: Acrocorinth, Argos, Methoni, Koroni, Mistra & Nafplion** (Peloponnese): Some of these castles have ancient foundations; all were added onto by the Franks, Venetians, Byzantines, and Turks. Several were used as fortresses as recently as World War II; one, Koroni, has a convent and settlement within its walls. See chapter 8.

- **A Profusion of Byzantine Churches in the Cyclades:** The fertile countryside of the island of Naxos is dotted by well-preserved Byzantine chapels. Parikia, the capital of Paros, has the Byzantine-era cathedral of Panagia Ekatondapiliani. Santorini boasts the 11th- to 12th-century church of the Panagia in the hamlet of Gonias Episkopi. See chapter 10.

4 The Best Beaches

- **Arvanitia** (Nafplion, Peloponnese): After a vigorous and tiring day of sightseeing, this convenient little municipal beach can seem like the best in Greece. Handy changing rooms and showers make this a great place for a quick break between exploring the ruins at Mycenae and taking in a play at Epidaurus. See p. 276.

- **Plaka** (Naxos, Cyclades): Naxos has the longest stretches of sea and sand in the Cyclades, and 4.8km (3-mile) Plaka is the most beautiful and pristine beach on the island. If you need abundant amenities and a more active social scene, you can always head north to Ayia Anna or Ayios Prokopios. See chapter 10.

- **Paradise** (Mykonos, Cyclades): Paradise is the quintessential party beach, known for wild revelry that continues through the night. An extensive complex built on the beach includes a bar, taverna, changing rooms, and souvenir shops. This is a place to see and be seen, a place to show off muscles laboriously acquired during the long winter months. See p. 426.

- **Lalaria Beach** (Skiathos, Sporades): This gleaming, white-pebble beach boasts vivid aquamarine water and white limestone cliffs with natural arches cut into them by the elements. Lalaria is neither nearly as popular nor as accessible as Skiathos's famous Koukounaries, which is one of the reasons it's still gorgeous and pristine. See p. 536.

- **Myrtos** (Kefalonia, Ionian Islands): Although remote enough to require you come with your own wheels, this isolated sand-pebble beach has long charmed countless visitors. It does lack shade and it offers limited refreshments—perhaps bring a picnic—but the setting makes up for these deficiencies. See p. 595.

- **Vroulidia** (Hios, Northeastern Aegean): White sand, a cliff-rimmed cove, and a remote location at the southern tip of the island of Hios combine to make this one of the most exquisite small beaches in the northeastern Aegean. The rocky coast conceals many cove beaches similar to this one, and they rarely become crowded. See p. 659.

5 The Best Islands

- **Hydra** (Saronic Gulf Islands): Old-timers keep waiting for Hydra, with its handsome stone mansions overlooking a picture-postcard harbor, to be spoiled. After all, even before Mykonos and Santorini, Hydra was one of the first Greek islands to be "discovered." So far, so good: Donkeys still outnumber motorcycles, and the day-trippers who blitz through the appealing harborside shops leave at twilight. That means you can almost always find the table you want at one of Hydra's pleasant small restaurants. See p. 255.

- **Crete:** Whether for its rugged mountains or its countless beaches, its ancient remains or its ultramodern hotels, its layered history or its intense people, Crete cannot be denied. It is not just a distinctive Greek island—it is a world unto itself. See chapter 9.

- **Santorini** (Cyclades): This is undoubtedly one of the most spectacular islands in the world. The streets of Fira and Ia are carved into the face of a high cliff, overlooking the circular caldera left by an ancient volcanic eruption and now filled with the deep-blue waters of the Aegean. The site of Akrotiri offers a unique glimpse into life in a Minoan city, frozen in time by the eruption 3,600 years ago. Be sure to find out if this spectacular site, which was partly closed to the public at press time, has completely reopened when you visit. Add to this the Fira nightlife scene, and you'll see why this is one of the most popular (and overcrowded) summer vacation spots in the Aegean. See p. 371.

- **Siros** (Cyclades): This tiny island has it all: a vivacious, cosmopolitan capital town; thriving beach resorts; and a starkly beautiful region of farming communities, archaeological remains, and remote beaches to the north. Siros is also one of the centers of *rembetika,* a form of Greek traditional music with roots in Asia Minor. The *Fragosiriani,* a classic known throughout Greece, was composed by the Siriot Markos Vamvakaris, and you're sure to hear its simple and infectious rhythms many times during your stay here. See p. 453.

- **Tinos** (Cyclades): The island often called the "Lourdes of Greece," because of the church, Panagia Evangelistria (Our Lady of Good Tidings) with its healing icon, also has Venetian dovecotes; farm fields set off with handsome stone boundary walls; and Pirgos, the village of marble. See chapter 10.

- **Rhodes** (Dodecanese): The island of Rhodes has everything a visitor could want—dazzling ancient and medieval ruins, great food, spectacular beaches, and some of the hottest nightlife outside of Athens—the one drawback being that everyone knows it. See chapter 11.

- **Skyros** (Sporades): Winding roads and remote beaches, one main town and a few minor villages, some ancient legends and 20th-century tales: Skyros's charms remain perhaps the most elusive of the four Northern Sporades. But though the island remains a bit difficult to access and not overstocked with touristy amenities, Skyros also offers both a living local culture and some natural wildness. See chapter 13.

- **Corfu** (Ionian Islands): With lush vegetation, some still-undeveloped interior and unspoiled coast, ancient sites and a 19th-century presence, a dash of Italy and a dose of the cosmopolitan, Corfu is a Greek island like no other. Tourism may be rampant, but Corfu's attractions have survived worse. See chapter 15.

- **Hios** (Northeastern Aegean): You'd think that an island with such gorgeous beaches, exquisite medieval towns, and remarkable scenery wouldn't remain a secret for long. Despite the qualities that attract a small group of devotees year after year, Hios remains surprisingly quiet. If you like the idea of getting away from the tour buses, being alone on a beach to rival any in the Cyclades, and exploring towns that preserve the contours of medieval life, Hios is for you. Another benefit: The local hospitality hasn't worn thin here, as it has on many of the more heavily toured islands. See chapter 17.

- **Sifnos** (Cyclades): Sifnos is a green island of ravines, mountaintops, and pristine beaches. Despite its small size (a hardy walker can explore the entire island on foot), Sifnos has numerous attractive small towns which can be used as bases for your explorations. Apollonia, in the central hills, offers elegant small-town civility, with the added benefit of being the hub of an excellent public transportation system. The *kastro* (castle), on its seaside rock, is the medieval locus of the island, whereas Platis Yialos is a bustling beach resort. Don't visit in August, when the island is mobbed with vacationing Athenians. See chapter 10.

6 The Best Places to Get Away from It All

- **National and Zappeion Gardens** (Athens): It's all too easy to overlook this oasis of calm and cool in the heart of Athens. In 2006, more than a thousand new trees and hundreds of roses were planted in the National Garden in its first major makeover since 1854. You'll discover shady benches, a small cafe, the excellent Aegli restaurant in the adjacent Zappeion Gardens, and lots of opportunities to enjoy watching Greek families out for a stroll. Keep an eye out for the balloon sellers on weekends. See p. 210.

- **Mount Likavitos, aka Mount Lycabettus** (Athens): Walk up Likavitos at dawn and enjoy the sunrise over the hills that surround Athens. Come back for sunset, and you may encounter others strolling here, but the sounds (and smells!) of Athens's ferocious traffic will be pleasantly distant. See p. 214.

- **Folegandros** (Cyclades): Most visitors to Greece once sailed past the formidable Folegandros cliffs en route from the mainland to Santorini and other islands; they'd catch a glimpse of the whitewashed kastro walls perched 300m (984 ft.) above the sea. The beauty of Hora, the fine beaches, and the great walking trails are no longer secrets, but if you arrive during the off season, Folegandros still offers a restful retreat. Largely free of the commercialism that has engulfed so many Aegean isles, Folegandros is now appearing on insider lists as *the* new place to visit. See p. 388.

- **Milia** (Crete): Here is a true retreat from not only the hustle and bustle of mass tourism but of most modern distractions: a once-abandoned village off in the mountains of western Crete where you live in a renovated stone house and spend your days hiking, enjoying the wildlife, eating simple meals, and just plain relaxing. See p. 344.

- **Zagori & Vikos Gorge** (Western Greece): If the 40-some tiny villages linked by roads lined with spectacular terrain are not enough, you can venture into at least a section of one of the most spectacular gorges in Europe. Greeks and some Europeans have long appreciated this undeveloped corner of northwestern Greece known as the Zagoria. See p. 570.

- **The Road Not Taken** (Greece): Don't fret if you take a wrong turn in Greece, whether it is on a street in Athens or a road somewhere in the country. Go with it! This may be the highlight of your trip—the Athenian shop-owner who shows you pictures of his aunt's family in Chicago when you stop to ask for directions; the *yiayia* (granny) next to you on that boat that you caught after the boat you wanted to catch had left; the schoolchild who quizzes you about why you came to Greece when you bump into him at an ancient site; the little village you chance upon because you stumbled onto the road you did not mean to take.

7 The Best Museums

- **National Archaeological Museum** (Athens): This stunning collection, which reopened after a major renovation in 2004, has it all: superb red- and black-figured vases, bronze statues, Mycenaean gold, marble reliefs of gods and goddesses, and the hauntingly beautiful frescoes from Akrotiri, the Minoan site on the island of Santorini. See p. 203.

- **Museum of Popular Greek Musical Instruments** (Athens): Life-size photos of musicians beside their actual instruments and recordings of traditional Greek music make this one of the country's most charming museums. On our last visit, an elderly Greek gentleman listened to some music, transcribed it, stepped into the courtyard, and played it on his own violin! See p. 202.
- **Archaeological Museum of Iraklion** (Crete): Few museums in the world can boast of holding virtually all the important remains of a major culture. This museum can do just that with its Minoan collection, including superb frescoes from Knossos, elegant bronze and stone figurines, and exquisite gold jewelry. The museum also contains Neolithic, Archaic

Greek, and Roman finds from throughout Crete. See p. 331.
- **Archaeological Museum of Chania** (Crete): Let's hear it for a truly engaging provincial museum, not one full of masterworks but rather of representative works from thousands of years, a collection that lets us see how many people experienced their different worlds. All this, in a former Italian Renaissance church that feels like a special place. See p. 345.
- **Archaeological Museum of Thessaloniki & Museum of Byzantine Culture** (Northern Greece): These side-by-side museums showcase the art and architecture of Thessaloniki and Northern Greece from the earliest days to the Byzantine era and its legacy. See p. 609 and 610.

8 The Best Resorts & Hotels

- **Andromeda Hotel** (Athens; ✆ 210/643-7302): The city's first serious boutique hotel, located on a wonderfully quiet side street, the classy Andromeda offers charm, comfort, and a reassuringly helpful staff. See p. 168.
- **Grande Bretagne** (Athens; ✆ 210/333-0000): Back for a return engagement and better than ever, Athens's premiere hotel still overlooks the best view in town if you have the right room: Syntagma Square, the Houses of Parliament and, in case you wondered, the Acropolis. See p. 165.
- **Malvasia** (Monemvassia, Peloponnese; ✆ 27320/61-113): The Malvasia brought the concept of the boutique hotel to the Peloponnese. Each room in the Malvasia is different, with some of the best overlooking the sea; all are tastefully furnished with hand-loomed rugs and antiques. A visit here gives you the illusion of staying in the home of wealthy Greek

friends who have enormously good taste—and who just happen to be away and have left the staff behind to tend to your needs. See p. 303.
- **Atlantis Hotel** (Iraklion, Crete; ✆ 2810/229-103): There are many more luxurious hotels in Greece, but few can beat the Atlantis's urban attractions: a central location, modern facilities, and views over a busy harbor. You can swim in the pool, work out in the fitness center, send e-mail via your laptop, and then within minutes enjoy a fine meal or visit a museum. See p. 335.
- **Doma** (Chania, Crete; ✆ 28210/51-772): A former neoclassical mansion east of downtown, the Doma has been converted into a comfortable and charming hotel, furnished with the proprietor's family heirlooms. Although it's not for those seeking the most luxurious amenities, its atmosphere appeals to many. See p. 348.

- **Astra Apartments** (Santorini, Cyclades; ℂ 22860/23-641): This small hotel with handsomely appointed apartments looks like a miniature whitewashed village—and has spectacular views over Santorini's famous caldera. The sunsets here are not to be believed, the staff is incredibly helpful, and the village of Imerovigli itself offers an escape from the tourist madness that overwhelms the island each summer. This is a spot to get married at—or celebrate any special occasion. See p. 383.
- **Anemomilos Apartments** (Folegandros, Cyclades; ℂ 22860/41-309) and **Castro Hotel** (Folegandros, Cyclades; ℂ 22860/41-230): The small island of Folegandros has two of the nicest hotels in the Cyclades, both with terrific cliff-top locations. The Anemomilos has all the creature comforts, traditional decor, and a good location (it's just out of town), with a pool and sea views that seem to stretch forever. The Castro, built into the walls of the 12th-century Venetian castle that encircles the village, has lots of character and the necessary modern comforts. See p. 390.
- **S. Nikolis Hotel** (Rhodes, Dodecanese; ℂ 22410/34-561) This small hotel in the Old Town of Rhodes combines such modern amenities as Internet access and Jacuzzis with the experience of living in a renovated centuries-old Venetian mansion. The

decor and furnishings maintain the sense that you are indeed in a special place and the proprietors' warm hospitality enhances this feeling. See p. 471.
- **Hotel Nireus** (Simi, Dodecanese; ℂ 22410/72-400): Perfect island, perfect location, unpretentious, and tasteful. The views from the sea-facing rooms, framed by the fluid swirls of the wrought-iron balcony, define the spell of this little gem of an island. You'll never regret one more night on Simi, and here's the place to spend it. See p. 486.
- **White Rocks Hotel & Bungalows** (Kefalonia, Ionian Islands; ℂ 26710/28-332): For those who appreciate understated elegance, a shady retreat from all that sunshine, a private beach, and quiet but attentive service, this hotel, a couple of miles outside Argostoli, can be paradise. See p. 592.
- **Mediterranean Palace Hotel** (Thessaloniki; ℂ 2310/552-554). This hotel has it all: location (overlooking the harbor, in the trendy Ladadika district) and luxury. The lobby is, as you might expect, seriously glitzy—but the really pleasant surprise is the comfort and elegance of the guest rooms. The service is usually excellent. The two restaurants are good enough to tempt you to dine here at least 1 night rather than explore the hot spots of Ladadika. See p. 624.

9 The Best Restaurants

- **Varoulko** (Athens; ℂ 210/522-8400): In its new Athens location, with a menu that adds tasty meat dishes to its signature seafood, Varoulko continues to win plaudits. Everything here is so good that many Athenians believe chef/owner Lefteris Lazarou serves not only the finest

seafood in Athens, but some of the best food in all of Greece. See p. 181.
- **Vlassis** (Athens; ℂ 210/646-3060): This small restaurant with a loyal following (ranging from prominent ambassadors to struggling artists) serves traditional *(paradisiako)* Greek cooking at its very best. A tempting

choice if you have only 1 night in Athens—but be sure to make a reservation. See p. 190.

- **Fish Taverna Takis To Limeni** (Limeni, Mani, Peloponnese; ℂ **27330/ 51-327**): Visitors to Greece dream of finding the perfect open-air fish taverna perched by the sea serving fish that were swimming in the sea earlier the same day. Here it is—with some of the fish still swimming in the underwater storage cages they're plopped into from the fishing boats. Everything here is fresh and delicious. See p. 308.

- **Selene** (Santorini, Cyclades; ℂ **22860/ 22-249**): The best restaurant on an island with lots of good places to eat, Selene is one of the finest restaurants in all Greece. The reason: Owner George Haziyannakis constantly experiments with local produce to turn out innovative versions of traditional dishes. Inside, the dining room is elegant, while the terrace has a wonderful view over the caldera. See p. 386.

- **Brillant Gourmet** (Iraklion, Crete; ℂ **2810/334-959**): Only opened in 2007, this restaurant immediately positioned itself as the most stylish restaurant on Crete, with food and

wine to match its decor. Admittedly, a restaurant for special treats or occasions, but it's worth inventing one for yourself at least once. See p. 337.

- **Mavrikos** (Lindos, Rhodes; ℂ **22440/ 31-232**): Don't be fooled by its location at the crossroads of tourists and its moderate prices—this 70-year-old family restaurant serves some of the most elegant and innovative dishes in all of Greece. See p. 480.

- **Petrino** (Kos, Dodecanese; ℂ **22420/ 27-251**): When royalty come to Kos, this is where they dine. Housed in an exquisitely restored, two-story, century-old stone *(petrino)* private residence, this is hands-down the most elegant taverna in Kos, with cuisine to match. This is what Greek home cooking would be if your mother were part divine. See p. 495.

- **Venetian Well** (Corfu, Ionian Islands; ℂ **26610/44-761**): A bit severe in its setting at the edge of a small enclosed square in Corfu town, with no attempt at the picturesque, this restaurant gets by on its more esoteric, international, and delicate menu. It's for those seeking a break from the standard Greek scene. See p. 584.

10 The Best Nightlife

- **Theater under the Stars** (Athens and Epidaurus, Peloponnese): If you can, take in a performance of whatever is on at Odeion of Herodes Atticus theater in Athens or the theater at Epidaurus. You'll be sitting where people have sat for thousands of years to enjoy a play beneath Greece's night sky. See chapters 6 and 8.

- **Mykonos** (Cyclades): Mykonos isn't the only island town in Greece with nightlife that continues through the morning, but it was the first and still offers the most abundant, varied

scene in the Aegean. Year-round, the town's narrow, labyrinthine streets play host to a remarkably diverse crowd—Mykonos's unlimited ability to reinvent itself has assured it of continued popularity. Spring and fall tend to be more sober and sophisticated, whereas the 3 months of summer are reserved for unrestrained revelry. See chapter 10.

- **Rhodes** (Dodecanese): From cafes to casinos, Rhodes has not only the reputation but also the stuff to back it up. A good nightlife scene is ultimately a matter of who shows up—and this, too, is where Rhodes stands out. It's the place to be seen, and if nobody seems to be looking, you can always watch. See chapter 11.

- **Skiathos** (Sporades): With as many as 50,000 foreigners packing this tiny island during the high season, the many nightspots in Skiathos town are often jammed with the mostly younger set. If you don't like the music at one club, cross the street. See chapter 13.

- **Corfu** (Ionian Islands): If raucous nightspots are what you look for on a holiday, Corfu offers probably the largest concentration in Greece. Most of these are beach resorts frequented by young foreigners. More sedate locales can be found in Corfu town. Put simply, Corfu hosts a variety of music, dancing, and "socializing" opportunities. See chapter 15.

- **Thessaloniki** (Macedonia, Northern Greece). You knew something was up in 2007 when the *New York Times* dubbed Greece's "Second City" the "Seattle of the Balkans" and praised its vibrant cafe life that goes round-the-clock, but is especially lively after dark. See chapter 16.

11 The Best Shopping

- **Traditional Arts & Crafts:** So many places in Greece pride themselves on their needlework that it is hard to single out even a few, but among those few would be Crete, Rhodes, and Skyros. Two places in Athens deserve mention: **The Center of Hellenic Tradition** (59 Mitropoleos and 36 Pandrossou) and the **National Welfare Organization** (6 Ipatias and Apollonos). The Center offers ceramics, woodcarvings, prints—and one of the finest views of the Acropolis in Athens. The National Welfare Organization contains hand-loomed rugs and silk embroidery done by village women, as well as excellent copperwork and ceramics.

- **Leatherwork:** Both Rhodes and Crete feature local leatherwork, from sandals to handbags, from belts to jackets. Pay attention to quality.

- **Furs:** Kastoria, in northwestern Greece, is the center of the fur trade, and fur products are everywhere. Athens, of course, sells expensive fur coats. Rhodes also features fur coats. Wherever furs are sold, be sure you know what you are buying.

- **Jewelry:** It now seems that half of Greece's retail stores sell jewelry, so shop around. Much of it is really no different than what can be found in cities all over the world, but Athens does have major, internationally known jewelers such as LALAoUNIS and Zolotas. Try Chania, Crete, for sophisticated local artisans' work. Islands such as Hydra, Mykonos, Santorini, Skiathos, and Rhodes have scores of stores appealing to the tourist trade.

- **Ceramics:** As with needlework, pots and ceramics of all kinds are to be found throughout Greece. Some of the more traditional may be found on Chios, Crete, Mitilini, Sifnos, and Skopelos.

- **Rugs/Weavings:** Crete probably offers the largest variety of rugs and weavings. Metsovo has some distinctive textiles. If you like rag rugs, keep an eye out for *kourouloudes* on sale at small shops as you travel the Peloponnese.

- **Wood:** Corfu seems to be the center of olive-wood products—carving boards, bowls, and utensils. Rethymnon, Crete, also has a selection. In the

Peloponnese, woodcarvings and utensils are often found in the villages of Arcadia. Chios and Mitilini also boast wood-carving traditions.

- **Icons and Ecclesiastical Books & Items:** On the streets around the Greek Orthodox Cathedral (Metropolitan) in Athens, you'll find many shops selling votive offerings, candles, and reproductions of icons. In Thessaloniki, **Apostolic Diakonta Bookstore** (⌀ **2310/275-126**) has a wide selection of religious items. Many of the most important religious shrines, such as Panagia Evangelistria on Tinos, and many convents and monasteries, including most of the Meteora monasteries, sell reproductions of icons and other religious items. On Crete, the Petrakis couple in Elounda paint internationally sought traditional icons.

- **Museum Reproductions:** Officially approved, fine replicas of many famous museum pieces may be purchased at the Archaeological, Byzantine, Benaki, Goulandris, and LALAoUNIS museums in Athens; at the Archaeological and Byzantine museums in Thessaloniki; and at official archaeological service stores in Rhodes Old Town and in Chania and Rethymnon, Crete.

- **Books:** Whether you're looking for books about Greece or books for vacation reading, in Athens the places to go are **Eleftheroudakis, Compendium, Reymondos,** and **Folia tou Bibliou.** In Thessaloniki, head for the excellent **Molho.**

- **Natural Products:** In the last few years, Greece has begun to produce superb organic and natural products, including olive oil, honey, jams, and cosmetics. Keep an eye out for food products with the Peloponnese, Gaea, Milelia, Nefeli, Yiam, and Stater labels in groceries and delis. Good places to look in Athens include most specialty food shops in Kolonaki, and the Mesogaia delicatessen in the Plaka section of Athens. **Green Farm** in Kolonaki sells only organic produce. **Korres Natural Products** (www.korres.com), including a wide range of herbal shampoos and lotions, and **Apivita's Aromatherapy Essential Oils** (www.apivita.gr), are now carried in many pharmacies and cosmetics stores (such as the widespread Hondos Centers) throughout Greece. And, more than 10 **Mastihashops** in Greece sell natural mastic products from liqueur and gum to toothpaste and soaps.

2

Planning Your Trip to Greece

by John S. Bowman

To get the most out of your trip to Greece, some advance planning is in order. The best time to go? What are things going to cost? Will there be a special holiday when I visit? What insider tips or special moments might I appreciate? We'll answer these and other questions for you in this chapter.

1 The Regions in Brief

Greece is a land of sea and mountains. Over a fifth of the Greek landmass is islands, numbering several thousand if you count every floating crag—and nowhere in Greece will you find yourself more than 96km (60 miles) from the sea. It should come as no surprise, then, that the sea has shaped the Greek imagination, as well as its history.

So, too, have the mountains. Mainland Greece is a great vertebrate, with the Pindos range reaching from north to south, and continuing, like a tail, through the Peloponnese. The highest of its peaks is Mount Olympus, the seat of the gods, nearly 3,000m (10,000 ft.) above sea level. Eighty percent of the Greek mainland is mountainous, which you will rapidly discover whether you make your way on foot or on wheels.

ATHENS Whether you arrive by sea or by air, chances are you'll debark in Athens. The city is not always pleasant and is sometimes exhausting—just to be clear, it's the noise level and traffic—yet it's unavoidable. Its **archaeological sites** and its **museums** alone warrant a couple of days of exploration. Between visits to the sites, a stroll in the **National Garden** will prove reviving. Then, after dark as the city cools, the old streets of the **Plaka**

district at the foot of the Acropolis offer you chances to stroll, shop, and have dinner with an Acropolis view. The central square, pedestrianized side streets, and residential streets of **Kolonaki** are where fashionable Athenians head to see and be seen—and to do some serious shopping. **Piraeus,** as in antiquity, serves as the port of Athens and the jumping-off point to most of the islands.

Athens is also a great base for day trips and overnight excursions, whether to the Temple of Poseidon at **Cape Sounion,** the forested slopes of **Mount Hymettus (Imittos),** the Monastery of **Kaisariani (Kessariani),** the Byzantine Monastery of **Daphni,** the legendary plains of **Marathon,** or the ruins of **Eleusis,** place of ancient mysteries.

THE SARONIC GULF ISLANDS Cupped between Attica and the Peloponnese, in the sheltering Saronic Gulf, these islands offer both proximity and retreat for Athenians who, like their visitors, long for calming waters and cooler breezes. In high season, the accessibility of these islands on any given day, especially on weekends, can be their downfall. Choose carefully your day and island, or you may be part of the crowd you're trying to avoid.

Aegina, so close to Athens it can be a daily commute, is the most besieged island, yet it possesses character and charm. The main port town of Aegina is picturesque and pleasant, while across the island to the east, set atop a pine-crested hill, stands the remarkably preserved Temple of Aphaia, a Doric gem. **Poros,** the next island in line proceeding south, is convenient to both Athens and the Peloponnese. Its beaches and lively port are each a draw, with the picturesque rubble of an ancient, scenically situated temple thrown in. Still farther south lies vehicle-free **Hydra,** remarkable for its natural beauty and handsome stone mansions built by sea captains. The port of Hydra has a lot to offer and knows it, all of which is reflected in the prices. It's a great place for pleasant strolls, views, and a swim off the rocks. **Spetses,** the farthest of these islands from Athens, offers glades of pine trees and fine beaches—and a great many hotels catering to package holiday tours from Europe.

THE PELOPONNESE Crossing the narrow isthmus—less than 6.5km (4 miles) across at its narrowest point—from the mainland onto the southern peninsula of Greece is a move you will never regret. The Peloponnese retains a sense of separation from the north and from the rest of Greece. Its often barren landscape is virtually forested with stunning archaeological remains, each with a richly evocative past: **Mycenae,** the mountain citadel of Agamemnon; **Olympia,** birthplace of the Olympic Games; **Sparta,** home of Helen and Menelaus; the palace of Nestor at **Pylos;** the magnificent and still-used theater of **Epidaurus;** the temple and stadium at **Nemea;** and the Bema at **Corinth,** where St. Paul addressed the Corinthians. The small but stately port of **Nafplion** provides a comfortable, convenient base from which to explore surrounding sights.

The mountain and seaside roads of the Peloponnese are unrivalled in Greece. There are several particularly spectacular routes we suggest you take. The vertiginous route from **Sparta** to Kalamata passes the Byzantine ghost town of **Mistra** and continues on through the twists and turns of Langada Pass, one of Greece's most beautiful routes. Follow the excellent road from Tripolis to **Olympia** that cuts through some of the most beautiful mountain scenery in Arcadia, passing traditional villages that are among the region's loveliest. And allow yourself a day or two to head to **The Mani,** the southernmost region of the Peloponnese, where tower-villages dot the hillsides, and coastal roads wind high above the sea.

CRETE The largest of the Greek islands, birthplace of the painter El Greco (and Zeus, they claim!), possesses a landscape so diverse, concentrated, and enchanting that no description is likely to do it justice. Especially if you rent a car and do your own exploring, a week will pass like a day. More or less circling the island on the national highway (don't imagine an interstate), you'll drive a line of inviting ports like **Iraklion,** the capital, **Chania, Rethymnon,** and **Ayios Nikolaos.**

Venturing into the heartland of Crete—not far, since Crete's width ranges from 12 to 56km (7½–35 miles)—you'll find the legendary palaces of the Minoans: **Knossos, Phaestos,** and **Ayia Triadha,** to mention only a few. This is not to say that Crete is without classical sites, Byzantine monasteries, Venetian structures, and Turkish remains. It's Greece, after all. Other excursions might include the **Lasithi Plain** or the **Amari Valley,** and for the energetic, the **Gorge of Samaria** is indispensable.

Crete is a culinary mecca. For thousands of years its wines were sent all over the ancient world. Today, they complement the fresh goat cheese and olives—all local and all part of Crete's spell.

THE CYCLADES   In antiquity, the *Cyclades*—the "encirclers" or "circling islands"—had at their center the small island of **Delos,** where mythology tells us that Apollo and his sister Artemis were born. Declared a sanctuary where both birth and death were prohibited, Delos was an important spiritual, cultural, and commercial hub of the Aegean. Today, its extensive remains remind visitors of its former importance. It's easy to make a day trip here from **Mykonos,** whose white, cubelike houses and narrow, twisting streets began to attract first a trickle and then a flood of visitors in the 1960s. Today, almost every cruise ship puts in at Mykonos for at least a few hours, so that visitors can take in the proliferation of cafes, restaurants, and shops. Those who spend a few days here can stay in boutique hotels, sip martinis in sophisticated bars—or head inland to visit the island's less-visited villages.

Paros (sometimes called "the poor man's Mykonos"), is the transport hub of the Cyclades, with a gentle landscape, appealing villages, good beaches, and opportunities for windsurfing. From here you can get to **Tinos,** home to perhaps the most revered of all Greek Orthodox churches; **Naxos,** whose fertile valleys and high mountains lure hikers and campers; **Folegandros,** much of whose capital Hora is built within the walls of a medieval *kastro* (castle); and **Santorini,** which some believe to be the lost Atlantis. On Santorini you'll find a black lava beach, the impressive remains of the Minoan settlement at Akrotiri, chic restaurants, boutique hotels—and the most spectacular sunsets in all of Greece.

THE DODECANESE   This string of islands, named "the 12" despite the fact that they number more than that, nearly touch the Turkish shoreline. Except for Rhodes and Kos, all of the Dodecanese are deforested, bare bones exposed to sun and sea. But what bones! Far to the north lies **Patmos** (already in the 5th c. nicknamed "the Jerusalem of the Aegean"), a holy island where the Book of Revelation is said to have been penned and where the Monastery of St. John still dominates the land. Far to the south basks **Rhodes,** "City of the Sun," with more than 300 days of sunshine per year. For obvious reasons, it's the most touristed of the islands. Rhodes has it all: history and resorts, ruins and nightlife. There's even peace and quiet—we'll tell you where to find it.

Between these two lie an array of possibilities, from the uncompromised traditional charm of tiny **Simi** to the ruins and well-known beaches of **Kos.** And with Turkey so close, you may want to consider an easily arranged side trip.

CENTRAL GREECE   Central Greece, for our purposes, stretches from the Corinth Canal to Mount Olympus. Its landscape is vastly diverse, from the fertile Boetian plains to the snowy peaks of **Parnassus** and **Olympus.** Also here are the legendary battlegrounds of **Thermopylae** (where the Spartans under Leonidas delayed the Persian invasion in 480 B.C.) and **Chaironeia** (where Philip of Macedon defeated the Greeks in 338 B.C.).

Central Greece's best-known site is the sanctuary of **Delphi,** whose imposing ruins and spectacular mountainside location dazzle visitors. Farther north, in Thessaly, the monasteries on the lofty otherworldly heights of **Meteora** offer glimpses into the Byzantine and modern Greek world of the Orthodox Church. If you have a less austere retreat in mind, the traditional villages on the lush, gentle slopes of **Pelion**—where centaurs once roamed—are ideal places to relax under chestnut trees and read up on all that you've seen, and all that you plan to see, in Greece.

THE SPORADES Whether by air, ferry, or hydrofoil, the Sporades, strewn north and east of the island of Evvia (Euboea), are readily accessible from the mainland and offer verdant forest landscapes, gold-sand beaches, and crystalline waters. That's the good news. The bad news is that they are no secret. **Skiathos** is the most popular. **Skopelos,** whose lovely port is one of the most striking in Greece, is more rugged and remote than Skiathos, with more trails and fewer nightclubs. Relatively far-off **Skyros** is well worth a visit, offering fishing and diving, sandy beaches, and luminously clear waters.

WESTERN GREECE Northwestern Greece, or **Epirus,** is predominantly mountainous and mostly cut off by those mountains from the sea. It is unlikely that you will encounter many tourists. Nature lovers and trekkers venture here to challenge themselves hiking **Vikos Gorge** and the mountainous **Zagori** region. Epirus is not, however, without amenities and attractions.

Ioannina, on the shores of Lake Pamvotis, is the largest and most appealing city in the region; it is one of the few places in Greece where the long Muslim occupation is still manifestly visible. The traditional mountain village of **Metsovo,** perched several thousand feet high in the Pindos Mountains, offers a number of local attractions and hikes replete with vistas.

Only 32km (20 miles) from Ioannina lie the ruins of one of the most famous of ancient shrines, the Oracle of Zeus at **Dodona,** where the voice of the great lord of Olympus was believed to speak through the rustling leaves of a sacred oak tree.

THE IONIAN ISLANDS Across centuries, these islands have been the apple of more than one empire's eye. Lush, temperate, blessed with ample rain and sun, and tended like architectural gardens, they are splendid. **Corfu,** the most noted and ornamented, is a gem, and is sought after accordingly. **Ithaka** is as yet somewhat out of the tourist loop, but needs no

---

⌒Tips   Greece on the Web

Anyone with access to the Web can obtain a fair amount of information about Greece. Remember that these sources cannot necessarily be counted on for the most up-to-date, definitive, or complete information. We advise you to use computer searches as *supplements only,* and then check out specific "facts" on which you are going to base your travel plans. Websites are continually being changed and added, but among the most useful for broad-based searches are:

- www.frommers.com (practical travel information)
- www.greekembassy.org (official Greek matters)
- www.gtp.gr (ship and air travel in Greece)
- www.maporama.com (online maps)
- www.salon.com/wanderlust (one of many travel blogs)
- www.phantis.com (current news about Greece)
- www.culture.gr (official site for Greek's cultural attractions)
- www.perseus.tufts.edu (classical Greek texts)

introduction for readers of the *Odyssey*. With adjustments for the nearly 3,000 years that have elapsed, Homer's descriptions of the island still hold their own. If you can do without name recognition, **Kefalonia,** relatively inconspicuous and unspoiled, has a lot to offer: picturesque traditional villages, steep rocks plunging into the sea, fine beaches, and excellent local wine.

THESSALONIKI & NORTHERN GREECE   Just as it once was the urban understudy of Constantinople, **Thessaloniki** is modern Greece's second city. With less than 20% of Athens's population, however, it is not a close second. Even so, among Greece's major cities, it may be second to none in visual appeal and international flair. Among the city's many attractions are the legendary White Tower and its archaeological and Byzantine museums. As a home base, it offers comfortable proximity to many of Macedonia's major sites.

Macedonia is Greece's largest geographical region—rich in natural beauty, soaked in history, and mostly removed from the epicenters of the tourist explosion that, in places, has almost leveled the diverse traditions and cultures of Greece. Besides Thessaloniki, Macedonia is home to three major archaeological sites associated with Alexander and his father— **Pella, Vergina,** and **Dion**—as well as the location of the independent religious state of **Mount Athos.** This mountaintop theocracy, off-limits to women since the year 1060, may be viewed from cruise ships (departing from Thessaloniki) or visited with special permission—but only by men.

THE NORTHEASTERN AEGEAN ISLANDS   The four major islands comprising this group form Europe's traditional sea border with the East. Beyond their strategic and thus richly historic location, they offer a taste of Greece that is less compromised by tourism and more deeply influenced by nearby Asia Minor and modern Turkey. **Samos,** unique among the islands in the extent to which it is covered with trees, produces excellent local wine. Its important archaeological sites and opportunities for outdoor activities make it a congenial and interesting destination, and it is an ideal place from which to enter and explore the northwestern Turkish coast. **Hios** is unspoiled and welcoming, offering isolated and spectacular beaches, as well as the stunning monastery of Nea Moni and some of Greece's most striking village architecture. The remaining islands of **Lesvos** and **Limnos,** for various reasons not major tourist destinations, have their ways of inviting and rewarding those who explore them.

Security in Greece

Inevitably and understandably, travelers might be concerned about the threat of terrorists in Greece. As for Al Qaeda or Islamic militants, there has never been any indication that they have a presence, let alone an agenda, in Greece. For one thing, Greece is pro-Palestinian, and militant Muslims have no desire to offend. This is not to say that there might not be angry and anti-American Middle Easterners in Greece. In fact, many Greeks oppose U.S. foreign policies; most particularly, the war in Iraq. But in all locales where tourists are apt to be, you will find at least formal politeness.

Tips **Site and Museum Hours**

If you visit Greece during the summer, check carefully on the visiting hours for major sites and museums. According to the official postings, they should be open from 8am to 7:30pm, but some may close earlier in the day or even be closed 1 day a week. All are closed on major holidays.

---

2 Visitor Information

The **Greek National Tourism Organization** (**GNTO** or **EOT** in Greece—and increasingly referred to as the Hellenic Tourism Organization) has offices throughout the world that can provide you with information concerning all aspects of travel to and in Greece. Look for them at **www.gnto.gr** or contact one of the following GNTO offices:

UNITED STATES Olympic Tower, 645 Fifth Ave., 5th Floor, New York, NY 10022 (*©* **212/421-5777;** fax 212/826-6940).

AUSTRALIA & NEW ZEALAND 37–49 Pitt St., Sydney, NSW 2000 (*©* **29/241-1663;** fax 29/241-2499).

CANADA 1500 Donmills Road, Toronto, ON M3B 3K4 (*©* **416/968-2220;** fax 416/968-6533).

UNITED KINGDOM & IRELAND 4 Conduit St., London W1S 2DJ (*©* **207/495-9300;** fax 207/287-1369).

For the latest information on security issues, health risks, and similar issues, in the U.S., you can call, fax, or send a self-addressed, stamped envelope to the **Overseas Citizens Emergency Center,** Department of State, Room 4811, Washington, DC 20520 (*©* **202/647-5225;** www.travel.state.gov); ask for Consular Information Sheets. You can also get the latest information by contacting any U.S. embassy, consulate, or passport office.

---

3 Entry Requirements & Customs

PASSPORTS

For information on how to get a passport, go to "Passports" in the "Fast Facts: Greece" section, later in this chapter—the websites listed provide downloadable passport applications as well as the current fees for processing passport applications. For an up-to-date country-by-country listing of passport requirements around the world, go to the "Foreign Entry Requirement" Web page of the U.S. State Department at **http://travel.state.gov**.

For entry into Greece, citizens of Australia, Canada, New Zealand, South Africa, the United States, and almost all other non-E.U. countries are required to have a **valid passport,** which is stamped upon entry and exit, for stays up to 90 days. All U.S. citizens, even infants, must have a valid passport, but Canadian children under 16 may travel without a passport if accompanied by either parent.

Citizens of the United Kingdom and other members of the European Union are required to have only a valid passport for entry into Greece, and it is no longer stamped upon entry; you may stay an unlimited period (although you should inquire about this at a Greek consulate or at your embassy in Greece). Children under 16 from E.U. countries may travel without a passport if accompanied by either parent. All E.U. citizens are reminded that they should check the requirements for non-E.U. countries through which you might travel to get to Greece.

VISAS

For stays longer than 90 days, all non-E.U. citizens will require visas from the Greek embassies or consuls in their home countries. If already in Greece, arrangements must be made with the **Bureau of Aliens,** 173 Leoforos Alexandras, 11522 Athens (© **210/770-5711**).

MEDICAL REQUIREMENTS

For information on medical requirements and recommendations, see "Health" p. 40.

CUSTOMS

For information on what you can bring in and take out of Greece, go to "Customs" in "Fast Facts: Greece" later in this chapter.

4 When to Go

WEATHER   Greece has a generally mild climate, though in the mountainous northern interior the winters are rather harsh and summers brief. Southern Greece enjoys a relatively mild winter, with temperatures averaging around 55° to 60°F (13°–16°C) in Athens. Summers are generally hot and dry, with daytime temperatures rising to 85° to 95°F (30°–35°C), usually cooled by prevailing north winds *(meltemi),* especially on the islands, which often cool appreciably in the evenings. And at some point in most summers, usually July, the temperature will rise to over 100°F (38°C).

For weather forecasts for major cities in Greece, try **www.accuweather.com**.

The best time to visit is **late April to mid-June** before summer arrives in force with hordes of tourists, higher prices, overbooked facilities, and strained services. **September** to **mid-October** is another time to avoid the crowds and yet enjoy comfortable weather. **Orthodox Easter Week**—which takes place close to but not exactly concurrent with Easter in Western countries—falls sometime in the Spring period.

Average Monthly Temperatures & Precipitation

		Jan	Feb	Mar	Apr	May	June	July	Aug	Sept	Oct	Nov	Dec
Athens	Temp °F	52	54	58	65	74	86	92	92	82	72	63	56
	Temp °C	12	13	15	19	24	30	33	33	28	23	18	14
	Precip. (in.)	2.4	2.0	1.3	0.9	0.8	0.2	0.1	0.2	1.1	2.0	2.9	4.1
Crete	Temp °F	52	54	57	62	68	74	78	78	75	69	63	58
	Temp °C	13	13	14	17	20	24	26	26	24	21	18	15
	Precip. (in.)	2.4	2.0	1.3	0.9	0.8	0.2	0.1	0.2	1.1	2.0	2.9	4.1

If you possibly can, avoid traveling in **July and August** (especially around Aug 15). The crowds from Europe overwhelm facilities. In overcrowded southern Greece and the islands, midday temperatures are too high for much except beach and water activities. We strongly recommend that you not go unless you have firm reservations and enjoy close encounters with masses of fellow tourists and footloose students. Of course, the higher elevations remain cooler and less crowded, a plus for

hikers, bikers, and those who don't demand sophisticated pleasures.

By **mid-September,** temperatures begin to fall and crowds thin, but it can still be hot. The weather remains generally calm and balmy well into October. If you can't get to Greece in the spring, and beaches are not your primary goal, this is a fine time to visit.

By **late October,** ferry service and flights are cut back and most facilities on the islands begin to close for the winter,

> **Tips Two Holidays to Stay Put**
>
> Greece observes a number of holidays during which museums, sites, government offices, banks, and such are closed. But during several days around Easter (a fluctuating holiday) and August 15, not only do many places shut down, but internal transportation is overwhelmed by Greeks returning to their hometowns and villages. So although it is great to be in Greece to observe these occasions, do not plan to do much moving around.

but the cooler fall atmosphere makes Athens and the mainland all the more pleasant. If you have the time, visit the islands first, then return for a tour of the mainland archaeological sites.

Winter (Nov–Mar) is not the time to visit Greece unless you want to join the Greeks for skiing in the mountains. However, some hotels and many good tavernas stay open, prices are at their lowest, and the southern mainland and Crete remain inviting, especially for those interested in archaeology and authentic local culture.

HOLIDAYS The legal national holidays of Greece are: **New Year's Day,** January 1; **Epiphany** (Baptism of Christ), January 6; **Clean Monday (Kathari Deftera),** day before Shrove Tuesday, 41 days before Easter (which in Greece may come in late Mar to late Apr; every few years it coincides with Easter Sunday in Western countries); **Independence Day,** March 25; **Good Friday to Easter,** including the Monday after Easter Sunday; **May Day** (Labor Day), May 1; **Whitmonday** (Holy Spirit Monday), day after Whitsunday (Pentecost), the seventh Sunday after Easter; **Assumption of the Virgin,** August 15; **Ochi Day,** October 28; **Christmas,** December 25 and 26.

On these holidays, government offices, banks, post offices, most stores, and many restaurants are closed; a few museums and attractions may remain open on several of the lesser holidays. But if you are intent on seeing a specific museum or site, be sure to find out before you leave home whether the place will be open.

Meanwhile, visitors are often included in the celebration. Consult the "Greece Calendar of Events," below, if you are in the planning stage. If you are already in Greece, ask at your hotel or find one of the current English-language publications, such as the *Athens News,* the *Kathimerini* insert in the *International Herald Tribune,* the weekly brochure *Athens Today,* or the *Athenscope* section of the weekly *Hellenic Times.*

GREECE CALENDAR OF EVENTS

For an exhaustive list of events beyond those listed here, check http://events.frommers.com where you'll find a searchable, up-to-the-minute roster of what's happening in cities all over the world.

January

Feast of St. Basil (Ayios Vassilios). St. Basil is the Greek equivalent of Santa Claus. The holiday is marked by the exchange of gifts and a special cake, *vassilopita,* made with a coin in it; the person who gets the piece with the coin will have good luck. January 1.

Epiphany (Baptism of Christ). Baptismal fonts and water are blessed. A priest may throw a cross into the harbor and young men will try to recover it; the finder wins a special blessing. Children, who have been kept good during Christmas with threats of the *kalikantzari* (goblins), are allowed on the 12th day to help chase them away. January 6.

Holy Week Celebrations

Orthodox Easter, a time of extraordinary festivities in Greece, usually falls one or more weeks after Easter in the West; inquire ahead! The Good Friday exodus from Athens is truly amazing, and you can remain and enjoy the deserted city or, if you're fortunate and have made reservations, because Greeks take up most of the travel facilities, you can be among the celebrants in any town or village. Holy Week is usually marked by impressive solemn services and processions; serious feasting on roasted lamb, the traditional *margaritsa* soup, and homemade wine. Dancing takes place, often in traditional costumes. In a unique celebration on Patmos, the Last Supper is reenacted at the Monastery of St. John the Divine. *Tip:* Tourists must dress appropriately during this special time. Shorts, miniskirts, and sleeveless shirts will not only offend Greeks, but will prohibit your entry to religious sites.

Gynecocracy (Gynaikokratia, Rule of Women). In some villages in Thrace, the women take over the cafes while the men stay home and do the housework. January 8.

February

Carnival (Karnavali). Be ready for parades, marching bands, costumes, drinking, dancing, and general loosening of inhibitions, depending on the locale. Some scholars say the name comes from the Latin for "farewell meat," while others hold that it comes from "car naval," the chariots celebrating the ancient sea god Poseidon (Saturn, to the Romans). The city of Patras shows its support of the latter theory with its famous chariot parade and wild Saturnalia, private parties, and public celebrations. Masked revels are widely held in Macedonia. On the island of Skyros, the pagan "Goat Dance" is performed, reminding us of the primitive Dionysiac nature of the festivities. Crete has its own colorful versions, whereas in the Ionian Islands, festivities are more Italian. In Athens, people bop each other on their heads with plastic hammers. Celebrations last the 3 weeks before the beginning of Lent.

March

Independence Day and the Feast of the Annunciation. The two holidays are celebrated simultaneously with military parades, especially in Athens. The religious celebration is particularly important on the islands of Tinos and Hydra and in churches or monasteries named *Evangelismos* (Bringer of Good News) or *Evangelistria* (the feminine form of the name). March 25.

April

Sound-and-Light Performances. These begin on the Acropolis in Athens and in the Old Town on Rhodes. Nightly through October.

Procession of St. Spyridon (Ayios Spyridon). On Palm Sunday, the procession is held in Corfu town. St. Spyridon's remains are also paraded through the streets of Corfu town on Holy Saturday, August 1, and on the first Sunday in November.

Feast of St. George (Ayios Yioryios). The feast day of the patron saint of shepherds is an important rural celebration with dancing and feasting. Arachova, near Delphi, is famous for its festivities. The island of Skyros also gives its patron saint a big party on

April 23. (If the 23rd comes before Easter, the celebration is postponed until the Mon after Easter.)

May

May Day. On this important urban holiday, families have picnics in the country and pick wildflowers, which are woven into wreaths and hung from balconies and over doorways. May Day is still celebrated by Greek communists and socialists as a working-class holiday. May 1.

Folk-Dance Performances. Dances begins in the amphitheater on Filopappos Hill in Athens and continue to September. Among the most regular and popular groups is the Dora Stratou Dance Troupe.

Hippocratic Oath. Ritual recitations of the oath by the citizens of Kos honor their favorite son, Hippocrates. Young girls in ancient dress, playing flutes, accompany a young boy in procession until he stops and recites in Greek the timeless oath of physicians everywhere. May through September.

Sound-and-Light Shows. The shows begin in Corfu town and continue to the end of September.

Feast of St. Constantine (Ayios Konstandinos). The first Orthodox emperor, Constantine, and his mother, **St. Helen (Ayia Eleni),** are honored, most interestingly, by fire-walking rituals *(anastenaria)* in four villages in Macedonian Greece: Ayia Eleni, Ayios Petros, Langada, and Meliki. It's a big party night for everyone named Costa and Eleni. (Name-days, rather than birthdays, are celebrated in Greece.) The anniversary of the Ionian reunion with Greece is also celebrated, mainly in Corfu. May 21.

June

Athens Festival. Featured are superb productions of ancient drama, opera, orchestra performances, ballet, modern dance, and popular entertainers. The festival takes place in the handsome Odeum of Herodes Atticus, on the southwest side of the Acropolis. June to early October.

Folk-Dance Performances. The site of these performances is the theater in the Old Town of Rhodes.

Wine Festival. This festival is held annually at Daphni, about 10km (7 miles) west of Athens; wine festivals are also held on Rhodes and elsewhere.

Simi Festival. The 4-month feast features concerts, theater, storytelling, and dance, starring acclaimed Greek and international artists. With its epicenter on the tiny island of Simi, the events spill over onto seven neighboring islands: Astypalea, Halki, Kastellorizo, Karpathos, Kassos, Nissiros, and Tilos. June through September.

Lycabettus Theater. A variety of performances is presented at the amphitheater on Mount Likavitos (Lycabettus) overlooking Athens. Mid-June to late August.

Miaoulia. This celebration on Hydra honors Hydriot Admiral Miaoulis, who set much of the Turkish fleet on fire by ramming it with explosives-filled fireboats. Weekend in mid-June.

Aegean Festival. In the harbor of Skiathos town, the Bourtzi Cultural Center presents ancient drama, modern dance, folk music and folk dance, concerts, and art exhibits. June through September.

International Classical Musical Festival. This annual festival takes place at Nafplion, in the Peloponnese. One week in June or July.

Midsummer Eve. The now-dried wreaths of flowers picked on May Day are burned to drive away witches, in a version of pagan ceremonies now associated with the birth of John the Baptist on June 24, Midsummer Day. June 23 to June 24.

The Feast of the Holy Apostles (Ayii Apostoli, Petros, and Pavlos). Another important name-day. June 29.

Navy Week. The celebration takes place throughout Greece. In Volos, the voyage of the Argonauts is reenacted. On Hydra, the exploits of Adm. Andreas Miaoulis, naval hero of the War of Independence, are celebrated. Fishermen at Plomari on Lesvos stage a festival. End of June and beginning of July.

July

Puppet Festival. Hydra's annual festival has drawn puppeteers from countries as far away as Togo and Brazil. Early July.

Dodoni Festival. Classical dramas are presented at the ancient theater of Dodoni, south of Ioannina. For information, call ℂ **26510/20-090.** July through September.

Epidaurus Festival. Performances of classical Greek drama take place in the famous amphitheater. For information, contact the **Greek Festival Office,** 4 Stadiou (ℂ **210/322-1459** or 210/322-3111 to -3119, **ext. 137**). July to early September.

International Folklore Festival. At Naoussa, in Northern Greece, both amateur and professional dance companies gather from all over the world. For information, call ℂ **23320/20-211** or e-mail cioff@nao.forthnet.gr. July.

Northern Greece National Theater. Classical drama is performed in the amphitheaters in Phillipi and on the island of Thasos. You will be able to see these productions without the hassles of Athens performances. For information, call ℂ **2510/223-504.** July and August.

Hippokrateia Festival. Art, music, and theater come to the medieval castle of the Knights of St. John, in the main harbor of Kos. July and August.

Kalamata International Dance Festival. In Kalamata, in the southern Peloponnese, performances are given by prestigious dance companies from all over the world. Usually during mid-July.

Dionysia Wine Festival. This is not a major event, but it's fun if you happen to find yourself on the island of Naxos. For information, call ℂ **22850/22-923.** Mid-July.

Wine Festival at Rethymnon, Crete. Rethymnon hosts a wine festival as well as a **Renaissance Festival.** There are now wine festivals and arts festivals all over Greece, but among the more engaging are those held in Rethymnon. Sample the wines, then sample the Renaissance theatrical and musical performances. Mid-July to early September.

Feast of Ayia Marina. The feast of the protector of crops is widely celebrated in rural areas. July 17.

Feast of the Prophet Elijah (Profitis Elias). The prophet's feast day is celebrated in the hilltop shrines formerly sacred to the sun god Helios. The most famous shrine is on Mount Taygetos, near Sparta. July 18 to July 20.

Feast of Ayia Paraskevi. The succession of Saint Days continues to be celebrated at the height of summer, when agricultural work is put on hold. July 26.

August

Feast of the Transfiguration (Metamorphosi). This feast day is observed in the numerous churches and monasteries of that name, though they aren't much for parties. August 6.

Aeschylia Festival of Ancient Drama. Classical dramas are staged at the archaeological site of Eleusis, home of the ancient Mysteries and birthplace of Aeschylus, west of Athens. August to mid-September.

Feast of the Assumption of the Virgin (Apokimisis tis Panayias). On this important day of religious pilgrimage, many come home to visit, so rooms are particularly hard to find. The holiday reaches monumental proportions in Tinos; thousands of people descend on the small port town to participate in an all-night vigil at the cathedral of Panagia Evangelistria, in the procession of the town's miraculous icon, and in the requiem for the soldiers who died aboard the Greek battleship *Elli* on this day in 1940. August 15.

Epirotika Festival. Ioannina presents theatrical performances, concerts, and exhibitions. August to early September.

Olympus Festival. Cultural events take place in several sites around Mt. Olympus, in particular at the ancient theater of Dion and in the Venetian castle of Platamonas. Throughout August.

Santorini Festival of Classical Music. International musicians and singers give outdoor performances for 2 weeks. End of August.

September

Feast of the Birth of the Virgin (Yenisis tis Panayias). Another major festival, especially on Spetses, the anniversary of the Battle of the Straits of Spetses is celebrated with a reenactment in the harbor, fireworks, and an all-night bash. September 8.

Feast of the Exaltation of the Cross (Ipsosi to Stavrou). This marks the end of summer's stretch of feasts, and even Stavros has had enough for a while. September 14.

Thessaloniki International Trade Fair. This is one of the world's major trade fairs. Rooms are scarce in the city,

so if the fair's not your destination, try to come to Thessaloniki at another time. For information, call (?) **2310/ 271-888.** Mid-September.

Thessaloniki Film Festival and Festival of Popular Song. That lively and sophisticated city continues to live it up. End of September.

October

Feast of St. Demetrius (Ayios Dimitrios). Particularly important in Thessaloniki, where he is the patron saint, the Demetrius Festival features music, opera, and ballet. New wine is traditionally untapped. October 26.

Ochi Day. General Metaxa's negative reply (*ochi* is Greek for "no") to Mussolini's demands in 1940 conveniently extends the feast-day party with patriotic outpourings, including parades, folk music and folk dancing, and general festivity. October 28.

November

Feast of the Archangels Gabriel and Michael (Gavriel and Mihail). Ceremonies are held in the many churches named for the two archangels. November 8.

Feast of St. Andrew (Ayios Andreas). The patron saint of Patras provides another reason for a party in this swinging city. November 30.

December

Feast of St. Nikolaos (Ayios Nikolaos). This St. Nick is the patron saint of sailors. Numerous processions head down to the sea and to the many chapels dedicated to him. December 6.

Christmas. The day after Christmas honors the Gathering Around the Holy Family (Synaksis tis Panayias). December 25 and 26.

New Year's Eve. Children sing Christmas carols (*kalanda*) outdoors while their elders play cards, talk, smoke, eat, and imbibe. December 31.

5 Getting There

BY PLANE

The vast majority of travelers reach Greece by plane, and most of them arrive at the new Athens airport—officially Eleftherios Venizelos International Airport (**ATH** is its code when searching online), sometimes referred to by its new location as the Spata airport. Thessaloniki (**SKG** is its code) in northeastern Greece is an alternative for those who might like to make their way south but it has far fewer connecting flights to foreign cities.

FROM NORTH AMERICA

UNITED STATES   At press time, only four regularly scheduled airlines offer direct, nonstop flights from the States to Athens: Olympic, Delta, US Air, and Continental. **Olympic Airways** (✆ 800/ 223-1226; www.olympicairlines.com) offers nonstop service daily from New York and twice weekly from Montréal and Toronto. Olympic will make arrangements to have your luggage transferred from other airlines arriving at New York for your connection. Also, if you fly Olympic transatlantic, it offers reduced fares to all its destinations within Greece. **Delta Air Lines** (✆ 800/241-4141; www. delta.com) offers service from throughout the United States, with all flights connecting to their nonstop Athens flights at JFK in New York (and in Atlanta during the summer). **US Air** (✆ 800/428-4322; www.usair.com) instituted its direct flights only in 2007; its daily flights leave from Philadelphia. And **Continental** (✆ 800/231-0856; www.continental.com) also commenced service in 2007 by offering daily flights from Newark Airport. Many airlines these days belong to an alliance or code-sharing group so you might be able to use or earn frequent flyer miles with one of the other members.

All the other airlines make stops at some major European airport, where a change of planes is usually required. **Alitalia** (✆ 800/223-5730; www.alitalia. com) offers flights from JFK that go to Greece via Rome. **British Airways** (✆ 800/247-9297; www.britishairways. com) has service to Athens from a number of major U.S. cities, all stopping in London (most at Heathrow, but some at Gatwick). **Lufthansa** (✆ 800/645-3880; www.lufthansa.com) provides service to Athens, Thessaloniki, and Crete from 10 U.S. cities, most via Frankfurt. **Northwest/ KLM/Northwest** (✆ 800/447-4747; www.nwa.com) has service from 10 major cities in the United States to Athens, with all flights stopping in Amsterdam. **Swiss International Airlines** (✆ 877/359-7947; www.swiss.com) offers service from Boston as well as New York, with all flights connecting to Athens at Zurich. **Virgin Atlantic Airways** (✆ 800/862-8621; www.virgin-atlantic.com) offers flights via London, with daily flights from Los Angeles and the New York area, and less frequent service from several other cities.

CANADA   In addition to the various airlines flying out of the United States, Canadians have a number of choices. **Olympic Airways** (✆ 800/223-1226; www.olympicairlines.com) offers the only direct flights from Canada to Athens— two flights a week from Montréal and Toronto. **Air Canada** (✆ 888/247-2262; www.aircanada.ca) flies from Calgary, Montréal, Toronto, and Vancouver to various airports in Europe with connections on Olympic to Athens. **Air France** (✆ 800/237-2747; www.airfrance.com), **British Airways** (✆ 800/247-9297; www. ba.com), **Czech Airlines** (✆ 800/223-2365; www.czechairlines.com), **Iberia** (✆ 800/772-4642; www.iberia.com), **KLM Royal Dutch Airlines** (✆ 800/ 447-4747; www.klm.com), **Lufthansa** (✆ 800/645-3880; www.lufthansa.com)

and **Swiss International Airlines** (© 877/ 359-7947; www.swiss.com), have at least one flight per week from Calgary, Montréal, Toronto, or Vancouver via other European cities to Athens.

FROM EUROPE

IRELAND   Aer Lingus (© 01/836-5000 in Dublin; www.aerlingus.com) and **British Airways** (© 0345/222-111 in Belfast; www.britishairways.com) both fly to Athens via London's Heathrow. Less-expensive charters operate in the summer from Belfast and Dublin to Athens, less frequently to Corfu, Crete, Mykonos, and Rhodes. Contact any major travel agency for details. Students should contact **USIT,** at Aston Quay, Dublin 2 (© 01/602-1904), or at Fountain Centre, College Street, Belfast (© 02890/327-111).

UNITED KINGDOM   British Airways (© 0845/773-3377; www.ba.com), **Olympic Airways** (© 0870/606-0460; www.olympicairlines.com), and **Virgin Atlantic** (© 0870/380-2007; www.fly. virgin.com) offer several flights daily from London's Heathrow Airport. For the smaller companies offering no-frill flights, contact **EasyJet** (© 0870/600-0000; www.easyjet.com). Or consider the Flight Pass sold by **Europebyair** (in North America, © 888/321-4737; www.europe byair.com), which allows one-way flights for 129€ ($168) between Athens and several European cities (including Milan, Brussels, Bucharest). Several of the eastern European airlines, such as **CSA Czech Airlines** (© 0870/4443-747; www. czechairlines.co.uk), have offered cheaper alternatives, but in recent years the status of some has been in doubt; make inquiries at the time you are prepared to book. There are also connecting flights to Athens and to Thessaloniki via various airlines from Aberdeen, Belfast, Birmingham, Bristol, Edinburgh, Glasgow, Leeds, Liverpool, Newcastle, and Southampton, as well as flights to Athens and the major islands from Birmingham, Cardiff, Gatwick, Glasgow, Luton, and Manchester.

FROM AUSTRALIA & NEW ZEALAND

AUSTRALIA   Service to Athens is offered daily from Perth and Sydney and several times weekly from Brisbane and Melbourne by **Alitalia** (© 02/247-1308 in Sydney; www.alitalia.com), via Bangkok and Rome; **KLM Royal Dutch Airlines** (© 800/505-747 throughout Australia; www.klm.com), via Singapore and Amsterdam; **Lufthansa** (© 02/367-3800 in Sydney; www.lufthansa.com), via Frankfurt; and **Olympic Airways** (© 02/251-2204 in Sydney; www. olympicairlines.com), via Bangkok.

Generally, the lowest fares are offered by **Aeroflot** (© 02/233-7148 in Sydney; www.aeroflot.org), which provides weekly service from Sydney via Moscow; and by **Thai Airways** (© 02/844-0900 in Sydney; www.thaiair.com), which flies from Brisbane, Melbourne, Perth, and Sydney to Greece via Bangkok. **British Airways** (© 02/258-3000 in Sydney; www.british airways.com) and **Qantas Airways** (© 02/ 957-0111 in Sydney; www.qantas.com) have regular service to London; the "Global Explorer Pass" allows you to make up to six stopovers wherever the two airlines fly, except in South America.

NEW ZEALAND   Air New Zealand is the first choice (© 0800/737-000; www. airnewzealand.com). Other possibilities, which often involve stopovers and airline changes, include: **Singapore Airlines** (© 09/303-2506 in Auckland; www. singaporeair.com), with service via Singapore; **Thai Airways** (© 09/377-3886 in Auckland; www.thaiair.com), with service via Bangkok; **Qantas Airways** (© 09/ 303-3209 in Auckland; www.qantas. com); **Lufthansa** (© 09/303-1529 in Auckland); **British Airways** (© 09/367-7500 in Auckland; www.ba.com); and

Alitalia (© **09/379-4457** in Auckland; www.alitalia.com).

FROM SOUTH AFRICA

Olympic Airways (© **11/880-1614;** www.olympicairlines.com) offers the only direct flights to and from Johannesburg to Athens about three times a week. **Air France** (© **01/880-8040;** www.airfrance. com), **Alitalia** (© **01/880-9254;** www. alitalia.com), **British Airways** (© **01/ 975-3931;** www.ba.com), and **Ethiopian Airlines** (© 01/616-7624; www.ethiopian airlines.com) also offer occasional flights to and from Johannesburg, with connections via other foreign cities.

GETTING THERE BY SHIP

Most people who travel by ship to Greece from foreign ports come from Italy, although there is occasional service from Cyprus, Egypt, Israel, and Turkey. Brindisi to Patras is the most common ferry crossing, about a 10-hour voyage, with as many as seven departures a day in summer. There is also regular service, twice a day in summer, from Ancona and Bari, once daily from Otranto, and two or three times a week from Trieste or Venice. Most ferries stop at Corfu or Igoumenitsa, often at both; in summer, an occasional ship will also stop at Kefalonia.

If you want to learn more about the ferry services between Greece and foreign ports, the best website is Paleologos Agency's **www.ferries.gr**. Britons might try the London-based agency **Viamare Travel,** Graphic House, 2 Sumatra Rd., London NW6 1PU (© **0870/410-6040;** www.viamare.com). The **Superfast Ferries Line,** 157 Leoforos Alkyonidon, 16673 Athens (© **210/969-1100;** www. superfast.com), offers service between Ancona and Patras (17 hr.), or between Ancona and Igoumenitsa (15 hr.); also between Bari and Patras (12 hr.) or between Bari and Igoumenitsa (8 hr.). Not all these so-called superfast ferries actually save that much time if you take

into consideration boarding and debarking. In addition, their fares are almost twice as much as those of regular ferries.

On the regular ferries, one-way fares during high season from Brindisi to Patras at press time cost from about 75€ ($98) for a tourist-class deck chair to about 135€ ($176) per person to share an inside double cabin. Vehicles cost at least another 75€ to 150€ ($98–$195). *Note:* The lines usually offer considerable discounts on round-trip/return tickets. Fares to Igoumenitsa are considerably cheaper, but are by no means a better value unless your destination is nearby. Because of the number of shipping lines involved and the variations in schedules, we're not able to provide more concrete details. Consult a travel agent about the possibilities, book well ahead of time in summer, and reconfirm with the shipping line on the day of departure.

GETTING THERE BY CAR

It is unlikely that you will find it worthwhile to bring your own car all the way from North America to drive around Greece, but many Europeans do drive down into Greece—and perhaps some North Americans bring their rented cars in. Drivers often come from Italy via ferry, usually disembarking at Patras; the drive to Athens is about 210km (130 miles). Others enter from the former Yugoslavian Republic of Macedonia, or FYROM. (The road from Albania, although passable, doesn't attract many tourists.) There are no particular problems or delays at the border crossings, providing all your papers are in order.

If you come through Skopje, FYROM, the road via Titov Veles to the southeast leads to the border, where it picks up an expressway down to the edge of Thessaloniki (242km/150 miles). Over to the west, there is a decent enough road via Vitola, FYROM, that leads to Florina, Greece (290km/180 miles); that road

Street Names

The Greek word for "street" is *odos* and the word for "avenue" is *leoforos,* often abbreviated *Leof.,* usually applied to major thoroughfares. In practice, Greeks seldom employ either of those words—they just use the name. Also, Greeks customarily write the numbers after rather than before the street name. But in the interest of simplifying things, we provide the numbers before the names and drop the word "Odos" (as Greeks do). *Leoforos,* however, we retain as an indication of a major thoroughfare. By the way, *plateia*—think "place" or "plaza"—is Greek for "square," and usually means a large public square, such as Syntagma (Constitution) Square in Athens. Sometimes, however, a plateia may be little more than a wide area where important streets meet.

then continues east to Thessaloniki (another 161km/100 miles) or south to Kosani (another 89km/55 miles). A long day's drive!

In any case, arm yourself with a good up-to-date map such as the ones published by Baedeker, Hallwag, Michelin, or Freytag & Berndt.

DRIVING YOUR OWN VEHICLE To bring your own vehicle into Greece, valid registration papers, an international third-party insurance certificate, and a driver's license are required. Valid American and E.U. licenses are accepted in Greece. A free entry card allows you to keep your car in the country up to 4 months, after which another 8 months can be arranged without you paying import duty. Check with your own car insurance company to make sure you are fully covered.

CAR FERRIES Car ferry service is available on most larger ferries. There's regular service from Piraeus to Aegina and to Poros in the Saronic Gulf; most of the Cyclades; Chania and Iraklion on Crete; Hios; Kos; Lesvos; Rhodes; and Samos. For the Cyclades, crossing is shorter and less expensive from Rafina, an hour east of Athens. From Patras, there's daily service to Corfu, Ithaka, and Kefalonia. The Sporades have service from Ayios Konstandinos, Kimi, and

Volos (and then among the several islands). The short car ferry across the Gulf of Corinth from Rio to Antirio can save a lot of driving for those traveling between the northwest and the Peloponnese or Athens. There's also service between many of the islands, even between Crete and Rhodes, as well as car-crossing to and from Turkey between Hios and Çesme; Lesvos and Dikeli; and Samos and Kusadasi. (If you intend to continue on with your vehicle into Turkey or plan to enter Greece from Turkey, you should inquire long before setting off for either country, and make sure that you have all the necessary paperwork.)

GETTING THERE BY TRAIN

In the late 1990s, train service from western Europe was disrupted by the trouble in the Balkans. Even when running, the trains tend to be slow and also uncomfortable in the summer. But a Eurailpass is valid for connections all the way to Athens or Istanbul and includes the ferry service from Italy. Endless types of passes are now offered—long stays, short stays, and combinations with airlines, among others. Note that North Americans must purchase their Eurailpasses before arriving in Europe. For information, see **www. raileurope.com**, or call © **800/438-7245.**

6 Money & Costs

Greece is no longer the bargain country it once was, although it remains considerably cheaper than many major nations with advanced economies. Certainly for most visitors, the hotels and restaurants will be cheaper than in major cities such as New York or London. That said, you will be spending money day in and day out, so it is important to understand the ins and outs of how to handle your money.

CURRENCY

The currency in Greece is the **euro** (pronounced *evro* in Greek), abbreviated "Eu" and symbolized by €. (If you still own old Drachmas, it is no longer possible to exchange them.)

The euro € comes in 7 paper notes and 8 coins. The notes are in different sizes and colors. They are in the following denominations: 5, 10, 20, 50, 100, 200, and 500. (Considering that each euro is worth over $1, those last bills are quite pricey!) Six of the coins are officially "cents"—but in Greece they have become referred to as *lepta,* the old Greek name for sums smaller than the drachma. They come in different sizes and their value is: 1, 2, 5, 10, 20, and 50. There are also 1€ and 2€ coins.

Although one side of the coins differs in each of the member E.U. nations, all coins and bills are legal tender in all countries using the euro.

It's a good idea to exchange at least some money—just enough to cover airport incidentals and transportation to your hotel—before you leave home, so you can avoid lines at airport ATMs (automated teller machines). You can exchange money at your local American Express or Thomas Cook office or at some banks.

ATMs

The easiest and best way to get cash away from home is from an ATM. **Cirrus** (© 800/424-7787; www.mastercard. com) and **PLUS** (© 800/843-7587; www.visa.com) networks span the globe; look at the back of your bank card to see which network you're on, then call or check online for ATM locations at your destination. If your bank, credit, or debit card is affiliated with one of the major international credit cards (such as Master-Card or Visa), you should not have any trouble getting money in Greece; if in doubt, ask your bank or credit card company if your card will be acceptable in Greece. *Tip:* Greek ATMs use only numeric PINs (personal identification numbers), so you must know how to convert letters to numerals (see your familiar ATM). Also, Greek ATMs accept only a 4-digit PIN—you are advised to change yours before you go if yours is longer.

In commercial centers, airports, all cities and larger towns, and most tourist centers, you will find at least a couple of machines accepting a wide range of cards. Smaller towns will often have only one ATM—and it may not accept your card. **Commercial Bank (Emboriki Trapeza)**

(Tips) Small Change

When you change money, ask for some small bills or loose change. Petty cash will come in handy for tipping and public transportation. Consider keeping the change separate from your larger bills, so that it's readily accessible and you'll be less of a target for theft (by constantly revealing where on your person you are keeping your money).

Tips **Credit Cards in Greece**

Credit cards are effectively required for renting a car these days. In Greece, they are accepted in the better hotels and at most shops. *Note:* Even many of the better restaurants in major cities do *not* accept credit cards, and certainly most restaurants and smaller hotels in Greece do not accept them. Also, some hotels that require a credit card number when you make advance reservations will demand payment in cash; inquire beforehand if this will be the case.

services PLUS and Visa; **Credit Bank (Trapeza Pisteos)** accepts Visa and American Express; **National Bank (Ethiniki Trapeza)** takes Cirrus and MasterCard/Access.

Transaction fees are usually built into the exchange rate you get; in any case, exchange rates are usually based on the wholesale rates of the major banks, so you may actually save money by withdrawing larger sums and paying your bills in cash. However, just as at home, there is usually a limit on how much you can withdraw in a single day; find out what it is before departure. Note, too, that the sums withdrawn are designated on the ATM screen in euros, not other currencies. Also keep in mind that most banks now impose a fee every time a card is used at a different bank's ATM, and that fee can be higher for international transactions (up to $5 or more) than for domestic ones (where they're rarely more than $2). On top of this, the bank from which you are withdrawing the cash may charge its own fee. To compare banks' ATM fees within the U.S., use www.bankrate.com. For international withdrawal fees, ask your bank.

CURRENCY EXCHANGE OFFICES

Private and commercial foreign-exchange offices are found in major cities, larger towns, and centers of tourism throughout Greece. They are generally competitive, but their rates vary, so shop around if you must use one.

CREDIT & DEBIT CARDS

Credit cards are another safe way to carry money. They also provide a convenient record of all your expenses, and they generally offer relatively good exchange rates. You can withdraw cash advances from your credit cards at banks or ATMs provided you know your PIN. (If you've forgotten yours, or didn't even know you had one, call the number on the back of your credit card and ask the bank to send it to you. It usually takes 5 to 7 business days, though some banks will provide the number over the phone if you tell them your mother's maiden name or some other personal information.) Your credit card company will likely charge a commission (1% or 2%) on every foreign purchase you make, but you may be getting a good deal with credit cards when you factor in things like ATM fees and higher traveler's check exchange rates, but high fees make credit-card cash advances a pricey way to get cash. Keep in mind that you'll pay interest from the moment of your withdrawal, even if you pay your monthly bills on time. Also, note that many banks now assess a 1%-to-3% "transaction fee" on **all** charges you incur abroad (whether you're using the local currency or your native currency).

In Greece, Visa and MasterCard are the most widely accepted cards. Diners Club is less widely accepted. And American Express is still less frequently accepted because it charges a higher commission

---

Tips Dear Visa: I'm Off to Mykonos!

There are increasing reports of American travelers abroad who discover that their credit cards are invalidated after their first purchase: An automated security system "kicks in" to protect you on the assumption that your card has been stolen. To be sure this won't happen, call your credit card company or the bank that issued it and inform them of your impending trip. Even if you don't call your credit card company in advance, you can always call the card's toll-free emergency number (see "Fast Facts: Greece," at the end of this chapter) if a charge is refused—a good reason to carry the phone number with you. But perhaps the most important lesson is to carry more than one card on your trip. If one card doesn't work for any number of reasons, you'll have a backup.

---

and is more protective of the cardholder in disagreements.

TRAVELER'S CHECKS

Traveler's checks are something of an anachronism from the days before the ATM made cash accessible at any time. Traveler's checks used to be the only sound alternative to traveling with dangerously large amounts of cash. They were as reliable as currency but, unlike cash, they could be replaced if lost or stolen.

It should also be said that although in Greece today most hotels and shops still accept traveler's checks, many no longer do, and in any case they usually charge a small commission or give a poor exchange rate. Do not expect any Greek operations to cash your traveler's checks, however, unless you are paying for their services or goods.

You can buy traveler's checks at most banks. They are offered in denominations of $20, $50, $100, $500, and sometimes $1,000. Generally, you'll pay a service charge ranging from 1% to 4%.

The most popular traveler's checks are offered by **American Express.** Visit **www. americanexpress.com** to order online or call *©* **800/221-7282;** this number accepts collect calls from Amex cardholders and offers service in several foreign languages; Amex gold and platinum cardholders are also exempted from the 1% fee); **Visa** (*©* **800/732-1322**)—AAA members can obtain Visa checks for a $9.95 fee (for checks up to $1,500) at most AAA offices or by calling *©* **866/ 339-3378;** and **MasterCard** (*©* **800/ 223-9920**).

American Express, Thomas Cook, Visa, and **MasterCard** offer **foreign currency traveler's checks,** useful if you're traveling to one country or to the euro zone; they're accepted at locations where dollar checks may not be.

Be sure to keep a record of the traveler's checks serial numbers separate from your checks in the event that they are stolen or lost. You'll get a refund faster if you know the numbers.

Another option is the new prepaid traveler's check cards, reloadable cards that work much like debit cards but aren't linked to your checking account. The **American Express Travelers Cheque Card,** for example, requires a minimum deposit, sets a maximum balance, and has a one-time issuance fee of $14.95. You can withdraw money from an ATM (for a fee of $2.50 per transaction, not including bank fees), and the funds can be purchased in dollars, euros, or pounds. If you lose the card, your available funds will be refunded within 24 hours.

EMERGENCY CASH

In an emergency, you can arrange to send money from home to a Greek bank. Telex transfers from the United Kingdom usually take at least 3 days and sometimes up to a week, with a charge of about 3%. Bank drafts are more expensive but potentially faster if you are in Athens. From Canada and the United States, money can be wired by **Western Union**

(✆ 800/325-6000) or **MoneyGram** (✆ 800/543-4080). In Greece, call Western Union in the United States (✆ 001-314/298-2313) to learn the location of an office. For MoneyGram, call the head office in Athens (✆ 01/322-0005). For a fee (4%–10%, depending on the sum involved), money can be available in minutes at an agent for Western Union or MoneyGram.

7 Travel Insurance

Greece presents no special problems when it comes to insurable "incidents," but it should be noted that most Greeks do not carry very much insurance so you will not be able to collect much if you are in an accident. Check your existing homeowner's, medical, and automobile insurance policies as well as your credit card coverage before you buy travel insurance. You may already be covered for lost luggage, canceled tickets, or medical expenses. If you are prepaying for your trip or taking a flight that has cancellation penalties, consider cancellation insurance.

The cost of travel insurance varies widely, depending on the destination, the cost and length of your trip, your age and health, and the type of trip you're taking, but expect to pay between 5% and 8% of the vacation itself. You can get estimates from various providers through **InsureMy Trip.com.** Enter your trip cost and dates, your age, and other information, for prices from more than a dozen companies.

U.K. citizens and their families who make more than one trip abroad per year may find an annual travel insurance policy works out cheaper. Check **www.money supermarket.com**, which compares prices across a wide range of providers for single- and multi-trip policies.

Most big travel agents offer their own insurance and will probably try to sell you their package when you book a holiday. Think before you sign. **Britain's Consumers' Association** recommends

that you insist on seeing the policy and reading the fine print before buying travel insurance. **The Association of British Insurers** (✆ 020/7600-3333; www.abi. org.uk) gives advice by phone and publishes *Holiday Insurance,* a free guide to policy provisions and prices. You might also shop around for better deals: Try **Columbus Direct** (✆ 0870/033-9988; www.columbusdirect.net).

TRIP-CANCELLATION INSURANCE

Trip-cancellation insurance will help retrieve your money if you have to back out of a trip or depart early, or if your travel supplier goes bankrupt. Trip cancellation traditionally covers such events as sickness, natural disasters, and State Department advisories. The latest news in trip-cancellation insurance is the availability of **expanded hurricane coverage** and the **"any-reason"** cancellation coverage—which costs more but covers cancellations made for any reason. You won't get back 100% of your prepaid trip cost, but you'll be refunded a substantial portion. **TravelSafe** (✆ 888/885-7233; www.travelsafe.com) offers both types of coverage. Expedia also offers any-reason cancellation coverage for its air-hotel packages.

For details, contact one of the following recommended insurers: **Access America** (✆ 866/807-3982; www.accessamerica. com); **Travel Guard International**

(© 800/826-4919; www.travelguard.com); **Travel Insured International** (© 800/243-3174; www.travelinsured.com); and **Travelex Insurance Services** (© 888/457-4602; www.travelex-insurance.com).

MEDICAL INSURANCE

For travel overseas, most U.S. health plans (including Medicare and Medicaid) do not provide coverage, and the ones that do often require you to pay for services upfront and reimburse you only after you return home.

As a safety net, you may want to buy travel medical insurance, particularly if you're traveling to a remote or high-risk area where emergency evacuation might be necessary. If you require additional medical insurance, try **MEDEX Assistance** (© 410/453-6300; www.medexassist.com) or **Travel Assistance International** (© 800/821-2828; www.travelassistance.com; for general information on services, call the company's **Worldwide Assistance Services, Inc.**, at © 800/777-8710).

Canadians should check with their provincial health plan offices or call

Health Canada (© 866/225-0709; www.hc-sc.gc.ca) to find out the extent of their coverage and what documentation and receipts they must take home in case they are treated overseas.

LOST-LUGGAGE INSURANCE

On international flights (including U.S. portions of international trips), baggage coverage is limited to approximately $9.07 per pound, up to approximately $635 per checked bag. If you plan to check items more valuable than what's covered by the standard liability, see if your homeowner's policy covers your valuables, get baggage insurance as part of your comprehensive travel-insurance package, or buy Travel Guard's "BagTrak" product.

If your luggage is lost, immediately file a lost-luggage claim at the airport, detailing the luggage contents. Most airlines require that you report delayed, damaged, or lost baggage within 4 hours of arrival. The airlines are required to deliver luggage, once found, directly to your house or destination free of charge.

8 Health

GENERAL AVAILABILITY OF HEALTHCARE

There are no immunization requirements for getting into Greece, though it's always a good idea to have polio, tetanus, and typhoid covered when traveling anywhere. In Greece, modern hospitals, clinics, and pharmacies are to be found everywhere, and personnel, equipment, and supplies ensure excellent treatment. Dental care is also widely available. Most doctors in Greece can speak English (having trained in England or the U.K.) or some other European language.

PRESCRIPTIONS Pack **prescription medications** in your carry-on luggage, and carry prescription medications in

their original containers, with pharmacy labels—otherwise they might not make it through airport security. (Even pills with codeine—such as those sold over-the-counter in Canada—might be questioned.) Also bring along copies of your prescriptions in case you lose your pills or run out. Don't forget an extra pair of contact lenses or prescription glasses. Carry the generic names of prescription medicines, in case a local pharmacist is unfamiliar with the brand name.

COMMON AILMENTS Diarrhea is no more a problem in Greece than it might be anytime you change diet and water supplies, but visitors occasionally experience it. Common over-the-counter

Avoiding "Economy-Class Syndrome"

Deep vein thrombosis, or as it's known in the world of flying, "economy-class syndrome," is a blood clot that develops in a deep vein. It's a potentially deadly condition that can be caused by sitting in cramped conditions—such as an airplane cabin—for too long. During a flight (especially a long-haul flight), get up, walk around, and stretch your legs every 60 to 90 minutes to keep your blood flowing. Other preventative measures include frequent flexing of the legs while sitting, drinking lots of water, and avoiding alcohol and sleeping pills. If you have a history of deep vein thrombosis, heart disease, or any other condition that puts you at high risk, some experts recommend wearing compression stockings or taking anticoagulants when you fly. Always ask your physician about the best course for you. Symptoms of deep vein thrombosis include leg pain or swelling, or even shortness of breath.

preventatives and cures are available in Greek pharmacies, but if you are concerned, bring your own. (Cola soft drinks are said to help those with digestive difficulties from too much olive oil in their food.) If you expect to be taking sea trips and are inclined to get seasick, bring a preventative. Allergy sufferers should carry antihistamines, especially in the spring.

SUN Between mid-June and September, too much exposure to the sun during midday could well lead to sunstroke or heatstroke. Sunscreen and a hat are strongly advised.

DIETARY RED FLAGS Nothing in the Greek diet requires any special warning. Greece's natural water is excellent, although these days you will usually be served—and charged for—bottled water. Milk is pasteurized, though refrigeration is sometimes not the best, especially in out-of-the-way places. Greece is not equipped to serve kosher meals.

BUGS, BITES & OTHER WILDLIFE CONCERNS There is no particular risk of poisonous bites, although mosquitoes can occasionally be a nuisance: You might well travel with some "bug-off" substance. Dogs, by the way, should not present a danger of rabies, but you are

strongly advised not to reach out and touch the dogs that roam around Greece.

WHAT TO DO IF YOU GET SICK AWAY FROM HOME

If you suffer from a chronic illness, consult your doctor about your travel plans before your departure. For conditions like epilepsy, diabetes, or heart problems, wear a **MedicAlert** identification tag (www.medicalert.org), which will immediately alert doctors to your condition and give them access to your records through MedicAlert's 24-hour hot line. Before setting off, contact **MedicAlert** (from within North America © **888/633-4298** or from abroad at 209/668-3333). If you have special concerns, before heading abroad you might check out the United States **Centers for Disease Control and Prevention** (© **800/311-3435**; www.cdc.gov/travel. You can find advice on health and medical situations in foreign lands as well as listings of reliable medical clinics overseas at the **International Society of Travel Medicine** (www.istm.org).

You can also contact the **International Association for Medical Assistance to Travelers** (IAMAT; © 716/754-4883 or, in Canada, 416/652-0137; www.iamat. org) for tips on travel and health concerns in the countries you're visiting, and for lists of local, English-speaking doctors. **Travel Health Online** (www.tripprep.com), sponsored by a consortium of travel medicine practitioners, may also offer helpful advice on traveling abroad.

Any foreign embassy or consulate can provide a list of area doctors who speak English. If you get sick, consider asking your hotel front desk to recommend a local doctor—even his or her own. You can also try the emergency room at a local hospital. In addition, many hospitals have walk-in clinics for emergency cases that are not life-threatening; you may not get immediate attention, but you won't pay the high price of an emergency room visit. For major cities in Greece, the phone numbers and addresses for hospitals or medical centers are given in the relevant "Fast Facts" section in each destination chapter. In an emergency, call a **first-aid center** (© **166**), the nearest **hospital** (© **106**), or the **tourist police** (© **171**).

Emergency treatment is usually given free of charge in state hospitals, but be warned that only basic needs are met. The care in outpatient clinics, which are usually open mornings (8am–noon), is often somewhat better; you can find them next to most major hospitals, on some islands, and occasionally in rural areas, usually indicated by prominent signs.

Greeks have national medical insurance. Citizens of other E.U. nations should inquire before leaving, but your policies will probably cover treatment in Greece. Non-E.U. travelers should check your health plan to see if it provides appropriate coverage; you may want to buy **travel medical insurance** instead. (See the section on insurance, above.) Bring your insurance ID card with you when you travel. Although you will receive emergency care with no questions asked, make sure you have coverage at home.

9 Safety

STAYING SAFE

Greece is undeniably exposed to earthquakes, but there are few known instances of tourists being injured or killed in one of these. Of far more potential danger are automobile accidents: Greece has one of the worst vehicle accident rates in Europe. You should exercise great caution when driving over unfamiliar, often winding, and often poorly maintained roads. This holds true especially when you're driving at night. As for those who insist on renting motorbikes or similar vehicles, at the very least wear a helmet.

Crime directed at tourists was traditionally unheard of in Greece but in more recent years there have been occasional reports of cars broken into, pickpockets, purse-snatchers, and the like. (Ask yourself whether it is necessary to travel with

irreplaceable valuables like jewelry.) Normal precautions are called for. For instance, if you have hand luggage containing truly expensive items, whether jewelry or cameras, never give it to an individual unless you are absolutely sure it will be safe with him or her. Tourists who report crimes to the local police will probably feel that they are not being taken all that seriously, but it is more likely that the Greek police have realized there is little they can do without solid identification of the culprits. As for the other side of the coin—police being exceptionally hard on foreigners, say, when enforcing traffic violations—although there is the rare reported incident, it does not seem to be widespread.

Drugs, however, are a different story: The Greek authorities and laws are extremely tough when it comes to foreigners with drugs—starting with marijuana. Do *not* attempt to bring any illicit drug into or out of Greece.

DEALING WITH HOSTILITY

There is no denying that many Greeks are opposed to American foreign policies in recent years, but there are no reported incidents of attacks on individual travelers.

That said, if you get to speaking with Greeks who dislike American policies, they will not be bashful about expressing their opinions or challenging yours.

10 Specialized Travel Resources

TRAVELERS WITH DISABILITIES

Increasingly, people with physical disabilities who travel abroad will find more options and resources out there than ever before. That said, few concessions exist for travelers with disabilities in Greece. Steep steps, uneven pavements, almost no cuts at curbstones, few ramps, narrow walks, slick stone, and traffic congestion can cause problems. Archaeological sites are, by their very nature, difficult to navigate, and crowded public transportation can be all but impossible.

The new airport and the new Athens Metro system are, however, wheelchair accessible, and thanks to the 2004 Olympics, an elevator now can take wheelchair-bound individuals to the top of the Acropolis; but even this requires that the wheelchair be pushed up a path. More modern and private facilities are only now beginning to provide ramps, but little else has been done. Increasingly, too, hotels are setting aside rooms that they advertise as "disability friendly" or "handicap accessible" but some of these may mean nothing more than handrails in the bathtub. That said, foreigners in wheelchairs accompanied by companions are becoming a more common sight in Greece. Several travel agencies now offer customized tours and itineraries for travelers with disabilities, but none as yet offer such services for Greece.

Organizations that offer a vast range of resources and assistance to disabled travelers include **MossRehab** (© **800/CALL-MOSS;** www.mossresourcenet.org); the **American Foundation for the Blind**

(AFB; © **800/232-5463;** www.afb.org); and **SATH** (Society for Accessible Travel & Hospitality; © **212/447-7284;** www.sath.org). **AirAmbulanceCard.com** is now partnered with SATH and allows you to preselect top-notch hospitals in case of an emergency.

Access-Able Travel Source (© **303/232-2979;** www.access-able.com) offers a comprehensive database on travel agents from around the world with experience in accessible travel; destination-specific access information; and links to such resources as service animals, equipment rentals, and access guides.

Many travel agencies offer customized tours and itineraries for travelers with disabilities. Among them are **Flying Wheels Travel** (© **507/451-5005;** www.flyingwheelstravel.com) and **Accessible Journeys** (© **800/846-4537** or 610/521-0339; www.disabilitytravel.com).

Flying with Disability (www.flying-with-disability.org) is a comprehensive information source on airplane travel. **Avis Rent a Car** (© **888/879-4273**) has an "Avis Access" program that offers services for customers with special travel needs. These include specially outfitted vehicles with swivel seats, spinner knobs, and hand controls; mobility scooter rentals; and accessible bus service. Be sure to reserve well in advance.

Also check out the quarterly magazine ***Emerging Horizons*** (www.emerginghorizons.com), available by subscription ($16.95 year U.S.; $21.95 outside the U.S.).

The "Accessible Travel" link at **Mobility-Advisor.com** (www.mobility-advisor.com) offers a variety of travel resources to disabled persons.

British travelers should contact **Holiday Care** (© 0845/124-9971 in the U.K. only; www.holidaycare.org.uk) to access a wide range of travel information and resources for disabled and elderly people.

GAY & LESBIAN TRAVELERS

Greece—or at least parts of Greece—has a long tradition of being tolerant of homosexual men and in recent years these locales, at least, have extended this tolerance to lesbians. But it should be said: Although Greeks in Athens, Piraeus, and a few other major cities may not care one way or the other, Greeks in small towns and villages—indeed, most Greeks—do not appreciate flagrant displays of dress or behavior. Among the best-known hangouts for gays and lesbians are Mykonos, Mitilini (Lesvos), and Chania, Crete, but gays and lesbians travel all over Greece without any particular issues. That said, the age of consent for sexual relations with homosexuals is 17 and this can be strictly enforced against foreigners.

The **International Gay and Lesbian Travel Association (IGLTA;** © 800/448-8550 or 954/776-2626; www.iglta.org) is the trade association for the gay and lesbian travel industry, and offers an online directory of gay- and lesbian-friendly travel businesses and tour operators.

Many agencies offer tours and travel itineraries specifically for gay and lesbian travelers. **Above and Beyond Tours** (© 800/397-2681; www.abovebeyond tours.com) are gay Australia tour specialists. San Francisco–based **Now, Voyager** (© 800/255-6951; www.nowvoyager. com) offers worldwide trips and cruises, and **Olivia** (© 800/631-6277; www. olivia.com) offers lesbian cruises and resort vacations.

Gay.com Travel (© 800/929-2268 or 415/644-8044; www.gay.com/travel or www.outandabout.com), is an excellent online successor to the popular *Out & About* print magazine. It provides regularly updated information about gay-owned, gay-oriented, and gay-friendly lodging, dining, sightseeing, nightlife, and shopping establishments in every important destination worldwide. British travelers should click on the "Travel" link at **www.uk.gay.com** for advice and gay-friendly trip ideas.

The Canadian website **GayTraveler (gaytraveler.ca)** offers ideas and advice for gay travel all over the world.

The following travel guides are available at many bookstores, or you can order them from any online bookseller: *Spartacus International Gay Guide, 35th Edition* (Bruno Gmünder Verlag; www. spartacusworld.com/gayguide) and *Odysseus: The International Gay Travel Planner, 17th Edition* (www.odyusa. com); and the *Damron* guides (www. damron.com), with separate, annual books for gay men and lesbians.

In Greece, the Athens, information about the **Hellenic Homosexual Liberation Movement (AKOE)** can be contacted at P.O. Box 26022 Athens 10022 (© 210/771/9221). The *Greek Gay Guide,* published by Kraximo Press, P.O. Box 4228, 10210 Athens (© 210/362-5249), can be purchased at some kiosks.

SENIOR TRAVEL

Greece does not offer many discounts for seniors. Some museums and archaeological sites offer discounts for those 60 and over, but the practice is unpredictable, and in general these are restricted to citizens of E.U. nations. *Tip:* We've heard reports of car rental agencies in Europe that will not rent to people over a certain age—usually 75 but as young as 70. Inquire beforehand.

For general information before you go, visit the U.S. Department of State website at http://travel.state.gov for information specifically for older Americans.

Try mentioning the fact that you're a senior when you make your travel reservations. Although almost all major U.S. airlines have canceled their senior discount and coupon-book programs, many hotels continue to offer discounts for seniors.

Members of **AARP** (formerly known as the American Association of Retired Persons), 601 E St. NW, Washington, DC 20049 (© **888/687-2277;** www.aarp.org), get discounts on hotels, airfares, and car rentals. AARP offers members a wide range of benefits, including *AARP: The Magazine* and a monthly newsletter. Anyone over 50 can join.

Many reliable agencies and organizations target the 50-plus market. **Elderhostel** (© **800/454-5768;** www.elderhostel.org) arranges study programs for those ages 55 and over (and a spouse or companion of any age) in the U.S. and in more than 80 countries around the world. Most courses last 5 to 7 days in the U.S. (2–4 weeks abroad), and many include airfare, accommodations in university dormitories or modest inns, meals, and tuition. In Greece, groups typically settle in one area for a week or so, with excursions that focus on getting to know the history and culture. **ElderTreks** (© **800/741-7956;** www.eldertreks.com) offers small-group tours to off-the-beaten-path or adventure-travel locations, restricted to travelers 50 and older. Britons might prefer to deal with **Saga Holidays** (Saga Building, Folkestone, Kent CT20 1AZ; © **0800/096-0084;** www.saga.co.uk), which offers all-inclusive tours in Greece for those ages 50 and older.

Recommended publications offering travel resources and discounts for seniors include *Travel 50 & Beyond* (www.travel50andbeyond.com) and the best-selling paperback *Unbelievably Good Deals and Great Adventures That You Absolutely Can't Get Unless You're Over 50* (McGraw-Hill, 2003) by Joan Rattner Heilman.

FAMILY TRAVEL

If you have enough trouble getting your kids out of the house in the morning, dragging them thousands of miles away may seem an insurmountable challenge. But family travel can be immensely rewarding, giving you new ways of seeing the world through smaller pairs of eyes.

How to Take Great Trips with Your Kids (Harvard Common Press)—published in 1983 but revised in 1995—is packed with good, still relevant general advice that can apply to travel anywhere.

Set goals for your family for your travels in Greece. The whole family can head for the beaches. At the other extreme, however, think twice about taking younger kids along on a full-day exploration of museums and archaeological sites. Travel with infants and very young children—say up to about age 5—can work; most children ages 6 to 16 become restless at historical sites. If you're lucky, your children may tune into history at some point in their teens.

There are the occasional "kid-friendly" distractions in Greece: playgrounds all over the place; water parks here and there; and zoos. Greeks boys now play pickup basketball even in small towns—if your kids go for that, it's a great way to be quickly accepted. The kid-friendly icons throughout the book indicate places we feel might appeal to young people.

Most hotels allow children under 6 a free bed or cot in your room, and offer reduced prices for children under about 12. Some museums have children's prices, but by and large, Greece is not set up to offer reductions at every turn.

As for passport requirements for children, see "Entry Requirements & Customs," earlier in this chapter (or go to the State Department's website, www.travel.state.gov). If you are traveling with children other than your own, you must be sure you have full identification as well as notarized authorization from their parents.

Familyhostel (© 800/733-9753) takes the whole family, including kids ages 8 to 15, on moderately priced domestic and international learning vacations. Lectures, field trips, and sightseeing are guided by a team of academics.

Recommended family-travel Internet sites are **Family Travel Forum** (www.familytravelforum.com), a comprehensive site that offers customized trip-planning; **Family Travel Network** (www.familytravelnetwork.com), an award-winning site that offers travel features, deals, and tips; **Traveling Internationally with Your Kids** (www.travelwithyourkids.com), a comprehensive site offering sound advice for long-distance and international travel with children; and **Family Travel Files** (www.thefamilytravelfiles.com), which offers an online magazine and a directory of off-the-beaten-path tours and tour operators for families.

To locate those accommodations, restaurants, and attractions in Greece that are particularly kid-friendly, look for the "Kids" icon throughout this guide.

FEMALE TRAVELERS

Women traveling in Greece will not run into any situations particularly different from those encountered by men except while visiting monasteries and some churches, when women will be held to stricter dress codes and may even be denied entry.

That said, young women—especially singles or small groups—may well find Greek men coming on to them, especially at beaches, clubs, and other tourist locales. But our informants tell us that, in general, Greek men (a) do not attempt any physical contact; and (b) respect "No." One tactic said to work for women is to say, "I'm a Greek-American." The other advice is not to leave well-attended locales with someone you don't really know. Women should also be aware that some cafes and even restaurants are effectively male-only haunts; the men will not appreciate attempts by foreign women to enter these places.

Women Welcome Women World Wide (www.womenwelcomewomen.org.uk) works to foster international friendships by enabling women of different countries to visit one another. (Men can come along on the trips; they just can't join the club.) The big, active organization has more than 3,500 members from all walks of life in some 70 countries.

Check out the award-winning website **Journeywoman** (www.journeywoman.com), a "real life" women's travel information network where you can sign up for a free e-mail newsletter and get advice on everything from etiquette to dress to safety; or try the travel guide *Safety and Security for Women Who Travel,* by Sheila Swan Laufer and Peter Laufer (Travelers' Tales, 1998), offering common-sense advice and tips on safe travel.

AFRICAN-AMERICAN TRAVELERS

African Americans (and other people of color) have not been traveling to Greece in large numbers but this has been gradually changing. In any case, they should not expect to experience any discrimination—rather, more a curiosity on the part of individual Greeks, who simply are not accustomed to dealing with African Americans. Outside major cities you might be stared at.

Go Girl: The Black Woman's Guide to Travel & Adventure (Eighth Mountain Press) is a compilation of travel essays by writers including Jill Nelson and Audre Lorde. *The African-American*

Travel Guide by Wayne C. Robinson (Hunter Publishing) was published in 1997, so it may be somewhat dated. *Travel and Enjoy Magazine* (ⓒ 866/266-6211; www.travelandenjoy.com) is a travel magazine and guide. The well-done *Pathfinders Magazine* (ⓒ 877/977-PATH; www.pathfinderstravel.com) includes articles on everything from Rio de Janeiro to Ghana to upcoming ski, diving, golf, and tennis trips.

STUDENT TRAVEL

In Greece, students with proper identification (ISIC and IYC cards) are given reduced entrance fees to archaeological sites and museums, as well as discounts on admission to most artistic events, theatrical performances, and festivals. So you'd be wise to arm yourself with an **International Student Identity Card (ISIC)**, which offers substantial savings on rail passes, plane tickets, and entrance fees. It also provides you with basic health and life insurance and a 24-hour help line. The card is available for $22 from **STA Travel** (ⓒ 800/781-4040; www.sta.com or www.statravel.com), the biggest student travel agency in the world.

The **International Student Travel Confederation** (ISTC; www.istc.org) was formed in 1949 to make travel around the world more affordable for students. Check out its website for comprehensive travel services information for students.

If you're no longer a student but are still under 26, you can get an **International Youth Travel Card (IYTC)** from the same people, which entitles you to some discounts. **Travel CUTS** (ⓒ 800/592-2887; www.travelcuts.com) offers similar services for both Canadians and U.S. residents. Irish students may prefer to turn to **USIT** (ⓒ 01/602-1904; www.usit.ie), an Ireland-based specialist in student, youth, and independent travel.

In the United States, one of the major organizations for arranging overseas study for college-age students is the **Council on International Education Exchange,** or **CIEE** (ⓒ 800/407-8839; www.ciee.org).

A Hostelling International membership can save students money in some 5,000 hostels in 70 countries, where sex-segregated, dormitory-style sleeping quarters cost about $15 to $35 per night. In the United States, membership is available through **Hostelling International–American Youth Hostels,** 8401 Colesville Rd., Silver Spring, MD 20910 (ⓒ 301/495-1240; www.hiayh.org). A 1-year membership is free for ages 17 and under; $28 for ages 18 to 54; $18 for ages 55 and over.

In Greece, an International Guest Card can be obtained at the **Greek Association of Youth Hostels (OESE),** in Athens at 75 Dhamereos Athens 11633 (ⓒ 210/751-9530; www.athens-yhostel.com).

SINGLE TRAVELERS

Single travelers are usually hit with a single supplement to the base price for package vacations and cruises, while the price of a single room is almost always well over half that for a double. To avoid such charges, you might consider agreeing to room with other single travelers or to find a compatible roommate from one of the many roommate locator agencies before you go.

Travel Buddies Singles Travel Club (ⓒ 800/998-9099; www.travelbuddies worldwide.com), based in Canada, runs small, intimate, single-friendly group trips and will match you with a roommate free of charge. **TravelChums** (ⓒ 212/787-2621; www.travelchums.com) is an Internet-only travel-companion matching service with elements of an online personals-type site, hosted by the respected New York–based Shaw Guides travel service.

Many reputable tour companies offer singles-only trips. **Singles Travel International** (ⓒ 877/765-6874; www.singles travelintl.com) offers singles-only escorted tours to places like the Greek Islands. **Backroads** (℡ **800/462-2848;** www.back roads.com) offers "Singles + Solos" active-travel trips to destinations worldwide.

For more information, check out Eleanor Berman's classic *Traveling Solo: Advice and Ideas for More Than 250 Great Vacations, 5th Edition* (Globe Pequot), updated in 2005.

VEGETARIAN TRAVELERS

Vegetarians should find the Greek menu especially varied, as so many tasty vegetables, grains, and fruits are available; all except vegans will also enjoy the seafood and yogurt.

Happy Cow's Vegetarian Guide to Restaurants & Health Food Stores (www.happycow.net) has a restaurant guide with more than 6,000 restaurants in 100 countries. **VegDining.com** also lists vegetarian restaurants (with profiles) around the world. **Vegetarian Vacations** (www.vegetarian-vacations.com) offers vegetarian tours and itineraries.

11 Sustainable Tourism/Ecotourism

Sustainable Tourism—aka Ecotourism, Responsible Travel, Green Travel, and Eco-Holidays—is fast becoming a major force in international tourism. It takes many forms. Thus, each time you take a flight or drive a car CO_2 is released into the atmosphere. You can help neutralize this danger to our planet through "carbon offsetting"—paying someone to reduce your CO_2 emissions by the same amount you've added. Carbon offsets can be purchased in the U.S. from companies such as **Carbonfund.org** (www.carbonfund.org) and **TerraPass** (www.terrapass.org), and from **Climate Care** (www.climate care.org) in the U.K.

Although one could argue that any vacation that includes an airplane flight can't be truly "green," you can go on holiday and still contribute positively to the environment. You can offset carbon emissions from your flight in other ways. Choose forward-looking companies that embrace responsible development practices, helping preserve destinations for the future by working alongside local people. An increasing number of sustainable tourism initiatives can help you plan a family trip and leave as small a "footprint" as possible on the places you visit.

Responsible Travel (www.responsible travel.com) contains a great source of sustainable travel ideas run by a spokesperson for responsible tourism in the travel industry. **Sustainable Travel International** (www.sustainabletravelinternational.org) promotes responsible tourism practices and issues an annual Green Gear & Gift Guide.

You can find eco-friendly travel tips, statistics, and touring companies and associations—listed by destination under "Travel Choice"—at the TIES website, www.ecotourism.org. Also check out **Conservation International** (www.conservation.org)—which, with *National Geographic Traveler,* annually presents **World Legacy Awards** (www.wlaward.org) to the travel tour operators, businesses, organizations, and places that have made a significant contribution to sustainable tourism. **Ecotravel.com** is part online magazine and part ecodirectory that lets you search for touring companies in several categories (water-based, land-based, spiritually oriented, and so on).

In the U.K., **Tourism Concern** (www.tourismconcern.org.uk) works to reduce social and environmental problems connected to tourism and find ways of improving tourism so that local benefits are increased.

The **Association of British Travel Agents** (**ABTA;** www.abtamembers.org) acts as a focal point for the U.K. travel

Frommers.com: The Complete Travel Resource

For an excellent travel-planning resource, we highly recommend Frommers. com (www.frommers.com), voted Best Travel Site by *PC Magazine*. We're a little biased, of course, but we guarantee that you'll find the travel tips, reviews, monthly vacation giveaways, bookstore, and online-booking capabilities indispensable. Among the special features are our popular **Destinations** section, where you'll get expert travel tips, hotel and dining recommendations, and advice on the sights to see for more than 3,500 destinations around the globe; **Frommers.com Newsletter,** with the latest deals, travel trends, and money-saving secrets; our **Community** area featuring **Message Boards,** where Frommer's readers post queries and share advice (sometimes our authors show up to answer questions); and our **Photo Center,** where you can post and share vacation tips. When your research is done, the **Online Reservations System** (www.frommers.com/ book_a_trip) takes you to Frommer's preferred online partners for booking your vacation at affordable prices.

industry and is one of the leading groups spearheading responsible tourism.

The **Association of Independent Tour Operators** (**AITO;** www.aito.co.uk) is a group of interesting specialist operators leading the field in making holidays sustainable.

12 Staying Connected ·

TELEPHONES

Until the late 1990s in Greece, most foreigners went to the offices of the Telecommunications Organization of Greece (OTE, pronounced oh-tay, or Organismos Tilepikinonion tis Ellados) to place most of their phone calls, especially overseas. But because phone cards are now so widespread throughout Greece, this is no longer necessary, once you get the hang of using them. You must first purchase a phone card at an OTE office or at most kiosks. (If you expect to make any phone calls while in Greece, buy one at the airport's OTE office upon arrival.) The cards come in various denominations, from 3€ ($3.90) to 25€ ($33). The more costly the card, the cheaper the units.

The cost of a call with a phone card varies greatly depending on local, domestic, and international rates. A local call of up to 3 minutes to a fixed phone costs about .10€ (13¢), which is 3 units from a phone card; for each minute beyond that, it costs another .06€ (10¢) or 2 units off the card (so that a 10-min. local call costs 17 units or .52€/.68¢).

All calls, even to the house next door, cost Greeks something, so if you use someone's telephone even for a local call, offer to pay the charges.

In cities and larger towns, kiosks have telephones from which you can make local calls for .10€ (13¢) for 3 minutes. (In remote areas, you can make long-distance calls from these phones.) A few of the older public pay phones that required coins are still around, but it's better to buy a phone card. If you must use an older pay phone, deposit the required coin and listen for a dial tone, an irregular beep. A regular beep indicates that the line is busy.

Note: As of November 2002, all phone numbers in Greece have 10 digits. All (except for mobile phones—see below) also precede the city/area code with a 2 and end that with a 0. For example, since the Athens city code was originally 1, it is now 210, followed by a seven-digit number, but most other numbers in Greece are six digits. In all cases, even if you are calling someone in the same building, you must dial all 10 digits.

Calling a mobile (cell) phone in Greece requires substituting a 6 for the 2 that precedes the area code.

Long-distance calls, both domestic and international, can be quite expensive in Greece, especially at hotels, which may add a surcharge of up to 100%, unless you have a telephone credit card from a major long-distance provider such as AT&T, MCI, or Sprint.

If you prefer to make your call from an OTE office, these are centrally and conveniently located. (Local office locations are given under "Essentials" for most destinations in the chapters that follow.) At OTE offices, a clerk will assign you a booth with a metered phone. You can pay with a phone card, international credit card, or cash. Collect calls take much longer.

To call Greece from the United States or Canada:

1. Dial the international access code: 011 from the U.S.; 00 from the U.K., Ireland, or New Zealand; or 0011 from Australia
2. Dial the country code 30
3. Dial the city code—three to five digits—and then the number. (*Note:* All numbers in Greece must have 10 digits, including the city code.)

If you are calling Greece from other countries, dial one of the following international access codes. From the United Kingdom, Ireland, and New Zealand, 00; from Australia, 0011. Then follow steps 2 and 3 above to complete the call.

To make international calls from within Greece: The easiest and cheapest way is to call your long-distance service provider before leaving home to determine the access number that you must dial in Greece. The principal access codes in Greece are: AT&T, ℂ 00800-1311; MCI, ℂ 00800-1211; and Sprint, ℂ 00800-1411. Most companies also offer a voice-mail service in case the number you call is busy or there's no answer.

If you must use the Greek phone system to make a direct call abroad—whether using an OTE office, a phone that takes cards, or a phone that takes coins—dial the country code plus the area code (omitting the initial zero, if any), then dial the number. Some country codes are: Australia, 0061; Canada, 001; Ireland, 00353; New Zealand, 0064; United Kingdom, 0044; and United States, 001. Thus if you wanted to call the British Embassy in Washington, D.C., you would dial 00-1-202-588-7800.

Note that if you are going to put all the charges on your phone card (that is, not on your long-distance provider), you will be charged at a high rate per minute (at least 3€/$3.90 to North America), so you should not make a call unless your phone card's remaining value can cover it.

For operator assistance: If you need operator assistance in making a call, dial 131 if you're trying to make an international call and 169 if you want to call a number in Greece.

Toll-free numbers: Numbers beginning with 080 within Greece are toll-free, but calling a 1-800 number in North America from Greece is not toll-free. In fact, it costs the same as an overseas call.

RECHARGEABLE PHONE CARDS

One of the newest, easiest, and cheapest ways to make calls while abroad is to sign on for a phone card that can be used in most countries and can be re-charged (that is, money and so minutes added from your charge card account). To learn more about this card and its various other features, see www.lonelyplanet.ekit.com.

CELLPHONES

The three letters that define much of the world's wireless capabilities are **GSM** (Global System for Mobile Communications), a big, seamless network that makes for easy cross-border cellphone use throughout Europe and dozens of other countries worldwide. In the U.S., T-Mobile, AT&T Wireless, and Cingular use this quasi-universal system; in Canada, Microcell and some Rogers customers are GSM, and all Europeans and most Australians use GSM. GSM phones function with a removable plastic SIM card, encoded with your phone number and account information. If your cellphone is on a GSM system, and you have a world-capable multiband phone such as many Sony Ericsson, Motorola, or Samsung models, you can make and receive calls across civilized areas around much of the globe. Just call your wireless operator and ask for "international roaming" to be activated on your account. Unfortunately, per-minute charges can be high—usually $1 to $1.50 in western Europe and up to $5 in places like Russia and Indonesia.

For many, **renting** a phone is a good idea. While you can rent a phone from any number of places in Greece— including kiosks at major airports, OTE offices, and cellphone stores—we suggest renting the phone before you leave home. North Americans can rent one before leaving home from **InTouch USA** (© 800/872-7626; www.intouchglobal.com) or **Road-Post** (© 888/290-1606 or 905/272-5665; www.roadpost.com). Give them your itinerary, and they'll tell you what wireless products you need. Both support wireless phones in Greece—and both

RoadPost and InTouch support Black-Berry. InTouch will also, for free, advise you on whether your existing phone will work overseas; simply call © **703/222-7161** between 9am and 4pm EST, or go to **http://intouchglobal.com/travel.htm**.

However, phone rental isn't cheap. You'll usually pay $50 to $75 per week, plus airtime fees of at least a dollar a minute. If you're traveling to Europe, though, local rental companies often offer free incoming calls within their home country, which can save you big bucks. The bottom line: Shop around.

Buying a phone can be economically attractive, as many nations have cheap prepaid phone systems. Once you arrive at your destination, stop by a local cellphone shop and get the cheapest package; you'll probably pay less than $100 for a phone and a starter calling card. Local calls may be as low as 10¢ per minute, and in many countries incoming calls are free. In all decent-size cities in Greece you can buy phones at many of the commercial retail electronic stores or at the OTE, the national telephone office.

True outdoor adventurers, or those heading to less-developed countries, might consider renting a **satellite phone (satphone),** which are different from cellphones in that they connect to satellites rather than ground-based towers. A satphone is more costly than a cellphone but works where there's no cellular signal and no towers. You can rent satellite phones from **RoadPost** (see above). InTouch USA (see above) offers a wider range of satphones but at higher rates. Per-minute call charges can be even cheaper than roaming charges with a regular cellphone, but the phone itself is more expensive (up to $150 per week), and depending on the service you choose, people calling you may incur high long-distance charges.

VOICE-OVER INERNET PROTOCOL (VOIP)

If you have Web access while traveling, you might consider a broadband-based telephone service (in technical terms, **Voice-over Internet protocol,** or **VoIP**) such as Skype (www.skype.com) or Vonage (www.vonage.com), which allows you to make free international calls if you use their services from your laptop or in a cybercafe.

INTERNET/E-MAIL WITHOUT YOUR OWN COMPUTER

To find cybercafes in your destination you might start by checking **www.cyber captive.com** and **www.cybercafe.com**. But quite frankly, these lists are by no means thorough or up-to-date when it comes to Greece. All decent-size cities now have Internet cafes in their centers; if you have trouble finding one, ask a young person or shop-owner.

Most major airports have **Internet kiosks** that provide basic Web access for a per-minute fee that's usually higher than cybercafe prices.

WITH YOUR OWN COMPUTER

More and more hotels, resorts, airports, cafes, and retailers are going **Wi-Fi** (wireless fidelity), becoming "hot spots" that offer free high-speed Wi-Fi access or charge a small fee for usage. Most laptops sold today have built-in wireless capability. To find public Wi-Fi hot spots at your destination, go to **www.jiwire.com**; its Hotspot Finder holds the world's largest directory of public wireless hot spots.

For dial-up access, most business-class hotels throughout the world offer dataports for laptop modems, and a few thousand hotels in Europe now offer free high-speed Internet access.

Wherever you go, bring a **connection kit** of the right power and phone adapters, a spare phone cord, and a spare Ethernet network cable—or find out whether your hotel supplies them to guests. In Greece, too, you need a **transformer** to convert from 220 volts to 110 (although some laptops now allow for this with a switch) as well as the plug with the **two round prongs** that fit into Greek outlets.

FAXES

Almost all hotels in the higher categories, many telephone offices, some post offices, and some travel agencies will send and receive faxes, locally or internationally for set fees. But don't forget that a fax is the equivalent of a phone call so you must be prepared to pay for that in addition to the office's fee.

13 Packages for the Independent Traveler

Package tours are simply a way to buy the airfare, accommodations, and other elements of your trip (such as car rentals, airport transfers, and sometimes even activities) at the same time and often at discounted prices.

One good source of package deals is the airlines themselves. Most major airlines offer air/land packages, including **Delta Vacations** (© 800/654-6559; www.delta vacations.com) and **United Vacations** (© 888/854-3899; www.unitedvacations. com). Several big **online travel agencies**— Expedia, Travelocity, Orbitz, Site59, and Lastminute.com—also do a brisk business in packages.

Travel packages are also listed in the travel section of your local Sunday newspaper. Or check ads in national travel magazines such as *Arthur Frommer's Budget Travel Magazine, Travel + Leisure, National Geographic Traveler,* and *Condé Nast Traveler.*

14 Escorted General-Interest Tours

Escorted tours are structured group tours, with a group leader. The price usually includes everything from airfare to hotels, meals, tours, admission costs, and local transportation. Two of the major organizers of such tours in Greece are **Homeric Tours** (© **800/223-5570**; www.homeric tours.com) and **Tourlite International** (© **800/272-7600**; www.tourlite.com). All tours fall into the "moderate" category in pricing and accommodations, and both companies carry the risk of all charter flights—that is, delays. Both offer some variety—often these tours provide local guides, and often they include short cruises as part of the entire stay.

A more upscale agency is **TrueGreece** (in North America, © **800/817-7098** or in Greece 210/806-2619; www.truegreece. com), which escorts small groups on customized and more intimate tours to selected destinations.

Despite the fact that escorted tours usually require big deposits and predetermine hotels, restaurants, and itineraries, many people derive a certain ease and security from escorted trips. Escorted tours—whether they're navigated by bus, motorcoach, train, or boat—let travelers sit back and enjoy the trip without having to spend lots of time behind the wheel or worrying about details. All the details are taken care of; you know your costs upfront; and there are few surprises. Escorted tours can take you to the maximum number of sights in the minimum amount of time with the least amount of hassle—you don't have to sweat over the plotting and planning of a vacation schedule. Escorted tours are particularly convenient for people with limited mobility. They can also be a great way to make new friends.

On the downside, you'll have little opportunity for serendipitous interactions with locals. The tours can be jam-packed with activities, leaving you little time for individual sightseeing, whim, or adventure—plus they often focus only on the heavily touristed sites, so you miss out on the lesser-known gems.

15 Special-Interest Trips

ACTIVE TRAVELERS

Increasing numbers of travelers of all ages are seeking more active ways to experience Greece. We advise you to investigate closely what an activity involves—the level of difficulty, for example.

BICYCLING   Although some publicity suggests that more and more tourists are biking around Greece, the casual or occasional bicyclist is advised to think twice before attempting to bicycle in Greece. Traffic in the cities—where Greeks themselves do not bicycle and motorists are not accustomed to accommodating bicyclists—is downright dangerous. Outside towns and cities, the terrain—with occasional exceptions—is so mountainous that, again, the casual bicyclist would not

find it appealing. You would want to have a multi-geared bicycle (24–27 speeds) and be highly conditioned to cover any distances; otherwise you would find yourself walking uphill half the time. Also roads are often not that well maintained; many potholes, few shoulders.

Confirmation of this is the fact that it is not all that easy to rent bicycles throughout Greece. Major tourist centers will have possibilities; you can ask at local travel agencies and they should be able to direct you to a local firm. But the bicycles will not always be lightweight, multi-geared bikes. Be sure, too, to rent a helmet.

Most of the outfits that promote bike riding in Greece are aimed at young people and/or fairly experienced riders. In any case, those who are serious about biking in Greece should consider signing on for one of the tours arranged by such outfits as **Classic Adventures,** Box 143, Hamlin, NY 14464 (© **800/777-8090;** www.classicadventures.com). This firm has been around since 1979 and often offers bicycle tours in Greece, such as a 12-day tour of Crete; or an 11-day coastal excursion that includes Corinth, Epidaurus, Mycenae, Olympia, and the island of Zakinthos. Crete is a particularly popular place for serious bicyclists: contact **Trekking Plan** (www.cycling.gr), based outside Chania, Crete. In Greece itself, you can contact the **Hellenic Cycling Association,** National Velodrome, 15123 Marousi-Athens (© **210/689-3403**). **Trekking Hellas,** 7 Filellinon, 10557 Athens (© **210/331-0323;** www.trekking.gr), may also assist in arranging mountain-biking trips. *Note:* Many firms that speak of "bikes" in their websites are referring to motorbikes.

Should you bring your own bicycle to Greece, you can take it on Greek ferries and on trains, usually at no extra cost; you can also take it on planes, but it is not that easy to make the arrangements. You should also bring along spare parts, as they are rarely available outside the major cities. And don't forget your helmet!

CAMPING   Greece offers a wide variety of camping facilities throughout the country. Rough or freelance camping—setting up your camp on apparently unoccupied land—is forbidden by law but may be overlooked by local authorities. The **Greek National Tourism Organization** should have further information on its many licensed facilities, as well as a very informative booklet, *Camping in Greece,* published by the **Panhellenic Camping Association,** 102 Solonos, 10680 Athens (© **210/362-1560**).

DIVING   Scuba diving is currently restricted throughout most of Greece because of potential harm to sunken antiquities and the environment. That said, many locales now allow diving under supervision by accredited "schools." On the mainland, these may be found along the coast of Attica, off the Peloponnese peninsula, and off Halkidiki and a few other places in the north. There is also limited diving off the islands of Corfu, Crete, Hydra, Kalimnos, Kefalonia, Mykonos, Paros, Rhodes, Santorini, Skiathos, and Zakinthos.

To single out a few at the more popular locales, on Corfu there is **Calypso Scuba Divers,** Ayios Gordis (© 26610/53-101); on Rhodes, the **Dive Med Center,** 5 Dragoumi, Rhodes town (© 22410/33-654); on Crete, **Paradise Dive Center,** 51 Giamboudaki, Rethymnon (©/fax 28310/53-258); and on Mykonos, **Lucky Scuba Divers,** Ornos Beach (© 22890/22-813). Even if you are qualified, you must dive under supervision. Above all, you are forbidden to photograph, let alone remove, anything that might possibly be regarded as an antiquity.

For more information, contact the **Organization of Underwater Activities** (© 210/982-3840) or the **Union of Greek Diving Centers** (© 210/922-9532). If you're a serious underwater explorer, contact the **Department of Underwater Archaeology,** 4 Al Soutsou, 10671 Athens (© **210/360-3662**).

Snorkeling, however, is permitted, and the unusually clear waters make it a special pleasure. Simple equipment is widely available for rent or for sale.

FISHING   Opportunities for fishing abound. Contact **Amateur Anglers and Maritime Sports Club,** Akti Moutsopoulou, 18537 Piraeus (© **210/451-5731**).

GOLF   The Greek government is encouraging the construction of golf courses—as many as 30 are said to be planned!—but for now there are only five international standard 18-hole courses: at Glifada (along the coast outside Athens),

---

Tips Travel Tip

If you walk through any Greek countryside where there are apt to be sheep—and that means much of Greece!—there are also apt to be aggressive sheepdogs. Carry a walking stick for last-minute protection, but it's best to stay well away from the sheep, then stop and make sure that a shepherd is controlling his dogs. In any case, do not run; just walk slowly to the nearest safe point—other people, habitations, fences.

Halkidiki, Corfu, Rhodes, and Chersonnisos (Crete). There is a 9-hole course at Elounda. A travel agent can supply the details.

HIKING Greece offers endless opportunities for hiking, trekking, and walking. Greeks themselves are now showing interest in walking for pleasure, and there are a number of well-mapped and even signed walking routes.

Probably the best and most up-to-date source of information on nature-oriented tours or groups is the ads in magazines geared toward people with these interests—*Audubon Magazine,* for instance, for birders. But you need not sign up for special (and expensive!) tours to enjoy Greece's wildlife. Bring your own binoculars, and buy one of the many illustrated handbooks such as *Wildflowers of Greece,* by George Sfikas (Efstathiadis Books, Athens); or *Birds of Europe,* by Bertel Brun (McGraw-Hill).

In Greece, we recommend **Trekking Hellas,** in Athens at 7 Filellinon (© 210/331-0323), and in Thessaloniki at 71 Tsimiski (© 2310/222-128), for either guided tours or for help in planning your private trek. Other Greek travel agencies specializing in nature tours include: **Adrenaline Team,** 2 Kornarou and 28 Hermou, 10563 Athens (© 210/331-1777); **Athenogenes,** 18 Plateia Kolonaki, 10673 Athens (© 210/361-4829); and **F-Zein Active,** no longer based in Athens so start with the website (www.active.com.gr). In the Sporades, try **Ikos**

Travel, Patitiri, 37005 Alonissos (facing the quay; © 24240/65-320).

In the United States, **Appalachian Mountain Club,** 5 Joy St., Boston, MA 02108 (© 617/523-0636; www.outdoors.org), often organizes hiking tours in Greece. **Classic Adventures,** Box 143, Hamlin, NY 14464 (© 800/777-8090; www.classicadventures.com), sometimes offers hiking tours in regions of Greece. **Mountain Travel-Sobek,** 1266 66th St., Emeryville, CA 94608 (© 800/687-6235; www.mtsobek.com), sometimes conducts summer hikes and kayaking trips in the Greek mountains. **Country Walkers,** P.O. Box 180, Waterbury, VT 05676 (© 800/464-9255; www.countrywalkers.com), is another company that conducts occasional walking tours through regions of Greece. **Ecogreece,** P.O. Box 2614, Rancho Palo Verdes, CA 90275 (© 877/838-7748; www.ecogreece.com), conducts tours in Greece centered around activities such as sailing, hiking, diving, or riding.

Birders and nature lovers should contact the **Hellenic Ornithological Society,** 24 Vassiliou Irakleiou, 10682 Athens (© 210/822-7937; www.ornithologiki.gr). Also specializing in walking tours is **Alternative Travel Group,** 69–71 Banbury Rd., Oxford, OX2 6PJ England (© 44/1865-315678, or 800/527-5997 in the U.S; www.atg-oxford.co.uk); and **Naturetrek,** Cheriton, Alresford, Hants, England, S024 0NG (© 1982/733-051; www.naturetrek.co.uk).

HORSEBACK RIDING You can go horseback riding in Greece at a fair number of places. Near Athens you'll find the **Athletic Riding Club** of Ekali (© 210/813-5576) and the **Hellenic Riding Club** in Maroussi (© 210/681-2506). Call for directions and reservations. Good facilities are also located near Thessaloniki and on the islands of Corfu, Crete, Rhodes, and Skiathos, with smaller stables elsewhere (inquire at local travel agencies).

As for extended trips through various regions of Greece on horseback, several companies specialize in these. In North America, try **Equitours,** Box 807, Dubois, WY 82513 (© 800/545-0019; www.ridingtours.com); or **Hidden Trails,** 202–380 W. 1st Ave., Vancouver, BC V58 377 (© 888-987-2457; www.hiddentrails.com). In Europe, try **Equitour,** based in Switzerland (© 0041/61-303-3108; www.equitour.com).

MOUNTAINEERING If you're interested in more strenuous trekking and mountain-climbing, contact the **Hellenic Federation of Mountaineering & Climbing,** 5 Milioni, 10673 Athens (© 210/364-5904).

SKIING There are a number of attractive skiing centers in Greece. They can't compare to those located farther north with deep snow and posh facilities, but they don't approach them in steep prices, either. You may find the little hotels and lively après-ski life charming. The season generally begins after Christmas and continues until the end of April, depending on the weather.

The best-developed is **Parnassos Ski Center,** near Arachova, on Mount Parnassus (© 22340/22-694), with 20 runs, chairlifts, tow bars, classes, equipment rental, snack bars, restaurants, and even child care. There is also skiing on the gentler slopes of Mount Pelion and at charming Metsovo, in Epirus northeast of Ioannina, where the season is somewhat

shorter. Other centers are found on the Peloponnese at Helmos, near Kalavrita; in Central Greece at Velouhi, near Karpenissi; and in Macedonia, at Pisoderi, near Florina, and at Vermion, near Naoussa. For more information, contact the **Greek Skiers Organization,** P.O. Box 8037, 10010 Athens (© 210/524-0057).

SPELUNKING If you don't know what the word refers to, then don't do it. It refers to exploring caves, which are fragile environments that can be harmed easily. Visitors can fall prey to hypothermia if they go exploring without a guide. There are numerous caves in Greece and numerous individuals skilled in exploring them. For details, contact the **Hellenic Speleological Society,** 32 Sina, Athens (© 210/361-7824).

WATERSPORTS Watersports of various kinds are available at most major resort areas, and we mention the more important facilities in the relevant chapters that follow. **Parasailing** is possible at the larger resorts in summer. Although some of these facilities are limited to patrons of hotels and resorts, in many places they are available to anyone willing to pay.

River rafting and kayaking are definite possibilities, especially in Epirus, with more limited opportunities on the Peloponnese peninsula. Contact **Alpine Club,** 2 Plateia Kapnikareas, 11743 Athens (© 210/321-2355). One quite special opportunity is the kayaking trip occasionally conducted by the American agency **Mountain Travel-Sobek,** 1266 66th St., Emeryville, CA 94608 (© 800/687-6235; www.mtsobek.com).

Water-skiing facilities are widely available; there are several schools at Vouliagmeni, south of Athens, and usually at least one on each of the major islands. Contact the **Hellenic Water-Ski Federation,** Leoforos Poseidonos, 16777 Glyfada (© 210/894-7413).

Windsurfing is becoming more popular in Greece, and boards are widely available for rent. The many coves and small bays along Greece's convoluted coastline are ideal for beginners. Instruction is available at reasonable prices. The best conditions and facilities are found on the islands of Corfu, Crete, Lefkada, Lesvos, Naxos, Paros, Samos, and Zakinthos. Contact the **Hellenic Wind-Surfing Association,** 7 Filellinon, 10557 Athens (✆ **210/323-0068**), for details about the many excellent schools in Greece.

EXTENDING THE MIND

AGROTOURISM Agrotouristiki (✆ **210/331-4 117;** www.agrotravel.gr) promotes stays at small inns and villas with a focus on local food and genuine cultural or nature-oriented activities as a way to educate visitors about traditional life in Greece and stimulate rural economies.

ARCHAEOLOGICAL DIGS The **American School of Classical Studies at Athens,** 6–8 Charlton St., Princeton, NJ 08540 (✆ **609/683-0800;** www.ascsa.edu.gr), often sponsors tours in Greece and adjacent Mediterranean lands guided by archaeologists and historians. **Archaeological Tours,** 271 Madison Ave., Suite 904, New York, NY 10016 (✆ **866/740-5130;** www.archaeologicaltrs.com), offers tours led by expert guides; typical tours might be to classical Greek sites or to Cyprus, Crete, and Santorini. **Free-Gate Tourism,** 585 Stewart Ave., Suite 310, Garden City, NY 11530 (✆ **888/373-3428;** www.freegatetours.com), also specializes in guided trips in Greece. And **Dick Caldwell,** a retired USC classic professor, leads highly personal tours that mix ancient sites with a feel for modern Greece (**www.greecetravel.com/sporades tours**).

ART Group International Study Tours, 494 Eighth Ave., New York, NY 10001 (✆ **800/833-2111;** www.groupist.com), offers studies in the architecture, art, and culture of Greece, led by professionals. Especially attractive are the **Aegean Workshops** run by Harry Danos, a Greek-American architect and watercolorist. In spring and autumn, he leads groups to various regions of Greece, where he provides instruction in drawing and watercolor painting (and also ends up teaching the language). To learn more, call ✆ **860/739-0378** mid-May through October, or ✆ **239/455-2623** from November to mid-May. You can also e-mail hkdanos@copper.net.

Athens Center for the Creative Arts, 48 Archimidou, Pangrati, 11636 Athens (✆ **210/701-2268**), offers summer programs. **Hellas Art Club** on the island of Hydra, at the Leto Hotel, 18040 Hydra (✆ **22980/53-385**), offers classes in painting, ceramics, music, theater, photography, Greek dancing, and cooking. An especially attractive possibility is the American-run **Island Center for the Arts** that conducts classes in painting, photography, and Greek culture on Skopelos between June and September (✆ **617/623-6538;** www.islandcenter.org). As it is affiliated with the Massachusetts College of Art, some educational institutions grant credits for its courses.

MODERN GREEK Formal educational institutions and private language institutes throughout the English-speaking world offer many courses. There are also decent courses on tape for self-study. Be sure it is modern Greek you study—not classical Greek! If you are already in Greece, **Athens Center for the Creative Arts,** 48 Archimidou, Pangrati, 11636 Athens (✆ **210/701-2268**), is highly recommended. **School of Modern Greek Language of Aristotle University in Thessaloniki** also offers summer courses (www.auth.gr/smg). For basic vocabulary and phrases, see the **appendix** in this book.

PERSONAL GROWTH Skyros Center, which can be contacted in the United

Kingdom at 92 Prince of Wales Rd., London NW5 3NE (© 020/7267-4424; www.skyros.com), offers "personal growth" vacations on the island of Skyros, with courses in fitness, holistic health, creative writing, and handicrafts.

COOKING   Rosemary Barron, a food expert based in England, has for many years run a cooking school, Kandra Kitchen—usually on Santorini—in which participants learn not only how to prepare and appreciate Greek foods but also about the history of Greek food across the centuries and its value to us today (www.rosemarybarron.com). Diane Kochilas, a Greek-American expert on Greek foods, offers a variety of activities, including cooking classes in Athens and on Ikaria and culinary tours in Athens or throughout Greece (**www.dianekochilas. com**). Aglai Kremezi, an American-educated Greek authority on Greek food, runs a cooking school on the island of Kea (**www.keaartisinal.com**). And Nikki Rose, a Cretan-American professional chef, operates "seminars" on Crete that combine some travel with cooking lessons and investigations of Crete's diet (**www.cookingincrete.com**).

16 Getting Around Greece

BY PLANE

Compared to the cheaper classes on ships and ferries, air travel within Greece can be expensive, but we recommend it for those pressed for time and/or heading for more distant destinations (even if the planes don't always hold strictly to their schedules). Until the late 1990s, **Olympic Airways** (© 210/966-6666; www. olympicairlines.com) maintained a monopoly on domestic air travel and thus had little incentive to improve service. In the end, it declared bankruptcy and was placed under new management, which has steadily improved service. Better computerized booking has reduced the number of last-minute discoveries that you don't have a seat. Delayed flights are still common, although the quality of the service, which was criticized for some years, is reportedly better. (For some reason, Olympic's domestic flight attendants seem to be more helpful than their international counterparts.) Also, Olympic has one of the best safety records of any major airline.

Book as far ahead of time as possible (especially in summer), reconfirm your booking before leaving for the airport, and arrive at the airport at least an hour before departure; the scene at a check-in counter can be quite hectic.

Olympic Airways has a number of offices in Athens, though most travel agents sell tickets as well. It offers **mainland** service to Aktaion Preveza, Alexandroupolis, Ioannina, Kalamata, Kavala, Kastoria, Kozani, and Thessaloniki. As for **islands,** Olympic services Astipalea; Corfu (aka Kerkira); Iraklion, Chania, and Sitia, Crete; Hios (aka Chios); Ikaria; Karpathos; Kassos; Kastellorizo; Kefalonia; Kos; Kithira; Leros; Limnos; Milos; Mykonos; Mitilini (aka Lesvos); Naxos; Paros; Rhodes; Samos; Santorini (aka Thira); Skiathos; Skyros; Siros; and Zakinthos. All of Olympic's domestic flights leave from the new international airport at Spata. Most flights are to or from Athens, although during the summer there may be some inter-island service. The baggage allowance is 15 kilos (33 lb.) per passenger, except with a connecting international flight; even the domestic flights generally ignore the weight limit unless you are way over. Smoking is prohibited on all domestic flights.

A round-trip ticket costs double the one-way fare. Sample round-trip fares (including taxes) at this writing are:

Athens-Santorini (Thira) 220€ ($286); Athens-Iraklion, Chania, 210€ ($273); Athens-Ioannina, 215€ ($280); Athens-Mykonos, 215€ ($280); Athens-Mitilini (Lesvos), 200€ ($260); Athens-Skiathos, 135€ ($176). As you can see, even the shorter trips are not especially cheap, but there's no denying that for those with limited time, air travel is the best way to go. Ask, too, if Olympic still offers reduced fares for trips Monday through Thursday and trips that include a Saturday-night stay.

Over the years, several private airlines have tried to compete with Olympic, but only one has survived to provide a real alternative: **Aegean Airlines.** From abroad, dial the code for Greece, then © 210/626-1000; within Greece, dial © 801/112-0000. You can also check www.aegeanair.com, which allows you to order e-tickets online. Its prices now pretty much match those of Olympic. Their service is limited but includes Alexandroupolis, Chania, Chios, Corfu, Ioannina, Iraklion, Kavala, Kos Mitilini, Mykonos, Patras, Rhodes, Samos, Santorini, and Thessaloniki. (They also offer direct flights to Rome, Milan, several major German cities, and Cyprus.) Foreign travel agents may not be aware of Aegean Airlines, so check out their website. People who have been flying Aegean for several years now find the airline reliable, safe, and hospitable.

As of 2007, two more competitors are emerging—**Airsea Lines,** which flies hydroplanes between selected points, and **Sky Express,** which flies small (18-seater) planes between Crete and several Aegean islands. Airsea Lines claims to be operating out of are two principal bases—one at Lavrion on the coast of Attika to the southeast of Athens, and Gouvia, a few miles outside Corfu's capital city. (A third base has also been planned for Faliron, the coast just south of Athens.) The connections from Attika are with Ios, Kalymnos, Kos, Mykonos, Paros, Santorini, Tinos; from Corfu with Ithaka, Lefkada, Kefalonia, Patras, Paxoi, and to Brindisi in Italy. Fares range from 40€ to 120€ ($52–$156).

Sky Express claims that it will be offering flights between Crete and several Aegean islands. A typical fare is 79€ ($107) from Heraklion, Crete, to Rhodes—quite reasonable when one considers the time saved.

Both these lines have limited schedules and very low limits on luggage so anything over could increase the fare considerably. Also, as these are new outfits and much was still being worked out as we went to press, you are advised to consult their websites, www.airsealines.com and www.skyexpress.gr. If in Greece, call Airsea Lines at their toll-free number © **801/1180-0600** or Sky Express at © **2810/223-500.**

Note: Most Greek domestic tickets are nonrefundable, and changing your flight can cost you up to 30% within 24 hours of departure and 50% within 12 hours.

BY BOAT

BY FERRY Ferries are the most common, cheapest, and generally most "authentic" way to visit the islands, though the slow roll of a ferry can be also be stomach-churning. A wide variety of vessels sail Greek waters—some huge, sleek, and new, with comfortable TV lounges, discos, and good restaurants; some old and ill-kept, but pleasant enough if you stay on deck.

So-called "Flying Catamarans" and hydrofoils dubbed "Flying Dolphins" also serve many of the major islands. (See below.) Undoubtedly faster, they cost almost twice as much as regular ferries, and their schedules are often interrupted by weather conditions. (Never rely on a tight connection between a hydrofoil and, say, an airplane flight.) Ferries, too, often don't hold exactly to their schedules, but

Early- and Late-Season Ferries

In the early and late weeks of the tourist season—from April to early May, and September to November—boat service can be unpredictable. Boat schedules, at the best of times, are tentative—but during this time, they are wish lists, nothing more. Our best advice is that you wait until you get to Greece, then go to a major travel agency and ask for help.

they can be fun if you enjoy opportunities to meet people. Drinks and snacks are almost always sold, but the prices and selection are not that good, so you may want to bring along your own.

The map of Greece offered by the Greek National Tourism Organization (EOT), which indicates the common boat routes, is very useful in planning your sea travels. Once you've learned what is possible, you can turn your attention to what is available. Remember that the summer schedule is the fullest, spring and fall bring reduced service, and winter schedules are skeletal.

There are dozens of shipping companies, each with its own schedule—which are regulated by the government. Your travel agent might have a copy of the monthly schedule, *Greek Travel Pages,* or you can search online at **www.gtp.gr**, **www.ferries.gr**, or **www.allgreekferies. com**. When in Greece it's best to go straight to an official information office, a travel agency, or the port authority as soon as you arrive at the place that you intend to leave via ferry.

Photos can give you some idea of the ships, but remember that any photo displayed was probably taken when the ship was new, and it is unlikely that anyone will be able (or willing) to tell you its actual age. The bigger ferries offer greater stability during rough weather. Except in summer, you can usually depend on getting aboard a ferry by showing up about an hour before scheduled departure— inter-island boats sometimes depart before their scheduled times—and purchasing a ticket from a dockside agent or

aboard the ship itself, though this is often more expensive.

Your best bet is to buy a ticket from an agent ahead of time. In Athens, we recommend **Galaxy Travel,** 35 Voulis, near Syntagma Square (© **210/322-5960;** www.galaxytravel.gr); and **Alkyon Travel,** 97 Akademias, near Kanigos Square (© **210/383-2545**). During the high season, both agencies keep long hours Monday through Saturday.

Note: Different travel agencies sell tickets to different lines—this is usually the policy of the line itself—and one agent might not know or bother to find out what else is offered. However, if you press reputable agencies like those above, they will at least tell you the options. The port authority is the most reliable source of information, and the shipping company itself or its agents usually offer better prices and may have tickets when other agents have exhausted their allotment. It often pays to compare vessels and prices.

First class usually means roomy air-conditioned cabins and its own lounge; on some routes it costs almost as much as flying. However, on longer overnight hauls, you're on a comfortable floating hotel and thus save the cost of lodging. Second class means smaller cabins (which you will probably have to share with strangers) and its own lounge. The tourist-class fare entitles you to a seat on the deck or in a lounge. (Tourists usually head for the deck, while Greeks stay inside, watch TV, and smoke copiously.) Hold onto your ticket; crews conduct ticket-control sweeps.

Greek Ferry Routes

Note: Those taking a ferry to Turkey from one of the Dodecanese islands must submit passport and payment to an agent the day before departure.

We include more details on service and schedules in the relevant chapters that follow, as well as suggested travel agencies and sources of local information. To give you some sense of the fares, here are examples for standard accommodations from Piraeus at press time (compare with airfares during this same time, p. 32): to Crete (Iraklion), 80€–110€ ($104–$143); Kos, 55€ ($72); Mitilini (Lesvos), 62€ ($81); Mykonos, 60€ ($78); Rhodes, 95€ ($124); Santorini, 60€ ($78). Don't be surprised if small taxes get added on at the last minute.

BY HYDROFOIL Hydrofoils (often referred to by the principal line's trade name, Flying Dolphins, or by Greeks as *to flying*) are faster than ferries, and have comfortable airline-style seats. Their stops are much shorter, and they are less likely to cause seasickness (but they are noisy!). They cost somewhat more than ferries, are frequently fully booked in summer, can be quite bumpy during rough weather, and give little or no view of the passing scenery. In short, they're the best choice if your time is limited.

There is regular hydrofoil service to many of the major islands; new routes and new schedules appear often. Longer trips over open sea, such as between Santorini and Iraklion, Crete, may make them well worth the extra expense. (A one-way fare from Heraklion to Santorini in high season, for instance, is 35€– 50€/$46–$65.) Smoking is prohibited, and actually less likely to be indulged in, possibly because the cabins seem so much like those of an aircraft. The forward compartment offers better views but is also bumpy.

The Flying Dolphins are now operated by **Hellenic Seaways** Akti Kondyli and 2 Aitolikou, 18545 Piraeus (© **210/419-9000;** www.hellenicseaways.gr). The service from Zea Marina in Piraeus to the Saronic Gulf islands and throughout the Sporades is recommended for its speed and regularity. There is also service from Rafina, on the east coast of Attika, to several of the Cyclades islands.

BY SAILBOAT & YACHT Many more tourists are choosing to explore Greece by sailboat or yacht. There are numerous facilities and options for both. Experienced sailors interested in renting a boat in Greece can contact the **Hellenic Professional and Bareboat Yacht Owners' Association,** A8–A9 Zea Marina, 18536 Piraeus (© **210/452-6335**). Less experienced sailors should consider signing up for one of the flotillas—a group of 12 or more boats sailing as a group led by a boat crewed by experienced sailors; the largest of such organizations is **Sunsail,** 980 Awald Rd., Annapolis, MD 21403 (© **888/350-3568;** www.sunsail.com). However, travel agencies should be able to put you in touch with other such outfits.

At the other extreme, those who want to charter a yacht with anything from a basic skipper to a full crew should first contact the **Hellenic Professional and Bareboat Yacht Owners' Association** (listed above), or **Ghiolman Yachts,** 4 Filellinon, 10557 Athens (© **210/323-0330;** www.ghiolman.com). If you feel competent enough to make your own arrangements, contact **Valef Yachts Ltd.,** P.O. Box 385, Ambler, PA 19002

(© **800/223-3845;** www.valefyachts.com). In Greece, you can contact one of these associations or try a private agency such as **Alpha Yachting,** 67 Leoforos Possidonos, 16674 Glyfada (© **210/968-0486;** www.alphayachting.com).

BY CAR

Driving in Greece is a bit of an adventure, but it's the best way to see the country at your own pace. *Note:* Greece has one of the highest accident rates in Europe, probably due somewhat to treacherous roads, mountain terrain, and poor maintenance of older cars as much as to reckless driving—although Greeks are certainly aggressive drivers. Athens is a particularly intimidating place in which to drive at first, and parking spaces are practically nonexistent in the center of town. (Main routes in and out of cities are sometimes signed by white arrows on blue markers.) Several of the major cities are linked by modern expressways with tolls; the toll for Athens to Thessaloniki, for instance, is expected to go up to 30€ ($39). Accidents must be reported to the police for insurance claims.

If you do intend to do a fair amount of driving, acquire a good up-to-date map before you set off. The best source is a British shop that allows for online ordering, **www.themapstore.com.**

The **Greek Automobile Touring Club (ELPA),** 395 Mesoyion, 11343 Athens (© **210/606-8800**), with offices in most cities, can help you with all matters relating to your car, issue **International Driver's Licenses,** and provide **maps and information** (© **174,** 24 hr. daily). ELPA's emergency road service number is © **104.** Though the service provided by the able ELPA mechanics is free for light repairs, definitely give a generous tip.

The price of gasoline fluctuates considerably from week to week and from service station to service station, but it

Warning on Licenses

Legally, all non-E.U. drivers in Greece are required to carry an International Driver's License. In practice, most car rental agencies will rent to Americans and other non-E.U. drivers carrying their national driver's licenses, although they usually have to have been licensed for at least 1 year. (One major exception is on the island of Hios, where the International License is usually required.) This is fine so long as you don't get involved in an accident—especially one involving personal injury. Then you could discover that your insurance is voided on a technicality. Meanwhile, you run the risk of an individual policeman insisting that you must have the international license. Obtain one before leaving home (from the national automobile association) or from the Greek Automobile Touring Club (see above).

remains consistently expensive: about 1.05€ ($1.35) a liter, which works out to about $5.25 for an American gallon. There is no shortage of gasoline stations in all cities, good-size towns, and major tourist centers, but if you are setting off for an excursion into one of the more remote mountain areas or to an isolated beach, fill up on gas before setting out.

CAR RENTALS   You will find no end of rental cars throughout Greece, and almost as much variation in prices. Many cars have a standard shift; if you must have an automatic, make sure in advance that one is available. In high season you are strongly advised to make your reservation before leaving home and well in advance. Always ask if the quoted price includes insurance; many credit cards make the collision-damage waiver unnecessary, but you will find that most rental agencies automatically include this in their rates. You can sometimes save by booking at home before you leave; this is especially advisable in summer. If you are shopping around, let the agents see the number of competitors' brochures you're carrying.

Most companies require that the renter be at least 21 years old (25 for some car models). An occasional company won't rent to anyone older than 70 or 75. Definitely inquire beforehand! You must

possess a valid Australian, Canadian, E.U.-nation, U.S., or International Driver's License. You must also have a major credit card (or be prepared to leave a large cash deposit).

The major car rental companies in Athens are **Avis** (© 210/322-4951), **Budget** (© 210/349-8700), **Hertz** (© 210/922-0102), **National** (© 210/349-3400), and **AutoEurope** (© 00800/11574-0300 toll-free from Greece), all with additional offices in major cities, at most airports, and on most islands. Smaller local companies usually have lower rates, but their vehicles are often older and not as well maintained. If you prefer to combine your car rental with your other travel arrangements, we recommend **Galaxy Travel,** 35 Voulis, near Syntagma Square (© 210/322-2091; www.galaxytravel. gr). It's open Monday through Saturday during the tourist season.

Rental rates vary widely—definitely inquire around. In high season, the daily rates will be about 45€ ($59) for a compact and 65€ ($85) for a full-size—but you will usually have to pay some cents per kilometer; weekly rates with unlimited mileage might run 250€ ($325) for a compact and 450€ ($585) for a fullsize. In low season, rates are often negotiable in Greece when you show up in person. And be prepared for the addition of 19% in VAT taxes plus 2% in munici-pal taxes to the quoted price (as above). (And there's usually a surcharge for pickup and drop-off at airports.)

Note: You must have written permis-sion from the car rental agency to take your rental car on a ferry or into a foreign country.

DRIVING RULES In Greece, you drive on the right, pass on the left, and yield right of way to vehicles approaching from the right except where otherwise posted. Greece has adopted international road signs, though many Greeks appar-ently haven't learned what they mean yet. The maximum speed limit is 100kmph (65 mph) on open roads, and 50kmph (30 mph) in town, unless otherwise posted. Seat belts are required. The police have become stricter in recent years, espe-cially with foreigners in rental cars; alco-hol tests can be given and fines imposed on the spot. (If you feel you have been stopped or treated unfairly, get the offi-cer's name and report him at the nearest tourist police station.) Honking is illegal in Athens, but you can hear that law bro-ken by tarrying at a traffic signal.

PARKING Parking a car has become a serious challenge in the cities and towns of Greece. The better hotels provide parking, either on their premises or by arrange-ment with a nearby lot. Greece has few public parking garages or lots. Follow the blue signs with the white P and you may be lucky enough to find a space. Most Greek city streets have restricted parking of one kind or another. In some cities, signs—usually yellow, and with the direc-tions in English as well as in Greek—will indicate that you can park along the street but must purchase a ticket from the near-est kiosk. Otherwise, be prepared to park fairly far from your base or destination. If you lock the car and remove valuables from sight, you should not have to worry about a break-in.

BY TRAIN

Greek trains are generally slow but are inexpensive and fairly pleasant. The **Hel-lenic State Railway (OSE)** also offers bus service from stations adjacent to major train terminals. (Bus service is faster, but second-class train fare is nearly 50% cheaper, and trains offer more com-fortable and scenic rides.) If you are inter-ested in special arrangements involving rail passes for Greece (sometimes in com-bination with Olympic Airlines flights within Greece), check out **www.rail europe.com** or call ℭ **888/382-7245** in the U.S. and **800/361-7245** in Canada.

For information and tickets in Athens, visit the **OSE office** at 1–3 Karolou (ℭ **210/522-4563**), or at 6 Sina (ℭ **210/ 362-4402**), both near Omonia Square.

Purchase your ticket and reserve a seat ahead of time, as a 50% surcharge is added to tickets purchased on the train, and some lines are packed, especially in summer. A first-class ticket may be worth the extra cost, as seats are more comfort-able and less crowded. There is sleeper service on the Athens-Thessaloniki run. Though the costly sleepers are a good value, you must be prepared to share a compartment with three to five others. Express service (6 hr.) runs twice a day, at 7am and 1pm.

Trains to Northern Greece (Alexan-droupolis, Florina, Kalambaka, Lamia, Larissa, Thessaloniki, Volos, and other towns) leave from the Larissa station (Stathmos Larissis). **Trains to the Pelo-ponnese** (Argos, Corinth, Patras) leave from the Peloponnese station (Stathmos Peloponnisou). Take trolley no. 1 or 5 from Syntagma Square to either station.

The Peloponnese circuit from Corinth to Patras, Pirgos (near Olympia), Tripolis, and Argos is one way to experience this scenic region, though the Athens-Patras stretch is often crowded. The spectacular spur between Diakofto and Kalavrita is particularly recommended for train enthusiasts.

BY BUS

Public buses are inexpensive but often overcrowded. Local bus lines vary from place to place, but on most islands the bus stop is in a central location with a posted schedule. Destinations are usually displayed on the front of the bus, but you might have to ask. The conductor will collect your fare after departure.

Note that in Athens and other large cities, a bus ticket *must* be purchased before *and* validated after boarding. Kiosks usually offer bus tickets as well as schedules. Bus tickets cost about .50€ (65¢). Tram tickets cost some .60€/78¢ while the Athens metro ticket's cost is based on the destination.

Note: Save your ticket in case an inspector comes aboard. If you don't have a ticket, the fine can be at least 30 times the price of the ticket!

Greece has an extensive **long-distance bus service (KTEL),** an association of regional operators with green-and-yellow buses that leave from convenient central stations. For information about the long-distance-bus offices, contact the KTEL office in Athens (✆ **210/512-4910).**

In Athens, most buses heading to destinations within **Attica** leave from the Mavromate terminal, north of the National Archaeological Museum. Most buses to **Central Greece** leave from 260 Liossion, 5km (3 miles) north of Omonia Square (take local bus no. 024 from Leoforos Amalias in front of the entrance to the National Garden and tell the driver your destination). Most buses to the **Peloponnese, Western, and Northern Greece** leave from the long-distance bus terminal at 100 Kifissou, 4km (2½ miles) northeast of Omonia Square. To get to the long-distance bus terminal, take local bus no. 051 from the stop 2 blocks west of Omonia, near the big

church of Ayios Konstandinos, at Zinonos and Menandrou.

Express buses between major cities, usually air-conditioned, can be booked through travel agencies. Make sure that your destination is understood—you wouldn't be the first to see a bit more of Greece than bargained for—and determine the bus's schedule and comforts before purchasing your ticket. Many buses are not air-conditioned, take torturous routes, and make frequent stops. (NO SMOKING signs are generally disregarded by drivers and conductors, as well as by many older male passengers.)

Organized and guided **bus tours** are widely available. Some of them will pick you up at your hotel; ask the hotel staff or any travel agent in Athens. We especially recommend **CHAT Tours,** the oldest and probably most experienced provider of a wide selection of bus tours led by highly articulate guides. Almost any travel agent can book a CHAT tour, but if you want to deal with the company directly, contact them through their website, www. chatours.gr; in Athens, the CHAT office is at 9 Xenofontos, 10557 Athens (✆ **210/ 323-0827).** Then there is the longtime favorite, **American Express,** with offices all over North America and Europe; the Athens office (✆ **210/325-4690)** is located at 31 Panepistimiou, right on the corner of Syntagma Square.

Note: Readers have complained that some bus groups are so large they feel removed from the leader; inquire about group size if this concerns you.

BY TAXI

Taxis are one of the most convenient means of getting about in Greece. They can also be the most exasperating, although there have been improvements in recent years. For instance, you no longer have to fight for a cab at most airports; just find the line. Official fares are considerably lower in Athens than in

Taxi Tips

- Taxi rates are in constant (upward!) flux, so we provide the rates as we go to press. First, though, check to see that the little window next to the euro display on the meter is "1" and not "2"—which is the setting for midnight-to-6am or outside-the-city-limits rates (which are about double the regular rate). If that's not the case, reach over and indicate that you notice.

- Then check that the meter starts at no more than .85€ ($1.10) as you set off—that is the maximum starting rate. Drivers have been known to start with a much higher number already registered; or they leave the meter off, then try to extort a much larger fare from you. Even if you don't speak a word of Greek besides "taxi," point at the meter and say "meter." The rate per kilometer has been about .34€ (44¢) within the city during daylight hours, and about .60€ (80¢) outside city limits or at night. The minimum fare for any trip is 2.50€ ($3.25).

- For a group of tourists, a driver may insist that each person pay the full metered fare. Pay only your proportion of the fare if all of you have the same destination. Pairs or groups of tourists should have a designated arguer; the others can write down names and numbers, stick with the luggage, or look for help—from a policeman, maitre d', or desk clerk.

- Late at night, especially at airports, ferry stops, and bus and railroad stations, a driver may refuse to use his meter and demand an exorbitant fare. Smile, shake your head, and look for another cab; if none are available, start writing down the driver's license number and he will probably relent.

London, New York, or Toronto. At some major tourist locales the fixed charges for rides to select destinations are posted (from an airport to the city center, for instance). But there is no denying that many drivers take advantage of foreigners. That said, perhaps there is no greater percentage of cheats among Greece's cabdrivers than in all major cities around the world—and many Greek taxi drivers are good-natured, helpful, and informative. Foreigners' language limitations and unfamiliarity with the official regulations, however, can make it easier for some of them to gouge you.

The converse is also true: Language gaps can lead to genuine misunderstandings. And several legitimate surcharges do apply—for heavy luggage, for rides from midnight to 6am (almost twice the regular rate!), for rides on holidays, and for rides from and to airports. Ask to see the official rate sheet that the driver is required to carry.

Get your hotel desk to help you hail or book a taxi. Radio cabs cost 3€ ($3.90) extra, but you'll have some leverage. Restaurants and businesses can also help you call or hail a cab, negotiate a fare, and make sure your destination is understood. Using a card from your hotel, write down your destination (or learn to pronounce it). Be willing to share a cab with other passengers picked up on the way, especially during rush hour; think of it as your contribution to better efficiency and less pollution. Be aware that you pay only your proportion of the shared fare.

- Legal surcharges include: 3€ ($3.90) from and to the main Athens airport; .90€ ($1.20) pickup at other airports, ports, bus terminals, or train terminals; .35€ (45¢) per piece of luggage over 10 kilos (22 lb.). (Road tolls are charged to the passengers—for example, you will pay 2€ ($2.60) for the new road from the airport to Athens.)
- A driver may say that your hotel is full, but that he knows a better and cheaper one. Laugh, and insist you'll take your chances at your hotel.
- A driver may want to let you off where it's most convenient for him. Be cooperative if it's easier and quicker for you to cross a busy avenue than for him to get you to the other side, but you don't have to get out of the cab until you're ready.

If things are obviously not going well for you, conspicuously write down the driver's name and number and by all means report him to the **tourist police** (℡ **171**) if he has the nerve to call your bluff. One of the best countertactics is to simply reach for the door latch and open the door slightly; he won't want to risk damaging it. (Two passengers can each open a door.)

Our final advice: Don't sweat the small change. So the driver is charging you 13€ ($17) for a ride you have been told should be about 10€ ($13); are you prepared to go to court for 3€ ($3.90)? Any difference above 5€ ($6.50) probably should be questioned—but it may have to do with traffic delays when the meter ticks at the rate of 7.25€ ($9.40) per hour. Most cabbies are honest—just be aware of the possibilities. And be sure to reward good service with a tip.

Always have at least a vague idea of your destination as indicated by a map, so that you don't end up going to Plaka from Syntagma by way of Kolonaki. (There are, however, several ways of getting to Plaka from Syntagma.) Don't be bothered by bullying or bluster; counter with your own bluff, showing your self-confidence by keeping your cool. See also "Taxi Tips," above.

BY MOPED, MOTORBIKE & MOTORCYCLE

There seems to be no end to the number of mopeds, motorbikes, motorcycles, and related vehicles available for rent in Greece. They can be an inexpensive way to get around, especially in the islands, but they are not recommended for everyone: Greek hospitals admit scores of

tourists injured on mopeds or motorbikes every summer, and there are a number of fatalities. Roads are often poorly paved and without shoulders; loose gravel or stones are another common problem. Meanwhile, as of 2000, Greek law requires that all renters of mopeds and motorcycles be licensed to operate such vehicles. Make sure you have insurance and that the machine is in good working condition before you take it. Helmets are required by law and strongly recommended, although you will rarely see Greeks wearing them.

You might wish that the larger motorbikes and motorcycles were forbidden on all the islands, as Greek youths seem to delight in punching holes in the mufflers and tearing around at all hours. (Some

Moped Warning

Although mopeds are the vehicle of choice in Greece, especially on the islands, be aware that there is a Greek law (prompted by a huge number of accidents) requiring that anyone driving a moped must have a motorcycle license. Agencies offering moped rentals rarely tell tourists this because very few tourists have motorcycle licenses. This makes for serious troubles if an accident occurs and you are not a licensed motorcycle driver: You will have broken the law and will not be covered by insurance. Check with your own auto and/or medical insurance plan to see if you are covered for such an eventuality.

islands are wisely banning them from certain areas and restricting the hours of their use, as they are the single most common cause of complaints from tourists and residents alike.) The motorcycles rented to tourists are usually a bit quieter, but they are more expensive and at least as dangerous.

BY BICYCLE

Bicycles are not nearly as common in Greece as they are throughout most of Europe, since they are not well suited to Greek terrain or temperament and would be downright dangerous in traffic. In less hectic towns and in the countryside, however, a bicycle might be fine for short distances. Older bikes are usually available for rent at modest prices in most resort areas, and good mountain bikes are increasingly available. (See "Active Travelers," earlier in this chapter, for more information.)

17 Tips on Accommodations

Greece now offers a full spectrum of accommodations ranging from the extravagant to the basic. Within a given locale, of course, not all options are available, but most readers will find something that appeals to them.

Hotels used to be required to publicize a grading system imposed by the Greek government. Classes still exist and are indicated by stars, but these are based more on facilities such as public areas, pools, and in-room amenities than on any comfort or service ratings. Basically it is a market economy, for hotels know better than to ask for too much because competitors will undercut them. Frommer's own rating system of stars and icons for special features takes care of all such differences.

International travelers will be familiar with some of the major chains—the Hilton, Best Western. A number of Greek chains, such as Louis and Chandris, also own numerous hotels, while several hotels now belong to the Luxury Collection of Starwood Hotels and Resorts. These latter tend to be extremely upscale hotels. However, most Greek hotels are independent lodgings run by hands-on owners.

SURFING FOR HOTELS

In addition to the online travel booking sites **Travelocity, Expedia, Orbitz, Priceline,** and **Hotwire,** you can book hotels through **Hotels.com; Quikbook** (www.quikbook.com); and **Travelaxe** (www.travelaxe.net). Especially strong for hotels in Greece is **www.dilos.com.** An excellent free program, **TravelAxe** (www.travelaxe.net), can help you search hotel sites in a few Greek cities, but it conveniently compares the total room prices, including taxes and service charges. The competitiveness of these major sites can be a boon to consumers who have the patience and time to shop and compare the online sites for good deals—but shop you must, for prices can vary considerably from site to site. And keep in mind that hotels at the top of a site's listing may be there for no other reason than that they paid money to get the placement.

HotelChatter.com is a daily webzine offering smart coverage and critiques of hotels worldwide. Go to **TripAdvisor.com** or **HotelShark.com** for helpful independent consumer reviews of hotels and resort properties.

It's a good idea to **get a confirmation number** and **make a printout** of any online booking transaction.

Note: Some hotels do not provide loyalty program credits or points or other frequent-stay amenities when you book a room through opaque online services.

SAVING ON YOUR HOTEL ROOM

The **rack rate** is the maximum rate that a hotel charges for a room. Hardly anybody pays full rate, however, except in high season or holidays. To lower the cost of your room:

- **Ask about special rates or other discounts.** Always ask whether a room less expensive than the first one quoted is available, or whether any special rates apply to you. You may qualify for corporate, student, military, senior, or other discounts. Find

out the hotel policy on children—do kids stay free in the room or is there a special rate?

- **Dial direct.** When booking a room in a chain hotel, you'll often get a better deal by calling the individual hotel's reservations desk rather than the chain's main number.
- **Book online.** Many hotels offer Internet-only discounts, or supply rooms to Priceline, Hotwire, or Expedia at rates much lower than the ones you can get through the hotel itself. Shop around. And if you have special needs—a quiet room, a room with a view—call the hotel directly and make your needs known after you've booked online.
- **Remember the law of supply and demand.** Resort hotels are most crowded and therefore most expensive on weekends, so discounts are usually available for midweek stays. Business hotels in downtown locations are busiest during the week, so you can expect big discounts on weekends. Many hotels have high-season and low-season rates, so booking the day after high season ends can mean big discounts.
- **Look into group or long-stay discounts.** If you are with a large group, you should be able to negotiate a bargain rate, since the hotel can then guarantee occupancy in a number of rooms. Likewise, if you're planning a

---

(Tips **Hotel Bathrooms**

The bathrooms in all the newer and higher-grade Greek hotels are now practically state-of-the-art, but travelers might appreciate knowing a few things that apply to all except the more upscale hotels. Few hotels provide washcloths, and small bar soap is the standard. Many hotels don't offer generously sized towels, and many midprice hotels provide only cramped showers. As it happens, the two things in generous supply are slippery marble and glass shower doors: Be very careful getting in and out of tubs or showers.

Tips Booking a Room

Try to make reservations by fax so that you have a written record of the room and price agreed upon. Be aware that a double room in Greece does not always mean a room with a double bed, but a room with twin beds. Double beds in Greece are called "matrimonial beds," and rooms with such beds are often designated "honeymoon rooms." This can lead to misunderstandings.

Note that in a few instances—usually at the most expensive hotels—the prices quoted are per person. Note, too, that room prices, no matter what people say officially, are often negotiable, especially at the edges of the season. Because of Greek law and EOT regulations, hotel keepers are often reluctant to provide rates far in advance and often quote prices higher than their actual rates. When you bargain, don't cite our prices, which may be too high, but ask instead for the best current rate. Actual off-season prices may be as much as 25% lower than the lowest rate given to us for this book.

long stay (at least 5 days), you might qualify for a discount. As a general rule, expect 1 night free after a 7-night stay.

LANDING THE BEST ROOM

Somebody has to get the best room in the house. It might as well be you. Although it is unlikely that the average visitor to Greece will be staying at a hotel with a "frequent-guest" program, inquire if you think it might be a possibility. Always ask about a corner room. They're often larger and quieter, with more windows and light, and they often cost the same as standard rooms. When you make your reservation, ask if the hotel is renovating; if it is, request a room away from the construction. Ask about nonsmoking rooms; rooms with views; rooms with twin, queen-, or king-size beds. If you're a light sleeper, request a quiet room away from vending machines, elevators, restaurants, bars, and discos. Ask for one of the rooms that have been most recently renovated or redecorated.

If you aren't happy with your room when you arrive, ask for another. If another room is available, most lodgings will be willing to accommodate you.

Rentals (Apartments & Houses)   An increasingly popular way to experience Greece is to rent an apartment or a house; the advantages include freedom from the formalities of a hotel, often a more desirable location, and a kitchen that allows you to avoid the costs and occasional crush of restaurants. Such rentals do not come cheap, but if you calculate what two or more people might pay for a decent hotel, not to mention all the meals eaten out, a rental can turn out to be a good deal. (Cost per person per day in a really nice apartment runs about 100€/$130; a fancier villa with two bedrooms might cost about 200€/$260 per person per day.) Any full-service travel agency in your home country or in Greece should be able to put you in touch with an agency specializing in such rentals.

The fact is that the British dominate this field in Greece, both in terms of experience and sheer numbers of offerings. So via the Internet, anyone can now see what's offered and contact such outfits as **Simply Travel Ltd.,** Columbus House, Westwood Way, Westwood Business Park Coventry CV4 877 (© **0870/381-0201;** www.simplytravel.co.uk); or **Pure Crete,**

79 George St., Croydon, Surrey CRO 1LD (📞 **020/8760-0879;** www.pure-crete.com). Among those in the United States are **Villas International,** 17 Fox Lane, Anselmo CA 94960 (📞 **800/221-2260;** www.villasintl.com) and **Villas and Apartments Abroad,** 183 Madison Ave., Suite 201, New York, NY 10016 (📞 **212/213-6435;** www.vaanyc.com). In Canada, try **Grecian Holidays,** 75 The Donaway W., Don Mills, Ontario M3C 2E9 (📞 **800/268-6786;** www.grecianholidays.com). For those interested in investigating further on the Web, try **www.thehotel.gr** or **www.vacation homes.com**.

For apartment, farmhouse, or cottage stays of 2 weeks or more, **Idyll Untours** (**888-868-6871;** www.untours.com) provides exceptional vacation rentals for a reasonable price—which includes air/ground transportation, cooking facilities, and on-call support from a local resident. Best of all: Untours—named the "Most Generous Company in America" by Newman's Own—donates most profits to provide low-interest loans to underprivileged entrepreneurs around the world (see website for details).

Another option is to rent a traditional house in one of about 12 relatively rural or remote villages or settlements throughout Greece. These small traditional houses have been restored by the Greek National Tourism Organization (GNTO or EOT); to learn more about this possibility, contact the GNTO office nearest you. (See "Visitor Information," earlier in this chapter, or go to **www.dilos.com** or **www.thehotel.gr**.)

18 Tips on Dining

Descriptions of Greek food and the dining experience can—and do—fill entire books. Here, we've focused on distinctive highlights of dining in Greece. Greek meals, for instance, usually start off with appetizers known as *mezedes*—small plates of hot and cold selections shared from the center of the table. A notable aspect of restaurants in Greece is that you can make a meal out of as little or as much as you want from any section of the menu—all *mezedes,* if you wish.

In most restaurants, the fresh fish entree is priced "per kilo." Remember that a kilo is 2.21 pounds—so although expensive, it's a lot of fish! In the case of a smallish fish that you intend to order grilled, you can do nothing about the weight except ask for a smaller (or larger) one; realize, too, that with grilled fish, the weight includes the whole fish. If your portion is being cut from a really large fish, you can ask for the approximate weight. (A ½-lb. serving would be about a quarter of a kilo.)

Another distinction of Greek restaurants is that you can order at almost any hour of the day. Not in every little village and not in the more stylish restaurants, but many will start serving meal courses by late morning and on through the day to late at night. Greeks eat their evening meal quite late—usually not before 8pm—but restaurants are prepared to accommodate foreigners who like to sit down as early as 5:30pm. Room rates at most hotels now include satisfying buffet breakfasts. If you miss the buffet, you can usually find an outside cafe that can come up with the basics. Don't expect fresh orange juice, though. And if you have definite preferences for tea—especially herbal—consider bringing your own tea bags.

Most restaurants now have a "cover charge" that includes the table setting and a small basket of bread. (In some city cafes, you can pick up your drinks and snacks and eat them standing up at a table and avoid a cover charge.) It used to be that Greek waiters brought ice-cold

> ## (Tips Greek Siesta
>
> The combination of hot climate, heavy lunches, and plain old tradition means that most Greeks take siestas. So keep siesta hours, about 2 to 5pm, in mind when planning your own day. Even in Athens, you should be considerate about contacting friends or acquaintances at home during these hours.

pitchers of fresh water to each table without being asked to, but this custom has pretty much vanished. If you request "natural water," they may bring tap water to your table, but if you ask for "water," you will be brought a plastic bottle of water—and charged for it. (By Greek law, they are supposed to open the sealed top in your presence.)

Only the rare expensive restaurant in Athens and a few resorts expect advance reservations. During the height of the tourist season, however, anyone with a tight schedule should try to secure reservations.

19 Recommended Books, Films & Music

BOOKS   It seems only proper to begin with **Homer,** who though reputedly blind, will open your eyes to a Greece that is timeless. The *Iliad* and the *Odyssey* remain *the* imaginative gateways to Greece. Of the many fine translations, we favor those of Richmond Lattimore (Perennial, 1999). And lest you have any doubts that Homer was describing the same landscape you'll be seeing, you might want to read, as a companion to the epics, John V. Luce's *Celebrating Homer's Landscapes* (Yale Univ. Press, 1998). As for the more recent claim that Odysseus's home island of Ithaka was actually what has become a peninsula of Kefalonia, see *Odysseus Unbound* by Robert Bittlestone (Cambridge Univ. Press, 2006).

For a glimpse into **ancient Greek history,** the men reporting at the time are still the most exciting. *The History* by Herodotus and Thucydides's *Peloponnesian War* hold their own as consummate storytelling and will place you firmly in classical Greece. Among many fine translations, the most accessible are those of Aubrey de Selincourt (Penguin, 2003). *A Basic Survey of Greek Art* is a

good resource by John Boardman (Thames & Hudson, 4th rev. edition, 1996). For an in-depth but readable account of ancient Greece's major monument, try Mary Beard's *The Parthenon* (Harvard Univ. Press, 2003).

If you plan to attend any of the country's drama festivals, you will want to become familiar in advance with the play(s) you will see and perhaps bring along your favorite translation. For the tragedies, try those translated by David Grene and Richmond Lattimore (University of Chicago Press, 1991); for the comedies of Aristophanes, look for the translations by Paul Roche (Plume Books, 1984).

To be enlightened on the **Byzantine period,** you'd do well to start with Steven Runciman's *Byzantine Civilization* (North American Library, 2000) and Robin Cormack's *Byzantine Art* (Oxford Univ. Press, 2000). For an insider's account of scandal and splendor at the court of Justinian, pick up *The Secret History* of Procopius, translated by G. A. Williamson (Penguin, 1982). To put all this in quick perspective, as well as to follow the full sweep of Greek history to the present decade,

A Traveller's History of Greece, by Boatswain and Nicolson (Interlink, 4th rev. ed., 2000), is a pocket-size, helpful book. For just modern Greece, try Richard Clogg's *Concise History of Greece* (Cambridge, Univ. Press, 2nd ed. 2002).

In the **modern period,** Nikos Kazantzakis is the author who most appeals to foreigners. His *Zorba the Greek* (Touchstone, 1998) and *The Greek Passion* (Touchstone, 1959) are guaranteed to deliver you to Greece before your plane lands. Of the many travel books by foreigners, one still regarded as the most insightful is Henry Miller's *Colossus of Maroussi* (New Directions, 1975). Two classics by Patrick Leigh Fermor are *Mani: Travels in Southern Greece* (Murray, 1958) and *Rouneli: Travels in Northern Greece* (Murray, 1966). A fine book about modern Greece is Patricia Storace's *Dinner with Persephone* (Pantheon, 1996). And before taking on one of Lawrence Durrell's complete books about Greece, try the *Lawrence Durrell Travel Reader* (Carroll & Graf, 2004). For beach reading, John Fowles's *The Magus* (Laurel, 1985) is engaging. In a more serious vein concerning recent Greece, Nicholas Gage's *Eleni* (Ballantine, 1996) and Louis de Bernières's *Captain Corelli's Mandolin* (Vintage, 1995) are both extremely captivating.

FILMS Of the many films made in and about Greece, several come to mind, all more or less readily available on video or DVD. The films of Michael Cacoyannis—from his Euripides trilogy, including *Trojan Women* and *Iphigenia,* to his famed *Zorba the Greek*—are essential viewing. So too is Costa-Gavras's *Z,* a gripping political thriller inspired by the assassination of Grigorios Lambrakis in 1963. The film version of Nicholas Gage's *Eleni* manages to be nearly as disturbing as the book. There is no avoiding—and no reason to avoid—*Never on Sunday* and *Captain Corelli's Mandolin.* Finally, for a good laugh and to enjoy the Greek scenery,

Jacqueline Bisset and Irene Papas team up to confront *High Season* on the island of Rhodes. The even sillier *Summer Lovers* (1982) is set on Santorini. And don't forget, 007 has "done" Greece *(For Your Eyes Only),* as did Gregory Peck in *The Guns of Navarone.*

MUSIC There is no denying that most non-Greeks have not been exposed to much Greek music (Yanni doesn't count!). But Greece has a long and distinguished—and beautiful—musical tradition that will repay those with inquisitive musical tastes. (Where recordings are available online, their labels and numbers are given here. Recordings of others are probably to be found only in Greece.) Each region—indeed, many an island—has its own variation of traditional folk music. The most complete collection is issued by the Greek Society for the Dissemination of National Music—over 30 CDs under its SDNM label. More easily acquired is Legacy's *Authentic Greek Folk Songs and Dances* (no. 318). If you want to focus on two especially strong regional traditions, Lyra Records (no. 0168) has a fine selection of Cretan and Dodecanese folk music. The clarinet has long been one of the most popular instruments for traditional Greek music and one of the finest modern players Petros Loukas Hlakias, can be heard on *Clarinet* (FM688).

The more recent *rembetika* music emerged at the time of the American jazz, to which it is often compared. Without intimate knowledge of the language, you lose the lyrics, but the emotion comes through. Lyra has a fine four-CD anthology (nos. 4635–4637 and 4644). Rounder Select (no. 1079) offers another option. Easydisc presents *The Athenians: Greek Songs, Dances and Rembetika* (no. 369019). Two of the great singers of *rembetika* are Domna Samiou (numerous CDs on various labels) and Sotira Bellou (try Lyra 0766). For those who like the twangy-metallic sound of *bouzoukia* music, Rounder Select (no. 1139) offers one of its masters, Markos Vamvakaris.

Often drawing on folk music, *rembetika*, or *bouzoukia*, a more sophisticated "classical" music emerged by the 1950s. The two practitioners of *entekhno* (artistic) best known to the world at large are Manos Hatzidhakis and Mikis Theodorakis. The former is famed for his music for the film *Never on Sunday,* but would prefer to be known for more serious work such as his songs (try Columbia GCX 107). Theodorakis is also best known abroad for his music for the movie *Zorba,* but his masterwork is his soundtrack of the Nobel prize–winner Odysseus Elytis's *To Axion Esti* (EMI International no. 483759). Yannis Markopoulos, George Tsontakis, Stavros Xylouris, Nikolas Labrinakos, and Christos Hatzis are other contemporary "high art" Greek musicians whose works are worth seeking out. And Iannis Xenakis's demanding compositions have become part of the modern avant-garde repertory. You might start with his orchestral and chamber music on Col-Legno (no. 20504).

Greece, of course, has its homegrown pop music, but it has been greatly influenced by international trends, including rock and, more recently, rap. One Greek pop star has an international following—Nana Mouskouri. And one of the more popular of contemporary Greek singers can be heard on *The Very Best of George Dalaras* (Ark 21).

FAST FACTS: Greece

American Express Amex maintains an extensive network of offices and agents throughout Greece. The Athens office ((C) **210/325-4690**) is located at 31 Panepistimiou, overlooking Syntagma Square. We indicate the locations of these offices and agencies throughout this book, as well as describe the various travel arrangements and financial services offered by American Express.

Area Codes Area codes within Greece range from three digits in Athens (210) to as many as five digits in less populated locales. All phone numbers provided in the text start with the proper area code.

ATM Networks See "Money & Costs," p. 36.

Banks Banks are open to the public Monday through Thursday from 8am to 2pm, Friday from 8am to 1:30pm. Some banks have additional hours for foreign-currency exchange. All banks are closed on the long list of Greek holidays. (See "When to Go," earlier in this chapter.)

Business Hours Greek business and office hours take some getting used to, especially in the afternoon, when most English-speaking people are accustomed to getting things done in high gear. Compounding the problem is that it is virtually impossible to pin down the precise hours of opening. We can start by saying that almost all stores and services are closed on Sunday—except, of course, tourist-oriented shops and services. On Monday, Wednesday, and Saturday, hours are usually 9am to 3pm; Tuesday, Thursday, and Friday, 9am to 2pm and 5 to 7pm. The afternoon siesta is generally observed from 3 to 5pm, though many tourist-oriented businesses have a minimal crew on duty during naptime, and they may keep extended hours, often from 8am to 10pm. (In fact, in tourist centers, shops may be open at all kinds of hours.) Most government offices are open Monday through Friday only, from 8am to 3pm. Call ahead to check the hours of businesses you *must* deal with, and try not to disturb Greek friends during siesta hours. ***Final advice:*** Anything you really need to accomplish in a government office, business, or store should be done on weekdays between about 9am and 1pm.

Car Rentals See "Getting Around Greece," p. 58.

Cashpoints See "Money & Costs," p. 36.

Climate Control Almost all Greek hotels recommended in this guide now promise air-conditioning in the hot season and heating in the colder months. The equipment is indeed there, but you should be aware that—except in the most expensive hotels—neither will necessarily be as adequate as you might like.

Crime Crimes against tourists are not a significant concern in Greece. Athens is probably the safest capital in Europe. Pickpocketing and purse-snatching may be slightly on the rise, especially in heavily touristed areas, but breaking into cars remains rare. Tourists, however, are conspicuous and much more likely to carry valuables, so take normal precautions—lock the car, don't leave cameras and such gear visible, and so on. Also, it is no longer safe to leave valuables unattended on all beaches. And young women should observe the obvious precautions in dealing with men in isolated locales.

Currency See "Money & Costs," p. 36.

Customs **What You Can Bring into Greece.**

Passengers from North America arriving in Athens aboard international flights are generally not searched, and if you have nothing to declare, continue through the green lane. (Because of the continuing threat of terrorism, baggage is X-rayed before boarding of domestic flights.) However, citizens of the United States, Canada, Australia, New Zealand, and other non-E.U. countries do face a few common-sensical restrictions on what you can bring into Greece. Clearly, no narcotics: Greece is *very* tough on drug users! No explosives or weapons—although upon application, a sportsman might be able to bring in a legitimate hunting weapon. Only medications for amounts properly prescribed for your own use are allowed. Plants with soil are not. Dogs and cats can be brought in, but they must have proof of recent rabies and other health shots. No parrots are allowed.

You are allowed to bring into Greece duty-free personal belongings including clothes, camping gear, and most sports equipment. (Certain watersports equipment, such as windsurfers, can be brought in only if a Greek citizen residing in Greece guarantees they will be re-exported.) If you are traveling with your own scuba tank, you must have it sealed upon entry; it will be unsealed at recognized scuba locales. Visitors from outside the European Union are allowed up to 10 kilos of food and beverage, 200 cigarettes, 50 cigars, 250 grams of tobacco, 1 liter of distilled alcohol or 2 liters of wine, 50 grams of perfume, 500 grams of coffee, and 100 grams of tea.

You may bring two cameras with 10 rolls of film each, a movie or video camera, a portable radio, a phonograph or tape recorder, a typewriter, and a laptop computer. These will probably not be inspected, but in some cases they can be written into your passport, so you'd better have them when you leave! In fact, it is unlikely that you will be stopped at entry points, but if you are, and it is discovered that you are carrying much more than $1,000 in cash, this might be written in your passport. You will then be expected to produce receipts if you intend to leave without the same amount. Entering with your own car or other motor vehicle requires a fair amount of paperwork: Check with Greek embassy or consular authorities before setting out.

There are presently no restrictions on the amount of traveler's checks you may carry upon either arrival or departure, although technically, amounts over $1,000 should be declared. If you plan to leave the country with more than $1,000 in bank notes (or its equivalent in other currency), technically you must declare at least that sum upon entry. No more than 1,000€ ($1,300) per traveler may be imported or exported.

U.K. citizens and those of other E.U. nations are relatively free from most of these restrictions, but you still must comply with some, such as those pertaining to drugs, firearms, certain plants, some animals, and scuba tanks. There are also restrictions on young people importing alcohol and tobacco. Even large sums of currency or unusual amounts of electronic equipment might warrant notice. Basically, you are allowed to bring in what is reasonable for personal use but not for engagement in a business.

What You Can Take Out of Greece

All Nationalities: Greek antiquities are strictly protected by law. No genuine antiquities may be taken out of Greece without prior special permission from the **Archaeological Service,** 3 Polignotou, Athens. Also, you must be able to explain how you acquired any genuinely old objects—in particular, icons or religious articles. A dealer or shopkeeper must provide you with an export certificate for any object dating from before 1830.

And in general, keep all receipts for major purchases in order to clear Customs on your return home. To avoid having to pay duty on foreign-made personal items you owned before you left on your trip, bring along a bill of sale, an insurance policy, a jeweler's appraisal, or purchase receipts. You can register items readily identifiable by a permanently affixed serial number or marking—think laptop computers, cameras, and CD players—with Customs before you leave. Take the items to the nearest Customs office or register them with Customs at the airport from which you're departing. You'll receive, at no cost, a Certificate of Registration, which allows duty-free entry for the life of the item.

U.S. citizens: For specifics on what you can bring back, download the invaluable free pamphlet *Know Before You Go* online at **www.cbp.gov**. (Click on "Travel," and then click on "Know Before You Go Online Brochure.") Or request the pamphlet from the **U.S. Customs & Border Protection (CBP),** 1300 Pennsylvania Ave. NW, Washington, DC 20229 (© 877/287-8667).

Canadian Citizens: For a clear summary of **Canadian** rules, write for the booklet *I Declare,* issued by the **Canada Customs and Revenue Agency** (© 800/461-9999 in Canada, or 204/983-3500; www.ccra-adrc.gc.ca).

U.K. Citizens: For information, contact HM Customs & Excise at © 0845/10-9000 (from outside the U.K., 020/8929-0152) or consult their website at www.hmce.uk.

Australian Citizens: A helpful brochure available from Australian consulates or Customs offices is *Know Before You Go.* For more information, call the **Australian Customs Service** at ℂ **1300/363-263;** or go to www.customs.gov.au.

New Zealand Citizens: Most questions are answered in a free pamphlet available at New Zealand consulates and Customs offices: *New Zealand Customs Guide for Travellers, Notice no. 4.* For more information, contact **New Zealand Customs,** The Customhouse, 17–21 Whitmore St., Box 2218, Wellington (ℂ **04/473-6099** or 0800/428-786; www.customs.govt.nz).

Driving Rules See "Getting Around Greece," p. 58.

Drugstores These are called *pharmikon* in Greek; aside from the obvious indications in windows and interiors, they are identified by a green cross. For minor medical problems, go first to the nearest **pharmacy.** Pharmacists usually speak English, and many medications can be dispensed without prescription. In the larger cities, if it is closed, there should be a sign in the window directing you to the nearest open one. Newspapers also list the pharmacies that are open late or all night.

Electricity Electric current in Greece is 220 volts AC, alternating at 50 cycles. (Some larger hotels have 110-volt low-wattage outlets for electric shavers, but they aren't good for hair dryers and most other appliances.) Electrical outlets require Continental-type plugs with two round prongs. U.S. travelers will need an adapter plug *and* a transformer/converter, unless their appliances are dual-voltage. (Such transformers can be bought in stores like Radio Shack.) Laptop computer users will want to check their requirements; a transformer may be necessary, and surge protectors are recommended. But increasingly various appliances—including laptops and hair dryers—allow for a simple switch to the 220 volts.

Embassies & Consulates See "Fast Facts: Athens" in chapter 5 for a list of embassies and consulates. United Kingdom citizens can get emergency aid by calling ℂ **210/727-2600** during the day; at night, try ℂ **210/723-7727.** United States citizens can get emergency aid by calling ℂ **210/721-2951** during the day; at night, try ℂ **210/729-4301.**

Emergencies If there is no tourist police officer available (ℂ **171**), contact the local **police,** ℂ **100.** For **fire,** call ℂ **199.** For **medical emergencies** and/or first aid and/or an ambulance, call ℂ **166.** For **hospitals,** call ℂ **106.** For **automobile emergencies,** put out a triangular danger sign and call ℂ **104** or 154. Embassies, consulates, and many hotels can recommend an English-speaking **doctor.**

Etiquette Greeks generally observe the same practices with which most of us are familiar, but there are a few special variations.

APPROPRIATE ATTIRE Dress—or undress!—codes have been greatly relaxed at Greek beach resorts in recent years, but Greeks remain uncomfortable with beachwear or slovenly garb in villages and cities. Women are expected—indeed, often required—to cover their arms and upper legs before entering monasteries and churches. Some priests and monks are stricter than others and may flatly bar men as well as women if they feel that the men are not dressed suitably.

GESTURES Greeks wave goodbye with the back of the hand—to hold up the open palm is to give the "evil eye"! Either wave sideways or in a little circle, but always with the palm turned away. When you are introduced to a Greek for the first time, a handshake is normal. When you get to know Greeks fairly well, the kiss on both cheeks is the accepted greeting. When Greeks meet small children, they tend to pinch them on the cheeks or pat them a bit harder than most of us would.

AVOIDING OFFENSE Greeks do not put a priority on punctuality, so do not be offended if they do not show up until well after the appointed time. Meanwhile, many Greeks observe a siesta between the hours of about 1pm and about 5pm so you are advised not to call on them at their homes during those hours unless invited to do so.

HOSPITALITY Greeks consider it a point of honor to treat foreigners to a coffee or drink: You should ask to pay your share or to pick up the tab for both, but once the Greek has insisted, you should stop insisting and simply thank them. However, if you are invited to a Greek's home for a meal or social event, flowers or chocolates are appropriate gifts. And by the way, Greeks make less of their birthday than their name day—that is, the day assigned to the saint after whom they have been named.

Here are three books that discuss some situations you might encounter as you make your way around Greece:

• *The Global Etiquette Guide to Europe* (Wiley Publishing, Inc.)
• *Kiss, Bow or Shake Hands: How to Do Business in 60 Countries* (Adams Media)
• *Culture Shock: Greece!* (Graphic Arts Center Publishing Co.)

Guides You may prefer to employ local guides to take you and/or a small circle of fellow travelers to visit sites or cities. Professional guides in Greece are thoroughly trained, and the fees they charge are well regulated. Most reputable travel agencies can arrange for such guides. You can also contact the **Union of Official Guides,** 9A Apollonos, 10557 Athens (⟨©⟩ **210/322-9705**). Our only caution is that as good as these official guides are, they are trained to produce a stream of facts, not make small talk.

Haggling Greek merchants resent foreigners who try to haggle over prices. In general, the marked price is the cost of the item. That said, some "games" can be played. Hesitate, consult with your companions with the appropriate expressions of regret, set the object down—with thanks!—and head for the exit. You may well be offered a lower price. But that is the merchant's prerogative, and all depends upon the manner in which this behavior is conducted. If you come across as demanding or disapproving, you can forget any further negotiating.

Holidays See "When to Go," p. 26 and the "Greece Calendar of Events," p. 27.

Hospitals Addresses of hospitals in all major cities are indicated under the "Fast Facts" for those cities.

Internet Access See "Staying Connected," p. 49.

Language Language is usually not a problem for English speakers in Greece, as so much of the population has lived abroad, where English is the primary language. Young people learn it in school, from Anglo-American–dominated pop culture, and in special classes meant to prepare them for the contemporary world of business. Many television programs are also broadcast in their original languages, and American prime-time soaps are very popular, nearly inescapable. Even advertisements have an increasingly high English content. Don't let all this keep you from trying to pick up at least a few words of Greek; your effort will be rewarded by your hosts, who realize how difficult their language is for foreigners and will patiently help you improve your pronunciation and usage. Look for books and audio courses on learning Greek, including *Berlitz's Greek for Travelers, Passport's Conversational Greek in 7 Days,* and *Teach Yourself Greek Complete Course* (book and CD pack). The appendix, "The Greek Language," can give you some basics.

Laundromats, Laundries & Dry Cleaning All cities and towns of any size will have laundromats, laundries, and dry-cleaning establishments. The addresses of laundromats in all major cities are provided under the "Fast Facts" sections for those cities. Many travelers prefer to make arrangements through their hotel desks; this is fine, but be prepared to pay heavily for even the smallest bundle. (Then again, everything, including socks, will have been ironed!). If you leave your laundry or dry cleaning, be sure you are in agreement as to the time it will be ready, especially if you must leave town. A medium-size bag of laundry may cost about 15€ ($20), washed, dried, and neatly folded.

Legal Aid If you need legal assistance, contact your own or another English-speaking embassy or consulate; their addresses and phone numbers are provided under the "Fast Facts" sections of major cities.

Liquor Laws The minimum age for being served alcohol in public locales is 18. Wine and beer are generally available in eating places but not in all coffeehouses or dessert cafes. Alcoholic beverages are sold in food stores as well as liquor stores. Although a certain amount of high spirits is appreciated, Greeks do *not* appreciate public drunkenness. The resort centers where mobs of young foreigners party every night are tolerated as necessary for the tourist trade, but the behavior wins no respect for foreigners.

Lost & Found Be sure to contact all of your credit card companies the minute you discover your wallet has been lost or stolen, and file a report at the nearest police precinct. Your credit card company or insurer may require a police report number or record of the loss. Most credit card companies have an emergency toll-free number to call if your card is lost or stolen; they may be able to wire you a cash advance immediately or deliver an emergency credit card in a day or two. From Greece, Visa's U.S. emergency number is ℂ **001-800-11-638-0304**; within North America, it's ℂ **800/847-2911**. American Express cardholders and traveler's check holders call ℂ **001-336/393-1111**; within North America call ℂ **800/992-3404**. MasterCard holders call ℂ **001-800/11-887-0303**; within North America call ℂ **800/307-7309**. For other credit cards, call the toll-free number directory at ℂ **800/555-1212**.

If you need emergency cash over the weekend when banks and American Express offices are closed, you can have money wired to you via **Western Union** (ℂ **800/325-6000**; www.westernunion.com).

Identity theft and fraud are potential consequences of losing your wallet, especially if you've lost your driver's license along with your cash and credit cards. Notify the major credit-reporting bureaus immediately; placing a fraud alert on your records may protect you against liability for criminal activity. The three major U.S. credit-reporting agencies are **Equifax** (© **888/766-0008**; www.equifax.com), **Experian** (© **888/397-3742**; www.experian.com), and **TransUnion** (© **800/680-7289**; www.transunion.com). Finally, if you've lost all forms of photo ID, call your airline and explain the situation; they might allow you to board the plane if you have a copy of your passport or birth certificate and a copy of the police report you've filed.

Mail The mail service of Greece is reliable—but slow. (Postcards usually arrive weeks after you have arrived home.) You can receive mail addressed to you c/o Poste Restante, General Post Office, City (or Town), Island (or Province), Greece. You will need your passport to collect this mail. Many hotels will accept, hold, and even forward mail for you also; ask first. American Express clients can receive mail at any Amex office in Athens, Corfu, Iraklion, Mykonos, Patras, Rhodes, Santorini, Skiathos, and Thessaloniki, for a nominal fee and with proper identification. If you are in a particular hurry, try FedEx or one of the other major international private carriers; travel agencies can direct you to these.

Postage rates have been going up in Greece, as they are elsewhere. At press time, a postcard or a letter under 20 grams (about .7 oz.) costs .65€ (85¢) to North America and Europe; 20 to 50 grams (up to 1.75 oz.), 1.15€ ($1.50); 50 to 100 grams (3.5 oz.) 1.60€ ($2.10). Rates for packages depend on size as well as weight, but are reasonable. *Note:* Do not wrap or seal any package—you must be prepared to show the contents to a postal clerk.

Measurements See the chart on the inside cover of this book for details on converting metric measurements to nonmetric equivalents.

Newspapers & Magazines All cities, large towns, and major tourist centers have at least one shop or kiosk that carries a selection of foreign-language publications; most of these are flown or shipped in on the very day of publication. English-language readers have a wide selection, including most of the British papers (*Daily Telegraph, Financial Times, Guardian, Independent, Times),* the *International Herald Tribune* (with its English-language insert of the well-known Athens newspaper, *Kathimerini*), and *USA Today.* A decent (and cheaper!) alternative is the English-language paper published in Athens, *Athens News,* widely available throughout Greece.

Passports Allow plenty of time before your trip to apply for a passport; processing normally takes at least 3 to 5 weeks and can take longer during busy periods (especially spring). If you need a passport in a hurry, you'll pay a significantly higher processing fee.

For Residents of Australia: You can pick up an application from your local post office or any branch of **Passports Australia,** but you must schedule an interview at the passport office to present your application materials. Call the **Australian Passport Information Service** at © **131-232,** or visit the government website at www.passports.gov.au.

For Residents of Canada: Passport applications are available at travel agencies throughout Canada or from the central **Passport Office,** Department of Foreign Affairs and International Trade, Ottawa, ON K1A 0G3 (✆ **800/567-6868;** www.dfait-maeci.gc.ca/passport).

For Residents of Ireland: You can apply for a 10-year passport at the **Passport Office,** Setanta Centre, Molesworth Street, Dublin 2 (✆ **01/671-1633;** www.irlgov.ie/iveagh). Those under age 18 and over 65 must apply for a €12 ($16) 3-year passport. You can also apply at 1A S. Mall, Cork (✆ **021/272-525**); or at most main post offices.

For Residents of New Zealand: You can pick up a passport application at any **New Zealand Passports Office** or download it from their website. Contact the Passports Office at ✆ **0800/225-050** in New Zealand or 04/474-8100; or go to www.passports.govt.nz.

For Residents of the United Kingdom: To pick up an application for a standard 10-year passport (5-year passport for children under 16), visit your nearest passport office, major post office, or travel agency. You can also contact the **United Kingdom Passport Service** at ✆ **0870/521-0410;** or search its website at www.ukpa.gov.uk.

For Residents of the United States: If you are applying for your first passport, you must go in person to one of 6,000 passport desks across the country (most convenient are those in post offices). Passports can be renewed by downloading the appropriate form on the website of the U.S. Information Center, **http://travel.state.gov.** For general information, call the **National Passport Information Center** (✆ **877/487-2778**); or go to that State Department website listed above.

Photocopying In most Greek cities, the bookstores offer commercial photocopying services.

Photography In several locales around Greece, photographing military or police installations is forbidden. These locales are posted and you are expected to observe the law. Cameras, film, accessories, and photo developing (including express service) are widely available, though slightly more expensive, in Greece.

Police To report a crime or medical emergency, or for information or other assistance, first contact the local **tourist police** (telephone numbers are under "Essentials" in the destination chapters that follow), where an English-speaking officer is more likely to be found. If there is no tourist police officer available (✆ **171**), contact the **local police** at ✆ **100.**

Radio & Television The Greek ERT 1 radio station has weather and news in English at 7:40am. The BBC World Service can be picked up on shortwave frequencies, often at 9.140, 15.07, and 12.09 Mhz; on FM it is usually at 107.1. Antenna TV, CNN, Eurochannel, and other cable networks are widely available. Many better hotels offer cable television.

Reservations During the height of the tourist season, anyone with a tight schedule or strict preferences should definitely secure reservations at hotels, airlines, ship lines, and major festival performances.

Restrooms Public restrooms are generally available in any good-size Greek town, and though they are sometimes rather crude, they usually do work. (Old-fashioned stand-up/squat facilities are still found.) Carry tissue or toilet paper with you at all times. In some places—even modern restaurants and hotels—you are told not to flush the paper down the toilet, but to use the receptacles provided. In an emergency, you can ask to use the facilities of a restaurant or shop; however, near major attractions, the facilities are denied to all but customers because traffic is too heavy. If you use any such facilities, respect its sponsor and give an attendant a tip.

Safety See "Health" and "Safety," p. 40 and 42.

Smoking Greeks continue to be among the most persistent smokers. Smoking is prohibited on all domestic flights, in certain areas or types of ships, and in some public buildings (such as post offices), but except on airplanes, many Greeks—and some foreigners—feel free to puff away at will. (The airport in Athens is practically a cancer culture lab.) Hotels are only beginning to claim that they have set aside rooms or even floors for nonsmokers, so ask about them, if it matters to you. If you are really bothered by smoke while eating, about all you can do is position yourself as best as possible—and then be prepared to leave if it gets really bad.

Taxes & Service Charges Unless otherwise noted, all hotel prices include a service charge of usually 12%, a 6% value-added tax (VAT), and a 4.5% community tax. In most restaurants, a 13% service charge, an 8% VAT, and some kind of municipal tax (in Athens it is 5%) are included in the prices and final bill. (Don't confuse any of these charges with a standard "cover charge" that may be .50€ to 2€ (65¢–$2.60) per place setting. Also see "Tipping," below.) A VAT of 19% is added to rental-car rates.

All purchases include a VAT of anywhere from 4% to 18%. If you have purchased an item that costs 100€ ($130) or more and are a citizen of a non–European Union nation, you can get most of this refunded (provided you export it within 90 days of purchase). It's easiest to shop at stores that display the sign TAX-FREE FOR TOURISTS. However, any store should be able to provide you with a Tax-Free Check Form, which you complete in the store. If you use your charge card, the receipt will list the VAT separately from the cost of the item. As you are leaving the country, present a copy of this form to the refund desk (usually at the Customs office). Be prepared to show both the goods and the receipt as proof of purchase. Also be prepared to wait a fair amount of time before you get the refund. (In fact, the process at the airport seems designed to discourage you from trying to obtain the refund.)

Time The European 24-hour clock is officially used to measure time, so on schedules you'll see noon as 1200, 3:30pm as 1530, and 11pm as 2300. In informal conversation, however, Greeks express time much as we do—though noon may mean anywhere from noon to 3pm, afternoon is 3 to 7pm, and evening is 7pm to midnight.

Time Zone Greece is 2 hours ahead of Greenwich Mean Time. In reference to North American time zones, it's 7 hours ahead of Eastern Standard Time, 8 hours ahead of Central Standard Time, 9 hours ahead of Mountain Standard

Time, and 10 hours ahead of Pacific Standard Time. Note that Greece does observe daylight saving time, although it may not start and stop on the same days as in North America.

Tipping Restaurant bills, including the VAT and any local taxes, now include a 10% to 15% service charge. Nevertheless, it's customary to leave an additional 5% to 10% for the waiter, especially if he or she has provided special service. Certainly round off on larger bills; even on small bills, leave change up to the nearest 1€ ($1.30). Good taxi service merits a tip of 5% to 10%. (Greeks rarely tip taxi drivers, but tourists are expected to.) Hotel chambermaids should be left about 2€ ($2.60) per night per couple. Bellhops and doormen should be tipped 1€ ($1.30) to 5€ ($6.50), depending on the services they provide.

Useful Phone Numbers **U.S. Department of State Overseas Citizens Services** (such as travel advisories and medical emergencies) are as follows. From abroad, © **001-317/472-2328.** From North America, during East Coast daylight hours, © **888/407-4747.** For 24-hour service, © **202-647-4000.**

   U.S. Passport Agency can be reached at © **877/487-2778.**

International Traveler's Hot Line for U.S. Centers for Disease Control is © 877/394-8747.

Water The public drinking water in Greece is safe to drink, although it can be slightly brackish in some locales near the sea. For that reason, many people prefer the bottled water commonly available at restaurants, hotels, cafes, food stores, and kiosks. The days when Greek restaurants automatically served glasses of cold fresh water are gone; you can try to insist on simply the tap water but you are now usually made to feel that you must order bottled water, at which point you will have to choose between natural or carbonated *(metalliko),* and domestic or imported. Cafes, however, tend to provide a glass of natural water.

3

Suggested Greece Itineraries

Greece is such a small country—its total area is about the state of Alabama's—that you might think it's possible to see much of it in a relatively short visit. Not so. Its mountainous terrain makes distances deceptive. Many desirable destinations are located on islands, requiring many hours of travel back and forth. And so many destinations are desirable. But with special planning, you can get the most out of whatever limited time you have.

The itineraries laid out below require from 8 to 16 days on the ground in Greece. (In addition, plan on spending the better part of a day to get to Greece and another day to return home.) The itineraries mix modes of transportation: You'll take buses, trains, cars, ships, and planes. Greek public transportation—intercity buses and trains—is now fairly comfortable and reliable. It's also a great way to meet locals. Schedules, however, often meet the needs of workers, not tourists. Although isolating, driving a car provides you with the greatest flexibility. Thousands of travelers choose this option, but make sure you feel comfortable driving a rented car in Greece.

When choosing your jaunt, you have to balance cost with time. Some islands are served only by ship; others, by ship and plane. Because these itineraries include islands, they work best in the summer, May through September. In the off season, the weather is not dependable, many hotels and restaurants close, and

airline and ferry schedules to some of these places become extremely limited. The converse of that also applies: The closer to high season you intend to travel, the more imperative it is to make reservations in advance.

All of the itineraries below end up in Athens and, in theory, you have 24 hours of leeway to allow for any unanticipated travel delays such as weather, accidents, or strikes. We must admit, though, that Greece keeps its own schedule. On any given day, a museum or archaeological site may be closed without notice. Call in advance to make sure that a destination will be open while you're traveling, and double-check your reservations, especially during special occasions such as Greek Easter week. We strongly advise you to avoid Greek Orthodox Easter; much of Greece shuts down and accommodations and transportation are on overload.

You can also sign up for one of the standard cruises that stop at several of the major islands and occasionally put into the mainland; as these last about 7 days, this would mean sailing off on your first day in Greece and then having only the last day for Athens. (Such cruises are described in detail in chapter 4.) Another alternative is to sign up for one of the bus tours, from 3 to 7 days, that visit the major mainland sites. Use the itineraries below, though, if you want to set your own pace and choose what you see. *Kalo taxidi* (have a good trip)!

1 Greece in 1 Week

Ideally, everyone should have a whole summer for Greece. But let's face it, most people leave home on a Friday evening and then fly back to work the next Sunday. That's 8 full days on the ground. We've included two weekends, but any 8 days will work. This itinerary is for those interested in sampling the distinctive "historical" Greece. Mold this to your needs. You can always drop a museum or site and take time to relax on a beach. However, this particular itinerary involves a fair amount of moving about and checking in and out of hotels: Maximum Greece in a minimum of time.

Day ❶: Athens & the Acropolis

Arrive in Athens and get settled in your hotel. Then, walk to the **Acropolis** ✿✿✿ (p. 194) to see the **Parthenon,** arguably the world's number-one destination. Make time for the **Acropolis Museum** (art-course sculptures!) and the **Theater of Dionysos** ✿✿ (ground zero of Greek drama!). For a modest dinner, head to **Platanos Taverna** ✿✿ (p. 177) or another of the restaurants in the Plaka (p. 176).

Day ❷: Athens & Santorini

Check out the gold masks, jewelry, sculptures, and other highlights at the **National Archaeological Museum** ✿✿✿ (p. 203). Then head to the **Ancient Agora** ✿✿ (p. 199) to experience the more down-to-earth ancient Athens. Imagine the individuals' lives when you visit the ancient **Kerameikos Cemetery** ✿ (p. 199). Any cafe nearby will do for a cool drink. Then hit the museum trail again (p. 201). Plan to lunch at **Oraia Ellada** ✿✿ in the Plaka (p. 183). Explore **Syntagma Square** (p. 147). Take the evening flight or overnight ferry to Santorini. Get a taxi to Oia (Ia) and, after checking in at a hotel there, try **Skala** ✿ for dinner (p. 387).

Days ❸ & ❹: Santorini & Crete

Whether **Ancient Akrotiri** ✿✿✿ is totally, or only partially, open, you must see it! (p. 372). Spend the rest of the day at Kamari beach, with no end of cafes for snacks. Have lunch on the beach at **Camille Stefani** (p. 386). Later, take in the restored mansion as you dine formally at **Restaurant-Bar 1800** ✿✿ (p. 387) in Oia. On Day 4, look for the ancient cave houses hollowed into the solidified ash (p. 381) before flying via Athens or taking the ferry directly to Iraklion, Crete (p. 327). Check into your hotel, then enjoy a stroll around town and grab a patio table for an Italian-Greek dinner in the heart of the city at **Loukoulos** ✿ (p. 338).

Days ❺ & ❻: Crete

Go early to visit **Knossos** ✿✿✿ (p. 332), then see the snake goddesses and rich Minoan artifacts at the **Archaeological Museum** ✿✿✿ (p. 331). Go where the archaeologists used to go, and have lunch at the **Ionia** (p. 338). After a siesta, take the walking tour of Iraklion (p. 333) before treating yourself to a superb meal at the **Brillant Gourmet** ✿✿ (p. 337). Spend Day 6 touring **Chania** ✿✿ (by rental car, public transportation, or escorted tour), with its relatively intact Venetian-Turkish old town (p. 341); or **Phaestos** ✿✿, the second-most ambitious Minoan palace (p. 340). Expect to be on the road for 5 hours round-trip for each. Eat lunch at the restaurant at Phaetos site or if you didn't take that trip, along Chania's harbor at the **Amphora** (p. 350). Take an evening flight back to Athens.

Day ❼: Athens or Delphi?

You may prefer to relax and spend a leisurely day taking in more of Athens, its museums, and its street life. Otherwise, we suggest a 1-day excursion to **Delphi** ✿✿✿ (177km/110 miles). (Your hotel can make the arrangements.) At Delphi, in

Greece in 1 Week

addition to major attractions such as the **Sanctuary of Apollo** ✹✹✹ and the **Delphi Museum** ✹✹✹ (p. 513), you'll be treated to breathtaking vistas. If that's too far, take the much shorter excursion to **Marathon** (p. 241). Then, in the late afternoon, you could go to the **Temple of Poseidon** ✹✹ at Sounion (p. 238). Stay for sunset before heading back to Athens.

Whatever you've chosen to do, treat yourself to a leisurely dinner when you get back to Athens; if you want to admire the Acropolis while you eat, try a rooftop table at **Strofi Tavern** ✹ (p. 188).

Day ❽: Flight Home
Go to the airport and fly home.

2 Greece in 2 Weeks

Two weeks is enough time to at least taste the different flavors of Greece. From the must-see ancient monuments (the Acropolis in Athens, the stadium in Olympia, and the site of the Delphic Oracle on the slopes of Mount Parnassus) to the famous isles (Mykonos, with its snow-white houses and trendy all-night bars; and volcanic Santorini, with its amazing harbor and sheer cliffs) to less-famous places that not all visitors know about when they come to Greece (but fall in love with when they discover them)—we're going to show you how to see all this and leave time for discoveries of your own. If you have the time and the energy, take our suggestions for little, off-the-beaten-track sites near the more well-known places.

Day ❶: Athens & The Archaeological Parkway

Settle into your hotel, then go for a get-acquainted walk along **The Archaeological Park,** which runs from Syntagma Square around the **Acropolis** ✦✦✦, past the **Agora** ✦✦, and into the **Plaka,** the heart of old—and touristy—Athens (p. 147). Do what the Athenians do and stop for cappuccino, pastries, cheese, or yogurt at **Oraia Ellada** ✦✦ (p. 183), a Plaka shop with a restaurant that offers a drop-dead-gorgeous Acropolis view. Browse through the old and new Greek folk art before continuing your walk. (If you get really tired, hop the Metro back to your hotel.) For lunch, sit under the plane tree as you enjoy roast lamb at **Platanos Taverna** ✦✦ (p. 177). Feeling revived? Stop at the little **Museum of Popular Greek Musical Instruments** ✦✦ (p. 202), just a few feet away. Listen to Greek music and enjoy the peaceful garden. The slumbering tortoises there may remind you it's siesta time. Go to your hotel for a nap before you head out again for a nighttime stroll back to the Acropolis (even if it's closed) and dinner. If you're hungry, have a bite at one of the many fast-food cafeterias on Syntagma Square. Point to what you want and leave your phrase book in your pocket. If you've feeling energetic, head into the Plaka and eat at **Platanos Taverna** ✦✦ (p. 177), one of the nicest old-time "authentic" tavernas.

Day ❷: Museums & Mount Likavitos

Visit the **National Archaeological Museum** ✦✦✦ to see art-course sculptures, gold, and other incredible artifacts (p. 204). Then head to the Acropolis, but first grab a snack at one of the kiosks on the slopes. Spend the rest of the day enjoying Athens's sprawling **National Garden** (p. 210) and watching Greek families. Then have dinner at nearby **Aegli** ✦✦ (p. 184). Or ride the cable car up **Mount Likavitos** (p. 214) before dinner at **To Kafeneio** ✦✦ (p. 186). Located in Kolonaki, the restaurant near the mountain is a great place to enjoy the bustle of Athens's most fashionable neighborhood.

Day ❸: Mykonos & Paradise

By plane or ship, go to Mykonos. Settle into your hotel, then take a bus to one of the beaches outside town—**Paradise** ✦ (p. 426) attracts partyers who love loud beach-bar music with their sun and sand, while **Ornos** is a quieter beach preferred by families (p. 425). Buy something for lunch on the beach. Back in town, get lost in the town's winding streets; end up at **Caprice** in "Little Venice" for a dry martini and good people-watching (p. 439). Before dinner, walk to Mykonos's famous three waterside windmills to take in the view back across the harbor. You'll see Little Venice's bars, perched vertiginously over the sea. The fish is fresh at **Kounelas** ✦ on the harbor (p. 436), where you'll vie for a table with locals.

Day ❹: Mykonos & Delos

Take an early excursion boat from Mykonos to **Delos** ✦✦✦ (p. 441) and spend several hours admiring the acres of marble ruins. There's a little snack bar by the museum, but you'll probably do better bringing your own food from Mykonos and picnicking in a patch of shade cast by the ancient monuments. When you get back to Mykonos, tarry in its excellent shops, which include some of the best jewelers in Greece. Be sure to stop at the LALAoUNIS shop here (p. 429). For dinner, sample the *mezedes* and grilled fish (or meat) at the **Sea Satin Market** ✦✦, past the windmills at Kato Myli, overlooking the sea (p. 438).

Day ❺: Santorini & Akrotiri

Head to Santorini next, by plane or ship (p. 372). If you go by ship, you'll sail into the deep harbor with its high cliffs streaked with lava from the volcanic eruption that tore the island in half around 1450 B.C.—this is one of the world's great travel experiences. Check into your hotel and rent a car or sign up for a tour of the ancient site of **Akrotiri** 𝄢𝄢𝄢, often called the "Pompeii of Greece" (p. 375). Then take in the **Boutari Winery** 𝄢, where your tour includes enough snacks and samples of local wines for a light lunch (p. 377). In the evening, do what everyone does in Fira, Santorini's capital: Wander down the narrow streets before having drinks and dinner. For an inventive, memorable meal in a beautiful setting, make reservations at one of the best restaurants in all of Greece: **Selene** 𝄢𝄢𝄢 (p. 386).

Day ❻: Ancient Thira & Kamari

Explore the island by car, tour, or the excellent local bus system. See the dramatic cliff-top site of **Ancient Thira** 𝄢𝄢 (p. 376) before heading down to the famous black-sand beach at Kamari for a swim and lunch at **Camille Stefani taverna,** a longtime favorite (p. 386). Back in Fira, see the fantastic reproductions of the beautiful Minoan wall paintings of Akrotiri in the **Thira Foundation** 𝄢𝄢 (p. 377). If you're here in season, watch the sun set from the village of **Imerovigli** (p. 382). Try **Katina's** 𝄢 or **Captain Dimitri's,** two excellent fish places in Ammoudi, the minuscule port of little Oia (Ia) (p. 387).

Day ❼: Athens to Olympia

Return to Athens early, and pick up your reserved rental car. (You'll drop it off in Thessaloniki.) Head across the isthmus of Corinth into the Peloponnese for a night in **Olympia.** En route, make a quick detour to **Ancient Corinth** for a glimpse of the massive **Temple of Apollo** and a snack at one of the restaurants ringing the site (p. 270). Back on the road, stop for a swim; the beaches at Rio, outside Patras, have better-than-usual parking. After your long drive, check in at Olympia's **Hotel Europa** 𝄢𝄢𝄢, which has a refreshing swimming pool and its own restaurant, which is currently one of the best in the area (p. 318).

Day ❽: Ancient Olympia

Fill up on the buffet breakfast at the hotel. Spend the entire day seeing the three superb museums and the site of **ancient Olympia** 𝄢𝄢𝄢 (p. 316). Look for the newly reerected column of the Temple of Zeus; the little **Museum of the History of the Excavations in Olympia** 𝄢, with its 19th-century photos documenting the temple's discovery (p. 317); the **Archaeological Museum** 𝄢𝄢𝄢 (p. 315); and the astonishing wealth of bronze dedications now on view in the new **Museum of the History of the Olympic Games in Antiquity** 𝄢𝄢𝄢 (p. 317). The hotel's evening meal will be better than any served at the tourist-trap places in the village of Olympia.

Day ❾: Olympia to Delphi

Drive from Olympia past the splendid new bridge that soars across the Gulf of Corinth, then head inland to **Delphi** 𝄢𝄢𝄢 (p. 510). Along the way, pick one of the many beaches on either side of the Gulf of Corinth for lunch and a swim. In Delphi, stroll past the ancient site and enjoy the view down across the olive groves to the sea, but save your exploring for tomorrow. For dinner, go to the village of Arachova to sit outdoors and enjoy the succulent grills at **Taverna Karathanassi** or **Taverna Dasaryiris** (p. 518), by the cafes in the main square with its lovely freshwater springs.

Greece in 2 Weeks

Day 10: Sanctuary of Apollo

At Delphi, you'll see the **Sanctuary of Apollo** ✹✹✹ and **Delphi Museum** ✹✹✹, newly reopened and expanded in 2004. After a full day's exploration, drive north toward Kalambaka, site of the monasteries of the **Meteora** ✹✹✹ (p. 524). Spend the night someplace en route (ask your hotel in Delphi to make a reservation for you) unless you don't mind driving at night.

Day 11: The Meteora & Dion

See the monasteries of the Meteora and get a glimpse of what monastic life must be like—in a setting of incredible natural beauty. The buildings seem to grow from the craggy rocks that soar up to 300m (984 ft.). Don't miss the frescoes of the

Garden of Eden in the 14th-century monastery of **Ayios Nikolaos Anapaphsas** ✹ (p. 526). Drive next to Dion and spend the night either in the modest little Hotel Dion or the more sybaritic **Dion Palace Resort Hotel** ✹ (p. 640) on the beach at Litochoro. The **Dionysos** restaurant across from the site is a good choice for lunch or dinner (p. 639). See the site of **Dion** ✹✹, in the foothills of Mount Olympus, where Philip and Alexander trained their armies (p. 638). Bring a picnic lunch; it's usually not crowded.

Day 12: Vergina & Pella

Drive from Dion to **Thessaloniki** ✹✹✹, stopping en route at the royal tombs at **Vergina** ✹✹✹ and **Pella** ✹, former Macedonian capital and the birthplace of

Philip of Macedon and his son Alexander the Great (p. 633). The museum at Vergina exhibits the stunning gold items found in the royal tombs. As soon as you get to Thessaloniki (p. 601), drop off your rental car: Having one here is a real inconvenience! Enjoy a drink in Aristotelous Square and a stroll along the harbor. Then settle into your hotel before heading out for good, home-style cooking at **Thanasis** 𝒦𝒦𝒦 (p. 629).

Day ⓭: Thessaloniki

Spend the day strolling the city's streets, taking in the famous **White Tower** 𝒦, ancient monuments, and enchanting **Byzantine churches** 𝒦𝒦𝒦 (p. 613).

Make a visit to the **Archaeological and Byzantine museums** 𝒦𝒦𝒦, handily located next to each other (p. 609). Take a bus or cab up to **Ano Poli** 𝒦𝒦𝒦, the old Turkish quarter above the modern city (p. 615). Enjoy the lovingly restored houses, the little churches, and the views over the city and out to sea. Stop for lunch in a cafe before strolling back down to the harbor. For dinner, try **Krikelas** 𝒦𝒦, one of the trendy places in the Ladadika district, where old warehouses are now boutiques, cafes, and restaurants (p. 627).

Day ⓮:

Fly back to Athens. End your trip with a final stroll beneath the Acropolis.

3 Greece with a Family

This itinerary works well for families with kids between 7 and 15 years old. We tried to balance the adults' reasons for coming all the way to Greece (seeing unique sites) with the children's desires (swimming in hotel pools). As for food? The varied Greek menu should provide something for everyone's taste. And for better or worse, fast food is increasingly available all over Greece. Heat, especially in high season, should be a concern for travelers of all ages. Stay out of the midday sun, especially on the beach. Most forms of transportation offer reduced rates for kids under 12, as do most hotels, museums, and archaeological sites. Our itinerary assumes that you will rent a car for touring the Greek mainland. We also recognized that children wilt faster while traveling than adults do.

Days ❶ & ❷: Athens

After you arrive in Athens, settle in to offset jet lag. Cool off by getting a day pass to the Athens Hilton pool (p. 168). By late afternoon, stroll over to the **Acropolis** 𝒦𝒦𝒦 (p. 194). Before and after dinner at **Taverna Sigalas** (p. 179), walk around the Plaka/Monasteraki district (p. 147). On Day 2, visit the **National Archaeological Museum** 𝒦𝒦𝒦 (p. 203)—forget the vases and go straight to the gold objects and the statues! Have lunch at the museum's outdoor cafe, or head to the National Garden with its cool paths, small zoo, and outdoor dining (p. 185). Later, take in the changing of the guard at the Tomb of the Unknown Soldier on Syntagma Square. If no one in your family

group is flagging, check out **Attica Zoological Park** 𝒦𝒦 (p. 211), which is open until 7pm, or the multimedia Hellenic Cosmos museum (p. 205) and its interactive exhibits (hours vary). After a rest at your hotel, ride the cable-car up Mount Likavitos. And treat yourself to a traditional Greek dinner at the **Rhodia** 𝒦 (p. 185).

Day ❸: Mycenae & Nafplion

Rent a car and drive via the Corinth Canal to Nafplion. Early risers might stop at **Water Fun,** a water park near the canal. Otherwise, take at least an hour's detour to visit the **Citadel and the Treasury of Atreus** 𝒦𝒦𝒦 (p. 284) at Mycenae. Tell the kids about the Trojan War before coming, so they can appreciate the

tombs here. Plan to eat at **La Petite Plan-
ete** ✦ just below the site (p. 286). At Nafplion, settle in to your hotel, then either
visit the impressive fortress or swim at the
town's Arvanitia beach (p. 276).

Day ❹: Epidaurus & Luna Park
Drive to the **Theater at Epidaurus** ✦✦
(p. 287) and amaze your kids by demonstrating its incredible acoustics. Get
snacks and drinks at the site; for lunch,
we recommend **Leonidas** on the approach
road (p. 288). Return to Nafplion to
swim, then take time to walk around Nafplion before or after dinner at **Hellas
Restaurant** ✦ (p. 281).

Day ❺: Olympia
Set off across the interior highway to
Olympia ✦✦✦, the site of the original

Olympic Games (p. 313). For lunch, stop
at one of the restaurants along the road.
Check into **Grecotel Lakopetra Beach** ✦✦
(p. 322); take a dip in its pool before (and
after, too!) visiting ancient Olympia. Cheer
your children on if they want to run the
dash in the original Olympic Stadium. It
might be easiest to dine at the hotel.

Day ❻: Delphi & the
Sanctuary of Apollo
Drive along the coast road to Rio, with its
spectacular new bridge across the Gulf of
Corinth, then proceed to Delphi. Check
into **Amalia Hotel** ✦ (p. 516); have lunch
there and relax in its pool. In the cool of
the evening, take an introductory walk
around the **Sanctuary of Apollo** ✦✦✦
(p. 514). Make sure you walk along the

two thousand-year-old marble path, the Sacred Way. Then dine at the **Taverna Skala** ⚓ (p. 517).

Day ❼: Delphi & Crete
Spend the morning exploring Delphi and its museums. Drive to the Athens airport, lunching en route. Take a late-afternoon flight to **Iraklion.** Hit the lovely beach soon after checking into the **Xenia-Helios** hotel ⚓ (p. 337); it's right out the door. The kids can also play basketball, tennis, or Ping-Pong here. Dine at the hotel or, if you are up to it, go into Iraklion for an early dinner at **Ippocampus** (p. 339). The kids should love the fried zucchini and potato slices. You'll like the seafood.

Day ❽: Knossos & Water City
Your hotel can arrange for you to visit the Minoan **Palace of Knossos** ⚓⚓⚓ (p. 332), one of the great archaeological sites of the world. Kids will appreciate the sheer complexity of the site. Reward them with time back at the hotel's beach or a visit to **Water City,** a water park at Kokkini Hani. That night, try dinner at the **Pantheon** (p. 338) in Iraklion's famous "Dirty Alley"—no longer "dirty" but still atmospheric.

Day ❾: Matala/Chania
In a rental car, drive to the caves and bluff-enclosed cove beach at **Matala** ⚓⚓, once a major hippie destination (p. 340). Then take the mid-island route, with its spectacular scenery, to your hotel on the coast west of **Chania** ⚓⚓ (p. 341). Savor the stuffed crab at **Antigone** ⚓ (p. 350), along the harbor of Chania (p. 345). Preparing for Day 10, sign up for a day-long trek through the **Samaria Gorge** ⚓⚓ (p. 352) or for the half-day *Evangelos* boat excursion (p. 344)

Day ❿: Samaria Gorge
Get up early and don good hiking shoes before you take the bus to undertake the 18km (11-mile) excursion through **Samaria Gorge** ⚓⚓ (p. 352). It's a long day, and you should make sure your children have hiked before (and that you know their limits). Carry water and snacks, although cafes await you at the end of the gorge. A boat makes the leg from the gorge to a bus that will return you to your hotel. Most likely you will be too exhausted to dine anywhere except at the hotel. Or if all this seems too demanding, head to the glass-bottomed boat, the *Evangelos* (p. 344), for a tour of this area's underwater life.

Day ⓫: Santorini
Take the ferry to Santorini (a 5-hr. trip). Check in at a hotel at Kamari, if you prefer a beach (p. 385); or at Oia (Ia), if you prefer a spectacular view (p. 383). In the evening, dine on the terrace overlooking the caldera at **Koukoumavlos** ⚓⚓ (p. 386) in Fira town. Try the yogurt panna cotta with pistachios, honey, and sour cherries for dessert.

Days ⓬ & ⓭: Akrotiri & Fira
On Day 12, visit the unique excavated ancient city (nicknamed the "Minoan Pompeii") at **Akrotiri** ⚓⚓⚓: Even jaded kids will be impressed by the three-story, 3,500-year-old houses (p. 375). Then snorkel (or relax) at the beach at **Kamari** (p. 379); or take in the sights of Fira town (p. 377). On Day 13, wake up in time to take the excursion to the volcanic islet in the caldera—it will probably be your only chance ever to walk on an emerging volcano (p. 379)! You should also have time to take the cable car from **Fira** town down to the shore and then come back up by donkey (p. 379) before flying to Athens in the early evening.

Day ⓮: Athens
Back in Athens for your final day, you have many choices—strolling, window-shopping, another museum. As a reward for struggling with all those Greek menus, take the kids to one of the recommended

restaurants in the Plaka (p. 176). If you're up to renting a car again, head to the **Temple of Poseidon at Sounion** 𝄞𝄞 for the day and for the sunset (p. 239). Otherwise, take in any of the places in Athens that you missed on your first days. Top off your stay with dinner at **Thanasis** 𝄞 (p. 179) in the Plaka.

Day ⓯: Flight Home

Take a taxi to the airport for the flight home.

4 In the Footsteps of the Apostle Paul

This itinerary is designed not just for Christians but for anyone interested in a major chapter of early Western history. The Apostle Paul visited a number of Greek sites linked to the New Testament and the earliest years of Christianity. Paul visited territories belonging to modern Greece on at least three different journeys—and most of the places still bear the same names. These visits are accounted for in the Book of Acts in the Bible; we recommend reading the section beforehand—perhaps even taking along a copy of the New Testament. Due to the exigencies of modern travel and time, we can't plot a trip that follows Paul's exact itinerary, just highlights.

Days ❶ & ❷: Athens

Spend as in **Day 1** and the Athens part of **Day 2** in "Greece in 1 Week," earlier in this chapter. Include a walk to the hill opposite the Acropolis known as the **Pnyx** (p. 209); this was the meeting place of the Areopagus (the Athenian Assembly), which Paul addressed on his first journey to Greece. Also, when you visit the **Ancient Agora** 𝄞𝄞 (p. 199), imagine Paul conversing with the people of Athens here.

Days ❸ & ❹: Thessaloniki & Paul's Sites

Head next to **Thessaloniki** 𝄞𝄞𝄞. Although there are no remains with any specific link to Paul, visit at least one or two of the earliest Christian churches (both 5th c.)—**Panagia Acheiropoietos** 𝄞 (p. 615) and **Ayios Dimitrios** 𝄞 (p. 614). Those dedicated to tracking Paul's footsteps should arrange with a travel agency to visit nearby locales he visited— Philippi, Apollonia, or Verria (Berea). Others may prefer to spend the second day as described for **Day 12** or **Day 13** in "Greece in 2 Weeks," above.

Days ❺ & ❻: Rhodes & Lindos

Fly from Thessaloniki to Rhodes 𝄞𝄞 (p. 462). You may have to go via Athens. For local color, try the **S. Nikolis Hotel** 𝄞𝄞 (p. 471). The Old Town of Rhodes is the oldest inhabited medieval town in Europe (p. 466). Don't miss the **Street of the Knights** 𝄞𝄞, a 600m-long (1,968-ft.) cobblestone street from the early 16th century. Take up Paul's journey by spending the day at picturesque **Lindos** (p. 478), where Paul is said to have landed. Explore the **Acropolis** 𝄞 and the Byzantine **Church of the Panagia** 𝄞 (p. 479). Have lunch at **Mavrikos** 𝄞 (p. 480) for a French twist on Greek food. Back in Rhodes Town, try for a garden table at the **Romeo** 𝄞 restaurant (p. 475).

Days ❼ & ❽: Patmos

On **Day 7**, set out for **Patmos** 𝄞 (p. 497), either by ferry direct from Rhodes or by plane to Kos, and take the ferry from there to Patmos. If you arrive at Kos at lunchtime, try the **Platanos** 𝄞 (p. 495); if already on Patmos, go to **Pantelis** (p. 504) in the port town, Skala. Check in at either **Skala Hotel** or **Blue Bay** 𝄞

(p. 502). After dinner at **Grigoris Grill** (p. 504), you can wander through town. Patmos has 30-plus churches. Nothing remains on Patmos to testify to Paul's visit, but a must-see for Christians is the **Cave of the Apocalypse** 🏛🏛, where John the Divine is said to have written the Book of Revelation (p. 500). Everyone will want to visit the nearby **Monastery of St. John** 🏛, built to withstand pirates (around 1090). It contains frescoes from the 12th century (p. 500). While at the monastery, lunch at the **Vagelis** (p. 504) and take in the view. In the evening, dine at the restaurant in the **Skala** Hotel (p. 503).

Day ⑨: Patmos to Crete

You'll spend most of the day returning to Rhodes by ferry and then flying on to **Iraklion,** Crete (p. 327). You can't go wrong with the **Lato Boutique Hotel** 🏛 or at the **Loukoulos** 🏛, with its delicious Greek/Italian fare. Try to get a patio table (p. 338). Paul never made it to Iraklion, of course, but you can visit the **Church of Ayios Titos,** patron saint of the island because Paul named him leader of the first Christian community.

Day ⑩: Iraklion

Take a day off from Paul in recognition of this island's unique heritage. To fully explore Crete would take many weeks, what with its Minoan, Roman, Byzantine, Venetian, Turkish, and 19th-century remains. Your hotel can arrange for you to visit the Minoan **Palace of Knossos** 🏛🏛🏛 (p. 332), one of the great archaeological sites of the world. And don't miss the **Archaeological Museum** 🏛🏛🏛 (p. 331). You can lunch at one of the many **tavernas** across from the entrance to Knossos or return to town and try the **Ippocampus** (p. 339). After a siesta, take the walking tour of Iraklion (p. 333) before treating yourself to a gourmet dinner at the **Brillant** 🏛🏛 (p. 337).

Day ⑪: Gortyna

Travelers focused on following Paul will definitely want to rent a car and take a day trip to visit **Gortyna.** There you'll see the ruins of the **Basilica of Ayios Titos** (p. 340); in the New Testament, this is the "Titus" appointed by Paul to head the Christian community of Crete (and still the patron saint of the island). The palace of **Phaestos** 🏛🏛 and the caves and beach at **Matala** 🏛 are definitely worth detours (p. 340). You can lunch at Phaestos itself or at one of the many restaurants at Matala. In the evening, back in Iraklion, dine outdoors at the **Pantheon** (p. 338) in "Dirty Alley"—no longer "dirty" but still atmospheric.

Day ⑫: Fair Havens or Chania

Those truly dedicated to tracking down Paul could ask a travel agency to arrange for a trip to **Kaloi Limines** on the south coast, said to be the "Fair Havens" where Paul put in to escape a storm. Others may decide to visit **Chania** 🏛🏛, Crete's second city (p. 341). After checking into your hotel and exploring some of the old town, take lunch at the **Amphora** on the harbor (p. 350). Continue your exploration of the town as described on p. 345 and be sure to set aside time for a visit to the **Archaeological Museum** 🏛. That evening, take dinner at **The Well of the Turk** 🏛🏛 (p. 350) before driving back to your hotel in Iraklion (although you could overnight in Chania and fly out of its airport; make such arrangements well in advance).

Days ⑬ & ⑭: Athens & Ancient Corinth

Fly back to the Athens airport in time to rent a car to drive to Corinth (p. 268). **Ancient Corinth** 🏛🏛 is one of the major sites of ancient Greece, with numerous Roman remains that date from the time of Paul's visit. In particular, ask to see the

In the Footsteps of the Apostle Paul

Roman bema, or rostrum, said to be on the site where the Roman governor Gallio defended Paul. In addition to the link to Paul, the area stands on its own with a 6th-century Temple of Apollo and wide, marble-paved roads. It's easiest to eat lunch at one of the many restaurants adjacent to the site. Back in Athens, in the evening, treat yourself to dinner and people-watching at **Aegli** ★★, in the Zappeion Gardens (p. 184).

Day ⓯: Flight Home

Take a taxi to the airport and fly home.

4

Cruising the Greek Islands

by Rebecca Tobin

Imagine standing on the sun deck, drink in hand, as your ship pulls away from the island of Rhodes; or picture yourself sitting back on your private balcony, sea breeze on your face as you survey a blue sea and islands crowned with white-washed villages. Cruising in Greece is all about gorgeous scenery, ancient historic sites, and lots of local culture. And not having to worry about deciphering ferry schedules, driving a car, or changing hotel rooms. You get on the ship, you unpack once, and the vessel goes with you as your floating hotel. It's your familiar retreat after a long day of touring or a place to kick back and bask in the Greek sun. Greece is practically tailor-made for cruising. Among the most beautiful regions to cruise in all the world, the seas are relatively calm and the islands are individual in character, offering travelers a satisfying mix of local culture, stunning scenery, and ancient and medieval ruins to explore.

Most Greek island itineraries highlight the region's history with optional guided **shore excursions** that take in the major sights, spicing up the vacation brew with other, less history-minded excursions such as visits to beaches, meals at local restaurants, and fishing or sailing excursions.

Of course, you can choose to get off the ship at each port of call and head off on your own to explore the sights, hit the beach, or check out the local color at the nearest taverna. Solo is often the best way to go.

If cruising sounds like a good deal to you, you're in luck. The region, which was hit hard by 9/11 and the Iraq war, now has many, many cruising options. You can go ultra-luxe on a small, yacht-like ship like the SeaDream I or go über-casual on the easyCruiseOne. You can choose a classic vessel or an ultra-modern megaship. There are options from cruise lines that are making new inroads into Greece; other companies are continuing to build on their previous offerings and adding new ports.

1 Choosing the Right Cruise for You

In choosing your cruise, you need to think about what you want to see and at what level of comfort you want to see it.

We recommend you first decide **what you want to see.** Are you looking to visit the most popular islands—Mykonos, Santorini, and Rhodes—or are you interested in places off the beaten path? Whichever it is, you'll want to make sure the itinerary you choose allows you enough time to experience the place or places that really take your fancy. Some ships visit a port and spend the full day, while others visit two ports in 1 day, which limits your sightseeing time in each (but gives you more overall visits to different places).

In the past, Greek law was designed so that only Greek-flagged ships could cruise between Greek ports, meaning that foreign-flagged vessels had to visit en route between other European ports, usually in Italy or Turkey. This law officially changed in 1999, but many Greek islands cruises maintain a similar routing, either beginning or ending their itineraries elsewhere. You'll have to consider embarkation and disembarkation points in making your decision. Do you mind flying to Venice or Istanbul to catch your ship?

Greece is also visited by ships as part of European itineraries where Greece is not the sole focus, but only one of several countries visited. Most cruise lines like to give their passengers a bit of variety in the itinerary, which means the Greek Isles itinerary you're considering might include a day in Alexandria, Egypt, or Dubrovnik, Croatia. This chapter focuses on cruises that spend the better part of the itinerary in Greece and Turkey, but there are a myriad of other options for Mediterranean cruises that include a sprinkling of Greek ports in a more varied lineup.

You'll also want to think about **what you want out of the cruise experience.** Is the purpose of your cruise to see as much as you can of the islands, or to relax by the ship's pool? And what level of comfort, entertainment, onboard activities, and so forth do you require? Some ships spend a day or more at sea, meaning they don't visit a port at all that day, and while some experienced cruisers enjoy those days the most, treasuring the opportunity they offer for real relaxation, they won't do you much good if your goal is seeing as much of Greece as you can.

Next, consider **how long you want to spend cruising the islands**—3 days, a week, 2 weeks? If you have the time, you may want to consider a **cruisetour,** which combines a cruise to the islands with a guided tour of important sights on the mainland. This is made easy in Greece by the fact that some lines offer cruises of only 3 or 4 days, which you can combine with a land tour into a 1-week vacation, and 1-week cruises you can combine with a land tour to make a 2-week vacation.

Also consider **when you want to cruise.** Most of the action on the islands takes place in the warmer months, late May through October; traveling in early spring and late fall has its own special charms, including the fact it allows you to avoid the tourist crush (although some visitor facilities may be closed in the off season) and the hottest months (in July and Aug, temperatures can reach 100°F/38°C). For the record, August is the month the islands are most crowded with vacationers (expect beaches, bars, and discos to be either lively or packed, depending on your point of view). April and November are the rainiest months. May and October are relatively problem-free, making them particularly nice times to sail in Greece.

CHOOSING YOUR SHIP

Not surprisingly, the onboard experience changes dramatically depending on how many people and amenities you can fit onto your ship. You can choose anything from a 16-deck, 3,000 passenger ship with a three-story restaurant, ice-skating rink and minigolf course, down to a yacht-like ship for 100 or 200 people where the idea of entertainment is an open sun deck, a novel, and an attendant who drops by periodically with your sunscreen. Which you choose has a lot to do with your personality and vacation goals.

MEGASHIPS & LARGE SHIPS   Cruises aboard these vessels focus as much on onboard activities as they do on their destination. The ships are floating resorts—sometimes glitzy—offering American-style luxury and amenities along with attentive service.

These ships, which tend to be newer, feature Las Vegas–style shows, lavish casinos, big spas and gyms, plenty of bars and restaurants, extravagant meals, and lots of daytime activities. You or your children can take part in games, contests, cooking lessons, wine tastings, and sports tournaments—although generally few ethnic Greek activities are offered.

CLASSIC & MIDSIZE SHIPS   Ships in this category include older, classic vessels as well as newer ships. Destination is more a focus than on the bigger ships, and itineraries may be very busy, with the ship visiting an island a day, or sometimes two. This leaves little time for onboard daytime activities, although some will be offered. In the Greek market, some of these ships feature Greek crews and cuisine, and service tends to be a big area of focus. Because some of these ships are often sold heavily in the European markets, you may hear many languages spoken onboard. The ships offer a variety of bars and lounges, at least one swimming pool and a small casino, a spa and gym, and plenty of open deck space. Entertainment is generally offered in a main show lounge; some ships have cinemas featuring recently released films. Some of the ships in this category fall in the luxury camp and offer upscale restaurants, modern spas and cabins with lavish touches, and big, private balconies; other ships are older and definitely more modest.

SMALL & YACHT-LIKE SHIPS   Small ships and yachts tend to offer a more relaxed pace and may seek itineraries that focus on smaller, alternative ports, which they can get into because of their small size and shallow draft (the amount of ship that rides beneath the waterline). They may offer "soft adventure" cruise experiences focused on nature- and outdoor-oriented activities; or they may offer an experience more like that of a luxury yacht. Some of the ships feature Greek crews and Greek cuisine. On these small ships, there will typically be more interaction with fellow passengers than on larger ships—there's fewer faces to keep track of. There will be fewer entertainment options compared with the big ships, and there may or may not be a swimming pool, casino, spa, or gym. Both cabins and public rooms range from small and serviceable to large and luxurious, depending on which ship you choose. Some ships are fully engine-powered while others are sailing vessels (even though these sails are typically more for show than for power).

In addition to the small ships we mention in depth later in this chapter, you may want to look into even smaller yachts, especially if you're seeking a charter or a truly private yacht-like experience. We'll explore this option later in the chapter.

2 Calculating the Cost

Cruises in the Greek islands range from 3 nights to 2 weeks, with starting prices per day ranging from around 87€ to more than 580€ ($120–$800) per person, double occupancy, and going up from there. These days, you're still almost always going to get a rate that's substantially **less than brochure prices.** Like new-car sticker prices, brochure rates are notoriously inflated. You can get a good price, as well a shot at the best cabins on the ship, if you book early; alternatively, you might be able to get a good price if you wait until the last minute, when the lines are trying to top-up their sailings (unlike a hotel, cruise ships almost always sail full). In this chapter, we've asked the cruise lines to supply introductory or "early booking" rates, which are the rates quoted in most brochures for guests who book early. These rates are sometimes based on a booking window, say, reserving your tickets 6 months in advance; other times they're capacity controlled, which means if the voyage is really popular the early-booking rates will sell out quickly.

Travel agencies and Web-based agencies offer the best and "real" prices (see "Booking Your Cruise," below). Depending on demand, you may snag a two-for-one deal or free airfare or hotel stays. No matter what price you end up paying, rates include three meals a day (with a couple of exceptions, which we've noted in the ship reviews below), accommodations, most of the onboard activities and entertainment, and if you book your airfare through the cruise line, a transfer from the airport to the ship. Some rates even include airfare (the inclusion of airfare is more common on European cruises than Caribbean cruises), and in rare cases the fare may include tips, shore excursions, and/or pre- and/or post-cruise hotel stays. Some cruises are packaged as cruise tours, meaning the price includes both hotel stays and land tours. Rarely included in the price are alcoholic beverages; almost never included are charges for spa and beauty treatments, Internet access, shore excursions, and tips for the crew.

Port charges can run anywhere from around $60 to upwards of $500 per person, depending on the length of your cruise and which ports you visit. These charges will be part of your cruise fare, but be aware when you're pricing your cruise that although some lines include these charges in the initial base price, some do not. Government taxes and fees are usually excluded from the base rate but will be assessed when your final payment is due.

Cruise prices are based on two people sharing a cabin. Most lines have special **single supplement** prices for solo passengers wishing to have a cabin to themselves. The "supplement," in this case, goes to the cruise line as their compensation for not getting two passenger fares for the cabin. At the opposite end, most lines offer highly discounted rates for a third or fourth person sharing a cabin with two full-fare passengers.

Seniors may be able to get extra savings on their cruise. Some lines will take 5% off the top for those 55 and over, and the senior rate applies even if the second person in the cabin is younger. Membership in groups such as AARP is not required, but such membership may bring additional savings.

If your package does not include **airfare,** you might want to consider booking air transportation through the cruise line. While the rates offered by the lines may or may not be as low as you can find on your own, booking through the line allows the cruise company to keep track of you if, for instance, your flight is delayed. In this case, the ship may be able to wait for you, and if it can't wait, it will arrange transportation for you to the next port of call. The cruise lines also negotiate special deals with hotels at port cities if you want to come in a few days before your cruise or stay after it.

Several lines have also added a **fuel surcharge** to 2008 cruises, which typically ranges from 3.40€ to 6.80€ ($5–$10) per person, per day.

3 Booking Your Cruise

Today, practically everybody has a website, and the difference between so-called **Web-based cruise sellers** and more **traditional travel agencies** is that the former rely on their sites for most of their actual bookings, while the latter use theirs as glorified advertising space to promote their offerings and do most of their actual business in person or over the phone. As far as cruise prices go, there's no absolutely quantifiable difference between the real live travel agents and Internet-based cruise sellers. Sometimes you'll get the best price on the Web, and sometimes you'll get it through an agent—and some lines tout a "level playing field," where everybody gets the same price and agents aren't allowed to advertise discounted rates.

In deciding how to book your cruise, consider your level of experience as a cruiser and as an Internet user. Most websites give you a menu of ships and itineraries to select from, plus a basic search capability that takes into account destination, price, length of trip, and date; some sites aid your search with sophisticated options such as interactive deck plans and ship reviews. If you've cruised before and know what you want, no problem. If, on the other hand, you have limited experience with cruising or with booking on the Web, it may be better to go through a traditional agent, who can help you wade through the choices and answer your questions, from which cabins have their views obstructed by lifeboats to information on dining, tuxedo rentals, onboard kids programs, and cuisine. No matter which way you wind up booking your cruise, you may want to first check out the cruise-line websites and browse the Internet for ship reviews, virtual tours, chats, and industry news.

To find an agent, rely on referrals from trusted friends and colleagues. Some agents really know the business—they travel themselves to sample what they sell and can reel off the differences between cabins on Deck 7 and Deck 8 down to where the towel racks are placed—while others are not much more than order-takers. Start looking as soon as you can, which can result in early-booking rates and the best cabin choices.

CHOOSING A CABIN

One of your biggest decisions is what type of cabin you need. Will you be happy with a slightly cramped space without a window (the most budget-minded choice); a cabin with a private balcony; or a suite with a separate dining room, hot tub, and a personal butler on call?

Obviously, price will determine your choice. If you don't plan to spend time in your cabin except to sleep, shower, and change clothes, an **inside cabin** (that is, one without a porthole or window) might do just fine. If you get claustrophobic, however; or if you insist on sunshine first thing in the morning; or if you intend to hole up in your cabin for extended periods, pay a bit more and take an **outside cabin,** which have windows—or even better, pay a bit more and take one with a **private balcony,** where you can open the door and feel the sea breezes. On smaller or older ships, your choice might be limited to inside and outside cabins, some with the old-style porthole windows.

One concern if you do go the window route is **obstructed views.** This isn't an issue with newer ships because the lifeboats now are housed on the decks containing the public spaces like restaurants and lounges; the passenger cabins are either above or below those decks. But check to make sure none of the cabins in the category you've selected has windows that directly face lifeboats or other objects that may block your view of the clear blue sea. You can determine this by looking at a diagram of the ship (included in the cruise brochure or found online) or by consulting with your travel agent.

Most ships offer cabins for two with private bathroom and shower. (Bathtubs are considered a luxury on most ships and are usually offered only in the most expensive cabins.) These days, most ships have a double bed, or twin beds that may be convertible to a queen-size. Other variations are cabins with bunk beds (referred to in the brochures as "upper and lower berths"), cabins designed for three or four people, and connecting cabins for families. Several lines, including Oceania, Holland America, and Regent have upgraded their bedding in recent years to feature fluffy mattresses and soft, down duvets.

Cabin amenities vary by line, and often include TVs (with a closed system of programmed movies and features and the occasional news channel like CNN), VCRs or DVD players, hair dryers, safes, and mini-refrigerators. If any of these are must-haves, let your agent know. Cruise lines tend to one-up their amenities pretty often, so it's possible your cabin may have a flat-panel LCD TV, a powerful hair dryer, brand-name toiletries, and fresh flowers or fruit awaiting you on arrival.

Usually the higher on the ship the cabin is located, the more expensive it is. But upper decks also tend to be rockier in rough seas than the middle or lower parts of the ship, a factor to consider if you're prone to seasickness.

The **size of a cabin** is determined by square feet. Keep in mind that ship cabins are generally smaller than the equivalent hotel rooms you'd find on land. As a rough guide, 11 sq. m (120 sq. ft.) is low-end and cramped, 17 sq. m (180 sq. ft.) is midrange and fairly roomy, and 23 sq. m (250 sq. ft.) and larger is suite-size and very comfortable.

If noise bothers you, pick a cabin far from the engine room and nowhere near the disco.

MEALTIMES: EARLY, LATE, OR ANY TIME

Dining on cruise ships has undergone a revolution in the past 10 years. Traditionally, guests ate in the large dining room, at the same time and at the same table every night. Today, you can still dine the traditional way—many ships offer that as the default preference (or the only preference). But there are several variations on the mealtime theme now, from complete open seating to separate restaurants specializing in seafood or steaks to proper en suite dining.

Traditional dining is still the norm. Because most ship dining rooms are not large enough to accommodate all passengers at one dinner seating, dining times and tables are assigned. When you book your trip, you will also indicate your preferred mealtime. Early, or "main," seating is usually at 6 or 6:30pm, late seating at 8 or 8:30pm. Lines catering to a majority of European clientele may offer seatings an hour or so later than these. Some of the bigger lines offer four staggered seatings, which gives you more choice and eliminates some of the crowding at the dining room door.

There are advantages to both times. **Early seating** is usually less crowded, and it's the preferred time for families and older passengers who want to get to bed early. Food items are fresher (they don't have to sit in warmers), but the waiters know that the second wave is coming, so they may be rushed. Early diners get first dibs on nighttime entertainment venues, and might be hungry enough in a few hours to take advantage of a midnight buffet. **Late seating** allows time for a nap or late spa appointment before dinner, especially if you're returning to the ship from a full day in port. Service is slower paced, and you can linger with after-dinner drinks, then catch the late show at 10pm.

When choosing a mealtime, you also need to consider **table size** (on most ships, you can request to be at a table for 2, 4, 8, 10, or 12), though sometimes it's tough to snag a table for 2 since they're usually in great demand. On the other hand, many cruisers appreciate the fun that comes from sitting around a big table and talking up your adventures of the day. Most dining rooms are completely **nonsmoking,** so there's generally no need to request a smoking or nonsmoking table. You can request a different table when you get onboard, too.

If your ship has **open seating** arrangements you can dine at any hour the restaurant is open. You also choose your dinner partners, or you can ask the maitre d' to sit you with other guests. Open seating can feel more casual and less regimented. Open seating arrangements are typically offered on the smaller and/or most upscale lines, although now some of the majors offer this option as well. The pioneer in the big-ship category is Norwegian Cruise Line, which now builds its ships with up to 10 different restaurants. Princess Cruises, and now Holland America Line, have a hybrid dining policy: Passengers choose whether they want the traditional seating or the open plan, and then show up at the restaurants accordingly.

Most ships now also have one or two restaurants separate—in location, cuisine, and atmosphere—from the main dining room. These so-called **specialty restaurants** or **alternative restaurants** are open-seating, so you can choose your dinnertime and dining companions. If you'd like to try an evening or two at these restaurants, make reservations in advance. A per-person cover charge, typically in the $15 to $30 range, often applies, so you should check in advance.

On most ships, **breakfast** and **lunch** are open seating. Most vessels also have buffet restaurants, where you can choose to have both meals at any time during open hours.

Inform the cruise line at the time you make your reservations if you have any **special dietary requests.** Kosher menus, vegetarian, low-fat, low-salt, low-carb, "spa," and sugar-free are some of the options available.

DEPOSITS, CANCELLATIONS & EXTRAS

After you've made your decision as to which ship you will vacation on, you will be required to put down a deposit if you're booking 2 or more months in advance (with the remaining fare usually paid no later than 2 months in advance of your departure date); or you must pay the entire fare if you're booking within 60 or 70 days of your sailing date.

Cruise lines have varying policies regarding cancellations, and it's important to look at the fine print in the line's brochure to make sure you understand the policy. Most lines allow you to cancel for a full refund on your deposit and payment any time up to about 70 days before the sailing, after which you have to pay a penalty (a few lines charge an administrative fee if you cancel your cruise less than 120 days before departure). If you cancel at the last minute, you likely will lose the entire fare you paid.

An agent will discuss with you optional **airline arrangements** offered by the lines, **transfers** from the airport to the pier, and any pre- or post-cruise **hotel or tour programs.** Some lines also let you purchase **shore excursions** in advance (for more on shore excursions, see the section later in this chapter). And you may also be able to pre-book certain onboard spa services.

If you are not booking airfare through the cruise line, make sure to allow several hours between the plane's arrival and the time you must board the ship. To reduce anxiety, it may be best to fly in the day before and spend the night in a hotel.

4 Cruise Preparation Practicalities

About 1 month before your cruise and no later than 1 week before, you should receive your **cruise documents,** including your airline tickets (if you purchased them from the cruise line), a boarding document with your cabin number and sometimes dining choices on it, boarding forms to fill out, luggage tags, and your prearranged bus-transfer vouchers and hotel vouchers (if applicable). Some lines offer some of these forms online.

There will also be information about **shore excursions** and additional material detailing things you need to know before you sail. Most lines also list excursions on their websites and allow you to book shore excursions in advance of your sailing online, which will give you first dibs at popular offerings that may sell out later.

Read all of this pre-trip information carefully. Make sure your cabin category and dining preferences are what you requested, and that your airline flight and arrival times are what you were told. If there are problems, call your agent immediately. Make sure there is enough time so you can arrive at the port no later than an hour before departure time.

You will be required to have a passport for your trip (see chapter 2 for more on this). If you are flying into Istanbul, you will also be required to have a Turkish visa, which can be obtained at Istanbul airport once you arrive.

Confirm your flight 3 days before departure. Also, before you leave for the airport, tie the tags provided by the cruise line onto your luggage and fill in your boarding cards. This will save you time when you arrive at the ship.

CASH MATTERS

You already paid for a good portion of your vacation when you paid for your cruise, but you will still need a credit card or traveler's checks to handle your **onboard expenses** such as bar drinks, dry cleaning and laundry, e-mail, spa services, beauty-parlor services, photos taken by the ship's photographer, babysitting, wine at dinner, souvenirs, shore excursions, specialty restaurant charges, and tips (see below for more on tipping). On most lines, you'll use your cabin key card as a charge card. Prepare to spend between 147€ and 440€ ($200–$600) per person on a weeklong cruise for "extras"—or more, depending on how much you drink, shop, and spend in the casino, and how many shore excursions you purchase during the cruise. One travel agent we talked to suggested setting aside the equivalent of 25% of your cruise fare, or 364€ ($500), whichever is greater, for the expenses on a weeklong cruise.

Some ships (but not all) will take a personal check for onboard expenses. If you want to pay in cash or by traveler's check, you will be asked to leave a deposit. Some ships have ATMs if you need to get cash while aboard, and some (but not all) offer currency-exchange services.

We suggest you keep careful track of your onboard expenses to avoid an unpleasant surprise at the end of your cruise. Some ships make this particularly easy by offering interactive TVs in the cabins: By pushing the right buttons, you can check your account from the comfort of your stateroom. On other ships, you can get this information at the purser's office or guest-relations desk.

You will want to have some cash in hand when going ashore for expenses, including taxis, snacks or meals, drinks, small purchases, and tips for guides.

PACKING

Generally, ships describe their **daily recommended evening attire** as casual, informal, and formal, prompting many people to think they'll have to bring a steamer trunk full of clothes just to get through the trip. Not true; you can probably get along with about half of what you think you need. Almost all ships offer laundry and dry-cleaning services, and some have coin-operated self-serve laundries aboard, so you have the option of packing less and having your clothes cleaned midway through your trip.

During the day, the onboard style is casual, but keep in mind that some ships do not allow swimsuits or tank tops in the dining room. If your ship operates under the "traditional" dress codes, you can expect two formal dinners and two informal nights during a 5- to 7-day cruise, with the rest casual. There will usually be proportionally more formal nights on longer cruises.

The daily bulletin delivered to your cabin each day will advise you of the proper dress code for the evening. **Formal** means a tux or dark suit with tie for men and a cocktail dress, long dress, gown, or dressy pantsuit for women. **Informal** is a jacket, tie, and dress slacks or a light suit for men and a dress, skirt with blouse, or pants outfit for women. **Casual** means different things to different people. Typically it means a sports shirt or open dress shirt with slacks for men; women can wear skirts, dresses, or pants outfits. Jeans and shorts are usually frowned upon.

Check your cruise documents to determine the number of formal nights (if any) during your cruise. Men who don't own a tuxedo might be able to rent one in advance through the cruise line's preferred supplier (who delivers the tux right to the ship). Information on this service often is sent with your cruise documents. Also, some cruises offer **theme nights,** so you may want to check your cruise documents to see if there are any you'll want to bring special clothes for. (For instance, "Greek Night" means everyone wears blue and white—the Greek national colors.)

Having said all this about formal and informal, you might not even need to know about it: A few lines, especially the smaller, more casual ships, have an all-casual policy, meaning slacks and sundresses at night are as dressy as you need to be; others are "formal-optional," which gives you the option of dressing up (or not). If you're one of those people who absolutely refuses to wear a tie on vacation, consider that many lines also offer a casual-alternative during formal evenings, such as dining in the buffet restaurant or in your cabin.

If you want to bring the crown jewels, be careful. If you're not wearing them, leave them either in your in-room safe (if there is one) or with the purser.

In general, during the day in Greece you're best off packing loose and comfortable cotton or other lightweight fabrics. You'll also want to pack a swimsuit, a sun hat, sunglasses, and plenty of sunscreen—the Greek sun can be intense. Obviously, you should adjust your wardrobe depending on when you plan to travel. Even if you're traveling in August, though, you should bring a sweater, as you'll be in and out of air-conditioning. And don't forget an umbrella.

For shore excursions, comfortable walking shoes are a must, as some excursions involve walking on stone or marble. Also, some tours may visit religious sites that have a "no shorts or bare shoulders" policy, so it's best to bring something to cover up with. (If you're taking the tour through the cruise line, you'll be advised of this before you go.)

If you plan on bringing your own hair dryer, electric razor, curling iron, or other electrical device, check out the ship's electric current in advance. An adapter may be required. Because of the risk of fire, items like irons are prohibited; ask your cabin steward about pressing services or bring a portable steamer.

5 Embarkation

Check-in is usually 2 to 3 hours before sailing. You will not be able to board the ship before the scheduled embarkation time. You have up until a half-hour (on some ships it's 1 hr.) before sailing to embark.

At check-in, your boarding documents will be checked and your passport will likely be taken for immigration processing. You will get it back sometime during the cruise. (Make a photocopy and carry that as backup.) Depending on the cruise line, you may establish your **onboard credit account** at this point by presenting a major credit card

> *Tips* **Dealing with Seasickness**
>
> If you suffer from seasickness, plan on packing **Bonine** or **Dramamine** in case your ship encounters rough seas. Keep in mind that with both these medications, it is recommended you not drink alcohol; Dramamine in particular can make you drowsy. Both can be bought over-the-counter. Ships stock supplies onboard, either at the purser's office, at the medical center, or in the gift shop.
>
> Another option is the **Transderm patch,** available by prescription only, which goes behind your ear and time-releases medication. The patch can be worn for up to 3 days, but it comes with all sorts of side-effect warnings. Some people have had success in curbing seasickness with **ginger capsules** available at health-food stores. If you prefer not to ingest anything, you might try the **acupressure wristbands** available at most pharmacies. When set in the proper spot on the wrist, they effectively ease seasickness, although if the seas are particularly rough they may have to be supplemented with medication.

or making a deposit in cash or traveler's checks. On other ships you need to go to the purser's office onboard to establish your account.

You may be given your **dining-room table assignment** in advance of your sailing (on your tickets) or as you check in, or find a card with your table number waiting for you in your stateroom. If you do not receive an assignment by the time you get to your stateroom, you will be directed to a maitre d's desk. This is also the place to make any changes if your assignment does not meet with your approval.

Once you're aboard, a crew member will show you to your cabin and will probably offer to carry your hand luggage. No tip is required for this service, though feel free to slip the steward a few bucks if you're feeling generous.

In your cabin, you will find a **daily program** detailing the day's events, mealtimes, and so forth, as well as important information on the ship's **safety procedures** and possibly its **deck plan.** Deck plans and directional signs are posted around the ship, generally at main stairways and elevators.

Tip: If you plan to use the ship's **spa services,** it's best to stop by as soon as you board the ship to make appointments so you can get your preferred times. (The best times, particularly the slots during the days at sea, go fast, and some popular treatments sell out.) Ditto dropping by the **shore excursions desk** if you plan to purchase an excursion. Even better, some lines allow you to pre-book shore excursions or spa treatments online before you board the ship.

Note: The ship's casino and shops are always closed when the ship is in port, and the fresh- or saltwater swimming pool(s) could be tarped.

Some lines offer **escorted tours** of the public rooms to get you acquainted with the ship. Check the daily program in your cabin for details.

LIFEBOAT/SAFETY DRILL

Ships are required by law to conduct safety drills the first day out. Most do this either right before the ship sails or shortly thereafter. At the start of the drill, the ship will broadcast its emergency signal. You will then be required to return to your cabin (if you're not there), grab your **life jacket** (which you're shown as soon as you arrive in your cabin), and report to your assigned muster station—outside along the promenade deck, or in a lounge or other public room. A notice on the back of your cabin door will list the procedures and advise you as to your assigned **muster station** and how to get there. You will also find directions to the muster station in the hallway. You will be alerted as to the time of the drill in both the daily program and in repeated public announcements (and probably by your cabin steward as well). If you hide out in your cabin to avoid the drill, you'll likely get a knock by the cabin steward reminding you to please join the others.

If you're **traveling with children,** make sure your cabin is equipped with special children's life jackets. If not, alert your steward.

6 End-of-Cruise Procedures

Your shipboard account will close in the wee hours before departure, but prior to that time you will receive a preliminary bill in your cabin. If you are settling your account with your credit card, you don't have to do anything except make sure all the charges are correct. If there is a problem, report it to the purser's office.

If you are paying by cash or traveler's check, you will be asked to settle your account either during the day or night before you leave the ship. This will require a trip to the purser's office. A final invoice will be delivered to your room before departure.

TIPS

You will typically find tipping suggestions in your cabin on the last day of your cruise. These are only suggestions, but since service personnel make most (or all) of their salaries through tips, we don't recommend tipping less—unless, of course, bad service warrants it. (On some very upscale lines, acceptance of tips is strictly forbidden.)

Most cruise lines now **automatically add gratuities** to your shipboard account; and other lines will add gratuities to your bill on a request basis. It typically adds up to about 7.25€ ($10) per person, per day. This takes a little of the personal touch out of tipping, but then again, you don't have to worry about running around with envelopes of cash on the last night of your vacation. Check with your cruise line to see if they offer automatic tipping. If you prefer to tip the crew in person or in cash, your ship should be able to cancel the automatic tips. There's also nothing wrong with tipping your cabin steward or waiter on top of the automatic tips.

If you do decide to tip the crew on your own, the cruise line will provide suggested minimums. Generally, each passenger should usually tip his or her cabin steward and waiter about 2.90€ ($4) per day each, and the assistant waiter about 1.45€ ($2). That minimum comes to about 51€ ($70) for a 7-day cruise. You are, of course, free to tip more. On some European ships, the suggested minimums are even less. The reason: Europeans aren't as used to tipping as Americans. On some ships you are encouraged to tip the maitre d' and headwaiter. You may also encounter cases where tips are pooled: You hand over a suggested amount and it's up to the crew to divide it among themselves. Bar bills often automatically include a 15% tip, but if the wine steward, for instance, has served you exceptionally well, you can slip him or her a bill, too. If you have spa or beauty treatments, you can tip that person at the time of the service (you can even do so on your shipboard charge account).

Don't tip the captain or other officers. They're professional, salaried employees.

The porters who carry your bags at the pier will expect a tip.

PACKING UP

Because of the number of bags being handled, big ships require guests to pack the night before departure and leave their bags in the hallway, usually by midnight. (Be sure they're tagged with the cruise line's luggage tags, which are color-coded to indicate deck number and disembarkation order.) The bags will be picked up overnight and removed from the ship before passengers are allowed to disembark. (Don't pack bottles or other breakables; luggage is often thrown from bin to bin as it's being off-loaded.) You'll see them again in the cruise terminal, where they'll most likely be arranged by deck number. *Reminder:* When you're packing that last night, be sure to leave at least one extra change of clothing, as well as necessary toiletries, in the cabin with you.

Tip: Pack all your purchases in one suitcase. This way you can easily retrieve them if you're stopped at Customs.

7 The Cruise Lines & Their Ships: Large & Midsize Ships

In this section, we describe the ships offering cruises with predominantly Greek islands itineraries; that is, itineraries where at least half of the port calls are in Greece and Turkey. We've broken the offerings up into two categories, based on ship size: Mega and midsize ships (more than 400 passengers), and small and yacht-like vessels (anywhere from 40 passengers to 400).

The lines are listed alphabetically within each category. Rates are starting 2008 **introductory or early-booking brochure prices per person,** based on two people sharing a cabin, unless otherwise noted. With a few exceptions, most of these rates were quoted in U.S. dollars, and were converted to euros using July 2007 exchange rates.

The **itineraries** we list are also for the 2008 season. Both prices and itineraries are subject to change.

We've listed the **sizes of ships** in two ways: **passenger capacity** and **gross registered tons (GRTs).** Rather than describing actual weight, the latter is a measure of interior space used to produce revenue on a vessel. One GRT = 100 cubic feet of enclosed, revenue-generating space.

Note that we've listed Athens as a port of call for many cruises, but in most cases you'll actually be calling in **Piraeus,** the port city for Athens. Other popular embarkation ports include Istanbul, Turkey; Venice, Italy; and Civitavecchia, Italy, about an hour's drive from Rome.

CELEBRITY CRUISES

1050 Caribbean Way, Miami, FL 33132. ✆ 800/327-6700. www.celebrity.com.

Celebrity is a decently priced yet upscale U.S. operator that offers eastern Mediterranean itineraries that, for the most part, operate on *Galaxy* (built in 1996; 1,870 passengers; 77,713 GRTs). The line's ships are big but not mega-size; they're sophisticated, not staid or super flashy. *Galaxy,* for example, is outfitted in muted woods, golds, and silvers. The ship has plenty of spots in which to relax, including Michael's cigar bar or the Oasis pool, with its retractable roof. If you're splurging, book a Sky Suite on Deck 12 for their extra-large, 179-square-foot balconies.

Service and cuisine are keys with Celebrity. Little luxuries on its cruises include chilled towels when you return from a long day of port exploration and sorbets at poolside. The line, long known for its culinary focus, has signed a new contract with Las Vegas–based dining company Blau & Associates, which has worked with restaurants in the Bellagio and MGM Grand.

ITINERARIES & RATES

GALAXY   **Eleven-day Civitavecchia round-trip** calls at Mykonos, Rhodes, Santorini, Istanbul (Turkey), Kusadasi (Turkey), Athens, and Naples (Italy). May 19, June 9 and 30, July 21, August 11, September 1 and 22, October 13, and November 3 and 24. **Rates:** From 796€ ($1,099). **Ten-day round-trip from Civitavecchia (Italy)** calls at Messina (Italy), Athens, Mykonos, Kusadasi (Turkey), Rhodes, Santorini, and Naples (Italy). June 20, July 11, August 1 and 22, September 12, October 3 and 24, and November 14. **Rates:** From 723€ ($999).

COSTA CRUISE LINES

Venture Corporate Center II, 200 S. Park Road, Hollywood, FL 33021. ℭ 877/88-COSTA. www.costacruises.com.

This Italian line traces its origins back to 1860 and the Italian olive-oil business. Today, Carnival Corporation, parent of Carnival Cruise Lines, is the owner. Costa is a very modern cruise brand; its megaships beat several companies' ships in size, and the fact that the man who handles the interior design of Costa's new ships is the same interior designer who designs Carnival's "fun ships" has led some folks to compare the two. However, they differ when it comes to the onboard product. Italy shows through in nearly everything Costa offers, from the food to the Italian-speaking crew (although they are not all from Italy), to the mostly Italian entertainers.

The line's ships represent one of the newer fleets in the industry, sporting blue-and-yellow smokestacks emblazoned with a huge letter *C*. And the fleet is growing fast: Costa has added six new ships in 7 years, with another on the way in 2008. The product is popular in the U.S./Caribbean market but is not designed strictly for a North American audience, and therein lies the charm. In Europe, the ships attract a good share of Italian and French passengers, so don't be surprised if your tablemates speak limited English.

Entertainment includes Italian cooking and language classes. The line also offers an activities program for kids and teens.

Costa Classica (built in 1991; 1,308 passengers; 54,000 GRTs) offers spacious public rooms done in contemporary Italian design, with Italian marble and original artwork. The ship's 446 cabins average almost 19 sq. m (200 sq. ft.) each (that's big by industry standards). *CostaRomantica* (built in 1991; 1,344 passengers; 53,000 GRTs) is a sister ship to the Classica. Both ships have a circular observatory-by-day-*discoteca*-by-night located above the pool deck.

CostaFortuna (built in 2004; 2,720 passengers; 105,000 GRTs) is a new, glitzy, modern cruise vessel that counts among its attributes cabins with balconies; multiple bars, lounges, and eateries; swimming pools; a large kids' play area; and a themed decor—in this case, the great Italian ocean liners of yore. Public rooms are named after legendary Italian ships, such as the Rex Theater and the Restaurant Michelangelo. Check out the miniature fleet of Costa ships affixed to the ceiling of the bar in *Fortuna's* atrium.

ITINERARIES & RATES

COSTA ROMANTICA   **Seven-day round-trip Civitavecchia** cruise visits Catania (Italy), Patmos, Mykonos, Izmir (Turkey), and Santorini. May 5, 12, and 26; June 2, 16, and 23; July 7, 14, and 28; August 4, 18, and 25; September 8, 15, and 29; and October 6, 20, and 27. **Rates:** From 651€ ($899).

COSTA CLASSICA   **Seven-day round-trip from Trieste (Italy)** cruise calls at Ancona (Italy), Santorini, Mykonos, Athens, Corfu, and Dubrovnik (Croatia). Sundays, June 15 through September 21. **Rates:** From 651€ ($899).

COSTA FORTUNA   **Seven-day round-trip from Venice (Italy)** visits Bari (Italy), Katakolon, Santorini, Mykonos, Rhodes, and Dubrovnik (Croatia). Mondays, May 5 through November 3. **Rates:** From 651€ ($899).

CRYSTAL CRUISES

2049 Century Park E., Suite 1400, Los Angeles, CA 90067. ✆ 310/785-9300. www.crystalcruises.com.

Crystal's ships offer a cultured, elegant atmosphere and unobtrusive service. Its parent company, NYK, is a Japanese firm, the cruise line itself is based in Los Angeles, and you can see a kind of upscale, tranquil, and elegant California-influenced design to these ships, especially in the feng shui–designed spas, the Japanese cuisine (chef Nobu Matsuhisa of *Nobu* restaurant fame designed the menus in the ship's sushi restaurants) and some of its more modern interior looks, especially on the *Crystal Serenity* (built in 2003; 1,080 passengers, 68,000 GRTs).

This operator offers luxury, but on a slightly larger and less-inclusive scale than lines like Silversea and Seabourn—alcohol, for example, is an a la carte purchase, but sodas are complimentary. It still preserves a traditional, two-seating dining pattern in its main restaurant and does formal nights. Crystal has invested heavily in education and enrichment. During the daytimes, passengers can take a financial planning class or pick up a new recipe or two. Cabins are spacious; the ship's upper-level penthouse suites (especially the top-of-the-line Crystal Penthouses) are top-notch.

ITINERARY & RATES

CRYSTAL SERENITY   **Seven-day Venice-to-Athens** cruise overnights in Venice and calls at Katakolon, Santorini, Kusadasi (Turkey), and Mykonos. May 30. **Rates:** From 2,491€ ($3,440). **Twelve-day Venice-to-Athens** cruise overnights in Venice and calls at Katakolon, Santorini, Samos, Kusadasi (Turkey), and overnights in Istanbul (Turkey) and Athens. July 7. **Rates:** From 4,157€ ($5,740). **Twelve-day Athens-to-Civitavecchia** (Italy) cruise calls at Kusadasi (Turkey), Santorini, Rhodes, Aghios Nikolaos, Corfu, Taormina (Italy), and overnights in Sorrento (Italy). August 24. **Rates:** From 4,157€ ($5,740). Port charges are not included in these rates.

GOLDEN STAR CRUISES

85 Akti Miaouli, Piraeus, Greece. ✆ 210/429-0650. www.goldenstarcruises.com.

Golden Star offers short cruises of 3 and 4 days around the Greek Isles. The line's ship, the *Aegean Two* (built in 1957; 496 passengers; 12,609 GRTs) isn't brand-new, but it was fully refurbished in 2006. The line touts a friendly Greek staff, hospitality, and activities, such as Greek language and dancing lessons. Other onboard activities include bingo and board games, wine-tasting, the casino and catching rays on the pool deck. Like other Greece-based and Greece-focused lines, the emphasis is on the destination, with as many as five calls in a 3-day cruise; most passengers will likely be on and off the ship throughout the day, as the *Aegean Two* typically is in port daily from 7am until noon, and then makes a second stop at a second island from 4 to 9pm. Food choices include Greek specialties alongside international cuisine.

ITINERARIES & RATES

AEGEAN TWO: **Three-day round-trip Athens** cruise calls at Mykonos, Kusadasi (Turkey), Patmos, Crete, and Santorini. Fridays between March 28 and November 7. **Rates:** from 388€ ($530). **Four-day round-trip Athens** cruise calls at Mykonos, Kusadasi (Turkey), Patmos, Rhodes, Crete, and Santorini. Mondays between March 31 and November 3. **Rates:** From 608€ ($830).

HOLLAND AMERICA LINE

300 Elliott Ave. W., Seattle, WA 98119. (*) 877/SAIL-HAL. www.hollandamerica.com.

Holland America is a premium-level line that offers a more traditional cruise flavor onboard new, modern cruise ships. The line takes pride in its Dutch heritage—the tradition of naming its ships with a "dam" suffix goes back to 1883—and in offering good service in a refined setting: Teak deck chairs around the promenade deck, classical music in the Explorers Lounge after dinner, formal nights, and a collection of art and artifacts from around the world. A few changes are in the mix, including a new dinner plan—guests can choose whether they'd like the traditional, two-seating dinner experience or eat at any time during restaurant hours. A few years ago, Holland America embarked on a plan to enhance its onboard experience, and the well-publicized "Signature of Excellence" program resulted in new Culinary Arts centers where passengers can go for cooking classes, bars with mixology classes, bigger-than-ever children's facilities, a specialty Pinnacle Grill restaurant on every ship, and big, comfortable lounges that encompass the library, game room, and specialty coffee shop.

The *Zuiderdam* (built in 2002; 1,848 passengers; 82,000 GRTs) was the first of a larger class of ships for Holland America, and it's a roomy ship with a fun, bright design scheme and a lot of cabins with balconies.

ITINERARIES & RATES

ZUIDERDAM **Twelve-day round-trip Venice** cruises call in Split (Croatia), Athens, Istanbul (Turkey), Mykonos, Kusadasi (Turkey), Santorini, and Katakolon. April 26, June 1, July 7, August 12, and September 17. **Rates:** 1,375€ ($1,899).

LOUIS CRUISE LINES

8 Antoniou Ambatielou St., Piraeus, Greece. www.louiscruises.com.

The Louis Group has been in the passenger shipping business for 70 years, but this Cyprus-based company got into cruising in earnest in 1986 when it purchased *Princesa Marissa* and set up Louis Cruise Lines. In late 2004, Louis started another cruise division called Louis Hellenic Cruises; in 2008 it's dedicating 4 of its 13-plus ships to the Greek islands.

The *Perla* (built in 1968; 780 passengers; 16,710 GRTs), the *Aquamarine* (built in 1971; 1,268 passengers, 23,149 GRTs), and the recently acquired *Cristal* (built in 1992; 1,278 passengers; 25,661 GRTs) are the line's main ships in Greece, with the *Orient Queen* (built in 1968; 912 passengers; 15,781 GRTs) offering longer cruises that embark from either Athens, Marseille (France), or Genoa (Italy).

The bulk of Louis's fleet consists of older, more classic-style vessels that have been rebuilt and refurbished. It charters several of them to European cruise lines and then operates the rest out of Cyprus, Athens, Genoa, and Marseille. The ships aren't as flashy or as new as the ones used by the major U.S.-based cruise lines, so you won't find state-of-the art amenities, or rows of balconies, though the *Cristal* is a newer, more modern vessel. However, these are cruises that concentrate on the destination: The itineraries are extremely port intensive, and the ships will sometimes visit more than one island in a day. Embarkations are somewhat flexible, as Louis permits cruisers to pick up the ships in Mykonos, or disembark early in order to stay a few days on Santorini or Crete. Its ships fly the Greek flag, and its officers are Greek, but Louis also is increasingly designing its ships, cuisine and entertainment to appeal to an American market: 60% to 65% of its clientele is North American.

Tragedy struck in 2007 when Louis ship the **Sea Diamond** sank after scraping its side on a volcanic reef in Santorini; all passengers were evacuated except for two, who were reported missing. The company, however, has continued its commitment to the Greece market, spending $49 million to acquire the *Cristal* as a replacement to the *Sea Diamond* and maintaining a four-ship deployment to the region in 2008.

Louis's strategy in the U.S. is to sell through tour operators, who will typically package a Louis cruise with a land tour. It currently does not deal directly with individual passengers or with travel agents—although agents can work through tour operators. Rates for land-cruise packages are set by individual tour operators. The rates below vary depending on the season.

ITINERARY & RATES
CRISTAL   **Seven-day round-trip Athens** cruises overnight in Istanbul (Turkey) and call in Mykonos, Patmos, Kusadasi (Turkey), Rhodes, Iraklion, and Santorini. Fridays, from April 11 through October 24. **Rates:** Start at 1,090€ to 1,266€ ($1,485–$1,725). **Seven-day round-trip Athens** cruise calls at Istanbul, Kusadasi (Turkey), Rhodes, overnights in Alexandria (Egypt) and Santorini. October 31; and November 7, 14, and 21. **Rates:** Start at 1,090€ to 1,266€ ($1,485–$1,725).

PERLA   **Three-day round-trip Athens** cruise calls at Mykonos, Kusadasi (Turkey), Patmos, Iraklion, and Santorini. Fridays from May 23 through October 17. **Rates:** Start at 400€ to 481€ ($545–$655). **Four-day round-trip Athens** cruise calls at Mykonos, Patmos, Kusadasi (Turkey), Rhodes, Iraklion, and Santorini. Mondays from May 19 through October 20. **Rates:** Start at 605€ to 723€ ($825–$985).

AQUAMARINE   **Three-day round-trip Athens** cruise calls at Mykonos, Rhodes, Patmos, and Kusadasi (Turkey). Fridays from March 7 through November 14. **Rates:** Start at 400€ to 481€ ($545–$655). **Four-day round-trip Athens** cruise calls at Mykonos, Kusadasi, Patmos, Rhodes, Iraklion, and Santorini. Mondays from March 10 through November 10. **Rates:** Start at 605€ to 723€ ($825–$985).

ORIENT QUEEN   **Ten-day round-trip Athens** cruise calls in Kusadasi (Turkey), Patmos, Mykonos, Santorini, Katakolon, Messina (Italy), Marseilles (France), Genoa (France), and Naples (Italy). May 11, 21, and 31; June 10, 20, and 30; July 10, 20, and 30; August 9, 19, and 29; September 8, 18, and 28; and October 8 and 18. Embarkations also permitted for round-trip cruises from Marseille and Genoa. **Rates:** Start at 1,255€ to 1,313€ ($1,710–$1,790).

MONARCH CLASSIC CRUISES
645 Fifth Ave., Suite 902A, New York, NY 10022. ℭ **800/881-2377**. www.mccruises.gr.

Monarch Classic Cruises is another Greece-based cruise line that plies the Aegean on older, classic-style vessels that have been updated for cruise-ship service. The company began service in 2006, so they're the new kids on the block, relatively speaking. All three of the company's ships were refurbished in 2007. The *Blue Monarch* (built in 1966; 452 passengers; 11,429 GRTs) offers seven port calls on its 7-day service, and the *Ocean Countess* (built in 1976; 800 passengers; 17,593 GRTs) and *Ocean Monarch* (built in 1955; 518 passengers; 15,800 GRTs) both offer 3- and 4-day cruises that pack five and six calls into the itinerary, respectively. In sum: These cruises are for visitors who want to see as much of the Greek Isles as they can in a relatively short time frame. According to the line, it draws an international crowd (about half of the passengers are American), from students to seniors.

Onboard, the line says, visitors can expect the environment to be comfortable and clean, with all the standard cruise-ship amenities (beauty salon, pool, and so on). The ships offer one open-seating dinner service a night in order to accommodate passengers who are arriving back from various shore activities—the ships are typically in port until 8pm or 9pm. A Greek Night is held once on each voyage.

ITINERARIES & RATES

BLUE MONARCH **Seven-day Athens round-trip** cruise calls in Santorini, Iraklion, Rhodes, Patmos, Kusadasi (Turkey), overnights in Istanbul (Turkey) and calls at Mykonos. April 4 and 18; May 2, 16, and 30; June 13 and 27; July 11 and 25; August 8 and 22; September 5 and 19; and October 3, 17, and 31. **Rates:** From 829€ ($1,131) to 955€ ($1,303), depending on the season.

OCEAN COUNTESS **Three-day Athens round-trip** cruise calls at Mykonos, Kusadasi (Turkey), Patmos, Iraklion, and Santorini. Fridays from May 2 through October 17. **Rates:** Start at 334€ ($455) to 404€ ($551), depending on the season. **Four-day Athens round-trip** cruise calls at Mykonos, Kusadasi (Turkey), Patmos, Rhodes, Iraklion, and Santorini. Mondays between April 28 and October 13. **Rates:** Start at 510€ ($695) to 620€ ($846), depending on the season.

OCEAN MONARCH **Three-day Athens round-trip** cruise calls at Mykonos, Kusadasi (Turkey), Patmos, Iraklion, and Santorini. April 25, October 24, October 31, and November 7. **Rates:** Start at 334€ ($455) to 404€ ($551), depending on the season. **Four-day Athens round-trip** cruise calls at Mykonos, Kusadasi (Turkey), Patmos, Rhodes, Iraklion, and Santorini. April 21, October 20 and 27, and November 3. **Rates:** Start at 510€ ($695) to 620€ ($846), depending on the season.

MSC CRUISES

6750 N. Andrews Ave., Fort Lauderdale, FL 33309. (C) 800/666-9333. www.msccruises.com.

MSC Cruises, a line with Italian heritage and a subsidiary of shipping giant Mediterranean Shipping Co., is one of the fastest-growing cruise lines out there. A few years ago MSC was an up-and-coming player, mixing a fleet of older, classic style ships with mostly midsize vessels. These days the line is adding megaships to its fleet that compete on size and amenities with the biggest cruise companies, has made a big push into the U.S. market, and has firmly established itself in the contemporary cruise market.

The company offers what it calls "classic Italian cruising," focusing on service and playing up its Italian ambience—Italian actress Sophia Loren is the godmother to four MSC Cruises ships. The line was trying to "Americanize" some aspects of the voyages in order to make the Continental vibe seem more familiar to U.S. passengers, such as offering coffee along with dessert (instead of afterward) and adding more items to the breakfast buffet. Still, the passenger mix is more international than many other lines. Itineraries are port-intensive, and the onboard experience friendly and fun.

The *MSC Musica* (built in 2006; 2,550 passengers; 89,000 GRTs), is a good example of where MSC Cruises is headed, hardware-wise: It's got room for a minigolf course, a sushi bar, an Internet cafe, a solarium, yoga classes, a wine bar and a children's playroom in addition to all the usual activities you'll find on ships (a casino, gym, sauna, and so on). Nearly 830 of the 1,275 suites and cabins have private balconies.

ITINERARY & RATES

MSC MUSICA   **Seven-day round-trip cruise from Venice** calls at Bari (Italy), Katakolon, Santorini, Mykonos, Athens, Corfu, and Dubrovnik (Croatia). Sundays, March 16 through November 2. **Rates:** from 650€ ($899).

NORWEGIAN CRUISE LINE

7665 Corporate Center Dr. Miami, FL 33126. ℂ 866/625-1166. www.ncl.com.

Many mega-cruise lines operate with dinner seatings at set times and offer an alternative restaurant or two for a change of pace. Not so NCL; this company pushed the envelope a few years ago with a concept called Freestyle Dining: Pick one of several restaurants and make a reservation for dinner or stroll in whenever, just as you would at a shoreside restaurant. NCL started building its ships to take advantage of the Freestyle concept, and the result is a fleet of new ships that offer about 10 restaurant choices. Another difference: No required formal nights.

The *Norwegian Jade* (built in 2006; 2,400 passengers; 93,500 GRTs) has 10 restaurants, ranging from Japanese teppanyaki to steaks to French fare; plus a collection of themed bars, a karaoke lounge, an observation lounge, and all the other regular goodies of a modern cruise ship. Although NCL operates in the contemporary, big-ship business, it has a couple of surprises when it comes to the very best suites, The Garden Villas: two 4,390-square-foot apartments with three bedrooms, a living/dining room overlooking the pool deck, a private, outdoor courtyard with a hot tub, and a sun deck with loungers.

ITINERARIES & RATES

NORWEGIAN JADE   **Twelve-day Istanbul-to-Athens** cruise overnights in Istanbul and calls at Izmir (Turkey), Mykonos, Santorini, Iraklion, overnights in Alexandria (Egypt), and calls at Corfu and Katakolon. April 11, September 19, and October 13. Operates the itinerary in reverse order on April 23 and October 1 and 25. **Rates:** From 1,013€ ($1,399).

OCEAN VILLAGE

Richmond House, Terminus Terrace, Southampton, U.K. SO14 3PN. ℂ +44 845/075-0032. www.oceanvillage holidays.co.uk.

Ocean Village's tagline is that it's a cruise line "for people who don't do cruises." It's a vibrant line (from its bright website to its fun-colored cruise ships) for a primarily British audience of vacationers who aren't into the two-dinner-seating-dress-codes-and-formality of a more traditional cruise. Its two ships, the *Ocean Village* (built in 1989; 1,578 passengers; 63,500 GRTs) and *Ocean Village Two* (built in 1990; 1,708 passengers; 63,524 GRTs), boast a fun, relaxed atmosphere—there's no formal dress code, for example. The ships even pack a few mountain bikes onboard for passengers who want to check out the ports on two wheels.

ITINERARIES & RATES

OCEAN VILLAGE **Seven-night round-trip Iraklion** cruise calls at Dubrovnik (Croatia), Corfu, Cephalonia, Katakolon, and Athens every other Thursday, from April 17 through October 16. **Rates:** from £599 ($1,228) **Seven-night round-trip Iraklion** cruise calls at Limassol (Cyprus), Rhodes, Ephesus (Turkey), Mykonos, and Santorini. Alternating Thursdays from April 24 to October 23. **Rates:** From £659 ($1,352). A **14-night cruise** encompassing both routes starts at £949 ($1,946).

OCEANIA CRUISES

8300 NW 33rd St., Suite 308 Miami, FL 33122. ✆ **800/531-5619.** www.oceaniacruises.com.

This cruise line has grown quickly since its 2003 debut. It now boasts three ships, and it has orders in for two new 1,260-passenger ships. The current vessels are identical in layout, and their sizes, at 680 passengers each, make them cozy and intimate but able to stock a lot of amenities like multiple restaurants and big spas. Oceania straddles the line between the small luxury players and the larger, though less pricey, premium cruise lines. It tries to offer a reasonably priced yet intimate, casual, upscale experience.

Insignia and *Nautica* (built in 1998–2000; 684 passengers; 30,277 GRTs), are the two ships sailing in Greece. The emphasis is on casual, so you won't need to dress up (or even bring a tie or fancy dress). Many of the outside cabins have nice-size balconies. Public rooms, too, are of the big-but-not-too-big mold, and there are nice touches throughout the ships like teak decks and DVD players in the cabins. Eight private cabanas at the very top of the ship can be reserved for the day or for the whole cruise and come with a dedicated attendant and food and beverage services. Two restaurants, the Polo steakhouse and Toscana Italian trattoria, are fine complements to the main restaurant.

ITINERARY & RATES

INSIGNIA **Twelve-day Istanbul-to-Athens** cruise overnights in Istanbul and calls at Kusadasi (Turkey), Rhodes, Delos, Mykonos, Santorini, Katakolon, Corfu, Sarande (Albania), Dubrovnik (Croatia), and overnights in Athens. August 20. **Rates:** Two-for-one pricing starts at 2,388€ ($3,299) per person. **Fourteen-day Istanbul-to-Venice** cruise overnights in Istanbul and calls at Mitilini, Kusadasi (Turkey), Rhodes, Delos, Mykonos, Santorini, Athens, Positano (Italy), Taormina (Italy), Kotor (Montenegro), Dubrovnik (Croatia), and overnights in Venice. May 10. **Rates:** Two-for-one pricing starts at 2,531€ ($3,499) per person.

NAUTICA **Twelve-day Istanbul-to-Athens** cruise overnights in Istanbul and calls at Kusadasi (Turkey), Rhodes, Delos, Mykonos, Santorini, Katakolon, Corfu, Sarande (Albania), Dubrovnik (Croatia), and overnights in Athens. May 20, July 19, September 5 and 17, and October 25. **Rates:** Two-for-one pricing starts from 2,170€ to 2,388€ ($2,999–$3,299) per person. **Fourteen-day Istanbul-to-Venice** cruise overnights in Istanbul and calls at Mitilini, Kusadasi (Turkey), Rhodes, Delos, Mykonos, Santorini, Athens, Positano (Italy), Taormina (Italy), Kotor (Montenegro), Dubrovnik (Croatia), and overnights in Venice. September 29. **Rates:** Two-for-one pricing starts at 2,895€ ($3,999) per person. **Twelve-day Istanbul-to-Civitavecchia (Italy) cruise** overnights in Istanbul and calls at Mitilini, Kusadasi (Turkey), Rhodes, Santorini, Delos, Mykonos, Athens, Positano (Italy), Portofino (Italy), and Livorno (Italy). July 31. **Rates:** Two-for-one pricing starts at 2,388€ ($3,299) per person. **Twelve-day Venice-to-Athens cruise** overnights in Venice and calls at Pula (Croatia),

Umbria (Italy), Dubrovnik (Croatia) Kotor (Montenegro), Sarande (Albania), Corfu, Aghios Nikolaos, Santorini, Kusadasi (Turkey), Delos, and Mykonos. October 13. **Rates:** Two-for-one pricing starts at 2,170€ ($2,999) per person.

PRINCESS CRUISES

24844 Ave. Rockefeller, Santa Clarita, CA 91355. © 800/PRINCESS. www.princess.com.

Premium U.S. operator Princess hasn't completely shed its "Love Boat" past. Captain Stubing still makes appearances on behalf of the line now and then, but it's grown up into a multi-destination, multi-megaship line that blends California-style casual with elegance and sophistication. Princess has been raising its profile in the Eastern Med; last year it christened one of its biggest ships, the **Emerald Princess** (built in 2007; 3,080 passengers; 113,000 GRTs), in Athens, and the *Emerald* will be returning in 2008. The line's Grand-class ships, which are the inspiration for *Emerald Princess* and her sisters, are fixtures in Europe during the summers. **Grand Princess** (built in 1998; 2,600 passengers; 109,000 GRTs) also will ply Mediterranean and Greek waters.

You can easily recognize the *Grand* and her sisters because the stern (the rear of the ship) is straight up and down, and a horizontal bar stretches across the top, like a giant cruise-ship sports-car spoiler. It's the ship's nightclub and the highest perch, affording views all around (and down!). These ships have other features—as well they should, since they'll be some of the largest cruise ships in Greece in 2008. You can choose between eating at a fixed time each night a la traditional cruise-ship dining, or dining at a different time and table every night. Two good features on the *Emerald:* The adults-only, shaded relaxation grotto at the top of the ship called the Sanctuary, and a minigolf course (called Princess Links). Throw in good-size kids and teens zones and a plethora of show lounges, bars, and pools, and you've got ships that can keep you busy for a week, never mind the destination.

ITINERARIES & RATES

GRAND PRINCESS **Twelve-day Venice-to-Civitavecchia** cruise overnights in Venice and calls at Dubrovnik (Croatia), Corfu, Katkolon, Athens, Mykonos, Kusadasi (Turkey), Rhodes, Santorini, and Naples (Italy). May 14, September 23, and October 29. **Rates:** Starting from 1,368€ to 1,548€ ($1,890–$2,140). **Twelve-day Civitavec-chia-to-Venice** cruise calls at Monte Carlo (Monaco), Livorno (Italy), Naples (Italy), Santorini, Kusadasi (Turkey), Mykonos, Athens, Katakolon, and Corfu. May 2, September 11, and October 17. **Rates:** Starting from 1,368€ to 1,585€ ($1,890–$2,190).

EMERALD PRINCESS **Twelve-day Civitavecchia-to-Venice** cruise calls at Monte Carlo (Monaco), Livorno (Italy), Naples (Italy), Santorini, Kusadasi (Turkey), Mykonos, Athens, Katakolon, and Corfu. June 17 and August 4. **Rates:** From 1,766€ ($2,440). **Twelve-day Venice-to-Civitavecchia** cruise overnights in Venice and calls at Dubrovnik (Croatia), Corfu, Katakolon, Athens, Mykonos, Kusadasi (Turkey), Rhodes, Santorini, and Naples (Italy). June 5 and July 23. **Rates:** Starting from 1,730€ to 1,766€ ($2,390–$2,440).

REGENT SEVEN SEAS CRUISES

1000 Corporate Dr., Suite 500, Fort Lauderdale, FL 33334. © 800/285-1835. www.rssc.com.

In 1992, Radisson Hotels Worldwide decided to translate its hospitality experience to the cruise industry, offering to manage and market upscale ships for their international owners. Two years ago the company exchanged the name Radisson Seven Seas Cruises for Regent Seven Seas Cruises, but its commitment to luxury cruises has remained the same. The line has gradually downsized over the past few years, but it's left a core fleet of similar, small-to-midsize vessels, including *Seven Seas Voyager* (built in 2003; 700 passengers; 50,000 GRTs) and *Seven Seas Navigator* (built in 1999; 490 passengers; 33,000 GRTs).

Seven Seas Voyager is an all-suite, all-balcony luxury vessel. It's both larger and faster than the earlier Regent ships. Decor is muted and sophisticated. The ship's size means it's easy to get around to the different restaurants and bars. Select alcoholic beverages are included in the rates. The four restaurants onboard·(five if you count the Pool Grill) include Signatures, operated by Le Cordon Bleu of Paris. Another draw is the cabin configurations: walk-in closets, big bathrooms, lots of space to spread out, and a balcony with every cabin.

Seven Seas Navigator also will be in Greece. *Navigator* is a smaller, cozier sister to *Voyager*. All of its cabins have ocean views, and 90% of them have balconies. As on *Voyager*, the word on interior design is soft and neutral tones.

ITINERARIES & RATES

SEVEN SEAS NAVIGATOR **Eleven-day Istanbul-to-Athens** cruise calls at Kusadasi, Rhodes, overnights in Alexandria (Egypt), and calls at Iraklion, Nafplion, Santorini, and Mykonos. September 9. **Rates:** From 5,102€ ($7,050). **Eleven-day Monte Carlo-to-Athens** cruise calls at Civitavecchia (Italy), Sorrento (Italy), Naxos (Italy) Mitilini, Istanbul (Turkey), Kusadasi (Turkey), Mykonos, Nafplion. September 27. **Rates:** From 4,773€ ($6,595). These rates include economy air; port charges not included.

SEVEN SEAS VOYAGER **Seven-day Venice-to-Istanbul** voyage calls at Dubrovnik (Croatia), Kotor (Montenegro), Katakolon, Santorini, Kos, Bodrum (Turkey), and Mitilini. September 27. **Rates:** 4,193€ ($5,795). **Seven-day Istanbul-to-Athens** cruise calls at Mykonos, Rhodes, Kusadasi (Turkey), Santorini, and Nafplion. October 4 and 18. Cruise operates in the reverse order October 11. **Rates:** From 3,904€ ($5,395). These rates include economy air; port charges not included.

ROYAL CARIBBEAN INTERNATIONAL

1050 Caribbean Way, Miami, FL 33132. ✆ 866/562-7625. www.royalcaribbean.com.

Heard about those megaships carrying the rock-climbing walls? Those are the vessels of Royal Caribbean International, which has made its unusual onboard features—ice-skating rinks and self-leveling billiards tables, for example—a benchmark for other companies in the cruise-vacation business. Royal Caribbean sells a reasonably priced, big-ship, American-style experience. And they do it very well: The line's ships are consistent and well run, and there are a lot of things to do onboard, from wine tastings to climbing the ubiquitous rock wall at the rear of the ship. Royal Caribbean cultivates an active, fun image, most typified through advertising that urges would-be cruisers to "get out there."

Royal Caribbean's behemoth Voyager-class ships, with room for 3,114 passengers and 138,000 GRTs will be sailing in Europe this summer, and one of them, the *Navigator of the Seas* (built in 2002) will be cruising to the Eastern Mediterranean; a few late-summer cruises will touch on ports in Turkey and in Athens and Thessoloniki. The ship that will be in the Ionian sea more often, however, is the *Splendour of the Seas* (built in 1996; 2,076 passengers; 70,000 GRTs). The vessel has an indoor-outdoor pool in the relaxing Solarium, the nautically themed Schooner Bar, an 18-hole miniature golf course and the Viking Crown Lounge, the observatory and disco perched at the very top of the ship.

ITINERARIES & RATES

SPLENDOUR OF THE SEAS   **Seven-day round-trip Venice** cruises call at Athens, Mykonos, Katakolon, Corfu, and Split (Croatia). May 3, 17, and 31; June 14 and 28; July 26; August 9 and 23; September 6 and 20; October 4 and 18; and November 1 and 15. **Rates:** From 506€ ($699). **Eight-day round-trip Venice** cruise calls at Dubrovnik (Croatia), Iraklion, Kusadasi (Turkey), Santorini, and Corfu. July 11. **Rates:** Start at 868€ ($1,199).

8 The Cruise Lines: Small & Yacht-like Ships

EASYCRUISE

The Rotunda, 42/43 Gloucester Crescent, London, U.K., NW17DL. ✆ 211/211-6211. www.easycruise.com.

easyCruise breaks just about every rule in the cruise book. Instead of arriving in the morning and departing in the evening, why not pull in port around lunchtime and stay into the early morning the next day, in order to enjoy the nightlife? Why not charge only for the room and let passengers choose to eat ashore or pay for meals onboard like regular hotels do? Why not offer Greek cruises for 29€ to 37€ ($40–$50) a night? The line, the brainchild of Greek shipping heir Stelios Haji-Ioan-nou, who founded ultra-low cost carrier EasyJet, set out to offer the anti-cruise, where passengers pay a la carte. And so far, it's succeeded.

The line's made some changes since its birth in 2005. The vessel, the *easyCruiseOne* (built in 1990; 232 passengers; 4,077 GRTs), was initially painted a bright orange. Now it's a more subdued gray with orange trim. The simple cabins have received a new, muted color scheme and more windows have been added to the cabins. The ship now has a spa and more dining options: In its maiden year in Greece the line offered ethnic food and drink choices, such as tzatziki, roasted vegetable and lamb kabob, Greek wine, and Mythos beer. The line attracts a young crowd—it says the average age of its passengers is 32. Because there are no set mealtimes, and a lot of passengers are off the ship during the day to see ruins or hit the beach, and off in the evenings for dinner, barhopping, and dancing, the atmosphere is quite different from a regular cruise ship. easyCruiseOne's Fusionon4 bar and restaurant doubles as the ship's late-night disco, and the line advertises aromatherapy massages for under 30€ ($41).

Rates are for a cabin with twin beds and a window, exclusive of services like food and housekeeping.

As this book was going to press, easyCruise announced that it was bringing on another ship, to be called the *easyCruise Life* (built in 1981; 540 passengers; 12,711 GRTs), that would offer 7-day cruises from Athens and Bodrum, Turkey.

ITINERARIES & RATES

EASYCRUISE ONE   **Seven-day round-trip Athens** cruise calls at Corinth, Ithaki, Katakolon, Itea, Aegina, and overnights in Athens. Sundays from February 24 through April 6. **Rates:** From 146€ ($201). **Eleven-day round-trip Athens** cruise calls at Itea, Ithaki, Paxos, Agioi Santara (Albania), Corfu, Preveza, Kefallonia, Zakynthos, Corinth, and Aegina. April 13. **Rates:** From 296€ ($407). **Ten-day round-trip Athens** cruise calls at Itea, Ithaki, Paxos, Agioi Saranta (Albania), Corfu, Preveza, Kefallonia, Zakynthos, and Corinth. Alternating Mondays from June 23 through September 29.

Rates: From 302€ ($415). **Four-day round-trip Athens** cruise calls at Poros, Mykonos, Paros, and Sifnos. Alternating Thursdays from July 3 through September 25. **Rates:** From 143€ ($197).

EASYCRUISE LIFE **Seven-day round-trip cruises from Athens** call in Syros, Kalymnos, Bodrum (Turkey), Kos, Samos, Mykonos, and Paros. Saturdays from April 19 through October 11. Also offers embarkations from Bodrum for 7-day cruises on Mondays from April 21 through October 6. **Rates:** From 200€ ($282).

SEABOURN CRUISE LINE

6100 Blue Lagoon Dr., Suite 400, Miami, FL 33126. 📞 **800/929-9391**. www.seabourn.com.

Seabourn excels in many areas, including food, service, itineraries, and a luxurious and refined environment. These cruises are pricey, and the customers who can afford them are often very discriminating. Discretion is key on these vessels, and the sophisticated environment and decor prove it.

Although the ambience aboard the ships can be casual during the day, it becomes decidedly more formal in the evening, although new dining options with modern cuisine and an "always informal" option at the restaurant at the top of the ship will go a way to making it feel more casual. There's an open bar policy and lots of open, teak decks, which make these ships very yacht-like.

Nighttime entertainment is low-key, though cabaret nights with themes like 1950s rock 'n' roll can get the audience going.

Seabourn has three nearly identical ships, but the *Seabourn Spirit* (built in 1989; 208 passengers; 10,000 GRTs) is handling the line's Greece offerings this year.

All cabins on the *Seabourn Spirit* are outside suites. Each cabin's fully stocked bar is complimentary. The ships were built before private balconies were a must-have amenity, so the must-get cabins are the ones with French balconies—sliding doors you can open to let in the ocean breezes (two new ships on order for Seabourn will have balconies, but they won't be in service until 2009). The other cabins have 1.5m-wide (5-ft.) picture windows, plenty big enough to make the room bright and airy. Owner's suites are very plush and offer private verandas.

The ships come equipped with a floating marina that, when lowered, provides a platform for watersports. Sunfish, kayaks, snorkeling gear, high-speed banana boats, and water skis are available for passenger use. There's also a mesh net that becomes a saltwater swimming pool.

ITINERARIES & RATES

SEABOURN SPIRIT **Eleven-day Alexandria (Egypt)-to-Athens** cruise calls at Rhodes, Bodrum (Turkey), Santorini, Chania, Gythion, Pylos, Katakolon, Corinth Canal, Itea, and Nafplion. May 13. **Rates:** from 4,773€ ($6,598). **Seven-day Athens-to-Istanbul** cruise calls at Mykonos, Mylos, Patmos, Fethiye (Turkey), and Kusadasi (Turkey). May 24, July 12, August 16, September 27, and November 1. **Rates:** From 3,093€ to 3,566€ ($4,275–$4,929). **Seven-day cruise from Istanbul to Athens** calls at Kusadasi (Turkey), Bodrum (Turkey), Santorini, Aghios Nikolaos, and Nafplion. October 4. **Rates:** From 3,326€ ($4,598). **Seven-day Istanbul-to-Alexandria** cruise calls at Athens, Nafplion, Aghios Nikolaos, and Rhodes. November 8. **Rates:** From 3,093€ ($4,275).

— I don't speak sign language.

A hotel can close for all kinds of reasons.

Our Guarantee ensures that if your hotel's undergoing construction, we'll let you know in advance. In fact, we cover your entire travel experience. See www.travelocity.com/guarantee for details.

travelocity®
You'll never roam alone.

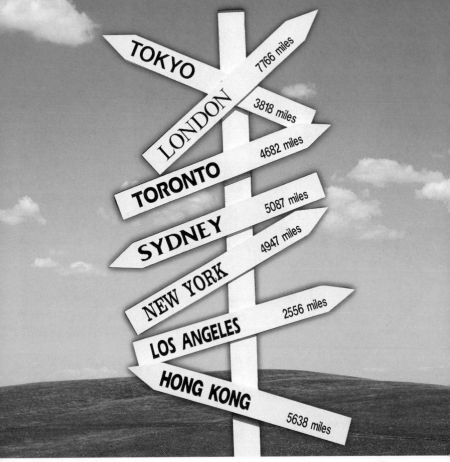

SEA CLOUD CRUISES

32-40 North Dean St., Englewood, NJ 07631 ✆ 888/732-2568. www.seacloud.com.

The flagship vessel **Sea Cloud** (built in 1931, 64 passengers; 2,532 GRTs) was built for heiress Marjorie Merriweather Post, who was involved in the design and construction of the sailing ship, planning the layout of the vessel right down to where the antiques would be placed. At the time it was the largest sailing yacht to be built. The *Sea Cloud* also served as a military support ship during World War II, was briefly owned by Dominican Republic dictator Rafael Trujillo, and sat tied up in Colon for 8 years before it was bought by a Hamburg-based group in the late 1970s and given a new, luxurious lease on life.

Guests can still see the care that Post originally put into the ship: Fireplaces in the cabins, antiques, marble, and shining wood. In the owner's suite, guests sleep in a Louis XIV–style bed next to a decorative marble fireplace; the bathroom alone is 9 sq. m (97 sq. ft.). The Category 5 cabins, on the other hand, are upper-and-lower berths, but Sea Cloud points out that since the cabins open to the promenade deck guests can sleep with the doors open to let in the sea air. Sailing buffs will be happy to gaze up at the 3,973 sq. m (32,000 sq. ft.) of sail—it has 36 separate sails, from the flying jib to the mizzen royal to the jigger gaff.

Sea Cloud is often chartered out by tour operators, who set their own itineraries for the ship; contact Sea Cloud for information on possible 2008 Greece cruises through tour operators.

ITINERARIES & RATES

SEA CLOUD   **Seven-day Athens-to-Istanbul** cruise visits Skyros, Skiathos, Volos, and Canakkale (Turkey). July 15. **Rates:** From 3,015€ ($4,160). **Seven-day Athens round-trip** calls in Kusadasi (Turkey), Patmos, Naxos, Milos, and Syros. August 3. **Rates:** From 3,015€ ($4,160).

SEADREAM YACHT CLUB

2601 S. Bayshore Dr., Penthouse 1B, Coconut Grove, FL 33133. ✆ 800/707-4911 www.seadreamyachtclub.com.

The owner and the operator of SeaDream Yacht Club both have luxury-line pedigrees: Seabourn Cruise Line founder Atle Brynestad and former Seabourn president Larry Pimentel. For the past 7 years, the two have been carrying on the Seabourn tradition of luxury and elegance, albeit on a smaller, more casual yachtlike scale. SeaDream in 2001 purchased the *Sea Goddess I* and *Sea Goddess II* from Seabourn, and after renovations renamed them **SeaDream I** and **SeaDream II** (built in 1984; 116 passengers; 4,260 GRTs).

The company defines itself not as a cruise line but an ultra-luxury yacht company whose vessels journey to smaller, less-charted destinations. Guests are offered an unstructured, casually elegant vacation (no formal nights) with no shortage of diversions. Toys carried aboard include jet skis and mountain bikes. You can choose to dine outdoors or indoors; there are enough tables to accommodate all the passengers in one outdoor lunch seating. None of the cabins have private balconies, but the line often urges guests to treat the teak decks as one large veranda where you can sprawl on bed-size Balinese loungers and congregate for a drink at the Top of the Yacht Bar—SeaDream has an open bar policy.

ITINERARIES & RATES

SEADREAM I   Seven-day Istanbul-to-Athens cruise calls at Mitilini, Molivos, Pythagoria, Kusadasi (Turkey), Patmos, Santorini, Naousa, and Mykonos. June 14. **Rates:** From 3,979€ ($5,499). **Seven-day Athens-to-Venice** cruise calls at Hydra, Corinth Canal, Itea, Fiskardo, Corfu, Dubrovnik (Croatia), and Hvar (Croatia). June 21. **Rates:** From 3,399€ ($4,699). **Seven-day Venice-to-Athens** cruise calls at Hvar (Croatia), Dubrovnik (Croatia), Corfu, Itea, Corinth Canal, Naousa, Mykonos, and Santorini. July 26. **Rates:** From 3,472€ ($4,799). **Seven-day Athens-to-Istanbul** cruise calls at Hydra, Santorini, Mykonos, Volos, Skiathos, and Mitilini. August 16. **Rates:** From 3,328€ ($4,599). **Seven-day Istanbul-to-Athens** calls at Mitilini, Molivos, Samos, Kusadasi (Turkey), Patmos, Santorini, Naousa, and Mykonos. August 30. **Rates:** From 3,328€ ($4,599). **Seven-day Athens-to-Civitavecchia** cruise calls at Hydra, Corinth Canal, Itea, Fiskardo, Taormina (Italy), Sorrento (Italy), and Capri (Italy). September 6. **Rates:** Start at 3,328€ ($4,599). Port charges are not included in these rates.

SEADREAM II   Seven-day Athens-to-Dubrovnik cruise calls at Mykonos, Santorini, Hydra, Corinth Canal, Zakynthos, Corfu, and Korcula (Croatia). June 14. **Rates:** From 3,472€ ($4,799). **Seven-day Venice-to-Athens** cruise calls at Hvar (Croatia), Dubrovnik (Croatia), Corfu, Itea, Corinth Canal, Naousa, Mykonos, and Santorini. August 30 and September 13. **Rates:** From 3,399€ ($4,699) to 3,472€ ($4,799). **Seven-day Athens-to-Venice** cruise calls at Hydra, Corinth Canal, Itea, Fiskardo, Corfu, Dubrovnik (Croatia), and Hvar (Croatia). September 6. **Rates:** From 3,328€ ($4,599). Port charges are not included in these rates.

SILVERSEA CRUISES

110 E. Broward Blvd., Fort Lauderdale, FL 33301. ℭ 800/722-9055. www.silversea.com.

The luxurious sister ships *Silver Cloud* and *Silver Wind* (built in 1994 and 1995; 296 passengers; 16,800 GRTs), *Silver Shadow* and *Silver Whisper* (built in 2000 and 2001; 382 passengers; 28,258 GRTs), carry their guests in splendor and elegance. Passengers are generally experienced cruisers, and are well traveled.

On *Silver Cloud* and *Silver Wind,* accommodations are outside suites with writing tables, sofas, walk-in closets, marble bathrooms, and all the amenities you'd expect of a top-of-the-line ship. Throughout, both vessels allot more space to each passenger than most other ships. There's also more crew, with the large staff at your service, ready to cater to your every desire on a 24-hour basis.

The newer *Silver Shadow* and *Silver Whisper* carry on the fine tradition in a slightly larger format. The all-suite vessels also feature verandas, poolside dining venues, a larger spa facility, a cigar lounge, and other niceties.

The ships offer five-star cuisine; guests can dine when, where, and with whom they choose. In the evening, the elegant buffet restaurant is open for a single-seating dinner on most nights.

The rates listed for Silversea are regular brochure prices, but the line offers a Silver Sailings saving program on some of its cruises that can result in up to 50% off cruise-only fares; the program is based on availability and time of booking. Port charges are not included in the rates listed.

ITINERARIES & RATES

SILVER CLOUD   Seven-day Athens-to-Istanbul voyage calls at Nafplion, Santorini, Rhodes, Kusadasi (Turkey), Mykonos, and overnights in Istanbul. April 10.

Rates: From 3,396€ ($4,695). **Seven-day Istanbul-to-Athens** cruise overnights in Istanbul and calls at Kusadasi (Turkey), Patmos, Rhodes, Mykonos, and Santorini. October 6. **Rates:** From 3,903€ ($5,395).

SILVER WIND **Nine-day Athens-to-Civitavecchia** cruise calls at Mykonos, Rhodes, Iraklion, Katakolon, Itea, Corfu, and Sorrento (Italy). October 17. **Rates:** From 5,060€ ($6,995) per person.

SILVER WHISPER **Twelve-day Athens-to-Civitavecchia** cruise overnights in Istanbul (Turkey) and calls at Kusadasi (Turkey), Patmos, Mykonos, Santorini, Valletta (Malta), Taormina (Italy), and Sorrento (Italy). May 5. **Rates:** From 7,014€ ($9,695). **Seven-day Civitavecchia-to-Athens** cruise calls at Sorrento (Italy), Dubrovnik (Croatia), Corfu, Kythira, and Mykonos. June 28. **Rates:** From 4,409€ ($6,095). **Seven-day Civitavecchia-to-Athens** cruise calls at Sorrento (Italy), Siracusa (Italy), Aghios Nikolaos, Rhodes, Tinos, and Mykonos. August 23. **Rates:** From 4,699€ ($6,495). **Seven-day Istanbul-to-Athens** cruise calls at Iraklion, Nafplion, Volos, Patmos, and Mykonos. September 21. **Rates:** From 4,337€ ($5,995).

STAR CLIPPERS
7200 NW 19th St., Suite 206, Miami, FL 33126. (*C*) 800/442-0550. www.starclippers.com.

Star Clipper (built in 1991; 170 passengers; 2,298 GRTs), is the name of the vessel this three-ship line, named Star Clippers, is sending to Greece in 2008. It is a replica of the big 19th-century clipper sailing ships (or barkentines) that once circled the globe. Its tall square rigs carry enormous sails, are glorious to look at, and are a particular thrill for history buffs.

And on this ship, the 36,000 square feet of billowing sails are more than window dressing. The *Star Clipper* was constructed using original drawings and specifications of a leading 19th-century naval architect, but updated with modern touches so that today it is among the tallest (226 ft.) and fastest clipper ships built.

The atmosphere onboard is akin to being on a private yacht rather than a mainstream cruise ship. It's active and casual in an L.L. Bean sort of way, and friendly.

Cabins are decorated with wood accents; the top categories have doors that open up directly onto the deck. There is one owner's suite. The public rooms include a writing room, an open-seating dining room, and an Edwardian-style library with a Belle Epoque fireplace and bookshelf-lined walls. There are two small swimming pools.

Local entertainment is sometimes brought aboard. Other activities on the ship tend toward the nautical, such as visiting the bridge, observing the crew handle the sails, and participating in knot-tying classes. Or just padding around the decks and lying in a deck chair underneath the sails. When seas are calm you can lie in the rigging.

ITINERARIES & RATES
STAR CLIPPER **Seven-day round-trip Athens cruise to the Northern Cyclades** calls at Kusadasi (Turkey), Pythagoria, Patmos, Delos, Mykonos, and Sifnos. Alternating most Saturdays, May 24 through September 27. **Rates:** From 1,334€ ($1,820). **Seven-day round-trip Athens-to–the Southern Cyclades** cruise calls at Rhodes, Bodrum (Turkey), Dalyan River (Turkey), Santorini, and Hydra. Alternating most Saturdays, May 17 through October 4. **Rates:** From 1,334€ ($1,820). **Five-day Athens round-trip** voyage calls at Delos, Mykonos, Santorini, Bodrum (Turkey), and Sifnos. May 12 and October 11. **Rates:** From 858€ ($1,170) per person.

Tips Booking Your Private Yacht Charter

Do you imagine yourself cruising the Greek Isles on a boat built for two? Or six? Maybe you fancy taking a more active role in itinerary planning? Do you love the idea of requesting that you cruise for a few hours and stop in a secluded cove for swimming? Or do you relish the thought of stepping off your 80-foot sailing vessel in the marina and heading off to a nearby beachfront restaurant for dinner?

Greece is a great place for a private yacht charter. Altogether, there are about 6,000 isles and islands in Greek territory. You're as free as a bird; you can cruise to an island and stay as long as you like (as long as the captain says it's okay). And although yacht cruising can be expensive, it doesn't have to be. But there are a few things to keep in mind.

You could go through a travel agent who's familiar with yacht chartering, or you could find a **yacht charter broker** on your own. Yacht charter brokers are a link between yacht owners and you—they're the ones who know the boats and the crew, the ones who will guide you through the chartering process and take your booking. Charter brokers go to boat shows around the world to check up on yachts and companies and crew; they might have personally sailed within the area you want to go to (or know someone who has).

For more information about charter brokers, visit the Charter Yacht Brokers Association, at www.cyba.net. The site has a page for prospective clients to request more information by describing their plans for a charter. Other associations for charter brokers include the Mediterranean Yacht Brokers Association and the American Yacht Brokers Association. The Greek Tourism Organization (www.gnto.org) can also be a resource.

The yacht broker should ask questions and listen as you describe what you're looking for in a vacation. How many people are you traveling with? What are their ages—are there kids involved? Where are you interested in cruising, and when? Do you care more about visiting Greek towns and historic sites, or do you want to kick back on the boat and relax? Do you want to go ultra-luxe, or are you on a tight budget? Do you want a power yacht, which is faster, or a sailing yacht, which burns less fuel? All these questions will help them plan the best route for you.

Here are a few tips:

• Be reasonable in your **itinerary planning.** A yacht probably won't be able to get you comfortably from Athens to Mykonos to Rhodes and back in a week. Generally speaking, you'll want to stick to nearby groups of

TRAVEL DYNAMICS INTERNATIONAL

132 E. 70th St., New York, NY 10021. © **800/257-5767.** www.traveldynamicsinternational.com.

This operator of small ships offers a number of interesting itineraries that include Greek ports, and no wonder: The co-founders of Travel Dynamics are two Greek brothers from the island of Rhodes. The journeys are tailored to be unique, visiting some of the smaller and lesser-known ports. Top-notch onboard educational programs islands, such as the Ionian, Dodecanese, Cyclades, and Sporades. If you're sailing from Athens, the Saronic Gulf and the Cyclades are close cruising areas. Many yachts are based in Athens, but sometimes you can have a specific yacht sent up to an island group, as long as you're willing to pay a relocation fee, plus fuel, in order to get it there.

- Who's driving? There are two basic types of charters. **Crewed** means there's a crew onboard. How many crew depends on the size of the boat, as well as your own personal needs. You'll need a captain and maybe a cook, a hostess and/or a guide. A **bareboat** charter means there's no crew, and you'll do the sailing or provide your own crew.

- Champagne and caviar? Well, that's all part of the provisioning and the charter's costs. Different charters work differently. Some vessels work on a **half-board** basis; in other words, breakfast and lunch are included in the cost, under the assumption that passengers will want to venture off the boat in the evenings for dinner and nightlife. Another way of determining costs is an **advance provisioning amount,** or APA. The APA is an amount of money paid upfront for costs associated with the charter, and it's on average about 30% of the base rate for the charter. The APA could include fuel, crew costs, food and beverages, marina fees, Corinth Canal fees and other extras. At the end of the cruise the costs are tallied and the passenger either gets money back or has to pay a little more. In either case, crew gratuity is not included. Be sure to work out with your charter broker exactly what's included and what's not.

- Party of eight: You can rent a yacht for a cozy party of two, or bring a group of friends onboard—typically, the more people onboard the cheaper the cruise price works out per person. However, you're more limited in the choice of vessel once you go above 12 people. One solution for a big party: Charter two yachts and split up the party (or if you have *lots* of friends, think about chartering one of the cruise ships listed in this chapter).

- Vessel style. You can get a 40-foot yacht or a 100-foot yacht, in as modest or luxurious style as you can imagine (and afford). Another important consideration is whether you want a sleek, graceful sailing vessel or a modern, upscale power boat. Whatever you decide, there's probably a yacht out there that suits your style.

complement the itineraries, and shore excursions are included in the cruise price. This line won't attract the budget-minded passenger or the folks who want to laze around. Itineraries are fast-paced and educational. Each day has several components: a museum in the morning and an archaeological site in the afternoon, for example. The company's itineraries often include references to the nearby sites (Iraklion for Knossos or Gortyn, for example).

Callisto (rebuilt in 2000; 34 passengers; 499 GRTs) is a cozy little yacht. All the cabins have picture windows or portholes. There's a lot of blue-and-white in the design, but it's all very tasteful. The blue-and-white striped cushions on the deck chairs match the Greek flag flying from the ship.

The larger *Corinthian II* (built in 1992; 114 passengers; 4,200 GRTs) is the newest addition to Travel Dynamics' fleet. Luxe touches include marble bathrooms, minifridges, and private balconies. An outdoor bar and cafe accommodates alfresco diners. The ship also has a gym, salon, sun deck with hot tub, and Internet cafe.

The line has several Eastern European itineraries that include ample time in Turkey and Italy as well as Greece.

ITINERARIES & RATES

CORINTHIAN II   **Ten-day Athens-to-Civitavecchia** cruise overnights in Athens and calls at Kusadasi (Turkey), Rhodes, Lindos, Santorini, Rethymnon, Gytheion, Katakolon, Taormina (Italy), and Sorrento (Italy). June 29 and July 9. **Rates:** From 4,336€ ($5,995). *Note:* This cruise is billed as a "family learning adventure"; kids' rates start at 3,106€ ($4,295). **Nine-day Athens round-trip** cruise calls at Iraklion, Rhodes, Patmos, Kusadasi (Turkey), Kavalla, Thessaloniki, and overnights in Athens. July 19. **Rates:** From 4,697€ ($6,495).

WINDSTAR CRUISES

2101 Fourth Ave., Suite 1150, Seattle, WA 98121. ℭ **87-STAR-SAIL**. www.windstarcruises.com.

Although they look like sailing ships of yore, *Wind Star* and *Wind Spirit* (built in 1986 and 1988; 144 passengers; 5,350 GRTs) and their bigger sister *Wind Surf* (built in 1990; 312 passengers; 14,745 GRTs) are more like floating luxury hotels with the flair of sailing ships. These vessels feature top-notch service and cuisine. Million-dollar computers operate the sails, and stabilizers allow for a smooth ride.

Windstar deploys its two smaller vessels, *Wind Spirit* and *Wind Star*, in the Greek islands. Casual, low-key elegance is the watchword. There's no set regime and no dress code above "resort casual." Most of the passengers are well-heeled; the ships appeal to all ages except children. (There are no dedicated kids' facilities onboard the ships.)

None of the roomy outside cabins has balconies, but they do have large portholes. The top-level owner's cabins are slightly bigger. Refurbishments completed a few years ago added flatscreen TVs and DVD players; new mattresses, bedding, carpet, and curtains to the cabins; an expanded gym; and an updated spa.

A watersports platform at the stern allows for a variety of activities when the ships are docked. Entertainment is low-key and sometimes includes local entertainers brought aboard at ports of call. Most of the onboard time revolves around the sun deck, plunge pool, and outdoor bar. The ships also have small casinos.

In 2007 the Windstar ships were sold to Ambassadors International, a California-based company that owns several U.S. river cruising brands.

ITINERARIES & RATES

WIND SPIRIT   **Seven-day Civitavecchia-to-Athens** cruise calls at Capri (Italy), Messina (Italy), Gythion, Nafplion, and Ermoupolis. May 10. Operates in the reverse order October 18. **Rates:** Start at 1,880€ ($2,599). **Seven-day Athens-to-Istanbul** cruise calls at Mykonos, Santorini, Rhodes, Bodrum (Turkey), and Kusadasi (Turkey). Sundays between May 17 and October 11. Cruises run in the reverse order on alternating weeks. **Rates:** From 2,314€ ($3,199) to 2,458€ ($3,399). The prices listed do not include port charges.

WIND STAR   **Seven-day Athens-to-Istanbul cruise** calls at Mykonos, Santorini, Rhodes, Bodrum (Turkey), and Kusadasi (Italy). Saturdays between May 24 through October 18, except for July 19, July 26, August 2, and August 9. Cruises run in the reverse order on alternating weeks. **Rates:** From 2,314€ ($3,199) to 2,458€ ($3,399). **Seven-day Athens-to-Civitavecchia cruise** calls at Ermoupolis, Nafplion, Gythion, Messina (Italy), and Capri (Italy) October 25. **Rates:** From 1,880€ ($2,599). These prices do not include port charges.

VARIETY CRUISES
2 Papada Street, Athens, Greece. ✆ 210/691-9191. www.varietycruises.com.

These Greek-flagged and -operated yachts might be just the ticket if you're looking for a casual, intimate experience with a more international flavor. Formerly known as Zeus Tours, the cruise portion of the company has been around since the mid-1960s when it chartered the yacht *Eleftherios;* it began scheduled weekly cruise service in 1973. Today, it divides its ships into three divisions. The more upmarket Variety Cruises division emphasizes a blend of cruising and yachting, relaxing, and exploring Greece's historical treasures. Ships in this fleet include the yachts *Harmony G* (built in 2003; 46 passengers; 490 GRTs) and *Harmony V* (built in 1985; 50 passengers; 495 GRTs), which underwent a major refurbishment in 2007. The Zeus Casual Cruises skews a little more in the sun-'n-fun direction, with beach barbecues and free drinks during the day; this fleet counts the motor sailboats *Viking Star* (built in 1991; 50 passengers; 248 GRTs) and *H&B I and H&B II* (built in 2001–02; 42 passengers; 390 GRTs) and yacht *Zeus II* (built in 1982; 38 passengers; 204 GRTs). The third division is Variety Yachts, which operates vessels for charter that sleep 8 to 12 guests.

These lines don't promote an ultra-luxury experience; the word on all these small ships is casual. There are sun decks but no pools except for the surrounding Mediterranean: passengers can swim right off the side of the ships during swim stops. On the Variety Cruises ships the price includes only two meals a day, breakfast, and then either lunch or dinner, depending on the itinerary, which gives guests the chance to eat and drink in port (local wine and refreshments are included with meals onboard). Zeus Casual Cruises, meanwhile, includes three meals a day and local wine, beer, and soft drinks between 11am and 11pm. On both lines there's no organized onboard entertainment per se, except for chatting with other guests in the saloon or while catching rays up on deck. And with only a couple dozen other guests with you, you'll probably get to know everyone within a day. Open-seating dinner helps with the mingling.

The cuisine is international and Mediterranean. Zeus Casual itineraries offer a "famous" Greek night, with themed food and music; their brochures also promise that the crew will help with the basics of Greek conversation and dancing.

ITINERARIES & RATES
HARMONY G and *HARMONY V*   **Seven-day Athens round-trip cruises** call in Kea, Delos, Mykonos, Santorini, Iraklion, Rethymnon, Monemvassia, Nafplion, and Spetses. Fridays from April 25 through October 31. Also allows embarkations for 7-day round-trips in Iraklion on Mondays and Rethymnon on Tuesdays. **Rates:** From 1,495€ ($2,040). (20% off the cruise-only portion of the fare on Apr 25 and Oct 31 cruises.)

H&B I and *H&B II* **Seven-day Athens round-trip cruises** call in Santorini, Ios, Paros, Mykonos, Syros, Kea, Sounion, and an overnight in Athens. Fridays from April 4 through October 31. **Rates:** From 902€ ($1,230). (10% off the cruise-only portion of the fare on Apr 4, 11, and 18, and Oct 24 and 31 cruises.)

ZEUS II **Seven-day round-trip Corfu** cruise calls at Sivota, Paxi, Antipaxi, Lefkas, Kefalonia, Ithaca, Zakynthos, and Parga. Saturdays between May 10 and October 11. Also allows embarkations for 7-day round-trips from Zakynthos on Thursdays. **Rates:** From 880€ ($1,200). (10% off the cruise-only portion of the fare on May 10, May 17, Oct 4, and Oct 11 cruises.)

VIKING STAR **Seven-day Rhodes round-trip** cruise calls at Nissiros, Kalymnos, Kos, Halki, Symi, and Lindos. Thursdays between May 8 and October 23. Also allows embarkations for 7-day round-trips from Lindos on Wednesdays. **Rates:** From 880€ ($1,200). (10% off the cruise-only portion of the fare on May 8, May 15, Oct 16, and Oct 23 cruises.)

9 Best Shore Excursions in the Ports of Call: Greece

Shore excursions are designed to help you make the most of your limited time in port by transporting you to sites of historical or cultural value, or of natural or artistic beauty. The tours are usually booked online in advance of the cruise or on the first day of your cruise; are sold on a first-come, first-served basis; and are nonrefundable. Some lines—but not many—include shore excursions in their cruise fares.

Generally, shore excursions that take you well beyond the port area are the ones most worth taking. You'll get professional commentary and avoid hassles with local transportation. In ports where the attractions are all within walking distance of the pier, however, you may be best off touring on your own. In other cases, it may be more enjoyable to take a taxi to an attraction and skip the crowded bus tours.

A few tips on choosing the best shore excursion for you, as you look through your cruise line's shore excursion booklet: Look at the description and see if it includes sites of interest to you. Check the activity level of the tour: a "level 1" or "moderate" tour means minimal walking; a "level 3" or "strenuous" marker means you may be climbing steep steps or walking long distances—be especially aware of this in Greece, as some tours of sites and ruins require a lot of walking up steps or over uneven ground. And check the tour's length and price tag—the longer and/or more expensive the tour, in general, the more comprehensive it tends to be.

When touring in Greece, remember to wear comfortable walking shoes and bring a hat, sunscreen, and bottled water to ward off the effects of the hot sun. Most lines offer bottled water for a fee as you disembark.

Also, keep in mind that some churches and other religious sites require modest attire, which means shoulders and knees should be covered.

Cruise lines tend to set shore excursion pricing and options closer to the sail-date. We've included 2007 prices here to give you a general idea of how much each shore tour will cost. Shore excursions are a revenue-generating area for the cruise lines, and the tours may be heavily promoted aboard the ship. They aren't always offered at bargain prices.

Below are selected shore excursion offerings at the major cruise ports. Keep in mind that not all the tours will be offered by every line, and prices will vary. The tour may also show up on different lines with a few variations and a different name. For more information on many of these ports, consult the relevant chapters in this book.

CORFU (KERKIRA)

See chapter 15 for complete sightseeing information.

MOUNTAIN BIKE EXPEDITION (4 hr., 86€/$119): Travel from the port by coach to the town of Dassia, where you'll pick up your bike. The bike tour starts with an uphill ride to Kato Korakiana, where you'll stop at a coffee shop. Bike through a narrow, paved alley to get to the town of Saint Marcos, with stone houses and a Byzantine chapel. Stop here for a Greek snack and then bike downhill.

PALEOKASTRITSA (half-day, 29€/$40): Visit the hilltop town of Paleokastritsa on the western side of Corfu, punctuated with olive, lemon, and cypress trees and bays and coves. Stop at the 13th-century Monastery of the Virgin Mary, on the edge of a promontory. The monastery is about a mile from the beach, and participants have the option of swapping the visit to the monastery with a visit to the beach. The tour includes free time in Corfu town.

THE ACHILLEION & PAELOKASTRITSA (7½ hr., 77€/$106): This tour includes a visit to the town of Paleokastritsa and the Monastery of the Holy Virgin Mary, as well as Achilleion Palace, which was built in the late 19th century as the home of Empress Elizabeth of Austria; the palace, now owned by the Greek government, has been renovated and guests can visit the home and the gardens, which boast views of the island. The tour continues to Perama and the monastery of Vlacherna; after a lunch break in a traditional Greek restaurant the coach returns to Corfu town for a tour of the city on foot.

4×4 ADVENTURE (4½ hr., 109€/$149): Get behind the wheel of a four-wheel-drive for this tour around Corfu (drivers must bring a driver's license and be familiar with driving a manual transmission). Following a guide vehicle, you'll drive, caravan-style, to different towns on the island of Corfu, stopping in some for sightseeing and snacks.

IRAKLION & AYIOS NIKOLAOS (CRETE)

See chapter 9 for complete sightseeing information.

KNOSSOS & THE MINOTAUR (3 hr., 44€/$62): Knossos was once the center of the prehistoric Minoan civilization; it is thought to be the basis for the original mythological Minotaur's labyrinth. Today it is one of the great archaeological sites. What remains are portions of two major palaces, plus several restorations made between 2000 B.C. and 1250 B.C.; parts of the palace were rebuilt in the 20th century. Visit the excavation of the palace of King Minos; view the royal quarter, the throne room, and the queen's quarters, with its dolphin frescoes above the door. Other sites include the house of the high priest and the "small palace." Some tours include a visit to the archaeological museum, which includes artifacts from the Minoan civilization, or a stop in the town of Iraklion.

WINDMILLS & LASSITHI PLATEAU (4½ hr., 58€/$79): This tour takes participants up Mount Dikti to the Lassithi plateau. On the way you'll stop at the monastery of Kera, which houses Byzantine-era icons. The plateau boasts views of other nearby mountains and the sailclothed windmills that irrigate the land. The tour includes about 2 hours of walking and standing, and there's considerable climbing involved. The tour includes a stop at a local restaurant.

ITEA (DELPHI)

THE MYTHOLOGY OF DELPHI (4 hr., 58€/$79): Delphi was the ancient home of the Oracle, where pilgrims came to ask questions of the Greek god Apollo. Visit the Sanctuary of Apollo to see the Temple of Apollo where one of three Pythian priestesses gave voice to Apollo's oracles; the well-preserved amphitheater; and the Castalian Spring and the Sacred Way. Be sure to visit the museum as well. The tour includes time to shop in the village of Delphi.

KATAKOLON (OLYMPIA)

ANCIENT OLYMPIA & ARCHAEOLOGICAL MUSEUM (4 hr., 46€/$64): Visit the site of the original Olympic Games, held from 776 B.C. to A.D. 393 (and most recently used in the 2004 Olympics). View temples and altars, including the Temple of Zeus, which once housed the gold-and-ivory statue of Zeus that was one of the Seven Wonders of the Ancient World; and the original stadium, which could seat 20,000. Also included is the temple of Hera, the shrine of Pelops, the Treasuries, the gymnasium, and the Council House, where athletes took the Olympic Oath. You'll spend about an hour in the museum, viewing artifacts and sculpture and conclude the tour with a visit to the village of Olympia. Some tours feature a folkloric show or snacks in Katakolon.

MYKONOS & DELOS

See chapter 10 for complete sightseeing information.

A VISIT TO DELOS (4 hr., 43€/$59): Delos is the small, uninhabited island just off the coast of Mykonos where, according to mythology, the gods Apollo and Artemis were born. The island was a religious center and a pilgrimage destination. Excavations have uncovered the city of Delos, and the tour explores the site, which includes marble lions, three temples dedicated to Apollo, the theater district, and the Sacred Lake, which dried up in 1926.

HISTORIC WALKING TOUR OF MYKONOS (2½ hr., 36€/$49): A downhill walking tour of Mykonos town takes in the Archaeological Museum, the Maritime Museum, and Lena's Traditional House, which re-creates the home of a 19th-century Mykonos family.

A DAY AT THE BEACH (3½ hr., 50€/$69): This tour takes participants to one of Mykonos's hotels on the beach of Platis Gialos. A sun bed, umbrella, and welcome cocktail or coffee will be offered to guests. Access is provided to the hotel's pool and facilities as well as a 10% discount on beach activities such as water-skiing and WaveRunners.

NAFPLION

MYCENAE & PALAMIDI CASTLE (3½ hr., 72€/$99): The area is rich with the remains of the ancient Mycenaean civilization. Drive by the ancient sites of Tiryns and come to the ruins of the ancient city of Mycenae, where excavation work begun in the late 19th century eventually exposed the Lions Gate, the entrance to the city. Also visit the Beehive Tomb, which gets its name from its shape. Take a shopping break at Fithia Village, then return to Nafplion and to the Palamidi Castle, which was built as a fortress by the Turks and Venetians (and later used as a prison). The castle offers views of the Argolic Gulf. *Note:* The path up consists of nearly a thousand steps (buses can drive up to the gate).

PATMOS
See chapter 11 for complete sightseeing information.

ST. JOHN'S MONASTERY & CAVE OF THE REVELATION (3 hr., 40€/$55): Depart the Port of Scala and travel by bus to the village of Chora and the 900-year-old, fortress-like Monastery of St. John, which overlooks the main harbor and is enclosed by fortified walls. You'll see the main church and the ecclesiastical treasures in the church and museum, including Byzantine icons, 6th-century Gospels, and frescoes in the chapel. Continue on by bus to the nearby Cave of the Apocalypse. Niches in the wall mark the pillow and ledge used as a desk by St. John, said to have written the Book of Revelations here; a crack in the wall was said to have been made by the Voice of God. Refreshments are served in Scala. Visitors to the monastery must cover their shoulders; shorts are not allowed.

PIRAEUS/ATHENS
See chapter 5 for complete sightseeing information.

ATHENS & CAPE SOUNION (8 hr., 95€–97€/$131–$134): This tour visits the Acropolis, Athens's most prominent historical and architectural site, in the morning; after lunch the tour continues to Cape Sounion (about a 1½–2 hr. drive from Athens), the most southern tip of the European landmass. Participants can explore the Temple of Poseidon, which is located at the top of a 180-foot cliff and offers a panoramic view of the Saronic Gulf and the Cyclades.

ACROPOLIS & CORINTH CANAL TRANSIT (9 hr., 79€/$109): The first stop on the tour is the Acropolis, where participants get a guided walking tour. Then drive past the coves of the Saronic Gulf to Isthmia, where you'll transit the Corinth Canal, a slim (30 meter/90-ft.-wide) waterway blasted through sheer rock in the 19th century. Other sites you'll see on the tour include the temple of Athena Nike, the Parthenon, the Porch of the Caryatids, Hadrian's Arch, Constitution Square, the Tomb of the Unknown Warrior, the Presidential Palace, and the National Gardens. Lunch is included in the tour.

RHODES
See chapter 11 for complete sightseeing information.

LINDOS ACROPOLIS (4 hr., 65€/$89): Travel through the scenic countryside to Lindos, an important city in ancient times. At Lindos, view the medieval walls, which were constructed by the Knights of St. John in the 14th century. Walk or take a donkey up to the ancient acropolis. Once you've reached the summit, visit the Doric Temple of Athena Lindia, built in 4th century B.C. The acropolis includes a double-winged portico, Byzantine church, and remains of the governor's quarters. The ruins are a backdrop for great views; souvenir shops can be found in the town of Lindos.

FILERIMOS LOCAL MEZES & WINE OUTING (3¾ hr., 40€/$55): Participants get a quick look at Rhodes Town before being driven to Filerimos, where hills are dotted with cypress, oaks, and pines. Visit Moni Filerimou and Lady of Filerimos, an Italian reconstruction of the Knights of St. John's 14th-century church, and nearby ruins of the Temple of Athena. The tour continues to Kalithea Resort, where the thermal water was, according to story, once recommended by Hippocrates for its healing qualities; today the thermal springs have dried up, but the area is known for swimming and scenery. There will be some time for shopping in Kalithea before participants are taken to a seaside taverna for local food and wine.

WALKING TOUR OF HISTORIC RHODES (3 hr., 33€/$45): Rhodes, which boasts one of the oldest inhabited medieval towns in Europe, is a great city for walking. This tour takes guests through the Old Town, a rambling collection of nearly 200 different, unnamed streets (and thus a good place to have a guide). You'll see churches, the Jewish quarter, the Inns of the Knights, and other spots; you'll tour the rebuilt Palace of the Grand Masters and the Hospital of the Knights, now a museum. And you'll walk down the cobblestoned Street of the Knights, an old pathway leading from the Acropolis of Rhodes down to the port and lined with medieval towers and architecturally interesting facades.

SANTORINI (THIRA)

See chapter 10 for complete sightseeing information.

SANTORINI VOLCANO HIKING (2¾ hr., 47€/$65): A caique, or wooden fishing boat, picks up participants for a 15-minute ride to Nea Kameni, along the shores where volcanic rock has formed unique shapes. A half-hour hike up the crater of the volcano follows. Once you reach the crater you can rest and enjoy the views of Santorini and the caldera's cliffs. Then hike back down to the caique and sail to Palea Kemeni, a thermal spring. Here, sulfur pools can reach 98°F. There's a chance of swimming if time permits, so wear a bathing suit and bring a towel. The boat returns you to the port.

VILLAGE OF OIA & SANTORINI ISLAND (4 hr., 47€/$65): Another white-washed hilltop town is Oia, the town where so many postcard-perfect photos are taken of blue-domed, whitewashed buildings and the blue sea beyond. There are small cobblestone streets to explore; pop in at shops and cafes. A wine tasting is offered to tour-goers, as well as a walk to the cable car station at the top of Fira.

10 Best Shore Excursions in the Ports of Call: Turkey

The following Turkish ports of call are commonly visited on Greek itineraries.

ISTANBUL

GRAND ISTANBUL WITH LUNCH IN AN OTTOMAN HOME (8½ hr., 120€/$165): Includes the Hippodrome, once the largest chariot race grounds of the Byzantine empire; Sultan Ahmet Mosque, also known as the Blue Mosque for its 21,000 blue Iznik tiles; the famous St. Sophia, once the largest church of the Christian world; the underground cistern, a reservoir held up by more than 300 Corinthian columns; and Topkapi Palace, the official residence of the Ottoman Sultans and home to treasures that include Spoonmaker's Diamond, one of the biggest diamonds in the world. Also visit the Grand Bazaar, with its 4,000 shops. In this version of the tour, stop for lunch in the gardens of an Ottoman house; other tours include lunch in a hotel, and/or a carpet-making demonstration.

THE BLUE MOSQUE, HAGIA SOPHIA & THE BAZAAR (4 hr., 53€/$73): An example of an abbreviated tour of the above, which visits the Blue Mosque, the Hippodrome, the Hagia Sophia, and the Grand Bazaar, as well as a carpet-making demonstration.

TURKISH DINNER & ENTERTAINMENT (4 hr., 54€/$75): A motorcoach will bring participants to a local nightclub, where a dinner of traditional Turkish cuisine will be accompanied by different types of entertainment: belly dancing, folk dancing, and a group of performers who sing phonetically in different languages. A viewing of the Bosphorus Bridge by night wraps up the evening. Available only if you're in town for the evening or overnight.

SCENIC BOSPHORUS CRUISE & LUNCH (6½ hr., 43€/$59): A narrated cruise up the famous Bosphorus includes lunch and a chance to view the city's most famous landmarks from the water. A visit to the Sadberk Hanim Museum is included, as well as a trip to the Grand Bazaar for shopping.

MAGNIFICENT LEGACIES WITH VISIT TO SPICE MARKET (4 hr., 43€/$59): Start with a visit to the Suleymaniye Mosque, built by the architect Sinan. Continue to the Church of the Savior in Chora, now the Chora Museum, near the city's old Byzantine walls, which features mosaics and frescoes depicting biblical scenes. This tour also includes the underground cistern, where 300-plus columns support the vaulted roof. At the end of the excursion you'll hit the famous spice market, where you can browse for all kinds of exotic items, from jewelry to spices and herbs.

KUSADASI

ANCIENT EPHESUS (3 hr.; 36€/$49): Visit one of the best-preserved ancient cities in the world. Your guide will take you through the Magnesia gate and down the city's marble streets to the Temple of Hadrian, the Trajan Fountain, the baths of Scoloastika, the theater, and the incredible library building, and along the way you'll pass columns, mosaics, monuments, and ruins. Some time for shopping in Kusadasi is provided.

EPHESUS, ST. JOHN'S BASILICA & VIRGIN MARY SHRINE (4½ hr., 43€/$59): This tour combines a visit to Ephesus with the House of the Virgin Mary, a humble chapel located in the valley of Bulbuldagi. Located here is the site where the Virgin Mary is believed to have spent her last days. The site was officially sanctioned for pilgrimage in 1892. The tour also includes a visit to St. John's Basilica, another holy pilgrimage site. It is believed to be the site where St. John wrote the fourth book of the New Testament. A church at the site, which is now in ruins, was built by Justinian over a 2nd-century tomb believed to contain St. John the Apostle. This tour may also be offered as a full-day excursion, including lunch at a local restaurant and a visit to the museum of Ephesus.

EPHESUS & TERRACED HOUSES (4 hr.; 55€/$76): You'll see the Ephesus highlights on this tour, including the Celsus Library facade and Hadrian's Temple. You'll also view the Terrace Houses, a newly excavated area opposite Hadrian's Temple. The houses were once inhabited by Ephesus's rich and are decorated with mosaics and frescoes. The area can only be accessed by special permission, such as part of a shore excursion group.

RUINS OF MILETUS & DIDYMA (6½–7 hr., 62€/$85): This tour takes in the ruins that surround the region of Ephesus: Didyma, known for its Temple of Apollo; and Miletus, which includes the Bath of Faustina and a stadium built by the Greeks and expanded by the Romans to hold 15,000 spectators. A lunch at a restaurant in Didyma is included. Some tours also will include visits to Ephesus or the ancient village of Priene.

Settling into Athens

by Peter Kerasiotis

Not too long ago, Athens used to be the city Greeks loved to hate. Expensive, polluted, overcrowded, and bursting at the seams with more than 5 million inhabitants—over 40% of the entire country's population. However, the preparations for the 2004 homecoming Olympics brought forth many changes to the city and the successful staging of the Games imbued the ancient city and her residents with a newfound confidence that acted like a catalyst for the many changes that are continuing to take place. Much like Barcelona, the Olympics were just what Athens needed to get its groove back. The city suddenly, unexpectedly, and almost unabashedly feels young again. Forever the city of a thousand contradictions, Athens is one of the few ancient cities in the world where the cutting edge, the hip, and the modern can suddenly coexist so harmoniously with the classical and complement each other to near perfection.

Athens today is a strikingly wealthier, more sophisticated and cosmopolitan city than it was pre-Olympics and most certainly than it was when I was growing up in the '80s, but no matter how fascinating its current renaissance is, one must keep in mind that this is a city that has gone through countless transformations throughout its long and turbulent history. When I was talking with my grandmother about how different the Athens of today is to that of my childhood, I paused to ask her what the biggest difference was between the Athens she had known as a young woman and the Athens of today. "People used to say 'I'm hungry'" she said. "Now they say 'I'm bored.'" She had been a young woman in Athens during the famine, poverty, and horrors of World War II; the images of the Nazi flag on the Acropolis and finding friends and neighbors dead in the streets were etched in her memory.

The dawn of the 21st century found the ancient city with a multitude of much-needed changes: a vast new infrastructure system; a sparkling and continuously expanding new Metro and immaculate stations, many of which display the artifacts found during its construction; a new international airport named one of the world's finest by the International Air Transport Association; miles of new roads and a sorely needed beltway around the city that has eased the city's infamous traffic and has significantly reduced the city's equally infamous smog. The ancient sites have been linked together by a promenade, a unique city boardwalk around classical Athens with antiquities on one side and modern-day sidewalk cafes, galleries, renovated mansions, and rotating outdoor art installations on the other. All in all, 10 miles of downtown Athens's notoriously traffic-clogged streets have been pedestrianized, transforming one of the most pedestrian-unfriendly cities in the world into a stroller's delight and into a much more charming, accessible, and enjoyable city than before. Pavements have been widened and squares refurbished or redesigned. The capital's coastline has also been revived, with a dizzying selection of cafes, restaurants, and open-air nightclubs by the sea and in marinas; the coast also has a multitude of sporting facilities, pedestrian shopping districts, and pristine beaches—all a mere tram ride from downtown.

The city's hotels also underwent major renovations that changed the landscape dramatically in just a couple of years. Not only were classic hotels restored to their former glory with all the modern comforts and luxuries, but new boutique hotels appeared that set the bar higher than one could have thought possible just a few years ago.

Greek cuisine is undergoing its own renaissance at the hands of talented new chefs, making Athens a haven for foodies worldwide (three restaurants have already been awarded a prestigious Michelin star); museums were renovated and expanded while several new and exceptional smaller museums have also joined the already impressive lineup (the stunning new Acropolis museum will steal the show for many years to come and will hopefully see the return of the Parthenon Marbles to their home), and many galleries and art and exhibition centers have sprung up all over the city—the majority of them housed in former warehouses and factories. The numerous industrial-to-art conversions have been among the most pleasant surprises for the city, for they led almost immediately to the rebirth of formerly run down and all-but-abandoned neighborhoods. Following the lead of Psirri and Thissio—two ancient neighborhoods neglected in more recent years that are now the hippest downtown destinations—Gazi and Kerameikos have also risen from the ashes, going from gritty to urban chic.

As you explore Athens, try to make the city your own. Walk its streets, take in its scents, linger in its sidewalk cafes, squares, and rooftop terraces, take in a show in an ancient open-air theater, or an avant-garde performance, concert, or art exhibition at one of the new multipurpose arts complexes, or enjoy a movie under the stars. Climb its mountains, swim in its waters, visit its ancient temples and Byzantine churches, try its food and its nightlife, and see as many museums as you can. Take a stroll along the Archaeological Promenade, inside the lush National Gardens and Zappeio gardens, through the many neighborhoods and ports, and find yourself at the top of Lycabettus Mountain or Cape Sounion at dusk for two of the most spectacular sunsets outside of Santorini. Explore its ancient districts and its most modern ones to witness an ancient city discovering its modern soul in front of your very eyes. Take the bad in stride as well—long-term problems have been addressed, not eradicated. The smog does return from time to time (especially during heat waves) and traffic can still be fierce—so feel free to yell at the taxi driver who refuses to stop for you in a torrential rain or packs you into his taxi with many other passengers in the stifling summer heat; to mutter obscenities to yourself for getting stuck in traffic when you could have easily taken the Metro instead; and to throw your hands up in exasperation as a strike threatens to ruin your holiday—a glimpse of the floodlit Parthenon or a glass of wine on a rooftop, in an ancient quarter, or by the sea will have you back to your old self in no time. Long after you have gone, you may feel a strange call, a certain nostalgia for something you will not be able to explain at first. You will soon realize it is Athens calling you back like a siren as she has done to so many of us that have tried to leave her. For anybody that has taken the time to truly get to know her, you will find yourself longing to return to her embrace. Exciting and exasperating, ancient and modern, seductive and unforgettable—welcome to my Athens.

STRATEGIES FOR SEEING THE REGION

For good ideas on how to approach the city, take a look at the "Suggested Itineraries" in chapter 3.

From mid-March through May the weather is almost always pleasant in Athens, although Greeks rightly say that the March wind has "teeth." Between June and August, the temperature usually rises steadily, making August a good month to emulate the Athenian practice of avoiding the city. If you do come here in August, you'll find that Athens, like Paris, belongs to the tourists: Some 60% of all Athenians take their summer holiday between the 1st and 15th of August. Stretches when it's well over 100°F (38°C) are not uncommon in August, when anyone with health problems such as asthma should be wary of Athens's *nefos* (smog). Because the city can be hot and exhausting, give yourself time off for a coffee or a cold drink in a cafe. After all, you're on vacation!

September is usually balmy, with occasional light rain, although it's not unknown for August heat to spill over well into September. October usually offers beautiful summer/autumn weather, although with rain and some wind likely. It might even be intermittently chilly.

Most rain falls between November and February, when Athens can be colder and windier than you might expect. Average daytime temperatures range from 52°F (11°C) in January to 92°F (33°C) in August.

1 Orientation

ARRIVING & DEPARTING
BY PLANE

The new **Athens International Airport Eleftherios Venizelos** (© 210/353-0000; www.aia.gr), 27km (17 miles) northeast of Athens at Spata, opened in 2001. The airport is usually called "Venizelos" or "Spata," after its nearest town. Time will tell whether the airport will meet its goal of handling 50 million passengers annually and become the leading airport in southeastern Europe. The good news about the new airport is that in contrast to the old Hellenikon Airport, Venizelos is a large, modern facility, with ample restrooms, interesting shops, and acceptable restaurants. The bad news is that it is a serious slog from Athens; you no longer have the option of heading back into the city for a few extra hours of sightseeing if your flight is delayed. The airport has plenty to keep you busy anyway, including a small museum with ruins found during the airport's construction and rotating art exhibits.

Look for free brochures that describe the airport's facilities at stands throughout the airport. Neither these publications, however, nor the airport's website, can be relied on for accurate up-to-date information. Here is a basic introduction to Athens's airport, based on information that was up-to-date at press time.

ARRIVALS   Most flights arrive at the main terminal, which has both an "A" and "B" area, but some flights—including most charter flights—arrive and depart from Spata's first of a projected cluster of satellite terminals. In addition, you may deplane down a steep flight of stairs onto the tarmac, where a bus will take you to the terminal. When planning what carry-on luggage to bring, keep in mind that it can be quite a trek from your arrival point to the baggage claim area and Customs hall.

The baggage claim area has ATMs, telephones, restrooms, and luggage carts. Luggage carts cost 1€ ($1.30); if you see a cart attendant, he or she can make change for

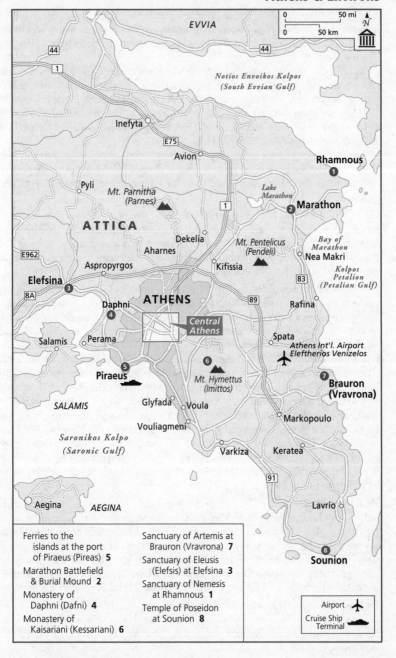

0   50 mi
0   50 km

EVVIA

44   44

1

*Notios Envoikos Kolpos
(South Evvian Gulf)*

Inefyta

E75

Avion

Rhamnous
1

Pyli

*Mt. Parnitha
(Parnes)*

*Lake
Marathon*

Marathon
2

ATTICA

Dekelia

1

Aharnes

*Mt. Pentelicus
(Pendeli)*

*Bay of
Marathon*

Nea Makri

E962

Aspropyrgos

Kifissia

83

*Kolpos
Petalion
(Petalian Gulf)*

Elefsina
3

8A

ATHENS

89

Rafina

Daphni
4

*Central
Athens*

Salamis

Perama

Spata

*Athens Int'l. Airport
Eleftherios Venizelos*

Piraeus
5

6

*Mt. Hymettus
(Imittos)*

7

**Brauron
(Vravrona)**

SALAMIS

Glyfada

Voula

Markopoulo

Vouliagmeni

*Saronikos Kolpo
(Saronic Gulf)*

Varkiza

Keratea

91

Aegina

AEGINA

Lavrio

8

Sounion

Ferries to the
islands at the port
of Piraeus (Pireas) **5**

Marathon Battlefield
& Burial Mound **2**

Monastery of
Daphni (Dafni) **4**

Monastery of
Kaisariani (Kessariani) **6**

Sanctuary of Artemis at
Brauron (Vravrona) **7**

Sanctuary of Eleusis
(Elefsis) at Elefsina **3**

Sanctuary of Nemesis
at Rhamnous **1**

Temple of Poseidon
at Sounion **8**

Airport ✈
Cruise Ship
Terminal

you. You can also use one of several free telephones in the baggage claim area to call for a porter. When we last passed through the airport, porters' fees were highly negotiable.

If your suitcases do not greet you in the baggage claim area, proceed to a "Baggage Tracing" desk.

Signs in the baggage claim area indicate which route to use for Customs. Citizens of Common Market countries (EEC) do not have to go through Passport Control; citizens of non-EEC countries, such as the U.S., must go through Passport Control.

If you are being met, you may want to rendezvous at the clearly marked Meeting Point (across from the Greek National Tourism Organization desk) between exits 2 and 3 in the main terminal Arrivals Hall.

The Pacific baggage storage (left luggage) facility is in the main terminal arrivals area; this service is officially open 24 hours a day and charges 2€ ($2.60) per piece per day.

Exits from the main terminal are signposted for taxi and bus connections into Athens.

GETTING INTO ATHENS   Getting into post-Olympics Athens is an entirely different experience than what it used to be. The airport is linked to the city with a six-lane expressway (Attiki Odos), Metro, buses, and taxis. Public transportation to and from the airport is excellent and advised (especially the Metro because buses can be slow and get stuck in traffic during rush hour once they enter the city).

By Metro   Line 3 of the Metro (6€/$7.80 single, 10€/$13 return—valid for 48 hr.; one-way fare for two people is 10€/$13 and 15€/$20 for three) is more convenient, less expensive, and faster than any other way of getting from the airport to downtown or vice versa. Unless you have a lot of luggage or simply just want to get in a car and go after a long flight, the Metro is the perfect option. The Metro line 3 serves the city center (where you can switch to the other lines at either Monastiraki or Syntagma stations) from the airport. The trip takes roughly 35 minutes and trains run every half-hour from 6:30am to 11:30pm. From the city to the airport (leaving from Syntagma and Monastiraki) trains run from 5:50am to 10:50pm. To get to Piraeus switch at Monastiraki station to line 1; total travel time is about 1 hour. At press time line 3 was set to reach the port of Piraeus, reducing travel time to the port to 50 minutes and not requiring a switch. Ask at the airport to see if the station has been opened upon your arrival. The airport ticket is valid for all forms of public transportation for 90 minutes; if you're approaching 90 minutes and are still in transit simply re-validate your ticket by having it punched again.

By Suburban Railroad   The suburban railroad train runs to and from the Larissa station, Doukissis Plakentias, with a connection to Metro line 1 at Nerantziotissa (at the Athens Mall in Marousi near the Athens Olympic Complex). It might not be as convenient as line 3 but it is more comfortable, not as crowded, and runs longer hours. Trains to the airport run from 4:30am to midnight while the trains from the airport to the city run from 5am to 1:20am. The suburban railroad has the same pricing as the Metro, the only difference is that the return ticket is valid for a month.

By Bus   Buses are far slower than the Metro but they are cheaper, run 24 hours, and can reach areas the Metro does not, such as the coast. If you want to take a **bus** from the airport into central Athens, be prepared for what may be a substantial wait and a slow journey.

There are several bus lines to and from the airport to destinations throughout the city. All buses depart from the designated area outside the Arrivals Terminal of the

Main Terminal Building (Doors 4 and 5). **Bus service** from the airport to Syntagma Square or to Piraeus costs about 4€ ($5.20). You can buy the ticket from a booth beside the bus stop or on the bus. Do *not* assume that the destination indicated on the front of the bus, or on the sign at the bus stop, is the actual destination of the bus. Always ask the driver where the bus is going. In theory, bus no. 95 (and, confusingly, sometimes bus no. 091) runs to Syntagma and Omonia squares before continuing to Piraeus every half-hour from 7am to 10pm (1€/$1.30), and then every hour from about 10:15pm to 6:30am (3€/$3.90).

By Taxi The easiest way to get to town logically, you would assume, would be to take a taxi from immediately outside the terminal. This is not as simple as it sounds: Greeks regard waiting in line with amusement, and getting a cab as a fiercely competitive sport. A taxi should cost anywhere between 20€ and 30€ ($26–$39) depending on traffic to reach the city center. Athenian taxi drivers have an awful reputation (and deservedly so) with locals and tourists alike; the usual complaint aside from the rudeness and the smoking is the ripping off. With many mandatory etiquette classes before and after the Olympics, things are supposedly better, but be alert, never get into a taxi if the meter isn't turned on; if the driver refuses to do so, simply find another taxi. Once you are certain the meter is on, check to see that it's set on the correct tariff (tariff 1 is for the day: 5am–midnight, tariff 2 for night: midnight–5am). Keep in mind you will have to pay an additional 3€ ($4) airport surcharge and an additional 2.50€ ($3.25) on tolls (as well as .30€ (39¢) for each piece of luggage over 10 kilograms). Depending on traffic, the cab ride can take under 30 minutes or well over an hour—something to remember when you return to the airport. Most likely you will not encounter any problems aside from city traffic. In the unlikelihood of an unpleasant experience you can threaten to call the police (© **100**).

By Car Even though post-Olympics Athens is a radically different city, with the Metro, the railroad, and a new network of ring roads that have eased the city's notorious traffic, make no mistake about it, it is not an easy city to drive in and if you're unfamiliar with the streets, it can be downright horrific. If you still choose to drive into Athens, you'll pass through the region known as *Mesogeia* (the inland). Until the new airport was built, this was one of the loveliest sections of Greece, with vineyards stretching for miles, sleepy country villages, and handsome chapels. Much of the area constituted the protected "Attic Park"; now, the once-protected wetlands and vineyards are busily being turned into new towns, sub-developments, malls—and yet more roads. Numerous exits serve the most important areas of Athens.

If you plan to rent a car and head north or south and plan on avoiding the city altogether, its easier than ever to do thanks to the new National Road. If you're headed for Peloponnese simply follow the signs for Elefsina. If you're headed toward northern Greece (including the city of Thessaloniki) get off at the Lamia exit.

DEPARTURES If you are taking a taxi to the airport, ask the desk clerk at your hotel to reserve it for you well in advance of your departure. Many taxis refuse to go to the airport, fearing that they will have a long wait before they get a return fare. Allow a minimum of an hour for the ride plus 2 hours for check-in for an international flight. Once again you can hop on Metro line 3 at Syntagma or Monastiraki or take line 1 at Monastiraki and switch at Nerantziotissa for the suburban railroad.

.For information on taxi fares to the airport, see above under "Getting into Athens."

For information on bus service to the airport from Syntagma, Ethniki Amyna, and Piraeus, see above under "Arrivals." For precise details on where to catch the airport

> ⌐ *Tips* **Arriving in Greece**
>
> If you plan to travel by air in Greece or elsewhere in Europe, keep in mind that the luggage allowance for most flights within Greece and Europe is 20 kilos (44 lb.) This is almost certainly less than you would have been allowed if you have flown to Greece from the U.S. or Canada.

bus from Athens to the airport, check with your hotel, the Greek National Tourism Organization, or—if you are very well organized and not too tired!—at an information desk when you arrive at the airport.

The flight information screens should indicate where you check in and what departure gate to go to. Make sure that the information on your boarding pass agrees with the information on the flight information screen. There have been frequent complaints that adequate information on arrivals, departures, cancellations, delays, and gate changes is not always posted. Nonetheless, it is important to check these screens and ask at the information desks, as there are *no* flight announcements.

Last-minute changes in your departure gate are not unknown; arrive at your gate as early as possible. Your best chance of finding out about a change is at the original gate.

CONNECTING FLIGHTS   The airport authority advises you to allow a minimum of 45 minutes to make a flight connection; this should be adequate if you arrive and depart from the main terminal and do *not* have to clear Customs. Allow at least an hour (1½ hr. is even better) if you have to clear Customs or if you arrive or depart from the satellite terminal. At present, many charter flights use the satellite terminal.

AIRPORT FACILITIES   The airport has about 35 shops ranging from chic boutiques to Travel Value to duty-free shops. There are 10 restaurants and cafes, including a Food Village with seven food "hubs" in the main departure lounge. A McDonald's overlooking the runways perches on the upper level of the main terminal building. As with airports around the world, both food and goods are overpriced, although the prices of books, newspapers, and magazines are reasonable.

Duty-free shops have different regulations for Intra-Schengen and Extra-Schengen passengers. In short, Intra-Schengen refers to flights within the Common Market (EEC); Extra-Schengen refers to flights outside the EEC. If you are flying from Athens to a country outside the EEC, you may find it worthwhile to check out the duty-free prices on perfumes and spirits.

The **Greek National Tourism Organization** (abbreviated GNTO in English-speaking countries and EOT in Greece) has an information desk in the Arrivals Hall.

Hertz, Avis, and Alamo rental cars are available at the airport. *Note:* All these companies levy a steep surcharge (at least 10%) if you collect your car at the airport rather than at their in-town offices.

Both short-term (3€/$3.90 per hour) and long-term (12€/$16 per day) parking is available at the airport. Much of the long-term parking is a serious walk from the main terminal. If you have the proper change (unlikely), you can use a machine to pay for your ticket; otherwise, join the queue at the payment booth.

Useful telephone numbers at Athens International Airport include: Information ℂ 210/353-0000; Customs ℂ 210/353-2014; Police ℂ 210/663-5140; First Aid ℂ 166 (from airport courtesy phones and information desks) and ℂ 210/353-9408 (from pay phones).

GETTING BETWEEN THE AIRPORT & PIRAEUS (PIREAS)   By the time you read this, line 3 of the Metro (the same line that goes to and from the airport into the city center) may have reached the port of Piraeus in a new Metro station. In that case, it will be a 50-minute ride from the airport to the port and the ticket will be 6€ ($7.80)

At press time, taking the Metro from the airport to Piraeus (1 hour) requires a change at Monastiraki, so this is not recommended if you have a lot of luggage. A taxi from the airport to Piraeus should cost 20€ to 35€ ($26–$46). It's important to know that boats to the islands leave from several **different** Piraeus harbors. Most ferryboats and hydrofoils (Flying Dolphins) for Aegina leave from the **Main Harbor.** Hydrofoils for other islands leave from **Marina Zea,** a vigorous half-hour walk from the Main Harbor. If you don't know from which harbor your boat is leaving, tell your taxi driver your final destination and he can probably find out which harbor and even which pier you are leaving from.

In theory, buses leave the airport for Piraeus every hour (4€/$5.20). The bus usually leaves passengers in Karaiskaki Square, several blocks from the harbor. The official schedule is as follows: **Spata-Piraeus** (E96): Every 20 minutes from 5am to 7pm; every 30 minutes from 7pm to 8:30pm; every 40 minutes from 8:30pm to 5am.

AIRLINE OFFICES   Most international carriers have ticket offices in or near Syntagma Square. Find out the location of your airline's Athens office before you leave home, as these offices can move without warning. **Air Canada** is at 10 Othonos (✆ 210/322-3206). **American Airlines** is at 15 Panepistimiou (✆ 210/331-1045 or 210/331-1046). **British Airways** is at 1 Themistokleous, at 130 Leoforos Vouliagmenis, Glyfada (✆ 210/890-6666). **Delta Air Lines** is at 4 Othonos (✆ 800/4412-9506). **Lufthansa Airlines** is at 11 Leoforos Vas. Sofias (✆ 210/617-5200). **Qantas Airways** is at 2 Nikodimou (✆ 210/323-9063). **Swissair** is at 4 Othonos (✆ 210/323-5811). **Turkish Airlines** is at 19 Filellinon (✆ 210/324-6024).

Olympic, the national carrier, offers both international and domestic service and has offices just off Syntagma Square at 15 Filellinon (✆ 210/926-7555); at 6 Othonos (✆ 210/926-7444); and at 96 Leoforos Syngrou (✆ 210/926-7251 to -7254). The main reservations and information numbers are ✆ 210/966-6666 and 210/936-9111; the website is www.olympic-airways.gr.

BY CAR

If you arrive by car from **Corinth** (to the southwest), the signs into Athens will direct you fairly clearly to Omonia Square, which you will enter from the west along Ayiou Konstantinou. In Omonia, signs *should* direct you on toward Syntagma Square and other points in central Athens (signs in Omonia disappear mysteriously). If you arrive from **Thessaloniki** (to the north), the signs pointing you into central Athens are few

---

⎛Tips Taking a Taxi

If you decide to take a taxi from the airport into Athens, ask an airline official or a policeman what the fare should be, and let the taxi driver know you've been told the official rate before you begin your journey. If you're taking a taxi from Athens to the airport, have the desk clerk at your hotel order it for you well in advance of your departure. Many taxis refuse to go to the airport, fearing that they'll have a long wait before they get a return fare.

> ⌢ *Tips*   **The Attica Zoological Park**
>
> If you find yourself with 2 or more hours to kill at the Venezelios Airport at
> Spata, consider taking a taxi (12€/$16) to the nearby Attica Zoological Park in
> Spata. Unlike the grim zoo in Athens's National Gardens, this one—with 2,000
> birds from more than 300 species—is a delight. Hours are daily from 10am to
> 5pm, October through April; and daily 9am to 7:30pm, May through Septem-
> ber. Admission is 8€ ($11).

and far between. It is not a good idea to attempt this for the first time after dark, as
you may well miss the turn for Omonia Square. If this happens, your best bet is to
look for the Acropolis and head toward it until you pick up signs for Omonia or Syntagma squares.

BY BUS
Before you start out on any bus trip, check with the **tourist police** (⟁ **210/171**) or
the **Greek National Tourism Organization (EOT)** office (⟁ **210/870-0000;** www.
gnto.gr) for current schedules and fares. As the new Metro continues to open stations,
bus routes and fares will change. It's best to double-check all routes and to be prepared
for fare increases. If possible, get someone to write down the name and address of your
bus station in Greek; this will be a great help when you take a taxi or bus. Keep in mind
that many buses run both with and without a "0" prefix: 024 and 24, for example.

There are two principal stations for **KTEL,** the national bus company. **Terminal A,**
100 Kifissou (⟁ **210/512-9233**), off the road out of Athens toward Corinth, handles
buses to and from **the Peloponnese** and parts of **Northern Greece.** A taxi here from
Syntagma Square should cost 4€ to 6€ ($5.20–$7.80); if traffic is light, the journey
is less than 20 minutes, but it can take an hour. If you don't have much to carry, take
public bus no. 051 to the terminal (.50€/65¢). It leaves from the corner of Zinonos
and Menandrou, several blocks off Omonia Square; you can catch the same bus at the
terminal for the trip into town.

Terminal B (⟁ **210/831-7096**) handles buses to and from **Central Greece**
(including Delphi, Thebes, Evvia, and Meteora) and some destinations **to the north
and east of Athens.** The GNTO, for reasons known best to itself, lists the address for
Terminal B as 260 Liossion; this is where the bus for the terminal stops. To get to the
terminal itself after you get off the bus, turn right onto Yousiou and you will see the
terminal at the end of the street. Bus no. 024, which stops at Leoforos Amalias in front
of the entrance to the National Garden (a block south of Syntagma Sq.), will take you
to and from the terminal for .50€ (65¢). If you take this bus, tell the driver you want
to get off at the bus terminal and then head right to Yousiou to reach the terminal.
The **Mavromateon terminal** at Patission and Alexandras, a few hundred meters north
of the Archaeological Museum, handles buses for most destinations in **Attica.**

BY TRAIN
Trains **from the south and west,** including Eurail connections via Patras, arrive at the
Peloponnese station (Stathmos Peloponnisou; ⟁ **210/513-1601**), about a mile
northwest of Omonia Square on Sidirodromeon. Trains **from the north** arrive at
Larissa station (Stathmos Larissis; ⟁ **210/529-8837**), just across the tracks from the

Peloponnese station on Deligianni. The Larissa station has both an exchange office (daily 8am–9:15pm) and luggage storage (daily 6:30am–9pm).

To get to the train stations, you can take the **Metro** (subway) to Larissa (line 2), close to both stations. A taxi from the center of town should cost about 5€ ($6.50). The Metro runs from Omonia, Syntagma, and Koukaki to the Larissa Metro station, which is near the train stations. The most central place to catch the Metro is the stop in front of the Parliament Building on Syntagma Square.

You can purchase train tickets just before your journey at the train station (running the risk that all seats may be sold); at the Omonia Square ticket office, 1 Karolou (© 210/524-0647); at 17 Filellinon, off Syntagma Square (© 210/323-6747); or from most travel agents. Information (in theory in English) on timetables is available by dialing © 145 or 147.

BY BOAT

Piraeus, the main harbor of Athens's main seaport, 11km (7 miles) southwest of central Athens, is a 15-minute Metro ride from Monastiraki and Omonia squares. The subway runs from about 5am to midnight and costs 2€ ($2.60). The far slower bus no. 040 runs from Piraeus to central Athens (with a stop at Filellinon, off Syntagma Sq.) every 15 minutes between 5am and 1am and hourly from 1am to 5am for .70€ (90¢).

You may prefer to take a **taxi** to avoid what can be a long hike from your boat to the bus stop or subway terminal. Be prepared for serious bargaining. The normal fare on the meter from Piraeus to Syntagma should be about 8€ to 13€ ($11–$17), but many drivers offer a flat fare, which can easily be as much as 20€ ($26). Pay it if you're desperate; or walk to a nearby street, hail another taxi, and insist that the meter be turned on.

If you arrive at Piraeus by hydrofoil (Flying Dolphin), you'll probably arrive at **Zea Marina** harbor, about a dozen blocks south across the peninsula from the main harbor. Even our Greek friends admit that getting a taxi from Zea Marina into Athens can involve a wait of an hour or more—and that drivers usually drive hard (and exorbitant) bargains. To avoid both the wait and big fare, you can walk up the hill from the hydrofoil station and catch bus no. 905 for 1€ ($1.30), which connects Zea to the Piraeus Metro (subway) station, where you can complete your journey into Athens.

Tips Hotels Near the Airport

Have an early flight out of Spata? You might consider spending the night at **Hotel Avra** (© 22940/22-780), 30 to 45 minutes by taxi from the airport on the waterfront in the nearby port of Rafina. The Avra was completely remodeled in 2004 and has a decent restaurant (sometimes with live music). Even better, you can stroll to one of Rafina's many harborside restaurants and watch the fishing boats and ferries come and go as you enjoy fresh seafood. Doubles start at 100€ ($130). If you want to be at the airport itself because you have an early flight or because you arrive late, the 345-room **Sofitel Athens Airport Hotel** (© 210/681-0882; www.sofitel.com), considered one of the finest airport hotels in Europe, with creature comforts such as its own restaurants, fitness club, and swimming pool, is the logical place to stay. Rates are from 140€ to 220€ ($182–$286) double.

Tips   Boat-to-Plane Connections

A word about making air connections after an island trip: It is unwise—even foolhardy—to allow anything less than 24 hours between your return to Piraeus by island boat and your departure by air, as rough seas can significantly delay the trip.

You must buy a ticket at the small stand near the bus stop or at a newsstand before boarding the bus. *Warning:* If you arrive late at night, you may not be able to do this, as both the newsstand and the ticket stand may be closed.

If you've disembarked at the port of **Rafina** (about an hour's bus ride east of Athens), you'll see a bus stop up the hill from the ferryboat pier. Inquire about the bus to Athens; it runs often and will take you within the hour to the **Areos Park bus terminal,** 29 Mavromateon, near the junction of Leoforos Alexandras and Patission. The Areos Park terminal is 1 block from the Victoria Square Metro stop and about 25 minutes by trolley from Syntagma Square. From the bus terminal, there are buses to Rafina every half-hour.

By spring 2007, the port of Lavrion (© **22920/25-249**), 52km (32 miles) southeast of Athens, began to take over some of the itineraries from the port of Piraeus including daily ferries and speedboats to Agios Efstratios, Alexandroupoli, Andros, Folegandros, Ios, Katapola, Kavala, Kea, Kythnos, Limnos, Milos, Mykonos, Naxos, Paros, Sikinos, Syros, and Tinos. The port's official website, www.oll.gr, is in Greek only so check the GNTO site (see below) for more info. A taxi to Lavrio port from downtown Athens shouldn't cost you more than 15€ ($20). You can also get to the port by bus: Use the express lines of the interurban buses (KTEL) "Koropi station-Porto Rafti/Avlaki" or the urban buses of the area to reach the port. The price of the ticket is 5€ ($6.50). Also there is a bus that can transfer you from the following Metro and suburban railway stations directly to the port: Pallini, Kantza, and Koropi.

VISITOR INFORMATION

The **Greek National Tourism Organization (EOT** or **GNTO)** is located at 7 Tsochas St., Ambelokipi (© **210/870-0000;** www.gnto.gr), well out of central Athens. The office is officially open Monday through Friday 8am to 3pm and is closed on weekends. At press time it was unclear whether the GNTO office at 26 Amalias, in central Athens, would remain open.

Information about Athens, free city maps, transportation schedules, hotel lists, and other booklets on many regions of Greece are available at the office in Greek, English, French, and German—although when we stop by, many publications we ask for are described as "all gone"—even when we can see them on display just out of reach. The staff members often appear bored with their jobs and irritated by questions; be persistent.

Information on Greece is also available on the Internet; see chapter 2 for details.

Available 24 hours a day, the **tourist police** (© **210/171**) speak English, as well as other languages, and will help you with problems or emergencies.

CITY LAYOUT

As you begin to explore Athens, you may find it helpful to look up to the **Acropolis,** west of Syntagma Square, and to **Mount Likavitos** (Lycabettus), to the northeast.

From most parts of the city, you can see both the Acropolis and Likavitos, whose marble lower slopes give way to pine trees and a summit crowned with a small white church.

Think of central Athens as an almost perfect equilateral triangle, with its points at **Syntagma (Constitution) Square, Omonia (Harmony) Square,** and **Monastiraki (Little Monastery) Square,** near the **Acropolis.** In government jargon, the area bounded by Syntagma, Omonia, and Monastiraki squares is defined as the commercial center, from which cars are banned except for several cross streets. Most Greeks think of **Omonia Square**—Athens's commercial hub—as the city center. Most visitors, however, take their bearings from **Syntagma Square,** site of the House of Parliament. The two squares are connected by parallel streets, **Stadiou** and **Panepistimiou,** and where you will find the stunning **Neoclassical University Trilogy.** (Panepistimiou is also known as Eleftheriou Venizelou.)

Flanking the Parliament Building is Athens's most beautiful park, the **National Garden.** Right adjacent is the **Zappeio Hall and gardens,** another beautiful oasis in the center of the city. West of Syntagma Square, **Ermou** and **Mitropoleos** lead slightly downhill to **Monastiraki Square,** home of the city's famous flea market. From Monastiraki Square, **Athinas** leads north back to Omonia past the modern Central Market. The old warehouse district of **Psirri**—now the home of many chic galleries, cafes, and restaurants—is between Athinas and Ermou.

If you stand in Monastiraki Square and look south, you'll see the Acropolis. At its foot are the **Ancient Agora (Market)** and the **Plaka,** Athens's oldest neighborhood, many of whose street names honor Greek heroes from either classical antiquity or the Greek War of Independence. The twisting labyrinth of streets in the Plaka can challenge even the best navigators. Don't panic: The Plaka is small enough that you can't go far astray, and its side streets with small houses and neighborhood churches are so charming that you won't mind being lost. An excellent map may help (see "Street Maps" below for info). Also, many Athenians speak some English, and almost all are helpful to direction-seeking strangers—unless you happen to be the 10th person in as many minutes to ask where the Acropolis is when it is clearly visible!

FINDING AN ADDRESS   If possible, have the address you want to find written out in Greek so that you can show it to your taxi driver, or ask for help from pedestrians. Most street signs are given both in Greek and a transliteration, which is a great help. Most taxi drivers carry a good Athens street guide in the glove compartment and can usually find any destination. Increasingly, however, some Athenian cabbies are newcomers themselves to the capital and may have trouble with out-of-the-way addresses.

STREET MAPS   The free maps handed out at branches of the **Greek National Tourism Organization** have small print and poor-quality paper. You may prefer to stop at a newspaper kiosk or bookstore to pick up a copy of the Greek Archaeological Service's *Historical Map of Athens* (with maps of the Plaka and of the city center showing the major archaeological sites). The map costs about 4€ ($5.20). For other city map recommendations, see "Books" under "Shopping A to Z," in chapter 6.

NEIGHBORHOODS IN BRIEF

Athens might seem like a huge city to the first-time visitor but what one must always keep in mind is that in reality Athens is a collection of many different neighborhoods, each with its own distinctive flair and things to offer that make the city such a fascinating and exciting place to visit and live in. If you have the time to explore Athens, here are some of the neighborhoods that await you.

Athens Accommodations

Acropolis House Hotel **22**
Andromeda Hotel **30**
Astor Hotel **15**
Athens Art Hotel **2**
Athens Cypria **13**
Athens Plaza **25**
Attalos Hotel **7**
Cecil Hotel **8**
Central **18**
Electra Hotel **16**
Electra Palace **19**
Fresh Hotel **6**
Grande Bretagne **27**
Hilton **31**
Hotel Achilleas **14**
Hotel Adonis **21**

Hotel Carolina **10**
Hotel Dioskouros **24**
Hotel Iridanus **3**
Hermes Hotel **17**
Hotel Plaka **11**
Hotel Tempi **9**
Jason Inn Hotel **4**
King George II **26**
Magna Grecia **12**
Nefeli Hotel **20**
Ochre & Brown **5**
Periscope **29**
Residence Giorgio **1**
St. George Lycabettus **28**
Student and
    Traveller's Inn **23**

EXARCHEIA

NEAPOLIS

Theatre of Likavitos

LIKAVITOS HILL

Rack Railway (Funicular)

Doras D'Istria

National Library

University of Athens

Athens Academy

PANEPISTIMIO

Aristippou
Kleomenous
Deinokratous

Souidias

KOLONAKI

Patriarchi Iokeim

Alopekis

Alopekis
Karneadou

EVANGELISMOS

SYNTAGMA

Georgiou A'

SYNTAGMA

Syntagma Square

Parliament

Kolonaki Square

Vas. Sofias

Vas. Sofias

National Art Gallery

Mitropoleos Othonos

NATIONAL GARDEN

Vasil. Georgiou II

Presidential Palace

Zappeion

ZAPPEION

GRAND PROMENADE (Vas. Olgas)

Temple of Olympian Zeus

Panathenian Stadium

Streets labeled: Stournari, Solomou, Themistokleous, Benaki, Arachovis, Dervenion, Eresou, Methonis, Kallidromiou, Isavron, Smolenski, Tsimiski, Ippokratous, Vatatzi, Laskareos, Asklipiou, Sarantapichou, Zoodhou Pigis, Charliou Trikoupi, Mavromichali, N. Ouranou, Dafnomilis, Ippokratous, Asklipiou, Anagnostopoulou, Sina, Chesonos, Rogakou, Massalias, Skoufa, Solonos, Omirou, Akadimias, Lykavittou, Dimokritou, Fokylidou, Loukianou, Spefsippou, Aristodimou, Aristippou, Marsali, Ioannou Gennardiou, Sina, (Panipistimiou), Amerikis, Voukourestiou, Solonos, Pindarou, Skoufa, Kanari, Irodotou, Ploutarchou, Sina, Stadiou, Niks, Filellinon, Amalias, Mitropoleos, Kidathineon, Dedalou, Amalias, Irodou Attikou, Rigilis, Rizari, Vas. Konstandinou, Rizari, Spyrou Merkouri, Eratesthenou, Diakou, Ardittou

Legend

(i) Information

Metro:
- (M) — Line 1
- (M) — Line 2
- (M) — Line 3
- (L) — Light Rail

0 — 1/4 mile
0 — 1/4 km

Map markers: 30, 28, 29, 31, 25, 26, 27, 21, 22, 23, 24

Unless you have a specific goal and limited time, why not just stroll, get lost, and be pleasantly surprised when you discover that you're on a street where almost off of the shops sell only icons or sugared almonds (an essential gift for guests at weddings and baptisms), or where there's a little park with a bench where you can sit and study your map. And don't forget to take in the "Archaeological Park," the pedestrianized walkways that stretch from Hadrian's Gate past the Acropolis on Dionissiou Areopagitou to the Ancient Agora and on to the Kerameikos.

Central Athens

Commercial Center The commercial center (as you might suspect, a bureaucratic name no one uses, and that appears on no map) lies between **Omonia, Syntagma,** and **Monastiraki** squares, and includes the **Plaka** and **Psirri** districts. Certain streets are for pedestrians only, which can be quite pleasant, but keep in mind that many motorists and almost all motorcycle riders assume that pedestrian-only regulations do not apply to them.

Omonia Square. My grandmother always used to tell me how beautiful Omonia Square used to be; a grand plateia (square), surrounded by elegant neoclassical buildings and couples strolling along. I never got to see that. For me Omonia was never a destination but rather a place you couldn't avoid. There wasn't anything in particular to see there either (except some good Acropolis views); it was gritty and grungy and not very pretty but always interesting to wander through. The redesign of the square is a rather unimaginative disappointment but the pre-Olympic cleanup got rid of all the unsightly billboards, restored buildings' neoclassical facades, and paved the way for trendy design hotels, chic boutiques, and edgy galleries to set up shop. (The "redesigned" square has not been popular with anybody and was being prepared, at press time, to be redone once more). Near the stock exchange as well, the area now is home to an Asian quarter ("Athens Chinatown") and several Bangladeshi shops. From the square you can head in six different directions; take Athinas street (or better yet, pedestrianized Aiolou

with its charming cafes and shops that end right at the Roman Forum), which leads you eventually to Monastiraki. For a look at grand Old Athens of the 19th century check out the beautifully restored **Kotzia Square** with its grand neoclassical buildings including the **Athens City Hall** designed in 1874 and the **National Bank of Greece Cultural Center.** In the middle of the square a large portion of an ancient road has been uncovered (found when building the new Stock Exchange) and can be seen in a fenced-off area where several ancient tombs and small buildings are also visible. The square is even more beautiful at night when it is dramatically lit so be sure to include it in an evening stroll.

Athinas Street, which links Omonia and Monastiraki squares, has Athens's **Central Market.** This is where you can browse fish and meat halls, buy vegetables and fruit from all over Greece, sample cheeses from distant islands—or buy a pair of shoes or sunglasses from a street vendor. Across from the markets, formerly bleak **Varvakeios Square** is now landscaped, has several cafes, and offers an opportunity to take a break from the frenzy of the market. The revamping of Varvakeios Square is indicative of just how much the transformation of the Psirri district—once deserted, now chic—has affected neighboring areas. Another nearby square, **Klaftmonos** has also been redesigned and now from it you can see the grand **Neoclassical University Trilogy** as it was meant to be seen—another glimpse at grand and elegant 19th-century Athens.

By day, Athinas is the best street in town to get a sense of Athens's nonstop bustle. By night, most of the Omonia area has retained some of its tacky New York Times Square ambience of the mid-1980s, although it has been considerably smartened up in the last few years and with its many chic new arrivals is changing rapidly. However, you might still be approached with offers of cheap sex or drugs in or around Omonia. You may also encounter street vendors from Albania, Eastern Europe, and Africa, who will try to sell you pirated CDs/DVDs, leather jackets, and sometimes themselves.

Syntagma (Constitution) Square is, for most visitors, the heart of Athens. This is where you'll find the major banks, travel agencies, American Express and Thomas Cook, and several fine hotels, including the **Grande Bretagne,** the grande dame of Greek hotels. The Grande Bretagne underwent an extensive face-lift in 2003 and is now more splendid than ever. If you are not staying here, take a discreet peak at the magnificent Beaux Arts lobby, head into the **Alexander bar** for a drink (dress smartly), and take in the exceptionally restored old-world elegance and glamour. The excellent **GB** restaurant on the terrace has some of the most stunning views of the city, but to enjoy the sweeping view and tempting menu you will need a reservation and a burning desire to spend lots of money. You might want to try however, to reserve a seat at the small terrace bar (if it's early enough) and enjoy the view with a pricey drink.

The **central post office** is at the corner of Mitropoleos. For years, the sidewalk cafes here were popular places from which to watch the world go by, but with the proliferation of the fast-food joints that attract teeny-bopper Athenians and bands of student travelers, you may not want to linger. That

said, beautifully restored Syntagma Square, the plateia in front of the Syntagma Metro, with two cafes across from one another, is a convenient central meeting point. This square as well is even more beautiful at night when it is brilliantly lit.

Syntagma is the home of much of governmental Athens: The handsome neoclassical building at the head of the square is the **Greek Parliament building,** formerly the Royal Palace. The most impressive thing about this grand building—and I urge you to pay close attention to this—is the buildings' stone and how it changes color throughout the day; from off-white to gold to a light blush mauve before it is lit dramatically at night. During the day this is where you'll see the **Changing of the Guard** several times a day and may hear a band playing on Sunday around 11am. The soldiers who march in front of the parliament building and the **Tomb of the Unknown Soldier** often wear the *evzone* uniform (frilly white skirts and pom-pommed red shoes) of their ancestors who fought to gain Greece's freedom during the War of Independence (1821–28). (Be sure to spend some time in the beautiful National and Zappeion Gardens adjacent to the Parliament.) South of Syntagma Square, **Monastiraki Square** and the **Plaka** area are Athens's two main tourist destinations.

Plaka is the most tourist-heavy neighborhood in the city. Right below the Acropolis, its maze of narrow medieval streets twist their way through ancient sites, Byzantine churches, offbeat museums, and 19th-century homes. Restaurants and cafes line many streets of this pedestrian neighborhood that is rich in history and character and is undeniably atmospheric, romantic, and nostalgia-inducing. Feel free to lose yourself in the labyrinthine streets because you never know what you'll find just around the next corner. Maybe you will find the tiny village within a village of Anafiotika, a Cycladic town at the very base of the Acropolis. Strolling through this quirky area will likely be one of the most beautiful moments you will have during your entire stay so take your time and explore.

Monastiraki fringes the **Agora** and the **Roman Forum,** and the flea markets are open every day but are usually best—and most crowded—on Sunday. Many tavernas, cafes, and shops line the streets but my favorite street by far is Adrianou, the street that links Monastiraki to beautifully restored Thissio, with restored houses as restaurants and cafes on one side and the Agora on the other—and Acropolis views as well. Certain areas of Monastiraki—most notably the bazaar—have a Middle Eastern look and feel.

Psirri, between Athinas and Ermou, was once derelict and forgotten. Now it's one of the city's hottest destinations after dark. Slick warehouse conversions, restored neoclassical houses, trendy restaurants, bars, cafes, tavernas and mezedopoleia (smaller dishes of samplings rather than main courses) with live music, clubs and galleries side by side with some still-remaining workshops and dilapidated buildings—this area comes alive in the late afternoon until the early morning hours. It is such a popular destination and with so much going on that it has its own website.

Back on the **Archaeological Promenade** (just cut across Ermou to get back on the Promenade) you will find the ancient neighborhood of **Kerameikos** undergoing its own reinvention. The little-visited ancient Athenian cemetery is peaceful and green and a delight to visit with many stunningly beautiful classical sculptures and part of the city's ancient walls. Psirri and

Kerameikos are linked by yet another restored square: **Koumoundourou.** More famous in recent years for its male prostitutes and even more recently for being the sleeping grounds for hundreds Kurdish refugees, Koumoundourou received the most extreme makeover of all the squares and is virtually unrecognizable today having also acquired new trees and nearly 2,000 plants.

The promenade ends right after Kerameikos and directly across busy **Pireos Avenue,** is **Technopolis** ("Art City") or better known as **Gazi**—once an industrial wasteland that spewed black gas fumes (thus the name "Gazi," which means gas) from the foundry's smokestacks. When the factory was closed in 1984, the entire area became an urban wasteland—forgotten, neglected and never visited except by low-income families (mostly immigrants) who lived in its old houses on forgotten streets. But when the city of Athens bought the old foundry and turned it into a stunning multipurpose art and exhibition center, it kickstarted the revival of the neighborhood in a shocking way. Today the old foundry's smokestacks are illuminated in arty neon red and they navigate you through streets with the edgiest and hippest nightlife in the city and a real downtown vibe—edgy arts spaces, fusion restaurants, art galleries, theaters, bars, cafes, and a gay "village"— the revival is beginning to spread well beyond the neighborhood's borders into other long-forgotten urban areas where closed factories are becoming the hottest clubs in town (due to their sheer size) or brilliantly transformed into museums, multipurpose arts centers, and exhibition halls—this is the birthplace of 21st-century Athens.

A must-see on your stroll here is the beautifully re-imagined Technopolis center which has retained much of its original industrial architecture, converted brilliantly to a multipurpose complex for shows, festivals, and exhibitions. It also has a cafe and a courtyard used for concerts. The one permanent exhibition here is the small **Maria Callas Museum.**

To truly understand the renaissance that Gazi started, apart from the many cutting-edge multiuse spaces and sophisticated dining and nightlife options, see the ripple effects it has had on the neighboring areas creating with it new architectural landmarks. Within walking distance of Gazi (along **Pireos Avenue**) you will find the **School of Fine Arts,** the glossy **Foundation of the Hellenic World** (converted from an old warehouse and featuring interactive and virtual tours of Ancient Greece) with its striking ribbed dome meant to evoke a Bronze Age beehive tomb. Farther along is the **Pantheon,** a 24-hour multiplex that houses a hotel, spa, theater, cinema, restaurants, galleries, bars, and a roof garden. Another new architectural landmark is the new **Benaki Museum** (called the "beautiful red box" for reasons you will understand once you see it), which holds temporary exhibitions, film screenings, and theater performances and concerts in its awesome internal courtyard. Farther down is the **Athinais,** a magnificent restoration of a former silk factory into a sophisticated arts complex. Here you will find the **Museum of Ancient Cypriot Art,** galleries, a concert hall, a theater and cinema, and two excellent restaurants, **Red** and **Votanikos,** and the cool **Boiler Bar.** At night, be sure to take in the extraordinary buzz of this lively neighborhood. Walk the streets and hop in and out of as many bars as you can or join the locals as they enjoy their drinks out in the streets after bar capacity has reached its limit; the Kerameikos Metro station smack in the middle of Gazi is a landscaped park/square surrounded by some of the city's coolest bars and its where locals socialize (drink in hand) when the bars are full, creating a scene that can only be found in the most popular islands at the height of summer. Gazi is where Athens's modern heart beats to its own rhythm.

Back on the Archaeological Promenade, across Ermou from Psirri is **Thissio**—my favorite downtown neighborhood. Right on the pedestrianized **Apostolou Pavlou,** Thissio with its restored neoclassical buildings, uninterrupted Acropolis views, the temple of Hephaestos, and some of the city's best places to hang out, is the place to be. Charming and old-fashioned, modern and happening, it's unlike any other neighborhood. With hip places to hang out at such as **Stavlos,** the former royal stables that have been converted into an all-day cafe/bar/restaurant with indoor and outdoor seating, an internal courtyard, a terrace, a gallery, and a dance- and live-performance area for late at night. Also be sure to check out the grand **National Observatory,** a beautiful neoclassical mansion from the late 1800s.

Kolonaki Forever posh, elegant, and happening, this neighborhood tucked beneath the slopes of Lycabettus Mountain has long been the favorite address of the socialites. The streets (many pedestrianized) are jampacked with boutiques, designer houses, private art galleries, and dozens of restaurants, cafes, and cooler-than-thou night and day spots. Leof Vasiliss Sofias is one of the most imposing streets in Athens, with beautiful neoclassical mansions that have been converted into museums (a few embassies as well) thus earning the nickname "The Museum

Mile" or "The Embassy District." Kolonaki is a great area to explore, through its happening streets, its busy plateias, boutiques, galleries, and restaurants, so take your time to soak in all the urban chic you can before making your way to the top of Lycabettus mountain for an extraordinary sunset with Athens laid under your feet like a sparkling map. If you walk down, you'll pass through some of central Athens's nicest and greenest streets winding around Likavitos's lower slopes.

If you're in Kolonaki on a Saturday, don't miss the beautiful people and the wannabes promenading up and down the streets, thronging in front of favorite boutiques to ogle the latest fashions, and collapsing at street cafes to revive their spirits with cool drinks. There are more shoe stores per inch in Kolonaki than almost anywhere else in Greece, a nation that takes its footwear very seriously.

Kolonaki gradually merges to the northwest with the university area, which is spread loosely between the 19th-century university buildings (the Neoclassical University Complex or Trilogy) on Panepistimiou and the **Polytechnic** some 10 blocks to the northwest. Many publishers have their offices around here, and bibliophiles may enjoy the window displays of everything from children's books about Hercules to mathematical texts. A few blocks from the Polytechnic—where countless students were killed in 1973 during a protest against the ruling junta—and near the excellent **National Archaeological Museum,** is **Exarchia.**

Long before Gazi, this was the closest thing Athens had to an "alternative" neighborhood, which is kind of funny since its neighbor is none other than posh Kolonaki. This bohemian neighborhood—covering 50 city blocks—is a lively area to spend a few hours in,

with excellent tavernas on a buzzing square and pedestrian streets, great lounges and bars, plus the city's finest rock clubs and live music venues. If you have the time, explore **Streffi Hill,** a little-visited hill, green and lovely, which offers incredible views of the city and the Acropolis all the way to the Saronic Gulf once you reach its top. Across busy **Leoforos Alexandros** is Athens's largest park, **Pedion Areos.**

Koukaki & Makrigianni   Once the working-class counterpart to Kolonaki, **Koukaki** has been thoroughly gentrified and is one of Athens's most desirable neighborhoods. The district lies at the base of **Lofos Filopappou (Filopappos Hill),** also known as the Lofos Mousseon (Hill of the Muses). A number of pleasant paths lead from streets at the base of Filopappos up through its pine-clad slopes, some ending at the **Dora Stratou Theater** or the Observatory. Buses and trolleys run along Veikou, the main road through Koukaki, home to unpretentious cafes and restaurants as well as reasonably priced hotels. Stay here if you want to be out of touristy Athens, enjoy shopping in neighborhood groceries and shops, and don't mind the 15- to 20-minute walk back into the city center.

Makrigianni, the upscale neighborhood just north of Koukaki, at the southern base of the Acropolis, has more office buildings, shops, and hotels than apartments. You'll find a few luxurious hotels, and several good restaurants, including the popular **Strofi** and **Socrates's Prison** (also known as the Samaria). Makrigianni used to be, along with Kolonaki, the city's main gay-friendly neighborhood before Gazi took over (many of the old gay bars are still here and remain very popular). This is a good area in which to stay if you want to be almost as centrally located as you would be in the Plaka or Syntagma, but a bit out of the tourist maelstrom. Of course, with the opening of the **New Acropolis Museum** in Makrigianni and of the **Contemporary Art Museum** at the Syngrou-Fix Metro and tram stops on the fringes of Koukaki, that will most likely change.

Pangrati & Mets Surrounding the reconstructed Athens Stadium known to the Greeks as **Kallimarmaro (Beautiful Marble),** where the first modern Olympics were held in 1896, you will find two lovely and lively residential areas with excellent dining and nightlife options. To the south of the stadium is the steep and beautiful street of **Markou Mousourou,** shaded by flowering trees, lined with neoclassical houses, and filled with the scent of jasmine and bougainvillea. Mets is a taste of old Athens, full of pre–World War II houses with tiled roofs and charming courtyards. It's one of the most beautiful neighborhoods to explore in the city, and the nightlife isn't bad either. To the south of the stadium is Pangrati, a residential area popular with those who can't afford Kolonaki. Foreigners, including academics attached to various schools of archaeology, often set up temporary roots here. If you enjoy baroque funerary monuments, don't miss the **First Cemetery,** where anybody who was anybody in 19th- and 20th-century Greece is buried among the tall cypress trees and many exceptional century-old marble statues. Be sure not to miss the splendid **"Koimomeni"** (Sleeping Girl), considered by many to be a high-art masterpiece by Ianoulis Halepas, a sculptor from Tinos, who battled mental illness most of his adult life and died in extreme poverty during World War II. If you prefer your green spaces without tombs, explore Pangrati's lovely green **park,** almost a miniforest in the heart

of Athens. There are also lots of neighborhood restaurants (the excellent **Spondi** for starters) and many charming traditional tavernas scattered in Pangrati.

The Embassy District Leoforos Vas. Sofias (Queen Sophia Blvd.) runs from Syntagma Square toward Athens's fashionable northeastern suburb of Kifissia. If you walk along Vas. Sofias and explore the side streets that run uphill from it into Kolonaki, you'll notice the national flags on elegant office buildings and town houses. This Embassy District stretches as far as the **Hilton,** where many embassy workers head for lunch or drinks after work—you should consider doing the same at least once either for lunch or dinner at the excellent **Milos** seafood restaurant or for a drink at around sunset on the rooftop's bar **Galaxy** with its jaw-dropping views of the city. The Embassy District is also known as the **Museum Mile** for the many excellent museums found here just downhill from Kolonaki: The **Benaki Museum,** the **Goulandris Museum of Cycladic Art**, the **Byzantine Museum,** the **National War Museum,** and the **National Gallery.**

The Northeast Suburbs

Athens is growing every-which-way, but much of its expansion is to the northeast, in the valley between the mountains of **Penteli** to the east and **Parnitha** to the west. Going north on **Leoforos Kifissias,** you will pass by Kolonaki, **Ampelokipi** (with its many first-rate bar/restaurants such as **Baraonda, 48,** and **Balthazar**), **Neo Psihiko** (check out the **Deste Foundation**), and you will find yourself in **Marousi** and **Kifissia.**

Marousi is home to Santiago Calatrava's redesigned **Athens Olympics Sports Complex,** the elegant and soaring modernist complex that stole the show during the 2004 Olympics and the stadiums that became the architectural landmarks of the new city; beautiful glass and steel arches over the main stadium, a gorgeous velodrome, the **Athens Tennis Academy** in a landscaped park filled with sculptures and lined with glass-covered walkways and a steel arched "Agora." This is a breathtaking place to visit, easily accessible by Metro line 1 at the **Irini** stop.

The last stop on line 1 is elegant **Kifissia.** Cooler than downtown Athens, thanks to its elevation, **Kifissia** was fashionable enough for the Royal Family to have a villa here. With elegant 19th-century neoclassical mansions, outrageous 21st-century ones, graceful tree-lined streets, excellent shopping options, lovely parks, two very good museums (the **Goulandris Museum of Natural History** and the **Gaia Center**), three of the city's best trendy hotels (the must-be-seen **Semiramis, 21,** and **Life Gallery**), and one of the best hotels, period, the **Pentillikon** with its Michelin-starred restaurant **Vardis.** Add these to countless bars, lounges, and clubs—and the charming open-air cinema dating from 1919—Kifissia is a delight to spend some time in if you've already spent some time in central Athens.

Piraeus (Pireas)

The main port of Athens, Piraeus is a city very much in its own right—although even locals have trouble telling precisely where Athens ends and Piraeus begins. Piraeus prides itself on being rough and tough—a stronghold of communism, the home of *rembetika* (the Greek "blues" born out of the population exchange between Greece and Turkey in 1922), and the workplace of a profusion of prostitutes. Probably none of this will be particularly obvious when you come here to

catch a boat to the islands from the **main harbor (Megas Limani or Great Harbor),** or from **Zea Marina,** also called Pasalimani. (For ferry information, see "Getting Around," below.) What will be obvious if you go to one of the many fish tavernas in **Mikrolimani (Little Harbor),** also called Turkolimani (Turkish Harbor), a picturesque harbor with eateries and cafes by the marina, are the prices, which can range from exorbitant to extortionate, but deals can still be found and the location is hard to beat.

The Southern Suburbs— Coastal Athens

The coastal avenue **Leoforos Poseidonos** begins where Syngrou ends—right by the sea. Easily accessible from downtown Athens via the tram (up to Glyfada) and farther via bus, this is where Athenians love to hang out and party during the hot summer months. Coastal Athens begins at the Metro line 1 stop Faliro and the tram stop SEF (at the revamped for the 2004 Games Stadium of Peace and Friendship). Nearby, the revitalized yacht marina of Flisvos is a delight for strolling, with a grand promenade and stores, malls, cafes, multiplexes, bars, restaurants, and even an open-air cinema. As you continue down Leoforos Poseidonos, be sure to take in all the revived coastline has to offer: beaches (which consistently score high on the E.U.'s "Blue Flag" list of clean beaches), boardwalks, esplanades, marinas, and open-air mega clubs (**Akrotiri, Bo, Envy,** and **Mao**) that are as luxurious and glamorous as they are fun. First-rate restaurants (**Ithaki**), excellent shopping on the pedestrian **Ioannou Metaxa** in **Glyfada,** top hotels throughout the coast (such as the **Astir Palace,** the **Divani Athens Spa and Thalassio Centre,** the **Magri,** and **Grand Beach**

Lagonissi), sports facilities, watersports, and a sizzling fashionable and addictively fun scene. If you're on a tight schedule and can't spend any time on the capital's coast, be sure to at least have dinner in the city's most romantic venue: **Island.**

2 Getting Around

BY PUBLIC TRANSPORTATION

BY METRO

Stop at the Syntagma station or go to the GNTO for a map of the Metro to learn what stations have opened by the time of your visit. To travel on the Metro, buy your ticket at the station, validate it in the machines as you enter, and hang onto it until you get off. A ticket on the old line costs .60€ (80¢); a ticket on the new line costs .75€ (95¢); a day pass costs 3€ ($3.90). Validate your ticket in the machine as you enter the waiting platform, or you'll risk a fine. Metro and bus tickets are not interchangeable but may be soon.

Even if you do not use the Metro to get around Athens, you may want to take it from Omonia or Monastiraki to Piraeus to catch a boat to the islands. (Don't miss the spectacular view of the Acropolis as the subway comes aboveground by the Agora.) The harbor in Piraeus is a 5-minute walk from the Metro station (head left).

BY BUS & TROLLEY BUS

The public transportation system is cheap—and, if you use it, you may think it's deservedly so. Although you can get almost everywhere you want to in central Athens and the suburbs by bus or trolley, it takes an excruciatingly long time to figure out which bus to take. This is especially true now, when many bus routes change as new Metro stations open. Even if you know which bus to take, you may have to wait a long time until the bus appears—usually stuffed with passengers. The bus service does have an information number (© **210/185**), but it's often busy.

If you find none of this daunting, tickets cost .50€ (65¢) each and can be bought from *periptera* (kiosks) scattered throughout the city. The tickets are sold individually or in packets of 10. Tickets are good for rides anywhere on the system. Be certain to validate yours when you get on. *Tip:* Hold on to your ticket. Uniformed and plainclothes inspectors periodically check tickets and can levy a basic fine of 5€ ($6.50) or a more punitive fine of 20€ ($26) on the spot.

If you're heading out of town and take a blue A-line bus to transfer to another blue A-line bus, your ticket will still be valid on the transfer bus. In central Athens, minibus nos. 60 and 150 serve the commercial area free of charge.

Buses headed to farther points of Attica leave from **Mavromateon** on the western edge of Pedion tou Areos Park, at the western end of Leoforos Alexandras.

BY TAXI

It's rumored that there are more than 15,000 taxis in Athens, but finding an empty one is almost never easy. Especially if you have travel connections to make, it's a good idea to reserve a radio taxi (see below). Fortunately, taxis are inexpensive in Athens, and most drivers are honest men trying to wrest a living by maneuvering through the city's endemic gridlock. However, some drivers, notably those working Piraeus, the airports, and popular tourist destinations, can't resist trying to overcharge obvious foreigners.

(Tips **Cultured Commuting**

Allow extra time when you catch the Metro in central Athens: Two stations—
Syntagma Square and Acropolis in particular—handsomely display finds from
the subway excavations in what amount to Athens's newest small museums.
You can get advance information on the Athens Metro at www.ametro.gr.

When you get into a taxi, check the meter. Make sure it is turned on and set to "1"
rather than "2." The meter will register 1€ ($1.30). The meter should be set on "2"
(double fare) only between midnight and 5am or if you take a taxi outside the city
limits; if you plan to do this, negotiate a flat rate in advance. The "1" meter rate is
.30€ (40¢) per kilometer. There's a surcharge of 2€ ($2.60) for service from a port,
from a rail or bus station, or from the airport. Luggage costs .50€ (65¢) per 10 kilograms (22 lb.). Unless your cab is caught in very heavy traffic, a trip to the center of
town from the airport between 5am and midnight should not cost more than 20€ to
30€ ($26–$39). Don't be surprised if the driver picks up other passengers en route;
he will work out everyone's share of the fare. The minimum fare is 2€ ($2.60). These
prices will almost certainly be higher by the time you visit Greece.

If you suspect that you have been overcharged, ask for help at your hotel or destination before you pay the fare.

Your driver may find it difficult to understand your pronunciation of your destination; ask a hotel staff member to speak to the driver directly or write down the address
so you can show it to the driver. Carry a business card from your hotel with you, so
you can show it to the taxi driver on your return.

There are about 15 **radio taxi** companies in Athens; their phone numbers change
often, so it's worth checking the daily listing in "Your Guide" in the *Athens News.*
Some established companies include **Athina** (𝒞 210/921-7942), **Express** (𝒞 210/
993-4812), **Parthenon** (𝒞 210/532-3300), and **Piraeus** (𝒞 210/418-2333). If you're
trying to make travel connections or are traveling during rush hour, a radio taxi is well
worth the 2€ ($2.60) surcharge. Your hotel can call for you and make sure that the
driver knows where you want to go. Most restaurants will call a taxi for you without
charge.

The GNTO's pamphlet *Helpful Hints for Taxi Users* has information on taxi fares as
well as a complaint form, which you can send to the **Ministry of Transport and
Communication,** 13 Xenophondos, 10191 Athens. Replies to complaints should be
forwarded to the *Guinness Book of World Records.*

BY CAR

In Athens, a car is more trouble than convenience. The traffic is heavy, and finding a
parking place is difficult. Keep in mind that if you pick up your rental car at the airport, you may pay a hefty (sometimes daily) surcharge. Picking up a car in town
involves struggling through Athens's traffic to get out of town. That said, we do have
some suggestions to follow.

Alamo, Avis, Budget, Dollar, Hertz, and National all have offices at Athens International Airport.

Tip: Renting a car from abroad is invariably cheaper than negotiating for one on
the spot in Athens. In fact, the savings in the rental rate usually make it worth your
while to telephone or e-mail a major car rental firm in the U.S. from Greece.

If you do decide on the spur of the moment to rent a car in Athens, you'll find many rental agencies south of Syntagma Square. Some of the better agencies include: **Athens Cars,** 10 Filellinon (℗ 210/323-3783 or 210/324-8870); **Autorental,** 11 Leoforos Syngrou (℗ 210/923-2514); **Avis,** 46–48 Leoforos Amalias (℗ 210/322-4951 to -4957); **Budget Rent a Car,** 8 Leoforos Syngrou (℗ 210/921-4771 to -4773); **Eurodollar Rent a Car,** 29 Leoforos Syngrou (℗ 210/922-9672 or 210/923-0548); **Hellascars,** 148 Leoforos Syngrou (℗ 210/923-5353 to -5359); **Hertz,** 12 Leoforos Syngrou (℗ 210/922-0102 to -0104), and 71 Leoforos Vas. Sofias (℗ 210/724-7071 or 210/722-7391); **Interrent-Europcar/Batek SA,** 4 Leoforos Syngrou (℗ 210/921-5789); and **Thrifty Hellas Rent a Car,** 24 Leoforos Syngrou (℗ 210/922-1211 to -1213). Prices for rentals range from 50€ to 100€ ($65–$130) per day. *Warning:* Be sure to take full insurance and ask if the price you are quoted includes everything— taxes, drop-off fee, gasoline charges, and other fees.

ON FOOT

Since most of what you'll want to see and do in Athens is in the city center, it's easy to do most of your sightseeing on foot. Fortunately, Athens has created pedestrian zones in sections of the **Commercial Triangle** (the area bounded by Omonia, Syntagma, and Monastiraki squares), the **Plaka,** and **Kolonaki,** making strolling, window-shopping, and sightseeing infinitely more pleasant. Dionissiou Areopagitou, at the southern foot of the Acropolis, was also pedestrianized, with links to walkways past the Ancient Agora and Kerameikos. Still, don't relax completely even on pedestrian streets: Athens's multitude of motorcyclists seldom respect the rules, and a red traffic light or STOP sign is no guarantee that vehicles will stop for pedestrians.

Wheelchair-users will find Athens challenging even though the 2004 Paralympics brought some improvements. For one, the Acropolis is finally wheelchair accessible. Ramps and platforms have been added to bus stops, railway stations, and ports, while Metro stations and sports venues are wheelchair accessible. Most central Athens streets, sites, and Metro stations have special sidewalks for the visually impaired.

FAST FACTS: Athens

ATMs Automated teller machines are increasingly common at banks throughout Athens. The **National Bank of Greece** operates a 24-hour ATM in Syntagma Square.

Banks Banks are generally open Monday through Thursday from 8am to 2pm and Friday from 8am to 1:30pm. In summer, the exchange office at the **National Bank of Greece** in Syntagma Square (℗ **210/334-0015**) is open Monday through Thursday from 3:30 to 6:30pm, Friday from 3 to 6:30pm, Saturday from 9am to 3pm, and Sunday from 9am to 1pm. Other centrally located banks include **Citibank,** in Syntagma Square (℗ **210/322-7471**); **Bank of America,** 39 Panepistimiou (℗ **210/324-4975**); and **Barclays Bank,** 15 Voukourestiou (℗ **210/364-4311**). All banks are closed on the long list of Greek holidays. (See "When to Go," in chapter 2.) Most banks exchange currency at the rate set daily by the government. This rate is often more favorable than that offered at unofficial exchange bureaus. Still, a little comparison-shopping is worthwhile. Some hotels offer better-than-official rates, though only for cash, as do some stores, usually when you are making an expensive purchase.

Business Hours Even Greeks get confused by their complicated and changeable business hours. In winter, Athens's shops are generally open Monday and Wednesday from 9am to 5pm; Tuesday, Thursday, and Friday from 10am to 7pm; and Saturday from 8:30am to 3:30pm. In summer, shops are generally open Monday, Wednesday, and Saturday from 8am to 3pm; and Tuesday, Thursday, and Friday from 8am to 2pm and 5:30 to 10pm.

Most food stores are open Monday and Wednesday from 9am to 4:30pm; Tuesday from 9am to 6pm; Thursday from 9:30am to 6:30pm; Friday from 9:30am to 7pm; and Saturday from 8:30am to 4:30pm.

Many shops geared to tourists stay open late into the night—but only if the shop-owner thinks that business will be good. In other words, the shop that was open late yesterday may close early today.

Dentists & Doctors Embassies (see below) may have lists of dentists and doctors. Some English-speaking physicians advertise in the daily *Athens News.*

Drugstores See "Pharmacies," below.

Embassies & Consulates Locations are: **Australia,** 37 Leoforos Dimitriou Soutsou (© 210/870-4000); **Canada,** 4 Ioannou Yenadiou (© 210/727-3400 or 210/725-4011); **Ireland,** 7 Vas. Konstantinou (© 210/723-2771); **New Zealand,** Xenias 24, Ambelokipi (© 210/771-0112); **South Africa,** 60 Kifissias, Maroussi (© 210/680-6645); **United Kingdom,** 1 Ploutarchou (© 210/723-6211); **United States,** 91 Leoforos Vas. Sofias (© 210/721-2951, or 210/729-4301 for emergencies). Be sure to phone ahead before you go to any embassy; most keep limited hours and are usually closed on their own holidays as well as Greek ones.

Emergencies In an emergency, dial © **100** for the **police** and © **171** for the **tourist police.** Dial © **199** to report a **fire** and © **166** for an **ambulance** and the **hospital.** If you need an English-speaking doctor or dentist, call your embassy for advice, or try **SOS Doctor** (© **210/331-0310** or 210/331-0311). There are two medical hot lines for foreigners: © **210/721-2951** (day) and 210/729-4301 (night) for U.S. citizens; and © **210/723-6211** (day) and 210/723-7727 (night) for British citizens. The English-language *Athens News* (published Fri) lists some American- and British-trained doctors and hospitals offering emergency services. Most of the larger hotels can call a doctor for you in an emergency, and embassies will sometimes recommend local doctors.

KAT, the emergency hospital in Kifissia (© **210/801-4411** to -4419), and **Asklepion Voulas,** the emergency hospital in Voula (© **210/895-3416** to -3418), both have emergency rooms open 24 hours a day. **Evangelismos,** a respected centrally located hospital below the Kolonaki district on 9 Vas. Sophias (© **210/722-0101**), usually has English-speaking staff on duty. If you need medical attention fast, don't waste time trying to call these hospitals: Just go. Their doors are open and they will see to you as soon as possible.

In addition, each major hospital takes its turn each day being on emergency duty. A recorded message in Greek at © **210/106** tells which hospital is open for emergency services and gives the telephone number.

Eyeglasses If anything happens to your glasses, **Artemiadis,** which has two branches (4 Hermou, Syntagma, ☎ **210/323-8555;** and 3 Stadiou, in the Kalliga Arcade, Syntagma, ☎ **210/324-7043**) as well as an e-mail address, info@artemiadis. gr, offers next-day, sometimes even same-day, replacement service, as does **Optical,** 2 Patriarchou Ioakim, Kolonaki (☎ **210/724-3564**). Both sell sunglasses and have English-speaking staff.

Hospitals Except for emergencies, hospital admittance is gained through a physician. See "Dentists & Doctors," above.

Information See "Visitor Information," earlier in this chapter.

Internet Access Internet cafes, where you can check and send e-mail, have proliferated in Athens almost as fast as cellular telephones. For a current list of Athenian cybercafes, check out www.athensinfoguide.com/geninternet.htm.

As a general rule, most cybercafes charge about 5€ ($6.50) an hour. The efficient **Sofokleous.com Internet C@fe,** 5 Stadiou, a block off Syntagma Square (☎/fax **210/324-8105**), is open daily from 10am to 10pm. **Astor Internet Cafés,** 17 Patission, a block off Omonia Square (☎ **210/523-8546**), is open Monday through Saturday from 10am to 10pm and Sunday from 10am to 4pm. Across from the National Archaeological Museum is the **Central Music Coffee Shop,** 28 Octobriou, also called Patission (☎ **210/883-3418**), with daily hours from 9am to 11pm. In Plaka, **Plaka Internet World** (☎ **210/331-6056**), 29 Pandrossou, offers air-conditioned chat rooms and an Acropolis view!

Laundry & Dry Cleaning The **self-service launderette** at 10 Angelou Yeronda, in Filomouson Square, off Kidathineon, Plaka, is open daily from 8:30am to 7pm; it charges 7€ ($9.10) per load, including wash, dry, and soap. **National Dry Cleaners and Laundry Service,** 17 Apollonos (☎ **210/323-2226**), next to the Hermes Hotel, is open Monday and Wednesday from 7am to 4pm, and Tuesday, Thursday, and Friday from 7am to 8pm; laundry costs 5€ ($6.50) per kilo (2.2 lb.). Hotel chambermaids will often do laundry as well. Dry cleaning in Athens is reasonable, at about 4€ ($5.20) for a pair of slacks. Next-day service is usually possible.

Lost & Found If you lose something on the street or on public transportation, it is probably gone for good, just as it would be in any large city. If you wish, contact the police's **Lost and Found,** 173 Leoforos Alexandras (☎ **210/642-1616**), open Monday through Saturday from 9am to 3pm. Lost passports and other documents may be returned by the police to the appropriate embassy, so check there as well. It's an excellent idea to travel with photocopies of your important documents, including passport, prescriptions, tickets, phone numbers, and addresses.

Luggage Storage & Lockers If you're coming back to stay, many hotels will store excess luggage while you travel. There are storage facilities at Athens International Airport, at the Metro station in Piraeus, and at both of Athens's train stations.

Newspapers & Magazines The *Athens News* is published every Friday in English, with a weekend section listing events of interest; it's available at kiosks everywhere. Most central Athens newsstands also carry the *International*

Herald Tribune, which has an English-language insert of highlights from the Greek daily *Kathimerini,* and *USA Today.* Local weeklies include the *Hellenic Times,* with entertainment listings; and *Athinorama* (in Greek), which has comprehensive listings of events. *Athens Best Of* (monthly) and *Now in Athens,* published every other month, have information on restaurants, shopping, museums, and galleries, and are available free in major hotels and sometimes from the Greek National Tourism Organization.

Pharmacies Pharmakia, identified by green crosses, are scattered throughout Athens. Hours are usually Monday through Friday from 8am to 2pm. In the evenings and on weekends, most are closed, but each posts a notice listing the names and addresses of pharmacies that are open or will open in an emergency. Newspapers such as the *Athens News* list the pharmacies open outside regular hours.

Police In an **emergency,** dial ✆ **100.** For help dealing with a troublesome taxi driver, hotel staff, restaurant staff, or shop-owner, stand your ground and call the **tourist police** at ✆ **171.**

Post Offices The main post offices in central Athens are at 100 Eolou, just south of Omonia Square; and in Syntagma Square, at the corner of Mitropoleos. They are open Monday through Friday from 7:30am to 8pm, Saturday from 7:30am to 2pm, and Sunday from 9am to 1pm.

All of the post offices accept parcels, but the **Parcel Post Office** is at 4 Stadiou inside the arcade (✆ **210/322-8940**). It's open Monday through Friday from 7:30am to 8pm. It usually sells twine and cardboard shipping boxes in four sizes. Parcels must remain open for inspection before you seal them at the post office.

You can receive correspondence in Athens c/o **American Express,** 2 Ermou, 10225 Athens, Greece (✆ **210/324-4975**), near the southwest corner of Syntagma Square, open Monday through Friday from 8:30am to 4pm and Saturday from 8:30am to 1:30pm. If you have an American Express card or traveler's checks, the service is free; otherwise, each article costs 2€ ($2.60).

Radio & Television Generally, English-language radio—BBC and Voice of America—is available only via shortwave radio. CNN and various European channels such as STAR are available on cable TV. The NET channel has daily news summaries in English, usually at 6pm. Most foreign-language films shown on Greek TV are not dubbed, but feature the original soundtracks with Greek subtitles. All current-release foreign-language films shown in Greek cinemas have the original soundtracks with Greek subtitles.

Restrooms There are public restrooms in the underground station beneath Omonia and Syntagma squares and beneath Kolonaki Square, but you'll probably prefer a hotel or restaurant restroom. (Toilet paper is often not available, so carry tissue with you. Do not flush paper down the commode; use the receptacle provided.)

Safety Athens is among the safest capitals in Europe, and there are few reports of violent crimes. **Pickpocketing,** however, is not uncommon, especially in the Plaka and Omonia Square areas, on the Metro and buses, and in Piraeus.

Unfortunately, it is a good idea to be wary of Gypsy children. We advise travelers to avoid the side streets of Omonia and Piraeus at night. As always, leave your passport and valuables in a security box at the hotel. Carry a photocopy of your passport, not the original.

Taxes A VAT (value-added tax) of between 4% and 18% is added onto everything you buy. Some shops will attempt to cheat you by quoting one price and then, when you hand over your credit card, they will add on a hefty VAT charge. Be wary. In theory, if you are not a member of a Common Market/E.U. country, you can get a refund on major purchases at the Athens airport when you leave Greece. In practice, you would have to arrive at the airport a day before your flight to get to the head of the line, do the paperwork, get a refund, and catch your flight.

Telephone, Telegram & Fax Many of the city's public phones now accept only phone cards, available at newsstands and the **Telecommunications Organization of Greece (OTE)** offices in several denominations, currently starting at 3€ ($3.90). Most OTE offices now sell cellphones and phone cards at very reasonable prices; if you are in Greece for a month, you may find this a good option. Some kiosks still have metered phones; you pay what the meter records. North Americans can phone home directly by contacting **AT&T** (② 00/800-1311), **MCI** (② 00/800-1211), or **Sprint** (② 00/800-1411); calls can be collect or billed to your phone charge card. You can send a telegram or fax from OTE offices. The OTE office at 15 Stadiou, near Syntagma, is open 24 hours a day. The Omonia Square OTE, at 50 Athinas, and the Victoria Square OTE, at 85 Patission, are open Monday through Friday from 7am to 9pm, Saturday from 9am to 3pm, and Sunday from 9am to 2pm. Outside Athens, most OTEs are closed on weekends.

Tipping Athenian restaurants include a service charge in the bill, but many visitors add a 10% tip. Most Greeks do not give a percentage tip to taxi drivers, but often round up the fare; for example, you would round up a fare of 2.80€ ($3.65) to 3€ ($3.90).

3 Where to Stay

The preparations for the 2004 Olympics gave the Athenian hotel industry the opportunity to finally reinvent itself. Most hotels were renovated and many new ones appeared, and the landscape now is strikingly different that it was before the Games with new hotels popping up seemingly weekly. Apart from the renovated favorites, now there are ultra-modern cutting-edge hotels and boutique hotels. Nearly all hotels have greatly improved their facilities and services; features that were once found only in luxury hotels can now be found even in budget hotels. And travelers have noticed: In 2006 tourism in Athens rose 20% from the year before. Even so, Athens hotels have some of the lowest average room prices in Europe, so even during peak season you can often find very good deals. Most hotels consider Easter through October high season; you can easily find discounts of 25% to 35% during low season. Interestingly enough, the opposite occurs with expensive and deluxe hotels downtown as upscale visitors tend to avoid Athens during the tourist rush of July and August, so you can find significant reductions in their prices during those 2 months. The hotels below concentrate mostly

---

> ## Tips   A Warning About ATMs
>
> It is *not* a good idea to rely on exclusive use of ATMs in Athens, since the machines here are often out of service when you need them most, particularly on holidays or during bank strikes.
>
> If your PIN includes letters, be sure that you know their numerical equivalent, as Greek ATMs do not have letters.

---

on the closest neighborhoods to the sites and attractions. Keep in mind that Athens is a city in the midst of an incredibly rapid urban transformation. As recently as 5 years ago nobody would recommend a hotel in areas such as Gazi or Psirri, for example. Even though Makrigianni has always been a semi-popular tourist destination due to its proximity to the sites and charming residential feel, the opening of the new Acropolis Museum will significantly change that as well. I have also listed some hotels in the northern suburb of Kifissia and by the coast. One interesting development in the Athenian hotel scene is that some of the most popular lounges, bars, and restaurants are now in hotels. The Galaxy bar atop the Hilton, the Frame lounge at St. George Lycabettus, the lounges in Fresh Hotel and Ochre & Brown, the rooftop bar of Hera Hotel, and the restaurant/bar on top of Electra Palace are just a few to check out. Be advised that reservations are essential any time you're going to Athens (particularly in summer).

THE PLAKA
EXPENSIVE

Electra Palace 𝒜𝒜   The Electra, just a few blocks southwest of Syntagma Square on a relatively quiet side street, is the most modern and stylish Plaka hotel. The rooms on the fifth, sixth, and seventh floors are smaller than those on lower floors, but a top-floor room is where you want to be, both for the terrific view of the Acropolis and to escape traffic noise. (Ask for a top-floor unit when you make your reservation. Your request will be honored "subject to availability.") Guest rooms here are hardly drop-dead elegant, but they are pleasant and decorated in soft pastels. Don't miss the rooftop pool. The hotel restaurant has become one of the best and most sought after restaurants in town with a view as sublime as the food. Note that the restaurant is closed Sunday, however.

18 Nikodimou, Plaka, 10557 Athens. 𝒞 **210/324-1401** or 210/324-1407. Fax 210/324-1975. 106 units. www.electra hotels.gr. 160€ ($208) single; 180€ ($234) double; 232€ ($302) triple. Rates include breakfast buffet. AE, DC, MC, V. The Electra is about 2 blocks down on the left as you walk along Ermou with Syntagma Sq. behind you. **Amenities:** Restaurant; bar; rooftop pool; indoor pool; gym; spa; parking (12€/$16) a day. *In room:* A/C, pay TV, dataport, minibar, hair dryer.

MODERATE

Acropolis House Hotel 𝒜   This small hotel in a handsomely restored 150-year-old villa retains many of its original classical architectural details. It offers a central location—just off Kidathineon in the heart of the Plaka, a 5-minute walk from Syntagma Square—and the charm of being on a quiet pedestrian side street. Room nos. 401 and 402 have good views and can be requested (but not guaranteed) when making a reservation. The newer wing, only 60 years old, isn't architecturally special; each unit's spartan bathroom is across the hall.

Accommodations & Dining South of the Acropolis

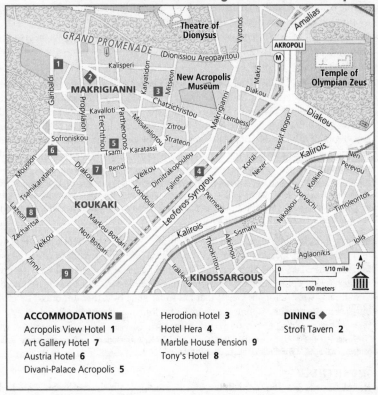

ACCOMMODATIONS ■
Acropolis View Hotel **1**
Art Gallery Hotel **7**
Austria Hotel **6**
Divani-Palace Acropolis **5**

Herodion Hotel **3**
Hotel Hera **4**
Marble House Pension **9**
Tony's Hotel **8**

DINING ◆
Strofi Tavern **2**

If the Acropolis House is full, try **Adonis Hotel,** on the same street at 3 Kodrou (© **210/324-9737**); it's architecturally undistinguished, but it does have an appealing location and a rooftop garden cafe with a view of the Acropolis. A few steps away, **Kouros Hotel,** 11 Kodrou (© **210/322-7431**), is very basic and can be noisy.

6-8 Kodrou, 10558 Athens. © **210/322-2344.** Fax 210/324-4143. www.acropolishouse.gr. 25 units, 15 with bathroom. 70€ ($91) double without bathroom; 80€ ($104) double with bathroom; 104€ ($135) triple. 10€ ($13) surcharge for A/C. Rates include continental breakfast. V. Walk 2 blocks out of Syntagma Sq. on Mitropoleos and turn left on Voulis, which becomes Kodrou. **Amenities:** Washing machine (small fee; free after 4-day stay); book swap. *In room:* A/C, TV, Internet.

Central ☆☆ Completely refurbished, this stylish, elegant hotel features wonderful seagrass or wooden floors, marble bathrooms, and excellent soundproofing. Family and interconnecting rooms are also available and the large roof has superb Acropolis views and a hot tub.

21 Apollonos, 10557 Athens. © **210/323-4357** www.centralhotel.gr. 84 units. 77€–120€ ($100–$156) double. AE, DC, MC, V. **Amenities:** Bar; rooftop terrace; hot tub; conference and meeting facilities; private parking; nonsmoking rooms available upon request. *In room:* A/C, TV, Internet, hair dryer.

Hermes Hotel ☆☆ Exceptionally well renovated for the 2004 Olympics, the Hermes Hotel has designer touches in every room, including polished wood floors, marble bathrooms, and large balconies. Interconnecting rooms are also available. The rooftop terrace has excellent Acropolis views.

19 Apollonos, 10557 Athens. © **210/323-5514.** Fax 210/322-2412. www.hermes-athens.com. 45 units. 115€ ($150) single; 145€ ($189) double; 165€ ($215) triple. AE, MC, V. **Amenities:** Cafe/bar; rooftop terrace; nonsmoking rooms. *In room:* A/C, TV.

Hotel Plaka 🌟🌟   This hotel is popular with Greeks, who prefer its modern conveniences to the old-fashioned charms of most other hotels in the Plaka area. It has a terrific location just off Syntagma Square. Most guest rooms have balconies; those on the fifth and sixth floors in the rear, where it's usually quieter, have views of the Plaka and the Acropolis (also visible from the roof-garden snack bar). Friends who stayed here recently were not charmed by the service, but they enjoyed the location and the rooftop bar.

7 Mitropoleos and Kapnikareas, 10556 Athens. © **210/322-2096.** Fax 210/322-2412. www.plakahotel.gr. 67 units, 38 with shower only. 115€ ($150) single; 145€ ($189) double; 165€ ($215) triple. Rates include breakfast. AE, MC, V. Follow Mitropoleos out of Syntagma Sq. past cathedral and turn left onto Kapnikareas. **Amenities:** Bar; roof garden. *In room:* A/C, TV, dataport, minibar, hair dryer.

Magna Grecia 🌟🌟   Located inside a beautiful 19th-century neoclassical building in a hard-to-beat location (right on Mitropoleos Sq.) this is easily one of the best hotels in the Plaka with high ceilings, French doors, and hardwood floors. All front rooms have sweeping Acropolis views, and there is a pleasant and relaxing rooftop bar as well (also with Acropolis views) that has so far gone by rather unnoticed by glamour-seeking Athenians. Rooms are named after Ionian and Aegean islands.

54 Mitropoleos, 10563 Plaka. © **210/324-0314.** Fax 210/324-0317. www.magnagreciahotel.com. 12 rooms. 125€ ($162) single; 140€ ($182) double; 160€ ($208) triple. AE, DC, MC, V. **Amenities:** Cafe/bar; room service; rooftop garden. *In room:* A/C, TV, dvd/cd/mp3 player, Internet, safe.

INEXPENSIVE

Hotel Adonis 🌟   Rather plain but efficient rooms (with tiny bathrooms) are highlighted by large balconies and breakfast in the rather unimaginative rooftop cafe/bar. You need only look over at the adjacent balcony for one of the most striking Acropolis views in the entire city. The hotel staff is rather stern but very efficient.

6 Kodrou and Voulis, 10558 Athens. © **210/322-2344.** Fax 210/324-4143. www.adonishotel.gr. 26 units. 55€ ($72) single; 80€ ($104) double; 108€ ($141) triple. No credit cards. **Amenities:** Cafe/bar; rooftop garden. *In room:* A/C, TV.

Hotel Dioskouros (aka Dioskouros Guest House)   As far as hostels go, this one is pretty hard to beat. It's a small and intimate choice. There are no en suite bathrooms, but the place is clean and has a very friendly staff, a peaceful garden, and an excellent location. Roughing it suddenly isn't so rough.

6 Pitakou, 10558 Plaka. © **210/324-8165.** Fax 210-321-9991. 12 units, all with shared bathrooms. 35€–40€ ($45–$52) single; 50€–60€ ($65–$78) double; 60€–80€ ($78–$104) triple. AE, MC, V. Free parking. **Amenities:** Bar; garden; cooking facilities (Oct–May); Internet; TV area. *In room:* A/C.

Student and Traveller's Inn   On a quiet pedestrian street on the outskirts of the Plaka, the inn features a charming, casual look with four- and eight-bed dorm rooms with shared facilities but also the option of single, double, and triple rooms (some with en suite facilities) and a pleasant green courtyard, plus Internet access. What else do you need when you're young and on the go?

16 Kydathinaion, 10558 Athens. © **210/324-4808.** Fax 210/321-0065. www.studenttravellersinn.com. Private bathroom 55€ ($71) single; 65€ ($85) double; 78€ ($101) triple. Shared bathroom 50€ ($650) single; 55€ ($72)

double; 72€ ($93) triple. No credit cards. **Amenities:** Internet (shared terminals); courtyard; vending machines; TV area. *In room:* A/C.

MONASTIRAKI
MODERATE

Attalos Hotel ⚐   The six-story Attalos is well situated for visitors wanting to take in the frenzied daytime street life of the nearby Central Market and the Psirri district's exuberant nighttime scene at the cafes and restaurants. Forty of the plain yet pleasant rooms have balconies and 12 have Acropolis views. The roof garden also offers fine views of the city and the Acropolis. The Attalos (whose staff is very helpful) often gives Frommer's readers a 10% discount. *Caution:* Drug dealing and prostitution are not unknown on Athinas Street.

29 Athinas, 10554 Athens. © 210/391-2801. Fax 210/324-3124. www.attalos.gr. 80 units. 72€ ($94) single; 96€ ($125) double; 120€ ($156) triple; 147€ ($192) quad. Rates include buffet breakfast. AE, MC, V. From Monastiraki Sq., walk about 1½ blocks north on Athinas. **Amenities:** Luggage storage; nonsmoking rooms. *In room:* A/C, TV, Internet, hair dryer (most rooms), lock boxes.

Cecil Hotel ⚐   A reasonably priced hotel with 36 rooms in a beautifully restored neoclassical town house with great architectural details—the rooms might be small but they all have polished wood floors, high ceilings, and are soundproof. Full breakfast is served and there's also a welcoming roof garden restaurant.

39 Athinas, 10554 Athens. © 210/321-7079. Fax 210/321-8005. www.cecil.gr. 65€ ($85) single; 99€ ($130) double; 110€ ($143) triple; 145€ ($189) suite. AE, MC, V. **Amenities:** Roof garden restaurant/cafe; bar; full breakfast. *In room:* A/C, TV.

Jason Inn Hotel ⚐ *Value*   On a dull street, but just a few blocks from the Agora, the Plaka, and the Psirri district, this renovated hotel offers attractive, comfortable rooms with double-paned windows for extra quiet. If you don't mind walking a few extra blocks to Syntagma, this is currently one of the best values in Athens, with an eager-to-help staff. If the Jason Inn is full, the staff may be able to find you a room in one of their other hotels: the similarly priced **Adrian Hotel,** on busy Hadrian in the Plaka; or the slightly less expensive **King Jason** or **Jason** hotels, both a few blocks from Omonia Square.

12 Ayion Assomaton, 10553 Athens. © 210/325-1106. Fax 210/523-4786. www.douros-hotels.com. 57 units. 90€ ($117) single; 110€ ($143) double; 135€ ($176) triple. Rates include American buffet breakfast. AE, MC, V. From Monastiraki Sq., head west on Ermou, turn right at Thissio Metro station, pass small below-ground church, and bear left. **Amenities:** Breakfast room; bar. *In room:* A/C, TV, minibar.

INEXPENSIVE

Hotel Tempi ⚐   If you believe that location is everything for a hotel, consider the three-story Tempi, which faces the flower market by the Church of Ayia Irini on a basically pedestrian-only street. The Tempi has simply furnished rooms (bed, table, chair), the mattresses are overdue for replacement, and plumbing here can be a problem—hot water is intermittent and the toilets can smell. But you can see the Acropolis from 10 of its balconied rooms (if you lean). This hotel is very popular with students and other spartan travelers able to ignore the Tempi's drawbacks and focus on its location, rates, and handy communal kitchen facilities.

29 Eolou, 10551 Athens. © 210/321-3175. Fax 210/325-4179. www.travelling.gr/tempihotel. 24 units, 8 with bathroom. 38€ ($50) single without bathroom; 50€–58€ ($65–$76) double with bathroom; 70€ ($91) triple with bathroom. AE, MC, V. From Syntagma Sq., take Ermou to Eolou.

PSIRRI
EXPENSIVE

Ochre & Brown 🐾🐾   This trendy, stylish, and small boutique hotel in the heart of Psirri opened in 2006 and has already found its niche for fashion-conscious and experienced travelers looking for style, highly personalized service, hi-tech comforts, and a chic urban experience. Some rooms have Thissio views but the finest room by far is the junior suite with Acropolis views from its terrace. Rooms have stylish furnishings, large work desks with Internet access, and marble bathrooms with custom-designed glass-enclosed showers. The hotel's lounge/bar and restaurant has quickly become one of the city's favorite haunts.

7 Leokoriou, 10554 Athens. ✆ 210/331-2950. Fax 210-331-2942. www.ochreandbrown.com. 11 units. 170€–190€ ($221–$247) double; 300€ ($390) junior suite. AE, MC, V. **Amenities:** Restaurant; lounge bar. *In room:* A/C, TV, Wi-Fi, safe.

KERAMEIKOS
MODERATE

Hotel Iridanos (Eridanus) 🐾   Another new boutique hotel arrives in Athens and this one feels and looks like an art gallery with colors that alternate between the shockingly bright and the deeply soothing. The rooms have been tastefully furnished with modern designer touches including funky furniture, stunning luxurious dark green marble Indian bathrooms, Web TV, original artwork, and huge beds. The well-known fish restaurant Varoulko next door is associated with the hotel. Some rooms have Acropolis views. The walk from here to Omonia or Syntagma takes about 10 minutes but the Metro stop Kerameikos is right next door. This probably not the place to stay on your first trip to Athens, when you may wish to be closer to the center and in a neighborhood not in the process of being gentrified, but you are within a short walking distance of the city's best nightlife in Gazi, Thissio, and Psirri and the new line 3 (airport line) Metro stop at Kerameikos virtually next door to the hotel, making it the most easily accessible non-airport hotel from the airport in the entire city.

80 Piraeus, 10551 Athens. ✆ 210/520-5360. www.eridanus.gr. 38 units. 100€–120€ ($130–$156) double; 160€ ($208) double with Acropolis views; 180€ ($234) junior suite. AE, MC, V. From Syntagma Sq., take the Archaeological Park walkway to Piraeus Ave. or get off at Kerameikos Metro station. Free parking. **Amenities:** Restaurant; breakfast room; bar; business center. *In room:* A/C, Web TV, Internet, minibar, safe.

OMONIA
MODERATE/EXPENSIVE

Fresh Hotel 🐾🐾   What was once an undistinguished (well, ugly) hotel from the '70s has morphed into one of the coolest and most stylish designer hotels in the city. A black vertical fireplace in the reception area sets the tone for what is an ideally modern urban experience. The rooms aren't huge but they are stylish and modern with many interesting choices such as the armchairs that open into beds, blinds controlled from your bed, and funky colored glass dividers in the bathrooms. One of the many assets of the Fresh Hotel is that it is a hip destination for Athenians to lounge around at as well. The Magenta Restaurant offers many healthy options during the day; on the 9th floor the beautiful Air Lounge Bar with its wooden deck and swimming pool has great city panoramas and very good drinks, but the entire scene belongs almost exclusively to the very popular Orange Bar Restaurant that is busy and hopping well into the early-morning hours. Located near the Athens stock exchange and Athens's little Chinatown and little Bangladesh, this is a true urban experience in a part of the city that used to be visited only by necessity.

26 Sofokleous and 2 Klisthenous, 10564 Athens. ✆ **210/524-8511.** Fax 210/524-8517 www.freshhotel.gr. 133 units. 150€–170€ ($195–$221) double. AE, DC, MC, V. From Omonia Sq., head south along Athinas until you reach Sofokleus. From Monastiraki Sq., head north along Athinias until you reach Sofokleus. Pay parking 12€ ($16) per day. **Amenities:** Restaurant/bar; swimming pool; minispa. *In room:* A/C, plasma TV, Wi-Fi.

Residence Georgio 🕐🕐 A great new hotel near Omonia Square, the Residence Georgio, is a sight to behold and experience, from its bustling sidewalk cafe, stylish decor, spacious rooms with beautiful pearwood decor, stunning marble bathrooms with Jacuzzis, complimentary wine, and fruit baskets in every room. The spacious, smartly designed suites steal the show with their deluxe furnishings and plasma TVs. The hotel also has a cool rooftop pool (home of the Captain's Bar) with great city views, and a very nice health club/spa. The lobby is home to a popular piano bar.

28 Octovriou and 14 Halkokndili, 10677 Athens. ✆ **210/332-0100.** www.residencegeorgio.com. 136 units. 130€ ($169) single; 145€ ($189) double; 230€–245€ ($299–$319) suite. AE, DC, MC, V. **Amenities:** 2 bars; rooftop pool; spa; health club; nonsmoking floors. *In room:* A/C, plasma TV, Internet, Jacuzzi.

INEXPENSIVE

Athens Art Hotel 🕐🕐 *Value* Opened in 2004, the Athens Art Hotel has been booked solid ever since. It's in a strikingly beautiful neoclassical building, dramatically lit at night; you might just want to sit and stare at it for a while before you go inside. The interior will not disappoint either. Modern and colorful, yet classic, this stylish boutique hotel features individually designed rooms with pinewood floors, well-designed features and spacious, marble bathrooms. It is a great value for your money, plus the staff is very friendly and knowledgeable about the city. One of the best deals in the city.

27 Marni, 10432 Athens. ✆ **210/524-0501.** Fax 210/524-3384. www.arthotelathens.gr. 30 units. 79€–90€ ($103–$117) single; 85€–105€ ($111–$137) double; 95€–120€ ($124–$156) triple; 120€-140€ ($156–$182) suite. AE, MC, V. **Amenities:** Restaurant; cafe/bar; business center. *In room:* A/C, TV, Internet:, safe.

SYNTAGMA
VERY EXPENSIVE

Athens Plaza 🕐🕐 The Athens Plaza, managed by the Grecotel group, reopened its glitzy doors in March 1998 after a complete remodeling, and we were pretty excited to stay here shortly thereafter. Acres of marble adorn the lobby, and there's almost as much in some bathrooms, which have their own phones and hair dryers. Many of the guest rooms are larger than most living rooms, and many have balconies overlooking Syntagma Square. That said, the service, although perfectly professional, lacks the personal touch.

Syntagma Sq., 10564 Athens. ✆ **210/325-5301.** Fax 210/323-5856. www.grecotel.gr. 207 units. 300€–400€ ($390–$520) double. AE, DC, MC, V. **Amenities:** 2 restaurants; 2 bars; health club and spa w/Jacuzzi; concierge; tour desk; car rental desk; courtesy car or airport pickup arranged; business center; 24-hr. room service; same-day laundry/dry-cleaning services; nonsmoking rooms; 1 room for those w/limited mobility. *In room:* A/C, TV, dataport, minibar, hair dryer, iron, safe.

Grande Bretagne 🕐🕐★ The legendary Grande Bretagne, one of Athens's most distinguished 19th-century buildings, is back after a $70-million, 2-year renovation. The changes preserved the exquisite Beaux Arts lobby, made dingy rooms grand once more, and added indoor and outdoor swimming pools. From Winston Churchill to Sting, the guests who stay here expect the highest level of attention. The Grande Bretagne prides itself on its service; you are unlikely to be disappointed. Ask for a room with a balcony overlooking Syntagma Square, the Parliament building, and the Acropolis.

Syntagma Sq., 10564 Athens. ℂ **210/333-000.** Fax 210/333-0160. www.grandebretagne.gr. 328 units. 225€–255€ ($293–$332) single; 277€–285€ ($360–$371) double; 330€–345€ ($429–$449) junior suite; 800€ ($1,040) suite. AE, DC, MC, V. **Amenities:** 2 restaurants; 2 bars; 2 pools (indoors and outdoors); health club and spa w/Jacuzzi; concierge; tour desk; car rental desk; courtesy car or airport pickup arranged; business center; 24-hr. room service; same-day laundry/dry-cleaning services; nonsmoking rooms; 1 room for those w/limited mobility. *In room:* A/C, TV, DSL, minibar, hair dryer, iron, safe.

King George II 🏵🏵🏵 Right next door to the strikingly beautiful Hotel Grande Bretagne, the King George II is one of Athens's great historical hotels, opulent and classy, which fell into hard times and disrepair in the '80s and was forced to close its doors for almost 15 years. Fast-forward to 2004 and after an intense, extremely expensive 3-year renovation, it opened its doors once again just in time for the Olympics. Although it looks extremely opulent, the hotel has only 102 rooms, which can also make it feel like a personalized boutique hotel rather than an Athenian landmark (like next door). The renovation has left the hotel better than it was even in its heyday (as is also the case with its more famous neighbor). Everything is immaculate from the antiques to the modern gym/health club. The rooms are individually designed with handmade furniture, silk and satin upholstery, and spacious, gray marbled bathrooms with sunken tubs and glass-encased showers. The Tudor Bar on the rooftop has excellent views of the city and its landmarks while the power Greek-dining Tudor restaurant is sublime. The infamous 9th-floor penthouse suite whose occupiers have included Aristotle Onassis, Maria Callas, Grace Kelly and Prince Rainier, Marilyn Monroe, and Frank Sinatra among others is said to be spectacular, and at $10,000 a night it should be!

Vas Georgiou A2, Syntagma Sq., 10564 Athens. ℂ **210/322-2210** or 210/728-0350. Fax 210/325-0564 or 210/728-0351. www.grecohotel.gr. 220€–260€ ($286–$338) double; 310€–360€ ($403–$468) junior suite. AE, DC, MC, V. **Amenities:** Rooftop bar/restaurant; bar; indoor swimming pool; health club; spa; pool; nonsmoking rooms; rooms for those with limited mobility. *In room:* A/C, TV, DSL.

EXPENSIVE

Electra Hotel 🏵 (Value On pedestrian Ermou, the Electra boasts a location that is quiet and central—steps from Syntagma Square. Most of the guest rooms have comfortable armchairs, large windows, and modern bathrooms. Take a look at your room before you accept it: Although most are large, some are quite tiny. The front desk is sometimes understaffed but the service is generally acceptable, although it can be brusque when groups are checking in and out.

5 Ermou, 10563 Athens. ℂ **210/322-3223.** Fax 210/322-0310. electrahotels@ath.forthnet.gr. 110 units. 152€ ($198) single; 174€ ($226) double; 250€ ($325) suite. Rates include buffet breakfast. AE, DC, MC, V. The Electra is about 2 blocks down on the left as you walk along Ermou with Syntagma Sq. behind you. **Amenities:** Restaurant; bar. *In room:* A/C, TV, Internet, minibar, hair dryer.

MODERATE

Astor Hotel We've never been very impressed with this hotel, which does a heavy business in tour groups and has service that is impersonal at best. That said, a well-traveled journalist tells me that he always stays here when in Athens because of the central location (Karayioryi Servias runs into Syntagma Sq.), bright rooms (some with Acropolis views), and efficient (if not pleasant) front desk staff. He sometimes succeeds in bargaining down the room price.

16 Karayioryi Servias, 10562 Athens. ℂ **210/335-1000.** Fax 210/325-5115. www.astorhotel.gr. 131 units. 62€–90€ ($81–$117) single; 100€–112€ ($130–$146) double; 94€–138€ ($122–$180) triple. Rates include buffet breakfast. AE, V. **Amenities:** Restaurant; bar. *In room:* A/C, TV.

Athens Cypria ⭐⭐   In a convenient central location on a (usually) quiet street, the renovated Cypria overlooks the Acropolis from unit nos. 603 to 607. With bright white halls and rooms, cheerful floral bedspreads and curtains, and freshly tiled bathrooms with new fixtures, the Cypria is a welcome addition to the city's moderately priced hotels. The breakfast buffet offers hot and cold dishes from 7 to 10am. The hotel can be infuriatingly slow in responding to faxed reservation requests.

5 Diomias, 10562 Athens. ⓒ 210/323-8034. Fax 210/324-8792. www.athenscypria.gr. 115 units. 72€–81€ ($94–$105) single; 103€–113€ ($134–$147) double; 126€–135€ ($164–$176) triple; 144€–198€ ($188–$257) quad. Reductions possible off season. Rates include buffet breakfast. AE, MC, V. Take Karayioryi Servias out of Syntagma Sq; Diomias is on the left, after Lekka. **Amenities:** Breakfast room; bar; snack bar; luggage storage. *In room:* A/C, TV, minibar, hair dryer.

Hotel Achilleas   The Achilleas (Achilles), on a relatively quiet side street steps from Syntagma Square, underwent a total renovation in 2001. The good-size guest rooms are now bright and cheerful, and the beds have new mattresses. Some rear rooms have small balconies; several on the fifth floor can be used as interconnecting family suites. The central location of Hotel Achilleas and its fair prices make it a good choice. If you want a room with a safe or a hair dryer, ask at the main desk upon check-in.

21 Lekka, 10562 Athens. ⓒ 210/323-3197. Fax 210/322-2412. www.achilleashotel.gr. 34 units. 100€ ($130) single; 125€ ($163) double; 145€ ($189) triple; 165€ ($215) quad. Rates include breakfast. AE, DC, MC, V. Take Karayioryi Servias out of Syntagma Sq. for 2 blocks and turn right onto Lekka. **Amenities:** Breakfast room; snack bar. *In room:* A/C, TV, minibar, hair dryer (in some), safe (in some).

INEXPENSIVE

Hotel Carolina ⭐⭐   The friendly, family-owned and -operated Carolina, on the outskirts of the Plaka, is a brisk 5-minute walk from Syntagma and has always been popular with students. In the last few years, the Carolina has undertaken extensive remodeling and now attracts a wide range of frugal travelers. Double-glazed windows and air-conditioning make the guest rooms especially comfortable. Many rooms have large balconies, and several (such as no. 308) with four or five beds are popular with families and students. The congenial atmosphere may be a bit too noisy for some.

55 Kolokotroni, 10560 Athens. ⓒ 210/324-3551. Fax 210/324-3350. www.hotelcarolina.gr. 31 units. 60€–80€ ($78–$104) single; 75€–85€ ($91–$111) double; 90€–120€ ($117–$156) triple; 90€–150€ ($117–$203) quad. Breakfast is negotiable 5€ ($6.50). MC, V. Take Stadiou out of Syntagma Sq. to Kolokotroni (on left). **Amenities:** Breakfast room; bar. *In room:* A/C, TV, Internet, safe.

KOLONAKI
VERY EXPENSIVE

St. George Lycabettus Hotel ⭐⭐   As yet, the distinctive, classy St. George does not get many tour groups, which contributes to its tranquil and sophisticated tone. The rooftop pool is a real plus, as is the excellently redesigned rooftop restaurant, the Le Grand Balcon, much-favored by wealthy Greeks for private events. Floors have differing decorative motifs, from baroque to modern Italian. Most rooms look toward pine-clad Mount Likavitos; some have views of the Acropolis. Others overlook a small park or have interior views. This impeccable boutique hotel is located in the posh city quarter of Kolonaki just steps from chic restaurants, cafes, lounges, and shops. Check out the fabulous Frame lounge in the hotel lobby after dark; this ultra-hip lounge/bar is one of the hottest Athenian destinations—people swore to me they saw Madonna there one night in the spring.

2 Kleomenous, 10675 Athens. ⓒ 210/729-0711. Fax 210/721-0439. www.sglycabettus.gr. 167 units. 139€–206€ ($181–$235) double; 315€–370€ ($410–$481) suite. Compulsory breakfast 20€ ($26). AE, DC, MC, V. From

Kolonaki Sq., take Patriarchou Ioachim to Loukianou and follow Loukianou uphill to Kleomenous. Turn left on Kleomenous; the hotel overlooks Dexamini Park. Pay parking 14€ ($18) per day. **Amenities:** 2 restaurants; 2 bars; pool; concierge; business center; 24-hr. room service; same-day laundry/dry-cleaning services; nonsmoking rooms; rooms for those with limited mobility. *In room:* A/C, TV, Internet, minibar, hair dryer.

Periscope 𝒜𝒜   A popular concept hotel with an unusual concept: surveillance. The 22 guest rooms, spread over 6 floors, are all black and white with large beds, industrial-style bathrooms, and ceilings decorated with aerial pictures of Athens taken from a helicopter. The top-floor penthouse suite has exclusive use of the rooftop deck with its Jacuzzi and breathtaking views of the city including the Acropolis, and Mt. Lycabettus all the way to the port of Piraeus. The lobby bar broadcasts live images of the city on huge flatscreen monitors—the images are shot from the rooftop bar which is controlled by loungers in the lobby area. This has led to a very lively bar scene. The neighborhood it's located in is upscale, posh with many boutiques and stylish cafes nearby.

22 Haritos, 10675 Athens. ℂ **210/623-6320.** Fax 210-729-7206. www.periscope.gr. 22 units. 135€–155€ ($176–$202) single; 155€–195€ ($221–$254) double; 225€–270€ ($293–$351) junior suite; 400€–450€ ($520–$585) penthouse. AE, DC, MC, V. **Amenities:** Cafe/bar; business center; gym; nonsmoking rooms. *In room:* A/C, TV, Wi-Fi, DVD player, minibar.

EMBASSY DISTRICT (MUSEUM MILE)
VERY EXPENSIVE
Hilton 𝒜𝒜𝒜   When the Hilton opened in 1963, it was the tallest building on the horizon—and the most modern hotel in town. In 2001, it closed for a long-overdue renovation, and 3 years and 96 million euros later, it reopened. Everything that was tired is again new and fresh. As before, small shops, a salon, and cafes and restaurants surround the glitzy lobby. The guest rooms (looking toward either the hills outside Athens or the Acropolis) have large marble bathrooms and are decorated in the generic but comfortable international Hilton style, with some Greek touches. The Plaza Executive floor of rooms and suites offers a separate business center and a higher level of service. Facilities include a large outdoor pool, conference rooms, and a spa. Even if you're not staying here, make sure to dine at the superb Milos seafood restaurant and have a drink around sunset at the Galaxy rooftop with its amazing city views. For 10€ ($13) visitors can use you can use the pool for the day. The Hilton often runs promotions, so ask about special rates before booking.

46 Leoforos Vas. Sofias, 11528 Athens. ℂ **800/445-8667** in the U.S., or 210/728-1000. Fax 210/728-1111. www.hilton.com. 249€–339€ ($324–$441) single/double; 274€ ($356) triple; 870€ ($1,131) junior suite. AE, DC, MC, V. Pay parking 27€ ($35) per day. **Amenities:** 4 restaurants; 3 bars; outdoor pool; indoor pool; health club and spa w/Jacuzzi; game room; concierge; tour desk; car rental desk; airport pickup arranged; business center; secretarial services; shopping arcade; salon; 24-hr. room service; babysitting; same-day laundry/dry-cleaning services; nonsmoking rooms/floors; rooms for those with limited mobility. *In room:* A/C, TV, Internet, Web TV, minibar, hair dryer, safe.

MODERATE
Andromeda Hotel 𝒜𝒜𝒜   The city's first boutique hotel is easily one of the most charming in Athens, with a staff that makes you feel as if this is your home away from home. This quiet sanctuary overlooks the garden of the American ambassador's home. Guest rooms are large and elegantly decorated, with furniture and paintings you'd be happy to live with. Marvelous breakfasts and snacks are served. The only drawback: The Andromeda is a serious hike (20–30 min.) or a 10-minute taxi ride to Syntagma, but the walk is pleasant and easily done plus very easily accessible by bus and trolley bus. You're also close to the Athens Music Hall and some great restaurants/nightlife such as The Park, Balthazar, 48, and Baraonda. The Hilton isn't too far, either.

22 Timoleontos Vassou, Ambelokipi (off Plateia Mavili), 11521 Athens. ℭ **210/643-7302.** Fax 210/646-6361. www. andromedahotels.gr. 42 units. 100€–120€ ($130–$156) single; 125€–150€ ($163–$195) double; 145€–160€ ($189–$208) triple/junior suite. Rates include breakfast. Special rates sometimes available. AE, DC, MC, V. **Amenities:** Restaurant; breakfast room; bar. *In room:* A/C, TV, Internet, minibar, hair dryer, wall safe.

KOUKAKI & MAKRIGIANNI (NEAR THE ACROPOLIS)

With all the Koukaki and Makrigianni hotels, you'll do some extra walking to get to most places you'll want to visit, but you will also be rewarded with a more quiet, tourist-free atmosphere—at least until the opening of the New Acropolis Museum will change all that.

VERY EXPENSIVE

Divani-Palace Acropolis ✮✮ Just 3 blocks south of the Acropolis, in a quiet residential neighborhood, the Divani Palace Acropolis does a brisk tour business but also welcomes independent travelers. The blandly decorated guest rooms are large and comfortable, and some of the large bathrooms even have two wash basins. The cavernous marble-and-glass lobby contains copies of classical sculpture; a section of Athens's 5th-century-B.C. defensive wall is preserved behind glass in the basement by the gift shop. The breakfast buffet is extensive. (There's also a handy SPAR supermarket a block away at 4 Parthenos, as well as a shop at 7 Parthenos that sells English-language newspapers.) The same hotel group operates **Divani Caravel Hotel,** near the National Art Gallery and the **Hilton** at 2 Leoforos Vas. Alexandrou (ℭ **210/725-3725**).

19–25 Parthenonos, Makrigianni, 11742 Athens. ℭ **210/922-2945.** Fax 210/921-4993. www.divaniacropolis.gr. 253 units. 170€ ($221) single; 180€ ($234) double; 300€ ($390) suite. Rates include breakfast buffet. AE, DC, MC, V. From Syntagma Sq., take Amalias to Dionissiou Areopagitou; turn left onto Parthenos. The hotel is on your left after 3 blocks. **Amenities:** 2 restaurants; 2 bars; outdoor pool; concierge; business center; 24-hr. room service; nonsmoking rooms. *In room:* A/C, TV, Internet, minibar, hair dryer, safe.

MODERATE

Acropolis View Hotel ✮ This nicely maintained hotel is on a residential side street off Rovertou Galli, not far from the Herodes Atticus theater. The usually quiet neighborhood, at the base of Filopappos Hill (itself a pleasant area to explore) is a 10- to 15-minute walk from the heart of the Plaka. Many of the small but appealing guest rooms are freshly painted each year. All units have good bathrooms as well as balconies. Some, such as room no. 405, overlook Filopappos Hill, while others, such as room no. 407, face the Acropolis. A big plus is the rooftop garden with awesome Acropolis views.

Rovertou Galli and 10 Webster, 11742 Athens. ℭ **210/921-7303.** Fax 210/923-0705. www.acropolisview.gr. 32 units. 125€ ($163) double. Rates include buffet breakfast. Substantial reductions Nov–Apr 1. AE, MC, V. From Syntagma Sq. take Amalias to Dionissiou Areopagitou; head west past Herodes Atticus theater to Rovertou Galli. Webster (Gouemster on some maps) is the little street intersecting Rovertou Galli between Propilion and Garabaldi. **Amenities:** Breakfast room; bar; roof garden. *In room:* A/C, TV, minibar.

Art Gallery Hotel Once home to several artists, this small hotel in a half-century-old house maintains an artistic flair (and a nice old-fashioned cage elevator). Rooms are small and plain but comfortable, many with polished hardwood floors and ceiling fans. A nice Victorian-style breakfast room on the fourth floor is furnished with heavy marble-topped tables and old velvet-covered chairs. Rooms were spruced up in 2004 (including polished wooden floors and new bathrooms), but happily, the essential ambience remains. The top-floor bar-lounge has beautiful views of Filopappou Hill and the Acropolis.

5 Erechthiou, Koukaki, 11742 Athens. ℰ **210/923-8376.** Fax 210/923-3025. www.artgalleryhotel.gr. 22 units. 70€ ($91) single; 100€ ($130) double; 120€ ($156) triple. 7€ ($9) buffet breakfast. Hotel sometimes closed Nov–Mar; when open then, prices reduced. AE, MC, V. *In room:* A/C, TV.

Austria Hotel ℱ

This very well-maintained hotel at the base of wooded Filopappos Hill is operated by a Greek-Austrian family who can point you to local sites (including a convenient neighborhood laundry!). The Austria's guest rooms and bathrooms are rather spartan (the linoleum floors aren't enchanting) but are more than acceptable—and the efficient staff is a real plus. You can sun yourself or sit under an awning on the rooftop and enjoy a great view over Athens and out to sea. (I could see the island of Aegina when last there.)

7 Mousson, Filopappou, 11742 Athens. ℰ **210/923-5151.** Fax 210/924-7350. www.austriahotel.com. 36 units, 11 with shower only. 125€ ($163) double. Rates include breakfast. AE, DC, MC, V. Follow Dionissiou Areopagitou around the south side of the Acropolis to where it meets Roverto Galli; take Garibaldi around the base of Filopappou Hill until you reach Mousson. **Amenities:** Breakfast room; rooftop terrace. *In room:* A/C, TV.

Hera Hotel ℱ *Value*

The Hera has a stunning indoor courtyard behind its breakfast room and great views of the Acropolis from its rooftop garden where the elegant Peacock Lounge has become one of the most popular bar/restaurants in the city—especially a little after sunset for its breathtaking views. The units are perfectly comfortable. You may find that the Hera's location outside the heart of tourist Athens is just what you want. If you have a car, you'll appreciate the garage. The Hera is a great value for the money, but the New Acropolis Museum will no doubt make this hotel a sought-after commodity in no time.

9 Falirou, Makrigianni 11742 Athens. ℰ **210/923-6682.** Fax 210/923-8269. www.herahotel.gr. 38 units. 90€–120€ ($117–$156) single; 100€–135€ ($130–$176) double; 180€ ($234) junior suite. AE, DC, MC, V. Free parking. **Amenities:** 2 cafe/bar/restaurants (1 on the rooftop); business center; shared Internet terminal; nonsmoking rooms; rooms for those with limited mobility. *In room:* A/C, TV.

Herodion Hotel

An archaeologist friend who always stays at this attractive hotel a block south of the Acropolis, near the Herodes Atticus theater, reports that there's considerably more traffic noise on Rovertou Galli since Dionissiou Areopagitou became a pedestrian street. Still, the rooms here are a good size, many with balconies. The lobby leads to a lounge and patio garden where you can have drinks and snacks under the trees. The same owners run nearby **Hotel Philippos,** 3 Mitseon, Makrigianni (ℰ **210/922-3611**).

4 Rovertou Gall, Makrigianni, 11742 Athens. ℰ **210/923-6832** or 210/923-6836. Fax 210/921-6150. www.herodion.gr. 90 units. 200€ ($260) single; 252€ ($327) double; 272€ ($354) junior suite. Rates include breakfast. AE, DC, MC, V. **Amenities:** Breakfast room; bar. *In room:* A/C, TV.

Marble House Pension ℱℱ

Named for its marble facade, which is usually covered with bougainvillea, this small hotel, whose front rooms offer balconies overlooking quiet Zinni Street, is famous among budget travelers (including many teachers) for its friendly staff. Over the last several years, the pension has been remodeled and redecorated, gaining new bathrooms and guest-room furniture (including small fridges). Two units have kitchenettes. If you're spending more than a few days in Athens and don't mind being outside the center (and a partly uphill 15-20-min. walk to the hotel from the Plaka), this is a homey base.

35 A. Zinni, Koukaki, 11741 Athens. ℰ **210/923-4058.** Fax 210/922-6461. www.marblehouse.gr. 16 units, 12 with bathroom. 42€ ($55) double without bathroom; 48€ ($63) double with bathroom. 9€ ($12) supplement for A/C.

Monthly rates available off season. No credit cards. From Syntagma Sq. take Amalias to Syngrou; turn right onto Zinni; the hotel is in the cul-de-sac beside the small church. **Amenities:** 2 rooms for those w/limited mobility. *In room:* A/C (9 units), TV, minibar.

Tony's Hotel (aka Tony's Pension)   Travelers planning a long stay in Athens should consider Tony's, which is popular with students and frugal travelers. Located between Filopappos Hill and Leoforos Syngrou, Tony's has communal lounges, kitchens, and a roof garden with a barbecue grill. It's nothing fancy but its friendly, charming, and homey.

26 Zacharitsa, Koukaki, 11741 Athens. (℃) **210/923-6370** or 210/923-5761. 21 units, including 11 studio apts. 55€–85€ ($72–$111). No credit cards. **Amenities:** Communal lounges; kitchens; roof garden w/barbecue grill. *In room:* A/C.

HERE & THERE—WORTH THE JOURNEY

This following selections are most likely to appeal to travelers seeking a different kind of Athenian experience, away from the downtown scene but not having to travel too far to get to the city center. The northern suburbs—lush, aristocratic, and green—and the coastal suburbs with their beaches and buzzing summer nightlife are two excellent options, depending which time of year you are in Athens. Kifissia is a half-hour train ride from downtown on Metro line 1, and the coast is accessible by tram (up to Glyfada) and farther out (from the center or Glyfada) either by bus or taxi.

KIFISSIA

Leafy and aristocratic Kifissia has long been the favorite destination of the rich and famous, thus its many elegant 19th-century neoclassical mansions found in tree-lined streets and squares, alongside audacious modern mansions and modern apartment buildings. The streets and squares are jampacked with people, cafes, restaurants, and clubs, but the side streets are charming and ideal for strolling. Although the scene is more low-key than downtown, it definitely isn't any less fun. Kifissia also has two excellent museums (Goulandris Museum of Natural History and the Gaia Center), a wonderful outdoor cinema dating back to 1919, and ample elegance to spare (even the local Pizza Hut is housed in a beautifully restored neoclassical mansion). Despite its high profile and outrageous real estate prices, Kifissia is surprisingly relaxed and (mostly) attitude-free, making it pleasant and accessible to all.

Hotel 21 👸👸   Ultra-cool Hotel 21 features spacious rooms with giant beds and large glass-encased bathrooms in more moderate prices. Paintings in each room tell part of a story (the story in its entirety is featured in the reception); split-level loft suites have sunroofs. Many guests come here for the popular scene at the gigantic outdoor cafe or bar inside the hotel.

21 Kolokotroni and Mykonou, 14562 Kifissia. (℃) **210/623-3521.** Fax 210/623-3821. www.twentyone.gr. 21 units. 160€ ($208) single/double; 200€ ($260) loft suite. AE, DC, MC, V. Metro: Kifissia, then 5-min. taxi ride, 25-min. walk to Kefalari Sq. or Kefalari bus. Free parking. **Amenities:** 2 restaurants/bars. *In room:* A/C, TV/DVD, Wi-Fi, safe.

Pentelikon 👸👸   Looking more like a private estate than a hotel—with its immaculately kept gardens—the Pentelikon, full of old-world glamour, was built in 1929 and features grand staircases and gigantic ballrooms of a long-gone era. Elegance and impeccable style can be found around every corner, and to make it even more appealing the hotel also houses the Michelin-starred restaurant Vardis. Both are a very brief walk from the Semiramis hotel. (Right next door to the Pentelikon is my high school housed in another old hotel, not nearly a quarter as grand of course as its neighbor).

66 Deligianni, 14562 Kifissia. © **210/623-0650.** Fax 210/801-0314. www.hotelpentelikon.gr. 101 units. 235€ ($306) single; 250€ ($325) double; 513€–1,900€ ($667–$2,470) suite. AE, DC, MC, V. Metro: Kifissia, then 5-min. taxi ride, 25-min. walk to Kefalari Square or Kefalari bus. Free parking. **Amenities:** Restaurant; bar; outdoor pool. *In room:* A/C, TV, safe.

Semiramis 🌟🌟 By far the most stunning of all the new designer hotels (if you approach the hotel at night you will think you suddenly made a wrong turn and found yourself in Miami when it is lit dramatically in changing colors that include magenta, lime, orange and yellow). New York–based British-Egyptian designer Karim Rashid, has created a modern artistic masterpiece with original touches throughout: symbols on room doors instead of numbers, hallways that glow different colors, LCD displays outside the rooms, and an ultra-stylish shoehorn-shaped pool. The hotel also has two popular bars and a great restaurant. The 51 units include 5 pool-side bungalows overlooking a giant waterfall while the suites command exceptional views from their terraces of the bustling city and nearby peaceful and serene Penteli mountain.

48 Harilaou Trikoupi, 14562 Kifissia. © **210/623-3521.** Fax 210/628-4499. www.semiramisathens.com. 51 units. 180€–265€ ($234–$345) single; 230€–265€ ($299–$345) double; 260€–300€ ($338–$390) bungalow. AE, DC, MC, V. Metro: Kifissia, then 5-min. taxi ride, 25-min. walk to Kefalari Sq. or Kefalari bus. **Amenities:** Restaurant; 2 bars; pool; gym. *In room:* A/C, LCD/plasma/pay TV, Wi-Fi, remote-controlled curtains, digital locks.

THE COAST

Athens has many beaches—nearly all of them have been awarded the E.U. blue flag for clear waters—but the coast is not only for swimming and watersports. Excellent restaurants and open-air clubs and bars by the sea as well as excellent shopping options make the coast irresistible during the summer and are a good choice if you won't have time to make it to the islands. The hotels below epitomize the best this area has to offer.

Astir Palace Resort 🌟🌟 Tranquil and beautiful, with sea vistas, the Astir Palace is actually a series of secluded bungalows and three hotels with their own private beaches on 75 acres with plenty of activity from windsurfing to private Pilates lessons. Seven well-regarded restaurants ranging from the beachside Taverna 37 to the Polynesian Sao Restaurant are on-site. The Arion hotel offers a more classical aesthetic and its sea-view rooms are arranged in such a way so that even the bathtubs have prime water views; in 2006 Starwood Hotels and Resorts of the St. Regis in NYC fame raised its luxury flag on the Arion, while the Westin was formerly known as the Nafsika. All rooms in the Westin have sea views while the rooms are elegant and modern, and the new W hotel (formerly Aphrodite) will open in 2008, following a long and extensive renovation that is expected to be spectacular when it is done.

40 Apollonos, 16671 Vouliagmeni. © **210/890-2000.** Fax 210/896-2582. www.astir.gr. 526 units. Arion: 350€–430€ ($455–$559) single; 380€–460€ ($494–$598) double. Westin: 310€–380€ ($403–$494) single; 340€–410€ ($403–$533) double. AE, DC, MC, V. Tram to Glyfada, then either taxi or bus 114. Free parking. **Amenities:** 7 restaurants; 7 bars; 3 pools; 3 tennis courts. *In room:* A/C, Web TV, Internet.

Divani Apollon Palace & Spa 🌟🌟 In a prime location on Kavouri beach with towering palm trees, picturesque gardens, and two large swimming pools, this is as close to a secluded island experience as you are likely to get in any large city. With sea views from every room, large balconies and green marble bathrooms, and a private beach, this is perhaps the most romantic of Athens's hotels. Complementing the romantic ambience is the well-regarded on-site seafood restaurant, Mythos tis Thalassas (Legend of the Sea), with seafront tables, accessible for the guests of the hotel via an underground tunnel.

10 Agiou Nikolaou and Iliou, 16671 Vouliagmeni. ℂ 210/891-1100. Fax 210/965-8010. www.divaniapollon.gr. 286 units. 200€ ($260) single; 320€ ($416) executive single; 220€ ($286) double; 340€ ($442) executive double; 1,600€ ($2,080) suite. AE, DC, MC, V. Tram to Glyfada, then either taxi or bus 114. Free parking. **Amenities:** 3 restaurants; bar; 2 pools; gym; spa; tennis court w/flood lighting; free shuttle bus to Glyfada and/or Syntagma Sq. *In room:* A/C, Web TV, Internet.

Margi 🐀🐀 Wonderfully stylish and atmospheric with colonial-style decor, this 88-room hotel—which looks like a Moorish castle with its stone walls and outdoor arches—has spacious rooms where contemporary design and antiques blend seamlessly, elegant gray marble bathrooms equipped with Bulgari products, and views overlooking either the pool, the sea, or the mountains. The Oriental-style candlelit pool bar and restaurant is a major plus.

11 Litous, 16671 Vouliagmeni. ℂ **210/896-2061.** Fax 210/896-0229. www.themargi.gr. 88 units. 220€ ($286) single; 250€ ($325) double; 600€ ($780) executive suite. AE, DC, MC, V. Tram to Glyfada, then either taxi or bus 114. Free parking. **Amenities:** Restaurant; 2 bars; pool. *In room:* A/C, Web TV, Internet.

4 Where to Dine

If you are in Athens during warm weather—and you more than likely will be—you will quickly discover that to the Athenians (as to most Greeks) dining outdoors is just as important as the meal itself. As with the rest of the rebirth that the ancient city is experiencing culinary offerings are undergoing a renaissance. Traditional Greek cuisine is undergoing its own reinvention in the hands of new chefs (most of them trained abroad) while classic foreign cuisines are also becoming well represented. Three new restaurants have been awarded the prestigious Michelin star. However, those seeking authentic Greek cuisine have no reason to worry: In spite of the booming restaurant industry's recent love affair with the new and trendy, traditional tavernas have not gone out of style, and indeed have been cropping up all over the place (with the excellent Mamakas restaurant in Gazi being the trailblazer when it first opened its doors in 1998). These tavernas put an edgier spin on their predecessors with lighter fare, catering to a mostly younger clientele, and pay more attention to pleasing the city's increasingly refined palates. Even though it is impossible to cover the entire city's offerings in such limited space, I have tried to highlight the best and most exciting restaurants, from the traditional tavernas and *mezodopoleia* or *ouzeri*, where you can enjoy many small dishes, to new tavernas, fusion restaurants, and more.

Be aware though that dining in Athens (like in any other European capital) will rarely come cheap at the quality restaurants. If you wish to dine with the locals, keep in mind that Athenians do not dine before 10pm, so plan accordingly. Your tip should be 10% to 15% on top of the bill (check first if it is included or not in the bill). Menus can be found in both Greek and English (if not, the waiter will help you with suggestions.) Since 2002 restaurants are required by law to offer nonsmoking seating. You may or may not find this law enforced.

Tips **Dining Out**

Because many of the city's finest nightlife options are found in bar-restaurants these days, I have included those options under the nightlife section of chapter 6. At these places you can enjoy a lively scene and great music with a small meal or well-prepared finger food.

Athens Dining

48 the Restaurant **47**	Elihrison **17**
Abyssinia Cafe **11**	Filipou **45**
Aegli **57**	Filistron **9**
Archaion Gefsis **1**	Furin Kazan **33**
Athinaikon **23**	Giouvetsakia **32**
Bar Guru Bar **19**	Godzilla **18**
Chez Lucien **5**	Ideal **25**
Cosa Nostra **15**	Ithaki **40**
Damigos **39**	Kalliste **44**
Daphne's **37**	Kotsoyannis **42**
Diporto **26**	Kouklis Ouzeri **38**
Eden Vegetarian	Mamakas **4**
Restaurant **35**	Meson el Mirador **21**
El Bandoneon **2**	Milos **49**
El Pecado **12**	Nefli **30**

Neon (Kolonaki) 53
Neon (Omonia) 24
Neon (Syntagma) 55
Nikitas 13
Noodle Bar 40
Oineas 14
Pak Indian 20
Papandreou 27
Paradosiako 41
Pica Pica 16
Platanos Taverna 34
Prosopa 3
Rhodia 52
Spondi 58
Strofi Tavern 31

Taverna Sigalas 43
Taverna Xinos 56
Taygetos 22
Tellis 28
Thalatta 7
Thanasis 29
The Park 48
To Kafeneio 50
To Kouti 10
To Ouzadiko 53
To Prytaneion 54
To Steki Tou Ilia 8
Tou Psara 36
Varoulko 6
Vlassis 46

EXARCHEIA

NEAPOLIS

National Library

University of Athens

Athens Academy

LIKAVITOS HILL

KOLONAKI

Kolonaki Square

SYNTAGMA

Syntagma Square

Parliament

National Art Gallery

EVANGELISMOS

NATIONAL GARDEN

Presidential Palace

Zappeion

Temple of Olympian Zeus

Panathenian Stadium

GRAND PROMENADE (Vas. Olgas)

Rack Railway (Funicular)

ℹ Information

Metro:
Ⓜ Line 1
Ⓜ Line 2
Ⓜ Line 3
Ⓛ Light Rail

0   1/4 mile
0   1/4 km

Tips **A Note on Credit Cards**

Much has changed in Athens but one thing remains the same: Many Athenian restaurants still do not accept credit cards, especially tavernas and "lower brow" places. Consider yourself warned.

THE PLAKA

Some of the most charming old restaurants in Athens are in the Plaka—as are some of the worst tourist traps. Here are a few things to keep in mind when you head off for a meal in the Plaka.

Some Plaka restaurants station waiters outside who don't just urge you to come in and sit down, but who pursue you with an unrelenting sales pitch. The hard sell is almost always a giveaway that the place caters to tourists. (That said, remember that announcements of what's for sale are not invariably ploys reserved for tourists. If you visit the Central Market, you'll see and hear stall owners calling out the attractions of their meat, fish, and produce to passersby—even waving particularly tempting fish and fowl in front of potential customers.)

In general, it's a good idea to avoid places with floor shows; many charge outrageous amounts (and levy surcharges not always openly stated on menus) for drinks and food. If you get burned, stand your ground, phone the **tourist police** (© 171), and pay nothing before they arrive. Often the mere threat of calling the tourist police has the miraculous effect of causing a bill to be lowered.

MODERATE/EXPENSIVE

Daphne's *ƒƒ* ELEGANT GREEK   Frescoes adorn the walls of this neoclassical 1830s home, which includes a shady garden courtyard displaying bits of ancient marble found on-site. Diners from around the world sit at Daphne's tables. The courtyard makes it a real oasis in Athens, especially when summer nights are hot. The food here—recommended by the *New York Times, Travel + Leisure,* and just about everyone else—gives you all the old favorites with new distinction (try the zesty eggplant salad), and combines familiar ingredients in innovative ways (delicious hot pepper and feta cheese dip). We could cheerfully eat the hors d'oeuvres all night. We have also enjoyed the *stifado* (stew) of rabbit in *mavrodaphne* (sweet-wine) sauce and the tasty prawns with toasted almonds. Live music plays unobtrusively in the background on some nights. The staff is attentive, endearing, and beyond excellent.

4 Lysikratous. ©/fax 210/322-7971. Reservations recommended. Main courses 16€–30€ ($21–$39), with some fish priced by the kilo. AE, DC, MC, V. Daily 7pm–1am. Closed Dec 20–Jan 15.

Eden Vegetarian Restaurant *ƒ* VEGETARIAN   You can find vegetarian dishes at almost every Greek restaurant, but if you want to experience organically grown products, soy (rather than eggplant) moussaka, mushroom pie with a whole-wheat crust, freshly squeezed juices, and salads with bean sprouts, join the young Athenians and Europeans who patronize the Eden. The prices are reasonable, if not cheap, and the decor is engaging, with 1920s-style prints and mirrors and wrought-iron lamps.

12 Lissiou. ©/fax 210/324-8858. Main courses 8€–15€ ($10–$20). AE, MC, V. Daily noon–midnight. Closed Tues and usually closed Aug. From Syntagma Sq., head south on Filellinon or Nikis to Kidathineon, which intersects Adrianou; turn right on Adrianou and take Mnissikleos up 2 blocks toward Acropolis to Lissiou.

Paradosiako ⭐ TRADITIONAL GREEK   Off the fringes of Plaka, removed from the tourist traps, is this great little place offering traditional fare (thus its name which translates to Traditional). We recommend the inexpensive and quite delicious whole grilled calamari and the baked chickpeas, but everything on the menu is quite tasty.

44A Voulis. ⓒ 210/321 4121. Main courses 7€–15€ ($9–$20). No credit cards. Mon–Sat 10am–2am; Sun 10am–9pm.

Platanos Taverna ⭐⭐ TRADITIONAL GREEK   In good weather, this taverna on a quiet pedestrian square puts its tables beneath a spreading plane tree (*platanos* means plane tree). Inside, where locals usually congregate to escape the summer sun at midday and where tourists gather in the evening, you can enjoy the old paintings and photos on the walls. The Platanos has been serving good *spitiko fageto* (home cooking) since 1932 and has managed to keep steady customers happy while enchanting visitors. If artichokes or spinach with lamb are on the menu, you're in luck: They're delicious. The casseroles (either lamb or veal with spinach or eggplant) are especially tasty. The wine list includes a wide choice of bottled wines from many regions of Greece, although the house wine is tasty. Plan to come here and relax, not rush, through a meal.

4 Diogenous. ⓒ 210/322-0666. Fax 210/322-8624. Main courses 7€–15€ ($9–$20). No credit cards. Mon–Sat noon–4:30pm and 8pm–midnight; Sun in Mar–May and Sept–Oct noon–4:30pm. From Syntagma Sq., head south on Filellinon or Nikis to Kidathineon. Turn right on Adrianou, and take Mnissikleos up 1 block toward the Acropolis; turn right onto Diogenous.

Taverna Xinos ⭐ TRADITIONAL GREEK   Despite the forgivable spelling lapse, Xinos's business card says it best: "In the heart of old Athens there is still a place where the traditional Greek way of cooking is upheld." Hidden away just off Plaka's main square, where it has been run for over 70 years by the same family, is this wonderful little gem, offering traditional, home-cooked meals specializing in lamb dishes. Try it fricasseed (with lemon sauce) or stewed with pasta (Giouvetsi) or grilled. According to family lore, this taverna is where my grandfather proposed to my grandmother as a strolling duo serenaded them with Greek love songs accompanied by the accordion. Though I am certain it isn't the same duo, a duo still serenades diners nightly with beautiful love songs of a long gone but not quite forgotten era. In warm weather you can dine in the charming tree-lined courtyard; in winter, warm yourself by the coal-burning stove and admire the frescoes.

4 Geronta. ⓒ 210/322-1065. Main courses 6€–15€ ($7.80–$20). No credit cards. Daily 8pm to any time from 11pm–1am; sometimes closed Sun. Usually closed part of July and Aug. From Syntagma Sq., head south on Filellinon or Nikis to Kidathineon; turn right on Geronta and look for the xinos sign in the cul-de-sac.

Tou Psara ⭐ GREEK SEAFOOD   One of the few remaining places in the touristy Plaka that remains a cut above its tourist-trap neighbors, this spot is tucked away in a quiet corner under blooming mulberry trees. This might just be the only seafood option in Plaka seriously worth considering. The marinated octopus is truly out of this world.

16 Erechtheos and 12 Erotokritou. ⓒ 210/321-8733. Main courses 7€–15€ ($9–$20). No credit cards. Daily noon–2am.

INEXPENSIVE

Damigos (The Bakaliarakia) ⭐⭐⭐ GREEK/CODFISH   This basement taverna, with enormous wine barrels in the back room and an ancient column supporting the roof in the front room, has been serving delicious deep-fried codfish and eggplant, as well as chops and stews, since 1865. The wine comes from the family vineyards. There are few pleasures greater than sipping retsina (if you wish, you can buy a bottle to take away) while you watch the cook turn out meal after meal in his absurdly small kitchen. Don't miss the delicious *skordalia* (garlic sauce), equally good with cod, eggplant, bread—well, you get the idea.

41 Kidathineon. (𝄖 210/322-5084. Main courses 6€–10€ ($7.80–$13). No credit cards. Daily 7pm to any time from 11pm–1am. Usually closed June–Sept. From Syntagma Sq., head south on Filellinon or Nikis to Kidathineon; Damigos is downstairs on the left just before Adrianou.

Giouvetsakia ✦ TRADITIONAL GREEK   Run by the same family since 1950, this traditional taverna at a bustling junction is perfect for people-watching in a scenic environment while enjoying some delicious, traditional fare. Try the Giouvetsi pasta (still the house's specialty and its namesake) and be sure to leave room for the complimentary fruit dish topped with cinnamon.

144 Adrianou and Thespidos. (𝄖 210/322-7033. Main courses 6€–15€ ($7.80–$20). MC, V. Daily 10am–2am.

Kouklis Ouzeri (To Yerani) ✦ GREEK/MEZEDES   Besides Kouklis Ouzeri and To Yerani, Greeks call this popular old favorite with its winding staircase to the second floor the "Skolario" because of the nearby school. Sit down at one of the small tables and a waiter will present a large tray with about a dozen plates of *mezedes*— appetizer portions of fried fish, beans, grilled eggplant, taramosalata, cucumber-and-tomato salad, olives, fried cheese, sausages, and other seasonal specialties. Choose the ones that appeal to you. If you don't order all 12, you can enjoy a tasty and inexpensive meal, washed down with the house *krasi* (wine). No prices are posted, but the waiter will help you if you ask. Now if only the staff could be a bit more patient when foreigners are trying to decide what to order . . .

14 Tripodon. (𝄖 210/324-7605. Appetizers 5€–15€ ($6.50–$20). No credit cards. Daily 11am–2am. From Syntagma Sq., head south on Filellinon or Nikis to Kidathineon; take Kidathineon across Adrianou to Thespidos and climb toward Acropolis; Tripodon is 1st street on right after Adrianou.

MONASTIRAKI
EXPENSIVE
Cosa Nostra ✦ ITALIAN-AMERICAN   For those of you that have been to New York's Little Italy, once you step into Cosa Nostra, you will swear you never left or that you found yourself on a set from the *Sopranos* that somehow found its way to Athens. The interior, with pictures of Mafia families, Prohibition-era liquor boxes, a jukebox playing classic "Rat Pack" fare, and a bathroom decorated like an old barbershop, is completely trippy. The food, classic Italian-American fare, is quite good (dependable comfort food) but it is the inspired decor in the most unlikely of places that captures the attention and imagination. You will swear Martin Scorcese is somewhere at a nearby table.

5 Agias Theklas, Monastiraki. (𝄖 210/331-0900. Main courses 35€–45€ ($46–$59). AE, MC. Daily 8pm–1am.

EXPENSIVE/MODERATE
Abyssinia Cafe ✦ GREEK   This small cafe in a ramshackle building sports a nicely restored interior featuring lots of gleaming dark wood and polished copper. It faces lopsided Abyssinia Square off Ifaistou, where furniture restorers ply their trade and antiques shops sell everything from gramophones to hubcaps. You can sit indoors or out with a coffee, but it's tempting to snack on Cheese Abyssinia (feta scrambled with

spices and garlic), mussels and rice pilaf, or *keftedes* (meatballs). Everything is reasonably priced here, but it's easy to run up quite a tab, because everything is so good.

Plateia Abyssinia, Monastiraki. © 210/321-7047. Appetizers and main courses 5€–15€ ($6.50–$20). No credit cards. Tues–Sun 10:30am–2pm (often open evenings as well). Usually closed for a week at Christmas and Easter; sometimes closed part of Jan and Feb and mid-July to mid-Aug. Abyssinia Sq. is just off Ifaistou (Hephaistos) across from Ancient Agora's entrance on Adrianou.

To Kouti ☆☆ CONTEMPORARY GREEK   Located along Adrianou Street next to the Ancient Agora, this place is great for people-watching as well. To Kouti (The Box) stands head and shoulders above its neighboring restaurants that seem to rely too much on their location. The place looks like children decorated it with bright-colored crayons—even the menu is handwritten in brightly illustrated children's books. Beyond decor, To Kouti has an unusual but very tasty menu: Try the beef in garlic and honey or the shrimp in carrots or opt for some of its exceptional vegetarian dishes. The homemade bread is served in (of course!) boxes.

23 Adrianou, Monastiraki. © 210/321-3229. Main courses 17€–30€ ($22–$39). AE, MC, V. Daily 1pm–1am.

INEXPENSIVE

Diporto GREEK   This little place, sandwiched between olive shops, serves salads, stews, and delicious *revithia* (chickpeas) and *gigantes* (butter beans), both popular Greek winter dishes among stall owners, shoppers, and Athenians who make their way to the market for cheap and delicious food.

Central Market, Athinas. No phone. Main courses 4€–8€ ($5.20–$10). No credit cards. Mon–Sat 6am–6pm.

Papandreou GREEK   The butcher, the baker, and the office worker duck past the sides of beef hanging in the Meat Hall and head to this hole in the wall for zesty tripe dishes. Don't like tripe? Don't worry: Their menu offers choices that don't involve it. Papandreou has a virtually all-male clientele, but a woman alone need not hesitate to eat here.

Central Market, Athinas. © 210/321-4970. Main courses 5€–8€ ($6.50–$10). No credit cards. Mon–Sat about 8am–5pm.

Taverna Sigalas GREEK   This longtime Plaka taverna, housed in a vintage 1879 commercial building with a newer outdoor pavilion, boasts that it has been run by the same family for a century and is open 365 days a year. Huge old retsina kegs stand piled against the back walls; black-and-white photos of Greek movie stars are everywhere. After 8pm, Greek Muzak plays. At all hours, both Greeks and tourists wolf down large portions of stews, moussaka, grilled meatballs, baked tomatoes, and gyros, washing it all down with the house red and white retsinas.

2 Plateia Monastiraki. © 210/321-3036. Main courses 6€–15€ ($7.80–$20). No credit cards. Daily 7am–2am. Sigalas is across Monastiraki Sq. from the Metro station.

Thanasis ☆ GREEK/SOUVLAKI   Thanasis serves terrific souvlaki and pita—and exceptionally good french fries—both to go and at its outdoor and indoor tables. As always, prices are higher if you sit down to eat. On weekends, it often takes the strength and determination of an Olympic athlete to get through the door and place an order here. It's worth the effort: This is both a great budget choice and a great place to take in the local scene, which often includes a fair sprinkling of Gypsies.

69 Mitropoleos (just off the northeast corner of Monastiraki Sq.). © 210/324-4705. Main courses 4€–10€ ($5.20–$13). No credit cards. Daily 9am–2am.

PSIRRI

EXPENSIVE

El Pecado 👁👁 SPANISH/LATIN AMERICAN   "The Sin" came about from the unorthodox union of a medieval Spanish-style church and erotic murals inspired by Bible themes. Confused? Don't be. Follow the fun into the sinfully enjoyable bar-restaurant, enjoy the exceptional Spanish and South American cuisine (the chicken Teriyaki with beans and rice, the honey-barbecued chicken, the empanadas diegito, grilled vegetables, and the chocolate soufflé are all excellent), and enjoy the fine wine and the utterly seductive scene. Soon enough you will most likely begin to feel the urge to dance to the outrageously sexy music ranging from flamenco and tango to techno. Only a sin could be this much fun. In summer the fun moves to the even more sinful branch on the island of Mykonos.

11 Tournavitou and Sarri, Psirri. 📞 **210/324-4049**. Main courses 40€–50€ ($52–$65). AE, MC, V. Oct–May Mon–Sat 10pm–3am.

MODERATE/EXPENSIVE

Bar Guru Bar 👁👁 THAI   I've included this bar-restaurant here because even though the scene there gets livelier as the night gets older, it was difficult for me to ignore it for the many fine nights I have enjoyed there. It's still a favorite Athenian destination after a successful decade, offering excellent Asian dishes (the gean gai rama—Burmese chicken with caramelized onions and coconut milk—is an absolute must), an exciting setting with a bustling bar that offers fantastic frozen Margaritas and Thai Martinis, and an excellent top-floor jazz club. Great food, great setting, and great drinks, what more could you ask for?

10 Plateia Theatrou, Psirri. 📞 **210/324-6530**. Main courses 18€–40€ ($23–$52). Closed late July to late Aug. AE, MC, V. Daily 9:30pm–1:30am (restaurant); 9:30pm–4am (bar)

Elihrison 👁 GREEK   This brand-new large restaurant in the heart of trendy Psirri features mostly classic dishes in a beautifully restored building (it was a Turkish justice hall in the early 1800s) that includes both roof garden seating and indoor courtyard seating. Although the location and setting is what gets you, the mostly traditional fare is also quite exceptional.

6 Agion Anargiton, Psirri. 📞 **210/321-5220**. Main courses 15€–30€ ($20–$39). AE, MC, V. Mon–Fri 8pm–2am; Sat–Sun noon–2am.

Pak Indian 👁 INDIAN/PAKISTANI   Behind city hall and Omonia Square on the borders of Psirri hides perhaps the best Indian restaurant in the city. It is always busy with South Asian immigrants and Athenians alike, and the dishes are traditional (if less spicy than their authentic recipe dictates). Owned and run by Pakistanis, the upstairs floor has low tables and huge pillows to sit on.

13 Menandrou, Psirri. 📞 **210/324-2225**. Main courses 18€–25€ ($23–$33). MC, V. Daily 2pm–2am.

Pica Pica 👁👁 SPANISH   Inside a restored neoclassical house on busy Agion Anargiron, you will find this fun place serving up tasty fare. The ground floor houses a smart tapas bar with great cocktails. The dining floor upstairs features beautiful light fixtures, large mirrors, two windows that look directly into the kitchen, and a glass dome so you can see what's going on in the downstairs bar area. Delicious tapas include *jamon serano*, empanadas, *pinchos,* paella valenciana, and *chorizo con puernos* as well as the very tasty (but lethal!) sangria.

8 Agion Anargiron, Psirri. ✆ **210/325-1663**. Main courses 18€–35€ ($24–$46). MC, V. Mon–Sat 6pm–2am; Sat–Sun noon–midnight.

INEXPENSIVE

Godzilla ☆ SUSHI   For those late nights where drinking has left you ravenous but you can't stomach another souvlaki, Godzilla is the perfect option. Decorated like a Tokyo subway station, Godzilla is a great sushi bar with winning prices just off Agion Anargiron.

5 Riga Palamidou, Psirri. ✆ **210/322-1086**. Main courses 6.50€–18€ ($8–$23). MC, V. Daily 9pm–2:30am.

Nikitas ☆☆ TRADITIONAL GREEK   Amid all the new and glitzy bars and bar-restaurants of this hip area, Nikitas stands alone as an old-time, traditional taverna featuring its delicious classic fare all throughout the day and late into the night. A must.

19 Agion Anargyron, Psirri. ✆ **210/325-2591**. Main courses 4€–10€ ($5.20–$13). No credit cards. Daily 10am–7pm.

Oineas ☆☆ TRADITIONAL GREEK   Absolutely delightful and delicious, this taverna in Psirri is popular with tourists and locals alike—the stamp of approval from both camps is richly deserved. The unusual appetizers (fried feta in light honey) will conspire to make you forget to order any main dishes, but don't—you cannot go wrong in any of your selections here.

9 Aisopou. Psirri. ✆ **210/321-5614**. Main courses 8€–15€ ($10–$20). DC, MC, V. Mon–Fri 6pm–2am; Sat–Sun noon–2am.

Tellis ☆ TRADITIONAL GREEK   It lacks style and decor (to put it mildly) but the hoards of locals could care less with delicious fare in this extraordinary meaterie which serves gigantic portions at budget prices. The grilled lamb chops with oven-roasted lemon potatoes are simply amazing. Salads are good, too.

86 Evripidou, Psirri. ✆ **210/324-2775**. Main courses 4€–10€ ($5.20–$13). No credit cards. Mon–Sat 9am–1am.

GAZI-KERAMEIKOS-THISSIO

VERY EXPENSIVE

Varoulko ☆☆☆ INTERNATIONAL/SEAFOOD   After years in an unlikely location on a Piraeus side street, chef-owner Lefteris Lazarou has moved what many already consider the greater Athens area's finest seafood restaurant into more fitting digs in central Athens with a drop-dead gorgeous view of the Acropolis. I had one of the best meals of my life here—smoked eel; artichokes with fish roe; crayfish with sun-dried tomatoes; monkfish livers with soy sauce, honey, and balsamic vinegar—and the best sea bass and monkfish I have ever eaten. Sweetbreads, goat stew, and tripe soup have joined seafood on the menu.

80 Piraios, Athens. ✆ **210/522-8400**. www.varoulko.gr. Reservations necessary several days in advance. Dinner for 2 from about 120€ ($156); fish priced by the kilo. No credit cards. Mon–Sat about 8pm–midnight. Closed Sun. Metro: Kerameikos.

EXPENSIVE

Thalatta ☆☆ SEAFOOD   This fancy fish restaurant off Pireos Avenue features excellent sea fare (try the impressive selection of shellfish or the salmon in champagne sauce) in a romantic courtyard where the owner Yannis Safos will no doubt visit your table to make his recommendations on the catch of the day. If you're lucky (like I was) you will get the chance to try the exceptional seafood linguini, the sea bass carpaccio plus the best *melitzanosalata* (aubergine paste) I have had in years.

Moments The Best-Kept Secret in Athens

In an obscure location and difficult to find, the taverna I'm about to mention is so off the beaten path it doesn't even have a name, but its prices are so low and its food so exceptional that it is truly Athens's best-kept secret.

When my grandfather was still alive he would often muse about the old days, about how much smaller and friendlier Athens used to be, about how in its zeal to become a modern European capital it had lost its unique flavor. When he told me about this little taverna in Gazi, it must have been 1985 or 1986, only a couple of years after the toxic spewing gasworks had been shut down, turning Gazi and its surrounding areas of hat and silk factories into an urban wasteland. He and his friends would go there during the war for shelter, warm meals, and barrel wine. This was during the beginning of the Nazi occupation and before the famine, though even the Nazis couldn't find it on their nightly patrols despite the many nights with live music. He never went searching for the taverna after the war. I think he doubted it would still be there, so imagine my surprise a few months ago when I came across a site online where people were talking about an obscure little taverna that was hard to find, with no name, close to the popular Mamakas restaurant and the Benaki Annex building on Pireos Avenue in Gazi.

Intrigued, I went searching for it myself. The area is a ghost town during the day (but for how long is anyone's guess given how popular the area is becoming and the Metro stop Kerameikos just a couple of blocks away). Eventually, I finally arrived, finding a taverna specializing in Byzantine cuisine that opens only for dinner. There is no name, no telephone number, no reservations, and credit cards are not accepted. But what you will find is one of the most delicious meals you have ever had. I had a slow-roasted lamb on parchment and *politiki salata* (Constantinople Salad) that floored me. The following night I brought my mother for dinner and for drinks afterward at Mamakas. We paid far more for four drinks than we did for two meals, four appetizers, two salads, and four glasses of wine.

So how do you get there? Begin at Mamakas restaurant on Persephone's Street. Walk down a couple of blocks until you reach the block before the train tracks. Turn left on Dekeleon Street and follow it a couple of blocks to a little triangular square. At the corner (the street is still Dekeleon) is a Turkish cafe. Descend the stairs below the cafe and you'll found this little treasure.

---

5 Vitonos, Gazi. ⓒ **210/346-4202**. Main courses 34€–40€ ($44–$52). Early May to mid-Nov Mon–Sat 8pm–1am. Closed on Sun. Mid-Nov to early May Mon-Sat 8pm–1am; Sun 1–5pm. AE, DC, MC, V. Metro: Kerameikos.

EXPENSIVE/MODERATE

Chez Lucien ✹✹ FRENCH Off pedestrian Apostolou Pavlou and tucked away in one of many of Thissio's charming side streets you will find this very good and very popular French bistro with a small but excellent menu. There are no reservations so be prepared to wait and even share a table if need be. It's definitely worth it.

32 Troon, Thissio. ⓒ **210/346-4236**. Main courses 20€–25€ ($26–$33). No credit cards. Tues–Sat 8:30pm–1am.

Mamakas ✸✸ GREEK If any restaurant can be credited for kick-starting the transformation of Gazi from gritty to urban chic, it is Mamakas. A famous restaurant on the cosmopolitan island of Mykonos since 1997, Mamakas has been irresistible to Athenians since it first opened its doors in 1998. With its modern, delicious twist on old favorites, whitewashed walls, chic clientele and impossibly good-looking staff, Mamacas is still one of the best the ancient city has to offer. Check out the trays of cooked dishes *(magirefta)* and a range of dependable and delicious grills and appetizers (the spicy meatballs or *keftedakia* are a must!). After dinner linger around a little at the bar as it picks up heat after midnight or watch the world go by outside in what is now the hippest place to be in the city.

41 Persophonous, Gazi. ✆ **210/346-4984**. Main courses 14€–30€ ($18–$39). AE, MC, V. Daily 1:30pm–1:30am. Walk all the way down the pedestrianized walkway to the illuminated smokestacks of Technopolis; make a left on Piraeos Ave., cross over onto Persephones St. or Metro: Kerameikos.

Meson el Mirador ✸✸ MEXICAN Finally! After years of pseudo Mexican fare, I finally had a genuine Mexican meal in Athens smack in the middle of Kerameikos, right off the ancient cemetery in a beautifully restored mansion. Top-notch enchiladas, quesadillas, and pork chops with beans, plus a vegetarian menu, excellent sangria, and margaritas blow the would-be competitors out of the water. With the

---

Quick Bites in Syntagma

In general, Syntagma Square is not known for good food, but the area has a number of places to get a snack. **Apollonion Bakery,** 10 Nikis, and **Elleniki Gonia,** 10 Karayioryi Servias, make sandwiches to order and sell croissants, both stuffed and plain. **Ariston** is a small chain of *zaharoplastia* (confectioners) with a branch at the corner of Karayioryi Servias and Voulis (just off Syntagma Sq.); it sells snacks as well as pastries.

For the quintessentially Greek *loukoumades* (round doughnut center–like pastries that are deep-fried, then drenched with honey and topped with powdered sugar and cinnamon), try **Doris,** 30 Praxitelous, a continuation of Lekka, a few blocks from Syntagma Square. If you're still hungry, Doris serves hearty stews and pasta dishes for absurdly low prices Monday through Saturday until 3:30pm. If you're nearer Omonia Square when you feel the need for *loukoumades* or a soothing dish of rice pudding, try **Aigina** ✸, 46 Panepistimiou.

Everest is another chain worth trying; there's one a block north of Kolonaki Square at Tsakalof and Iraklitou. Also in Kolonaki Square, **To Kotopolo** serves succulent grilled chicken to take out or eat in. In the Plaka, **K. Kotsolis Pastry Shop,** 112 Adrianou, serves excellent coffee and sweets; it's an oasis of old-fashioned charm in the midst of souvenir shops. **Oraia Ellada (Beautiful Greece)** ✸✸ a cafe at the Center of Hellenic Tradition, opens onto both 36 Pandrossou and 59 Mitropoleos near the flea market and has a spectacular view of the Acropolis. You can revive yourself here with a cappuccino and pastries.

surroundings, food, and music in this very atmospheric part of town, you can't go wrong. In summer there is a beautiful roof terrace with Acropolis views.

88 Agisilaou, corner Salaminas, Kerameikos. ✆ 210/342-0007. Main courses 20€–30€ ($26–$39). Mon–Sat noon–2am. MC, V. Metro: Thissio/Kerameikos.

Prosopa 😀😀 MEDITERRANEAN   This little restaurant beside the train tracks on the outskirts of Gazi has plenty of atmosphere going for it in this once-forgotten section of the city. Wonderful Mediterranean fare including a wide array of pasta and risotto entrees and some exceptional beef, chicken, and seafood dishes as well make "Faces" a wonderful little place to discover. Leave enough room for the complimentary "trio of death"—cheesecake, chocolate brownie, and banana cream pie.

84 Konstantinoupoleos, Gazi. ✆ 210/341-3433. www.prosopa.gr. Main courses 18€–30€ ($24–$39). Daily 8:30pm–2:30am. No credit cards. Metro: Kerameikos, then walk down to Konstantinoupoleos by the train tracks.

INEXPENSIVE

Filistron 😀😀 GREEK MEZEDEPOLEIO   For me this place can do no wrong. First of all, it's in my favorite Athens neighborhood. Recently restored Thissio is trendy yet picturesque with a plethora of options, pedestrian streets full of excellent cafes and bars. It manages to be both hip and romantic at the same time. Secondly, once on its rooftop terrace with views of the dramatically lit Parthenon against the starry night sky, you won't want to leave. Third, its delicious offerings are (mostly) *mezedes*, which means you can have many different dishes and try as many specialties as you'd like. And it's reasonably priced to boot. You can reserve a table on its roof terrace (a must in good weather, so be sure to do so) and have as many people come and go as you please. I recommend beginning with a glass of wine at dusk and watching the sky turn dark as the lights on the Acropolis come to life. After that, begin sampling the restaurant's many *mezedes*—my favorites are the island pies, the Byzantine salad, and the special grilled potatoes with smoked cheese. If you like all things salty, do as my friend Sophia and order the salted sardines from Spain, which she claims are out of this world.

23 Apostolou Pavlou, Thissio. ✆ 210/346-7554. www.filistron.com. Appetizers 7€–18€ ($9–$23). DC, MC, V. Mon–Sat 8pm–1am. Sun 1:30–5pm.

To Steki Tou Ilia 😀 TRADITIONAL GREEK GRILLHOUSE   On a quiet pedestrian street away from the bustling cafes and bars of lively Thissio with its majestic views of the Acropolis, you can find this gem of a grillhouse (Ilias' hangout). The house specialty its irresistible *paidakia*, chargrilled lamb chops served the old-fashioned way with grilled bread sprinkled with olive oil and oregano.

7 Thessalonikis, Thissio. ✆ 210/342-2407. Main courses 8€–16€ ($10–$21). Mid-June to mid-Sept Tues–Sat 8pm–1am; Sun 1:30–5pm. Closed 2 weeks in Aug. No credit cards. 2nd location at 5 Eptachalkou St., Thisio. ✆ 210/345-8052.

SYNTAGMA
EXPENSIVE

Aegli 😀😀 INTERNATIONAL   For years, the bistro in the Zappeion Gardens was a popular meeting spot; when it closed in the 1970s, it was sorely missed. Now it's back, along with a cinema, a hip and highly recommended outdoor bar/club, and a fine restaurant. Once more, chic Athenian families head here, to the cool of the Zappeion Gardens, for the frequently changing menu. Some of the specialties include foie gras, oysters, tenderloin with ginger and coffee sauce, profiteroles, fresh sorbets, strawberry soup, and delicious yogurt crème brûlée. Tables indoors or outdoors by the trees offer places to relax with coffee. In the evening, take in a movie at the open-air cinema here before dinner, or have a drink and a snack at one of the nearby cafes. In short, this is a wonderful spot to while away an afternoon or evening—and a definite destination for a special occasion.

Zappeion Gardens (adjacent to the National Gardens fronting Vas. Amalias Blvd.). © **210/336-9363**. Reservations recommended. Main courses 38€–44€ ($49–$57). No credit cards. Daily 10am–midnight. Sometimes closed in Aug.

MODERATE

Furin Kazan ⊛ JAPANESE   Unlike the super-expensive Japanese restaurants in nearby Kolonaki, Furin Kazan is reasonably priced, delicious, and swarming with a mostly Japanese clientele—a sure stamp of approval. Try the noodle and rice dishes, but it's the sushi and sashimi it's best known for.

2 Appolonos, Synatgma. © **210/322-9170**. Main courses 6.50€–24€ ($9–$31). MC, V. Mon–Sat 11:30am–11pm.

Noodle Bar ⊛ ASIAN   When you're searching for something other than Greek fare, this cheap and cheerful place is ideal for a quick and tasty lunch featuring every noodle dish you can think of and a wide and satisfying selection of Asian soups and spring rolls.

11 Apollonos, Syntagma. © **210/331-8585**. Main courses 10€–21€ ($13–$27). No credit cards. Mon–Sat 11am–midnight; Sun 5pm–midnight.

INEXPENSIVE

Neon ⊛ *Value* GREEK/INTERNATIONAL   If you're tired of practicing your restaurant Greek, the Neon restaurants are good places to eat as they are mostly self-service. You'll find lots of tourists here, as well as Athenians in a rush to get a bite, and a fair number of elderly Greeks who come here for a bit of companionship. This centrally located member of the chain is very convenient, although not as pleasant as the original on Omonia Square. There is also a handy Neon a block north of Kolonaki Square at Tsakalof and Iraklitou. You're sure to find something to your taste at any of the branches—maybe a Mexican omelet, spaghetti Bolognese, selections from the salad bar, or sweets ranging from Black Forest cake to tiramisu.

Mitropoleos 3 (on the southwest corner of Syntagma Sq.). © **210/322-8155**. Snacks 5€–8€ ($6.50–$10); sandwiches 5€–10€ ($6.50–$13); main courses 5€–15€ ($6.50–$20). No credit cards. Daily 9am–midnight.

KOLONAKI
MODERATE

Filipou ⊛ TRADITIONAL GREEK   This longtime Athenian favorite almost never disappoints. The traditional dishes such as stuffed cabbage, stuffed vine leaves, vegetable stews, and fresh salads are consistently good. In the heart of Kolonaki, near the fashionable St. George Lykabettus Hotel, this is a place to head when you want good *spitiko* (home cooking) in the company of the Greeks and resident expatriates who prize the food.

19 Xenokratous. © **210/721-6390**. Main courses 6€–20€ ($7.80–$26). No credit cards. Mon–Fri 8:30pm–midnight; Sat lunch 1–5pm. Closed Sun. From Kolonaki Sq., take Patriarch Ioakim to Ploutarchou, turn left on Ploutarchou, and then turn right onto Xenokratous.

Rhodia ⊛ TRADITIONAL GREEK   This respected taverna is located in a handsome old Kolonaki house. In good weather, tables are set up in its small garden—although the interior, with its tile floor and old prints, is equally charming. The

Rhodia is a favorite of visiting archaeologists from the nearby British and American Schools of Classical Studies, as well as of Kolonaki residents. It may not sound like just what you've always hoped to have for dinner, but the octopus in mustard sauce is terrific, as are the veal and dolmades (stuffed grape leaves) in egg-lemon sauce. The house wine is excellent, as is the halva, which manages to be both creamy and crunchy.

44 Aristipou. © 210/722-9883. Main courses 8€–18€ ($10–$23). No credit cards. Mon–Sat 8pm–2am. From Kolonaki Sq., take Patriarkou Ioakim uphill to Loukianou; turn left on Loukianou, climb steeply uphill to Aristipou, and turn right.

To Kafeneio ★★ GREEK/INTERNATIONAL This is hardly a typical *kafeneio* (coffee shop/cafe). If you relax, you can easily run up a tab of 50€ ($65) for lunch or dinner for two, but you can also eat more modestly, yet equally elegantly. If you have something light, like the artichokes *a la polita,* leeks in crème fraîche, or onion pie (one, not all three!), washed down with draft beer or the house wine, you can finish with profiteroles and not put too big a dent in your budget. I've always found this an especially congenial spot when I'm eating alone (perhaps because I love people-watching and profiteroles).

26 Loukianou. © 210/722-9056. Reservations recommended. Main courses 8€–25€ ($10–$33). No credit cards. Mon–Sat 11am–midnight or later. Closed Sun and most of Aug. From Kolonaki Sq., follow Patriarkou Ioakim several blocks uphill to Loukianou, and turn right.

To Ouzadiko ★★ GREEK/MEZEDES This ouzo bar offers at least 40 kinds of ouzo and as many *mezedes,* including fluffy *keftedes* (meatballs) that make all others taste leaden. To Ouzadiko is very popular with Athenians young and old who come to see and be seen while having a snack or a full meal, often after concerts and plays. A serious foodie friend of mine comes here especially for the wide variety of *horta* (greens), which she says are the best she's ever tasted. If you see someone at a nearby table eating something you want and aren't sure what it is, ask your waiter and it will appear for you—sometimes after a bit of a wait, as the staff here is often seriously overworked.

25–29 Karneadou (in the Lemos International Shopping Center). © 210/729-5484. Reservations recommended. Most *mezedes* and main courses 8€–20€ ($10–$26). No credit cards. Tues–Sat 1pm–12:30am. Closed Aug. From Kolonaki Sq. take Kapsali across Irodotou into Karneadou. The Lemos Center is the mini-skyscraper on your left.

To Prytaneion ★ GREEK/INTERNATIONAL The trendy bare stone walls here are decorated with movie posters and illuminated by baby spotlights. Waiters with cellphones serve customers with cellphones tempting plates of some of Athens's most expensive and eclectic *mezedes,* including beef carpaccio, smoked salmon, bruschetta, and shrimp in fresh cream, as well as grilled veggies and that international favorite, the hamburger. This place is so chic that it's a pleasant surprise to learn that it functioned as a neighborhood hangout during the earthquake of 1999 and during the snow storm that shut down Athens in 2001.

7 Milioni. © 01/364-3353. Prytaniou@otenet.gr. Reservations recommended. *Mezedes* and snacks 8€–30€ ($10–$39). No credit cards. Mon–Sat 10am–3am. From Kolonaki Sq., head downhill a block or 2 until you hit Milioni on your right. To Prytaneion is on your left.

INEXPENSIVE

Neon GREEK/INTERNATIONAL The Kolonaki Neon serves the same food as the Syntagma and Omonia branches, but the reasonable prices are especially welcome in this pricey neighborhood. Tsakalof is a shady pedestrian arcade, and the Neon has tables inside and outdoors.

6 Tsakalof, Kolonaki Sq. (C) **210/364-6873.** Snacks 5€–8€ ($6.50–$10); sandwiches 5€–10€ ($6.50–$13); main courses 5€–15€ ($6.50–$20). No credit cards. Daily 9am–midnight.

OMONIA SQUARE, METAXOURGEIO & UNIVERSITY AREA (NEAR EXARCHIA SQUARE/ARCHAEOLOGICAL MUSEUM)

EXPENSIVE

El Bandoneon 🎭🎭 ARGENTINE   In a beautiful theatrical space, this fine Argentine restaurant with its excellent meat selection, is dominated by a large central dance floor where professional tango dancers spin to tango rhythms and offer the diners free lessons. Many well-known Argentine singers and dancers often perform here. Lots of fun, great food, and an exceptional bar. An absolute must!

7 Virginias Benaki, Metaxourgeio. (C) **210/522-4346.** Main courses 40€–45€ ($52–$59). AE, DC, MC, V. Wed–Sat 8pm–1:30am; Sun 8pm–2am (operates only as a bar and offers tango lessons). Metro: Metaxourgeio.

MODERATE/EXPENSIVE

Archaion Gefsis (Ancient Flavors) 🎭🎭 ANCIENT GREEK CUISINE   A little on the kitsch side (columns, torches, and waitresses in togas) but a brilliant idea nonetheless. With recipes from ancient Greece (recorded by the poet Archestratos) this is your one chance to dine like the ancients did. Offerings include cuttlefish in ink with pine nuts, wild-boar cutlets, goat leg with mashed vegetables, and pork with prunes and thyme, among other such delicious fare. Just remember: You may use a spoon and a knife but no fork(!)—ancient Greeks did not use them. Equally adored by locals, foodies, and tourists alike, evenings here make for a unique dining experience.

22 Kodratou, Plateia Karaiskaki, Metaxourgeio. (C) **210/523-9661.** Main courses 22€–35€ ($29–$46). AE, DC, MC, V. Metro: Metaxourgeio.

Athinaikon 🎭🎭 GREEK/OUZERIE   Not many tourists come to this favorite haunt of lawyers and businesspeople who work in the Omonia Square area. You can stick to appetizers (technically, this *is* an ouzeri) or have a full meal. Appetizers include delicious *loukanika* (sausages) and *keftedes* (meatballs); pass up the more expensive grilled shrimp and the seafood paella. The adventurous can try *ameletita* (lamb's testicles). Whatever you have, you'll enjoy taking in the old photos on the walls, the handsome tiled floor, the marble-topped tables and bentwood chairs, and the regular customers, who combine serious eating with animated conversation.

2 Themistokleous. (C) **210/383-8485.** Appetizers and main courses 5€–16€ ($6.50–$21). No credit cards. Mon–Sat 11am–midnight. Closed Sun and usually in Aug. From Omonia Sq., take Panepistimou a block to Themistokleous; the Athinaikon is almost immediately on your right.

Ideal 🎭 TRADITIONAL GREEK   The oldest restaurant in the heart of Athens, today's Ideal has an Art Deco decor and lots of old favorites, from egg-lemon soup to stuffed peppers, from pork with celery to lamb with spinach. Ideal is a favorite of businesspeople, and the service is usually brisk, especially at lunchtime. Not the place for a quiet or romantic rendezvous, but definitely the place for good, hearty Greek cooking.

46 Panepistimiou. (C) **210/330-3000.** Reservations recommended. Main courses 8€–15€ ($10–$20). AE, DC, MC, V. Mon–Sat noon–midnight. From Omonia or Syntagma, take Panepistimiou (the Ideal is just outside Omonia Sq.).

INEXPENSIVE

Neon *Value* GREEK/INTERNATIONAL   In a handsome 1920s building, the Neon serves up cafeteria-style food, including cooked-to-order pasta, omelets, and grills, as well as salads and sweets. Equally good for a meal or a snack, the Omonia Neon proves that fast food doesn't have to be junk food. Prices here are a bit lower than those at the Syntagma and Kolonaki branches.

1 Dorou, Omonia Sq. © 210/522-9939. Snacks 5€–8€ ($6.50–$10); sandwiches 5€–10€; ($6.50–$13); main courses 5€–15€ ($6.50–$20). No credit cards. Daily 9am–midnight.

Taygetos ⟨Ⓐ Value⟩ GREEK/SOUVLAKI   This is a great place to stop for a quick meal on your way to or from the National Archaeological Museum. The service is swift and the souvlaki and fried potatoes are excellent, as are the chicken and the grilled lamb. The menu sometimes features delicious *kokoretsi* (grilled entrails). The Ellinikon Restaurant next door is also a good value.

4 Satovriandou. © 210/523-5352. Grilled lamb and chicken priced by the kilo. No credit cards. Mon–Sat 9am–1am. From Omonia Sq. take Patision toward National Museum; Satovriandou is the 3rd major turn on your left.

KOUKAKI & MAKRIGIANNI (NEAR THE ACROPOLIS)

See the "Accommodations & Dining South of the Acropolis" map on p. 161 to locate these restaurants.

MODERATE

Strofi Tavern ⟨Ⓐ⟩ GREEK   The Strofi serves standard Greek taverna fare (the *mezedes* and lamb and goat dishes are especially good here), but the view of the Acropolis is so terrific that everything seems to taste particularly good. Keep this place in mind if you're staying south of the Acropolis, an area not packed with restaurants. Strofi is popular with the after-theater crowd that pours out of the nearby Herodes Atticus Theater during the Athens Festival.

25 Rovertou Galli, Makriyianni. © 210/921-4130. Reservations recommended. Main courses 8€–20€ ($10–$26). DC, MC, V. Mon–Sat 8pm–2am. Located 2 blocks south of Acropolis.

HERE & THERE—WORTH THE JOURNEY

48 The Restaurant ⟨ⒶⒶⒶ⟩ GREEK/INTERNATIONAL   One of the most popular places in the city, with a clientele of the famous and infamous. This former art gallery has high ceilings and a big industrial space with fantastic design and lighting. The food here is exceptional—inspired dishes use traditional Greek ingredients in new ways. The menu changes daily according to the find of the day from the local markets. The wine list alone offers more than 500 labels from the owner's private vault in Paris.

Armatolon and 48 Klefton, Ambelokipi. © 210/641-1082. Main courses 26€–47€ ($33–$61). Mon–Sat 9pm–1am. AE, DC, MC, V.

Ithaki ⟨ⒶⒶ⟩ GREEK SEAFOOD   Exceptional seafood in an equally exceptional location on the coast, with tremendous sea vistas and an immaculate setting. With three levels of glass and wood, the restaurant opens onto a landscaped terrace set on a cliff. Between the views and the food, this is an ideal setting for an ultra-romantic dinner—definitely worth the 25km (15-mile) ride to the coast.

28 Apollonos, Voulaigmeni. © 210/896-3747. Main courses 50€–60€ ($65–$78). AE, MC, V. Daily 1pm–1:30am. Tram to Glyfada, then taxi from the square.

Kalliste ⟨ⒶⒶ⟩ ELEGANT GREEK   In a beautifully restored 19th-century house with polished wood floors and ornamental plaster ceilings, Kalliste manages to be both cozy and elegant. The constantly changing menu usually includes traditional dishes with a distinctive flair, such as lentil soup with pomegranate, and chicken with hazelnuts and celery purée. Even that old standby, crème caramel, is enlivened by the addition of rose liqueur. It would be difficult to improve on this lovely refuge well away from the bustle of Athens.

137 Asklepiou, off Akadimias above the University of Athens. © 210/645-3179. Reservations recommended. Main courses 15€–25€ ($20–$33). No credit cards. Mon–Sat about noon–2pm and 8pm–midnight.

Kostoyiannis ✶✶ TRADITIONAL GREEK   Kostoyiannis has been doing every-thing right since the 1950s, serving a wide range of fresh seafood, grills, sweetbreads, and their signature *stifados* (rabbit or veal stews). Arriving here is a joy, as you walk past a display of what can be cooked to perfection for you. Inside the bustling restau-rant, contented diners tuck into their choices. This is one of the nicest places in town to spend a leisurely evening watching more and more people arrive as concerts and theater performances let out across Athens.

37 Zaimi, Pedion Areos, behind the National Archaeological Museum. © 210/822-0624. Reservations recom-mended. Main courses 15€–25€ ($20–$33); fish and shellfish by the kilo. No credit cards. Mon–Sat 8pm–midnight. Closed Sun and late July to Aug.

Milos ✶✶✶ SEAFOOD   After two successful locations in Montreal and New York, Milos arrives at its birthplace and is better than ever. Housed in the ground floor of the Hilton hotel, this is an absolute must for any seafood lover. The main draw here is the freshness of the ingredients supplied from all over the country, sent directly to the restaurant via airplane from the fishing boats. The prices are a bit high but it is truly worth it.

Athens Hilton, 46 Vas Sofias, Ilissia. © 210/724-4400. Main courses 40€–85€ ($52–$111). AE, DC, MC, V. Daily noon–4:30pm; 7:30pm–midnight.

The Park ✶✶ ELEGANT GREEK   The most remarkable thing about this remark-able place is that it has managed to remain a secret from tourists for so long. Tucked inside the Eleftherias Park, adjacent to the Athens Music/Concert Hall, The Park restaurant, frequented only by Athenians in the know, is one of the city's more charm-ing places. During the day it functions as a lovely cafe set among the shady plane trees. At night it evolves into a romantic restaurant (with an always exceptional menu that changes daily). The adjoining bar/lounge heats up after 10pm with great music and clientele. Either before or after dinner stop by at the Galaxy bar on top of the Hilton hotel (a short walk away)—combined they make the ultimate chic urban experience. For those seeking to continue the night in trendy Athens, venture to **Balthazar** (p. 228), a beautiful mansion with a gorgeous courtyard that gets crowded after 1am—a very brief taxi ride away from either The Park or the Hilton.

Eleftherias Park, Vassiliss Sofias 11521. © 210/722-3784. Main courses 25€–35€ ($33–$53). AE, DC, MC, V. Metro: Megaro Mousikis.

Spondi ✶✶✶ INTERNATIONAL   *Athinorama,* the weekly review of the Athenian scene, has chosen Spondi several years running as the best place in town. The menu features light dishes—the fresh fish, especially the salmon, is superb—as well as dishes that you will find delightful (roast pork with myzithra cheese and a fig-and-yogurt sauce). The setting, a handsome 19th-century town house with a courtyard, is lovely; the wine list, extensive; the service, excellent; and the desserts, divine. You'll probably want to take a cab here that would cost you (from Syntagma Sq.) around 6€ ($7.80) It was voted the best restaurant in Greece for 6 consecutive years (2001–06).

5 Pyrronos, Pangrati. © 210/752-0658. Reservations recommended. Main courses 30€–80€ ($39–$104). No credit cards. Mon–Sat 8pm–1am. Pyrronos runs between Empedokleous and Dikearchou, behind the Olympic Stadium.

Vlassis ★★★ TRADITIONAL GREEK Greeks call this kind of food *paradisiako* (traditional), but paradisiacal is just as good a description. This reasonably priced food is fit for the gods: delicious fluffy vegetable croquettes, a unique eggplant salad, and hauntingly tender lamb in egg-lemon sauce. Vlassis is so popular with Athenians that it doesn't need even a discreet sign to announce its presence—which is in an old mansion around the corner from the American Embassy on hard-to-find Paster. Figure the price of a taxi (no more than 10€/$13) into your meal tab, although you may feel so giddy with delight after eating that you won't mind the half-hour walk back to Syntagma.

8 Paster (off Plateia Mavili), Ampelokipi. ☎ 210/646-3060. Reservations recommended. Main courses 13€–23€ ($17–$30). No credit cards. Mon–Sat 8pm–1am. Closed much of June–Sept. From Syntagma Sq., take Vas. south to Plateia Mavili, and follow D. Tsoustou out of Plateia Mavili to Chatzikosta; Paster is the cul-de-sac on the left after you turn right onto Chatzikosta.

Exploring Athens

by Peter Kerasiotis with Sherry Marker

It's quite likely that you'll arrive in Athens in the late afternoon, groggy and disoriented after a seriously long flight. The ride into town from the airport is unlikely to help your spirits. You'll whiz along an efficient but anonymous highway that could be anywhere, before being fed into Athens's ferocious traffic or you'll be underground in the Metro, itching to get to your hotel just so you can finally take a shower and wash the flight away. Somewhere, you know, not far away, must be the blue Aegean and the lofty Acropolis. But where?

When you get to your hotel, jump in the shower, take a nap, and then set off for an evening stroll through elegant **Syntagma (Constitution) Square** past the House of Parliament. Take a few minutes to explore Syntagma's handsome marble **Metro** station, with its display of finds from the excavations here. Sit on a bench or at one of the cafes and have a cup of coffee or a snack as you take in the city, its citizens, and your surroundings. (Syntagma Sq. has free wireless Internet so you have many reasons to return here and linger during your stay.) If it's too warm out, escape into the shade of the **National Gardens**—it's all too easy to overlook this oasis of calm and cool in the heart of Athens. In 2006 and 2007 more than a thousand new trees (and some 350 rose bushes) were planted in the Gardens after already having been spruced up in 2004 for the Olympics. You'll discover shady benches, a small cafe, the excellent Aigli restaurant in the adjacent, wider and more formal Zappeion Gardens, and lots of opportunities to watch Greek families out for a stroll. Keep an eye out for the newly found and shockingly well-preserved Roman Baths (another important discovery during the Metro's construction), have a seat and linger by the Zappeion's handsome fountain for a while and then head into the **Plaka,** the old neighborhood on the slopes of the Acropolis that has more restaurants, cafes, and souvenir shops than private homes. If you get off the Plaka's main drags, Kidathineon and Adrianou, and follow one of the streets such as Thespidos that runs up the slope of the Acropolis, you'll find yourself in **Anafiotika.** This Plaka district, built in the 19th century by immigrants from the Cycladic island of Anafi, retains much of its old village character. From time to time as you stroll, look up: You're bound to see the Acropolis, perhaps floodlit—the best reminder of why you came. French designer Pierre Bideau has radically and brilliantly altered the lighting of the Acropolis and many other key monuments across the city, so be sure to admire his work.

After you have had your first Greek meal, take a little stroll on the Archaeological Promenade, stop by Thisio (at the grand cafe/bar/restaurant Athinaion Politeia, a grand 19th-c. building) for a glass of wine with an excellent view of the floodlit Acropolis, and slowly head back to your hotel and get a good night's rest so that you'll be ready for your first real day in Athens.

Athens Attractions

Acropolis Archaeological
  Museum **14**
Athens City Museum **17**
Ayios Yioryios **27**
Benaki Museum **23**
Byzantine and Christian
  Museum **26**
Foundation of the Hellenic World
  (Hellenic Cosmos) **1**
Goulandris Museum of
  Cycladic Art **24**
Greek Folk Art Museum **20**
Hadrian's Arch **21**
Ilias LALAoUNIS
  Jewelry Museum **16**
Jewish Museum **19**
Kanellopoulos Museum **11**
Kerameikos Cemetery **2**

Metropolitan Cathedral **7**
Monastiraki Church **6**
Museum of Popular Greek
  Musical Instruments **9**
National Archaeological
  Museum **28**
National Gallery **25**
Numismatic Museum **18**
Odeion of Herodes Atticus **12**
Parthenon **13**
Roman Agora (Forum) **10**
Stoa of Attalos **5**
Stoa of Zeus **4**
Temple of Olympian Zeus **22**
Theater of Dionysos **15**
Theseion **3**
Tower of Winds (Aerides) **8**

1 The Top Attractions

Ask about a discounted ticket if you are a student or a senior. Often these discounts apply only to members of Common Market countries. Also, ask for the handy information brochure available at most sites and museums; ticket sellers do not always hand it over unless reminded.

The Acropolis ✮✮✮   The Acropolis is one of a handful of places in the world that is so well known, you may be anxious when you finally get here. Will it be as beautiful as its photographs? Will it be, ever so slightly, a disappointment? Rest assured: The Acropolis does not disappoint—but it *is* infuriatingly crowded. What you want here is time—time to watch the Parthenon's columns appear first beige, then golden, then rose, then stark white in changing light; time to stand on the Belvedere and take in the view over Athens (and listen to the muted conversations floating up from the Plaka); time to think of all those who have been here before you. *Tip:* There is no reason to head to the Acropolis during the day in summer when the crowds and the heat will take away some of the magic. The best time to visit during the summer is after 5pm—the brilliant light of the late-afternoon hours will only enhance your experience.

When you climb the Acropolis—the heights above the city—you know that you're on your way to see Greece's most famous temple, the **Parthenon.** What you may not know is that people lived on the Acropolis as early as 5,000 B.C. The Acropolis's sheer sides made it a superb natural defense, just the place to avoid enemies and to be able to see invaders coming across the sea or the plains of Attica. And it helped that in antiquity there was a spring here.

In classical times, when Athens's population had grown to around 250,000, people moved down from the Acropolis, which had become the city's most important religious center. The city's **civic and business center**—the **Agora**—and its **cultural center,** with several theaters and concert halls, bracketed the Acropolis. When you peer over the sides of the Acropolis at the houses in the Plaka, and the remains of the

Ancient Agora and the theater of Dionysos, you'll see the layout of the ancient city. Syntagma and Omonia squares, the heart of today's Athens, were well out of the ancient city center.

Even the Acropolis's superb heights couldn't protect it from the Persian assault of 480 B.C., when invaders burned and destroyed most of its monuments. Look for the immense column drums built into the Acropolis's walls. They are from the destroyed Parthenon. When the Athenian statesman Pericles ordered the Acropolis rebuilt, he had these drums built into the walls lest Athenians forget what had happened, and so that they would remember that they had rebuilt what they had lost. Pericles's rebuilding program began about 448 B.C.; the new Parthenon was dedicated 10 years later, but work on other monuments continued for a century.

You'll enter the Acropolis through **Beulé Gate,** built by the Romans and named for the French archaeologist who discovered it in 1852. You'll then pass through the **Propylaia,** the monumental 5th-century-B.C. entrance. It's characteristic of the Roman mania for building that they found it necessary to build an entrance to an entrance!

Just above the Propylaia is the elegant little **Temple of Athena Nike (Athena of Victory);** this beautifully proportioned Ionic temple was built in 424 B.C. and heavily restored in the 1930s. To the left of the Parthenon is the **Erechtheion,** which the Athenians honored as the tomb of Erechtheus, a legendary king of Athens. A hole in the ceiling and floor of the northern porch indicates where Poseidon's trident struck to make a spring gush forth during his contest with Athena to have the city named in his or her honor. Athena countered with an olive tree; the olive tree planted beside the Erechtheion reminds visitors of her victory—as, of course, does Athens's name.

Give yourself time to enjoy the delicate carving on the Erechtheion, and be sure to see the original **Caryatids** in the New Acropolis Museum. The Caryatids presently holding up the porch of the Erechtheion are the casts put there when the originals were moved to prevent further erosion by Athens's acid *nefos* (smog).

The **Parthenon** is dedicated to Athena Parthenos (Athena the Virgin, patron goddess of Athens) and is, of course, the most important religious shrine here. Visitors are not allowed inside, both to protect the monument and to allow restoration work to proceed safely. If you're disappointed, keep in mind that in antiquity only priests and honored visitors were allowed in to see the monumental—about 11m-tall (36-ft.)—statue of Athena designed by the great Phidias, who supervised Pericles's building program. Nothing of the huge gold-and-ivory statue remains, but there's a small Roman copy in the National Archaeological Museum—and horrific renditions on souvenirs ranging from T-shirts to ouzo bottles. Admittedly, the gold-and-ivory statue was not understood; the 2nd-century-A.D. traveler Pausanias, one of the first guidebook writers, recorded that the statue stood "upright in an ankle-length tunic with a head of Medusa carved in ivory on her breast. She has a Victory about 2.5m (8 ft.) high, and a spear in her hand and a shield at her feet, with a snake beside the shield, possibly representing Erechtheus."

Look over the edge of the Acropolis toward the **Temple of Hephaistos** (now called the **Theseion**) in the Ancient Agora, and then at the Parthenon, and notice how much lighter and more graceful the Parthenon appears. Scholars tell us that this is because Ictinus, the Parthenon's architect, was something of a magician of optical illusions. The columns and stairs—the very floor—of the Parthenon all appear straight, because all are minutely curved. Each exterior column is slightly thicker in the middle (a device known as *entasis*), which makes the entire column appear straight. That's why the Parthenon, with 17 columns on each side and eight at each end (creating an exterior colonnade of 46 relatively slender columns), looks so graceful, while the Temple of Hephaistos, with only 6 columns at each end and 13 along each side, seems squat and stolid.

The other reason the Parthenon looks so airy is that it is, quite literally, open to the elements. In 1687, the Venetians, in an attempt to capture the Acropolis from the Turks, blew the Parthenon's entire roof (and much of its interior) to smithereens. A shell fired from nearby Mouseion Hill struck the Parthenon—where the Turks were storing gunpowder and munitions—and caused appalling damage to the building and its sculptures.

A Britisher, Lord Elgin, carted off most of the remaining sculptures to London in the early 19th century. Those surviving sculptures—known as the **Elgin Marbles**— are on display in the British Museum, causing ongoing pain to generations of Greeks, who continue to press for their return. Things heated up again in the summer of 1988, when English historian William St. Clair's book *Lord Elgin and the Marbles* received a fair amount of publicity. According to St. Clair, the British Museum "over-cleaned" the marbles in the 1930s, removing not only the outer patina, but many sculptural details. The museum countered that the damage wasn't that bad—and that the marbles would remain in London.

The Parthenon originally had sculptures on both of its pediments, as well as a frieze running around the entire temple. The frieze was made of alternating **triglyphs** (panels with three incised grooves) and **metopes** (sculptured panels). The east pediment showed scenes from the birth of Athena, while the west pediment showed Athena and Poseidon's contest for possession of Athens. The long frieze showed the battle of the Athenians against the Amazons, scenes from the Trojan War, and struggles of the Olympian gods against giants and centaurs. The message of most of this sculpture was the triumph of knowledge and civilization—that is, Athens—over the forces of darkness and barbarians. An interior frieze showed scenes from the Panathenaic Festival held each August, when citizens paraded through the streets with a new tunic for the statue of Athena. Only a few fragments of these sculptures remain in place, and you will have to decide for yourself whether it's a good or a bad thing that Lord Elgin removed so much before the smog became endemic in Athens and ate away much of what he left here.

If you're lucky enough to visit the Acropolis on a smog-free and sunny day, you'll see the gold and cream tones of the Parthenon's handsome Pentelic marble at their most subtle. It may come as something of a shock to realize that in antiquity, the Parthenon—like most other monuments here—was painted gay colors that have since faded, revealing the natural marble. If the day is a clear one, you'll get a superb view of Athens from the Belvedere at the Acropolis's east end.

Tips Acropolis Renovations

At press time, the monuments of the Acropolis were undergoing extensive renovation. The Temple of Nike had been entirely dismantled for restoration. Scaffolding encased the Proplyaia and the Parthenon. The descriptions later in this chapter will explain what you should see when the renovations are complete. The climb up to the Acropolis is steep; if you don't want to walk, an elevator has been installed and the sacred hill is now wheelchair accessible as well.

Tips **The Archaeological Park** ☞☞☞

One of the great pleasures in Athens is strolling through what's been dubbed the "Archaeological Park." It takes visitors past the most important of the city's ancient monuments. Thanks to the 2004 Olympics, the city laid out walkways stretching from Hadrian's Gate past the Acropolis on Dionissiou Areopagitou to the Ancient Agora, and on to the Kerameikos. Athenians use the walkways for their evening *volta* (stroll); the walkways have transformed much of central Athens from a traffic-ridden horror to a delight.

Almost all of what you see comes from Athens's heyday in the mid–5th century B.C., when Pericles rebuilt what the Persians destroyed. In the following centuries, every invader who came built monuments, most of which were resolutely destroyed by the next wave of invaders. If you had been here a century ago, you would have seen the remains of mosques and churches, plus a Frankish bell tower. The great archaeologist Heinrich Schliemann, discoverer of Troy and excavator of Mycenae, was so offended by the bell tower that he paid to have it torn down.

If you'd like to know more about the Acropolis and its history, as well as the Elgin Marbles controversy, you can check the **Center for Acropolis Studies,** on Makrigianni just southeast of the Acropolis (☎ 210/923-9381; 9am–2:30pm; free admission). The center closes intermittently. It houses artifacts, reconstructions, photographs, drawings, and plaster casts of the Elgin Marbles—and hopes, one day, to house the "Parthenon" marbles (see **The New Acropolis Museum** below).

If you find the Acropolis too crowded, you can usually get a peaceful view of its monuments from one of three nearby hills (all signposted from the Acropolis): the **Hill of the Pnyx,** where the Athenian Assembly met; **Hill of the Areopagus,** where the Athenian Upper House met; and **Hill of Filopappos** (also known as the Hill of the Muses), named after the 2nd-century-A.D. philhellene Filopappos, whose funeral monument tops the hill.

Dionissiou Areopagitou. ☎ 210/321-0219. Admission 12€ ($16) adults. Free Sun. Ticket, valid for 1 week, includes admission to the Acropolis, Acropolis Museum, Ancient Agora, Theater of Dionysos, Karameikos Cemetery, Roman Forum, Tower of the Winds, and Temple of Olympian Zeus. Individual tickets may be bought (6€/$7.80) at the other sites. Acropolis hours are summer daily 8am–7pm; winter daily 8:30am–6pm or as early as 2:30pm. Ticket booth, small post office, and snack bar are located slightly below the Acropolis entrance. From Syntagma Sq., take Amalias into Dionissiou Areopagitou, and follow the marble path up to the Acropolis. Metro: Acropolis.

The New Acropolis Museum As gigantic cranes surrounded the Acropolis during the summer of 2007, what had been thought of as unlikely was finally happening. In post-Olympics Athens change has been everywhere, including the Acropolis. The old Acropolis Museum, first opened in 1876, closed its doors to the public and the cranes were there to carry out the treasures from within the badly lit and inadequate museum that had more treasures in storage than on display. A dream for many was to see this new museum open in time for the 2004 Olympics in order to put even more pressure on the British Museum to return the "Elgin Marbles" under the glare of the international spotlight. For decades the British had claimed Athens didn't have the necessary facilities to properly display the Marbles. When shown the plans of the grand new museum, they even claimed to have a receipt from the Ottoman Turks (who controlled Greece in 1801) and who allowed then British ambassador to Constantinople

Lord Eligin to remove whatever he wanted from the Acropolis—including one Caryatid that was meant to decorate his Scottish mansion! As ridiculous as the receipt argument may be, the New Acropolis Museum failed to open in time for the Games due to legal fighting and important archaeological finds at the site. The excavations unearthed ruins including private houses of the early Christian era (A.D. 400–600), and more than 50,000 portable antiquities, sculptures, lamps, vases, coins, and domestic artifacts.

Three years later, the cranes finally made their way to the Acropolis ready to transfer the priceless treasures to their new 129€-million ($174-million) home, a mere 400 meters (1,312 feet) away. Designed by Swiss-American architect Bernard Tschumi, the new museum promises to be nothing short of spectacular. In a recent book, the architect wrote: "How to make an architectural statement at the foot of one of the most influential buildings of all time; how to design a building on a site already occupied by extensive archaeological excavations and in an earthquake-prone region; and how to design a museum to contain an important collection of classical Greek sculptures and a singular masterpiece, the Parthenon frieze, currently still housed in the British Museum?" With all that in mind, Tschumi designed the 12,078-sq.-m (150,000-sq.-ft.) museum to take full advantage of the ample natural sunlight of the Attica region; he used seismic technology in the museum's foundations to absorb up to 70% of the power of earthquake tremors and even more impressively, designed the internal "cella" to mirror in perfection (accurate to the last millimeter it is said) the orientation of the Parthenon by featuring the same number of columns (this time in stainless steel instead of marble). The ground floor of the museum has been fitted with a series of glazed floor panels through which visitors can see the recently discovered antiquities right beneath their feet. The middle section has been designed as a large trapezoid plate to accommodate the Archaic Collection, permanent galleries, and a restaurant among other things. Visitors will be guided from level to level via a series of elegant, gentle ramps said to mirror the approach to the Acropolis in order to reach the majestic top floor. It will be here, in the upper galleries, that the Parthenon treasures will be displayed.

In contrast to the British Museum's Duveen Galleries the sculptures will be displayed for the first time in strict relation to their original arrangement on the Parthenon, which will be visible though the surrounding windows. Among the painstakingly rearranged sculptures will be stark empty spaces of blank walls and windows; the door cavities will represent the 1687 destruction of the temple by the Venetians, and the vacant walls will be the country's most eloquent appeal yet to London for unification by returning the Marbles to their home.

Dionisiou Aeropagitou. (To open in winter 2008.) Metro: Acropolis.

Tips **The August Full Moon**

For the past few years, 55 ancient sites throughout Greece—including, of course, the Acropolis—were open to the public on the night of the August full moon. The Culture Ministry plans to do this every August—and to stage free concerts at some of the moonlit sites. There is nothing quite like a moonlit stroll by the floodlit Acropolis.

Ancient Agora ✿✿   The Agora was Athens's commercial and civic center. People used these buildings for a wide range of political, educational, philosophical, theatrical, and athletic purposes—which may be why it now seems such a jumble of ancient buildings, inscriptions, and fragments of sculpture. This is a pleasant place to wander, enjoy the views up toward the Acropolis, and take in the herb garden and flowers planted around the amazingly well-preserved 5th-century-B.C. Temple of Hephaistos and Athena (the Theseion).

Find a shady spot by the temple, sit a while, and imagine the Agora teeming with merchants, legislators, and philosophers—but very few women. Women did not regularly go into public places. Athens's best-known philosopher, **Socrates,** often strolled here with his disciples, including **Plato,** in the shade of the Stoa of Zeus Eleutherios. In 399 B.C., Socrates, accused of "introducing strange gods and corrupting youth," was sentenced to death. He drank his cup of hemlock in a prison at the southwest corner of the Agora—where excavators centuries later found small clay cups, just the right size for a fatal drink. **St. Paul** also spoke in the Agora; he irritated many Athenians because he rebuked them as superstitious when he saw an inscription here to the "Unknown God."

The one monument you can't miss in the Ancient Agora is the 2nd-century-B.C. **Stoa of Attalos,** built by King Attalos of Pergamon in Asia Minor, and completely reconstructed by American archaeologists in the 1950s. (You may be grateful that they included an excellent modern restroom there.) The museum on the stoa's ground floor contains finds from 5,000 years of Athenian history, including sculpture and pottery, a voting machine, and a child's potty seat, all labeled in English. The stoa is open Tuesday through Sunday from 8:30am to 2:45pm.

As you leave the stoa, take a moment to look at the charming little 11th-century Byzantine **Church of the Holy Apostles,** also restored by the Americans. The church is almost always closed, but its delicate proportions are a relief after the somewhat heartless—too new and too well restored—facade of the Stoa of Attalos.

Below the Acropolis at the edge of Monastiraki. (Entrance is on Adrianou, near Ayiou Philippou Sq., east of Monastiraki Sq. and on Ayiou Apostoli, the road leading down into Plaka from the Acropolis.) ✆ 210/321-0185. Admission (includes museum) 4€ ($5.20), or free with purchase of 12€ ($16) Acropolis ticket. Agora hours are summer daily 8am–7pm; winter daily 8:30am–6pm, although it may close then as early as 2:30pm. Metro: Monastiraki.

Kerameikos Cemetery ✿   Ancient Athens's most famous cemetery, located just outside the city walls, is a lovely spot. Many handsome monuments from the 4th century B.C. and later still line the Street of the Tombs, which has relatively few visitors. You can sit quietly and imagine **Pericles** putting the final touches on his **Funeral Oration** for the Athenian soldiers killed during the first year of fighting in the Peloponnesian War. Athens, Pericles said, was the "school of Hellas" and a "pattern to others rather than an imitator of any." Offering comfort to the families of the fallen, he urged the widows to remember that the greatest glory belonged to the woman who was "least talked of among men either for good or for bad"—which must have caused a few snickers in the audience, since Pericles's own mistress, Aspasia, was the subject of considerable gossip.

Ancient Greek words very often hide in familiar English words, and that's true of Kerameikos. The name honors the hero Keramos, who was something of a patron saint of potters, giving his name both to the ceramics made here and to the district itself. The Kerameikos was a major crossroads in antiquity, rather like today's Omonia Square, where major roads from outside Athens intersected before continuing into the city. You can see remains of the massive **Dipylon Gate,** where most roads converged, and the **Sacred Gate,** where marchers in the Panathenaic Festival gathered before heading through the Ancient Agora and climbing to the Parthenon. What you can't see are the remains of **Plato's Academy,** which was located in this district but thus far has eluded archaeologists. The well-preserved statue of a *kouros,* found in the Kerameikos in 2000, is now on display in the Kerameikos Museum, along with photographs showing its discovery

The **Oberlaender Museum,** with a collection of finds from the Kerameikos, including terra-cotta figurines, vases, and funerary sculptures, is usually open when the site is. Be sure to see the handsome classical statue of a youth known as the Kerameikos Kouros and the lion and sphinx pieces. You may also want to visit Athens's enormous **First Cemetery,** near Athens Stadium; it has acres of monuments, many as elaborate as anything you'll see at the Kerameikos.

148 Ermou. ✆ **210/346-3553.** Admission 2€ ($2.60), or free with purchase of 12€ ($16) Acropolis ticket. The Kerameikos and the Oberlaender Museum are usually open in summer Tues–Sun 8am–7pm; winter Tues–Sun 8:30am–6pm, although in winter it may close as early as 2:30pm. Walk west from Monastiraki Sq. on Ermou past Thisio Metro station; cemetery is on the right. Metro: Monastiraki or Thisio on line 1 or Kerameikos at line 3.

Roman Agora (Forum) 𝄐   One of the nicest things about the Roman Agora is that if you don't want to inspect it closely, you can take it in from one of the Plaka cafes and restaurants on its periphery.

In addition to building a number of monuments on the Acropolis and in the Ancient Agora, Roman leaders, beginning with Julius Caesar, built their own agora, or forum, as an extension of the Greek agora. Archaeologists want to explore the area between the Greek and Roman agoras; Plaka merchants and fans of the district do not want more digging. At present, the Roman Agora is a pleasant mélange of monuments from different eras, including a mosque built here after the Byzantine Empire was conquered by Mehmet II in 1453.

The Roman Agora's most endearing monument is the octagonal **Tower of the Winds (Aerides),** with its relief sculptures of eight gods of the winds, including Boreas blowing on a shell. Like so many monuments in Athens—the Parthenon itself had a church inside it for centuries—the Tower of the Winds has had a varied history. Built by a 1st-century-B.C. astronomer as a combination sundial and water-powered clock, it became a home for whirling dervishes in the 18th century. When Lord Byron visited Athens, he lodged near the tower, spending much of his time writing lovesick poetry to the beautiful "Maid of Athens."

You can usually find the remains of the Roman latrine near Tower of the Winds by following the sound of giggles to people taking pictures of each other in the seated position. The less-well-preserved remains of the enormous and once-famous **library of Emperor Hadrian** go largely unnoticed. Draw your own conclusions.

Enter from corner of Pelopida and Eolou. Admission 2€ ($2.60) or free with 12€ ($16) Acropolis ticket. Roman Agora (Forum) hours usually summer Tues–Sun 8am–7pm; winter Tues–Sun 8:30am–6pm, although in winter it may close as early as 2:30pm. Metro: Acropolis.

Theater of Dionysos & Odeion (Odeum) of Herodes Atticus 𝄐𝄐   This theater of Dionysos was built in the 4th century B.C. to replace and enlarge the earlier theater in which the plays of the great Athenian dramatists were first performed. The new theater seated some 17,000 spectators in 64 rows of seats, 20 of which survive. Most spectators sat on limestone seats—and probably envied the 67 grandees who got to sit in the front row on thronelike seats of handsome Pentelic marble. The most elegant throne belonged to the priest of Dionysos (god of wine, revels, and theater); carved satyrs and bunches of grapes appropriately ornament the priest's throne.

Herodes Atticus, a wealthy 2nd-century-A.D. philhellene, built the Odeion—also known as the Odeum or Irodio (Music Hall). It is one of an astonishing number of monuments funded by him. If you think it looks suspiciously well preserved, you're right: It was reconstructed in the 19th century.

Although your 2€ ($2.60) entrance ticket for the Theater of Dionysos in theory allows you entrance to the Odeion, this is misleading. The Odeion is open only for performances—when, obviously, you cannot wander around freely. The best ways to see the Odeion are by looking down from the Acropolis or, better yet, by attending one of the performances staged here during the Athens Festival each summer. If you do this, bring a cushion: Marble seats are as hard as you'd expect, and the cushions provided are lousy.

Dionissiou Areopagitou, on the south slope of the Acropolis. ℂ 210/322-4625. Admission 2€ ($2.60) for both monuments; free with purchase of 12€ ($16) Acropolis ticket. Theater of Dionysos: summer Tues–Sun 8am–7pm; winter Tues–Sun 8:30am–6pm, although it may close as early as 2:30pm. Odeion open during performances and sometimes on performance day. Metro: Acropolis.

Temple of Olympian Zeus (Olympieion) ⟨⟨   Hadrian built this massive tem-

ple—or rather, he finished the construction that began in the 6th century B.C. and continued on and off (more off than on) for 700 years. At 108m long and 43m wide (360×143 ft.), the **Olympieion,** also known as **The Kolonnes (The Columns),** was one of the largest temples in the ancient world. The 1,317m-high (56-ft.) Pentelic marble columns that remain standing, as well as the one sprawled on the ground, give a good idea of how impressive this forest of columns must have been—although it may be more appealing as a ruin than it ever was as a contender for the title "mother of all temples." Inside, side by side, were once statues of Zeus and of Hadrian.

At Leoforos Vas. Olgas and Amalias, easily seen from the street. ℂ 210/922-6330. Admission 2€ ($2.60). Summer Tues–Sun 8am–7pm; winter Tues–Sun 8:30am–6pm. In winter it may close as early as 2:30pm. Metro: Syntagma or Acropolis.

Hadrian's Arch ⟨   The Roman emperor Hadrian built a number of monuments in

Athens, including this enormous triumphal arch with its robust, highly ornamental Corinthian columns. Although Hadrian was a philhellene, he didn't hesitate to use his arch to let the Athenians know who was boss: An inscription facing the Acropolis side reads THIS IS ATHENS, THE ANCIENT CITY OF THESEUS. On the other side it states THIS IS THE CITY OF HADRIAN, NOT OF THESEUS. Ironically, much more of ancient Athens is visible today than of Hadrian's Athens, and much of Roman Athens lies unexcavated under modern Athens.

Hadrian's Arch is still a symbolic entrance to Athens: A number of times when demonstrations blocked traffic from the airport into central Athens, taxi drivers told us that they could get us as far as Hadrian's Gate, from which we'd have to walk into town.

On Leoforos Amalias, near Temple of Olympian Zeus, easily seen from the street. Free admission. Summer daily 8am–7pm; winter daily 8:30am–6pm, though it may close as early as 2:30pm. Metro: Syntagma or Acropolis.

THE TOP MUSEUMS

Benaki Museum ⟨⟨   Housed in an elegant neoclassical mansion, the Benaki

Museum was founded by art collector Antoni Benaki in 1931. This stunning private collection of about 20,000 small and large works of art includes treasures from the Neolithic era to the 20th century. The folk art collection (including magnificent costumes and icons) is superb, as are the two entire rooms from 18th-century Northern Greek mansions, ancient Greek bronzes, gold cups, Fayum portraits, and rare early Christian textiles. The new wing that opened in 2003 doubled the exhibition space of the original 20th-century neoclassical town house belonging to the wealthy Benaki family. The new galleries will house special exhibitions. The museum shop is excellent. The cafe on the roof garden offers a spectacular view over Athens, as well as a 25€ ($33) buffet dinner Thursday. This is a very pleasant place to spend several hours—as many lucky Athenians do, as often as possible. After you visit the Benaki, take in its new branch, Benaki Museum of Islamic Art (see box below on Athens's new museums).

1 Koumbari (at Leoforos Vasilissis Sofias, Kolonaki, 5 blocks east of Syntagma Sq.). ☎ 210/367-1000. www.benaki. gr. Admission 6€ ($7.80); free Thurs. Mon, Wed, and Fri–Sat 9am–5pm; Thurs 9am–midnight; Sun 9am–3pm. Closed Tues. Metro: Syntagma or Evangelismos.

Byzantine and Christian Museum ★★
If you love icons (paintings, usually of saints and usually on wood) or want to find out about them, this is the place to go. As its name makes clear, this museum is devoted to the art and history of the Byzantine era (roughly 4th–15th c. A.D.). You'll find selections from Greece's most important collection of icons and religious art, along with sculptures, altars, mosaics, religious vestments, Bibles, and a small-scale reconstruction of an early Christian basilica. The museum originally occupied the beautiful 19th-century Florentine-style villa overlooking the new galleries now used for special exhibits. Allow at least an hour for your visit; two are better if a special exhibit is featured. And three is even better. The small museum shop sells books, CDs of Byzantine music, and icon reproductions.

22 Vasilissis Sofias Ave. ☎ 210/723-1570 or 210/721-1027. Admission 4€ ($5.20). Tues–Sun 9am–3pm (Wed until 9pm). From Syntagma Sq., walk along Queen Sophias about 15 min. Museum is on your right. If you get to the Hilton Hotel, you've gone too far. Metro: Syntagma or Evangelismos.

Greek Folk Art Museum ★★
This endearing small museum showcases dazzling embroideries and costumes from all over the country. Seek out the small room with zany frescoes of gods and heroes done by the eccentric artist Theofilos Hadjimichael, who painted in the early part of the 20th century. We stop by here every time we're in Athens, always finding something new, always looking forward to our next visit—and always glad we weren't born Greek women 100 years ago, when we would have spent endless hours embroidering, crocheting, and weaving. Much of what is on display was made by young women for their *proikas* (dowries) in the days when a bride was supposed to arrive at the altar with enough embroidered linen, rugs, and blankets to last a lifetime. The museum shop is small but good.

17 Kidathineon, Plaka. ☎ 210/322-9031. Admission 2€ ($2.60). Summer Mon noon–7pm; Tues–Sun 8am–7pm (in winter 8:30am–3pm). Metro: Syntagma or Acropolis.

Museum of Popular Greek Musical Instruments ★★
Photographs show the musicians, while recordings let you listen to the tambourines, Cretan lyres, lutes, pottery drums, and clarinets on display. Not only that, but this museum is steps from the excellent Platanos taverna, so you can alternate the pleasures of food, drink, and music. When we were here, an elderly Greek gentleman listened to some music, transcribed it, stepped out into the courtyard, and played it on his own violin! The shop has a wide selection of CDs and cassettes.

1–3 Diogenous (around the corner from Tower of the Winds). ☎ 210/325-0198. Free admission. Tues and Thurs–Sun 10am–2pm; Wed noon–6pm. Metro: Acropolis or Monastiraki.

National Archaeological Museum 🏛🏛🏛   Renovated and expanded just before the 2004 Olympics, this is the museum to see if you only have time to see one museum when you are in Athens. Considered one of the top 10 museums in the world, its collection of ancient Greek antiquities is unrivaled and stunning even to those of us that have been there quite a few times. The Akrotiri frescoes are in display again (after being damaged in the 1999 earthquake and removed) as are two new items: two ancient treasures that have been returned to Greece by the J. Paul Getty Museum in Los Angeles—a 4th-century B.C. gold wreath and a 6th-century B.C. marble statue of a young woman's torso. In order to appreciate the museum and its many treasures, try to be at the door when it opens, so you can see the exhibits and not the backs of other visitors. Early arrival, except in high summer, should give you at least an hour before most tour groups arrive; alternatively, get here an hour before closing or at lunchtime, when the tour groups may not be as dense. If you can come more than once, your experience here will be a pleasure rather than an endurance contest. *Tip:* Be sure to get the brochure on the collection when you buy your ticket; it has a handy and largely accurate description of the exhibits.

The **Mycenaean Collection** includes gold masks, cups, dishes, and jewelry unearthed from the site of Mycenae by Heinrich Schliemann in 1876. Many of these objects are small, delicate, and very hard to see when the museum is crowded. Don't miss the stunning **burial mask** that Schliemann misnamed the "Mask of Agamemnon." Archaeologists are sure that the mask is not Agamemnon's, but belonged to an earlier, unknown monarch. Also not to be missed are the stunning **Vaphio cups,** showing mighty bulls, unearthed in a tomb at a seemingly insignificant site in the Peloponnese. If little Vaphio could produce these riches, what remains to be found in future excavations?

The museum also has a stunning collection of **Cycladic figurines,** named after the island chain. Although these figurines are among the earliest known Greek sculptures (about 2,000 B.C.), you'll be struck by how modern the idols' faces look compared to

---

The Vases & Frescoes of Santorini

One of the museum's greatest treasures is its vast collection—not surprisingly, the finest in the world—of Greek vases and a wonderful group of frescoes from the Akrotiri site on the island of Santorini (Thira).

Around 1450 B.C., the volcanic island exploded, destroying not only most of the island but also, some say, the Minoan civilization on nearby Crete. Could Santorini's abrupt disappearance have created the myth of Atlantis? Perhaps. Fortunately, these beautiful frescoes survived and were brought to Athens for safekeeping and display.

Just as Athens wants the Elgin Marbles back, the present-day inhabitants of Santorini want their frescoes back, hoping that the crowds who come to see them in Athens will come instead to Santorini. There are as many theories on what these frescoes show as there are tourists in the museum on any given day. Who were the boxing boys? Were there monkeys on Santorini, or does the scene show another land? Are the ships sailing off to war, or returning home? No one knows, but it's impossible to see these lilting frescoes and not envy the people of Akrotiri who looked at such beauty every day.

those wrought by Modigliani. One figure, a musician with a lyre, seems to be concentrating on his music, cheerfully oblivious to his onlookers. If you are fond of these Cycladic sculptures, be sure to take in the superb collection at the N. P. Goulandris Foundation Museum of Cycladic Art (see below).

The museum's staggeringly large sculpture collection invites you to wander, stopping when something catches your fancy. We stop for the **bronzes,** from the tiny jockey to the monumental figure variously identified as Zeus or Poseidon. Much ink has been spilled trying to prove that the god was holding either a thunderbolt (Zeus) or a trident (Poseidon). And who can resist the bronze figures of the handsome young men, perhaps athletes, seemingly about to step forward and sprint through the crowds?

44 Patission. ✆ 210/821-7724. Fax 210/821-3573. Admission 6€ ($7.80) or 12€ ($16) with admission to the Acropolis. Mon 12:30–5pm; Tues–Fri 8am–5pm; Sat–Sun and holidays 8:30am–3pm. (Sometimes open to 7pm, but you can't count on this.) The museum is ½ mile (10 min. on foot) north of Omonia Sq. on the road named Leoforos 28 Octobriou, but usually called Patission. Metro: Omonia or Biktoria.

N. P. Goulandris Foundation Museum of Cycladic Art 🏛️🏛️   Come here to see the largest collection of Modigliani-like Cycladic art outside the National Archaeological Museum. This handsome museum—the astonishing collection of Nicolas and Aikaterini Goulandris—opened its doors in 1986 and displays more than 200 stone and pottery vessels and figurines from the 3rd millennium B.C. This museum is as satisfying as the National Museum is overwhelming. It helps that the Goulandris does not get the same huge crowds, and it also helps that the galleries here are small and well lit, with labels throughout in Greek and English. The collection of Greek vases is small and exquisite—the ideal place to find out if you prefer black or red figure vases. The museum's elegant little shop has a wide selection of books on ancient art, as well as reproductions of items from the collection, including a pert Cycladic pig.

When you've seen all you want to (and have perhaps refreshed yourself at the basement snack bar), walk through the courtyard into the museum's newest acquisition, the elegant 19th-century **Stathatos Mansion.** The mansion, with some of its original furnishings, provides a glimpse of how wealthy Athenians lived a hundred years ago.

4 Neophytou Douka. ✆ 210/722-8321. www.cycladic-m.gr. Admission 4€ ($5.20). Mon and Wed–Fri 10am–4pm; Sat 10am–3pm. Metro: Syntagma.

2 More Museums & Galleries

MORE MUSEUMS

The Athens City Museum   Modern Greece's first king, Otto, and his bride, Amalia, lived in this restored 19th-century Athenian town house while a more spacious royal palace (now the Parliament) was built. Poor Otto (a Bavarian princelet) attempted to ingratiate himself with his Greek subjects by wearing the traditional *foustanella* (short pleated skirt); most thought him dotty. He and Amalia were sent packing in 1862 and Greece imported a new king, George I, from Denmark.

The museum's wonderful collection of watercolors of 19th-century Athens includes works by English painter—and author of *The Owl and the Pussy-Cat*—Edward Lear. Amalia's piano is still here, along with portraits of the royal couple. A mini–throne room shows where the royal couple received important visitors, and a model shows in detail the small town of Athens of 1842. Special exhibits, usually small and very well done, focus on aspects of 19th- or 20th-century Athens.

7 Paparigopoulou (Klathmonos Sq., off Stadiou). ✆ 210/323-0168. Fax 210/322-0765. www.athenscitymuseum.gr. Admission 2€ ($2.60). Mon, Wed, and Fri–Sat 9am–1:30pm. Possible Sun openings. Metro: Syntagma.

Foundation of the Hellenic World 🎨🎨 *Kids*   Also known as the Hellenic Cosmos, this high-tech museum should spark kids' interest in history, with its interactive displays and virtual tours of Greece that allow visitors to call up and "see" moments in Greek history from ancient to modern times. Housed in a former factory, it also offers an Internet cafe and museum shop. Call ahead to make sure an English-speaking guide will be on duty. The museum frequently hosts visiting school groups. The ribbed dome—a hi-fi reinterpretation of a Bronze Age beehive tomb—has a 3-D and virtual reality exploration of the Ancient Agora (among other things) that at 10€ ($13) for adults and 5€ ($6.50) for children might be a little pricey but it is worth every penny. The center is set to keep expanding with new attractions every year such as the creation of a lake that visitors can paddle through and a train ride through Ancient Greece. A very ambitious project in a neighborhood that continues to impress with its ongoing transformation.

254 Pireos, Tavros (near Kallithea Metro station). 🎵 **210/483-5300.** www.fhw.gr. Free admission. Hours in flux. Check before visiting. Metro: Kallithea.

Ilias LALAoUNIS Jewelry Museum 🎨   The 3,000 pieces of jewelry on display here are so spectacular that even those with no special interest in baubles will enjoy this glitzy new museum, founded by one of Greece's most successful jewelry designers. The first floor contains a boutique and small workshop. The second and third floors display pieces honoring ancient, Byzantine, and Cycladic designs, as well as plants, animals, and insects. The shop carries copies of some of the displays, and jewelers in the museum's workshop take orders, in case you want your own gold necklace inspired by insect vertebrae.

12 Kalisperi (at Karyatidon). 🎵 **210/922-1044.** Fax 210/923-7358. www.lalaounis-jewelrymuseum.gr. Admission 4€ ($5.20). Mon and Thurs–Sat 9am–4pm; Wed 9am–9pm (free after 3pm); Sun 10am–4pm. Walk 1 block south of the Acropolis between Theater of Dionysos and Odeion of Herodes Atticus. Metro: Acropolis.

Jewish Museum 🎨🎨   Greece's Jewish community, a strong presence throughout the country and a dominant force in Thessaloniki, was essentially obliterated in the Holocaust. Heart-rending exhibits here include the wedding photograph of Yosef Levy and Dona Habif, who married in April 1944 and a month later were sent to Auschwitz, where they were killed. Articles of daily life and religious ceremony include children's toys and special Passover china. Perhaps the most impressive exhibit is the handsome reconstruction of the Patras synagogue. Most exhibits have English labels. If you contact museum curator Zanet Battinou in advance of your visit, she will try to have a staff member take you through the collection. The small shop carries books and museum reproductions, including lovely note cards reproducing manuscripts and prints.

39 Nikis (on the left side of Nikis as you walk away from Syntagma Sq.). 🎵 **210/322-5582.** Fax 210/323-1577. www.jewishmuseum.gr. Admission 3€ ($3.90). Mon–Fri 9am–2:30pm; Sun 10am–2pm. Metro: Syntagma.

Kanellopoulos Museum   The Kanellopoulos, in a former private home with a wonderful position high on the slopes of the Acropolis, is another nice place to visit when you've had your fill of big museums. This private collection highlights superb red and black figure vases, stunning Byzantine and post-Byzantine icons, and even a few Mycenaean pottery baby bottles. The house itself, with some fine painted ceilings, is a delight.

Theorias and Panos, Plaka. 🎵 **210/321-2313.** Admission 2€ ($2.60). Tues–Sun 8:30am–3pm.

Athens's New Museums
In the last few years, a number of new and quite wonderful museums have opened in Athens. The most impressive is **Benaki Museum of Islamic Art.** The stunning collection, housed in a 19th-century town house, displays Islamic art (ceramics, carpets, woodcarvings, and other objects, plus two excellent reconstructed living rooms from the Ottoman times) that date from the 14th century to the present. Labels are in Greek and English. (At Agio Asomaton and Dipylou, Psirri; ℭ 210/367-1000; www.benaki.gr; admission 6€/$7.80; Mon, Wed, and Fri 9am–5pm, Sat 9am–midnight, Thurs and Sun 9am–3pm; Metro: Monastiraki.) A block away, **The Museum of Traditional Pottery** has a wide-ranging display of traditional and contemporary Greek pottery, labeled in Greek and English. (At 4–6 Melidoni, Kerameikos; ℭ 210/331-8491; Mon, Thurs, and Fri 9am–3pm, Wed 9am–8pm, Sat 10am–3pm, Sun 10am–4pm, Tues 9am–3pm; small cafe.) In nearby Plaka, **Frissiras Museum** has innovative and excellent special exhibits as well as a permanent collection of 20th-century and later European art, with labels in English. (At 3–7 Moni Asteriou; ℭ 210/323-4678; admission 6€/$7.80; Wed–Thurs 11am–7pm, Fri–Sun 11am–5pm; small cafe; Metro: Akropolis.) **Pierides Museum of Ancient Cypriot Art** does just what it says: it records the art—and politics—of Cyprus. (At 34–35 Kastorias, Votanikos; ℭ 210/348-0000; www.athinais.com.gr; free admission; daily 10am–9pm.)

National Gallery   The core collection here is small, and of that, little is on display. Still, you'll find it worthwhile if there's a special exhibit: The El Greco exhibit in 1999 and 2000 was a blockbuster.

50 Vasileos Konstantinou. ℭ 210/723-5857. Admission 6€ ($7.80). Mon and Wed–Sat 9am–3pm; Sun 10am–2pm. Sometimes open Mon and Wed 6–9pm during special exhibits. Metro: Evangelismos.

Numismatic Museum   Many Greek coins were works of art. You can see examples attractively displayed in the magnificent 19th-century town house of the great archaeologist Heinrich Schliemann. Until this museum opened in 1999, visitors could only imagine the decor behind the ornate arcaded facade. Lest anyone forget that he had discovered Troy, Schliemann emblazoned the inscription *Iliou Melathron* (Palace of Troy) across the front of his town house. The interior is equally impressive, as are the more than 60,000 ancient bronze, silver, and gold coins on view (many displayed with helpful magnifying lenses).

12 Panepistimiou. ℭ 210/364-3774. Admission 3€ ($3.90); free Sun. Tues–Sun 8am–2:30pm. Metro: Syntagma.

GALLERIES
One of the great pleasures of visiting Athens is browsing in its small art galleries, getting a sense of the contemporary Greek art scene, and possibly buying something to take home. Stop in at an opening, if you see a notice—most are free to the public. For listings, pick up complimentary copies of the quarterlies *Art and the City* and *The Athens Contemporary Art Map* (both in Greek and English); both are available in hotels and galleries. Here are some galleries to keep an eye out for.

In trendy Psirri, **AD Gallery,** 3 Pallados (ℭ 210/322-8785), focuses on modern and conceptual Greek art. **a.antonopoulou.art,** 20 Aristofanous (ℭ 210/321-4994), is one of the most stunning art spaces in the city concentrating on Greek contemporary artists. **The Breeder,** 6 Eumorfopoulou (℡ **210/331-7527** www.thebreedersystem. com), showcases some of the more interesting up-and-coming artists in solo shows, group shows, and gallery swaps. **Els Hanappe Underground,** 2 Melanthiou (℡ **210/ 325-0364;** http://els.hanappe.com) showcases young artists from Glasgow, London, and Los Angeles. **Epistrofi Gallery,** 6–8 Taki (℡ **210/321-8640;** www.epistrofi.gr), has occasional concerts as well as shows. **Epikentro Gallery,** 10 Armodiou (℡ **210/ 331-2187**), stages frequent exhibits in its improbable location in the Athens Central Market. Not far away is one of the city's best-known galleries, **Rebecca Kamhi Gallery,** 23 Sofokleus (℡ **210/321-0448**). **Bernier/Eliades Gallery,** 11 Eptachalkou, Theseion (℡ **210/341-3935**), stages group exhibitions, as does **Kappatos,** 6 Agias Irenes (℡ **210/321-7931**). Frequent shows are held at **Melina Mercouri Cultural Center,** Iraklidon and 66 Thessalonikis (℡ **210/345-2150**), near the Theseion; and at **Melina Mercouri Foundation,** 9–11 Polygnotou (℡ **210/331-5601**), in Plaka.

The **National Museum of Contemporary Art** is set to open in its new Syngrou-Fix location in 2008 in what appears to be yet another brilliant industrial-to-art conversion. The highway formerly known as the "industrial wasteland highway" (Pireos Ave.) is gaining momentum as one of the city's main culture zones. The stunning **Benaki Museum-Pireos Street Annexe,** 138 Pireos and Andronikou (℡ **210/345-3111;** www.benaki.gr), stages exhibitions as does the huge multipurpose **Technopolis,** 100 Pireos (℡ **210/346-0981;** www.culture.gr), while the **School of Fine Arts** (256 Pireos; ℡ **210/480-1315**) stages exhibitions by new artists as well as retrospectives by top contemporary Greek artists. **Athinais,** 34-36 Kastorias (℡ **210/348-0000;** www.athinais.com.gr), the former silk factory brilliantly restored into a multipurpose arts center, also stages exhibitions and shows.

The fashionable Kolonaki district is chockablock with galleries: **Athens Art Center,** 4 Glyconos, Dexameni (℡ **210/721-3938**); **Photohoros,** 44 Tsakalof (℡ **210/ 321-0448**); and **Medussa,** 7 Xenokratous (℡ **210/724-4552**), are three to look for. **Athens Arts and Technology School** (℡ **210/381-3700**) usually stages shows around town in July and August, when many galleries close or move out of town. The **Medusa Art Gallery,** 7 Xenokratous (℡ **210/724-4552;** www.medusaartgallery.com) features the work of tomorrow's stars today and showcases everything from video to photography, painting, and sculpture. Another gallery open year-round and well worth a visit (in part for its great cafe and shop) is **Deste Foundation for Contemporary Art** ⚡, 8 Omirou, Neo Psychico (℡ **210/672-9460;** www.deste.gr), a 20-minute cab ride from Syntagma. Deste, owned by collector Dakis Joannou, showcases cutting-edge works from the international scene.

3 Ancient Monuments

One small, graceful monument you might easily miss is the 4th-century-B.C. **Choregic Monument of Lysikrates,** on Lysikratous in the Plaka, handily located a few steps from the justly famous and excellent **Daphne's** restaurant (p. 176). This circular monument with Corinthian columns and a domed roof bears an inscription stating that Lysikrates erected it when he won the award in 334 B.C. for the best musical performance with a "chorus of boys." A lovely frieze shows Dionysos busily trying to turn evil pirates into friendly dolphins.

Three hills near the Acropolis deserve at least a respectful glance: **Areopagus, Pnyx,** and **Filopappos. Areopagus** is the bald marble hill across from the entrance to the

Acropolis; it is so slippery, despite its marble steps, that it is never an easy climb, and it is positively treacherous in the rain. This makes it hard to imagine the distinguished Athenians who served on the Council and Court making their way up here to try homicide cases. Still harder to imagine is St. Paul on this slippery perch thundering out criticisms of the Athenians for their superstitions.

From the Areopagus and Acropolis, you can see two nearby wooded hills. The one with the monument visible on its summit is **Filopappos (Hill of the Muses).** The monument is the funeral stele of the Roman consul after whom the hill is named. You can take pleasant walks on the hill's wooded slopes; view a nice Byzantine church, **Ayios Demetrios;** and see **Dora Stratou Theater,** where you can watch folk dances being performed (p. 224). If you climb to the summit (at night, don't try this alone or wander here or on Pnyx hill) and face the Acropolis, you can imagine the wretched moment in 1687 when the Venetian commander Morosini shouted "Fire!"—and cannon shells struck the Parthenon.

Pnyx hill, crowned by the Athens Observatory, is where Athens's citizen assembly met. Pnyx hill, as much as any spot in Athens—which is to say, any place in the world—is the "birthplace of democracy." Here, for the first time in history, every citizen could vote on every matter of common importance. True, citizens did not include women, and there were far more slaves than citizens in Athens—as was the case in most of the world for a very long time after this democracy was born.

4 Historic Buildings

Athens was a small village well into the mid–19th century and did not begin to grow until it became capital of Independent Greece in 1834. This fact is hard to believe when you look at today's traffic-clogged Athens, but the recently restored and expanded **Byzantine and Christian Museum,** at 22 Vas. Sofias, occupies the Renaissance-style villa built by the Duchess of Plaisance as her country retreat in the 1840s. Syntagma Square is home to several other buildings from the same period, including **Parliament House** (the former royal palace); **Grande Bretagne Hotel** (a former mansion); and Schliemann's house, **Iliou Melathron** (see the Numismatic Museum, above). Many neoclassical 19th-century buildings fell in Athens's rapid expansion after World War II, but thankfully a large number of them still survive all over the city from downtown right into Kifissia. Watch for surviving buildings, described below, as you explore central Athens.

In the Plaka, several 19th-century buildings have survived, tucked between the T-shirt shops and restaurants at busy Adrianou (Hadrian) and Kidathineon. One of the oldest surviving pre-revolutionary houses in Athens, **96 Adrianou** dates from the Turkish occupation. The nearby 19th-century **Demotic School** has a distinguished neoclassical facade. On Kidathineon is the house in which **King Ludwig** of Bavaria stayed when he visited Athens in 1835; there's no number on the house, but a small plaque identifies it. Several other former houses date from the same period.

Finally, if you climb through the Plaka to the **Anafiotika district** on the slopes of the Acropolis, you'll find yourself in a delightful neighborhood with many small 19th-century homes. This district is often compared to an island village, and small wonder: Most of the homes were built by stonemasons from the Cycladic island of Anafi, who came to Athens to work on the buildings of the new capital of independent Greece.

Syntagma Square & Plaka

Grande Bretagne **1**
Greek Folk Art Museum **5**
Greek Orthodox Cathedral
(Metropolis) **3**
Hadrian's Gate **7**
Monument of Lysikrates **6**
Panayia Gorgoepikoos **4**
Tomb of the Unknown
Soldier & Parliament **2**

Metro:
Ⓜ Line 1
Ⓜ Line 2
Ⓜ Line 3
Ⓛ Light Rail

5 Churches & Synagogues

As you stroll through Athens, you'll discover scores of charming churches. Many date from the Byzantine era of A.D. 330 to A.D. 1453—although almost nothing survives from the early centuries of that Christian empire. Alas, vandals and thieves have forced many churches to lock their doors, so you may not be able to go inside unless a caretaker is present. If you do go inside, **dress suitably:** Shorts, miniskirts, and sleeveless shirts are not appropriate. You can leave a donation in one of the collection boxes. Below we list a few churches to keep an eye out for.

Athens's 19th-century **Greek Orthodox (Metropolis)** on Mitropoleos gets almost universally bad press: too big, too new, too . . . well, ugly. It also suffers terribly in comparison with the adjacent 12th-century **Little Metropolis,** with the wonderful name **Panayia Gorgoepikoos (Virgin Who Answers Prayers Quickly).** Fragments of classical masonry (including inscriptions), built into the walls of this little church, create a delightful crazy-quilt effect.

The square in front of the cathedral is a great place to people-watch on summer weekends, when weddings often take place nonstop at evening. As one bride leaves the church, the next bride (and her flowers, attendants, and guests) is poised to enter. It's a very Greek assembly line, with limousines pulling up, horns blaring, and everyone having a fantastic time.

Also on Mitropoleos, crouched on the sidewalk below an ugly modern building, is the minuscule chapel of **Ayia Dynamis,** where women who want to become pregnant light candles.

If you like spying (from a respectful distance) on weddings and baptisms, continue on to the 12th-century **Church of Ayia Aikaterini,** in the little square off Frinihou. The church sits well below ground level, an indication of how much Athens has grown over the centuries. You'll notice ancient columns strewn around the courtyard; you may even decide to sit on one to watch the comings and goings.

If you walk from Syntagma to Monastiraki Square, you can take in a few more churches. A few blocks from Syntagma Square, on Skouleniou, the little 11th-century **Church of St. Theodore** is also below street level. On Hrissopileotissis, the small **Church of the Virgin** is a good place to buy incense from street vendors. Check out the flower market at the **Square of St. Irene,** off Eolou. On Monastiraki Square, **Church of the Pantanassa** is all that remains of a convent on this spot. A short walk away on Ermou, 11th-century **Kapnikarea Church** sits right in the middle of the road.

If you're walking along busy Leoforos Vas. Sofias, you may want to rest a bit in the courtyard of the **Church of Ayios Nikolaos.** A few blocks farther along on Gennadius, the 12th-century **Church of the Taxarchi** is set in a small park.

Beth Shalom, the Athens synagogue on Melidoni, stands in what was, before World War II, a vibrant Jewish neighborhood. Across the street from Beth Shalom's marble facade is the old synagogue it replaced. You can get information on synagogue visits and services from the **Jewish Museum,** 39 Nikis (© **210/322-5582**).

6 Parks & Gardens

In addition to the parks and gardens listed here, see "Especially for Kids," below.

The lush **National Gardens,** between Leoforos Amalias and Irodou Attikou, south of Vas. Sofias, was once the Royal Family's palace garden. Now a public park, the area combines a park, gardens, meandering paths, many quaint bridges over ponds and small lakes favored by ducks, swans, and peacocks and a small zoo with shade trees and benches. Thousands of new trees and shrubs were planted here before the summer 2004 Olympics and in 2006 and 2007 more than a thousand new trees were planted. Look for one of the several cafes tucked away in the gardens; you can also picnic here or stop by the elegant **Aigli** cafe/restaurant. The large neoclassical exhibition/reception hall in the adjacent more orderly and wide gardens (the **Zappeion Gardens**) were built by the brothers Zappas and so are known as the **Zappeion.** The National Gardens are open daily from 7am to 10pm. *Note:* At night, it becomes a spot for prostitutes, gay cruising, and pickups, but by daytime it is a wonderful little oasis in the city center.

Mount Likavitos (Lycabettus) dominates the city's northeast. It is a favorite retreat for Athenians, and a great place from which to get a bird's-eye view of the city as it spreads before you all the way to the Saronic Gulf. Even when the smog is bad, sunsets can be spectacular here and the glittering city beckoning you from below is at its most seductive. A small **Chapel of Ayios Yioryios (St. George)** sits at the top. Catch a summer performance at the Likavitos Theater here. You can take the funicular (which leaves every 20 min. in summer) from the top of Ploutarchou (2€/$2.60), or you can walk up from Dexameni Square using the route preferred by young lovers, the energetic, and all too many who abandon kittens, dump garbage, or use drugs.

Pedion tou Areos (Plain of Mars) is Athens's largest park on busy Leoforos Alexandras. Large trees, benches, gardens, and meandering paths all offer escape from the bustling city; a long boulevard lined with statues of the heroes of the Greek War of Independence bisects the park. Near the park and across the busy avenue is the wonderful and little visited **Lofos tou Strefi (Strefis Hill)** where a labyrinth of green paths lead you to the summit with spectacular vistas of the city and the Acropolis all the way to the Saronic Gulf.

In the city center is **Fillopapou Hill** (also known as Hill of the Muses), a wonderful landscaped park with cypresses, pine trees, indigenous flora, joggers, dog-walkers, lovers, and some important archaeological finds. It features the perfect vantage point from which to snap that postcard-perfect picture of the Acropolis. Along the way uphill you will walk by ancient walls, a 16th-century church (Agios Dimitiros-St. Demetrios), and a cave dwelling thought to be Socrates's prison. **The Hill of the Pnyx** (the meeting place of the democratic assembly) also has breathtaking vistas of the Acropolis and beyond. Farther to the west, there is a third hill, **Hill of the Nymphs,** said to be the location of William Shakespeare's Midnight Summer's Dream.

7 Especially for Kids

The **National Gardens** off Syntagma Square have a small **zoo,** several duck ponds, a playground, and lots of room to run around. There's also a **Children's Library** with books in English and some toys and coloring materials. The library is usually open Tuesday through Saturday from 8:30am to 3pm, and is closed in August. The National Gardens are open from sunrise to well after sunset.

Among the many small parks and gardens scattered throughout Athens, the National Gardens are the best for children. That said, if you're staying in Kolonaki, try **Dexamini Square,** which has a small playground and several cafes. (It's below the St. George Lycabettus hotel off Kleomenous.)

The very impressive privately operated **Attica Zoological Park** ��� (© 210/663-4724; atticapark@internet.gr), Spata, is home to more than 2,000 birds from some

Athens's Urban Beaches

A string of popular beaches stretches along the Saronic Gulf from Athens to Cape Sounion; nearly all of them have been awarded the E.U. blue flag for clear waters. The beaches are easily accessible by bus, tram, and taxi. The tram reaches Glyfada, from there you can continue to the farther-away beaches via bus or taxi. *Tip:* To shorten your tram ride from downtown to the coast by 20 minutes, hop on Metro line 1 and get off at Faliro. Across the street is the tram stop, right outside the Peace and Friendship Olympic Stadium Complex. From here you can just hop on the SEF tram line to Glyfada. For beaches farther away from Glyfada, you can take a bus or taxi from Glyfada Square. Long administered by the Greek National Tourism Organization, the beaches are now run by private companies and charge admission, ranging from 4€ to 20€ ($5.20–$26) per person, per day. Entrance rates are always higher on weekends and holidays. Athens's privatized beaches resemble stylish clubs. For the admission price you get a chair, umbrella, changing rooms, showers, and restrooms. Some have water parks, children's play areas, snack bars, lifeguards, beach volleyball and racket-ball areas—a few even have guest rooms in quaint bungalows for those wishing to have a siesta. The first beach off the tram from Syntagma, **Edem,** is quite a good public beach, which means there is no fee even though there is a private beach section within the same beach, managed by the hotel Poseidon across the street and a nice seaside taverna. Edem is Athens's most urban beach but it is clean and free and due to its proximity to downtown very popular with tourists.

Some of the best beaches along the coast are:

Agios Kosmas (second Agios Kosmas tram stop; weekdays: 5€ ($6.50), weekends: 8€/$10). A little difficult to find, but worth it, it's a small, quiet beach, clean and well-managed and perfect if you have little children. **Asteria,** take tram to either the Glyfada stop at "Palio Dimarheio" and walk along the coast or at the last stop in Glyfada on Ioanou Metaxas, walk across Plateia Kritis, cross Leoforos Poseidonos and take a right and walk to the entrance. Weekdays: 7€/($9); weekends: 10€/$13). A scene beach with huge landscaped gardens, a nightclub, several cafes, boutiques and shops, a playground for children, volleyball court, and a plethora of watersports options; this is one happening beach, ideal for upscale families and scenesters. **Voula A,** Thallaseo. (The tram has been extended from Glyfada and stops right outside this beach.) Weekdays: 5€/$6.50) Quiet, pretty, and clean, with a waterslide, ample space, and a snack bar. Next door are two upscale yet reasonably priced and delicious restaurants (one for meat lovers, the other for seafood lovers). This beach is more for families seeking a quiet time, older folk, or for anyone looking to spend the day on a quiet, inexpensive, scene-free, and clean beach. **Voula B** (Tram to Glyfada then bus no. A1, A2, or E1. 5€/$6.50). Palm trees, a spacious beach, a cafe, self-service restaurant, sports facilities and some great bungalows to rent out make Voula B an excellent urban beach. **Astir Beach** (Tram to Glyfada then bus no. 114 or 116). This, the "sceniest" beach of all has a 15€ ($20) entrance fee on weekdays (weekends vary). Nestled in a sheltered bay, the beach is clean and pleasant with many amenities (shops, cafe, restaurant, and sport facilities) and even ruins—a Temple to Apollo. **Attica Vouliagmeni Beach** (Tram to Glyfada then bus no. 114 or 116; 5€/$6.50). Set on an enormous stretch of sand on a beautiful coastline with playgrounds, tennis courts, basketball courts, all the usual beach amenities and a beautiful coastline, this is the best-value beach for your money. You can also swim in the springs at **Lake Vouliagmeni** (open year-round; ☎ 210/896-2239; 7am–7:30pm; admission: 6€/$7.80, children under 5 free). The setting is strikingly beautiful (a huge cave-like rock) where the blue-green mineral water remains the same temperature year-round and is said to have many healing properties. **Varkiza Beach** (Tram to Glyfada then bus no. 116, 125, or 171; ☎ 210/897-2414; 12€/$16). Varkiza Beach is one of the fanciest beaches with pristine waters and a lot of fun for both adults and children with beach bars, a water park, volleyball and tennis courts, and private cabanas. Though the beach gets very busy during the weekends, it can be delightfully quiet during the weekdays. On your way back downtown from the beach, linger around in Glyfada for a while before catching the tram to explore this popular neighborhood. Pedestrian Metaxa runs through central Glyfada alongside the tram line and combined with its side streets offers excellent shopping options, lively cafes, and fine restaurants. Walking down Metaxa, check out Zisimopoulou street, with more upscale cafes than you could ever need, but ideal for a stop to linger at, chill, and take in the scene with a cool drink. Walk down the street and you will reach beautiful Kiprou street. At first glance you will think this street—tree lined and full of handsomely restored old mansions—is strictly residential but you will quickly realize the mansions now house beer gardens and restaurants in their candlelit courtyards and terraces. **Amigos** (52 Kiprou; ☎ 210/898-3167) serves good Mexican food and excellent margaritas but it is **Buffalo Bill's** (14 Kiprou; ☎ 210/894-3128) with its excellent Tex-Mex food (superb chili and T-bone steaks) that is one of the most popular restaurants in the area.

When your time in Glyfada is up, head back to Metaxa to catch the tram. Once again if you're heading back into the city center and want to shave off at least 20 minutes from the ride, hop on the SEF tram, get off at the last stop (Faliro—Peace and Friendship Stadium) and hop on Metro line 1 (Kifissia).

320 species, a butterfly garden, and a small farm. The zoo, which plans to add more exhibits, is open daily from 10am to 7pm and charges 8€ ($10) admission for adults, 4€ ($5.20) for children. The zoo is not far from the new airport at Spata; given the state of most airports in the summer, the zoo might seem an oasis of tranquillity.

The ride up **Mount Likavitos** on the cable-car railway *(teleferique)* is often a hit with kids. It operates every 20 minutes in summer (2€/$2.60). A cafe at the top sells ice cream, and children can let off steam by running around on the paths.

The **Museum of Greek Children's Art** often hosts special activities and workshops (conducted in Greek). If your children might enjoy seeing what Greek kids like to draw, stop by 9 Kodrou, Plaka (© **210/331-2621;** 2€/$2.60; Tues–Sat 10am–2pm, Sun 11am–2pm; closed Aug). This small museum has changing displays of children's art from throughout Greece. The **Children's Museum,** around the corner at 14 Kidathineon, also runs workshops but has no exhibitions. In addition, sometimes **Karaghiozis Puppet Shows** (shadow theater) set up a few doors away at the **Greek Folk Art Museum,** 17 Kidathineon. You don't have to understand Greek to appreciate the slapstick comedy of Karaghiozis. In leafy and aristocratic Kifissia you will find two excellent museums that the entire family will enjoy. At the **Goulandris Museum of Natural History** (13 Levidou, Kifissia; (© **210/801-5870;** www.culture.gr; 5€/ $6.50; Mon–Thurs and Sat 9am–2:30pm, Sun 10:30am–2:30pm; Metro line 1: Kifissia) you will find a flawlessly researched exhibit on Greece's wildlife including mammals, birds, and reptiles. Down the street is the equally impressive **Gaia Center** (Earth Center) 100 Othonos (© **210/801-5870;** 5€/$6.50; Mon–Thurs and Sat 9am–2:30pm, Sun 10:30am–2:30pm). The two museums are affiliated with one another so if you wish to visit them both on the same day you can purchase a ticket (at either museum) that will include access to both for 7€ ($9). The Gaia Center features three floors of interactive video, computer, and tactile displays of our planet, our systems, and how we have slowly ruined what we were given and how to prevent further damage.

The multimedia center **Hellenic Cosmos** is an excellent, ultra-modern living museum that offers interactive exhibits that focus on Greek history and culture through the ages. You can visit ancient Miletus via virtual reality, take a 3-D journey through the Ancient Agora in Ancient Athens, visit ancient cities and civilizations, browse the Web in the Internet cafe, and in the more traditional way, view a collection of Greek costumes. The center was founded in 1998 by the **Foundation for the Hellenic World.** (At 254 Pireos, Tavros; © **210/342-2292** or 210/483-5300; www. fhw.gr; free admission for now; Mon, Tues, and Thurs 9am–6pm, Wed and Fri 11am–9pm, Sat and Sun 11am–3pm; Metro: Kallithea.) The "Dome" is 10€ ($13) for adults and 5€ ($6.50) for children but is worth every penny. The nearest Metro station is a 10-minute walk away, so if you're bringing small children, you might want to take a taxi.

It might surprise some of you to know that Athens has the world's finest, most modern and well-equipped planetarium. The **New Eugenides Digital Planetarium** is a 280-seat ultra-modern auditorium with many shows daily. Call © **210/9469-641** for the latest program schedule. 387 Syngrou Ave. (Bus: 126, B2, 550, and A2.)

Allou Fun Park (Kifissou and Petrou Ralli, Rendi; © **210/425-6999;** www.allou funpark.gr; Mon–Fri 5pm–1am; Sat–Sun 10am–2am; Tram 21 from Omonoia [Kan Kan stop]) is a large amusement park for all ages and a fun way to spend a family evening. Free-fall from a 40m shock tower, ride roller coasters and take in an amazing

view of the city from the large Panorama Ferris wheel. Next
ment park run by the same company especially for younge
Kidom.

Check the English-language daily *Athens News* (www.a
Kathimerini insert in the *International Herald Tribune* for
American **movies.** A couple of hours in an air-conditioned
pass a hot afternoon.

The "Scope" section's "Kids' Corner" in the weekly *Hellenic Times* lists activities of interest to children in Athens, including Girl Scout meetings, hiking excursions, and day camps.

8 Organized Tours

Many independent travelers (ourselves included) turn up their noses at organized tours. Nonetheless, such a tour can be an efficient and easy way to get an overview of an unfamiliar city. We're impressed by the number of people we know who confess that they are very glad they took one of these tours, which helped them get oriented and figure out which sights they wanted to see more thoroughly. Most of the tour guides pass stiff tests to get their licenses.

A new addition in Athens is the **Sightseeing Bus** (© 185; www.oasa.gr; 5€/ $6.50). An initiative of the Athens Urban Transport Organization, the route begins and ends outside the National Archaeological Museum with stops at the Acropolis, Temple of Zeus, Plaka, Syntagma-Parliament, the university, Omonia Square, Kerameikos, Monastiraki, Psirri, Thission, the Benaki Museum, the National Gallery, the Central Market and the Panathenaiko Stadium. The bus (with a tour guide) leaves every half-hour from the museum from 7am to 9pm and takes about 90 minutes if you stay on board during the entire trip. This is a hop-on, hop-off bus so you can get off at any site you choose and catch the next bus to your next destination. Tickets can only be purchased from the bus driver and are valid for 24 hours.

The best-known Athens-based tour groups are **CHAT Tours,** 4 Stadiou (© 210/ 322-3137 or 210/322-3886); and **Key Tours,** 4 Kalliroïs (© 210/923-3166; www. keytours.gr). Each offers half- and full-day tours of the city, "Athens by Night" tours, and day excursions from Athens. Expect to pay about 50€ ($65) for a half-day tour, 80€ ($104) for a full-day tour, and around 100€ ($130) for "Athens by Night" (including dinner and sometimes a folk-dance performance at the Dora Stratou Theater). To take any of these tours, you must book and pay in advance. At that time, you will be told when you will be picked up at your hotel, or where you should meet the tour.

Each company also offers excursions from Athens. A visit to the very popular **Temple of Poseidon at Sounion** costs about 60€ ($78) for a half-day trip, including swimming and a meal. A trip to **Delphi** usually costs about 110€ ($143) for a full day, which often includes stops at the Monastery of Osios Loukas and Arachova village. If you want to spend the night in Delphi (included are hotel, site, and museum admissions, as well as dinner, breakfast, and sometimes lunch), the price ranges from 50€ to 160€ ($65–$208). Rates for excursions to the **Peloponnese,** taking in Corinth, Mycenae, and Epidaurus, are similar to those for Delphi. If your time in Greece is limited, you may find one of these day trips considerably less stressful than renting a car for the day and driving yourself.

Visiting the Olympic Sports Complex

...u have the chance to see a concert or catch a match at the **Athens Olympic Sports Complex (OAKA;** ✆ **210-683-4777;** www.oaka.com.gr; Metro line 1 to Irini), do it. Otherwise, call to organize a tour of Athens's newest landmark. To see this massive complex up close you have to call and arrange to join an organized tour for 3€ ($3.90). If you're traveling alone and want to see the complex and the showcase stadiums e-mail oakapre1@otenet.gr with a request to join another tour. Open daily 8am to 8pm. No admission fee for those who wish to visit without a guided tour.

If you want to hire a private guide, speak to the concierge at your hotel or contact the **Association of Official Guides,** 9a Apollonas (✆ **210/322-9705**). Expect to pay from 100€ ($130) for a 5-hour tour.

For the more adventurous there are two ways of sightseeing that will offer you a unique perspective on the city. The first one is on the ground and the second above.

Pame Volta (Let's go for a Ride), 20 Hadjichristou, Acropolis (✆ **210/922-1578;** www.pamevolta.gr; Wed–Fri 9am–5pm; Sat–Sun 11am–7pm), has taken advantage of post-Olympics pedestrian-friendly Athens and offers bicycles for rent and bicycle tours around the city. A very unique and fun way to explore the city.

Much more expensive but also much more spectacular is the Helicopter Sightseeing Tour of Athens by **Hop In Zinon Tours** (29 Zanni St., Piraeus Athens, 185 36 Greece ✆ 210/428 5500). Seeing Athens from above, especially at night when all the monuments are lit, is an unforgettable (if pricey) experience.

9 Spectator Sports

The Greeks are passionately devoted to soccer and basketball, and betting (legal and nationwide) on sports events is popular. All sports events are listed in the Greek press and sometimes in the English-language daily *Athens News.* The concierge or desk clerk at your hotel should know what's on. The best-known soccer teams are the fierce rivals **Olympiakos** (Piraeus) and **Panathanaikos** (Athens). Greece's World Cup Victory in 2004 brought the entire nation first to its feet and then to a halt for weeklong celebrations.

The Greek national basketball team endeared itself to the nation when it won the European Championship by defeating Russia in 1987. Celebrations went on all night. The championships take place in July or August at different venues in Europe. You may also be able to catch a game between Greek teams in Athens.

If you're in Greece when major international soccer or basketball events take place, you probably will be able to see them on Greek television or CNN. If you're in Greece during Wimbledon and not staying in a hotel with CNN or STAR cable service, you may have to settle for the BBC's live radio coverage.

10 Shopping

THE SHOPPING SCENE

Your hotel room may have a copy of the monthly magazines *Athens Today* or *Now in Athens,* both of which have a shopping section. The **Greek National Tourism**

Organization, at 2 Amerikis, may also give away copies. Keep in mind that most of the restaurants and shops featured in the sections pay for the privilege.

You're in luck shopping in Athens, because much of what tourists want can be found in the central city, bounded by Omonia, Syntagma, and Monastiraki squares. You'll also find most of the shops frequented by Athenians, including a number of large **department stores.**

Monastiraki has a famous **flea market,** which is especially lively on Sunday. Although there's a vast amount of ticky-tacky stuff for sale here, you can uncover real finds, including retro clothes and old copper. Many Athenians furnishing new homes head here to pick up old treasures.

The **Plaka** has pretty much cornered the market on souvenir shops, with T-shirts, reproductions of antiquities (including antique imagery reproduced on obscene playing cards, drink coasters, bottle openers, and more), fishermen's sweaters (increasingly made in the Far East), and jewelry (often not real gold)—enough souvenirs to encircle the globe.

In the Plaka-Monastiraki area, shops worth seeking amid the endlessly repetitive souvenir shops include **Stavros Melissinos,** the Poet-Sandalmaker of Athens, relocated after 50 years on Pandrossou to his new location at 12 Agias Theklas (© **210/ 321-9247**); **Iphanta,** a weaving workshop, 6 Selleu (© **210/322-3628**); **Emanuel Masmanidis' Gold Rose Jewelry Shop,** 85 Pandrossou (© **210/321-5662**); the **Center of Hellenic Tradition,** 59 Mitropoleos and 36 Pandrossou (© **210/321-3023**), which sells arts and crafts; and the **National Welfare Organization,** 6 Ipatias and Apollonos, Plaka (© **210/325-0524**), where a portion of the proceeds from everything sold (including handsome woven and embroidered carpets) goes to the National Welfare Organization, which encourages traditional crafts.

Kolonaki, on the slopes of Mount Likavitos, is boutique heaven. However, it's a better place to window-shop than to buy, since much of what you see here is imported and heavily taxed. During the January and August sales, you may discover bargains. If not, it's still fun to work your way up pedestrian Voukourestiou and along Tsakalof and Anagnostopoulou (location of probably the most expensive boutiques in Athens) before you collapse at a cafe by one of the pedestrian shopping streets in Kolonaki Square—perhaps the very fashionable Milioni. Then you can engage in the other really serious business of Kolonaki: people-watching. Give yourself about 15 minutes to figure out the season's must-have accessory. If you want to make a small, traditional purchase, have a look at the "worry beads" at **Kombologadiko,** 6 Koumbari (© **210/362-4267**); or check out charms that ward off the evil eye at **To Fylakto Mou,** 20 Solonos (© **210/364-7610**).

Pedestrianized Ermou Street is the prime shopping district in the city with more stores than you will ever have the time to visit but if you want to do all your shopping in one take and not walk around outdoors, check our listings under "Department Stores" below.

SHOPPING A TO Z
ANTIQUES
Warning: If you hope to take home an antique—perhaps an icon or a woodcarving—know in advance that not everything sold as "antique" is genuine, and that it's illegal to take antiquities and icons more than 100 years old out of Greece without a hard-to-obtain export license.

If you're looking for first editions, prints showing 19th-century Athens, a silver sword, or amber worry beads, try **Antiqua,** 2–4 Leoforos Vas. Sofias, off Syntagma Square (© **210/323-2220**). This is one of Athens's oldest antiques stores, and perhaps the best. It also features handsome ancient coins and old icons—but take heed of the warning above.

Also near Syntagma Square, **Giannoukos,** 4 Vas. Amalias (℃ **210/324-1700**), has a sound reputation. If you're near Syntagma and looking for antiquarian books, maps, and prints, try **Salaminia,** with branches at 47 Panepistimiou (℃ **210/321-8155**) and 22 Stadiou (℃ **210/331-3944**).

Over in Monastiraki on Pandrossou, of the many pseudo-antiques shops, you'll find one or two good ones. **Martinos,** 50 Pandrossou (℃ **210/321-3110**), has Venetian and ancient glass, embroidery and kilims, swords, and side tables. **Anita Patrikiadon,** 58 Pandrossou (℃ **210/324-6325**), also offers a good selection of weavings and woodcarvings. Also in Monastiraki be sure to check out **Byzantino,** 120 Adrianou (℃ **210/324-6605**) for certified handmade replicas of stunning, intricate gold designs of Byzantine and Hellenistic jewelry in addition to original works. In Kolonaki, the eponymous proprietor of **Argyriadis,** 42 Patriarchou Ioakim (℃ **210/725-1727**), specializes in 18th-century furniture and a variety of more easily transported bibelots. **Mihalarias Art,** 1–3 Alopekis (℃ **210/721-3079**), in a gorgeous neoclassical Kolonaki mansion, offers museum-quality furniture, paintings, and just about any bauble you can imagine. And be sure to visit the excellent **Benaki Museum Gift Shop,** 1 Koumbari (℃ **210/367-1000;** www.benaki.gr) for high-quality prints, jewelry, ceramics, and books, plus stunning replicas of Greek artifacts.

BOOKS

Eleftheroudakis ⨁, with its old quarters still open at 4 Nikis (℃ **210/322-2255**), has new eight-story headquarters at 17 Leoforos Panepistimiou (℃ **210/331-4480**). It sells Athens's widest selection of English-language books and a good range of CDs, including Greek music. The cafe's staff doesn't mind when readers stop by here to rest, pick up a free newspaper or journal, or use the clean restrooms. The store is amazingly tolerant of tourists who read, but don't buy, the wide selection of books on Greece. Check the bulletin board by the cafe for readings by local authors (sometimes in English) or upcoming concerts.

Compendium, 28 Nikis (℃ **210/322-1248**), on the edge of the Plaka near Syntagma Square, is a small but fine English-language bookstore, selling both new and used fiction and nonfiction, plus magazines and maps. Local writers sometimes hold readings here. Just off Panepistimiou and steps from Syntagma Square, **Reymondos,** 18 Voukourestiou (℃ **210/364-8189**), has a good selection in English (including dazzling photography books on Greece), stocks English-language magazines and newspapers, and is often open after usual shop hours. In the stoa, one floor up, **Folia tou Bibliou (The Book Nest),** 25–29 Panepistimiou (℃ **210/323-1703**), stocks lots of English fiction and a wide selection of maps and books on Greece, as does **Pantelis,** 11 Amerikis, up from Panepistimiou (℃ **210/362-3673**).

In Kolonaki, try **Rombos,** 6 Kapsali, off Kolonaki Square (℃ **210/724-2082**), for English-language books, including books on Greece.

CRAFTS

There are lots of mass-produced so-called "crafts" for sale in Athens, which is why it's good to know which shops offer quality work. The **Center of Hellenic Tradition,** 3 Mitropoleos and 36 Pandrossou in the Plaka (℃ **210/321-3023**), is a wonderful place for quality traditional Greek art, including icons, pottery, woodcarvings, embroideries, and prints. Best of all, you can take a break from shopping and look at the Acropolis

---

Tips Insider Shopping

Serious shoppers should look for the "Best of Athens" issue of the English-language magazine, *Odyssey*. Usually published in July or August and available at
bookstores and kiosks, the issue is filled with shopping tips—and scoops on
what's "in" and what's "out" in Athens.

---

while you have coffee and a snack at the cafe here. While you are on and around
Mitropoleos, named after Athens's Metropolitan cathedral, keep an eye out for the
shops where craftspeople still turn out decent reproductions of icons for the faithful.

Also in the Plaka, **Anoyi,** 1 Sotiros (☎ **210/322-6487**), is an absolute delight, with
old prints, furniture, reproduced icons, and fabrics. On the fringes of the Plaka, the
National Welfare Organization (Ethnikos Organismos Pronias), 6 Ypatias and
Apollonos, just east of the cathedral (☎ **210/325-0524**), has gorgeous embroideries,
rugs, pottery, icons, and very bored, unhelpful salespeople. The **Greek Women's Institution,** 3 Kolokotroni (☎ **210/325-0524**), specializes in embroidery from the islands
and copies of embroideries from the Benaki Museum.

DEPARTMENT STORES

Head toward Omonia Square to see the city's best-known department stores: The
Attica department store in the beautiful CityLink building (9 Panepistimiou; ☎ **210/
180-2500**), has the best window displays in the entire city and over 300 stores in its
eight floors, with 800 different brands of clothing, accessories, cosmetics, and home-
wares. **Notos Galleries,** 99 Eolou and 2–6 Lykourgou (☎ **210/324-5811**) has seven
floors of clothing, cosmetics, sportswear, and more. **Hondos Center,** 4 Platieia Omo-
nias, smack in the middle of Omonia Square, is reasonably priced and has just about
everything you could want plus a rooftop cafe with Acropolis views. **Lambropoulos,**
9 Eolou (☎ **210/324-5811**) is the city's oldest department store. For smaller shops,
wander along Ermou, off Syntagma, where you'll find enough shoe shops to outfit the
world. When you tire of shoes, explore the side streets of Emou, such as Mitropoleos,
Voulis, and Praxitelous, where you can buy everything from chocolates and curtains,
to doorknobs and dust bins, to buttons and baptism dresses. Outside the center,
coastal Glyfada and leafy Kifissia also offer excellent (but more high-end) shopping. If
you want to shop in a mega mall with 15 movie theaters, 25 restaurants, and 300
shops hop on Metro line 1 and get off at Nerantziotissa station, right in front of the
Athens Mall (called The Mall Athens in Greece; Mon–Sat 9am–9pm, Sun 9am–8pm).
When you're done shopping, go the top-floor balcony and have a cold drink while you
take in the view of Northern Athens and the magnificent Athens Olympic Sports
Complex, the city's newest landmark.

FASHION

If you do any window-shopping in Athens, you'll soon see how expensive most things
are, except during the January and August sales. Not surprisingly, Athens's most posh
clothing stores are in **Kolonaki.** Much of what you'll see is American or European and
often carries a hefty import duty; the other selections are mostly Greek designer wear.
Good streets to browse are Voukourestiou, Kanari, Milioni, Tsakalof, Patriarchou
Ioakim, and perhaps the most expensive street in town, Anagnostopoulou—where

Versace, Ferre, Lagerfeld, and Guy Laroche have boutiques, as do well-known Athenian designers such as Aslanis, Nikos, Filemon, and Sofos. If shoes are your thing, head for Tsakalof, with its heavy concentration of the shoe stores that most Athenians find irresistible.

A few individual shops near Kolonaki Square to check out: **Artisti Italiani,** 5 Kanari (© 210/363-9085), has Italian-designed clothes for men and women. Head to the **Bettina Boutique,** 40 Pindarou and 29 Anagnostopoulou (© 210/339-2094) for Greek designer Sophia Kokosalaki, whose sexy and edgy work has made her the toast of Paris. The well-known French firm **Lacoste** sells men's and women's sportswear at 5 Solonos (© 210/361-8030). **Jade,** 3 Anagnostopoulou (© 210/364-5922); **Ritsi,** 13 Tsakalof (© 210/363-8677); and **Sofos,** 5 Anagnostopoulou (© 210/361-8713), all sell designer women's clothing. **Elina Lembessi,** 13 Irakleitou (© 210/363-1731), has elegantly casual tops, bottoms, and accessories. **Desmina,** 5 Koubare (© 210/364-1010), offers sportier women's clothing, with lots of pantsuits and casual wear. **New Man,** 25 Solonos at Voukourestiou (© 210/360-8876), has casual men's clothes, while nearby **Berto Lucci,** 8 Solonos (© 210/360-3775), carries more trendy attire. Greek designer **Yiorgos Eleftheriades,** 13 Agion Anargiron (© 210/331-2622; www.yiorgoseleftheriades.gr), well known in Greece and abroad for his casual yet elegant designs for both men and women has recently moved his studio/store from Kolonaki to Psirri. It is well worth a visit. Back in Kolonaki, check out **Christos Veloudakis,** 22a Tsakalof (© 210/364-1764) where long, red velvet curtains lead you into an impeccably stylish boutique right on Tsakalof street. For men and women. See also "Shoes" and "Sweaters," below.

In pharmacies, keep an eye out for the **Korres** line of natural beauty products, now being sold in smart shops abroad such as Liberty of London. The soaps and lotions make lovely gifts. If you want to visit Korres's mother store, go to the corner of 8 Ivikou and Erathosthenous (© 210/722-2774).

JEWELRY

All that glitters most definitely is not gold in Athens's myriad of jewelry shops. Unless you know your gold very well, you'll want to exercise caution when shopping here, especially in the Plaka and Monastiraki stores that cater to tourists.

Greece's best-known jewelry stores are **Zolotas,** with branches at 10 Panepistimiou (© 210/361-3782) and at 10 Stadiou (© 210/322-1212); and **LALAoUNIS,** 6 Panepistimiou (© 210/362-1371). Both firms have gorgeous reproductions of ancient and Byzantine jewelry, as well as their own designs. You can see more of the LALAoUNIS designs at the LALAoUNIS museum (see "More Museums & Galleries," earlier in this chapter).

For serious window-shopping for gold and silver, crisscross pedestrian Voukourestiou, which is dripping with jewelry shops. Then head to Kolonaki Square along Patriarchou Ioakim, where still more ornate and serious baubles are on display. Don't miss **J. Vourakis** (© 210/3311-1087) at 8 Voukourestiou; and **Fanourakis** (© 210/234-6624) at 23 Patriiarchou Ioakeim.

One of the best shops for silver is **Nisiotis,** 23 Lekka, just off Syntagma Square (© 210/324-4183). Off Syntagma, but toward Plaka, **Pantelis Mountis,** 27 Apollonos (©/fax 210/324-4574), sells reproductions of Byzantine icons and religious medals.

We've been pleased with the quality and prices at Emanuel Masmanidis's small **Gold Rose Jewelry** shop, 85 Pandrossou (© 210/321-5662). Others report satisfaction in dealings with **Stathis,** 2 Venizelou, Mitropoleos Square (© 210/322-4691).

MARKETS & GROCERIES

The **Central Market** ✦ on Athinas is open Monday through Saturday from about 8am to 6pm. You may not want to take advantage of all of the bargain prices (two sheep's heads for the price of one is our all-time favorite), but this is a great place to buy Greek spices, herbs, cheeses, and sweets—and to see how Athens is fed.

Every Friday from about 8am until 2pm, **Xenokratous** in Kolonaki turns into a street market selling flowers, fruits, and vegetables. This is a very different scene from the rowdy turmoil of the Central Market, although it's lively enough. Kolonaki matrons come here with their Filipino servants, who lug their purchases home while the ladies head off for shopping and light lunches (perhaps at fashionable **To Kafenio,** ℂ 210/722-9056). Every neighborhood has a weekly market; if you want to take in a number of them, ask at your hotel. **Green Farm** (ℂ 210/361-4001), also in Kolonaki, sells only organic produce.

In Plaka, **Mesogeia,** 52 Nikkis (ℂ 210/322-9146), with organic produce, is one of a number of small "boutique" groceries springing up in Athens.

MUSIC

You won't have trouble finding **Metropolis,** 66 Panepistimiou and 15 Tsakalof (ℂ 210/361-1463), Athens's largest music store: Follow the booming vibrations. At **Slammin',** 22 Asklepiou (ℂ 210/361-3611), you can buy CDs and clothes. The excellent bookstore **Eleftheroudakis** (see above) has a wide selection of CDs, as does the **Virgin Megastore** at 7 Stadiou (ℂ 210/361-8080).

SHOES

If you walk along Tsakalof or Patriarchou Ioakim in Kolonaki, or along almost any street in central Athens, you'll get an idea of how serious Greeks are about their footwear. Sometimes the biggest crowds in town on a Saturday night are the window-shoppers eyeing the shoes on Ermou off Syntagma Square. Good-quality stores include **Kaloyirou,** at 12 Pandrossou, Plaka (ℂ 210/331-0727), and at 4 Patriarchou Ioakim, Kolonaki (ℂ 210/722-8804). The Kolonaki branch, housed inside an elegant 19th-century mansion, offers four floors of shoes for women for all occasions (plus bags and accessories on the first floor) and a separate entrance for the men's store. It is an Athenian institution; **Mouriadis,** 4 Stadiou (ℂ 210/322-1229); and **Moschoutis,** 12 Voulis at Ermou (ℂ 210/324-6504).

SWEATERS

Several travelers recommend **Nick's Corner,** 48 Pandrossou, Monastiraki (ℂ 210/321-2990), for the heavy knit sweaters considered bargains in Greece (look downstairs). You'll see many more sweaters along Adrianou in the Plaka and, if you don't mind that many of these "authentic" Greek sweaters are made by machines and imported from Third World countries, you can find decent prices almost everywhere.

SWEETS

You'll have no problem satisfying your sweet tooth in Athens. If anything, you'll come up gasping for air as you eat the seriously sweet sweets adored by most Greeks.

The long-established **Aristokratikon,** 9 Karayioryi Servias, just off Syntagma Square (ℂ 210/322-0546), makes excellent chocolates, glazed pistachio nuts, and *loukoumia* (Turkish delight). Beware—even chocoholics may find the truffles coated with white chocolate too sweet. **Karavan,** the hole in the wall at 11 Voukourestiou (no phone), has the best Levantine delights in town. Serving excellent coffee and sweets, **K. Kotsolis Pastry Shop,** 112 Adrianou, is an oasis of old-fashioned charm in the midst of the Plaka souvenir shops.

Loukoumades are the Greek doughnuts with a difference—each is about the size of an American doughnut hole, drenched in honey, covered with cinnamon, and served hot. Delicious. If you're near Syntagma Square, try **Doris,** 30 Praxitelous (© **210/ 323-2671**). If you're nearer Omonia Square, try **Aigina,** 46 Panepistimiou (© **210/ 381-4621**). Better yet, try both.

11 Athens After Dark

Greeks enjoy their nightlife so much that they take an afternoon nap to rest up for it. The evening often begins with a leisurely *volta* (stroll); you'll see this in most neighborhoods, including the main drags through the Plaka and Kolonaki Square. Most Greeks don't think of dinner until at least 9pm in winter, 10pm in summer. Around midnight, the party may move on to a club for music and dancing.

Check the *Athens News* (published Fri) or the daily *Kathimerini* insert in the *International Herald Tribune* for listings of current cultural and entertainment events, including films, lectures, theater, music, and dance. The weekly *Hellenic Times* and monthly *Now in Athens* list nightspots, restaurants, movies, theater, and much more.

FESTIVALS

New festivals spring up every year in Athens and throughout Greece. You may want to check with the Greek National Tourism Organization to see what's new at your destination.

HELLENIC FESTIVAL   Early June through September, the Athens Festival (also known as the **Athens or Greek Festival**) features famous Greek and foreign artists

---

Tips **Ticket Information for the Athens (Hellenic), Lycabettus & Epidaurus Festivals**

Tickets for the Athens, Lycabettus, and Epidaurus festivals are available at the Hellenic Festival Box Office, 39 Panepistimiou (in the arcade; © **210/ 928/2900**). Hours are Monday through Friday 8:30am to 4pm, Saturday 9am to 2:30pm. (The name "Hellenic Festival" is an umbrella term for a number of summer festivals, including the Athens and Epidaurus festivals.) Advance booking for most events in the Hellenic Festival starts 3 weeks before each performance, 10 days before each event for the Lycabettus Festival. Ticket reservation and telephone booking (as below) are also possible by credit card (MasterCard or Visa), with the exact date and performance, number and category of tickets, and number and expiration date of the credit card. Tickets (if available) also go on sale at the box offices at each theater 2 hours before each performance. Events at the Odeion of Herodes Atticus on the slopes of the Acropolis are usually sold out by the day of the performance; for information, call © **210/323-2771.**

Additional information is available at www.hellenicfestival.gr, www.athens infoguide.com, and www.greektourism.com.

from Elton John to Placido Domingo performing on the slopes of the Acropolis. You may catch an opera, concert, drama, or ballet here—and see the Acropolis illuminated over your shoulder at the same time. To enjoy the performance to the fullest, bring a cushion to sit on (the cushions available are often minimal). Schedules are usually available at the **Hellenic Festival Office,** 39 Panepistimiou (in the arcade; ✆ **210/928-2900**). The office is usually open Monday through Saturday from 8:30am to 2pm and 5 to 7pm, Sunday from 10am to 1pm. You will have better luck if you come here in person rather than try to reach the office by phone. If available—and that's a big "if"—tickets can be purchased at the **Odeion of Herodes Atticus** (✆ **210/323-2771** or 210/323-5582) several hours before the performance. Again, you will have better luck going to the ticket office than phoning, although if your hotel has a concierge, he or she may be able to obtain tickets (15€–50€/$20–$65) over the phone. Shows begin at 9pm.

LYCABETTUS (LIKAVITOS) FESTIVAL   The Pet Shop Boys, Buena Vista Social Club, and other pop musicians make appearances here at the outdoor amphitheater near the top of Likavitos during the summer. For information on music and special events, check with the **Hellenic Festival Office** (see above) or **Likavitos Theater** (✆ **210/722-7209**). Tickets may also be available at **Ticket House,** 42 Panepistimiou (✆ **210/618-9300** or 210/360-8366).

EPIDAURUS FESTIVAL   From late June to late August, performances of ancient Greek tragedies and comedies (usually given in modern Greek translations) take place at Epidaurus, in Greece's most beautiful ancient theater. This makes for a long evening, but a memorable one. If you purchase bus service along with your ticket (about 2 hr. each way), the evening doesn't have to be exhausting. You may want to inquire as to whether the bus/boat excursion from Piraeus to Epidaurus offered in 2002 has been reinstituted; contact the **Greek National Tourism Organization,** the **Hellenic Festival Office** (see above), or the **Rex Theater** box office (✆ **210/330-1881**) on Panepistimiou just outside Spiromilios Arcade.

ROCKWAVE FESTIVAL   What started as a one-time event in 1996 has taken place every summer since, with concerts at various venues in and around Athens. Popular groups from around the world perform each year. For more information on what's taking place during your visit, check with the Greek National Tourism Organization, Ticket House (see above), or visit their website at www.rockwavefestival.gr.

ATHENS INTERNATIONAL DANCE FESTIVAL   Founded in 2003, this festival takes place during the first 2 weeks in July at the Technopolis arts complex, 100 Piraeus, Gazi. This is not the place to go for a traditional rendition of Swan Lake; groups performing here push the envelope of contemporary dance. The 2005 festival featured the American Pretty Ugly Dance Company. Schedule and ticket information at ✆ **210/346-1589** or 210/346-7322.

THE PERFORMING ARTS

The acoustically marvelous new **Megaron Mousikis Concert Hall,** 89 Leoforos Vas. Sofias (✆ **210/729-0391** or 210/728-2333), hosts a wide range of classical music programs that include quartets, operas in concert, symphonies, and recitals. On performance nights, the box office is open Monday through Friday from 10am to 6pm, Saturday from 10am to 2pm, and Sunday from 6 to 10:30pm. Tickets are also sold Monday through Friday from 10am to 5pm in the Megaron's convenient downtown kiosk in the Spiromillios Arcade, 4 Stadiou. Ticket prices run from 5€ ($6.50) to as much as 100€ ($130), depending on the performance. The Megaron has a limited summer season but is in full swing the rest of the year.

The **Greek National Opera** performs at **Olympia Theater,** 59 Akadimias at Mavromihali (© 210/361-2461). The summer months are usually off season.

Pallas Theater, 1 Voukourestiou (© 210/322-8275), hosts many jazz and rock concerts, as well as some classical performances. Prices vary from performance to performance, but you can get a cheap ticket from about 10€ ($13).

The **Hellenic American Union,** 22 Massalias between Kolonaki and Omonia squares (© 210/362-9886), often hosts performances of English-language theater and American-style music (tickets 10€/$13 and up). If you arrive early, check out the art shows or photo exhibitions in the adjacent gallery.

The **Athens Center,** 48 Archimidous (© 210/701-8603), often stages free performances of ancient Greek and contemporary international plays in June and July.

Since 1953, **Dora Stratou Folk Dance Theater** has been giving performances of traditional Greek folk dances on Filopappos Hill. At present, performances take place May through September, Tuesday through Sunday at 9:30pm, with additional performances at 8:15pm on Wednesday and Sunday. There are no performances on Monday. You can buy tickets at the **box office,** 8 Scholio, Plaka, from 8am to 2pm (© 210/924-4395 or 210/921-4650 after 5:30pm; www.grdance.org). Prices range from 12€ to 25€ ($16–$33). Tickets are also available at the theater before the performances. The program changes every 2 or 3 weeks.

Seen from Pnyx hill, **sound-and-light** shows illuminate Athens's history by telling the story of the Acropolis. As lights pick out monuments on the Acropolis and the music swells, the narrator tells of the Persian attack, the Periclean days of glory, the invidious Turkish occupation—you get the idea. Shows are held April through October. The 45-minute performances in English are given at 9pm on Monday, Wednesday, Thursday, Saturday, and Sunday. Tickets (10€/$13) can be purchased at the **Hellenic Festival Office,** 39 Panepistimiou (© 210/928-2900), or at the entrance to the sound-and-light show (© 210/922-6210). You'll hear the narrative best if you don't sit too close to the loud public-address system.

THE CLUB, MUSIC & BAR SCENE

Given the vicissitudes of Athens nightlife, your best bet here is to have a local friend; failing that, you have this guide and you can always ask someone at your hotel for a recommendation. The listings in the weekly *Athinorama* (Greek) or in publications such as the English-language *Athens News,* the *Kathimerini* insert in the *Herald Tribune,* and hotel handouts such as *Best of Athens* and *Welcome to Athens,* can be very helpful. If you ask a taxi driver, he's likely to take you to either his cousin's joint or the place that gives him drinks for bringing you.

If you head to a large club, you're likely to face a cover charge of at least 10€ to 20€ ($13–$26). Thereafter, each drink will probably cost over 10€ ($13). It's best to go only to clubs with or recommended by someone *trustworthy* who knows the scene or that have come recommended from reliable sources (such as this guide). In large clubs, don't sit at a table unless you want to purchase a bottle of alcohol (100€/$130), whether you want it or not. If you hear music you simply must have, **Metropolis** (© 210/380-8549) in Omonia Square has a wide choice of CDs and tapes of Greek music.

TRADITIONAL MUSIC

Walk the streets of the Plaka on any night and you'll find plenty of tavernas offering pseudo-traditional live music. As noted, many are serious clip joints, where if you sit down and ask for a glass of water, you'll be charged 100€ ($130) for a bottle of scotch. At most of these places, there's a cover of 10€ ($13). We've had good reports on **Taverna Mostrou,** 22 Mnissikleos (© **210/324-2441**), which is large, old, and best known for traditional Greek music and dancing. Shows begin around 11pm and can last until 2am. The cover of 30€ ($39) includes a fixed-menu supper. A la carte fare is available but expensive (as are drinks). Nearby, **Palia Taverna Kritikou,** 24 Mnissikleos (© **210/-322-2809**), is another lively open-air taverna with music and dancing.

Appealing tavernas offering low-key music include fashionable **Daphne's,** 4 Lysikratous (© **210/322-7971**); **Nefeli,** 24 Panos (© **210/321-2475**); **Dioyenis,** 4 Sellei (Shelley; © **210/324-7933**); **Stamatopoulou,** 26 Lissiou (© **210/322-8722**); and longtime favorites **Klimataria,** 5 Klepsidras (© **210/324-1809**), and **Xinos,** 4 Agelou Geronta (© **210/322-1065**).

BARS/CLUBS

Greek nightlife has a reputation for just getting started when the rest of Europe has already gone to bed. It's true. The nightlife in Athens is very sophisticated and varied. It used to be that during the summer the coast stole the show with its large and luxurious waterfront clubs but with the resurrection of Gazi, Psiri, and Thisio, Athenians now head to the coastal clubs mostly on weekends during the summer. Most will begin their night downtown and make their way to the coast later. Keep in mind that with the tram, reaching these clubs is easier than ever. Because it runs on a 24-hour schedule on weekends during the summer, you will have no problem getting back to the center inexpensively. Even though I recommend you visit at least one of these clubs, to avoid velvet ropes and lines, you can make a reservation for dinner (they have amazingly tasty menus) and you can dine by the sea before the party gets started and linger until the club heats up. Apart from a few waterfront choices I will list, visitors will find most places conveniently located in the center. Some of the best lounges/bars in the city these days are found in hotels. Don't forget to have a drink at the top-floor **Galaxy** bar at the **Hilton** hotel for an amazing city view you won't find anywhere else. For the best Acropolis view head to the **Hera Hotel's Peacock Lounge;** for the most happening scene visit the **Frame Bar-Lounge** at **St. George Lycabettus Hotel,** the **Fresh Hotel's Air Lounge Bar,** and **Ochre & Brown** lounge. Okay, let's get going.

MONASTIRAKI

(Metro: Monastiraki)

Gallery Café (cafe/bar), 33 Adrianou (© **210/324-9080**). On busy Adrianou, Gallery Café is a delightful and edgy cafe serving breakfast and snacks throughout the day. At night, the lights dim and it morphs into an equally charming bar. You can enjoy your drink on the busy sidewalk as you watch the city go by or sit inside and check out its various exhibitions and sometimes live shows. **Inoteka** (bar), 3 Plateia Avyssinias (© **210/324-6446**). When electronica-loving hipsters bought this old restaurant all they wanted was a cool place to play their music to an appreciative crowd in a funky space. They redid the space into a funky bar. During the summer, the candlelit tables spill out on the plateia—a great place to linger at all night long.

PSIRRI
(Metro: Monastiraki)

Bar Guru Bar (restaurant/bar/club), 10 Plateia Theatrou, ✆ **210/324-6530.** Closed mid-July to mid-August. Apart from being a fine Thai restaurant, Guru also offers an infectious good time as a bar/club. Upstairs hosts live jazz and downstairs is reserved for funky dance hits. **Hamam** (cafe/bar), Plateia Agion Anrgiron. A cafe for most of the day, this former hamam (equipped with hubble-bubble pipes) turns to a chill bar at night with outdoor and rooftop seating. **Candy Bar/Danze** (club), 11 Aristofanous, ✆ **210/331-7105.** Hang out at the bar and take in the hip and fun scene; then move upstairs to the popular club **Danza** where rotating guest DJs spin everything from house to rock and everything in between. **Corto Maltese** (club), 33 Karaiskaki (open only in winter) Named after an obscure cult comic book character, this is a great club with mostly alternative or indie rock music. Some live performances also. Admission is 6€ ($7.80) but includes a drink. **Cubanita** (restaurant/bar/club), 28 Karaiskaki, ✆ **210/331-4605.** May close in July and August. Hands down one of the most fun nights to be had in the city where Latin beats and excellent Cuban cuisine combine to make a great place to party until the early morning hours. On some nights there's live Cuban music. **Soul Garden** (bar/restaurant/club), 65 Evripidou, ✆ **210/331-0907.** Inside a restored house, you can have the best Mojitos in this part of town and excellent Thai finger food in the beautiful candlelit, Chinese lantern–filled courtyard or just chill out to the soundtrack inside and out. Unpretentious, stylish, and fun, the upstairs club opens late.

THISSIO
(Metro: Thissio)

Athinaion Politeia (cafe/bar/restaurant), 30 Apostolou Pavlou and 1 Akamanthos, ✆ **210/341-3794.** My favorite cafe in Athens, this grand restored building (once a grocery store in 19th-c. Athens) has the perfect location right on the Promenade with uninterrupted views of the Acropolis and passersby. **Space by Avli** (cafe/bar/club), 14 Iraklidon. This charming daytime cafe slowly evolves into a bar/club over its three stylish floors with a mostly soul and jazz soundtrack. **Stavlos** (multi-functional urban coolness), 10 Iraklidon, ✆ **210/346-7206.** Off the Archaeological Promenade on pedestrian Iraklidon Street, Stavlos was the royal stables in the 1880s. Now it is a cafe during the day with an Italian restaurant, outdoor seating in either the terrace, the tree-lined courtyard or on the sidewalk. Good music and a laid-back pace guarantee a good time day and night when it turns into a bar/club.

GAZI
(Metro: Kerameikos)

And here we are: nightlife central. Trying to pick a place here is tricky because most of the bars and clubs in Gazi are good. For starters, take a leisurely stroll to scope out the scene. Walk down Persefonis Street and Triptopolemou on either direction: The Kerameikos Metro station is a large landscaped plateia that covers an entire city block and is surrounded on either side by extremely popular bars. Once the bars reach full capacity, patrons head to the street and the plateia, drinks in hand. **Bios** (multi-purpose venue), 84 Pireos, ✆ **210/342-5335.** There is always something cool going on in this art-space/cafe/bar/club, from avant-garde performances to exhibitions and foreign art film showings. A basement nightclub sways to a mostly rock soundtrack.

Brothel (bar/restaurant), 33 Orfeos and Dekeleion, ℂ **210/347-0505.** Dark, stylish, and welcoming, Brothel has a great soundtrack, smooth cocktails and tasty Mediterranean dishes (25€–35€/$33–$46) plus the ambience and dark charm of an old-world cabaret. **45 degrees** (bar/club), 18 Iakhou, corner Voutadhon ℂ **210/347-2729.** An excellent place to begin the night, this rock bar/club has a stunning rooftop terrace overlooking Gazi and the Acropolis in the distance. **Gazaki** (bar), 31 Triptopolemou, ℂ **210/346-0901.** The oldest bar in Gazi remains one of the best, having recently added a very nice roof terrace. The music is always excellent as are the drinks. The no-pretense mixed-crowd makes this a sure bet for any night of the week. Across from Gazaki, you will find **Tapas Bar and Dirty-Ginger** (bar/restaurant), 46 Triptopolemou, ℂ **210/342-3809.** With table seating right on one of the most active streets in the city, a beautiful palm tree–lined garden, and excellent Mediterranean cuisine and pumping soundtrack, this mixed-crowd bar/restaurant is fun for everyone that visits. You are guaranteed to return. **Gazarte** (bar/restaurant/exhibition-conference center), 32–34 Voutadon, ℂ **210/346-0347.** Three-level urban chic space with various weekly art exhibitions, a very good restaurant, and a lovely bar on the roof terrace with sweeping views. **Hoxton** (bar), 42 Voutadon, ℂ **210/341-3395.** Beautiful, edgy, arty, and hip with a seriously addictive rock/new wave soundtrack, Hoxton is the place to be night after night. (Across the park from Hoxton, is **Mad,** 53 Persefonis, ℂ **210/346-2027;** an ideal late-night location for indie rock.) **Tapas Bar,** 44 Triptopolemou, ℂ **210/347-1844,** is one of the most interesting bars in Gazi at press time; the space is rather tiny and always packed. The action begins in the bar with light snacks and a rather jazzy soundtrack that segues into Latin beats as patrons down the margaritas, mojitos, and rum-based drinks that ensure an amazing time. **Nipiagogio (Kindergarten;** bar/club), Elasidon and 8 Kleanthous, ℂ **210/345-8534.** What was once an elementary school has been turned into one of the hottest bar/clubs in the city. On Saturday nights the former classrooms and playground stay hot until 6am! **Villa Milioni** (club), Andronikou and 11 Jafferi, ℂ **210/342-3606.** This impressive nightclub with many rooms and an internal courtyard (plus a restaurant) is always fun to check out and has no cover charge. *Tip:* Any night you're in Gazi, stop by **Mamacas** bar/lounge (inside the popular modern taverna) and have a drink at the bar to check out the scene. Something interesting is always going on here.

ZAPPEIO
(Metro: Syntagma)

Inside the Aigli complex you will find the **Lallabai** (lounge/club), 9 Zappeion, ℂ **210/336-9340.** Tastefully decorated, this is a great place to chill out and soak up the serene garden surroundings or the boisterous scene as the lounge turns into a club. **On the Road** (bar/club), 1 Adrittou, ℂ **210/347-8716.** From as far back as I can remember I had always wanted to visit this club. Driving with my dad I would always wonder how they ever build a bar right in the middle of the avenue. Great music and decor and a wonderfully rowdy atmosphere plus the bizarre location, make this an absolute must. Plus, it is refreshingly attitude free. Right across the street is another great club named **Exo (Outdoors),** 1 Markou Mousourou, ℂ **210/923-7109.** Admission is 15€ ($20). These days it's a club/restaurant with outdoor seating during summer with amazing views of the city—including the Acropolis and Lycabettus.

OMONIA/METAXOURGEIO
(For Omonia, Metro to: Omonia; for Metaxourgeio: Metaxourgeio)

Bacaro (cafe/bar/restaurant/gallery), 1 Sofokleous and 11 Aristidou, ✆ 210/321-1882. Across from the Athens Stock Exchange, this is one of the hippest, not to mention most stylish places in the middle of the city. Delicious Italian fare (for those choosing to have dinner here), cool art exhibitions, excellent decor, and a popular bar show off modern Athens at its best. **Cabaret Voltaire** (bar/club), 30 Marathonos, Metaxourgeio, ✆ **210/522-7046.** In formerly run-down Metaxourgeio, the cabaret has a cool scene, industrial-to-arts surroundings, well-known DJs, organic wine, art exhibitions, and live jazz every Sunday.

EXARHEIA
(Metro: Omonia/Panepistimio)

Decadence (bar/club), 69 Voulgaroktonou and 2 Poliherias, Stroffi Lofos, ✆ 210/882-7045. Landmark Athenian rock club housed in a beautiful neoclassical mansion that used to belong to royalty. It's popular with all ages and touring bands that stop in after their shows. This year it joined forces with Kipos (see below) and they co-sponsor many events and theme nights. **Kipos** (bar/cafe/club), 87 Emmanouil Benaki, ✆ 210/3813685. Housed in an elegant old mansion with many rooms, each one of a different musical genre. Live shows and special events weekly. **Mo Better** (club), 32 Koletti, ✆ **210/381-2981.** Admission of 6€ ($8) includes drink. This wildly popular club housed in the first floor of a neoclassical building has DJs spinning everything from house to punk rock. **Resital** (club), 64 Eressou, ✆ **210/380-5556.** This place has been around forever (I hear it was the place to be on the Grand Opening Day of the Acropolis). The ivy-covered mansion hosts live performances by Greek and foreign rock bands; it's a smart choice for listening to music or hanging out on the terrace. **Texas** (bar), 56 Ippokratous, ✆ **697/280-2171.** This retro scene of a time gone by but not forgotten by everyone hosts heavy metal, goth and glam rock. **Gagarin 205** (live rock venue), 205 Liossion, ✆ **210/854-7601;** www.gagarin205.gr. Catch a rock concert in this large space in the winter or its other space on the coast in the summer. Check its website to find out who is performing.

KOLONAKI/AMBELOKIPI
(Metro for Kolonaki: Syntagma or Evaggelismos; for Ambelokipi: Megaro Mousikis or Ambelokipi)

Balthazar (bar/restaurant), 27 Tsoha and Soutsou, Ambelokipi, ✆ **210/644-1215.** Having been a favorite Athenian destination since the '80s, this beautiful mansion also has a fine restaurant, but it is the bar in the mansion's beautiful lantern-lit courtyard that is the favorite destination. Show up late (after midnight) for drinks in this incredibly romantic location with the pretty people. **Baraonda** (restaurant/bar/club), 43 Tsoha, Ambelokipi, ✆ **210/644-4308.** An atmospheric establishment with red velvet curtains, candles, stone and tiled walls, chandeliers, two bars, a VIP section, and a summer courtyard complement the energetic music, the fun-loving clientele, and the exceptional Mediterranean cuisine which tends to be on the expensive side (45€–50€/$59–$65). **Memphis** (bar/club), 5 Vendiri, Ilisia (behind the Hilton hotel), ✆ **210/722-4104.** Memphis has been popular for decades for its Indie rock sounds. **Mike's Irish Bar** (Irish bar), 6 Sinopis, Ambelokipi, ✆ **210/777-6797.** Insanely popular Irish pub that's packed with ex-patriots longing for a non-glamorous bar setting. Right by the Athens Tower, this bar has gotten more expensive lately with certain nights (such as karaoke night) having an admission fee, but still it's a lot of fun. **Mommy** (bar/restaurant), 4 Delfon, Kolonaki, ✆ **210/361-9682.** One of the most popular places of the moment, this impressive space with a smart decor, contemporary art exhibitions, excellent Mediterranean menu, and great drinks, gets pumping after midnight when the fun spills out to its summer terrace. **Rock n' Roll** (bar/restaurant/club), 6 Loukianou and Ypsilantou, ✆ **210/721-7127.** A legendary Kolonaki haunt year after year (it's closed during the summer). On the upper level the restaurant has incredible views whereas on the lower floor you can enjoy a drink in one of the most stylish bars in town.

SEASIDE CLUBS

Akrotiri Club Restaurant (club/restaurant), Leof Vas Georgiou B5, Agios Kosmas (tram to Elliniko stop), ✆ 210/985-9147; www.akrotirilounge.gr. Admission is from 11pm to 5am Monday through Thursday and Sunday 10€ ($13) and includes a drink. Friday and Saturday is 15€ ($20) including a drink. This massive (capacity 3,000), ridiculously beautiful and stylish open-air club next to the beach, with an elegant tropical decor, a huge pool, dance floors, deck seating by the beach, sea views, excellent (but pricey) Med fusion cuisine (50€–70€/$65–$91) has been popular since the '80s and shows no signs of stopping.

Bo (cafe/bar/restaurant/club), 14 Karamanli, Voula, ✆ 210/895-9645. Open daily 11am to 4am. Take the Tram to Glyfada then bus no. A2 from Plateia Glyfadas. This longtime Athenian favorite is housed in a beautiful seafront mansion with a huge terrace right above the waves. During the day it is a trendy cafe then slowly morphs into a lounge/restaurant until its final reincarnation as a pumping club.

Mao Summer (club/restaurant), Diadohou Pavlou, Glyfada, ✆ **210/894-4048.** Tram to Paralia Glyfadas. Admission is 10€ ($13) weeknights but includes a drink; 15€ ($20) Friday and Saturday includes a drink. It's a massive open-air club (with a capacity of 5,000), impeccably decorated and featuring a large swimming pool surrounded by recliners and sofas. On Sundays there's a pool party.

If you only visit one summer coastal club/restaurant, romantic **Island** ⚑ should be it. Limanakia Vouliagmenis, ✆ **210/965-3563.** Take the tram to Glyfada (Paleio Dimarheio) and from there take a taxi or bus no. 114 and get off at Limanakia. It is out-of-the-way but worth the trip. Set on a breathtaking cliff-top with sea vistas, excellent finger food, sushi, and Mediterranean dishes, this is the quintessential Athenian summer nightspot. Things get louder after 1am. Show up early or make dinner reservations—prices are moderate (20€–50€/$26–$68). No admission fee but annoying door policy—if you arrive on foot you won't get in unless it's very early (10pm) or you have dinner reservations.

REMBETIKA & BOUZOUKIA

Visitors interested in authentic *rembetika* (music of the urban poor and dispossessed) and *bouzoukia* (traditional and pop music featuring the *bouzouki,* a kind of guitar, today almost always loudly amplified) should consult their hotel concierge or check the listings in *Athinorama,* the weekly *Hellenic Times,* or *Kathimerini* (the daily insert in the *International Herald Tribune*). Another good place to ask is at the shop of the Museum of Popular Greek Musical Instruments (see "The Top Museums," earlier in this chapter). *Rembetika* performances usually don't start until nearly midnight, and though there's rarely a cover, drinks can cost as much as 20€ ($26). Many clubs close during the summer.

One of the more central places for *rembetika* is **Stoa Athanaton,** 19 Sofokleous, in the Central Meat Market (✆ **210/321-4362**), which serves good food and has live music from 3 to 6pm and after midnight. It's closed Sunday. **Taximi,** 29 Isavron, Exarchia (✆ **210/363-9919**), is consistently popular. Drinks cost 12€ ($16). It's closed Sunday and during July and August. Open Wednesday through Monday, **Frangosyriani,** 57 Arachovis, Exarchia (✆ **210/360-0693**), specializes in the music of *rembetika* legend Markos Vamvakaris. The downscale, smoke-filled **Rebetiki Istoria,** in a neoclassical building at 181 Ippokratous (✆ **210/642-4967**), features old-style *rembetika,* played to a mixed crowd of older regulars and younger students and intellectuals. The music usually starts at 11pm, but arrive earlier to get a seat. The legendary Maryo I Thessaloniki (Maryo from Thessaloniki), described as the Bessie Smith of Greece, sometimes sings *rembetika* at **Perivoli t'Ouranou,** 19 Lysikratous (✆ **210/323-5517** or 210/322-2048), in Plaka. Expect to pay at least 10€ ($13) per drink in these places, most of which have a cover from 25€ ($33).

JAZZ

A number of clubs and cafes specialize in jazz, but they also offer everything from Indian sitar music to rock to punk. The very popular—and very well-thought of— **Half Note Jazz Club,** 17 Trivonianou, Mets (✆ **210/921-3310**), schedules performers who play everything from medieval music to jazz; set times vary from 8 to 11pm and later. **Café Asante,** 78 Damareos (✆ **210/756-0102**), in Pangrati, has music most nights from 11pm. At the **House of Art,** Sahtouri and 4 Sari (✆ **210/321-7678**), and at **Pinakothiki,** 5 Ayias Theklas (✆ **210/324-7741**), both in newly fashionable Psirri, you can often hear jazz from 11pm. You'll pay the same here as at the *rembetika* clubs—from 10€ ($13) per drink and a cover of at least 25€ ($33).

MOVIES

Central Athens has lots of air-conditioned theaters (mostly multiplexes now) showing new-release Greek, American, and European films. Listings appear in the *Athens News,* in *Kathimerini* (the English-language insert in the *International Herald Tribune*), and in the weekly *Hellenic Times.*

If you're in Athens in summer, look for listings of neighborhood open-air cinemas; it's a pleasant way to pass an evening, although some old favorites have closed in recent years. Many of the open-air cinemas are family-owned and -run, and all are great places to watch Athenian families watching films—which is to say, talking to each other, pursuing runaway toddlers, munching snacks, and sipping cold drinks, all the while keeping up a running commentary on the film. We're fond of **Dexameni** (✆ **210/ 362-3942**) in Dexameni Square, Kolonaki, where there always seems to be a breeze on a hot evening. **Cine Paris** (✆ **210/322-2071**), on Kidathineon in the Plaka, is one of the oldest in town—and has great views of the Acropolis, as does charming **Thission** (✆ **210/342-0864**) on Apostolou Pavlou, just off the pedestrian walkway that runs around the Acropolis to the Ancient Agora. Don't be surprised if the phone is not answered at these places; times are not always posted at the theater, either. Most shows begin sometime after 9pm.

GAY & LESBIAN ATHENS

You will not find a shortage of gay bars, cafes, and clubs in Athens even though the gay male venues by far outnumber the lesbian ones. The scene used to be in Makrigianni and Kolonaki but Gazi has taken over here as well with the hippest gay or gay-friendly establishments within walking distance from one another. The legendary gay bars and clubs of the past still remain in Makrigianni and are still popular, but the real scene has moved to Gazi. The weekly publications *Athinorama* and *Time Out* often list gay bars, discos, and special events in the nightlife section. Get-togethers are sometimes advertised in the English-language press, such as the weekly *Athens News*. Information is also available from the **Greek National Gay & Lesbian Organization,** or **EOK** (✆ 210/253-7333; www.eok.gr). You can also look for the Greek publication **Deon Magazine** (✆ 210/953-6479; www.deon.gr) or surf the web at www.gay greece.gr. **Gay Travel Greece,** at 377 Syngrou Ave. in central Athens (✆ 210/948-4385), specializes, as its name proclaims, in travel for gay and lesbian visitors.

Gay and lesbian travelers will not encounter difficulties at any Athenian hotel, but one with a largely gay and lesbian clientele is 41-room **Hotel Rio Athens** (www.hotel-rio.gr), at 13 Odysseos off Karaiskaki Square in a nicely restored neoclassical building. Below are some selections we have made of the city's more fun gay bars/clubs. For a complete listing of all the gay fun the metropolis has to offer, check out www. athensinfoguide.com and www.gaytravel-greece.com.

GAY & LESBIAN BARS/CLUBS

Blue Train, 84 Konstantinoupoleos, Gazi (✆ 210/346-0677; www.bluetrain.gr), is right by the railway tracks on the edge of Gazi. The friendly scene here is a great place to begin the evening, preferably in the sidewalk seating where you can watch the trains and the boys go by. Daily 8pm to 4am. **Eyeland,** 24 Ikarion, Gazi (✆ 694615-0196), is a large industrial space converted to a club for women, with wall projections, techno, house, and R&B all night long. The girls here range from butch dykes to lipstick chicks, but they are all friendly and fun to be around and there is no attitude. Once a month it hosts gay film screenings and other special events so be sure to call ahead for the schedule of the particular night you're planning to visit. Tuesday through Sunday 10pm to 4am. **Kazarma,** 1st floor, 84 Konstantinoupoleos, Gazi (✆ 210/346-0667), is above Blue Train, one of the best gay clubs in the city. During summer the fun moves to the terrace. Wednesday though Sunday midnight to 5am. **Lamda,** 15 Lembessi and 9 Syngrou, Makrigianni (✆ 210/922-4202; www.lamdaclub.gr) has been popular for so long, it has become an Athenian institution. The energy on the ground floor is mostly laid-back while things in the basement get far rowdier. Perhaps the cave-like dark room (the only one in town) is to blame. Daily 11pm to 5am. **Mayo,** 33 Persefonis, Gazi (✆ 210/342-3066) is a quiet bar with a great inner courtyard and a rooftop terrace with a killer view. An excellent place to begin your evening with a couple of drinks on the balcony before hitting the more rowdy places. Daily 8pm to 4am. **Micraasia,** 70 Konstantinopoleos, Gazi (✆ 210/346-4851), whose name means "Asia Minor" and the decor has something of the Middle Eastern vibe of the old Greek world in that region (now Turkey). Red lighting, colored tiles, chaises, and belly dancers all contribute to making this a unique, atmospheric, and interesting venue (mostly for girls). There is also seating on its "secret" rooftop. Open daily 7:30pm to 4am. **Moe,** 1–5 Keleou, Gazi is open from midnight to 6am daily. The small after-hours bar gets busy after 4am just when most of the other gay bars in the city have given up. It's the place to go when the drinks, loud music, and flirting refuse to call it a night. **Noiz,** 41 Evmolpidon and Konstantinoupoleos, Gazi (✆ 210/342-4771; www.noizclub.gr). With its good music and dynamic scene, the girls have made Noiz into the most popular lesbian bar/club in town. The ultimate lesbian party. Weeknights 10:30pm to 4am; weekends 10:30pm to 6am. **So Bar So Food,** 23 Persefonis, Gazi (✆ 210/341-7774), is a popular lesbian bar with a great garden for the girls that want to chill out with their friends before hitting the clubs. Nice soundtrack, chill-out ambience, lesbian has rarely been so chic (sorry, couldn't resist). Open Tuesday though Sunday 10pm to 4am. **Sodade,** 10 Triptopolemou, Gazi (*©* **210/346-8657;** www.sodade.gr), Much like Lamda, Sodade has also become an institution in Athenian gay nightlife. Owned by two lesbians who had the foresight over a decade ago to take a chance in a forgotten part of the city with a gay bar. Sodade was that unique place where gay boys and girls and their straight friends partied and fell in love together. It remains extremely popular every day of the week but is unbearably packed on weekends. Weeknights 10:30pm to 4am; weekends 10:30pm to 6am. **S'Cape,** Iera Odos and 139 Meg. Alexandrou, Gazi (*©* **210/345-2751**), is a large club housed in the space formerly occupied by one of the city's best straight summer clubs. With army bunks, military-style motif, and a very sexy crowd, the place is fun and very cruisy but never takes itself too seriously. Monday is Karaoke night, Thursday is Greek night. Weeknights 10:30pm to 4am; weekends 10:30pm to 6am.

RESTAURANTS
Myrovolos, 12 Giatrakou, Metaxourgeio (*©* **210/522-8806**). This popular gay restaurant is a wonderful venue in a large piazza that opens at 11am every day as a cafe. It then becomes a very good restaurant before morphing into a very busy bar for girls who love other girls and their guy friends. **Sapho,** 35 Megalou Alexandrou, Metaxourgeio (*©* **210/523-6447**), is owned by two lesbians from the island of Lesbos. They serve traditional and delicious dishes from their island at very reasonable prices. Also, don't forget to check out the very popular restaurants **Mamakas** and **Prosopa,** both mainstream but still very gay-friendly; check out the dining section in chapter 5 for more information.

BEACH
Not a typical beach as there is no sand, **Limanakia B** is a series of beautiful rocky coves. Nearby Limanakia A is far more popular, with a cafe/bar built right inside the rock and a rowdy, party crowd of teenagers and 20-somethings. Limanakia B is more forlorn and has no such features. If you take the tram to Glyfada then bus no. E22 to Limanakia (third stop), once you get off the bus you will see a roadside canteen with outdoor seating on a wooden deck. This is where you can stock up on snacks and water before descending down to the water and where, after sunning and swimming, you can linger for the sunset. Visitors follow the steep trail down to the water and claim their own rock. The water is beautiful and so are some of the other visitors. Nudity and public sex are common, especially late in the day when men get to know each other in private caves.

BOOKSTORE
Even though **Colorful Planet,** 6 Antoniadou, Plateia Victoria (*©* **210/882-6600;** www.colourfulplanet.gr; Metro: Victoria), caters mostly to a Greek gay and lesbian clientele with many Greek and international (translated) works of gay literature, there is still enough here to browse through such as DVDs, calendars, gay foreign press, gay guides to Greece, and many other goodies.

12 Piraeus: A Jumping-Off Point to the Islands

Piraeus has been the port of Athens since antiquity, and it is still where you catch most island boats and cruise ships. What's confusing is that Piraeus has **three harbors: Megas Limani (Main Harbor),** where you'll see everything from tankers to cruise ships; beautiful **Zea Limani (Zea Marina),** the port for most of the swift hydrofoils

Papastratou
Gravias

Train Station
(Peloponnese)

Akti Kondhili

Metro Station

Train Station
(Northern
Greece)

Plateia
Karaiskaki

Bus
Station

Market

Platía
Themistokleous

Plateia
Korai

Megas Limani
(Main Harbor)

Thivon

Moutsopoulou

Dodekanisou

Athinon

Ikonomidou

Retsina

Alipedou

34

Sintagmatos

Venizelou

Evanyelistrias

Gr. Lambraki

M. Assias

Karaoli-Dimitriou

Demokratias

Tzavela

Maritime Museum

Plateia
Kanari

Archaeological
Museum

Zea Limani
(Zea's Harbor)

Mikrolimano

(Little Harbor/
Turkish Harbor)

Plateia
Alexandras

Hatzikiriakou

Akti Xaverou

Akti Miaouli

Iroon Politehniou

Moutsopoulou

Akti Koundourioti

Koumoundourou

Vas. Pavlou

Plateia
Freatidas

Greece

Athens

Aegean
Sea

Piraeus

Mediterranean
Sea

CRETE

Akti Themistokleous

Amos **4**
Flying Dolphins to
    Poros, Hydra, Spetses **2**
International Ferries **1**
Istioploikos **5**
Jimmy and the Fish **6**
Pisina **3**

that dart to the islands; and **Mikrolimano (Little Harbor),** also called Turkolimano, or Turkish Harbor by the old-timers), one of the most charming and picturesque harbors in the Mediterranean, lined with a number of fish restaurants, cafes, and bars.

The absence of helpful signs at both the Main Harbor and Zea Limani however, along with their constant hustle and bustle, means that this is not an easy place to navigate. To be on the safe side, even if you have your tickets, get there an hour before your ship is scheduled to sail—and don't be surprised if you curse this advice because your ship sails later than announced.

As in antiquity, today's Piraeus has the seamier side of a sailors' port of call as well as the color and bustle of an active harbor—both aspects, somewhat sanitized, were portrayed in the 1960 film *Never on Sunday* that made Melina Mercouri an international star. Piraeus also has a sprawling street market just off the Main Harbor, where you can buy produce brought each day on island boats, including bread baked that morning on distant islands. If you find yourself here with some time to spare, keep in mind to take a stroll along Mikrolimano, Zea Marina (otherwise known as Pasalimani, with countless cafes and shopping stores) and the beautiful residential area of Kastella.

ESSENTIALS

As always, keep in mind that these prices were accurate at press time and probably will have gone up by the time you arrive here.

Tips **For the Insider**

From mid-July through the end of August, boats leaving Piraeus for the islands are heavily booked, and often overbooked. It is sometimes possible to get deck passage without a reservation, but even that can be difficult when as many as 100,000 passengers leave Piraeus on a summer weekend (as often happens in July and Aug). Most ships will not allow passengers to board without a ticket, so buy your tickets in advance.

   Because schedules depend on the weather, and sailings are often delayed or canceled, it's not a good idea to plan to return to Athens by boat less than 24 hours before your flight home. Also, as with most ports, this is not a good place to wander around in the wee hours—unless you are looking for a walk on the wild side.

GETTING THERE   By Metro   The fastest and easiest way to Piraeus is to take the Metro from Omonia Square or Monastiraki to the last stop (1€/$1.30), which will leave you a block from the domestic port. (This can feel like a very long block if you are carrying heavy luggage.)

By Bus   From Syntagma Square, take the (very slow) Green Depot bus no. 40 from the corner of Filellinon; it will leave you a block from the international port, about a 10-minute walk along the water from the domestic port. From the airport, bus no. 19 goes to Piraeus; the fare is 1€ ($1.30).

By Taxi   A taxi from Syntagma Square will cost up to 10€ ($13). A taxi from Athens International Airport to the port costs 15€ to 25€ ($20–$33).

RETURNING TO ATHENS   The easiest route is to take the Metro to central Athens, to either Monastiraki or Omonia squares. Most taxi drivers will try to overcharge tourists disembarking from the boats. They often offer a flat rate two or three times the legal fare. If you stand on the dock, you'll get no mercy. The options are to pay up, get a policeman to help you, or walk to a nearby street, hail a cab, and hope for a fair rate.

VISITOR INFORMATION   For boat schedules, transit information, and other tourist information 24 hours a day, dial © 171 or 1441. The **Piraeus Port Authority** can be reached at © 210/451-1311 to -1317. The *Athens News* and the *Kathimerini* insert in the *International Herald Tribune* print major ferry schedules. The **Greek National Tourism Organization (EOT)** office (© 210/452-2591) is inconveniently located on the street above Zea Marina (the hydrofoil port), on the second floor of a shopping arcade stocked with yacht supplies. It's open Monday through Friday from 9am to 2:30pm, but its limited resources probably won't warrant the 20-minute walk from the ferry piers. The small **tourist office** (© 210/412-1181) in the Piraeus Metro station on Akti Poseidonos is open from 8am to 8pm. The numbers for the **harbor police** are © 210/412-2501 or 210/451-1311.

FAST FACTS   Several **banks** are along the waterfront. **National Bank,** on Ethniki Antistaseos, has extended hours in summer. A portable **post office** opposite the Aegina ferry pier offers currency exchange; it's open Monday through Saturday from 8am to 8pm, Sunday from 8am to 6pm. The **main post office** is on Tsamadoy; it's usually open from 8am to 4pm. There is also a substation in the Metro office on Akti Poseidonos. The **telephone office (OTE)** is a block away from the post office and is open 24 hours. There is another branch by the water, on Akti Miaouli at Merarchias, open daily from 7am to 9:30pm. You'll find secure **luggage storage** in the Metro station at the **Central Travel Agency** (© 210/411-5611); hours are from 6am to 8pm.

TICKETS TO THE ISLANDS   The quay of the Main Harbor is lined with **ticket agents,** many concentrated in Plateia Karaiskaki; some sell tickets for one or two lines or destinations only, some for more. A sign in the window should tell you what the agent sells. Almost every agent will tell you that you're getting a good deal; almost no agent will give you one.

FERRIES TO THE ISLANDS   You will be confused as to where to catch your boat; this is inevitable. Allow yourself plenty of time. Even the person you buy your ticket from may give you a bum steer. *Tip:* Information below may change at any moment. Sorry—but we thought you should know the truth!

Ferry tickets can be purchased at a ticket office up to 1 hour before departure; after that they can usually be bought on the boat. To book first-class cabins or buy advance-sale tickets, see one of the **harborside travel agents** (around Karaiskaki Sq. by the domestic ferries and along Akti Miaouli, opposite the Crete ferries). Most open at 6am, and some will hold your baggage for the day (but without security). The **Greek National Tourism Organization** publishes a list of weekly sailings. The **tourist police** (© 171) or the **Port Authority** (© 210/451-1311 to -1317) can provide you with schedule information.

Boats for the eastern Cyclades (including Mykonos and Santorini) leave in the morning from Akti Tzelepi across from Plateia Karaiskaki. Aegina boats leave from Akti Poseidonos. Boats for Rhodes sail in the afternoon from Akti Miaouli. Boats for the western Cyclades (including Sifnos) sail in the early evening from Akti Kalimassi-oti near Plateia Karaiskaki. Boats for Crete sail in the early evening from Akti Kondyli. Many additional island boats leave from the quay opposite the Metro station. Boats heading out of Greece depart the quay on Akti Miaouli farthest away from the quays near the Metro and train stations. Boats for Aegina, Poros, Hydra, Spetses, Peloponnesian ports, and Kithira depart from Zea Marina, which is across the Piraeus peninsula and opposite the Main Harbor; the walk there takes 30 minutes.

WHAT TO SEE & DO

If you're stuck between boats, you may not want to do anything except pass the time as quietly as possible. If so, the walk inland from the harbor on Demosthenous or Vas. Georgiou to Plateia Korai leads to a cafe where you can sit with a book. If you want to be by the sea, stroll or take the no. 904 bus (.50€/65¢) from the Main Harbor to Akti Themistokleous, where you can also find cafes.

If you're in Piraeus in the summer, a more energetic suggestion is an **open-air theatrical performance** at the Kastella Theater, a few blocks inland from Mikrolimano. In 2000, the first **Poseidon Festival,** with a wide range of concerts, took place in Piraeus; it's on its way to becoming an annual event. Get details at **Piraeus Municipal Theater,** Ayiou Konstantinou (© 210/419-4550).

In the winter, performances are staged indoors, at the **Public Theater** on the green at Leoforos King Constantine. The Sunday **flea market** on and around Alipedou and Skylitsi is an equally crowded variation on the Monastiraki flea market, with generally lower-quality goods. The daily **street market** just off the Main Harbor is a good place to get **picnic supplies** for your boat trip.

The **Maritime Museum,** Akti Themistokleous, near the pier for hydrofoils (© **210/452-1598**), has handsome models of ancient and modern ships. Don't miss the classical warship *(trireme);* scholars still don't know how all those oarsmen rowed in unison. The museum is open Tuesday through Saturday from 9am to 2pm; admission is 2€ ($2.60). If you have time, stop by the **Archaeological Museum,** 32 Harilaou Trikoupi (© **210/452-1598**), to see three superb monumental bronzes, one depicting a youth (some say Apollo) and two of goddesses (some say Athena and Artemis). Museum hours are Tuesday through Sunday from 8:30am to 3pm; admission is 3€ ($3.90).

WHERE TO STAY

Because Athens is so accessible by Metro, we don't recommend an overnight stay in Piraeus. However, if it makes sense in your travel plans, try one of the decent, moderately priced choices below (usually no more than 100€/$130 double). The 74-unit **Hotel Mistral,** 105 Vas. Pavlou, Kastella (© **210/411-7150**), has a nice roof garden. Recently renovated, the 31-unit **Ideal Hotel** is at 142 Notara (© **210/429-4050**). If you want something a bit nicer, try 32-unit **Hotel Castella,** 75 Vas. Pavlou (© **210/411-4735**); or 74-unit **Cavo D'Oro,** 19 Vas. Pavlou (© **210/411-3744**). Cavo D'Oro has a pool, but it also has a disco that can be very noisy. Frugal traveling friends who visit Greece every year always stay at 56-unit **Hotel Triton,** 8 Tsamadou (© **210/4173-4578**), which they praise for its relatively quiet location—and double-glazed windows that cut down what noise there is.

WHERE TO DINE

While there are some good restaurants in Piraeus, most of the places to eat along the harbor are mediocre at best. You'll do better if you walk a few blocks along Demosthenous to Plateia Korai, location of small cafes and restaurants actually patronized by Greeks. If you do decide on one of the seafood restaurants in central Piraeus or Mikrolimano, make sure you know the price before ordering; some of these places prey on the unwary. If the final tab seems out of line, insist on a receipt, phone the tourist police, and sit tight. Despite that warning, however, it would be a shame if such a postcard-perfect spot such as Mikrolimano had nothing to offer but ambience. Ignore the aggressive restaurant staff that try to get you to dine in their establishments by all means possible (far worse than their Plaka counterparts) and try either of the two restaurants in the area I have listed there for you. You will not regret it.

Ammos ✿ SEAFOOD/MEZEDES Very reasonably priced and delicious seafood restaurant (with a large selection of *mezedes*) and a low-key island feel (great outdoor seating as well right on the marina) plus a younger crowd than the other restaurants around it.

44 Akti Koumoundourou, Mikrolimano. © 210/422-4633. Appetizers and salads 4€–14€ ($5.20–$18). Fish prices (by the kilo) change daily. MC. V.

Dourambeis SEAFOOD This fish taverna near the Delphinario theater in Piraeus is where many locals go when they want a good fish dinner. The decor is simple, the food excellent. The crayfish soup alone is worth the trip, but the whole point of going is for the excellent grilled fish.

29 Dilaveri. © 210/412-2092. Reservations suggested. Fish prices (by the kilo) change daily. No credit cards. Mon–Sat noon–5pm and 8pm–1am.

Jimmy & the Fish ✿✿ SEAFOOD More than its excellent location and its great summer deck right by the marina, you will also find excellent food here and impeccable service. The lobster spaghetti is out of this world as is the octopus in red wine and virtually everything on the menu.

46 Akti Koumoundourou, Mikrolimano. © 210/412-4417. www.jimmyandthefish.gr. Reservations recommended. 35€–40€ ($46–$52). MC, V.

Margaro 🎯 *(Value)* SEAFOOD   This fish taverna near the Main Harbor offers unusually good value (along with excellent cooking) by keeping the menu simple: fish (large or small), crayfish, and salads. Service is brisk, although this place gets very crowded.

126 Hatzikyriakou. © 210/451-4226. Fish prices (by the kilo) change frequently. No credit cards. Mon–Sat 11am–midnight; Sun lunch only.

Vassilenas 🎯 SEAFOOD/GREEK   Vassilenas has been serving its flat-fee menu for decades. Come here hungry, and even then you probably won't be able to eat everything in the more than 15 courses set before you. There's plenty of seafood, plus good Greek dishes. This is a great place to bring friends, so you can compare notes on favorite dishes or share them. Since Vassilenas is a fair hike from the waterfront, you may want to take a taxi.

72 Etolikou, Ayia Sofia. © 210/461-2457. Reservations recommended Fri–Sat. Meals 25€ ($33). No credit cards. Mon–Sat 8pm–midnight. Closed Aug.

WHERE TO HANG OUT & HAVE FUN

Istioploikos   Surrounded by sailboats right on picturesque Mikrolimano, Istioploikos (named after the private Yacht Club of Greece), features delicious variations on classic Greek cuisine, but it is the cafe that steals the show with its incredible vistas. Later on in the night, the cafe turns into a bar.

Akti Mikrolomano. © 210/413-4084. www.istioploikos.gr. Main courses 35€–40€ ($46–$52). AE, DC, MC, V.

Pisina (The Swimming Pool)   Ultra-trendy and ultra-hip, Pisina is centered around a large swimming pool (thus its name), offering amazing views of Zea Marina throughout the day and night. This is a great place to sit by the pool during the day, overlooking the yachts and to dine and/or enjoy drinks by the candlelight at night.

Zea Marina. © 210/451-1324. www.pisinacafe.gr. Main courses 22€–26€ ($29–$34). AE, DC, MC, V.

13 Day Trips from Athens

Although there are a number of tempting excursions from Athens, getting in and out of the city is so unpleasant that we suggest you visit most of the following places as you head off to the Peloponnese (Daphni and Eleusis are on the way) or to Central or Northern Greece (you can take in Marathon or Brauron). Nonetheless, two excursions—the Monastery at Kaisariani and the Temple of Poseidon at Sounion—can be more easily done as day trips from Athens.

All these excursions take you into Attica—today, as in antiquity, the countryside around Athens. According to legend, the hero Theseus unified the 12 towns of Attica under Athens. Although by no means one of the most fertile areas of Greece, the Attic countryside provided Athens with wine grapes, olives, honey, grains, fruit, marvelous marble from **Mount Pentelicus (Pendeli)** and **Mount Hymettus (Imittos),** and silver from the mines at Laurium, near Sounion. Today the Attic *Mesogeion* ("the middle of the earth," or the Attic plain) is still known for its fine grapes, most often used in making white retsina.

Serious fires have raged through much of Attica every summer since 1995. Some forests on Mounts Pentelicus and Hymettus have been totally destroyed, as were many vineyards. In addition, the new road system, engendered by the Athens International Airport at Spata—and for some Olympic events—has accelerated the transformation of Attica into a spreading suburb of Athens.

TEMPLE OF POSEIDON AT SOUNION ★★

One of the easiest and most popular day trips from Athens is to the 5th-century-B.C. Temple of Poseidon on the cliffs above Cape Sounion, 70km (43 miles) east of Athens (about 2 hr. by bus). This place is very popular at sunset—so popular that, if at all possible, you should not come on a weekend.

The easiest way to visit Sounion is on an **organized tour** (see "Organized Tours," earlier in this chapter). If you want to go on your own for far less money, take the Sounion **bus** leaving from Mavromateon along the west side of Pedion tou Areos Park (off the eastern end of Leoforos Alexandras). Buses leave about every half-hour, take 2 hours to reach Sounion, and cost less than 5€ ($6.50). To verify times, ask a Greek speaker to telephone the local **ticket office** (© 210/823-0179). Once you're in Sounion, you can catch a cab or walk the remaining kilometer to the temple. If you go to Sounion **by car,** heading out of Athens on Syngrou or Vouliagmenis boulevards, you'll probably fight your way through heavy traffic almost all the way, in both directions.

Temple of Poseidon ★★   Cape Sounion is the southernmost point of Attica, and in antiquity, as today, sailors knew they were getting near Athens when they caught sight of the Temple of Poseidon's slender Doric columns. According to legend, it was at Sounion that the great Athenian hero Theseus's father, King Aegeus, awaited his son's return from his journey to Crete to slay the Minotaur. The king had told his son to have his ship return with white sails if he survived the encounter, with black sails if he met death in the Cretan labyrinth. In the excitement of his victory, Theseus forgot his father's words, and the ship returned with black sails. When Aegeus saw the black sails, he threw himself, heartbroken, into the sea—forever afterward known as the Aegean.

One of the reasons Sounion is so spectacular, other than its site, is that 15 of the temple's original 34 columns are still standing. A popular pastime here is trying to find the spot on one column where Lord Byron carved his name. After you find Byron's name, you may wish to sit in the shade of a column, enjoy the spectacular view over the sea, envy the solitude and quiet Byron found here, and recite these lines on Sounion from the poet's *Don Juan:*

> *Place me on Sunium's marbled steep,*
> *Where nothing, save the waves and I*
> *May hear our mutual murmurs sweep . . .*

There was also a Temple of Athena here (almost entirely destroyed); it's easy to think of Sounion as purely a religious spot in antiquity. Nothing could be more wrong: The entire sanctuary (of which little remains other than the Poseidon Temple itself) was heavily fortified during the Peloponnesian War because of its strategic importance overlooking the sea routes. Much of the grain that fed Athens arrived from outside Attica in ships that had to sail past Cape Sounion. In fact, Sounion had something of an unsavory reputation as the haunt of pirates in antiquity; it would be uncharitable to think that their descendants run today's nearby souvenir shops, restaurants, and cafes.

If you wish, you can swim in the sea below Sounion and grab a snack at one of the overpriced seaside restaurants, of which the Akrogiali (here since 1887), by the Aegeon

Hotel, is a favorite. Or bring a picnic to enjoy on the beach. If you want to spend the night, the large **Grecotel Cape Sounio** (✆ **22920/39-010;** www.grecotel.gr) has all the creature comforts for a minimum of 100€ ($130) a night.

Cape Sounion. ✆ **22920/39-363.** Admission 4€ ($5.20). Daily 10am–sunset (sometimes in summer 8am–sunset).

MONASTERY OF KAISARIANI (KESSARIANI) & MOUNT HYMETTUS (IMITTOS)

Beautiful Kaisariani Monastery stands in a cool, bird-inhabited grove of pines and cypresses on the lower slopes of Mount Hymettus, famous for its beautiful marble and delicious honey. In fact, the 4th-century-A.D. philosopher Synesius of Cyrene tells the story that the Sophists lured students to their lectures "not by the fame of their eloquence, but by pots of honey from Hymettus." This has long been a lovely place to escape the heat of Athens, especially after most of the bees left Hymettus and no longer vexed visitors. Unfortunately, the forests were damaged in the fires of 1998. Keep in mind that the remaining pine groves here are a potential tinderbox. As always, be very careful if you smoke or use matches.

Kaisariani is 8km (5 miles) east of central Athens. The easiest way to visit is to take a **taxi** from Athens for about 15€ ($20). Then, if you wish, you can return by bus, having spotted the bus stop on your way up to Kaisariani. If you want the cab to wait while you visit the monastery, negotiate a price in advance. Every 20 minutes, **bus no. 224** leaves from Plateia Kaningos on Academias and from Panepistimiou and Vas. Sofias, northeast of Syntagma Square, for the suburb of Kaisariani. If the day isn't hot, the monastery's wooded site is a pleasant 2km (1-mile) walk (follow the signs) up the road; or you can take one of the cabs by the bus stop.

We suggest that you do not drive unless you want to explore Mount Hymettus, which is no longer the woodsy place fabled in antiquity, but which has become bleak after its recent fires. Kaisariani is poorly signposted so you may have trouble finding it, even with a good map.

At press time, fires had raged through part of Penteli mountain. The total damage was unknown even though the fire was under control during the same day. Earlier in the summer (in one of the worst summers in over a decade in regards to fires in the entire country), Mount Parnitha, the most beautiful and largest national park in Athens (well known for its hiking trials, ski resort, and casino) was severely damaged during a fire that raged for days during a heat wave in late June 2007. About a third of the forest (referred to as the "lungs of Athens") has either been destroyed or severely damaged.

Kaisariani Monastery ✦   When a spot is holy in Greece, it has usually been holy for a very long time indeed. Today's monastery occupies the site of an ancient temple to Aphrodite, probably built here because of the spring, part of the headwaters of the River Ilissos that flowed through Athens in antiquity. You'll see the water pouring forth through the open mouth of the marble goat's head at the monastery's entrance. Incredibly, this spring once supplied much of Athens with drinking water. Now, Greek brides who wish to become pregnant often journey here to drink from the spring, whose waters are believed to speed conception.

The monastery was built in the 11th century over the ruins of a 5th-century Christian church, itself built over the temple. The monks supported themselves by keeping bees and selling the honey, much as some religious orders today sell jams or liqueurs. The monastery's kitchen and refectory, which now house sculptural fragments, are on the west side of a paved, flower-filled courtyard. To the south, the old monks' cells and

---

Tips **Reminder**

Kaisariani is still an active church. Remember to dress appropriately: Shorts, miniskirts, and sleeveless or skimpy shirts are considered offensive.

---

a bathhouse are being restored (exploration at your own risk is usually permitted). The well-preserved church, built like so many others in Greece in the shape of a Greek cross, has a dome supported by four ancient Roman columns. Most of the frescoes are relatively late, dating from the 17th and 18th centuries; the distinctive bell tower is from the 19th century.

Kaisariani. ℃ 210/723-6619. Admission 4€ ($5.20). Tues–Sun 8:30am–3pm; often later in summer.

SANCTUARY OF ARTEMIS AT BRAURON (VRAVRONA)

Most visitors do not come to this little shrine to Artemis in the Attic hills. It's a lovely, tranquil spot—in danger of losing its peace to the proliferating roads and increasing overhead noise from planes heading into and out of the new international airport. Brauron is 38km (22 miles) east of central Athens between Porto Rafti and Loutsa, on the east coast of Attica.

Take **bus no. 304** for the Zappion to the village of Loutsa, which is about 2km (about a mile) from the site. **By car,** from Athens, head toward Porto Rafti. In Porto Rafti, follow signs for Vravrona and Artemida. On the left, about 600m (1,968 ft.) before the site, are the remains of a 6th-century church. Traffic often backs up on the road between Stavrou and Markopoulo, particularly in Peania, so the trip will probably last the better part of an hour. You can also take the new highway from Athens to the airport and continue on to Rafina, where you can ask for directions to Brauron.

Sanctuary of Artemis ⚐   Just when you think that you're beginning to understand the ancient Greeks, you encounter something like the cult of Artemis at Brauron. According to legend, Agamemnon's ill-fated daughter Iphigenia served as a priestess here—and was buried here after her ritual sacrifice on the eve of the expedition to Troy. Little girls in modern times dress themselves as bear cubs for a quadrennial festival here to honor Iphigenia and Artemis. According to one story, the custom began when an epidemic broke out after a youth killed a bear that had attacked his sister. An oracle suggested that a purifying ceremony take place in which young girls dress like bears; this practice continued every 4 years throughout antiquity. As you sit on a shady slope, you may want to imagine the bearlike antics of the little girls as they parade here in bear masks and saffron-colored robes. To confuse matters further, these ceremonies were believed to assist women in childbirth.

The most striking structure at Brauron is the **stoa,** restored in 1961. The stoa was built in the shape of an incomplete Greek letter "p" facing south toward the hill. Six rooms on the stoa's north side contained 11 small beds for the children, with stone tables by the beds. Four rooms on the stoa's west side may also have been used as bedrooms for the children. The foundations of the 5th-century **Temple of Artemis** are located here as well, along with a cave called the **Tomb of Iphigenia.** There's also a sacred spring and two chapels at this altogether delightful spot.

This small, well-lit **museum** has some especially charming displays, including marble portrait heads of the little girls, plus bear masks, handsome geometric vases from the nearby cemetery at Anavyssos, and grave markers found in the surrounding area.

Vraona. (℗ **22990/27-020.** Site and museum admission 4€ ($5.20). Tues–Sun 8:30am–3pm in winter; often later in summer.

MARATHON

In 490 B.C., the vastly outnumbered Athenians and their allies from the little Boeotian town of Plataea defeated the invading Persian army on the plain of Marathon, and saved Athens and much of Greece (and, some say, much of Europe) from Persian rule. In honor of their valor, the 192 Athenians who fell here were buried on the battlefield in an enormous burial mound. Beyond that, there's little to see at Marathon, as there is little to see at Gettysburg and Runnymede, but such sites are moving because of the battles that shaped the course of history. When Lord Byron came to Greece to fight in the War of Independence, he visited Marathon and wrote:

> *The mountains look on Marathon,*
> *And Marathon looks on the sea.*
> *And musing there an hour alone,*
> *I dreamed that Greece might still be free . . .*

Alas, before he could fight to free Greece, Byron succumbed to fever in the boggy, cholera-infested town of Mesolongi, where he died on April 19, 1824.

Marathon is 42km (26 miles) northeast of Athens between the villages of Nea Makri and Marathona. **Buses** leave Athens from Mavromati along the east side of Pedion tou Areos Park every half-hour in the morning and every hour in the afternoon. The trip costs 4€ ($5.20) and takes 2½ hours. For departure times, call the **tourist police** (℗ **171**) or ask a Greek speaker to call the local **ticket office** (℗ **210/821-0872**). **By car,** drive north from Athens along Leoforos Kifissias, the more scenic route that circles Mount Pendeli through Dionissiou to the sea at Nea Makri; or drive along the National Highway toward Thessaloniki, from where signs direct you to Marathon.

Marathon Battlefield & Burial Mound ☀

By September of 490 B.C., the advancing force of Persia—then the most powerful empire in the world—reached Marathon, anchored its fleet in the bay, and made plans to attack Athens by land and by sea. The Athenians sent their swiftest runner, Pheidippides, to Sparta to ask for help, and marched their entire army of about 9,000 men north to Marathon. When Pheidippides reached Sparta (some say that it took him about a day and a half—clearly the gods were on his side), the Spartans said they would be delighted to join the Athenians, after the conclusion of an important Spartan religious festival observing the full moon. This was widely thought to be a delaying tactic, and Athens prepared to stand alone—and did, except for a small contingent of about 1,000 soldiers from the little town of Plataea in Boeotia. The Persian force was at least 24,000 strong.

For some days, the two forces eyed each other, but neither attacked. Then, before dawn on September 12, the Athenians launched a surprise attack. As the Athenian right and left wings forged forward, the center gave way—but when the Persians pressed forward, the Athenian flanks surrounded them and the serious slaughter began. Many of the Persians tried to flee to the safety of their ships, anchored offshore, but were cut down in the marshy plain that lay between the battlefield and the sea. By nightfall, the victory was won, and Pheidippides was again dispatched, this time to run to Athens with news of the victory at Marathon. Pheidippides ran flat out, burst into the Athenian Agora, shouted, "We have won," and fell dead from exhaustion. Today's marathons commemorate Pheidippides's run. (If you want information on the annual rerunning of the Marathon in Nov, check out www.athensmarathon.com.)

Although the Athenians won the battle at Marathon, the Persian navy had not been harmed, and it set sail for Athens. The weary Athenian army marched posthaste back to Athens and prepared to do battle again, but the Persians, for whatever reason, after sailing up and down the coast of Attica, reversed course and returned to Asia Minor. Ten years later, they would be back—only to be defeated decisively in the Battle of Salamis.

The Athenian victory at Marathon, against such great odds, became the stuff of legend. Some said that the Athenian hero Theseus himself fought alongside his descendants. Others said that the god Pan had bewitched and confused the Persians, leading them to plunge to their deaths in the marshy swamp—leading them, in short, to panic, the word derived from the god's name. According to one of the legends, Pan appeared to Pheidippides as he ran with news of the victory to Athens. Pointedly, Pan asked why the Athenians built so few shrines to him—a situation that was quickly rectified throughout Attica.

Although it was customary to bury war casualties in the Kerameikos cemetery in Athens, the 192 Athenian dead from this astonishing victory were cremated and buried together in the mound that still stands on the battlefield. When the Athenian mound was excavated in the late 19th century, quantities of ashes and burned bones were found.

Half a millennium after the battle, when the traveler Pausanias visited Marathon, he wrote, "Here every night you can hear the noise of whinnying horses and of men fighting." Indeed, there are those today who claim to have heard sounds of battle on moonlit nights at Marathon.

The excellent little Marathon museum is several kilometers from the battlefield but is signposted both there and on the main road. The collection includes finds from the battlefield and other sites in the area, including startling imitation Egyptian statues from a local shrine, possibly built by Herodes Atticus, the great 2nd-century-A.D. benefactor born near Marathon. Herodes Atticus, who owned a number of luxurious villas in Greece, was almost incapable of taking a day trip without building a fountain, shrine, or temple to commemorate his visit.

If you're not bothered by swimming near the marshy swamp where so many Persians drowned, you can take a dip and enjoy a bite at a taverna along the coast. Most tavernas close off season, although some open on the weekend.

If you want to see the part of the plain that was transformed into a lake for the Olympic rowing venue in 2004, look for signs for Schinias. You can decide whether holding a sporting event on the battlefield of Marathon is analogous to turning part of the Gettysburg battlefield into a bowling alley.

Marathonas. (✆ 0294/55-155. Admission of 3€ ($3.90) includes both the mound and museum. Museum and battle site Tues–Sun 8:30am–3pm; often later in summer.

MONASTERY OF DAPHNI (DAFNI)

If you've never seen Byzantine mosaics and wonder what all the fuss is about, Daphni is the place to come. Daphni is one of the greatest masterpieces of the Byzantine Empire, which was founded by the first Christian emperor, Constantine, in the 4th century A.D. and conquered by the Turks in 1453. The great art historian of Byzantine Greece, Sir David Talbot-Rice, has called Daphni "the most perfect monument" of the 11th century—and this sober scholar was not given to hyperbole.

Unfortunately, getting here is an ordeal. If possible, see Daphni on your way to or from the Peloponnese. If you're driving, you can easily stop here; if you're traveling with a tour, most stop at Daphni. You could brave a taxi, but it's a very ugly ride—and the 9km (5½-mile) trip west of Athens can take an hour. Coming by bus involves numerous changes. It is best to take the Metro to the Daphni station and continue by bus or taxi. A visit to Daphni can be combined with a stop at Eleusis (see below).

If you're **driving,** follow the signs for Corinth out of Omonia Square. You will be on a very ugly and very crowded road for the entire journey of at least half an hour (an hour is not unusual). After you cross an overpass of the National Road that runs north to Thessaloniki (Salonika), the road rises steadily for 5km (3 miles) to the gentle crest of a hill. There is a traffic light just over the crest and another traffic light approximately half a kilometer (1,500 ft.) farther on. Turn left at the second light and then right along the parallel road about a third of kilometer (about 900 ft.) to the monastery. *Warning:* Due to the heavy traffic, turning off the National Road is not always easy, so allow yourself plenty of time to get to the left to make the turn.

Monastery of Daphni 🏛🏛   When you reach Daphni, you may want to take a few minutes in the courtyard to look at the church's lovely brickwork and think about the long history of this sacred spot. There have been shrines here since antiquity, when there was a temple to Apollo. The temple is long since gone (except one column near the entrance), but the name *Daphni* (Greek for "laurel," Apollo's favorite plant) still honors that god.

In the 6th century, a small monastery was built here, later greatly expanded in the 11th century. The monastic buildings have been almost entirely destroyed, but the domed church dedicated to the Virgin Mary remains. This is something of a miracle: Over the centuries, Daphni has been repeatedly damaged by invaders and earthquakes, and repeatedly rebuilt. You'll see an example of that rebuilding in the twin Gothic arches in front of the church's west entrance. These were added by the Cistercian monks who turned Daphni into a Catholic monastery after the Crusaders captured Constantinople in 1204. During the long period of the Turkish occupation, there was no functioning monastery here—indeed, for a while, the buildings were used as army barracks. After the Greek War of Independence, Daphni was reclaimed by the Greek Orthodox church and restored to its former glory.

A severe earthquake in the 1980s prompted another round of restoration in which the church was strengthened and its dazzling mosaic cycle repaired. Step inside and let your eyes become accustomed to the dark. On the **central dome** is the commanding mosaic of Christ Pantocrator (the Almighty). This image of Christ as an awesome judge is quite different from the Western image of Christ as a suffering mortal. If you're familiar with the Old and New Testaments, you'll be able to pick out familiar stories in the mosaics throughout the rest of the church. As is traditional in Greek Orthodox churches, the Annunciation, Nativity, Baptism, and Transfiguration are in the squinches supporting the dome, and the 16 major prophets are displayed between the windows of the dome. The Adoration of the Magi and the Resurrection are in the **barrel vault** inside the main (southern) entrance of the church, and the Entry into Jerusalem and the Crucifixion are in the **northern barrel vault.** Mosaics showing scenes from the life of the Virgin are in the **south bay** of the narthex (a passage between the entrance and nave). Even if you're not familiar with the stories, and even if you find the mosaic of Christ Pantocrator grim rather than awesome, you may well be enchanted by the charming details in scenes such as the Adoration of the Magi.

Daphni. ☎ 210/581-1558. Admission 3€ ($3.90). Daily (except major holidays) 8:30am–2:45pm.

SANCTUARY OF ELEUSIS (ELEFSIS)

Although Eleusis was the site of the most famous and revered of all the ancient Mysteries, the present-day site is so grim (surrounded by the horrors, and horrible smells, of the industrial city of Elefsina) that you'll need a very keen interest in either archaeology, mystery cults, or oil refineries to enjoy a visit here. That said, we must admit that one friend says that Eleusis is her favorite site near Athens. This makes absolutely no sense to us, but if you come here, you can decide for yourself.

Eleusis is 23km (14 miles) west of Athens. To get here **by bus,** take no. A16, 853, or 862 from Eleftherias Square off Leoforos Pireos near Omonia. (This trip can be combined with a visit to Daphni Monastery.) Ask the driver to let you off at the Sanctuary (Heron), which is off to the left of the main road, before the center of town. If you're **driving,** take the National Road and exit at Elefsina. There are almost no signs for this important site; you may have to ask repeatedly for directions. You'll know you're close when you pass through a small, pleasantly wooded square with several restaurants and can catch a glimpse of the site off to the side.

Sanctuary of Eleusis ⚐ The unknown and the famous were initiated into the sacred rites here, yet we know almost nothing about the Eleusinian Mysteries. What we do know is that the Mysteries commemorated the abduction of Demeter's daughter Persephone by the god of the underworld, Hades (Pluto). Demeter was able to strike a bargain with the god, who allowed Persephone to leave the underworld and rejoin her mother for 6 months each year. The Mysteries celebrated this—and the cycle of growth, death, and rebirth of each year's crops.

Despite its substantial remains and glorious past—this was already a religious site in Mycenaean times—the sanctuary's present surroundings make it difficult to warm to the spot. Admittedly, there are the considerable remains of a **Temple of Artemis,** a 2nd-century-A.D. **Roman Propylaea** (monumental entrance), and **triumphal arches** dedicated to the Great Goddesses and to the emperor Hadrian. Hadrian's arch here, by the way, inspired the Arc de Triomphe on Paris's Champs-Elysées. Nearby is the **Telesterion,** the Temple of Demeter, where only initiates of the cult knew what happened at the sacred rites—and they kept their silence.

One poignant spot at the sanctuary is **Kallichoron Well,** where the goddess Demeter wept over the loss of her daughter, whom Hades (Pluto) spirited away. The dark god may have dragged Persephone with him through the cave here known as **Ploutonion,** which was believed to be an entrance to the underworld. It seems ironic that modern Elefsina itself is so ghastly that it has become something of a hell on earth.

If you're in luck, the small **museum** (closed since the 1999 earthquake but open intermittently of late) will be open. It contains finds from the site, including several **figures of Demeter** and a lithe **statue of Antinous,** the beautiful boy who won the emperor Hadrian's heart.

Elefsina. ☎ 210/554-6019. Admission 3€ ($3.90); free Sun. Tues–Sun 8:30am–3pm; often open later in summer.

The Saronic Gulf Islands

by Sherry Marker

The islands of the Saronic Gulf are so close to Athens that each summer Athenians flee there for some relief from the heat and the crowds in Athens. If the summer of 2007—the hottest in at least 90 years—really is a sign of the future, more and more Athenians will head for the Saronic Gulf islands each year. In addition, these islands are popular destinations for European and American travelers with limited time who are determined not to go home without seeing at least one Greek island. You can make a day trip to any of these islands, and some day cruises out of Piraeus rush you on and off three islands! Usually, that involves quick stops at Hydra, Poros, and Spetses before you're deposited back on the mainland. If you plan to spend the night on any of these islands in summer, book well in advance. The website **www.saronicnet.com** is a useful resource for all the islands.

The easiest island to visit is **Aegina,** a mere 30km (17 nautical miles) from Piraeus. The main attractions—in addition to the ease of the journey—are the graceful Doric **Temple of Aphaia,** one of the best-preserved Greek temples; several good beaches; and verdant pine and pistachio groves. That's the good news. The bad news is that Aegina is so close to the metropolitan sprawl of Athens and Piraeus that it's not easy here to get a clear idea of why the Greek islands are so beloved as refuges from urban life. Aegina has become a bedroom suburb for Athens,

with many of its 10,000 inhabitants commuting to work by boat. That said, Aegina town still has its pleasures; and both the Temple of Aphaia and deserted medieval town of **Paleohora** are terrific.

Poros is hardly an island at all; only a narrow (370m/1,214-ft.) inlet separates it from the Peloponnese. There are several decent beaches, and the landscape is wooded, gentle, and rolling, like the landscape of the adjacent mainland. Alas, Poros's pine groves were damaged by the summer fires that swept through Greece in 2007. Poros is popular with tour groups as well as young Athenians (in part because the Naval Cadets' Training School here means that there are lots of young men eager to party). On summer nights, the waterfront is either very lively or hideously crowded, depending on your point of view.

Hydra (Idra), with its bare hills, superb natural harbor, and elegant stone mansions, is the most strikingly beautiful of the Saronic Gulf islands. One of the first Greek islands to be "discovered" by artists, writers, and bon vivants in the '50s, Hydra, like Mykonos, is not the place to experience traditional village life. The island has been declared a national monument from which cars have been banished. Its relative quiet is increasingly being infiltrated by motorcycles. A major drawback: Few of the beaches are very good for swimming, although you can swim from the rocks in and just out of Hydra town. **Spetses** has always been

Easy Cruising

In 2007, Sir Stelios Haji-Ioannou, the endlessly energetic Greek founder of easy-Jet and a myriad other easy-companies, added Greece to his easyCruise options. For detailed itineraries and prices, check out www.easycruise.com.

popular with wealthy Athenians, who built—and continue to build—handsome villas here. If you like wooded islands, you'll love Spetses, although summer forest fires over the last few years have destroyed some of Spetses's pine groves. This gentle, forested island is very unlike the images of most Greek islands shown on countless tourist posters that depict the Cycladic isles with their bare, austere landscapes and simple whitewashed houses. The island has some good beaches; alas, several of the best have been taken over by large hotels.

If possible, avoid June through August unless you have a hotel reservation and think that you'd enjoy the hustle and bustle of high season. Also, mid-July through August, boats leaving Piraeus for the islands are heavily booked—often overbooked. It is sometimes possible to get a deck passage without a reservation, but even that can be difficult when as many as 100,000 Athenians leave Piraeus on a

summer weekend. Most ships will not allow passengers to board without a ticket.

Something to keep in mind: Some hydrofoils leave from the Piraeus Main Harbor while others leave from the Piraeus Marina Zea Harbor—and some leave from both harbors!

If you go to one of these islands on a **day trip,** remember that, unlike the more sturdy ferryboats, hydrofoils cannot travel when the sea is rough. You may find yourself an unwilling overnight island visitor, grateful to be given the still-warm bed in a private home surrendered by a family member to make some money. I speak from experience. For more information, see "Getting There," below. *Greek Island Hopping,* published annually by Thomas Cook, is, by its own admission, out of date by the time it sees print. That said, it's a very useful volume for finding out where (if not when) you can travel among the Greek islands.

1 Aegina

30km (17 nautical miles) SW of Piraeus

More travelers come to Aegina (Egina), the largest of the Saronic Gulf islands, than to any of the other Greek islands. Why? The answer, as so often, is Location, Location, Location. Aegina is so close to Athens that it draws thousands of day-trippers. As the day-trippers arrive, many of the 10,000 who live on Aegina and commute daily to work in Athens depart. If you have only 1 day for one island, you may decide on Aegina, where you can see one famous temple (the Doric **Temple of Aphaia**) visit one romantic medieval hill town **(Paleochora),** have lunch at one of the harborside tavernas in Aegina town, and munch the island's famous pistachio nuts as you sail back to Athens.

Most ships arrive and depart from the main port and capital of **Aegina town** on the west coast, though a few stop at the resort town of **Souvala** on the north coast and at the port of **Ayia Marina** on the east coast. Ayia Marina is about as charmless as it's possible to be, but this port is your best choice if your principal destination is the Temple of Aphaia.

The Saronic Gulf Islands

0   50 mi
0   50 km

Salamis
Perama
To Athens
Ambelakia
Piraeus
SALAMIS
Perani
Glyfada
Peristeria

Saronikos Kolpos
(Saronic Gulf)

DIAPORIA

IPSILI
Souvala
Vaia
Korfos
Aegina
Messagros
Ayia
Marina
Paleohora
KIRA
Marathonas
Portes
Epidaurus
AEGINA
ANGISTRI
MONI
Perdika
Kounoupitsa

Epidaurikos
Kolpos
Vathy
(Gulf of
Epidaurus)
Methana

PELOPONNESE
POROS
Kaloni
Poros
Trizina
(Ancient Troezen)
Galatas
Didima
TSELEVINIA
Loukaiti
Piepi
Metochi
Ermioni
Zourvas
Kranidi
Dokos
Hydra
Episkopi
DOKOS
HYDRA
SPETSES
Spetses
SPETSOPOULA

Ferry Routes
Ruins/Archeological Site

Lemon Groves of Limonodassos **5**
Monastery of Ayios Nektarios **1**
Monastery of the Prophet Elijah (Profitis Elias) **6**
Monastery of Zoodoches Piyi **4**
Temple of Aphaia **2**
Temple of Poseidon **3**

Greece
Athens
Aegean
Sea
The
Saronic
Gulf
Mediterranean
Sea   **CRETE**

Despite massive tourism and the rapid development devouring much farmland, the area still has its share of almond, olive, and especially **pistachio** orchards. In fact, the island has an endemic water problem simply because of the water necessary for the pistachio groves. Wherever you buy pistachios in Greece, the vendor may assure you that they are from Aegina to indicate their superior quality.

ESSENTIALS

GETTING THERE   **Car ferries** and **excursion boats** to Aegina usually leave from Piraeus's Main Harbor; confusingly, **hydrofoils** leave both from the Main Harbor and from Marina Zea Harbor. Hydrofoil service is at least twice as fast as ferries and at least 40% more expensive (except to Aegina, for which the charge is only about 10% more). The sleek little hydrofoils are outfitted like broad aircraft with airline seats, toilets, and a minimum of luggage facilities. (The fore sections offer better views, but they're also bumpier.) The newer Super Cats are bigger, faster, and more comfortable, with food and beverage service. Reservations are recommended on weekends. Often, in order to continue to another Saronic Gulf island by hydrofoil, you must return to Piraeus and change to another hydrofoil. Some ferries go from Aegina to the other Saronic Gulf islands. **Warning:** As we mentioned above, schedules—and even carriers—can change, so double-check information you get from anyone other than the **Greek National Tourism Organization** (© 210/870-0000; www.gnto.gr)—and remain prepared for schedule and carrier changes.

Daily hydrofoil and ferry service to the Saronic Gulf islands is offered by **Hellenic Seaways** (© 210/419-9200; www.hellenicseaways.gr). **Saronikos Ferries** (© 210/417-1190) takes passengers and cars to Aegina, Poros, and Spetses; cars are not allowed to disembark on Hydra. **Euroseas** (© 210/411-3108) has speedy catamaran service from Piraeus to Poros, Hydra, and Spetses. You can usually visit any one of the Saronics for between 20€ and 65€ ($26–$85) day return; the faster the ship, the higher the price. Several cruises offer day trips to Hydra, Poros, and Aegina; for details, see chapter 4, "Cruising the Greek Islands."

For information on schedules for most Argo-Saronic ferries, you can try one of the various numbers of the **Piraeus Port Authority:** © 210/422-6000, 210/410-1480, or 210/410-1441, but phones are not always answered. On Aegina, try © **22970/22-328.**

VISITOR INFORMATION   **Aegina Tourist Office** (© **22970/22-220**) is in Aegina Town Hall. There's a string of travel agencies at the harbor, including the usually efficient **Aegina Island Holidays,** 47 Demokratias (© **22970/26-439;** fax 22970/26-430). To learn a little about Aegina's history, look for Anne Yannoulis's *Aegina* (Lycabettus Press), usually on sale at **Kalezis Boatokshop** on the harbor (© **22970/25-956**),

---

⌒Tips Booking Your Return Trip

With virtually all of the hydrofoils and ferries that serve the Saronic Gulf islands, it is impossible to book a round-trip. As soon as you arrive at your island destination, head for the ticket office and book your return ticket. If you do not do this, you may end up spending longer than you planned—or wished—on one or more of the islands. At press time, both Minoan Flying Dolphins and Ceres Flying Dolphins had been absorbed by Hellas Flying Dolphins (www.dolphins.gr), but there may be more ownership and name changes by the time you arrive.

Tips **Culture Calls**

If you visit the islands of the Saronic Gulf in July and August, keep an eye out for posters announcing exhibitions at local museums and galleries. There are often exhibits at the **Citronne Gallery** (© 22980-22-401) on Poros and at the **Koundouriotis Mansion** (© 22980/52-210) on Hydra. In addition, many Athenian galleries close for parts of July and August, and some have shows on the islands. The **Athens Center,** 48 Archimidous (© **210/701-2268;** www.athens centre.gr), sometimes stages plays on Spetses and Hydra. The center offers a Modern Greek Language Summer Program on Spetses in June and July.

---

which stocks foreign newspapers. Check the websites **www.aeginagreece.com** and **www.greeka.com/saronic/aegina** for info in English.

GETTING AROUND A left turn as you disembark takes you east to the **bus station** on Plateia Ethatneyersias. There's good service to most of the island, with trips every hour in summer to the Temple of Aphaia and Ayia Marina (2€/$2.60); tickets must be purchased before boarding. **Taxis** are available nearby; the fare to the temple should be about 12€ ($16). You can sometimes negotiate a decent rate for a round-trip by taxi with an hour's wait at the temple. **Bicycles** and **mopeds** can be rented at the opposite end of the waterfront, near the beach. *Tip:* Prices can be exorbitant. An ordinary bike should cost about 10€ ($13) per day; mopeds, from 25€ ($33).

FAST FACTS The **National Bank of Greece** is one of four waterfront banks with currency-exchange service and ATMs; some travel agents, including **Island Holidays** (© **22970/23-333**), often exchange money both during and after normal bank hours, usually at less favorable rates. The island **clinic** (© **22970/22-251**) is on the northeast edge of town; for **first aid,** dial © **22970/22-222.** The **police** (© **22970/23-343**) and the **tourist police** (© **22970/27-777**) share a building on Leonardou Lada, about 200m (656 ft.) inland from the port. The **port authority** (© **22970/22-328**) is on the waterfront. The **post office** is in Plateia Ethatneyersias, around the corner from the hydrofoil pier. The **telephone office** (**OTE**) is 5 blocks inland from the port, on Aiakou. There are several Internet cafes, including **Prestige** and **Nesant,** on and just off the waterfront. *Tip:* Before you head out, try to pick up the useful pamphlet *Essential Aegina,* often available from travel agents, hotels, and the tourist police.

WHAT TO SEE & DO
EXPLORING AEGINA TOWN

Aegina town's neoclassical buildings date from its brief stint as the first capital of newly independent Greece (1826–28). Most people's first impression of this harbor town, though, is that of fishing boats and the small cargo vessels that ply back and forth to the mainland. Have a snack at one of the little restaurants in the **fish market** (follow your nose!) just off the harbor. This is where the men who catch your snacks of octopus and fried sprats come to eat their catches. The food is usually much better here than the food at the harborfront places catering to tourists.

If you take a horse-drawn carriage (15€–25€/$20–$33) or wander the streets back from the port, you'll easily spot neoclassical buildings, including the **Markelos Tower,** near the Cathedral of **Ayios Demetrios,** with its square bell towers. In 1827, the first government of independent Greece held sessions both in the tower and at the cathedral.

Fans of Nikos Kazantzakis may want to take a cab to **Livadi,** just north of town, to see the house where he lived when he wrote *Zorba the Greek.* North of the harbor, behind the town beach, and sometimes visible from boats entering the harbor, is the lone worn Doric column that marks the site of the **Temple of Apollo,** open Tuesday through Sunday from 8:30am to 3pm; admission is 2€ ($2.60). The view here is nice, the ruins very ruined. The small museum (✆ **22970/22-637**) has finds from the site, notably pottery; open Tuesday through Sunday 8:30am to 3pm; admission is 3€ ($3.90).

About 4.8km (3 miles) out of Aegina town, the ruins of **Paleohora,** capital of the island from the 9th to the 19th centuries, sprawl over a steep hillside. During the centuries when pirate raids threatened seaside towns, the people of Aegina chose to live inland. This is a wonderful spot to explore (be sure to wear sturdy shoes and a sun hat). You'll see ruined houses and a number of carefully preserved churches and have fine views over the island. The bus to Ayia Marina makes a stop in Paleohora. If you come here, allow several hours for the excursion.

SEEING THE TEMPLE OF APHAIA ⭐⭐

The 5th-century-B.C. **Temple of Aphaia,** set on a pine-covered hill 12km (7½ miles) east of Aegina town (✆ **22970/32-398**), is one of the best-preserved and most handsome Greek temples. No one really knows who Aphaia was, although it seems that she was a very old, even prehistoric, goddess who eventually became associated both with the huntress goddess Artemis and with Athena, the goddess of wisdom. According to some legends, Aphaia lived on Crete, where King Minos, usually preoccupied with his labyrinth and Minotaur, fell in love with her. When she fled Crete, he pursued her, and she finally threw herself into the sea off Aegina to escape him. At some point in the late 6th or early 5th century B.C., this temple was built, on the site of earlier shrines, to honor Aphaia.

Thanks to the work of restorers, 25 of the original 32 Doric columns still stand. The pedimental sculpture, showing scenes from the Trojan War, was carted off in 1812 by King Ludwig of Bavaria. Whatever you think about the removal of art treasures from their original homes, Ludwig probably did us a favor by taking the sculptures to the Glyptothek in Munich: While he was doing this, locals were busily burning much of the temple to make lime and hacking up other bits to use in building their homes. Admission to the site is 4€ ($5.20); it's open Monday through Friday from 8:30am to 7pm, Saturday and Sunday from 8:30am to 3pm. Allow at least 4 hours for your visit if you come here by the hourly bus from Aegina town; by taxi, you might spend only 2 hours.

⟨Tips⟩ A Swim and a Snack

There's a small beach in the seaside, still charming, village of **Perdika** (served by bus from Aegina town). This is also a good place to have a meal by the sea; **Antonis** (✆ **22970/61-443**) is the best-known and priciest place, but there are lots of other appealing (and much cheaper) places, including **Saronis.** If you visit Aegina with children, you may want to head to **Faros** (also served by bus from Aegina town) to the **Aegina Water Park** (✆ **22970/22-540**). There are several pools, waterslides, snack bars, and lots of over-excited children; on hot days, this is a very popular destination for Athenian families.

WHERE TO STAY

In addition to the places mentioned below, you might consider two hotels in restored buildings in Aegina town: **Stone House** (✆ **22970/23-970**), and **Hotel Brown** (✆ **22970/22-271**); the Brown also has bungalow-like units in its garden. Both hotels charge from 90€ to 120€ ($117–$156) for a double or a studio. If you're planning a longish stay, consider the 12-unit family-run **To Petrino Spiti** (✆ **22970/23-837**), which has well-designed and carefully maintained studio apartments with harbor views from 90€($117).

Eginitiko Archontiko 🏆🏆   This mansion near the cathedral, only a couple of hundred feet from the harbor, was built in 1820, and later renovations have preserved much original detail, including some walls and ceilings with paintings; the suite is especially charming. The small guest rooms are traditionally furnished, comfortable, and quiet (although here, as elsewhere in Greece, motorcycle noise can be irritating). The pleasant downstairs lobby retains much 19th-century charm, and the glassed-in sunroom is a delight. The owners care about this handsome building and make guests comfortable.

Ag. Nikolaou and 1 Eakou, 18010 Aegina. ✆ **22970/24-968.** www.lodgings.gr. 12 units. 80€ ($111) double; 130€ ($169) 2-room suite. AE, MC, V. **Amenities:** Breakfast room; garden; sunroom; communal kitchen. *In room:* A/C.

Hotel Apollo 🏆 🄺ids   Ayia Marina, along with lots of resort hotels, is not our cup of tea. That said, friends with small children who stayed at this beach hotel were pleased with the large bathrooms and simple bedrooms, most with balconies. If you come for a long stay, ask about renting a fridge for your room.

Ayia Marina, 18010 Aegina. ✆ **22970/32-271.** www.apollo-hotel.de. 107 units. 90€–150€ ($117–$195) double. Compulsory breakfast buffet 8€ ($10); daily and weekly meal plans available. AE, DC, MC, V. Closed Nov–Mar. **Amenities:** Restaurant; bar; fresh- and saltwater pools; tennis. *In room:* A/C, TV, minibar, hair dryer.

WHERE TO DINE

Keep in mind that fish is priced by the kilo at most restaurants. The price varies from catch to catch, so it's a good idea to ask before you order.

Maridaki 🏆 GREEK   This lively portside spot offers a wide selection of fish, grilled octopus, and the usual taverna fare of souvlaki and moussaka. The *mezedes* here are usually very good, and you can make an entire meal of them if you wish. Come on a quiet evening and you will have the sense of going back in time to an earlier Greece.

Demokratias. ✆ **22970/25-869.** Main courses 10€–20€ ($13–$26); seafood priced by the kilo. DC, MC. Daily 8am–midnight.

Mezedopoleio To Steki 🏆🏆 SEAFOOD   Locals and Athenians head to this little place by the fish market for its delicious *mezedes*, including succulent grilled octopus. You can make a meal of *mezedes* here. If you eat as the Greeks do, wash it all down with ouzo. (If you're not used to ouzo, wash the ouzo down with lots of water.)

45 Pan Irioti. ✆ **22970/23-910.** *Mezedes* 6€–15€ ($7.80–$20). No credit cards. Daily 8am–midnight.

AEGINA AFTER DARK

At sunset, the harbor scene gets livelier as everyone comes out for an evening *volta* (stroll). As always, this year's hot spot may be closed by the next season. As no one answers the phones at these places, we do not list phones. In Aegina town, **Avli** and **Perdikiotika,** in another one of Aegina's handsome 19th-century houses, are durable favorites. On summer weekends, **En Egina** and **Kyvrenio** have live music and occasional traditional *rembetika* music—often from around midnight 'til dawn. On summer weekends, **Armida,** a bar/restaurant in a converted caique moored at the harbor, is open from breakfast until, well, breakfast. There are also several outdoor cinemas in town, including the **Olympia** and the **Faneromeni.**

2 Poros·

55km (31 nautical miles) SW of Piraeus

Poros shares the gentle, rolling landscape of the adjacent Peloponnesian coastline, and has several good beaches, some decent tavernas, and lively summer nightlife. If that sounds like lukewarm praise, it just may be. Poros lacks the sense of being a world unto itself that makes most Greek islands so delicious to visit. And, in July and August, the island virtually sinks under the weight of day-trippers and tour groups.

As someone once said, "Geography is destiny." Poros (the word means "straits" or "ford") is separated from the Peloponnese by a narrow channel only 370m (1,214 ft.) wide. Poros is so easy to reach from the mainland that weekending Athenians and many tourists flock here each summer. In fact, a car ferry across the straits from Galatas to Poros town leaves almost every 20 minutes in summer—which means there are a *lot* of cars here.

Technically, Poros is separated by a narrow canal into two islands: little **Sferia,** where Poros town is, and larger **Kalavria,** where everything else is. If you wish, you can use Poros as a base for visiting the nearby attractions on the mainland, including Epidaurus, ancient Troezen (modern Trizina), and the lemon groves of Limonodassos. In a long day trip, you can visit Nafplion (Nafplio) and Epidauros; in a very long day trip, you could also see Mycenae and Tiryns.

ESSENTIALS

GETTING THERE   Daily hydrofoil and ferry service to Poros and other Saronic Gulf islands is offered by **Hellenic Seaways** (© 210/419-9200; www.hellenic seaways.gr). **Saronikos Ferries** (© 210/417/1190) takes passengers and cars to Aegina, Poros, and Spetses; cars are not allowed to disembark on Hydra. **Euroseas** (© 210/ 411-3108) has speedy catamaran service from Piraeus to Poros, Hydra, and Spetses. For information on schedules for most Argo-Saronic ferries, you can try one of the various numbers of the **Piraeus Port Authority:** © 210/422-6000, 210/410-1480, or 210/410-1441, but phones are not always answered. On Poros, try © 22980/22-274.

The other Saronic Gulf islands are all easy to reach from Poros. In addition, in summer **Marinos Tours** (© 22980/22-297) offers a excursions to Saronic and Cycladic islands.

VISITOR INFORMATION   The waterfront hotels are generally too noisy for all except heavy sleepers, so if you want to stay in town, we suggest you check with **Marinos Tours** (© 22980/22-297), which handles several hundred rooms and apartments, as well as many island hotels. We've had good reports of **Saronic Gulf Travel** (© 22980/24-555; www.saronicgulftravel.gr), which usually has an excellent free map of the island. To learn more about Poros, look for Niki Stavrolakes's enduring classic, *Poros* (Lycabettus Press), for sale on the island. The websites **www.poros. com.gr** and **www.greeka.com/saronic/poros** have information in Greek and English.

GETTING AROUND   You can walk anywhere in Poros town. The island's **bus** can take you to the beaches or to the **Monastery of the Zoodhochou Pigis** and the remains of the **Temple of Poseidon;** the conductor will charge you according to your destination. The **taxi station** is near the hydrofoil dock, or you can call for one at *©* **22980/23-003;** the fare to or from the Askeli beach should cost about 8€ ($10). **Kostas Bikes** (*©* **22980/23-565**), opposite the Galas ferry pier, rents bicycles for about 8€ ($10) per day, and mopeds from about 15€ ($20) per day. (Motorcycle and moped agents are required to, but do not always, ask for proof that you are licensed to drive such vehicles and give you a helmet.)

FAST FACTS   The **National Bank of Greece** is one of a handful of waterfront banks with an ATM where you can also exchange money. The **police** (*©* **22980/ 22-256**) and **tourist police** (*©* **22980/22-462**) are on the paralia (harbor). The **port authority** (*©* **22980/22-274**) is on the harborfront. For **first aid,** call *©* **22980/22- 254.** The **post office** and **telephone office (OTE)** are also on the waterfront; their hours are Monday through Friday from 8am to 2pm. In summer, in addition to normal weekday hours, the OTE is open Sunday 8am to 1pm and 5 to 10pm. **Coconuts Internet Café** and **Kentrou Typou** (also a newsagent with foreign newspapers) are both on the harborfront and offer Internet service for about 5€ ($6.50) per hour.

WHAT TO SEE & DO
ATTRACTIONS IN POROS TOWN
As you make the crossing to the island, you'll see the streets of Poros town, the capital, climbing a hill topped with a clock tower. Poros town is itself an island, joined to the rest of Poros by a causeway. (In short, the island of Poros is made up of two linked islands.) The narrow streets along the harbor are usually crowded with visitors inching their ways up and down past the restaurants, cafes, and shops. At night, the adjacent hills are, indeed, alive with the sound of music; the "Greek" music is usually heavily amplified pop.

Poros town has a **Naval Cadets' Training School**—which means that a lot of young men are looking for company here. Anyone wishing to avoid their attention can visit the small **Archaeological Museum** (*©* **22980/23-276**), with finds from ancient Troezen. It's usually open daily from 9am to 3pm; admission is free.

EXPLORING THE ISLAND
By car or moped, it's easy to make a circuit of the island in half a day. What remains of the 6th-century-B.C. **Temple of Poseidon** is scattered beneath pine trees on the low plateau of Palatia, east of Poros town. The site is usually open dawn to dusk; admission is free. The ruins are scant, largely because the inhabitants of the nearby island of Hydra plundered the temple and hauled away most of the marble to build their harborside Monastery of the Virgin.

The Temple of Poseidon was the scene of a famous moment in Greek history in 322 B.C. when Demosthenes, the Athenian 4th-century orator and statesman, fled here for sanctuary from Athens's Macedonian enemies. When his enemies tracked him down, the great speechwriter asked for time to write a last letter—and then bit off his pen nib, which contained poison. Even in his death agonies, Demosthenes had the presence of mind to leave the temple, lest his death defile the sanctuary. It seems fitting that Demosthenes, who lived by his pen, died by the same instrument.

Those who enjoy monasteries can continue on the road that winds through the island's interior to the 18th-century **Monastery of the Zoodhochou Pigis (Monastery of the Life-Giving Spring),** south of Poros town. There are usually no monks in residence, but the caretaker should let you in from about 9am to 2pm and from 4 to

7pm. It's appropriate to leave a small donation in the offerings box. There's a little taverna nearby.

Poros's beaches are not enchanting. The beach easiest to visit after seeing the temple of Poseidon is Vagonia, one of the nicer ones. Both the sea and beach at **Neorio,** northwest of town, are sometimes polluted.

OFF THE ISLAND: A FESTIVAL, ANCIENT TROEZEN & LEMON GROVES

If you're in Poros in mid-June, you might want to catch the ferry across to Galatas and take in the annual **Flower Festival,** with its floral displays and parades of floats and marching bands. (Lots of posters in Poros town advertise the festival.)

From Galatas, you can catch a bus the 8km (5 miles) west to **Trizina** (ancient Troezen), birthplace of the great Athenian hero Theseus. It's also where his wife, Phaedra, tragically fell in love with her stepson, Hippolytus. When the dust settled, both she and Hippolytus were dead and Theseus was bereft. There are the remains of a temple to Asclepius here—but again, these ruins are very ruined.

About 4km (2½ miles) south of Galatas near the beach of Aliki, you'll find the olfactory wonder of **Limonodassos (Lemon Grove),** where more than 25,000 lemon trees fill the air with their fragrance each spring. Alas, many were harmed in a harsh storm in March 1998, and in yet another storm in 2002. Some trees survived, and more were planted. Several cafes nearby serve freshly squeezed lemonade. When the trees aren't in bloom, there's not much point in visiting here, as several readers have irately brought to our attention!

WHERE TO STAY

There are a great many places to stay on Poros, in Poros town, from which we want to single out two fine choices.

Hotel Seven Brothers ★★   This small hotel has been around for quite a while (the building, if not the hotel itself, since 1901). The simple rooms have balconies, the hospitality is old-fashioned, the tips on what to see and do are up-to-date. An excellent choice, it was charming when I first stayed there a number of years ago and is still charming today.

18020 Poros Island. ℭ **22980/23-412.** nikos@7brothers.gr. 16 units. 75€ ($98) double. DC, V. **Amenities:** Breakfast. *In room:* A/C.

Sto Roloi ★★   Another small hotel with charm: Sto Roli is a 2-century-old town house near the island's famous *roloi* (clock tower). The owner rents the building as two suites: a garden apartment and a terrace apartment. A separate garden studio is also available. Many of the original details of the building (tiles, woodwork) have been preserved, and a serious attempt has been made to furnish Sto Roloi with appropriate island furniture (rather than the flashy modern furnishings often used in upmarket island hotels). This would be a very good place to spend a week; you can take advantage of the substantial price reduction for a week's stay, watch performances at Epidaurus, tour the eastern Peloponnese, or simply relax. The owners will arrange caique excursions for guests and will help watersports enthusiasts hook up with Passage Watersports.

13 Karra, 18020 Poros, Trizinias. ℭ **22980/25-808.** www.storoloi-poros.gr. 3 units. 100€ ($130) studio; 150€ ($195) garden apt; 175€ ($228) terrace apt. No credit cards. **Amenities:** Breakfast room; bar. *In room:* Kitchen.

WHERE TO DINE

If you're willing to give up your view of the harbor, head into town, a bit uphill, and try one of the restaurants near the church of Ayios Yeorgios, such as **Platanos, Dimitris,** or **Kipos.** As is often the case, these places tend to draw a more Greek crowd than the harborside spots. Fish is priced by the kilo at most restaurants; ask for prices before you order.

Caravella Restaurant GREEK   This portside taverna prides itself on serving organic homegrown vegetables and local (not frozen) fish. Specialties include traditional dishes such as snails, veal *stifado*, moussaka, souvlaki, and stuffed eggplant, as well as seafood and lobster.

Paralia, Poros town. © **22980/23-666.** Main courses 6€–18€ ($7.80–$23). AE, MC, V. Daily 11am–1am.

Taverna Grill Oasis ✦ GREEK   This taverna has been here since the mid-1960s. Its harborside location with indoor and outdoor tables, the excellent fresh fish, and a cheerful staff make it live up to its name as a pleasant oasis for lunch or dinner. One not-so-traditional item on the menu: pasta with lobster.

Paralia, Poros town. © **22980/22-955.** Main courses 6€–19€ ($7.80–$25); seafood priced by the kilo. No credit cards. Daily 11am–midnight.

POROS AFTER DARK

There's plenty of evening entertainment in Poros town, including strolls up and down the harborside past solid bar/disco/restaurant territory, while people-watching. As always, this year's hot spot may be closed by the next season. As no one answers the phones at these places, we do not list phones. If you want to dance, try **Lithos, Orion** in town, and **Poseidon** about 2km (1¼ miles) out of town; all are popular discos.

3 Hydra (Idra)

65km (35 nautical miles) S of Piraeus

Hydra is one of a handful of places in Greece that seemingly can't be spoiled. Along with Mykonos, this was one of the first Greek islands to be "discovered" by the beautiful people back in the '50s and '60s. Today, there are often more day-trippers here than beautiful people, although when elegant Athenians flee their stuffy apartments for their Hydriote hideaway each summer, the harborfront turns into an impromptu fashion show. If you can, arrive here in the evening, when most of the day visitors have left. Whatever you do, be sure to be out on the deck of your ship as you arrive, so you can see Hydra's bleak mountain hills suddenly revealing a perfect horseshoe harbor overlooked by the 18th-century clock tower of the Church of the Dormition. This truly is a place where arrival is half the fun.

With the exception of a handful of municipal vehicles, there are no cars on Hydra. You'll probably encounter at least one example of a popular form of local transportation: the donkey. When you see Hydra's splendid 18th- and 19th-century stone *archontika* (mansions) along the waterfront and on the steep streets above, you won't be surprised to learn that the entire island has been declared a national treasure by both the Greek government and the Council of Europe. You'll probably find Hydra town so charming that you'll forgive its one serious flaw: no top-notch beach. Do as the Hydriots do, and swim from the rocks at Spilia and Hydronetta, just beyond the main harbor.

ESSENTIALS

GETTING THERE   Daily hydrofoil and ferry service to Hydra and other Saronic Gulf islands is offered by **Hellenic Seaways** (© 210/419-9200; www.hellenic seaways.gr). **Saronikos Ferries** (© 210/417/1190) takes passengers and cars to Aegina, Poros, and Spetses; cars are not allowed to disembark on Hydra. **Euroseas** (© 210/411-3108) has speedy catamaran service from Piraeus to Poros, Hydra, and Spetses. For information on schedules for most Argo-Saronic ferries, you can try one of the various numbers of the **Piraeus Port Authority:** © 210/412/4585, 210/422-6000, or 210/410-1480, but phones are not always answered. On Hydra, try © 22980/52-279. Reservations are a must on summer and on holiday weekends.

VISITOR INFORMATION   The free publications *Holidays in Hydra* and *This Summer in Hydra* are widely available and contain much useful information, including maps and lists of rooms to rent; shops and restaurants pay to appear in these publications. **Saitis Tours** (© 22980/52-184), in the middle of the harborfront, can exchange money, provide information on rooms and villas, book excursions, and help you make long-distance calls or send faxes. For those wanting to pursue Hydra's history, we recommend Catherine Vanderpool's *Hydra* (Lycabettus Press), on sale on the island. You may also want to check **www.greeka.com/saronic/hydra** or **www.hydra direct.com**.

GETTING AROUND   Walking is the only means of getting around on the island itself, unless you bring or rent a donkey or a bicycle. **Caiques** provide water-taxi service to the island's beaches (Bisti has extensive watersport facilities) and to the little offshore islands of Dokos, Kivotos, and Petasi, as well as to secluded restaurants in the evening; rates run from around 10€ ($13) to outrageously steep amounts, depending on destination, time of day, and whether or not business is slow.

FAST FACTS   The **National Bank of Greece** and **Commercial Bank** are on the harbor; both have ATMs. Travel agents at the harbor will exchange money from about 9am to 8pm, usually at less favorable rates. The small **health clinic** is signposted at the harbor; cases requiring complicated treatment are taken by boat or helicopter to the mainland. The police and tourist **police** (© 22980/52-205) share quarters on the second floor at 9 Votsi (signposted at the harbor). The **port authority** (© 22980/53-150) is on the harborside. The **post office** is just off the harborfront on Ikonomou, the street between the two banks. The **telephone office (OTE),** across from the police station on Votsi, is open Monday through Saturday from 7:30am to 10pm, Sunday from 8am to 1pm and 5 to 10pm. For **Internet access,** try HydraNet (© 22980/54-150), signposted by the OTE.

Festivals in Hydra

On a mid-June weekend, Hydra celebrates **Miaoulia,** honoring Hydriot Admiral Miaoulis, who set much of the Turkish fleet on fire by ramming it with explosives-filled fireboats. Celebrations include a reenactment of the sinking of a model warship. In early July, Hydra has an annual **puppet festival** that, in recent years, has drawn puppeteers from countries as far away as Togo and Brazil. As these two festivals are not on set dates, check for schedules with the **Greek National Tourist Office** (© 210/870-0000; www.gnto.gr) or the **Hydra tourist police** (© 22980/52-205).

WHAT TO SEE & DO
ATTRACTIONS IN HYDRA TOWN

Why did all those "beautiful people" begin to come to Hydra in the '50s and '60s and why is the island so popular today? As with the hill towns of Italy, the main attraction here is the architecture and setting of the town itself—and all the chic shops, restaurants, hotels, and bars that have taken up quarters in the handsome old stone buildings. In the 18th and 19th centuries, ships from Hydra transported cargo around the world and made this island very rich indeed. Like ship captains on the American island of Nantucket, Hydra's ship captains demonstrated their wealth by building the fanciest houses money could buy. The captains' lasting legacy: the handsome stone *archontika* (mansions) overlooking the harbor that give Hydra town its distinctive character.

One archontiko that you can hardly miss is the **Tombazi mansion,** which dominates the hill that stands directly across the harbor from the main ferry quay. This is now a branch of the School of Fine Arts, with a hostel for students, and you can usually get a peek inside. Call the mansion (✆ **22980/52-291**) or **Athens Polytechnic** (✆ **210/619-2119**) for information about the program or exhibits.

The nearby **Ikonomou-Miriklis mansion** (also called the **Voulgaris**) is not open to the public, but the hilltop **Koundouriotis mansion,** built by an Albanian family who contributed generously to the cause of independence, is now a house museum. The mansion, with period furnishings and costumes, is usually open from April until October, Tuesday to Sunday 10am to 4pm. If you wander the side streets on this side of the harbor, you will see many more handsome houses, some of which are being restored so that they can once again be private homes, while others are being converted into still more "boutique" hotels.

Hydra's waterfront is a mixed bag, with a number of ho-hum shops selling nothing of distinction—and a handful of elegant boutiques and jewelry shops, especially in the area below the Tombazi mansion. **Hermes Art Shop** (✆ **22980/52-689**) has a wide array of jewelry, some good antique reproductions, and a few interesting textiles. **Domna Needlepoint** (✆ **22980/52-959**) offers engaging needlepoint rugs and cushion covers, with Greek motifs of dolphins, birds, and flowers. **Vangelis Rafalias's Pharmacy** is a lovely place to stop in, even if you don't need anything, just to see the jars of remedies from the 19th century.

When you've finished with the waterfront, walk uphill on Iconomou (it's steep) to browse in more shops. **Meltemi** (✆ **22980/54-138**) sells original jewelry (including drop-dead gorgeous earrings) and ceramics. Although the shop is small, just about everything here is borderline irresistible—especially the winsome blue ceramic fish. Across from Meltemi, **Emporium** (no phone) shows and sells works by Hydriot and other artists. If you want to take home a painting or a wood or ceramic model of an island boat, try here.

Like many islands, Hydra boasts that it has 365 churches, one for every day of the year. The most impressive, the mid-18th-century **Monastery of the Dormition of the Virgin Mary (E Kimisis tis Panagias)** is by the clock tower on the harborfront. This is the monastery built of the marble blocks hacked out of the (until then) well-preserved Temple of Poseidon on the nearby island of Poros. The buildings here no longer function as a monastery, and the cells are now municipal offices. The church itself has rather undistinguished 19th-century frescoes, but the elaborate 18th-century marble iconostasis (altar screen) is terrific. Like the marble from Poros, this altar screen was "borrowed" from another church and brought here. Seeing it is well worth the suggested donation.

EXPLORING THE ISLAND: A MONASTERY, A CONVENT & BEACHES

If you want to take a vigorous uphill walk (with no shade), head up Miaouli past Kala Pigadia (Good Wells), still the town's best local source of water. A walk of an hour or two, depending on your pace, will bring you to the **Convent of Ayia Efpraxia** and **Monastery of the Prophet Elijah (Profitis Elias).** Both have superb views, both are still active, and the nuns sell their hand-woven fabrics. (*Note:* Both nuns and monks observe the midday siesta 1–5pm. Dress appropriately—no shorts or tank tops.)

Unfortunately, must of Hydra's best **beach** at **Mandraki,** a 20-minute walk east of town, is the private preserve of the Miramare Hotel. If you're on Hydra briefly, your best bet is to swim off the rocks just west of Hydra town at **Spilia, Hydrometta,** or **Kamini.** Still farther west are the pretty pine-lined cove of **Molos** and **Bisti,** best reached by water taxi from the main harbor. The **Kallianos Dive Center** (www. kallianosdivingcenter.gr) offers PADI scuba lessons and excursions off Kapari island near Hydra.

The island of **Dokos,** northwest off the tip of Hydra, an hour's boat ride from town, has a good beach and excellent diving conditions; it was here that Jacques Cousteau found a sunken ship with cargo still aboard, believed to be 3,000 years old. You may want to take a picnic with you, as the taverna here keeps unpredictable hours.

WHERE TO STAY

Hydra has an impressive number of small, charming hotels in thoughtfully restored 19th-century buildings. In addition to the following choices, you might try the 19-unit **Hotel Greco,** Kouloura (© **22980/53-200;** fax 22980/53-511), in a former fishing-net factory in a quiet neighborhood, or the 20-unit **Misral Hotel** (© **22980/52-509)** a restored island home off the harbor, or the 27-unit **Hotel Leto** (© **22980/53-385;** www.letohydra.gr), which is airy and bright, with large bedrooms, a large garden courtyard, and one wheelchair-accessible room. If you're traveling with friends, you might investigate the **Kiafa,** once a 19th-century sea captain's mansion, now a boutique hotel with a pool, in the Historic Hotels of Europe group, that rents to groups of up to nine people (© **210/364-0441;** www.yadeshotels.gr).

Hotel Angelica 🏵   The whitewashed Angelica complex continues to expand its cluster of red tile–roofed buildings offering accommodations ranging from the very nice (standard doubles and an apartment) to the luxurious VIP rooms and a villa, which share a pool. Almost all the rooms have high ceilings and a balcony or terrace, with rooms in the pension annex more simply furnished than the VIP units. The apartment has no kitchen, but a fridge and electric kettle. If you stay here, try to splurge on the VIP quarters so that you are not tormented by the sounds of other guests splashing in that pool while you stand under your shower to cool down. The breakfast buffet is highly praised.

42 Miaouli, 18040 Hydra. © **22980/53-264.** www.angelica.gr. 10 units in Building 1 (Pension/Annex) 100€–120€ ($130–$156) double; 8 units in Building 2 (VIP); doubles from 170€ ($221). Angelica Apartment from 140€ ($182); Villa Angelica from 300€ ($990). MC, V. **Amenities:** Breakfast room; VIP pool; garden. *In room:* A/C, TV, fridge.

Hotel Bratsera 🏵   The Bratsera, in a restored 1860s sponge factory a short stroll from the harbor, keeps turning up on everyone's list of the best hotels in Greece; unfortunately, this is a telling comment on the state of most Greek hotels. Throughout, there's lots of wood and stone, many distinctive Hydriot touches (paintings, engravings, ceramics), and many units with antique four-poster beds. The small pool with wisteria-covered trellises is very attractive; meals are sometimes served poolside in fair weather. Unfortunately, we've had reports that room-service trays left in the hall after breakfast were still not collected by dinnertime, and I know from personal experience that messages left for guests aren't always delivered—nor does staff express any surprise or chagrin when this is brought to their attention. That said, many readers report having a lovely stay here; for others, cavalier service and high prices are their most lasting memory.

Tombazi, 18040 Hydra. © **22980/53-971.** Fax 22980/53-626. www.bratserahotel.com. 23 units. 165€–250€ ($215–$325) double; suites from 300€ ($390). Rates include breakfast. AE, DC, MC, V. Closed mid-Jan to mid-Feb. **Amenities:** Restaurant; bar; pool. *In room:* A/C, minibar, hair dryer.

Hotel Hydra *Value* This is one of the best bargains in town if you don't mind the steep walk up to the beautifully restored two-story, gray-stone mansion on the western cliff, to the right as you get off the ferry. The guest rooms have high ceilings and are simply furnished; many have balconies overlooking the town and harbor.

8 Voulgari, 18040 Hydra. © **22980/52-102.** Fax 22980/53-330. hydrahotel@aig.forthnet.gr. 12 units, 8 with bathroom. 80€ ($104) double without bathroom; 90€–110€ ($117–$143) double with bathroom. MC, V. Open year-round. **Amenities:** Breakfast room. *In room:* TV.

Hotel Miranda Once, when we were trapped for the night on Hydra by bad weather, we were lucky enough to get the last guest room at the Miranda. The unit was small, with a tiny bathroom and no real view—so it's a tribute to this hotel that we have wonderful memories of that visit. Most of the guest rooms here are decent-size, with nice views of the lovely garden courtyard and town. The handsome 1820 captain's mansion is decorated throughout with Oriental rugs, antique cabinets, worn wooden chests, marble tables, contemporary paintings, and period naval engravings. There's even a small art gallery—in short, this is a very classy place. We're distressed at one recent report of indifferent service; please let us know how you find things here.

Miaouli, 18040 Hydra. © **22980/52-230.** Fax 22980/53-510. Mirandahydra@hol.gr. 14 units. 140€–180€ ($182–$234) double. Compulsory breakfast 10€ ($13). AE, V. Closed Nov–Mar. **Amenities:** Breakfast room. *In room:* A/C, TV, minibar.

Hotel Orloff This restored mansion, just a short walk from the port, on one of Hydra town's main squares, was built in the 18th century by the Russian admiral Count Orloff, who led a naval campaign against the Turks. Today it's a comfortable small hotel, distinctively decorated with antique furnishings. The basement lounge has a bar. Breakfast is excellent.

9 Rafalia, 18040 Hydra. © **22980/52-564.** Fax 22980/53-532. www.orloff.gr. 10 units. 120€–170€ ($156–$221). Rates include buffet breakfast. AE, MC, V. Closed Nov–Mar. **Amenities:** Dining room; bar. *In room:* A/C.

WHERE TO DINE

The harborside eateries are predictably expensive and mostly not very good, although the views are such that you may not care. Two longtime favorites off the harbor are still going strong: **Manolis** (© **22890/29-631**) and **Kyria Sophia** (© **22980/53-097**), both with lots of vegetable dishes, as well as stews and grills. A number of cafes also lie along the waterfront, including **To Roloi (The Clock),** by the clock tower. The cost of fish, priced by the kilo at most restaurants, varies from catch to catch, so it's a good idea to ask the price before you order.

Marina's Taverna GREEK Several readers report that they have enjoyed both the food and the spectacular sunset at this seaside taverna, appropriately nicknamed

"Iliovasilema" ("Sunset"). Perched on the rocks west of town, it's a 10€ ($13) water-taxi ride from town. The menu is basic, but the food is fresh and carefully prepared by Marina; her *klefltiko* (pork pie), an island specialty, is renowned.

Vlihos. ℂ 22980/52-496. Main courses 10€–15€ ($13–$20). No credit cards. Daily noon–11pm.

To Steki *(Value* GREEK   This small taverna, a few blocks up from the quay end of the harbor, has simple food and reasonable prices. The walls inside have framed murals showing a rather idealized traditional island life. The daily specials, such as moussaka and stuffed tomatoes, come with salad, vegetables, and dessert. The fish soup is memorable.

Miaouli. ℂ 22980/53-517. Main courses 6€–18€ ($7.80–$23); daily specials 8€–15€ ($10–$20); seafood priced by the kilo. No credit cards. Daily noon–3pm and 7–11pm.

HYDRA AFTER DARK

Hydra has a very energetic nightlife, with restaurants, bars, and discos all going full steam ahead in summer. In theory, bars close at 2am. As always, this year's hot spot may be closed by the next season. Portside, there are plenty of bars. As no one answers the phones at these places, we do not list phones. **The Pirate,** near the clock tower, is one of the most durable and best. **Veranda** (up from the west end of the harbor, near the Hotel Hydra) is a wonderful place to escape the full frenzy of the Hydra harbor scene, sip a glass of wine, and watch the sunset. **Hydronetta** tends to play more Western than Greek music—although the music at all these places is so loud that it's hard to be sure. Friends report enjoying drinks at the **Amalour** just off the harbor, where they were surrounded by hip, black-clad 30-somethings. There are still a few local haunts left around the harbor; you'll be able to recognize them easily. You'll also easily spot the **Saronicos:** If you don't hear the music, just look for the fishing boat outside the front door.

4 Spetses 🅐🅐

98km (53 nautical miles) SW of Piraeus; 3km (2 nautical miles) from Ermioni

First: One real plus—with quibbles—for visitors to Spetses: Cars are not allowed to circulate freely in Spetses town. Here's the quibble: This would make for admirable tranquillity if motorcycles were not increasingly endemic. Now, a closer look at the island:

Despite a recent series of dreadful forest fires, Spetses's pine groves still make it the greenest of the Saronic Gulf islands. Even, in antiquity this island was called *Pityoussa* (Pine-Tree Island). Over the centuries, many of Spetses's pine trees became the masts and hulls of the island's successive fleets of fishing, commercial, and military vessels. In time, Spetses was almost as deforested as its rocky neighbor Hydra is to this day.

In the early 20th century, the wealthy local philanthropist Sotiris Anargyros bought up more than half the island and replanted barren slopes with pine trees. Anargyros also built himself one of the island's most ostentatious mansions, flanked by palm trees, which you can see just off Spetses's main harbor, the Dapia. Amargyros also built the massive harborfront Hotel Poseidon to jump-start upper-class tourism. Then he built Anargyros College (modeled on England's famous Eton College) to give the island a first-class prep school; John Knowles taught here in the early 1950s and set his cult novel *The Magus* on Spetses.

Today, Spetses's pine groves and wonderful architecture are its greatest treasures: The island has an unusual number of handsome *archontika* (mansions) built by wealthy residents, many of them shipping magnates. Many Spetses homes have lush gardens and handsome pebble mosaic courtyards; if you're lucky, you'll catch a glimpse of some when garden gates are ajar. Like Andros, another island beloved of wealthy Athenians, Spetses communicates a sense that there's a world of private privilege that exists undisturbed by the rough-and-tumble of tourism, which—let's not mince words—means you and me.

Fortunately for attentive visitors, a number of Spetses's dignified villas have been converted into appealing small hotels where it's possible to escape the world of the package tour, mostly based at Ayia Marina.

ESSENTIALS

GETTING THERE   Daily hydrofoil and ferry service to Spetses and other Saronic Gulf islands is offered by **Hellenic Seaways** (© 210/419-9200; www.hellenic seaways.gr). **Saronikos Ferries** (© 210/417-1190) takes passengers and cars to Aegina, Poros, and Spetses; cars are not allowed to disembark on Hydra. **Euroseas** (© 210/411-3108) has speedy catamaran service from Piraeus to Poros, Hydra, and Spetses. For information on schedules for most Argo-Saronic ferries, you can try one of the various numbers of the **Piraeus Port Authority:** © 210/412-4585, 210/422-6000, or 210/410-1480, but phones are not always answered. On Spetses, try © 22980/72-245.

VISITOR INFORMATION   The island's travel agencies include **Alasia Travel** (© 22980/74-098) and **Spetses & Takis Travel** (© 22980/72-215). Andrew Thatomas's *Spetses* (Lycabettus Press), usually on sale on the island, is the book to get if you want to pursue Spetses's history. You can also check out **www.greeka.com/saronic/spetses** and the very helpful **www.spetsesdirect.com**.

GETTING AROUND   The island's limited public transportation consists of several municipal **buses** and a handful of **taxis. Mopeds** can be rented everywhere, beginning at 15€ ($20); be sure to check the brakes and get a helmet. **Bikes** are also widely available, and the terrain along the road around the island makes them a good means of transportation; three-speed bikes cost about 10€ ($13) per day, while newer 21-speed models go for about 15€ ($20). **Horse-drawn carriages** can take you from the busy port into the quieter back streets, where most of the island's handsome old mansions are located. Take your time choosing a driver; some are friendly and informative, others are surly. Fares are highly negotiable.

The best way to get to the various beaches around the island is by **water taxi.** Locals call it a *venzina* (gasoline); each little boat holds about 8 to 10 people. Here, too, fares are negotiable. A tour around the island costs about 40€ ($52). Schedules are posted on the pier. You can also hire a water taxi to take you anywhere on the island, to another island, or to the mainland. Again, prices are highly negotiable.

FAST FACTS   The **National Bank of Greece** is one of several banks on the harbor with an ATM. Most travel agencies (9am–8pm) will also exchange money, usually at less favorable rates than banks. The local health **clinic** (© 22980/72-201) is inland from the east side of the port. The **police** (© 22980/73-100) and **tourist police** (© 22980/73-744) are to the left off the Dapia pier, where the hydrofoils dock, on Boattassi. The **port authority** (© 22980/72-245) is on the harborfront. The **post office** is on Boattassi near the police station; it's open from 8am to 2pm Monday to Friday. The **telephone office (OTE),** open Monday to Friday from 7:30am to 3pm, is to the right off the Dapia pier, behind Hotel Soleil. **Internet access** is available at Delphina Net-Café on the harborfront.

WHAT TO SEE & DO
EXPLORING SPETSES TOWN (KASTELLI)

Spetses town (aka Kastelli) meanders along the harbor and inland in a lazy fashion, with most of its neoclassical mansions partly hidden from envious eyes by high walls and greenery. Much of the town's street life takes place on the main square, the **Dapia,** the name also given to the harbor where the ferries and hydrofoils now arrive. The massive bulk of the 19th-century Poseidon Hotel dominates the west end of the harbor. The Old Harbor, **Baltiza,** largely silted up, lies just east of town, before the popular swimming spots at **Ayia Marina.**

If you sit at a cafe on the Dapia, you'll eventually see pretty much everyone in town passing by. The handsome black-and-white pebble mosaic commemorates the moment during the War of Independence when the first flag with the motto "Freedom or Death" was raised. Thanks to its large fleet, Spetses played an important part in the War of Independence, routing the Turks in the Straits of Spetses on September 8, 1822. The victory is commemorated every year on the weekend closest to **September 8** with celebrations, church services, and the burning of a ship that symbolizes the defeated Turkish fleet.

As you stroll along the waterfront, you'll notice the monumental bronze statue of a woman, her left arm shielding her eyes as she looks out to sea. The statue honors one of the greatest heroes of the War of Independence, **Laskarina Bouboulina,** the daughter of a naval captain from Hydra. Bouboulina financed the warship *Agamemnon,* oversaw its construction, served as its captain, and was responsible for several naval victories. She was said to be able to drink any man under the table, and strait-laced citizens sniped that she was so ugly, the only way she could keep a lover was with a gun. You can see where Bouboulina lived when she was ashore by visiting **Laskarina Bouboulina House** (© 22980/72-077) in Pefkakia, just off the port. It keeps flexible hours (posted on the house) but is usually open mornings and afternoons from Easter until October. An English-speaking guide often gives a half-hour tour. Admission is 4€ ($5.20). If you wish, you can even see Bouboulina's bones, along with archaeological finds and mementos of the War of Independence, at **Spetses Mexis Museum,** in the handsome stone Mexis mansion (signposted on the waterfront). Hours are Tuesday to Sunday 9:30am to 2:30pm; admission is 3€ ($3.90).

If you head east away from the Dapia, you'll come to the picturesque **Paleo Limani** (aka the Baltiza or **Old Harbor**), where many wealthy yacht owners moor their boats and live nearby in villas hidden behind high walls. The **Cathedral of Ayios Nikolaos (St. Nicholas)** was built in the 17th century as the church of a monastery, now no longer functioning. The great moment here took place on April 3, 1821, when the flag of Spetses first flew from Saint Nicolas's campanile to support for the War of Independence against the Turks. A bronze flag beside the church's war memorial commemorates this moment and a pebble mosaic commemorates the War of Independence (look for the figure of Bouboulina). While you're at the Old Harbor, have a look at the boatyards, where you can usually see *kaikia* (caiques) being made with tools little different from those used when Bouboulina's mighty *Agamemnon* was built here.

BEACHES

Ayia Marina, signposted and about a 30-minute walk east of Spetses town, is the best, and busiest, town beach. It has a number of tavernas, cafes, and discos. West of

Spetses town, **Paradise beach** is crowded, littered, and to be avoided. On the south side of the island, **Ayii Anaryiri** has one of the best sandy beaches anywhere in the Saronic Gulf, a perfect C-shaped cove lined with trees, bars, and tavernas. The best way to get here is by water taxi. Whichever beach you pick, go early, as beaches here get seriously crowded by midday.

Fans of *The Magus* may want to have a look at the beach at **Ayia Paraskevi,** which is bordered by pine trees. Located here are a cantina and **Villa Yasemia,** residence of The Magus himself. West over some rocks is the island's official nudist beach.

WHERE TO STAY

Check to see whether the **Hotel Posidonion,** situated on the harbor and impossible to miss, has reopened before you visit. If the ambitious restorations (spa facilities are promised) have taken place, the Posidonion should be worth serious consideration.

Finding a good, quiet, centrally located room in Spetses is not easy. If you are planning a lengthy stay, check out **Hotel Nissia** (ⓒ **22980/75-000;** www.nissia.gr), open all year. It has a wide range of accommodations, including 40 rooms, maisonettes, studios, and flats clustered around a pool to simulate traditional village residences. Doubles cost from 180€ ($234); the Presidential suite is 600€/$780. The hotel is a 10-minute walk from the center of Spetses town. Below, we have tried to suggest several budget options, as well as more upmarket possibilities.

Economou Mansion ★★★ Small and elegant, this 19th-century sea captain's mansion has mosaics with sea motifs in the garden and views far out to sea from most rooms. Unlike many boutique hotels, where you feel almost smothered in muslin curtains and embroidery, the Economous Mansion rooms are cozy, elegant, but never pretentious. The owners are attentive, but never intrusive. The breakfast buffet is extensive and delicious. Friends who had never been particularly enamored of Spetses stayed here in 2006 and report that the hotel made them fall in love with the island itself.

Kounoupitsa, Spetses town. 18050 Spetses. ⓒ **22980/73-400;** www.spetsesyc.gr/economoumansion.htm. 8 units (5 doubles, 1 studio, 2 suites). $180€ ($234) double; 205€ ($267) studio; 240€ ($312) deluxe suite. DC, MC, V. **Amenities:** Breakfast room, pool, Wi-Fi. *In room:* Kitchens in suites, fridge in rooms.

Hotel Faros ★ (Value) Though there's no *faros* (lighthouse) nearby, this older hotel shares the busy central square with a Taverna Faros, a Faros Pizzeria, and other establishments whose tables and chairs curb the flow of vehicular traffic. Try for the top floor, where the simple, comfortable, twin-bedded rooms are quietest, with balcony views of the island.

Plateia Kentriki (Central Sq.), 18050 Spetses. ⓒ **22980/72-613.** Fax 22980/74-728. 50 units. 85€ ($111) double. No credit cards. **Amenities:** Breakfast room.

Orloff Resort ★★★ This elegant little resort, about a 10-minute walk from the Old Harbor, was built in 1975, totally renovated in 2004, and won a place in *Odyssey* magazine's selection of the best hotels in Greece in 2007. The complex, with a swimming pool and sea and garden views, occupies the land and some of the buildings of the 1865 Orloff estate. Accommodations range from rooms, suites, and maisonettes (some with kitchenettes) to a self-contained house. The decor is simple, but not stark, with red accents perking up the pristine white and understated grays and beiges. If you play tennis and pull a muscle, not to worry: aromatherapy and massage are available.

18050 Spetses. ℭ **22980/75-444.** www.orloffresort.com. 22 units. 190€–230€ ($247–$299) double; 400€ ($520) suite; 480€ ($624) maisonette for 4; 1,000€ ($1,300) house. Rates include breakfast. DC, MC, V. **Amenities:** Restaurant; bar; pool; tennis; spa facilities; babysitting. *In room:* A/C, TV, minibar, safe.

Star Hotel ★ *Value*   This blue-shuttered, five-story hotel—the best in its price range—is flanked by a pebble mosaic, making it off-limits to vehicles. All guest rooms have balconies, the front ones with views of the harbor. Each large bathroom has a tub, shower, and bidet. Breakfast is available a la carte in the large lobby.

Plateia Dapia, 18050 Spetses. ℭ **22980/72-214** or 22980/72-728. Fax 22980/72-872. 37 units. 85€ ($111) double. No credit cards. **Amenities:** Breakfast room. *In room:* A/C, TV.

WHERE TO DINE

Spetses's restaurants can be packed with Athenians on weekend evenings, so you may want to eat unfashionably early; about 9pm, to avoid the crush. If the price of your fish is not on the menu, ask for it; fish is usually expensive and priced by the kilo. Note that the island's considerable popularity with tour groups seems to have led to a decline in the quality of restaurant fare.

For standard Greek taverna food, including a number of vegetable dishes, try the rooftop taverna **Lirakis,** Dapia, over the Lirakis supermarket (ℭ **22980/72-188**), with a nice view of the harbor. **To Kafeneio,** a long-established coffeehouse and ouzo joint on the harborfront, is a good place in which to sit and watch the passing scene, as is **To Byzantino. Orloff,** on the road to the Old Harbor, which has a wide variety of *mezedes.*

Spetses has some of the best **bakeries** in the Saronic Gulf; all serve a Greek specialty especially beloved on the islands: *amygdalota,* small usually crescent-shaped almond cakes flavored with rosewater and covered with powdered sugar. You'll see why this is usually served with a tall glass of cold water when you bite into all that powdered sugar.

The Bakery Restaurant GREEK/CONTINENTAL   This restaurant is on the deck above one of the island's more popular patisseries. There are a few ready-made dishes, but most of your choices are prepared when you order them. The chef obviously understands foreign palates and offers smoked trout salad, grilled steak, and roasted lamb with peas, in addition to the usual Greek dishes.

Dapia. No phone. Main courses 8€–20€ ($10–$26). MC, V. Daily 6:30pm–midnight.

Exedra Taverna ★ GREEK/SEAFOOD   This traditional taverna on the Old Harbor, where yachts from all over Europe moor, is also known by locals as Sioras or Giorgos. This is a good place to try fish Spetsiota (a broiled fish-and-tomato casserole). The freshly cooked zucchini, eggplant, and other seasonal vegetables are also excellent. If you can't find a table for supper, try the nearby **Taverna Liyeri,** also known for good seafood.

Paleo Limani. ℭ **22980/73-497.** Main courses 8€–20€ ($10–$26); fish priced by the kilo. No credit cards. Daily noon–3pm and 7pm–midnight. Closed Feb–Nov.

Lazaros Taverna ★ GREEK   Another traditional place, catering less to the yachties than Exedra does and more to locals. Lazaros is decorated with potted ivy, family photos, and big kegs of homemade retsina lining the walls. It's popular with locals (always a good sign) who come here for the good, fresh, reasonably priced food. The small menu features grilled meats and daily specials, such as goat in lemon sauce.

Dapia. No phone. Main courses 6€–14€ ($8–$18). No credit cards. Daily 6:30pm–midnight. Closed mid-Nov to mid-Mar. Inland and uphill about 400m (1,312 ft.) from the water.

SPETSES AFTER DARK

There's plenty of nightlife on Spetses, with bars, discos, and bouzouki clubs from the **Dapia** to the Old Harbor to Ayia Marina, and even to the more remote beaches. As always, this year's hot spot may be closed by the next season. For bars, try **Bratsera** in the heart of Dapia. As for discos, there's **Figaro,** with a seaside patio and international funk until midnight, when the music switches to Greek and the dancing follows step, often until dawn. The **1800 Bar & Internet Café** in Kounoupitsa, Spetses town, is the place to go if you want to listen to music, keep an eye on the 52-inch flatscreen TV, check your e-mail, and take in the narghile lounge, where you can have a water pipe and some flavored tobacco for 2 hours (8€/$10). **Fox** often has live Greek music and dancing; obvious tourists are encouraged to join the dancing—information that may help you decide whether or not to come here!

8

The Peloponnese

by Sherry Marker

What's special about the Peloponnese? It's tempting to answer, "Everything." Virtually every famous ancient site in Greece is in the Peloponnese—the awesome Mycenaean palaces of Kings Agamemnon and Nestor at Mycenae and Pylos (Pilos); the mysterious thick-walled Mycenaean fortress at Tiryns; the magnificent classical temples at Corinth, Nemea, Vassae, and Olympia; and the monumental theaters at Argos and Epidaurus, still used for performances today.

But the Peloponnese isn't just a grab bag of famous ancient sites. This peninsula, divided from the mainland by the Corinth Canal, is studded with great sand beaches, boutique hotels, fine restaurants, and two of Greece's most impressive mountain ranges: Taygetos and Parnon. Tucked away in the valleys and hanging precipitously from the mountainsides are the villages that are among the Peloponnese's greatest treasures. An evening under the plane trees in tiny Andritsena, where the sheep bells are usually the loudest sounds at night, and where oregano and flowering broom scent the hills, is every bit as memorable as a visit to one of the famous ancient sites. This is perhaps especially true in the mountains of Arcadia and deep in the Mani peninsula, where traditional Greek hospitality hasn't been eroded by too many busloads of visitors.

Let's face it: even the most avid travelers do not live by culture alone, and one of the great delights of seeing the Peloponnese comes from the quiet hours spent in seaside cafes, watching fishermen mend their nets while Greek families settle down for leisurely meals. *Leisurely* is the word to remember in the Peloponnese, an ideal place to make haste slowly. And what better place to watch shepherds on the hills or fishing boats on the horizon as you wait for dinner?

Peloponnesian culinary favorites include *kouneli stifado* (rabbit stew) with a surprising hint of cinnamon; and fish *a la Spetsai* (baked with tomato sauce). In summer—when it seems that every tree on the plain of Argos hangs with apricots and every vine is heavy with tomatoes—Peloponnesian food is at its freshest and best. If you're here in spring, look for delicious fresh artichokes and delicate little strawberries. The fresh lettuce grown here during the cool winter months is superb and Greek hothouses produce excellent tomatoes year-round. And don't forget to sample the local wines; the vineyards at Nemea, Patras, and Mantinia are famous. You can find out more about local cuisine at **www.kerasma.gr** and wines at **www.greekwinemakers. com** and **www.greekwine.gr**.

A few suggestions for your trip to the Peloponnese: While many of the Aegean islands sag under the weight of tourists from May until September, the Peloponnese is still relatively uncrowded, even in midsummer. That doesn't mean that you're going to have Olympia all to yourself if you arrive at high noon in August, but it does mean that if you get to

Peloponnese

Olympia early in the morning, you may have a quiet hour under the pine trees. If you're traveling with a car and can set your own pace, you can avoid the crowds at the most popular tourist destinations of Corinth, Mycenae, Epidaurus, and Olympia by visiting early in the morning or late in the afternoon.

So, *kalo taxidi* (bon voyage) on your trip to the Peloponnese, the most beautiful and historic part of Greece.

STRATEGIES FOR SEEING THE REGION

You can easily tour the region in either a clockwise or counterclockwise direction. Whichever approach you choose, at some point you'll probably head into the center of the Peloponnese, either to see the Byzantine ghost town of **Mistra** outside ancient

---

Tips **Museum Hours Update**

If you visit Greece during the summer, check to see when sites and museums are open. According to the tourist office, they should be open from 8am to 7:30pm, but some may close earlier in the day or even be closed 1 day a week.

Sparta, or to take in some of the mountain villages of Arcadia and the **Temple of Vassae** dedicated to Apollo. Here's one suggested itinerary based on the assumption that you have your own car and are setting out from Athens. If you're traveling by public transportation, you'd be wise to double the time allowed. Even if you do have a car, don't let yourself be deceived by the short distances between what you want to see in the Peloponnese. You'll be astonished at how long even a short drive on a winding mountain road can take—especially when you have to stop repeatedly to let flocks of goats cross that road!

If you have 2 days, head from Athens to **Corinth,** have a look at the canal, and visit the sprawling ancient site with its impressive temple as well as **Acrocorinth,** the sugarloaf mountain that looms over the plain of Corinth. Head on to **Mycenae** to see the citadel and chamber tombs before ending up for the night in **Nafplion,** which just about everyone calls *oraia* (beautiful); refresh yourself with a swim at the public bathing beach, some window-shopping along Nafplion's pedestrianized streets, and dinner. In the morning, explore Nafplion's museums and monuments and drive over to **Epidaurus** to see the famous theater before heading back along the coast to Athens.

If you have a few more days to spend here, you can head from Nafplion to **Olympia,** taking in some of the Arcadian mountain villages, including **Andritsena,** with the **Temple of Vassae.** Then you can head back to Athens along the **Gulf of Corinth,** which offers lots of chances for lunch and a swim at seaside resorts such as **Xylokastro.** There's still lots more to see in the Peloponnese—so let's hope that you have at least a week to spend here and can take in **Sparta** and Byzantine **Mistra** and the fortress (and chic hotels) of **Monemvassia** and the tower house villages of the **Mani.** And remember: If you are heading from the Peloponnese into Central Greece, the **Rio-AntiRio** suspension bridge which opened in 2004 makes a journey from, for example, Olympia to Delphi, very easy.

Many of the best-known ancient sites in the Peloponnese, including Olympia, Corinth, and Epidauros, were threatened by the forest fires that raged through Greece in the summer of 2007. The ancient sites were undamaged, but as you travel, you may see once green hillsides with stands of blackened tree trunks left behind by the fires.

1 Corinth ★★

89km (55 miles) W of Athens

Today, as in antiquity, Corinth, along with Patras, is one of the two major gateways to the Peloponnese. Still, gates are for passage, not for lingering. Corinth (pop. 24,000) was moved to its present location in 1834, after an earthquake devastated the 19th-century town that sprawled around ancient Corinth. Today, Corinth is a thicket of undistinguished, flat-roofed concrete buildings, supposedly built to withstand future quakes.

Stop to see the ships slipping through the impressive Corinth Canal that cuts across the isthmus, then head straight for ancient Corinth, in the hamlet of Archaia Korinthos

(Old Corinth), bypassing the unappealing modern city altogether. When you've seen ancient Corinth, head for Mycenae or Nafplion, both less than an hour away and both with excellent hotels and restaurants.

A LOOK AT THE PAST   Historians say fondly that "geography is destiny," and much of Corinth's power and prosperity came from its strategic location overlooking the sea and land routes into the Peloponnese. No enemy could sneak across the isthmus without being spotted by the soldiers stationed on Corinth's towering acropolis, Acrocorinth (559m/1,863 ft.).

During the 8th and 7th centuries B.C., Corinth controlled much of the trade in the Mediterranean and founded colonies as far away as Syracuse in Sicily. This was when Corinth made and exported the distinctive red-and-black figured pottery decorated with lively animal motifs, examples of which are on display in the excavation museum. Great sailors, the Corinthians were credited with refining the design of the *trireme,* the standard warship in Greek antiquity. The only obstacle Corinth couldn't overcome was the isthmus itself: there were only two ways for ships to get around the Peloponnese. Either they were dragged between the ports of Kenchreai on the east and Lechaion on the west, or they sailed around the entire Peloponnese.

Although Corinth's greatest period of prosperity was between the 8th and 5th centuries B.C., most of the ancient remains here are from the Roman period. Razed and destroyed when the Romans conquered Greece in 146 B.C., Corinth was refounded by Julius Caesar in 44 B.C. and began a second period of wealth and prosperity. When St. Paul visited here in A.D. 52, he found Corinth all too sophisticated, and chastised the Corinthians for their wanton ways.

By the 2nd century A.D., with some 300,000 citizens and 500,000 slaves, Corinth was much larger and more powerful than Athens—and much larger than any city in the Peloponnese today. As one Greek proverb had it, "See Corinth and die," suggesting that there was nothing to look forward to after visiting the monuments (and fleshpots) of the city that dominated trade in Greece for much of the 8th and 7th centuries B.C. and that had a second golden age under the Romans in the 2nd century A.D.

ESSENTIALS

GETTING THERE   By Train   There are several trains a day from Athens's Stathmos Peloponnisou (train station for the Peloponnese) to the Corinth train station off Demokratias (© **27410/22-522** or 27410/22-523). These trains are almost invariably late, often taking 3 hours or more. For information on schedules and fares, call © **210/529-8735** or 11100; www.ose.gr.

By Bus   There are at least 15 buses a day, taking 2 to 2½ hours, from the Stathmos Leoforia Peloponnisou (bus station for the Peloponnese) in Athens, 100 Kifissou (© **210/512-4910;** www.ktel.org), to Corinth, where you can catch a bus for the short (15–20 min.) trip to Archaia Korinthos. For general information on Athens-Peloponnese schedules and fares, call © **210/512-4910;** or check www.ktel.org. *Warning:* Buses from Athens to Corinth sometimes terminate at the canal; from there, another bus will run into Corinth itself. From Corinth itself, you can continue to Ancient Corinth.

Confusingly, buses for destinations in the Peloponnese leave Corinth from one of two badly signposted stations: one at the corner of Kolokotroni and Koilatsou (© **27410/24-444**) and the other at the corner of Ethnikis Konstantinou and Aratou (© **27410/24-403**). For most destinations in the Peloponnese beyond Tripolis, you'll find yourself changing buses at Tripolis.

The Corinth Canal

The French engineers who built the Corinth Canal between 1881 and 1893 used dynamite to blast through 86m (285 ft.) of sheer rock to make this 6.4km-long (4-mile), 27m-wide (90-ft.) passageway. This revolutionized shipping in the Mediterranean: Ships that previously had made their way laboriously around Cape Matapan at the southern tip of the Peloponnese could dart through the canal. The journey from Brindisi, Italy, to Athens was shortened by more than 320km (200 miles).

Although it took modern technology to build the canal, the Roman emperors Caligula and Nero had tried, and failed, to dig a canal with slave labor. Nero was obsessed with the project, going so far as to lift the first shovelful of earth with a dainty golden trowel. That done, he headed back to Rome and left the real work to the 6,000 Jewish slaves he had brought from Judea.

By Car   The National Highway runs from Athens to Corinth. The highway, which has been widened over the last decade, still contains some nasty three-lane stretches. The highway now sweeps over the Corinth Canal; if you want to stop here, look for the signs indicating the Canal Tourist Area. Shortly after the canal, you'll see signs for Corinth (the modern town and ancient site), Isthmia (site of the Isthmian Games), and Patras. Allow about 1½ hours for the journey from Athens.

WHAT TO SEE & DO

The new highway rushes you over the **Corinth Canal** very quickly, and unless you're vigilant you can miss the turnoff to the **Canal Tourist Area.** Before the new road was completed in 1997, almost everyone stopped here for a coffee, a souvlaki, and a look at the canal that separates the Peloponnese from the mainland. Now, traffic hurtles past, and the cafes, restaurants, and shops here are hurting. There's a small post office at the canal, along with a kiosk with postcards and English-language newspapers; most of the large souvlaki places have clean toilet facilities (but tough souvlaki). *Warning:* Be sure to lock your car door. This is a popular spot for thieves who prey on unwary tourists.

Ancient Corinth ★★   If you visit in summer, try to come here first thing in the morning or late in the afternoon: The sun on this virtually shadeless site will be less fierce, and fewer tourists will clog the area. Excavations continue at Corinth (you may see American and Greek archaeologists at work here) and since 1995 have unearthed remains of an extensive Roman villa of the 4th century A.D. as well as imported English china of the 19th century A.D.—important suggestions that Corinth's prosperity did not die in antiquity.

The most conspicuous—and the most handsome—surviving building at ancient Corinth is clearly the 6th-century-B.C. **Temple of Apollo,** which stands on a low hill overlooking the extensive remains of the **Roman Agora** (the Roman forum, or marketplace). Only seven of the temple's 38 monolithic Doric columns are standing, the others having long since been toppled by earthquakes.

From the temple, ancient Corinth's main drag, a 12m (40-ft.) marble-paved road that ran from the port of Lechaion into the heart of the marketplace, is clearly visible. Pottery from Corinth was carried down this road to the ships that took it around the world; back along the same road came the goods Corinthian merchants bought in every corner of the Mediterranean. Everything made and brought here was for sale in countless shops, many of whose foundations are still clearly visible in the agora.

Two spots in the agora are especially famous: the **Bema** and the **Fountain of Peirene.** In the 2nd century A.D., the famous Roman traveler, philhellene (lover of Greeks), and benefactor Herodes Atticus rebuilt the original modest fountain house. Like most Romans, Herodes seemed to think that bigger was better: When he was done, the spring was encased in an elaborate two-storied building with arches and arcades and a 4.6-sq.-m (50-sq.-ft.) courtyard. Peirene was a woman who wept so hard when she lost her son that she finally dissolved into the spring that still flows here. As for the Bema, this was the public platform where St. Paul had to plead his case when the Corinthians, irritated by his constant criticisms, hauled him in front of the Roman governor Gallo in A.D. 52.

Old Corinth. ✆ 27410/31-443. Admission 6€ ($7.80), which includes the museum (see below). Summer daily 8am–8pm; winter daily 8am–3pm.

Acrocorinth ✸✸   A road twists from the ancient site to the summit of Acrocorinth, the rugged limestone sugarloaf mountain that looms 566m (1,885 ft.) above the plain. This is a stiff climb; if you don't have a car, allow several hours for the ascent, or grab a taxi by the ancient site; it's about 8€ ($10) for the round-trip, with a half-hour wait—less if you decide to walk back (it's really downhill all the way!). On a clear day, the views from the summit are splendid, although it's been a long time since the atmosphere was clear enough to spot the glistening columns of the Parthenon on the Athenian Acropolis.

A superb natural acropolis, Acrocorinth was first fortified by the ancient Greeks. Everyone who came later—the Byzantines, Franks, Venetians, and Turks—simply added to the original walls. Today, there are three courses of outer walls; massive gates with towers; and a jumble of ruined houses, churches, and barracks. Before you head down, you can stop for a cold drink at the small cafe here and reflect on the fact that there was a Temple of Aphrodite on this summit in antiquity, staffed by an estimated 1,000 temple prostitutes—some of whom worked the streets in town but others who worked here, awaiting those hardy customers who walked up from Corinth.

Old Corinth. ✆ 27410/31-966. Free admission. Usually summer daily 8:30am–7pm; winter daily 9am–3pm.

The Archaeological Museum ✸   As you'd expect, this museum has a particularly fine collection of the famous Corinthian pottery that is often decorated with charming red-and-black figures of birds and animals. In addition, there are a number of statues of Roman worthies and several mosaics, including one in which Pan is shown piping away to a clutch of cows. When you visit, be sure to see the display of sculpture and vases stolen from the museum in 1990. In a bizarre happy ending, the treasures were found in 1998 packed in plastic containers in a fish warehouse in Miami, Florida, and returned to Greece in 2001. The museum courtyard is a shady spot to sit and read; the toilet facilities are good.

Insider Tip: The Archaeological Museum has an extensive collection of finds from the Shrine of Asclepius; because many of these are graphic representations of intimate body parts, they are kept in a room that is usually locked. If you look solemn and express a scholarly interest, you may be able to persuade a guard to unlock the room for you.

Old Corinth, on the site of ancient Corinth. ✆ 27410/31-207. Admission 6€ ($7.80), which includes admission to the site (see above). Summer daily 8am–8pm; winter daily 8am–3pm.

WHERE TO STAY

In Old Corinth, the 20-unit **Marinos Rooms** (℡ 27410/31-209), about 300m (984 ft.) from the ancient site, has excellent home cooking and simple rooms from about 50€ ($72); reservations are vital in summer, when visiting archaeologists are much in evidence.

Kalamaki Beach Hotel ⚡ *Kids*   This sprawling beach resort, about 10km (6 miles) outside Corinth near Isthmia, might be just the place for a family with children to combine sightseeing with relaxation. There's good swimming both in the hotel pools and in the Gulf itself—and lots of Greek families, most of whom come for at least a week. Independent travelers are very much in the minority. The guest rooms are plainly furnished, with tile floors, decent beds, semi-comfortable reading chairs, and good-size balconies and bathrooms. The floor-to-ceiling sliding glass doors that open onto the balcony allow you to take in the view. The hotel offers demi and full pension; the food is ample but not particularly interesting.

P.O. Box 22, 20100 Corinth. ℡ **27410/37-653**, or 210/323-5605 in Athens. Fax 27410/37-652, or 210/324-1092 in Athens. www.kalamakibeach.gr. 82 units. 120€–220€ ($156–$286) double, including breakfast and dinner buffet; 600€ ($780) villa. MC, V. Parking. **Amenities:** Restaurant; 2 outdoor pools (freshwater, saltwater); tennis. *In room:* A/C, TV, minibar, hair dryer.

WHERE TO DINE

None of the cafes or restaurants along the Corinth Canal out of town or along the waterfront in town deserves to be singled out; most deserve to be avoided. Similarly, the restaurants near the ancient site tend to have high prices and mediocre food. That said, following are a couple suggestions if you find yourself hungry in Old Corinth (and can't wait until you get to Nafplion, which has a number of good places to eat).

Locals speak well of the grandly named **Splendid** restaurant across from the site; a lunch or dinner of simple stews, chops, and salads costs around 15€ ($20). The **Ancient Corinth** on the main square offers much the same food at similar prices.

SIDE TRIPS FROM CORINTH
ISTHMIA

Isthmia was one of the four places in Greece where Panhellenic Games were held (the others being Delphi, Olympia, and Nemea). The Isthmian Games took place every 2 years at the Sanctuary of Poseidon, of which *very* little remains. To get here from ancient Corinth, drive back toward the canal. Isthmia is signposted on your right just before you reach the canal.

The **Site and Museum of Isthmia** (℡ 27410/37-244) were closed at press time, but are slated to have reopened by the time this edition hits the shelves. The projected visiting times are Tuesday through Sunday from 9am to 3pm. Admission was not decided at press time, perhaps 3€ ($3.90) for the site and museum. The principal **temple** in Isthmia was dedicated to Poseidon. Foundations remain of the structure built in the 7th century B.C., first rebuilt after a fire in the 5th century B.C., and then rebuilt once again when the Romans refounded Corinth in 44 B.C. Speaking of the temple, even the excavator, Oscar Broneer, admitted that "the casual visitor will marvel chiefly, perhaps, at the thoroughness of its destruction." Remains of the **ancient stadium's** elaborate starting gate were lovingly reconstructed by Broneer.

Isthmia's small **museum** has exhibits on the Isthmian Games, as well as handsome Roman **glass-mosaic panels** showing land- and townscapes and the figure of a philosopher, sometimes identified as Plato.

LOUTRAKI & PERACHORA ⟨⟩

To get to Loutraki from Corinth, cross the Corinth Canal. Once you're on the mainland, Loutraki will be signposted on your left. For Perachora, continue through Loutraki to Perachora, 32km (20 miles) or 30 minutes away by car.

Loutraki is the famous Greek spa whose springs churn out a good deal of the bottled water you'll see in restaurants. If possible, avoid visiting here on summer weekends when Loutraki bursts at the seams with Athenian day-trippers and busloads of Russian visitors who stream here to gamble at the huge **Casino,** 48 Posidonos ⟨⟩ **27440/ 65-501**(open round-the-clock). If you come here, you might want to emulate Greek visitors and "take the waters" (and have a massage) at the **Hydrotherapy Thermal Spa,** 26 G. Lekka (⟨⟩ **27440/22-215**); open Monday through Saturday from 7am to 2pm. Off season, the seaside promenades and leafy parks are quite charming; information available at www.loutraki.gr.

En route to Perachora from Loutraki is **Lake Vouliagmeni,** a saltwater inlet from the Gulf of Corinth. You'll find a number of seafood restaurants along the lake; make your choice depending on where the most Greeks are eating and what looks good in the kitchen.

After sprawling Corinth, **Perachora** ⟨⟩ will seem like a miniature model of an ancient site, with just enough fallen walls and columns to be picturesque. This is an ideal spot to spend a few lazy hours swimming and picnicking (but not on weekends, when too many other people have the same idea). You may prefer to dangle your toes in the water and not swim in the cove, although the snorkeling is good. Sharks are not unknown just outside the harbor in the gulf.

Perachora is situated at the end of the peninsula, around a tiny cove with a picturesque lighthouse chapel. The ancient Corinthians rather self-referentially named this place Perachora, which means "the land beyond"—in this case, the land beyond the Gulf, as seen from Corinth. Views are superb south across the Gulf of Acrocorinth and the mountains of the Peloponnese, and along the north coast to the mountains of Central Greece.

Founded in the 8th century B.C., the **site of Perachora** had several temples to Zeus's wife, Hera, several stoas, and a number of useful water cisterns. Little was left standing after the Romans dismantled the temples and stoas and ferried the stones across the gulf to rebuild Corinth after they destroyed that city in 146 B.C.

The site is open daily: in summer from 8am to 7pm, in winter from 8am to 3pm. Admission is free.

2 Nafplion ⟨⟩⟨⟩⟨⟩

145km (90 miles) SW of Athens

Nafplion is far and away the most charming town in the Peloponnese, with stepped streets overhung with balconies dripping with bougainvillea, handsome neoclassical buildings, and enticing shops, restaurants, cafes, and, for that matter, two fine museums! You could spend several pleasant days here simply enjoying exploring this port town itself, but you'll probably want to use Nafplion as your home base for day trips to the ancient sites at Argos, Nemea, Mycenae, Tiryns, Epidaurus, and—if you didn't see it on the way here—Corinth. Keep in mind that *lots* of Athenians come here year-round on weekends. It's important to reserve your hotel in advance.

Nafplion (pop. 10,000) brings you face to face with the beginnings of modern Greece. For several years after the Greek War of Independence (1821–28), this was

Greece's first capital. Although the palace of Greece's young King Otto—a mail-order monarch from Bavaria—burned down in the 19th century, you can see the former mosque off Plateia Syntagma (Constitution Sq.) where Greece's first parliament met. Another legacy of those years is the impressive number of commemorative statues of revolutionary heroes in Nafplion's squares and parks.

All this would be reason enough to visit this port on the east coast of the Gulf of Argos, but Nafplion also has two hilltop Venetian fortresses, a miniature castle on an island in the harbor, shady parks, and the best ice cream in the entire Peloponnese (see Antica Gelateria di Roma, later in this chapter).

ESSENTIALS

GETTING THERE   By Car   From Athens, head south to the Corinth Canal. If you want to stop at Epidaurus en route, turn left just after the canal at the sign for Epidaurus. If you want to stop at Mycenae en route, take the winding old Corinth-Argos road and the signposted Mycenae bypass. If you want to stop at Nemea en route, take the new Corinth-Tripolis road to the Nemea exit. If you want to get to Nafplion as quickly as possible, take the new Corinth-Nafplion road to the Argos exit. Follow the signs first into Argos itself, about 10km (6 miles) from the exit, and thence on to Nafplion. You will almost certainly get lost at least once in Argos, which has an abysmal system of directional signs. Allow at least 3 hours for the drive from Athens to Nafplion, including a brief stop at the Corinth Canal and some time thrashing around in Argos. When you reach Nafplion, leave your car—and be sure to lock it— in the large municipal **parking lot** (no charge) by the harbor.

By Train   Unless you are a totally dedicated train buff, it makes no sense to come here by train. That said, there are several trains a day from Athens to Corinth and Argos, where you can catch a bus to Nafplion. Information on schedules and fares is available from the Stathmos Peloponnisou (train station for the Peloponnese) in Athens (© **210/529-8735**; www.ose.gr).

By Bus   There are at least a dozen buses a day to Nafplion from the Stathmos Leoforia Peloponnisou (bus station for the Peloponnese) in Athens, 100 Kifissou (© **210/ 512-4910**; www.ktel.org). The trip is a slow one (about 4 hr.) because the bus goes into both Corinth and Argos before reaching the Nafplion station on Syngrou Street (by Plateia Kapodistrias; © **27520/28-555**). For general information on Athens-Peloponnese schedules and fares, call © **210/512-4910;** or go to www.ktel.org.

VISITOR INFORMATION   The **Municipal Tourist Office** is at 25 Martiou (© **27520/24-444**), diagonally across from the bus station. It's usually open Monday through Friday from 9am to 1pm and 5 to 8pm (but is often mysteriously closed during work hours). Ask for the useful brochure *Nafplion Day and Night*. The website www.nafplion.gr is helpful when functioning. Information and tickets for special

---

Tips Hairdressers

Female travelers might like to know that several of the staff at **AD Hair Studio** (© **27520/24-861**), at the corner of Ypsilanti and 5 Kotsonopoulou, speak English and do good work. There's another hairdresser nearby, so make sure that you get this one.

events, such as the concerts in the June **Nafplion Music Festival,** are sometimes available from the Town Hall (Demarkeion) in the old high-school building on Iatrou Square (© 27520/23-332); you can also check at www.nafplionfestival.gr. There are a number of travel agencies in Nafplion, such as **Staikos Travel,** by the harbor (© 27520/27-950); and **Yiannopoulos Travel,** on Plateia Syntagma (© 27520/28-054), where you can get information on car rentals and day trips from Nafplion.

FAST FACTS The **National Bank of Greece,** on Plateia Syntagma (Constitution Sq.), has an ATM and currency exchange, as do most other banks in town. The **hospital** (© 27520/27-309) is at Kolokotroni and Asklipiou streets. The **police** (© 27520/27-776) and **tourist police** (© 27520/98-729) are now also on Asklipiou, just outside the town center. The **post office,** on Plateia Kapodistrias, and the **telephone office (OTE),** on 25 Martiou flanking Plateia Kapodistrias, are both signposted from the bus station. **Internet access** is available at a number of cafes, including DADIS, 15 Asklipiou (© 27520/29-688); and at the Diplo-Internet Cafe, 43 Bouboulinas (© 27520/21-280). Both charge 5€ ($6.50) an hour.

WHAT TO SEE & DO

Nafplion is a stroller's delight. One of the great pleasures here is to wander with no particular destination through parks (Kolokotronis and Kapodistrias parks run into each other), up and down the stepped side streets, and along the harbor, discovering unexpected Turkish fountains, small churches, and tempting cafes. Don't make the mistake of ending your harborside stroll when you come to the last of the large seaside cafes facing the miniature island fortress known as the Bourtzi. If you continue on, you can watch fishing boats putting in at the pier, explore several cliff-side chapels, and wind your way past the small beach on a cliff-side path under the Acronafplia. Nafplion is so small that you can't get seriously lost, so have fun exploring. Below are some suggestions on how to take in the official sights after you've had your initial stroll.

ACRONAFPLIA & PALAMIDI 🍲

Nafplion's two massive fortifications, the **Acronafplia** and the **Palamidi,** dominate the skyline and, as usual with fortresses, are most impressive when seen from afar. It's a very stiff climb to either fortress, and you may prefer to take a taxi up (around 5€/$6.50) and walk back down.

As you'll realize when you visit these fortresses, whoever held the heights here could keep a close watch on both the gulf and the plain of Argos. The Greeks began to fortify Acronafplia and Palamidi, and the Romans, Byzantines, Venetians, Franks, and Turks added a wall here and a turret there, with the results you see today. If you're here in the summer, try to visit the fortresses in the relative cool of either morning or evening; the sunsets are usually spectacular. If you're in Nafplion during the June **Music Festival,** find out if any evening concerts are being held at the **Palamidi,** which is open in summer, Monday through Friday from 8am to 7pm, and Saturday and Sunday from 8am to 3pm; in winter, daily from 8am to 3pm. Admission is 3€ ($3.90).

If you're not in the mood to climb the 800-plus steps from Polyzoidhou Street to the **summit of Palamidi,** you can take a taxi up and then walk down. The Venetians spent 3 years building the Palamidi, only to be conquered the next year by the Turks in 1715. You'll enter the fortress the way the Turkish attackers did, through the main gate to the east. Once inside, you can trace the course of the massive wall that encircled the entire summit and wander through the considerable remains of the five defense fortresses that failed to stop the Turkish attack. Kolokotronis, the hero of the

Tips **Take a Dip**

The best place to swim is at Arvanitia Beach beneath the Palamidi. With the Bourtzi on your right, walk south along the quay until you come to the beach, which has changing facilities and chairs and great views of the sunset.

Greek War of Independence who later tried to subvert the new nation and seize power for himself, was held prisoner for 20 months in **Fort Miltiades,** the structure to your right as you enter the Palamidi.

Compared to huffing and puffing up all those steps to the **Palamadi,** the ascent of **Acronafplia** (not enclosed and no charge) can be a leisurely—if always higher!—stroll through the upper city. If this still seems like work, you can either take a taxi up or take the elevator that runs from Koustouros Street up through the cliff-side and deposits you on the summit at the Nafplia Palace Hotel.

If you're walking, follow signs in the lower town to the **Church of St. Spyridon;** one wall has the mark left by one of the bullets fired when Ioannis Kapodistrias, the first governor of modern Greece, was assassinated here in 1831. From there, continue up to the Catholic **Church of the Transfiguration,** a fitting symbol of Nafplion's vexed history. Built by the Venetians, it was converted into a mosque by the Turks, and then reconsecrated as a church after the War of Independence. Inside, an ornamental doorway has an inscription listing philhellenes who died for Greece, including nephews of both Lord Byron and George Washington. Greece's first king, young Otto of Bavaria, worshiped here wearing the Greek national costume, known as the *foustanella* (short pleated skirt for men), which he adopted to show solidarity with his new subjects. Ironically, while Otto wore his foustanella, the more fashion-conscious of his subjects abandoned their Greek costumes and copied the Western clothes worn by most members of Otto's court.

As you continue to climb toward Acronafplia, you may see several **carvings of the winged lion** that was the symbol of St. Mark, the protector of Venice. The most important fortifications on Acronafplia were built during the first (1388–1540) and second (1686–1715) Venetian occupations. In the days before the birth of today's Greek historical preservation movement, both the Xenia and the Xenia Palace Hotels were built over the fortifications, one reason that the original structures have been obscured.

THE BOURTZI ⭐

Everyone's favorite fortress—and perhaps the only one to evoke squeals of "how cute" from tourists—the miniature **Bourtzi Fortress** was built by Venetians in the 15th century to guard the entrance to Nafplion's harbor. Since then, it's had a checkered career, serving as a home for retired executioners in the 19th century and as a small hotel in the 20th century. Small boats ply back and forth between the harbor and the Bourtzi (5€/$6.50 round-trip); usually, you can stay as long as you wish, explore, and return with the same or a different boat. Take something to drink and a snack with you, as the small cafe here is often closed.

MUSEUMS

Keep an eye out in museums, galleries, and hotels for the elusive brochure *Artspotting Nafplion,* billed as a "guide to the best art spots in Nafplion," which lists local museums, galleries, and shops. Two of the best are the **Nafplion Art Gallery,** 5 Vassileos

Alexandrou St. (✆ **27520/25-385**), which features the work of Greek and foreign artists, and **The Art Shop,** 14 Ipsilandou St. (✆ **27520/29-546**), featuring clothing, jewelry, toys and books by Greek and foreign artists.

The Archaeological Museum ✦   *Note:* The museum is slated to reopen in 2008 after extensive renovations. It is housed in the handsome 18th-century Venetian arsenal that dominates Plateia Syntagma. The thick walls make this a deliciously cool place to visit on even the hottest day. The collection, from sites in the area, includes pottery, jewelry, and some quite terrifying Mycenaean terra-cotta idols as well as a handsome bronze Mycenaean suit of armor.

Plateia Syntagma (Constitution Sq.). ✆ 27520/27-502. Admission 2€ ($2.60). Projected hours Tues–Sun 8:30am–1pm.

The Peloponnesian Folklore Foundation ✦✦✦   Shortly after it opened in 1981, this museum—with its astonishingly rich collection of traditional Greek costumes—won the European Museum of the Year Award. The museum occupies three full floors in an elegant 18th-century house with a shady courtyard and a welcome snack bar and excellent shop. In 2005, the museum installed a new permanent exhibition focusing not on rural but on urban Greece, particularly Nafplion in the 19th and 20th centuries. Dioramas show elegant town-house parlors stuffed with marble-topped furniture, Persian carpets, and ornate silver and china bibelots.

1 V. Alexandros. ✆ 27520/28-947. Fax 27520/27-960. www.pli.gr. Admission 4€ ($5.20). Museum Wed–Mon 9am–3pm; shop daily 9am–2pm and 6–10pm. Closed Feb.

The National Gallery-Alexandros Soutzos Museum, Nafplion Annex ✦   The National Gallery in Athens has begun an ambitious scheme to open branches throughout Greece. This one, in a former neoclassical 19th-century town house, has a permanent exhibit of paintings showing scenes from the Greek War of Independence, including young warriors lounging by classical remains and wounded veterans begging alms. There are frequently changing temporary exhibits, sometimes featuring local artists, and a small shop.

23 Sidiras Merarhias St. ✆ 27520/21-915. Admission 4€ ($5.20); Monday free. Mon, Thurs 10am–3pm; Wed and Fri 10am–3pm and 5–8pm; Sat 10am–2pm. Closed Tues.

SHOPPING

Nafplion has not escaped the invasion of mass-produced souvenirs that threatens to overwhelm Greece, but you'll also find some genuinely fine handicrafts for sale here. No shop that I recommend is more than a 5-minute walk from the central square, **Plateia Syntagma.** As in most Greek towns heavily dependent on tourism, some of these shops close in winter. Year-round, the weekly Saturday **market** occupies most of the road alongside Kolokotronis Park, from around 7am to 1pm. You can buy everything from handsaws to garlic here.

For a wide range of handsome handcrafted jewelry, try **Preludio,** 2 Vas. Konstantinou just off Plateia Syntagma (✆ **27520/25-277**). Almost everything sold here is made and designed by the very helpful owners, who travel as far away as Afghanistan and Australia to find fine gemstones. Just two doors away at 4 Vas. Konstantinou, Cleopatra Pomoni at **Morphes** sells handsome wooden chests, antique locks and keys, jewelry, and other objets d'art.

You'll know that you've found **To Enotion,** on Staikopoulou St. (no phone and no visible street number), when you see a window filled with handsome museum-quality reproductions of characters from the Greek shadow theater—from country bumpkins to damsels in distress. The smallest of the colorful marionettes begins at about 20€ ($26). A few doors along, **Nafplio tou Nafpliou,** 56A Staikopoulou (no phone), sells icons showing virtually every saint in the Greek Orthodox church.

The **Komboloi Museum,** 25 Staikopoulou (✆/fax **27520/21-618;** www.cs-net. gr/komboloi), is on the second floor of a shop selling *komboloi,* usually referred to as "worry beads" (and priced from a few to many thousand euros); museum admission is 2€ ($2.60). **Premier Jewellery,** at 19 Vas. Konstantinou (✆ **27520/22-324**), also has a wide selection of *komboloi.*

Konstantine Beselmes, 7 Ath. Siokou (✆ **27520/25-842**), offers magical paintings of village scenes, sailing ships, and idyllic landscapes. Although new, the paintings are done on weathered boards, which gives each a pleasantly aged look. A few doors away, **Agynthes,** 10 Siokou (✆ **27520/21-704**) has hand-loomed fabrics that look and feel wonderful; some are fashioned into throws, bags, and scarves.

The **Odyssey,** Plateia Syntagma (✆ **27520/23-4300**), has a wide selection of newspapers, magazines, and books in English, as well as a startling collection of pornographic drink coasters. This is also a good place to pick up a copy of Timothy Gregory's *Nafplion* (Lycabettus Press); although printed in 1980, this remains the best guide to the city's history and monuments.

The **Wine Shop,** 5 Amalias (✆/fax **27520/24-446**), is one of the best wine shops in the Peloponnese and an excellent place to head if you want to browse and learn about Greek wines from owner Dimitris Karonis. If your tastes run to honey, stop at **Nektar and Ambrosia,** 6 Pharmakopoulou (✆ **27520/43-001**), for a wide selection of delicious organic honey products and herbs.

WHERE TO STAY

Popular year-round with Greeks, as well as with summer travelers, Nafplion has some of the best hotels in the Peloponnese, ranging from charming small boutique hotels to large luxury establishments. Be sure to make a reservation if you want a view of the harbor or if you will be here during a scheduled performance at Epidaurus, when tour groups reserve entire hotels. Otherwise, Nafplion has enough hotels that you can usually find a room, although you may end up on the outskirts of town in high season. If you arrive without a reservation and have trouble finding a room, try the Municipal Tourist Office, 25 Martiou (✆ **27520/24-444**), across from the bus station. They sometimes can find rooms in small pensions. If you feel like a serious splurge, check out the completely renovated 42-unit **Amphitryon,** transformed from its down-at-the-heels days into a five-star member of the Leading Small Hotels of the World (✆ **27520/70-700;** www.amphitryon.gr or www.helioshotels.gr). The Amphitryon has drop-dead-gorgeous flower arrangements, enormous bathrooms with fiendishly clever showers, and promises "romantic moments in an ambience of privileged scenery"; doubles from 320€ ($416). If you'd prefer the ambience of the pleasant residential neighborhood around Ayios Spiridon church, try the 21-unit **Pension Acronafplia** (www.pensionacronafplia.gr). The pension occupies four thoughtfully restored town houses whose very congenial accommodations range from quite simple (small room, no private bathroom) to quite elegant (large room, private bathroom and balcony with harbor view); doubles from 65€ to 130€ ($85–$169).

EXPENSIVE

Hotel Ilion ★★   You'll have to decide whether you find the decor in this boutique hotel (a member of the Historic Hotels of Europe) in a restored 19th-century town house on a stepped street above Plateia Syntagma engaging or overwhelming. Virtually every ceiling is painted (often with cupids), and wall frescoes with scenes from Greek mythology alternate with borders of fruits and flowers. Many walls are deep rose or gold. Windows and beds alike are draped with filmy hangings. The mattresses are excellent. A friend who spent a happy week here reported that the service was top-notch, the neighborhood quiet, and the breakfasts delicious.

4 Efthimiopoulou and 6 Kapodistriou sts., 21100 Nafplion. ℭ **27520/25-114.** Fax 27520/24-497. www.ilionhotel.gr. 15 units (3 doubles, 7 suites, 5 studios). 100€–115€ ($130–$150) double; 140€–180€ ($182–$234) suite; 110€–120€ ($143–$156) studio. Breakfast 10€ ($13). No credit cards. Amenities: Bar/breakfast room. In room: A/C, TV, minibar.

Hotel Nafsimedon 🖈
Another boutique hotel, this one is in a handsome mid-19th-century neoclassical house with a small garden with palm trees overlooking relatively quiet Kolokotronis Park. The guest rooms, many done in shades of apricot and peach, have handsome chandeliers, marble-topped tables, some old paintings—and good-size bathrooms and beds with firm mattresses. When the Nafsimedon is full, rooms are sometimes found at its younger sister hotel, the **Ippoliti** (www.ippoliti.gr), also a boutique hotel in a restored 19th-century town house at 9 Ilia Miniati and Aristidou just off the harbor (some rooms have harbor views) with a small outdoor pool (doubles 130€–190€/$169–$247).

Nafsimedon, 9 Sidiras Merarhias (on Kolokotronis Park), 21100 Nafplion. ℭ **27520/25-060.** Fax 27520/26-913. www.nafsimedon.gr. 13 units. 95€–125€ ($124–$163) double. No credit cards. **Amenities:** Bar/breakfast room; courtyard. In room: A/C, TV.

Nafplia Palace Hotel (formerly Xenia Palace Hotel) 🖈
Atop Acronafplia, the Nafplia Palace has the best view in town, not only of Nafplion itself, but across the bay to the mountains of the Peloponnese. That view and complete renovations in 1999 and 2005 have earned the villas and suites here high praise in *Odyssey* magazine's "Best Hotels" issues. Though it is true that the bungalow villas are glamorous, with bathrooms the size of battleships, throughout the hotel the service remains lax, the room decor bland, the lobby sterile, and the food ranges from tedious to pretentious. In short, I find this a seriously overrated hotel—with a view to die for.

Acronafplia, 21000 Nafplion. ℭ **27520/28-981** or 27522/89-815. Fax 27520/28-783. www.helioshotels.gr. 51 units, 54 bungalows. 250€ ($325) double; 260€ ($468) bungalow. Significant off-season reductions possible. Rates include breakfast. AE, DC, MC, V. **Amenities:** 2 restaurants; 2 snack bars; 2 pools. In room: A/C, TV, DVD, minibar.

MODERATE
Byron Hotel 🖈🖈
The Byron was one of the first hotels in town to attempt to add individual charm and creature comfort to a pleasant location, and has since been frequently redecorated. It's almost impossible to stay here in July or August without a reservation, especially on weekends, when the entire hotel can be taken over by Athenians. The hotel is in a quiet, breezy location overlooking the Church of Agiou Spiridona, a short but steep hike from the main plateia. Sitting rooms and guest rooms contain nice bits of Victoriana, as well as modern conveniences. The cheapest rooms are quite small with no view; usually, for another 15€ ($20), you'll can get a view of Nafplion—and enough space that you won't feel the burden of togetherness with your roommate.

2 Platonos, Plateia Agiou Spiridona, 21100 Nafplion. ℭ **27520/22-351.** Fax 27520/26-338. www.byronhotel.gr. 17 units. 80€–100€ ($104–$130) double. AE, MC, V. **Amenities:** Breakfast room; terrace. In room: A/C, TV, minibar, hair dryer.

Hotel Leto ⚜ Value   Your effort in climbing up to the Leto, perched under Acronafplia, is rewarded with fine views over Nafplion. Guest units are simply furnished, with decent-size bathrooms; ask for a room with a balcony. The staff here has been praised as very helpful.

28 Zigomala, 21100 Nafplion. © 27520/28-098. Fax 27520/29-588. 15 units. 75€–95€ ($96–$124) double. No credit cards. *In room:* A/C, TV, minibar.

King Otho I and **II** ⚜⚜   The King Otho I, a longtime favorite, was getting down-at-the-heels before its completely successful renovation in 2000. In 2002, the owners bought and restored another wonderful town house a few blocks up the hill on Staikopoulou. Now, Nafplion has two small hotels that contend for the honor of the most breathtaking curved staircase in the Peloponnese. Both hotels have high ceilings (some with frescoes), wood floors, and period furniture, including marble-topped tables. The new Otho is more expensive, because every guest room has a view (of Nafplion, or of Nafplion and the harbor). Each hotel has a garden, a real plus for breakfast or a quiet hour's reading. Both sometimes close in winter.

4 Farmakapoulou, 21100 Nafplion. © 27520/27-585. Fax 27520/27-595. 12 units. 90€ ($117) double. Rates include continental breakfast. No credit cards. **Amenities:** Breakfast room. *In room:* A/C, TV, minibar.

21 Staikopoulou, 21100 Nafplion. © 27520/97-790. Fax 27520/27-595. 10 units. 100€ ($130) double. Rates include continental breakfast. No credit cards. **Amenities:** Breakfast room. *In room:* A/C, TV, minibar.

INEXPENSIVE

Epidaurus Hotel ⚜   Rooms here are small but acceptable, with good, firm beds, small bathrooms, and wooden hanging cupboards; each unit is large enough for a stay of at least a month. The location, on a quiet street just off the main square, is excellent and usually quiet, although adjacent nightclubs, restaurants, and bars can make things noisy on summer weekends. Service here is rather unpredictable, ranging from hospitable and efficient to cursory. The Epidaurus also operates the slightly less expensive 12-room Tiryns nearby on Othonos Street and will try to get you a room there if it is full.

2 Kokkinou, 21100 Nafplion. ©/fax 27520/27-541. 30 units, 25 with full bathroom. 55€–65€ ($72–$85) double. No credit cards. **Amenities:** Bar.

Omorfi Poli Pension ⚜⚜   What a lovely place! This small pension/hotel above the charming cafe by the same name (Greek for "Beautiful City") has gone all out: The restoration of the building gives guests the sense that they are staying in a Nafplion home—but with privacy; when business is not brisk, you can sometimes get a suite at a double room price. The beds are good, the tile floors and prints on the walls are tasteful—there's nothing to fault here. This makes a pleasant base for touring the area. Families will like the rooms with fridges and sleeping lofts for children as well as the breakfasts with freshly baked bread. The **Omorfi** cafe on the ground floor is also very charming.

5 Sofroni, 21100 Nafplion. © 27520/21-565. www.greek-tourism.gr/nafplio/omorfi-poli. 9 units, all with shower only. 75€ ($98) double; 115€ ($150) family suite (for up to 5 persons). Rates include breakfast. No credit cards.

WHERE TO DINE

Oddly enough, not all the restaurants in and just off Plateia Syntagma (Constitution Sq.) are the tourist traps you'd expect. Furthermore, you'll see a good number of Greeks at the big harborside cafes on Akti Miaouli. In short, Nafplion has many good restaurants—and some excellent sweet shops, including the superb Antica Gelateria di Roma.

Hellas Restaurant *Kids* GREEK   Children who normally squirm in restaurants will enjoy the Hellas: Between courses, they can join the Greek kids kicking soccer balls and racing up and down Plateia Syntagma. Shady trees and awnings make this a cool spot to eat outdoors. Locals tend to congregate in the indoor dining room year-round. Reliable dolmades with egg-lemon sauce are usually on the menu, as well as stuffed tomatoes and peppers in season. Just about everyone in town passes through Plateia Syntagma, so this is a great spot to watch the world go by.

Plateia Syntagma. ✆ 27520/27-278. Main courses 6€–12€ ($8–$16). AE, MC, V. Daily 9am–midnight.

Karamanlis *Value* GREEK   This simple harborfront taverna several blocks east of the cluster of cafes tends to get fewer tourists than most of the places in town. It serves up good grills and several kinds of meatballs (*keftedes, sousoutakia,* and *yiouvarlakia*). If you like the food here, you'll probably also enjoy **Arapakos, Kanares Taverna,** and **Hundalos Taverna,** also on Bouboulinas.

1 Bouboulinas. ✆ 27520/27-668. Main courses 6€–15€ ($8–$20); fresh fish priced by the kilo. AE, MC, V. Usually daily 11am–midnight.

Ta Phanaria GREEK   A shaded table under Ta Phanaria's enormous scarlet bougainvillea makes for one of the prettiest places in the center of town for lunch or dinner. Ta Phanaria usually has several inventive vegetable dishes on the menu in addition to such standbys as moussaka. The stews and chops here are also good. In winter, hearty bean dishes are usually available. Like the Hellas, Ta Phanaria continues to attract steady customers, despite doing much of its business with tourists.

13 Staikopoulo. ✆ 27520/27-141. Main courses 6€–12€ ($7.80–$16). MC, V. Daily about noon–midnight.

Taverna Old Mansion (Paleo Archontiko) GREEK   Sometimes when it's snowing in New England, where I spend part of the year, I dream of spending the evening here. In summer, when I'm usually in Nafplion, tables spill out along Siokou Street. I also have happy memories of cozy winter evenings spent enjoying the good food and lively local scene. The menu offers consistently good traditional Greek *spitiko* (home) cooking: stews, chops, and usually several vegetarian choices. When live music is featured in the evening, tables are at a premium.

7 Siokou. ✆ 27520/22-449. Main courses 8€–15€ ($10–$20). MC, V. Daily 7pm–midnight; summer weekends noon–4pm.

OUZERIES, CAFES & SWEET SHOPS
Antica Gelateria di Roma SWEETS/ICE CREAM/COFFEES/DRINKS What a wonderful addition to Nafplion! Marcello and Claudia Raffo make and sell delicious ice cream and ices. You can have anything from a banana split to a tiny cup with just a taste. Don't miss the hazelnut, lemon, mango, strawberry, chocolate—well, you get the idea. If you tire of ice cream, you can always have a freshly made panini with tomato and mozzarella and finish off with a real espresso, while getting up-to-the-minute news of Italian soccer.

3 Pharmakopoulou and Komninou. ✆ 27520/23-520. spyde@tri.forthnet.gr. Sweets and sandwiches 4€–12€ ($5–$16). No credit cards. Daily about 10am–midnight.

Sokaki COFFEE/DRINKS/SNACKS/BREAKFAST   In the morning, tourists tuck into the full American breakfast here, while locals toy with tiny cups of Greek coffee.

In the evening, young men lounge, some eyeing the women who pass by, others eyeing the men. In short, great people-watching and good margaritas.

8 Ethniki Antistaseos. ℂ 27520/26-032. Drinks and snacks 2€–12€ ($2.60–$16). No credit cards. Daily about 8am–8pm; summer daily 8am–midnight.

NIGHTLIFE

In Nafplion itself, the Paleo Lichnari on Bouboulinas sometimes has live Greek music, including *rembetika*, the once revolutionary, now increasingly nostalgic songs of the urban poor. A number of nightclubs and discos cluster around Nea Chios on the coast road from Nafplion to Muloi; all are serious clip joints, often charging 100€ ($130) for a bottle of inferior Scotch. These places are popular with the sailors who turn up in Nafplion, and with area 20- and 30-somethings who come here for a night on the town. Some of the better-known places (with monumentally garish decor that has to be seen to be believed) include Shiva of Liquid Club, Liquid Live, and the Rusty Club. There's no point in phoning ahead: No one answers the phones at these places.

SIDE TRIP FROM NAFPLION
TIRYNS 𝓡𝓡

From the moment that you see Tiryns, you'll understand why Homer called this Mycenaean citadel "well-walled." The **Archaeological Site of Tiryns** (ℂ 27520/22-657) is usually open in summer, daily from 8am to 7pm; in winter, Monday through Saturday from 8am to 5pm. Admission is 2€ ($2.60). Tiryns is 5km (3 miles) outside Nafplion on the Argos road. If you have a car, this is an easy drive; if you don't, take one of the frequent Argos-Nafplion buses and ask to be let off at Tiryns. Taxi drivers will take you to Tiryns and wait while you visit; expect to pay around 25€ ($33) for an hour visit. A small stand by the ticket booth sometimes has cold drinks and postcards.

Tiryns is a good deal better preserved—and much less crowded and more pleasant to visit—than Mycenae. Most scholars assume that Tiryns was a friendly neighbor to the more powerful Mycenae, and some have suggested that Tiryns was Mycenae's port. Today, Tiryns is only a mile from the sea; in antiquity, before the plain silted up, it would have been virtually on the seashore.

Tiryns's citadel stands on a rocky outcropping 27m (87 ft.) high and about .3km (990 ft.) long and is encircled by the **massive walls** that so impressed Homer. Later Greeks thought that only the giants known as Cyclops could have positioned the wall's 13-metric-ton (14-U.S.-ton) red limestone blocks, and archaeologists still call these walls "cyclopean." Even today, Tiryns's walls stand more than 9m (30 ft.) high; originally, they were twice as tall—and as much as 18m (57 ft.) thick. Tiryns seems to have increased its fortifications around 1400 B.C., but to have been destroyed around 1200 B.C., whether by an enemy or an earthquake is not known.

Once you climb the ramp and pass through the two gates, you'll find yourself in an impressive series of **storage galleries and chambers** on the east side of the citadel. One long passageway with a corbeled arch has glistening walls that were rubbed smooth by the generations of sheep that took shelter here after Tiryns fell.

The citadel is crowned by the **palace,** whose **megaron** (great hall) has a well-preserved circular hearth and the base of a putative throne. This room would have been gaily decorated with frescoed walls; you can see the surviving frescoes, some with scenes of elegant women riding in a chariot, in the National Archaeological Museum in Athens. Lesser folk would have lived below the citadel on the plain. Two tunnels led from the lower slopes of Tiryns out into the plain to the large **subterranean cisterns,** which held the secret water supply that allowed Tiryns to withstand even lengthy sieges.

Insider Tip: If you want a quick dip after you visit Tirnys, take one of the side roads to the Gulf of Argos from the Nafplion-Argos road that Tirnys overlooks. A sandy beach stretches almost all the way from the outskirts of Nafplion to the hamlet of Nea Chios, where there are fresh fish restaurants. The water is shallow enough that you can wade a long way out, which makes this an ideal spot for families with young children. The men wading about with long-handled nets are rooting around in the sand for mussels. The families hanging their washing out to dry on trees and bushes are Gypsies. As always at a public beach, it's a good idea to lock your car and keep an eye on valuables.

AYIA MONI CONVENT ☙

This hillside convent is just a 3km (1½-mile) drive outside Nafplion. Until recently, much of the drive was through countryside. Now, the road to the convent winds uphill through a fast-growing suburb, where houses and small apartment blocks are fast replacing the olive groves. Still, the convent itself remains peaceful. To get here by car, head out of Nafplion on the Epidaurus road. Turn right at the sign for Ayia Moni and continue on a partly bumpy road uphill to Ayia Moni. The convent is usually open from about 9am to 5pm in winter, later in summer, but closed during the afternoon siesta (about 1–4pm).

Ayia Moni was founded in the 12th century, and the church is a fine example of Byzantine church architecture, with nice brickwork. Many of the other buildings here are modern and were built after a series of fires destroyed much of the original convent. If the main door is closed, knock.

The nuns sometimes have embroidery to sell and are usually more than willing to show you the church and garden and tell about the rich Greek-American benefactor who rebuilt the convent.

The spring that feeds a small pond just outside the convent walls is one of a number of springs in Greece identified as the place where Zeus's wife, Hera, took an annual bath to restore her virginity and renew Zeus's ardor. Today, the spring water is considered both holy and delicious; pilgrims often fill bottles to take home.

3 Mycenae ✪✪✪

50km (31 miles) S of Corinth; 115km (71 miles) SW of Athens

Virtually every visitor to the Peloponnese comes to Mycenae, which can make for bumper-to-bumper tour buses on the narrow roads to the citadel and wall-to-wall tourists inside the citadel itself. Why do they all come here? As the English philhellene Robert Liddell once wrote: "Mycenae is one of the most ancient and fabulous places in Europe. I think it should be visited first for the fable, next for the lovely landscape, and thirdly for the excavations."

According to Greek legend and the poet Homer, King Agamemnon of Mycenae was the most powerful leader in Greece at the time of the Trojan War. It was Agamemnon, Homer says, who led the Greeks from Mycenae, which he called "rich in gold," to Troy (around 1250 B.C.). There, the Greeks fought for 10 years to reclaim fair Helen, the wife of Agamemnon's brother Menelaus, from her seducer, the Trojan prince Paris.

The German archaeologist Heinrich Schliemann, who found and excavated Troy, began to dig at Mycenae in 1874. Did Schliemann's excavations here prove that what Homer wrote was based on an actual event—and not myth or legend? Scholars are suspicious, although most admit that Mycenae could have been built to order from Homer's descriptions of Mycenaean palaces. Displays at the **new site museum,** opened in 2004, help put flesh on the bones of the archaeological remains. Try very hard to visit the museum the minute it opens; it is small and gets very crowded as the day goes on. At press time, museum tickets and guidebooks were sold only at the ticket booth for the site itself.

ESSENTIALS

GETTING THERE By Car From Corinth, take the new national highway toll road to the Nemea exit, where you will join the old Corinth-Argos highway, which has a clearly marked turnoff for Mycenae. If you prefer, you can take the old Corinth-Argos road to the Mycenae turnoff. This takes longer and you may get stuck behind a bus or truck, but you will have a better sense of the countryside than on the elevated highway. Either way, Mycenae is about 90km (56 miles) south of Corinth. **From Nafplion,** take the road out of town toward Argos. When you reach the Corinth-Argos highway, turn right and then, after about 16km (10 miles), turn right again at the sign for Mycenae.

By Bus There is frequent bus service from the Stathmos Leoforia Peloponnisou (bus station for the Peloponnese), at 100 Kifissou in Athens (© **210/512-4910;** www.ktel. org), to Corinth, Argos, and Nafplion (allow 3–4 hr.). From any of these places you can travel on by bus to Mycenae (allow 1 hr.). The Athens-Argos bus is usually willing to drop Mycenae-bound travelers at the turnoff at Fihtia—but don't count on finding a taxi to take you the rest of the way (about 2km, a bit more than a mile). For general information on Athens-Peloponnese schedules and fares, call © **210/512-4910** or check www.ktel.org.

FAST FACTS You can buy stamps and change money at the **mobile post office** at the ancient site, Monday through Friday from 8am to 2pm. This office is sometimes open on weekends and after 2pm, but don't count on it. There is a **pay phone** near the mobile post office.

WHAT TO SEE & DO

The Citadel & the Treasury of Atreus ⭐⭐⭐ As you walk uphill to Mycenae, you begin to get an idea of why people settled here as long ago as 3000 B.C.: Mycenae straddles a low bluff between two protecting mountains and is a superb natural citadel. The site overlooks one of the richest plains in Greece, and whoever held Mycenae could control all the land between the narrow Dervenakia Pass to the north and the Gulf of Argos, some 16km (10 miles) to the south.

By about 1400 B.C., Mycenae controlled not just the Plain of Argos, but also much of mainland Greece, as well as Crete, many of the Aegean islands, and outposts in distant Italy and Asia Minor. Then, some unknown disaster struck Mycenaean Greece; by about 1100 B.C., the Mycenaeans were on the decline. By the time of the classical era, almost all memory of the Mycenaeans had been lost, and Greeks speculated that the massive walls of Mycenae and Tiryns had been built by the mythical Cyclops.

You'll enter Mycenae through just such a wall, passing beneath the arching **Lion Gate,** whose two lions probably symbolized Mycenae's strength. The door itself (missing, like the lions' heads) would have been of wood, probably covered with bronze for additional protection; cuttings for the door jambs and pivots are clearly visible in the lintel. Soldiers stationed in the **round tower** on your right would have shot arrows down at any attackers who tried to storm the citadel. Because soldiers carried their shields on their left arms, the tower's position made the attackers vulnerable to arrows aimed at their unprotected right sides.

One of the most famous spots at Mycenae is immediately ahead of the Lion Gate: the so-called **Grave Circle A,** where Schliemann found the gold jewelry now on display at the National Archaeological Museum in Athens. When Schliemann opened the tombs and found some 14 kilos (31 lb.) of gold here, including several solid-gold face masks, he concluded that he had found the grave of Agamemnon himself. At once, Schliemann exuberantly fired off a telegram to the king of Greece, saying, "I have looked upon the face of Agamemnon bare." More sober scholars have concluded that Schliemann was wrong, and that the kings buried here died long before Agamemnon was born.

From the grave circle, head uphill past the low remains of a number of **houses.** Mycenae was not merely a palace, but a small village with the palace at the crest of the hill and administrative buildings and homes on the slopes. The **palace** was considerably grander than these small houses and had several courtrooms, bedrooms, a throne room, and a large megaron (ceremonial hall). You can see the imprint of the **four columns** that held up the roof in the megaron, as well as the outline of a **circular altar** on the floor. And spare a glance for the palace's inconspicuous **little bathtub;** Schliemann thought this was the very bathtub where Agamemnon was stabbed to death by his wife, Clytemnestra.

If you're not claustrophobic, head to the northeast corner of the citadel and climb down the flight of stairs to have a look at Mycenae's enormous **cistern.** You may find someone here selling candles, but it's a good idea to bring your own flashlight. Along with Mycenae's great walls, this cistern, which held water secretly channeled from a spring 500m (1,640 ft.) away, ensured Mycenae a safe water supply even during long enemy sieges.

There's one more thing to see before you leave Mycenae: the massive tomb known as the **Treasury of Atreus,** the largest of the tholos (beehive) tombs found here. You'll see signs for it on your right as you head down the modern road away from Mycenae. This treasury may have been built around 1300 B.C., at about the same time as the Lion Gate, in the last century of Mycenae's real greatness. The enormous tomb, with its 107 metric-ton lintel, is 13m (43 ft.) high and 14m (47 ft.) wide. To build it, workers first cut the 35m (115-ft.) passageway into the hill and faced it with stone blocks. Then the tholos chamber itself was built, by placing slightly overlapping courses of stone one on top of the other until a capstone could close the final course. As you look up toward the ceiling, you'll see why this is called a beehive tomb. Once your eyes get accustomed to the tomb's poor lighting, you can make out the bronze nails that once held hundreds of bronze rosettes in place in the ceiling. This tomb was robbed even in antiquity, so we'll never know what it contained, although the contents of Grave Circle A give an idea of what riches must have been here. If this was the family vault of Atreus, it's entirely possible that Agamemnon himself was buried here—indeed, some still call this the Tomb of Agamemnon.

Admission 8€ ($10) includes Treasury of Atreus. Summer daily 8am–7pm; winter daily 8am–5pm.

Mycenae Archaeological Museum ✦✦✦

The museum, which opened in 2004, has a low blocky exterior which suggests the outline of the citadel itself—a point reinforced by the model of the citadel just inside the museum's entrance. Unfortunately, since the museum's galleries are quite small, both the displays and the labels (in Greek and English) are hard to see when the museum is crowded, which it often is.

Most objects are grouped with others found in the same area of the citadel in an attempt to show how people actually lived here. The so-called "Cult Center," for example, has alarming representations of snakes and wide-eyed figures found together. Still, it's an indication of how little is known of what went on at the Cult Center that it is not certain whether the figurines represent deities who were worshiped or the mortals who worshiped them. Copies of the famous gold masks and jewels found in Grave Circle A (the originals are in the National Archaeological Museum, in Athens) are reminders of the fabled wealth of Mycenae.

📞 27510/76-585. Admission 4€ ($5.20). Summer daily 8am–7pm; winter shorter hours.

WHERE TO STAY & DINE

Most of the restaurants in Mycenae specialize in serving set, fixed-price meals to groups. You won't starve if you eat at one of these big, impersonal roadside restaurants, but you're likely to be served a bland meal. You'll have better luck trying the smaller restaurants at one of the following hotels. It's also sometimes possible to avoid tour groups at the **Achilleus** (📞 27510/76-027) or **Mykinaiko** (📞 27510/76-724) both on the main drag, where you can eat lunch or dinner from about 12€ ($16).

La Belle Helene

The real reason to stay here is to add your name to that of Schliemann and other luminaries in the guest book. Sentiment aside, this small hotel, one of the most famous in Greece, is usually quiet (although it does do a brisk business with tour groups in its large restaurant). The simple rooms are clean and comfortable. If you stay here, be sure to drive or walk up to the ancient site at night, especially if the moon is full.

Mycenae, 21200 Argolis. 📞 **27510/76-225.** Fax 27510/76-179. 8 units, none with bathroom. 50€–65€ ($65–$85) double, sometimes lower off season. Rates include breakfast. DC, V. **Amenities:** Restaurant.

La Petite Planete ✦

This would be a nice place to stay even without its small swimming pool, which is irresistible after a hot day's trek around Mycenae. We've usually found it quieter here than at La Belle Helene, with very helpful owners, a decent restaurant, and fine views over the plain of Argos to the hills beyond (from the front rooms).

Mycenae, 21200 Argolis. 📞 **27510/76-240.** 30 units. 70€ ($91) double. AE, V. Usually closed Apr–Oct. **Amenities:** Restaurant; bar; outdoor freshwater pool. *In room:* A/C, TV.

4 Epidaurus ✦✦

32km (20 miles) E of Nafplion; 63km (39 miles) S of Corinth

The Theater of Epidaurus is one of the most impressive sights in Greece. Probably built in the 4th century, possibly by Polykleitos, the architect of the Tholos, this theater seated—and still seats—some 14,000 spectators. Unlike so many ancient buildings, including almost everything at the Sanctuary of Asclepius, the theater was not pillaged for building blocks in antiquity. As a result, it is astonishingly well-preserved; restorations have been both minimal and tactful.

The village of Palea Epidaurus, a beach resort 10km (6 miles) from Epidaurus, is confusingly sometimes signposted ANCIENT EPIDAURUS; the theater and sanctuary are usually signposted ANCIENT THEATER.

To confuse things further, Palea Epidaurus has its own small theater and festival. If you want a swim, Palea Epidaurus is the nearest beach—but it is often quite crowded.

ESSENTIALS

GETTING THERE   By Car   If you're coming from Athens or Corinth, turn left for Epidaurus immediately after the Corinth Canal and then follow the coast road to Ancient Epidaurus, not to Nea Epidaurus or Palea Epidaurus. From Nafplion, follow the signs for Epidaurus. If you drive to Epidaurus from Nafplion for a performance, be alert: The road will be clogged with tour buses and other travelers who are driving the road for the first time.

By Bus   Two buses a day run from the Stathmos Leoforia Peloponnisou (bus station for the Peloponnese), 100 Kifissou, Athens (© 210/512-4910; www.ktel.org), to Epidaurus. The trip takes about 3 hours. There are three buses a day from the Nafplion bus station, off Plateia Kapodistrias (© 27520/27-323), to Epidaurus, as well as extra buses when there are performances at the Theater of Epidaurus. This bus takes about an hour. For general information on Athens-Peloponnese schedules and fares, call © 210/512-4910; or check www.ktel.org.

FAST FACTS   The ancient site has both a **mobile post office** and a **pay phone.**

WHAT TO SEE & DO

The Sanctuary, Museum & Theater at Epidaurus ★★   Although it's pleasant to wander through the shady **Sanctuary of Asclepius,** it's not at all easy to decipher the scant remains here—visit the excavation museum first (see below). As at Olympia, the Asklepion had accommodations for visitors, several large bathhouses, civic buildings, a stadium, a gymnasium, and several temples and shrines. The remains here are so meager that you may have to take this on faith, but try to find the round Tholos that you'll pass about halfway into the sanctuary. The famous 4th-century-B.C. architect Polykleitos, who built similar round buildings at Olympia and Delphi, was the architect here. If you wonder why the inner foundations of the Tholos are so convoluted and labyrinthine, you're in good company: Scholars still aren't sure what went on here, although some suspect that Asclepius's healing serpents lived in the labyrinth. Keep an eye out to see if the long-standing plans to reconstruct 7 of the 26 columns of the Tholos's Doric colonnade are underway when you visit.

Next to the Tholos are the remains of two long **stoas,** where patients slept in the hope that Asclepius would reveal himself to them in a dream. Those who had dreams and cures dedicated the votive offerings and inscriptions now in the museum.

At the entrance to the site, the **Excavation Museum** helps put some flesh on the bones of the confusing remains of the sanctuary. It has an extensive collection of architectural fragments from the sanctuary, including lovely acanthus flowers from the mysterious tholos. The terra-cotta body parts are votive offerings that show precisely what part of the anatomy was cured. The display of surgical implements and intimate body parts will send you away grateful that you didn't have to go under the knife here, although hundreds of inscriptions record the gratitude of satisfied patients.

If you climb to the top of the **ancient theater,** seating 14,000, you can look down over the 55 rows of seats, divided into a lower section of 34 rows and an upper section with 21 rows. The upper seats were added when the original theater was enlarged to in the 2nd century B.C. The theater's acoustics are famous: You'll almost certainly see someone demonstrate how a whisper can be heard all the way from the round orchestra to the topmost row of seats. In 2007, researchers at the Georgia Institute of Technology demonstrated that the theater's superb acoustics are due to its limestone seats! The seats deaden the low-frequency murmurs of the audience while magnifying the higher-frequency voices of the actors. Just as the stadium at Olympia brings out the sprinter in many visitors, the theater at Epidaurus tempts many to step stage center and test the acoustics by reciting poetry or bursting into song. Still, there's a respectful silence here when a performance of a classical Greek play begins, as the sun sinks behind the orchestra and the first actor steps onto the stage (see "Epidaurus After Dark," below).

If you're a theater buff, be sure to take in the **Epidaurus Festival Museum,** near the entrance to the site, with its displays of props, costumes, programs, and memorabilia from past performances. It's usually open daily from May 1 until September 30 (when the site is open), and until 9pm on performance nights; free admission.

Be sure to check the opening hours as soon as you arrive, if not before; they change unpredictably.

(© 27530/23-009. Combined admission 6€ ($7.80). Site and theater summer daily 8am–7pm, winter daily 8am–5pm; Excavation Museum Mon 11am–5pm, Tues–Sun 8am–5pm.

WHERE TO STAY & DINE

We suggest that you stay in Nafplion when you visit Epidaurus. The small hotels closer to Epidaurus are usually booked by tour groups well in advance of theater performances and are not sufficiently charming to recommend if you visit when there is not a performance. As to food, several kiosks sell snacks and cold drinks near the ticket booth at Epidaurus. In Nea and Palea Epidaurus, you'll find a number of boring restaurants, most of which cater to large groups. In other words, you won't starve, but there's no place worth seeking out, with the exception of **Leonidas** (© 27530/22-115). This small restaurant with a garden on the main Epidaurus road is open for lunch and dinner year-round, has consistently good food, and attracts a post-theater crowd that often includes actors who relax here after performances.

EPIDAURUS AFTER DARK

Classical performances at the **ancient theater** are usually given Saturday and Sunday at around 9pm June through September. Many productions are staged by the **National Theater of Greece,** some by foreign companies. Ticket prices at press time ranged from 12€ to 35€ ($16–$46). For the latest ticket prices and other information, contact the **Hellenic Festival Box Office,** 39 Panepestimiou (in the arcade; © 210/928-2900; www.hellenicfestival.gr); or the **Epidaurus Festival Box Office** (© 27530/22-006). It's also possible to buy tickets at most of Nafplion's travel agencies and at the theater itself, starting at 5pm on the day of a performance. The ancient tragedies are usually performed either in classical or modern Greek; programs (4€/ $5.20) usually have a full translation or synopsis of the play. The excellent Odyssey bookstore in Nafplion (see "Shopping" under "What to See & Do" in section 2, earlier in this chapter) usually has English-language translations of the plays.

NEMEA   289

If you are in Epidaurus in July, check out the delightful **Musical July Festival** at the **Little Theater** of Ancient Epidaurus, 7km (4½ miles) from Epidaurus. Performances in the past have ranged from chamber music to flamenco. Information on ticket prices and chartered bus and excursion-boat transportation from Athens is usually available by June from the **Athens Concert Hall (Megaron Mousikis),** 1 Kokkali and Vas. Sophias (© **210/728-2000;** www.megaron.gr); the **Greek National Tourism Organization** (© **210/870-7000;** www.gnto.gr); or the **Municipality of Palea Epidaurus** (© **27530/41-250**).

5 Nemea ★★

25km (15 miles) SE of Corinth; 35km (21 miles) N of Argos

Nemea is a gem of a site, with a restored stadium, a temple with standing columns, and the most user-friendly museum in the Peloponnese. The most famous Panhellenic Games were held every 4 years at Olympia and Delphi, but there were also games every 2 years at Isthmia, near Corinth, and at Nemea, in a gentle valley in the eastern foothills of the Arcadian Mountains from about 573 B.C. to 100 B.C. Around 100 B.C., Nemea's powerful neighbor Argos moved the festival from Nemea to Argos itself, putting an end to the Games here. But, thanks to the Society for the Revival of the Nemean Games, the Games were held here for the first time in 2,000 years on June 1, 1996, when 1,000 contestants from around the world, ranging in age from 12 to 90, participated. The 2000 and 2004 Games drew even larger crowds, and the next Games are planned for 2008. So, when you visit Nemea, you won't see just the stadium where athletes once contended, but also the site of the new Nemean Games. Contestants run barefoot, as in antiquity, but wear short tunics rather than run naked. If you want to know more about the Nemean Games, contact the **Society for the Revival of the Nemean Games** (© **510/642-5924** in the U.S.; www.nemeagames.gr).

Two excellent site guides should be on sale at the museum: *Nemea* (10€/$13) and *The Ancient Stadium of Nemea* (2€/$2.60). You'll find shady spots to read them both at the site and at the stadium.

ESSENTIALS

GETTING THERE   By Car   From Athens, take the National Road to Corinth and then follow signs for Argos and Tripolis. The road divides just after the sign for Ancient Corinth. The speedy new Corinth-Tripolis toll road has green signposts depicting a highway. Take the Nemea turnoff and follow signs to the site. If you take the old Corinth-Argos road, the turnoff for Nemea is signposted. Allow 30 minutes from Corinth to Nemea on the new road and an hour on the old road.

Tips In Vino Veritas

Nemea is famous for its wines, especially its red wines, many known as the "blood of Heracles." Signs along local roads indicate "Wine Routes." On the road between Ancient and New Nemea, several vineyards, including Palivos (www.palivos.gr), offer tours and tastings of the excellent local wines most days in summer.

By Bus   There are about five buses a day from the Stathmos Leoforia Peloponnisou (bus station for the Peloponnese) in Athens, 100 Kifissou (© **210/512-4910;** www. ktel.org), to Nemea, usually via Corinth. Allow about 3 hours for the trip and ask to be let off at the ancient site of Nemea *(Ta Archaia)* on the outskirts of the hamlet of Archaia Nemea, not in the village of Nea Nemea. For general information on Athens-Peloponnese schedules and fares, call © **210/512-4910** or check www.ktel.org.

FAST FACTS   Nea Nemea has both a **post office** and a **telephone office,** but it's unlikely that you'll want to go there. There's a **pay phone** by the ancient site.

WHAT TO SEE & DO

The Museum & Ancient Site 𝆕𝆕   The Nemea Museum, set on an uncharacteristically Greek green lawn, is one of the most charming small museums in Greece (labels in Greek and English). You'll get an excellent sense of the history of the excavation of Nemea and the Nemean Games, as well as the early Christian village here, much of which was built from material pillaged from ancient Nemea.

A display map just inside the museum's main gallery shows all the cities in the Greek world whose coins were found at Nemea and illustrates just how far people came to see these Games. Just as today, most fans sat together—coins from each city were usually found in the same area of the stadium. You'll see excellent photographs of the excavations as well as enlarged photos of important finds, such as the small bronze figure of the infant Opheltes, in whose honor the Nemean Games may have been founded.

According to one legend, the Seven Theban Champions founded the Games in memory of the infant, who—not as agile as Heracles (Hercules)—was killed by a serpent. In honor of Opheltes, the judges wore black mourning robes, just as they do today at the revived Nemean Games. Another legend says that the Games were established not to honor Opheltes but to honor Heracles, who killed a fierce lion that had his lair in one of the caves in Evangelistria hill, just behind the stadium. Fortunately, lions are unknown in today's Greece.

While you're in the museum, be sure to take a look from one of the large picture windows that overlook the ancient site where the coins, vases, athletic gear, and architectural fragments on display were found. A raised stone path tactfully suggests the route from the museum to the site, passing a carefully preserved early Christian burial tomb and skirting a 4th-century-B.C. bath complex and the large 5th-century Christian basilica before arriving at the Temple of Zeus.

This temple was built of local limestone around 330 B.C. on the site of an earlier temple, which may have burned down. When Pausanias came by here in the 2nd century A.D., he felt that the temple was worth seeing but complained that "the roof has collapsed." Sometime later, the columns followed suit, perhaps when early Christians used the temple as a handy quarry for building material for their 5th-century basilica. For perhaps 1,500 years, only 3 of the original 32 exterior Doric columns were left standing; the drums of the others lay scattered on the ground. In 1999, University of California archaeologist Stephen Miller initiated an ambitious plan to reerect a number of the fallen columns, starting with two columns at the temple's north end.

Joint admission to site, museum, and stadium 7€ ($9). Tues–Sun 8:30am–3pm.

The Stadium 𝆕𝆕   To reach the stadium, leave the site and head back along the road that brought you into Nemea. *The Ancient Stadium of Nemea,* on sale at the ticket booth, contains a self-guided tour of the stadium. The locker room just outside the stadium caused quite a stir when it was discovered in 1991, with few journalists able to resist cracks about what a locker room must smell like after 2,500 years.

Athletes would have stripped down in the locker room, oiled their bodies with olive oil, and then entered the stadium through the vaulted tunnel, just as football players today rush onto the playing field. Once you pass through the tunnel, you'll see where the judges sat while spectators sprawled on earthen benches carved out of the hillside itself. When they got thirsty, they could have a drink from the water carried around the racetrack in a stone channel. If you wish, walk down onto the 178m (584-ft.) racecourse and stand at the stone starting line where the athletes took their places for the footraces. Running naked and barefoot, the athletes kept their balance at the starting line by gripping the indentations in the stone with their toes.

© 27460/22-739. Joint admission to site, museum, and stadium 7€ ($9). Tues–Sun 8:30am–3pm.

WHERE TO STAY & DINE

There's no hotel here as yet. **Nemeios Dias** (© 27450/24-244), a welcome cafe/restaurant signposted SNAK BAR/SOUVENIR is usually open from 10am to midafternoon; local wines are a tempting souvenir here.

6 Argos

48km (30 miles) S of Corinth

There should be lots of impressive remains to visit here, but because modern Argos (pop. 20,000) is built precisely on top of the ancient city, there's little to see in town except the 4th-century theater, a hodgepodge of rather tedious remains across from the theater, and the museum. Repeated earthquakes during the last century left modern Argos with an undistinguished agglomeration of flat-roofed concrete buildings, with only the occasional neoclassical house. That said, the central plateia is lively and the street market on Wednesday and Saturday mornings is one of the largest in the Peloponnese. Still, it takes a vigorous imagination to visualize Argos as it was in its heyday in the 7th century B.C. Then, under the tyrant Pheidon, who is often credited with inventing coinage in Greece, Argos was the most powerful city in the entire Peloponnese. Out of town is a different story: The fortifications on Argos's twin citadels, the Aspis and the Larissa, are very impressive.

If your time in the Peloponnese is limited, you might consider saving Argos for a return trip. If you can spend a few hours here, have a look at the theater, stop by the museum, and try to drive up to the Larissa and Aspis citadels to take in the Venetian fortifications and the view over the plain.

ESSENTIALS

GETTING THERE By Train There are about five trains a day from Athens to Argos. Information on schedules and fares is available from Stathmos Peloponnisou (railroad station for the Peloponnese) in Athens (© 210/513-1601 or 210/512-4910), or at the Corinth train station (© 27510/27-212). Trains take at least 3 hours. The Argos train station, on Leoforos Vas. Sofias (© 27510/67-212), is about a kilometer from the central square.

By Bus Five buses a day run to Argos from the Stathmos Leoforia Peloponnisou (bus station for the Peloponnese) in Athens, 100 Kifissou (© 210/512-4910; www.ktel.org). The bus ride usually takes just under 3 hours. Argos is also served by frequent buses from Nafplion (about 30 min.). Argos has two bus stations: the Athinon

A Word of Caution

Argos's confusing system of one-way streets and potentially lethal three-way intersections make driving almost as chaotic as the night in 272 B.C. when Pyrrus of Epirus stormed the city with a large force—including two war elephants, one of which overturned and blocked the main gate into the city. In short, drive with particular care here.

station (buses to and from Athens), on Leoforos Vas. Georgiou B. (© 27510/673-24); and the Arcadia-Laconia station (buses for Tripolis), at 24 Peithonos (© 27510/67-324). For general information on Athens-Peloponnese schedules and fares, call © 210/512-4910 or check www.ktel.org.

By Car   From Athens, take the National Road to Corinth, and then follow signs for Argos and Tripolis. The road divides just after the sign for Ancient Corinth. The speedy new Corinth-Tripolis toll road has green signposts with drawings of highways. Take the Argos exit and follow the exit road until it reaches an obvious main road (the old Corinth-Argos road). Turn right, cross the bridge, and you'll soon enter Argos. If you take the old road to Argos, it runs straight into the town. It's never easy to park in Argos, but you'll probably find a place on one of the side streets off the central square or by the ancient theater.

FAST FACTS   The **National Bank of Greece** and several others on the main square, Plateia Ayios Petros, all have ATMs. The **hospital** (© 27510/24-455) is signposted on the main road into town from Athens. The **police** are at 10 Agelou Bobou (© 27510/67-222). The **post office,** 16 Danaou, off the central square, is open Monday through Friday from 7am to 2pm. The **telephone office (OTE),** 8 Nikitara, is usually open Monday through Friday from 7am to midnight. **Café Net,** at 4 Oktavriou 28th, offers Internet access for 6€ ($7.80) per hour.

WHAT TO SEE & DO

The Theater at Argos ✪   If you've already seen the theater at Epidaurus, you'll find it hard to believe that Argos's 4th-century theater was not just larger, but probably the largest in classical Greece. Twenty thousand spectators could sit here, in 89 tiers of seats, many of which were carved from the hillside itself. The thronelike seats in the front rows were added by the Romans and reserved for visiting bigwigs, including the Roman emperor. The Romans remodeled the theater, so that the orchestra (stage) could be flooded and mock naval battles staged. Fortunately, they had a genius for building the aqueducts needed to channel enough water to create a temporary inland sea. There was enough water left over to service the baths, whose remains are next to the theater. Also near the theater are the minimal remains of the ancient agora, as yet largely unexcavated, as it lies beneath today's Argos.

© 27510/68-819. Admission 3€ ($3.90); joint admission to theater, agora, Heraion, Archaeological Museum 6€ ($7.80). Summer Tues–Sat 9am–6pm, Sun 10am–3pm; often open in winter as well. Sometimes closed unexpectedly (but clearly visible from the Argos-Tripolis road).

The Museum at Argos ✪   This small museum has a handful of superlative pieces that you'll want to take in, including the fragment of a 7th-century-B.C. clay krater (vessel) showing a determined Ulysses blinding the one-eyed Cyclops Polyphemus. Nearby are a handsome lyre made from a tortoise shell, and a stunning late geometric bronze helmet and suit of body armor. Downstairs, in the Lerna Room, the tiny, stout Neolithic clay figure of a woman or goddess found at Lerna is one of the oldest known sculptural representations of the human body yet found in Europe. Nearby is a handsome pitcher in the shape of a bird with its head thrown back in song—and ornamental breasts on its chest.

Outside, in the museum's shady courtyard, are some terrific Roman mosaics showing the god Dionysos and the seasons. The figures in the mosaics are bundled up in cloaks and heavy leggings in the cold months, and casually dressed in light tunics and filmy cloaks in the summer months.

If you visit the museum (which has a welcome icy-cold water fountain and clean toilets) on Wednesday or Saturday morning, don't miss the **street market** that runs for several blocks to your left as you leave. This is the place to get anything from water glasses, baseball caps, and farm implements to live chickens and every possible seasonal fruit and flower. If you're here on a nonmarket day and need supplies, there's a large **supermarket** just off the main square.

Elgas St. (no street no.), off the main square, Plateia Ayiou Petrou. ℭ 27510/68-819. Admission 2€ ($2.60); joint admission to theater, agora, Heraion, Archaeological Museum 6€ ($7.80). Tues–Sun 8:30am–3pm.

The Larissa & the Aspis ℱ   Argos was famous in antiquity for its two citadels; The Greek word *aspis* means "shield," which is what the Argives thought this hill (98m/328 ft. high) looked like. Now topped by a small chapel, the Aspis was Argos's first acropolis, abandoned when the higher (274m/905-ft.) Larissa was fortified in the 5th century B.C. You can still see some of the ancient blocks that were reused in Larissa's medieval battlements. There's an inner and outer system of walls, with several towers and the ruins of a church. The view's the thing here, and you get a bird's-eye view of the Aspis, the convent of Panaghia tou Vrakou (Virgin of the Rocks) on the lower slopes of the Larissa, Argos itself, with its fertile encircling, plain, and the blue waters of the Gulf of Nafplion.

The climb from Argos's ancient theater to the Larissa and Aspis is rigorous; allow several hours and take water. If you drive, ask for directions to the kastro, or castle, as the Larissa is called, at the theater, the Archaeological Museum, or the police station, as Argos roads are in a seemingly constant state of flux. Not many visitors come here, and you may have the place to yourself.

Free admission. Usually sunrise–sunset.

WHERE TO STAY & DINE

With Nafplion just down the road, there's really no reason to stay overnight in Argos unless you prefer the bustle of this crowded Greek market town to Nafplion's more sybaritic pleasures. If you do stay here, **Hotel Mycenae,** 10 Plateia Ayiou Petrou (ℭ 27510/68-754); and **Hotel Telesilla,** 2 Danaou and Plateia Ayiou Petrou

---

Tips **Argos Ouzo**

One of Greece's most distinguished ouzos, Mavrakis, has been made in Argos since 1864 and can be purchased in handsome metal bottles in the original shop (with many of its original furnishings) at 20 Vas. Konstantinou on the main plateia, Plateia Ayiou Petrou.

(ⓒ 27510/68-317), which cater to businesspeople, are probably your best bets. Both are on the main square, and both have air-conditioning, central heating, and TV. Doubles cost from 60€ ($78). None of the small cafes and restaurants in Argos is worth seeking out, but the conveniently located **Retro** and **Aigle,** on the main square, have the usual chops, salads, and souvlaki, as well as pizza and veal in lemon sauce *(moskari lemonato).* Lunch or dinner costs from 15€ ($20) with beer or wine.

7 Sparta (Sparti) ⓧ

248km (153 miles) SW of Athens; 58km (36 miles) S of Tripolis

Sparta is an energetic town, with lively street markets and a bustling main square flanked by restaurants, cafes, and shops where locals congregate and engage in the unofficial Greek national sport: talking politics and trading tidbits of gossip.

All around Sparta, lush olive and citrus groves spread across the rich plain watered by the bottle-green Eurotas River. The ornamental orange trees planted along Sparta's main avenues bring the country right into town.

Few sights in the Peloponnese are more imposing than the immense bulk of Mount Taygetos towering above Sparta along the western horizon. There's often snow on Taygetos until well into the summer, and when the sun sinks behind the mountain, the temperature seems to plummet instantly. To the east, the more gentle Parnon range brackets the Spartan plain. The ancient Spartans boasted that they didn't need fortifications because the Taygetos and Parnon mountains were their defense walls.

The ancient Spartans were as famous for courage as the Athenians were for intellectual bravado. Little Spartan boys were told to "come back with your shield or on it"— that is, victorious or dead. The Spartans first earned their reputation for courage and military heroism in 580 B.C., when the Spartan general Leonidas and a band of only 300 soldiers faced down the invading Persian army at Thermopylae—an event featured in the 2007 blockbuster film "300" that earned $130 million dollars in the first 10 days after its release! From 431 to 404 B.C., Sparta and Athens fought the Peloponnesian War; Sparta finally won, but was exhausted by the effort. From then on, Sparta was a sleepy provincial town with a great future behind it. Greece's first king, young Otto of Bavaria, paid tribute to Sparta's past by redesigning the city with the wide boulevards and large central square that still make it charming today.

In a famously accurate prediction, the 5th-century-B.C. Athenian historian Thucydides wrote that if Sparta were ever "to become desolate, and the temples and the foundations of the public buildings were left, no one in future times would believe that this had been one of the preeminent cities of Greece." The ancient remains here are so meager that only the truly dedicated will seek them out. Others will prefer to enjoy Spartan street life, eat Spartan *loukoumades,* take in the small archaeological museum and the engaging new museum of the Olive, and then head 8km (5 miles) down the road to the much more impressive remains of the Byzantine city of Mistra.

ESSENTIALS

GETTING THERE   By Bus   From Athens, seven buses a day depart from the Stathmos Leoforia Peloponnisou (bus station for the Peloponnese), 100 Kifissou (ⓒ **210/512-4910;** www.ktel.org) for the Sparta bus station on the east side of town at Lykourgou and Dafnou (ⓒ **27310/26-441).** There are frequent buses from Sparta to Mistra. For general information on Athens-Peloponnese schedules and fares, call ⓒ **210/512-4910** or check www.ktel.org.

By Car   From Athens, allow 5 hours; from Corinth, 3 hours; from Patras, 3 hours; from Tripolis, 2 hours. From Athens or Corinth, the new Corinth-Tripolis road is well worth taking for those not wishing to visit much en route.

VISITOR INFORMATION   It is usually possible to get visitor information in the Town Hall, on the main square (© **27310/26-517** or 27310/24-852); hours are Monday through Friday from 8am to 3pm. Ask whether the English-language pamphlet *Laconia Traveller* is available. In recent years, a **summer music and drama festival** has been held in Sparta. It is sometimes called Artistic Summer Sparta (fax 27310/82-470); inquire at the Town Hall.

FAST FACTS   Two **National Bank of Greece** branches on Paleologou exchange currency and have ATMs. The **hospital** (© **27310/28-671**) is signposted in town. The **police** and **tourist police** are at 8 Hilonos (© **27310/20-492** or 27310/89-583). Both the **post office,** on Kleombrotou, and the **telephone office (OTE),** at 11 Kleombrotou, are signposted. The **Cosmos Club Internet Café** (© **27310/21-500**) charges 6€ ($7.80) per hour of Internet access.

WHAT TO SEE & DO

The Acropolis & Ancient Theater
The acropolis is at the north end of town, just beyond the monumental statue of Leonidas near the supposed site of his tomb. The grove of trees here makes this a pleasant parklike place to sit at sunset, but you'll probably enjoy the view of Taygetos more than the scattered remains of the 2nd-century-B.C. theater. Originally, this was one of the largest theaters in Greece, seating 16,000. The theater was dismantled and the blocks were carted off for reuse when the Franks built Mistra in the 13th century. The theater is sometimes used during the summer festival here.

Free admission. Usually Tues–Sun 8:30am–3pm.

The Archaeological Museum ⚔
The prize of this museum is a handsome 5th-century marble bust, believed to show Leonidas and to have stood on his tomb. The Spartans, however, were famous as soldiers, not as artists, and for the most part the museum's collection reflects Sparta's lack of a lively artistic tradition. Still, a stop here is worthwhile to see the statue of Leonidas, several fine Roman mosaics, and a small collection of objects found at Mycenaean sites in the countryside near Sparta. The museum's rose garden, peopled with decapitated Roman statues, is a nice spot to sit and read. *Tip:* This museum has no restrooms.

On the square between Ayios Nikolaos and Paleologou sts. © **27310/28-575**. Admission 2€ ($2.60). Tues–Sat 8:30am–3pm; Sun 8:30am–12:30pm.

The Coumantaros Gallery
En route to the Acropolis, it's easy to stop in at this branch of the National Gallery, in a handsome early-20th-century neoclassical house. The gallery has a small permanent collection of western European 16th-to-20th century painters and temporary exhibits, usually of contemporary Greek artists.

Corner of Palaiologou and Thermopylon. Free admission. Tues–Sat 9am–3pm; Sun 10am–2pm. Closed Mon. Often closed in winter.

The Menelaion ⚔
To visit the Menelaion, take the Tripolis road north out of town and turn right immediately after the bridge; the Menelaion is signposted about 5km (3 miles) down the road. The shrine's three terraces of gray limestone blocks, in honor of Helen of Troy's long-suffering husband, Menelaus, is about a 10-minute walk uphill

from the chapel, where you can park your car. Next to the shrine are the low remains of several Mycenaean houses, none of which seems remotely grand enough to have belonged to Menelaus. Again, as with the acropolis of ancient Sparta, the real reason to come here is the view of the plain and Taygetos.

Free admission. Usually Tues–Sun 8:30am–3pm.

Museum of the Olive and Greek Olive Oil 🏛🏛 This small museum, in a handsome restored stone warehouse, opened in 2005 and focuses on the cultivation and use of the olive through the ages in Greece. Drawings and photographs of scenes on vases show how the olive was raised in antiquity, and exhibits of tools and machinery bring the story up to the present. The small shop sells lovely pure olive oil soap, postcards, and posters. This is one of several new industrial museums in Greece; others include the Museum of Hydroelectric Power in Dimitsana, and Arcadia and the Silk Museum, in Serres, Greece.

129 Odos Othonos-Amalias. ☎ 27310/89-315. Admission 2€ ($2.60). Mar 1–Oct 15 Wed–Mon 10am–6pm; Oct 16–Feb 28 Wed–Mon 10am–4pm. Closed Tues.

Mount Taygetos 🏛🏛🏛 The **Hellenic Alpine Club of Sparta** (near the central square) has information on climbing Mount Taygetos and on local hikes. *Taygetos,* published by the Municipality of Sparta, is an invaluable guide (9€/$12). **Trekking Hellas** offers a number of weekend and 1-week hikes in the Taygetos area.

Alpine Club: 97 Gortsologou. ☎ 27310/22-574. Trekking Hellas: www.trekking.gr.

The Temple of Artemis Orthia If you head out of Sparta on the Tripolis road, you'll see a small yellow sign for the Temple of Artemis Orthia, where little Spartan boys were whipped to learn courage and endurance. The site, which dates from the 10th century B.C. but was extensively remodeled by the Romans, is often crowded with Gypsy children aggressively begging for money. Consequently, this can be an unpleasant place to visit, especially alone.

Free admission. Usually Tues–Sun 8:30am–3pm.

WHERE TO STAY

There's only one special place to stay here, the little Xenonas Pyrgos Mystras, a 7-unit boutique hotel which opened in 2005 and is the antithesis of most large, impersonal Greek hotels (see below). Most hotels here offer substantial reductions off season.

Hotel Byzantion 🏛 This family-owned and -operated hotel is a great place to stay if you want to be poised to visit Mistra first thing in the morning. Guest rooms and bathrooms are on the small side and somewhat spartan (sorry!). Rooms in the back escape any sounds of traffic and overlook a pleasant garden. The staff is exceptionally helpful and the breakfast buffet is ample. The Mistra has several small taverns if you don't want to go to Sparta for dinner.

23100 Mistra, Laconia. ☎ 27310/83-309. Fax 27310/20-019. Byzanhtl@otenet.gr. 22 units. 65€–75€ ($85–$98) double. MC, V. Usually closed Dec–Mar 15. **Amenities:** Breakfast room; garden. *In room:* A/C, TV.

Hotel Maniatis Despite its central location at the corner of Paleologou and Lycourgou, Sparta's two main streets, the Maniatis is reasonably quiet (the rooms in back are smaller but quieter). The marble-and-glass lobby is considerably grander than the guest rooms which, if not spartan, are simple, with the pine paneling, functional bedside tables, straight chairs, and the small bathrooms endemic in Greek hotels. The food at the hotel restaurant, the **Dias,** is quite good, but the place is often filled with

---

Tips **Shopping in Sparta**

The weekly **market** in Sparta is on Saturday. **Lampropoulou** and **Liakos,** both on Paleologou, stock English-language guides, newspapers, magazines, and books. During the last week in August, farmers from across Laconia bring goods to sell at a lively street fair in Mistra.

---

noisy tour groups; you can walk a couple blocks to the excellent **Diethnes** restaurant (see below).

72 Paleologou, 23100 Sparta, Laconia. © **27310/22-665.** Fax 27310/29-994. 80 units. 75€–90€ ($98–$117) double. MC, V. **Amenities:** Restaurant; bar. *In room:* A/C, TV.

Hotel Melelaion ⭐ The Menelaion's location is almost too central: rooms fronting Paleologou get lots of traffic noise as well as noise from the main taxi stand. You may forgive the noise: The handsome neoclassical building now has a welcome swimming pool in its central courtyard. Rooms are good-size, bathrooms are decent, but both but could use some sprucing up.

1 Paleologou, 23100 Sparta, Laconia. © **27310/22-161.** Fax 27310/26-332. 48 units. 80€ ($104) double. Rates include breakfast. MC, V. **Amenities:** Restaurant; bar; pool. *In room:* A/C, TV, minibar.

Xenonas Pyrgos Mystra ⭐⭐ This 7-room boutique hotel may be the only place in Greece where you can stay in a handsomely restored traditional mid-19th-century tower house with flatscreen television and DVD in your room. Some rooms have drop-dead views of Byzantine Mistras, while others look out on the hotel's garden and the plain of Sparta. The units are painted in pastels and decorated with silks and other elegant fabrics, with comfortable armchairs and excellent reading lights. The breakfast buffet is extensive and has fresh baked goods, local honey, eggs cooked to order and an array of regional cheeses. The staff gets high praise from guests. Friends who decided to splurge and stay here 1 night found this such a haven that they stayed another 2 nights and can't wait to come back.

3 Manousaki, 23100 Mistra, Laconia. © **27310/20-970** or 27310/20-700. Fax 27310/20-774. www.pyrgosmystra. com. Doubles and suites 250€–400€ ($325–$520). AE, DISC, MC, V. **Amenities:** Breakfast room; garden. *In Room:* A/C, TV, Internet.

WHERE TO DINE

Diethnes ⭐⭐ GREEK On summer Saturdays, all of Sparta seems to eat lunch in the Diethnes's shady garden after shopping at the street market around the corner. If you're going to eat only one meal in Sparta, it should be here; in fact, unless you really don't like eating in the same place more than once, why go anywhere else? The grills (including local *loukanika* sausages) are excellent; the vegetables are drizzled, not drenched, in oil; the local wine is eminently drinkable; and the waiters move at the speed of light through the crowds. If the Diethnes is too crowded, try the similarly priced but less tasty **Elysee,** a few doors away at 113 Paleologou.

105 Paleologou. © **27310/28-636.** Main courses 6€–12€ ($8–$16). No credit cards. Daily about 8am–midnight.

The Stoa Cafeteria ⭐ LOUKOUMADES/SNACKS This little hole in the wall next to a florist is the place to go for a Greek favorite: *loukoumades,* airy deep-fried puffs of pastry drenched in honey syrup. I try to go at least twice when I'm in Sparta, even if I'm only there for a day.

140 Lycourgou. ⓒ **27310/23-237.** Coffee and *loukoumades* 6€ ($8). No credit cards. Mon–Fri 8am–evening; Sat 8am–noon.

MISTRA 𝕽𝕽𝕽
A LOOK AT THE PAST

In 1204, the Frankish leader William de Villehardouin chose this site as the headquarters for his Greek empire. De Villehardouin crowned Mistra with a fortress and defense walls, built himself a palace on the slopes below, and had 10 good years here until the Byzantine Greeks defeated him at the Battle of Pelagonia in 1259. According to legend, de Villehardouin would have escaped capture if a Greek soldier had not identified him by his famously protruding buckteeth.

Mistra's real heyday came under the Byzantine Greeks, when most of its churches and more than 2,000 houses, as well as the enormous Palace of the Despots, were built. Some 25,000 people lived in Mistra—twice the population of Sparta today. Among them were the philosophers, writers, architects, and artists who made Mistra something of an international center of culture.

Mistra was such an important city that many Byzantine emperors sent their heirs here for on-the-job training. After Constantinople and the Byzantine empire fell to the Turks in 1453, Mistra held out; the last emperor of Byzantium was crowned in the cathedral at Mistra, which finally fell to the Turks in 1460.

The Venetians captured Mistra from the Turks in 1687 and ruled here for a half-century, during which time Mistra swelled to an enormous city of more than 40,000, largely supported by a flourishing silk industry. When the Turks regained power, Mistra began its long decline into what it is today: Greece's most picturesque ghost town.

THE ARCHAEOLOGICAL SITE OF MISTRA

Be sure to bring water and wear a hat and sturdy shoes when you visit Mistra. If you start your tour of Mistra at the top, you can orient yourself by taking in the fine view over the entire site from de Villehardouin's **Castle** (kastro). The **Palace of the Despots,** which has been undergoing restoration for some years, stands out clearly, surrounded by the roofs of Mistra's magnificent **churches.** Despite what one scholar described as Mistra's "picturesque incoherence," you should be able to make out the tall walls of the once-handsome town houses of Mistra's nobility on the upper slopes; on the lower slopes are the remains of the more modest homes of laborers and shopkeepers. Here, and throughout the site, there are excellent information signs in Greek and English beside many monuments. As you head down from the kastro, you'll begin to pass some of the churches, most of which have elaborate brickwork decoration, a multiplicity of domes, and superb frescoes. Give your eyes time to adjust to the poor light inside the churches. Once they do, you'll be able to pick out vivid scenes, such as the *Raising of Lazarus* and the *Ascension* in the 15th-century frescoes in the **Pantannasa Monastery;**

Mistra's Earthly Delights

If you are lucky enough to visit Mistra in the spring or early summer, you'll find it carpeted with fragrant wildflowers and echoing with sheep bells from the flocks that are enjoying the fresh spring vegetation. This is the perfect place to take a break, smell the flowers, and enjoy the view down over the green plain of Sparta and up to the snow-clad peaks of Mount Taygetos.

---

the *Marriage of Cana* in the 14th-century **Panayia Hodegetria;** and the stunning *Birth of Christ* in the 14th-century **Peribleptos Monastery.** The frescoes that decorated Greek churches have been described as the "Books of the Illiterate"; any devout Byzantine Greek could have "read" these frescoes and identified every New and Old Testament scene, just as their descendants can today. Try also to sit for a quiet moment or two in the garden courtyard of the **Metropolis** (cathedral) **of Saint Dimitrios,** with its small museum, with exhibits on Mistra as a link between East and West. The site (© **27310/83-377**) is open from 8am to 3pm and sometimes later in summer. Admission is 5€ ($6.50).

8 Andritsena ★/★ & Vassae ★

45km (27 miles) from Megalopolis to Andritsena; 24km (15 miles) from Andritsena to Vassae

Andritsena, with the scent of oregano and the sound of sheep bells everywhere, is one of the most charming of the Peloponnesian mountain villages. After years with only the desultory Theoxenia Hotel, Andritsena now has two good places to stay and a number of small restaurants. The main street is punctuated by enormous plane trees, several of which have been fitted with pipes gushing forth the delicious local spring water. In the evening, villagers stroll the main street while sheep bells echo in the hills. If you want to get away from it all and spend the night in a Greek mountain village, make it Andritsena. If you can, plan to be in Andritsena on Saturday, when the main street is taken over by the weekly **market,** an excellent place to buy every manner of bell (for sheep, goat, or cow), as well as mountain tea and herbs.

  Vassae is one of the most impressive 5th-century Greek temples, its gray granite columns the perfect complement to its remote mountain setting. Unfortunately, the temple, badly damaged by time and earthquakes, is hidden under a bizarre protective tent that looks rather like the Sydney opera house. In short, the main reason to visit Vassae these days is to see the charming neighboring village of Andritsena.

ESSENTIALS
GETTING THERE   By Bus   Buses for Andritsena leave from the Stathmos Peloponnisiou (bus station for the Peloponnese) in Athens, 100 Kifisswiou (© **210/512-4910;** www.ktel.org). There are several buses a day to Andritsena from Athens and from Argos, Tripolis, Olympia, and Megalopolis. General information on Athens-Peloponnese schedules is available at © **210/512-4910** or www.ktel.org.

By Car   All the routes to Andritsena go through spectacular mountain countryside. The roads are excellent, but each winding mile takes about twice as long to drive as you might have anticipated.

FAST FACTS   Everything you might need—the **bus station, OTE, post office, bank, police**—is clearly signposted on or just off Andritsena's main street.

WHAT TO SEE & DO
THE TEMPLE OF VASSAE
Coming around the last turn in the road and suddenly seeing the severe gray limestone columns of this 5th-century Doric temple to Apollo used to be one of the great sights in the Peloponnese. It seemed almost impossible that such a staggeringly impressive building should have been built in such a remote location—and designed by none other than Ictinus, the architect of the Parthenon. Evidently, the temple was built by

the inhabitants of the tiny hamlet of Phigaleia, to thank Apollo for saving them from a severe plague.

If you saw the temple before it disappeared under its tent, cherish your memory and don't bother to visit now. The tent fits so snugly that the only way to get a sense of what the temple actually looks like is to buy a postcard.

Every year, the guard at Vassae says that he hopes that the temple will be mended and the tent removed "next year," a phrase that in Greek does not carry the specificity that its translation into English implies! In the summer of 2000, the Committee for the Preservation of the Temple announced government-funded plans to begin a 20-year restoration. Initially, the foundation along the temple's north end, along with 10 columns, will be restored. Of course, when this vital work begins—which it had not at press time—and while it goes on, the entire temple itself will be even less visible to visitors.

Visiting hours to the currently shrouded monument are usually daily from 8am to 7pm in summer, to 3pm in winter. Admission is 3€ ($3.90).

THE VILLAGE OF ANDRITSENA

Tiny Andritsena has one of the finest small libraries in Greece, the legacy of a 19th-century philhellene. If you like old books, check to see if the **library,** just off the main street, is open. If not, you can console yourself at the **Club Mylos Internet Café** on the plateia.

The small **folk museum,** on the plateia below the main street, is usually locked, despite its posted hours. Admission is 2€ ($2.60); contributions are welcome. To see the endearing collection of local wedding costumes, rugs, farm tools, and family photographs, ask to be let in at the house nearest to the museum. If the people there don't have the keys, they'll phone Kyria Vasso at the Sigouri restaurant (see below).

WHERE TO STAY

In addition to our recommendations, in a pinch, there's the 45-unit Theoxenia (© **26260/22-219**), which continues to need remodeling, as it has for several decades. Doubles from around 50€/$65; prices often negotiable. Restaurant to be avoided.

Avgerinou Syrrakou Inn 🏠🏠 Up a steep street, with views over the village and surrounding countryside, two restored stone houses are a small inn that opened in 2005. Rooms are small and charming, with wood floors, stone walls, and handwoven rugs. The large terrace (where breakfast is served in fine weather) is ideal for reading up on what you want to see next. Greek-speaking friends who stayed here were very happy, and felt very welcome; we'd like to hear from other visitors.

27061 Andritsena, Eleia. © **26260/22-314.** 9 units. 75€–95€ ($98–$124) double with breakfast. No credit cards. **Amenities:** Bar/terrace/breakfast room. *In room:* Heating in winter.

Epikourias Apollon Hotel 🏠 Frequent travelers to Andritsena rejoiced when this five-room hotel on the main plateia opened in 2002. The simple rooms have pleasant views over the town. Kuria Maria, who is in charge here, could not be more helpful. Since there are only five rooms, you probably should make a reservation, lest you be forced back on the Theoxenia or find yourself driving on to Olympia, the nearest place with a good number of hotels.

Plateia, 27061 Andritsena, Eleia. © **26260/22-840.** 6 units. 65€ ($85) double without breakfast; 70€ ($91) double with breakfast. No credit cards. **Amenities:** Breakfast room. *In room:* Heating in winter.

WHERE TO DINE

There are a number of pleasant places on and just off the main street, including **Andritsena Kafezakeroplasteion** (a coffee and sweet shop) and the Greek restaurants **Georgitsis** and **Trani Brisi**. Phone numbers are not useful for any of these—walk in and sit down. In addition, there is one place to seek out (see below).

Sigouri ☆☆ GREEK HOME COOKING   Kyria Vasso's *briam* (vegetable stew) is excellent, as are her stuffed tomatoes and barrel wine. A meal here consists of a salad, main course, and the local wine. If you like *kourouloudes* (rag rugs), ask to see the ones she makes and sells by the meter; from about 30€ ($39), you can take home a color-ful hand-loomed bedside rug. Kyria Vasso also usually has the keys to the Folk Museum. She may even have a Frommer's sticker on her window!

Sofokleos (across from the metalworker's shop above the main plateia), Andritsena. © 26260/22-197. Lunch or dinner from 10€ ($13). No credit cards. Lunch and dinner served most days; usually closes by 10pm.

9 Monemvassia ☆☆

97km (60 miles) S of Sparta; 340km (210 miles) S of Athens

In the Middle Ages, Monemvassia was nicknamed "the Gibraltar of Greece" because of its strategic importance overlooking the East-West sea routes. Centuries of decline followed and Monemvassia had become a virtual ghost town by the early 20th cen-tury, remembered largely for its once-famous sweet wine, Malmsey. Today, this rocky island just off the easternmost tip of the Peloponnese has a new lease on life: For some years, wealthy foreigners and Greeks have been buying and restoring old houses here. Furthermore, word is getting out that in addition to its medieval fortress, handsome churches, and drop-dead sunsets, Monemvassia has several of the most stylish small hotels in the Peloponnese (and increasingly good restaurants). Consequently, Monem-vassia draws visitors year-round; I've made several spur-of-the-moment midwinter trips here only to find both the hotels and restaurants crowded.

In addition to independent travelers, an increasing number of round-the-Pelopon-nese bus tours stop here for an hour or two. Try to arrive in the late afternoon or evening, so that early the next morning you can have a swim, relax, and do your sight-seeing before the first tour bus arrives.

Although Monemvassia is an island, it's connected to the mainland by a causeway across which you can drive or stroll. Once you step through the massive Venetian Gate that is Monemvassia's only entrance (*mone emvasis* means "one entrance" in Greek), you're in a separate world. Cars are banned here—a wise decision, since the only approximation of a street on "the rock" is barely wide enough for two donkeys (which bring in supplies) to squeeze past each other.

ESSENTIALS

GETTING THERE   By Bus   There is one direct bus a day from the Stathmos Leoforia Peloponnisou (bus station for the Peloponnese), at 100 Kifissou in Athens, to Gefyra (on the mainland directly across the causeway from Monemvassia); there are six daily buses via Sparta. Call © **210/512-4910;** www.ktel.gr for schedule informa-tion. General information on Athens-Peloponnese schedules is available at © **210/ 512-4910** or www.ktel.org.

By Car   Take the National Road from Athens-Corinth-Tripolis. Head south to Monemvassia via Sparta. Allow at least 6 hours for the trip.

By Boat   For information on hydrofoil (Flying Dolphin) service from Marina Zea in Piraeusto Monemvassia call ℭ **210/419-9200** or 210/419-9000, or check www. hellenicseaways.gr. Information in Monemvassia is available at the Port Authority (ℭ **27320/61-266**).

FAST FACTS   The **National Bank of Greece** in Gefyra (on the shore across the causeway from the old town) exchanges currency and has an ATM. You'll find the **post office** and the **OTE** in Gefyra. For **first aid,** call ℭ **27320/61-204.** The **police** are at 137 Spartis (ℭ **27320/61-210**). The **Malvasia Travel Agency** (ℭ **27320/61-752; fax** 27320/61-432) in Gefyra has several helpful English-speaking staff members.

WHAT TO SEE & DO
SIGHTSEEING AND SHOPPING
Monemvassia is a great place to wander. Sure, you'll get lost in the winding cobbled lanes, but how lost can you get on an island 1,600 feet long and half as wide? The answer (at least at night) is pretty lost. It's a good idea to wear decent walking shoes, bring along a flashlight, and save the 800-foot ascent of the citadel (the best path up is marked on Odos Ritsos, the main street) for daytime—preferably in the cool of the morning.

You might begin your visit at the **Momemvassia Archaeological Collection** (ℭ **27320/61-403**) located in the former mosque on the Plateia Dsami (Square of the Mosque). It's open daily from 8am to 7pm; admission is free. The exhibits of local architecture and artifacts include some elegant old clay pipes; try to pick up a copy of the excellent guide *The Castle of Monemvasia* (3€/$3.90), with its detailed map and explanations of the castle's elaborate fortifications.

From the **citadel,** there are truly spectacular views down to the red-tile roofs of Monemvassia, out across the sea and deep into the mountains of the Mani peninsula. While you're here, try to figure out how the 13th-century Church of Ayia Sophia (Holy Wisdom) was built not just on, but virtually over, the edge of the cliffs.

After exploring the citadel, you'll probably want a swim, so head down to the bathing jetty, signposted along the sea wall. En route, you'll probably pass through the main square again, with the church of Christos Elkomenos (Christ in Chains) across from a Venetian canon, as well as the Venetian chapel of Panagia Chryssafiotissa. The churches are sometimes locked; if locked, content yourself with the thought that the handsome stone houses lining Monemvassia's lanes are the real treat to see here.

The line of small shops along Ritsos Street, the main drag on "the rock," have thus far avoided the infestation of T-shirts and cheap museum reproductions so common elsewhere. **Ioanna Angelatou's shop,** next to the Byzantion hotel, has been here more than 20 years; it sells the deep-blue glassware made in Greece, jewelry, and well-done reproductions of antique woodcarvings and copper. Just inside Monemvassia's gate, **Costas Lekakis** has a good selection of books in English, including R. Klaus and U. Steinmuller's excellent guide *Monemvassia* (6€/$7.80). **Kelari** has a good selection of wines, including examples from the local Vatistas vineyards. Takis Papadakis at Kelari can often give you information on local rentals of rooms and small apartments (ℭ **27320/61-695**).

WHERE TO STAY
I always want to stay on the rock—especially at full moon—so that I can enjoy wandering along the winding stone lanes above the sea in the evening. There are so few rooms here that this is one place where it's essential to try to make a reservation. I say

"try" because records of reservations sometimes disappear mysteriously, even after several phone calls. If at all possible, avoid weekends and arrive here early in the day to be sure to get your room. If you can't find a room on the rock, a number of new hotels on the mainland are in and around Gefyra, including the 23-unit **Flower of Monemvassia (Louloudi tis Monemvasias),** completely remodeled in 2005 (✆ **27320/61-395;** fax 27320/61-391). Most of its rooms come with minifridges and with partial views (across a road) of the beach and of the rock. On the causeway itself, the elegant 14-unit **Lazarreto** has a large garden behind the tall stone walls that keep out most traffic noise; ✆ **23070/61-991.**

Ardamis Castle ⍟   This boutique hotel in an 800-year-old town house with a vast terrace overlooking the sea, had hardly opened when it started turning up on lists of the best hotels in Greece, heaped with adjectives like "romantic" and "distinctive." Units are furnished with antiques and embroideries (and ferociously energetic showers)—and most have sea views. The staff is not always noticeably attentive—or even in evidence.

23070 Monemvassia. ✆ **27320/61-887.** www.ardamis.gr. 6 units. 150€–200€ ($195–$260) double. DC, MC, V. **Amenities:** Breakfast room/bar. *In room:* A/C.

Kellia ⍟ (Value   It is nice to be able to recommend the Kellia again. This former convent, with a quiet location by the church of the Panagia Chrissafitissa, was (mis)managed as a hotel by the GNTO, but has perked up greatly now that it is operated privately. Kuria Athena is very helpful, and the once-neglected rooms and garden are now well tended.

By the Panayia Chrysafiotissa Church. 23070 Monemvassia. ✆ **27320/61-520.** 15 units. 75€–85€ ($85–$111) double. DC, V. **Amenities:** Restaurant; garden. *In room:* A/C.

Malvasia ⍟⍟   Monemvassia's first "boutique" hotel, the Malvasia remains charming—although service can be significantly haphazard. Over the years, the owners bought up a number of old houses, restored them, and furnished them with old copper pieces, hand-loomed rugs and bedspreads, and antique wood furniture. This would be a wonderful place to stay a week or even a month (long-term reduced rates are available). If you can't do that, at least stay for a night and hope for a sea-view room in the Stellaki Mansion on the ramparts or in the hotel's original building on Ritsos. If you're here in winter, ask for a room with a fireplace. Some units have phones and refrigerators; some suites have full kitchens.

Headquarters on Ritsos, 23070 Monemvassia. ✆ **27320/61-113.** Fax 27320/61-722. Malvazia@otenet.gr. 35 units. 60€–100€ ($78–$113) double; 85€–150€ ($111–$195) suite. MC, V. **Amenities:** Restaurant; breakfast room; gardens. *In room:* A/C, TV (in some rooms), kitchenette (in some rooms), minibar (in some rooms), hair dryer (in some rooms).

WHERE TO DINE

There are a number of cafes and restaurants strung out along Monemvassia's main drag, but it's hard to resist **Matoula's** (✆ **27320/61-660**), which has been serving up good *spitiko fageto* (home cooking) since the early 1960s. A few doors away, **To Kanoni** (✆ **27320/61-387**) has a somewhat more varied menu, including a rich spaghetti carbonara. Both restaurants have indoor and outdoor tables and wonderful views over the town and sea. Depending on what season and what time of day you eat here, you'll enjoy watching the chic young Athenians who flock here on weekends—or the rather less-chic middle-aged Europeans. They're the ones studying guidebooks, while the Athenians snap photos of each other with their *kineta* (cellphones). Lunch or dinner with wine from 15€ ($20).

10 The Mani ⟨★⟨★

Githio is 301km (186 miles) S of Athens and 45km (27 miles) S of Sparta; Areopoli is 32km (20 miles) W of Githio

The innermost of the Peloponnese's three tridentlike prongs, the Mani is still one of the least-visited areas in Greece. That's changing fast, as word gets out about the fine beaches near Githio and Kardamili and the haunting landscape of the Inner Mani (the southernmost Mani). Good new roads mean that you can drive the circuit of the entire Mani in a day, but it's more fun to spend at least a night here, perhaps in one of the restored tower-house hotels. Whatever you do, eat at least one meal in Limeni, the port of Areopoli, at the superb **Fish Taverna Takis To Limeni** (see below).

The Inner Mani's barren mountains are dotted with tiny olive trees and enormous prickly pear cacti. It's hard to believe that 100 years ago, this was a densely populated area and almost every hillside was cultivated. If you squint, you can make out the stone walls and terraces built by farmers on the deserted hillsides.

Originally, the Maniotes chose to live in tower houses because they were easy to defend, an important consideration for these constantly feuding Peloponnesians who spent much of their time until the early 20th century lobbing cannonballs at their neighbors. Fortunately, many tower houses survived. The towers of the virtually deserted villages of Koita and Nomia look like miniature skyscrapers from a distance.

When the Maniotes weren't trying to destroy their neighbors' homes, they seem to have atoned for their warfare by building churches: The area is dotted with tiny medieval chapels tucked in the folds of the hills. Keep an eye out for the stands of cypress trees that often mark the chapels, many of which have decorative brickwork and ornately carved marble doors. If you don't want to tramp around the countryside in search of chapels, at least take a look at the **Church of the Taxiarchoi (Archangels)** in Areopoli. Don't miss the droll figures of the saints and the signs of the zodiac carved on the church's facade.

After World War II, when most Maniotes moved away to Athens or abroad, entire villages of austere gray-stone tower houses became deserted. In recent years, many of these handsome houses have been restored as vacation or retirement houses by Maniotes, other Greeks, and foreigners. Villages that were ghost towns 10 years ago are gaining new leases on life in this austere and beautiful region.

Tip: University of Herefordshire professor and longtime hellenophile John Chapman's excellent and beautifully illustrated *Mani: A Guide and History* is available online at www.maniguide.info or www.zorbas.de/maniguide. Longtime Mani resident Patrick Leigh Fermor's *Mani* remains one of the best books on Greece ever written.

ESSENTIALS

GETTING THERE   By Car   This is a long trip but not as tedious as the ride by the bus, which makes many stops. Take the National Road Athens-Corinth-Tripolis, and then head south to Githio (Gythion) and Areopoli via Sparta.

By Bus   It's possible to travel from Athens to the Sparta bus station (✆ **27310/ 26-441**), and from Sparta to the Githio bus station (✆ **27330/22-228**) or the Areopoli bus station (✆ **27330/51-229**), but this is a full-day trip. For schedule information, call ✆ **210/512-9233**, 210/512-9410, or the numbers above for the bus stations in Sparta, Githio, and Areopoli. For general information on Athens-Peloponnese schedules, try ✆ **210/512-4910** or www.ktel.org.

By Ship   Githio is served by hydrofoil (Flying Dolphin) from Piraeus and interme-
diate stops (© **210/419-9000** or 210/419-9200; www.hellenicseaways.gr). Sailings
also depart from Githio to the islands of Kythera and Crete. The **Rozakis Ship Brokers & Travel Agency,** 5 Vas. Pavlou (the harborfront; © **27330/22-650;** fax 27330/
22-229; rosakigy@otenet.gr), has information on sailings (including the Patras-
Ancona Super Ferry service). The agency can make reservations and issue tickets.
Rozakis also rents cars from minis to vans at 40€ ($52) to 75€ ($98) per day.

GETTING AROUND   Longtime visitors to Greece wax nostalgic about the days
when they had to hoof it around the Mani. You can get around today by local bus,
but by car is the most efficient way.

FAST FACTS   Githio and Areopoli both have **banks** with ATMs. Don't count on
finding banks elsewhere in the Mani. In Areopoli, most services are on or just off the
main square: the **bank** (usually Mon–Fri 9am–noon), the **post office,** the **OTE,** the
bus station, several **restaurants,** and an excellent small **bookstore** called Mani
(© **27330/53-670**). At the bookstore you can pick up Patrick Leigh Fermor's enduring classic, *Mani,* and Bob Barrow and Mat Dean's *Inside the Mani.* The **police**
(© **27330/51-209**) are signposted on the main square in Areopoli.

WHAT TO SEE & DO

The Caves of Dirou (Glyfada & Alepotrypa) 🏛🏛   Here's the good news: The
crystal-studded stalactites (the ones hanging from the ceilings like icicles) and stalagmites (the ones rising from the cave's floor) are spectacular, in shades of rose, green,
amber, black, blood red, and purple. The bad news . . .

These caves, a very popular holiday destination for Greeks, are mobbed in summer,
so try to arrive as soon as they open. If you get here later in the day, buy your ticket
immediately; usually visitors are taken in some kind of order. As wonderful as they are,
these caves are not recommended for the claustrophobic. Guided tours through the
Glyfada Cave take about 30 minutes. The largest of the cave's passageways is 100m
(328 ft.) long; and although the trail is lit with multicolored lights, you are well aware
that you are far, far underground. Guides pole small boats (each holding up to a dozen
passengers) past the strange formations and call out the stalactites' and stalagmites'
nicknames (ranging from the reverential to the obscene). The guides also delight in
warning passengers not to trail their fingers in the cool subterranean waters that reach
depths of 20m (98 ft.): Giant eels are rumored to live just below the surface. Visitors
usually disembark from the boat for a short excursion on foot through a slippery segment of the cave.

The Pirgos Dirou Caves were discovered in 1955 by a dog that crawled through a
hole into the caves and returned several days later coated in red clay. Fortunately, its
owner, spelunker Anna Petroclides, was curious about the red clay and followed her
dog when it next set off on explorations. What she found was a vast network of caves,
of which some 5km (3 miles) have now been explored. The caves themselves are
impressive, but what has made them famous is the Paleolithic and Neolithic remains
found here. In short, the Pirgos Dirou Caves are one of the oldest inhabited spots in
Greece, and the pottery, bone tools, and even garbage found here have shed light on
Greece's earliest history.

Before you leave Pirgos Dirou, check to see if the small **Neolithic Museum**
(© **27330/52-233**), with displays of artifacts found in the caves, is open. Admission
is 2€ ($2.60).

Pirgos Dirou. 🕿 **27330/52-222.** Fax 27330/52-223. Admission 15€ ($20). Cave visiting hours vary; in general, daily 9am–5pm in summer, with shorter hours off season.

WHERE TO STAY

Our recommendations below are in the Mani itself, but if you want to stay on the outskirts of the Mani, here are some suggestions. In Githio, harborfront choices offering doubles from 70€ ($91) include the venerable (and restored) **Aktaion** (🕿 **27330/23-500;** fax 27330/22-294), our favorite with its seaside balconies; **Gythion** (🕿 **27330/23-452;** fax 27330/23-523), in a charming 19th-century former businessmen's club; **Pantheon** (🕿 **27330/22-289;** fax 27330/22-284); and **Leonidas** (🕿 **27330/22-389;** fax 27330/22-595). In Messenian Mani, at the seaside hamlet of Kardamili, **Kalamitsi Hotel & Bungalows** (🕿 **27210/73-131;** fax 27210/73-135; www.kalamitsi-hotel.gr) has doubles in the main building from 100€ ($130); suites and bungalows are also available. In the Mani itself, at Gerolimenas, the posh 25-unit **Kyrimai** (🕿 **27330/54-288;** www.kyrimai.gr or www.yadeshotels.gr), a member of the Historic Hotels of Europe, looks like a miniature seaside tower hamlet—albeit one with Jacuzzis and a swimming pool; doubles from 120€ ($156), suites from 300€ ($390). We've had disappointing reports on the food and service here and welcome readers' updates.

Akroyiali & Yerolimenas Hotels 🕿🕿 *Kids*   Over the years, the helpful multi-lingual Theodorakis family has expanded its empire from the original harborside 12-room Akroyiani with its excellent restaurant that serves fresh seafood. Now, the 23-unit Gerolimenas, a traditional stone building built in traditional Maniote style, stands beside the original hotel; just uphill are 20 furnished apartments in yet another traditionally stone-faced building. The new units have air-conditioning, while the furnished apartments also have TV and complete kitchenettes; many units have balconies. All these rooms are very popular in summer with vacationing Greek and European families who come for a week or more. Ask about long-term rates if you plan to do the same and do reserve ahead, especially if you'll be here July through August or on weekends. Keep in mind that the small beach in Gerolimenas is shadeless and rocky, although some good beaches are nearby.

Gerolimenas, 23062 Lakonia, Mani. 🕿 **27330/54-204.** Fax 27330/54-272. 12 original hotel units 50€–65€ ($65–$85) double; 23 added hotel units 85€ ($111) with breakfast; 20 1- and 2-room apts 55€–90€ ($72–$117). No credit cards. **Amenities:** Restaurant. *In room:* A/C (in most), TV (in most), kitchenettes (in some).

Hotel Itilo 🕿 *Kids*   This beachfront family-run hotel on the Gulf of Itilo, just north of Areopoli, attracts lots of families, whose children enjoy the little beachside playground. Many of the large guest rooms overlook the sea. If you show up here for just a night or two in high season, you may be relegated to the annex, across the road from the sandy beach. The hotel food, which includes lots of fresh fish, is excellent but, as always with fish, expensive. Children love the ice-cream sundaes served with little parasols and sometimes sparklers.

Neo Itilo, 23062 Lakonia, Mani. 🕿 **27330/59-222.** Fax 27330/29-234. 26 units. 80€ ($104) double. Rates include breakfast. AE, MC, V. **Amenities:** Restaurant; children's play area. *In room:* A/C, TV.

Kapetanakou Tower Hotel 🕿   This is a wonderful place to stay to get an idea of what it was like to live in a Maniote tower. (Noisy, for one thing: When the wind blows, or other guests walk on the wooden staircase, you know it!) One of the first of the traditional settlement hotels managed by the Greek National Tourism Organization, and now privately owned, the 180-year-old Kapetanakou Tower stands in a walled garden just off the main street in Areopoli. Some of the rooms have sleeping lofts, several have balconies or little patios, and most have colorful rag rugs and locally handmade weavings. The hotel serves breakfast, and it's only a 5-minute stroll to Areopoli's restaurants. The TV in the lobby is sometimes left on, but the manager will usually turn it down or off if you ask.

Areopoli, 26062 Laconia, Mani. (℃) 27330/51-233. 8 units, with 2 shared bathrooms on each floor. 65€–75€ ($85–$98) double. AE, MC, V. **Amenities:** Breakfast room.

Limeni Village Hotel 🏛🏛 Before I stayed here, I regarded this hotel, built as a Maniote tower village, a glaring example of bringing coals to Newcastle. But after enjoying the swimming pool each day before and after sightseeing, and taking in the sunset while sipping gin and tonics on the balcony, I was a convert. The guest rooms (two units to most bungalows; some bungalows rented as suites) are outfitted with rag rugs, stone floors, and balconies overlooking the Bay of Itilo. The breakfast buffet is fine, if not inspired; the restaurant is desultory (but the superb Fish Taverna Takis To Limeni is minutes away; see below). Most guests here seem to be Greek families visiting the Mani. Reservations essential in August and on summer weekends.

Limeni, Areopoli, 23062 Laconia, Mani. (℃) 27330/51-111. Fax 27330/51-182. 32 units. 130€ ($169); lower off season. AE, MC, V. **Amenities:** Restaurant; bar; pool. *In room:* A/C, TV, minibar.

Londas Tower Guesthouse 🏛🏛 Small and well-appointed, the Londas Guesthouse has three doubles and a triple in a restored 18th-century tower off Ayii Taxiarches Square. Each unit has an en suite bathroom, done with more attention to detail than is customary in this part of Greece (not to mention paintings done by one of the owners). There are views over the town from the rooms and their terraces. There's no air-conditioning (the winds here are so fierce that it is almost never needed) and, to ensure tranquillity, no TVs. Owner/managers Hans Kleiner and Iakovos Xenakis speak most of the languages you will probably need, are most helpful, serve wonderful homemade preserves at breakfast, and have great suggestions on how best to enjoy the Mani.

Limeni, Areopoli, 23062 Laconia, Mani. (℃) 27330/51-360. Fax 27330/51-012. www.londas.com. 4 units. 85€ ($111) double. AE, MC, V. **Amenities:** Breakfast room/bar.

WHERE TO DINE

In **Kardamili,** the food is good at **Lela's** (℃ 27210/73-541) by the sea, reached by the twisting road from the main plateia. When Lela's is closed, there's usually a sign posted with directions to another family-run place.

I've eaten at most of the seafood restaurants on the harbor in **Githio,** and find them pretty similar. You should get good, fresh fish at any one of these places, so you may want to make your choice based on other factors, such as atmosphere or noise level. If, like me, you like octopus, head for **Nautilia** (there are usually octopus strung up outside the restaurant). Just off the harborfront, by the minuscule traffic roundabout, are several ouzeries. **Korali** serves snacks and light meals at considerably lower prices than the seafood places. En route from Githio to Areopoli, in the narrow pass dominated by the castle of Passava, 10km (6 miles) out of Githio, the family-run **Kali Kardia** (℃ 27330/93-250) serves good *spitiko* (home-style) food. The owners can point out the path up to the castle if you feel energized by your meal.

The three basically interchangeable restaurants on **Areopoli's main square** serve pretty basic meals, featuring grilled meats and salads. Lunch or dinner at any one of these costs from about 10€ ($13). Unless you are in a terrible rush, head instead to the following:

Barba-Petros 🏵 GREEK This little taverna on Areopoli's sinuous main street, which runs from the main square to the cathedral, has a pleasant small garden and much better food than the restaurants on the square. If someone could only persuade the youths on motorcycles not to race up and down the street, this would be a totally gratifying place to sip the local wine and enjoy the tasty fried zucchini and eggplant, as well as chops and stews.

On the main street, Areopoli. 📞 27330/51-205. Main courses 6€–12€ ($7.80–$16). No credit cards. Usually daily noon–11pm (often closed midafternoon).

Fish Taverna Takis To Limeni 🏵🏵🏵 SEAFOOD The superb fresh fish at this small restaurant in Limeni, the port of Areopoli, draws customers from as far away as Kalamata, so be sure to make a reservation if you want a seaside table. This is not the place to eat if you are squeamish about seeing fish cleaned a few feet away from where you are eating. On the other hand, the seafood here is so good that you may find yourself coming back for meal after meal while you're in the Mani. The seafood's price per kilo varies from day to day and is never cheap; be sure to ask for prices unless price is no object. The lobster diavalo (lobster with spaghetti in a tangy sauce with green peppers) is among the memorable "fancy" dishes, but a plain grilled fish is equally delicious.

Limeni, Areopoli. 📞 27330/51-327. Fish and lobster priced by the kilo. No credit cards. Reservations recommended weekends. Usually daily noon–midnight; sometimes closed during the week in winter.

11 Pylos (Pilo/Navarino) 🏵

50km (31 miles) W of Kalamata; 108km (67 miles) W of Sparta; 317km (196 miles) SW of Athens

I spend as much time in Greece as I can, but I have to admit that all too often the modern village with a famous ancient name—Argos or Corinth, for example—is a disappointment. That's not the case at Pylos (also known as Navarino), where the modern harbor town has considerable charm. The harborfront, the tree-shaded main square with its statues and cafes, and the cobblestoned side streets all make Pylos an appealing place to wander, especially in the cool of the evening when breezes blow from the sea. Pylos is developing some sprawling suburbs, and a few of the nearby beaches are being developed with a vengeance, but the harbor and leafy main square are largely untouched.

In fact, it's so pleasant to sit at a harborside cafe that it's hard to realize that Pylos's harbor has seen some very bloody battles. The Athenians trapped a Spartan force on the offshore island of Sfaktiria in 424 B.C.; and in 1827, a combined French, Russian, and British armada defeated the massed Ottoman fleet here. More than 6,000 Ottoman sailors were butchered in what proved to be one of the critical battles of the Greek War of Independence. There's a monument to the three victorious admirals in Pylos's main square (understandably called the Sq. of the Three Admirals) as well as lots of cafes that stay open late for after-dinner wanderers.

Some memorabilia from the battle, as well as archaeological finds from the area, are on view in the little **Antonopouleion Museum,** just off the main square (usually Tues–Sun 8:30am–3pm; admission 2€/$2.60).

Ancient Pylos, site of the Mycenaean palace of garrulous old King Nestor, is located about 17km (10 miles) north of the town on the hill of Englianos. Homer described Pylos as "sandy Pylos, rich in cattle," and the hilltop palace still overlooks sandy beaches flanked by rich farmland. Ancient Pylos seems to be a site that people take to—or don't. For every visitor who complains about the protective plastic roof over the site, another raves about the palace's idyllic setting, with its views over farm fields and hills. Some call the remains here "scanty," while others find this the perfect place to imagine Nestor telling his tall tales (yet again!) while his courtiers sighed and cast surreptitious glances across the gentle countryside.

ESSENTIALS

GETTING THERE   By Bus   There are several buses a day from the Stathmos Leoforia Peloponnisou (bus station for the Peloponnese) in Athens, 100 Kifissou (© **210/512-9410**; www.ktel.org), to the Pylos station (© **27230/22-230**). For a general schedule of Athens-Peloponnese service, try © **210/512-4910** or www.ktel.org.

By Car   Pylos is a full day's drive from Athens and 3 to 4 hours from either Patras or Sparta. The drive from Sparta to Pylos via the **Langada Pass** to **Kalamata** takes in one of the most beautiful mountain roads in the Peloponnese.

FAST FACTS   Both **banks** in the main square offer currency exchange and have ATMs. The **hospital** (© **27230/22-315**) is signposted in town. The **post office, telephone office (OTE), police** (© **27230/22-316**), and **tourist police** (© **27230/23-733**) are all signposted in the main square.

WHAT TO SEE & DO

Ancient Pylos (Nestor's Palace) & Museum 🏛🏛   The palace at Pylos belonged to Nestor, the old king who told stories and gave unsolicited advice while the younger warriors fought at Troy. The palace was rediscovered in 1939 by the American archaeologist Carl Blegen, who had the unbelievable good fortune of discovering the palace archives on his first day of work here. Blegen uncovered some 600 clay tablets written in a mysterious language initially called Linear B and later shown to be an early form of Greek.

Unlike Mycenae and Tiryns, Pylos was not heavily fortified: You'll see a sentry box but no massive walls. The well-preserved royal apartments include a more-than-adequate bathroom with the tub still in place. Archaeologists have suggested that the small block beside the tub was a step, installed when the elderly King Nestor had trouble stepping into his bath. The palace, with its central courtyard, was originally two stories high and richly decorated with frescoes, some of which are on display at the small **archaeological museum** a mile away in the village of Hora.

Admission to each 3€ ($3.90). Tues–Sat 8:30am–3pm; Sun 9:30am–2:30pm. Head north out of Pylos on the main road and follow the signs for Hora.

Neokastro 🏛   The Turkish fortress above the harbor, known as Neokastro to distinguish it from an earlier fortress, now contains a splendid small museum in a restored 19th-century barracks. The museum features the extensive collection of maps, prints, and watercolors of the French philhellene Rene Puaux, as well as a number of

---

(Tips   Taking a Boat Tour

If you'd like to take a boat tour of the magnificent Pylos harbor and the island of Sfaktiria, look for signs advertising excursions, usually posted by the harbor. An hour-long trip should cost from 15€ ($20); if the water is calm, you may see some of the ships that were sunk here during the Battle of Navarino in 1827.

---

marvelously kitschy porcelain figurines of the English philhellene Lord Byron. Neokastro also contains a small church (clearly a former mosque), impressive fortification walls, shade trees, beds of vibrant geraniums and roses, and fine views over the harbor.

Admission 3€ ($3.90). Daily 8am–7pm.

WHERE TO STAY

The pleasant coast north of Pylos around the hamlet of Kinigou is about to change, as construction begins of Navarino Resorts, slated when finished in 2020 to include 11 hotels. 7 golf courses, a number of spas, and hundreds of holiday villas. It is difficult to be optimistic about the effect of so much construction and so many visitors on the nearby wildlife sanctuary at Voidhokilia. You may want to check on the progress of the construction before deciding to stay at our seaside recommendations.

Hotel Zoe ⓐ *Kids*   This pleasant seaside hotel about 5km (3 miles) north of Pylos is very popular with German families. If you're traveling with children, the chance to begin and end a day of sightseeing with a swim here might be the salvation of a family holiday. The guest rooms are decent in size, spare, and ferociously clean. Ask about long-term (a week or more) rates.

Gialova, 24001 Pylos, Messenia. ⓒ 27230/22-025. Fax 27230/22-026. 35 units. 60€–75€ ($78–$98) double. No credit cards. **Amenities:** Restaurant. *In room:* A/C, TV, some units with fridge.

Karalis Beach Hotel   With the best location in town, at the end of the harbor below the Turkish kastro, far from most traffic, this used to be the nicest place to stay in Pylos. But at some point, the management became haphazard. In short, the reason to stay here is the location, especially if you get one of the seaside rooms with a balcony.

The Karalis Beach Hotel often sends its overflow to the **Karalis Hotel,** Kalamateas 26 (ⓒ **27230/22-980**), which is under the same management. Rooms here are pleasant, but suffer from traffic noise.

Paralia, 24001 Pylos, Messenia. ⓒ **27230/23-021.** Fax 27230/22-970. 14 units, 4 with shower only. 70€ ($91) double. MC, V. Usually closed Nov–Apr. **Amenities:** Breakfast room; bar. *In room:* TV in some.

Navarone Hotel/Bungalows ⓐ   Friends who stayed here report enjoying this new hotel and its pool, about 5km (3 miles) north of Pylos and a 5-minute walk from an excellent sand beach. Many of the rooms have seafront balconies, and most have good reading lights and handy desks. Keep in mind that the Navarone gets lots of tour groups.

Petrochori, 24001 Pilias, Messenia. ⓒ **27230/41-571.** Fax 27230/41-575. navaron1@otenet.gr. 17 units, 41 bungalows. 60€–75€ ($78–$98). DC, MC, V. **Amenities:** Restaurant; pool. *In room:* TV.

WHERE TO DINE

Diethnes Taverna ⓐ GREEK/SEAFOOD   The Diethnes has been here forever, serving meals both indoors and at tables by the quay overlooking the harbor. As you'd expect from a restaurant on the sea and next to the government fish-inspection station, the seafood here is very fresh. There are usually a number of chicken and meat dishes on the menu, as well as a good *briam* (vegetable stew). If you like the food here and want to try different restaurants with similar menus, **Pende Adelphia** and **4 Epoches** are also located along the harborfront.

Paralia. ⓒ **27230/22-772.** Fish priced by the kilo. No credit cards. Mid-May to mid-Sept daily noon–11pm (and sometimes later).

A Little History

The Venetians built Methoni on the Ionian Sea and Koroni on the Gulf of Messenia in the 13th century to safeguard their newly acquired Greek empire. In some of the bloodiest fighting on record, the fortresses, almost immediately nicknamed "the twin eyes of empire," passed back and forth between various powers for the next several centuries: In 1500, the Turks slaughtered all 5,000 Venetian defenders at Methoni; in 1685, the Venetians wiped out the 1,500-man garrison at Koroni.

12 Side Trips from Pylos: Methoni & Koroni ✦✦

Methoni is 13km (8 miles) from Pylos; Koroni is 30km (18 miles) from Pylos

Methoni and Koroni are two of the most impressive medieval fortresses in Greece and would be worth seeing for that reason alone. But that's not the only reason to come here: Methoni has one of the best restaurants in the Peloponnese, and the drive through the lush Messenian countryside between Methoni and Koroni is ravishing. The route from Pylos to Koroni via Longa is especially blissful; by contrast, the southerly seaside route takes in the village of Finikounda, a windsurfers's paradise, and can be heavily trafficked on summer weekends. In a day trip, you can drive from Pylos to the convent and fortress at Koroni, have a swim and a bite near Finikounda, head to Methoni for another fortress, another swim, and dinner at the excellent **Klimataria** restaurant, before heading back to Pylos.

The fortress at **Koroni** encloses a number of whitewashed and pastel **village houses,** a flourishing **convent,** and several small **cemeteries.** Although the main road in town leads steeply uphill to the fortress gate, park in town, unless you'd enjoy backing up over a sheer drop to the sea if you meet a car heading downhill! The grounds inside the fortress walls are lovingly planted with roses and shade trees; piles of cannonballs and the occasional cannon remind visitors of Koroni's bloody past. There's a string of seafood restaurants at the harbor below, but nothing to compare with Methoni's Klimataria. This is a good place to avoid on summer weekends, when day-trippers from Kalamata head here for a fish lunch and a stroll through the village's stepped streets.

The long, sandy **Methoni beach** has won several awards for its eco-sensitivity, including Greece's Golden Starfish and the Common Market's Blue Flag. The seaside cafes and fish tavernas all have fine views of the fortress, which stands at the end of a low spit of land and covers enough ground to have contained a city of several thousand inhabitants during the Middle Ages. Methoni's **exterior walls** are stupendous, although little remains inside the fortress itself. Don't worry about being locked in here when the gates close at 7pm: An officious guard on a motorcycle usually rounds up any stragglers. The fortress is usually open from 8am to 7pm; admission is free. When it closes, you can head to the **Taverna Klimataria** (✆ **27230/31-544**), where the chef somehow manages to take standard dishes familiar from any Greek menu (fried zucchini, eggplant salad, *briam*) and turn them into elegant delights.

13 Messene (Ithomi/Mavromati) ⟨★⟨★

25km (16 miles) N of Kalamata; 60km (39 miles) E of Pylos

Even though Messene's walls and towers knock the socks off the remains at many bet-ter-known classical sites, not many visitors come here yet. Between 370 and 369 B.C., the great Theban general and statesman Epaminondas built the sprawling city of Messene. He hoped that its almost 9.5km (6 miles) of walls below Mount Ithomi would check Sparta's power. Today, the defense wall, with its two-story towers and tur-reted gates, is the best-preserved classical fortification in the Peloponnese, a startling sight standing alone in the lush Messenian countryside.

To get here by car from Pylos, Kalamata, or Tripolis, take the main Kalamata-Pylos road to the modern town of Messini, where the road to ancient Messene is (imper-fectly) signposted. The site of ancient Messene (also called Ithomi) is in the village of Mavromati, approximately 20km (13 miles) north of Messini.

WHAT TO SEE & DO

Ancient Messene ⟨★⟨★   The most impressive stretches of the ancient wall are out-side the site, north of the village of Mavromati. As you pass through Mavromati, pick up a copy of the excellent site guide at the postcard shop next to the village spring (4€/$5.20). Even at a distance, the sheer size of the wall, with its towers and gates, makes most visitors gasp. The **Arcadian Gate** is especially well-preserved; the grooves cut into the marble pavement by ancient chariot wheels are clearly visible. As you drive back toward Mavromati, you'll pass more of the defense wall and the site museum, which keeps irregular hours. Admission is 2€ ($2.60).

The excavated ruins of Messene are clearly signposted past the site museum (open Tues–Sun 8:30am–3pm; 2€/$2.60). This is a vast, sprawling site with a partially restored theater, an impressive **agora/forum** (marketplace), and a **Sanctuary of Ascle-pius** so large that it was originally thought to be the entire agora! The partially exca-vated **stadium,** with many of its marble benches well-preserved, lies along the dirt road beyond the Asklepeion. A walk through the entire site takes a minimum of sev-eral hours, but it's possible to see just the Asklepeion in an hour. Keep an ear cocked for the tuneful frogs that live in several wells and cisterns on the site.

Admission 3€ ($3.90). Usually Tues–Sun 8am–3pm.

WHERE TO STAY & DINE

Ithome Restaurant GREEK   This very simple restaurant has a terrific view over the ancient site and serves souvlaki, grills, salads, french fries, and the occasional veg-etable dish. If it is crowded, there are other spots nearby.

Special Moment: Top of the World

A rough, but adequate, road runs from the site of ancient Messene to the summit of Mount Ithomi (800m/2,624 ft.). The views of the districts of Messene and Lako-nia are spectacular. At Ithomi's summit are remains of a Temple of Zeus and the small medieval monastery of Voulkanos. The monks are long gone and visitors are few, so this is a place to feel that the view is yours and yours alone. At sunset, there are few more spectacular spots in Greece. The summit is presently unfenced, and there is no admission charge; this will no doubt change soon, so try to go now!

A Quick Visit to Kalamata

Accommodations are pretty basic in Mavromati, so after you visit ancient Messene you may prefer to head to Kalamata, only 31km (19 miles) to the south. The 193-unit **Filoxenia Hotel** on the beach outside Kalamata has all the creature comforts, including several swimming pools and restaurants (Navarinou St., 24100 Kalamata; ✆ **210-322-5891;** www.grecotel.gr); doubles around 200€ ($260). In Kalamata itself, the 7-unit **Hibiscus Hotel** occupies a 19th-century neoclassical house, is furnished with antiques, and has its own peaceful garden (196 Faron St., 24100 Kalamata; ✆ **27210/62-511;** www.traditional hotels.gr); doubles from 75€ ($98). If you get to Kalamata, try to eat the famous local figs and olives, take in the old market area, and visit the excellent **Benakion Archaeological Museum,** founded by the same family that gave Athens its Benaki museums. (Benaki and Papazoglou sts., 24100 Kalamata; ✆ **27210/26-209;** open Tues–Sun 8:30am–3pm).

Mavromati-Ithome (across from the Klepsidra Spring). ✆ **2724/51-498.** Fax 2724/51-298. Lunch or dinner with a beer from 10€ ($13). No credit cards. Summer daily 11am–10pm; shorter hours in winter.

Pension Zeus This small family-run pension—which is about as far from the Greece of tour-group hotels as you can get—has several small, pleasant guest rooms, some with balconies. The family is very helpful and nice. The only problem: You're on the one road through town, and from your room you will hear whatever traffic there is.

Mavromati-Ithome, 24200 Messenia. ✆ **2724/51-025.** 5 units, 3 with bathroom. 55€ ($72) double. Rates include breakfast. No credit cards.

14 Olympia ✶✶✶

311km (199 miles) W of Athens; 90km (55 miles) S of Patras; 21km (13 miles) E of Pirgos

With its shady groves of pine, olive, and oak trees; the considerable remains of two temples; and the stadium where the first Olympic races were run in 776 B.C., Olympia is the most beautiful major site in the Peloponnese. When you realize that both the archaeological museum and the new museum of the ancient Games are among the finest in Greece, you'll see why it's wonderful to have more than just 1 day here, especially if your hotel has a swimming pool!

A LOOK AT THE PAST There's really no modern equivalent for ancient Olympia, which was both a religious sanctuary and an athletic complex where the Games took place every 4 years from 776 B.C. to A.D. 393. Thereafter, the sanctuary slipped into oblivion, and buildings were repeatedly toppled by earthquakes and flooded by the Alfios and Kladeos rivers. When the English antiquarian Richard Chandler rediscovered the site in 1766, most of Olympia lay under 3m (10 ft.) of mud and silt. The Germans began to excavate here in 1852 and are still at it today.

Reports of the rediscovery of Olympia prompted the French Baron de Coubertin to work for the reestablishment of the Olympic Games in 1896. The first modern Games were held in Athens in 1896, and since then the Olympic torch has always been lit here at the beginning of the Olympic Games, wherever they are held. In 2004, Athens hosted the 2004 Olympics, with the shot put finals taking place in Olympia's ancient stadium.

The Ancient Olympic Games

The 5-day Olympic festival was held every 4 years between 776 B.C. and A.D. 393 at full moon in mid-August or September, after the summer harvest. Participants came from as far away as Asia Minor and Italy, and the entire Greek world observed a truce to allow athletes and spectators to make their way to Olympia safely. During all the years that the Games took place, the truce was broken only a handful of times.

By the time the Games opened, literally thousands of people had poured into Olympia; and much of the surrounding countryside was a tent city. Women were barred from watching or participating in the Games, although they had their own Games in honor of Hera, Zeus's wife, in non-Olympic years. Any woman caught sneaking into the Olympic Games was summarily thrown to her death from a nearby mountain.

No one knows precisely what the order of events was, but the 5 days included footraces, short and long jumps, wrestling and boxing contests, chariot races, the arduous pentathlon (discus, javelin, jumping, running, and wrestling), and the vicious pankration (which combined wrestling and boxing techniques).

The 3rd-century-A.D. writer Philostratos recorded that participants in the pentathlon "must have skill in various methods of strangling." The most prestigious event was the *stade*, or short footrace, which gave its name to the stadium. Each Olympiad was named after the winner of the stade, and athletes like the 2nd-century-B.C. Leonidas of Rhodes, who won at four successive Olympics, became international heroes. In addition to the glory, each victor won a crown made of olive branches and free meals for life in his hometown. In the Athens 2004 Summer Olympics, the shot put finals were held in Olympia's ancient stadium, which you can visit.

OLYMPIA TODAY   The straggling modern village of Olympia (confusingly known as Ancient Olympia) is bisected by its one main street, Leoforos Kondili. The town has the usual assortment of tourist shops selling jewelry, T-shirts, and reproductions of ancient pottery and statues, as well as more than a dozen hotels and restaurants. Two things worth visiting in town: the small **Museum of the Olympic Games** and the excellent **Galerie Orphee bookstore** (see below).

The ancient site of Olympia is an easily walkable 15 minutes south of the modern village, but if you have a car, you might as well drive: The road teems with tour buses and the walk is less than relaxing.

ESSENTIALS
GETTING THERE   By Train   There are several trains a day from Athens to Pirgos, where you change to the train for Olympia. Information on schedules and fares is available from the Stathmos Peloponnisou (train station for the Peloponnese) in Athens (© **210/513-1601**).

By Bus   There are three buses a day to Olympia from the Stathmos Leoforia Peloponnisou (bus station for the Peloponnese) in Athens, 100 Kifissou (ℭ **210/512-4910; www.ktel.org**). There are also frequent buses from Patras to Pirgos, with connecting service to Olympia. In Patras, KTEL buses leave from the intersection of Zaimi and Othonos (ℭ **2610/273-694**). For general schedule information for Athens-Peloponnese service, try **210/512-4910** or www.ktel.org.

By Car   Olympia is easily a 6-hour drive from Athens, whether you take the coastal road that links Athens-Corinth-Patras and Olympia, or head inland to Tripolis and Olympia on the new Corinth-Tripolis road. Heavy traffic in Patras means that the drive from Patras to Olympia can take 2 hours.

VISITOR INFORMATION   Olympia is basically a one-street town; the few things you do not find on **Praxitelous Kondili** will be just off it. The **tourist office,** on the way to the ancient site near the south end of the main street, is officially open daily, in summer from 9am to 10pm, and in winter from 11am to 6pm. Ask here for maps of the site and town, and for information on accommodations (ℭ **26240/23-100** or 26240/23-125).

FAST FACTS   The **National Bank of Greece,** on Praxitelous Kondili (the main drag), exchanges currency and has an ATM. The **health clinic** (ℭ **26240/22-222**) is signposted in town. The **police** (ℭ **26240/22-100**) are at 6 Ethnossinelefseos. The **tourist police** (ℭ **26240/22-550**) are handily located on a street behind the tourist office. Both the **post office** (on the main street) and the **telephone office** (just off the main street) are signposted.

WHAT TO SEE & DO

The Archaeological Museum ✫✫✫   Even though you'll be eager to see the ancient site, you might want first to visit the museum, which reopened after extensive renovations in 2004. The collection makes clear Olympia's astonishing wealth and importance in antiquity: Every victorious city and almost every victorious athlete dedicated a bronze or marble statue here and the site was something of an outdoor museum of the finest bronze and marble sculpture. Most of the exhibits are displayed in rooms to the right and left of the main entrance and follow an essentially chronological sequence, from severe Neolithic vases to baroque Roman imperial statues, neither of which will probably tempt you from heading straight ahead to see the museum's superstars. Labels are in Greek, English, and German.

The monumental **sculpture from the Temple of Zeus** is probably the finest surviving example of Archaic Greek sculpture. The sculpture from the west pediment shows the battle of the Lapiths (Greeks who lived in Thessaly) and Centaurs raging around the magisterial figure of Apollo, the god of reason.

Most scholars think that the message here is the triumph of civilization (as represented by the Greek Lapiths) over barbarism—those brutish Centaurs. On the east pediment, Zeus oversees the chariot race between Oinomaos, the king of Pisa, and Pelops, the legendary figure who wooed and won Oinomaos's daughter by the unsporting expedient of loosening his opponent's chariot pins. Pelops not only won his bride, but went on to have the entire Peloponnese named in his honor. At either end of the room, sculptured metopes show scenes from the Labors of Hercules, including the one he performed at Olympia: cleansing the foul stables of King Augeus by diverting the Alfios River.

Just beyond the sculpture from the Temple of Zeus are the 5th-century-B.C. **Winged Victory,** done by the artist Paionios, and the 4th-century-B.C. figure of Hermes and the infant Dionysos, known as the **Hermes of Praxiteles.** The Hermes has a room to itself—or would, if tourists didn't make a beeline to admire Hermes smiling with amused tolerance at his chubby half-brother Dionysos. If you want to impress your companions, mention casually that many scholars think that this is not an original work by Praxitelous, but a Roman copy.

Admission to museum and site 9€ ($12). Summer Mon noon–6pm, Tues–Sat 8am–5pm; winter Mon noon–6pm, Tues–Sat 11am–5pm.

The Ancient Site ✹✹✹   In antiquity, every 4 years during the Olympic Games, so many people thronged here that it was said by the time the Games began, not even one more spectator could have wedged himself into the stadium. So if the site is very crowded when you visit, remember that it would have been much worse in antiquity.

Olympia's setting is magical. Pine trees shade the small valley, dominated by the conical Hill of Kronos that lies between the Alfios and Kladeos rivers. In July 2000, archaeologists excavating beside the Kladeos discovered a Mycenaean tholos (beehive) tomb with more than 100 amphorae, and they expect to find more tombs as excavations continue. The discovery was a reminder of how much is yet to be discovered here.

The handsome temples and the famous stadium that you've come to Olympia to see are not immediately apparent as you enter the site. Immediately to the left are the unimpressive low walls that are all that remain of the **Roman baths,** where athletes and spectators could enjoy hot and cold plunges. The considerably more impressive remains with the slender columns on your right mark the **gymnasium** and **palestra,** where athletes practiced their footracing and boxing skills. The enormous gymnasium had a roofed track, precisely twice the length of the stadium, where athletes could practice in bad weather. Still ahead on the right are the fairly meager remains of a number of structures, including a **swimming pool** and the large square **Leonidaion,** which served as a hotel for visiting dignitaries until a Roman governor decided it would do nicely as his villa.

The **religious sanctuary** was, and is, dominated by two temples: the good-size Temple of Hera and the massive Temple of Zeus. The **Temple of Hera,** with its three standing columns, is the older of the two, built around 600 B.C. If you look closely, you'll see that the temple's column capitals and drums are not uniform. That's because this temple was originally built with wooden columns, and as each column decayed, it was replaced; inevitably, the new columns had variations. The **Hermes of Praxiteles** was found here, buried under the mud that covered Olympia for so long due to the repeated flooding of the rivers.

The **Temple of Zeus** once had a veritable thicket of 34 stocky Doric columns; one was reerected in honor of the 2004 Olympic Games. Built around 456 B.C, the entire temple—so austere and gray today—was anything but austere in antiquity. Gold, red, and blue paint decorated it, and inside stood the enormous gold-and-ivory statue of Zeus, seated on an ivory-and-ebony throne. The statue was so ornate that it was considered one of the Seven Wonders of the Ancient World—and so large that people joked that if Zeus stood up, his head would go through the temple's roof. In fact, the antiquarian Philo of Byzantium suggested that Zeus had created elephants simply so that the sculptor Phidias would have the ivory with which to make the statue of Zeus.

Not only do we know that Phidias made the 13m-high (43-ft.) statue, we know where he made it: The **Workshop of Phidias** was on the site of the well-preserved brick building clearly visible west of the temple, just outside the sanctuary. How do we know that this was Phidias's workshop? Because a cup with "I belong to Phidias" written on it and artists' tools were found here—and are now on display in the Archaeological Museum.

Between the temples of Zeus and Hera, you can make out the low foundations of a round building; the three standing columns and their stylobate (base) were restored in honor of the 2004 Olympics. This is all that remains of the **shrine** that Philip of Macedon, never modest, built here to pat himself on the back after conquering Greece in 338 B.C.

Beyond the two temples, built up against the Hill of Kronos itself, are the curved remains of a once-elegant **Roman fountain** and the foundations of 11 **treasuries** where Greek cities stored votive offerings and money. In front of the treasuries are the low bases of a series of bronze **statues of Zeus,** dedicated not by victorious athletes but by those caught cheating in the stadium. These statues would have been the last things that competitors saw before they ran through the vaulted tunnel into the stadium.

Ancient tradition clearly shows that the Olympic Games began here, but it is less clear why they were held every 4 years. According to one legend, Herakles (Hercules) initiated the Games to celebrate the completion of his 12 labors. With the fetid Augean stables clean, Herakles paced off the stadium and then ran its entire length of 192m (600 Olympic ft.) without having to take a single breath.

Admission to site and museum 9€ ($12). Usually summer Mon–Fri 8:30am–7pm, Sat–Sun 8:30am–3pm; winter Mon–Fri 8am–5pm, Sat–Sun 8:30am–3pm.

The Museum of the History of the Olympic Games in Antiquity ✸✸✸   The museum, which opened in 2004, occupies the handsome neoclassical building that served as the site's original archaeological museum. The path to the museum is steep; it is sometimes possible to get permission to drive up and drop off passengers by the museum's entrance. The collection is superb; the text (Greek, English, German) posted on exhibits is extensive. Each of the 12 galleries has a theme, including "The Beginning of the Games," "Zeus and his Cults," "The Events," and Games at other ancient sites (Nemea, Isthmia, Delphi). Exhibits document the growth of the Games from a sprint on 1 day to 5 days of events for hundreds of athletes from around the Greek world. In wrestling, breaking fingers was forbidden, eye-gouging was permitted. In each event, there was only one winner: There were no runners-up at Olympia. Displays include massive chariot wheels, delicate musical instruments, statues of lithe athletes, and all manner of athletic gear.

© 26240/22-529. Free admission (but a fee is planned). Summer Mon noon–7pm, Tues–Sun 8am–7pm; winter, the museum usually closes by 5pm.

Museum of the History of the Excavations in Olympia ✸   This charming little museum occupies one of the original houses used by the German excavators (imagine them warming up by the large fireplace). Photographs and journals document the history of the excavations from 1766, when antiquarian Richard Chandler identified the site, to the present. Look for the 19th-century photograph showing the unearthing of the Temple of Zeus. The photo was taken as the structure was emerging from beneath 5m (16 ft.) of soil. Some of the shovels and whisk brooms used are on display.

© 26240/20-128. Free admission. Summer, Mon noon–7pm, Tues–Sun 8am–7pm; winter, the museum usually closes by 5pm.

Finds A Great Place for Books & Music

Galerie Orphee, Antonios Kosmopoulos's shop on the main street in Ancient Olympia (© 26240/23-555), has a wide selection of books, an extensive range of cassettes and CDs of Greek music, plus frequent displays of contemporary art. What a pleasant contrast to Olympia's other shops, which have all too many T-shirts, museum reproductions, and machine-made rugs and embroideries sold as "genuine handmade crafts."

The Museum of the Olympic Games ⋆   When you head back to town, try to set aside half an hour to visit this museum, which is signposted on the main drag. Not many tourists come here, and the guards are often glad to show visitors around. Displays include victors' medals, commemorative stamps, and photos of winning athletes, such as former king Constantine of Greece and the great African-American athlete Jesse Owens. There's also a photo of the bust of the founder of the modern Olympics, Baron de Coubertin. (The bust itself stands just off the main road east of the ancient site and marks the spot where de Coubertin's heart is buried.)

Admission 2€ ($2.60). Mon–Sat 8am–3:30pm; Sun and holidays 9am–2:30pm.

WHERE TO STAY

Olympia has more than 20 hotels, which means that you can almost always find a room—although if you arrive without a reservation in July or August, you probably won't get your first choice. As is often the case in major tourist centers, hotels here often raise or lower rates depending on the kind of season they're having. In winter, many hotels are closed. If you want to have the best of both worlds and stay by the sea, you can, but you will have to do some nasty driving on truck-infested main roads to get back and forth to Olympia. If this does not deter you, try the elegant **Grecotel Olympia Riviera Resort** (www.grecotel.gr) 45 minutes away on its own beach in Kyllini, with three hotel complexes (Mandola Rosa is the fanciest), 500 acres of gardens, six restaurants (one entirely organic), seven pools, and just about everything else you'd want.

Hotel Europa ⋆⋆⋆   The Europa is the best hotel in town—and one of the best in the Peloponnese. Part of the Best Western chain (but managed by a very helpful local family), it's a few minutes' drive out of town on a hill overlooking both the modern village and the ancient site. Most units overlook the large pool and garden, and several have views of a bit of the ancient site. The rooms are large, with extra-firm mattresses and sliding glass doors opening onto generously sized balconies. The two very professional restaurants include a taverna in the garden, which serves tasty grills and stews; the indoor breakfast buffet is extensive.

27065 Ancient Olympia, Peloponnese. © 800/528-1234 in the U.S., 26240/22-650 or 26240/22-700. Fax 26240/23-166. www.bestwestern.com. 80 units. 130€ ($169) double. Considerable reductions possible off season. Rates include breakfast. AE, DC, MC, V. **Amenities:** Restaurant; bar; pool. *In room:* A/C, TV, unstocked minifridge, hair dryer.

Hotel Olympia Palace ⋆   Frankly, I had looked forward to staying here again after the renovations and I was disappointed. It's true that the Olympia Palace, which was completely remodeled for the 2004 Olympics, is an excellent choice if you want to be poised on the main street in order to investigate the village. The guest rooms have good beds, cheerful prints on the walls, and nice rag rugs on the floor; the bathrooms are modern and good-size. However, street noise plagues the front rooms and a large parking lot flanks the side toward the ancient site; try for a rear room. Another problem: seriously ho-hum service.

2 Praxiteleous Kondili, 27065 Ancient Olympia. (©) **26240/23-101.** Fax 26240/22-525. 58 units. 100€–130€ ($130–$169) double. AE, MC, V. **Amenities:** Restaurant; bar; shops. *In room:* A/C, TV, minibar, hair dryer.

Hotel Pelops ✪✪✪   If you've heard how helpful Aussie expat Susanna Spiliopoulou and her Greek husband Theo are, believe every word! Susanna and her family make this one of the most welcoming hotels in Greece. Rooms are good-size, cheerful, and very comfy, unlike all too many Greek hotels. Check out their website to learn about their 3- and 4-day cooking, writing, and painting classes, usually offered off season. An added bonus: Guests here can use the dishy pool at the Europa Hotel and order up a Pelops Platter (a wide variety of Greek *mezedes*) for dinner back at the Pelops. But the real bonus here is leaving the all-too-often anonymous world of hotels and entering a welcoming haven, in the center of town, but on a blissfully quiet street.

2 Varela, 27065 Ancient Olympia. (©) **26240/22-543.** www.hotelpelops.gr. 25 units. 75€–85€ ($98–$111) double. MC, V. **Amenities:** Breakfast room. *In room:* A/C, TV.

WHERE TO DINE

Olympia has almost as many restaurants as hotels. The ones on and just off the main street with large signs in English and German tend to have indifferent food and service; the **Aegean, Zeus,** and the **4 Epoxei (4 Seasons),** are consistently better than average. The two restaurants of the Hotel Europa (see above) are far superior to most restaurants in town, but check to see if the excellent **Kladeos** restaurant has reopened. If you have a car, the family-operated **Taverna Bacchus,** some 5km (3 miles) outside Olympia in the village of Miraka, has long served up excellent country cooking. Phone first ((© **26240/22-498**) to make sure the Bacchus is open the night you want to go.

15 Patras (Patra)

207km (128 miles) SW of Athens

The third-largest city in Greece and far and away the largest in the Peloponnese, Patras's unappealing urban sprawl now extends for miles north and south of the city center. Patras has always had sights worth seeing—the Cathedral of St. Andrew, the Archaeological Museum, a Roman Odeon (music hall) on the slopes of the ancient acropolis, and a medieval castle on the summit. Still, this remains a better place to live than to visit; unless you are arriving or departing here by ship, love commercial ports, or have lots of time on your hands, you'll probably want to give Patras a miss.

If you do plan to spend time in Patras, here are some suggestions: In July and August, the **Patras International Festival of the Arts** ((© **2610/276-540** or 2610/279-008) brings performances of everything from ancient drama to popular music to the Roman Odeon and the Patras Municipal Theater ((© **2610/623-730**) and a number of locations around the city. Patras also has a vigorous **carnival** that lasts nearly a month, with parades, costumes, and floats, ending the Monday before Lent (www.carnivalpatras.gr). Whenever you are here, you may choose to sample local wines at the Achaia Clauss winery, 8km (5 miles) southeast of town ((© **2610/325-051**); check with the tourist office for directions, bus schedules, and hours.

ESSENTIALS

GETTING THERE   By Train   There are frequent trains from the Stathmos Pelo-ponnisou (railroad station for the Peloponnese) in Athens (© **210/513-1601** or 210/522-4302). The Patras train station, on Othonos and Amalias (© **2610/273-694**), is on the waterfront near the boat departure piers. If you're catching a ferryboat, keep in mind that Greek trains usually run late, and allow extra time for your journey.

By Bus   There are some 15 buses to Patras daily from the Stathmos Leoforia Pelo-ponnisou (bus station for the Peloponnese) in Athens, 100 Kifissou (© **210/ 512-4910;** www.ktel.org). The Patras bus station (© **2610/623-886**) is on Othonos and Amalias. For general Athens-Peloponnese schedule information, try © **210/ 512-4910** or www.ktel.org.

By Car   The drive on the National Highway from Athens to Patras takes about 5 hours. *Note:* In the Patras city center, the system of one-way streets, not always obvi-ously marked, along with the profusion of foreign drivers who have just arrived from Europe by car ferry, means that you should drive with particular care.

If you're heading from Patras across the Gulf of Corinth into Central Greece, you'll probably want to take the spectacular new Rio-AntiRio Bridge which opened in 2004 (10€/$13). If you prefer—and if it has not been discontinued, as threatened—you can still take the Rio-AntiRio car ferry, which runs twice an hour from early morning until about 11pm (3€/$3.90).

Tip: The bridge's official, and seldom used name, in honor of a 19th century states-man, is the Harilaos Trikoupis Bridge. Most people simply refer to simply call it "e gefyra" (the bridge).

VISITOR INFORMATION   There is a **tourist information** office in an old factory building at Othonos and 6 Amalias; it's usually open weekdays (8am–8pm; © **2610/461-740;** www.patras.gr). The **tourist police** are at 53 Patreos (© **2610/ 220-902** or 2610/451-833). The website of Patras's year as the European Capital of Culture, has some useful information at www.patras2006.gr.

FAST FACTS   A number of **banks** on the waterfront and on Plateia Georgiou exchange currency and have ATMs. The **post office** is signposted at the intersection of Mezonas and Zaimi. There is a **telephone office (OTE)** on the waterfront by the Customs sheds. Most of the **car-rental agencies** (Avis, Hertz, Kemwell) have clearly marked offices on the waterfront. The **hospital** (© **2610/22-3812**) is signposted in town. There is also an **emergency first-aid station** (© **2610/277-386**) at the corner of Karolou and Ayiou Dionysion. For Internet access, try **Netp@rk** (© **2610/ 279-699**), 37 Gerokostopoulou; or try **Netrino Internet Café** (© **2610/623-344**), 133 Karaiskaki. Both charge 5€ ($6.50) per hour, and both are off the waterfront; it is entirely possible that by the time you visit Patras, someone will have opened an Internet cafe on the harbor. Inquire at the tourist office (see above). English-language newspapers and magazines are widely available at kiosks along the waterfront.

WHAT TO SEE & DO

If you find yourself with a few hours in Patras, we suggest you head inland on Gerokostopoulou to **Plateia Yioryiou (George Sq.).** Sit at a cafe and take in the facades of the handsome neoclassical theater and banks on the square. Patras was burned by the Turks during the War of Independence and has been hit repeatedly by earthquakes. These buildings are among the few that remain from the 19th century when the city was famous for its arcaded streets and neoclassical architecture. Patras boasts other attractive squares: Plateia Olga and Plateia 25 Martiou have cafes, restaurants, and shops.

Then head down to the waterfront to the **Cathedral of St. Andrew.** Although the present (substantial, but undistinguished) church was built after World War II, the mosaics give a vivid picture of old Patras. It's important to dress appropriately to visit the cathedral, a major pilgrimage shrine thanks to the presence of St. Andrew's skull in an ornate gold reliquary to the right of the altar. Visitors will find several pleasant cafes in the shaded park across from the cathedral.

If you have an attack of conscience, check to see if the **Archaeological Museum,** 42 Mezonos (© **2610/220-829**) is open. It's been closed for renovations, but promises to be open Tuesday through Sunday from 8:30am to 5pm; free admission. If you're here on the weekend and feel energetic, have a look at the **Roman Odeon** off Platia Martiou; at night, pedestrianized streets such as Gerokostopoulou around the Plateia and the Odeon have lots of bars and cafes. There are also a number of small cafes and restaurants in the streets leading up to the **Patras Fortress,** a medieval castle on the ancient acropolis that's open Saturday and Sunday from about 8am to 7pm; admission is free. If you drive up, be pleasantly surprised if you don't get lost.

The Ferry to the Ionian Islands & Italy

The major ferryboat and shipping companies all have offices on the waterfront. There is usually daily ferry service from Patras to the **Ionian islands** and **Corfu**. There are many daily services from Patras to the Italian towns of **Brindisi** and **Ancona**. The fastest service to Italy is the 18-hour **Super Ferry Crossing** from Patras to Ancona, offered by **Superfast Ferries** (© **2610/622-500**, or 210/969-1100 in Athens; www.superfast.com). In 2007, a cabin for two cost 300€ ($390); a bunk in a shared four-bunk cabin cost 45€ ($59); price bargaining often possible on board.

If you take the Rio-AntiRio bridge or ferry from the Peloponnese across to Central Greece, you can see another fortress, the 15th-century **Fortress of Rio.** The fortress is open daily from 8am to 7pm; admission is free.

WHERE TO STAY

Astir Hotel   If you arrive too late to continue your journey or if you have an early-morning boat to catch, this is a convenient hotel whose best feature is its roof garden with pool. The guest rooms are nothing special, and many seem to have been decorated by someone who couldn't decide which color would go with which. Some units have harbor views, as does the rooftop terrace. For Patras, this is a quiet place to spend the night—which is to say that the street noise here is usually endurable.

16 Ayiou Andreas, 26223 Patras. © **2610/277-502.** Fax 2610/271-644. www.greekhotel.com. 120 units. 100€–150€ ($130–$195) double. MC, V. **Amenities:** Restaurant; bar; pool. *In room:* A/C, TV, minibar.

Grecotel Lakopetra Beach 🏖🏖 *(Kids)*   This resort hotel, with just about everything you would want at a resort after a long day of sightseeing, is set in extensive gardens a short walk from the beach. The large guest rooms come with balconies or terraces, and the bathrooms are well-appointed. If you are traveling with children, this could be the spot to compensate them for all those hours looking at what my own children called "those old things you want to see."

Kato Achaia, 25200 Achaia. © **26930/51-713.** Fax 26930/51-045. 192 units. 115€–150€ ($150–$195) double. Rates include breakfast. MC, V. **Amenities:** 2 restaurants; bar; pool; fitness center w/sauna; shops. *In room:* A/C, TV, minibar, hair dryer.

Primarolia Art Hotel 🏖🏖   This boutique hotel with its own art gallery and trendy modernistic furniture occupies an elegantly restored 19th-century building. The Primarolia is popular with business travelers on expense accounts and with couples in search of a romantic spot to spend the night before boarding a ship. If you have to spend the night in Patras and want to splurge, this is the place to stay. The guest rooms are elegant (especially those with balconies), have art on display, and also have all the modern conveniences you'd expect.

33 Othonos and Amalias, 26223 Patras. © **2610/624-900.** Fax 2610/623-559. www.arthotel.gr. 14 units. 200€–260€ ($260–$338) double or suite. AE, DC, V. **Amenities:** Restaurant; bar; sauna. *In room:* A/C, TV, fax, dataport, minibar, hair dryer, safe.

WHERE TO DINE

The restaurants along the harbor near the train station serve consistently mediocre food to the hordes of tourists arriving from and departing for Italy. You won't starve at any of these places, but you can do better. If, however, you are pressed for time, try **To Konaki,** across from the station; it serves dependably good food. (Unfortunately, for most of the summer, To Konaki moves shop to the beach at Rio.) If you want an ouzo before dinner or a sweet afterward, head for any of the cafes on the main square, Plateia Yioryiou. There are several old-fashioned tavernas along Ayiou Nikolaou, including the **Majestic** and **Nikolaras.** If you visit the kastro, you might have a meal at **Krini,** 57 Pandokratoros, which is usually open for lunch and dinner, has its own garden, and is popular with locals and Greek tourists.

One place I think of fondly is **Trikoyia,** 46 Otho and Amalias (no phone), a hole-in-the-wall taverna that serves excellent fresh fish and octopus. Chops and one or two other meat dishes are usually available as well. It's a 15-minute walk along the harbor from the main port.

Next door at 48 Otho and Amalias (the number is not posted on the building) is **Pharos Fish Taverna** (© **2610/336-500**), with equally fresh fish. There are usually lots of locals eating here—always a good sign. Head inside first and choose your fish; if you arrive and sit at a table, the waiter will probably ignore you, thinking that you're waiting for friends. If these places are too crowded, you'll find lots of other seafood tavernas on the harbor front, including **Dinos** at 102 Otho and Amalias and **Apameno** a few doors along at 107.

9

Crete

by John S. Bowman

Per square mile, Crete must be one of the most "loaded" places in the world—loaded, that is, in the diversity of its history, archaeological sites, natural attractions, tourist amenities, and just plain surprises. In a world where more and more travelers have "been there, done that," Crete remains an endlessly fascinating and satisfying destination.

Few travelers need to be sold on the glories of the Minoan culture of Crete. But Crete also offers cities layered with 4,000 years of continuous inhabitation, including the vibrant heritage of centuries-old Orthodox Christianity and the distinctive imprint left by almost 700 years of Venetian and Turkish rule. Not to mention endless beaches, magnificent mountains, intriguing caves, resonant gorges, and countless villages and sites

that provide unexpected and unforgettable experiences.

An elaborate service industry has developed to please the many thousands of foreigners who visit Crete each year. Facilities now exist to suit everyone's taste, ranging from luxury resorts to guest rooms in villages that have hardly changed over several centuries. You can spend a delightful day in a remote mountain town where you're treated to fresh goat cheese and olives, then be back at your hotel within an hour, enjoying a cool drink on the beach.

To be frank, Crete isn't always and everywhere a gentle Mediterranean idyll—its terrain can be raw, its sites austere, its tone brusque. But for those looking for a distinctive destination, Crete never fails to deliver.

STRATEGIES FOR SEEING THE ISLAND

If possible, go in June or September, even late May or early October, unless your goal is simply a sun-drenched beach: Crete has become an island on overload in July and August—and it's very hot! The overnight ferry from Piraeus is still the purist's way to go, but the 50-minute flight by plane from the Athens airport gives you more time for activities. The island offers enough to do to fill up a week, if not a lifetime of visits. By flying, you could actually see the major sites in 2 packed days. To make full use of your time, you can fly into Iraklion and out of Chania, or vice versa.

We recommend the following destinations if you have 5 to 7 days. This mix of activities even allows you time to collapse on a beach at the end of the day. Iraklion is a must, with its archaeological museum and nearby Knossos. An excursion to Phaestos, its associated sites, and the caves at Matala can easily occupy most of day 2. If you don't need to see that second Minoan palace, I recommend you move on at the end of the first day to overnight in Chania or Rethymnon—each or both can fill another day of strolling. Choose your route: The old road from Iraklion that winds through the mountains and villages has its charms, while the coastal expressway offers

Crete

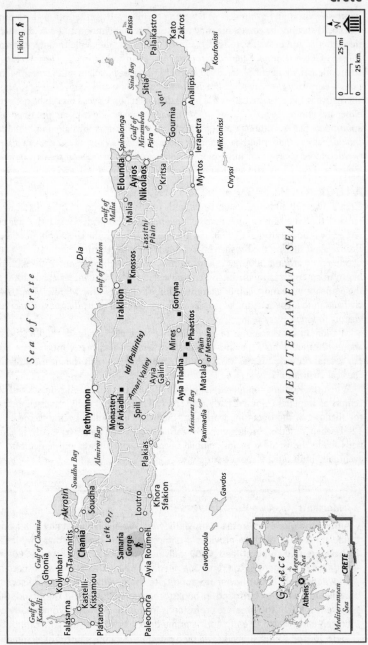

impressive vistas and a "tunnel" of flowering oleanders. If you set off in the morning, you could stay on the coastal highway to just before Rethymnon and take the side trip through the Amari Valley (p. 360). Once in Chania, the walk through the famed Samaria Gorge requires 1 long day for the total excursion (p. 352). Those seeking less strenuous activity might prefer a trip eastward to Ayios Nikolaos and its nearby attractions—especially the many fine beaches between Iraklion and Ayios Nikolaos. Another alternative is a visit to the Lasithi Plain and the Dhiktaion Cave: This can be taken from either Iraklion or Ayios Nikolaos (p. 341). Various other side trips are described in the appropriate places. Although public transportation or tour groups are possibilities, you should really rent a car (although not for use in the cities or towns!) so you can leave the overdeveloped tourist trail and explore countless villages, spectacular scenery, beaches at the ends of the roads, and lesser-known archaeological, historical, and cultural sites.

A LOOK AT THE PAST

Crete's diversity and distinction begin with its history, a past that has left far more remains than the Minoan sites many people first associate with the island. After being settled by humans around 6500 B.C., Crete passed through the late Neolithic and early Bronze ages, sharing the broader eastern Mediterranean culture.

Sometime around 3000 B.C., new immigrants arrived; by about 2500 B.C., there began to emerge a fairly distinctive culture called Early Minoan. By about 2000 B.C., the Minoans were moving into a far more ambitious phase, the Middle Minoan—the civilization that gave rise to the palaces and superb works of art that now attract many visitors to Crete every year.

Mycenaean Greeks appear to have taken over the palaces about 1500 B.C., but by about 1200 B.C., this Minoan-Mycenaean civilization had pretty much gone under. For several centuries, Crete was a relatively marginal player in the great era of Greek classical civilization.

When the Romans conquered the island in 67 B.C., they revived Knossos and other centers as imperial colonies. Early converts to Christianity, the Cretans slipped into the shadows of the Byzantine world, but the island was pulled back into the light in 1204, when Venetians broke up the Byzantine Empire and took over Crete. The Venetians made the island a major colonial outpost, revived trade and agriculture, and eventually built quite elaborate structures.

Moments Crete's Wildflowers

Among the glories of Crete are its wildflowers: A walk in almost any locale outside the center of cities provides a glimpse of their diversity and loveliness. There are said to be at least 1,500 individual species, of which some 200 are endemic or indigenous to Crete. One need not be a botanist or even especially knowledgeable about flowers to appreciate them, although there are several available guides to be found in bookstores and stalls around the island. But there is a hitch: the greatest profusion is in the spring, which comes early on Crete—early March to early April is prime time. However, those who cannot be there for the spring showing will be treated throughout much of the summer to the miles and miles of blooming oleanders that line the national highway from Chania to Ayios Nikolaos.

> **Tips** **Site and Museum Hours Update**
>
> If you visit Crete during the summer, check to see when major sites and muse-
> ums are open. According to the tourist office, they should be open from 8am
> to 7:30pm, but some may close earlier in the day and all are usually closed 1 day
> a week.

By the late 1500s, the Turks were conquering the Venetians' eastern Mediterranean
possessions, and in 1669 they captured the last major stronghold on Crete, the city of
Candia—now Iraklion. Cretans suffered considerably under the Turks, and although
some of Greece finally threw off the Turkish yoke in the late 1820s, Crete was left
behind. A series of rebellions marked the rest of the 19th century, resulting in a partly
independent Crete.

Finally, in 1913, Crete was for the first time formally joined to Greece. Crete had
yet another cameo role in history when the Germans invaded it in 1941 with gliders
and parachute troops; the ensuing occupation was another low point. Since 1945,
Crete has advanced amazingly in the economic sphere, powered by its agricultural
products—particularly olives, grapes, melons, and tomatoes—as well as by its tourist
industry. Not all Cretans are pleased by the impact of tourism, but all would agree
that, for better or for worse, Crete owes much to its history.

1 Iraklion (Heraklion)

Iraklion is the gateway to Knossos, the most impressive of the Minoan palace sites,
while the museum here is home to the world's only comprehensive collection of
Minoan artifacts. Beyond that, the town has magnificent fortified walls and several
other testimonies to the Venetians' time of power. Iraklion is also big enough (Greece's
fifth-largest city) and confident enough to have its own identity as a busy modern city.
It often gets bad press because it bustles with traffic and commerce and construction—the very things most travelers want to escape. At any rate, give Iraklion a chance.
Follow the advice below, and you just may come to like it.

ESSENTIALS

GETTING THERE   By Plane   Aside from the many who now fly from European
cities directly to Crete on charter/package tour flights, most visitors will take the
50-minute flight from Athens to Iraklion or Chania on **Olympic Airways** (✆ 210/
926-9111; www.olympicairlines.com) or **Aegean Airlines** (✆ 801/112-0000; www.
aegeanair.com) Fares vary greatly depending on time of year and time of day and so
can run from 50€ ($65) to 130€ ($169) round-trip. Olympic also offers a few direct
flights a week between Iraklion and Rhodes, and in high season the airline offers service between Athens and Sitia (in eastern Crete). Otherwise, flights between Crete and
other points in Greece (such as Santorini, Mykonos, Thessaloniki) go through Athens.
Reservations are a necessity in high season.

Iraklion's airport is about 5km (3 miles) east of the city, along the coast. Major car-
rental companies have desks at the airport. A taxi to Iraklion costs about 15€ ($20);
the public bus, 2€ ($2.60). To get back to the airport, you have the same two
choices—taxi or public bus no. 1. You can take either form of transport from Plateia

Eleftheria (Liberty Sq.) or from other points along the way. Inquire in advance at your hotel about the closest stop.

By Boat Throughout the year, there is at least one ship per day (and as many as two or three in high season) from Piraeus to Iraklion, and other ships to Chania and Rethymnon. Most trips take about 10 hours but as of 2007 there is a "high speed" service from Piraeus to Chania that is supposed to cut the trip down to under 5 hours. Check online at **www.ferries.gr**. Less frequent ships link Crete to Rhodes (and Karpathos, Kassos, and Khalki, the islands between the two); to Santorini and some of the other Cycladic islands en route to or from Piraeus; and even to Thessaloniki and various Greek ports en route. In high season, occasional ships from Italy, Cyprus, and Israel put into Iraklion. And now catamarans operated by **Hellenic Seaways** link Iraklion with several Cycladic islands (Santorini, Ios, Paros, Naxos, and Mykonos); these run daily in high season, four times weekly other times; check online (www.greek islands.gr) or contact their Athens office (© **210/419-9000**). For information on all ships, inquire at a travel agency, search online (www.gtp.gr), or contact **Paleologos Agency** (www.ferries.gr).

If you have arrived at Iraklion's harbor by ship, you'll most likely want to take a taxi up into the town, as it's a steep climb. Depending on where you want to go, the fare ranges from 4€ to 10€ ($5.20–$13). Or you can take a bus from the depot.

By Bus Visitors also come to Iraklion by public bus from other cities on the island. Where you arrive depends on where you've come from. Those arriving from points to the west, east, or southeast—Chania or Rethymnon, for instance, or Ayios Nikolaos or Sitia to the east—end up along the harbor. To get into the center of town, you must walk, take a taxi, or hop a public bus. The bus starts its route at the terminal where buses from the east and southeast stop; directly across the boulevard is the station for the Rethymnon-Chania buses. Visitors arriving from the south—Phaestos, Matala, and other towns—will end up at Chania Gate on the southwest edge of town; walking may not appeal to most people, but you can take a public bus or taxi.

VISITOR INFORMATION The **National Tourist Office** is at 1 Xanthoudidou, opposite the Archaeological Museum (© **2810/228-225;** fax 2810/226-020). Its hours are Monday through Friday 8am to 2:30pm. Quite frankly, the National Tourist service is so poor these days that you'd do better to contact one of the more reliable travel agencies in Iraklion: **Creta Travel Bureau,** 49B Dikeossinis (© **2810/300-610;** fax 2810/223-749); or **Arabatzoglou Travel,** 30 25th Avgusto (© **2810/301-398;** fax 2810/301-399). For those interested in renting an apartment or villa on Crete, see the agencies listed in chapter 2, p. 70.

GETTING AROUND   By Bus You can see much of Crete by using the public bus system. The buses are cheap, relatively frequent, and connect to all but the most isolated locales. The downside: Remote destinations often have schedules that cater to locals, not tourists. The long-distance bus system is operated by **KTEL,** which serves all of Greece. Ask your travel agent or call © **2810/221-765** to find out more about KTEL buses to Rethymnon-Chania and points west. For buses to Ayios Nikolaos, Sitia, Ierapetra, and points east, call © **2810/245-019.** For buses to Phaestos and other points south, call © **2810/255-965.**

By Car & Moped A car gives you maximum flexibility in seeing the island. All the familiar car-rental agencies are available at the main centers of Crete, including the airports, and most travelers have their preferences. In Iraklion, aside from these,

Iraklion

Harbor Fort (The Koules)

Sea of Crete

To Bus Terminals

Historical Museum of Crete

Sof. Venizelou
Skordilon
Sof. Venizelou
Theotokopoulou
Palelogou
Makariou
Kisssamou
Valestra
Papadopoulou
Delimarkou
Giamalaki
Odos 1878
Handaka
Idis
Kalokerinou
1821
Ioustinianou
Vikela
Giannikou
Vikela
Kounali
Giamboudi
Nikolaou Plastira
Nikolaou Plastira
Thenon
Kondilaki
Georgiadi
Grigoraki
Erofilis
25 Avgusto
Epimenidou
Plateia Venizelou
Police
Dikeossinis
Hatzimihali Gianari
Evans
1866
Averof
Evans
Pediados
Nikolaou Plastir
Xanthoudidou
Archaeological Museum
Akadimias
Neas Ionias
Papandreou G.
Knossou
Kastrinaki
Demokratias

Chania (Panigra) Gate

Kainouriya (Gesu) Gate

Tomb of Nikos Kazantzakis

N
0 — 250 m
0 — 250 y

Iraklion
CRETE

Church ✝
First Aid ✚
Information ⓘ
OTE
Post Office ✉

ACCOMMODATIONS ■
Atlantis Hotel 4
Atrion Hotel 1
Galaxy Hotel 9
Lato Hotel 3
Megaron Hotel 10

DINING ◆
Brillant 3
Giovanni 6
Ionia 7
Ippocampus 2
Loukoulos 5
Pantheon 8

Greece
Athens
Aegean Sea
Mediterranean Sea
CRETE Iraklion

Tips Biking on Crete

In general, I am reluctant to encourage the casual visitor to Greece to rent and ride a bicycle—whether it is to get around cities and towns or to set off for the countryside. In the former case, Greek drivers are not accustomed to bicycle riders and their driving habits make it extremely dangerous; in the latter case, the terrain is usually quite mountainous, roads are often not that well maintained, and there is little shoulder to ride on. That said, Crete has become a major attraction for serious bikers. Various specialized tour operators run bicycle tours on Crete—extending over several days, doing a segment each day, with accommodations at each stop over; you could bring your own but these firms rent them. Some of these tours are described as requiring truly top-level conditioning, others are less demanding, but all involve a lot of hills! (And in summer, any activity can be quite draining.) If you want to pursue this, try **Trekking Plan (www.cycling.gr)** to learn about their offerings. Or **www.peter-thomson.co.uk/crete/bicycles**. If you are intent on renting on your own for some limited excursion, major tourist centers usually have some outfit that will rent a bike (usually a mountain bike); **Trekking Plan** in Chania (above) will rent for the short term; in Iraklion, try **Blue Aegean Holidays (www.blueaegean.com)** or **MotoExpress (www.moto express.gr)**. Note that many online sites that advertise bikes for rent are referring to motorbikes.

I recommend the locally owned **Motor Club,** 18 Plateia Agglon at the bottom of 25th Avgusto, overlooking the harbor (© **2810/222-408;** www.motorclub.gr). If a moped or motorcycle looks tempting, be *very* sure you can control such a vehicle in chaotic urban traffic and on dangerous mountain roads (with few shoulders but lots of potholes and gravel). Try the Motor Club, above, for rentals.

By Taxi   Taxis are reasonable if two or three people share a trip to a site; no place on Crete is more than a day's round-trip from Iraklion. Ask a travel agent to find you a driver who speaks at least rudimentary English; he can then serve as your guide as well. You might spend 100€ ($130) for three or four to tour of the city and Knossos but for a party of three or four it is well worth it.

By Boat   Several excursion boats take day trips to offshore islands or to isolated beaches as well as to Santorini; inquire at a travel agency.

FAST FACTS   The official **American Express** agency is Adamis Travel Bureau, 23 25th Avgusto (© **2810/346-202;** fax 2810/224-717). There are numerous **banks** and **ATMs** (as well as several currency-exchange machines) throughout the center of Iraklion, with many along 25th Avgusto. The **British Consul** is at 16 Papa Alexandrou, opposite the Archaeological Museum (© **2810/224-012**); there is no American consulate in Iraklion. **Venizelou Hospital** (© **2810/237-502**) is on Knossos Road. For general **first-aid** information, call © **2810/222-222.** For Internet access, try the InSpot Cafe at 6 Korai or the Cyberpoint Cafe, 117 Paraskiyopoulou. Both open midmorning and close at midnight. The access fee at both is now about 4€ ($5.20) per hour.

The most convenient place to do **laundry** is at 25 Merebellou (behind the Archaeological Museum); its hours are Monday through Saturday from 9am to 9pm. You can leave **luggage** at the airport for 4€ ($5.20) per piece per day; most hotels will hold luggage for brief periods. The **tourist police** are at 10 Dikeossenis, on the main street linking 25th Avgusto to Plateia Eleftheria (© 2810/283-190); they are open daily from 7am to 11pm. The main **post office** (© 2810/289-995) is on Plateia Daskaloyiannis and is open daily from 7:30am to 8pm. The **telephone office (OTE),** 10 Minotaurou (far side of El Greco Park), is open daily from 6am to 11pm.

WHAT TO SEE & DO
ATTRACTIONS

The Archaeological Museum 𝕣𝕣𝕣   This—the world's premier collection of art and artifacts from the Minoan civilization—amazes most visitors who are surprised by the variety of objects, styles, and techniques of the treasures inside. Many of the most spectacular objects are from Knossos; the rest, from other sites on the island. Among the most prized objects are **snake goddesses** from Knossos, the **Phaestos Disc** (with its still-undeciphered inscription), the **bee pendant** from Mallia, **carved vases** from Ayia Triadha and Kato Zakros, and objects depicting young men leaping over the horns of charging bulls. Upstairs you'll find the **original frescoes from Knossos** and other sites, their restored sections clearly visible (the frescoes now at Knossos are copies of these). Most displays have decent labels in English, but you may want to invest in one of the guidebooks for sale in the lobby. You will need at least 1 hour for even a quick walk-through. To avoid the tour groups in high season, plan to visit very early, late in the day, or on Sunday.

1 Xanthoudidou. © **2810/226-092.** Admission 6€ ($7.80) adults, 3€ ($3.90) students with official ID and E.U. citizens 65 and over. Free on Sun Nov–Mar, and some Sun in summer. Apr to mid-Oct Tues–Sun 8am–8pm, Mon 12:30–8pm; mid-Oct to Mar, closes daily at 5pm. Far corner of Plateia Eleftheria. Parking in immediate area impossible—best is to park below along commercial harbor road. Note: Special combination ticket for the museum and Palace of Knossos (below) is 10€($13).

Harbor Fort (The Koules) (Kids)   You may feel as if you're walking through a Hollywood set—but this is the real thing! The harbor fort, built on the site of a series of earlier forts, went up between 1523 and 1540, and although greatly restored, it is essentially the Venetian original. Both its exterior and interior are impressive in their dimensions, workmanship, and details: thick walls, spacious chambers, great ramparts, cannon balls, and Lion of St. Mark plaques. It's well worth an hour's visit.

At breakwater on old harbor. © **2810/288-484.** Admission 4€ ($5.60). Daily 9am–1pm and 4–7pm.

(Tips) Museum's Temporary Display

When this edition went to press, Iraklion's Archaeological Museum was closed for major renovations and additions, and it was not certain when the new museum would be open. However, they have installed a wonderful selection of all the major holdings in a new building at the rear of the museum. The hours are the same as listed above; the admission fee is reduced to 4€. And to be frank, this greatly reduced selection is probably enough for most visitors—all the notable pieces are on display. One drawback is that the floor space is limited even more than usual, so try to visit there during off hours—very early in the morning or late in the day.

Historical Museum of Crete ⊛   This museum picks up where the Archaeological Museum leaves off, displaying artifacts and art from the early Christian era up to the present. You get some sense of the role the Cretans' long struggle for independence still plays in their identity. On display are traditional Cretan **folk arts;** the re-created study of **Nikos Kazantzakis,** Crete's great modern writer; and at least one work attributed to the painter **El Greco,** another of the island's admired sons. Even if you take only an hour for this museum, it will reward you with surprising insights about the island.

7 Lysimakos Kalokorinou (facing coast road 450m/1,500 ft. west of harbor). ℂ 2810/283-219. www.historical-museum.gr. Admission 4€ ($5.60) adults, 2€ ($2.60) students. Mar–Oct Mon–Fri 9am–5pm, Sat 9am–2pm; reduced hours in winter.

The Palace of Knossos ⊛⊛⊛ *Kids*   This is undeniably one of the great archaeological sites of the world, yet until Arthur Evans began excavating here in 1900, little was known about the ancient people who inhabited it. Using every possible clue and remnant, Evans rebuilt large parts of the palace—walls, floors, stairs, windows, and columns. Visitors must now stay on a walkway, but you still get a good sense of the structure's labyrinthine nature. You are looking at the remains of two major palaces plus several restorations made from about 2000 B.C. to 1250 B.C. This was not a palace in the modern sense of a royal residence, but a combination of that and the Minoans' chief religious-ceremonial center as well as their administrative headquarters and royal workshops. Take the time for a guided tour here; it's worth the expense (your hotel or a travel agency can arrange it). On your own, you'll need at least 2 hours for a cursory walk-through. The latter part of the day and Sunday tend to be less crowded.

Knossos Rd., 5km (3 miles) south of Iraklion. ℂ 2810/231-940. Admission 6€ ($7.80), 3€ ($3.90) students with official ID and E.U. citizens 65 or over. Free on Sun Nov–Mar and some Sun in summer. Apr to mid-Oct daily 8am–8pm; mid-Oct to Mar Mon–Fri 8am–5pm, Sat–Sun 8:30am–3pm. Frequent buses from center of Iraklion. Free parking down slope on left 90m (300 ft.) before main entrance. Note: Special combination ticket for the Palace of Knossos and Archaeological Museum (above) is 10€ ($13).

Venetian Walls & Tomb of Nikos Kazantzakis ⊛ *Kids*   These great walls and bastions were part of the fortress-city the Venetians called Candia. Two of the great city gates have survived fairly well: the Pantocrator or Panigra Gate, better known now as the Chania Gate (dating from about 1570), at the western edge; and the Gate of Gesu, or Kainouryia Gate (about 1587), at the southern edge. Walk around the outer perimeter of the walls to get a feel for their sheer massiveness. They were built by the forced labor of Cretans.

On the Martinengo Bastion at the southwestern corner of the great walls is the grave of Nikos Kazantzakis (1883–1947), a native of Iraklion and author of *Zorba the Greek* and *The Last Temptation of Christ.* Here, too, is one of the best views to the south. Mount Iouktas appears in profile as the head of a man—some say the head of the buried god Zeus. A dedicated visit here requires a solid hour from the center of the city, especially if you want to examine the nearby Kainouryia Gate and a segment of the wall.

The tomb is on the Martinengo Bastion, at the southwestern corner of the walls, along Plastira. Free admission. Sunrise–sunset.

Cretaquarium *Kids*   Not quite a world-class aquarium, but there's more than enough here to occupy your kids on a day when you need a break from the beach. Located on the edge of the former U.S. Air Force Station, its several tanks house over

2,500 specimens from some 200 Mediterranean species of fish and invertebrates—from hunter sharks to tiny sea horses to jellyfish. Various underwater terrains have also been replicated—it is definitely a professional operation. The whole complex, known as Thalassocosmos ("sea world"), belongs to the Hellenic Center for Marine Research. A restaurant and souvenir shop are also on the premises.

At Gournes, 16 km (10 miles) east of Iraklion. Public bus from bus station at port in Iraklion. (℃ 2810/337-788. www.cretaquarium.gr. Admission 8€ ($10), students and children 5–17 6€ ($7.80). May 1–Oct 15 daily 9am–9pm; Oct 16–April 30 daily 10am–5:30pm.

A STROLL AROUND IRAKLION

Start your stroll at **Fountain Square** (also known as Lions Sq., officially Plateia Venizelou), after trying a plate of *bougatsa* at one of the two cafes here serving this local pastry: Armenian Greeks introduced this cheese- or cream-filled delicacy to Crete. This square, long one big traffic jam, is now for pedestrians only. Francesco Morosini, Crete's Venetian governor, installed the **fountain** ⚓ here in 1628. Note the now fading but still elegant relief carvings around the basin. Across from the fountain is the **Basilica of St. Mark,** restored to its original 14th-century Italian style and used for exhibitions and concerts. And since the city of Iraklion acquired the painting at an auction in 2004, St. Mark's is now the home of native son El Greco's "The Baptism of Christ."

Proceeding south 50m (164 ft.) to the crossroads, you'll see the **market street** (officially from 1866); alas, it is increasingly taken over by tourist shops but is still a must-see with its purveyors of fresh fruits and vegetables, meats, and wines.

At the far end of the market street, look for **Kornarou Square,** with its lovely Turkish fountain; beside it is the **Venetian Bembo Fountain** (1588). The modern statue at the far side of the square commemorates the hero and heroine of Vincenzo Kornarou's Renaissance epic poem *Erotokritos,* a Cretan-Greek classic.

Turning right onto Vikela, proceed (always bearing right) until you come to the imposing, if not artistically notable, 19th-century **Cathedral of Ayios Menas,** dedicated to the patron saint of Iraklion. Below and to the left, the medieval **Church of Ayios Menas** boasts old woodcarvings and icons.

At the far corner of the cathedral (to the northeast) is the 15th-century **Church of St. Katherine.** During the 16th and 17th centuries, this church hosted the Mount Sinai Monastery School, where Domenico Theotokopoulou is alleged to have studied before moving on to Venice and Spain; there he became known as **El Greco.** The church houses a small museum of icons, frescoes, and woodcarvings. It's open Monday through Saturday from 10am to 1pm; and Tuesday, Thursday, and Friday from 4 to 6pm. Admission is 5€ ($6.50).

Take Ayii Dheka, the narrow street that leads directly away from the facade of St. Katherine's, and you'll arrive at **Leoforos Kalokerinou,** the main shopping street for locals. Turn right onto it and proceed up to the crossroads of the market street and 25 Avgusto—now set aside for pedestrians. Turn left to go back down past Fountain Square and, on the right, you'll see the totally reconstructed **Venetian Loggia,** originally dating from the early 1600s. Prominent Venetians once met here to conduct business affairs; it now houses city government offices.

A little farther down 25th Avgusto, also on the right, is the **Church of Ayios Titos,** dedicated to the patron saint of Crete (Titus of the Bible), who introduced Christianity to Crete. Head down to the **harbor,** with a side visit to the **Koules** (Venetian fort), if you have time (see above), then pass on the right the two sets of great **Venetian arsenali—**where ships were built and repaired. (The sea at that time came in this far.) Climbing the stairs just past the arsenali, turn left onto Bofort and curve up beneath the **Archaeological Museum** to **Plateia Eleftheria (Liberty Sq.),** where you can pride yourself on having seen the main attractions of Irakion and reward yourself with a refreshing drink at one of the many cafes on the far side.

SHOPPING

Costas Papadopoulos, the proprietor of **Daedalou Galerie,** 11 Daedalou (between Fountain Sq. and Plateia Eleftheria; ⓒ **2810/346-353**), has been offering his tasteful selection of traditional Cretan-Greek arts and crafts for several decades—icons, jewelry, porcelain, silverware, pistols, and more. Some of it is truly old, and he'll tell you when it isn't.

Eleni Kastrinoyanni-Cretan Folk Art, 3 Ikarou (opposite the Archaeological Museum; ⓒ **2810/226-186**), is the premier store in Iraklion for some of the finest in embroidery, weavings, ceramics, and jewelry. The work is new but reflects traditional Cretan folk methods and motifs. Get out your credit card and go for something you'll enjoy for years to come. It's closed October through February.

For one of Crete's finest selections of antique and old Cretan textiles (rugs, spreads, coverlets, and more), along with some unusual pieces of jewelry, try **Grimm's Handicrafts of Crete,** 96 25th Avgusto (opposite the Venetian Loggia; ⓒ **2810/282-547**). The finest objects are not cheap, but you get exactly what you pay for here; even the newer textiles can be stunning.

Stores that sell local agricultural products have sprung up all over Iraklion (as well as most of Crete!). Crete's olive oil—among the finest in the world—stands side by side with honey, wines and spirits, raisins, olives, herbs, and spices. One store is as good as the other.

WHERE TO STAY

In recent years, mass tourism on Crete has led to a demand for beach hotels outside of the cities, but Iraklion still offers a range of hotels. Reservations are a must in high season.

INSIDE THE CITY

Our search for a good hotel here tries hard to feature the criterion of quiet. Iraklion lies under the flight patterns of many commercial planes and the occasional Greek Air Force jet fighter. The noise factor probably adds up to less than 40 minutes every 24 hours, so the sounds of scooters and motorcycles outside your hotel at night will probably be more annoying. The city plans to add a runway out into the sea or build an airport far inland, but it will take some years for this to happen. Meanwhile, closed windows and air-conditioning promise the best defenses.

LUXURY

Megaron Hotel ⋆⋆⋆ Since 2004, this has become the "grand hotel" of Iraklion. After gutting an old and abandoned commercial/apartment building located on the site of a bastion of the old Venetian walls and high above the harbor, the new owners have installed a hotel that is elegant in its decor, facilities, and service. All rooms have an exterior view, leaving the core of the structure as a great atrium. All the public areas bespeak understated luxury and the guest rooms are more generous than in many Greek hotels as well as far more stylish. The various amenities and the service are of the highest standard. Special elements include a small library/reading area, plasma TV, free wireless in public areas, private dining options, rooms for those with disabilities—even dogs will be welcomed. The second floor is set aside for nonsmoking rooms—but smoking seems to be allowed in some of the public areas. There are conference rooms for up to 100 persons. Convenient for walking to anyplace in the core of the city, the Meagron has undeniably seized the high ground of Iraklion's hotels in every sense of that phrase.

9 Beaufort, 71202 Iraklion. © 2810/305-300. www.gdmmegaron.gr. 58 units. High and low seasons 182€–294€ ($237–$382) double. Rates include full breakfast. AE, DC, MC, V. Private parking arranged. Below the Archaeological Museum. **Amenities:** Restaurant; cafe; bar; rooftop pool and cafe; health club and gym w/Jacuzzi, steam bath, sauna, and massage room; concierge; tour desk; car-rental desk; airport pickup by arrangement; secretarial service; 24-hr. room service; babysitting; laundry service; dry cleaning; nonsmoking rooms. *In room:* A/C, TV, Internet service, minibar, fridge, hair dryer, safe.

EXPENSIVE

Atlantis Hotel 😊😊 *(Value)*   Although Iraklion now boasts of a more luxurious hotel, the Atlantis is probably more than adequate for most travelers' tastes. This superior Class A hotel is in the heart of Iraklion, yet removed from city noise (especially if you use the air-conditioning). The staff is friendly and helpful, and although the Atlantis is popular with conference groups—it has major conference facilities—individuals get personal attention. Guest rooms, although neither plush nor especially large, are comfortable. You can swim in the pool, send e-mail via your laptop, and then within minutes be out enjoying a fine meal or visiting a museum.

2 Iyias, 71202 Iraklion. © 2810/229-103. www.theatlantishotel.gr. 162 units. High season 145€ ($189) double; low season 130€ ($169) double. Rates include breakfast. Reduction possible for longer stays. Special rates for business travelers and half-board (breakfast and dinner). AE, DC, MC, V. Private parking arranged. Behind the Archaeological Museum. **Amenities:** Restaurant; 2 bars; small indoor pool; rooftop garden; tennis court across street; Jacuzzi; bike rental; children's playground (across street); video rentals; concierge; tour desk; car-rental desk; airport pickup by arrangement; secretarial service; salon; 24-hr. room service; massage; babysitting; laundry service; dry cleaning; nonsmoking rooms. *In room:* A/C, TV, minibar, fridge, hair dryer, safe.

Galaxy Hotel 😊   With a reputation as one of the finer hotels on Crete, the Galaxy is classy once you get past its rather forbidding gray exterior. The public areas are striking if airport-modern, and the Galaxy boasts (for now, at least) the largest indoor swimming pool in Iraklion. Guest rooms are stylish—international modern—but don't expect American-style size. Ask for an interior unit since you lose nothing in a view and gain in quiet. The hotel also offers several expensive suites. Although a reader once reported a less-than-gracious tone from desk staff, I have always found them courteous in handling requests for services. The Galaxy appeals most to travelers who prefer a familiar international ambience to folksiness. Although its restaurant serves the standard Greek/international menu, the pastry shop and ice-cream parlor attract locals, who consider the fare delicious.

67 Leoforos Demokratias, 71306 Iraklion. © 2810/238-812. www.galaxy-hotel.gr. 137 units, some with shower, some with tub. High season 150€ ($195) double; low season 120€ ($156) double. Rates include buffet breakfast. AE, DC, MC, V. Parking on adjacent streets. Frequent bus to town center within yards of entrance. About ½ mile out main road to Knossos. **Amenities:** Restaurant; pastry shop; bar; indoor pool; sauna; concierge; car-rental desk; 24-hr. room service; laundry service; dry cleaning; executive-level rooms; nonsmoking rooms. *In room:* A/C, TV, high-speed Internet, minibar, hair dryer.

MODERATE

Atrion Hotel   Nothing spectacular here, but I have liked this hotel for many years if only for its location. A recent renovation opened up the public areas and spruced up the rooms. It's in a quiet, seemingly remote corner that is in fact only a 10-minute walk to the center of town, and an even shorter walk to the coast road and the harbor. True, the adjacent streets are not that attractive, but they are perfectly safe; once inside the hotel, you can enjoy your oasis of comfort and peace. This hotel has well-appointed public areas—a lounge, a refreshing patio garden—and pleasant, good-size guest rooms.

9 Chronaki (behind the Historical Museum), 71202 Iraklion. © **2810/229-225.** Fax 2810/223-292. www.atrion.gr. 74 units, some with tub, some with shower. High season 130€ ($169) double; low season 115€ ($150) double. Rates include buffet breakfast. Reductions for children. AE, MC, V. Parking on street. Public bus within 200m (656 ft.). **Amenities:** Cafeteria; bar/restaurant; babysitting; laundry service; nonsmoking rooms. *In room:* A/C, TV, minibar.

Lato Boutique Hotel ☆ *Value* Long one of my favorites in all of Greece, the Lato has now jumped to the head of the line when it comes to providing value, a stylish environment, and warm hospitality. Renovations completed in 2007 have completely refurbished the public areas and transformed the rooms' decor and furnishings (including fire and smoke detectors and high-security door locks). A few rooms are a bit small, five are handsome suites, but all are perfectly adequate—and most have state-of-the-art bathrooms. The buffet breakfast is especially satisfying. Another major plus: its location, which is convenient to the town's center while offering rooms with harbor views (just ask for one). A rooftop restaurant is also one of the attractions of this hotel, combining alfresco dining with a spectacular view. Valet parking eliminates parking aggravation, and the staff is always ready to help you make the most of your stay in Iraklion.

15 Epimenidou, 71202 Iraklion. © **2810/228-103.** Fax 2810/240-350. www.lato.gr. 58 units, some with shower only. High season 140€ ($182) double; low season 105€ ($137) double. Rates include buffet breakfast. 10% discount for Internet reservations. 50% discount for children 6–12. AE, DC, MC, V. Parking on street. **Amenities:** Brillant Gourmet Restaurant (see below); breakfast room; rooftop restaurant; bar; fax and Internet facilities (free Internet in lobby); concierge; car-rental service; room service 8am–11pm; laundry service; dry cleaning; nonsmoking rooms. *In room:* A/C, TV, minibar, hair dryer, safe.

INEXPENSIVE

Poseidon *Value* This is not for everyone, but if there were a contest among longtime Frommer's Greece guidebook loyalists for a favorite hotel in Iraklion, the Poseidon would probably win. And it's not just because of good value for the money. Owner/host John Polychronides established a homey atmosphere, a tone maintained by the desk staff (fluent in English), who are always ready to provide useful information and support for your stay on Crete. In 2004, the hotel was renovated by installing an elevator and, in each unit, air-conditioning, a TV, and a fridge. Yes, the street is not especially attractive—but that's true at most of Iraklion's hotels, and few can match the fresh breezes and an unobstructed view over the port. All rooms have balconies, and the sound-insulated windows keep out most of the exterior noise but there's no denying that the overhead airplane traffic can be annoying at times. Rooms are on the small side and showers are basic, but everything is clean and functional. Frequent buses and cheap taxi fares let you come and go into Iraklion center, a 20-minute walk away. While not for those demanding luxury, this is an alternative to more expensive hotels.

54 Poseidonos, Poros, 71202 Iraklion. © **2810/222-545.** www.hotelposeidon.gr. 26 units, all with shower only. High season 85€ ($111) double; low season 72€ ($94) double. Rates include continental breakfast. A 10% discount for e-mail reservations, 5% discount for stays over 2 nights. AE, MC, V. Parking all around. Frequent public buses 180m (590 ft.) at top of street. About 2.5km (1½ miles) from Plateia Eleftheria, off the main road to the east. *In room:* A/C (7€/$9.10 daily surcharge), TV, fridge.

OUTSIDE THE CITY

Assuming you want to be fairly close to Iraklion, stay on the coast if you want to avoid city noise. If you just want to stay near a remote beach on Crete, such accommodations are described later in this chapter. Although the hotels below can be reached by public bus, a car or taxi will save you valuable time.

EXPENSIVE

Candia Maris ℛ The grandest of the resort hotels on the western edge of Iraklion, the deluxe-class Candia Maris had come in for some harsh criticism in recent years but a thorough renovation in 2006 seems to have taken care of the issues. Even those who complained praised many of its facilities and found it to be an especially good place for families with children. It offers just about everything, from special "Cretan nights" with traditional music and dancing to a squash court to the newest fad, thalassotherapy (sea-water treatment). Although the beach on the west coast is not as visually pleasing as those to the east, it's perfectly clean. And although you have to pass through a rather dreary edge of Iraklion to get here, this area is close to town and so allows for excursions. The exterior and layout are a bit severe, but the rooms are good-size and cheerful, the bathrooms up-to-date. Because you won't spend much time looking at the building's exterior, don't let it deter you from trying this first-class resort hotel. It was also one of the first hotels in Greece to offer accessibility for those with limited mobility.

Amoudara, Gazi, 71303 Iraklion. ℂ **2810/377-000.** Fax 2810/250-669. www.maris.gr. 252 units. High season 175€–380€ ($228–$494) double in hotel, 250€ ($325) seafront bungalow; low season 75€–160€ ($98–$208) double in hotel, 115€ ($150) bungalow. Rates include buffet breakfast. Varied fees for extra person in room and for children; half-board plan (including breakfast and dinner) available for additional 35€ ($46). AE, DC, MC, V. Public bus every half-hour to Iraklion. On beach about 6km (4 miles) west of Iraklion center. **Amenities:** 4 restaurants; 4 bars; 6 pools (2 outdoor, 4 indoor) plus children's pool; tennis courts; squash court; minigolf; volleyball; basketball; bowling; billiards; health club, spa, and thalassotherapy; watersports; bike rental; children's program; game room; concierge; tour arrangements; car-rental desk; airport transport arrangements; conference facilities; salon; room service 7am–noon; babysitting; laundry service; dry cleaning; Internet access; rooms for those w/limited mobility. *In room:* A/C, TV, minibar, fridge, hair dryer.

MODERATE

Xenia-Helios ℛ *Value* We single out the Xenia-Helios because here you can save a bit of money and feel you're contributing to the future of young Greeks. It's one of three such hotels run by the Greek Ministry of Tourism to train young people for careers in the hotel world. (Another is outside Athens, the other outside Thessaloniki.) The physical accommodations may not be quite as glitzy as some of the other beach resorts, but they're certainly first class and the service is especially friendly. The beach here is also especially lovely, and children will enjoy Water City, the water park just a mile or so east of the hotel.

Kokkini Hani, 71500 Iraklion. ℂ **2810/761-502.** Fax 2810/418-363. 108 units. High season 95€ ($124) double; low season 70€ ($91) double. All rates include half-board plan. AE, MC, V. Closed Oct–May. Buses every half-hour to Iraklion or points east. About 13km (8 miles) east of Iraklion. **Amenities:** Restaurant; bar; pool; tennis courts; watersports equipment; conference facilities; hair salon. *In room:* A/C.

WHERE TO DINE

Avoid eating a meal at either Fountain Square or Liberty Square (Plateia Eleftheria) unless you want the experience of being at the center of activity—the food at those areas' establishments is, to put it mildly, nothing special. Save these spots for a coffee or beer break.

EXPENSIVE

Brillant Gourmet Restaurant ℛℛ INTERNATIONAL Since opening in 2007, this restaurant has emerged as offering the finest dining experience in Iraklion. I put it that way because there is no denying that the decor of the dining room contributes greatly to the occasion. The decor is perhaps best described as "postmodern," with elements of Art Deco and "industrialism" making for an eye-catching environment. But this would mean nothing if it were not matched by the menu and service, which are in fact of the highest quality. The ingredients are basically Greek—even local Cretan—but prepared in combinations that make for some unexpected treats: Appetizers include a tomato-brie puff pie and goat cheese with prosciutto, while entrees include tender filets of beef or pork, as well as chicken and fish dishes. The basic menu changes twice a year and specials are offered most nights. The wine list is equally special—trust the waiter to suggest a wine appropriate for your entree and you may be surprised at how good, say, one of the better Cretan wines can be. It is not cheap— a couple should be prepared to spend between 90€ and 130€ ($117–$169) depending on the number of courses and the choice of wine.

15 Epimenidou. © 2810/334-959. Adjacent to the Lato Boutique Hotel. Reservations recommended for dinner in high season. Appetizers 8€–13€ ($11–$17); main courses 18€–25€ ($24–$33). Lobster dishes extra. AE, DC, MC, V. Daily throughout the year 7:30pm–12:30am. Lato Hotel desk can help with parking but best is just to walk here.

Loukoulos *ITALIAN/GREEK* Here's another restaurant that has gained a stylish reputation. It's in the very heart of the city on a back street, crammed into a tiny patio with fanciful umbrellas shading the tables. The chairs are comfortable, the table settings lovely, and the selection of *mezedes* (appetizers) varied. The creative Italian menu features lots of pasta dishes, such as a delicious rigatoni with a broccoli-and-Roquefort cream sauce. Treat yourself at least once to Iraklion's "in" place.

5 Korai (1 street behind Daedalou). © 2810/224-435. Reservations recommended for dinner in high season. Main courses 6€–20€ ($7.80–$26); fixed-price lunch about 16€ ($21). AE, DC, V. Mon–Sat noon–1am; Sun 6:30pm–midnight.

MODERATE

Giovanni GREEK A taverna with some pretensions to chic, this appeals to a slightly younger, more casual set than its neighbor, Loukoulos (see above). Its name may be Italian, but its fare is traditional Greek. House specialties include shrimp in tomato sauce with cheese, baked eggplant with tomato sauce, and *kokhoretsi* (a sort of oversize sausage made from lamb innards; much better than it may sound)—all quite tasty.

12 Korai (1 street behind Daedalou). © 2810/246-338. Main courses 5€–18€ ($6.50–$24). AE, MC, V. Mon–Sat 12:30pm–2am; Sun 5pm–1:30am.

Pantheon *Moments* GREEK Anyone who spends more than a few days in Iraklion should take at least one meal in "Dirty Alley," where this restaurant is a longtime favorite. Although it lost its rough-hewn atmosphere long ago, Dirty Alley still seems an indigenous locale. The menu at Pantheon (much the same as the menus at the other Dirty Alley places) offers taverna standards—meat stews; chunks of meat, chicken, or fish in tasty sauces; and vegetables such as okra, zucchini, or stuffed tomatoes. These places are not especially cheap—the proprietors know to charge for the atmosphere—but the food's tasty. And if you sit in the Pantheon, on the corner of the market street, you'll get a choice view of the scene outside.

2 Theodosaki ("Dirty Alley," connecting the market street and Evans). © 2810/241-652. Main courses 5€–16€ ($6.50–$21). No credit cards. Mon–Sat 11am–11pm.

INEXPENSIVE

Ionia GREEK Undistinguished as it now appears, this is in some respects the Nestor of Iraklion's restaurants. Founded in 1923, Ionia has served generations of Cretans as well as all the early archaeologists. Although it's greatly reduced in size, the food is as good as ever, and the staff encourages foreigners to step over to the kitchen area and select from the warming pans. You may find more refined food and fancier service elsewhere on Crete, but you won't taste heartier dishes than the Ionia's green beans in olive oil or lamb joints in sauce. For a cheap meal, I recommend a visit to what is clearly a fading tradition.

3 Evans (just to the left of the market street). © 2810/282-313. Main courses 4€–12€ ($5.20–$16). MC, V. Mon–Fri 8am–10:30pm; Sat 8am–4pm.

Ippocampus SEAFOOD/GREEK   This is an institution among locals, who line up for a typical Cretan meal solely of appetizers. The zucchini slices, dipped in batter and deep-fried, are fabulous. A plate of tomatoes and cukes, another of sliced fried potatoes, small fish, perhaps fried squid—that's it. A couple could assemble a meal for as little as 20€ ($26)—but go early. Ippocampus is down along the coast road. You can sit indoors or on the sidewalk, a bargain either way.

3 Mitsotaki (along the waterfront to left of traffic circle as you come down 25 Avgusto). © 2810/282-081. Main courses 2.50€–8€ ($3.25–$10). No credit cards. Mon–Fri 1–3:30pm and 7pm–midnight.

IRAKLION AFTER DARK

To spend an evening the way most Iraklians do, stroll and then sit in a cafe and watch others stroll by. The prime locations for the latter have been Plateia Eleftheria (Liberty Sq.) or Fountain Square, but the crowded atmosphere of these places—and some overly aggressive waiters—has considerably reduced their charm.

For a more relaxed atmosphere, go to **Marina Cafe** at the old harbor (directly across from the restored Venetian arsenali). For as little as 2€ ($2.60) for a coffee or as much as 9€ ($12) for an alcoholic drink, you can enjoy the breeze as you contemplate the illuminated Venetian fort, which looks much like a stage set.

An alternative is **Four Lions Roof-Garden Cafe** (© 2810/222-333); enter through an interior staircase in the shopping arcade on Fountain Square. It attracts younger Iraklians, but travelers are welcome. The background music is usually Greek. You get to sit above the crowded crossroads and, with no cover or minimum, enjoy anything from a coffee (2€/$2.60) or ice cream (from 3€/$3.90) to an alcoholic drink (from 4€/$5.20).

There is no end to the number of **bars** and **discos** featuring everything from international rock 'n' roll to Greek pop music, although they come and go from year to year to reflect the latest fads. **Disco Athina,** 9 Ikarou, just outside the wall on the way to the airport, is an old favorite with the young; or try any of the clubs along Epimenidou—the **Veneto Bar, Club Itan,** or **Gozo.**

Most Class A hotels now host a **Cretan Night,** when performers dance and play **traditional music.** For more of the same, take a taxi to either **Aposperides,** out on the road toward Knossos, or **Sordina,** about 5km (3 miles) to the southwest of town.

During the summer, Iraklion's **arts festival** (though hardly competitive with the major festivals of Europe) brings in world-class performers (ballet companies, pianists, and others), but mostly featured are ancient and medieval-Renaissance Greek dramas, Greek-themed dance, or traditional and modern Greek music. Many performances take place outdoors in one of three venues: on the roof of the **Koules** (the Venetian fort in the harbor), **Kazantzakis Garden Theater,** or **Hadzidaksis Theater.** Ticket prices vary from year to year and for individual events but are well below what you'd pay at such cultural events elsewhere. Maybe you didn't come to Crete expecting to hear Vivaldi, but why not enjoy it while you're here? The festival begins in late June and ends in mid-September.

SIDE TRIPS FROM IRAKLION

Travel agencies arrange excursions setting out from Iraklion to virtually every point of interest on Crete, such as **Samaria Gorge** in the far southwest (p. 352). In that sense, Iraklion can be used as the home base for all your touring on Crete. If you have only 1 extra day on Crete, I recommend the following trip.

GORTYNA, PHAESTOS, AYIA TRIADHA & MATALA 🏕🏕

If you have an interest in history and archaeology, and you've already seen Knossos and Iraklion's museum, this is the trip to make. The distance isn't that great—a round-trip of about 165km (100 miles)—but you'd want a full day to take it all in. A taxi or guided tour is advisable if you haven't rented a car. Bus schedules won't allow you to fit in all the stops. (You can, of course, stay at one of the hotels on the south coast, but they're usually booked long in advance of high season.)

The road south takes you up and across the **mountainous spine** of central Crete. At about the 25th mile, you'll leave behind the **Sea of Crete** (to the north) and see the **Libyan Sea** to the south. You then descend onto the **Messara,** the largest plain on Crete (about 32km/20 miles×5km/3 miles) and a major agricultural center. At about 45km (28 miles), you'll see on your right the **remains of Gortyna;** many more remnants lie scattered in the fields off to the left. Gortyna (or Gortyn or Gortys) first emerged as a center of the Dorian Greeks who moved to Crete after the end of the Minoan civilization. By 500 B.C., they had advanced enough to inscribe a code of law into stone. The stones were found in the late 19th century and reassembled here, where you can see this unique—and to scholars, invaluable—document testifying to the legal and social arrangements of this society.

Then, after the Romans took over Crete (67 B.C.), Gortyna enjoyed yet another period of glory when it served as the capital of Roman Crete and Cyrenaica (Libya). Roman structures—temples, a stadium, and more—litter the fields to the left. On the right, along with the **Code of Gortyna** 🏕, you'll see a small **Hellenistic Odeon,** or theater, as well as the remains of the **Basilica of Ayios Titos** (admission 5€/$6.50; daily 8am–7pm high season; reduced hours off season). Paul commissioned Titos (Titus) to lead the first Christians on Crete. The church, begun in the 6th century, was later greatly enlarged.

Proceed down the road another 15km (10 miles), turn left at the sign, and ascend to the ridge where the **palace of Phaestos** 🏕🏕 sits in all its splendor. (Admission is 6€/$7.80; daily 8am–7pm high season; reduced hours off season.) Scholars consider this the second-most powerful Minoan center; many visitors appreciate its attractive setting on a prow of land that seems to float between the plain and the sky. Italians began to excavate Phaestos soon after Evans began at Knossos, but they decided to leave the remains much as they found them. The **ceremonial staircase** is as awesome as it must have been to the ancients, while the **great court** remains one of the most resonant public spaces anywhere.

Leaving Phaestos, continue down the main road 4km (2½ miles) and turn left onto a side road. Park here and make your way to pay your respects to a Minoan minipalace complex known as **Ayia Triadha.** To this day, scholars aren't certain exactly what it was—something between a satellite of Phaestos and a semi-independent palace. Several of the most impressive artifacts in the Iraklion Museum, including the painted sarcophagus (on the second floor), were found here.

Back on the road, follow the signs to **Kamilari** and then **Pitsidia.** Now you've earned your rest and swim, and at no ordinary place: the nearby **beach at Matala** 🏕.

It's a small cove enclosed by bluffs of age-old packed earth. Explorers found **chambers,** some complete with bunk beds, that probably date back to the Romans (most likely no earlier than A.D. 500). Cretans used them as summer homes, the German soldiers used them as storerooms during World War II, and hippies took over them in the late 1960s. You can visit them during the day; otherwise, they are off-limits. Matala has become one more overcrowded beach in peak season, so after a dip and some refreshment, make your way back to Iraklion (straight up via **Mires,** so you avoid the turnoff back to Ayia Triadha and Phaestos).

LASITHI PLAIN 🦊

Here's an excursion that combines some spectacular scenery, a major mythological site, and an extraordinary view on a windy day! Long promoted as "the plain of 10,000 windmills," alas, the Lasithi Plain can no longer really boast of this: The many hundreds if not thousands of white-sailcloth–vaned windmills have largely been replaced by gasoline-powered generator windmills (and wooden or metal vanes) but it is still an impressive sight as you come over the ridge to see these windmills turning. What they are doing is pumping water to irrigate the crops that fill the entire plain: no buildings are allowed on this large plateau (some 40 sq. km/15 sq. miles) because its rich alluvial soil (washed down from the surrounding mountains) is ideal for cultivating potatoes and other crops. Having come this far—the plain is some 35 miles from Iraklion—you must go the next 10 miles to visit one of the major mythological sites of all Greece: the Dhiktaion Cave, regarded since ancient times as the birthplace of Zeus and the cave where he was hidden so that his father, Cronus, could not devour him. Driving around the outer edge of the plain (via Tzermiadhes, Drasi, Ayios Constantinos, and Ayios Georgiios) you come to the village of Psykhro on the slopes on the southern edge of the plain. Psykhro and the cave are geared for tourists who come from all over the world. After you reach the tourist pavilion, you still face a relatively steep climb to the cave; you are advised to take on one of the guides because the descent into the cave can be slippery and tricky (it's best to wear rubber-soled, sturdy footwear) and you will not know what you are looking at. Although long known as the cave associated with Zeus—it appears in numerous ancient myths and texts—it was not excavated until 1900 and successive "digs" in the decades since have turned up countless artifacts confirming that it was visited as a sacred shrine for many centuries. It should be admitted that other caves on Crete and elsewhere claim the honor of Zeus' birthplace but the Dhiktaion Cave seems to have won out, and having visited it, you can claim to have been at one of the more storied sites of the ancient world.

Lasithi Platin can also be visited as a side trip from Ayios Nikolaos (see later in this chapter); you head back westward on the old road to Iraklion and at about 8km (5 miles) turn left (signed Drasi) and climb another 25km (15 miles) up to the plain.

2 Chania (Hania/Xania/Canea) 🦊🦊

150km (95 miles) W of Iraklion

Until the 1980s, Chania was one of the best-kept secrets of the Mediterranean: a delightful provincial town nestled between mountains and sea, a labyrinth of atmospheric streets and structures from its Venetian-Turkish era. Since then, tourists have flocked here and there's hardly a square inch of the Old Town that's not dedicated to satisfying them. Chania was heavily bombed during World War II; ironically, some of its unique atmosphere is due to still-unreconstructed buildings that are now used as shops and restaurants.

What's amazing is how much of Chania's charm has persisted since the Venetians and Turks effectively stamped the old town in their own images between 1210 and 1898. Try to visit any time except July and August; whenever you come, dare to strike out on your own and see the old Chania.

ESSENTIALS

GETTING THERE   By Plane   Olympic Airways offers at least three flights daily to and from Athens in high season. (Flight time is about 50 min.) Flights to Chania from other points in Greece go through Athens. **Aegean Airlines** also offers a several flights daily to and from Athens. See "Getting There" in the section on Iraklion, earlier in this chapter, for contact information. The airport is located 15km (10 miles) out of town on the Akrotiri. Public buses meet all flights except the last one at night, but almost everyone takes a taxi (about 18€/$25).

By Boat   One ship makes the 10-hour trip daily between Piraeus and Chania, usually leaving early in the evening (www.ferries.gr). But as of 2007, during the tourist season **Hellenic Seaways** runs a once-daily high-speed catamaran between Piraeus and Chania that cuts the trip down to about 5 hours (www.greekislands.gr). All ships arrive at and depart from Soudha, a 20-minute bus ride from the stop outside the municipal market. Many travel agents around town sell tickets. In high season, if you're traveling with a car, make reservations in advance, or check with the **Paleologos Agency** (www.ferries.gr).

By Bus   Buses run almost hourly from early in the morning until about 10:30pm, depending on the season, connecting Chania to Rethymnon and Iraklion. There are less frequent, and often inconveniently timed, buses between destinations in western Crete. The main **bus station** to points all over Crete is at 25 Kidonias (© **28210/93-306**).

By Car   All the usual agencies can be found in the center of town, but we've always had reliable dealings with **Europrent** at 87 Halidon (© **28210/27-810;** www.europrent.gr).

VISITOR INFORMATION   The official Tourist Information office is at 40 Kriari, off 1866 Square (© **28210/92-943**) but it keeps unreliable hours. You're better off turning to private travel agencies. On the scene, I recommend **Lissos Travel,** Plateia 1866 (© **28210/93-917;** fax 28210/95-930); **Diktynna Travel,** 6 Archontaki (© **28210/43-930;** www.diktynna-travel.gr); from your home abroad, try **Crete Travel** in the nearby village of Monoho (© **28250/32-690;** www.cretetravel.com). A useful source of insider's information is **The Bazaar,** 46 Daskaloyiannis, on the main street down to the new harbor (to the right of the Municipal Market). This shop sells used foreign-language books and assorted "stuff." Owned and staffed by non-Greeks, it maintains a listing of all kinds of helpful services.

GETTING AROUND   You can walk to most tourist destinations in Chania. Public buses go to nearby points and to all the major destinations in western Crete. If you

---

A Taxi Tip

To get a taxi driver who is accustomed to dealing with English-speakers, call **Andreas** at © **28210/50-821;** you can also try © **69450/365-799** (his mobile phone number). With Andreas, you get an informative guide as well as a driver.

Chania

ATTRACTIONS ●
Archaeological Museum **5**
Mosque of Djamissis **8**
Naval Museum **1**
Orthodox Cathedral **6**

ACCOMMODATIONS ■
Casa Delfino **4**
Hotel Palazzo **2**
Hotel Porto Veneziano **13**
Palazzo di Pietro **9**

DINING ◆
Amphora Restaurant **3**
Antigone Restaurant **12**
Enomayirio **10**
Psitopoleio **11**
Remezzo Cafe **7**
The Well of the Turk **14**

Information ⓘ
Post Office ⊠
OTE ☎

> ### Finds Two Eco-Getaways
>
> I am pleased to be able to call attention to two new possibilities on Crete that should appeal to those who are into ecotourism and are also willing to rough it a bit. One is **Milia** (www.milia.gr), a long-abandoned village in the mountains of western Crete that has been converted into a retreat for those willing to stay in old stone houses, do without modern hotel facilities (although there is electricity), and eat a limited but delicious natural diet. It is operated by native Cretans and you are left pretty much on your own to enjoy the wild natural setting. The other, called **Footscapes** (www.footscapesofcrete.com), is in the hills just south of Rethymnon and comprises three small modern villas built by an English couple, the Marsdens; they will take you on various hikes and help you with other interests (bird-watching, and so forth) Both places require a vehicle to reach. Milia is a solid 2-hour drive from Chania and requires a rental car and a willingness to travel the last miles up a rather hairy dirt road; once there, you would probably want to take all your meals at the simple dining room. Footscapes is only a 20-minute drive from Rethymnon and although the Mardens advise you how to get to their place by combinations of public transport and taxi, you would probably want to rent a car to be able to get to the nearby villages to either buy food to cook or eat out. For those wavering between the two, note that at Milia you have no view but you step out of your cabin into a wooded area bursting with wildlife; at Footscapes you have to hike to get into the woods but you sit on a ridge with a 360-degree view.

want to explore the countryside or more remote parts of western Crete, I recommend that you rent a car to make the best use of your time.

FAST FACTS   Banks in the new city have ATMs. For the **tourist police,** dial ⓒ **171.** The **hospital** (ⓒ **28210/27-231**) is on Venizelou in the Halepa quarter. There are now several **Internet** cafes: I like the Vranas Studios Cafe, behind the cathedral and at the corner of Aghion Deka, or Cafe Santé (on the second floor at the far west corner of the old harbor). There are also several **laundromats** in the old town, including the ones at 38 Karoli and Dimitriou or 38 Kanevero. In the new town, Speedy Laundry at 17 Kordiki, is on the corner of Koroneou, a block west of Plateia 1866. If you prefer to leave your laundry off, you can't beat Oscar at 1 Kanevro at the corner of the harbor square. For **luggage storage,** try the KTEL bus station on Kidonias. The **post office** is at 6 Peridou (an extension of Plastira that leads directly away for the municipal market); hours are Monday through Friday from 8am to 8pm, Saturday from 8am to noon. The **telephone office (OTE),** is on Tzanakaki (leading diagonally way from the municipal market); it is open daily from 7:30am to 11:30pm. **Foreign-language publications** are available at 8 Skalidi (main street heading west at top of Halidon).

WHAT TO SEE & DO

In summer, several small **excursion ships** offer 3- to 5-hour trips to the waters and islets off Chania. These trips depart from the old and new harbors and include stops for swimming at one or another of the islets; some provide free snorkeling gear. On the glass-bottomed *Evangelos,* you can see underwater life. The cost is about 25€ ($33) adults, free for children under 12.

Archaeological Museum Ⓕ   Even short-term visitors should stop here, if only for a half-hour's walk-through. The museum, housed in the 16th-century Venetian Catholic Church of St. Francis, was carefully restored in the early 1980s and gives a fascinating glimpse of the different cultures that have played out on Crete, from the Neolithic through the Minoan and on to the Roman and early Christian. You'll come away with a sense of how typical people of these periods lived, as opposed to the elite classes featured in so many museums.

30 Halidon. Ⓒ **28210/90-334.** http://odysseus.culture.gr. Admission 5€ ($6.50). Mon 12:30–7pm; Tues–Sat 8am–7pm; Sun 8am–2:30pm. No parking.

A WALK AROUND OLD CHANIA

Start at **Plateia Venizelou,** the large clearing at the far curve of the old harbor—now distinguished by its marble fountain. Head along the east side to see the prominent domed **Mosque of Djamissis** (or of Hassan Pasha), erected soon after the Turks conquered Chania in 1645. Proceeding around the **waterfront** toward the **new harbor,** you'll come to what remains of the great **arsenali,** where the Venetians made and repaired ships; exhibitions are sometimes held inside. Go to the far end of this inner harbor and if you are lucky (due to unpredictable hours) you can enter the old arsenal and see the massive replica of a **Minoan ship** that was made to participate in the Athens Olympics of 2004; they actually got a crew of about 24 to row it (stage by stage) to Piraeus but the authorities deemed it not authentic and it never got much recognition. In any case, you can walk out along the breakwater to the 19th-century lighthouse (thoroughly restored in 2006). Go back to the far corner of the long set of arsenali and Arnoleon, where you turn inland and then proceed up Daskaloyiannis; on the left you'll come to **Plateia 1821** and the **Orthodox Church of St. Nicholas.** Begun as a Venetian Catholic monastery, it was converted by the Turks into a mosque—thus its campanile and minaret! (It has also been undergoing a major restoration which should be finished by 2008.) The square is a pleasant place to sit and have a cool drink. Go next to Tsouderon, where you turn right and (passing another minaret) arrive at the back steps of the great **municipal market** (ca. 1911)—worth wandering through, although, and alas, it too is being taken over by touristic shops.

If you exit at the opposite end of your entrance, you'll emerge at the edge of the **new town.** Go right along Hadzimikhali Giannari until you come to the top of **Halidon,** the main tourist-shopping street. The stylish **Municipal Art Gallery,** at no. 98, sits at the top right side (hours posted). As you continue to make your way, you'll pass on the right the famous **Skridlof,** with its leather workers; the **Orthodox Cathedral** or the Church of the Three Martyrs, from the 1860s; and on the left the **Archaeological Museum** (see earlier in this chapter).

As you come back to the edge of Plateia Venizelou, turn left one street before the harbor onto **Zambeliou.** Proceed along this street; you can then turn left onto any of the side streets and explore the **old quarter** (now, alas, overwhelmed by modern tourist enterprises). If you turn up at Kondilaki, follow the signs at the right alley for the **synagogue;** built in the 17th century and destroyed in World War II, it has now been beautifully restored and is well worth a visit. (Check www.etz-hayyim-hania.org to learn about the history and activities of the synagogue.) Continue along Zambeliou, but take a slight detour to Moskhou to view **Renieri Gate** from 1608. On Zambeliou again, you'll ascend a bit until you come to **Theotokopouli;** turn right here to enjoy the architecture and shops of this Venetian-style street as you make your way down to the sea.

Moments Coasting Down a Mountain

Everyone with time and an interest in experiencing the different facets of
Crete, should spend at least a day in the mountainous interior. Excursions to the
Lasithi Plain from Iraklion and the Amari Valley from Rethymnon are described
respectively on p. 341 and 360. For arranging day trips from Chania, customized
or in groups, I recommend contacting Maria Mylonaki of **Diktynna Travel**
(6 Archontaki; © **28210/43-930;** www.diktynna-travel.gr) She'll come to your
hotel the night before to map out plans and costs; her English is excellent. One
possibility is a bike trip for which you don't have to be in especially great shape.
The bikes will accompany you in a van on a narrow, winding, 45-minute uphill
drive to the mountain village of Zourva for a delicious, traditional Greek lunch
(lamb chops and Greek salad) at a taverna called Emilia's. From here you can
bike some 15 spectacular kilometers (10 miles) downhill, virtually without peddling once. Note, however, that this doesn't mean you don't have to exert
extreme caution and control on winding roads that lack shoulders and can
have potholes!

At the end of the street, on the right, the recently restored **Church of San Salva-
tore** was converted into a fine little museum of Byzantine and post-Byzantine art
(irregular hours; admission 2€/$2.60 (www.culture.gr). After the museum, you'll be
just outside the harbor; turn right and pass below the walls of the **Firkas,** the name
given to the fort that was a focal point in Crete's struggle for independence at the turn
of the 20th century. If you're into naval history, the **Naval Museum** (© **28210/
26-437**) here has some interesting displays and artifacts (daily 10am–4pm; admission
5€/$6.50); or you can take a seat for welcome refreshment at one of the cafes on the
slope before the museum entrance.

SHOPPING
Jewelers, leather-goods shops, and souvenir stores are everywhere—but it's hard to
find that very special item that's both tasteful and distinctively Cretan. Below, I point
out things you will not find anywhere else. Unless otherwise noted, the following
shops are open daily.

Carmela, at 7 Anghelou, the narrow street across from the Naval Museum's
entrance (© **28210/90-487**), has some of the finest ceramics, jewelry, and works of
art in Crete—all original, but inspired by ancient works of art and even employing
some of the old techniques.

Step into **Cretan Rugs and Blankets,** 3 Anghelou (© **28210/98-571**), to experience a realm not found anywhere else on Crete. It's an old Venetian structure filled
with gorgeously colored rugs, blankets, and kilims. Prices range from 100€ to 2,000€
($130–$2,600). Or visit **Roka Carpets,** 61 Zambeliou (© **28210/74-736**), where
you can watch a traditional weaver at his trade. The carpets come in patterns, colors,
and sizes to suit every taste; prices start at 15€ ($20). These are not artsy textiles, but
traditional Cretan weaving.

Although **Khalki,** 75 Zambeliou, near the far end of the street (© **28210/75-379**),
is one of many little shops that sell ceramics along with other trinkets and souvenirs.
It carries the work of several local and Greek ceramicists who draw on traditional

motifs and colors. For a more sophisticated selection of Greek handicrafts, try **Mitos** at 44 Halidon (opposite the Orthodox Cathedral; ℭ **28210/88-862**). For a varied selection by amateur Cretan artisans, visit the **Local Artistic Handicrafts Association** (ℭ **28210/41-885**), located just where the new harbor turns the corner into the old harbor.

Finally, for a truly different souvenir or gift, try **Orphanos,** 24 Tsopuderon (ℭ **28210/48-285**), by the stairs at the rear of the public market, with its unexpected collection of dolls and marionettes.

WHERE TO STAY
EXPENSIVE

Casa Delfino 🏵🏵   When did you last have the chance to stay in a 17th-century Venetian mansion, with fresh orange juice for breakfast? Its quiet neighborhood (also dating from the 1600s) is conveniently located a block from the harbor. The owners transformed the stately house into stylish independent suites and studios, whose taste-fully decorated rooms are among the most elegant you will find on Crete. All have modern bathrooms (nine with Jacuzzi), and three have kitchenettes. One potential drawback: Several rooms have beds on a second level—little more than sleeping lofts—that require you to go up and down stairs to get to the bathroom. (You can request other rooms.) And except for sitting in the courtyard, there's no public area in which to relax. The reception desk may be informal but the friendly staff will provide a wide range of services, from airport transport to tour arrangements.

8 Theofanous, 73100 Chania, Crete. ℭ 28210/87-400. Fax 28210/96-500. www.casadelfino.com. 22 units. High sea-son 200€–330€ ($260–$429) double; low season 150€–250€ ($195–$325) double. AE, MC, V. Free parking nearby. Open year-round (with central heating). **Amenities:** Courtyard breakfast area; small bar; Jacuzzi; tour desk; car-rental desk; courtesy car or airport pickup arranged; conference facilities for 24; Internet access; 24-hr. room service; babysit-ting; laundry service; dry cleaning. In room: A/C, TV, minibar, hair dryer, safe.

Creta Paradise Beach Resort Hotel 🏵🏵 *(Kids)*   This luxurious resort is a perfect place to take in the sun on a beach, or to take a tour of western Crete. The full-serv-ice resort offers minigolf, volleyball, water polo, billiards, table tennis, and lessons in shooting and archery. Guests can take part in weekly "theme nights" that feature Greek music and dancing. Families with young children will take delight in the small petting zoo as well as an active children's program. Guest rooms are a bit severe for Americans accustomed to upholstered luxury (don't expect overstuffed beds), but everything is tasteful and comfortable, and bathrooms are up-to-date. The only down-side: The hotel sometimes draws large international conferences with its high-tech facilities. Beautifully landscaped in the style of a Mediterranean villa, the resort lives up to its image. A special treat: Turtles come onto the hotel's beach to lay their eggs from May to June; these hatch in late August.

Gerani Beach, P.O. Box 89, 73100 Hania (14km/9 miles) west of Chania on coast road. ℭ 28210/61-315. Fax 28210/61-134. www.cretaparadise.gr. 230 units. High season 220€–275€ ($286–$358) double; low season 120€–160€ ($156–$208) double. Rates include buffet breakfast. Considerably lower rates for tour groups include half-board plan (breakfast and dinner). AE, DC, MC, V. Ample parking. Taxi or bus to Chania. **Amenities:** Restaurant; poolside taverna; 2 bars; 2 pools; 2 children's pools; tennis court; fully equipped gym w/sauna; aerobics; extensive watersports equipment rentals; children's program; game room (or video arcade); concierge; tour desk; car-rental desk; airport pickup arranged; secretarial services; shopping arcade; salon; 24-hr. room service; babysitting; laundry service; dry cleaning; nonsmoking rooms. In room: A/C, TV, minibar, fridge on request, hair dryer, safe.

MODERATE

Doma ★★ Long regarded as one of the most distinctive hotels on Crete, the neo-classical, turn-of-the-century Doma was once a fine mansion, former home of the British consulate. Authentic Cretan heirlooms and historical pictures decorate its public areas. Bedrooms and bathrooms are not especially large but are perfectly adequate. The four suites are roomier. All the rooms are plainly decorated—even a bit severe, with muted wall colors and rather old-fashioned furniture. Front rooms have great views of the sea but also the sounds of passing traffic, even though the hotel is far from the noisy town center. The third-story dining room offers fresh breezes and a superb view of Old Chania; breakfast here includes several homemade delights, while the evening dinner features Cretan specialties. An elevator provides access for those who can't take stairs. Among the hotel's special features is a museum-quality display of headdresses from all over the world. The Doma is not for those seeking luxury, but it appeals to travelers who appreciate a discreet old-world atmosphere.

24 Venizelou, 73100 Chania, Crete. ✆ **28210/51-772**. Fax 28210/41-578. www.hotel-doma.gr. 25 units, all with private bathroom (22 with shower only). 130€ ($169) double; 190€–280€ ($247–$364) suite. Rates include buffet breakfast. Special rates for more than 2 persons in suite; reduced rates for longer stays. AE, MC, V. Closed Nov–Mar. Free parking on nearby streets. Bus to Halepa or Chania center; can be reached on foot. 3km (2 miles) from the town center along the lower coastal road. **Amenities:** Restaurant; bar; concierge; tours and car rentals arranged; airport pickup arranged; laundry service; dry cleaning; nonsmoking rooms. *In room:* A/C, TV, hair dryer.

Hotel Palazzo di Pietro ★ Although I have been aware of this small hotel for some time, I never quite got around to checking it out. But several Frommer's fans have so praised it that now I have done so—and am pleased to recommend it. The seven suites and apartments distinguish themselves with kitchenettes—perfect for those who like to make breakfast, perhaps a light lunch, or even return home after a full day for a light supper. Three rooms have balconies, and one is accessible to those with disabilities. The building originally belonged to the aristocratic Venetian Renieri family and, after years of neglect, was restored with a concern for authentic detail; the furnishings also give you a sense that you are in an old mansion. A roof garden terrace offers superb views as well as a place to enjoy your own meals. Some of the owner/family speak English and will graciously help you with all your needs—including laundry service, car rentals, and tours. On a quiet alleyway, it has the minor downside of being close to the cathedral, whose bells strike until midnight and again at 6am, but these are heard all over town anyhow. Also, the only guaranteed parking is a 10-minute walk to the lot at the far end of the new harbor—but at least it's guaranteed and free. A final plus: A daughter of the family is an internationally commissioned painter of traditional icons and works away in her studio off the entryway.

13 Ayiou Dheka, 73100 Chania, Crete. ✆ **28210/20-410**. www.palazzodipietro.com. 7 units, 1 with shower, others with bathtubs and hand-held shower units. High season 120€–185€ ($156–$241) double; low season 90€–150€ ($117–$195) double. MC, V. Parking away. Closed Nov–Mar. Within easy walking distance of all of Chania. **Amenities:** Kitchenette. *In room:* A/C, TV, fridge, safe.

Hotel Porto Veneziano ★ Thanks to the owner/manager "on the scene," this hotel combines the best of old-fashioned Greek hospitality with good, modern service. As a member of the Best Western chain, it has to maintain certain standards. The tasteful bedrooms (standard international style) are relatively large; the bathrooms are modern. Many rooms have a fine view of the harbor. (Be warned—that can also mean harbor noise early in the morning!) Six suites offer even more space. Located at the far end of the so-called Old Harbor (follow the walkway from the main harbor all the way around to the east, or right), this hotel offers proximity to the town center with a sense that you're in old Chania. There are many restaurants within a few yards of the hotel. Refreshments from the hotel's own Cafe Veneto may be enjoyed in the garden or at the front overlooking the harbor. The desk personnel are genuinely hospitable and will make tour arrangements.

Akti Enosseos, 73100 Chania, Crete. (C) **28210/27-100.** Fax 28210/27-105. www.portoveneziano.gr. 57 units, all with private bathroom (48 with shower only). High season 140€ ($182) double; low season 110€ ($143) double. Rates include buffet breakfast. AE, DC, MC, V. Free parking nearby. Within walking distance of everything. **Amenities:** Breakfast room; cafe-bar; concierge; tours and car rentals arranged; airport pickup arranged; room service 7am–noon; babysitting; laundry service; dry cleaning. *In room:* A/C, TV, minibar, hair dryer.

INEXPENSIVE

Hotel Palazzo   This Venetian town house, now a handsome little hotel, delivers the feeling of old Crete without skimping on amenities. A fridge in every room, a TV in the bar, and a roof garden with a spectacular view of the mountains and sea make this a comfortable hotel. Nothing fancy about the rooms (furnishings are traditional Cretan rustic, knotty-pine style), but they are good-size; those at the front have balconies. The location is generally quiet, and if occasionally the still night air is broken by rowdy youths (true of all Greek cities), that seems a small price to pay for staying on Theotokopouli—the closest you may come to living on a Venetian canal. The owners speak English and will graciously help you with all your needs—including laundry service, car rentals, and tours. You can also drive up the street to unload and load but must park below.

54 Theotokopouli, 73100 Chania, Crete. (C) **28210/93-227.** www.palazzohotel.gr. 11 units, some with shower, some with tub. High season 85€ ($111) double; low season 60€ ($78) double. Rates include breakfast. MC, V. Ample parking 50m (114 ft.) away. Closed Nov–Mar (but will open for special groups). Within easy walking distance of all of Chania. Around the corner from the west arm of harbor. **Amenities:** Bar; car rentals arranged; laundry service. *In room:* A/C, TV, fridge, safe.

WHERE TO DINE

Chania offers a wide variety of dining experiences and all I can do is single out a few of them. But you will discover others—such as the **Taman** at 49 Zambeliou (the main street behind the Old Harbor), many people's favorite for reliable food and reasonable prices. Don't be afraid to take a chance here and there.

EXPENSIVE

Nykterida ★★ GREEK   Here is another of those restaurants where the location is a major part of the dining experience. It's on a high point with spectacular nighttime views of Chania and Soudha Bay—but be sure to insist on a table with that view—so save it for when you can dine outdoors on a summer evening. An institution in Chania since 1933, its founder claims to have taught Anthony Quinn the steps he danced in *Zorba*. The cuisine is traditional Cretan-Greek, but many of the dishes have an extra something. For an appetizer, try the *kalazounia* (cheese pie speckled with spinach) or the special *dolmades* (squash blossoms stuffed with spiced rice and served with yogurt). Any of the main courses will be well-done, from the basic steak filet to the chicken with okra. Complimentary *tsoukoudia* (a potent Cretan liquor) is served at the end of the meal. Traditional Cretan music is played on Monday, Thursday, and Friday evenings until the end of October.

Korakies, Crete. ⓒ **28210/64-215.** www.nykterida.gr. Reservations recommended for parties of 7 or more. Main courses 6€–20€ ($7.80–$26). MC, V. Mon–Sat 6pm–1am. Parking on-site. Open year-round. Taxi or car required. About 6.4km (4 miles) from town on road to airport; left turn opposite NAMFI Officers Club.

MODERATE

Amphora Restaurant GREEK   At some point, almost everyone who spends any time in Chania will want to eat a meal right on the old harbor. Frankly, most of the restaurants there are undistinguished at best, but this old favorite still offers a decent meal at a reasonable price. As with any Greek restaurant, if you order the lobster or steak, you'll pay a hefty price, but you can assemble a good meal here at modest prices. To start, try the aubergine croquettes and the specialty of the house, a lemony fish soup. The restaurant belongs to the adjacent Amphora Hotel (Category A) and this is probably what has maintained its food and friendly service.

49 Akti Koundouriotou. ⓒ **28210/93-224.** Fax 28210/93-226. Main courses 5€–18€ ($6.50–$24). AE, MC, V. Daily 11:30am–midnight. Closed Oct–Apr. Near the far right, western, curve of the harbor.

Antigone Restaurant ⓐ GREEK/SEAFOOD   One of the many better-than-average restaurants along the new harbor. Start off here with the unusual dip made of limpets and mussels, then move on to a specialty such as stuffed crab or the catch of the day. Many of the ingredients come fresh from the sea. Trust the staff to direct you to whatever is best that day. A colorful interior, fresh flowers on the tables, and a harbor view make this a most pleasant dining experience.

Akti Enoseos. ⓒ **28210/45-236.** Main courses 6€–18€ ($7.80–$24). No credit cards. Daily 10am–2am. Park at side of restaurant, or walk from harbor. At farthest corner of new harbor.

The Well of the Turk ⓐⓐ MIDDLE EASTERN/MEDITERRANEAN   Here's a restaurant that rises above others in Chania because of its unexpected menu, tasty cooking, and unusual setting. At the heart of the old Turkish quarter (Splanzia), in a historic building that contains a well, there is a quiet outside court where diners may sit in the summer. The chef's imaginative touches make the cuisine more than standard Middle Eastern. In addition to tasty kabobs, specialties include meatballs mixed with eggplant, and *laxma bi azeen* (a pita-style bread with a spicy topping). Middle Eastern musicians sometimes play here, and you can settle for a quiet drink at the bar.

1–3 Kalinikou Sarpaki. ⓒ **28210/54-547.** Reservations recommended for parties of 7 or more. Main courses 7€– 18€ ($9.10–$24). No credit cards. Wed–Mon 7pm–midnight. No parking in immediate area; leave car and walk into old quarter. On a small street off Daskaloyiannis.

INEXPENSIVE

Enomayirio SEAFOOD   Here's a special treat for diners who can handle eating in a cramped, unstylish restaurant smack in the center of Chania's public market. The fish and other seafood come from stalls barely 10 feet away. All the other ingredients also come straight from the nearby stands. Food doesn't get any fresher nor a dining experience more "immediate." Sit here and watch the world go by.

In the public market, at the "arm" with the fish vendors. Main courses 5€–15€ ($6.50–$20); gigantic platter of mixed fish for 2 is 24€ ($31). No credit cards. Mon–Sat 9am–3:30pm.

Psitopoleio ("The Grill") GREEK   Known to the foreign community of Chania as "The Meatery," this is not for the fainthearted (or vegetarians!). Its clientele is almost 100% Cretan. I have debated for years whether to include this place but have finally decided that some travelers will appreciate its distinctive ambience. To call its decor "basic" is a major understatement: It is a long, bare space, with the butcher's block at the rear and the grill at the front. Your meat course is butchered at the former and cooked at the latter. The specialties are lamb chops, pork chops, kidneys, spareribs, and sausages; excellent french fries; salads, both the standard Greek and a cabbage version; soup; and tzaziki. House wine, beers, and soft drinks help you wash down the tasty and unforgettable food. Go for it!

48 Apokorono. ℭ 28210/91-354. Main courses 4€–12€ ($5.20–$16). No credit cards. Daily noon–3pm and 7:30pm–1am. No parking nearby. With your back to the municipal market, walk along the main street leading diagonally away off to the right.

Remezzo Cafe INTERNATIONAL   Sooner or later, we say, "Enough Greek salads!" and want to indulge in a club sandwich or tuna salad. Remezzo, at the very center of the action—Venizelou Square—on the old harbor, is a great choice for breakfasts and light meals (omelets, salads, and so on). It also offers a full range of coffee, alcoholic drinks, and ice-cream desserts. Sitting in one of the heavily cushioned chairs as you sip your drink and observe the lively scene, you'll feel like you have the best seat in the house.

16A Venizelou. ℭ 28210/52-001. Main courses 5€–12€ ($6.60–$16). No credit cards. Daily 7am–2am. On corner of main square at old harbor.

CHANIA AFTER DARK

At night, instead of seeking out a packed club/bar/disco or walking around the harbor and Old Town, wander into Chania's back alleys to see the old Venetian and Turkish remains. Sit in a quayside cafe and enjoy a coffee or a drink, or treat yourself to a ride in a horse-drawn carriage at the harbor. At the other extreme, stroll through the new town; you might be surprised by the modernity and diversity (and prices) of the stores patronized by typical Chaniots.

Clubs come and go from year to year. Some popular spots include **El Mondo** and the **Happy Go Lucky,** both on Kondilaki (the street leading away from the center of the old harbor); **Idaeon Andron,** 26 Halidon; and **Ariadne,** on Akti Enoseos (around the corner where the old harbor becomes the new). On Anghelou (up from the Naval Museum) is **Fagotta,** a bar that sometimes offers jazz.

Cafes are everywhere but two stand out because of their special locations. You can take a little ferry to **Fortezza,** situated midway along the harbor's outer quay. And at **Pallas Roof Garden Cafe-Bar,** on Akti Tobazi (right at the corner where the new harbor meets the old harbor), you can sit high above the harbor, watch the blinking lights, listen to the murmur of the crowds below, and nurse a refreshing drink or ice cream. However, you must climb 44 stairs to get here; as the sign says, IT'S WORTH IT.

A more unusual cafe is **Tzamia-Krystalla,** at 35 Skalidi, the main street heading east out of 1866 Square (ℭ 28210/71-172; tza-ury@otenet.gr). A welcome addition to the usual tourist scene, it's a combination art gallery/cafe/performance space. The gallery hosts changing exhibits by Greek artists. The cafe serves a standard selection of alcoholic and non-alcoholic drinks (no cover or minimum), and at times offers live music. If you'd prefer to hear traditional Cretan songs, try **Cafe Lyriaka,** 22 Kalergon (behind the arsenali along the harbor).

The gay community in Chania does not seem to have any single gathering place but the **DioLuxe** cafe at 8 Sarpidonas (behind the Porto Veneziano hotel on the new harbor) is reported to be gay-friendly.

Movie houses around town—both outdoor and indoor—usually show foreign movies in their original language. The one in the public gardens is especially enjoyable. Watching a movie on a warm summer night in an outdoor cinema is one of life's simpler pleasures.

A **summer cultural festival** sometimes features dramas, symphonic music, jazz, dance, and traditional music. These performances take place from July to September at several venues: **Firka** fortress at the far left of the harbor; the **Venetian arsenali** along the old harbor; **East Moat Theater** along Nikiforou Phokas; or **Peace and Friendship Park Theater** on Demokratias, just beyond the public gardens. For details, inquire at one of the tourist information offices when you arrive in town.

A SIDE TRIP FROM CHANIA: SAMARIA GORGE 🌟🌟

Everyone with an extra day on Crete—and steady legs and solid walking shoes—should consider hiking through Samaria Gorge. The endeavor involves first getting to the top of the gorge, a trip of about 42km (26 miles) from Chania. Second comes the actual descent and hike through the gorge itself, some 18km (11 miles). Third, a boat takes you from the village of Ayia Roumeli, at the end of the gorge, to Khora Sfakion; from there, it's a bus ride of about 75km (46 miles) back to Chania. (Some boats go westward to Paleochora, approximately the same distance by road from Chania.)

Most visitors do it all in a long day, but you can put up for the night at one of the modest hotels and rooms at Ayia Roumeli, Paleochora (to its west), Souya (to its east), Khora Sfakion (main port to meet buses), and elsewhere along the south coast. But for most people I strongly advise signing up with one of the many travel agencies in Chania that get people to and from the gorge. This way, you are guaranteed seats on the bus and on the boat. One agency I recommend is **Diktynna Travel** (6 Archontaki St.; ℂ **28210/43-930;** www.diktynna-travel.gr); it offers group transportation to and from Samaria George for 42€ ($59) per person or private transportation at 300€ ($390) per tour (not per person).

In recent years, Samaria Gorge has been so successfully promoted as one of the great natural splendors of Europe that on certain days, it seems that half of the Continent is trekking through it. On the most crowded days, you can find yourself walking single file with several thousand other people. The gorge is open from about mid-April through mid-October (depending on weather conditions); the best chance for a bit of solitude means hiking near the beginning or end of the season. The hike is relatively taxing; and here and there, you will scramble over boulders. Bring water and snacks, and wear sturdy, comfortable shoes. Admission is 6€ ($7.80).

The gorge offers enough opportunities to break away from the crowds. You'll be treated to the fun of crisscrossing the water, not to mention the sights of wildflowers and dramatic geological formations, the sheer height of the gorge's sides, and several unexpected chapels—it will all add up to a worthwhile experience, one that many regard as the highlight of their visit to Crete.

3 Rethymnon (Rethimno)

72km (45 miles) E of Chania; 78km (50 miles) W of Iraklion

Whether visited on a day trip from Chania or Iraklion or used as a base for a stay in western Crete, Rethymnon can be a most pleasant town—provided you pick the right Rethymnon.

Rethymnon

Information **ⓘ**
Post Office ☒
OTE ☎

Sea of Crete

Greece

Aegean Sea

Athens ✪

Mediterranean Sea

CRETE • Rethymnon

Venetian Harbor 17

Petikhaki

Arkadiou

Venizelou

Kallergi

Afentouli

Gerakari

Plateia Iroon 10

14

Giaboudaki

Hortatzi

Iroon

Marouli

Kazantzaki

Demokratias

Prevelaki

Hatzidaki

Moatsou

Daskalaki

Zabeliou

Dimitrakaki

Municipal Gardens

Kountourioti

Dimakopoulou

Platonos

Antistaseos

Tobazi

8

9

Paleologou

Kornarou

Vernardou

4

18

6

7

Souliou

5

Salaminos

Damvergi

15

3

Mesologiou

Public Parking

13

16

Xanthoudidou

11

Arambatzoglou

Dikastiron

Nik Foka

Platonos

Patelarou

Navarinou

Grigoriou

Sofokleous

Smirnis

Plateia Georgiou

Melissinou

Plateon

Athinon 12

Katehaki

Plastira

Venetian Fortezza

2 1

Igoumenou Gavril

Trim Yasou

Bus Station

The town's defining centuries came under the Venetians in the late Middle Ages and the Renaissance, then under the Turks from the late 17th century to the late 19th century. Its maze of streets and alleys is now lined with shops, its old beachfront is home to restaurants and bars, and its new beach-resort facilities (to the east of the old town) offer a prime, some might say appalling, example of how a small town's modest seacoast can be exploited. Assuming you have not come to see these "developments," we'll help you focus your attention on the old town—the side of Rethymnon that can still work its charm on even the casual stroller.

ESSENTIALS

GETTING THERE   Rethymnon lacks an airport but is only about 1 hour from the Chania airport and 1½ hours from the Iraklion airport.

By Boat   Rethymnon does have its own ship line, which offers direct daily trips to and from Piraeus (about 10 hr.).

By Car   Many people visit Rethymnon by car, taking the highway from either Iraklion (about 79km/49 miles) or Chania (72km/45 miles). The public parking lot at Plateia Plastira, at the far western edge, just outside the old harbor, is best approached via the main east-west road along the south edge of the town.

By Bus   If you don't have your own vehicle, the bus offers frequent service to and from Iraklion and Chania—virtually every half-hour from early in the morning until mid-evening. In high season, buses depart Rethymnon as late as 10pm. The fare has been about 14€ ($18) round-trip. The **KTEL** bus line (© 28310/22-212) that provides service to and from Chania and Iraklion is located at Akti Kefaloyianithon, at the city's western edge (so allow an extra 10 min. to get there).

VISITOR INFORMATION   The **National Tourism Office** (© 28310/29-148) is on Venizelou, the main avenue that runs along the town beach. In high season, it's open Monday through Friday from 8am to 2:30pm; off season, its hours are unpredictable. But there are numerous private travel agencies in town that can arrange trips to virtually anywhere on the island. I recommend **Ellotia Tours** at 155 Arkadhiou (www.rethymnoatcrete.com).

GETTING AROUND   Rethymnon is a walker's town. Bringing a car into the maze of streets and alleys is more trouble than it's worth—in fact, it's virtually impossible. The sights you'll want to see are never more than a 20-minute walk from wherever you are.

To see the countryside of this part of Crete, unless you have unlimited time to use the buses, you'll need to rent a car. Among the many agencies with offices in Rethymnon are **Motor Club** (© 28310/54-253), **Budget** (© 28310/56-910), **Europeo** (© 28310/51-940), and **Hertz** (© 28310/26-286).

FAST FACTS   Several **banks** in both the old town and the new city have ATMs and currency-exchange machines. The **hospital** is at 7–9 Trantallidou in the new town

---

(Finds For Wine Lovers

Rethymnon's annual wine festival takes place for about 10 days starting near the end of July. It's centered around the public gardens, with music and dancing to accompany the samplings of local wines. The modest affair is a welcome change from larger, more staged festivals elsewhere.

(© 28310/27-491). For **Internet access,** try Caribbean Bar Cafe (behind Rimondi Fountain) or Alana Taverna (on Salaminas near Hotel Fortezza). The most convenient place to do **laundry** is next to the Youth Hostel, 45 Tombazi; its hours are Monday through Saturday from 8am to 8pm. The **tourist police** (© 28310/28-156) share the same building with the tourist office along the beach. The **post office** is east of the public gardens at 37 Moatsu (© 28310/22-571); its hours are Monday through Friday from 8am to 8pm, Saturday from 8am to noon. The **telephone office (OTE)** is at 40 Kountourioti; it's open daily from 7:30am to midnight.

WHAT TO SEE & DO
ATTRACTIONS
Archaeological Museum The exhibits here are not of much interest to any except specialists, and I recommend instead the little Folk Art Museum, described below.

© 28310/29-975. Admission 5€ ($6.50). Daily 8:30am–7pm. On foot, climb Katehaki, a fairly steep road opposite Hotel Fortezza on Melissinou; by car, ascend the adjacent Kheimara. Museum is in building just outside the fortress walls.

Historical and Folk Art Museum ✯ Housed in a centuries-old and architecturally significant Venetian mansion, this small museum displays ceramics, textiles, jewelry, artifacts, implements, clothing, and other vivid reminders of the traditional way of life of most Cretans across the centuries. Well worth a brief visit.

30 Vernardou. © 28310/23-398. Admission 3€ ($3.90) adults, 1€ ($1.30) students, free for children. Mon–Fri 10am–2pm.

The Venetian Fortezza ✯ Dominating the headland at the western edge of town, this massive fortress is the one site everyone should give at least an hour to visit. Built under the Venetians (but *by* Cretans) from about 1573 to 1580, its huge walls, about 1,130m (1,819 ft.) in perimeter, were designed to deflect the worst cannon fire of its day. In the end, of course, the Turks simply went around it and took the town by avoiding the fort. There's a partially restored mosque inside as well as a Greek Orthodox chapel. It's in this vast area that most of the performances of the annual **Rethymnon Renaissance Festival** take place (see below).

A STROLL THROUGH THE OLD TOWN
Rethymnon's attractions are best appreciated by walking through the old town. Start by getting a free map from the tourist office down along the beachfront, or follow the numbers on our Town Plan.

If you have limited time, first visit the **Venetian Fortress (1)** (see the "Rethymnon" map, p. 353). If you have the time or inclination, look into the **Archaeological Museum (2).** Then make your way down to Melissinou and turn left and proceed to the **Catholic Church (3)** at the corner of Mesologiou. Proceed down Salaminos to Arkadiou; make a left here to the western edge of the **old harbor.** Curving right down to the harbor is an unexpected sight: the wall of restaurants and bars that effectively obliterates the quaint harbor that drew them here in the first place. Making your way through this obstacle course, you'll emerge at the southeast corner of this curved harbor and come to a square that faces the town's long beach, its broad boulevard lined with even more restaurants and cafes. Turn right up Petikhaki, and at the first crossroads, you'll see the **Venetian Loggia** (ca. 1600) **(4)**—for many years the town's museum and now a Ministry of Culture gallery that sells officially approved reproductions of ancient Greek works of art. Continue up past it on Paleologou to the next crossroads. On the right is **Rimondi Fountain** (ca. 1623) **(5).**

> ## Moments   Rethymnon Renaissance Festival
>
> Rethymnon's cultural festival offers mostly musical and theatrical events from July to early September. Productions range from ancient Greek dramas to more contemporary artistic endeavors (and now include folk and rock concerts). Most performers are Greek; some are foreigners. The majority of performances are staged in the Fortezza itself; there's nothing quite like listening to 17th-century music or seeing a Renaissance drama in this setting. For details, inquire at the tourist information office.

Leaving the fountain, head onto Antistaseos toward the 17th-century **Mosque of Nerantzes (6)** (originally a Christian church) near the corner of Vernardou; you can climb the minaret Monday to Friday 11am to 7:30pm, Saturday 11am to 3pm (closed in Aug). Again, if you have the time, proceed up Vernardou to the **Historical and Folk Art Museum (7).** If you follow Antistaseos to its end, you'll come to **Porta Guora (8),** the only remnant of the Venetian city walls.

Emerging at that point onto the main east-west road, opposite and to the right are the **municipal gardens.** On your left is the **Orthodox Church of the Four Martyrs (9),** worth a peek as you walk east along Gerakari. You then come to **Platei Iroon,** the large circle that serves as the junction between the old town and the new beachfront development.

Turning back into the old town on Arkadiou, you'll see on your left the restored **Mosque of Kara Pasha (10),** now converted to a botanical museum (daily 9am–6pm). Continue along Arkadiou, and in addition to the modern shops, note the surviving remains of the Venetian era—particularly the **facade of no. 154.** From here, you're on your own to explore the narrow streets, go shopping, or head for the waterfront for something cool to drink.

OUTDOOR PURSUITS

If you're interested in horseback riding, try the **Riding Center,** southeast of town at Platanias, 39 N. Fokas (© **28310/28-907**) or the **Zoraida Horse Riding** at Georgioupolis, about midway between Chania and Rethymnon (© **28250/61-745**). Among the newer diversions offered in Rethymnon are the daily **excursion boats** that take people on day trips for **swimming** on the beach either at **Bali** (to the east) or **Marathi** (on the Akrotiri to the west). The price, which is about 30€ ($39) for adults, includes a midday meal at a local taverna as well as all the wine you care to drink. You can sign on at the far end of the harbor. **Manias Tours,** 5 Arkadiou (© **28310/56-400**), offers an **evening cruise** that provides a view of Rethymnon glittering in the night.

SHOPPING

Here, as in Chania and Iraklion, you may be overwhelmed by the sheer number of gift shops offering mostly souvenirs. Looking for something different? Try Nikolaos Papalasakis's **Palaiopoleiou,** 40 Souliou, which is crammed with some genuine antiques, old textiles, jewelry, and curiosities such as the stringed instruments made by the proprietor. At **Olive Tree Wood,** 35 Arabatzoglou, the name says it all—the store carries bowls, containers, and implements carved from olive wood. **Evangeline,** 36 Paleologlou, has a good selection of textiles while **Haroula Spridaki,** 36 Souliou, has a nice selection of Cretan embroidery. **Talisman,** 32 Arabatzoglou, sells an interesting selection of blown glass, ceramics, plaques, paintings, and other handmade articles. And **Avli "Raw Materials"** at 38–40 Arabatzoglou has a large and varied selection of Cretan natural products.

WHERE TO STAY

There is no shortage of accommodations in and around Rethymnon—but it has become hard to find a place in town that offers location, authentic atmosphere, and a quiet night's sleep. Our choices try to satisfy the last-mentioned criterion first. Note that many places in Rethymnon shut down in winter.

EXPENSIVE

AVLI Lounge Apartments ✿   This small boutique hotel is in a restored mansion dating back to 1530, now loaded with elements from various centuries and cultures, with eye-catching interior decorating, and with every possible modern convenience. The rooms are suites in the sense that they are large enough to be assigned to different functions—sleeping, office, relaxing; two even have working fireplaces. The chef at AVLI's in-house restaurant produces meals that utilize Cretan products and traditional dishes while treating them in innovative ways—although there's still nothing quite like a simple grilled fish. The restaurant will also provide private dinners, special celebration dinners, wine-tasting evenings, and even cooking lessons. But clients should be warned that some of the rooms are in a separate building across a narrow (pedestrian only) street and there are no elevators in either this or the main building. Rooms along the street are not well soundproof and should be avoided by light sleepers. Also, because there are only eight units, if you are for any reason dissatisfied with your room, you have little chance of switching. The point is: Insist on your room's location when making a reservation.

1622 Xanthoudidou, 74100 Rethymnon. ⓒ **28310/58-250.** www.avli.gr. 8 units. High season 210€–250€ ($273–$325) double; low season 145€–180€ ($189–$234) double. Rates include buffet breakfast. Surcharge for 3rd person sharing room; babies stay free. AE, DC, MC, V. Parking on public lot 10-min. walk away. **Amenities:** Restaurant; bar; pool; concierge; secretarial support; tour and car rentals arranged; 18-hr. room service; yoga and massage; babysitting; laundry. *In room:* A/C, TV, CD players, Internet, fridge, hair dryer, bathrobes, safe, Jacuzzi.

Palazzino di Corina ✿   Setting a new benchmark for stylish accommodations in Rethymnon, this boutique hotel is in a centuries-old Venetian mansion restored with taste and restraint, using natural and original building materials complemented by fine old furnishings. Each of the 21 rooms is named after one of the Greek gods or goddesses and each has some distinctive configuration and appearance; size varies considerably but all have comfortable beds and private bathrooms. A courtyard offers a delightful place to retreat from your city walks or wider excursions—plus a small pool in which to cool off. Its location offers closeness to the old town's center while providing a quiet night, but there is one drawback for some: There is no elevator and some rooms are on what Americans call a third floor; however, there is a room for those limited in their mobility. Definitely only for those who appreciate subdued luxury and are willing to spend this kind of money for such an environment.

7–9 Damvergi and A. Diakou, 74100 Rethymnon. ⓒ **28310/21-205.** Fax 28310/54-073. www.corina.gr. 21 units. High season 185€–280€ ($241–$364) double; low season 160€–235€ ($208–$306) double. Rates include buffet breakfast. Surcharge for 3rd person sharing room; babies stay free. AE, DC, MC, V. Parking nearby on public lot. **Amenities:** Restaurant; bar; pool; concierge; car rentals and tours arranged; 24-hr. room service; babysitting. *In room:* A/C, TV, Internet access, hydromassage, fridge, dryer, safe.

MODERATE

Hotel Fortezza ⚡ Fortezza is one of the more popular hotels in Rethymnon, mainly because of its location and moderate prices. You're only a few blocks from the inner old town and then another couple of blocks to the town beach and the Venetian Harbor. It's convenient, too, for driving and parking a car. The Venetian Fortezza rises just across the street. Guest rooms are decent-size with modern bathrooms (some with shower, some with tub); most have balconies. It is essential, however, to ask for one of its inside rooms, which overlook the small but welcome pool—street-side rooms can be noisy. This hotel has become so popular that you must make reservations for the high season.

16 Melissinou, 74100 Rethymnon. ⓒ **28310/55-551.** Fax 28310/54-073. 52 units. High season 120€ ($156) double; low season 95€ ($124) double. Rates include buffet breakfast. Surcharge for 3rd person sharing room; babies stay free. AE, DC, MC, V. Parking nearby. On the western edge of town, just below the Venetian Fortezza, which is approached by Melissinou. **Amenities:** Restaurant; bar; pool; TV room; card-playing room; concierge; tour and car rentals arranged; babysitting. *In room:* A/C, TV, dryer.

Mare Monte Beach Hotel ⚡ *Kids* Some 15 miles west of Rethymnon, you'll feel like you're living in a remote hideaway, with the sea before you and the mountains behind. This first-class resort hotel also boasts a beautiful beach. Guest rooms are of moderate size with basic Greek hotel furnishings but have fully modern bathrooms. Activities include minigolf, archery, horseback riding by arrangement, and table tennis. Although it lacks the luxury of the grand resorts to the east of Rethymnon, the Mare Monte is a good alternative for those who want to focus their Cretan stay on Rethymnon, Chania, and western Crete, yet prefer to be based well away from a noisy town. The village of Georgioupolis is close enough for an evening stroll.

73007 Georgioupolis, Crete. ⓒ **28250/61-390.** 200 units. High season 95€ ($124) double; low season 70€ ($91) double. Rates include breakfast. DC, MC, V. Parking on-site. Closed Nov–Mar. 25 min. west of Rethymnon, on the main road to Chania. **Amenities:** 2 restaurants; 2 bars; pool; children's pool; 2 night-lit tennis courts; extensive watersports; children's playground; concierge; tours and car rentals arranged; secretarial services; 24-hr. room service; babysitting; laundry and dry cleaning arranged. *In room:* A/C, TV, safe.

INEXPENSIVE

Hotel Ideon This longtime favorite is a solid choice for its location and price. It also boasts a pool with a sunbathing area as well as a conference room that can handle up to 50 people. The friendly desk staff will arrange for everything from laundry service to car rentals. The guest rooms are the standard modern of Greek hotels—but insist on one away from street as an adjacent area is popular gathering spot in summer. I like this place because it offers an increasingly rare combination in a Cretan hotel: It's near the active part of town and near the water (although it doesn't have a beach).

10 Plateia Plastira, 74100 Rethymnon. ⓒ **28310/28-667.** Fax 28310/28-670. www.hotelideon.gr. 86 units, some with shower, some with tub. High season 75€ ($98) double; low season 55€ ($72) double. Rates include buffet breakfast. Reduced rates for 3rd person in room or for child in parent's room. AE, DC, MC, V. Parking on adjacent street. Closed Nov to mid-Mar. On coast road just west of the Venetian Harbor. **Amenities:** 2 bars; pool; concierge; tours and car rentals arranged; babysitting. *In room:* A/C, TV in some, fridge, safe.

Kyma Beach Hotel This is a modern, city hotel—not a resort hotel—designed for people who want to take in Rethymnon and then retire to a beach at the end of the day. It's close to the attractions of old town and to the beach. The somewhat austere gray exterior might put off some people, but in fact the hotel is relatively well designed. Although rooms are hardly spacious, they are neatly furnished. Some have sleeping lofts, so if this doesn't appeal to you, speak up. Bathrooms are up-to-date. All rooms have balconies, but insist on a higher floor to escape street noise. The outdoor cafe is a popular watering hole for locals; you won't feel as if you're in a foreigners' compound.

Platai Iroon, 74111 Rethymnon. (C) 28310/55-503. Fax 28310/27-746. 35 units, some with tub, some with shower. High season 80€ ($104) double; low season 60€ ($78) double. Rates include continental breakfast. AE, MC, V. Parking nearby. Public buses nearby. At eastern edge of old town and its beach. **Amenities:** 2 restaurants; 2 bars; concierge; tours and car rentals arranged; babysitting; laundry service; dry cleaning; Internet access. *In room:* A/C, TV, minibar, safe.

WHERE TO DINE

For truly elegant—but not inexpensive—dining and wining, try the above-described **AVLI Lounge**'s restaurant or try the **Veneto,** a 600-year-old Venetian mansion at 4 Epimenidou (a small street halfway between Nerantzes Mosque and the Folk Museum).

EXPENSIVE

Knossos 👀 GREEK/SEAFOOD   Visitors who appreciate dining in a 600-year-old taverna little known to tourists sneak off to this small, charming family-owned find along the old Venetian harbor. Specializing in fish as fresh as the day's catch, all meals are lovingly prepared by Maria Stavroulaki and her mother. You can't go wrong with the grilled whole fish with fresh vegetables, or baked lobster with pasta. Happiness is snagging the single table on the open second-floor balcony overlooking the blinking harbor lights.

40 Nearchou (the old port) (C) 28310/25-582. Main courses 20€–40€ ($26–$52). MC, V. Daily 11am–midnight. Reservations recommended. Closed Nov–Mar.

MODERATE

Famagusta GREEK/INTERNATIONAL   This well-tested, sea-view restaurant is far from the hustle of the harbor yet convenient to the center's attractions. The menu offers Cretan specialties such as breaded, deep-fried zucchini with lightly flavored garlic yogurt or *halumi,* a grilled cheese. Grilled fish and filets are the core of the main courses, but the adventurous chef includes Chinese-style Mandarin beef and that old basic, chili con carne. Eating here makes you feel like you're at an old-fashioned seaside restaurant, not some touristic confection.

6 Plastira Sq., Rethymnon. (C) 28310/23-881. Main courses 6€–16€ ($7.80–$21). AE, DC, MC, V. Daily 10am–midnight. Closed Christmas through New Year's. Parking lot nearby. Near Ideon Hotel, on coast road just to west of Venetian Harbor.

Othonos GREEK   Just as Americans claim to trust a diner where the truckers are parked, you can trust a Greek restaurant where the locals gather, and the Othonos is such a place. It offers tasty taverna food and a front row seat for the passing scene. Minor variations—such as a Roquefort dressing on a salad, cheese and ham pies, artichokes with the lamb dish—liven up the traditional fare such as rabbit stifado. Just right for dropping in when you are on a walking tour of the town.

27 Pethihaki Sq., Rethymnon. (C) 28310/55-500. Main courses 6€–18€ ($7.80–$24). MC, V. Daily 10am–midnight. In center of Old Town so park on edge.

A SIDE TRIP FROM RETHYMNON: MONASTERY OF ARKADHI

The events that took place here can help put modern Cretan history in perspective. The **Monastery of Arkadhi** sits some 23km (15 miles) southeast of Rethymnon and can be reached by public bus. A taxi might be in order if you don't have a car. If you ask the driver to wait an hour, the fare should total about 80€ ($104). What you'll see is a surprisingly Italianate-looking church facade, for although it belongs to the Orthodox priesthood, it was built under Venetian influence in 1587.

Like many monasteries on Crete, Arkadhi provided support for the rebels against Turkish rule. During a major uprising on November 9, 1866, many Cretan insurgents—men, women, and children—took refuge here. Realizing they were doomed to fall to the far larger besieging Turkish force, the abbot, it is claimed, gave the command to blow up the powder storeroom. Whether it was an accident or not is debatable, but hundreds of Cretans and Turks died in the explosion. The event became known throughout the Western world, inspiring writers, revolutionaries, and statesmen of several nations to protest at least with words. To Cretans it became and remains the archetypal incident of their long struggle for "freedom or death." (An ossuary outside the monastery contains the skulls of many who died in the explosion.) Even if you never thought about Cretan history, a brief visit to Arkadhi should go a long way in explaining the Cretans you deal with.

AN EXCURSION FROM RETHYMNON: THE AMARI VALLEY

Everyone who has more than a few days to spend on Crete should try to make at least one excursion into the interior to experience three of the elements that have traditionally characterized the island: eons-old rugged mountains, age-old village life, and centuries-old chapels and monasteries. The Amari Valley, south of Rethymnon, offers just such an opportunity. It's not much more than a 100-mile round-trip but given the mountainous roads and allowing for at least some stops to see a few villages and chapels, a full day should be budgeted. Your own vehicle or a hired taxi is a must (unless of course you get a travel agency to arrange a tour); if you go on your own, a good map of Crete is also a necessity. Heading east out of Rethymon, some 3 miles along at Platanias, you take the road south to Prassies and Apostoli, always climbing and zigzagging. At Apostoli, a turnoff to the left leads to Thronos and its Chucrh of the Panayia, built on the mosaic floor of an early Christian church. Back on the main road, you proceed on toward Monasteraki but take the turnoff to the left to visit the Monastery of Asomatos; founded in the 10th century, its present building dates from the Venetian period; it served as a center of resistance and Greek culture under the Turks. Proceed on down to Fourfouras (a starting point for the ascent to Crete's highest peak, Psiloritis). Continue south to Nithavris and Ayios Ioannis, then head north via Ano Meros, Gerakari, Patsos, and Pantanassa until you rejoin the road where a left starts you back north and down to the coast. Along the way you will have passed through many other villages and be directed to other chapels but best of all you will have spent an unforgettable day in the Cretan mountains.

4 Ayios Nikolaos

69km (43 miles) E of Iraklion

Ayios Nikolaos tends to inspire strong reactions, depending on what you're looking for. Until the 1970s, it was a lazy little coastal settlement with no archaeological or historical structures of any interest. Then, the town got "discovered," and the rest is the history of organized tourism in our time.

For about 5 months of the year, Ayios Nikolaos becomes one gigantic resort town, taken over by the package-tour groups who stay in beach hotels along the adjacent coast and come into town to eat, shop, and stroll. During the day, Ayios Nikolaos vibrates with people. At night, it vibrates with music—the center down by the water is one communal nightclub.

Ayios Nikolaos

0   100 m
0   100 y

Sea of Crete

Archaeological Museum

To Bus Terminal

Miliatou

Koritsás

Koraka

Prigipos Georgiou

Paleologou

Akti Koundourou

Ethnikis Antistaseos

Theotokoulloud

Kobnarouv

D. Solonos

Kantanoleontos

Katehaki

Kondilaki

Quay

Koundourou

Lasthenous

Pasifias

Ariadhis

Milou

Ebans

M. Sfakianaki

Alexomanoli

K. Sfakianaki

Manousogianakis

Lake Voulismeni

Titou

Plastira

Filelinon

Omirou

28 Octobriou

Koundourou

25 Martiou

Polytechniou

Plateia Venizelou

El. Venizelou

Kitroplatia Beach

Bus Station

Tavla

Koziri

Akti Atlantidos

Information *(i)*
Post Office ✉
OTE ☏

Greece

Athens
Aegean Sea

Mediterranean Sea   CRETE

Ayios Nikolaos

ACCOMMODATIONS ■
Hotel Hermes **2**
Minos Beach **1**

DINING ◆
Hollands Restaurant—
   De Molen (The Mill) **4**
Itanos **6**
La Casa **5**
Pelagos **3**

Somehow, the town remains a pleasant place to visit, and it serves as a fine base for excursions to the east of Crete. And if you're willing to stay outside the very center, you can take only as much of Ayios Nikolaos as you want—then retreat to your beach or take off to explore the east end of the island. And anyone who's come as far as Ayios Nikolaos should get over to Elounda at least once: It's some 12km (8 miles) but in addition to taxis there are buses every hour back and forth. It's slower-paced and less fashionable than Ayios Nikolaos but all the more pleasant for being so.

ESSENTIALS

GETTING THERE   By Plane   Ayios Nikolaos does not have its own airport but can be reached in about 1 hour by taxi or bus (1½ hr.) from the Iraklion airport. During the high season, **Olympic Airways** offers a few flights weekly to Sitia, the town to the east of Ayios Nikolaos, but the drive from there to Ayios Nikolaos is also a solid 1½ hours.

By Boat   Several ships a week each way link Ayios Nikolaos and Piraeus (about 11 hr.). Ships also run from Ayios Nikolaos to Sitia (just east along the coast) and on to Rhodes via the islands of Kassos, Karpathos, and Khalki. In summer, several ships link Ayios Nikolaos to Santorini (4 hr.), and then to Piraeus via several other Cycladic islands. Schedules and even ship lines vary so much from year to year that you may want to wait until you get to Greece to make specific plans, but you can try checking www.gtp.gr in advance.

By Bus   Bus service almost every half-hour of the day each way (in high season) links Ayios Nikolaos to Iraklion; almost as many buses go to and from Sitia. The **KTEL** bus line (✆ 28410/22-234) has its terminal in the Lagos neighborhood (behind the city hospital, which is up past the Archaeological Museum).

VISITOR INFORMATION   The **Municipal Information Office** (✆ 28410/22-357; gr_tour_ag_nik@acn.gr) is one of the most helpful in all of Greece, perhaps because it's staffed by eager young seasonal employees (daily Apr 15–Oct 31, 8am–10pm). In addition to providing maps and brochures, it can help arrange accommodations and excursions. Of several travel agencies in town, I recommend **Nostos Tours,** 30 R. Koundourou (along the right arm of the harbor; ✆ 28410/26-383)

GETTING AROUND   The town is so small that you can walk to all points, although taxis are available. The KTEL buses (see above) serve towns, hotels, and other points in eastern Crete. If you want to explore this end of the island on your own, it seems as if car and moped/motorcycle rentals are at every other doorway. I found some of the best rates at **Alfa Rent a Car,** 3 Kap. Nik. Fafouti, the small street between the lake and the harbor road (✆ 28410/24-312; fax 28410/25-639).

FAST FACTS   Several **ATMs** and currency-exchange machines line the streets leading away from the harbor. The **hospital** (✆ 28410/22-369) is on the west edge of town, at the junction of Lasithiou and Paleologou. For **Internet access,** try either the bookstore/cafe **Polychromos** at 28 October or the **Atlantis Café,** 15 Akti Atlantidos; they tend to be open daily in high season from 9am to 11pm. The most convenient place to do **laundry** is Xionati Laundromat, 10 Chortatson (a small street leading up from beach on Akti Nearchou); it's open Monday through Friday from 8am to 2pm and 5 to 8pm, Saturday from 8am to 4pm. **Luggage storage** is available at the main bus station (see above). The **tourist police** (✆ 28410/26-900) are at 34 Koundoyianni. The **post office** is at 9 28th Octobriou (✆ 28410/22-276). In summer, it's open Monday through Saturday from 7:30am to 8pm; in winter, Monday through Saturday from 7:30am to 2pm. The **telephone office (OTE),** 10 Sfakinaki, at the corner of 25th Martiou, is open Monday through Saturday from 7am to midnight, Sunday from 7am to 10pm.

WHAT TO SEE & DO

The focal point in town is the small pool, formally called **Lake Voulismeni,** just inside the harbor. You can sit at its edge while enjoying a meal or a drink. Inevitably, it has given rise to all sorts of tales—that it's bottomless (it's known to be about 65m/213 ft. deep); that it's connected to Santorini, the island about 104km (65 miles) to the north; and that it was the "bath of Athena." Originally it was a freshwater pool, probably fed by a subterranean river that drained water from the mountains inland. A 20th-century channel now mixes the fresh water with sea water.

Archaeological Museum ✵   This is a fine example of one of the relatively new provincial museums that have opened up all over Greece—in an effort both to decentralize the country's rich holdings and to allow local communities to profit from the finds in their regions. It contains a growing collection of Minoan artifacts and art being excavated in eastern Crete. Its prize piece, the eerily modern ceramic **Goddess of Myrtos,** shows a woman clutching a jug; it was found at a Minoan site of this name down on the southeastern coast. The museum is worth at least a brief visit.

74 Paleologou. ✆ **28410/24-943.** Admission 4€ ($5.20). Tues–Sun 8:30am–3pm. Closed all holidays (reduced hours possible in low season, so call ahead).

SHOPPING

Definitely make time to visit **Ceramica,** 28 Paleologou (✆ **28410/24-075**). You will see many reproductions of ancient Greek vases and frescoes for sale throughout Greece, but seldom will you have a chance to visit the workshop of one of the masters of this art, Nikolaos Gabriel. His authentic and vivid vases range from 25€ to 300€ ($33–$390). He also carries a line of fine jewelry, made by others to his designs. Across the street, at no. 1A, **Xeiropoito** sells handmade rugs. **Pegasus,** 5 Sfakianakis, on the corner of Koundourou, the main street up from the harbor (✆ **28410/24-347**), offers a selection of jewelry, knives, icons, and trinkets—some old, some not. You'll have to trust the owner, Kostas Kounelakis, to tell you which is which.

For something truly Greek, what could be better than an icon—a religious or historic painting on a wooden plaque? The tradition is kept alive in Elounda at the studio/store **Petrakis Workshop for Icons,** 22 A. Papendreou, on the left as you come down the incline from Ayios Nikolaos, just before the town square (✆ **28410/41-669**). Georgia and Ioannis Petrakis work seriously at maintaining this art. Orthodox churches in North America as well as in Greece buy icons from them. Stop by and watch the artists at their painstaking work—you don't have to be Orthodox to admire or own one. The store also carries local artisans' jewelry, blown glass, and ceramics.

WHERE TO STAY

IN TOWN

Hotel Hermes   This is perhaps the best you can do if you want to stay close to the center of town yet be free from as much of the noise as possible. The Hermes is just far away enough, around the corner from the inner harbor, to escape the nightly din. This won't be in everyone's budget, but it's a compromise between the deluxe beach resorts and the cheaper in-town hotels. Guest rooms are done in the standard style, and most enjoy views over the sea. There's a private terrace (not a beach) on the shore, just across the boulevard. The roof has a pool, with plenty of space to sunbathe.

If the Hermes is booked, you might try **Hotel Coral,** Akti Koundourou next door (© **28410/28-253**). It's under the same management, almost as classy, and slightly cheaper.

Akti Koundourou, Ayios Nikolaos, 72100 Crete. © **28410/28-253**. www.hermes-hotels.gr. 206 units. High season 160€ ($208) double; low season 110€ ($143) double. Rates include buffet breakfast; special rate for longer stays. AE, DC, MC, V. Parking on opposite seawall (but beware of spray!). Closed Nov–Mar. On the shore road around from the inner harbor. **Amenities:** 2 restaurants; 2 bars; swimming pool; fitness center and sauna; billiards; video games; conference facilities; car rentals and tours arranged. In room: A/C, TV, fridge, hair dryer.

Minos Beach ★★

I have to admit that I recommend this place out of loyalty to the first of the luxury beach-bungalow resorts in all of Greece. It remains a favorite among many returnees, but I must also admit that the common areas are not as glitzy as those at newer resorts, and that its grounds now look a bit overgrown. But the individual accommodations are just fine, although as with almost all Greek deluxe hotels, the mattresses seem a bit thin—to Americans, at least. But the hotel does have a civilized air, which is enhanced by the original, modern works of sculptors (several world-famous) scattered around the grounds. It's a great place to enjoy complete peace and quiet not too far from Ayios Nikolaos. It will appeal to those who like a touch of the Old World when they go abroad.

Amoudi, Ayios Nikolaos, 72100 Crete. © 28410/22-345. Fax 28410/22-548. www.greekhotel.com/crete/agiosnikolaos. 12 units (in main building), 120 bungalows. High season per person rates 145€–210€ ($169–$273) double/bunga-low; low season per person rates 90€–165€ ($117–$215) double/bungalow. **Note:** Rates are per person but include buffet breakfast. Special rates for children. AE, DC, MC, V. Closed late Oct to late Apr. Frequent public buses to Ayios Nikolaos center or Elounda. A 10-min. walk from center. **Amenities:** 5 restaurants; 2 bars; saltwater pool; night-lit tennis court; health club and sauna; Jacuzzi in some bungalows; watersports equipment rentals; TV room; bike rentals; table tennis; concierge; tours and car rentals arranged; airport transport arranged; conference center; secre-tarial services; salon; room service 7:30am–9:30pm; babysitting; laundry service; dry cleaning; safe-deposit box at desk. In room: A/C, TV, minibar, hair dryer.

OUT OF TOWN

Elounda Beach ★★★

This world-class resort consistently appears on all the lists of "best," "top," and "great" hotels and resorts. Isolated on is own stretch of coast and built to suggest a Cycladic village, it is truly deluxe, yet understated. It offers more extras than I can list, including a gala dinner every Sunday and open-air movies on Monday. From the prunes at the lavish breakfast buffet to the mini-TV by your bath-room mirror—the management has thought of everything. Guest rooms and bath-rooms are appropriately luxuriously appointed. The restaurants serve haute cuisine. And in case you're concerned, the hotel does have its own heliport. Its clientele include the wealthy and well-known from all over the world, but if you go at low season and opt for the least expensive rooms, its rates are not extreme. Definitely a once-in-a-life-time experience.

72053 Elounda, Crete. © **28410/41-412**. Fax 28410/41-373. www.eloundabeach.gr. 243 units (including 21 suites and bungalows with private swimming pools). High season per person rates 340€–450€ ($442–$585) double; low season per person rates 245€–310€ ($319–$403) double. **Note:** Rates are per person per day and include break-fast. Bungalow rates available online. AE, DC, MC, V. Closed early Nov to early Apr. Public buses to Ayios Nikolaos or Elounda every hour; Elounda is 8km (5 miles) from the center of Ayios Nikolaos. **Amenities:** 4 restaurants; 4 bars; pool (and 25 suites w/own pools); 5 night-lit tennis courts; health club, sauna; watersports including scuba diving and sailing; bike rentals; volleyball; table tennis; billiards; children's program; concierge; tours and car rentals arranged; transport from airport arranged (car or helicopter); business center; secretarial services; shopping arcade; salon; 24-hr. room service; massage; babysitting; laundry service; dry cleaning. In room: A/C, TV, fridge, hair dryer, safe, Jacuzzi.

Istron Bay ✸✸   Another beautiful—and quiet—beach resort, this one is nestled against the slope on its own bay. The resort's location, plus its own beach and the tropical paradise atmosphere, makes the resort a special place. Family-owned, it maintains traditional Cretan hospitality; for example, newcomers are invited to a cocktail party to meet others. The comfortable guest rooms have modern bathrooms and spectacular views. If you can tear yourself away from here, you're well situated to take in all the sights of eastern Crete. The main dining room has a fabulous view to go with its award-winning cuisine; it takes special pride in offering choices based on the "Cretan diet," internationally recognized as especially healthy. The resort offers activities such as scuba diving at an authorized school, nature walks in the spring and autumn, wine tastings, fishing trips, and Greek lessons.

72100 Istro, Crete. ✆ 28410/61-347. Fax 28410/61-383. www.istronbay.com. 145 units (including 27 bungalows). High season 200€–240€ ($260–$312) double, 265€–310€ ($345–$403) suite or bungalow; low season 98€–126€ ($128–$164) double, 148€–204€($192–$265) suite or bungalow. Rates include half board with buffet breakfast. Special rates for extra beds in room, for children, for June, and for breakfast only. AE, DC, MC, V. Closed Nov–Mar. Public buses every hour to Ayios Nikolaos or Sitia. 12km (7 miles) east of Ayios Nikolaos. **Amenities:** 3 restaurants; 2 bars; seawater swimming pool and children's pool; night-lit tennis court; watersports equipment rentals; volleyball; table tennis; billiards; children's program; concierge; tours and car rentals arranged; airport transport arranged; conference facilities; salon; room service 7am–11pm; massage; babysitting; laundry and dry-cleaning service. *In room:* A/C, satellite TV, minibar, hair dryer, safe for rent, bathrobe service (some units).

WHERE TO DINE

Ayios Nikolaos and nearby Elounda have so many restaurants that it's hard to know where to start or stop. When deciding, consider location and atmosphere; those factors have governed our recommendations below.

MODERATE

Hollands Restaurant—De Molen (The Mill) DUTCH/INDONESIAN   Looking for a change from the basic Greek menu? Aside from offering a (possibly) new experience for your palate, this place commands the most dramatic nighttime view of Ayios Nikolaos. Specialties include pork filet in a cream sauce. Vegetarian? Try the crepe with eggplant, mushrooms, carrots, and cabbage, tied up with leeks. I sampled the popular Indonesian dish, *nasi goreng*—a plate heaped with rice, vegetables, and pork in a *satay* (peanut) sauce. It went well overlooking exotic Ayios Nikolaos.

10 Dionysos Solomos. ✆/fax 28410/25-582. Main courses 6€–17€ ($7.80–$22); combination plates offered. V. Daily 10am–11:30pm. Closed Nov–Mar. A taxi is your only choice if you can't make it up the hill. It's the road at the highest point above the lake.

La Casa GREEK/INTERNATIONAL   With its lakeside location, tasty menu, and friendly Greek-American proprietress, this might be many travelers' first choice in Ayios Nikolaos. You'll enjoy the fine meals Marie Daskaloyiannis cooks up, including such specialties as fried rice with shrimp, lamb with artichokes, and rabbit stifado. Or try the "Greek sampling" plate—moussaka, dolmades, stuffed tomato, meatballs, and whatever other goodies Marie heaps on. There's always a slightly special twist to the food here.

31 28th Octobriou. ✆ 28410/26-362. Main courses 6€–16€ ($7.80–$21). AE, DC, DISC, MC, V. Daily 9am–midnight. No parking in immediate area.

Pelagos ✸ GREEK/SEAFOOD   Looking for a change from the usual touristy seafront restaurant—something a bit more cosmopolitan? Try Pelagos, in a handsome old house a block up from the hustle and bustle of the harbor. As its name suggests, it specializes in seafood. From squid to lobster (expensive, as it always is in Greece), it's all done with flair. You can sit indoors in a subdued atmosphere or out in the secluded garden; either way you'll be served with style. This restaurant lets you get away from the crowd and share a more intimate meal.

10 Ketahaki. ✆ **28410/25-737.** doxan45@hotmail.com. Reservations recommended in high season. Main courses 6€–20€ ($7.80–$263); some fish by the kilo. MC, V. Daily noon–1am. Closed Nov–Feb. Parking on adjacent streets impossible in high season. At corner of Koraka, a block up from the waterfront.

Vritomartes GREEK/SEAFOOD   The 12km (8-mile) trip to get to this Elounda taverna takes a bit of effort, but a seat here by the water makes it worthwhile. You can't beat dining at this old favorite—there's been at least a lowly taverna here long before the beautiful people and tour groups discovered the area. (In high season, come early or make a reservation.) The specialty, no surprise, is seafood. (You may find the proprietor literally "out to sea," catching that night's fish dinners.) If you settle for the red mullet and a bottle of Cretan white Xerolithia, you can't go wrong. The dining area itself is plain, but this is one place you won't forget.

On the breakwater, Elounda. ✆ **28410/41-325.** Reservations recommended for dinner in high season. Main courses 6€–32€ ($7.80–$42); fish platter special for 2 58€ ($75). MC, V. Daily 10am–11pm. Closed Nov–Mar. Parking lot nearby.

INEXPENSIVE

Itanos GREEK   A now familiar story on Crete: A simple local taverna where you go to experience "authenticity" becomes overrun by tourists, changing the scene. But the fact is, the food and prices haven't changed *that* much. Standard taverna oven dishes are still served—grilled meats; or no-nonsense chicken, lamb, or beef in tasty sauces; and hearty helpings of vegetables. The house wine comes from barrels. Low seasons and during the day, you sit indoors, where you'll experience no-nonsense decor and service. But at night during the hot months, tables appear on the sidewalk, a roof garden opens up on the building across the narrow street, and fellow travelers take over. Come here if you need a break from the harbor scene and want to feel you're in a place that still exists when all the tourists go home.

1 Kyprou. ✆ **28410/25-340.** Reservations not accepted, so come early in high season. Main courses 6€–16€ ($7.80–$20). No credit cards. Daily 10am–midnight. Just off Plateia Venizelos, at top of Koundourou.

SIDE TRIPS FROM AYIOS NIKOLAOS

Almost everyone who spends any time in Ayios Nikolaos makes the two short excursions to Spinalonga and Kritsa. Each can easily be visited in a half-day.

SPINALONGA

Spinalonga is the **fortified islet** in the bay off Elounda. The Venetians built one of their many fortresses here in 1579, and it enjoyed the distinction of being their final outpost on Crete, not taken over by the Turks until 1715. When the Cretans took possession in 1903, it was turned into a leper colony, but this ended after World War II. Now Spinalonga is a major tourist attraction. In fact, there's not much to do here except walk around and soak in the atmosphere and ghosts of the past. Boats depart regularly from both Ayios Nikolaos harbor and Elounda as well as from certain hotels. It's not especially romantic, more like an abandoned site, so visitors are left to populate it with their own imaginations.

KRITSA ⭑

Although a walk through Spinalonga can resonate as a historical byway, if you have time to make only one of these short excursions, I advise taking the 12km (8-mile) trip into the hills behind Ayios Nikolaos to the village of Kritsa and its 14th-century **Church of Panagia Kera** ⭑. The church is architecturally interesting, and scholars regard its **frescoes,** dating from the 14th and 15th centuries, as among the jewels of Cretan-Byzantine art. They have been restored, but their impact still emanates from the original work. Scenes depict the life of Jesus, the life of Mary, and the Second Coming. Guides can be arranged at any travel agency or at the Municipal Information Office in Ayios Nikolaos. After seeing the church, visit the village of Kritsa itself and enjoy the view and the many fine handcrafted goods for sale.

10

The Cyclades

by Sherry Marker

When most people think of the "Isles of Greece," they're thinking of the Cyclades. This rugged, often barren, chain of islands in the Aegean sea has villages with dazzling white houses that from a distance look like so many sugar cubes. The Cyclades got their name from the ancient Greek word meaning "to circle," or "surround," because the islands encircle Delos, the birthplace of the god Apollo. Today, especially in the summer, it's the visitors who circle these islands, taking advantage of the swift boats and hydrofoils that link them. The visitors come to see the white villages, the blue-domed chapels, and the fiery sunsets over the cobalt blue sea. They also come to relax in chic boutique hotels, eat in varied and inventive restaurants—and to enjoy an ouzo—or a chocolate martini—in some of the best bars and cafes in Greece

When you visit the Cyclades, chances are that one island will turn out to be your favorite. Here are some of our favorites, for you to shortlist when you set out to explore the islands that lie in what Homer called the "wine dark sea." Our journey begins in the north Aegean and makes its way south, before circling back north.

Unlike many of the Cyclades, where you can easily hear more English, French, and German spoken in summer than Greek, almost everyone who comes to **Tinos** is Greek. The island is often nicknamed the "Lourdes of Greece" because its famous church of the Panagia Evangelistria is Greece's most important pilgrimage destination. Don't even think of coming here on the Feast of the Assumption of the Virgin (Aug 15) without a reservation unless you enjoy sleeping alfresco—with lots of company. Tinos is also famous for its villages ornamented with the marble doors and fanlights carved here. Tinos also has miniature villages, of intricate dovecotes, that cluster on the hills and in the valleys.

The Beautiful People discovered **Mykonos** back in the 1950s and 1960s, drawn by its perfect Cycladic architecture. Today, travelers still come to see the famous windmills and sugar-cube houses, but they also come for the boutique hotels, the all-night cafe life, and serious shopping. In short, Mykonos—along with Santorini—is still one of the Cyclades that just about everyone wants to see. If you come here in August, you'll think that just about everyone has arrived with you and finding a hotel, or even a place at one of the chic nouvelle Greek cuisine restaurants, will not be easy.

That's one reason some travelers prefer **Paros,** which has something of a reputation as the poor man's Mykonos, with excellent windsurfing and a profusion of restaurants and nightspots less pricey and crowded than those on its famous neighbor Mykonos. Paros also has one preposterously picturesque seaside village—Naoussa—and one perfect inland village—Lefkes.

The largest and most fertile of the Cyclades, **Naxos** somehow has yet to

The Cyclades

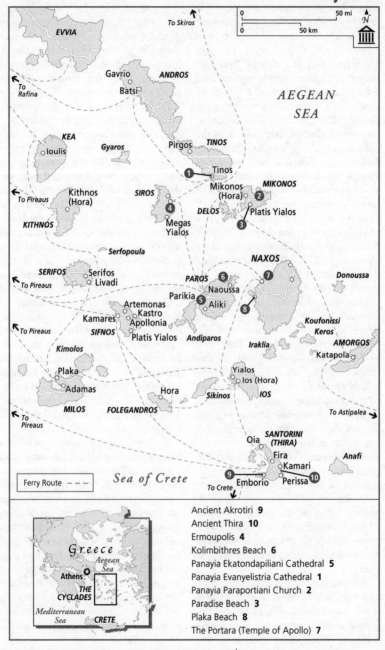

0   50 mi
0   50 km

To Skiros
To Rafina
To Pireaus
To Pireaus
To Pireaus
To Pireaus
To Astipalea
To Crete

AEGEAN SEA

Sea of Crete

EVVIA
ANDROS
Gavrio
Batsi
KEA
Ioulis
Gyaros
Pirgos
TINOS
Tinos
Kithnos (Hora)
KITHNOS
SIROS
Mikonos (Hora)
MIKONOS
Platis Yialos
DELOS
Megas Yialos
Serfopoula
SERIFOS
Serifos
Livadi
NAXOS
Donoussa
PAROS
Naoussa
Parikia
Aliki
Artemonas
Kastro
Kamares
Apollonia
SIFNOS
Platis Yialos
Andiparos
Iraklia
Koufonissi
Keros
AMORGOS
Katapola
Kimolos
Plaka
Adamas
MILOS
FOLEGANDROS
Hora
Sikinos
Yialos
Ios (Hora)
IOS
SANTORINI (THIRA)
Oia
Fira
Kamari
Emborio
Perissa
Anafi

Ferry Route - - - -

Greece
Athens
THE CYCLADES
Aegean Sea
Mediterranean Sea
CRETE

Ancient Akrotiri **9**
Ancient Thira **10**
Ermoupolis **4**
Kolimbithres Beach **6**
Panayia Ekatondapiliani Cathedral **5**
Panayia Evanyelistria Cathedral **1**
Panayia Paraportiani Church **2**
Paradise Beach **3**
Plaka Beach **8**
The Portara (Temple of Apollo) **7**

369

attract hordes of summer visitors. You know what that means: Go there soon! The hills—sometimes green well into June—are dotted both with dovecotes and a profusion of endearing Byzantine chapels. The main town is crowned by a splendid *kastro* (castle) and a number of stately houses that the Venetians built between the 12th and 16th centuries; some of the houses are still lived in by the descendants of those very Venetians. Furthermore, although Naxos is a rich enough island that it does not have to woo tourists, there are some good small hotels and restaurants here.

Santorini (Thira) is famous from a thousand travel posers showing its black lava pebble-and-sand beaches and sheer blood-red cliffs. Only a crescent-shaped sliver remains of the once-sizeable island that was blown apart in antiquity by the volcano that still steams and hisses today. The first serious tourist invasion here began in the 1970s, as word got out about Santorini's deep harbor, framed by its sheer cliffs and its odd villages, cut out of the lava. The first travelers here were willing to put up with the most modest of accommodations in local homes. (On my first visit here I was installed in a bed from which the owner's grandmother had just been ejected!). Today, Santorini gives Mykonos a serious run for the money as Boutique Hotel Central, with some of the best food in all Greece. Santorini also has one of the most impressive ancient sites in all Greece: ancient Akrotiri, where you can walk down streets some 3,500 years old. It is so well-preserved that it is often compared to Pompeii.

Folegandros is the perfect counterbalance to Santorini. As yet, this little island is not overwhelmed with visitors, but the helipad suggests that this generation's Beautiful People have discovered this still-tranquil spot. Folegandros's capital—many say it's the most beautiful in all the Cyclades—is largely built into the walls of a medieval *kastro* (castle). Just outside the kastro is another reason to come here: the elegant cliff-side Anemomilos Apartments Hotel.

Sifnos, long popular with Athenians, increasingly draws summer visitors to its handsome whitewashed villages, which many consider to have the finest architecture in all the Cyclades. In the spring this is one of the greenest and most fertile of the islands. In summer, it's a place for the young at heart: In the capital Apollonia, it's easier to count the buildings that have not (yet) been converted into discos than those that have been.

Siros, on the other hand, is as "undiscovered" as a large Cycladic island can be. Its distinguished capital, Ermoupolis, has a startling number of handsome neoclassical 19th-century buildings, including the Cyclades's only opera house, modeled on Milan's La Scala. Ano Siros, the district on the heights above the port, has sugar-cube Cycladic houses and both Catholic and Orthodox monasteries. Like Tinos and Naxos, Siros welcomes, but does not depend, on foreign tourists.

If you wanted to describe the Cyclades in their entirety, you could do worse than string together well-deserved superlatives: Wonderful! Magical! Spectacular! The sea and sky really are bluer here than elsewhere, the islands on the horizon always tantalizing. In short, the Cyclades are very "more-ish"—once you've visited one, you'll want to see another, and then another, and then, yes, yet another.

Tip: You can access a useful website for each of the Cyclades by entering "www.greeka.com/cyclades" and the name of the island. For example, www.greeka.com/cyclades/santorini.

> **Finds Foodie Alert!**
>
> Invest in a copy of Miles Lambert's *Greek Salad: A Dionysian Travelogue* (The Wine Appreciation Guild, 2004), which shows you where to find the tastiest local delicacies—here in the Cyclades and elsewhere in Greece. It's a travel guide, but it reads like a novel.

STRATEGIES FOR SEEING THE ISLANDS

A few practicalities: As you might expect, the Cyclades are crowded and expensive during high season—roughly mid-June to early September—and high season seems to get longer every year. If summer crowds and prices don't appeal to you, visit during the off season; the best times are mid-September to October or May to early June. April can still be very cold in these islands and winter winds can be unremittingly harsh. Should you visit in winter or spring, keep in mind that many island hotels have minimal heating; make sure that your hotel has genuine heat before you check in. And, keep in mind that island boat service is much less frequent off season and that many hotels, restaurants, and shops close for the winter (usually Nov–Mar). Whenever you visit, you'll discover that most hotels charge a **supplementary fee of 10%** for a stay of fewer than 3 nights. Finally, it's useful to remember that on most of these islands, the capital town has the name of the island itself. In addition, "Hora," or "Chora," meaning "the place," is commonly used for the capital. The capital of Paros, Parikia, for example, is also called Hora, as is Apollonia, the capital of Sifnos. Just to keep you on your toes, Apollonia/Hora is also called Stavri. When you're in island capitals, try to pick up the handy Sky Map, available at many travel agencies; there's a map for almost every Cycladic island. Although the businesses on these maps pay to be included, the maps are quite useful.

Although the Cyclades are bound by unmistakable family resemblance, each island is rigorously independent and unique, making this archipelago an island-hopper's paradise. Frequent ferry service makes travel easier—although changes in schedules can keep travelers on their toes (often on their toes as they pace harborside for ships to appear at unpredictable hours). Hydrofoils, in particular, are notoriously irregular, and even summer service is often canceled at the whim of the *meltemi* (blasting winds). Still, the growing fleet of catamarans is greatly facilitating travel between the ports of Piraeus and Rafina and the Cycladic islands.

1 Santorini (Thira) ✶✶✶

233km (126 nautical miles) SE of Piraeus

This is one of the most spectacular islands in the world. Many Greeks joke, somewhat begrudgingly, that there are foreigners who know where Santorini is—but are confused about where Greece is! Especially if you arrive by sea, you won't confuse Santorini with any of the other Cyclades. What will confuse you is that the island is also known as Thira. While large ships to Santorini (pop. 7,000) dock at the port of Athinios, many small ships arrive in Skala, a spectacular harbor that's part of the enormous caldera (crater) formed when a volcano blew out the island's center sometime between 1600 and 1500 B.C. To this day, some scholars speculate that this destruction gave birth to the myth of the lost continent of Atlantis.

The real wonder is that Santorini exceeds all glossy picture-postcard expectations. Like an enormous crescent moon, Santorini encloses the pure blue waters of its caldera, the core of an ancient volcano. Its two principal towns, **Fira** and **Oia** (also transliterated as **Ia**), perch at the summit of the caldera; as you approach by ship, bending back as far as possible to look as far up the cliffs as possible, whitewashed houses look like a dusting of new snow on the mountaintop. Up close, you'll find that both towns' main streets have more shops (*lots* of jewelery shops), restaurants, and discos than private homes. If you come here off season—say in early May—you'll still find Fira's streets, shops and restaurants crowded. In August, you'll experience gridlock.

Akrotiri is Santorini's principal archaeological wonder: a town destroyed by the volcano eruption here, but miraculously preserved under layers of lava. As soon as you reach Santorini, check to see if Akrotiri is open; the site's protective roof collapsed in 2005 and the site has been totally, or partially, closed since then. If Akrotiri is closed, don't despair: If it weren't that Akrotiri steals its thunder, the site of **Ancient Thira** would be the island's must-see destination. Spectacularly situated atop a high promontory, overlooking a black lava beach, the remains of this Greek, Roman, and Byzantine city sprawl over acres of rugged terrain. Ancient Thira is reached after a vertiginous hike or drive up (and up) to the acropolis itself.

Arid Santorini isn't known for the profusion of its agricultural products, but the rocky island soil has long produced a plentiful grape harvest, and the local wines are among the finest in Greece. Be sure to visit one of the island **wineries** for a tasting. And keep an eye out for the tasty, tiny unique Santorini tomatoes and white eggplants—and the unusually large and zesty capers. Most importantly, allow yourself time to see at least one sunset over the caldera; the best views are from the ramparts of the kastro and from the footpath between Fira and Oia.

The best advice we can offer is to avoid visiting during the months of July and August. Santorini experiences an even greater transformation during the peak season than other Cycladic isles. With visitors far in excess of the island's capacity, trash collects in the squares, and crowds make strolling the streets of Fira and Oia next to impossible. *Tip:* Some accommodations rates can be marked down by as much as 50% if you come off season. Virtually all accommodations are marked up by at least as much for desperate arrivals without reservations in July and August.

ESSENTIALS

GETTING THERE   By Plane   Olympic Airways (© 210/926-9111; www. olympic-airways.gr) offers daily flights between Athens and the Santorini airport Monolithos (© **22860/31-525**), which also receives European charters. There are frequent connections with Mykonos and Rhodes, and service two or three times per week to and from Iraklion, Crete. For information and reservations, check with the Olympic Airways office in Fira on Ayiou Athanassiou (© **22860/22-493**), just southeast of town on the road to Kamari; or in Athens at © **210/926/9111. Aegean Airlines** (© **210/998-2888** or 210/998-8300 in Athens), with an office at the Monolithos airport (© **22860/28-500**), also has several flights daily between Athens and Santorini. A bus to Fira (3€/$3.90) meets most flights; the schedule is posted at the bus stop, beside the airport entrance. A taxi to Fira costs about 10€ ($13).

By Boat   Ferry service runs to and from Piraeus at least twice daily; the trip takes 9 to 10 hours by car ferry on the Piraeus-Paros-Naxos-Ios-Santorini route, or 4 hours by catamaran if you go via Piraeus-Paros-Santorini. Boats are notoriously late

Santorini

and/or early; your travel or ticket agent will give you an estimate of times involved in the following journeys. Remember: That's estimate, as in guesstimate. In July and August, ferries connect several times a day with **Ios, Naxos, Paros,** and **Mykonos;** almost daily with **Anafi** and **Siros;** five times a week with **Sikinos** and **Folegandros,** and twice weekly with **Sifnos.** Service to **Thessaloniki** (17–24 hr.) is offered four to five times per week. There is an almost daily connection by excursion boat with **Iraklion** in Crete, but because this is an open sea route, the trip can be an ordeal in bad weather and is subject to frequent cancellation. Confirm ferry schedules with the Athens **GNTO** (210/870-0000; www.gnto.gr), the **Piraeus Port Authority** (© 210/451-1311 or 1440 or 1441; phone not always answered), or the **Santorini Port Authority** (© 22860/22-239).

Almost all ferries dock at **Athinios,** where buses meet each boat and then return directly to Fira (one-way to Fira costs 2€/$2.60); from the Fira dock, buses depart for many other island destinations. Taxis are also available from Athinios, at nearly five times the bus fare. Athinios is charmless; when you come here to catch a ferry, it's a good idea to bring munchies, water, and a good book.

The exposed port at **Skala,** directly below Fira, is unsafe for the larger ferries but is often used by small cruise ships, yachts, and excursion vessels. If your boat docks here, head to town either by cable car (5€/$6.50), mule, or donkey (5€/$6.50); or you can do the 45-minute uphill walk. Be prepared to share the narrow path with the mules. We recommend a mule up and the cable car down. If you suffer from acrophobia, try taking the cable car both ways with your eyes firmly shut.

VISITOR INFORMATION   Nomikos Travel (© 22860/23-660; www.nomikos villas.gr), **Bellonias Tours** (© 22860/22-469), and **Kamari Tours** (© 22860/31-390) are well-established on the island. Nomikos and Bellonias offer bus tours of the island, boat excursions around the caldera, and submarine tours beneath the caldera. Expect to pay about 30€ ($39) to join a bus tour to Akrotiri or Ancient Thira, about the same for a day-trip boat excursion to the caldera islands, and about twice that for the submarine excursion.

GETTING AROUND   By Bus   The **central bus station** is just south of the main square in Fira. Schedules are posted here: Most routes are served every hour or half-hour from 7am to 11pm in high season. A conductor on board will collect fares, which range from 1€ to 4€ ($1.30–$5.20). Destinations include Akrotiri, Athinios (the ferry pier), Oia, Kamari, Monolithos (the airport), Perissa, Perivolas Beach, Vlihada, and Vourvoulos. Excursion buses go to major attractions; ask a travel agent for details.

By Car   The travel agents listed above can help you rent a car. You might find that a local company such as **Zeus** (© 22860/24-013) offers better prices than the big names, although the quality might be a bit lower. Be sure to take full insurance. Of the better-known agencies, try **Budget Rent-A-Car,** at the airport (© 22860/33-290) or in Fira a block below the small square that the bus station is on (© 22860/22-900); a small car should cost about 60€ ($78) a day, with unlimited mileage. If you reserve in advance through Budget in the U.S. (© 800/527-0700), you should be able to beat that price.

Warning: If you park in town or in a no-parking area, the police will remove your license plates and you, not the car-rental office, will have to find the police station and pay a steep fine to get them back. There's free parking—often full—on the port's north side.

By Moped   Many roads on the island are narrow and winding; add local drivers who take the roads at high speed, and visiting drivers who aren't sure where they're going, and you'll understand the island's high accident rate. If you're determined to use two-wheeled transportation, expect to pay about 25€ ($33) per day, less during off season. Greek law now requires wearing a helmet; not all agents supply the helmet.

By Taxi   The taxi station is just south of the main square. In high season, book ahead by phone (© 22860/22-555 or 22860/23-951) if you want a taxi for an excursion; be sure that you agree on the price before you set out. For most point-to-point trips (Fira to Oia, for example), the prices are fixed. If you call for a taxi outside Fira, you'll be charged a pickup fee of at least 2€ ($2.60); also, you're required to pay the driver's

---

(*Tips* **Museum Hours Update**

If you visit Greece during the summer, check to see when sites and museums are open. According to the tourist office, they should be open from 8am to 7:30pm, but some may close earlier in the day or even be closed 1 day a week.

> **Tips** **Safety First**
>
> Use caution when walking around
> that many drivers on the roads are
> every twist and turn.

> **Fun Fact** **Akrotiri Trivia**
>
> In 1860, workers quarryi
> Canal—discovered an
> Who knows what
> the workers ha

fare from Fira to your pickup point.
taxi in advance if you'll need it late at

FAST FACTS The **American Ex**
(✆ **22860/22-624;** fax 22860/23-600
ing the caldera, above Franco's Bar. I
National Bank (Mon–Fri 8am–2pm)
square on the right near the taxi statio
the southeast edge of town on Ayiou A̲_____, immediately below the bus station
and the new archaeological museum.

There are a number of **Internet** cafes on the main square, including P.C. Club, in the Markozannes Tours office (✆ **22860/25-551**). There are several do-it-yourself launderettes in Fira; if you want your wash done for you, **Penguin Laundry** (✆ **22860/22-168**) is at the edge of Fira on the road to Oia, 200m (656 ft.) north of the main square. The **police** (✆ **22860/22-649**) are several blocks south of the main square, near the post office. For the **port police,** call ✆ **22860/22-239.** The **post office** (✆ **22860/22-238**), open Monday through Friday from 8am to 1pm, is south of the bus station. The **telephone office (OTE)** is off Ipapantis, up from the post office; hours are Monday through Saturday from 8am to 3pm.

THE TOP ATTRACTIONS

The top attraction here is the island itself; don't feel compelled to race from attraction to attraction. It's far better to make haste slowly, linger on the black beach at Kamares, and stroll Thira in the early morning when the town belongs to its inhabitants, who are buying loaves sprinkled with sesame seeds at the bakery and sweeping and washing the pavement outside all those jewelry shops. Most importantly, wherever you are, enjoy the view. There's nowhere else in the world, let alone in the Cyclades, with that caldera view.

Tip: If you plan to visit the ancient sites and their associated museums, get the economical 8€ ($10) ticket that's good for the Archaeological Museum, Ancient Akrotiri (if open), Prehistoric Thira, and Ancient Thira. Even if the ticket price goes up, as it almost certainly will, and even if Akrotiri is closed, as it may be, this will be a good buy.

Ancient Akrotiri 🕅🕅🕅 As noted, Akrotiri has been open only intermittently since the protective roof over the site collapsed in 2005. If even part of Akrotiri is open, go. If the entire site is closed when you want to visit, there's no point in coming here in the hopes of catching a glimpse of the remains: Unlike many sites, Akrotiri is *not* visible from the road.

Since excavations began in 1967, this site has presented the world with a fascinating look at life in the Minoan period. Akrotiri—sometimes nicknamed the "Minoan Pompeii"—was frozen in time sometime between 1600 and 1500 B.C. by a cataclysmic eruption of the island's volcano. Many scholars think that this powerful explosion destroyed the prosperous Minoan civilization on Crete. Pots and tools still lie

g blocks of volcanic ash—for use in building the Suez
_ient remains here. The excavation of Akrotiri followed.
_nnoticed treasures may have been walled into the canal if
_ not been alert!

_eir owners left them before abandoning the town; the absence of human
_ns indicates that the residents had ample warning of the town's destruction.
You enter the Akrotiri site along the ancient town's main street, on either side of
which are the stores or warehouses of the ancient commercial city. *Pithoi* (large
earthen jars) found here contained traces of olive oil, fish, and onion. To get the best
sense of the scale and urban nature of this town, go to the triangular plaza, near the
exit, where you'll see two-story buildings and a spacious gathering place. Imagine
yourself 3,000 years ago leaning over a balcony and spying on the passersby. As you
walk along the path through town, look for the descriptive plaques in four languages.
A few poor reproductions of the magnificent wall paintings are here; the best frescoes
were taken off to the National Archaeological Museum in Athens, although Santorini
continues to agitate for their return. For now, you can see some originals in the
Museum of Prehistoric Thira and a splendid recreation in the Thira Foundation. As
you leave the site, you may notice a cluster of flowers beside one of the ancient walls.
This marks the burial spot of Akrotiri's excavator, Professor S. Marinatos, who died in
a fall at Akrotiri. Allow at least an hour here.

Akrotiri. © 22860/81-366. Admission 6€ ($7.80). Tues–Sun 8:30am–3pm.

Ancient Thira 🎭🎭   A high rocky headland (Mesa Vouna) separates two popular
beaches (Kamari and Perissa), and at its top stand the ruins of Ancient Thira. It's an
incredible site, where cliffs drop precipitously to the sea on three sides and there are
dramatic views of Santorini and neighboring islands. This extensive group of ruins is
not easy to take in because of the many different periods on view—Roman baths jostle for space beside the remains of Byzantine walls and Hellenistic shops. One main
street runs the length of the site, passing first through two agoras. The arc of the theater embraces the town of Kamari, Fira beyond, and the open Aegean.

Greeks lived here as early as the 9th century B.C., though most buildings are much
later and date from the Hellenistic era (4th c. B.C.) You may not decipher everything,
but do take in the view from the large Terrace of the Festivals. This is where naked
lads danced to honor Apollo (inadvertently titillating, some of the graffiti suggests, a
number of the spectators).

You can reach the site by bus, car, or taxi or, if you wish, on foot, passing on the
way a cave that holds the island's only spring (see "Walking" under "Outdoor Pur-
suits," below). Excursion buses for the site of Thira leave from Fira and from the beach
at Kamari. Allow yourself at least 5 hours to view the site if you walk up there and
walk back down; if you come and go by transport, allow at least an hour at the site.

Kamari. © 22860/31-366. Admission 4€ ($5.20). Tues–Sun 8am–2:30pm; site sometimes open later in summer. On
a hilltop 3km (2 miles) south of Kamari by road.

Boutari Winery   Boutari is the island's largest winery, and Greece's best-known wine exporter. The admission includes a tour, video presentation, and tasting of about six wines, with *mezedes* (light snacks). This is a pleasant way to spend an hour or so.

Megalohori. ℭ 22860/81-011. Admission and tasting 8€ ($10). Daily 10am–sunset. 1.5km (1 mile) south of Akrotiri village. Just outside Megalohori, on the main road to Perissa.

Museum of Prehistoric Thira 𝔊   Come here to see frescoes and other finds from Ancient Akrotiri, along with objects imported from ancient Crete and the Northeastern Aegean Islands. Some of the pottery—cups, jugs, and *pithoi*—are delicately painted with motifs familiar to those of the wall paintings (see below). If possible, visit both the museum and the archaeological site at Ancient Akrotiri on the same day. Allow an hour here.

ℭ 22860/22-217. Admission 3€ ($3.90). Tues–Sun 8:30am–3pm. Across the street from the bus stop in Fira; entrance is behind the Orthodox Cathedral.

Thira Foundation: The Wall Paintings of Thira 𝔊𝔊   This exhibition created copies of the Akrotiri wall paintings, using a sophisticated technique of three-dimensional photographic reproduction that closely approximates the originals. The displays present some of the paintings in a re-creation of their original architectural context. The terrace in front of the foundation offers an astonishing view toward Fira and Imerovigli. Allow an hour here.

Petros Nomikos Conference Center, Fira. ℭ 22860/23-016. Admission 4€ ($5.20). Recorded tour 3€ ($3.90). On the caldera, 5 min. past the cable car on the way to Firostephani.

EXPLORING THE ISLAND
FIRA

Location, location, location: To put it mildly, Fira has a spectacular location on the edge of the caldera. Just when you think you've grown accustomed to the view down and out to sea and the offshore islands, you'll catch a glimpse of the caldera from a slightly different angle—and be awed yet again. If you're staying overnight on Santorini, take advantage of the fact that almost all the day-trippers from cruise ships leave in the late afternoon. Try to explore Santorini's capital, Fira, in the early evening, between the departure of the day-trippers and the onslaught of the evening revelers. As you stroll, you may be surprised to discover that, in addition to the predictable Greek Orthodox cathedral, Fira has a Roman Catholic cathedral and convent, legacies from the days when the Venetians controlled much of the Aegean. The name Santorini is, in fact, a Latinate corruption of the Greek for "Saint Irene." **Megaron Gyzi Museum** (ℭ 22860/22-244) in a stately old house by the cathedral has church and local memorabilia, including before-and-after photographs of the island at the time of the devastating earthquake of 1956. It is open Monday to Saturday 10:30am to 1pm and 5 to 8pm; Sunday 10:30am to 4:30pm. Admission is 3€ ($3.90).

⸢Tips⸣ A Different Santorini

A different way to explore Santorini is the 1-hour submarine tour beneath the caldera's surface. It sinks 25 to 30m (82–98 ft.) below the surface and offers you a glimpse into the submerged volcanic crater. The trip costs 50€ ($65); information is available at most travel agents and at ℭ 22860/28-900.

Not surprisingly, Fira is Santorini's busiest and most commercial town. The abundance of **jewelry stores** is matched in the Cyclades only by Mykonos—as are the crowds in July and August. At the north end of Ipapantis (also known as "Gold Street" for all those jewelry stores), you'll find the **cable-car station.** The Austrian-built system, the gift of wealthy ship owner Evangelos Nomikos, can zip you down to the port of Skala in 2 minutes. The cable car makes the trip every 15 minutes from 7:30am to 9pm for 3€ ($3.90), and it's worth every euro, especially on the way up.

Up and to the right of the cable-car station is the small **Archaeological Museum** (© 22860/22-217), which contains early Cycladic figurines, finds from Ancient Thira and erotic (or obscene, depending on the eye of the beholder) Dionysiac figures. It's open Tuesday through Sunday from 8:30am to 3pm. Admission is 3€ ($3.90) or free with a ticket to the Museum of Prehistoric Thira. You can easily spend a day or more enjoying Fira but don't count on getting much sleep: Fira has a wild all-night-every-night bar scene, with every bar seemingly competing for the award for the highest decibel level attainable with amplified music.

OIA ✦

Oia gets most visitors' votes as the most beautiful village on the island. The village made an amazing comeback from the 1956 earthquake which left it a virtual ghost town for decades. Several fine **19th-century mansions** survived the earthquake and have been restored, including the elegant **Restaurant-Bar 1800** and the **Naval Museum** (see below). Much of the reconstruction continues the ancient Santorini tradition of excavating dwellings from the cliff's face, and the island's most beautiful cliff dwellings can be found here. The village has basically two streets: one with traffic; and the much more pleasant inland pedestrian lane, paved with marble and lined with an increasing number of jewelry shops, tavernas, and bars.

The **Naval Museum** ✦ (© 22860/71-156) is a great introduction to this town where, until the advent of tourism, most young men found themselves working at sea and sending money home to their families. The museum, housed in a restored neoclassical mansion, was almost completely destroyed during the 1956 earthquake. Workers meticulously rebuilt the mansion using photographs of the original structure. The museum's collection includes ship models, figureheads, naval equipment, and fascinating old photographs. Its official hours are Wednesday through Monday from 12:30 to 4pm and 5 to 8:30pm, although this varies considerably. Admission is 3€ ($3.90).

The battlements of the ruined **kastro** (fortress) at the western end of town are the best place to catch the famous Oia sunset. Keep in mind that many cruise ships disgorge busloads of passengers who come here just to catch the sunset; unless you are here on a rainy February day, you may prefer to find a more secluded spot where the click of camera shutters is less deafening (see Imerovigli, below). Below the castle, a long flight of steps leads down to the pebble beach at **Ammoudi,** which is okay for swimming and sunning, and has some excellent fish tavernas (see "Where to Dine," later in this chapter). To the west is the more spacious and sandy **Koloumbos Beach.** To the southeast below Oia is the fishing port of **Armeni,** where ferries sometimes dock and you can catch an excursion boat around the caldera.

OUT ON THE ISLAND: SOME VILLAGES

It's easy to spend all your time in Fira and Oia, with excursions to the ancient sites and beaches, and to neglect other villages. Easy, but a shame, as there are some very charming villages on the island. As you travel, keep an eye out for the troglodytic **cave**

houses hollowed into solidified volcanic ash. Another thing to look for: In many fields, you'll see what look like large brown circles of intertwined sticks neatly placed on the ground. What you're looking at is a vineyard. Santorinians twist the grape vines into wreaths that encircle the grapes and protect them from the island's fierce winds.

At the south end of the island, on the road to Perissa, is the handsome old village of **Emborio.** The town was fortified in the 17th century, and you can see its towers, a graceful marble statue of the muse Polyhymnia in the cemetery, and modern-day homes built into the ruins of the citadel.

Pirgos, a village on a steep hill just above the island's port at Athinios, is a maze of narrow pathways, steps, chapels, and squares. Until the mid–19th century, this quiet hamlet hidden away behind the port was the island's capital. Near the summit of the village is the crumbling Venetian kastro, with sweeping views over the island. There is less tourism in Pirgos than in many island villages, and the central square, just off the main road, has just about all the shops and cafes. If you feel like a break try the **Café Kastelli,** with tasty snacks, *glyka tou koutalou* ("spoon sweets" of preserved fruits), and fine views. If you want a sweet-and-sour treat, try the preserved *nerangi* (bitter orange).

In the hamlet of **Gonias Episkopi** ⍟, the Church of the Panagia is an astonishingly well-preserved 11th- to 12th-century Byzantine church. As is often the case, the builders pillaged classical buildings. You will see the many fragments they appropriated incorporated into the walls—and two ancient marble altars supporting columns. Among the frescoes, keep an eye out for the figure of a dancing Salome.

THE CALDERA ISLETS ⍟

These tantalizing **islands** in the caldera are part of the glory of Santorini's seascape, reminders of the larger island that existed before the volcano left today's crescent in the sea. Fortunately, you can visit the islands and get a view of Santorini from there.

Thirassia is a small, inhabited island west across the caldera from Santorini; a cliff-top village of the same name faces the caldera, and is a relatively quiet retreat from Santorini's summer crowds. You can reach the village from the caldera side only by a long flight of steep steps. (Travelers once had to get to Fira and Oia the same way.) Full-day **boat excursions** departing daily from the port of Fira (accessible by cable car, donkey, or on foot) make brief stops at Thirassia, just long enough for you to have a quick lunch in the village; the cost of the excursion—which includes Nea Kameni, Palea Kameni, and Ia—is about 40€ ($52) per person. Another option is local **caiques,** which make the trip in summer from Armeni, the port of Oia; ask for information at one of the Fira travel agents (see "Visitor Information," earlier in this chapter).

The two smoldering dark islands in the middle of the caldera are **Palea Kameni (Old Burnt),** the smaller and more distant one, which appeared in A.D. 157; and **Nea Kameni (New Burnt),** which began to appear sometime in the early 18th century. The day excursion to Thirassia (a far more enjoyable destination) often includes these two (unfortunately often litter-strewn) volcanic isles.

OUTDOOR PURSUITS

BEACHES   Santorini's beaches may not be the best in the Cyclades, but the volcanic black and red sand here is unique in these isles—and gets very hot, very fast. **Kamari,** a little over halfway down the east coast, has the largest beach on the island. It's also the most developed, lined by hotels, restaurants, shops, and clubs. The natural setting is excellent, at the foot of cliffs rising precipitously toward Ancient Thira, but the black-pebbled beach becomes unpleasantly crowded in July and August. **Volcano**

Diving Center (© **22860/33-177;** www.scubagreece.com), at Kamari, offers guided snorkel swims for around 20€ ($26) and scuba lessons from around 50€ ($65). **Perissa,** to the south, is another increasingly crowded beach resort, albeit one with beautiful black sand. **Red beach (Paralia Kokkini),** at the end of the road to Ancient Akrotiri, gets its name from its small red volcanic pebbles; it is—but for how long?— usually much less crowded than Kamari and Perissa. All three beaches have accommodations, cafes, and tavernas.

BICYCLING Santorini's roads are in fairly good condition; it's the drivers you need to worry about: Local drivers know the roads with their eyes shut (and sometimes seem to drive that way) and visitors study maps as they drive. That said, you can rent high-quality suspension mountain bikes from 15€ ($20) per day from **Moto Chris** (© **22860/23-431**) in Fira and **Moto Piazza** (© **22860/71-055**) in Ia. It's a good idea to check the brakes and steering before you set off.

WALKING If it's not too hot when you are here, there are a great many walks you can enjoy. Here are a few.

FIRA TO OIA ✦ The path from Fira to Oia (10km/6 miles) follows the edge of the caldera, passes several churches, and climbs two substantial hills along the way. Beginning at Fira, take the pedestrian path on the caldera rim, climbing past the Catholic Cathedral to the villages of Firostephani and Imerovigli. In Imerovigli, signs on the path point the way to Oia; you'll be okay so long as you continue north, eventually reaching a dirt path along the caldera rim that parallels the vehicular road. The trail leaves the vicinity of the road with each of the next two ascents, returning to the road in the valleys. The descent into Oia eventually leads to the main pedestrian street in town. Allow yourself at least 2 hours. If you end up at Oia around sunset, you'll feel that every minute of the walk was worth it.

IMEROVIGLI & SKAROS ✦✦ In **Imerovigli,** a rocky promontory jutting into the sea is known locally as **Skaros.** From medieval times until the early 1800s, this absurdly small spot was home to the island's administrative offices. There is little to be seen of the Skaros castle now; it probably collapsed during a 19th-century earthquake. Skaros's fantastic view of the caldera is especially nice at sunset. Getting out on the promontory takes just enough effort that it is usually a tranquil haven from the crowds and bustle of the adjacent towns. The trail (signposted) descends steeply to the isthmus connecting Skaros with the mainland. The path wraps around the promontory, after a mile reaching a small chapel with a panoramic view of the caldera. On the way, note the cliffs of glassy black volcanic rock, beautifully reflecting the brilliant sunlight. People used this rock to decorate many of the older buildings in Santorini.

KAMARI TO ANCIENT THIRA ✦ The trail from Kamari to the site of **Ancient Thira** is steep but doable. It passes the beautiful site of Santorini's only freshwater spring, which you will wish to drink dry. To reach the trail head from Kamari, take the road (in the direction of Ancient Thira) past the Kamari beach parking, and turn right into the driveway of the hotel opposite Hotel Annetta, to the right of a minimarket. The trail begins behind the hotel. Climbing quickly by means of sharp switchbacks, the trail soon reaches a small chapel with a terrace and olive trees at the mouth of a cave. You can walk into the cave, which echoes with purling water, a surprising and miraculous sound in this arid place. Continuing upward, the trail rejoins the car road after a few more switchbacks, about 300m (984 ft.) from Ancient Thira. The full ascent from Kamari takes a good hour.

SHOPPING

If you're interested in fine **jewelry,** keep in mind that many prices in Fira are higher than in Athens, but the selection here is fantastic. **Porphyra** (© **22860/22-981**), in the Fabrica Shopping Center near the cathedral, has impressive work. Santorini's best-known jeweler is probably **Kostas Antoniou** (© **22860/22-633**), on Ayiou Ioannou north of the cable-car station. And there are plenty of shops between the two. Generally, the farther north you go, the higher the prices and the less certain the quality. In Firostephani, **Cava Sigalas Argiris** (© **22860/22-802**) stocks all the local **wines,** including their own. Also for sale are locally grown and **prepared foods,** often served as *mezedes*: *fava,* a spread made with chickpeas; *tomatahia,* small pickled tomatoes; and *kapari* (capers). The main street in Oia, facing the caldera, has many interesting stores, several with prints showing local scenes, in addition to the inevitable souvenir shops. **Replica** (© **22860/71-916**) is a source of contemporary statuary and pottery as well as museum replicas; it will ship purchases to your home at post-office rates. Farther south on the main street is **Nakis** (© **22860/71-813**), which specializes in amber jewelry and not surprisingly has a collection of insects in amber.

WHERE TO STAY

As noted, Santorini is stuffed to the gills with visitors in July and August; try to make a reservation with a deposit at least 2 months in advance; we hear travelers' tales of people sitting miserably in cafes all night. We also hear tales of hotels doubling the price on remaining rooms. Except in July and August, don't accept lodging offered at the port unless you're exhausted and don't care how meager the room is and how remote the village when you wake up the next morning. In July and August, be grateful for whatever you get if you show up without a reservation. *Tip:* If you made your reservation by e-mail, be sure to arrive with a printout of your reservation confirmation.

The island's unusual **cave houses** have inspired many hotel designers. Barrel-vaulted ceilings and perhaps even a bathroom carved into the rock distinguish a typical **cave house.** Built for earthquake resistance and economy, some of the spaces may at first strike you as cramped; like most newcomers, you'll soon see them as part of the island's special charm. The best of them are designed with high ceilings, airy rooms, and good cross-ventilation, and because they are carved into the cliff face, they remain relatively cool throughout the summer.

Many apartments and villas have efficiency kitchens, but the facilities may be minimal. If you plan to do much cooking, check first to see what's in the drawers and cupboards, or you may find yourself frustrated if you try to prepare anything more elaborate than a cup of coffee.

FIRA

In addition to the choices below, we've had good reports on the quiet **Hotel Atlantis** (© **22860/22-232**), where guests can spend the sunset hours with a bottle of wine on the balcony overlooking the caldera. *Note:* Due to the noise in Fira, you may want to consider staying in one of the villages out on the island, unless you stay in one of the quieter hotels suggested below.

Aigialos ⋆⋆   In a quiet caldera location, occupying 16 restored 18th- and 19th-century town houses, the Aigialos proclaims its intention to be a "Luxury Traditional Settlement." The oxymoron aside—rather few traditional settlements here or elsewhere have had Jacuzzis, swimming pools, and counter swim exercise pools—this is a nifty place. The units have all the mod cons and all the creature comforts. As the price goes up, you get more space (two bathrooms, not just one) and more privacy (your own, not a shared terrace or your own balcony). There's an extensive breakfast buffet and a highly praised in-house, guests-only, restaurant.

Fira, 84700 Santorini. ⒸChar 22860/25-191. www.aigialos.gr. 16 units. 375€–550€ ($488–$715) double; honeymoon suites 700€–1,300€ ($910–$1,690). Rates include breakfast. AE, DC, MC, V. Closed Nov–Mar. **Amenities:** Pool bar; pools; 24-hr. room service; twice-daily maid service. *In room:* A/C, TV, CD, DVD, Internet, fridge, safe.

Hotel Aressana ★★   This hotel (popular with Greek and foreign honeymooners) compensates for its lack of a caldera view with a large swimming pool and excellent location, tucked away behind the Orthodox Cathedral, in a relatively quiet location. Most rooms have balconies or terraces; many have the high barrel-vaulted ceilings typical of this island. Unusual in Greece are the nonsmoking rooms. The breakfast room opens onto the pool terrace, as do most of the guest rooms; the elaborate buffet breakfast includes numerous Santorinian specialties. The Aressana also maintains seven nearby apartments facing the caldera, starting at 250€ ($325), which includes use of the hotel pool.

Fira, 84700 Santorini. ⒸChar 22860/23-900. Fax 22860/23-902. www.aressana.gr. 50 units, 1 with shower. 250€–300€ ($325–$390) double; 320€–400€ ($416–$520) suite. Rates include full breakfast. AE, DC, MC, V. Closed mid-Nov to Feb. **Amenities:** Snack bar; bar; freshwater pool; room service 7am–noon. *In room:* A/C, TV, minibar.

Hotel Keti ★★ *Value*   This simple little hotel offers one of the best bargains on the caldera. All of the (smallish) rooms have traditional vaulted ceilings, white walls and coverlets, and open onto a shared terrace overlooking the caldera. The bathrooms, at the back of the rooms, are carved into the cliff face. Clearly, the Keti is doing something right: Not many places this modest make it into Alastair Sawday's *Special Places.* One drawback if you have trouble walking: It's a steep 5- to 10-minute walk from the Keti's quiet cliff-side location to Fira itself.

Fira, 84700 Santorini. ⒸChar 22860/22-324. www.hotelketi.gr. 7 units. 100€–120€ ($130–$156) double. No credit cards. Closed Nov to mid-Mar. **Amenities:** Breakfast room; bar. *In room:* A/C, fridge, TV, safe.

FIROSTEPHANI

This quieter and less expensive neighborhood is just a 10-minute walk from Fira. The views of the caldera are just as good, if not better.

Tsitouras Collection ★   This top-of-the-line luxury hotel will either dazzle or dismay you: Understatement is conspicuous by its absence here, where antiques and reproductions jostle for space in five themed villas (including "House of Portraits" and "House of Porcelain"). The villa you stay in is all yours, which ensures blissful privacy. Tranquillity is easy to achieve here thanks to the no-television policy. One astonishing drawback: Only the villa guests have a pool. Some spa services are available and guests are encouraged to meet with the chef to discuss "constructing" a meal. We've had almost as many thumbs-down for the indifferent service as we have had raves for the serious luxury and quiet location.

Firostefani, 84700 Santorini. ⒸChar 22860/23-747. Fax 22860/23-918. www.tsitouras.gr. 5 villas (each accommodating at least 4). 500€–800€ ($780–$1,040) for 2 sharing a villa; T.C. Villa (sleeps 1–6) 3,500€ ($4,550). MC, V. **Amenities:** Restaurant; cafe. *In room:* A/C, kitchenette, wet bar, CD, TV, DVD, safe.

IMEROVIGLI

The next village north along the caldera rim is so named because it is the first place on the island from which you can see the rising sun. The name translates as "day vigil." By virtue of its height, Imerovigli also has the best views on this part of the caldera.

While everyone else is jostling for a place to see the sunset at Oia, head to Imerovigli and take the path over to the promontory of Skaros, with the picturesque remains of its medieval kastro. Amazingly, this deserted and isolated spot was the island's medieval capital. It's a blissful place to watch the sunset.

Imerovigli and Oia have a considerable number of attractive and comfortable places to stay. In addition to the places listed below, you might want to consider **La Maltese** (© **22860/24-701;** www.lamaltese.com), a member of the Relais & Châteaux, in a restored sea captain's neoclassical mansion, now fitted out with indoor and outdoor pools, hammam and sauna, restaurant and piano bar, and, of course, that caldera view.

Astra Apartments 🏆🏆🏆 Perched on a cliff side, with spectacular views, this is one of the nicest places to stay in all of Greece. There are other places nearby which also have spectacular pools with spectacular views, but manager George Karayiannis is a large part of what makes Astra so special: He is always at the ready to arrange car rentals, recommend a wonderful beach or restaurant—or even help you plan your wedding and honeymoon here. The Astra Apartments look like a tiny, whitewashed village (with an elegant pool) set in the village of Imerovigli, which is still much less crowded than Fira or Oia. Nothing is flashy here; everything is just right. The vibrant blue of the bed coverlets is echoed in the blue paint on the cupboards. Although each unit has its own kitchenette, breakfast is served on your private terrace or balcony, and you can order delicious salads and sandwiches from the bar day and night.

Imerovigli, 84700 Santorini. © **22860/23-641.** Fax 22860/24-765. www.astra-apartments.com. 85 units. 230€–300€ ($299–$390) double; apt from 275€ ($378); 750€ ($975) apt with private pool. MC, V. **Amenities:** Bar; pool. *In room:* A/C, TV, CD, DVD, radio, Internet, kitchenette.

Chromata 🏆🏆 Here you'll get a wonderful view out over the island, an inviting pool, and excellent service. The lovely rooms sport comfortable, stylish chairs and hand-loomed rugs. If it weren't that George Karayiannis makes its neighbor, Astra, so special, Chromata would be the place to stay. If Astra is full, you'll be happy here.

Imerovigli, 84700 Santorini. © **22860/24-850.** 17 units. 150€–300€ ($195–$390) double. AE, MC, V. **Amenities:** Bar; pool. *In room:* A/C, TV, minibar.

KARTERADOS

About 2km (1 mile) southeast of Fira, this small village knows the tourist ropes, and has many new hotels and rooms to let. Buses stop at the top of Karterados's main street on their ways to Kamari, Perissa, and Akrotiri. Nevertheless, the location is somewhat inconvenient: not especially close to Fira or to the beach. Karterados beach is a 3km (2-mile) walk from the center of town. Get to Monolithos, a longer beach, by continuing south along the water's edge an additional half-mile.

Pension George 🏆 *Value* With a small pool, simple wood furnishings, attractive and reasonably priced rooms, and helpful owners, the Pension offers good value if you're on a budget. To save even more money, opt for a room without a balcony. George and Helen Halaris will help you arrange car and boat rentals.

P.O. Box 324, Karterados, 84700 Santorini. © **22860/22-351.** www.pensiongeorge.com. 25 units. 60€–90€ ($78–$117) double. No credit cards. Inquire about apts that sleep 2–5. **Amenities:** Breakfast on request; free transportation to airport or harbor. *In room:* A/C, TV (in some), fridge, safety-deposit box.

OIA

Oia's chic shops (check out **The Art Gallery** and **Art Gallery Oia** on Oia's meandering main drag), boutique hotels, and gorgeous sunsets make it an increasingly popular place to stay or to visit—especially for travelers who find Fira too frenetic.

If you're running low on reading material by the time you get to Santorini, head to **Atlantis Books** (*C* **22860/72-346;** www.atlantisbooks.org) in Oia, run by a group of expat Brits and Americans as well as several Greeks. You'll find everything from guidebooks and detective novels for the beach to poetry and philosophy.

Chelidonia ☆   Chelidonia (the Greek name for the swallows that you'll see here) is a carefully restored and reconstructed slice of Oia that was destroyed in the 1956 earthquake. Most units are former homes, each with its unique layout—another unit was a bakery, yet another a stable. Skylights illuminate many rooms from above. Most have truly private terraces, many with small gardens of flowering plants and herbs for cooking. The guest rooms are spacious, the bathrooms luxuriously large, and the interiors simple and very elegant. All units enjoy the famous Oia view across the caldera toward Imerovigli, Fira, and the southern end of the island. The Chelidonia is not a traditional hotel with room service, but its apartments have daily maid service, and the owner clearly understands what makes guests feel at home. There's usually a 3-night minimum for stays.

Ia, 84702 Santorini. *C* **22860/71-287.** Fax 22860/71-649. www.chelidonia.com. 10 units. 150€ ($195) studio; 165€–205€ ($215–$267) house. No credit cards. Open all year. *In room:* A/C, kitchenette.

Hotel Finikia *Value*   This small, appealing hotel has a number of rooms with the domed ceilings traditional to Santorini architecture. Some rooms boast local weavings and artifacts. Most units have semiprivate balconies or terraces with views toward the sea—the hotel is on the east slope of the island, so the view is gentle rather than spectacular. The pool is good-size and the restaurant/bar is open almost all day. Irene and Theodoris Andreadis are your very helpful and friendly hosts. They have adjacent apartments for rent as well.

Finikia, 84702 Santorini. *C* **22860/71-373** or 210/654-7944 in winter. Fax 22860/71-118. finikia@otenet.gr. 15 units. From 90€ ($117) double. Rates include breakfast. MC, V. Closed Nov–Mar. **Amenities:** Restaurant; bar; pool. *In room:* A/C, minibar.

Katikies ☆☆   If you find a more spectacular pool anywhere on the island, let us know. The main pool—one of four here—runs almost to the side of the caldera. You'll enjoy a world-class view. Katikies began as a small hotel, then added suites (some with their own plunge pools), and now has a seven-unit villa (with, of course, its own pool). The hotel's island-style architecture incorporates twists and turns, secluded patios, beamed ceilings, and antiques. If the people in the next room like to sing in the shower, you might hear them, but most people who stay here treasure the tranquillity. After all, this is a member of the Small Luxury Hotels of the World. The top-of-the-line honeymoon suite has its own Jacuzzi, just in case you can't be bothered going to either outdoor pool. The new White Cave restaurant has only a handful of tables, so be sure to book ahead! Or head to one of Katikies' three other restaurants. A masseur is on call at the small spa on-site.

Oia, 84702 Santorini. *C* **22860/71-401.** Fax 22860/71-129. www.katikies.com. 22 units. 300€–400€ ($390–$520) double; prices for suites on request. Rates include breakfast. MC, V. **Amenities:** 4 restaurants; bar; 4 pools; health club and spa; concierge; car rental; laundry service; currency exchange; library and Internet facilities. *In room:* A/C, TV, minibar, hair dryer.

Perivolas Traditional Settlement ☆☆   You could be forgiven for thinking that this is a pool with a nice little hotel attached: The *Conde Nast Traveler* cover photo of Perivolas's pool meeting the edge of the sky and the lip of the caldera put this place on the jet-setters' map. The 17 houses that make up the hotel offer studios and junior and superior suites. Price differences reflect the sizes of the three categories; each unit has a kitchenette and a terrace. The superior suites have a separate bedroom, whereas the other units are open plan. The architecture—wall niches, skylights, stonework—and some of the furnishings of these greatly enhanced cave dwellings are traditional. Everything is elegant—including the in-house library. The only downside: Few units have terraces with significant degrees of privacy—but that is true of almost every Santorini hotel—and certainly true of genuine traditional village settlements!

Ia, 84702 Santorini. © **22860/71-308.** Fax 22860/71-309. www.perivolas.gr. 19 units. 390€–600€ ($507–$780) double/suite; 700€–1,450€ ($910–$1,885) deluxe suite. Rates include buffet breakfast. No credit cards. Closed mid-Oct to mid-Apr. **Amenities:** Cafe; bar; pool. *In room:* A/C, full kitchen.

MEGALOHORI
Villa Vedema Hotel 🌟🌟   The sleepy village of Megalohori is not where you'd expect to find a luxury hotel, but Santorini is full of surprises. The hotel is a self-contained world, surrounded by a wall like a fortified town. A member of the Small Luxury Hotels of the World group, the Vedema is justly proud of its attentive but unobtrusive service. The residences are set around several irregular courtyards, much like those found in a village. Each apartment is comfortable, with sink-into-them chairs and at least one huge marble bathroom. The restaurant is excellent, and the candlelit wine bar is located in a 300-year-old wine cellar. The principal disadvantage of a stay here is the location: Megalohori is not a particularly convenient base for exploring the island. But with this amount of luxury, you may not want to budge!

Megalohori, 84700 Santorini. © **22860/81-796** or 22860/81-797. www.vedema.gr. 45 units. 400€–1,000€ ($520–$1,300) double/suite. Minimum 3-night stay. AE, DC, MC, V. Closed mid-Oct to mid-Apr. **Amenities:** Restaurant; bar; pool; concierge; airport pickup arranged; 24-hr. room service. *In room:* A/C, TV, CD, DVD, Internet, minibar.

PYRGOS
Zannos Melathron 🌟🌟   Relatively uncrowded Pyrgos sits inland between Megalohori and Kamari. This 12-room boutique hotel, on one of the highest points on the island, occupies an 18th-century and a 19th-century building. The rooms mix antiques with modern pieces, the island views are lovely, the pool is welcoming. If you want nightlife, this is not the place for you; if you want a peaceful retreat and near-perfect service, this may be just the spot. If you want a cigar bar, look no further.

Pyrgos, 84700 Santorini. © **22860/28-220.** www.zannos.gr. 12 units. 300€–440€ ($390–$572) double; 550€–1,000€ ($715–$1,300) suites. Cards to be accepted soon; reconfirm this when you make your reservation. **Amenities:** Restaurant; bar; pool; concierge; airport pickup; 24-hr. room service. *In room:* A/C, TV, minibar.

KAMARI
Tour groups book most of the hotels at Santorini's best and best-known beach resort in the summer. (Below we recommend one that is often group-free.) If you can't find a room, try the local office of **Kamari Tours** (© **22860/31-390** or 22860/31-455), which manages many of the hotels in Kamari and may be able to find you a vacancy. Many hotels here offer substantial discounts if you book online.

Hotel Astro 🌟   A perfectly decent hotel, near, but not on the beach, with a freshwater pool and a helpful owner. Rooms have balconies or terraces and you're near, but not smothered by, Kamari's discos, cafes, and tavernas.

Kamari, 84700 Santorini. © **22860/31-366.** www.astro-hotel.com. 35 units. 8 apartments. From 80€ ($104) double. MC, V. **Amenities:** Bar. *In room:* TV, Internet, fridge.

WHERE TO DINE
FIRA

As you might expect, restaurants here range from blah to beatific. The bad ones stint on quality and service because they know that most tourists are here today and gone tomorrow. The good places cater to the discriminating tourist and to Greek and foreign visitors who come back again and again.

If all you want is breakfast or a light, cheap meal, try **Corner Crepes,** just off the main square (no phone). The popular taverna **Camille Stefani** (© 22860/28-938) long in Kamari, is now in Fira, at the Fabrica shopping center.

Note: Many of the restaurants near the cable car fall into the forgettable category. In addition, some of these restaurants have been known to present menus without prices, and then charge exorbitantly for food and wine. If you are given a menu, make sure prices are listed.

Koukoumavlos ✿✿ GREEK   The terrace at Koukoumavlos enjoys the famous caldera view, but unlike most caldera restaurants where a spectacular view compensates for mediocre food, here the view is a distraction from the delights of the kitchen. The menu changes often, as the chef tries out new dishes with ingredients not always used in the islands (a wide variety of mushrooms, for example). Many dishes offer creative variations on traditional Greek food, like the shrimp poached in retsina; or the fava served hot in olive oil with grilled zucchini, onions, tomatoes, olives, and toasted almonds. That said, maybe crayfish with white chocolate–ginger–lemon sauce is one innovation too many.

Below the Hotel Atlantis, facing the caldera. © **22860/23-807.** Reservations recommended for dinner. Main courses 20€–35€ ($26–$46). AE, MC, V. Daily noon–3pm and 7:30pm–midnight.

Selene ✿✿✿ GREEK   If you eat only one meal on Santorini, eat it here. This is the best restaurant on Santorini—and one of the best in Greece. Selene uses local produce to highlight what owner George Haziyannakis call the "creative nature of Greek cuisine." The appetizers, often including a delicious sea urchin salad on artichokes and fluffy fava balls with caper sauce, are deservedly famous. Entrees include *brodero* (seafood stew). The baked mackerel with caper leaves and tomato wrapped in a crepe of fava beans will convert even the most dedicated flesh eaters. The local lamb, quail, rabbit, and beef are all excellent. In short, everything—location, ambience, view, service—comes together to form the perfect setting for the delicious, inventive food. The selection of cheeses from across the Cyclades is impressive. If you want to learn to make some of Selene's selections yourself, check out her cooking classes at www. selene.gr.

Fira. © **22860/22-249.** Fax 22860/24-395. Reservations recommended. Main courses 17€–30€ ($22–$39). AE, MC, V. Mid-Apr to mid-Oct daily 7pm–midnight. Closed late Oct to early Apr. In the passageway between the Atlantis and Aressana hotels.

Sphinx Restaurant ✿ INTERNATIONAL   Antiques, sculpture, and ceramics by local artists fill this restored mansion and large terrace with views of the caldera and the port at Skala Fira. You may not decide that you've come to Santorini to eat ostrich, but the fresh pasta is tasty, as is the seafood. Locals eat here—always a good sign.

Odos Mitropoleos. © **22860/23-823.** Reservations recommended. Main courses 15€–25€ ($20–$33); fish priced by the kilo. AE, DC, MC, V. Daily 11am–3pm and 7pm–1am. Near the Panagia Ypapantis Church.

Taverna Nikolas *Value* GREEK   This is another one of the few restaurants in Fira where locals queue up alongside throngs of travelers for a table—high praise, for a place that has been here forever. There aren't any surprises; you'll get traditional Greek dishes prepared very well. The lamb with greens in egg-lemon sauce is particularly delicious. The dining room is always busy, so arrive early or plan to wait.

Just up from the main square in Fira. No phone. Main courses 10€–15€ ($13–$20). No credit cards. Daily noon–midnight.

OIA

If you want to be by the sea, head down to **Ammoudi,** Oia's port, hundreds of feet below the village, huddled between the cliffs and the sea. We recommend Katina's fish taverna there; Captain Dimitri's, a long time favorite, is now at the other end of the island at Akrotiri. If you don't want to trek all the way down to the beach, stop along the way at **Kastro** (© 22860/71-045), where you'll still have a fine view and can enjoy Greek dishes, pasta, or fresh fish. To get there, follow the stepped path down from the vicinity of Lontza Castle, hire a donkey (5€/$6.50 one-way), or call a taxi. We recommend the walk down (to build an appetite) and a taxi or donkey up.

Katina's *Value* SEAFOOD   ) Fresh fish, grilled by the sea—what more could one ask for?

Ammoudi. © 22860/71-280. No credit cards. Daily 10am–midnight (usually).

Restaurant-Bar 1800 *Value Value* CONTINENTAL   For many years recognized as the best place in Oia for a formal dinner, the 1800 has a devoted following among visitors and locals. Many items are Greek dishes with a difference, such as the tender lamb chops with green applesauce and the cheese pie filled not just with feta, but with five cheeses. The restaurant, housed in a splendidly restored neoclassical captain's mansion, has undeniable romantic charm whether you eat indoors or on the rooftop terrace. After you eat, you can decide whether the owner (an architect and chef) deserves more praise for his skill with the decor or with the cuisine. "Each plate resembles a canvas," this restaurant proclaims.

Odos Nikolaos Nomikos. © 22860/71-485. www.oia-1800.com. Main courses 15€–30€ ($20–$39). AE, DC, MC, V. Daily 6pm–midnight.

Skala *Value* GREEK   Skala has perfectly fine taverna food, at prices that are less steep than those at many other places here. All the staples of traditional Greek (if not local Santorini) food are reliably good; the management is helpful and friendly. Veggies are not, as so often in Greece, overcooked, and the grills and stews are tasty.

Odos Nikolaos Nomikos. © 22860/71-362. Main courses 8€–15€ ($10–$20). MC. Daily 1pm–midnight.

SANTORINI AFTER DARK

The height of the tourist season is also the height of the music season in Santorini. If you are here in July, you may want to take in the annual Santorini Jazz Festival (www.jazzfestival.gr), which has been bringing international jazz bands and artists here every summer since 1997. Many performances are on Kamari beach. In August and September, the 2-week **Santorini International Music Festival** (© 22860/23-166), with international singers and musicians, gives performances of classical music at the Nomikos Centre in Fira. Admission to most events starts at 15€ ($20).

Fira has all-night nightlife; as always on the islands, places that are hot one season are gone the next. I'm not listing phone numbers here because phones simply are not answered. If you want to kick off your evening with a drink on the caldera, to watch the spectacular sunset **Franco's** and **Palaia Kameni** are still the most famous and best places for this magic hour; be prepared to pay 15€ ($20) and up (and up). If you are willing to forego the caldera view, you'll find almost too many spots to sample along the main drag and around the main square, including the inevitable Irish pub, **Murphy's.** **Kirathira Bar** plays jazz at a level that permits conversation, and the nearby **Art Café** offers muted music.

Discos come and go, and you need only follow your ears to find them. **Koo Club** is the biggest, whereas **Enigma** is thronged most nights. **Tithora** is popular with a young, heavy-drinking crowd. There's usually no cover, but the cheapest drinks at most places are at least 10€ ($13).

Out on the island, in Oia, **Zorba's** is a popular cliff-side pub. The fine restaurant/bar **1800** (see above) is a quiet and sophisticated place to stop in for a drink—and certainly for a meal.

Kamari has lots of disco bars, including **Disco Dom, Mango's, Yellow Donkey,** and **Valentino's,** all popular with the youngish tour groupers who grope about here.

2 Folegandros ★★

181km (98 nautical miles) SE of Piraeus

Tell people that you're off to Folegandros and you're likely to get one of two reactions: quizzical expressions from those who have not been here and envious glances from those who know the island. Folegandros has one of the most perfect settlements in the islands: More village than town, Folegandros's capital, Hora, huddles at the edge of cliffs some 250m (820 ft.) above the sea. One small, shaded square spills into the next, with green and blue paving slates outlined in brilliant white. As you prowl the streets, you'll gradually realize that much of Hora is built into the walls of the kastro, a medieval castle. Small houses with steep front staircases and overhanging wooden balconies weighed with pots of geraniums line the narrow lanes. What's more, cars and motorcycles are banned in **Hora.** Bliss.

As for the main port, **Karavostasi,** if you didn't know about Hora and the island's beguiling interior landscape, you could be forgiven for continuing to the next port of call and not getting off here: Karavostasi means "ferry stop" and the name really just about sums up all there is to say about this desultory little port.

If you want to explore Folegandros, you can do a good deal by local bus, but if you like to walk, this is a great place for it. The island's paved roads are minimal and there is still an elaborate network of foot and donkey paths over very beautiful terraced hillsides. Look closely and you'll see that some of these parths are paved with ancient marble blocks; others are hacked from the natural bedrock. Hills are crisscrossed with the stone walls that enclose the terraced fields that allow local farmers to grow barley on the island's steep slopes. Rocky coves shelter some appealing pebble beaches (best reached by caique). Try to allow at least a day and a night on Folegandros.

Tips Avoiding the easyCruisers

In 2007, easyCruise added Folegandros to its Aegean itinerary. If you want to see a tranquil Folegandros, you may want to check www.easycruise.com to see what day the ship will be here and come another day.

ESSENTIALS

GETTING THERE   By Boat   Three ferries a week stop at Folegandros on the San-torini-Folegandros-Sikinos-Ios-Naxos-Paros-Piraeus route; it's about 10 hours from Piraeus to Folegandros. Information is available at the **Piraeus Port Authority** (© 210/451-1311 or 1440 or 1441), which seldom answers the phone. Boats are notoriously late and/or early; your travel or ticket agent will give you an estimate of times involved in the following journeys. Remember: That's estimate, as in guesstimate. Several ferries per week stop on the Folegandros-Milos-Sifnos-Paros-Mykonos-Tinos-Siros hydrofoil run. During the off season, infrequent service and bad weather can easily keep you here longer than you intend. **Folegandros Port Police** are at © 22860/41-530.

VISITOR INFORMATION   Maraki Travel Agency (© 22860/41-273) and **Sottovento Travel** (© 22860/41-444; sottovento94@hotmail.com) exchange money, help with travel arrangements, sell maps of the island, and offer Internet facilities. Sottovento also serves as the local Italian consulate. You can buy ferry tickets at a branch of Maraki Travel at the port (© 22860/41-198).

GETTING AROUND   By Bus   The bus to Hora meets all ferries in peak season and most ferries during the rest of the year; it also makes eight or nine trips a day on the road running along the island's spine between Hora and Ano Meria at the island's northern end. The fare is 1.50€ ($1.95).

By Moped   There are two moped-rental outfits on Folegandros: **Jimmy's Motorcycle** (© 22860/41-448) in Karavostassi; and **Moto Rent** (© 22860/41-316) in Hora, near Sottovento Travel.

By Boat   Mid-June through August, boat taxis or caiques provide transport to the island's southern beaches. From Karavostassi, boats depart for Katergo and Angali (10€/$13 round-trip); another boat departs from Angali for Ayios Nikolaos, Livadaki, and Ambeli (10€/$13 round-trip). There is also a 7-hour tour of the island's beaches that departs from Karavostassi at least three times weekly in summer, and makes stops at five beaches; the cost is 25€ ($33) per person, including lunch. Reservations can be made at Diaplous or Sottovento Travel (see above); note that tickets must be purchased a day in advance.

FAST FACTS   Folegandros has neither bank nor ATM, but you can exchange money at travel agents and hotels. Commissions on money exchange can be steep, because you are something of a captive audience here. It may be wise to arrive with enough cash for your visit. The **post office** and **telephone office (OTE)** are right off the central square in Hora, open Monday through Friday from 8am to 3pm. The **police station** (© 22860/41-222) is behind the post office and OTE.

WHAT TO SEE & DO

You probably won't want to linger in **Karavostassi,** perhaps the least enticing port in the Cyclades. Best to hop on a local bus and chug the 4km (2½ miles) up to Hora.

Clifff-side **Hora** ✦✦ is centered around five closely connected squares, connected by meandering streets, lined with houses, restaurants, and shops. Even from the bus-stop square, the sheer drop of the cliff offers an awesome sight. On the right in the next square, you'll find the **Kastro:** two narrow pedestrian streets connected by tunnel-like walkways, squeezed between the town and the sea cliffs, with remnants of the medieval castle. One majestic church, **Kimisis Theotokou,** dominates the skyline of Hora. It's particularly beautiful at night, when it's illuminated. Built at the highest point in town—and with fine views over the island—it stands on the foundations of the ancient Greek town. Townspeople parade through the village with the church's icon of the Virgin with great ceremony each Easter Sunday. The other church to see here is the deserted **Monastery of the Panagia,** north of town, also with lovely views.

OUT ON THE ISLAND

As you rush from island to island, checking in and out of hotels, it's not always easy to feel the rhythm of island life. One great way to do that is to visit Folegandros's small **Folk Museum,** in Ano Meria. If you want to see some countryside, head west from Hora to the village of **Ano Meria.** This tiny hamlet of scattered farms is the island's second-largest village. Some of the tools and household items on view in the museum have been used for generations, and you can see some still in use today. The museum (no phone; free admission, but donation appropriate) is open 5 to 8pm weeknights in July and August, and the local bus can drop you a pleasant stroll away. If the museum turns out to be closed, console yourself that this, too, is an insight into the rhythms of island life!

BEACHES

You can swim at the port of Karavostasi, or get a caique (10€/$13 round-trip) from there to the island's best beach **Katergo** ✿, which is protected from the sometimes fierce winds here by rocky headlands. You can also get by caique to **Angali,** the largest and most crowded fine-sand beach on the island. There are a few tavernas on the beach and rooms to let.

WALKING

The footpaths through the northern part of the island are for the most part well used and easy to follow. Numerous paths branch off to the southwest from the paved road through Ano Meria; the hills traversed by these trails, between the road and the sea, are particularly beautiful. Here's one walk you may enjoy; if you want to try more walks, check with someone at the Sottovento Travel agency for tips. There may even be a walker's map by the time you visit.

Ayios Andreas to Ayios Yeoryios. An easy path leads you from **Ayios Andreas** to the bay at **Ayios Yeoryios.** Take the bus to the next-to-last stop, at the northern end of Ano Meria; it will let you off by the church of Ayios Andreas. At the stop, the sign AG. GEORGIOS 1.5, points to the right. Follow the sign, and continue along a road that quickly becomes a path and descends steeply toward the bay. Follow the main path at each of several intersections; you'll be able to see the bay for the last 20 minutes of the walk. You'll find a small pebble beach at the bay of Ayios Yeoryios, but no fresh water, so be sure to bring plenty. Allow 2 hours for the round-trip.

WHERE TO STAY

There are two special places to stay here; **Anemomilos Apartments** and the **Castro Hotel.** That said, the **Meltemi Hotel** (© **22860/41-425;** meltemihotel@yahoo.gr) across from Anemomilos is a good buy, with decent rooms, but no view or pool. The island's limited facilities are always fully booked in July and August, when advance reservations are essential; other times, reservations are recommended here.

Anemomilos Apartments ✿✿   This congenial place began to turn up on lists of the "best island retreats" soon after it opened in 1998—and made *Odyssey* magazine's best-of-the-year list again in 2007. Spectacularly situated at the edge of a cliff overlooking the sea, all but two of the units here have terraces; all units have either a full or partial sea view. A well-stocked kitchenette means you can actually cook here. If you don't want to make your own breakfast, Cornelia Patelis, who manages the hotel with her husband, Dimitris, makes a delicious sweet breakfast pie with local cheese. The hotel also serves breakfast and snacks throughout the day on the pool terrace. One apartment is accessible for travelers with disabilities. Transport to and from the port, arranged by the hotel, costs about 5€ ($6.50) per person one-way.

Hora, 84011 Folegandros. © 22860/41-309. www.AnemomilosApartments.com. 17 units. 160€–240€ ($208–$312) double. Breakfast 15€ ($20). V. Closed mid-Oct to Easter. Near the central bus stop. **Amenities:** Breakfast room/bar; pool. *In room:* A/C, Internet, kitchenette, fridge.

Castro Hotel ★★ The Castro is in a Venetian castle dating back to 1212; it's the oldest part of Hora, wedged against the cliffs and facing the Aegean 250m (820 ft.) below. Guest rooms are small but comfortable, and seven have phenomenal views. The two most desirable units have balconies surveying the extraordinary view; these don't cost extra and are a great bargain. (Try to reserve room no. 3, 4, 5, 13, 14, 15, or R1.) Even if you opt for a room without the view, you can enjoy it from the shared rooftop terrace. The charming Despo Danassi, whose family has owned this house for five generations, will make you feel at home. And her homemade fig jam is fabulous!

Hora, 84011 Folegandros. © 22860/41-230 or 210/778-1658 in Athens. Fax 22860/41-230 or 210/778-1658 in Athens. 12 units. 80€–125€ ($104–$163) double. Continental breakfast 10€ ($13). AE, V. Closed Nov–Apr. **Amenities:** Breakfast room.

WHERE TO DINE

Main courses for all the restaurants listed run about 5€ to 15€ ($6.50–$20); hours are generally from 9am to 3pm and 6pm to midnight.

The local specialty, *matsata,* is made with fresh pasta and rabbit or chicken. The best place to sample it is **Mimi's,** in Ano Meria (© **22860/41-377**), where the pasta is made on the premises. Look for two other restaurants in Ano Meria: **Sinandisi** (© **22860/41-208**), also known as Maria's, which has good *matsata* and swordfish (take the bus to the Ayios Andreas stop); and **Barbakosta** (© **22860/41-436**), a tiny room that serves triple duty as bar, taverna, and minimarket (the bus stop has no name, so ask the driver to alert you).

Hora has a number of tavernas, whose tables spill onto and partially fill the central squares. At the bus-stop square, **Pounda** (© **22860/41-063**) serves a delicious breakfast of crepes, omelets, yogurt, or coffeecake; lunch and dinner, including vegetarian dishes, are also available. **Silk** (© **22860/41-515**), on the *piatsa* (third) square, offers delicious variations on taverna fare, including numerous vegetarian options. **Piatsa** (© **22860/41-274**), also on the third square, is a simple taverna with tasty food. **O Kritikos** (© **22860/41-219**) is another local favorite, known for its grilled chicken. After dinner, if you want some nightlife, you'll find some bars and discos sprouting on the outskirts of Kastro.

3 Sifnos ★★

172km (93 nautical miles) SE of Piraeus

Just about everyone thinks that Sifnos is the most beautiful of the western Cyclades. This island has long been a favorite of Greeks, especially Athenians, but now in summer it is an all-too-popular destination for European tourists. August here can be more than hectic, with rooms hard to find, cars impossible to rent, and the village buses sardine-can full.

The mountains that frame Sifnos's deep harbor, Kamares, are barren, but once you've left the port, you will see elegantly ornamented dovecotes above cool green hollows, old (no one really knows just how old) fortified monasteries, and watchtowers that stand astride the summits of arid hills. The beautiful slate and marble paths across the island are miracles of care, although an increasing number are now covered over with concrete and asphalt to accommodate car traffic. The island is a hiker's—even a stroller's—delight and astonishingly green not only in spring but well into the summer. In addition, beaches along the southern coast offer long stretches of fine amber sand; several smaller rocky coves are also excellent for swimming.

Sifnos is small enough that any town can be used as a base for touring; the most beautiful are the **seven settlements** spread across the central hills—notably Apollonia (sometimes called Stavri) and Artemonas—and Kastro, a small medieval fortified town atop a rocky pinnacle on the eastern shore. Buses now run from Cheronissos in the north to Vathi in the south, and the bus, combined with some walking, will take you to the island's top attractions: the ancient acropolis at **Ayios Andreas,** the town of **Kastro** and its tiny but excellent **archaeological museum,** the southern **beaches,** the once isolated beaches at **Vathi** and **Cheronisso** and, for the ambitious, the walled **Monastery of Profitis Elias** on the summit of the island's highest mountain. Brown and gold signs in Greek and English now mark most places of archaeological and historical interest.

In Greece, Sifnos has long been famous for its ceramics, although fewer and fewer locals work as potters and fewer still use local clay. Some of the island's best potters are in Kamares and Platis Yialos. Sifnos is also famous for its olive oil and sophisticated cooking.

ESSENTIALS

GETTING THERE By Boat Weather permitting, there are at least four boats daily from Piraeus, including car ferries and HighSpeeds and SeaJets, some of which do and some of which do not take cars. Check ferry schedules with a travel agency or with the **Piraeus Port Authority** (© 210/451-1311 or 1440 or 1441; phone not always answered), or **Sifnos Port Authority** (© 22840/33-617). Ferries travel on ever-changing schedules to other islands, including **Serifos, Kimolos Milos, Paros,** and **Kithnos.** Boats are notoriously late and/or early; your travel or ticket agent will give you an estimate of times involved in above journeys

VISITOR INFORMATION The best place on the island for information and help getting a hotel room, boat tickets, car, or motorbike (and arranging excursions) is **Aegean Thesaurus Travel and Tourism** ✿✿ on the port (© 22840/32-152; www.thesaurus.gr). Aegean Thesaurus handles tickets for all hydrofoils and ferries. Check to see if the company, which also has an office on the main square in Apollonia (© 22840/33-151), has its excellent information packet on Sifnos for 2€ ($2.60).

GETTING AROUND By Bus Apollonia's central square, **Plateia Iroon** (which locals simply call the **Plateia** or **Stavri**), is the main bus stop for the island. Buses run regularly to and from the port at Kamares, north to Artemonas and Cheronisso, east to Kastro, and south to Faros, Platis Yialos, and Vathi. Pick up a schedule at Aegean Thesaurus Travel (see "Visitor Information," above).

By Car & Moped Many visitors come to Sifnos for the wonderful hiking and mountain trails. Though unnecessary, a car or moped can be rented at **Aegean Thesaurus** (© 22840/33-151) in Apollonia, or from Kostas Kalogirou (© 22840/33-791; www.protomotocar.gr) or Stavros Kalogirou (© 22840/33-383; www.sifnostravel.com) both in Kamares. In high season, you should reserve ahead. As always, exercise caution if you decide to rent a car or moped; many drivers, like you, will be unfamiliar with the island roads. The daily rate for an economy car with full insurance is about 50€ ($65); a moped rents for about 22€ ($29).

By Taxi   Apollonia's main square is the island's primary taxi stand. There are about 10 taxis on the island, each privately owned, so you'll have to get their **mobile phone numbers** available at travel agents. Most hotels, restaurants, and shops will call a taxi for you; offer to pay for the call.

FAST FACTS   Visitor services are centered in Apollonia. **National Bank (© 22840/ 31-317),** with an ATM, is just past Hotel Anthoussa on the road to Artemonas (Mon–Thurs 8am–2pm; Fri 8am–1:30pm). The **post office (© 22840/31-329),** on Plateia Iroon (Stavri to the islanders), the main square, is open in summer Monday through Friday from 8am to 2pm. The **telephone office (OTE),** just down the vehicle road, is open daily year-round from 8am to 3pm, and in summer from 5 to 10pm as well. You will find it most convenient to purchase a telephone card and use it at one of the pay phones on the island. The **police (© 22840/31-210)** are just east of the square, and a **first-aid station** is nearby; for **medical emergencies** call © 22840/ 31-315.

WHAT TO SEE & DO

The capital town of the island, **Apollonia** ✮ (also called Hora and Stavri) is the name given jointly to the **seven settlements** on these lovely interior hills. It's 5km (3 miles) inland from Kamares; a local bus makes the trip hourly (from about 6am–midnight) in summer. The town's central square is the transportation hub of the island. All vehicle roads converge here, and this is where you'll find the bus stop and taxi stand. The small **Popular and Folk Art Museum** is open July 1 to September 15 from 10am to 1pm and 6 to 10pm (admission is 1.50€/$1.95). From the square, pedestrian paths of flagstone and marble wind upward through the beautiful town. This is a great place to wander, admire the perfect whitewashed sugar-cube houses, and get a bit lost.

Kastro ✮✮ is one of the best-preserved medieval towns in the Cyclades, built on the dramatic site of an ancient acropolis. Until several decades ago, Kastro was almost entirely deserted; as tourists began to infiltrate the island, Kastro sprouted cafes, restaurants, and shops. The 2km (1-mile) walk from Apollonia is easy, except under the midday sun. Start out on the footpath that passes under the main road in front of Hotel Anthoussa, and continue through the tiny village of Kato Petali, finishing the walk into Kastro on a paved road, or the marked footpath. Whitewashed houses, some well-preserved and others eroding, adjoin one another in a defensive ring abutting a sheer cliff. Venetian coats of arms are still visible above doorways of older houses. Within the maze of streets are a few tavernas and some beautiful rooms to let. The little **Archaeological Museum (© 22840/31-022)** here has a good collection of pottery and sculpture found on the island; it's open Tuesday through Saturday from 9am to 2pm, Sunday and holidays from 10am to 2pm. Admission is free.

About 2km (1 mile) south of Apollonia on the road to Vathi is a trail leading to the hilltop church of **Ayios Andreas** and the excavations of an **ancient acropolis.** Broad stone steps begin a long climb to the summit; count on about 20 vigorous minutes to make the ascent. The acropolis ruins are at the top of the hill on your left. These ruins are made up of the outer walls and a block of houses from a Mycenaean fortified town.

Excavations haven't been completed and there's no interpretive information at the site, but the location is stirring. It's worth a visit if only for the view.

Well into the 1980s, pottery making flourished on Sifnos. Now, only a handful of potteries remain. The distinctive brown-and-blue glazed Sifnian pottery still being made has become something of a collector's item. If you fall for a piece, buy it—with more and more potteries closing down, you can't be sure you'll find this distinctive ware again.

BEACHES

Sifnos has a number of good beaches. If you're pressed for time, head east to **Platis Yialos,** easy to reach by taxi or public transportation, with tavernas where you can have a bite as well as a swim. (You can also hike from Platis Yialos to the Panagia tou Vounou monastery; see "Walking," below). Not surprisingly Platis Yialos—which boasts that it is the longest beach in the Cyclades—can be crowded in summer. If you have time, you may want to explore some of the island's other beaches. Here are some suggestions.

From Platis Yialos, it's a half-hour walk east through the olive groves and intoxicating oregano and thyme patches over the hill to **Panagia Chrissopiyi,** a double-vaulted whitewashed church on a tiny island. There's good swimming at **Apokofto,** a cove with a long sand beach and several shade trees just beyond the monastery, where rocky headlands protect swimmers from rough water. **Pharos** and **Fasolou,** two other east-coast beaches (reachable from Platis Yialos on foot by the resolute) are easier to get to by taking the bus from Apollonia. The excellent **Dimitris taverna (© 22840/71-493)** is by the sea at Fasolou.

Until 1997, the beach at **Vathi**—one of the best on the island—was accessible only on foot or by boat, but there's now a road and regular bus service. The elegant new resort, **Elies,** opened here in 2005. The beach does not have the dense development of the port of Kamares and Platis Yialos, but there's every sign that it may yet. Of the tavernas here, my friends with houses on Sifnos praise **To Livada (© 22840/71-123).** The beach at **Cheronisso,** at the island's northern end, is a spectacular spot to watch the sun go down.

WALKING

More and more asphalt roads are appearing on Sifnos to accommodate wheeled vehicles, but you'll still be able to do most of your walking on the island's distinctive flagstone and marble paths. You'll probably see village women whitewashing the edges of the paving stones, transforming the monochrome paths into elaborate abstract patterns. Throughout the island, you'll see dovecotes, windmills, and small white chapels in amazingly remote spots.

One wonderful walk on the island leads west from **Apollonia to Profitis Elias,** passing through a valley of extraordinary beauty to the summit of the island's highest mountain, with a short detour to the church and ruined monastery at Skafis. Pick up a walking map at one of the local travel agencies. The 12th-century walled monastery of Profitis Elias is a formidable citadel, its interior courtyard lined with the monks' cells. The lovely chapel has a fine marble iconostasis. Continue straight where the summit path branches right and walk through the next intersection. You'll soon reach the church of Skafis, situated within the ruins of an old monastery and overlooking a small valley shaded by olive trees. Look for the remains of paintings on the walls of the ruined monastery, in what must have been a tiny chapel. Allow about 4 hours for the round-trip to Profitis Elias, with an additional half-hour for the detour to Skafis.

From Platis Yialos (see **"Beaches,"** above), you can hike to the **Panagia tou Vounou,** by following a paved road that leads off the main road to Platis Yialos; although the monastery (which has fine views over the island) is signposted, it is best to have a good island map. The church here is usually unlocked in the morning, locked in the afternoons.

SHOPPING
Famed in antiquity first for its riches, then for its ceramics, Sifnos still produces wonderful pottery. In Kamares, **Antonis Kalogerou** (© **22840/31-651**) sells folk paintings of island life and the typical pottery of Sifnos, which is manufactured in his showroom from the deep gray or red clay mined in the inland hill region. In Platis Yialos, **Simos and John Apostolidis** (© **22840/71-258**) have a ceramics workshop. As you stroll the town's winding back streets, you'll find several other contemporary ceramics galleries featuring the excellent work of Greek artisans. For those in search of distinctive jewelry rather than ceramics, Spyros Koralis's **Ble** (© **22840/33-055**) in Apollonia does innovative work in silver and gold.

WHERE TO STAY
If you feel like a little serious indulgence, check out the top-of-the-line **Elies Resort** (© **22840/34-000;** www.eliesresorts.com), which opened in 2005 on the beach in Vathi and immediately appeared in *Odyssey* magazine's annual feature on the 50 best hotels in Greece. The resort, shaded by olive trees ("Elies" is Greek for olive trees), is designed to look like a traditional Cycladic village—albeit a village with tennis courts, villas with private pools, and a spa offering aromatherapy and massage. Doubles from 320€ ($416); suites from 500€ ($650); villas from 850€ ($1,105).

APOLLONIA
Apollonia is the most central place to use as a base on Sifnos. Buses depart from the central square to most island towns, and stone-paved paths lead to neighboring villages. Keep in mind that many Athenians vacation on Sifnos, particularly on summer weekends, when it can be virtually impossible to find a room, car, or, unless you start early, even a meal. If you plan to be in Apollonia or Kamares during the high season, be sure to make reservations by May. If you're here during off season, many hotels are closed, although some do remain open.

With advance notice, the efficient **Aegean Thesaurus Travel** (see "Visitor Information," earlier in this chapter) can usually place you in a rented room with your own bathroom, in a studio with a kitchenette, or in other, more stylish accommodations. A simple double can cost 100€ ($130) in high season.

Hotel Anthoussa   This hotel is above the excellent and popular Yerontopoulos cafe and patisserie, on the right past the main square. Although street-side rooms offer wonderful views over the hills, they overlook the late-night sweet-tooth crowd and can be recommended only to night owls. Back rooms are quieter and overlook a beautiful bower of bougainvillea.

Apollonia, 84003 Sifnos. © **22840/31-431.** 15 units. 80€ ($104) double. MC, V. **Amenities:** Breakfast room. *In room:* A/C, TV.

Hotel Petali 🖈🖈   Not far—but all uphill—from Apollonia's main square, on a pedestrianized side street, the Petali has lovely distant views of the sea beyond the town's many houses. After a day's sightseeing, it's especially nice to enjoy those views from the Petali's pool or poolside terrace. Each guest room has a large terrace, handsome and comfortable chairs, good beds, and modern bathrooms. A small restaurant serves delicious Sifnian specialties. Although the Hotel Petali does not accept credit cards, its managing office, **Aegean Thesaurus Travel Agency** (© **22840/32-152;** www. thesaurus.gr), accepts MasterCard and Visa.

Apollonia, 84003 Sifnos. ©/fax **22840/33-024.** www.hotelpetali.gr. 11 units. 160€–240€ ($208–$312) double. MC, V. **Amenities:** Restaurant; bar; pool; sauna; Jacuzzi; laundry facilities. *In room:* A/C, TV.

Hotel Sifnos 🌶🌶 The hospitable owners here have tried hard to make their hotel reflect island taste, using local pottery and weavings in the smallish but cheerful rooms. The hotel restaurant (see "Where to Dine," below) offers good basic meals beneath a broad arbor; it's just as popular with locals as it is with travelers and hotel guests.

Apollonia, 84003 Sifnos. © **22840/31-624.** 9 units. 90€ ($117) double. AE, MC, V. Usually open in winter. **Amenities:** Restaurant; bar. *In room:* A/C, TV.

KASTRO

Aris Rafeletos Apartments These traditional rooms and apartments are distributed throughout the medieval town of Kastro. Most have exposed ceiling beams, stone ceilings and floors, and the long narrow rooms typical of this fortified village. The two smallest units are somewhat dark and musty, but the three apartments are spacious and charming. All apartments have kitchenettes and terraces; three have splendid sea views. The largest apartment is on two levels and can comfortably sleep four. If the antiquity and charm of this hilltop medieval village appeals to you, then these accommodations may be the perfect base for your exploration of the island.

Kastro. ©/fax **22840/31-161.** 6 units. 80€–180€ ($104–$234) apts. No credit cards. The rental office is at the village's north end, about 50m (164 ft.) past the Archaeological Museum. **Amenities:** Breakfast room/bar. *In room:* Kitchenette in some units.

KAMARES

The port of Kamares has the greatest concentration of hotels and pensions on the island, but unfortunately, it has little of the beauty of Sifnos's traditional villages. You can swim here, but the water is not as clean as at the island's less commercial beaches. Two moderately priced hotels are the 14-unit harborside **Hotel Stavros** (doubles from 75€/$98) and the 18-unit **Hotel Kamari** (doubles from 65€/$85), a 10-minute walk from the beach and harbor. Information on both is available from Stavros and Sarah Kalogirou (© **22840/33-383;** www.sifnostravel.com). This helpful couple (Sarah is English) also has a car hire agency and the very attractive **Elonas** apartments to rent in Apollonia (units sleeping up to five from 110€/$130). They also run the YaMas Internet Cafe Bar in Kamares.

Hotel Boulis This hotel, capably managed by two more members of the Kalogirou family, Lyn and Antonis, is right on the port's beach. The large, carpeted rooms have balconies or patios, most with beach views; all have fridges and ceiling fans. The hotel has a spacious, cool, marble-floored reception area and a sunny breakfast room.

Kamares, 84003 Sifnos. © **22840/32-122.** www.hotelboulis.gr. 45 units. 100€–130€ ($130–$169) double. Rates include breakfast. AE. Closed Oct–Apr. Follow the main street 300m (984 ft.) from the ferry pier, turning left opposite the Boulis Taverna (operated by the same family). The hotel is on your left. **Amenities:** Breakfast room/bar. *In room:* Fridge.

PLATIS YIALOS

A busy beach resort on the island's south coast, Platis Yialos serves as a convenient base for visiting the southern beaches. The town exists for tourism during high season. If Hotel Platis Yialos is full, try little **Hotel Philoxenia** (© **22840/71-221**), whose rooms have refrigerators; doubles cost from 90€ ($117).

Hotel Platis Yialos ☆ *(Kids)*   The island's oldest hotel overlooks the beach on the west side of the cove, set apart from the rest of the town's densely populated beach strip. The hotel's location, on an excellent sand beach that slopes gently into the sea, and its popularity with families, makes this an ideal place to stay if you are traveling with young children. Originally a government-owned Xenia hotel, its design is functional rather than beautiful. The ground-floor guest rooms, with patios facing the garden and water, are especially desirable; rooms on the upper stories have balconies. A suite contains flagstone floors, beamed ceilings, beds for up to six people, and two bathrooms, one with Jacuzzi; it opens to a small terrace with views of the bay. Frescoes and small paintings by a local artist are displayed throughout the hotel. The Platis Yialos's flagstone sun deck extends from the beach to a dive platform at the end of the cove. A bar and restaurant share the same Aegean views.

Platis Yialos, 84003 Sifnos. ℂ **22840/71-324** or 28310/22-626 in winter. Fax 22840/71-325 or 2831/055-042 in winter. 29 units. 180€–230€ ($234–$299) double. Rates include breakfast. No credit cards. Closed Oct–Mar. **Amenities:** Restaurant; bar. *In room:* A/C, fridge.

WHERE TO DINE
APOLLONIA

If you want a snack, try Vegera or **Sifnos Café-Restaurant,** in Apollonia. Both serve breakfasts and sweets all day—and, along with many other places, has the island specialty of *revithia* (chickpeas) most Sundays. My Siphnian friends say that **Okyalos** (ℂ **22840/32-060**), on Apollonia's main drag, succeeds in its aim of serving "Mediterranean gourmet cuisine."

ARTEMONAS AND ENVIRONS

To Liotrivi (Manganas) ☆☆ GREEK   We're still mentioning To Liotrivi because it has been an island favorite for a long time. Unfortunately, recent reports from readers and friends suggest that this place is resting far too heavily on its laurels. It was one of the first restaurants on the island to have a varied and inventive menu.

Artemona. ℂ **22840/31-246.** Main courses 18€–86€ ($23–$112). No credit cards. Daily noon–midnight. From Apollonia, follow the pedestrian street north from the main plateia, past Mama Mia and Hotel Petali; the walk takes a pleasant 10–15 min.

Sunset (To Troullaki) ☆ GREEK   This is a good place to go at sunset or any other time. About 8km (5 miles) out of Apollonia in a peaceful setting by the road to Cheronisso, this family-run taverna serves delicious island food. The sunsets here are spectacular. Much of the meat and vegetables is organic. The *Mastello,* melt-in-the-mouth lamb on vine leaves, is slowly baked in a (local, of course!) earthenware pot.

Apollonia. ℂ **22840/31-970.** Main courses 7€–15€ ($9–$16). No credit cards. Lunch and dinner most days.

KAMARES

Boulis Taverna ☆ GREEK   With an unexceptional location at the top of the town's busy main street, this isn't the place to go for a romantic evening, but it does offer some very good food. The taverna is operated by Andonis Kalogirou of Hotel Boulis, who uses vegetables, cheeses, and meats raised on the organic family farm. The walls of the vast interior room are lined with wooden wine casks. Outside, lamb, chicken, and steak cook on the grill.

At the top of the main street through town. ℂ **22840/31-648.** Main courses 7€–15€ ($9–$20). No credit cards. Daily 11am–1am.

> ⌒ *Moments*   **A Special Feast**
>
> **Prophet Elijah's feast day** (between July 20 and 22) is one of the most impor-
> tant religious holidays on Sifnos, which has had a monastery dedicated to this
> saint for at least 800 years. The celebration begins with a mass outing to the
> monastery of Profitis Elias on the summit of the island's highest mountain, and
> continues through the night with dancing and feasting.

Kapitain Andreas ✿ SEAFOOD   This place, with its sometimes gruff host,
Andreas, who is both proprietor and fisherman, serves good food and grills.

On the town beach. ✆ 22840/32-356. Main courses 8€–15€ ($10–$20); fish priced by the kilo. No credit cards.
Daily 1–5pm and 7:30pm–12:30am.

Poseidonas (Sophia's) ✿✿ GREEK   The first restaurant you pass after disembarking the ferry is easily the best place to eat in Kamares: Sophia Patriarke and her
daughters are hospitable to strangers and serve tasty grills, truly fresh salads, and fabulous *rivithokeftedes rena* (chickpea croquettes).

✆ 22840/32-362. Fish priced by the kilo. No credit cards. Daily 1–5pm and 7pm–midnight.

PLATIS YIALOS
Sofia's (To Steki) ✿✿ GREEK   Platis Yialos's best restaurant for traditional Siphnian home cooking taverna fare is popular for its outdoor terrace with tamarik trees.

At the beach's east end. ✆ 22840/71-202. Main courses 6€–18€ ($8–$23). No credit cards. Daily 9pm–1am.

SIFNOS AFTER DARK
My friends who have houses on Sifnos remind me that bars come and go with amazing rapidity here; many don't last an entire season. I'm not listing phone numbers here
because phones simply are not answered. The main street of Apollonia vibrates to the
sound of music from virtually wall-to-wall bars all summer. Of these, the **Argo Bar**
has been around for years; it plays European and American pop music with some
Greek tunes thrown in.

In Kamares, there's another longtime survivor of the bar wars: the picturesque **Old
Captain's Bar.** For classical music, the **Cultural Society of Sifnos** sometimes schedules summer concerts in Artemonas.

4 Paros ✶✶

168km (91 nautical miles) SE of Piraeus

Paros is accurately (but hardly enticingly) known as the "transportation hub" of the
Cyclades: Almost all island boats stop here en route to someplace else. As a result, Paros
has suffered from the reputation of the place on the way to the place where you're
going. At present, Paros is still cheaper than either Mykonos or Santorini—in fact,
some call it the "poor man's Mykonos"—although rising prices are rapidly making that
nickname anachronistic. Comparisons aside, Paros's good beaches and nightlife have
made it a very popular destination in its own right. Because of the absence of any single five-star attraction—there's no antiquity here to rival Santorini's ancient Akrotiri
and nothing to rival the beauty of Mykonos's perfect Cycladic architecture—a lot of
visitors come here simply to have a good time, windsurfing, sunbathing, and partying.

Still others—not necessarily opposed to having a good time—are drawn back over and over again to Paros because of its other attractions. Admittedly, if you come by ship, your first impression after docking at the main port and capital **Parikia** will be of the kitsched-up windmill on the quay, travel agents, cafes, and the not terribly enticing fast-food joints lining the harborfront. Where, you'll wonder, is the town described as "charming?" Take a few steps inland, and you'll find it. **Parikia** has an energetic marketplace and the Eka-tondapiliani, the 100-doored church designed in the 6th century by the famous architect Isodore of Miletus. Winding streets, the paving stones meticulously marked off with whitewash, lead off from the main square. One street meanders up and up, passing marble fountains and modest houses with elaborate door frames, to the remains of a medieval castle, largely built with chunks pillaged from various local ancient temples.

Somehow, Parikia manages to be both cozy and cosmopolitan. The town has a lively cultural life: The Archilochos Cultural Society stages a winter film festival and hosts a summer music festival (www.archilochos.gr). This is also the home of the Aegean Center for the Fine Arts, which has exhibitions and lectures, and offers several 2-month-long sessions in painting and literature each year (www.aegeancenter.org). Not surprisingly, there are lots of shops selling local artwork.

Out on the island, there's a scattering of appealing villages and two must-see spots: the hillside village of Lefkes deep in the interior and the picture-postcard seaside hamlet of Naoussa. Paros also has enough good beaches to keep almost any visitor happy.

Paros is large enough that even if you're just here for a day, renting a car makes sense. Then, you can make an around-the-island tour that includes a morning visit to **Petaloudes (Valley of the Butterflies),** a visit to Lefkes, a stop for a good lunch in Naoussa, a swim at your beach of choice, and a night back in Parikia, where you can shop and stroll the evening away.

ESSENTIALS

GETTING THERE   By Plane   Olympic Airways (© **210/966-6666** or 210/936-9111; www.olympic-airways.gr) has at least two flights daily between Paros and Athens; in Parikia, call © **22840/21-900** for flight information.

By Boat   Paros has more connections with more ports than any other island in the Cyclades. The main port, Parikia, has connections at least once daily with Piraeus by ferry (5–6 hr.) and high-speed ferry (3–4 hr.). Confirm schedules with the Athens **GNTO** (© **210/327-1300** or 210/331-0562) or **Piraeus Port Authority** (© **210/ 926-9111**). Boats are notoriously late and/or early; your travel or ticket agent will give you an estimate of times involved in the following journeys. Remember: That's estimate, as in guesstimate. Daily ferry and hydrofoil service links Parikia with Ios,

---

Tips **Check Your Calendar**

The Feast of the Dormition of the Virgin (Aug 15) is one of the most important religious holidays in Greece—and the most important, after Easter, in Paros. Pilgrims come here from throughout the Cyclades to attend services at the Panagia Ekatondapiliani, which is dedicated to the Virgin. If you come here then, make reservations well in advance, or you will probably find yourself sleeping rough. And on the subject of dates: If you want to visit Paros to see its famous **butterflies,** remember that they come here in May and June.

> **Tips   American Students Here?**
>
> The Aegean Center for the Fine Arts (www.aegeancenter.org) offers courses in painting, photography, music, creative writing, and other artistic endeavors in a 13-week session here from March to June. You'll see the mostly teen and 20-something students all over Parikia and out on the island.

Mykonos, Santorini, and Tinos. Several times a week, boats depart for Folegandros, Sifnos, and Siros. There are daily excursion tours from Parikia or Naoussa (the north-coast port) to Mykonos. The high-speed services usually take half as long and cost twice as much as the slower ferries. There's also overnight service to Ikaria and Samos several times a week. (From Samos you can often arrange a next-day excursion to Ephesus, Turkey.) In high season, there's hourly caique service to Andiparos from Parikia and Pounda, a small port 6km (4 miles) south of Parikia, with regular connection by bus. The east-coast port of Piso Livadi is the point of departure for travelers heading to the "Little Cyclades." Ferries depart four times weekly for Heraklia, Schinoussa, Koufonissi, and Katapola.

For general ferry information, **Santorineos Travel** in Parikia (© 22840/24-245) is excellent, or try the **port authority** (© 22840/21-240). Many agents around Mavroyenous Square and along the port sell ferry tickets; schedules are posted along the sidewalk.

VISITOR INFORMATION   There is a **visitor information office** on Mavroyenous Square, just behind and to the right of the windmill at the end of the pier. This office is often closed, but there are numerous travel agencies on the seafront, including **Santorineos Travel** (© 22840/24-245; fax 22840/23-922; santorineos@travelling.gr) and **Parikia Tours** (© 22840/222-470). The municipality information office in the Parikia town hall can be reached at © 22840/22-078. The island has a number of helpful websites, including **www.parosweb.com** and **www.paroslife.com**. The monthly English-language newspaper *Paros Life* (2€/$2.60) is very useful.

GETTING AROUND   By Bus   The **bus station** (© 22840/21-395) in Parikia is on the waterfront, left from the windmill. There is often hourly service between Parikia and Naoussa from 8am to midnight in high season. The other buses from Parikia run frequently from 8am to 9pm in two general directions: south to Aliki or Pounda, and southeast to the beaches at Piso Livadi, Chrissi Akti, and Drios, passing the Marathi Quarries and the town of Lefkes along the way. Schedules (not always up-to-date) are posted at the stations.

By Car & Moped   Paros is large enough that renting a car makes sense. There are many agencies along the waterfront, and except in July and August, you should be able to bargain. **Iria Cars and Bikes** (© 22840/21-232) and **Santorineos Travel** (© 22840/24-245) get praise from travelers. Expect to pay from 50€ ($65) per day for a car and from 20€ ($26) per day for a moped. Be sure to get full insurance.

By Taxi   Taxis can be booked (© 22840/21-500) or hailed at the windmill taxi stand. Taxi fare to Naoussa with luggage should run about 12€ ($16).

FAST FACTS   The **American Express** agent is Santorineos Travel, on the seafront 100m (328 ft.) south of the pier (© 22840/24-245; fax 22840/23-922; santorineos@travelling.gr). There are five **banks** in Parikia on Mavroyenous Square, and one in

Naoussa; their hours are Monday through Thursday from 8am to 2pm, Friday from 8am to 1:30pm. The private **Medical Center of Paros** (✆ **22840/24-410**) is to the north of the pier, across from the post office; the public **Parikia Health Clinic** (✆ **22840/22-500**) is on the central square, down the road from the Ekatondapiliani Cathedral. **Internet access** is available on the Wired Network (www.parosweb.com) at eight locations around the island; you can buy a "smart card" that stores your personal settings and provides access at any of these locations for about 6€ ($7.80) per hour. The main Wired Network location—often noisy and crowded—is in Parikia on Market Street (✆ **22840/22-003**). **Cyber Cookies** (✆ **22840/21-610**), just past the square with the ficus tree and Distrato Cafe on the nameless street that runs from the cathedral into Market Street, is much nicer and charges nothing for Internet use when you eat there.

The **Laundry House** is on the paralia (shore road) near the post office (✆ **22840/ 24-898**). For the Paraikia **police,** call ✆ **22840/23-333**; in Naoussa, ✆ **22840/ 51-202**. The **post office** in Parikia (✆ **22840/21-236**) is left of the windmill on the waterfront road, open Monday through Friday from 7:30am to 2pm, with extended hours in July and August. Parikia's **telephone office** (OTE; ✆ **22840/22-135**) is just to the right of the windmill; its hours are 7:30am to 2pm. (If the front door is closed, go around to the back, as wind direction determines which door is open.) A branch in Naoussa has similar hours. It is much easier to make a phone call with a phone card, on sale at almost all kiosks.

WHAT TO SEE & DO
THE TOP ATTRACTIONS IN PARIKIA
Archaeological Museum   The museum's most valued holding is a fragment of the famous Parian Chronicle, an ancient chronology. The Ashmolean Museum at Oxford University has a larger portion of the chronicle, which is carved on Parian marble tablets. Why is this document so important? Because it lists dates for actual and mythical events from the time of Cecrops (264–263 B.C.). Cecrops was the legendary first king of Athens, whose dates—indeed, existence—cannot be proven. Just to confuse and irritate historians, the chronicle gives information about artists, poets, and playwrights—but doesn't bother to mention many important political leaders or battles. The museum also contains a number of sculptural fragments as well as a splendid running Gorgon and a Winged Victory from the 5th century B.C. There's also part of a marble monument with a frieze of Archilochus, the important 7th-century-B.C. lyric poet known as the inventor of iambic meter and for his ironic detachment. ("What breaks me, young friend, is tasteless desire, lifeless verse, boring dinners.")

Parikia. ✆ **22840/21-231**. Admission 2€ ($2.60). Tues–Sun 8:30am–3pm. Behind the cathedral, opposite the playing fields of the local school.

Finds **The Ancient Cemetery**

Ask at the Archaeological Museum for directions to Paros's ancient cemetery on the waterfront. Excavations here since the 1980s have revealed much about the island's history between the 11th century B.C. and the Roman period. Many of the graves contained the bones and weapons of warriors, often buried in handsome ceramic jars and marble urns, some of which are on view at the Archaeological Museum.

Murder in the Cathedral

As you visit the Panagia Ekatondapiliani Cathedral, keep an eye out for the two squat sculptured figures that support the columns of the monumental gate by the chapel of St. Theodosia. According to popular legend, the two figures are Isidore of Miletus, the best-known architect here and his pupil Ignatius. As the story has it, Isodore was so envious of Ignatius's talent that he pushed him off scaffolding high inside the church's dome. As he fell, Ignatius grabbed onto Isidore and they both tumbled to their deaths. The sculptor has shown Isidore pulling on his beard (evidently a sign of apology) and Ignatius rubbing his head—perhaps in pain, perhaps as he cogitates on revenge. It's a nice story, but, in fact archaeologists think that the two figures come from a temple of Dionysos that stood here and represent two satyrs—yet another example of how often successive generations reused building materials and re-created appropriate legends.

Panagia Ekatondapiliani Cathedral *GG*   This is a magical spot. According to tradition, the Byzantine cathedral of Panagia Ekatondapiliani (Our Lady of a Hundred Doors) was founded by Saint Helen, the mother of Constantine the Great, the emperor whose conversion to Christianity led to its establishment as the official religion of the Roman Empire. Saint Helen is said to have stopped on Paros en route to the Holy Land, where the faithful believe that she found the True Cross. Fragments of the Cross are revered relics in many a church. Heleni's son fulfilled her vow to found a church here, and successive emperors and rulers expanded it—which may in part explain the church's confusing layout, an inevitable result of centuries of renovations and expansions, which include the six side chapels. The work has not stopped: The cathedral was extensively restored in the 1960s, and the large square in front was expanded in 1996 for the church's 1,700th birthday.

A high white wall built as protection from pirates surrounds the cathedral; in the thickness of the wall are rows of monks' cells, which now house a small shop and small ecclesiastical museum. After you step through the outer gate, the noise of the town vanishes, and you enter a garden with lemon trees and flowering shrubs. Ahead is the cathedral, its elegant arched facade a memento both of the Venetian period and of classical times (several of the columns were brought here from ancient temples).

Inside, the cathedral is surprisingly spacious. Almost every visitor instinctively looks up to the massive dome, supported on vaults ornamented with painted six-winged seraphim. Take time to find the handsome icons, including several set in the iconostasis (altar screen), side chapels, and an elegant little 4th-century baptistery, with a baptismal font in the shape of a cross. In the arcade, the museum contains a small but superb collection of 15th- to 19th-century icons, religious vestments, and beautiful objects used in Orthodox Church ceremonies. Everything is labeled in Greek and in English.

The small shop, also in the arcade, features religious books and memorabilia, as well as books on Paros. Panayotis Patellis's *Guide Through Ekatontapiliani* (4€/$5.20) is both useful and charming. When you leave the cathedral precincts, turn left slightly uphill toward the Archaeological Museum for a fine view of the entire cathedral complex with its red-tile roofs.

Parikia. No admission fee for cathedral, although it is customary to leave a small offering. Daily 8am–8pm, but usually closed 2–5pm in winter. Museum © **22840/21-243**. Admission 2€ ($2.60). Daily 10am–2pm and 6–9pm. On Parikia's central square opposite and north of the ferry pier.

THE TOP ATTRACTIONS OUT ON THE ISLAND

Marathi Marble Quarries   The inland road to Lefkes and Marpissa will take you up the side of a mountain to the marble quarries at Marathi, source of the famous Parian marble. Ancient sculptors prized Parian marble for its translucency and fine, soft texture, and they used it for much of their best work, including the *Hermes* of Praxiteles and the *Venus de Milo*. The turnoff to the quarries is signposted, and an odd, rather foolishly monumental path paved with marble leads up the valley toward (but not to) a group of deserted buildings and the ancient quarries. The buildings, to the right of the path, once belonged to a French mining company, which in 1844 quarried the marble for Napoleon's tomb; the company was the last to operate here. The quarry entrances are about 46m (150 ft.) beyond the marble path's end, on the left. The second, very wide quarry on the left has a 3rd-century-B.C. relief of the gods at its entrance, encased in a protective cage. In Roman times, as many as 150,000 slaves labored here, working day and night to the flickering lights of thousands of oil lamps. There isn't much to see today inside the quarries unless you're a spelunker at heart, in which case you'll find it irresistible to explore the deep caverns opened by the miners high above the valley. Bring a flashlight, wear appropriate clothing, and don't explore alone.

Marathi. Open site.

The Valley of Petaloudes & Convent of Christou stou Dhassous ✮   Another name for this oasis of plum, pear, fig, and pomegranate trees is Psychopiani (Soul Softs). The butterflies, actually tiger moths *(Panaxia quadripunctaria poda),* look like black-and-white-striped arrowheads until they fly up to reveal their bright red underwings. They have been coming here for at least 300 years because of the freshwater spring, flowering trees, dense foliage, and cool shade; they're usually most numerous in early mornings or evenings in June. Donkey or mule rides from Parikia to the site along a back road cost about 12€ ($16). You can take the Pounda and Aliki bus, which drops you off at the turnoff to the nunnery; you'll have to walk the remaining 2.5km (1½ miles) in to Petaloudes. Be sure to scowl at any visitors who clap and shout to alarm the butterflies and make them fly, often causing the fragile insects to collapse. A small snack bar serves refreshments; men can wait here, while women visit the nearby Convent of Christou stou Dhassous, which does not welcome male visitors. (Cooling their heels in the courtyard, the men can console themselves by thinking of visiting Mount Athos, which is forbidden to female visitors.)

Tips **Studio Detour**

En route to or from Marathi, consider a detour to the nearby **Studio Yria** (© **22840/29-007**), signposted by the village of Kostos. A number of artists, including sculptors, painters, and potters have set up shop here and their wares are impressive. Many works draw on traditional Byzantine and island designs, whereas others are modern.

Petaloudes. Admission 3€ ($3.90). Daily 9am–1pm and 4–8pm. Closed Oct–May. Head 4km (2½ miles) south of
Parikia on the coast road, turn left at the sign for the nunnery of Christou stou Dhassous, and continue another 2.5km
(1½ miles).

BEACHES

Paros has some fine sand beaches. If you only have time to visit a couple, here are some
suggestions. All have chairs and umbrellas to rent and lots of tavernas and cafes. **Chrissi
Akti (Golden Beach)** ✿, on the island's southeast coast, is a kilometer of fine golden
sand (with umbrellas and chairs to rent, tavernas, and cafes), is generally considered the
best beach on the island. It's also the windiest, although the wind is usually offshore.
As a result, this has become the island's primary windsurfing center and has hosted the
World Cup championship every year since 1993. **Aegean Diving School** (☎ 22840/
92-071; www.eurodivers.gr) offers scuba instruction and guided dives here. There's frequent bus service here from both Parikia and Naoussa. If you're interested in kiteboard-
ing, try (crowded, built up) **Pounda** (see "Windsurfing & Scuba," below).

One of the island's best and most famous, picturesque **Kolimbithres** ✿, is also
served by bus from Parikia and Naoussa. It has smooth giant rocks that divide the
gold-sand beach into several tiny coves—and appear on lots of island postcards. As at
Golden Beach, there are umbrellas and chairs to rent and lots of places to have a bite.

There's bus and caique service from Naoussa to **Santa Maria beach** ✿, one of the
most beautiful on the island. It has particularly clear water and shallow dunes (rare in
Greece) of fine sand along the irregular coastline. It also offers some of the best windsurfing on Paros. The **Santa Maria Surf Club** (☎ 22840/52-490) provides windsurfing gear and lessons for about 20€ ($26) per hour.

TOWNS & VILLAGES: NAOUSSA, LEFKES

If your time on Paros is limited, do try to see Naoussa and Lefkes. If you have more
time, you'll enjoy rambling about the island discovering other villages. One to keep in
mind is **Marpissa** and the nearby monastery of **Agios Antonios,** from which there are
fine views over the island.

Until recently, the fishing village of **Naoussa** remained relatively undisturbed, with
simple white houses in a labyrinth of narrow streets, but it's now a growing resort center with increasingly fancy restaurants, trendy bars, boutiques, and galleries. Most of
the new building here is concentrated along the nearby beaches, so the town itself
retains its charm—but for how long? Colorful fishing boats fill the harbor, and fishermen calmly go about their work on the docks, all in the shadow of a half-submerged
ruined Venetian minifortress—and, increasingly, tour buses. Signs along the harbor
advertise caique service to nearby beaches.

A narrow causeway links the Venetian fortress with the quay; the little kastro is
absurdly picturesque when illuminated at night. The best night of all to see the fortress
is during the **festival** held on or about each **August 23,** when the battle against the
pirate Barbarossa is reenacted by torch-lit boats converging on the harbor. Much feasting and dancing follows. On July 2, The Festival of Fish and Wine is celebrated here
and elsewhere on Paros.

There's frequent bus service from Parikia to Naoussa in summer. Daily excursion
tours from Naoussa to Mykonos are usually offered in summer; inquire at any of the
travel agencies in Parikia or here at any local travel agency, such as **Nissiotissa Tours**
(☎ **22840/51-480;** fax 22840/51-189).

Hilltop **Lefkes** ❦ is the medieval capital of the island. Its whitewashed houses with red-tile roofs form a maze around the central square, with its *kafeneion* with its imposing neoclassical facade. A kafeneion, a barbershop, a shop selling crafts, a plateia paved with stone slabs accented with fresh whitewash—this is surely the most perfect little plateia in the Cyclades—unless the plateia in Pyrgos on Tinos has a slight edge because of its fountain house! Lefkes was purposely built in an inaccessible location and with an intentionally confusing pattern of streets to thwart pirates. Test your own powers of navigation by finding **Ayia Triada (Holy Trinity) Church,** whose carved marble towers are visible above the town. The Lefkes Village Hotel is one of the nicest places on the island to stay (see "Where to Stay," below).

OUTDOOR PURSUITS

WALKING   Paros has numerous old stone-paved roads connecting the interior towns, many of which are in good condition and perfect for walking. One of the best-known trails is the **Byzantine Road** between Lefkes and Prodromos, a narrow path paved along much of its 4km (2½-mile) length with marble slabs. Begin in Lefkes, since from here the way is mostly downhill. There isn't an easy way to find the beginning of the Byzantine Road among the labyrinthine streets of Lefkes; we suggest starting at the church square, from which point you can see the flagstone-paved road in a valley at the edge of the town, to the west. Having fixed your bearings, plunge into the maze of streets and spiral your way down and to the right. After a 2-minute descent, you emerge into a ravine, with open fields beyond, and a sign indicates the beginning of the Byzantine Road. It's easy going through terraced fields, a leisurely hour's walk to the Marpissa Road, from which point you can catch the bus back to Parikia. Check the schedule and exact pickup point beforehand.

WINDSURFING & SCUBA ❦❦   The continuous winds on Paros's east coast have made it a favorite destination for windsurfers. Golden beach has hosted the **World Cup** for the past 7 years. The best months are July and August, but serious windsurfers may want to visit earlier or later in the season to avoid the crowds. The free *Paros Windsurfing Guide* is available at most tourist offices in Parikia or Naoussa. On Golden Beach, the **F2 Windsurfing Center** (© 22840/41-878) has lessons and sponsors the **Windsurfing World Cup.** The **Aegean Diving College** (© 22840/43-347) offers scuba instruction; director and marine archaeologist Peter Nikolaides is also connected with the Aegean Center in Parikia. At the port town of **Pounda,** the **Paros Kite Pro Center** (© 22840/92-071; www.windsurfingholidays.net) rents equipment from 25€ ($33) and gives kiteboarding lessons (from 85€/$111 for 3 hours).

SHOPPING

Market Street in Parikia is the shopping hub of the island, with many interesting alternatives to the ubiquitous souvenir stores. Yvonne von der Decken's shop **Palaio Poleio** ❦ (© 22840/21-909), opposite the Apollon Restaurant, has a fine selection of antique vernacular furniture and household items from the islands and the Greek mainland; it stays open all winter. **Ta Tsila Pou Efere O Notias (The Wood that the South Wind Brings)** ❦ (© 22840/24-669) sells enchanting paintings on wood, some of which are done by Clea Hatzinikolakis, the talented co-owner of Hotel Petres (see "Where to Stay," below); you'll find the shop on the lane on the right just past Hotel Dina. **Audiophile** (© 22840/22-357) has an extensive collection of CDs of Greek and international music, at prices a bit higher than you might pay in Athens.

The Cave of Andiparos

There was a time, not so long ago, when people went to little Andiparos, the islet about a nautical mile off Paros, for two reasons: to see the famous cave and to get away from all the crowds on Paros. The cave is still a good reason to come here, but Andiparos has been put firmly on the tourist map. Tom Cruise cruised by here, other stars followed in their yachts, and then the wannabes began to come by ferryboat. There's been a lot of charmless building here to accommodate holiday makers, and it's hard to think of a reason to linger here after you see the cave.

The cave (3€/$3.90) is open in summer from 11am to 3pm; excursion caiques run hourly from 9am from Parikia and Pounda to Andiparos (3€/$3.90) one-way. A shuttle barge, for vehicles as well as passengers, crosses the channel between Paros's southern port of Pounda and Andiparos continuously from 9am; the fare is 2€ ($2.60) or 10€ ($13) with a car; you can take along a bicycle for free. Buses (1.50€/$2) run back and forth from the port to the cave. Something to keep in mind: Greeks have a soft spot for caves (see the Caves of Dirou, chapter 8) and the Andiparos cave is often as crowded as an Athens bus.

Tourists once entered the cave by rope, but today's concrete staircase offers more convenient—if less adventuresome—access. The cave is about 90m (300 ft.) deep, but the farthest reaches are closed to visitors. Through the centuries, visitors have broken off parts of the massive stalactites as souvenirs and left graffiti to commemorate their visits, but the cool, mysterious cavern is still worth exploring. As usual, Lord Byron, who carved his name into a temple column at Sounion, left his signature here. The Marquis de Nointel celebrated Christmas Mass here in 1673 with 500 attendants; a large stalagmite served as the altar and the service was concluded with fireworks and explosions at the stroke of midnight.

Several shops that sell local produce, including cheeses, honey, and wine, all merit stars. **Pariana Proionta (Parian Produce)** ✸ (© 22840/22-181), run by the Agricultural Collective, is on Manto Mavroyennis Square; **Topika Proionta (Local Produce)** ✸ (© 22840/24-940) is on Market Street. **Distrato Café** ✸ (© 22840/24-789), on the unnamed street that runs from the cathedral to Market Street, has its own shop with organic produce from Paros and elsewhere in Greece. On the harbor, **News Stand** (no phone) sells international newspapers, guidebooks, maps, and some novels.

Across the island in the old part of Naoussa, **Metaxas Gallery** (© 22840/52-667) holds exhibitions of paintings by local artists, which are sometimes for sale; you can also find locally crafted jewelry here. **Hera,** just down the lane from the **Naoussa Sweet Shop** (© 22840/53-566), sells local pottery, jewelry, carpets from Greece and Turkey, and fine-arts books of local interest. Owner Hera Papamihail is a talented photographer whose prints are available for purchase. The **kiosk** on the main plateia has some international newspapers. **Paria Lexis Bookstore** (© **22840/51-121**) offers a selection of travel guides, maps, and novels.

In Lefkes, **Anemi** (© **22840/41-182**), by the *kafeneion* on the plateia, has hand-loomed and embroidered fabrics. In addition, nuns in several of the island's convents often sell crafts. **Market Street** in Parikia is the shopping hub of the island, with many interesting alternatives to the ubiquitous souvenir stores. At **Geteki** (© **22840/21-855**), you'll find paintings and sculpture by French artist Jacques Fleureaux, now a full-time resident of Paros. He makes use of local materials (clay and driftwood) and motifs (Cycladic figurines) in his work. Also for sale at Geteki are Afghani rugs and local ceramics by other artists.

WHERE TO STAY
PARIKIA

The port town has three basic hotel zones: **agora** (the market area), **harbor,** and **beach;** alas, all can be very noisy. Here are some suggestions for potentially quiet places to stay. In addition to the places listed below, the **Pandrossos** (© **22840/22-903**; www.pandrossoshotel.gr), on a hill overlooking Parikia and the harbor, has a pool and a quiet location. The hotel is within walking distance of town, but on hot days—with apologies to Al Gore—I'd rather drive up the hill; doubles from 130€ ($169).

Captain Manolis Hotel ⭐ A tempting flower-covered entrance on Market Street by the National Bank leads into a passageway to this small hotel, with its own garden. Rooms have balconies or terraces, the lobby is perfectly pleasant, and friends who have stayed here praise the staff and say that they were astonished at the tranquillity of this hotel in the heart of Market Street. I was impressed every time I stopped in here, because someone was usually sweeping and washing the passage.

Market St., Parikia, 84400 Paros. © **22840/21-244**. Fax 22840/25-264. 14 units. 90€ ($117) double. No credit cards. **Amenities:** Breakfast room. *In room:* A/C, TV, fridge.

Hotel Dina ⭐⭐ *Value* This is a charming place run by a charming couple. More pension than hotel, it was renovated in 2005. You reach the cozy rooms through a narrow, plant-filled courtyard at the quiet end of Market Street. Dina Patellis has been the friendly proprietor for nearly 3 decades, and her personal touch keeps guests coming back year after year. Her husband wrote the excellent *Guide Through Ekatontapiliani,* available in local bookshops. Three bedrooms overlook Market Street (no. 2 has a balcony). The balcony in room no. 8 looks onto a quintessentially Greek blue-domed church across a narrow lane; the other rooms face a small garden courtyard. As always in Greece, bring ear plugs, in case people walking the streets talk louder than you'd wish after you've gone to bed.

Market St., Parikia, 84400 Paros. © **22840/21-325** or 22840/21-345. Fax 22840/23-525. 8 units. 65€–70€ ($85–$91) double. No credit cards. The entrance is just off Market St., next to the Apollon Restaurant and across from the Pirate Bar. *In room:* A/C.

SOUTH OF PARIKIA
Hotel Iria ⭐ *Kids* This new bungalow resort complex (completely renovated in 2003) is just the place to head for if you are traveling with young children. A playground, a pool—and a beach about 150m (492 ft.) away—make this a persuasive choice for families. The architecture follows a villagelike plan, and while not all rooms

have a sea view, the grounds are so nicely landscaped that you won't feel deprived if your room faces inward. The staff has been praised as helpful.

Parasporos, 84400 Paros. (℧) **22840/24-154.** Fax 22840/21-167. Info@yriahotel.gr. 68 units. 180€–250€ ($234– $325) double. Rates include full buffet breakfast. Lunch or dinner 25€ ($33). AE, DC, MC, V. Closed mid-Nov to Apr. Located 2.5km (1½ miles) south of the port. **Amenities:** Restaurant; bar; freshwater pool; tennis; concierge; car rental; laundry. *In room:* A/C, TV, minibar, hair dryer.

NAOUSSA

In addition to the places listed below, you might consider the coyly named **Heaven Naoussa,** (℧) **22840/51-549;** www.heaven-naoussa.com) with 4 doubles, 5 suites, and 2 maisonettes (with pool); doubles from 110€ ($143); suites from 150€ ($195); maisonettes 1,600€ ($2,080) per week. The architecture is, appropriately, Cycladic, the decor is eclectic and stylishly casual, restaurants and the harbor are steps away. If you're unable to find a room, try **Nissiotissa Tours** (℧) **22840/51-480),** just off the east (left) side of the main square.

Astir of Paros ⚜ The most luxurious hotel on the island is built like a self-contained Cycladic village within a luxurious garden, with a private beach, 3-hole golf course, good pool, tennis court, gym, and efficient staff. What the Astir does not have is something to make it really memorable. Double rooms are unexceptional, with simple bed, table, and chair. The spacious suites have a bit more personality, with armchairs, desks, and attempts at fancy window drapes. Four units are equipped for travelers with disabilities. Produce for the two hotel restaurants is grown on a nearby farm; the breakfast buffet (not included in the room rates) features more than 70 items.

Kolimbithres Beach, 84401 Paros. (℧) **22840/51-976** or 22840/51-707. Fax 22840/51-985. Astir@otenet.gr. 61 units. 200€–240€ ($260–$312) double; 210€–450€ ($273–$585) suite. Rates include continental breakfast. AE, DC, MC, V. Closed Oct 20–Easter. West of Naoussa, off the south end of the beach. **Amenities:** Restaurant; bar; freshwater pool; 3-hole golf course; tennis; health club; concierge; 4 rooms for those w/limited mobility. *In room:* A/C, TV, DVD, Internet, minibar.

Hotel Petres ⚜⚜ Clea and Sotiris Hatzinikolakis combine warm hospitality with helpful efficiency to ensure that their guests' needs are met. The large, comfortable rooms, with private terraces or balconies, cluster around the big pool. Throughout, antiques and charming paintings, many done by Clea herself, give the Petres the charm and comfort so sadly lacking in most Greek hotels. The extensive, inventive, and delectable buffet breakfast-brunch served from 9 to 11:30am may well be the highlight of your stay on Paros! Dinner is usually available on request; and most Saturdays in summer there's a barbecue at the poolside grill. The view is of farm fields, with the sea in the distance and the location is blissfully quiet; if you want to get into Naoussa, the hotel offers a frequent, free minibus shuttle. A floodlit tennis court, sauna, and Jacuzzi will tempt many. In short, the only drawback to the Petres is that its comforts may entice you to put off sightseeing until *aurio* (tomorrow).

Naoussa, 84401 Paros. (℧) **22840/52-467.** Fax 22840/52-759. www.petres.gr. 16 units. From 120€ ($156) double. Rates vary depending on location and length of stay and include extensive buffet breakfast. DC, MC, V. Closed Nov–Mar. 3km (5 miles) from town. **Amenities:** Breakfast room/bar; freshwater pool; tennis; Jacuzzi; sauna; airport/port pickup. *In room:* A/C, TV, minibar.

Papadakis Hotel ⚜ The Papadakis has terrific views over the village from every room as well as from the pool with Jacuzzi. The large guest rooms have rather heavy, dark walnut wardrobes, beds, and desks; some rooms also have sofa beds. The excellent breakfast includes homemade baked goods prepared by owner Argyro Barbarigou, who happens to be an excellent cook—be sure to visit the Papadakis fish taverna (see "Where to Dine," below).

Naoussa, 84401 Paros. ✆ **22840/51-269**. Fax 22840/51-269. 19 units. 75€ ($98) double. Breakfast 10€ ($13). No credit cards. A 5-min. walk uphill from the main square. **Amenities:** Restaurant; bar; freshwater pool; Jacuzzi. *In room:* A/C, TV, minibar.

LEFKES

The Lefkes Village Hotel is quite special, but if it is full when you visit, or if you want to spend less, the 14-unit **Pantheon** (✆ **22840/41-646**) is perfectly decent and a lot cheaper; doubles from 60€ ($78).

Lefkes Village Hotel ✸✸✸   This handsome new hotel 10km (6 miles) from Parikia is designed to look like a small island village. It helps that Lefkes is probably the most charming inland village on the island. The spectacular views reach across the countryside to the sea. The pool is so nice that you don't mind not being on the ocean. Guest rooms are light and bright, with good bathrooms; some have balconies. In addition to all the things you'd expect in a tasteful hotel, there's a small Museum of Popular Aegean Culture and a winery. It's a popular place for wedding receptions and honeymoons.

P.O. Box 71, Lefkes Village, 84400 Paros. ✆ **22840/41-827** or 210/251-6497. Fax 2284/41-0827. www.lefkes village.gr. 25 units. 100€–210€ ($30–$273) double. MC, V. Rates include buffet breakfast. **Amenities:** Restaurant; bar; freshwater pool; Jacuzzi. *In room:* A/C, TV, minibar.

WHERE TO DINE
PARIKIA

Apollon Garden ✸ GREEK   THE PLACE TO GO, THE PLACE TO BE SEEN says the business card, and while that may be true, this is also a place with a lovely garden and excellent food. You will find all the Greek standards here—stuffed vegetables in season, grills, stews—and the quality is consistently good.

Market St., Parikia. ✆ **22840/21-875**. Main courses 8€–20€ ($10–$26). No credit cards. Daily 7pm–midnight. On Market St. just past the HOTEL DINA sign.

Bountaraki ✸ GREEK   Many small details set this taverna apart from its neighbors: fresh brown bread that's refreshingly flavorful, and simple main courses that aren't overwhelmed by olive oil. There's a small porch in front, facing the quieter southern end of the paralia. As with most tavernas, don't bother with the desserts, which are clearly an afterthought.

Paralia (shore road). ✆ **22840/22-297**. Main courses 8€–20€ ($10–$26). No credit cards. Daily 1–5pm and 7pm–midnight. At the southeast end of the waterfront, just over the bridge.

Distrato ✸✸ GREEK/INTERNATIONAL   On the street that runs from the cathedral to Market Street, beneath the spreading branches of a ficus tree, this is as nice a place as any to spend an hour or two, or an entire afternoon. Distrato serves crepes, sandwiches, ice creams, and inventive salads. If you're still hungry when you leave, the shop stocks nicely packaged organic Greek produce. (If there are no tables at Distrato, try **Symposio,** a few steps away, with tasty snacks but no shady tree.)

Paralia. ✆ **22840/22-311**. Snacks and main courses 8€–15€ ($10–$20). No credit cards. Daily 10am–midnight. Look for the ficus tree as you walk from the cathedral to Market St.

Levantis ✸ GREEK/INTERNATIONAL   This place gets high praise for its offbeat dishes that combine local produce with international ingredients. Where else on the island will you find Thai dishes alongside stuffed eggplant? Owner-chef George Mavridis likes to cook and likes to talk food, so you can enjoy what you eat while learning about the kitchen. The desserts are well worth saving room for, especially if you're a chocoholic. If you're too full for dessert, you can relax and enjoy the pleasant garden.

Paralia. ✆ 22840/23-613. Main courses 8€–20€ ($10–$26). AE, V. Daily 7pm–midnight. On Market St.

Porphyra ⟡⟡ GREEK/FISH   Locals say Porphyra serves the best fish in town. It's small, and the nondescript, utilitarian service and decor are typical of your average taverna. The difference here is that the owner cultivates the shellfish himself, resulting in an exceptional mussels Saganaki (mussels cooked with tomato, feta, and wine). The tzatziki and other traditional cold appetizers are also very good. The fish is predictably fresh, and offerings vary with the season. The same owners operate the nearby **Art Café;** drinks and snacks are served at the small gallery and cafe, which sometimes features live music.

Paralia. ✆ 22840/22-693. Main courses 8€–20€ ($10–$26); fish priced by the kilo. AE, V. Daily 6:30pm–midnight. Closed Jan–Feb. Between the pier and the post office, just back from the waterfront.

NAOUSSA

In addition to the places mentioned below, don't forget **Christos** ⟡⟡, uphill from the main square. It's not often that a restaurant maintains its quality and edge for a quarter of a century, but **Christos** (✆ **22840/51-442**) has done just that. The taverna food here is more elegant than at most places, with an inventive use of spices and herbs. Ask about the day's specials, which often include fresh fish (priced by the kilo) cooked with a deft touch.

Barbarossa Ouzeri ⟡ GREEK   This longtime local ouzeri is right on the port. Wind-burned fishermen and gaggles of chic Athenians sit for hours nursing their milky ouzo in water and their miniportions of grilled octopus and olives. If you want more of a meal, this is a fine fish restaurant. If you wonder what language the staff here is speaking, it's often Arabic or Russian—more evidence that the world is indeed becoming a global village.

Naoussa waterfront. ✆ 22840/51-391. Appetizers 4€–15€ ($5–$20). No credit cards. Daily 1pm–1am.

Christo's Taverna ⟡ GREEK/CONTINENTAL   Christo's has been here 25 years and is known for its eclectic menu and Euro-Greek style. A beautiful garden filled with red and pink geraniums serves as a backdrop for dinner. The color of the dark-purple grape clusters dripping through the trellised roof in late summer is unforgettable. When there's music, as often as not, it's classical. The veal dishes are usually very good here.

Archilochus. ✆ 22840/51-442. Reservations recommended July–Aug. Main courses 8€–18€ ($10–$23). No credit cards. Daily 7:30–11:30pm.

Le Sud ⟡ GREEK/INTERNATIONAL   This very ambitious place, which opened in 2003, has wooed diners away from the harbor to its garden with an inventive menu. There's often terrine of vegetables, bream with ginger, lamb with lemon and cardamom confit—and blinis. In short, although all the ingredients are fresh and almost all are local, the cuisine is eclectic. Try to reserve one of the handful of tables in the small garden; it's a good idea to call in advance in summer.

✆ 22840/51-547. Main courses 15€–25€ ($20–$33). No credit cards. Daily 7pm–midnight. About 200m (656 ft.) back from the port.

Tips **Beware the *Bomba***

Several places on the strip in Parikia offer very cheap drinks or "buy one, get one free." What you'll get, most likely, is locally brewed alcohol that the locals call *bomba*. This speak-easy brew is made privately and often illegally. It's a quick way to get drunk—and to feel awful after you get sober.

Mitsi's ⚔⚔ GREEK/SEAFOOD   This is the sort of seafood taverna you dream about finding and will always remember. We stopped at this little place on the beach beyond the harbor one evening just to have an ouzo and watch the sun set—and left 4 hours later after a number of ouzos and a leisurely dinner of fresh greens, fresh fish, and something tasty that the *patron* called "grandmother's stew." When we sat down, we were the only customers; by the time we left, every table was taken, about half by locals, half by visitors to the island. The retsina wine, which the engaging owner (Mitsi himself) makes, is terrific.

Harborside. ℂ **22840/51-302.** Main courses 8€–15€ ($10–$20); fish priced by the kilo. No credit cards. Daily 7pm–midnight.

Papadakis ⚔ INNOVATIVE GREEK   Fresh fish is one of the specialties here, but be sure not to rush to the main course—the appetizers are admirable: The tzatziki with dill is delicious and refreshingly different; the traditionally prepared *melitzanosalata* is redolent of wood-smoked eggplant. The desserts are worth sampling, especially *kataifi ekmek,* a confection conjured from honey, walnuts, cinnamon, custard, and cream.

Naoussa waterfront. ℂ **22840/51-047.** Reservations recommended. Main courses 10€–30€ ($13–$39). AE, V. Daily 7:30pm–midnight.

Pervolaria ⚔ GREEK   There's something for everyone here. The restaurant is set in a garden, lush with geraniums and grapevines, behind a white stucco house decorated with local ceramics. There's pasta and pizza, and schnitzel a la chef (veal in cream sauce with tomatoes and basil). If you want to eat Greek, order the souvlaki and varied appetizers' special.

ℂ **22840/51-598.** Main courses 6€–15€ ($7.80–$20). AE, V. Daily 7pm–midnight. About 100m (328 feet) back from the port.

PAROS AFTER DARK

As on all the islands, what's hot this year is often gone next year. You'll sense what the hot places are (they're the ones that are absolutely packed with customers and amplifiers). I'm not giving phones for these places because phones simply are not answered. Here are a few durable favorites. Just behind the windmill in Parikia is a local landmark, **Port Cafe,** a basic *kafenio* lit by bare incandescent bulbs and filled day and night with tourists waiting for a ferry, bus, taxi, or fellow traveler. The cafe serves coffee, pastry, and drinks; it's a good place for casual conversation.

Pebbles Bar ⚔ often has classical music and good jazz; as does the **Pirate Bar** ⚔, a few doors from Hotel Dina in the agora. Both are very congenial places, as popular with Greeks as with foreign visitors. **Alexandros,** in a restored windmill by the harbor, is awfully attractive and a perfect spot to enjoy being on an island, by the harbor, watching the passing scene.

In Naoussa, check out **Agosta** or **Café del Mar** by the harbor or for an after-dinner drink. You'll find the serious discos on the outskirts of town and by the bus station (**Vareladikos,** by the bus station, often goes all night.)

Music-Dance Naoussa (© **22840/52-284**) often performs Greek dances; the group wears costumes and is quite good. Look for posters around the island advertising upcoming performances. There seems to be little traditional Greek entertainment on Paros, but if you're interested, ask about performances by the local community dance group in Naoussa or inquire at **Nissiotissa Tours** in Naoussa (© **22840/51-480**).

5 Naxos ★★

191km (103 nautical miles) SE of Piraeus

Unlike many of its neighbors, green, fertile, largely self-sufficient Naxos has not needed to attract tourists. This does not mean that there is not a great deal here to charm visitors. The Venetians ruled this island from 1207 until the island fell to the Turks in 1566. The influence of **Venetian architecture** is obvious in the Hora's Kastro, some handsome mansions in town, and in the *piryi* (fortified Venetian towers) that punctuate the hillsides. The presence on the island of descendants of the Venetians means that Naxos has both Catholic and Orthodox churches. That said, the glory of Naxos's church architecture is the remarkable abundance of small **Byzantine chapels,** many of which contain exceptional frescoes dating from the 9th to the 13th centuries. These chapels escaped destruction by Naxos's various overlords and remain to charm visitors today.

The island's mountain villages, on the lower slopes of Mount Zas, the highest mountain in the Cyclades, preserve the rhythms of agrarian life. The area known as the **Tragea** has plains of olive trees, upland valleys, and a cluster of villages, Venetian towers, and Hellenistic watchtowers. Just about everybody's favorite village is **Apiranthos,** with some marble-paved streets, a particularly handsome Venetian tower, and small shaded plateias.

The airport, good inter-island ferry service, and speedy high-speed ferries make Naxos easy to visit. New hotels have appeared in the port, and more hotels cluster on island beaches—which are among the best in the Cyclades. In short, tourism has arrived—but, as yet, in a way that makes visiting here easy and pleasurable. As always, it is handy to have a car, although the local bus service is good, if leisurely. If you just want to see Naxos town, a day will do you; but, remember, Naxos is the largest of the Cyclades, with lots to see out on the island.

ESSENTIALS

GETTING THERE   By Plane   Olympic Airways (© **210/966-6666** or 210/ 936-9111; www.olympic-airways.gr) has at least one flight daily between Athens and Naxos Airport (© **22850/23-969**). For information and reservations on Naxos, call Olympic (see above). A bus meets most flights and takes passengers into Naxos town (2€/$2.60).

By Boat   From Piraeus, there is at least one daily ferry (6 hr.) and one daily high-speed ferry (4 hr.). Check schedules at the Athens **GNTO** (**210/870-0000;** www. gnto.gr), the **Piraeus Port Authority** (© **210/451-1311** or 1440 or 1441), or **Naxos Port Authority** (© **22850/22-300**). Boats are notoriously late and/or early; your travel or ticket agent will give you an estimate of times involved in the following journeys Remember: That's estimate, as in guesstimate. There is at least once-daily ferry connection with Ios, Mykonos, Paros, and Santorini. There is ferry connection several times weekly with Siros by high-speed ferry or hydrofoil; Tinos; and Samos; and somewhat less frequently with Sifnos and with Folegandros. For ferry tickets, try **Zas Travel** (© **22850/23-330**), on the paralia opposite the ferry pier.

VISITOR INFORMATION   The privately operated **Naxos Tourist Information Center** (© **22850/25-201;** fax 22850/25-200), across the plaza from the ferry pier, is the most reliable source of information and help. (Don't confuse it with the small office on the pier itself, which is often closed.) The center, run by the owner of the Chateau Zevgoli (see "Where to Stay," below) provides ferry information, books charter flights between various European airports and Athens, books accommodations, books cars and mopeds, arranges excursions, sells maps, exchanges money, holds luggage, assists with phone calls, provides 2-hour laundry service, and offers a **24-hour emergency number** (© **22850/24-525**) for travelers on Naxos who need immediate assistance.

Naxos has a helpful website, **www.naxos-island.com**, with maps, bus schedules, hotel listings, and a photo tour of the island.

You will want to find a good map as soon as possible, as Hora (Naxos town) is old, large, and complex, with a permanent population of more than 3,000. The free *Summer Naxos* magazine has the best map of the city. The *Harms-Verlag Naxos* is the best map of the island, but it's pricey at 7€ ($9.10). John Freely's *Naxos* (1976) remains delightful and helpful.

GETTING AROUND   By Bus   The bus station is on the harbor; bus schedules are often posted at the station, and free schedules are sometimes available. Regular bus service is offered throughout most of the island two or three times a day, more frequently to major destinations. In summer, there's service every 30 minutes to the nearby south-coast beaches at Ayios Prokopios and Ayia Anna. A popular day trip is to Apollonas, near the northern tip. In summer, the competition for seats on this route can be fierce, so get to the station well ahead of time.

In addition to the public buses, Zas Travel (© **22850/23-300**) offers day excursions around the island in season, usually for about 25€ ($33).

By Bicycle & Moped   Moto Naxos (© **22850/23-420**), on Protodikiou Square south of the paralia, has the best mountain bikes as well as mopeds for rent. A basic bike is about 10€ ($13) per day. For a moped, expect to pay from 20€ ($26) per day. Naxos has some major inclines that require a strong motor and good brakes, so a large bike (80cc or greater) is recommended (as is checking the brakes before you set off).

By Car   It's a good idea to inquire first about car rental at the Naxos Tourist Information Center (see "Visitor Information," above), which usually has the best deals. Car is the ideal mode of transport on this large island, and most travel agencies in Naxos town rent them, including **AutoTour** (© **22850/25-480**), **Auto Naxos** (© **22850/23-420**), and **Palladium** (© **22850/26-200**).

By Taxi   The taxi station (© **22850/22-444**) is at the port. A taxi trip within Naxos town shouldn't cost more than 4€ ($5.20). The fare to Ayia Anna Beach is about 8€ ($10); to the handsome inland village of Apiranthos, 20€ ($26).

FAST FACTS   Commercial Bank, on the paralia, has an ATM. It and other banks are open Monday through Thursday from 8am to 2pm, Friday from 8am to 1:30pm. Naxos has a good 24-hour **health center** (© **22850/23-333**) just outside Hora on the left off Papavasiliou, the main street off the port. **Holiday Laundry,** on Periferiakos Road, Grotta area (© **22850/23-988**), offers drop-off service. The **police** (© **22850/ 22-100**) are beyond Protodikiou Square, by the Galaxy Hotel. The **telephone office (OTE)** is at the port's south end; summer hours are daily from 7:30am to 2pm. The **post office** is south of the OTE by the basketball court; it's opposite the court on the left, on the second floor (Mon–Fri 8am–2pm).

WHAT TO SEE & DO: THE TOP ATTRACTIONS IN HORA ★★

Kastro is the name both for the 13th-century Venetian kastro (castle) which is Hora's greatest treasure, and also for the neighborhood around it where the Venetian nobility lived from the 13th to the 16th century. You should allow yourself several hours to explore the Kastro area of Hora—preferably by meandering and being pleasantly surprised at the architectural treasures (and nice little cafes) that you happen upon. If you take in Kastro's two museums, it's nice to have at least half a day here. To get to Kastro, you have to climb up from the **harbor,** through **Bourgo,** Hora's lower town. This route goes from harborside, through Bourgo, to Kastro. This is a pleasant way to spend a day—or, if pressed, several hours.

The Portara and Myrditiotissa ★★   If you come here by sea, you'll see two of Naxos's most famous monuments as you sail into the harbor: the little whitewashed **Myrditiotissa** chapel on an islet off the quay and the **Portara (Great Door),** connected to the quayside by a causeway. The Myrditiotissa was built around 1207 by the Venetian Marco Sanudo, a nephew of the Doge of Venice and ruler of the Venetian Duchy of the Archipelago. Sanudo also built much of the Kastro (see below). The massive Portara entrance door is all that remains of an obviously enormous Temple of Apollo. A 6th-century tyrant, Lygdamis, began the temple; when he died, construction stopped and demolition began. Over the centuries, most of the temple was carted away to build other monuments and buildings, including parts of both the Catholic and Orthodox cathedrals and much of the kastro. Fortunately, the massive posts and lintel of the Portara were too heavy for the Venetians to handle. Each of the four surviving blocks in the gates weighs about 20 tons.

Some scholars have thought that this temple was dedicated to the god Dionysos, who spent some time in his youth on Naxos dallying with local nymphs. Many locals believed that this was the palace of Ariadne, the Cretan princess who taught Theseus the mysteries of the labyrinth and helped him to slay the Minotaur. Her reward was to be abandoned here by Theseus as he sailed back to Athens, an event commemorated by Strauss in his opera *Ariadne auf Naxos.* Dionysos took pity on the discarded princess and married her, which gave rise to the nice legend that this great door was the entrance to the bridal palace. Now, most scholars think that the temple was dedicated to Apollo, in part because of a brief reference in the Delian Hymns and in part because it directly faces Delos, Apollo's birthplace.

One of the nicest ways to see the Portara is at sunset, from one of the harborside cafes.

Panagia Zoodochos Pigi Cathedral (Mitropolis) and Mitropolis Site Museum ★   As is so often the case in Greece, the modern town sits atop successive ancient settlements. Excavations undertaken around the Panagia Zoodochos Pigi Cathedral from 1982 to 1985 revealed a layered history of continuous occupation here from Mycenaean times to the present, with significant remains of the classical agora and the later Roman city. The Mitropolis museum, located in the square facing

What's in a Name?

There are many churches in Greece called Panagia Zoodochos Pigi ("Virgin of the life-giving spring"). Here, the name is especially appropriate: The church was built near the ancient Nymphaeum (fountain house). Much of the handsome marble in the Cathedral was pillaged from ancient buildings both on Naxos and from neighboring islands, including Delos. Since Venetian times, this neighborhood has been known as "Fontana," because of the spring that still flows here.

Naxos town's Mitropolis Cathedral, preserves the open space of the square while providing access to the excavated archaeological site below. You'll probably want to spend at least half an hour here.

Hora. ✆ **22850/24-151.** Free admission. Tues–Sun 8am–2:30pm. Turn in from the paralia at Zas Travel and continue about 100m (328 ft.) until you see the Mitropolis Cathedral Sq. on your right.

Bourgo/Kastro/Archaeological Museum/Venetian Museum ★★★   In Venetian times, the grandees lived at the top of the kill, in Kastro, and the Greeks lived down the hill, in Bourgo. To get to the Kastro, wend your way up through Bourgo, along one of the streets that snakes uphill from the Mitropolis (see above).

The Kastro had three main entryways, of which the most impressive today is the north entry, known as the **Trani Porta (Strong Gate),** signposted on Apollon St. This narrow marble arched threshold marks the transition from the commercial bustle of Bourgo to the Kastro's medieval world. Look for the incision on the right column of the arch, which marks the length of a Venetian yard, and was used to measure the cloth brought here for aristocratic Venetian ladies to consider purchasing. Exploring the Kastro's by-ways, it's hard not to wish to be able to levitate up over the lofty walls and have a look inside one of these Venetian mansions, with their walled gardens and coats of arms carved over doorways. Fortunately, one typical aristocratic Venetian house, the 800-year-old Della Roca family home, located just inside the Trani Porta, is open to the public. The 40-minute tour, offered in English and Greek, of the **Domus Venetian Museum** is a wonderful chance to get an inside look at one of the surviving great Venetian homes; you'll see and learn about the reception rooms, chapel, and vaults, and end in a small shop with local produce and handicrafts.

Be sure to find out whether any concerts are being given in the Venetian Museum's garden while you are on Naxos. You can ask at the museum or at the Naxos Tourist Information Center; or keep an eye out for posters. If there is a concert, you may get to spend a pleasant evening listening to Greek music, a string quartet, or some jazz. Whatever you hear, the setting could not be nicer.

At the center of the Kastro is the perhaps too heavily restored 13th-century **Catholic cathedral,** with its brilliant marble facade. To the right behind the cathedral is the French School of Commerce and the former **Ursuline Convent and School,** where young ladies of the Venetian aristocracy were educated. The nearby French School has housed schools run by several religious orders, and among its more famous students was the (famous irreligious) Cretan writer Nikos Kazantzakis, who studied here in 1896. The school now houses the **Archaeological Museum** ★. One of the highlights here is the group of white marble Cycladic figurines. These are the often violin-shaped marble figurines (dating from as long ago as 3000 B.C.) whose stark outlines some have compared to figures painted by Modigliani. The museum also has an extensive collection of late-Mycenaean-period (1400 B.C.–1100 B.C.) pottery found near Grotta, a district in the northern part of Hora, including vessels with the octopus motif that still appears in local art. The museum has a great view from its terrace and balconies to the hills of Naxos.

Hora. Archaeological Museum: (*C*) **22850/22-725.** Admission 4€ ($5.20). Tues–Sun 8am–2:30pm. Venetian Museum: (*C*) **22850/22-387.** Admission and tour 6€ ($7.80). Daily 10am–3pm and 6–10pm.

WHAT TO SEE & DO: THE TOP ATTRACTIONS OUT ON THE ISLAND
Naxos is generally thought to be the most beautiful of the Cyclades, with valleys and fertile farm fields. The island also has wonderful old chapels, absurdly picturesque villages, and—let's not mince words—often over-crowded beaches. You could spend a lifetime exploring this island. Here are just a few suggestions.

ANCIENT AND MEDIEVAL MONUMENTS
In addition to the Temple of Demeter, Naxos has two unfinished kouroi (monumental statues of men) that are well worth seeing in villages themselves worth seeing. See "The Villages," below, for the kouros of Apollonas and the kouros of Flerio.

Sangri & the Temple of Demeter ✦ The village of Sangri is an agglomeration of several villages in a valley below Mt. Profitias Elias. There's a deserted 16th-century monastery, Timios Stavros, on the mountain's lower slopes and the remains of a 13th-century Venetian kastro on its summit. The temple of Demeter is signposted (5km/3 miles) out of Stavri. Until about 10 years ago, the temple, built in the 6th century B.C., was in a state of complete ruin; it had been partially dismantled in the 6th century A.D. to build a chapel on the site, and what was left was plundered repeatedly over the years. Then, it was discovered that virtually all the pieces of the original temple were on the site, either buried or integrated into the chapel. A long process of reconstruction began. Most of the work has been completed, and it's possible to see the basic form of the temple—one of the few known square-plan temples.

Temple of Demeter at Ano Sangri. Free admission. Depart from Hora on the road to Filoti, and after about 10km (6 miles), turn onto the signposted road to Ano Sangri and the Temple of Demeter. From here it's another 3.5km (2 miles) to the temple, primarily on dirt roads (major turns are signposted).

THE BELLONIA, FRANGOPOULOS AND HIMARROS TOWERS ✦
The Naxian countryside is dotted with the towers (some defensive, some dwellings) that the Venetians built here. If you visit island villages, you'll inevitably see some of the towers, such as the 17th-century Frangopoulos tower in the hamlet of Chalki, some 17km (10 miles) south of Hora. The easiest to see from Hora is the Bellonia, just 5km (3 miles) south of town, outside the village of Galando. The tower, once the residence of the Catholic Archbishop of Naxos, is privately owned, but you can get a good look at the exterior without making the owners feel that they are under attack. The chapel beside the tower is really two chapels: one Catholic, one Orthodox; the arch between the chapels rests on an ancient column capital.

Lovers of Hellenistic fortifications and of hiking may wish to see the 20m-tall (45-ft.) Hellenistic Himaros tower, outside the hamlet of Filoti; the tower is signposted in Filoti as "Pirgos Himarou," but ask for supplementary directions locally and allow at least 3 hours to hike there and back from Filoti.

BYZANTINE CHURCHES ⭐⭐

You can easily spend a week seeing the Byzantine churches of Naxos; or you can see the handful mentioned below in a day. Getting to each one involves at least some walking. In order to see the interiors, allow time to find the caretaker. The churches are kept locked, due to increasing theft, although the caretaker often makes an early-morning or early-evening visit.

The remarkable number of small Byzantine chapels on Naxos mostly date from the 9th to the 15th centuries, many in or near some of the island's loveliest villages (see below). The prosperity of Naxos during this period of Byzantine and Venetian rule meant that wealthy patrons funded elaborate frescoes, many of which can still be seen on the interior walls of the chapels. Restoration has revealed multiple layers of frescoes and, whenever possible, the more recent ones have been removed intact during the process of revealing the initial paintings. Several frescoes removed in this way from the churches of Naxos can be seen at the Byzantine Museum in Athens. Anyone with a particular interest in Byzantine churches here and elsewhere would enjoy Paul Hetherington's *The Greek Islands: Guide to the Byzantine and Medieval Buildings and their Art.*

Just south of Moni (23km/14 miles east of Hora), near the middle of the island, is the important 7th-century monastery of **Panagia Drossiani (Our Lady of Refreshment)** ⭐, which contains some of the finest—and oldest, dating from the 7th century—frescoes on Naxos (St. George and his dragon are easy to spot). Locals believe the icon of the Virgin ended a severe drought on the island shortly after the frescoes were painted. The church is all that survives of what we are told was an extensive monastery; what an appealing place for a contemplative life! Visits are allowed at all hours during the day; when the door is locked, ring the church bell to summon the caretaker (remember to dress appropriately). To get here, drive about 1km (½ mile) south from Moni and look for the low, gray, rounded form of the church on your left.

About 8km (5 miles) from Hora along the road to Sangri, you'll see a sign on the left for the 8th-century Byzantine cathedral of **Ayios Mamas,** which fell into disrepair during the Venetian occupation but has recently been partly restored. The **view** alone from this charming church *vaut le voyage!* Sangri (the Greek contraction of Sainte Croix) today is made up of three villages, and includes the ruins of a medieval castle. The church of Ayios Nikolaos, which dates to the 13th century, has well-preserved frescoes, with a lovely figure of the personified River Jordan. To view them, ask around to find out which villager has the keys.

THE VILLAGES ⭐⭐

Many of the nicest villages are in the lush **Tragaea Valley** ⭐ at the center of the island. Each village is unique, and you can easily spend several days, or several years, exploring them. The bus between Hora and Apollonas makes stops at each of the villages mentioned below, but you'll have considerably more freedom if you rent a car. You'll find cafes all the villages and restaurants in most.

SOME TRAGAEA VALLEY VILLAGES

Halki, 16km (10 miles) from Hora, has a lovely central square shaded by a magnificent plane tree. Side streets have some rather grand 19th-century neoclassical homes. The fine 11th-century white church with the red-tiled roof, **Panagia Protothronos (Our Lady Before the Throne),** has well-preserved frescoes and is sometimes open in the morning. Turn right to reach the **Frankopoulos (Grazia) Tower.** The name is Frankish, but it was originally Byzantine; a marble crest on the tower indicates 1742, when it was renovated by the Venetians. Climb the steps for an excellent view of Filoti, one of the island's largest inland villages.

The brilliant white houses of **Filoti,** 2km (1 mile) up the road from Halki, elegantly drape the lower slopes of **Mount Zas,** the highest peak in the Cyclades. This is the largest town in the Tragaea, and the center of town life is the main square, shaded like Halki's square by a massive plane tree. There's a *kafenion* at the center of the square and two tavernas within 50m (164 ft.). In the town's center, the church of **Kimisis tis Theotokou (Assumption of the Mother of God)** has a lovely marble iconostasis and a Venetian tower.

Apiranthos ⚘, 10km (6 miles) beyond Filoti, the most enchanting of the mountain villages, is remarkable in that its buildings, streets, and even domestic walls are built of the brilliant white Naxos marble. The people of Apiranthos were originally from Crete; they fled their homes during a time of Turkish oppression. Be sure to visit **Taverna Lefteris,** the excellent cafe/restaurant just off the main square (see "Where to Dine," below); day tours of the island often stop here, so you may want to eat early or late.

THE VILLAGES WITH THE KOUROI ⚘

Apollon, at the northern tip of the island (54km/40 miles from Hora) is a small fishing village on the verge of becoming a rather depressing resort. It has a sand cove, a pebbled beach, plenty of places to eat, rooms to let, and a few hotels. From the town, you can drive or take the path that leads about 1km (½ mile) south to the famous **kouros** (a monumental statue of a nude young man). The kouros, about 10m tall (33 ft.), was begun in the 7th century B.C. and abandoned probably because the stone cracked during carving. Some archaeologists believe the statue was meant for the nearby temple of Apollo, but the kouros's beard suggests that it may be Dionysos. Naxos's other kouros is in the village of **Flerio** (also known as Melanes), about 7km (4 miles) east of Naxos town. The 8m (26-ft.) probably 6th-century-B.C. kouros lies abandoned in a lovely garden. Both kouroi sites are open to the public and free; in Flerio you can sip refreshments (including the local *kitron,* a lemon liqueur) served at the cafe run by the family that owns the garden. When you visit the National Museum in Athens, you can view a number of successfully completed kouroi statues.

BEACHES ⚘⚘

Naxos has the longest and some of the best beaches in the Cyclades, although you wouldn't know it from crowded **Ayios Yeoryios** beach just south of Hora. Windsurfing equipment and lessons are available at Ayios Yeoryios from Naxos Surf Club (© **22850/ 29-170**). **Ayios Prokopios,** just beyond Ayios Yeorgios, is another sand beach, some of which is now dominated by the new Lagos Mare Hotel (see "Where to Stay," below). **Kastraki Beach** is 7km long (4½ miles) and has won awards for its clean waters.

Tips **Walking Tours**

If you're going to spend some time on the island, we recommend buying a copy of Christian Ucke's excellent guide, *Walking Tours on Naxos.* You can take an island bus to reach most of the start and finish points for the walks. It's available for 15€ ($20) at **Naxos Tourist Information Center** on the paralia. As with all off-the-beaten-track walks, be equipped with water, a hat, good shoes, sunblock, a map, a compass—and a good sense of direction.

SHOPPING

Hora is a fine place for shopping, both for value and variety. **Zoom** (© 22850/ 23-675), on the waterfront, is the place to head for books and magazines. To the right and up from the entrance to the Old Market is **Techni** ✸ (© 22850/24-767), which has two shops within 20m (66 ft.) of each other. The first shop contains a good array of silver jewelry at fair prices; farther along the street, the second and more interesting of the two features textiles, many hand-woven (including some antiques) by island women. Nearby, **Loom** (© 22850/25-531), as its name suggests, has hand-woven fabrics and garments.

On the paralia next to Grotta Tours is tiny **Galini** (© 22850/24-785), with a collection of local ceramics. Also on the paralia, the venerable **Pamponas Wines** (© 22850/ 22-258) has been here since 1915; the local citron liqueur is a house specialty, along with a wide variety of Naxian wines. If you want something to eat with your wine, head along the paralia to the OTE, turn left on the main inland street, Papavasiliou, and proceed up the left side of the street until your nose leads you into **Tirokomika Proïonda Naxou** ✸ (© 22850/22-230). This delightful old store is filled with excellent local cheeses (*kephalotiri*, a superb sharp cheese, and milder *graviera*), barrels of olives, local wines, honey, spices, and dried comestibles.

In the kastro itself, **Antico Veneziano** ✸ (© 22850/26-206) has just that— antiques from the island's Venetian period—as well as glassware, woodcarvings, and old weavings from throughout Greece. This is a lovely place to browse; it's in a handsome Venetian-period house.

WHERE TO STAY

Hora's harbor is too busy for quiet accommodations; the following hotels in Kastro and Bourgo are within a 10-minute walk of the port; hotels in Grotta are a bit farther away, and places in Ayios Yeoryios are just outside of Hora. Insect repellent is advised wherever you stay. In addition to the following, you might consider the 19-unit **Hotel Anixis** (© 22850/22-112), near the Kastro's Venetian tower. Rooms are small, but about half have balconies and the Kastro location is appealing; as always with a Kastro, the walk there is steep. If you want to be on a beach, consider Anixis's the sister hotel, the seven-unit Anixis Resort (© 22850/26-475), a 10 minute walk from town, 30m (98 feet) from Ayios Yiorgos Beach. The friendly family management at both is highly praised. Prices from 60€ ($78). www.hotel-anixis.gr.

KASTRO

Castro ✸   Not quite a B&B, not quite self-catering flats, the two units here are rather fey studio apartments just inside the Kastro, with a shared terrace and a view across town to the Portara and the sea—and that's quite a view! This is the sort of place that makes you have pleasant fantasies of holing up and writing a novel (or at least a novella) and spending enough time exploring Kastro neighborhood that you would get lost only once a day! Try to get the top-floor unit with its own balcony so that you can watch the passing scene. Both units have wrought-iron beds and plenty of shelf space with interesting nick-nacks; you can add to the collections of sea shells if you wish. The Castro also rents several nearby apartments (usually by the week).

Kastro, Hora, 84300 Naxos. © 22850/25-201. www.naxostownhotels.com. 2 units. 80€–100€ ($104–$130) studios; 110€–130€($143–$169) apts. No credit cards. Closed Nov–Apr. **Amenities:** Terrace. *In room:* Kitchenette.

BOURGO

Apollon ★ What more appropriate spot to stay, on an island famous for its marble, than in a former marble workshop—one that has taken advantage of its quiet location and been transformed into a small, tasteful hotel? The rooms have verandas or balconies (always a big plus) and are simply furnished (twin beds, table, chair). Although there is no garden to speak of, there are plants everywhere. In short, Apollon offers welcoming lodging in Naxos town—just behind the imposing Orthodox Cathedral. Try to get one of the seaview rooms.

Fontana, Hora, 84300 Naxos. ✆ **22850/22-468.** www.naxostownhotels.com. 13 units. 120€–150€ ($156–$195) double. Rates include breakfast. DC, MC. Closed Nov–Mar. **Amenities:** Breakfast room/bar. *In room:* A/C, TV.

Chateau Zevgoli ★★ This small hotel, easily the most attractive in Naxos, lies at the foot of the 13th-century kastro walls. The Chateau is often fully booked months in advance; plan well ahead if you want to stay here. The energetic and helpful owner, Despina Kitini, decorated the lobby and dining area with antiques and family heirlooms. All guest rooms open onto a central atrium with a lush garden; there's also a roof terrace. The units are small but distinctively furnished with dark wood and drapes. Room no. 8, for example, features a canopy bed and a private terrace. Several rooms have views of the harbor. Ms. Kitini also rents four apartments in her house, also within the kastro walls and only 100m (328 ft.) from the hotel. These share a large, central sitting room; throughout are handsome stone walls and floors. The honeymoon suite has a balcony overlooking the town and the sea. Ms. Kitini also sometimes has studios for rent in town, often at excellent long-term rates.

Bourgo, Hora, 84300 Naxos. ✆ **22850/25-201** or 22850/22-993. Fax 22850/25-200. www.naxostownhotels.com. 14 units. 90€–120€ ($117–$195) double. Hotel rates include breakfast. AE, MC, V. Closed Nov–Mar. **Amenities:** Breakfast room/bar.

OUT ON THE ISLAND

Hora makes a pleasant base, but if you want to be near a pool or the sea, here are three places to check: Ayios Prokopios Beach, about 5km (2 miles) out of Hora, has two good choices. The 42-unit **Lianos Village Hotel** (✆ **22850/26-362;** www.lianos village.com) has a pool, is a 15-minute walk from the beach, has a snack bar, Internet cafe, and good views out toward the sea; doubles from 130€ ($182). The fancier 30-unit **Lagos Mare** (✆ **22850/42-844;** www.lagosmare.gr) opened in 2006, with two restaurants, spa facilities, Internet hookup, children's playground, snorkeling lessons, and a beachside position; doubles from 180€ ($234). Some 18km (11 miles) out of Hora at Mikri Vigli bay, **Orkos Village Hotel** ★ (✆ **22850/75-321;** www. orkoshotel.gr), is a 28-unit apartment complex (mostly bungalows) constructed to suggest a small Cycladic village. The hotel has a small library, its own excellent restaurant, genial Norwegian owners, and a location only 100m (328 ft.) from the beach; doubles from 110€ ($143); reductions for long stays.

WHERE TO DINE
HORA

The Bakery, on the paralia (✆ **22850/22-613**), sells baked goods at fair prices. Farther north, across from the bus station, **Bikini** (✆ **22850/24-701**) is a good place for breakfast and crepes. **Meltemi** (✆ **22850/22-654**) and **Apolafsis** (✆ **22850/22-178**) on the waterfront both offer all the Greek staples; Apolafsis also features live music many nights in summer.

Nikos ⍟ GREEK   This is one of the most popular restaurants in town. The owner, Nikos Katsayannis, is a fisherman, and usually has whatever is available. Those not in the mood for fish can try the *eksohiko,* fresh lamb and vegetables with fragrant spices wrapped in crisp filo (pastry leaves). The wine list is quite long, with lots of local and Cyclades choices.

Paralia, above Commercial Bank. ⍟ 22850/23-153. Main courses 6€–14€ ($7.80–$18); fish priced by the kilo. MC, V. Daily 8am–1am.

The Old Inn ⍟⍟ INTERNATIONAL   Yearning for some homemade pâté, or sausages? Dieter Ranizewski, who for many years operated the popular Faros Restaurant on the paralia, makes them at The Old Inn. The Germanic menu (this is one of relatively few places in the Cyclades where you can get jellied or smoked pork) offers an alternative to standard taverna fare. The food is simple, hearty, and abundant. As for the decor, the courtyard offers a green haven from the noise and crowds of the paralia. The restaurant, once a small monastery, inhabits several buildings surrounding a courtyard. The wine cellar is situated in a former chapel. Another vaulted room houses an eclectic collection of old objects from the island and from Dieter's native Berlin.

⍟ 22850/26-093. Main courses 8€–20€ ($10–$26). No credit cards. Daily 6pm–2am. 100m (328 ft.) in from the port.

Taverna To Kastro ⍟ GREEK   Just outside the kastro's south gate, you'll find small Braduna Square, which is packed with tables on summer evenings. There's an excellent view toward the bay and St. George's beach, and at dusk a pacifying calm pervades the place. The specialty here is rabbit stewed in red wine with onions, spiced with pepper and a suggestion of cinnamon. The local wines are light and delicious.

Braduna Sq. ⍟ 22850/22-005. Main courses 7€–15€ ($9–$20). No credit cards. Daily 7pm–2am.

APIRANTHOS

Taverna Lefteris ⍟⍟ GREEK   One of the island's best restaurants is in Apiranthos, perhaps Naxos's most beautiful town. The menu features the staples of Greek cooking, prepared in a way that shows you how good this food can be. The dishes highlight the freshest of vegetables and meats, prepared with admirable subtlety; the hearty homemade bread is delicious. A cozy marble-floored room faces the street, and in back is a flagstone terrace shaded by two massive trees. The homemade sweets are an exception to the rule that you should avoid dessert in tavernas—the trip here is worth making for the sweets alone.

Apiranthos. ⍟ 22850/61-333. Main courses 6€–10€ ($7.80–$13). No credit cards. Daily 11am–11pm.

NAXOS AFTER DARK

Naxos certainly doesn't compete with Mykonos and Paros for wild nightlife, but it has a lively and varied scene. As always on the islands, places that are hot one season are often closed the next year. We're not listing phones, because they are never answered at these places. **Portara,** by its namesake at the far end of the harbor, is an excellent place to enjoy the sunset. Next, you can join the evening **volta** (stroll) along the paralia. **Fragile,** through the arch in the entrance to the Old Town, is one of the older bars in town and worth a stop. **Lakridi,** off the paralia and not easy to find (ask someone to point the way), often has jazz, classical, and other mellow selections. On the paralia, **Ocean Dance** and **Super Island** are reliably lively and usually go all night in summer.

6 Mykonos (Mikonos)

177km (96 nautical miles) SE of Piraeus

By Peter Kerasiotis

What is it about Mykonos that has captured the world's imagination for over 40 years and refuses to let go? Though it is an undeniably beautiful island, it isn't the prettiest Greek island, or even of the Cyclades for that matter. Santorini is far more striking and Folegandros and Naxos have prettier towns and beaches than Mykonos does and are green and lush compared to Mykonos's barren land. It used to be it was the island's cosmopolitan lifestyle, luxury hotels, and nightlife, but today many of the more popular islands claim to be able to compete with that. It used to be its title as the party capital of all Mediterranean islands that set it apart, yet today Spain's Ibiza shares that title. So what is it then?

It all began with the picture-perfect town of labyrinthine roads leading you in circles around the beautiful cubist Cycladic architecture that attracted the likes of Jackie Kennedy and Aristotle Onassis in the '60s. With their stamp of approval, Mykonos became *the* place to be for anybody who was anybody. Soon in the hedonistic '70s, it became the island version of Studio 54 making world headlines on celebrity pages and magazines; the sheer contrast of a traditional Greek fishing village and the type of tourists it attracted: gay partyers, international jet setters, celebrities, and models made the island a unique place to visit and it captured the world's imagination.

The town, with its exceptionally handsome Cycladic architecture is still as pretty, romantic, and happening as ever; the beaches remain pristine, the prices keep climbing, and visitors still cannot get enough. Mykonos has that intangible, inexplicable, undeniable, impossible-to-resist "something" and it has it in spades.

If this is your first visit, you'll find lots to enjoy—especially if you avoid mid-July and August, when it seems that every one of the island's million annual visitors is here. Then again, what is Mykonos if you can't experience some of its legendary nighttime vibe for yourself? I suggest (for first timers) an early July visit. It's busy enough so you can understand what all the fuss is about but not choked with visitors like late July and August, when even finding a table at a restaurant can be difficult. Keep in mind that it's **very important** to arrive here with reservations in the high season, unless you enjoy sleeping outdoors and don't mind being moved from your sleeping spot by the police, who are not always charmed to find foreigners alfresco.

If you come in mid-September or October, you'll find a quieter Mykonos, with a pleasant buzz of activity, and streets and restaurants that are less clogged. Unlike many of the islands, Mykonos remains active year-round. In winter it hosts numerous cultural events, including a small film festival. Many who are scared off by the summer crowds find a different, tranquil Mykonos during this off season, demonstrating Hora's deserved reputation as one of the most beautiful towns in the Cyclades.

ESSENTIALS

GETTING THERE By Plane Olympic Airways (© **210/966-6666** or 210/936-9111; www.olympic-airways.gr) has several flights daily (once daily in off season) between Mykonos and Athens, and one flight daily from Mykonos to Iraklion (Crete) and Santorini. Book flights in advance and reconfirm with Olympic in Athens or on Mykonos (© **22890/22-490** or 22890/22-237). The Mykonos office is near the south bus station; it's open Monday through Friday from 8am to 3:30pm. Travel agencies on the port sell Olympic tickets as well. **Aegean Airlines** (© **210/998-8300** or 210/998-2888; www.aegeanair.com) has initiated service to Mykonos, daily in summer.

By Boat   Mykonos now has two ports: the old port in Mykonos town, and the new port north of Mykonos town at Tourlos. Check before you travel to find out which port your boat will use. From Piraeus, **The Blue Star Ithaki** (www.ferries.gr) has departures once daily at 7:30am. The **Pegasus** has two afternoon departures during summer at 7:30pm (Mon and Sat). The **High Speed** has two departures daily, one at 7:15am and 4:45pm and the **Marina** has three departures weekly at 11:50pm on Tuesdays, and 5pm Thursday and Saturday. From Rafina, **the Super Ferry** has one departure at 8am daily; the **Super Jet 2** has two departures daily at 7:40am and 4pm. The **Aqua Jewel** has one departure daily at 5pm while the **Penelope** leaves at 7:35pm daily. **High Speed** boats line **2** and **3** have daily afternoon departures at 7:30pm and 4:30pm respectively. Schedules can be checked with the **port police** (© **22890/22-218**). There are daily ferry connections between Mykonos and Andros, Paros, Syros, and Tinos; five to seven trips a week to Ios; four a week to Iraklio, Crete; several a week to Kos and Rhodes; and two a week to Ikaria, Samos, Skiathos, Skyros, and Thessaloniki. **Hellas Flying Dolphins** offers service from **Piraeus** (© **210/419-9100** or 210/419-9000; www.dolphins.gr) in summer. From the port of Lavrio, the Fly Cat 3 has an 11:15am departure daily to Mykonos.

On Mykonos, your best bet for getting up-to-date lists of sailings is to check at individual agencies. Or you can check with the **port authority** by National Bank (© **22890/22-218**), **tourist police** at the north end of the harbor (© **22890/22-482**), or **tourist office,** also on the harbor (© **22890/23-990;** fax 22890/22-229).

Hydrofoil service to Crete, Ios, Paros, and Santorini is often irregular. For information, check at **Piraeus Port Authority** (© **210/451-1311** or 210/422-6000; phone seldom answered); **Piraeus Port Police** (© **210/451-1310**); Rafina Port Police (© **22940/23-300**), or Mykonos Port Police (© **22890/22-218**).

Warning: Check each travel agency's current schedule, because most ferry tickets are not interchangeable. Reputable agencies on the main square in Mykonos (Hora) town include **Sunspots Travel** (© **22890/24-196;** fax 22890/23-790); **Delia Travel** (© **22890/22-490;** fax 22890/24-440); **Sea & Sky Travel** (© **22890/22-853;** fax 22890/24-753); and **Veronis Agency** (© **22890/22-687;** fax 22890/23-763).

VISITOR INFORMATION   **Mykonos Accommodations Center,** at the corner of Enoplon Dhinameon and Malamatenias (© **22890/23-160;** www.mykonos-accommodation.com), helps visitors find accommodations. It also functions as a tourist information center. **Windmills Travel** ✷ (© **22890/23-877;** www.windmills.gr) has an office at Fabrica Square where you can get general information, book accommodations, arrange excursions, and rent a car or moped. Look for the free *Mykonos Summertime* magazine, available in cafes, shops, and hotels throughout the island.

GETTING AROUND   One of the best things to happen to Mykonos was the government decree that made Hora an architectural landmark and prohibited motorized traffic from its streets. You will see a few small delivery vehicles, but the only ways to get around town are to walk—or to ride a bike or donkey! Many of the town's large hotels ring the busy peripheral road, and a good transportation system serves much of the rest of the island.

By Bus   Mykonos has one of the best bus systems in the Greek islands; the buses run frequently and on schedule. Depending on your destination, a ticket costs about .50€

Tips Finding an Address

Although some shops hand out maps of Mykonos town, you'll probably do better finding restaurants, hotels, and attractions by asking people to point you in the right direction—and saying *efcharisto* (thank you) when they do. Don't panic at how to pronounce *efcharisto*; think of it as a name and say "F. Harry Stowe." Most streets do not have their names posted. Also, maps leave off lots of small, twisting, streets—and Mykonos has almost nothing but small, twisting, streets! The map published by **Stamatis Bozinakis,** sold at most kiosks for 2€ ($2.60), is quite decent. The useful **Mykonos Sky Map** is free at some hotels and shops.

---

to 4€ (65¢–$5.20). There are two bus stations in Hora: one near the archaeological museum and one near the Olympic Airways office (follow the helpful blue signs). At the tourist office, find out from which station the bus you want leaves, or look for schedules in hotels. Bus information in English is sometimes available from the **KTEL** office (© **22890/23-360**).

By Boat Caiques to Super Paradise, Agrari, and Elia depart from Platis Yialos every morning, weather permitting; there is also service from Ornos in high season (July and Aug) only. Caique service is highly seasonal, with almost continuous service in high season and no caiques October through May. Excursion boats to Delos depart Tuesday through Sunday between 8:30am and 1pm, from the west side of the harbor near the tourist office. (For more information, see a travel agent; guided tours are available.)

By Car & Moped Rental cars are available from about 50€ ($65) per day, including insurance, in high season; most agencies are near one of the two bus stops in town. **Windmills Travel** (see "Visitor Information" above) can arrange a car rental for you and get good prices. The largest concentration of moped shops is just beyond the south bus station. Expect to pay about 15€ to 30€ ($20–$39) per day, depending on the moped's engine size. Take great care when driving: Island roads can be treacherous.

Warning: If you park in town or in a no-parking area, the police will remove your license plates. You—not the rental office—will have to find the police station and pay a steep fine to get them back.

By Taxi There are two types of taxis in Mykonos: standard **car taxis** for destinations outside town, and tiny, cart-towing **scooters** that buzz through the narrow streets of Hora. The latter are seen primarily at the port, where they wait to bring new arrivals to their lodgings in town—a good idea, since most in-town hotels are a challenge to find. Getting a car taxi in Hora is easy: Walk to Taxi (Mavro) Square, near the statue, and join the line. A notice board gives rates for various destinations. You can also call **Mykonos Radio Taxi** (© **22890/22-400**).

FAST FACTS   Commercial Bank and **National Bank of Greece** are on the harbor a couple blocks west of Taxi Square; both are open Monday through Friday from 8am to 2pm. ATMs are available throughout town. **Mykonos Health Center** (© **22890/23-994** or 22890/23-996) handles routine medical complaints; serious cases are usually airlifted to the mainland. The **tourist police** (© **22890/22-482**) are on the west side of the port near the ferries to Delos; the local **police** (© **22890/22-235**) are behind the grammar school, near Plateia Laka. The **post office** (© **22890/22-238**) is next to the police station; it's open Monday through Friday from 7:30am to 2pm. The **telephone office (OTE)** is on the north side of the harbor beyond the Hotel Leto (© **22890/22-499**), open Monday through Friday 7:30am to 3pm. **Internet access** is expensive here: Mykonos Cyber Cafe, 26 M. Axioti, on the road between the south bus station and the windmills (© **22890/27-684**), is open daily 9am to 10pm and charges 16€ ($21) per hour or 5€ ($6.50) for 15 minutes. Angelo's Internet Cafe, on the same road (© **22890/24-106**), may have lower rates.

WHAT TO SEE & DO
BEACHES
The beaches on the island's **south shore** have the best sand, views, and wind protection. However, these days they are so popular that you'll have to navigate through a forest of beach umbrellas to find your square meter of sand. A few **(Paradise, Super Paradise)** are known as party beaches, and guarantee throbbing music and loud revelry until late at night. Others **(Platis Yialos** and **Ornos)** are quieter and more popular with families. **Psarrou** has gone from being a family beach to being perhaps the sceniest beach of them all (for visiting Athenians mostly). With all the south-coast beaches, keep in mind that most people begin to arrive in the early afternoon, and you can avoid the worst of the crowds by going in the morning. The **north-coast beaches** are less developed but just as beautiful. Because the buses and caiques don't yet make the trip, you'll have to rent a car or scooter; you'll be more than compensated for the trouble by the quiet and the lack of commercial development.

For those who can't wait to hit the beach, the closest to Mykonos town is **Megali Ammos (Big Sand)**, about a 10-minute walk south—it's very crowded and not particularly scenic. To the north, the beach nearest town is 2km (1 mile) away at **Tourlos;** however, since this is now where many ships dock at the new harbor, it's not a place for a relaxing swim. **Ornos** is popular with families; it's about 2.5km (1½ miles) south of town, and has a fine-sand beach in a sheltered bay with extensive hotel development along the shore. Buses to Ornos run hourly from the south station between 8am and 11pm.

With back-to-back hotels and tavernas along its long sandy beach, **Platis Yialos** is extremely easy to get to from the town and has pristine aqua-blue waters and a variety of watersports. Due to its proximity to town however, it is always crowded and lacks character. It's ideal for a swim if you're too hung over to make it to farther beaches. Here you can catch a caique to the more distant beaches of Paradise, Super Paradise, Agrari, and Elia as well as a small boat to Delos. The bus runs every 15 minutes from 8am to 8pm, then every 30 minutes until midnight. Nearby **Psarou** is the first stop on the bus from town to Platis Yialos and it is a much higher-brow version of its neighbor. It is actually a beautiful stretch of beach, with white sand and greenery, overlooked by the terraces of tavernas and hotels. The excellent **N'Ammos** restaurant is right here as is the sublime hotel **Mykonos Blu** of the Grecotel chain. A rowdy and beach bar here has patrons dancing on whatever free inch of space they can find. During high season and especially during the weekends when the trendy Athenians flock to this beach, even chaise longues require reservations! Psarou is also popular when the meltemi winds strike the island as it offers protection in its bay to many yachts, boats, and swimmers. Its watersports facilities include **Diving Center Psarou,** water-skiing, and windsurfing. **Paranga,** farther east, is small and picturesque and can be reached easily on foot via an inland path from Platis Yialos; this small cove is popular for nude sunbathing and doesn't get too crowded, but is never too quiet either as the loud music from the neighboring beaches can be heard. From here you can take a hill path that will lead you to another beach, **Agia Anna (St. Anne).** Agia Anna is a shingle beach with a beautiful landscape and sweeping views from the top of the hill.

Reach **Paradise** *⊛*, the island's most famous beach, on foot from Platis Yialos (about 2km/1 mile), by bus, or by caique. The more adventurous arrive by moped on roads that are incredibly narrow and steep. Seeing how very few leave this beach sober, it is in your best interest (even if you have rented a moped) to get back to town by bus. This is the island's original nude beach, and it still attracts many nudists. A stand of small trees provides some shade, and the beach is well protected from the predominant north winds. Lined with bars, tavernas, and clubs, Paradise is never a quiet experience but it is the premiere party beach of the island and shows no signs of stopping. The **Tropicana Beach Bar** and the **Sunrise Bar** are both havens for the party crowd that go all day, long after the sun has set. On top of the hill, the popular and internationally known **Cavo Paradiso Club,** is a large, open-air nightclub with rotating international DJs and doors that do not open until after 2am. In fact the "cool crowd" begins to arrive only after 5am. On the beach Paradise Club is the club destination from 6pm to midnight and then reopens again from 2am to 6am. One beach party on Paradise you shouldn't miss is the **Full Moon Party,** once a month. The only other party that compares to it is the **Closing Party** every September that has become an island institution. As in most of the island, the water here is breathtakingly beautiful, but hardly anybody comes to Paradise for the sea.

Super Paradise (Plindri) is in a rocky cove just around the headland from Paradise; it's somewhat less developed than its neighbor, but no less crowded. You can get to the beach on foot, by bus, or by caique; if you go by car or moped, be very careful on the extremely steep and narrow access road. The left side of the beach is a nonstop party in summer, with loud music and dancing, while the right side is mostly nude and gay, with the exclusive **Coco Club** providing a relaxed ambience for its chic clientele until after 5pm when things get rowdy and loud. On the right side, there are similar party bars for the straight crowd. The waters here are beautiful but very deep so it isn't the best swimming option for families with small children. Farther east across the little peninsula is **Agrari,** a lovely cove sheltered by lush foliage, with a good little taverna and a beach that welcomes bathers in all modes of dress and undress.

Elia, a 45-minute caique ride from Platis Yialos and the last regular stop (also accessible by bus from the town), is a sand-and-pebble beach with crowds nearly as overwhelming as at Paradise and minimal shade and bamboo wind-breaks. Nevertheless, this beautiful beach is one of the longest on the island. The beach is surrounded by a circle of steep hills, has an attractive restaurant/cafe/bar, and offers umbrellas, sunbeds, and watersports. There is also a gay section to this beach that is also clothing optional. Despite its popularity however, there is no loud bar/club here, so the atmosphere is much more sedate than the Paradise beaches. The next major beach is **Kalo Livadi (Good Pasture).** Located in a farming valley, this long, beautiful beach is about as quiet as a beach on Mykonos's southern coast gets. There's bus service from Mykonos town's north station. Adjacent to the beach are a taverna and a few villas and hotels on the hills.

The last resort area on the southern coast accessible by bus from the north station is **Kalafatis** *⊛*. This fishing village was once the port of the ancient citadel of Mykonos, which dominated the little peninsula to the west. A line of trees separates the beach from the rows of buildings that have grown up along the road. This is one

Beach Notes

Activity on the beaches is highly seasonal, and all the information offered here pertains only to the months of June through September. The prevailing winds on Mykonos (and throughout the Cyclades) blow from the north, which is why the southern beaches are the most protected and calm. The exception to this rule is a southern wind that occurs periodically during the summer, making the northern beaches more desirable for sunning and swimming. In Mykonos town, this southern wind is heralded by particularly hot temperatures and perfect calm in the harbor. On such days, those in the know will avoid Paradise, Super Paradise, and Elia, heading instead to the northern beaches of Ayios Sostis and Panormos—or simply choose another activity for the day.

of the longest beaches on Mykonos, and its days of being uncrowded are, alas, over. The waters are pristine, however, and the hotels offer water ski, surfing, and windsurfing lessons. Here you will also find a good beach restaurant and bar and many boats throughout the day to take you to **Dragonisi,** an islet that has many caves ideal for swimming and exploring. You might also catch a glimpse of rare monk seals as the islet and its caves are reportedly a breeding ground for them. Adjacent to Kalafatis in a tiny cove is lovely **Ayia Anna** (not to be confused with the other beach of the same name by Paranga beach), a short stretch of sand with a score of umbrellas. Several kilometers farther east, accessible by a fairly good road from Kalafatis, is **Lia,** which has fine sand, clear water, bamboo windbreaks, and a small, exceptional, and shockingly low-priced taverna.

Most of the north-coast beaches are too windy to be of interest to anyone other than windsurfers and surfers. Though windsurfing has always been extremely popular in Greece, surfing is a relatively new sport there and Greece is a newly discovered destination for many surfers. All over the country, from Athens to beach towns and villages that line both coasts and many islands, surfers are suddenly realizing Greece with its many coasts has more to offer than clear waters that aren't shark-infested. Though Mykonos doesn't appear in the top 10 list of favorite places to surf in Greece, it should; already many of the island's wind-battered north-coast beaches attract many of European surfers in the know. When the north winds hit the island relentlessly, waves can swell up to impressive sizes and the lack of competition provides an uninterrupted haven for surfers and windsurfers alike. In order to enjoy this scene, however, you have to either have a car or a moped as public transportation, regrettably or not, hasn't made it here yet. **Fokos** is a superb sandy beach that has only recently begun to get noticed by tourists. The scenery is raw, wild, and beautiful and there is a small taverna here that is quite good. Fokos was the first beach to get noticed by the surfers. The huge Panormos Bay has three main beaches. The one closest to town is **Ftelia** and it is a long fine-sand beach, easily one of the best on the island but for the force of the north wind that has made it popular with surfers and windsurfers. There are, however, two well-sheltered northern beaches, and because you can only reach them by car or moped, they're much less crowded than the southern beaches. Head east from Mykonos town on the road to Ano Mera, turning left after 1.5km (1 mile) on the road to Ayios Sostis and Panormos. At **Panormos,** you'll find a cove with 100m (328 ft.) of fine sand backed by low dunes. Another 1km (¾ mile) down the road is **Ayios Sostis** ✸, a lovely small beach that sits just below a village. There isn't any parking, so it's best to leave your vehicle along the main road and walk 200m (656 ft.) down through the village. An excellent small taverna just up from the beach operates without electricity, so it's open only during daylight hours. Both Panormos and Ayios Sostis have few amenities—no beach umbrellas, bars, or snack shops—but they do offer a break from the crowds. Ayios Sostis is wild, windswept, and beautiful as are all north coast beaches, offering a completely different landscape than their far more popular southern counterparts. When the meltemi winds are at their strongest, during July and August into September, the waves can be awesome and unrelenting and the water is filled with surfers. Ayios Sostis, however, is becoming the new "in" beach during the high season when the visiting Athenians escape here when the winds aren't too strong.

Beaches to avoid on Mykonos because of pollution, noise, and crowds include **Tourlos** and **Korfos Bay.**

With so many sun-worshipers on Mykonos, local merchants have figured out that they can charge pretty steep prices for suntan lotions and sunscreens. You probably want to bring some with you. If you want to try a Greek brand, the oddly named Carrot Milk is excellent.

DIVING

Mykonos is known throughout the Aegean as one of *the* places for diving. Scuba diving on many islands is prohibited to protect undersea archaeological treasures from plunder. The best month is September, when the water temperature is typically 75°F (24°C) and visibility is 30m (98 ft.). Certified divers can rent equipment and participate in guided dives; first-time divers can rent snorkeling gear or take an introductory beach dive. The best established dive center is **Mykonos Diving Centre,** at Paradise beach (©/fax **22890/24-808**), which offers 5-day PADI certification courses in English from about 500€ ($650), including equipment. **Psarou Diving Center** in Mykonos town (© **22890/24-808**) has also been around for a long time. As always, before you sign up for lessons, be sure that all instructors are PADI certified. The **Union of Diving Centers in Athens** (© **210/411-8909**) usually has up-to-date information. In general, certified divers can join guided dives from 50€ ($65) per dive; beginners can take a 2-hour class and beach dive from 60€ ($78). There's a nearby wreck at a depth of 20 to 35m (65–114 ft.); wreck dives run from 60€ ($78).

ATTRACTIONS

Ask anybody who has visited the Greek islands and they will tell you that apart from the beaches, nothing compares to the early-evening stroll in the islands' towns. The light of the late hour, the pleasant buzz, the narrow streets filled with locals and tourists alike, and the romantic ambience in the air as you stroll along streets can lead you to anything from a modern restaurant, a pleasant taverna, a fortress, or an ancient, unassuming site.

Despite its intense commercialism and seething crowds in high season, Hora is still the quintessential Cycladic town and is worth a visit to the island in itself. The best way to see the town is to venture inland from the port and wander. Browse the window displays, go inside an art gallery, a store, or an old church that may be open but empty inside. Keep in mind that the town is bounded on two sides by the bay, and on the other two by the busy vehicular District Road, and that all paths funnel eventually into one of the main squares: **Plateia Mantos Mavroyenous,** on the port (called **Taxi Square** because it's the main taxi stand); **Plateia Tria Pigadia;** and **Plateia Laka,** near the south bus station.

Hora also has the remains of a small **Venetian kastro** (fortress) and the island's most famous church, **Panagia Paraportiani (Our Lady of the Postern Gate),** a thickly whitewashed asymmetrical edifice made up of four small chapels. Beyond the Panagia Paraportiani is the **Alefkandra** quarter, better known as **Little Venice** 𝕬𝕬, for its cluster of homes built overhanging the sea. Many buildings here have been converted into fashionable bars prized for their sunset views; you can sip a margarita and listen to Mozart most nights at the **Montparnasse** or **Kastro Bar** or check out the sunset and stay all night at **Caprice.** (See "Mykonos After Dark," later in this chapter.)

Another nearby watering spot is the famous **Tria Pigadia (Three Wells)** 𝕬𝕬. Local legend says that if a virgin drinks from all three, she is sure to find a husband, but it's probably not a good idea to test this hypothesis by drinking the brackish well water. After your visit, you may want to take in the famous **windmills of Kato Myli** and enjoy the views back toward Little Venice.

Save time to visit the island's clutch of pleasant small museums. **The Archaeological Museum** (© 22890/22-325), near the harbor, displays finds from Delos; it's open Wednesday to Monday 9am to 3:30pm. Admission is 3€ ($3.90); free on Sunday. **Nautical Museum of the Aegean** (© 22890/22-700), across from the park on Enoplon Dinameon Street, has just what you'd expect, including handsome ship models. It's open Tuesday to Sunday 10:30am to 1pm and 6 to 9pm; admission is 3€ ($3.90). Also on Enoplon Dinameon Street, **Lena's House** (© 22890/22-591) re-creates the home of a middle-class 19th-century Mykonos family. It's usually open daily Easter through October; free admission. **Museum of Folklore** (© 22890/25-591), in a 19th-century sea captain's mansion near the quay, displays examples of local crafts and furnishings. On show is a 19th-century island kitchen. It's open Monday to Saturday 4 to 8pm, Sunday 5 to 8pm; admission is free.

When you've spent some time in Hora, you may want to visit **Ano Mera,** 7km (4 miles) east of Hora near the center of the island, a quick bus ride from the north station. Ano Mera is the island's only other real town, and we especially recommend this trip for those interested in religious sites—the **Monastery of Panagia Tourliani** southeast of town dates from the 18th century and has a marble bell tower with intricate folk carvings. Inside the church are a huge Italian baroque iconostasis (altar screen) with icons of the Cretan school; an 18th-century marble baptismal font; and a small museum containing liturgical vestments, needlework, and woodcarvings. One kilometer (½ mile) southeast is the 12th-century **Monastery of Paleokastro,** in one of the island's greenest spots. Ano Mera also has the island's most traditional atmosphere; a fresh-produce market on the main square sells excellent local cheeses. This is the island's place of choice for Sunday brunch.

SHOPPING

Mykonos has a lot of shops, many selling overpriced souvenirs, clothing, and jewelry to cruise-ship day-trippers. That said, there are also a number of serious shops here, selling serious wares—at serious prices. **Soho-Soho** is by far the most well known clothing store on the island; pictures of its famous clientele (Tom Hanks, Sarah Jessica Parker, and so forth) carrying the store's bags have been in gossip publications around the world. Maria will help the female clientele find the perfect outfit while just across the street, at the men's store, Bill will recommend the latest men's arrivals. 81 Matoyanni (© **22890/26-760**). The finest jewelry shop is **LALAoUNIS** 𝕬, 14 Polykandrioti (© **22890/22-444**), associated with the famous LALAoUNIS museum and shops in Athens. It has superb reproductions of ancient and Byzantine jewelry as well as original designs. When you leave LALAoUNIS, have a look at **Yiannis Galantis** (✆ **22890/22-255**), which sells clothing designed by the owner. If you can't afford LALAoUNIS, you might check out one of the island's oldest jewelry shops, the **Gold Store,** right on the waterfront (✆ **22890/22-397**). **Delos Dolphins,** Matoyanni at Enoplon Dimameon (✆ **22890/22-765**), specializes in copies of museum pieces; **Vildiridis,** 12 Matoyianni (✆ **22890/23-245**), also has jewelry based on ancient designs.

Mykonos has lots of art galleries, including some based in Athens that move here for the summer season. **Scala Gallery** ✿, 48 Matoyianni (✆ **22890/23-407;** fax 22890/26-993; www.scalagallery.gr), is one of the best galleries in town. All the artists represented are from Greece, many of them quite well known. There is a selection of jewelry, plus an interesting collection of recent works by Yorgos Kypris, an Athenian sculptor and ceramic artist. Nearby on Panahrandou is **Scala II Gallery** (✆ **22890/26-993**), where the overflow from the Scala Gallery is sold at reduced prices. In addition, manager **Dimitris Roussounelos** (✆/fax **22890/26-993;** scala@otenet.gr) of Scala Gallery manages a number of studios and apartments in Hora, so you might find lodgings as well as art at Scala!

There was a time when Mykonos was world-famous for its vegetable-dyed hand-loomed weavings, especially those of the legendary Kuria Vienoula. Today, **Nikoletta** (✆ **22890/27-503**) is one of the few shops where you can still see the island's traditional loomed goods. Eleni Kontiza's tiny shop **Hand Made** (✆ **22890/27-512**), on a lane between Plateia Tria Pigadia and Plateia Laka, has a good selection of hand-woven scarves, rugs, and tablecloths from around Greece.

The best bookstore on Mykonos is **To Vivlio** ✿ (✆ **22890/27-737**), on Zouganeli, one street over from Matoyianni. It carries a good selection of books in English, including many works of Greek writers in translation, plus some art and architecture books and a few travel guides.

Works of culinary art can be found at **Skaropoulos** (✆ **22890/24-983**), 1.5km (1 mile) out of Hora on the road to Ano Mera, featuring the Mykonian specialties of Nikos and Frantzeska Koukas. Nikos's grandfather started making confections here in 1921, winning prizes and earning a personal commendation from Winston Churchill. Try their famed *amygdalota* (an almond sweet) or the almond biscuits (Churchill's favorite). You can also find Skaropoulos sweets at **Pantopoleion,** 24 Kaloyerou (✆ **22890/22-078**), along with Greek organic foods and natural cosmetics; the shop is in a beautifully restored 300-year-old Mykonian house.

When you finish your shopping, treat yourself to another almond biscuit (or two or three) from **Efthemios,** 4 Florou Zouganeli (✆ **22890/22-281**), just off the harborfront, where biscuits have been made since the 1950s.

WHERE TO STAY

In summer, reserve a room 1 to 3 months in advance (or more), if possible. Ferry arrivals are often met by a throng of people hawking rooms, some in small hotels, others in private homes. If you don't have a hotel reservation, one of these rooms may be very welcome. Otherwise, book as early as you can. Many hotels are fully booked all summer by tour groups or regular patrons. Keep in mind that Mykonos is an easier, more pleasant place to visit in the late spring or early fall. Off-season hotel rates are sometimes half the quoted high-season rate. Also note that many small hotels, restaurants, and shops close in winter, especially if business is slow.

Mykonos Accommodations Center (MAC), 10 Enoplon Dinameon (© **22890/ 23-160** or 22890/23-408; fax 22890/24-137; www.mykonos-accommodation.com), is a very helpful service, especially if you are looking for hard-to-find inexpensive lodgings. The service is free when you book a hotel stay of 3 nights or longer. If you plan a shorter stay, ask about the fee, which is sometimes a percentage of the tab and sometimes a flat fee.

IN HORA

Andronikos Hotel 🦋🦋   Beautiful, elegant, and right in town, this impeccably designed hotel offers spacious verandas or terraces with incredible vistas of the sea and the town, a very good in-site restaurant, an edgy gallery, and a spa at affordable (for Mykonos) prices.

Hora 86400, Mykonos. © **22890/24-231.** Fax 22890/24-691. www.andronikoshotel.com. 53 units. 180€–230€ ($234–$299) double without Jacuzzi; 240€–290€ ($312–$377) double with Jacuzzi; 310€-380€ ($403–$494) suite. AE, DC, MC, V. **Amenities:** Restaurant; bar; pool; spa; gym; gallery. *In room:* A/C, TV, Internet, DVD player, minibar, hair dryer, Jacuzzi (in some rooms).

Apanema Resort Hotel 🦋🦋   This intimate and pretty boutique hotel is also ideally located only a 10-minute walk from town. The young owner has decorated her hotel in impeccable taste with personal touches throughout such as handcrafted pottery and rugs creating a homey feeling amid the elegance. Another big plus (apart from the stunning view from the pool) is the hotel's ample and delicious American buffet breakfast, served from 7am to 2pm, for those that cannot get out of bed before 1pm. The on-site Med fusion restaurant, Apanema, is also another excuse to stay.

Hora, Tagoo 84600 Mykonos. © **22890/28-590.** Fax 22890/79-250. www.apanemaresort.com. 17 units. 179€– 220€ ($232–$286) double; 510€ ($663) suite. Rates include American buffet breakfast. Considerable off-season reductions. AE, MC, V. Free parking. **Amenities:** Restaurant; bar; pool; tennis court. *In room:* A/C, TV, Internet, minibar, hair dryer, safe.

Apollon Hotel _Value_   No-nonsense, no-frills hotels in Mykonos are hard to come by. Rooms are basic yet comfortable and very well kept. But it's the price that is by far its biggest attraction.

Hora, 84600 Mykonos. © **22890/22-223.** Fax 22890/2437. 10 units. 50€–65€ ($65–$84) single/double with shower. No credit cards. *In room:* A/C, TV.

Belvedere Hotel 🦋🦋   The all-white oasis of the Belvedere, in part occupying a handsomely restored 1850s town house on the main road into town, has stunning views over the town and harbor, a few minutes' walk away. Rooms are nicely, if not distinctively, furnished. Stay here if you want many of the creature comforts of Mykonos's beach resorts, but prefer to be within walking distance of Hora. The ultrachic poolside scene buzzes all night and day, in part due to Nobu Matsuhisa's only open-air restaurant, the impeccable **Matsuhisa Mykonos.** In season, the hotel often offers massage, salon, and barber service. Off season, look for excellent specials; after a 4-night stay, this might be a free jeep for a day or a fifth night free. This is the Delano of Mykonos; stylish, always popular, and in a class of its own.

Hora, 84600 Mykonos. © **22890/25-122.** Fax 22890/25-126. www.belvederehotel.com. 48 units. 230€–460€ ($299–$600) double; 650€ ($832) suites. Rates include American buffet breakfast. Considerable off-season reductions. AE, DC, MC, V. **Amenities:** 2 restaurants; bar; pool; fitness center; Jacuzzi; sauna. *In room:* A/C, TV, Internet, minibar, hair dryer.

Cavo Tagoo 𝒢𝒢   This exceptional hotel set into a cliff with stunning views over Mykonos town is hard to resist—and consistently makes it onto *Odyssey* magazine's list of 10 best Greek hotels. Cavo Tagoo's island-style architecture has won awards, and its gleaming marble floors, nicely crafted wooden furniture, queen- and king-size beds, and local-style weavings are a genuine pleasure. An impressive redesign has left it better than ever before. Elegantly minimalist with marble, spacious bathrooms and large balconies with stunning sea vistas, Cavo Tagoo features suites with private pools, a Spa Center, stunning lounge, and pool areas. Hora's harbor is only a 15-minute walk away, although you may find it hard to budge: A saltwater pool and a good restaurant are located at the hotel.

Hora, 84600 Mykonos. ℭ **22890/23-692** to -695. Fax 22890/24-923. www.cavotagoo.gr. 69 units. 225€–420€ ($293–$546) double. Rates include buffet breakfast. AE, DC, MC, V. Closed Nov–Mar. **Amenities:** Restaurant; bar; saltwater pool; gym; sauna. *In room:* A/C, TV, Internet, minibar, hair dryer.

Elysium 𝒢𝒢   The smartest gay hotel on the island is located on a steep hillside right in the old town; a walk down the steep hill will have you back in town in 3 minutes. Gardens, a pool, great views, a gym, sauna, and a very relaxed atmosphere keep guests coming again and again.

Mykonos Old Town, 84600 Mykonos. ℭ **22890/23-952.** Fax 22890/23-747. www.elysiumhotel.com. 42 units. 101€ ($131) single; 180€ ($234) double; 246€ ($320) suite; 800€–1,126€ ($1,040–$1,464) royal suite. AE, DC, MC, V. **Amenities:** Bar/cafe; pool; gym; sauna; spa; hydro-massage. *In room:* A/C, TV, Internet, bathtub, hair dryer, safe.

Hermes Hotel 𝒢   Atop a hill with stunning vistas of the town, the port, the windmills, and the sea, Hermes Hotel has clean and comfortable rooms, a breakfast area, and a lovely pool with breathtaking views. The 10-minute walk down the hill to town is effortless but the same walk on your way back up can easily run you longer and can be exhausting—the only drawback to this charming hotel. However, the magnificent views and good value compensate for the extra calories burned.

Drosopezoula, Hora, 84600 Mykonos. ℭ **22890/24-242.** Fax 22890/25-640. www.greekhotel.com. 24 units. 72€– 126€ ($93–$164) single; 83€–147€ ($108–$191) double; 98€–189€ ($127–$246) triple. AE, MC, V. **Amenities:** Cafe/bar; breakfast; pool. *In room:* A/C, TV.

Mykonos Theoxenia 𝒢𝒢   When the Mykonos Theoxenia reopened its doors in 2004 after an extensive makeover, it quickly became the talk of the town once again as it was in the '60s. With its stone-clad walls and orange and turquoise fabrics, the mood is already set before you venture beyond the reception. In the 52 rooms and suites, funky '60s-inspired furniture and loud colors dominate the decor with spacious bathrooms (stuffed with luxuries) enclosed in glass walls. The location, right by the windmills and impossibly romantic Little Venice, could not be any more ideal. A wonderful pool and restaurant are the perfect finishing touches. When you arrive at the hotel you will be treated to a welcoming drink, a fruit basket, and bottle of wine.

Kato Mili, Hora, 84600 Mykonos. ℭ **22890/22-230.** www.mykonostheoxenia.com. 52 units. 282€–420€ ($367– $546) single/double depending on balcony and view; 625€ ($813) junior suite; 830€ ($1,079) 2-bedroom suite. AE, DC, MC, V. Free parking. **Amenities:** Restaurant; bar; pool. *In room:* A/C, TV, Internet, hair dryer, safe.

Mykonos View 𝒢   With a view that you'll be hard-pressed to beat, the Mykonos View, is ideally situated on a hill above the town is a complex of apartments (independent studios, apartments and maisonettes) all connected via cobblestone paths that give you the sense of having your own island apartment which is infinitely more alluring for some than feeling they are in a hotel. The swimming pool hangs over the

Aegean and the town. The hotel's awesome **Oneiro Bar** (Dream Bar) has become an island-must sunset destination.

Hora, 84600 Mykonos. ℂ **22890/24-045.** Fax 22890/26445. www.mykonosview.gr. units. 130€–160€ ($169–$208) studio; 160€–220€ ($208–$286) superior studio; 180€–250€ ($234–$325) apartment; 200€–280€ ($260–$364) maisonette. AE, DC, MC, V. **Amenities:** Restaurant; bar; pool. *In room:* A/C, TV, Internet, hair dryer, safe.

Ostraco Suites ✪   This mod-meets-island decor is ideal for young, hip couples or a group of young friends who are looking for something stylish (but not outrageously pricey or chic) and a 5 minute walk to town. It consists of five white villas, and manages to be affordable and trendy at the same time. Two of the suites were renovated by the late renowned Greek interior designer Angelos Angelopoulos.

Drafaki, 84600 Mykonos. ℂ **22890/23-396.** Fax 22890/27-123. www.ostraco.gr. 21 units. 185€–230€ ($241–$299) double; 305€–380€ ($397–$494) suite. AE, DC, MC, V. **Amenities:** Restaurant; bar; cafe; American buffet breakfast; pool; sun deck; spa. *In room:* A/C, LCD TV, DVD, minibar, hair dryer.

Philippi Hotel   Each room in this homey little hotel in the heart of Mykonos town is different, so you might want to have a look at several before choosing yours. The owner tends a lush garden that often provides flowers for her son's restaurant, the elegant Philippi (see "Where to Dine," below), which can be reached through the garden.

25 Kaloyera, Hora, 84600 Mykonos. ℂ **22890/22-294.** Fax 22890/24-680. 13 units. 90€ ($117) double. No credit cards. **Amenities:** Restaurant; breakfast room.

Porto Mykonos ✪   Just above the old port with vistas in every direction and an enviable location, this boutique hotel has minimalist rooms, new bathrooms, and great views from its front and side balconies (be sure not to get the back rooms as they look into a parking lot). There is some noise here (as it is near the port) but you will be compensated by the comfortable rooms, a wonderful saltwater pool and Jacuzzi, and direct access to the action any time of the day and night. The very good a la Carte restaurant is also another plus.

Palio Limani, Hora, 84600 Mykonos. ℂ **22890/22-454.** www.portomykonos.gr. 59 units. 226€ ($294) single/double/triple; 363€ ($472) suite. AE, DC, MC, V. **Amenities:** Restaurant; bar; cafe; saltwater pool and Jacuzzi; gym; spa. *In room:* A/C, TV, Internet.

Tharraoe of Mykonos ✪✪   Built on top of a hill, this small boutique hotel has spacious rooms with stunning sea and town vistas from the balconies; clean-lined wooden furniture; colorful bathrooms with funky, spacious tubs; and a wonderful pool area overlooking the sea and town. Top-notch **Barbarossa** restaurant and the in-house beauty salon and Ayurvedic Spa complete the picture.

Hora, 84600 Mykonos. ℂ **22890/27-370 ext. 4.** Fax 22890/27-375. www.tharroeofmykonos.gr. 24 units. 200€ ($260) double with island view; 226€ ($294) double with sea view; 380€–460€ ($494–$598) suite. AE, DC, MC, V. Free parking. **Amenities:** Restaurant; bar; cafe; pool; gym; spa. *In room:* A/C, TV, Internet, minibar, hair dryer, safe.

Zorzis Hotel   Confused by all the posh boutiques in town? Don't know quite what to choose? For a completely different experience, you might like to try this unique option in town. Set inside a traditional 16th-century building in the center of town, the rooms at Zorzis have Casablanca ceiling fans, wooden antique furniture, and antique Louis XV beds; this is truly like taking a few stylish steps back in time.

30 Kalogear Street, Hora, 84600 Mykonos. ℂ **22890/22-167.** Fax 22890/24-168. www.zorzishotel.com. 10 units. 200€ ($260) double with island view; 121€ ($157) single; 152€–460€ ($494–$598) suite. AE, DC, MC, V. Free parking. **Amenities:** Restaurant; bar; cafe; pool; gym; spa. *In room:* A/C, TV, Internet, minibar, hair dryer, safe.

OUT ON THE ISLAND

Although most visitors prefer to stay in Hora and commute to the beaches, there are some truly spectacular hotels on or near many of the more popular island beaches and many more affordable ones.

The beaches at Paradise and Super Paradise have private studios and simple pensions, but rooms are almost impossible to get, and prices more than double in July and August. Contact **Mykonos Accommodations Center** (© 22890/23-160) or, for Super Paradise, **GATS Travel** (© 22890/22-404), for information on the properties they represent. The tavernas at each beach may also have suggestions.

AT KALAFATI   The sprawling **Aphrodite Hotel** (© 22890/71-367) has a large pool, two restaurants, and 150 rooms. It's a good value in May, June, and October, when a double costs about 100€ ($130). The hotel is popular with tour groups and Greek families.

AT ORNOS BAY ★★   Elegant **Kivotos Club Hotel** ★★, Ornos Bay, 84600 Mykonos (© **22890/25-795;** fax 22890/22-844; www.kivotosclubhotel.gr), is a small, superb luxury hotel about 3km (2 miles) outside Mykonos town. Most of the 45 individually decorated units overlook the Bay of Ormos, but if you don't want to walk that far for a swim, head for the saltwater or freshwater pool, the Jacuzzi and sauna, or the pool with an underwater sound system piping in music! Kivotos Clubhouse is small enough to be intimate and tranquil; the service (including frozen towels for poolside guests on hot days) gets raves from guests. If you're ever tempted to leave (and you may not be), the hotel minibus will whisk you into town. You can easily dine at the several restaurants on-site. The hotel also has a traditional sailing ship, at the ready for spur-of-the moment sails. In short, it's no surprise that this popular honeymoon destination appears often on *Odyssey* magazine's annual list of the best hotels in Greece. Doubles cost 290€ to 390€ ($377–$507); suites are priced from 650€ to 1,000€ ($845–$1,300). The enormous **Santa Marina,** also at Ornos Bay (© **22890/23-200;** fax 22890/23-412; info@santa-marina.gr), has 90 suites and villas in 20 landscaped acres overlooking the bay. If you don't want to swim in the sea, two pools and spa facilities are available at the hotel, which has its own restaurant as well. Suites with private pool are available from 1,500€ ($1,950). If you wish, you can arrive here by helicopter and land on the hotel pad. Doubles cost from 395€ to 600€ ($514–$780); suites and villas from 625€ to 2,400€ ($813–$3,120). The more modest 25-unit **Best Western Dionysos Hotel** (© 22890/23-313) is steps from the beach and has a pool, restaurant, bar, and air-conditioned rooms with fridges and TV; doubles cost from 190€ ($247). The even more modest 42-unit **Hotel Yiannaki** (© **22890/23-393**) is about 200m (656 ft.) away from the beach and has its own pool and restaurant; doubles begin at 125€ ($163). The nicest units have sea views and balconies.

Families traveling with children will find staying at one of the Ornos Bay hotels especially appealing. The beach is excellent and slopes into shallow, calm water. Furthermore, this is not one of Mykonos's all-night party beaches. If your hotel does not have watersports facilities, several of the local tavernas have surfboards and pedal boats to rent, as well as umbrellas. One minus: The beach is close to the airport, so you will hear planes come and go.

AT PLATI YIALOS   The large and comfortable rooms of the 82-unit **Hotel Petassos Bay,** Plati Yialos, 84600 Mykonos (© **22890/23-737;** fax 22890/24-101), all have air-conditioning and minibars. Doubles go for about 150€ ($195). Each has a balcony overlooking the relatively secluded beach, which is less than 36m (132 ft.) away. The hotel has a good-size pool, sun deck, Jacuzzi, gym, and sauna. It offers free round-trip transportation to and from the harbor or airport, safety-deposit boxes, and laundry service. The new seaside restaurant has a great view and serves a big buffet breakfast (a smaller continental breakfast is included in the room rate).

AT AYIOS IOANNIS   Mykonos Grand is a 100-room luxury resort a few kilometers out of Hora in Ayios Ioannis, 84600 Mykonos (✆ **22890/25-555;** www.mykonosgrand.gr). With its own beach and many amenities—pools, tennis, squash, Jacuzzis, a spa—this is a very sybaritic place. The Mykonos Grand regularly appears on *Odyssey* magazine's list of the 50 best hotels in Greece and is popular with Greeks, Europeans, and Americans. Doubles start at 225€ ($293). The **St. John Hotel,** Ayios Ioannis, 84600 Mykonos (✆ **22890/28-752;** fax 22890/28-751; www.saintjohn.gr) has doubles from 310€ ($403) and suites from 590€ ($767). It's a breathtaking hotel on a hillside over the Aegean with spectacular sea vistas and a stunning infinity pool with views over the cliff and into the sea. The St. John resembles a traditional blue-and-white village complete with its own chapel. With 148 guest rooms and 9 opulent suites, the rooms are huge, stylishly decorated in warm hues of deep peach, with simple and elegant furniture, large marble bathrooms overflowing with products and with their own Jacuzzi, and grand balconies with sea vistas as far as the eye can see. With a superb restaurant and fitness spa, three pools and its own private beach, this is an experience in itself.

AT AYIOS STEPHANOS   This popular resort, about 4km (2½ miles) north of Hora, has a number of hotels. Most close from November to March. The 38-unit **Princess of Mykonos,** Ayios Stephanos beach, 84600 Mykonos (✆ **22890/23-806;** fax 22890/23-031), is lovely. The Princess has bungalows, a gym, a pool, and an excellent beach; doubles cost from 180€ ($234). **Hotel Artemis,** Ayios Stephanos, 84600 Mykonos (✆ **22890/22-345**), near the beach and bus stop, offers 23 units from 115€ ($150), breakfast included. Small **Hotel Mina,** Ayios Stephanos, 84600 Mykonos (✆ **22890/23-024**), uphill behind the Artemis, has 15 doubles that go for 80€ ($104). **Mykonos Grace** ✮✮, Ayios Stefanos, 84600 Mykonos (✆ **22890/26-690;** www.mykonosgrace.com), 230€ to 330€ ($299–$429) double; 320€ to 420€ ($416–$546) junior suite, is an intimate yet undeniably stunning boutique hotel. Some of the hotel's 39 rooms might be on the small side but the glass that separates the bathroom from the bedroom adds depth and the illusion of extra space, and huge balconies with stunning views more than compensate. Rooms range from standard to VIP suites, all with minimalistic design. Elegant and sophisticated, the Mykonos Grace won *Odyssey* magazine's "Best New Entry" award for 2007 and was singled out by The *London Sunday Times* as one of the hippest new hotels of 2007 after its complete face-lift that year. Guests can swim in the sea off Ayios Stephanos beach, or in one of several hotel pools, or soak in the spa Jacuzzis or their suite's hot tub. Decor, food, privacy all get high marks—as do the prices, which are less extravagant than at some of Mykonos's other boutique hotels. It's only a 5-minute walk to town to boot.

AT PSARROU BEACH   Grecotel Mykonos Blu ✮✮, Psarrou Beach, 84600 Mykonos (✆ **22890/27-900;** fax 22890/27-783; www.grecotel.gr), is another of the island's serious luxury hotels with award-winning Cyclades-inspired architecture. Like Cavo Tagoo and Kivotos, this place is popular with wealthy Greeks, honeymooners, and jet-setters. The private beach, large pool, and in-house Poets of the Aegean restaurant allow guests to be as lazy as they wish (although there is a fitness club and spa for the energetic). Doubles run from 250€ to 450€ ($325–$585).

WHERE TO DINE

Camares Cafe (✆ **22890/28-570**), on Mavroyenous (Taxi) Square, has light meals and a fine view of the harbor from its terrace. It's open 24 hours and, for Mykonos, is very reasonably priced. Try the "striftopita" or crispy fried "xinotiro" (bitter cheese) and the thyme-scented grilled lamb chops (9am–2am; no credit cards). As is usual on the islands, most of the harborside tavernas are expensive and mediocre, although **Kounelas** ✿ on the harbor (no phone; no credit cards) is still a good value for fresh fish—as attested to by the presence of locals dining here.

Restaurants come and go here, so check with other travelers or locals as to what's just opened and is getting good reviews.

Antonini's GREEK   Antonini's is one of the oldest of Mykonos's restaurants. It serves consistently decent stews, chops, and *mezedes*. Locals eat here, although in summer they tend to leave the place to tourists.

Plateia Manto, Hora. ✆ **22890/22-319**. Main courses 9€–18€ ($12–$23). No credit cards. Summer daily noon–3pm and 7pm–1am. Usually closed Nov–Mar.

Aqua Taverna ✿✿ MEDITERRANEAN/ITALIAN   Aqua, in Little Venice, has the ideal location, right by the sea with a view of the windmills and the sea. It's an impossible location to beat, picture-perfect, romantic, and serene, so it's a surprise that this Mediterranean/Italian restaurant doesn't rely on its location but rather has excellent food. Specials vary from day to day depending on the catch of the day; however, some dishes are staples. The spaghetti with lemon, olive oil, and parmeggiano cheese; the seafood pasta; the lobster pasta; and the risotto and steamed mussels are all excellent.

Little Venice, Hora. ✆ **22890/26-083**. Main courses 18€–35€ ($23–$45). AE, DC, MC, V. Summer daily 7pm–1am.

Avra Restaurant (the Breeze) ✿ GREEK-MEDITERRANEAN   You can dine in this wonderful restaurant on either its busy terrace, in its more intimate interior, or in its lovely private garden. Try the octopus in white sauce, the stuffed chicken (with cheese, vegetables and apricots), the stuffed lamb (with cheese, vegetables, and mustard) or the salmon risotto—all are excellent choices.

Garden Kalogera St. (behind Alpha Bank on Matoyanni St.), Hora. ✆ **22890/22-298**. Main courses 20€–40€ ($26–$52). DC, V. Daily 7pm–2am. Closed Nov–Mar.

Casa di Giorgio ✿ ITALIAN   Right behind the Catholic Catedral, Giorgio's grandson transformed his grandfather's old village house into an exceptional Italian restaurant. Excellent risotto and linguini; traditional oven-baked thin-crust pizza, succulent sausages, and shrimp pasta are just the highlights.

1 Mitropoleos St., Hora. ✆ **69325/61-998**. Main courses 12€–25€ ($16–$33). AE, DC, MC, V.

Chez Catrine ✿✿ GREEK/FRENCH   This is a pleasant place to spend the evening, enjoy a seafood soufflé or a seafood pasta, or try the chateaubriand. The candlelit dining room is so elegant that you won't mind being indoors. In addition to a wide variety of entrees, there is a range of excellent desserts. The feisty 70-year-old owner still makes her rounds night after night.

1 Nikiou St., Hora. ✆ **22890/22-169**. Reservations recommended July–Aug. Main courses 22€–44€ ($29–$53). AE, DC, MC, V. Daily 7pm–1am.

Chez Marinas GREEK   Formerly known as "Maria's Garden," this is another longtime favorite, with a lovely, lantern- and candlelit garden full of bougainvilleas and cacti, often animated by live music and fits of dancing. The vegetable dishes are always fresh and tasty, the lamb succulent, and the seafood enticing. In short, this is a place where ambience and cuisine come together to make a very successful restaurant. There's often a good-value set menu for around 25€ ($33).

27 Kaloyera, Hora. ⓒ 22890/27-565. Reservations recommended July–Aug. Main courses 15€–30€ ($20–$39). DC, V. Daily 7pm–1am.

Danielle's Restaurant GREEK/MEDITERRANEAN   On the road from town to Ano Mera, this wonderful restaurant (completely renovated during the winter of 2006) has excellent fare, combining traditional Greek island dishes with Mediterranean cuisine to stunning results. The salads are fresh and delicious, the pasta dishes are all excellent, and the wine is exceptional. Hands down one of the best restaurants in Mykonos.

On the road to Ano Mera, Hora. ⓒ 22890/71-513. Main courses 25€–40€ ($32–$52). MC, V. Daily 7pm–1am. Closed Nov–Feb.

Edem Restaurant GREEK/CONTINENTAL   This is one of the oldest restaurants in Hora, with a reputation for good food built over 30 years. Tables are clustered around a courtyard pool—diners have been known to make a splash upon arrival with a preprandial swim—and the sunny courtyard is a pleasant place to enjoy a leisurely dinner even if you aren't dressed for the water. Edem is known especially for its variety of lamb dishes and fresh fish—but the eclectic menu includes steak, pasta, and a variety of traditional Greek and Continental dishes. The service is good and the produce as fresh as you'll see on Mykonos.

Above Panachra Church, Hora. ⓒ 22890/23-355. Reservations recommended July–Aug. Main courses 8€–30€ ($10–$39); fish priced by the kilo. AE, DC, MC, V. Daily 6pm–1am. In off season, sometimes open for lunch. Walk up Matoyianni, turn left on Kaloyera, and follow the signs up and to the left.

El Greco/Yorgos GREEK/CONTINENTAL   Put aside your suspicions of a place called El Greco and be prepared to enjoy traditional recipes collected from various regions of Greece. The eclectic menu includes traditional dishes; from Kerkira, for example, *bourdeto* is a monkfish-and-shellfish stew in tomato-and-wine sauce. Many concoctions feature such local produce as mushrooms with Mykonian cheese. This place is doing something right: It's been here since the 1960s.

Plateia Tria Pigadia, Hora. ⓒ 22890/22-074. Main courses 9€–30€ ($12–$39); fish priced by the kilo. AE, DC, MC, V. Daily 7pm–1am.

Interni ASIAN FUSION   With its avant-garde space and exceptional fusion cuisine, Interni is one of the island's most fashionable restaurants. A happening bar scene is popular with affluent young Athenians, but the attraction here is the cuisine. Consider the marinated salmon and stir-fried seafood noodles and you will see what all the fuss is about.

Hora, Matoyanni. ⓒ 22890/26-333. www.interni.gr. Main courses 18€–40€ ($23–$52). DC, V. Daily 8pm–2am.

Mamakas Mykonos GREEK/MODERN   This is a branch of the Mamakas that opened its second location in the down-at-the-heels area of Gazi in Athens in 1998 and helped transform the area from gritty to chic, managed to start a new trend, traditional taverna fare with modern twists. This is where it all started, right by the Taxi Square, inside a lovely house built in 1845. You can dine in the courtyard (the terra-cotta planters were a gift from the Princess of Malta to the present owner's grandmother) or indoors. The meals are just as delicious and reasonably priced as ever. Check out the trays of cooked dishes (magirefta) and a range of dependable and delicious grills and appetizers—the spicy meatballs (keftedakia)—are a must!

Hora, Mykonos. © **22890/26-120.** www.mamakas.gr. Main courses 14€–30€ ($18–$39). AE, MC, V. Daily 8pm–1:30am.

Matsuhisa Mykonos ⭐⭐ JAPANESE/SOUTH AMERICAN   Nobu Matsuhisa has extended his sushi empire to this, his only open-air restaurant in the most happening hotel in town, the Belvedere. Right by the hotel's pool, with views of the sea and town, try the exceptional Japanese cuisine with Latin influences that will have you yearning for more, despite the high prices. Top-quality ingredients and sushi are flown in daily from Japan. Begin with a Sakepirnha, the famous Brazilian cocktail made with sake instead of cachaca and then continue to pick your way through the chef's choice tasting menu.

At the Belvedere Hotel, Hora. © **22890/25-122.** Reservations essential July–Sept. Main courses 68€–82€ ($88–$107). AE, DC, MC, V. Daily 8pm–1am.

Philippi ⭐ GREEK/CONTINENTAL   One of the island's most romantic dining experiences, Philippi is in a quiet garden. Old Greek favorites share space on the menu with French dishes and a more than usually impressive wine list. What this restaurant provides in abundance is *atmosphere,* and that's what has made it a perennial favorite.

Just off Matoyianni and Kaloyera behind the eponymous hotel, Hora. © **22890/22-294.** Reservations recommended July–Aug. Main courses 10€–25€ ($13–$33). AE, MC, V. Daily 7pm–1am.

Sea Satin Market ⭐⭐ GREEK/SEAFOOD   Below the windmills, beyond the small beach adjacent to Little Venice, the paralia ends in a rocky headland facing the open sea. This is the remarkable location of one of Hora's most charming restaurants. Set apart from the clamor of the town, it's one of the quietest spots in the area. On a still summer night just after sunset, the atmosphere is all you could hope for on a Greek island. At the front of the restaurant, the kitchen activity is on view along with the day's catch sizzling on the grill. You can make a modest meal on *mezedes* here, or let it rip with grilled bon filet. A couple of readers have recently mentioned "nonchalant" and "slow" service; let us know what you think.

Near the Mitropolis Cathedral, Hora. © **22890/24-676.** Main courses 20€–45€ ($26–$59). No credit cards. Daily 6:30pm–12:30am.

Sesame Kitchen GREEK/CONTINENTAL   This small, health-conscious taverna, which serves some vegetarian specialties, is next to the Naval Museum. Fresh spinach, vegetable, cheese, and chicken pies are baked daily. A large variety of salads, brown rice, and soy dishes are offered, as well as a vegetable moussaka and stir-fried veggies. Lightly grilled and seasoned meat dishes are available.

Plateia Tria Pigadia, Hora. © **22890/24-710.** Main courses 8€–18€ ($10–$23). AE, V. Daily 7pm–midnight.

OUT-OF-TOWN DELIGHTS
PSAROU
N'Ammos ⭐⭐ GREEK   On hip and happening Psarou beach, N'Ammos with its casual elegance and beachfront setting is one of the island's finest restaurants. Wealthy Athenians stop by Mykonos just to have lunch here and taste the incredible lobster-pumpkin risotto. Other highlights are the spicy Mykonian meatballs, the marinated anchovies, fresh fish, and T-bone steaks.

Psarou Beach. © **22890/22-440.** Main courses 25€–45€ ($33–$59). AE, DC, MC, V. Daily 1pm–1am.

AYIOS SOSTIS

Kiki's Taverna GREEK   A small, delightful, unspoiled taverna (with no sign, telephone number, or electricity!) is open only until sundown. Adjacent the secluded Ayios Sostis beach, they serve island food the way it should taste. Meat and fish are grilled on a charcoal barbecue and served in the restaurant's shady courtyard. Be sure to try the tasty salad, too.

Ayios Sostis beach. Main courses 8€–18€ ($10–$23). Daily 11am–6pm.

FOKOS BEACH

Fokos GREEK   On a secluded beach adored by surfers, Fokos serves up excellent traditional Greek cuisine that's unpretentious and delicious. Fresh local meat, fish of the day, and vegetables flown in daily from the owners' garden on the island of Crete make the unpretentious meals here some of Mykonos's best.

Fokos Beach. © **22890/23-205.** Main courses 8€–18€ ($10–$23). No credit cards. Daily 10am–7pm.

MYKONOS AFTER DARK

Once you arrive on Mykonos you will realize that the day has just as many party options as the night. As such, I've organized this section to give you party options for both day life and nightlife. Drinks in Mykonos are expensive; rarely will they cost less than 9€ ($12), but the good news is, if you are planning to head out at night, there are many supermarkets all over where you can buy a decent bottle of wine for no more than 6€ ($8) and begin your own party in your room, or on your balcony before hitting the town. As in previous sections, I do not give phone numbers or addresses for clubs and bars as phones are never answered and the clubs and bars are located virtually on top of one another in Mykonos town.

DAY

Beach parties dominate the scene during the day. The most famous parties happen at Psarrou beach where a hopping bar/club keeps the (mostly) Athenian crowd joyful. On Paradise beach, the **Tropicana Bar** and the **Sunrise Bar** cater to a more mixed crowd, and at Super Paradise, two loud bar/clubs on opposite sides of the beach cater to gay and mixed crowds, respectively. All three beaches have sunset parties starting around 6pm, but it is Paradise Beach's **Paradise Club,** with its gigantic swimming pool in the middle of the club, that steals the show with its nightly fireworks and a wild party that lasts until midnight.

SUNSET

Back in town, things are less wild and more sophisticated around sunset. For over quarter of a century, **Caprice** has been the island's sunset institution, with chairs lined along its narrow porch overlooking Little Venice, the windmills, and the sea. It is extremely popular with the Athenians (but it has caught on with the rest of the tourists as well). It isn't rare to come straight from the beach for the sunset and spend the entire night. The indoor area (set like a series of caves, with candlelit corners and a window opening up directly to the sea) is intimate and romantic. The newest arrival-destination for sunsets is the **Oneiro Bar** perched on a beautiful wooden deck overlooking the sea. Coming here will also give you a chance to check out the bar scene at the Mykonos View hotel. Back in Little Venice, or sunset-central as it's sometimes called, **Kastro,** near the Paraportiani Church, is famous for its classical music and frozen daiquiris. This is a great spot to watch or join handsome young men flirting with each other. **Montparnasse** is cozier, with classical music and Toulouse-Lautrec posters. At night this becomes a very popular (mostly with a gay crowd) piano bar. **Veranda,** in an old mansion overlooking the water with a good view of the windmills, is as laid-back as its name might imply. **Galeraki** has a wide variety of exotic cocktails (and customers); the in-house art gallery gives this popular spot its name, "Little Gallery." After dark, it turns to a loud and fun bar/club.

With sunset out of the way, most head back to their rooms for a quick shower and change of wardrobe before heading out to dinner and then for after-dark fun.

AFTER DINNER

Aroma bar is popular day and night as it occupies one of the finest people-watching locations, right on busy Matoyanni street. It's a great place for an after-dinner drink. **Astra** is a legendary bar and elegant lounge with groovy modernist rooms with wonderful indoor and outdoor seating and the perfect place to begin the night, or stay all night as it morphs from a casual lounge to a pumping dance club when some of Athens's top DJs take over. Right in the entrance of town from the old harbor, the Athenian hot spot Spanish restaurant/bar/club **El Pecado (The Sin)** moves to Mykonos in the summer and has taken over the old space occupied by the infamous Remezzo. El Pecado has a great tapas bar and very good cuisine but it is the sangria and the rum-based drinks combined with the Latin beats (with some Greek as well) that make this such a fun place. Just follow the music. **Uno,** a tiny bar on Matoyanni, is a popular destination for Athenians—peek inside to see why or join in the fun. **New Faces,** formerly known as Down Under, is popular with a northern European and American crowd under 25, in large part because their happy hour extends from 9pm to midnight. On busy Matoyanni, **Pierro's,** is extremely popular with gay visitors and rocks all night long to American and European music. Adjacent **Icarus** is best known for its terrace and late-night drag shows. During the early-evening hours, both bars are so popular that sometimes just walking by is difficult. In Taxi Square, another popular gay club, **Ramrod,** has a terrace with a view over the harbor and live drag shows after midnight. Even though the island used to have a loud and large gay club, it no longer does, so Pierro's after 2am is the closest you get, which quite frankly, is pretty close, as is **Yacht Club** (see below in "After Hours"). **Porta** (© 22890/27-807), a popular gay cruising spot, is busy from 9pm onward.

The **Anchor** plays blues, jazz, and classic rock for its 30-something clients, as do **Argo, Stavros Irish Bar, Celebrities Bar,** and **Scandinavian Bar-Disco.** They draw customers from Ireland, Scandinavia, and quite possibly as far away as Antarctica. If you'd like to sample Greek music and dancing, try **Thalami,** a small club underneath the town hall. For a more intense Greek night out, head to **Guzel**—at Gialos, by the waterfront and near the Taxi Square—the place to experience a super trendy hang out populated mostly by trendy Athenians with Greek and international hits that drive the crowd into a frenzy, with people dancing on the tables and on the bars. It's the sort of place that by the end of the night, you feel like you have partied with a group of close friends. Don't be intimidated if you aren't Greek. Go and have a blast! If you're looking for a club before 4am, try **Space Club** by Lekka Square. It's extremely popular with the under-30 crowd, with a large dance floor and theme nights. The 10€ to 20€ ($13–$26) entrance fee includes a drink.

If having a quiet evening and catching a movie is more your speed, head for **Cinemanto** (© 22890/27-190), which shows films nightly around 9pm. Many films are American; most Greek films have English subtitles.

AFTER HOURS

To continue late into the night, head for Paradise beach (take the bus from town) to either **Cavo Paradiso** on the hill (cover 25€–50€/$32–$65 depending on DJ and event; nightly 2am–10am) or to **Paradise Club,** a large club by the beach (cover 15€–20€/$19–$26; nightly 2am–6am) Both clubs are extremely popular, have rotating international DJ's, theme nights, huge pools, and great views. If you last until they close, you can just go for a swim and begin the day all over again. After all, sunset is only a few hours away.

For those that want to continue their partying after 4am but don't want to go all the way to Paradise beach to do so, there is **Yacht Club,** which is really the cafe by the old port that for some reason turns to a very popular mixed bar/club after-hours. Wild flirting, drinking, and dancing ensue—this is the perfect place to end the night and to finally get together with the object of your affection. Being a mixed place, there is something for everybody here.

If you're visiting between July and September, find out what's happening at **Anemo Theatre** (© 22890/23-944), an outdoor venue for the performing arts in a garden in Rohari, just above town. A wide variety of concerts, performances, and talks are usually planned.

7 Delos ★★★

There is as much to see at **Delos** as at Olympia and Delphi, and there is absolutely no shade on this blindlingly white marble island covered with shining marble monuments. Just 3km (2 miles) from Mykonos, little Delos was considered by the ancient Greeks to be one of the holiest of sanctuaries, the fixed point around which the other Cycladic islands circled. It was Poseidon who anchored Delos to make a sanctuary for Leto, impregnated (like so many other maidens) by Zeus and pursued (like so many of those other maidens) by Zeus's aggrieved wife Hera. Here, on Delos, Leto gave birth to Apollo and his sister Artemis; thereafter, Delos was sacred to both gods, although Apollo's sanctuary was the more important. For much of antiquity, people were not allowed to die or be born on this sacred island, but were bundled off to the nearby islet of Rinia.

Delos was not exclusively a religious sanctuary: For much of its history, the island was a thriving commercial port, especially under the Romans in the 3rd and 2nd centuries B.C. As many as 10,000 slaves a day were sold here on some days; the island's prosperity went into a steep decline after Mithridates of Pontus, an Asia Minor monarch at war with Rome, attacked Delos in 88 B.C., slaughtered its 20,000 inhabitants, and sailed home with as much booty as he could stuff into his fleet of ships.

The easiest way to get to Delos is by caique from Mykonos; in summer, there are sometimes excursion boats here from Tinos and Paros. Try not to have a late night before you come here and catch the first boat of the day (usually around 8:30am). As

---

Tips Carpe Diem

Heavy seas can suddenly prevent boats docking at Delos. Follow the advice of the Roman poet Horace and Carpe Diem (Seize the day). Come here as soon as possible; if you decide to save your visit here for your last day in the area, rough seas may leave you stranded ashore.

the day goes on, the heat and crowds here can be overwhelming. On summer afternoons, when cruise ships disgorge their passengers, Delos can make the Acropolis look shady and deserted. Sturdy shoes are a good idea here; a hat, water, munchies, and sunscreen are a necessity. There is a cafe near the museum, but the prices are high, the quality poor, and the service even worse. Nor are the toilets great.

ESSENTIALS

GETTING THERE   From Mykonos, organized guided and unguided excursions leave starting about 8:30am about four times a day Tuesday through Sunday at the harbor's west end. Every travel agency in town advertises its Delos excursions (some with guides). Individual caique owners also have signs stating their prices and schedules. The trip takes about 30 minutes and costs about 10€ ($13) round-trip; as long as you return with the boat that brought you, you can (space available) decide which return trip you want to take when you've had enough. The last boat for Mykonos usually leaves by 4pm. The site is **closed** on Mondays.

EXPLORING THE SITE

Entrance to the site and museum costs 6€ ($7.80), unless this was included in the price of your excursion. At the ticket kiosk, you'll see a number of site plans and picture guides for sale; *Delos & Mykonos: A* Guide *to the History and Archaeology,* by Konstantinos Tsakos (Hesperos Editions), is a reliable guide to the site and the museum. Signs throughout the site are in Greek and French (the French have excavated here since the late 19th c.).

To the left (north) of the jetty where your boat will dock is the **Sacred Harbor,** now too silted for use, where pilgrims, merchants, and sailors from throughout the Mediterranean used to land. The commercial importance of the island in ancient times was due to its harbor, which made Delos an excellent stopping-off-point between mainland Greece and its colonies and trading partners in Asia Minor.

The remains at Delos are not easy to decipher, but when you come ashore, you can head right toward the theater and residential area or left to the more public area of ancient Delos, the famous avenue of the lions, and the museum. Let's head left, toward the **Agora of the Competialists,** built in the 2nd century B.C. when the island was a bustling free port under Rome. The agora's name comes from the *lares competales,* who were minor "crossroad" deities associated with the Greek god Hermes, patron of travelers and commerce. This made them popular deities with the Roman citizens here, mostly former slaves engaged in commerce. The agora dates from the period when Delos's importance as a port had superceded its importance as a religious sanctuary. To reach the earlier religious sanctuary, take the **Sacred Way**—once lined with statues and votive monuments—north from the agora toward the Sanctuary of Apollo. Although the entire island was sacred to Apollo, during Greek antiquity, this was where his sanctuary and temples were. By retracing the steps of ancient pilgrims along it, you will pass the scant remains of several temples (most of the stone from the site was taken away for buildings on neighboring islands, including Naxos, Mykonos, and Tinos). At the far end of the Sacred Way was the **Propylaea,** a monumental marble gateway that led into the sanctuary. As at Delphi and Olympia, the sanctuary here on Delos would have been chockablock with temples, altars, statues, and votive offerings. You can see some of what remains in the **museum,** which has finds from the various excavations on the island. Admission to the museum is included in the site's entrance fee. Beside the

Delos

museum, the remains of the Sanctuary of Dionysos are usually identifiable by the crowd snapping shots of the display of marble phalluses, many on tall plinths.

North of the museum and the adjacent Tourist Pavilion is the **Sacred Lake,** where swans credited with powers of uttering oracles once swam. The lake is now little more than a dusty indentation most of the year, surrounded by a low wall. Beyond it is the famous **Avenue of the Lions** ✿, made of Naxian marble and erected in the 7th century B.C. There were originally at least nine lions. One was taken away to Venice in the 17th century and now stands before the arsenali there. The whereabouts of the others lost in antiquity remains a mystery; five were carted off to the museum for restoration some years ago and replaced by replicas. Beyond the lake to the northeast is the large square courtyard of the gymnasium and the long narrow stadium, where the athletic competitions of the Delian Games were held.

If you stroll back along the Sacred Way to the harbor, you can head next to the **Maritime quarter,** a residential area with the remains of houses from the Hellenistic and Roman eras, when the island reached its peak in wealth and prestige. Several houses contain brilliant **mosaics** ⚑, and in most houses the cistern and sewer systems can be seen. Among the numerous small dwellings are several magnificent villas, built around a central court and connected to the street by a narrow passage. The mosaics in the palace courtyards are particularly dazzling, and include such famous images as Dionysos riding a panther in the **House of the Masks,** and a similar depiction in the **House of Dionysos.** Farther to the south is the massive **Theater,** which seated 5,500 people and was the site of choral competitions during the Delian Festivals, an event held every 4 years that included athletic competitions in addition to musical contests. Behind the theater is a fine arched **cistern,** which was the water supply for the city. If you visit here in spring, the wildflowers are especially beautiful, and the chorus of frogs that live in and around the cisterns will be at its peak.

If you're not on a tour and have the energy, consider wrapping up your visit by getting an overview of the site—and of the Cyclades—from **Mount Kinthos** ⚑, the highest point on the island. On many days, nearby Mykonos, as well as Siros to the west, Tinos to the north, and Naxos and Paros to the south are easy to spot. On your way down, keep an eye out for the **Grotto of Hercules,** a small temple built into a natural crevice in the mountainside—the roof is formed of massive granite slabs held up by their own enormous weight.

8 Tinos ⚑⚑

161km (87 nautical miles) SE of Piraeus

Tinos has some very good restaurants, some good beaches, exquisite dovecotes, and handsome villages with houses decorated with locally carved marble doorways and fanlights. But that's not why most people come here. Each year, thousands of pilgrims come here to pray before the icon of the Virgin Mary in the church of the **Panagia Evangelistria (Our Lady of Good Tidings)**—sometimes called the "Lourdes of Greece." Although Tinos is the most important destination in all of Greece for religious pilgrims, it remains one of the least commercialized islands of the Cyclades—and a joy to visit for that reason.

From well out to sea, **Panagia Evangelistria**—illuminated at night—is visible atop a hill overlooking Tinos town. Almost any day of the year you can see people, particularly elderly women, crawling from the port on hands and knees up Megalocharis, the long, steep street that leads to the red-carpeted steps that are the final approach to the cathedral. Adjacent pedestrian-only Evangelistria is a market street, as well as a pilgrimage route for those who choose to walk it. The street is lined with stalls selling vials of holy water, incense, candles (up to 2m/7 ft. long), and mass-produced icons. There are also several jewelry and handicraft shops, one or two cafes, groceries, old-fashioned dry-goods stores—and a surprising number of shops selling both incense and battery-powered kittens that roll over and meow.

Don't even think about arriving on Tinos without a reservation around **August 15** (Feast of the Assumption of the Virgin), when thousands of pilgrims travel here to celebrate the occasion. **March 25** (Feast of the Annunciation) is the second-most important feast day here, but it draws fewer pilgrims because it is less easy to travel by sea in March. Pilgrims also come here on July 23 (the anniversary of St. Pelagia's vision of the icon) and on January 30 (the anniversary of the finding of the icon).

Remember that Tinos *is a pilgrimage place:* It is considered very disrespectful to wear shorts, short skirts, halters, or sleeveless shirts in the precincts of the Evangelistria (or any other church, for that matter). Photographing the pilgrims, especially those approaching the shrine on hands and knees, is not appreciated.

Like Naxos, Tinos was ruled by Venice for several centuries and, like Naxos, Tinos still has a sizeable Catholic population. You'll see signs of Tinos's Venetian heritage in the number of fine old Venetian mansions (locally known as *pallada,* the word also used for the harborfront), located on the streets off the harbor. Tinos town has a clutch of Catholic churches, including the harborfront churches of St. Anthony and St. Nicolas; out on the island, the **Church of the Virgin Mary Vrisiotissa** near the village of Ag. Romanos on the main Hora-Pirgos road is an important Catholic pilgrimage shrine. The village of **Loutra** (see "Exploring the Island," later in this chapter) has a folk-art museum in a Jesuit monastery, staffed by monks who come here from around the world.

The villages of Tinos are some of the most beautiful in the Cyclades. Many of the most picturesque are nestled into the slopes of **Exobourgo,** the rocky pinnacle crowned by a Venetian castle that is visible from the port. Many villages are connected by a network of walking paths that make this island a hiker's paradise. In these villages and dotting the countryside, you'll see the ornately decorated medieval *peristerionades* (dovecotes) for which the island is famous, as well as elaborately carved marble lintels, door jambs, and fan windows on village houses. According to one tradition (popular on virtually every one of the Cyclades), there are 365 churches scattered across the island, one for every day of the year; others boast that the island has 1,000 churches. The island's beaches aren't worthy of superlatives, but they are plentiful and uncrowded throughout the summer. All this may change if an airport is built here—all the more reason to visit Tinos now. If you want to do as the Greeks do, you'll spend a day or two here; do that once, and you may find that you keep coming back to this *very* Greek island.

ESSENTIALS

GETTING THERE   Several ferries travel to Tinos daily from Piraeus (5 hr.). Catamaran (1½ hr.) and ferry services (4 hr.) are available daily in summer from Rafina. Check schedules at the Athens **GNTO** (© 210/331-0562); **Piraeus Port Authority** (© 210/459-3223 or 210/422-6000; phone seldom answered); or **Rafina Port Authority** (© 22940/22-300). Several times a day, boats connect Tinos with nearby Mykonos and Siros (20–50 min.; there's usually daily service to Santorini Paros and Naxos in summer. Tinos has more winter connections than most Cycladic isles due to its religious tourism, which continues throughout the year. In summer, a day excursion to Delos and Mykonos usually departs from the old pier in Tinos harbor at 10am Tuesday through Sunday, returning to Tinos at 7pm; the fare is 25€ ($33) adult and 9€ ($12) children under 11.

There are three ports in Tinos harbor. Be sure to find out from which pier your ship will depart—and be prepared for last-minute changes. Most ferries, the small catamarans (Seajet, Flying Cat, and Jet One), as well as the excursion boat to Delos/Mykonos, dock at the old pier in the town center; some use the new pier to the north, on the side of town in the direction of Kionia. **Tinos Port Authority** (not guaranteed to be helpful) can be reached at © 22830/22-348.

Fun Fact **Looking for Dove ...**

Tinos is famous for its **dovecotes,** stout stone towers elaborately ornamented with slabs of the local shale, with ornamental perches and passageways for the doves. Venetians built the first dovecotes here. They brought with them the dovecote's distinctive miniature tower architecture. They used the doves' droppings as fertilizer, and the birds soon became an important part of the local diet. Locals still sometimes cook them, often in tomato sauce, as a winter dish. Some of the most elaborate of these birdhouses grace the towns of **Tarambados** and **Smardakito;** keep your eyes open. It is said that the island is home to 2,000 of them. Look for signs announcing detours to TRADITIONAL DOVECOTES as you explore the island.

VISITOR INFORMATION   For information on accommodations, car rentals, island tours, and Tinos in general, head to **Windmills Travel** ★★★ (© **22830/23-398;** fax 22830/23-327; www.windmills.gr), on the harbor by the new port, next to St. Anthony's Catholic church. The office has a large painting of a windmill's round, spoked pinwheel on its exterior. Sharon Turner is the friendly, amazingly helpful, and efficient manager, with unparalleled knowledge of Tinos and its neighboring islands. She also runs a terrific book exchange out of her office. What's more, Turner can often get you substantial discounts on island accommodations, transportation, and tours.

GETTING AROUND   By Bus   The **bus station** (© **22830/22-440**) is on the harbor, opposite the National Bank of Greece. Schedules are usually posted or available here. (You can also ask about bus times at Windmills Travel.) There are frequent daily buses to most island villages.

By Car & Moped   Again, inquire at Windmills Travel and follow the advice you get there. Expect to pay from 30€ ($39) per day for a car and half that for a moped.

By Taxi   Taxis hang out on Trion Ierarchon, which runs uphill from the harbor just before Palamaris supermarket and Hotel Tinion.

FAST FACTS   There are several **banks** on the harbor, open Monday through Thursday from 8am to 2pm and Friday from 8am to 1:30pm; all have ATMs. The **first-aid center** can be reached at © **22830/22-210.** There's a drop-off **laundry** service (© **22830/32-765**) behind the Lito Hotel—but be forewarned that it can be slow, up to 3 days in peak season. For **luggage storage,** try Windmills Travel (© **22830/23-398**). The **police** (© **22830/22-348**) are located just past the new pier, past Lito Hotel and Windmills Travel. The **post office** (© **22830/22-247**), open Monday through Friday from 7:30am to 2pm, is at the harbor's south end next to Tinion Hotel. The **telephone office (OTE),** open Monday through Friday from 7:30am to 12:30pm, is on the main street leading to the church of Panagia Evangelistria, about halfway up on the right (© **22830/22-399**). The harborside Cultural Foundation (© **22830/29-070**) has art exhibitions; admission sometimes charged.

WHAT TO SEE & DO
Panagia Evangelistria Cathedral and Museums ★★★   Each year, the **Church of Panagia Evangelistria (Our Lady of Good Tidings)** draws thousands of pilgrims seeking the aid of the church's miraculous icon. According to local lore, in 1882 a nun

named Pelagia repeatedly dreamed that the Virgin appeared to her and told her where to find a miraculous icon. A modest woman, Pelagia could not believe the Virgin would appear to her, but when the dreams did not stop, Pelagia finally sought out the Bishop of Tinos, whom she hesitantly informed of her dreams. The bishop, convinced of her piety, ordered excavations to begin. Before long, the remains first of a Byzantine church and then of the icon itself were unearthed. As is the case with many of the most holy icons, this one is believed to be the work of Saint Luke. The icon was initially housed where it was found, in the chapel of the Zoodohos Pigi, under the present Cathedral. Astonishingly on such a small and poor island, the Parians built the massive church of the Panagia in just 2 years. The church is made of gleaming marble from Paros and Tinos, with a tall slender bell tower, and handsome black-and-white pebble mosaics in the exterior courtyard.

At the end of Evangelistria Street, a broad flight of marble stairs leads you up to the church. Inside, hundreds of gold and silver hanging lamps illuminate the icon of the Virgin, to the left of the entrance. The icon is almost entirely hidden by votive offerings of gold, silver, diamonds, and precious gems dedicated by the faithful. Even those who do not make a lavish gift customarily make a small offering and light a candle. Keep an eye out for the silver ship with a fish hanging beneath it. According to tradition, a fierce storm threatened to sink a ship, which was taking in water through a breach in its hull. When the captain and crew called out to the Virgin for help, the storm abated and the ship reached harbor safely. When it was taken ashore for repairs, an enormous fish was discovered plugging the hole in the hull.

Beneath the church is the crypt with the chapel where the icon was found, surrounded by smaller chapels. The crypt is often crowded with Greek parents waiting to have their (usually howling) toddlers baptized here. Others come to fill vials with holy water from the spring.

Keep in mind that to enter the cathedral, men must wear long pants and shirts with sleeves, and women must wear dresses or skirts and blouses with sleeves. If there is a church service while you are here, you will hear the beautiful, resonant chanting that typifies a Greek Orthodox service—but remember that it's not appropriate to explore the church during a service. Services are usually held just after the church opens, just before it closes, and at other times during the day. A schedule of services is usually posted outside the main entrance.

Within the high walls that surround the church are various museums and galleries, each of which is worth a quick visit: a gallery of 14th- to 19th-century religious art, a gallery of more modern Tinian artists, and a sculpture museum. Admission is sometimes charged at these places.

Hora, Tinos. Free admission. Cathedral: daily 8am–7pm (off-season hours vary). Galleries: Sat–Sun (some weekdays during July–Aug) 8am–8pm (off season usually noon–6pm).

Tips Trying Your Hand at Marble Carving

Tinos has a long tradition of marble carving. If you want to try your hand, the **Dellatos Marble Sculpture School** (© 22830/23-664; www.tinosmarble.com), just outside Tinos town in Spitalia, offers 1- and 2-week workshops for would-be marble workers from May through October.

A Swim, a Snack, an Ancient Site

If you're staying in Tinos town, the easiest place to take a dip is the beach at Kionia, about 3km (2 miles) west of Hora. Just across from the pebble and sand strand where you'll swim are the island's only excavated antiquities, the modest remains of the Temple of Poseidon and one of his many conquests, Amphitrite, a semi-divine sea nymph (Tues–Sun 8:30am–3pm; admission 3€/$3.90). When sheep or the custodians have trimmed the vegetation at the site, you can clearly make out the foundations of the 4th-century-B.C. temple, and a large altar and long stoa, both built in the 1st century B.C. As is inevitable with a site where Romans lived, there are the remains of a bath. Finds from the site are on display at the Tinos town Archaeological Museum (Tues–Sun 8:30am–3pm; admission 3€/$3.90). When you head back to town, you can have a drink and a snack at either the Mistral or Tsambia taverna, both on the main road near the site. Closer to town, also on the main road, you can check your e-mail at the Para Pende cafe. Depending on your mood, you can do this excursion on foot, by public bus, or taxi. If on foot, keep to the side of the road and don't expect the trucks and motorcycles to cut you much slack.

EXPLORING THE ISLAND

If it's a clear day, one of your first sights of Tinos from the ferry will be the odd mountain with a bare summit that looks bizarrely like a twisted fist. This is **Exobourgo** ✸✸, a mountain eminence crowned by the remains of a Venetian kastro (castle) about 15km (9 miles) outside of Hora. Sheer rock walls surround the fortress on three sides; the only path to the summit starts behind a Catholic church at the base of the rock, on the road between Mesi and Koumaros. As you make the 15-minute ascent, you'll pass several lines of fortification—the entire hill is riddled with walls and hollowed with chambers. As you might expect, the view over the Cyclades is superb from the summit (565m/1,854 ft.). The fortress itself has long been in ruins—and was never as imposing as, for example, the massive Venetian fortress at Nafplion in the Peloponnese. The Turks defeated the Venetians here in 1714 and drove them from the island.

The towns circling Exobourgo are among the most picturesque on the island; you can visit them by car or on foot (see "Walking," below). **Dio Horia** and **Monastiri** have beautiful village houses. In Dio Horia's main square is a spring where some villagers still wash their clothes by hand.

There's a town bus to the nearby **Convent of Kechrovouniou** ✸✸, one of the largest in Greece—almost a town in its own right. It dates from the 10th century and was the home of Pelagia, the nun whose vision revealed the location of the island's famed icon; you can visit her cell and see a small museum of 18th- and 19th-century icons.

Loutra ✸ is an especially attractive village with many *stegasti*, tunnel-like streets formed by the overhanging second-floor rooms of village houses. Expanding over the street below was a clever way to have as much house as possible on a small amount of land. An imposing 17th-century Jesuit monastery contains a small museum of village life; implements for making olive oil and wine are on display alongside old manuscripts and maps. It's usually open mid-June to mid-September from about 10:30am to 3:30pm (no phone). **Volax** is in a remote valley known for a bizarre lunar landscape of rotund granite boulders. The villagers constructed a stone amphitheater for theatrical productions there, so be sure to ask **Windmills Travel** (②/fax **22830/23-398**) for a schedule of performances, most of which occur in August. Volax is also known for its local basket weavers, whose baskets are remarkably durable and attractive; ask for directions to their workshops. Be sure to visit the town spring, down a short flight of steps at the bottom of the village. Channels direct the water to the fields, and the basket weavers' reeds soak in multiple stone basins. If you're hungry here, you might want to try the local *loukanika* (sausages) at the **Taverna Volax** (② **22830/41-021. Koumaros** is a beautiful small village on the road between Volax and Mesi, both of which have many of the arched *stegasti* passageways.

Pirgos ⑅⑅, at the western end of the island, is one of Tinos's most beautiful villages, with an enchanting small plateia with trees, a marble fountain, several cafes, and a taverna that is usually open for lunch and dinner in summer, less regularly off season. Renowned for its school of fine arts, Pirgos is a center for marble sculpting, and many of the finest sculptors of Greece have trained here. The Museum of Yiannoulis Chalepas and Museum of Panormian Artists occupy adjacent houses, and give visitors a chance not only to see sculpture by local artists, but to step into an island house. After you see the small rooms on the ground floor, you'll be surprised at how large the cool, flag-stoned lower story with the kitchen is. The museums are located near the bus station, on the main lane leading toward the village. Both are open Tuesday through Sunday from 11am to 1:30pm and 5:30 to 6:30pm; admission is 2€ ($2.60).

Although you may be tempted by the sculptures you see on sale in local workshops, even a small marble relief is not easy to slip into a suitcase. In a small hardware shop across from Pirgos's two museums, **Nikolaos Panorios** ⑅⑅⑅ makes and sells whimsical tin funnels, boxes, spoon holders, and dustpans, as well as dovecotes, windmills, and sailing ships. Each item is made of tin salvaged from olive oil and other containers, and every one is unique (some with scenes of Pallas Athena, others with friezes of sunflowers, olive gatherers, fruits, or vegetables). All are delightful; they cost from 10€ ($13). Eugenia and Nikolaos Panorios are usually in their shop mornings (② **22830/ 32-263**) from about 9am to 1pm.

BEACHES

The easiest place to take a dip from Tinos town is at **Kionia,** across from the site of the Temple of Poseidon, 3km/2m west of Tinos town (see "A Swim, a Snack, an Ancient Site" box, earlier in this chapter). Another beach close to town lies 2km (1¼ miles) east of town at busy **Ayios Fokas.** West of Tinos town, a series of hairpin-turn paved and unpaved roads lead down—and when we say "down," we mean "way down"—to beaches at Ayiou Petrou, Kalivia, and Giannaki. From Tinos, there's bus service on the south beach road (usually four times a day) to the resort of **Porto,** 8km (5 miles) to the east. Porto offers several long stretches of uncrowded sand, a few hotel

---

⸜Finds⸝ Taverna Special

When you finish climbing Exobourgo, reward yourself with a *froutalia,* a local specialty: a pizza-size omelet with cheese, sausage, tomatoes, vegetables, and herbs. You can't beat eating it under the grape arbor at the roadside **Taverna Gourni** (② **22830-51-274**) in the hamlet of Skalados. If you are traveling with small children, they'll love the play area, with its slides and toys.

complexes, and numerous tavernas, several at or near the beach. The beach at Ayios Ioannis facing the town of Porto is okay, but you'd be better off walking west across the small headland to a longer, less popular beach, extending from this headland to the church or Ayios Sostis at its western extremity; you can also get here by driving or taking the bus to Ayios Sostis. There are two beaches at **Kolimbithres** on the north side of the island, easily accessed by car, although protection from the *meltemi* winds can be a problem. The second is better, with fine sand in a small rocky cove and two tavernas. Just beyond Pirgos, the beach at **Panormos** is on the verge of turning into a holiday resort, but has a decent (usually windy) beach and one of the island's best tavernas, the *Psarokokkalo* (Fishbone).

WALKING

Tinos is a walker's paradise, with a good network of paths and remote interior regions waiting to be explored. Some of the best walks are in the vicinity of **Exobourgo**— paths connect the cluster of villages circling this craggy fortress, offering great views and many places to stop for refreshment along the way. There isn't a current English-language guide to walks in Tinos, but you can ask for information at **Windmills Travel** (©/fax 22830/23-398) in Tinos town.

SHOPPING

In Hora, the **flea market** on Evangelistria Street is a pleasant place for a ramble. Pedestrianized Evangelistria parallels Megaloharis, the main street from the harbor up to the cathedral. Shops and stalls lining Evangelistria Street sell icons, incense, candles, medallions, and *tamata* (tin, silver, and gold votives). You'll also find local embroidery, weavings, and the delicious local nougat, as well as *loukoumia* (Turkish delight) from Siros. Weekdays, a **fish market** and a **farmer's market** set up in the square by the docks. Keep an eye out for the rather pink-plumed pelican who hangs out nearby. A **Palamaris** supermarket on the harbor is handy to have nearby, and an even larger Palamaris is just outside Tinos town on the road to Pirgos.

Two fine jewelry shops stand side by side on Evangelistria: **Artemis,** 18 Evangelistria (© 22830/23-781); and **Harris Prassas Ostria-Tinos,** 20 Evangelistria (© 22830/23-893; fax 22830/24-568). Both have jewelry in contemporary, Byzantine, and classical styles; silverwork; and religious objects, including reproductions of the miraculous icon. Near the top of the street on the left in a neoclassical building, the small **Evangelismos Biotechni Shop,** the outlet of a local weaving school (© 22830/22-894), sells reasonably priced table and bed linens, as well as rugs.

Those interested in local produce should head a few steps up and cross over to 16 Megaloharis, the shop of the local **agricultural cooperative,** where pungent capers, creamy cheeses, olive oil, and the fiery local *tsiporo* liqueur are on sale (© 22830/21-184). If you like capers, stock up; we got ours safely back to Massachusetts and enjoyed them for months.

Several shops along the harbor sell international newspapers, local travel guides, maps, and some novels. The newspapers are on stands outside the shops.

WHERE TO STAY

Unless you have reservations, avoid Tinos during important religious holidays, especially **March 25** (Feast of the Annunciation) and **August 15** (Feast of the Assumption). It is also advisable to have reservations for summer weekends, when Greeks travel here by the thousands for baptisms and pilgrimages. For those planning to stay a week or longer, contact **Windmills Travel** (see "Exploring the Island," above), which rents out apartments and houses from about 55€ to 85€ ($72–$111) a day in several villages—a great way to see more of the island and get a taste for village life.

Oceanis Hotel ☆   This 10-year-old hotel is on the harbor but not where the boats dock, so it is quieter than other lodgings by the port. The balconies, with views of Siros in the distance, are a real plus. The hotel is often taken over by Greek groups visiting the island's religious shrines. As an independent traveler, you may feel a bit odd-man-out. The rooms are simply furnished, with good-size bathrooms. Don't bother with the restaurant. The Oceanis stays open all year and has reliable heat in the winter.

Akti G. Drossou, Hora, 84200 Tinos. ℂ 22830/22-452. Fax 22830/25-402. 47 units. From 80€ ($104) double. No credit cards. From the old harbor, walk south (right) along the paralia until you come to the Oceanis, whose large sign is clearly visible from the harbor. **Amenities:** Restaurant; bar. *In room:* A/C, TV.

Porto Tango ☆   This place has all the frills—restaurant, sauna, spa, health club, pool, and more. But—and this is a very big "but"—the beach is an irritating 10-minute walk away. Many rooms have balconies or terraces with sea views; some have both. There are lots of antiques and antique reproductions throughout: chests, glass-globed lamps, and other almost-pseudo French Provincial decor that jar with island touches such as rough-wood beamed ceilings.

Porto, 84200 Tinos. ℂ 22830/24-411. Fax 22830/24-416. www.portotango.gr. 61 units. 150€ ($195) double; 250€ ($325) suite. Breakfast buffet included. AE, MC, V. **Amenities:** 2 restaurants; bar; pool; health club; spa. *In room:* A/C, TV, minibar.

Tinos Beach Hotel ☆☆ *Kids*   Despite a somewhat impersonal character this is the best choice in a beachfront hotel, especially after its renovations in 2006. The decent-size rooms all have balconies, most with views of the sea and pool. The suites are especially pleasant—large sitting rooms open onto poolside balconies. The pool is the longest on the island, and there's a separate children's pool as well. No one seems to praise either the ambience or the service here, but if you want to be on Tinos, near Tinos town but on the beach, this is the place to be.

Kionia, 84200 Tinos. ℂ 22830/22-626 or 22830/22-627. Fax 22830/23-153. www.tinosbeach.gr. 180 units. 140€–160€ ($182–$208) double. Rates include breakfast. Children 7 and under stay free in parent's room. AE, DC, MC, V. Closed Nov–Mar. 4km (2½ miles) west of Tinos town on the coast road. **Amenities:** Restaurant; bar; saltwater pool; children's pool; tennis courts; watersports equipment for rent. *In room:* A/C, TV, minifridge.

WHERE TO DINE

As usual, it's a good idea to avoid most harborfront joints, where food is generally inferior and service can be rushed. If you find yourself hungry when you're out on the island, **Agoni Grammi** ☆ (℃ 22830/31-689) and **Psarokokkalo** ☆☆ (℃ 22830/31-364) are excellent fish tavernas in Panormos.

Metaxi Mas ☆ GREEK   It breaks my heart to report that my favorite restaurant on Tinos is going through what I hope is a brief bad patch. It's hard to pin down, but prices have gone up and the zest that made the cooking at this longtime distinctive *mezedopoleio* (hors d'oeuvres place) is muted. That said, the *mezedes* are still tasty, especially the vegetable croquettes, fried sun-dried tomatoes, piquant fried cheeses, and succulent octopus. There's a cozy interior dining room with a fireplace for when it's chilly, and tables outside in the pedestrianized lane for good weather

Kontoyioryi, Paralia, Hora. ℂ 22830/24-857. Main courses 8€–20€ ($10–$26). No credit cards. Daily noon–midnight. Off the harbor, in a lane between the old and new harbors. Look for the sign over the door. Sometimes a METAXI MAS banner is strung across the lane.

Special Moments in Tinos Town

If you're lucky, while you're trying to decide what to have for lunch or dinner at a restaurant in Tinos town, you'll become aware of family celebrations taking place at other tables. Why, you may wonder, is that young couple dancing on one of the tables and passing their screaming toddler from guest to guest? Why is everyone kissing him and pinching his cheeks? Families come from all over Greece to baptize their children at the Panagia Evangelistria Cathedral. After the ceremony, it's time to celebrate (which means lots of food, wine, and dancing). If you're lucky, you may get to kiss the baby and toast the occasion. Be sure to say "Na Sas Zee-see" ("May he live for you") to the proud parents.

Palaia Pallada 🏵🏵 GREEK   Palaia Pallada, next to Metaxi Mas, is a bit more down-home, a bit less inventive, and consistently good. There are fewer ruffles and flourishes here, but the food (grills, stews, salads) in this family-run place is excellent, as is the local wine. You can eat indoors or outside in the lane.

Kontoyioryi, Paralia, Hora. ✆ **22830/23-516.** Main courses 7€–15€ ($9–$20). No credit cards. Daily noon–midnight. Off the harbor, in a lane between the old and new harbors. Look for the sign over the door, and the sign that overhangs the lane.

Taverna Drosia 🏵 GREEK   This taverna, perched at the head of a steep valley overlooking the sea, seems a world away from the crowds and traffic of the harbor. From the shaded flagstone terrace, you can watch ships slowly approaching. Siros sits across the water, and your view takes in terraced fields, dovecotes, and an old windmill in the valley. The food is basic taverna fare, though considerably better than average—bread arrives at the table in thick wholesome slabs, salads are sprinkled with succulent capers, and everything is very fresh.

Ktikades. ✆ **22830/41-387.** Main courses 5€–12€ ($6.50–$16). No credit cards. Daily 11am–midnight. 5km (3 miles) from Tinos town.

To Koutouki tis Eleni 🏵 GREEK   There's usually no menu at this excellent small taverna, known in town simply as To Koutouki. Basic ingredients are cooked up into simple meals that remind you how delightful Greek food can be. Local cheese and wine, fresh fish and meats, delicious vegetables—these are the staples that come together so well in this taverna.

Paralia, Hora. ✆ **22830/24-857.** Main courses 5€–15€ ($6.50–$20). No credit cards. Daily noon–midnight. From the harbor, turn onto Evangelistria, the market street; take the 1st right up a narrow lane with 3 tavernas. Koutouki is the 1st on the left.

TINOS AFTER DARK

As we've mentioned, Tinos is a place of pilgrimage, and there's less nightlife here than on many islands; as always on the islands, places that are hot one season are often gone the next. I'm not listing phone numbers here because phones simply are not answered. Two sweets shops, **Epilekto** and **Meskiles** (fantastic *loukoumades* with ice cream), both on the waterfront, stay open late. At the end of town near the new (largest) quay, there is a clutch of bars with music, TV, and sometimes dancing, including **Kaktos** and **Syvilla,** and, on the road toward Kiona, **Paradise.** If you want a late-night (or early-morning) coffee, try **Monopolio** (✆ **22830/25-770**) on the harborfront;

instead of a cup, this place brings you a delicious full pot of French filtered coffee. If you want to check your e-mail while you drink your coffee, try **Symposio** (© **22830/ 24-368**), which bills itself as a cafe-bar-restaurant. If you walk on the main road at night, watch out for the kamikaze motorcycles.

9 Siros (Syros) ★/★

144km (78 nautical miles) SE of Piraeus

Siros is very different from the other Cycladic islands. The capital, **Ermoupolis,** is not a twee Cycladic sugar-cube miniature town, but the administrative capital of the Cyclades. If you live anywhere in the Cyclades and need a building permit, or a license, or a lawyer, you'll end up making at least one trip here. Consequently, Ermoupolis has a year-round businesslike bustle totally unlike any other town in the Cyclades. Ermoupolis has been the most important town in the Cyclades almost since it was founded in the 1820s by refugees from Asia Minor and the eastern Aegean islands. The settlers named the town after Hermes, the god of merchants. The name seems to have been an excellent choice: Soon, this was the busiest port in Greece—far busier than Piraeus—and a center of shipbuilding. You'll see several still- functioning shipyards and dry docks along the harbor. Just inland are neighborhoods with hand-some neoclassical mansions built by shipping magnates. When you walk into Plateia Miaoulis, the main square in town, you may find it hard to believe you're still in the Cyclades: The square is lined with truly grandiose public buildings, including a town hall that could hold its own beside any government building in Athens. Just off the Plateia is the Apollon Theater, a miniature of Milan's La Scala Opera House, with a summer music festival. Climb uphill from the Plateia Miaoulis and you'll find your-self in the oldest part of town, Ano Syros, which just happens to be a perfect little sugar-cube Cycladic neighborhood, albeit one with both a Capuchin and a Jesuit monastery. Although Ermoupolis saw a considerable period of decline in the 20th century, recent restoration efforts have brought back much of the city's glory; the entire town is now a UNESCO World Heritage Site.

I have to confess that Siros is one island where the capital town's pleasures are so considerable that I don't mind neglecting the island itself. That said, the north end of Syros is a starkly beautiful region of widely dispersed farms, multilayered terraced fields, and village-to-village donkey and foot paths. Some of the island's best beaches are here, many accessible only on foot or by boat. The south is more gentle, with a number of villages with the 19th-century country villas of the wealthy shipping mag-nates who had both a town house and a summer retreat; the villages of Manna, Ano Manna, and Dellagrazia have especially impressive villas. Throughout the island, the San Mihali and kopanisti cheeses are made, as well as delicious thyme honey.

The best months to visit Siros are May, June, and September; the worst month is August, when vacationing Greeks fill every hotel room on the island. If you want to tour the island, having a car is the best way to get around, although bus service to the more settled southern part of the island is good.

ESSENTIALS
GETTING THERE   By Plane   In summer, there's at least one flight daily from Athens. Contact **Olympic Airways** in Athens (© **210/966-6666** or 210/936-9111; www.olympic-airways.gr) or at their office in Ermoupolis, 100m (328 ft.) from the port in the direction of Hotel Hermes (© **22810/88-018** or 22810/82-634).

> **Tips   Two Festivals, a Gallery & a Guidebook**
>
> Syros has two impressive summer festivals, the **Ermoupoleia** and the **Festival of the Aegean.** The Ermoupoleia runs almost all summer and has indoor and open-air concerts, plans, and performances. The **Festival of the Aegean** (www.festivaloftheaegean.com), usually held in July, has most of its performances—including several operas—at the Apollon Theater. You'll see posters advertising performances. Schedules for both festivals are available at island travel agencies and at city hall. You may also want to keep an eye out for posters announcing art exhibits at exhibitions at the Cyclades Gallery in the Old Customs Building on the harbor; the gallery also has a permanent collection of modern and folk art. If you're an architecture and history buff, be sure to buy a copy of the delightful handsomely illustrated *Ermoupoli-Syros A Historical Tour* (10€/$13), on sale at island bookstores and the Industrial Museum.

By Boat   Ferries connect Siros at least once daily with Piraeus, Naxos, Mykonos, Paros, Tinos, and Santorini. The ferries connect once or twice weekly with Folegandros, Sifnos, Iraklion, Samos, and Thessaloniki (12–15 hr.). There is service in summer from Rafina. Boats are notoriously late and/or early; your travel or ticket agent will give you an estimate of times involved in the following journeys. Remember: That's estimate, as in guesstimate. You'll find numerous ferry-ticket offices on the harborfront: **Alpha Syros** (② 22810/81-185), opposite the ferry pier, and its sister company **Teamwork Holidays** (② 22810/83-400; www.teamwork.gr) sell tickets for all the ferries (and also handles plane tickets and hotel reservations). Ferry information can be verified with the Ermoupolis **port authority** (② 22810/88-888 or 22810/82-690). Piraeus ferry schedules can be confirmed with the **GNTO** in Athens (210/870-0000; www.gnto.gr), the **Piraeus Port Authority** (② 210/451-1311 or 1440 or 1441; phone not always answered). For Rafina schedules, call **Rafina Port Authority** (② 22940/28-888).

VISITOR INFORMATION   The **Hoteliers Association of Siros** operates an information booth at the pier in summer; it's open daily from 9am to 10pm. Note that the list of hotels they offer includes only hotels registered with their service.

GETTING AROUND   By Bus   The **bus stop** in Ermoupolis is at the pier, where the schedule is posted. Buses circle the southern half of Siros hourly in summer between 8am and midnight. There is minimal bus service to the northern part of the island. Teamwork Holidays offers a **bus tour of the island** for 20€ ($26) that starts at 9am by touring Ermoupoli and then heads out on the island for a visit to some southern villages, lunch (a la carte) and a swim, before returning to town at 4:30pm.

By Car & Moped   Of the several car-rental places along the harbor in the vicinity of the pier, a reliable choice is **Siros Rent A Car** (② 22810/80-409), next to the GNTO office on Dodekanisou, a side street just to the left of the pier. A small car will cost from 55€ ($72) per day, including insurance. A 50cc scooter rents from 25€ ($33) per day.

By Taxi   The taxi stand is on the main square, Plateia Miaoulis (② 2810/86-222).

FAST FACTS   Several **banks** on the harbor have ATMs. The Ermoupolis hospital (② 22810/86-666) is the largest in the Cyclades; it's just outside town to the west near Plateia Iroon. For free **luggage storage,** ask at Teamwork Holidays (© 22810/83-400). The **police** (© 22810/82-610) are on the south side of Miaoulis Square. The **port authority** (© 22810/88-888 or 22810/82-690) is on the long pier at the far end of the harbor, beyond Hotel Hermes. The **post office** (© 22810/82-596) is between Miaoulis Square and the harbor on Protopapadaki; it's open Monday through Friday from 7:30am to 2pm. The **telephone office (OTE)** is on the east side of Miaoulis Square (© 22810/87-399); it's open Monday through Saturday from 7:30am to 3pm. Bizanas is an **Internet cafe** on Plateia Miaoulis, on the harbor, **Multirama** has Internet service.

WHAT TO SEE & DO
MUSEUMS
Archaeological Museum ✮ The highlight of this museum's small collection is a room containing finds, including pottery and several fine Cycladic figurines, from Halandriani and Kastri, prehistoric sites in the northern hills of Siros. There are also finds from the Greek and Roman city here, which lies under modern Ermoupolis. Since Ermoupolis is the capital of the Cyclades, the archaeological museum has holdings from many of the smaller Cycladic islands. Allow half an hour for your visit.

On the west side of the town hall below the clock tower, Ermoupolis. © 22810/86-900. Admission 3€ ($3.90). Tues–Sun 8:30am–3pm.

Ermoupolis Industrial Museum ✮✮ Behind the cranes and warehouses of the Neorion Shipyard at the southern end of the port, you'll find the Industrial Museum of Ermoupolis, which opened in a restored paint-works factory in 2000. If you have any fondness for industrial history, you're going to love this museum. There's an extensive collection of artifacts from the town's industrial past: weaving machines, metalworking tools, and, of course, items related to the town's famed shipyards (compasses, anchors, ships models). Also check out the fine collection of original drawings by the architects of Ermoupolis's neoclassical heyday, the wonderful old photographs and engravings depicting various aspects of island life, and the old maps of Siros and the Cyclades. The museum is a 20-minute walk or a short bus ride from the harbor. Allow an hour for your visit.

Ermoupolis. Just off Plateia Iroon and opposite the hospital. © 22810/86-900. Admission 3€ ($3.90); free on Wed. Tues–Sun 10am–2pm and 6–9pm.

EXPLORING ERMOUPOLIS ✮✮
If you arrive on Siros by boat, you'll immediately be aware of the two steep hills that tower over Ermoupolis. Originally, the term **Ano Siros** (which means "the area above Siros") was used to describe the peaks of both hills. Today, the term Ano Siros describes the taller hill seen to the left of Ermoupolis as you enter the harbor. This was, and still is, the Catholic quarter of the town, settled by the Venetians in the 13th century. Much of the intricate maze of narrow streets from that period remains today; cars are not allowed. There's a **Jesuit Monastery** and a **Capuchin Monastery** as well as the elaborately decorated **Church of Ayios Yeoryios** (Mass Sun at 11am) at the crest of the hill. The real joy of visiting Ano Siros comes from wandering along its narrow lanes, peeking surreptitiously into courtyards, and stumbling across a tiny shop or cafe. Needless to say, there are great views over Ermoupolis and the island. Omirou, one of the streets that run uphill, is probably your best bet for an assault on foot on

(Tips **Aegean Casino**

Ermoupolis has the only **casino** (© **22810/84-400**) in the Cyclades. The main entrance is directly opposite the bus station and ferry pier. The management is British, and most of the staff speak English. The entrance fee is 25€ ($33). There's no cover charge for the restaurant and bar. The casino is open daily from 8pm to 6am in summer; slot machines are open from 2pm. The casino is hardly black tie, but there is a dress code of sorts to weed out the ostentatiously underdressed.

Ano Siros; you can also drive up, park outside one of the gates into the quarter (as residents here do), and then explore on foot.

Ermoupolis's other hill, **Vrondado,** is crowned by the massive 19th-century blue-domed Greek Orthodox **Church of the Resurrection (Anastasi).** There's a fine view of Ermoupolis and the neighboring islands from the church's terrace. This area was built up as the town grew when Greeks from other islands, especially Chios, moved here at the time of the Greek War of Independence in the 1820s. Narrow streets, marble-paved squares, and dignified pedimented mansions with elegant balconies make this neighborhood a quiet refuge from the bustling inner city.

Ermoupolis's central square, **Plateia Miaoulis,** and the elaborately elegant neoclassical **Town Hall** (designed by Ernst Ziller, who designed the Grande Bretagne Hotel in Athens) are conspicuous reminders of Ermoupolis's heyday. Ringed by high palm trees and facing the town hall, you really can't miss Plateia Miaoulis; if you do, go back to the harbor and head inland on Venizelou. This is the heart of Ermoupolis; this is where the island's most vigorous *volta* (promenade) takes place even if it takes place under umbrellas. Any of the cafes here is a nice place to sit, preferably with an elaborate ice-cream sundae, and watch the promenade.

A couple of blocks northeast of the town hall is the recently restored 19th-century **Apollon Theater** ✫, a smaller version of Milan's La Scala, hence nicknamed "la piccola Scala." The theater is home to the Festival of the Aegean (www.festivaloftheaegean.com), with its summer opera, classical, and pop music performances. Even if you can't go to a performance here, step inside to see the elaborate painted ceilings and crystal chandeliers (entrance fee 2€/$2.60). To the northeast is the imposing Greek Orthodox church of **Ayios Nikolaos.** The green marble iconostasis and the touching monument to the Unknown Soldier in the park across from the church were both done by Vitalis, a famed 19th-century marble carver from Tinos. A short stroll beyond the church will bring you to the neighborhood called **Vaporia,** appropriately named after the steamships that brought it great prosperity. Many of the town houses are built on the edge of the rocks that plunge into the sea. One other church on nearby Omirou Street is especially worth seeing: the Cathedral church of the Transfiguration (Metamorphosi), with its glistening marble floors and precinct with wonderful pebble mosaics. This church, with its imposing arcade, is a grand tribute to the 19th-century prosperity of the Ermoupolis. One more church to visit: the Church of the Koimisis (Dormition), just off the harbor, a block of so from the Casino. This 19th-century church, with a very cheerful blue and gold pulpit, houses (among much else) an icon of the virgin painted by Domenico Theotokopoulos, better known as El Greco. Exploring Ermoupolis is a very nice way to spend a day, or parts of any number of days.

BEACHES

Beaches are not the island's strongest suit, but there are a number of good places to swim and sun. **Megas Yialos,** as its name states, is the largest beach on the island and, not surprisingly, the most developed. Hotels there include the **Alexandra** (© 22810/ 42-540; www.hotelalexandra.gr).

On the west coast, **Galissas** (with its still charming village) has one of the best beaches on the island, a crescent of sand bordered by tamarisks. It also has a large campsite (for info, contact www.twohearts-camping.com) and a number of small hotels. Also on the west coast, **Finikas** has a slender beach and a cluster of hotels and restaurants. A few kilometers to the south, **Poseidonia** and **Agathopes** have sand beaches and less competition for a place in the sun. A bonus if you go to Poseidonia and Agathopes is that you can take in the charming village of Dellagrazia-Poseidonia, with its cluster of 19th-century villas.

WHERE TO STAY

As you come off the ferry in Ermoupolis, you'll see the kiosk of the **Hoteliers Association of Siros,** which provides a list of island hotels. Note that hotels pay to become members of this association, so not all of the island's best lodgings are represented. In August, when vacationing Greeks pack the island, don't even think of arriving without a reservation. In addition to the following, you may want to consider the 16-unit **Syrou Melathron** (© 22810/85-963; syroumel@otenet.gr), in a handsome 19th-century town house. Only reports of indifferent service keep us from recommending this handsome little hotel wholeheartedly; doubles from 130€ ($169).

Hotel Apollonos ☆   This small hotel on the water in Vaporia is one of the best of the town's restored mansion hotels. Those looking for a fully authentic restoration might be disappointed—the furnishings and lighting are contemporary in style—but the overall effect creates a mood of understated elegance. The best guest rooms are the two facing the water at the back of the house: Both are quite spacious, and one has a loft sleeping area with sitting room below. Bathrooms are large, with tile and wood floors. A large common sitting room faces the bay, while a breakfast room faces the street.

8 Apollonos, Ermoupolis, 84100 Siros. © **22810/81-387** or 22810/80-842. Fax 22810/81-681. 3 units. 185€ ($241) double. Rates include breakfast. No credit cards. **Amenities:** Breakfast room/bar. *In room:* A/C.

Hotel Ethrion ☆ *Value*   This small family-run hotel with a quiet location in the heart of town has rooms and studios (one with kitchenette) with terraces or balconies; five units have sea views from the balconies. The rooms are comfortably and pleasantly furnished (the ones on the top floors have fancier decor), the owners are very helpful, and the price is right. This is the sort of homey place that can tempt you to relax into getting to know Ermoupolis *siga, siga* (slowly, slowly).

24 J. Kosma, Ermoupolis 84100, Siros. © **22819/89-006.** www.ethrion.gr. 8 doubles, 4 studios (1 with kitchenette). 55€–75€ ($72–$98). MC, V. **Amenities:** Internet. *In room:* A/C.

Hotel Hermes ☆ *Value*   The Hermes presents a bright, modern facade to busy Plateia Kanari at the harbor's east end. What you can't see from the street is that many of the better rooms directly face a quiet stretch of rocky coast at the back of the building. The functional, rather dull standard rooms have shower-only bathrooms and views of the street or a back garden. The rooms in the new wing are worth the extra money for their size, furnishings, and balconies that allow early risers to see the sunrise. If you get a room here on a summer weekend, be prepared to be the only guest

Shopping in Ermoupolis

The shops here tend to be functional rather than funky, and there aren't any that stand out. However, just about anything you need can be found somewhere in town. The best street for shopping is **Protopapadaki**, two streets from the port, which is open to car traffic and the location of the post office. The town's **produce market** is on **Hios**, west of the main square. It's open daily, but is particularly lively on Saturday. Don't leave the market without trying two local specialties: *loukoumia*, better known as Turkish delight; and *halvodopita*, a sort of nougat.

not in a wedding party—and to see the sun rise from your balcony as the wedding reception winds down.

Plateia Kanari, Ermoupolis, 84100 Siros. ✆ **22810/83-011** or 22810/83-012. Fax 22810/87-412. 51 units. 85€–100€ ($111–$130) double. Continental breakfast 5€ ($6.50). AE, DC, MC, V. **Amenities:** Restaurant; bar. *In room:* A/C, TV.

Hotel Omiros 🏵️   The Omiros is one of the most appealing of the neoclassical mansion hotels in Ermoupolis. Rooms are furnished with simple antiques. Some details from the original building have been retained, such as marble hand basins and massive fireplaces. The architectural highlight of the building is the spiral staircase that climbs through a shaft of light to the glass roof. Breakfast, drinks, and light meals are served in a small walled garden. The hotel is on a hill above Miaoulis Square—the climb from the port is steep, so it's best to take a taxi. There is parking, although the route from the port is complex and difficult to follow; call ahead for directions.

43 Omirou, Ermoupolis, 84100 Siros. ✆ **22810/84-910** or 22810/88-756. Fax 22810/86-266. 13 units. From 130€ ($169) double. Continental breakfast 10€ ($13). MC, V.

Hotel Vourlis 🏵️🏵️   On a hill overlooking the fashionable Vaporia district, the elegant Hotel Vourlis occupies one of the finest of the city's mansions. Built in 1888, the house has retained its grandeur and charm. The fine details that have sadly been lost in many other restored mansions are here in all their glory. The plaster ceilings in the front rooms are especially resplendent. Most furniture also dates to the 19th century, creating a period setting that incorporates all the comforts you expect from a fine hotel. Bathrooms are spacious and come with tubs. The two front rooms on the second floor have great sea views. Winter guests will be glad to know that the house is centrally heated. The adjacent five-unit **Ipatia Guesthouse** (✆ **22810/83-575**) is in a nicely restored town house.

5 Mavrokordatou, Ermoupolis, 84100 Siros. ✆/fax **22810/88-440** or 22810/81-682. 8 units. 135€–200€ ($176–$260) double. Continental breakfast 9€ ($12). MC, V. **Amenities:** Breakfast room/bar. *In room:* A/C, TV.

WHERE TO DINE

There are numerous excellent tavernas in and around Ermoupolis. **Boubas Ouzeri** and **Yacht Club of Siros** are both known for ouzo and *mezedes*. In addition to the tavernas mentioned below, try the consistently good **Petrino Taverna** (✆ **22810/84-427**), around the corner from To Arhontariki; and **Fragosiriani** (✆ **22810/84-888**), with a great view from its high terrace in Ano Siros (down the street from Taverna Lilis).

Taverna Lilis ★★ GREEK/SEAFOOD   Lilis is one of the best of the tavernas in Ano Siros, the quarter cresting the high conical hill behind Ermoupolis. From the terrace, there's a stellar view of Ermoupolis, the bay, distant Tinos and, even farther out, the shores of Mykonos. The food is better-than-average taverna fare—meats and fish are grilled on a wood fire, and the ingredients are reliably fresh. There's sometimes *rembetika* music here (see "Siros After Dark," below).

Ano Siros. ℭ 22810/88-087. Reservations recommended in July–Aug. Main courses 8€–20€ ($10–$26). No credit cards. Daily 7pm–midnight. Follow Omirou from the center of Ermoupolis, past the Hotel Omiros, and continue straight up the long flight of steps that leads to Lilis's brightly lit terrace. You can also call a taxi.

To Arhontariki GREEK   This small place fills the narrow street with tables precariously perched on cobblestones and is probably the best of the tavernas in Ermoupolis center. It's easy to find—just plunge into the maze of streets at the corner of Miaoulis Square between Pyramid Pizzeria and Loukas Restaurant, and weave your way left—it's 2 blocks or so in, between Miaoulis and the harbor. The menu is largely composed of specials (several vegetarian) that change daily.

Ermoupolis. ℭ 22810/81-744. Main courses 8€–18€ ($10–$23). Daily noon–midnight.

To Koutaki Tou Liberi ★ GREEK   Take a taxi to this out-of-the-way place that is definitely worthwhile. There is no menu—the night's offerings are brought out to you on a massive tray, and each dish is explained in turn. The food is often innovative, making slight but significant departures from traditional recipes. The spicing is subtle, and good use is made of the season's best ingredients. The owner is renowned locally for his *bouzouki* playing—late at night, after the last diners have finished their meals, impromptu traditional music sessions sometimes take place. Did we mention the view? It's terrific.

Kaminia. ℭ 22810/85-580. Reservations recommended several days in advance in high season. Main courses 8€–18€ ($10–$23). No credit cards. Fri–Sat 9pm–1am. 2km (1¼ miles) from Ermoupolis center.

SIROS AFTER DARK

Siros was among the most fertile grounds for *rembetika,* the haunting songs of the dispossessed, marginally criminal underclasses that probably began in Asia Minor in the early 20th century. Markos Vambakaris, the Bob Dylan, as it were, of *rembetika,* was born on Siros, which still prizes his music. You can hear *rembetika* at **Xanthomalis** (no phone; closed in summer) and at **Lilis** (ℭ 22810/28-087) in Ano Siros, which sometimes have late-night performances on the weekends; reservations are a must.

As always on the islands, places that are hot one season are often gone the next. I'm not listing phone numbers here because phones simply are not answered. Stick your head into any of the many bars along the waterfront to see which is playing music that suits your taste. You can also join in the evening *volta* **(stroll)** around Plateia Miaoulis, take a seat to watch it, or drop in at **Piramatiko, Agora,** or **Bizanas,** longtime music joints. The outdoor **Pallas Cinema,** east of the main square, has one nightly showing, often in English.

The Dodecanese

By John S. Bowman

"The Dodecanese"—the very name suggests someplace exotic (in fact it is merely the Greek for "twelve islands"!) and these islands, if not exotic, certainly have been providing visitors for many, many centuries a range of extraordinary attractions and experiences.

Part of their special appeal comes from the fact that the Dodecanese mostly hug the coast of Asia Minor, far from the Greek mainland. As frontier or borderline territories, their struggles to remain free and Greek have been intense and prolonged. Although they have been recognizably Greek for millennia, only in 1948 were the Dodecanese formally reunited with the Greek nation.

By the way, "the Twelve Islands" are in fact an archipelago of 32 islands: 14 inhabited and 18 uninhabited. But they have been known collectively as the Dodecanese since 1908, when 12 of them joined forces to resist the revocation of the special status they had long enjoyed under the Ottoman sultans.

The four islands selected for this chapter are certainly the most engaging of the Dodecanese. From south to north, they are **Rhodes, Simi, Kos,** and **Patmos.** Patmos and Simi are relatively barren in summer, while the interiors of Rhodes and Kos remain fertile and forested. Spectacular historical sights such as ancient ruins and medieval fortresses are concentrated on Patmos, Kos, and Rhodes; so are the tourists. Simi is the no-longer-quite-secret getaway you will not soon forget.

Long accustomed to watching the seas for invaders, these islands now spend their time awaiting the tourists who show up each spring and stay until October. The beginning of the tourist season sets into motion a pattern of activity largely contrived to attract and entertain outsiders. Such is the reality of island life today. As in the past, however, the islanders proudly retain their own character even as they accommodate an onslaught of visitors.

STRATEGIES FOR SEEING THE ISLANDS

In planning a visit to the Dodecanese, keep in mind that Rhodes has the longest tourist season. So, if you're rushing into the season in April, begin in Rhodes; if you're stretching the season into October, end up in Rhodes. If you can, avoid the Dodecanese July through August, when they are so crowded with tourists that they nearly sink.

In high season, at least, you can travel easily from one to the other of the three principal islands described here—**Rhodes, Kos,** and **Patmos.** From the mainland, all are best reached by air. Rhodes and Kos have airports; Patmos is a short jaunt by hydrofoil from Samos, which also has an airport. From Kos and Rhodes, you can get just about anywhere in the eastern Aegean, including nearby **Turkey,** which is worth at

The Dodecanese

Ancient Lindos **6**
Asklepion **2**
Monastery of St. John
 and the Cave of the Apocalypse **1**
Monolithos Castle **5**
Panormitis Monastery **3**
Petaloudes (Valley of the Butterflies) **4**

PATMOS
Arki
Marathos
Kampos
Skala
1
Lipsi
Parthenie
LEROS
Lakki
Ksirokampos
Levitha
Emborios
Arginonta
Telendos
Massouri
Mirties
KALIMNOS
Kalimnos
Psarimos
Lambi
Tigaki
Mastihari
Kos
2
Asfendiou
Ayios Fokas
Kefalos
Kardamena
KOS
Agathonisi
Megalo Horio
Farmakonisi

Greece
Aegean Sea
Athens
The Dodecanese
Mediterranean Sea
CRETE

Nimos
Yiali
Loutra
Mandraki
Emborios
Avlaki
Nisyros
Simi
Pedi
SIMI
3
Vathys
Analipsi
Astypalea
Astypalea
Megalo Horio
Livadia
Tilos
Rhodes
Sirna
Tria Nissia
Halki
Alimia
Mandriko
RHODES
4
Ialisos
Maritsa
Soroni
Fanes
Kalithea
Faliraki
Afandou
Embonas
Archangelos
Monolithos **5**
Laerma
6 Lindos
Apolakia
Messanagros
Gennadio
Kattavia
Plimiri

Sea of Crete

Saria
Diafani
Olymbos
KARPATHOS
Spoa
Piles
Arkassa
Karpathos
Armathia
Fri
Kassos
To Crete

MEDITERRANEAN

SEA

Airport
Ferry Routes

0   25 mi
0   25 km

N

> **Tips Museum and Site Hours Update**
>
> If you visit Greece during the summer, check to see when museums and sites are open. According to the official listings, they should be open from 8am to 7:30pm, but some may close earlier in the day and almost all are closed 1 day a week.

least a day's excursion. **Simi** can be reached by ferry from Piraeus but most people will approach it by boat as an excursion from Rhodes.

1 Rhodes (Rodos) ✸✸

250km (135 nautical miles) E of Piraeus

Selecting a divine patron was serious business for an ancient city. Most Greek cities played it safe and chose a mainstream god or goddess, a ranking Olympian: someone like Athena or Apollo or Artemis, or Zeus himself. It's revealing that the people of Rhodes chose **Helios,** the sun, as their signature god.

Indeed, millennia later the cult of the sun is alive and well on Rhodes, and no wonder: The island receives on average more than 300 days of sunshine a year. What's more, Rhodes is a destination for sun-worshipers from colder, darker, wetter lands around the globe.

But Rhodes gives visitors more than a mere tan. A location at the intersection of the East and West propelled the island into the thick of both commerce and conflicts. The scars left by its rich and turbulent history have become its treasures. Hellenistic Greeks, Romans, Crusader Knights, Turks, Italians—all invaders who brought some destruction—also left behind fascinating artifacts.

Through it all, Rhodes has remained beautiful. Its beaches are among the cleanest in the Aegean, and its interior is still home to unspoiled mountain villages, rich fertile plains—and beautiful butterflies. Several days in Rhodes will allow you to appreciate its marvels, relax in the sun, and perhaps add a day trip to the idyllic island of Simi or to the coast of Turkey. If Rhodes is your last port of call, it will make a grand finale; if it is your point of departure, you can launch forth happily from here to just about anywhere in the Aegean or Mediterranean.

ESSENTIALS

GETTING THERE By Plane In addition to its year-round service between Rhodes and Athens and Thessaloniki, **Olympic Airways** offers summer service between Rhodes and the following Greek locales: Iraklion (Crete), Karpathos, and Santorini. The local Olympic office is at 9 Ierou Lohou (✆ 22410/24-571 or 22410/24-555). Flights fill quickly, so reserve in advance. **Aegean Airlines** (within Greece ✆ 801/112-0000; www.aegeanair.com), in addition to flights to Rhodes, offers at least high-season flights between Rhodes and Thessaloniki and Iraklion, Crete. Tickets for any flight in or out of Rhodes can be purchased directly from **Triton Holidays,** near Mandraki Harbor, 9 Plastira, Rhodes city (✆ 22410/21-690; fax 22410/31-625; www.tritondmc.gr). Triton will either send your tickets to you or have them waiting for you at the airport.

The Rhodes **Paradissi Airport** (✆ 22410/83-214) is 13km (8 miles) southwest of the city and is served from 6am to 10:30pm by bus. The bus to the city center (Plateia

Rhodes Attractions

Rhodes

RHODES

Greece

Athens

Aegean Sea

Mediterranean Sea

Rhodes

Acropolis of Rhodes **8**
Archeological Museum
  of Rhodes **2**
Church of Our Lady
  of the Castle/
  Byzantine Museum **4**
Clock Tower **5**
Hospice of St. Catherine **9**
Mosque of Suleiman **6**
Municipal Art Gallery **3**
Municipal Baths **7**
Square of the Jewish
  Martyrs **10**
Street of the Knights **1**

Aquarium

100 PALMS

Vas. Konstantinou

Orthonos
Kritis
Akti Miaouli
Octobriou
Dragoumi
Ioannou Kazouli
Amalias

Government
Buildings

Fort St. Nicholas
Lighthouse

Mandraki
Harbor

NEW
TOWN

Metaxa
Ioannou
Alexandrou
Amerikis
Vas. Marias
Martiou
Vas. Sofias
Amerikis
Diakou

Papalouka

Market

Plateia
Rimini

Palace
of the
Knights

Windmills

Eleftheria
(Liberty)
Gate

Akandia
Harbor

Mill
Tower

Commercial
Harbor

Customs
House

Ippoton

Sokratous

Kennedy
Them. Sofouli
Pindou
Riga Fereou

Enoplon Dynameon
President
Chimairas
Pavlou Mela
Ioannou
Demokratias
Diagondon
Aviou
Komninon

Ippodamou
Fanouriou
Omirou
Pythagora
Perikleous

OLD
TOWN

City Walls

City Walls

Mount Smith

Fitellinon

Vyronon

Rimini) is 5€ ($6.50). A taxi costs about 20€ ($26). By the way, some taxi drivers resist taking passengers to hotels in the Old City (because of the slow going in the old streets); note their number and threaten to report them, and they will usually relent.

By Boat Rhodes is a major port with sea links not only to Athens, Crete, and the islands of the Aegean, but also to Cyprus, Turkey, and Israel. Service and schedules are always changing; check with the tourist office or a travel agency for the latest information.

In late spring and throughout the summer there are daily sailings—some with high-speed hydrofoils or catamarans—from and to Rhodes and many of the Dodecanense and other islands in the eastern Aegean: Kos, Kalimnos, Kastellorizo, Leros, Nissiros, Patmos, Samos, and Simi, and Tilos. The advantage of hydrofoils and catamarans is that they make the voyage in half the time, but when the wind blows, the sailings are canceled. Air quality is also poor, especially compared to that on larger open-deck excursion boats or ferries. For more detailed information about the most active ship line, **Dodekanisos Seaways,** see www.12ne.gr.

Wherever it is you want to go, whether by ferry, hydrofoil, catamaran, or excursion boat, schedules and tickets are available from **Triton Holidays,** 9 Plastira (© **22410/ 21-690;** fax 22410/31-625; www.tritondmc.gr). Although travel agents throughout

Rhodes city and island can issue air and sea tickets, we like Triton Holidays' focus on independent travelers.

VISITOR INFORMATION   The staff at the **South Aegean Tourist Office,** at the intersection of Makariou and Papagou (© **22410/23-255;** www.ando.gr/eot), can provide advice and help for all the Dodecanese islands, including Rhodes. Hours are Monday through Friday from 8am to 3pm. During the high season only, you'll find a helpful **Rhodes Municipal Tourist Office** down the hill at Plateia Rimini near the port taxi stand (© **22410/35-945**). It dispenses information on local excursions, buses, ferries, and accommodations, and offers currency exchange as well. Its hours are Monday through Saturday from about 9am to 9pm and Sunday from 9am to 2pm. The earlier-recommended **Triton Holidays** (© 22410/21-690; www.tritondmc.gr) is also willing to answer any traveler's question, free of obligation, and is sometimes open when the tourist offices are closed.

GETTING AROUND   Rhodes is not an island you can see on foot. You need wheels of some sort: public bus, group-shared taxi, rental car, or organized bus tour for around-the-island excursions. Rhodes City is a different story. Walking is the best and most pleasurable mode of transport; you'll need a taxi only if you're going to treat yourself to a meal at one of the farther-flung restaurants or if you're decked out for the casino and don't want to walk. Note that wheeled vehicles, except those driven by permanent Old Town residents, are not allowed within the walls. This goes for all taxis, unless you have luggage and are arriving or leaving.

By Bus   Public buses provide good service throughout the island; the tourist office publishes a schedule of routes and times. Buses to points **east** (except for the eastern coastal road as far as Falilraki) leave from the East Side Bus Station on Plateia Rimini, whereas buses to points **west,** including the airport, leave from the nearby West Side Bus Station on Averof. Buses for the eastern coastal road as far as Falilraki also leave from the West Side Bus Station. Island fares range from 1€ ($1.30) within the city to 15€ ($20) for the most remote destinations. The city bus system also offers six different tours; details are available from the tourist office.

By Bicycle, Moped & Motorcycle   Even where there are strips set aside for bicyclists, it can be risky cycling on Greek highways. You must have a proper license to rent anything motorized. We can recommend several outfits that rent motorbikes and bicycles: **Bicycle Center,** 39 Griva (© **22410/28-315**); **Mike's Motor Club,** 23 Kazouli (© **22410/37-420**); **Moto Pilot,** 12 Kritis (© **22410/32-285**). Starting prices per day are roughly 10€ ($13) for a mountain bike; from 15€ ($20) for a moped; and 30€ to 40€ ($39–$52) for a motorcycle.

By Taxi   In Rhodes city, the largest of many taxi stands is in front of the old town, on the harborfront in Plateia Rimini (© **22410/27-666**). There, posted for all to see, are the set fares for one-way trips throughout the island. (A sample fare to Lindos is 40€/$52.) Since many of the cabdrivers speak sightseer English, a few friends can be chauffeured and lectured at a reasonable cost. Taxis are metered, but fares should not exceed the minimum on short round-the-city jaunts. For longer trips, negotiate directly with the drivers. Better yet, **Triton Holidays** (see above), will at no extra charge arrange for a private full- or half-day taxi with a driver who not only speaks fluent English, but will also respect your wishes regarding smoking or nonsmoking en route. For **radio taxis,** call © **22410/64-712.** There is a slight additional pickup charge when you call for a taxi.

Tips **A Helping Hand**

The **Dodecanese Association for People with Special Needs** (© 22410/73-109; mobile 6940/463810) provides free minibus door-to-door service from the port, airport, and hotels—or even if you want to go out for coffee or a swim.

By Car   Apart from the array of international companies—among them **Alamo/National** (© 22410/73-570), **Avis** (© 22410/82-896), **Europcar** (© 22410/21-958), and **Hertz** (© 22410/21-819)—there is a large number of local companies. The latter may offer the lowest rates but have only a handful of cars, so they may be unable to back you up in the event of an accident. Be very certain that you are fully covered, for all minor scrapes as well as major accidents, before signing anything. An established Greek company with some 300 cars—reputedly the newest fleet on Rhodes—is **DRIVE Rent-a-Car** (© 22410/68-243; www.driverentacar.gr). It has an excellent reputation for personal service, as well as low prices from about 60€ ($78) per day. Keep in mind that some of the more remote roads on Rhodes require all-terrain vehicles and Rhodian rental-car companies usually stipulate that their standard vehicles be driven only on fully paved roads.

By Organized Tour & Excursion Boats   Several operators feature nature, archaeology, shopping, and beach tours. In Rhodes city, **Triton Holidays** (see earlier) is one of the largest and most reliable agencies and specializes in trips designed for independent travelers. Triton offers day and evening cruises, hiking tours, and excursions in Rhodes, as well as in the other Dodecanese islands and in Mamaris in Turkey. We recommend the full-day guided tours, either the one to Lindos (40€/$52); or the "Island Tour" (45€/$59), which takes you to small villages, churches, and monasteries, and includes lunch in the village of **Embonas,** known for its local wines and fresh-grilled meat. There is also a fascinating half-day guided tour to Filerimos Monastery, Valley of the Butterflies, and the ancient city of Kamiros for 35€ ($46). Along Mandraki Harbor, you can find excursion boats that leave for **Lindos** at 9am and return around 6pm, costing 25€ ($33); and daily excursions to **Simi** for 35€ ($46). For an in-depth island experience, Triton Holidays also offers a combination package of car rental and hotel accommodations in four small villages around the island (Kalavarda, Monolithos, Prasonisi, and Asklepion), ranging from 4 to 10 nights.

CITY LAYOUT   Rhodes is not the worst offender in Greece, but it does share the country's widespread aversion to street signs. This means that you need a map marked with every lane, so that you can count your way from one place to another. We recommend the two maps drawn and published by Mario Camerini in 1995, of which the mini-atlas entitled *Map of Rhodes Town* is the best. It's available at kiosks and tourist bookstalls.

Rhodes city (pop. 45,000) is divided into two sections: the Old Town, dating from medieval days, and the New Town. Overlooking the harbor, the **Old Town** ✶✶ is surrounded by massive walls—4km (2½ miles) around and in certain places nearly 12m (40 ft.) thick—built by the Knights of St. John. The **New Town** embraces the old one and extends south to meet the **Rhodian Riviera,** a strip of luxury resort hotels. At its northern tip is the city beach, in the area called 100 Palms, and famed **Mandraki Harbor,** now used as a mooring for private yachts and tour boats.

Walking away from Mandraki Harbor on Plastira, you'll come to **Cyprus Square,** where many of the New Town hotels are clustered. Veer left and continue to the park where the mighty fortress (the city walls) begins. Down the slope is Plateia Rimini and the Municipal Tourist Office (see "Visitor Information," earlier in this chapter).

FAST FACTS The local **American Express** agent is Rhodos Tours, 29 Ammochos-tou (© 22410/21-010), in the New Town; it's open Monday through Saturday from 8:30am to 1:30pm and 5 to 8:30pm. The **National Bank of Greece,** on Cyprus Square, exchanges currency Monday through Thursday from 8am to 2pm, Friday from 8am to 1:30pm, and Saturday from 9am to 1pm. There are other currency-exchange offices throughout the Old Town and New Town, often with rates better than those of the banks. For emergency care, call the **hospital** (© 22410/80-000) or, if necessary, an **ambulance** (© 166).

The oldest established **Internet access** in the Old Town is **Cosmonet Internet Cafe,** at 45B Evreon Martyron Sq. Open from May 1 to November 15, its daily hours are 9am to 7pm. You may see other Internet cafes around town. **Express Laundry,** 5 Kosti Palama, behind Plateia Rimini (© 22410/22-514), is open daily from 8am to 11pm. **Wash-O-Matic** on 33 Platonos (leading off Sokratous) keeps the same hours. **International Pharmacy,** 22 A. Kiakou (© 22410/75-331), is near Thermai Hotel. There are **public toilets** at 2 Papagou and across from 10 Papagou; there is also one just outside the wall at the Marine Gate by the Old Harbor. The **police** (© 22410/23-849) in the Old Town can handle any complaints from 10am to midnight. The **tourist police** (© 22410/27-423), on the edge of the Old Town near the port, address tourists' queries, concerns, and grievances. The main **post office** on Mandraki Harbor is open Monday through Friday from 7am to 8pm. A smaller office is on Orfeon in the Old Town, open daily with shorter hours.

WHAT TO SEE & DO IN RHODES CITY

Rhodes is blessed with first-rate sights and entertainment. As an international play-ground and a museum of both antiquity and the medieval era, Rhodes has no serious competitors in the Dodecanese and few peers in the eastern Mediterranean. Conse-quently, in singling out its highlights, we necessarily pass over sights that on lesser islands would be main attractions.

EXPLORING THE OLD TOWN

Best to know one thing from the start about Old Town: It's not laid out on a grid—not even close. There are roughly 200 streets or lanes that simply have no name. Get-ting lost here, however, is an opportunity to explore. Whenever you feel the need to find your bearings, you can ask for **Sokratous,** which is the closest Old Town comes to having a main street.

When you approach the walls of Old Town, you are about to enter arguably the oldest continuously inhabited medieval town in Europe. It's a thrill to behold. Although there are many gates, we suggest that you first enter through **Eleftheria (Liberty) Gate,** where you'll come to **Plateia Simi,** containing ruins of the **Temple of Venus,** identified by the votive offerings found here, which may date from the 3rd century B.C. The remains of the temple are next to a parking lot (driving is restricted in the Old Town), which rather diminishes the impact of the few stones and columns still standing. Nevertheless, the ruins are a reminder that a great Hellenistic city once stood here and encompassed the entire area now occupied by the city, including the old and new towns. The population of the Hellenistic city of Rhodes is thought to have equaled the current population of the whole island (roughly 100,000).

Plateia Simi is also home to the **Municipal Art Gallery of Rhodes,** above the Museum Reproduction Shop (generally Mon–Sat 8am–2pm); admission is 4€ ($5.20). Its impressive collection comprises mostly works by eminent modern Greek artists. The gallery now has a second beautifully restored venue in the Old Town (across from the Mosque of Suleiman) to house its collection of antique and rare maps and engravings (Mon–Fri 8am–2pm). One block farther on is the **Museum of Decorative Arts,** which contains finely made objects and crafts from Rhodes and other islands, most notably Simi (Tues–Sun 8:30am–3pm). Admission is 3€ ($3.90). Continue through the gate until you reach Ippoton, also known as the Street of the Knights. *Note:* If you are ready for serious sightseeing, purchase a ticket for 12€ ($16) that includes admissions to the Museum of Decorative Arts, Archaeological Museum, Church of our Lady of the Castle, and Palace of the Knights. It's available at all of the museums.

Street of the Knights ✦✦ (Ippoton on maps) is one of the best-preserved and most delightful medieval relics in the world. The 600m-long (1,968-ft.) cobble-paved street was constructed over an ancient pathway that led in a straight line from the Acropolis of Rhodes to the port. In the early 16th century, it became the address for most of the inns of each nation (and known as "tongues" because if the languages they spoke), which housed Knights who belonged to the Order of St. John. The inns were used as eating clubs and temporary residences for visiting dignitaries, and their facades reflect the architectural details of their respective countries.

Begin at the lowest point on the hill at **Spanish House,** now used by a bank. Next door is **Inn of the Order of the Tongue of Italy,** built in 1519 (as can be seen on the shield of the order above the door). Then comes the **Palace of the Villiers of the Isle of Adam,** built in 1521, housing the Archaeological Service of the Dodecanese. The **Inn of France,** constructed in 1492, now hosts the French Language Institute. It's one of the most ornate inns, with the shield of three lilies (fleur-de-lis), royal crown, and crown of the Magister d'Aubusson (the cardinal's hat above four crosses) off center, over the middle door. Typical of the late Gothic period, the architectural and decorative elements are all somewhat asymmetrical, lending grace to the squat building.

Opposite these inns is one side of the **Hospital of the Knights,** now the **Archaeological Museum,** whose entrance is on Museum Square. The grand and fascinating structure is well worth a visit. (As with so many public buildings in Rhodes, its hours are subject to change, but summer hours are generally Tues–Fri 8am–7pm and Sat–Sun 8:30am–3pm.) Admission is 4€ ($5.20). Across from the Archaeological Museum is the **Byzantine Museum,** housed in the **Church of Our Lady of the Castle** ✦ (the Roman Catholic Cathedral of the Knights); it often hosts rotating exhibits

---

⌒Tips From the Outside Looking In

Of all the inns on the Street of the Knights, only the **Inn of France** is open to the public (Mon–Fri 8am–noon). The ground floor houses the Institut Français, but you can see its garden as well as an occasional art show in the second-floor gallery. The other inns are now offices or private residences and are closed to the public.

of Christian art. Its hours vary but are generally Tuesday through Sunday from 8am to 7pm or later; admission is 3€ ($3.90).

The church farther on the right is **Ayia Triada** (open when it's open), next to the Italian consulate. Above its door are three coats of arms: those of France, England, and the pope. Past the arch that spans the street, still on the right, is the **Inn of the Tongue of Provence,** which was partially destroyed in 1856 and is now shorter than it once was. Opposite it on the left is the traditionally Gothic **Inn of the Tongue of Spain,** with vertical columns elongating its facade and a lovely garden in the back.

The culmination of this impressive procession should be **Palace of the Knights** ✸✸✸ (also known as Palace of the Grand Masters), but it was destroyed in a catastrophic accidental explosion in 1856. What you see before you now is a grandiose palace built in the 1930s to accommodate Mussolini's visits and fantasies. Its scale and grandeur are more reflective of a future that failed to materialize than of a vanished past. Today it houses mosaics stolen from Kos by the Italian military as well as a collection of antique furniture. Hours vary, but in summer are Monday from 12:30 to 7pm, Tuesday through Sunday from 8am to 7pm. Admission is 6€ ($7.80).

The **Mosque of Suleiman** and the public baths are two reminders of the Turkish presence in Old Rhodes. Follow Sokratous west away from the harbor or walk a couple of blocks south from the Palace of the Knights, and you can't miss the mosque with its slender, though incomplete, minaret and pink-striped Venetian exterior.

The **Municipal Baths** (what the Greeks call the "Turkish baths") are housed in a 7th-century Byzantine structure and have been considerably upgraded since 2000. They merit a visit by anyone interested in vestiges of Turkish culture that remain in the Old Town, and cost less than the showers in most pensions. The *hamam* (most locals use this Turkish word for "bath") is in Plateia Arionos, between a large old mosque and the Folk Dance Theater. Throughout the day, men and women go in via their separate entrances and disrobe in private shuttered cubicles. A walk across cool marble floors leads you to the bath area—many domed, round chambers sunlit by tiny glass panes in the roof. Through the steam you'll see people seated around large marble basins, chatting while ladling bowls of water over their heads. The baths are open Tuesday through Saturday from 11am to 7pm. Tuesday, Thursday, and Friday, their use costs 3€ ($3.90), but on Wednesday and Saturday the cost is only 2€ ($2.60). Note that on Saturday, the baths are extremely crowded with locals.

The Old Town was also home to the Jewish community, whose origins date to the days of the ancient Greeks. Little survives in the northeast or Jewish Quarter of the Old Town other than a few homes with Hebrew inscriptions, the Jewish cemetery, and the **Square of the Jewish Martyrs** (**Plateia ton Martiron Evreon,** also known as Sea Horse Sq. because of the sea-horse fountain). The square is dedicated to the 1,604 Jews who were rounded up here and sent to their deaths at Auschwitz. On Dosiadou, leading off the square (signed) is a lovely synagogue, where services are held on Friday night; it is usually open daily from 10am to 1pm. A small museum is attached to it (open Apr–Oct, Sun–Fri 10am–4pm; free admission). While at the Square of the Jewish Martyrs, be sure to visit the **Hospice of St. Catherine** ✸ (Mon–Fri 8am–2pm; free admission). Built in the late 14th century by the Order of the Knights of St. John (Knights Hospitaller) to house and entertain esteemed guests, it apparently lived up to its mission; one such guest, Niccole de Martoni, described it in the 1390s as "beautiful and splendid, with many handsome rooms, containing many and good beds." The description still fits, though only one "good bed" can be seen today. The restored hospice has exceptionally beautiful sea-pebble and mosaic floors, carved and intricately painted wooden ceilings, a grand hall and lavish bedchamber, and engaging exhibits. There's a lot here to excite the eyes and the imagination.

After touring the sites of the Old Town, you might want to walk around the **walls.** The fortification has a series of magnificent gates and towers, and is a remarkable example of a fully intact medieval structure. Much of the structure can be viewed by walking around the outside, but to walk along the top of the walls requires an admission fee of 4€ ($5.20) for adults, 2€ ($2.60) for students. The museum operates a 1-hour tour (6€/$7.80) on Tuesday and Saturday at 3pm, beginning at the Palace of the Knights.

EXPLORING THE NEW TOWN

The New Town is best explored after dark, since it houses most of the bars, discos, and nightclubs, as well as innumerable tavernas. In the heat of the day, its beaches—**Elli beach** and the **municipal beach**—are also popular. What few people make a point of seeking out but also can't miss are landmarks such as **Mandraki Harbor** and the "neo-imperial" architecture (culminating in the Nomarhia or Prefecture) along the harbor, all of which date from the Italian occupation. Other draws are the lovely park and ancient burial site at **Rodini** (2km/1¼ miles south of the city), and the impressive ancient **Acropolis of Rhodes** on Mount Smith.

The remains of the ancient Rhodian acropolis stand high atop the north end of the island above the modern city, with the sea visible on two sides. This is a pleasant site to explore leisurely with a picnic; there's plenty of shade. The restored stadium and small theater are particularly impressive, as are the remains of the Temple of Pythian Apollo. Although just a few pillars and a portion of the architrave still stand, they are provocative and pleasing, giving fodder to the imagination. The open site has no admission fee.

SHOPPING

In Rhodes city, it's the Old Town that is most interesting to shoppers. (But be warned: Most of these shops close at the end of Nov and don't reopen until Mar.) You'll find classic and contemporary **gold and silver jewelry** almost everywhere. The top-of-the-line Greek designer **Ilias Lalaounis** has a boutique on Plateia Alexandrou. **Alexandra Gold,** at 18 Sokratous next to the Alexis Restaurant, offers stylish European work, elegant gold and platinum link bracelets, and beautifully set precious gems. For a dazzling collection of authentic antique and reproduction jewelry, as well as ceramics, silver, glass, and everything you'd expect to find in a bazaar, drop in at **Royal Silver,** 15 Apellou (off Sokratous).

For imported **leather goods** and **furs** (the former often from nearby Turkey and the latter from northern Greece), stroll the length of Sokratous. Antiquity buffs should drop by the **Ministry of Culture Museum Reproduction Shop,** on Plateia Simi, which sells excellent reproductions of ancient sculptures, friezes, and tiles. True **antiques**—furniture, carpets, porcelain, and paintings—can be found at **Kalogirou Art,** 30 Panetiou, in a wonderful old building with a pebble-mosaic floor and an exotic banana-tree garden opposite the entrance to the Knights Palace.

Although most of what you find on Rhodes can be found throughout Greece, several products bear a special Rhodian mark. **Rhodian wine** has a fine reputation, and on weekdays you can visit two distinguished island wineries: **Cair,** at its winery 2km (1¼ miles) outside of Rhodes city on the way to Lindo (www.cair.gr); and **Emery,** in the village of Embonas (www.emery.gr). Another distinctive product of Rhodes is a rare form of **honey** made by bees committed to thimati (like oregano). To get this you may have to drive to the villages of Siana or Vati and ask if anyone has some to sell. It's mostly sold out of private homes, as locals are in no hurry to give it up. **Olive oil** is another local art, and again the best is sold out of private homes, meaning that you have to make discreet inquiries to discover the current sources.

Rhodes is also famed for handmade **carpets** and **kilims,** an enduring legacy from centuries of Ottoman occupation. Some 40 women around the island currently make carpets in their homes; some monasteries are also in on the act. There's a local carpet factory known as **Kleopatra** at Ayios Anthonias, on the main road to Lindos near Afandou. In the Old Town, these and other Rhodian handmade carpets and kilims are sold at **Royal Carpet** at 45 Aristotelos and 15 Apellou. At **Pazari,** 1 Aristoteous and Dimokritou, you can watch carpets being made. Finally, there is "Rhodian" **lace** and **embroidery,** much of which, alas, now comes from Hong Kong. Ask for help to learn the difference between what's local and what's imported.

SPORTS & OUTDOOR PURSUITS

Most outdoor activities on Rhodes are beach- and sea-related. For everything from **parasailing** to **jet skis** to **canoes,** you'll find what you need at **Faliraki beach** (see "Sights & Beaches Elsewhere on the Island," later in this chapter), if you can tolerate the crowds.

No license is required for **fishing;** the best grounds are reputed to be off Kamiros Skala, Kalithea, and Lindos. Try hitching a ride with the fishing boats that moor opposite Ayia Katerina's Gate. For sailing and yachting information, call the **Yacht Agency Rhodes** (© 22410/22-927; fax 22410/23-393), the center for all yachting needs.

If you've always wanted to try scuba diving, both **Waterhoppers Diving Schools** (©/fax **22410/38-146;** www.waterhoppers.com) and **Dive Med** (© **22410/61-115;** fax 22410/66-584; www.divemedcollege.com) offer 1-day introductory dives for beginners, diving expeditions for experienced divers, and 4- to 5-day courses leading to various certifications.

Other sports are available at **Rhodes Tennis Club** (© 22410/25-705) in the resort of Elli, or at **Rhodes-Afandu Golf Club** (© 22410/51-225), 19km (12 miles) south of the port. A centrally located, fully equipped fitness center can be found at the **Fitness Factory** (© 22410/37-667) at 17 Akti Kanari (www.rodosnet.gr/fitnessfactory).

If you want to get some culture as you get in shape, information on traditional **Greek folk-dance lessons** can be obtained from the **Old Town Theater** (© 22410/ 29-085), where Nelly Dimoglou and her entertaining troupe perform. Or contact the **Traditional Dance Center,** 87 Dekelias, Athens (© 210/251-1080); they usually offer summer classes each week to teach dances from different regions of Greece.

WHERE TO STAY IN RHODES CITY
IN THE OLD TOWN

Accommodations in the Old Town have an atmosphere of ages past, but character does not always equal charm. There are few really attractive options here, and they are in considerable demand, with all of the attending complications. One is that some hosts will hold you to the letter of your intent—so if you need or wish to cancel a day or more of your stay, they will do their best to extract every last pence. And there is some hedging, which means that the exact room agreed upon may be "unavailable" at the end of the day. Be explicit and keep a paper trail.

Rhodes Accommodations & Dining

ACCOMMODATIONS ■
Andreas Hotel **20**
Esperia **3**
Hotel La Luna **8**
Hotel Mediterranean **2**
Ibiscus **1**
Marco Polo Mansion **14**
Maria's Rooms **9**
Rodos Palace **4**
Rodos Park **7**
S. Nikolis Hotel **17**
Spot Hotel **21**

DINING ◆
Alexis Taverna **11**
Diafani Garden
   Restaurant **16**
Goniako Palati **5**
Hatzikelis **22**
Iannis Taverna **15**
Kafenio Turkiko **10**
Kioupia **18**
Kon Tiki Floating
   Restaurant **6**
Manolis Dinoris Fish
   Taverna **12**
Palia Historia **19**
Romeo **15**

Expensive

S. Nikolis Hotel and Apartments ★★   If you are determined to stay within the walls of the Old Town—which you really should do if you've come to experience Rhodes—and if you are willing and able to pay a premium, this is the place. Proprietor Sotiris Nikolis is a true artisan as well as genial host. Here, on the site of an ancient Hellenistic agora, he has restored several medieval structures using the original stones and remaining as faithful as possible to the original style. The result is immensely pleasing but not to be confused with the gaudiness of modern luxury hotels. Many of the furnishings are true antiques. Some rooms have sleeping lofts; some suites and studios have Jacuzzis; some studios have basic kitchenettes; a special business suite comes with two bedrooms, two bathrooms, and a small office area with fax and computer (contact for rates). The S. Nikolis also has some less-expensive, but equally pleasant, units in a nearby annex, the Hippodamou Hamam.

In the hotel's enclosed garden are a small fitness center and a computer nook with Internet access. Be sure to check out its adjacent **Ancient Agora Bar and Restaurant** where, in 1990, a 10-ton marble pediment dating from the 2nd century was found beneath the medieval foundations. Note that smoking is not permitted here.

61 Ippodamou, 85100 Rhodes. ℂ 22410/34-561. www.s-nikolis.gr. 12 units. 190€–200€ ($247–$260) double; 225€–350€ ($293–$445) suites; 140€–160€ ($182–$208) annex rooms. Rates include breakfast. AE, MC, V. Parking within

reasonable distance. Open year-round (but call ahead Nov–Mar). **Amenities:** Restaurant; bar; Jacuzzi in some suites; concierge; tours and car rentals arranged; Internet access. *In room:* A/C, TV, fridge, hair dryer.

Moderate

Marco Polo Mansion 🖈   Come here if you want a history lesson as well as a room with a touch of the exotic. Featured in glossy fashion and travel magazines, the Marco Polo Mansion has captured attention with its timeless style and good taste. As if squeezed from tubes of ancient pigments and weathered in the bleaching sun, the color palate here is all deep blues, mustard, wine, and pitch-black. Each guest room is steeped in a history of its own and furnished with antiques and folk art. One was a harem, another a *hamam* (Turkish bath). The "Imperial Room" has six windows, whereas the "Antika 2" room, lined with kilims, has a view of minarets. The smaller garden rooms, nestled in fragrant greenery, reflect the house's Italian period. Ceiling fans and cross breezes protect you from the heat of the day.

42 A. Fanouriou, 85100 Rhodes. ℂ/fax **22410/25-562.** www.marcopolomansion.web.com. 7 units. 90€–180€ ($117–$234) double. Rates include breakfast. V. No parking in the immediate area. Closed Nov–Mar.

Inexpensive

Hotel Andreas   This exceptionally well-run hotel (actually under Belgian owner-ship) offers relief from the cardboard walls and linoleum floors that haunt many of the town's budget choices. Housed in a restored 400-year-old Turkish sultan's house, it offers attractive rooms, some with panoramic views of the town. Others have wooden lofts, which can comfortably sleep a family of four. The bedrooms (with commend-ably firm beds) were once occupied by the sultan's harem, while the sultan held forth in room no. 11, a spacious corner unit with three windows and extra privacy. Break-fast is served on a shaded terrace that boasts gorgeous vistas of the town and the har-bor—some of the best views in Old Town. The full bar has a wide-screen TV, and laundry service is provided. Room nos. 10 and 11 have the best views; room nos. 8 and 9 have private terraces.

28D Omirou (located between Omirou 23 and 20, *not* just before 29), 85100 Rhodes. ℂ **22410/34-156.** Fax 22410/74-285. www.hotelandreas.com. 12 units, 6 with private bathroom. 55€–75€ ($72–$98) double with bath-room. Breakfast 10€ ($13) per person extra. AE, V. No parking in immediate area. Closed Nov–Feb.

Hotel La Luna 🖈   This small hotel is a block in from taverna-lined, touristy Orfeos, nestled between two churches in a calm residential neighborhood (but near the clock tower!). It features a large shaded garden with a bar and breakfast tables. Looking at the clean, modest rooms, all without toilet or tub, you may wonder why this is a prime spot in Old Town, patronized by various celebrities The answer is charm, which the ancient Greek poets knew to be capricious and inscrutable. It also has a lot to do with the private 300-year-old Turkish bath, which more than makes up for the one you don't have in your room. This is a place for visitors who want and respect quiet; blast your radio or make a ruckus, and you'll be asked to leave. Our favorite double is room no. 2 Just beyond the encircling walls of La Luna is a fascinating archaeological site encompassing two ancient churches, a traditional Turkish residence and garden, a Byzantine monastery, and more, making this a particularly intriguing corner of Old Town in which to base yourself.

21 Ilerokleous, 85100 Rhodes. ℂ/fax **22410/25-856.** www.helios.gr/exr. 7 rooms, none with bathroom. 75€–85€ ($98–$111) double. Rates include breakfast. No credit cards. No parking in immediate area. Closed Nov–Mar. Turn off Orfeos between the halves of Don Kichotis taverna.

Maria's Rooms   This pristine little pension near the Archontiko Restaurant merits high marks for both price and quality. The accommodations are sparkling white and squeaky clean, and Maria is a warm and welcoming hostess. Even without air-conditioning the rooms are cool, and they are secluded enough from the bustle of the Old Town to be surprisingly quiet.

147–Z Menekleous, 85100 Rhodes. ℭ 22410/22-169. vasilpyrgos@hotmail.com. 8 units, 3 with bathroom. 38€– 53€ ($49–$69) double with private bathroom. No credit cards. No parking in immediate area. Closed Nov–Easter.

Spot Hotel   Spotless would be a more suitable name for this small hotel. By Old Town standards, this building is an infant, barely 50 years old, but the proprietors have gradually added architectural enhancements that provide the hotel an island and medieval atmosphere more in keeping with its location. The garden and terrace sitting areas have also been enlarged. The rooms are simple and tasteful if not especially bright. Guests enjoy a large communal fridge, access to a phone for free local calls, free limited use of a PC for e-mail, and free luggage storage. Spot is near the harbor right off Plateia Martiron Hevreon, so breakfast is available at nearby cafes.

21 Perikleous, 85100 Rhodes. ℭ 22410/34-737. www.islandsinblue.gr. 9 units. 60€–70€ ($76–$91) double. No credit cards. No parking in immediate area. *In room:* A/C in some units.

IN THE NEW TOWN & ENVIRONS

Unlike the Old Town, the New Town doesn't prohibit new construction. You'll find a wild array of options, from boardinghouses to package-tour hotels to luxury resorts. Some are dazzling—take a look at the **Rodos Palace** on the west-coast road running out of town if your taste runs that way—but many are dull and so indistinguishable that you may forget which one you're in. I've tried to make a selection of those in different prices ranges that stand out.

Very Expensive

Rodos Park ⚓   This superb New Town luxury hotel, with gleaming marble and polished wood interiors, enjoys a uniquely convenient yet secluded location. Guests are within a short stroll of the city's attractions: only a few minutes from the Old Town and Mandraki Harbor, yet conveniently close to the New Town shopping and dining areas. Some might regard the rooms as over-decorated in terms of colors and textiles, but they are comfortable and have all the amenities you'd expect to find in a first-class hotel. This is not a beach resort—it's a fine city hotel open year-round. If you want a Jacuzzi in your room, opt for a suite, preferably one with a superb view of the Old Town walls. If you want to work off surplus calories from the 24-hour room service or the in-house gourmet restaurant, head down to the fitness center, then pamper yourself with a Swedish massage, sauna, or steam bath. A dip in the outdoor pool will offer the perfect finish to your regime.

12 Riga Fereou, 85100 Rhodes. ℭ 800/525-4800 in the U.S., or 22410/89-700. Fax 22410/24-613. www.rodos park.gr. 60 units. High season 460€ ($546) double, 510€ ($663) suite; low season 400€ ($520) double, 445€ ($579) suite. Rates include breakfast. AE, MC, V. Parking nearby. **Amenities:** 3 restaurants; 2 bars; pool; health club; Jacuzzi in suites; concierge; tours and car-rental arrangements; conference facilities; fax and computer facilities; 24-hr. room service; babysitting; same-day laundry/dry-cleaning service. *In room:* A/C, TV, minibar, hair dryer.

Moderate

Hotel Mediterranean ⚓ *Kids*   Directly across from Kos beach and next to Rodos Casino, this location speaks for itself (the Aquarium, a great spot for kids, is also nearby; admission fee 4€/$5.20). The year-round hotel's interior, from the common to the private rooms, is stylish and sophisticated. Doubles have adjoining twin beds, pullout sofas, and spacious tiled bathrooms. Rates vary according to the view: Of the three exposers, the spectacular sea view far outshines the garden (pool and veranda) or side (city) view. All suites have sea views, sitting areas, and king-size beds. All units have balconies. Rooms for travelers with disabilities are available upon request.

35 Kos beach, 85100 Rhodes. (© 22410/22-410. Fax 22410/22-828. www.mediterranean.gr. 241 units. 140€ ($182) double; 155€ ($202) suite. Rates include breakfast. AE, DC, MC, V. Free parking. Frequent public buses. **Amenities:** 2 restaurants; bar; outdoor freshwater pool; night-lit tennis court nearby; watersports equipment rentals; concierge; tours and car rentals arranged; airport pickup arranged; conference facilities; 24-hr. room service; babysitting; same-day laundry/dry-cleaning services; rooms for those w/limited mobility on request. *In room:* A/C, TV, minibar, hair dryer.

Ibiscus ⊛ The Ibiscus was a well-situated beachfront hotel when it underwent a makeover in 2000 that took it from attractive to striking. The spacious marble entrance hall opens into a stylish cafe bar; you can take your drinks out front to the beach or back onto the poolside garden veranda. The large, tasteful, fully carpeted double rooms have king-size orthopedic beds, large wardrobes, ample desk areas, tile and marble bathrooms, and hair dryers. The suites are especially appealing, with rich wood paneling, parquet floors, and two bedrooms (one with a king-size bed and one with twin beds). Every unit has a balcony, many of which face the sea.

Kos beach, 85100 Rhodes. (© 22410/24-421. Fax 22410/27-283. 205 units. 180€ ($234) double; 210€ ($273) suite. Rates include breakfast. AE, DC, MC, V. Free parking. Closed Nov–Mar. Frequent public buses. **Amenities:** Restaurant; bar; dipping pool; concierge; tours and car rentals arranged; shops. *In room:* A/C, TV, minibar, hair dryer.

Inexpensive

Esperia (Value) This hotel, open year-round, will probably appeal most to budget-conscious travelers. The guest rooms are tasteful and exceptionally clean, most with a large balcony with pleasant views. New double-glazed sliding balcony doors effectively seal the rooms from most of the town's noise. TVs are available on request at a small additional cost. The bar, lounge, and breakfast room are inviting, and the walled outdoor pool and poolside bar are well above average for a modest hotel. The hotel is located near the restaurant district and only a short walk from the beach.

7 Griva, 85100 Rhodes. (© 22410/23-941. Fax 22410/77-501. 171 units. 90€ ($117) double. Rates include breakfast. AE, DC, MC, V. **Amenities:** Breakfast room; bar; pool. *In room:* A/C, fridge, hair dryer.

WHERE TO DINE IN RHODES CITY
IN THE OLD TOWN

The Old Town is thick with tavernas, restaurants, and fast-food nooks, all doing their best to lure you into places that might be where you want to be. If not, the more brazen their overtures, the more adamant you must be in holding to your course. Don't imagine, however, that all Old Town restaurants are tourist traps. Many Rhodians come to this area for what they consider the island's best food, particularly fish. Don't even think of driving to these places; walk through an entrance to the Old City.

Very Expensive

Alexis Taverna ⊛ GREEK/SEAFOOD For more than 50 years, this fine restaurant has been the one to beat in Old Town, setting the standard by which the other seafood restaurants are judged. But you do have to be prepared to abandon restraint. The proprietors preserve the traditions established by their grandfather to devise a seafood feast for you, accompanied by the perfect wine from the cellar (which represents vineyards all over Greece). The fish is selected daily day down at the harbor—the best of the catch—and the proprietors have their own greenhouse on the outskirts of town to cultivate organic vegetables. Start with a bounteous seafood platter of delicately flavored sea urchins, fresh clams, and tender octopus carpaccio. Try the sargos, a sea-bream-type fish, charcoal-grilled to perfection. The creamy Greek yogurt with homemade green-walnut jam is a perfect ending for a superb culinary experience. Every meal here begins with a chef's consultation and should end with applause.

18 Sokratous. ☏ 22410/29-347. Reservations recommended. Individually prepared dinners without wine average 65€ ($85). AE, V. Mon–Sat 10am–4pm and 7pm–1am.

Manolis Dinoris Fish Taverna ☞ GREEK/SEAFOOD   This restaurant, housed in the former stables of the 13th-century Knights of St. John's Inn, provides a unique setting to enjoy delicious and fresh seafood delights. You can order either a la carte or from the set menu of coquille St. Jacques, Greek salad, grilled prawns, swordfish, baklava, coffee, and brandy. In warm weather, the quiet side garden is delightful; in winter, a fire roars in the old stone hearth indoors.

14A Museum Sq. ☏ 22410/25-824. Main courses 25€–60€ ($33–$78); set menu 70€ ($91). AE, MC, V. Year-round daily noon–midnight.

Expensive

Goniako Palati (Corner Palace) GREEK   The new Goniako Palati may not be a palace, but it is on the corner—a busy corner you overlook once the food arrives. Great canvas awnings cover the seating area, raised above street level. The extensive taverna menu is basic Greek, fresh and skillfully prepared in a slightly upscale environment at reasonable prices. This is one place local New Towners go for reliable, and then some, taverna fare. The grilled swordfish souvlaki, served with a medley of steamed vegetables, is quite tasty. The *saganaki* (grilled cheese) here is a performance art, and delicious to boot.

110 Griva (corner of Griva and 28 Oktobriou). ☏ 22410/33-167. Main courses 8€–26€ ($10–$34). AE, MC, V. Year-round daily 9am–midnight.

Kon Tiki Floating Restaurant ☞ GREEK/INTERNATIONAL   Still floating after 40 years of serving good food, this was one of Rhodes's first decent restaurants. It's a great place to watch the yachts bobbing alongside while you enjoy well-prepared, creative dishes such as sole *valevska* (filet of sole with shrimp, crab, and mushrooms gratinéed in a béchamel sauce). The saganaki shrimp—prepared with feta cheese, local herbs, and tomato sauce—is an exceptional dish. Count on the chef to offer "fushion" cuisine, which blends Polynesian, international, and Greek techniques and tastes. The restaurant is also open for breakfast and for coffee or a drink at the bar, if that's all you want.

Mandraki Harbor. ☏ 22410/22-477. Main courses 7€–26€ ($9.10–$34). AE, MC, V. Year-round daily 8am–midnight.

Romeo ☞ GREEK/SEAFOOD   Though under siege by tourists, many locals gladly frequent the Romeo, as there is a good deal that's authentic within its walls. (For one thing, the walls themselves are roughly 500 years old.) More important, besides the predictable taverna fare, are the number of local dishes on offer—including vegetarian options. Two house specialties are the mixed fish grill and the stuffed souvlaki. For the grill, you select your own fish from a generous array of fresh deep-sea options—the tender grilled octopus is especially good. The finely cut grilled souvlaki stuffed with melted cheese and tomatoes is a regional dish from the north end of the island. The very reasonably priced dry house wines go quite nicely with each entree. Set back in a quiet enclave, just off and out of the crush of Sokratous, Romeo offers both courtyard and roof-garden seating, as well as tasteful live traditional Greek music and song. If you're keen on a smoke-free environment, the air on the breezy roof garden is particularly fresh.

7–9 Menekleous (off Sokratous). ℭ **22410/25-186.** Main courses 6€–22€ ($7.80–$29). AE, MC, V. Mid-Mar to mid-Nov daily 10am–1am.

Moderate

Hatzikelis ⍟ GREEK/SEAFOOD   This delightful fish taverna enjoys a peaceful and pleasant setting in the midst of a small neighborhood park just behind the Church of Our Lady of the Burgh in the Square of the Jewish Martyrs. Although there is an extensive a la carte menu, the special dinners for two are irresistible. The Fisherman's Plate consists of lobster, shrimp, mussels, octopus, squid, and a liter of wine, while the plates of traditional Rhodian dishes include specialties like pumpkin balls and shrimp saganaki. The portions are challenging, but the quality of the cuisine and the fact that you have until 2am to do your duty increase the odds in your favor. To find Hatzikelis easily without winding your way through the Old Town, enter the walls at Pili Panagias (St. Mary's Gate).

9 Alhadeff. ℭ **22410/27-215.** Main courses 8€–19€ ($10–$25). No credit cards. Year-round daily 11am–2am.

Diafani Garden Restaurant (Value) GREEK   Several locals recommended this family-operated taverna, which cooks up fine traditional Greek fare at bargain prices. You won't find better authentic Greek home cooking than this anywhere in Rhodes, especially at lunch. Sitting under the spreading walnut tree in the vine-shaded courtyard, we enjoyed the splendid *papoutsaki,* braised eggplant slices layered with chopped meat and a thick, cheesy béchamel sauce, delicately flavored with nutmeg and coriander.

3 Plateia Arionos (opposite the Turkish bath). ℭ **22410/26-053.** Main courses 5€–17€ ($7–$22). No credit cards. Year-round daily noon–midnight.

Iannis Taverna ⍟ GREEK   For a budget Greek meal, visit chef Iannis's small place on a quiet back lane. The moussaka, stuffed vegetables, and meat dishes are flavorful and well prepared by a man who spent 14 years as a chef in the Greek diners of New York. His Greek plate is one of the best to be found in Rhodes, with an unbelievably large variety of tasty foods. Portions are hearty and cheap, and the friendly service is a welcome relief from service at nearby establishments. The breakfast omelets are a great deal.

41 Platonos. ℭ **22410/36-535.** Main courses 4€–15€ ($5.20–$20). No credit cards. Year-round daily 9am–midnight.

Kafenio Turkiko GREEK/SNACKS   Located in a Crusader structure, this is the only authentic place left on touristy Sokratous, otherwise replete with Swatch, Body Shop, Van Cleef, and a multitude of souvenir shops. Each rickety wooden table comes with a backgammon board for idling away the hours while you sip a Greek coffee or juice. The old pictures, mirrors, and bric-a-brac on the walls enhanced our feeling of bygone times.

76 Sokratous. No phone. Drinks/snacks 2€–7€ ($2.60–$9). No credit cards. Year-round daily 11am–midnight.

IN THE NEW TOWN & ENVIRONS
Expensive

Kioupia ⍟⍟ GREEK   Once rated by the *London Guardian* as one of the world's 10 best restaurants, this unique place offers an exquisite gourmet experience. Much-lauded Greek chef Michael Koumbiadis founded it in 1972 and he has uncovered the true harmonies of traditional Greek cuisine, using the best local ingredients and village recipes. In this elegantly decorated, rustic old house, the meal might begin with a choice of three soups, including the unusual *trahanas,* a Greek wheat-and-cheese soup. Soup is followed by an amazing array of appetizers: sautéed wild mushrooms, pumpkin *beignee* (dumplings), and savory braised red peppers in olive oil, accompanied by home-baked carrot bread and pastrami bread. The main dishes are equally superb—broiled veal stuffed with cheese and sprinkled with pistachio nuts in yogurt sauce; or delectable pork souvlaki with yogurt and paprika sauce on the side. For dessert, try the light crepes filled with sour cherries and covered with chocolate sauce and vanilla crème. Many of the foods are prepared in clay pots in a traditional wood-burning oven, source of the faint woodsy scent permeating the restaurant. The grand fixed-price meal, like the Orthodox liturgy, requires fasting, devotion, and time (roughly 3 hr.).

Tris Village, 9km (6 miles) south of Rhodes Town. (C) 22410/91-824. Reservations required. Fixed-price meals 35€ ($46) or 65€ ($85) per person; wine and service extra. A la carte available. MC, V. Year-round Mon–Sat 8pm–midnight; Sun noon–3pm.

Moderate

Palia Historia (The Old Story) ✦ GREEK   If you're maxed out on run-of-the-mill Greek taverna fare, this is a good place to come—well worth a taxi ride from wherever you're staying. Most of the clientele is Greek, drawn by the subtle cuisine and lack of tourists. The marinated salmon and capers are worthy of the finest Dublin restaurant, and the broccoli with oil, mustard, and roasted almonds is inspired. As a main course, the shrimp saganaki leave nothing to the imagination. With fish, the dry white Spiropoulos from Mantinia is perfect. For a great finish, go for the banana flambé.

108 Mitropoleos (south in New Town, below modern stadium). (C) 22410/32-421. Reservations recommended. Main courses 10€–24€ ($13–$31). AE, MC, V. Year-round daily 7pm–midnight.

RHODES CITY AFTER DARK

During the high season, Rhodes claims one of the most active nighttime scenes in Greece outside of Athens. Granted, some of that energy is grounded in the resort complexes north of the city, but there is enough to go around.

Your own common sense is as good a guide as any in this ever-changing scene. In a city as compact as Rhodes, it's best to follow the lights and noise, and get a little lost. When you decide to call it quits, shout down a taxi (if you're outside the Old Town) to bring you back—just remember where you're staying.

As a rule of thumb, the younger set will find the **New Town** livelier than the Old Town. **Cafe scenes** are located on the harbor, behind Academy Square, or on Galias near New Market. The **bar scene** tends to line up along Diakonou. In the Old Town, most of the clubs and bars are found along Miltiadhou. There must be at least 100 **nightclubs** on Rhodes, so you're sure to find one to your liking.

Gambling is a popular nighttime activity in Greece. Rhodes for many years housed one of Greece's six legal casinos, a government-operated roulette and blackjack house adjoining the Grand Hotel. Now in private hands and known as the **Casino Rodos,** it is located in the **Grande Albergo delle Rose** in the New Town; admission coasts 15€/$20 and the patrons must be at least 23 years old.

The **sound-and-light** *(Son et Lumière)* presentation at Papagou, south of Plateia Rimini ((C) 22410/21-922), dramatizes the life of a youth admitted into the monastery in 1522, the year before Rhodes fell to invading Turks. In contrast to Athens's Acropolis show, the dialogue here is more illuminating, though the lighting is unimaginative. Nevertheless, sitting in the lush gardens below the palace on a warm evening can be pleasant, and I recommend the experience to those smitten by the medieval Old Town. Check the posted schedule for English-language performances. Admission is 6€ ($7.80) for adults, 2€ ($2.60) for youths, and free for children under 11.

I also recommend the **Traditional Folk Dance Theater,** presented by the Nelly Dimoglou Dance Company, Adronikou, off Plateia Arionos, Old Town (© **22410/ 20-157**). This internationally acclaimed company is always lively, colorful, and utterly entertaining. Twenty spirited men and women perform dances from many areas of Greece in often embroidered flouncy costumes. The five-man band plays an inspired repertoire. Performances take place May through early October: Monday, Wednesday, and Friday at 9:15pm. Admission is 12€ ($16) for adults.

EXPLORING THE ISLAND

Sun, sand . . . and the rest is history. Nowhere is that more true than on Rhodes, where ruins and beaches lure visitors out of Rhodes city. For the best **beaches,** head to the island's east coast. Visitors also flock to archaeological sites identical to the three original Dorian city-states, all nearly 3,000 years old: **Lindos, Kamiros,** and **Ialisos.** Of these, Lindos was and is preeminent; it is by far the top tourist destination outside of Old Town. So we begin here with Lindos, and explore the island counterclockwise.

LINDOS

Lindos is without question the most picturesque town on the island of Rhodes. Because Lindos has been designated a historic settlement, the Archaeological Society controls development in the village, and the traditional white-stucco homes, shops, and restaurants form the most unified, classically Greek expression in the Dodecanese. Be warned, however, that Lindos is often deluged with tourists, and your first visit may be unforgettable for the wrong reasons. Avoid the crush of mid-July to August, if at all possible.

Frequent public buses leave Plateia Rimini for a fare of 6€ ($7.80); a taxi will cost 40€ ($52) one-way. There are two entrances to the town. The first and northernmost leads down a steep hill to the bus stop and taxi stand, then veers downhill again to the beach. (If you're driving, park in the lot above the town.) At this square from April through October, daily from 9am to 10pm, you'll find the **Tourist Information Kiosk** (© **22440/31-900;** fax 22410/31-288). Here, too, is the commercial heart of the village, with the Acropolis looming above. The rural **medical clinic** (© **22410/ 31-224**), **post office,** and **telephone office (OTE)** are nearby. The second road into town leads beyond it and into the upper village, blessedly removed from the hordes. This is the better route for people more aesthetically minded. Follow signs to the Acropolis. You'll pass a stand where, for 7€ ($9), you can ride a donkey (also known as a Lindian taxi) all the way to the top. Along the way, the sides of your path will be strewn with embroidery and lace for sale, which may or may not be the handiwork of local women. Embroidery from Rhodes was highly coveted in the ancient world. In fact, it is claimed that Alexander the Great wore a grand Rhodian robe into battle at Gaugemila, and in Renaissance Europe French ladies used to yearn for a bit of Lindos lace. Much of what is for sale in Lindos today, however, is from Asia.

Before you start the final ascent to the Acropolis, be sure to inspect the famous **relief carving of a trireme** ⊛, or three-banked ship, dating from the 2nd century B.C. At the top, from the fortress ramparts, are glorious views of medieval Lindos below, where most homes date from the 15th century. To the south you can see the lovely beach at St. Paul's Bay—legend claims St. Paul put ashore here—along with Rhodes's less-developed eastern coastline. Across to the southwest rises Mount Krana, where caves, dug out to serve as ancient tombs, are thought to have sheltered cults to Athena well into the Christian period.

The **Acropolis** ⟨⟩ (℗ **22410/27-674**) is open Tuesday through Sunday from 8am to 7pm, Monday from 12:30 to 7pm. Admission is 6€ ($7.80) for adults and 3€ ($3.90) for students and children. This is one of three original Dorian acropolises in Rhodes. Within the much-later medieval walls stand the impressive remains of the **Sanctuary of Athena Lindos,** with its large Doric portico from the 4th century B.C. St. John's Knights refortified the Acropolis with monumental turreted walls and built a small church to St. John inside. Today, stones and columns are strewn everywhere as the site undergoes extensive restoration.

On your descent, as you explore the labyrinthine lanes of medieval Lindos, you will come to the exquisite late-14th- or early-15th-century **Byzantine Church of the Panagia** ⟨⟩. Still the local parish church (admission 2€/$2.60), its more than 200 iconic frescoes cover every inch of the walls and arched ceilings. Dating from the 18th century, all of the frescoes have been painstakingly restored at great expense and with stunning results. Be sure to spend some time here; many of these icons are sequentially narrative, depicting the Creation, the Nativity, the Christian Passover, and the Last Judgment. And after you've given yourself a stiff neck from looking up, look down at the extraordinary floor, made of sea pebbles.

Adjoining the Church of the Panagia is the **Church Museum** (℗ **22440/32-020**), open April through October daily from 9am to 3pm; admission is 2€ ($2.60). The historical and architectural exhibits and collected ecclesiastical items, including frescoes, icons, texts, chalices, and liturgical embroidery, comprise a collection.

Then, of course, there's the inviting **beach** below, lined with cafes and tavernas.

Where to Stay & Dine in Lindos & Environs

In high season, Lindos marks the spot where up to 10,000 day-trippers from Rhodes city converge with 4,000 resident tourists. As no hotel construction is permitted, almost all of the old homes have been converted into pensions (called "villas" in the brochures) by English charter companies. **Triton Holidays** (℗ **22410/21-690;** www. tritondmc.gr) books six-person villas, including kitchen facilities (reservations are often made a year in advance). In peak season, the local **Tourist Information Kiosk** (℗ **22440/31-900;** fax 22440/31-288) has a list of homes that rent rooms. Plan to pay 50€ ($65) for a double and 70€ to 95€ ($91–$124) for a studio apartment.

Melenos Hotel, in an authentically Lindian-style villa, with hand-painted tiles, local antiques, handcrafted lamps—in short, traditional splendor combined with contemporary comforts and convenience—charges hefty prices (suites in high season run 360€–650€/$455–$845). If you're up for this, check it out at **www.melenoslindos. com** and then contact Michalis Melenos.

Atrium Palace ⟨⟩   Just over 6.4km (4 miles) out of Lindos on the long beach of crystal-clear Kalathos Bay, this luxurious resort hotel features an eclectic architectural design—a neo-Greek, Roman, Crusader, and Italian pastel extravaganza. The rooms are colorful and comfortable—they are especially proud of their wooden floors. The inner atrium is an exotic, tropical garden of pools and waterfalls. The beautifully landscaped outdoor pool complex is a nice alternative to the nearby beach, and the indoor pool, sauna, and fitness club will keep you busy. To fully entertain the whole family on the rainy days that seldom occur, there are game rooms, a miniclub for young children, and an arcade of shops. Despite the hotel's five-star status, the atmosphere here is relaxed, unpretentious, and friendly, all perhaps due to the Atrium Palace's excellent staff.

Kalathos beach, 85100 Rhodes. (℗ **22440/31-601.** Fax 22440/31-600. 256 units. 100€–170€ ($130–$221) double; 120€–360€ ($156–$468) suite for 2. Rates include breakfast. AE, DC, MC, V. Closed Nov–Mar. *In room:* A/C, TV, minibar.

Ladiko Bungalows Hotel   Anthony Quinn obtained permission to build a retirement home for actors on this pretty little bay on the road to Lindos, 3km (2 miles) south of the swinging beach resort of Faliraki, but never realized his plans. The location *is* exceptional—both quiet and convenient. This friendly family-operated lodge has activities for nature lovers (swimming, fishing, and hiking to nearby ruins and less-frequented beaches) but is just a 20-minute walk to noisy, bustling Faliraki. The outside terrace bar and dining area with a splendid view of Ladiko Bay provide lovely tranquil spots for a drink or a meal. The guest rooms are not exceptional, but are quite comfortable. Fourteen rooms come with fridges.

Faliraki, P.O. Box 236, 85100 Rhodes. ⓒ **22410/85-560.** Fax 22410/80-241. 42 units. 60€–90€ ($78–$117) double. Rates include breakfast. MC, V. Closed Nov–Mar. *In room:* A/C.

Lindos Mare ⍟   This relatively small and classy cliff-side resort hotel is a prime site at which to drop anchor on the east shore. The rooms are a notch above those of comparable luxury hotels on the coast, and the views of the bay below are glorious. A tram descends from the upper lobby, restaurant, and pool area to the lower levels of attractive Aegean-style bungalows, and continues onward down to the beach area, where you'll find umbrellas and watersports. The hotel is only a 2km (1¼-mile) walk or ride into Lindos, although you might want to stay put in the evenings to enjoy in-house social activities, such as barbecues, folklore evenings, or dancing.

You'll have a paralyzing array of restaurants and tavernas to choose from in tiny Lindos. On the beach, the expansive **Triton Restaurant** gets a nod because you can easily change into your swimsuit in the bathroom, essential for nonresidents who want to splash in the gorgeous water across the way. The restaurant is also not as pricey as the others.

Lindos Bay 85100 Rhodes. ⓒ **22440/31-130.** Fax 22440/31-131. www.lindosmare.gr. 138 units. 60€–95€ ($24) double; 180€ ($234) junior suite for 2 with half-board plan (breakfast and dinner). AE, DC, MC, V. Closed Nov–Mar. *In room:* TV.

Argo Fish Taverna ⍟ GREEK/SEAFOOD   Haraki Bay is a quiet fishing hamlet with a gorgeous, crescent-shaped pebbly beach and this excellent seafood taverna. Consider stopping here for a swim and lunch on a day trip to Lindos. We appreciated the freshness of the food, as well as a creative variation on a Greek salad that added mint, dandelion leaves, and other fresh herbs and was served with whole-wheat bread. The lightly battered fried calamari was tasty and a welcome relief from the standard over-battered fare. The mussels, baked with fresh tomatoes and feta cheese, were also right on.

Haraki beach (10km/6 miles north of Lindos). ⓒ **22440/51-410.** Reservations recommended. Main courses 13€–55€ ($17–$72). AE, MC, V. Easter–Oct daily noon–1am.

Mavrikos ⍟ GREEK/FRENCH   There's no denying that this is the most celebrated restaurant in Lindos—arguably in all of Rhodes—as attested to by the various rich and famous who have dined here in recent decades. And it deserves this reputation by combining elegant food with the rustic charm of the tree-shaded terrace. The brothers Michalis and Dimitri Mavrikos continue a now 70-year-old family tradition of fine Greek and French cuisine, such as their oven-baked lamb and fine beef filets, or the perfectly grilled and seasoned fresh red snapper. The food is especially distinguished the subtle flavors provided by seasonings—butter beans in a sauce with carobs, beef in a casserole with bergamot, tuna with fenugreek. And for something truly special, try their appetizer of shrimp paste. The brothers Mavrikos also run a great ice-cream parlor, **Geloblu,** serving homemade frozen concoctions and cakes. It's within the labyrinth of the old town near the church.

Main Sq., Lindos. (○ **22440/31-232.** Reservations recommended. Main courses 8€–20€ ($10–$26) V. Year-round daily noon–midnight.

SIGHTS & BEACHES ELSEWHERE ON THE ISLAND

A tour around the island provides you with a chance to view the wonderful variations of Rhodes's scenery. The sights described below, with the exception of Ialisos and Kamiros, are not of significant historical or cultural importance, but if you're tired of lying on the beach, they provide a pleasant diversion. The route outlined below traces the island counterclockwise from Rhodes city, with a number of suggested sorties to the interior. Even a cursory glance at a map of Rhodes will explain the many zigs and zags in this itinerary. Keep in mind that not all roads are equal; all-terrain vehicles are required for some of the detours suggested below.

Ialisos was the staging ground for the four major powers that were to control the island. The ancient ruins and monastery on Mount Filerimos reflect the presence of two of these groups. The Dorians ousted the Phoenicians from Rhodes in the 10th century B.C. (An oracle had predicted that white ravens and fish swimming in wine would be the final signs before the Phoenicians were annihilated. The Dorians, quick to spot opportunity, painted enough birds and threw enough fish into wine jugs that the Phoenicians left without raising their arms.) Most of the Dorians left Ialisos for other parts of the island; many settled in the new city of Rhodes. During the 3rd to 2nd centuries B.C., the Dorians constructed a temple to Athena and Zeus Polios, whose ruins are still visible, below the monastery. Walking south of the site will lead you to a well-preserved 4th-century-B.C. fountain.

When the Knights of St. John invaded the island, they, too, started from Ialisos, a minor town in Byzantine times. They built a small, subterranean chapel decorated with frescoes of Jesus and heroic knights. Their little whitewashed church is built right into the hillside above the Doric temple. Over it, the Italians constructed the **Monastery of Filerimos,** which remains a lovely spot to visit. Finally, Suleiman the Magnificent moved into Ialisos (1522) with his army of 100,000 and used it as a base for his eventual takeover of the island.

In summer, the site of Ialisos is open Monday through Saturday from 8am to 7pm; hours are irregular the rest of the year. Proper dress is required. Admission is 3€ ($3.90). Ancient Ialisos is 6km (3½ miles) inland from Trianda on the island's northwest coast; buses leave from Rhodes frequently for the 14km (8½-mile) ride.

Petaloudes is a popular attraction because of the millions of black-and-white-striped "butterflies" (actually a species of moth) that overtake this verdant valley in July and August. When resting quietly on plants or leaves, the moths are well camouflaged. Only the wailing of infants and the Greek rock blaring from portable radios disturbs them. Then the sky is filled with a flurry of red, the moths' underbellies exposed as they try to hide from the summer crush. The setting, with its many ponds, bamboo bridges, and rock displays, is admittedly a bit too precious. Petaloudes is 25km (16 miles) south of Rhodes and inland; it can be reached by bus but is most easily seen on a guided tour. It's open daily from 8:30am to 6:30pm; admission is 3€ ($3.90) from mid-June to late September, and 1€ ($1.30) the rest of the year.

The ruins at **Kamiros** are much more extensive than those at Ialisos, perhaps because this city remained an important outpost after the new Rhodes was completed in 408 B.C. The site is divided into two segments: the upper porch and the lower valley. The porch served as a place of religious practice and provided the height needed for the city's water supply. Climb to the top and you'll see two aqueducts, which assured the Dorians of a year-round supply of water. The small valley contains ruins of homes and streets, as well as the foundations of a large temple. The site is well enough preserved to visualize what life in this ancient Doric city was like more than 2,000 years ago. Think about wearing a swimsuit under your clothes: Across from the site is a good stretch of **beach,** where there are some rooms to let, a few tavernas, and the bus stop. The site is open Tuesday through Sunday from 8:30am to 3pm. Admission is 4€ ($5.20). Kamiros is 34km (21 miles) southwest of Rhodes city, with regular bus service.

Driving south along the western coast from Kamiros, you'll come to the late-15th-century Knights castle of **Kastellos (Kritinias Castle),** dominating the sea below. From here, heading south and then cutting up to the northeast, make your way inland to **Embonas,** the wine capital of the island and home to several tavernas famed for their fresh meat barbecues. This village is on the tour-group circuit, and numerous tavernas offer feasts accompanied by live music and folklore performances. If you then circle the island's highest mountain, **Attaviros** (1,196m/3,986 ft.), you come to the village of **Ayios Issidoros,** where devoted trekkers can ask directions to the summit. (It's a 5-hr., round-trip hike from Ayios Issidoros to the top of Mount Attaviros.) Otherwise, proceed to the picturesque village of **Siana,** nestled on the mountainside. From here, head to **Monolithos,** with its spectacularly sited crusader castle perched on the pinnacle of a coastal mountain.

If, to reach the eastern coast, you now decide to retrace your path back through Siana and Ayios Issidoros, you will eventually reach **Laerma,** where you might consider taking a 5km (3-mile) seasonal road to **Thami Monastery,** the oldest functioning monastery on the island, with beautiful though weather-damaged frescoes. From Laerma, it's another 10km (6 miles) to Lardos and the eastern coastal road, where you can either head straight to **Lindos** (see above) or take another detour to **Asklipio,** with its ruined castle and impressive Byzantine church. The church has a mosaic-pebbled floor and gorgeous cartoon-style frescoes, which depict the 7 days of Creation (check out the octopus) and the life of Jesus.

The **beaches** south of Lindos, from Lardos Bay to Plimmiri (26km/16 miles in all), are among the best on Rhodes, especially the short stretch between Lahania and Plimmiri. At the southernmost tip of the island, for those who seek off-the-beaten-track places, is **Prasonisi (Green Island),** connected to the main island by a narrow sandy isthmus, with waves and world-class windsurfing on one side and calm waters on the other.

From Lindos to Faliraki, there are a number of sandy, sheltered beaches with relatively little development. **Faliraki beach** is the island's most developed beach resort, offering every possible vacation distraction imaginable—from bungee jumping to laser clay shooting. The southern end of the beach is less crowded and frequented by nude bathers.

North of Faliraki, the once-healing thermal waters of **Kalithea,** praised for their therapeutic qualities by Hippocrates, have long since dried up—but this small bay, only 10km (6 miles) from Rhodes city, is still a great place to swim and snorkel. Mussolini built a fabulous Art Deco spa here; the abandoned derelict retains an odd grandeur evoking an era thankfully long gone.

2 Simi (Symi)

11km (7 miles) N of Rhodes

Tiny, rugged Simi is often called "the jewel of the Dodecanese." Arrival by boat affords you a view of pastel-colored neoclassical mansions climbing the steep hills above the broad, horseshoe-shaped harbor. Yialos is Simi's port, and Horio its old capital. The welcome absence of nontraditional buildings is due to an archaeological decree that severely regulates the style and methods of construction and restoration of all old and new buildings. Simi's long and prosperous tradition of shipbuilding, trading, and sponge diving is evident in its gracious mansions and richly ornamented churches. Islanders proudly boast that there are so many churches and monasteries that you can worship in a different sanctuary every day of the year.

During the first half of this century, Simi's economy gradually deteriorated as the shipbuilding industry declined, the maritime business soured, and somebody went and invented a synthetic sponge. Simiots left their homes to find work on nearby Rhodes or in North America and Australia (a startling 70% eventually returned). Today, the island's picture-perfect traditional-style houses have become a magnet for moneyed Athenians in search of real-estate investments, and Simi is a highly touted "off-the-beaten-path" resort for European tour groups trying to avoid other tour groups. The onslaught of tourists for the most part arrives at 10:30am and departs by 4pm.

In recent years, the **Simi Festival,** running June through September, has put Simi on the cultural map as a serious seasonal contender offering an exciting menu of international music, theater, and cinema. In July, August, and September, there's something happening virtually every night.

By the way, Simi has no natural source of water—all water has to be transported by boat from nearby islands. Day visitors will scarcely be aware of this, but everyone is asked to be careful to conserve water.

ESSENTIALS

GETTING THERE   Many (if not most) visitors to Simi arrive by boat from Rhodes. Several **excursion boats** arrive daily from Rhodes; round-trip fares run from 8€ to 30€ ($10–$39) depending on the type (and speed!) of the ship. The schedules and itineraries for the boats vary, but all leave in the morning from Mandraki Harbor and stop at the main port of Simi, Yialos, often with an additional stop at Panormitis Monastery or the beach at Pedi, before returning to Rhodes later in the day. Currently, there are daily **car ferries** from Piraeus, and two **local ferries** weekly via Tilos, Nissiros, Kos, and Kalimnos. From late spring to summer, **hydrofoils** and a **catamaran** skim the waters daily from Rhodes to Simi, usually making both morning and afternoon runs. Most travel agencies could make arrangements; in Rhodes Town, use **Triton Holidays (© 22410/21-690;** www.tritondmc.gr).

VISITOR INFORMATION   Check out the wonderfully helpful website operated by Simi's delightful and informative independent monthly, *The Symi Visitor* (**www.symivisitor.com**). Through the site's e-mail option, you can request information on accommodations, buses, weather, and more. Or you can address your queries to *The Symi Visitor,* P.O. Box 64, Simi, 85600 Dodecanese. Don't ask them, however, to recommend one hotel over another; explain exactly what you're looking for and they'll provide suggestions. Once you're on Simi, you'll find free copies of the latest *Symi Visitor* at tourist spots.

The resourceful George Kalodoukas of **Kalodoukas Holidays** (© 22410/71-077; www.kalodoukas.gr), just off the harbor up the steps from the Cafe Helena, can help with everything from booking accommodations (often at reduced rates) to chartering a boat. Once you've arrived on Simi, drop by the office (Mon–Sat 9am–1pm and 5–9pm). In summer, George plans a special outing for every day of the week, from cruises to explorations of the island. Most involve a swim and a healthy meal.

A **tourist information kiosk** on the harbor keeps hours that remain a mystery. Information and a free pamphlet may also be obtained at the **town hall,** located on the town square behind the bridge.

GETTING AROUND   Ferries and excursion boats dock first at hilly **Yialos** on the barren, rocky, northern half of the island. Yialos is the liveliest village on the island and the venue for most overnighters. The clock tower, on the right as you enter the port, is used as a landmark when negotiating the maze of car-free lanes and stairs. Another landmark used in giving directions is the bridge in the center of the harbor.

Simi's main road leads to **Pedi,** a developing beach resort one cove east of Yialos, and a new road rises to **Horio,** the old capital and now overshadowed by Yialos. (You can also climb the 375 or so stone steps, known as the Kali Strata, from Yialos up to Horio.) The island's 4,000 daily visitors most often take an excursion boat that stops at Panormitis Monastery or at Pedi beach. **Buses** leave every hour from 8am until 11pm for Pedi via Horio (1€/$1.30). There are only about six **taxis** on the island— leaving from the taxi stand at the center of the harbor and charging a set fee of 3€ ($3.90) to Horio and 4€ ($5.20) to Pedi. **Mopeds** are also available, but due to the limited network of roads, you'll do better relying on public transportation and your own two feet. **Caiques** (converted fishing boats) shuttle people to various beaches: Nimborios, Ayia Marina, Ayios Nikolaos, and Nanou; prices range from 8€ to 12€ ($10–$16), depending on distance; you can rent sunbeds at these beaches.

FAST FACTS   For a **doctor,** call © 22410/71-316; for a dentist, call © 22410/ 71-272; for the **police,** © 22410/71-11. The **post office** (© 22410/71-315) and **telephone office (OTE;** © 22410/71-212) are located about 100m (330 ft.) behind the waterfront; both open Monday through Friday from 7:30am to 3pm. For **Internet access,** try Vapori Bar (vapori@otenet.gr), just in from the harbor at the taxi stand and next to Bella Napoli Restaurant, open most evenings.

WHAT TO SEE & DO

Simi's southwestern portion is hilly and green. Located here is the medieval **Panormitis Monastery,** dedicated to St. Michael, the patron saint of seafaring Greeks. The monastery is popular with Greeks as a place of pilgrimage and of refuge from modern life; young Athenian businessmen speak lovingly of the monks' cells and small apartments that can be rented for rest and renewal. There is also an "alms house" that provides a home for the elderly. Call the **guest office** (© 22410/72-414) to book accommodations, ranging from 30€ to 65€ ($39–$85) for an apartment or house. All units are self-contained, with their own stove and fridge. The least expensive units have shared outdoor toilets. Most sleep at least four people.

The whitewashed compound has a verdant, shaded setting and a 16th-century gem of a church inside. **Taxiarchis Mishail of Panormitis** boasts icons of St. Michael and St. Gabriel adorned in silver and jewels. The combined folk and ecclesiastical museums are well worth the 2€ ($2.60) entrance fee, which goes to support the "alms house" mentioned above.

Local Industries

One skill still practiced on Simi is **shipbuilding.** If you walk along the water toward Nos beach, you'll probably see boats under construction or repair. It's a treat to watch the men fashion planed boards into graceful boats. Simi was a boat-building center in the days of the Peloponnesian War, when spirited sea battles were waged off its shores.

Sponge fishing is almost a dead industry in Greece. Only a generation ago, 2,000 divers worked waters around the island; today only a handful undertake this dangerous work, and most do so in the waters around Italy and Africa. In the old days divers often went without any apparatus. Working at depths of 50 to 60m (164–197 ft.), many divers were crippled or killed by the turbulent sea and too-rapid depressurization. The few sponges that are still harvested around Simi—and many more imported from Asia or Florida—are sold at shops along the port. Even if they're not from Simi's waters, they make inexpensive and lightweight gifts. For guaranteed-quality merchandise and an informative explanation and demonstration of sponge treatment, we recommend the **Aegean Sponge Centre (℗ 22410/ 71-260),** operated by Kyprios and his British wife, Leslie.

The town of **Panormitis Mihailis** is at its most lively and interesting during the annual November 8 festival, but it can be explored year-round via local boats or bus tours from Yialos. The hardy can hike here—it's 10km (6 miles), about 3 hours from town—and then enjoy a refreshing dip in the sheltered harbor and a meal in the taverna. In Yialos, by all means hike the gnarled, chipped stone steps of the **Kali Strate** ("the good steps"). This wide stairway ascends to Horio, a picturesque community that reflects a Greece in many ways long departed. Old women sweep the whitewashed stone paths outside their homes, and occasionally a young boy or very old man can be seen retouching the neon-blue trim over doorways and shutters. Nestled among the immaculately kept homes, which date back to the 18th century, are renovated villas now rented to an increasing number of tourists. And where tourists roam, tavernas, souvenir shops, and *bouzouki* bars soon follow. Commercialization has hit once-pristine Simi, but it remains at a bearable level despite constant pressure to transform the island for the worse.

Horio has an excellent small **Archaeological Museum** that houses archaeological and folklore artifacts that the islanders consider important enough for public exhibition. You can't miss the blue arrows that point the way. It's open Tuesday through Saturday from 9am to 2pm. Admission is 2€ ($2.60). The **Maritime Museum** in the port also costs 2€ ($2.60) and is open daily from 11am to 2:30pm.

Crowning Horio is the **Church of the Panagia.** The church is surrounded by a fortified wall and is therefore called the kastro (castle). It's adorned with the most glorious frescoes on the island, which can be viewed only when services are held (Mon–Fri 7–8am; all morning Sun).

Simi is blessed with many beaches, though they are not wide or sandy. Close to Yialos are two: **Nos,** a 15m-long (50-ft.) rocky stretch; and **Nimborios,** a pebble beach.

A bus to **Pedi** followed by a short walk takes you to **St. Nikolaos beach,** with shady trees and a good taverna, or to **St. Marina,** a small beach with little shade but stunning turquoise waters as well as views of the St. Marina islet and its cute church.

The summertime cornucopia of outings provided by Kalodoukas Holidays has already been mentioned; but if you want to set out on your own, be sure to pick up a copy of *Walking on Symi: A Pocket Guide,* a private publication of George Kalodoukas (7€/$9.10). It outlines 25 walks to help you discover and enjoy Simi's historic sites, interior forests, and mountain vistas.

WHERE TO STAY

Many travelers bypass hotels for private apartments or houses. Between April and October, rooms for two with shower and kitchen access go for 35€ to 70€ ($46–$92). More luxurious villa-style houses with daily maid service rent for 80€ to 130€ ($104–$169). To explore this alternative, contact Kalodoukas Holidays or the Simi website (see "Visitor Information," above).

Aliki Hotel ⭐ This grand Italianate sea captain's mansion, dating from 1895, is the most elegant and exclusive tourist address on Simi. It has the atmosphere of a boutique guesthouse, intimate and charming, and offers tastefully styled accommodations furnished with Italian antiques. Four rooms and two separate large apartments (added in 2007; for four to six persons) have balconies. Several units enjoy dramatic waterfront views, and the roof garden provides a spectacular 360-degree vista of the sea, town, and mountains. Because the Aliki has become a chic overnight getaway from bustling Rhodes, reservations are absolutely required, but be aware: If you cancel, none of the money you have been charged will be refunded.

Akti Gennimata, Yialos, 85600 Simi. ℂ 22410/71-665. Fax 22410/71-655. 17 units. 110€–135€ ($143–$176) standard double; 130€–150€ ($169–$195) suite. Rates include breakfast. MC, V. Closed mid-Nov to Mar. *In room:* A/C, fridge, hot plate.

Dorian Studios In a beautiful part of town, only 10m (33 ft.) from the sea, this rustically furnished hotel offers comfortable lodging (orthopedic beds!) and a kitchenette in every room. Some of the studios have vaulted beamed ceilings as well as balconies or terraces overlooking the harbor, where you can enjoy your morning coffee or evening ouzo.

Yialos, 85600 Simi. ℂ 22410/71-181. 10 units. 50€–70€ ($65–$91) double. MC, V. Closed Nov to mid-Apr. Just up from the Akti Gennimata at the Aliki Hotel. *In room:* A/C in 5 units.

Hotel Nireus ⭐ This beautifully maintained hotel right on the waterfront is gracious and inviting, with its own shaded seafront cafe and restaurant, sunning dock, and swimming area. Its location, amenities, and price make it a personal favorite on Simi—and it has become a popular venue for vacationing Greeks as well. The traditional Simiot-style facade has been preserved, while the spacious guest rooms are contemporary and comfortable. All have fridges, and the beds are among the most comfortable we've found in Greece. Ask for one of the 18 units that faces the sea and offers stunning views; if you're fortunate, you might get one with a balcony. All four suites front on the sea.

Akti Gennimata, Yialos, 85600 Simi. ℂ 22410/72-400. nireus@rho.forthnet.gr. 37 units. 90€ ($117) double; 110€ ($143) suite. Rates include buffet breakfast. MC, V. Closed Nov–Easter. *In room:* A/C, TV.

Hotel Nirides If you crave tranquil seclusion, this small cluster of apartments, on a rise overlooking Nimborios Bay and only minutes on foot from the one-taverna-town of Nimborios, may be exactly what you're seeking. It's about 35 minutes from Yialos on foot and appreciably less by land or sea taxi. Each attractive and spotless apartment sleeps four (two in beds and two on couches) and has a bedroom, bathroom, salon, and kitchenette. Seven apartments have balconies, three have terraces, and all face the sea. The Nirides has its own small bar and rents bicycles for excursions to town or beyond. There's a small beach with pristine water just a few minutes down the hill.

Nimborios Bay, 85600 Simi. ©/fax **22410/71-784.** 11 units. 65€–90€ ($85–$117) double. Rates include breakfast. MC, V. Closed Nov–Mar. *In room:* A/C.

WHERE TO DINE

For traditional home cooking and a respite from the crowds, look for the tiny **Family Taverna Meraklis,** hidden on a back lane behind Alpha Credit Bank and the National Bank (© **22410/71-003**).

Hellenikon (The Wine Restaurant of Simi) ⚔ GREEK/MEDITERRANEAN
If you have the impression that the Greek culinary imagination spins on a predictable wheel, you need a night at the Hellenikon. In addition to spectacular fare, this diminutive open-air restaurant on the Yialos town square often provides, by virtue of its location, free evening concerts, compliments of the Simi Festival.

Start with one of the imaginative combination-appetizers plates. The chef's fish soup is spectacular, as are the grilled vegetables. In addition to a piquant array of traditional Greek entrees, you can select one of seven homemade pastas and combine it with one of numerous sauces. Meanwhile, host Nikos Psarros is a wine master who has over 150 Greek wines in his cellar, all from small independent wineries. Every meal here begins with a personal consultation with Nikos in his cellar, where he will help you select the perfect wine to complement your meal.

Yialos. © **22410/72-455.** psarrosn@otenet.gr. Main courses 10€–20€ ($13–$26). MC, V. May–Oct daily 8pm–midnight.

Muragio Restaurant ⚔ GREEK/SEAFOOD
This restaurant, which opened in 1995, has become a big hit among locals, who praise the generous main courses and the quality of the food. Try the *bourekakia,* skinned eggplant stuffed with a special cheese sauce and then fried in a batter of eggs and bread crumbs. The lemon lamb is extremely popular but you might also consider the saganaki shrimp in tomato sauce and feta cheese.

Yialos. © **22410/72-133.** Main courses 7€–28€ ($9–$36). V. Year-round daily 11am–midnight.

Mylopetra (The Mill Stone) ⚔ MEDITERRANEAN
Owners Eva and Hans converted this 200-year-old flour mill into an exquisite setting for a gourmet dining experience. Their collection of antique Greek furniture and fabrics graces this most unusual space simply yet elegantly. (Note the 2,000-year-old grave visible through a glass window in the floor; it's made of pebble mosaic and rose marble.) Find an excuse to ascend to the toilet on the upper veranda, where you can get an overall view of the wonderful interior. Guests dine outdoors on the patio or inside by the open kitchen, enjoying a different menu every day. The lamb and fish dishes, made with wonderful Simiot hill spices, are especially impressive, as are the homemade pastas, such as ravioli Larissa, filled with potatoes and homemade cheese and served in sage butter.

Yialos. © **22410/72-333.** Fax 22410/72-194. Main courses 15€–36€ ($20–$47). V. May–Oct daily 7pm–midnight.

Nireus Restaurant ⚔ GREEK
Michalis, the chef of this superior restaurant in the Nireus Hotel on the waterfront, has gained quite a reputation in recent years. Kudos

to his *frito misto,* a mixed seafood plate with tiny, naturally sweet Simi shrimp and other local delicacies. The savory filet of beef served with a Madeira sauce is also recommended. They say you can't eat the scenery, but the view from here is delicious all the same.

Yialos. ✆ **22410/72-400.** Main courses 6€–19€ ($7.80–$25). MC, V. Easter–Oct daily 11am–11pm.

Taverna Neraida *(Value* SEAFOOD   Proving the rule that fish is cheaper far from the port, this homey taverna on the town square has among the best fresh-fish prices on the island, as well as a wonderful range of *mezedes.* Try the black-eyed-pea salad and *skordalia* (garlic sauce). The grilled daily fish is delicious, while the typical ambience is a treat.

Yialos. ✆ **22410/71-841.** Main courses 5€–20€ ($6.50–$26). No credit cards. Year-round daily 11am–midnight.

3 Kos

370km (230 miles) E of Piraeus

Kos today is identified with and at times nearly consumed by tourism, but the island and its people have endured, and so will you, with a little initiative and independence.

Almost three-quarters of the island's working people are directly engaged in tourism, and the scale of demand tells you something about Kos's beauty and attractions.

Kos has been inhabited for roughly 10,000 years, and has for a significant portion of that time been both an important center of commerce and a line of defense. Its population in ancient times may have reached 100,000, but today it is less than a third of that number. Across the millennia, the unchallenged favorite son of the island has been Hippocrates, the father of Western medicine, who has left his mark not only on Kos but also on the world.

The principal attractions of Kos are its **antiquities**—most notably the Asklepion—and its **beaches.** You can guess which are more swamped in summer. But the taste of most tour groups is thankfully predictable and limited. The congestion can be evaded, if that's your preference.

Kos town is still quite vital. Because the island is small, you can base yourself in the town, in an authentic neighborhood if possible, and venture out from there. You'll get the most out of Kos by following the locals—especially when it comes to restaurants. If you think you're in a village and see no schools or churches, and no old people, chances are you're not in a village at all, but in a resort. Kos has many, especially along its coasts.

ESSENTIALS

GETTING THERE   By Plane   Kos is now serviced by both **Olympic Airways** (Kos town office, 22 Vas. Pavlou; ✆ **22420/28-331**) and **Aegean Airlines** (✆ **22420/51-654**). Although Olympic has experimented with expanded service and may do so again, at present its only direct flights to Kos are from Athens and Rhodes. From **Hippocrates Airport** (✆ **22420/51-229**), a public bus will take you the 26km (16 miles) to the town center for 4€ ($5.20); or you can take a taxi for about 18€ ($23).

By Boat   As the transportation hub of the Dodecanese, Kos offers (weather permitting) a full menu of options: car ferries, passenger ferries, hydrofoils (Flying Dolphins), excursion boats, and caiques. Though most schedules and routes are always in flux, the good news is that you can, with more or less patience, make your way to Kos from virtually anywhere in the Aegean. Currently, the only ports linked to Kos with year-round nonstop and at least daily ferry service are Piraeus, Rhodes, Kalimnos, and Bodrum. Leros and Patmos enjoy the same frequency but with a stop or two along the way. The Kos harbor is strewn with travel agents who can assist you; or check current schedules with the Municipal Tourism Office (see below).

VISITOR INFORMATION   The **Municipal Tourism Office** (© **22420/24-460;** fax 22420/21-111), on Vas. Yioryiou, facing the harbor near the hydrofoil pier, is your one-stop source of information in Kos. It's open May through October, Monday to Friday from 8am to 2:30pm and 5 to 8pm, and Saturday and Sunday from 9am to 2pm; and November through April, Monday to Friday from 8am to 2:30pm. Hotel and pension owners keep the office informed of what rooms are available in the town and environs; you must, however, book your room directly with the hotel. Be sure to pick up a free map of Kos. For a more extensive and detailed guide to Kos—beaches, archaeological sites, birds, wildflowers, tavernas, and much more—pick up a copy of *Where and How in Kos,* available at most news kiosks for 4€ ($5.20).

GETTING AROUND   By Bus   The **Kos town (DEAS) buses** offer service within roughly 6.4km (4 miles) of the town center, whereas the **Kos island (KTEL) buses** will get you nearly everywhere else. For the latest schedules, consult the **town bus office,** on the harbor at 7 Akti Kountourioti (© **22420/26-276**); or the **island bus station,** at 7 Kleopatras (© **22420/22-292**), around the corner from the Olympic Airways office. The majority of DEAS town buses leave from the central bus stop on the south side of the harbor.

By Bicycle   This is a congenial island for cyclists. Much of Kos is quite flat, and the one main road from Kos town to Kefalos has all but emptied the older competing routes of traffic. As bike trails are provided until well beyond Kos town, you can also avoid the congested east-end beach roads. But don't expect to pedal one-way and then hoist your bike onto a bus, because that won't work here. Rentals are available throughout Kos town and can be arranged through your hotel. Prices range from 5€ to 15€ ($6.50–$20) per day.

By Moped & Motorcycle   It's easy to rent a moped through your hotel or a travel agent. Or, as with bicycles, you can walk toward the harbor and look for an agency. Rentals range from 18€ to 25€ ($23–$33). You can also call **Motoway,** 9 Vas. Yioryiou (© **22420/20-031**), for mopeds and motorcycles.

By Car   It's unlikely that you'd need to rent a car for more than 1 or 2 days on Kos, even if you wanted to see all its sights and never lift a foot. Numerous companies, including **Avis** (© **22420/24-272**), **Europcar** (© **22420/24-070**), and **Hertz** (© **22420/28-002**), rent cars and all-terrain vehicles. Expect to pay at least 95€ ($124) per day including insurance and fuel. Gas stations are open Monday through Saturday from 7am to 7pm; there are also several stations open (in rotation) in Kos town on Sunday; ask your hotelier or the tourist office for directions.

By Taxi   For a taxi, drop by or call the **harbor taxi stand** beneath the minaret and across from the castle (© **22420/23-333** or 22420/27-777). All Kos drivers are required to know English, but then again, you were once required to know trigonometry.

ORIENTATION   Kos town is built around the harbor from which the town fans out. In the center are an **ancient city** *(polis)* consisting of ruins, an old city limited mostly to pedestrians, and the new city with wide, tree-lined streets. Most of the town's hotels are near the water, either on the road north to Lambi or on the road

---

Moments **The Oldest Tree in Europe?**

From the Kos Museum, you might want to walk directly across to the **Municipal Fruit Market,** then have a picnic at the foot of the oldest tree in Europe, only a short walk toward the harbor at the entrance bridge to the castle. The bizarre-looking tree standing with extensive support is said to be the **Tree of Hippocrates** ✿, where he once instructed his students in the arts of empirical medicine and its attending moral responsibilities. Botanists may not endorse this claim but why not enjoy the legend!

---

south and east to Psalidi. If you stand facing the harbor, with the castle on your right, **Lambi** is to your left and **Psalidi** on your right. In general, the neighborhoods to your right are less overrun and defined by tourists. This area, although quite central, is overall more residential and pleasant. The relatively uncontrolled area to your left (except for the occasional calm oasis, like that occupied by the Pension Alexis) has been largely given over to tourism. Knowing this will help you find most of the tourist-oriented services by day and action by night, as well as where to find a bit of calm when you want to call it quits. Most recommended places to stay lie to your left, east of the castle.

FAST FACTS   Of the three banks that exchange currency, **Ionian Bank of Greece,** El. Venizelou, has the most extensive hours: Monday through Friday from 8am to 2pm and 6 to 8pm. The **hospital** is at 32 Hippokratous (© 22420/22-300). **Del Mare Internet Cafe,** 4a Megalo Alexandrou (© 22420/24-244; www.cybercafe.gr) is open daily from 9am to 2am. **Happy Wash,** 20 Mitropoleos, across from Ayios Nikolaos (© 22420/23-424), is open May through October, daily from 8am to 9pm; and November through April, daily from 9am to 1:30pm and 4 to 9pm. The **post office** on Vas. Pavlou (at El. Venizelou) is open Monday through Friday from 7:30am to 2:30pm. Across from the castle, the **tourist police** (© 22420/22-444) are available 24 hours to address any outstanding need or emergency, even trouble finding a room.

WHAT TO SEE & DO
ATTRACTIONS IN KOS TOWN

Dominating the harbor, the **Castle of the Knights** stands in and atop a long line of fortresses defending Kos since ancient times. What you see today was constructed by the Knights of St. John in the 15th century and fell to the Turks in 1522. Satisfying your curiosity is perhaps the only compelling reason to pay the 4€ ($5.20) admission fee. The castle is a hollow shell, with nothing of interest inside that you can't imagine from the outside, except when it serves as a venue for concerts. Best to stand back and admire from a distance this massive reminder of the vigilance that has been a part of life in Kos from prehistory to the present.

At the intersection of Vas. Pavlou and E. Grigoriou stands the **Casa Romana** (© 22420/23-234), a restored 3rd-century Roman villa that straddles what appears to have been an earlier Hellenistic residence. It's open Tuesday through Sunday from 8:30am to 3pm and costs 3€ ($3.90) for adults. If you carry no flame for ruins, this won't ignite one. Nearby, however, to the east and west of the Casa Romana, are a number of interesting open sites, comprising what is in effect a small archaeological park. Entrance is free. To the east lie the remains of a **Hellenistic temple** and the **Altar of Dionysos,** and to the west and south a number of impressive excavations and remains, the jewel of which is the **Roman Odeon,** with 18 intact levels of seats. The other extensive area of ruins is in the agora of the **ancient town** just in from Akti Miaouli. Kos town is strewn with archaeological sites opening like fissures and interrupting the flow of pedestrian traffic. Rarely is anything identified for passersby, so they seem like mere barriers or building sites, which is precisely what they were. The rich architectural tradition of Kos did not cease with the eclipse of antiquity—Kos is adorned with a surprising number of striking and significant structures, sacred and secular, enfolded unselfconsciously into the modern town.

While you're strolling about town, note the **sculptures** by Alexandros Alwyn in the Garden of Hippocrates opposite Dolphins Square, down along the Old Harbor. An English painter and sculptor with something of an international reputation, Alwyn long maintained a studio in the village of Evangelistra on Kos.

Asklepeion ✺   Unless you have only beaches on the brain, Asklepeion is reason enough to come to Kos. On an elevated site with grand views of Kos town, the sea, and the Turkish coastline, this is the Mecca of modern Western medicine, where Hippocrates—said to have lived to the age of 104—founded the first medical school in the late 5th century B.C. (In case your mythology is a bit rusty, Asclepius was the Greek god of healing.) For nearly a thousand years after his death, this was a place of healing where physicians were consulted and gods invoked in equal measure. The ruins date from the 4th century B.C. to the 2nd century A.D. Systematic excavation of the site was not begun until 1902. Truth be told, this is one of those archaeological sites that work best for those who bring something to them—namely some associations, some knowledge, some respect for the history behind the ruins. In this case, a sense of the role of Hippocrates in our own lives.

Located 4km (2½ miles) southwest of Kos town. ☎ 22420/28-763. Admission 4€ ($5.20) adults, 2€ ($2.60) seniors and students, free for children under 17. Oct to mid-June Tues–Sun 8:30am–3pm; mid-June to Sept Tues–Fri 8:30am–7pm, Sat 8:30am–3pm.

Kos Museum   For a town the size of Kos, this is an impressive archaeological museum, built by the Italians in the 1930s to display mostly Hellenistic and Roman sculptures and mosaics uncovered on the island. Although there is nothing startling or enduringly memorable in the collection, a visit reminds visitors of the former greatness of this now quite modest port town. Look in the museum's atrium for the lovely 3rd-century mosaic showing how Hippocrates and Pan once welcomed Asclepius, the god of healing, to this, the birthplace of Western medicine.

Plateia Eleftherias (across from the municipal market). ☎ 22420/28-326. Admission 3€ ($3.90) adults, 2€ ($2.60) seniors and students, free for children under 17. Year-round Tues–Sun 8:30am–3pm.

SHOPPING

Kos town is compact and the central shopping area all but fits in the palm of your hand, so you can explore every lane and see what strikes you. If you've grown attached to the traditional music you've been hearing since your arrival in Greece and want some help in making the right selection, stop by either of the **Ti Amo Music Stores,** 11 El. Venizelou and 4 Ipsilandou, where Giorgos Hatzidimitris will help you find traditional or modern Greek music. At either shop you may sit and listen before making a purchase.

Even if you're unwilling to pack another thing, you won't notice the weight of the unique handmade gold medallions at the jewelry shop of **N. Reissi,** opposite the museum at 1 Plateia Kazouli (☎ **22420/28-229**). Especially striking are the Kos medallions designed and crafted by Ms. Reissi's father (60€–125€/$78–$163). Handcrafted rings, charms, and earrings are also on display. For unusual ceramic pieces, visit the shop of **Lambis Pittas** at 6 Kanari (leading away from the inner harbor), or his factory at G. Papendreou (on the coast leaving town for the southeast).

Another sort of treasure to bring home is a hand-painted Greek icon. **Panajiotis Katapodis** has been painting icons for over 40 years, both for churches and for individuals. His studio and home are on a lovely hillside little more than a mile west of Kos center at Ayios Nektarios, and visitors are welcome April through October, Monday through Saturday from 9am to 1pm and 4 to 9pm. The way is signposted from just east of the Casa Romana.

BEACHES & OUTDOOR PURSUITS

The beaches of Kos are no secret. Every foot of the 290km (180 miles) of mostly sandy coastline has been discovered. Even so, for some reason, people pack themselves together in tight spaces. You can spot the package-tour sites from afar by their umbrellas, dividing the beach into plots measured in centimeters. **Tingaki** and **Kardamena** epitomize this avoidable phenomenon. Following are a few guidelines to help you in your quest for uncolonized sand.

The beaches 3 to 5km (2–3 miles) east of Kos town are among the least congested on the island, probably because they're pebbled rather than sandy. Even so, the view is splendid and the nearby hot springs worth a good soak. In summer, the water on the northern coast of the island is warmer and shallower than that on the south, though less clear due to stronger winds. If you walk down from the resorts and umbrellas, you'll find some relatively open stretches between **Tingaki** and **Mastihari.** The north side of the island is also best for **windsurfing;** try Tingaki and Marmara, where everything you need can be rented on the beach. A perfect day at the northwestern tip of the island would consist of a swim at **Limnionas Bay** followed by grilled red mullet at Taverna Miltos.

Opposite, on the southern coast, **Kamel beach** and **Magic beach** are less congested than **Paradise beach,** which lies between them. Either can be reached on foot from Paradise beach, a stop for the Kefalos bus. The southwestern waters are cooler yet calmer than those along the northern shore; and apart from Kardamena and Kefalos Bay, the beaches on this side of the island are less dominated by package tours. Note that practically every sort of watersport, including jet-skiing, can be found at **Kardamena.** The extreme southwestern tip of the island, on the **Kefalos peninsula** near Ayios Theologos, offers remote shoreline ideal for surfing. You can end the day watching the sunset at **Sunset Wave beach,** where you can also enjoy a not-soon-forgotten family-cooked feast at **Agios Theologos Restaurant,** which rents molded plastic surfboards as well.

For yachting and sailing, call the **Yachting Club of Kos** (© **22420/20-055**) or **Istion Sailing Holidays** (© **22420/22-195;** fax 22420/26-777). For diving, contact **Kos Diving Centre,** 5 Plateia Koritsas (© **22420/20-269** or 22420/22-782), **Dolphin Divers** (© **2940/548-149**), or **Waterhoppers** (© **22420/27-815;** mobile 69440/130533).

As already outlined (see "Getting Around," above), the island is especially good for **bicycling,** and rentals are widely available. If horseback riding is your thing, you can arrange guided excursions through the **Marmari Riding Centre** (© **22420/41-783**), which offers 1-hour beach rides and 4-hour mountain trail rides. **Bird-watchers** will be interested in the wild peacocks in the forests at Skala, and the migrating flamingos that frequent the salt-lake preserve just west of Tingaki.

EXPLORING THE HINTERLANDS

The most remote and authentic region of the island is comprised of the forests and mountains stretching roughly from beyond Platani all the way to Plaka in the south. The highest point is Mount Dikeos, reaching nearly 900m (3,000 ft.). The mountain villages of this region were once the true center of the island. Only in the last 30 years or so have they been all but abandoned for the lure of more level, fertile land and, since the 1970s, the cash crop of tourism.

There are many ways to explore this region, which begins little more than a mile beyond the center of Kos town. Trekkers will not find this daunting, and by car or motorbike it's a cinch, but peddling a mountain bike the ups and downs may be a challenge. Regardless of which way you go, the point is to take your time. You could take a bus from Kos to Zia and walk from Zia to Pili, returning then from Pili to Kos town by bus. The 5km (3-mile) walk from Zia to Pili will take you through a number of traditional island villages. Along the way you'll pass the ruins of **old Pili,** a mountaintop castle growing so organically out of the rock that you might miss it. As your reward at day's end, have **dinner in Zia** at **Sunset Taverna,** where at dusk the view of Kos island and the sea is magnificent. Zia also has a ceramics shop and a Greek art shop to occupy you as you wait for your taxi. For those looking to get away from the crowds, an hour's drive from Kos town all the way to the southwest coast leads to **Sunset Wave beach** below Ayios Theologos. There the Vavithis family, including some repatriated from North America, maintain a restaurant that makes for a most enjoyable setting and meal.

VENTURING OFFSHORE

Two interesting offshore options lie within easy reach of Kos. Hop one of the daily ferries from Kardamena and Kefalos to the small island of **Nissiros.** Nissiros, while not too attractive, has at its center an active volcano, which blew the top off the island in 600 B.C. and last erupted in 1873. There are also daily ferries from Kos harbor to **Bodrum, Turkey** (ancient Halikarnassos). Note that you must bring your passport to the boat an hour before sailing so that the captain can draw up the necessary documents for the Turkish port police.

WHERE TO STAY

Plan ahead and make a reservation well in advance. Most places are booked solid in summer and closed tight in winter.

EXPENSIVE

Hotel Kipriotis Village *(Kids)*   Here's a resort hotel that will appeal to families willing to spend at least part of a vacation amid loads of fun-seeking Europeans with all the possible holiday facilities. Only 4km (2½ miles) from Kos and right on the beach, it is constructed as a village of sorts, with its two-story bungalows and apartments surrounding an attractively designed sports area. The attractive rooms vaguely suggest an Ikea-modern style with a Greek touch. Kids can take part in a full day of supervised activities. If you're here to soak up the sun, you'll never have to leave the premises; meals, however, as might be predicted for such a large institution, are not especially imaginative, but there is public transportation every 15 minutes into Kos town. While this place is relatively classy, it does tend to be booked by groups, so don't expect a cozy atmosphere.

P.O. Box 206, Psalidi beach, 85200 Kos (5km/3 miles south of Kos town). ℭ **22420/27-640.** Fax 22420/23-590. 512 units. 175€ ($228) double; 200€ ($260) bungalow for 2 (including breakfast). AE, MC, V. Closed mid-Oct to mid-Apr. Parking on premises. **Amenities:** 3 restaurants; 4 bars; 2 outdoor pools; 1 heated indoor pool; tennis; health center w/sauna and hydromassage; Turkish bath; solarium; watersports equipment; minigolf, volleyball, basketball, billiards, and table tennis; children's program; tours and car rentals arranged; salon; babysitting; same-day laundry and dry cleaning. *In room:* A/C (July–Aug only), TV, fridge, hair dryer.

MODERATE

Hotel Astron ✵   This is the most attractive hotel directly on Kos Town's harbor yet only some 360m/1,181 ft. from a swimming beach—although the hotel does have its own generous sized pool and pleasant patio. The entrance and lobby—a mélange of glass, marble, and Minoan columns—are quite striking and suggest an elegance that does not in fact extend to the rooms and suites. All units are, however, tasteful and clean, with firm beds and balconies. The pricier units include extras such as harbor views and Jacuzzis. In the larger and more expensive suites, the extra space is designed to accommodate a third person and is wasted if you intend to use it as a sitting area. One extra that might be worth the money is a harbor view, but remember that by night you are facing the action. Kos is no retirement community: In summer, about 65% of the rooms in town are allotted to package tour groups who come to live it up.

31 Akti Kountourioti, 85300 Kos. ℭ **22420/23-703.** Fax 22420/22-814. 80 units. 115€ ($150) double; 140€ ($182) suite. Rates include breakfast. AE, MC, V. Open year-round. **Amenities:** Restaurant; bar; swimming pool; children's pool; Jacuzzi; tours and car rentals arranged. *In room:* A/C, TV, fridge.

INEXPENSIVE

Hotel Afendoulis *(Value)*   Nowhere in Kos do you receive so much for so little. Nestled in a gracious residential neighborhood a few hundred yards from the water and less than 10 minutes on foot from the very center of Kos, Afendoulis offers the magical combination of convenience and calm. The rooms are clean and altogether welcoming, with firm beds. Nearly all units have private balconies, and most have views of the sea. Whatever room you have, you can't go wrong. Note that the hotel has an elevator. This is a long-established family-run place, and the Zikas family—Alexis, Hippocrates, Dionisia, and Kiriaki—spare nothing to create a very special holiday community in which guests enjoy and respect one another. If you are coming to Kos to raise hell, do it elsewhere.

Although this is likely to be many people's non-negotiable first choice in Kos, don't despair if you haven't made a reservation. Alexis Zikas holds several extra rooms, including a two-room apartment, open and unreserved in order to accommodate such emergencies. He also owns the Pension Alexis (see below) several blocks away and can usually accommodate someone who shows up at the last minute.

1 Evrepilou, 85300 Kos. ℭ **22420/25-321.** afendoulishotel@kos.forthnet.gr. 17 units. 50€–65€ ($65–$85). MC, V. Closed mid-Oct to mid-Apr.

Hotel Yiorgos   This inviting, family-run hotel is a block from the sea and no more than a 15-minute walk from the center of Kos town. Although the immediate neighborhood is not residential, the hotel enjoys relative quiet year-round. Guest rooms are modest and very clean. All units have balconies, most with pleasant but not spectacular views of either sea or mountains. Individually controlled central heating makes this an exceptionally cozy small hotel at the chilly edges of the tourist season. Convenience, hospitality, and affordability have created a place to which guests happily return.

9 Harmilou, 85300 Kos. © 22420/23-297. Fax 22420/27-710. yiorgos@kos.forthnet.gr. 35 units. 40€–65€ ($52–$85) double. Rates include breakfast. No credit cards. *In room:* Fridge, coffeemaker.

Pension Alexis   Ensconced in a quiet residential neighborhood only a stone's throw from the harbor, Pension Alexis feels like a home because it is one, or was until it opened as a guesthouse. This is a gracious dwelling, with parquet floors and many tasteful architectural touches. The expansive rooms have high ceilings and open onto shared balconies. Most have sweeping views of the harbor and the Castle of the Knights. Individual rooms are separated from the halls by sliding doors, and share three large bathrooms. Room no. 4 is a truly grand corner space with knockout views. What was a great location became even better when the town created the Hippocrates Gardens just across from the pension, closing the one street to cars. In summer, the heart of the pension is the covered veranda facing private gardens, where in the morning guests can enjoy breakfast and at dusk can share stories late into the night.

9 Irodotou, 85300 Kos. © 22420/28-798 or 22420/25-594. Fax 22420/25-797. 14 units. 35€–45€ ($46–$59) double. No credit cards. Closed mid-Oct to mid-Apr.

WHERE TO DINE

In Kos, as at all popular Greek tourist destinations these days, there's a lot of routine food and even fast food. But there's no need to make eating on Kos a Greek tragedy; the key is to eat where the locals do. Along with your meals, you may want to try some of the local wines: dry **Glafkos,** red **Appelis,** or crisp **Theokritos** retsina.

EXPENSIVE

Petrino ⧫ GREEK   When royalty come to Kos, this is where they dine—so why not live the fantasy yourself? Housed in an exquisitely restored, century-old, two-story stone *(petrino)* private residence, this is hands-down the most elegant taverna in Kos, with food to match. In summer, sit outside on the spacious three-level terrace overlooking the ancient agora; but be sure to take a look at the splendid architecture inside, especially upstairs.

   Although the menu focuses on Greek specialties, it is vast enough to include lobster, filet mignon, and other Western staples. But don't waste this opportunity to experience Greek traditional cuisine at its best (and not necessarily all that expensive). The stuffed peppers, grilled octopus, and *beki meze* (marinated pork) are perfection. More than 50 carefully selected wines, all Greek, line the cellar—this is your chance to learn why Greece was once synonymous with wine. The dry red kalliga from Kefalonia is exceptional.

1 Plateia Theologou (abutting agora's east extremity). © 22420/27-251. Reservations recommended. Main courses 9€–48€ ($12–$62). AE, DC, MC, V. Mid-Dec to Nov daily 5pm–midnight.

Platanos Restaurant ⧫ GREEK/INTERNATIONAL   Not only is Platanos in one of Kos's best locations, overlooking the Hippocrates Tree, it is in a handsome building, a former Italian officers' club replete with arches and the original tile floor. Try reserving a place on the upstairs balcony with its impressive vista. Among the creatively prepared appetizers is chicken stuffed with dates in a spicy sauce. If you're tired of Greek salads, try the mixed vegetable salad. For a main course, try the souvlaki, a combination of chicken, lamb, and beef; or the duck Dijonnaise, served with a tasty sauce and a selection of seasonable vegetables. A generous selection of choice wines, live music, and gracious service makes for a splendid evening.

Plateia Platanos. ℂ **22420/28-991.** Main courses 14€–30€ ($18–$39). AE, MC, V. Apr–Oct daily noon–11:30pm.

MODERATE

Taverna Mavromatis ℛ GREEK   One of the best choices in town is this 40-year-old vine- and geranium-covered beachside taverna run by the Mavromati brothers. Their food is what you came to Greece for: melt-in-your-mouth saganaki, mint- and garlic-spiced *sousoutakia* (meatballs in red sauce), tender grilled lamb chops, moist beef souvlaki, and perfectly grilled fresh fish. In summer, the taverna spills out along the beach; you'll find yourself sitting only feet from the water watching the sunset and gazing at the nearby Turkish coast. A dinner here can be quite magical, something locals know very well; so arrive early to ensure a spot by the water.

Psalidi beach. ℂ **22420/22-433.** Main courses 5€–18€ ($6.50–$23). AE, MC, V. Year-round Wed–Sun 11am–11pm. A 20-min. walk southeast of the ferry port; or accessible by the local Psalidi Beach bus.

INEXPENSIVE

Arap (Platanio) Taverna GREEK/TURKISH   Like the population of Platinos, the food here is a splendid mix of Greek and Turkish. The spirit of this unpretentious family restaurant is contagious. Whatever you order from the extensive menu, it's impossible for you to choose wrong. Although there are many meat dishes, vegetarians will have a feast. The roasted red peppers stuffed with feta and the zucchini flowers stuffed with rice are splendid, as is the *bourekakia* (a kind of fried pastry roll stuffed with cheese). For a really top-notch meal, put yourself in the hands of the Memis brothers and let them order for you. Afterward, you can walk across the street for the best homemade ice cream on Kos, an island legend since 1955. This combination is well worth the walk or taxi ride.

Platinos-Kermetes. ℂ **22420/28-442.** Main courses 5€–16€ ($6.50–$21). No credit cards. Apr–Oct daily 10am–midnight. Located 2km (1¼ miles) south of town on the road to the Asklepion.

Olimpiada (Value) GREEK   Around the corner from the Olympic Airways office, this is one of the best values in town for simple Greek fare. The food is fresh, flavorful, and inexpensive, and the staff is remarkably courteous and friendly. The vegetable dishes, including okra in tomato sauce, are a treat.

2 Kleopatras. ℂ **22420/23-031.** Main courses 5€–15€ ($6.50–$20). MC, V. Year-round daily 11am–11pm.

Taverna Ampavris ℛ GREEK   This is undoubtedly one of the best tavernas on Kos. It's outside the bustling town center on the way to the Asklepion, down a quiet village lane. In the courtyard of this 130-year-old house, you can feast on local dishes from Kos island. The *salamura* from Kefalos is mouthwatering pork stewed with onions and coriander; the *lahano dolmades* (stuffed cabbage with rice, minced meat, and herbs) is delicate, light, and not at all oily. The *faskebab* (veal stew on rice) is tender and lean, while the vegetable dishes, such as the broad string beans cooked and served cold in garlic and olive-oil dressing, are out of this world.

Ampavris. ℂ **22420/25-696.** Main courses 5€–14€ ($6.50–$18). No credit cards. Apr–Oct daily 5:30pm–1am. Take a taxi.

Taverna Ampeli ℛ GREEK   This is as close as you come in Kos to authentic Greek home cooking. Facing the sea and ensconced in its own vineyard, Ampeli is delightful even before you taste the food. The interior is unusually tasteful, with high-beamed ceilings, and the outside setting is even better. The dolmades rate with the best in Greece. Other excellent specialties are *pliogouri* (gruel), *giouvetsi* (casserole), and *revithokefteves* (meatballs). Even the fried potatoes set a new standard. The house retsina is unusually sweet, almost like a sherry; the house white wine, made from the grapes before your eyes, is dry and light and quite pleasing—the red, however, is less memorable. If you're here on Saturday or midday on Sunday, the Easter-style goat, baked overnight in a low oven, is not to be missed.

Tzitzifies, Zipari village (8km/5 miles from Kos town). ☎ 22420/69-682. Main courses 6€–18€ ($7.80–$23). MC, V. Apr–Oct daily 10am–midnight; Nov–Mar daily 6–11pm. Closed Easter week and 10 days in early Nov. Off the beach road 1km (½ mile) east of Tingaki. Take a bus to Tingaki and walk, or take a taxi.

Taverna Nikolas *Value* GREEK/SEAFOOD   Known on the street as Nick the Fisherman's, this is one taverna in Kos that wasn't designed with tourists in mind. Off season, it's a favorite haunt for locals, with whom you'll have to compete for one of eight tables. In summer, however, seating spills freely onto the street. Although you can order anything from filet mignon to goulash, the point of coming here is the seafood. If the Aegean has it, you'll find it here: grilled octopus, shrimp in vinegar and lemon, calamari stuffed with cheese, and mussels souvlaki, for example. The menu is extensive, so come with an appetite.

21 G. Averof. ☎ 22420/23-098. Main courses 5€–13€ ($6.50–$17); fixed-price dinners 10€–16€ ($10–$21), with a seafood dinner for 2 32€ ($42). No credit cards. Year-round daily noon–midnight.

KOS AFTER DARK

Kos nightlife is no more difficult to find than your own ears. Just go down to the harbor and follow the noise. Names change but the scene remains. The **portside cafes** opposite the daily excursion boats to Kalimnos are best in the early morning. **Platanos,** across from the Hippocrates Tree, has live music, often jazz; and just across from Platanos is the beginning of **Bar Street,** which needs no further introduction. The lively **Fashion Club,** Kanari 2 Dolphins Sq., has the most impressive light-and-laser show. On Akti Zouroudi there are two popular discos, **Heaven** and **Calua,** with a swimming pool. If you want to hit the bar scene, try **Hamam Club** on Akti Kountourioti or **Beach Boys** at 57 Kanari. Another option is an old-fashioned outdoor movie theater, Kos style, at **Open Cine Orfeas,** 10 Vasileos Yioryiou. Relatively recent films, often in English, cost 6€ ($7.80).

4 Patmos ⋆

302km (187 miles) E of Piraeus

If a musician were to compose and dedicate a piece to Patmos, it might be a suite for rooster, moped, and bells (church and goat), for these are the sounds that fill the air. But just because Patmos is wonderfully unspoiled, don't imagine that it's "primitive." In fact, in recent years it has developed quite sophisticated tourist facilities and attracted a large following. The saving grace for those who come seeking a bit of quiet is that most visitors either come for a day or settle in a couple of beach resorts.

Architects sometimes speak of "charged sites," places where something so powerful happened that its memory must always be preserved. Patmos is such a place. It is where **St. John the Divine** ⋆, traditionally identified with the Apostle John, spent several years in exile, dwelling in a cave and composing the Book of Revelation, also known as the Apocalypse. From that time on, the island has been regarded as hallowed ground, re-consecrated through the centuries by the erection of more than 300 churches, one for every 10 residents.

Neither the people of Patmos nor their visitors are expected to spend their days in prayer, but the Patmians expect—and deserve—a heavy dose of respect for their traditions. Patmos is a place for those seeking a "retreat," and by that, we do not mean a religious calling, but a more subdued, civilized alternative to major tourist destinations. Some guidebooks highlight the island's prohibitions on nude bathing and how to get around them—but if this is a priority for you, then you've stumbled onto the wrong island. Enjoy your stay on Patmos, by all means, but don't expect raucous nightlife.

ESSENTIALS

GETTING THERE   By Plane   Patmos has no airport, but it is convenient (especially by hydrofoil and catamaran in spring and summer) to three islands which do: Samos, Kos, and Leros. Rather than endure the all-but interminable ferry ride from Piraeus, fly from Athens to one of these, then hop a boat or hydrofoil the rest of the way to Patmos. Samos is your best bet: With the right schedule, you can get from the Athens airport to Patmos in 3 hours via Samos.

By Boat   Patmos, the northernmost of the Dodecanese Islands, is on the daily ferry line from Piraeus to Rhodes—confirm schedules with **Piraeus Port Authority** (© 210/417-2657 or 210/451-1310) or **Rhodes Port Authority** (© 22410/23-693 or 22410/27-695). Patmos has numerous sea links with the larger islands of the Dodecanese, as well as with the islands of the northeast Aegean. Options are limited from late fall to early spring, but Easter through September, sea connections with most of the islands of the eastern Aegean are numerous and convenient. With **Blue Star Line's** (www.bluestarferries.com) new high-speed ferries, the travel time from Piraeus has been reduced to about 7 hours.

VISITOR INFORMATION   The **tourism office** (© 22470/31-666) in the port town of Skala is directly in front of you as you disembark from your ship; it's open June through August daily from 9am to 10pm. It shares the Italianate "municipal palace" with the post office and the **tourist police** (© 22470/31-303), who take over when the tourism office is closed. The **port police** (© 22470/31-231), in the first building on your left on the main ferry pier, are very helpful for boat schedules and whatever else ails or concerns you; the building is open year-round, 24 hours a day. There is also a host of helpful information about Patmos at **www.travelpoint.gr**.

Apollon Tourist and Shipping Agency, on the harbor near the central square (© 22470/31-724; fax 22470/31-819), can book excursion boats and hydrofoils and arrange lodging in hotels, rental houses, and apartments throughout the island. It's open year-round from 8am to noon and 4 to 6pm, with extended summer hours. **Astoria Tourist and Shipping Agency** (© 22470/31-205; www.astoriatravel.gr) is also helpful. For the "do-it-yourselfer" in you, pick up a free copy of *Patmos Summertime. Warning:* The map of the island provided in that publication is not particularly accurate—as is true of many other tourist maps of Patmos.

GETTING AROUND   By Moped & Bicycle   Mopeds are definitely the vehicle of choice on the island, provided you have a proper license. At the shops that line the harbor, 1-day rentals start at around 20€ ($26) and go up to 40€ ($52). **Australis Motor Rent** (© 22470/32-723), in Skala's new port, is a first-rate shop and you can usually rent for less than a full day at a discounted rate. You can also contact **Billis**

(© **22470/32-218**) on the harbor in Skala. Bicycles are hard to come by on the island, but Theo & Georgio's has 18-speed mountain bikes for 10€ ($13) per day.

By Car Two convenient car-rental offices, both in Skala, are **Patmos Rent-a-Car,** just behind the police station (© **22470/32-203**); and **Avis,** on the new port (© **22470/33-095**). Daily rentals in high season start about 50€ ($65). The island does not have that many gas stations, so be sure you watch your gas tank gauge.

By Taxi The island's main taxi stand is on the pier in Skala Harbor, right before your eyes as you get off the boat. From anywhere on the island, you can request a taxi by calling © **22470/31-225.** As the island is quite small, it's much cheaper to hire a taxi than to rent a car.

By Bus The entire island has a single bus, whose current schedule is available at the tourist office and is posted at locations around the island. Needless to say, it provides very limited service—to Skala, Hora, Grikos, and Kambos—so it's best to use another method to get around.

ORIENTATION Patmos lies along a north-south axis; were it not for a narrow central isthmus, it would be two islands, north and south. **Skala,** the island's only town of any size, is situated near that isthmus joining the north island to the south. Above Skala looms the hilltop capital of **Hora,** comprising a mazelike medieval village and the fortified monastery of St. John the Divine. There are really only two other towns on Patmos: **Kambos** to the north and **Grikou** to the south. While Kambos is a real village of roughly 500 inhabitants, Grikou is mostly a resort, a creation of the tourist industry.

Most independent visitors to Patmos, especially first-timers, will choose to stay in Skala (Hora has no hotels) and explore the north and south from there. Patmos is genuinely addicting, an island to which visitors, Greek and foreign, return year after year. So while it makes sense on your first visit to Patmos to be centrally located, you may wish to stay elsewhere during future visits.

FAST FACTS **Commercial Bank of Greece** on the harbor and **National Bank of Greece** on the central square offer exchange services and ATMs. Both are open Monday through Thursday from 8am to 2pm and Friday from 8am to 1:30pm. You will also find an ATM where ferries and cruises dock at the main pier. For **dental or medical emergencies,** call © **22470/31-211;** for special **pharmaceutical needs,** call © **22470/31-500.** The **hospital** (© **22470/31-211**) is on the road to Hora. The **post office** on the harbor is open Monday through Friday from 8am to 1:30pm. The **tourist police** (© **22470/31-303**) are directly across from the port.

For **Internet access,** the Internet Cafe at Blue Bay (Blue Bay Hotel) is open April through October, daily from 8am to 8pm. Millennium Internet Cafe (on the lane to Horio, near the OTE office) is open year-round, daily from 9am to 10pm. A short walk down toward the new port will bring you to **Just Like Home** (© **22470/33-170**), where a load of laundry costs 15€ ($20). It's open daily until 9pm year-round,

---

⌕ Tips For Your Health

One essential you need to know about Patmos from the outset is that tap water is not for drinking. *Drink only bottled water.*

and until 10pm in July and August. Cold-water wash and rinse are available, as are hand washing and dry cleaning.

WHAT TO SEE & DO
THE TOP ATTRACTIONS

What Patmos lacks in quantity it makes up for in quality. Apart from its natural beauty and its 300-plus churches, to which we can't possibly provide a detailed guide here, there are several extraordinary sights: the **Monastery of St. John, Cave of the Apocalypse,** and medieval town of **Hora** ⚭. The latter is a labyrinthine maze of whitewashed stone homes, shops, and churches in which getting lost is the whole point.

Off season, the opening days and times for the **cave** and the **monastery** are unpredictable, as they are designed to accommodate groups of pilgrims and cruise-ship tours rather than individual visitors. Neither place is public. The cave is enclosed within a convent, and the monastery is just that. It's best to consult the tourist office or one of the travel agents listed above for the open hours on the day of your visit (the times given below are for the peak season May–Aug). To visit both places, appropriate attire is required, which means that women must wear full skirts or dresses and have covered shoulders, while men must wear long pants.

The road to Hora is well marked from Skala; but if you're walking, take the narrow lane to the left just past the central square. Once outside the town, you can mostly avoid the main road by following the uneven stone-paved donkey path, which is the traditional pilgrims' route to the sanctuaries above. And if you have taken this much trouble to get to Hora, hang around awhile—it is really quite a delightful old town with many mansions from the 17th and 18th centuries.

Cave of the Apocalypse ⚭⚭   Exiled to Patmos by the Roman emperor Domitian in A.D. 95, St. John the Divine is said to have made his home in this cave, though Patmians insist quite reasonably that he walked every inch of the small island, talking with its people. The cave is said to be the epicenter of his earth-shaking dreams, which he dictated to his disciple Prochoros and which has come down to present believers as the Book of the Apocalypse, or Revelation, the last book of the Christian Bible. The cave is now encased within a sanctuary, which is in turn encircled by a convent. A stirring brochure written by Archimandrite Koutsanellos, Superior of the Cave, provides an excellent description of the religious significance of each niche in the rocks, as well as the many icons in the cave. Other guides are available in local tourist shops. The best preparation, of course, is to bone up on the Book of Revelation.

On the road to Hora. © **22470/31-234.** Free admission. May–Aug Sun 8am–1pm and 2–6pm; Mon 8am–1:30pm; Tues–Wed 8am–1:30pm and 2–6pm; Thurs–Sat 8am–1:30pm. Otherwise, hours vary (as described above).

Monastery of St. John ⚭   Towering over Skala and, for that matter, over the south island, is the medieval Monastery of St. John, which looks far more like a fortress than a house of prayer. Built to withstand pirates, it is certainly up to the task of deterring runaway tourism. The monastery virtually controls the south island, where the mayor wears a hat but the monastic authority wears a miter. In 1088, with a hand-signed document from the Byzantine emperor Alexis I Comnenus ceding the entire island to the future monastery, Blessed Christodoulos arrived on Patmos to establish here what was to become an independent monastic state. The monastery chapel is stunning, as is the adjoining **Chapel of the Theotokos,** whose frescoes date from the 12th century. On display in the treasury is but a fraction of the monastery's exquisite Byzantine treasures—icons, vestments, rare books—which are second only to those of Mount Athos, a monastic state. One of the icons, by the way, is claimed to be by El Greco.

Hora. ✆ 22470/31-234. Free admission to monastery; 4€ ($5.20) to treasury. May–Aug Sun 8am–1pm and 2–6pm; Mon 8am–1:30pm; Tues–Wed 8am–1:30pm and 2–6pm; Thurs–Sat 8am–1:30pm. Otherwise, hours vary (as described above).

OUTDOOR PURSUITS

The principal outdoor activities on Patmos are walking and swimming. The best **beaches** are highlighted later in this chapter (see "Exploring the Island") and the best **walking trails** are the unmarked donkey paths, which crisscross the island. You won't find jet-skis or surfboards on Patmos, although limited **watersports** are available. Paddleboats and canoes can be rented and water-skiing arranged at Helen's Place on Agriolivada beach, while Elisabeth on Kampos Beach offers a variety of watersports (water-skiing, tubes, boards).

SHOPPING

Patmians are quick to lament and apologize for the fact that just about everything, from gas to toothpaste, is a bit more expensive here. Patmos doesn't even have its own drinking water, and import costs inevitably get passed along to the customer. That said, the price differences are much more evident to the locals than to tourists.

There are several excellent jewelry shops, like **Iphigenia** (✆ 22470/31-814) and **Midas** (✆ 22470/31-800), on the harbor, though **Filoxenia** (✆ 22470/31-667) and **Art Spot** (✆ 22470/32-243), both behind the main square in the direction of Hora, have more interesting contemporary designs, often influenced by ancient motifs. The Art Spot also sells ceramics and small sculptures, and is well worth seeking out. Farther down the same lane is **Parousia** (✆ 22470/32-549), the best single stop for hand-painted icons and a wide range of books on Byzantine subjects. The proprietor, Mr. Alafakis, is quite learned in the history and craft of icon painting and can tell you a great deal about the icons in his shop and the diverse traditions they represent.

The most fascinating shop on Patmos may be **Selene** (✆ 22470/31-742), directly across from the port authority office. The highly selective array of Greek handmade art and crafts here is extraordinary, from ceramics to hand-painted Russian and Greek icons to marionettes, some as tall as 1m (3 ft.). And be sure to notice Selene's structure, also a work of art. Built in 1835, it was once a storage space for sails and later a boat-building workshop. Look down at the shop's extraordinary floor made of hand-made stamped and scored bricks, quite special and traditional to Patmos.

WHERE TO STAY IN SKALA

There are no hotels, only pensions in Hora, but you will find many in Skala and elsewhere around the island. Unless you plan to visit Patmos during Greek or Christian Easter or late July through August, you should not have difficulty finding a room upon arrival, though it's always safer to book ahead. Residents offering private accommodations usually meet ferries at the harbor. If you're interested in renting a kitchenette apartment or villa, contact the **Apollon Agency** (© **22470/31-724;** fax 22470/31-819).

EXPENSIVE

Porto Scoutari ⚑ (Kids)   High on a bluff overlooking Meloï Bay, this luxury hotel is seductively gracious, with the largest rooms and pool on the island. Ground-level suites are designed with families in mind, whereas upper-level suites, with four-poster beds and bathtubs, have "honeymoon" written all over them. The decor, a blend of reproduction antiques and contemporary design, is both elegant and comfortable. Each bungalow-style studio has a kitchenette, year-round climate control, and a private balcony. The common areas—breakfast room, lounge, piano bar, and pool—are simultaneously informal and refined. This is the most ambitious "full-service" hotel on the island. If your stay on Patmos is brief, you probably wouldn't want to stay here, only because you're paying for facilities that you might not have time to use.

Scoutari, 85500 Patmos. © **22470/33-123.** Fax 22470/33-175. www.portoscoutari.com. 30 units. 250€–290€ ($325–$377) double; 340€–420€ ($442–$546) studio or suite. Rates include full breakfast buffet. Much cheaper rates for paying in advance or booking for a week. MC, V. Closed Nov–Easter. Note that this hotel overlooks, but is not in, Meloï Bay—so follow the signs to Kambos, not to Meloï Bay. It's less than 3km (2 miles) from the center of Skala. **Amenities:** Restaurant; pool; Internet and fax facilities; room service; transfers arranged; laundry and dry cleaning arranged. *In room:* A/C, TV, minibar, coffeemaker, hair dryer, safe.

MODERATE

Blue Bay Hotel ⚑   Two unique features distinguish this hotel (operated by a Greek-Australian couple): First, its stellar location on the southwest side of the harbor offers a rare fusion of convenience and quiet. Second, guests are requested not to smoke anywhere in the hotel except on the private balconies. The bedrooms are spacious, immaculate, and comfortable. Room nos. 114 and 115 share a terrace the size of a tennis court overlooking the sea. The hotel emphasizes service and gracious hospitality. The new Blue Bay Internet Cafe offers Internet access for 2€ ($2.60) per 20 minutes.

Skala, 85500 Patmos. © **22470/31-165.** www.bluebay.50g.com. 27 units. 120€ ($156) double; 170€ ($221) suite. Rates include buffet breakfast. MC, V. Closed Nov–Mar. **Amenities:** Breakfast room; bar; Internet access. *In room:* A/C.

Castelli Hotel   Guests stay in two white-stucco blocks framed with brown shutters. The large, spotless rooms have white walls, beige tile floors, fridges, and covered balconies. The common lounge and lobby areas are filled with photographs, flower-print sofas, seashells, fresh-cut flowers from the surrounding gardens, and other knickknacks of seaside life. The hotel's striking sea vista can be enjoyed from cushioned wrought-iron chairs on each room's balcony or from a pleasant covered terrace/bar. The price you pay for the view is a mildly challenging 5-minute climb from the harbor.

Skala, 85500 Patmos. © **22470/31-361**. Fax 22470/31-656. 45 units. 90€ ($117) double, year-round. Rates include breakfast. No credit cards. **Amenities:** Bar. *In room:* A/C, fridge.

Romeos Hotel

Of Skala's newer lodgings, this one, run by a Greek-American family from Virginia, is especially commodious, with a large pool and a quiet garden. The simply decorated, spotless rooms are built like semi-attached bungalows on a series of tiers, with balconies offering views across the countryside to Mount Kastelli. Large honeymoon suites, with double beds, full bathtubs, and small lounges, are available. One downside has been the unsightly lot in front of the property, though it's hardly a factor once you're inside the hotel compound.

Skala (in the back streets behind the OTE), 85500 Patmos. © **22470/31-962**. Fax 22470/31-070. romeosh@ 12net.gr. 60 units. 95€ ($124) double; 110€ ($143) suite. Rates include breakfast. MC, V. Closed Nov–Mar. **Amenities:** Pool. *In room:* A/C, minibar.

Skala Hotel

Tranquilly but conveniently situated well off the main harbor road behind a lush garden overflowing with arresting pink bougainvillea, this comfortable hotel has aged like a fine wine and become an established Skala favorite. Attractive features include a large pool with an inviting sun deck and bar, the large breakfast buffet, and personalized service. The three views to choose from are the sea, the western mountains, and the Monastery of St. John—and all are striking. If you want to stay here at Easter or in late July and August, you'll need advance reservations.

Skala, 85500 Patmos. © **22470/31-343**. Fax 22470/31-747. skalahtl@12net.gr. 78 units. 90€ ($117) double. Rates include breakfast. MC, V. Closed Nov–Mar. **Amenities:** Restaurant; 2 bars; pool; conference facilities. *In room:* A/C, TV, minibar.

INEXPENSIVE

Australis Hotel and Apartments ⓐ

On the approach, you may have misgivings regarding this hotel's location, down a less-than-charming lane off the new port area. Your doubts will vanish when you enter the hotel compound, a blooming hillside oasis. Once featured in *Garden Design* magazine, the grounds are covered with bougainvillea, fuchsias, dahlias, and roses. The pleasant communal porch, where breakfast is served, offers delightful views of the open harbor. The guest rooms are bright, tasteful, and impeccably clean (and with firm beds). Within the same compound and enjoying the same floral and sea vistas, four apartments offer spacious homes away from home for families or groups of four to six people; these are fully equipped with kitchenettes, TVs, and heat for the winter months. In addition to these apartments, the Fokas family has three handsome studios over a house on the old road to Hora; each has a well-stocked kitchen and goes for 40€ to 65€ ($52–$78) per day.

Skala (a 5-min. walk from the center), 85500 Patmos. © **22470/32-562**. Fax 22470/32-284. 29 units. 75€ ($98) double; 165€ ($215) apt, depending on size and season. Rates include breakfast. No credit cards. Closed Nov–Mar. *In room:* TV, fridge in some.

Villa Knossos

This small white villa off the new port is set within an abundant garden of palms, purple and pink bougainvillea, potted geraniums, and hibiscus. The tasteful, spacious guest rooms have high ceilings (making them cool even in the summer's heat). All rooms have their own fridges, and all but one have private balconies. The two units facing the back garden are the most quiet, while room no. 7 in front has a private veranda. Guests can use a comfortable sitting room.

Skala, 85500 Patmos. © **22470/32-189**. Fax 22470/32-284. 7 units. 50€–75€ ($65–$98) double. No credit cards. Closed Nov–Mar. *In room:* Fridge.

WHERE TO DINE IN SKALA & HORA

The culinary scene in Skala and Hora may not have any true standout restaurants, but there are many that will not disappoint. In Hora, on the path to the Monastery of St. John, you'll find **Pirgos; Balkoni** (with grand view of Skala Harbor); **Patmian House;** and (following signs from the monastery) **Vagelis** in the central square (Vagelis enjoys views of the south island). Two favorites in Skala are recommended (below) but you will want to browse for yourself. Alternatively, venture out to the north and south islands, which serve up some of Patmos's most enticing food. In particular, the restaurant at the Petra Hotel and Apartments (see "Exploring the Island," below) stands out.

Grigoris Grill GREEK   One of Skala's better-known eateries, this place was formerly the center of Patmian chic. Any of the grilled fish or meat dishes are recommended, particularly in the slow season, when more time and attention are lavished on the preparation. Well-cooked veal cutlets, tender lamb chops, and the swordfish souvlaki are favorites. Grigoris also offers several vegetarian specials. Both curbside seating and a more removed and quiet roof garden are available.

Opposite Skala car ferry pier. ℂ 22470/31-515. Main courses 6€–14€ ($7.80–$18). No credit cards. Easter–June and Sept–Oct 6pm–midnight; July–Aug 11am–midnight.

Pantelis Restaurant GREEK   Pantelis is a proven local favorite for no-frills Greek home cooking. The food here is consistently fresh and wholesome—the basics prepared so well that they surprise you. Daily specials augment the standard menu. Portions are generous, so pace yourself; and if you're not yet a convert to the Greek cult of olive oil, order something grilled. The lightly fried calamari, chickpea soup, swordfish kabob, and roasted lamb met all expectations. In winter, the spacious dining hall with high ceilings makes this a relatively benign environment for nonsmokers.

Skala (1 lane back from the port). ℂ 22470/31-922. Main courses 5€–17€ ($6.50–$22). No credit cards. Year-round daily 11am–11pm.

Vegghera Restaurant ⭐⭐ GREEK/MEDITERRANEAN   Vegghera has become the premier restaurant of Skala and deserves this status for its food, service, and ambience. Located in a handsome mansion overlooking the marina where yachts from distant ports dock, Vegghera carries this international flavor into its menu. George Grillis, proprietor and chef, combines traditional Greek fare with French-influenced Mediterranean cuisine such as salmon smoked with rose sticks or lobster with tagliatelle. Not unexpectedly, its specialties feature seafood from various parts, but the vegetables, pork, and rabbit are all raised by Grillis himself. The wine list is equally selective and desserts are to die for. It's not cheap, but once in a while, when you've come this far, you should just splurge. And you get a choice of eating on the shaded terrace or inside.

Nea Marina, Skala. ℂ 22470/32-988. Main courses 9€–30€ ($12–$39). MC, V. Easter–Oct daily 7:30pm–1am.

PATMOS AFTER DARK

The nightlife scene on Patmos, while not ecclesiastical, is a bit subdued compared to some Greek islands. Clubs tend to open for a few weeks in season, then close like flowers. In Hora at Plateia Agia Lesvias, there's **Kafe 1673,** locally known as **Astivi,** where you can dance to whatever the DJ spins. In Skala, a sturdy standby—never fully "in" and never fully "out"—that survives each year's fads is **Consolato Music Club,** to the left of the quay. Skala also has the **Kahlua Club,** at the far end of the new port; and

Sui Generis, behind the police station. Others recommended by visitors are **Pyrgos Bar, Kafe Aman, Café Arion, Isalos,** and **Celine.** On a more traditional note, **Aloni Restaurant** in Hora offers Greek music and dance performances in traditional costume a few nights each week in summer. Most clubs charge a modest admission and tend to stay open into the early hours of the morning. And for those who do come for a more "ecclesiastical" experience, Patmost hosts an annual **Festival of Religious Music** in early September, featuring music from the Balkans, Russia, and Turkey as well as Greece.

EXPLORING THE ISLAND

Apart from the seductive contours of the Patmian landscape, the myriad seascapes, and the seemingly countless churches, the **beaches** of Patmos draw most visitors beyond the island's core. Don't be tempted to think of the strand between the old and new ports in Skala as a beach. It's better and safer to take a shower in your bathroom. Most beaches have tavernas on or near them, as well as rooms to rent by the day or week. They're too numerous and similar to list here.

THE NORTH ISLAND

The nicest beaches in the north lie along the northeastern coastline from Lambi Bay to Meloï Bay. The northwestern coastline from Merika Bay to Lambi is too rocky, inaccessible, and exposed. The most desirable northern beaches are in the following bays (proceeding up the coast from south to north): **Meloï, Agriolivada,** and **Lambi.** Meloï has some shade and good snorkeling. **Kambos Bay** is particularly suitable for children and families, offering calm, shallow waters, rental umbrellas, and some tree cover, as well as a lively seaside scene with opportunities for windsurfing, paragliding, sailing, and canoeing. East of Kambos Bay at Livada, it's possible to swim or sometimes to walk across to **Ayiou Yioryiou Isle;** be sure to bring shoes or sandals, or the rocks will do a number on your feet. The stretch of shoreline from **Thermia to Lambi** is gorgeous, with crystalline waters and rocks from which you can safely dive. The drawback here is that access is only by caique from Skala. Also, avoid the north coast when the *meltemi* (severe north summer winds) are blowing.

Where to Stay & Dine

Aspri GREEK   Poised on a north island headland just minutes by taxi from Skala, this dramatically situated restaurant enjoys splendid views of Meloï Bay, Aspris Bay, and Skala and Hora from its multiple terraces. In addition to the standard taverna fare offered throughout the islands, which Aspris prepares with great skill, the menu has unusual, enticing items such as cuttlefish with Patmian rice. The portions are generous and attention is paid to presentation in this quite stylish and widely recommended spot.

Geranos Cape. ✆ **22470/32-240.** Main courses 6€–20€ ($7.80–$26). MC, V. June–Sept daily 7pm–midnight.

Patmos Paradise   Perched high above Kambos Bay, this is one of several upscale hotels on the island. The rooms are spacious and inviting, with private balconies that enjoy spectacular sea vistas, in some cases broken by a power line. This unpretentious place is exceptionally pleasant and quite chic. Down below, Kambos Bay has a modest strand, a handful of shops and tavernas, and rental outlets for windsurfing boards, paddleboats, and canoes. A hotel minibus transports you to and from Skala Harbor when you arrive at or depart from Patmos. Highly recommended if you want to stay close to Skala!

Kambos Bay, 85500 Patmos. (✆) **22470/32-590.** www.patmosparadise.com. 37 units. 150€–170€ ($195–$221) double; 165€–275€ ($215–$358) suites. Rates include breakfast. MC, V. Closed Nov–Eastger. **Amenities:** Restaurant, 2 bars, large saltwater terrace pool; outdoor tennis and indoor squash courts; sauna. *In room:* A/C, TV, minibar.

Taverna Leonida (✿) GREEK   At least one Patmian in the know claims "the best saganaki in the world" is served here. A taxi driver went further, calling this the "number-one taverna" as he dropped off his passengers on Leonida's pebble beach. The restaurant enjoys a dramatic location; at high tide it's just a few yards from the clear water of Lambi Bay. If the wind is high, the waves come pounding in. The drama continues with the arrival of your flaming *saganaki* (grilled cheese). Your next course should be the fresh catch of the day. But you can also order a steak, and there is a good selection of the standard Greek dishes.

Lambi Bay. (✆) **22470/31-490.** Main courses 6€–14€ ($7.80–$18). No credit cards. Easter–Oct daily noon–11pm.

Taverna Panagos & Sarandin GREEK   Eating here is an experience that goes beyond merely consuming food. Just above Kambos Bay sits the sleepy village of Kambos; and squarely on its pulse, directly across from the village church, sits the cafe-estiatorion-taverna Panagos. In this local hangout for everyone from children to cats to timeless, bent figures in black, the sea vistas are replaced by myriad glimpses into Patmian village life. The food is the same fare villagers eat at home, and the origins of the succulent daily specials are visible on the nearby hillsides: capons in wine, kid in tomato sauce, lamb in lemon sauce, Patmian goat cheese.

Kambos. (✆) **22470/31-570.** Main courses 6€–28€ ($7.80–$36). No credit cards. Year-round daily noon–midnight.

THE SOUTH ISLAND

The island's south end has two beaches, one at **Grikou Bay** and the other at **Psili Ammos.** Grikou Bay, only 4km (2½ miles) from Skala, is the most developed resort on Patmos and home to most of the package-tour groups on the island. Psili Ammos is another story, an extraordinary isolated fine-sand cove bordered by cliffs. Most people arrive by one of the caiques leaving Skala Harbor at 10am, and on arrival (at 10:45am) do battle for the very limited shade offered by some obliging tamarisks. The only way to ensure yourself of a place in the shade is to arrive before 10:30am; the best way to do that is to take a taxi to Diakofti for 15€ ($20) and ask the driver to point the way to Psili Ammos, which is about a 30-minute trek on goat paths (wear real shoes). The caiques returning to Skala leave Psili Ammos around 4 to 5pm. At any given time, a range of caiques provide this service. Round-trip fare is about 15€ ($20) and 10€ ($13) one-way.

Another reason to head south is to dine at Benetos, only a short taxi ride from Skala and known as the finest restaurant on the island.

Where to Stay & Dine

Benetos Restaurant (✿) MEDITERRANEAN   For fashionable, non-pretentious, fine dining on Patmos, this Tuscan villa at the sea's edge is the place. Where else could you find light jazz filling the air, a fresh arugula salad with shaved Parmesan, shrimp baked in filo, and filet mignon, all accompanied by an exclusively Greek wine list? Nowhere but Benetos, where the owners, Benetos and his American wife Susan Matthaiou, have made it their goal to give Greeks and their visitors "a night out" from what they will find anywhere else on these islands. Their winning recipe begins with the freshest and finest local ingredients, mostly from their own organic garden and from nearby waters. The regular menu strikes primarily Greek notes with its appetizers, and the occasional Asian note with its entrees; daily specials reflect the best fresh materials available. With only 12 tables on offer, you must reserve yours several days in advance during high season.

Sapsila. *©* **22470/33-089.** Reservations necessary in high season. Main courses 7€–20€ ($9–$26). No credit cards. June–Sept Tues–Sun 7:30pm–1am.

Joanna Hotel-Apartments   These comfortable, relatively spacious, and fully equipped apartments are just a few minutes on foot from the beach. Each has a balcony. Rooms with air-conditioning cost extra. The layout and feel of the one-bedroom apartments is better than that of the two-bedroom apartments, which have very limited kitchen space. Room no. 15 has a large private deck with a sea view, but it is usually reserved for friends, clients, and guests staying 2 to 3 weeks—still, there's no harm in asking. A special feature is the attractive air-conditioned lounge with satellite TV and bar.

Grikos, 85500 Patmos. *©* **22470/31-031.** Fax 22470/32-031 or 210/981-2246 in Athens. 17 units. 65€–85€ ($85–$111) apt for 2 persons. Full hot breakfast 7€ ($9.10) extra. V. Closed mid-Oct–Easter. **Amenities:** Bar. *In room:* A/C (5€/$6.50 per day), fan, kitchenette, fridge.

Petra Hotel and Apartments *☆* *Kids*   Petra Hotel, true to its name, has long been a rock-solid sure thing. Since completing renovations in 2002, it has bolstered its position as one of the finest boutique hotels in Greece. The Stergiou family lavishes care on their stylish, spacious apartments. These one-and two-bedroom apartments come with handsome bathrooms. All except one unit have balconies that enjoy splendid views of Grikos Bay. Each is simply and handsomely decorated, with the necessities of home plus local touches. It's a perfect family place, just a 2-minute walk from the beach. It's also ideal for couples, who can enjoy a drink on Petra's elegant, romantic main veranda. The Stergious provide an intimate dining experience as well, with a menu that includes both Greek standards and gourmet offerings. Advance reservations are advised, especially in August.

Grikos, 85500 Patmos. *©* **22470/34-020.** Fax 22470/32-567. Off season *©*/fax **210/806-2697** Athens. www.petra hotel.gr. 13 units. 155€–185€ ($202–$241) doubles; 250€–320€ ($325–$416) suites for 2–4 persons. Rates include breakfast. AE, MC, V. Closed Oct–May. **Amenities:** Room service 8am–1am. *In room:* A/C, TV, Internet connection, kitchenette, fridge.

Stamatis Restaurant GREEK   Stamatis, serving consistently reliable taverna fare since 1965, is a landmark in Grikou. On its covered terrace practically at water's edge, diners enjoy drinks and consume prodigious amounts of fresh mullet while watching yachts and windsurfers. This is a pleasant spot at which the evening can unwind while you savor delicious island dishes.

Grikos beach. *©* **22470/31-302.** Main courses 5€–15€ ($6.50–$20). No credit cards. Easter–Oct daily 10am–11pm.

12

Central Greece

by Sherry Marker

Central Greece (Sterea Ellada) is best known as the home of Delphi, the famous ancient oracle and spectacular sanctuary that is one of Greece's "must see" destinations. Delphi has it all: a gravity-defying cliff-side location with the remains of treasuries, small temples, a stadium, and a theater—not to mention the massive temple of Apollo and a view over a plain of gnarled olive trees to the Gulf of Corinth. The star of the Delphi museum is the famous bronze statue of the charioteer who raced his horses to victory in Delphi's stadium. North of Delphi, in the dusty plain of Thessaly, improbable cliffs dominate the landscape. For a thousand years, pilgrims and tourists have tried to figure out just how monks built the vertiginous monasteries of the Meteora atop these seemingly unscalable cliffs. Yet farther north loom the snow-topped peaks of Mount Olympus, once home to Zeus and the other Olympian gods, today a destination for mountain climbers, hikers, and nature lovers. Central Greece is also home to two of Greece's most famous and bloody ancient battle sites—Thermopylae and Chaironeia—and one of its legendary beauty spots—the Vale of Tempe.

If you are a lover of vibrant nightlife, you may find that evenings in the neighborhood of the monasteries and ancient sanctuaries can be a bit tame. That said, the mountain village of Arakova, 10km (6 miles) from Delphi, has a lively (and very chic) après ski scene in winter.

Despite its famous sights and monuments, Central Greece is not as easy as some other sections of Greece to define: The Peloponnese, for example, is separated from the rest of the mainland by the narrow Isthmus of Corinth. Still, most Greeks would agree that Central Greece stretches from the Gulf of Corinth in the south to Mount Olympus in the north. As for the name itself, the term Central Greece (Sterea Ellada) dates from only 1821, when it was used as a shorthand term for the area of mainland Greece that had been liberated from the Turks.

If you're setting out from Athens, take the National Road toward Corinth and then the Thebes turnoff to Osios Loukas and Delphi; try to spend 2 nights in Delphi. Then, head north via Lamia to the Meteora for another night or two, before spending a night on or near Mount Olympos.

Tip: If you approach Delphi by car along the northern shore of the Gulf of Corinth, take a lunch-and-swim break at the miniature port of Galaxidi (35km/22 miles southwest of Delphi), but try not to do this on a weekend, when Galaxidi is taken over by excursion-loving Athenians.

Galaxidi is studded with the homes of 19th-century ship captains and seafarers, some of which are now restaurants, cafes, and small hotels on the narrow streets around the harbor. If you're tempted to stay the night, the eight-unit Hotel Ganimede, itself in a 19th-century sea captain's house, has a nice garden and comfortable rooms (© 22650/41-328; www.gsp.gr) from around 70€ ($91).

Central Greece

Delphi,
Site and Museum **4**

The Meteora
Monasteries of
Ayia Triada,
Ayios Nikolaos
Anapaphsas,
Ayiou Stefanou,
The Great Meteoron,
Roussanou,
and Varlaam **1**

Monastery of
Osios Loukas **5**

Mount Olympus **3**

The Vale of Tempe
and Ambelakia **2**

> ⌐ **Tips** **Museum Hours Update**
>
> If you visit Greece during the summer, check to see when sites and museums are open. According to the tourist office, they should be open from 8am to 7:30pm, but some may close earlier in the day or even be closed 1 day a week.

1 Delphi ⟨★⟩⟨★⟩⟨★⟩

178km (110 miles) NW of Athens

Delphi is the big enchilada of Greek sites. Even more than Olympia, this place has everything: a long and glorious history, spectacular ancient remains, a superb museum, and a heartbreakingly beautiful location on the slopes of Mount Parnassus. Look up and you see the cliffs and crags of Parnassus; look down, and Greece's most beautiful plain of olive trees stretches as far as your eyes can see, toward the town of Itea on the Gulf of Corinth.

Delphi is especially magical in the spring, when there are both snow and wildflowers on Parnassus—and relatively few tourists tramping around the site. But whenever you visit, you'll understand why the ancient Greeks believed that Delphi was the center of the world, the spot Apollo chose as the home of his most famous oracle.

As for the modern village of Delphi, the main drag is usually clogged with herds of tour groups migrating from hotel to restaurant to the generally indifferent souvenir shops; it's the side streets, clinging to the slopes of Parnassus, that give a sense of village life.

A LOOK AT THE PAST   Pilgrims came to Delphi from throughout the Greek world—and much of the non-Greek world—to ask Apollo's advice on affairs of state as well as small, personal matters. Unfortunately, the god's words were famously hard to interpret. "Invade and you will destroy a great empire," the oracle told Lydian King Croesus when he asked whether he should go to war with his Persian neighbors. Croesus invaded and destroyed a great empire: his own.

Delphi was also the site of the Pythian Games, the most famous festival in Greece after the Olympics. The Games commemorated Apollo's triumph over his oracular predecessor here, the snaky Python. Because Apollo was the god of music, the Pythian Games had more artistic contests than the Olympic Games. When you sit in the theater, you can imagine the flute and lyre contests and the dances and plays staged every 4 years throughout antiquity to honor Apollo.

Like so many ancient sites, Apollo's sanctuary at Delphi was first neglected, and then virtually forgotten during the Christian era. Kings and generals looted Delphi of its treasures; later, locals hacked up the buildings and used the blocks to build their own houses. The modern village of Delphi sat atop the ancient site until the 19th century, when the village was relocated down the road so that archaeologists could help ancient Delphi reclaim its past.

ESSENTIALS

GETTING THERE   By Bus   There are usually five buses daily to Delphi from the Athens bus station at 260 Liossion (© **210/831-7096** or 210/831-7179 in Athens, or 22650/82-317 in Delphi).

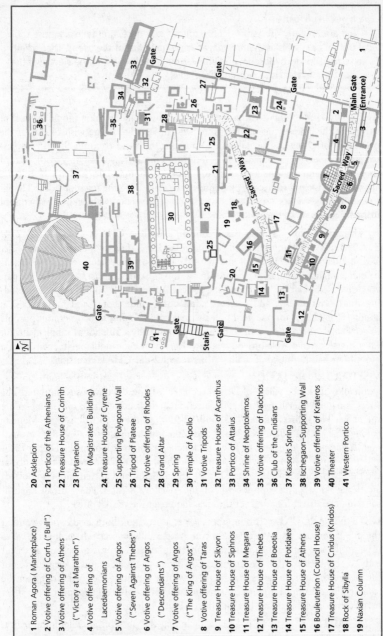

1 Roman Agora (Marketplace)
2 Votive offering of Corfu ("Bull")
3 Votive offering of Athens
  ("Victory at Marathon")
4 Votive offering of
  Lacedaemonians
5 Votive offering of Argos
  ("Seven Against Thebes")
6 Votive offering of Argos
  ("Descendants")
7 Votive offering of Argos
  ("The King of Argos")
8 Votive offering of Taras
9 Treasure House of Sikyon
10 Treasure House of Siphnos
11 Treasure House of Megara
12 Treasure House of Thebes
13 Treasure House of Boeotia
14 Treasure House of Potidaea
15 Treasure House of Athens
16 Bouleuterion (Council House)
17 Treasure House of Cnidus (Knidos)
18 Rock of Sibylla
19 Naxian Column

20 Asklepion
21 Portico of the Athenians
22 Treasure House of Corinth
23 Prytaneion
   (Magistrates' Building)
24 Treasure House of Cyrene
25 Supporting Polygonal Wall
26 Tripod of Plateae
27 Votive offering of Rhodes
28 Grand Altar
29 Spring
30 Temple of Apollo
31 Votive Tripods
32 Treasure House of Acanthus
33 Portico of Attalus
34 Shrine of Neoptolemos
35 Votive offering of Daochos
36 Club of the Cnidians
37 Kassotis Spring
38 Ischegaon–Supporting Wall
39 Votive offering of Krateros
40 Theater
41 Western Portico

A Special Moment

If you are an early riser, sniff deeply, follow your nose, and take a sunrise tour of Delphi's bakeries as the first loaves are coming out of the ovens. Then, climb up to the Sikelanos Museum and enjoy some fresh bread and the view over the ancient site in the early morning light. Bliss.

By Car   Take the Athens-Corinth National Highway about 74km (46 miles) west of Athens to the Thebes turnoff. Continue west to Levadia. If you wish to stop at the monastery of Osios Loukas, take the Distomo turnoff and continue 9km (5½ miles) to Osios Loukas (be prepared to meet tour buses thundering along this road). Return to Distomo and continue via Arachova 26km (16 miles) to Delphi. If you are approaching Delphi from the Peloponnese, the drive from the town of Itea to Delphi (65km/40 miles) takes a spectacular winding road that climbs higher and higher until it finally comes to Delphi.

By Organized Tour   Athens-based companies such as **CHAT,** 4 Stadiou (✆ 210/322-3137; www.chatours.gr) and **Key** (✆ 210/923-3166; www.keytours.com) offer 1- and 2-day trips to Delphi. If possible, take the 2-day trip. Most tours leave Athens by 8am and arrive at Delphi by 3pm after a stop at Osios Loukas. On the second day, you leave Delphi around 3pm, arriving back in Athens about 7pm. The price (including transportation, site and museum admissions, guide, hotel, and most meals) is about 150€ ($195) for one person in a shared double room; sometimes, it is possible to get a single room at the same rate, but there is usually a 50€ ($65) supplement. An exceptionally well-traveled friend who was leery of the inevitable regimentation of a group tour had nothing but praise for her recent 2-day CHAT excursion.

VISITOR INFORMATION   Most services, such as the post office, tourist office, and banks, are in the village of Delphi (pop. 2,500), on the obvious main street. The street is named after King Paul and Queen Frederika, although no one seems to use the name. The **tourist office** (✆ 22650/82-900), in the town hall, is open Monday through Friday from 8am to 2:30pm, and sometimes reopens from 6 to 8pm in summer. If you are here in June or July, check here for information on the Delphi Festival of ancient Greek drama. Performances are held either in the ancient theater or at the European Cultural Center of Delphi. The museum and ancient site (signposted) are about 1km (½ mile) out of town, on the Arachova Road. If you want an English-speaking taxi driver for a tour of the area, inquire at the tourist office.

GETTING AROUND   Parking spots are at a premium both in the village and at the site. If you can, park your car near your hotel and walk everywhere. If you have to drive to the site rather than walk the 5 to 10 minutes from town, be sure to set off early to get one of the few parking places. Whether you walk or drive, keep an eye out for the enormous tour buses that barrel down the center of the road. Traffic on the lower main street heads toward the site and Arachova; traffic on the upper main street heads out of Delphi toward Itea and the Gulf of Corinth.

FAST FACTS   Everything you need, including the **post office, telephone office,** and several banks with **ATM**s, including the **National Bank of Greece,** is on the main street. The **police** (✆ 22650/82-222) are in the town hall. For **first aid,** call ✆ 22650/82-307. In addition to normal weekday hours (Mon–Fri 8am–2pm), the post office and OTE are sometimes open Sunday from 9am to 1pm in summer.

WHAT TO SEE & DO

There's little in the modern village to tempt you away from the site, but stopping at the museum first can help you put flesh on the bones of the sanctuary's remains. After all, in antiquity Apollo's sanctuary was something of an unofficial outdoor museum, crammed with goodies from around the world. As at Olympia, begin your visit here as early as possible and hold onto your 9€ ($12) ticket; it's good for admission to both the museum and the site. *Tip:* Both site and museum can be relatively uncrowded an hour before closing time or during the midday lunch break.

The Angelos and Eva Sikelianos Museum   The road that leads steeply uphill through the village of Delphi ends at the handsome stone-and-brick Sikelianos home, now a museum commemorating the work of the eccentric Greek poet Sikelianos and his equally eccentric American wife, Eva Palmer. The couple's attempts to revive the Pythian Games were not long-lived, but their staging of Greek tragedies in Delphi's theater in the 1930s had lasting effects, as all who have seen plays performed here or at the theater at Epidaurus know. Few tourists visit this elegant home, which has spectacular views from most windows, a fine collection of Sikelianos-designed costumes, and the nicest bathroom in town. A pleasant place to spend an hour.

(C) **22650/82-173.** Fax 22650/82-722. epkdelfi@otenet.gr. Admission 2€ ($2.60). Wed–Mon 8:30am–3pm.

The Delphi Museum 𝒜𝒜𝒜   Almost everyone who was anyone in the ancient world sent gifts to Delphi. The remains of those dedications and of the sculpture that adorned the splendid buildings are some of the finest works that survive from classical antiquity. The star of the museum, with much of a room to himself, is the famous 5th-century-B.C. **Charioteer of Delphi,** a larger-than-life bronze figure that was originally part of a group that included a four-horse chariot. The wealthy Sicilian city of Gela dedicated this near-monumental work to honor its tyrant Polyzalos and his chariot victory here. It's an irresistible statue: Don't miss the handsome youth's delicate eyelashes shading wide enamel-and-stone eyes, or the realistic veins that stand out in his hands and feet. The graceful charioteer makes earlier statues on view here, such as the *kouroi* (monumental youths) Kleobis and Biton, look like stolid muscle-bound hulks. That's not far from the truth: According to Herodotus, the lads pulled their mother's cart to the Temple of Hera after the oxen fell ill. As they reached the temple, the boys collapsed—earning both good deaths and immortal fame.

Although the charioteer is the star of the collection, he's in good company here. Wealthy patron King Croesus of Lydia contributed the massive **silver-plated bull,** flanked by delicate gold and ivory dedications. Each of the museum's rooms has a specific focus, such as sculpture from the elegant **Siphnian** and **Athenian treasuries;** pedimental sculpture from the **Temple of Apollo;** works from the Roman period (including a marble sculpture of the Epicene youth **Antinous,** the beloved of the emperor Hadrian); and a rich array of bronze dedications.

Tips **The Delphi Tram**

Be sure to hop on the free new tram that leaves from the Hotel Vouzas and gives 30-minute rides around the village of Delphi nightly from about 8 to 11pm in the summer and on some off-season weekends.

Eggs and Eagles

At the museum, don't miss the 4th-century-B.C. **marble egg,** a copy of the yet older *omphalos* (egg) that symbolized Delphi's unique position as the center (or navel) of the world. According to legend, when Zeus wanted to determine the earth's center, he released two eagles from Olympus. When the eagles met over Delphi, Zeus had his answer. It's easy to see why the ancient Greeks thought that Delphi, straddling a cleft in the rocky slopes of the majestic Parnassus mountain range and looking out over the Corinthian Gulf, was so spectacular that it must be the center of the universe. You may still see eagles in the sky above Delphi, but more often than not, the large birds overhead are the less-distinguished Egyptian vultures.

You could spend hours here, but allow yourself at least 1 hour. If you need a break, a cafe and gift shop is located just outside the museum.

Delphi. ✆ **22650/82-312.** Admission 9€ ($12) includes admission to site. Museum only, 6€ ($7.80). Summer Mon 11am–7pm, Tues–Fri 8am–7pm, Sat–Sun and holidays 8am–3pm; winter daily 9:30am–3pm. (Be sure to check these hours when you arrive in Delphi, as they can change without warning.)

The Sanctuary of Apollo ★★★   The Sanctuary of Apollo is immediately beyond and just above the museum. The less-well-known Sanctuary of Athena on the lower slopes of Parnassus is a 10-minute walk past the museum. The Castalian Spring is between the two sanctuaries. If you can't visit everything, spend your time at the Sanctuary of Apollo, stroll to the Castalian Spring, and then cross the Delphi-Arachova Road to take a peek down at the Sanctuary of Athena. When you see hatless visitors in sling-back sandals huffing and puffing here, you'll be glad to have good shoes, a sun hat, and a bottle of water.

As you enter the Sanctuary of Apollo, you'll be on the marble **Sacred Way,** walked by visitors for thousands of years. The road runs uphill past the remains of **Roman stoas** and a number of **Greek treasuries,** including the restored **Athenian treasury.** Cities built these small, temple-like buildings at Delphi for several reasons: to impress their neighbors and to store riches and works of art dedicated to Apollo. Take a close look at the **treasury walls:** You'll see countless inscriptions. The Greeks were never shy about using the walls of their buildings as bulletin boards.

So many recent visitors were bent on adding their names to the ancient inscriptions that the Greek archaeological service no longer allows visitors inside the massive 4th-century-B.C. **Temple of Apollo,** which was built after the 7th- and 6th-century-B.C. temples were destroyed. In antiquity, one of the three Pythian priestesses on duty gave voice to Apollo's oracles from a room deep within the temple. That much is known, although the details of what precisely happened here are obscure. Did the priestess sit on a tripod balanced over a chasm, breathing in the hallucinatory fumes that may well have escaped from fissures in the rocks the temple rested on? Did she chew various herbs, including the laurel leaf sacred to Apollo, until she spoke in tongues, while priests interpreted her sayings? Perhaps wisely, the oracle has kept its secrets.

From the temple, it's a fairly steep uphill climb to the remarkably well-preserved 4th-century-B.C. **theater** and the **stadium,** which was extensively remodeled by the Romans. Events in the Pythian festival took place in both stadium and theater. In 1927, the Greek poet Angelos Sikelianos and his wife attempted to revive the ancient contests (see the Sikelianos Museum, above). Today, the theater and stadium are used most summers for the **Festival of Delphi** which has, on occasion, featured exceptionally nonclassical pop music.

Keep your ticket as you leave the Sanctuary of Apollo and head along the Arakova-Delphi road toward the Sanctuary of Athena (also called the Marmaria, which refers to all the marble found here). En route, you'll pass the famous **Castalian Spring,** where Apollo planted a laurel he brought from the Vale of Tempe. Drinking from the spring inspired legions of poets in antiquity; now, poets have to find their inspiration elsewhere, as the spring is off-limits, purportedly to allow repairs to the Roman fountain facade. (Once an antiquity is closed in Greece, it often stays closed quite a while.) Above are the rose-colored cliffs known as the **Phaedriades (Bright Ones),** famous for their reflection of the sun's rays.

North of the Castalian Spring, a path descends from the main road to the **Sanctuary of Athena,** the goddess of wisdom who shared the honors at Delphi with Apollo. Because the remains here are quite fragmentary, except for the 4th-century-B.C. **gymnasium,** you might want to wander about and enjoy the picturesque ruins without trying too hard to figure out what's what. The round 4th-century **tholos** with its three graceful Doric columns is easy to spot, though no one knows why it was built, why it was so lavishly decorated, or what went on inside. You can easily spend all day at Delphi; at the least, allow 3 hours and try to give yourself time to sit in a bit of shade and take in the view.

Sanctuary of Apollo, Castalian Spring, and Sanctuary of Athena Pronaia. ℂ **22650/82-313.** Admission 9€ ($12) includes site. Site only, 6€ ($7.80). Summer Mon 8am–7pm, Tues–Fri 8am–7pm, Sat–Sun and holidays 8am–3pm; winter daily 9:30am–3pm. (Check hours as soon as you arrive at Delphi, as they can change without warning.)

WHERE TO STAY

Delphi has no shortage of lodgings; you can usually find rooms even in July or August. When tourists are few, you may be able to improve on the rates below. Still, if you want to be sure that you get a room in a specific price category (or with a view or a pool), it's best to make a reservation in high season. With the growing popularity of skiing Parnassus, fewer and fewer of Delphi's hotels close for part of the winter, but summer is still high season here.

In addition to the following options, we've had good reports of **Apollo Hotel,** 59b Frederikis (ℂ **22650/82-244;** fax 22860/82-455), and its sister hotel, **Villa Filoxenia-Apollo** (ℂ **22650/83-114;** fax 22650/82-455); **Hermes Hotel,** 29 Vasileos Pavlou and Frederikis (ℂ **22650/82-318;** fax 22650/82-639); **Pan Hotel,** 53 Vasileos Pavlou and Frederikis (ℂ **22650/82-294**), and its annex, the **Artemis,** 53a Vasileos Pavlou and Frederikis (ℂ **22650/82-793;** fax 22650/82-780). The little **Odysseus Pension,** 1 Isea (ℂ 22650/82-235) has a garden and is a good budget choice (most rooms with shared bathroom).

The Festival of Delphi

Each summer (usually in June), the European Cultural Center of Delphi sponsors a festival featuring ancient Greek drama and works inspired by ancient drama. Tickets and schedules are usually available at the center's Athens office at 9 Frynihou, Plaka (ℂ **210/331-2781**), and at the center's Delphi office (ℂ **22650/82-731** to -732), just out of town set back from the Itea road in a grove of trees.

Tip: If you want a main street room with a view, be sure to ask for a back room with a balcony that faces the Gulf of Corinth. You may not always see the water, but from your balcony you will almost always see the magnificent valley of olive trees that leads down to the Gulf—and avoid the traffic noise of the main street.

Amalia Hotel ★ *Kids* The Pros: Like most of the Amalia chain hotels, the Delphi Amalia has good-size rooms with balconies and is outside town in a quiet location. If you are traveling with children, you may find the Amalia's garden and pool irresistible. The Cons: Most guest rooms are rather anonymous and the Amalia does most of its business with tour groups, many of whose members seem to find it impossible to resist shouting greetings from balcony to balcony.

Signposted on the Delphi-Itea road, 33054 Delphi. ℂ **22650/82-101.** Fax 22650/82-290. www.amalia.gr. 185 units. 200€ ($260) double. Rates include breakfast. AE, MC, V. **Amenities:** Restaurant; bar; pool; room service 7am–midnight. *In room:* A/C, TV, minibar, hair dryer.

Hotel Acropole ★★ *Value* The 42-room Hotel Acropole was completely redecorated in 2007, stays open year-round, and is owned and managed by the very helpful Kourelis family. One street below Vasileos Pavlou and Frederikis, the Acropole has one of the quietest locations and best views in town over private houses, gardens, and the olive groves that stretch beneath Delphi to the sea. If the Acropole is full, the staff can usually find you a room at their other Delphi hotel, the Parnassos. The Parnassos does not have the great view, but is less expensive (70€/$91), with a 10% discount usually available to Frommer's readers. Guests at both hotels have free use of the Internet cafe at the Parnassos.

13 Filellinon St., 33054 Delphi. ℂ **22650/82-675.** www.delphi.com.gr. 42 units. 80€ ($104) double. Rates include breakfast. Inquire about Frommer's discount. AE, MC, V. **Amenities:** Breakfast room; lounge w/fireplace. *In room:* A/C, TV, Internet.

Hotel Varonos ★ This small, family-owned hotel has minimalist (bed, table, chair) guest rooms with fine views over the olive plain. The family is very welcoming: We once arrived with an ailing gardenia plant, and the entire family pitched in to make sure it was well taken care of.

25 Vasileos Pavlou and Frederikis, 33054 Delphi. ℂ/fax **22650/82-345.** 11 units, 10 with shower, 1 with tub/shower. 80€–100€ ($104–$130) double. Rates include breakfast (room without breakfast sometimes possible). Inquire about a Frommer's 20% discount. MC, V. **Amenities:** Breakfast room; lounge w/fireplace. *In room:* A/C, TV.

Hotel Vouzas ★★ If you don't mind sacrificing the swimming pool at the Amalia, this is *the* place to stay—great location only a short walk from everything you're here to see and spectacular views from rear room balconies. The guest rooms and bathrooms are quite comfortable. Each unit has a balcony with table and chairs (and, in season, a welcoming pot of basil).

1 Frederikis (at Vasileos Pavlou), 33054 Delphi. ℂ **22650/82-232.** Fax 22650/82-033. 59 units. 145€–200€ ($188–$260) double. AE, DC, MC, V. **Amenities:** Restaurant; bar. *In room:* A/C, TV.

WHERE TO DINE

The problem with most of the Delphi restaurants that cater to tourists (and that includes most of the restaurants in town!) is that the restaurateurs know that they probably will never see you again. This does not inspire good service or loving food preparation. A happy exception to this general rule is the excellent **Epikouros Restaurant** (see below). If you like music, try the **Iniochos,** on the main drag, which serves good *mezedes* (appetizers), and where a piano player sometimes turns up after 10pm and gets a singalong going with guests both local and foreign. One other suggestion: If you have a car, consider eating in Arachova, 10km (6 miles) east of Delphi, where the restaurants cater to a more local crowd—or to the Athenians who come here to ski in winter and enjoy the mountain air in summer—and who know their Greek food. Especially at night, the drive to and from Arachova, along a switchback mountain road, is best taken *siga, siga* (slowly, slowly), as the Greeks say.

Epikouros Restaurant *☆☆☆* GREEK   Easily the best restaurant with a view in Delphi, with an astonishingly extensive and varied menu (including tasty veggie fritters, delicious local olives and formaella cheese, lamb with fresh tomato sauce, *keftedes* (grilled round meatballs) and sousoutakia (oval rice-and-meat-balls, stewed in tomato sauce) and, in season, wild boar, casseroled with tomatoes, onions, and herbs). If you come early, you may be one of few diners not with a tour group; come after 9pm and you may dine with Greek visitors and locals.

Vasileos Pavlou and Frederikis. ℂ **22650/83-250.** Main courses 9€–18€ ($12–$23). No credit cards.

Taverna Skala *☆* GREEK   This simple, year-round restaurant attracts locals in the summer and skiers in the winter. The menu is typical Greek taverna fare (grills and stews), but there's usually a wide variety of *mezedes,* and wood paneling (just about everything in Delphi that can be wood-paneled is!) makes the room cozy.

Vasileos Pavlou and Frederikis. ℂ **22650/82-762.** Main courses 6€–10€ ($8–$13). No credit cards. Daily noon to around midnight.

Taverna Vakchos *☆* *Value* GREEK   This small taverna gets many of its customers from the youth hostel. This means that the prices are very reasonable, the clientele casual, and the food basic (although they sometimes serve game in winter). The back room with its veranda has good views over Delphi, across the plain of olives, and to the Corinthian Gulf. The neighboring **Taverna Lekaria,** at 33 Apollonos, is a bit more ambitious and a bit more expensive and has a nice courtyard with flowering plants. The Lekaria usually has excellent local *loukanika* (sausages) and *briam* (a veggie stew steeped in olive oil) and sliced apple rounds sprinkled with cinnamon for a healthy dessert.

31 Apollonos. ℂ **22650/83-186.** Main courses 6€–10€ ($8–$13). No credit cards. Daily noon to around midnight.

SIDE TRIPS FROM DELPHI
ARACHOVA *☆*

The mountain village of **Arachova,** 10km (6 miles) east of Delphi, clings to Mount Parnassus about 950m (3,116 ft.) above sea level. Generations of Greeks and tourists have bought hand-loomed fluffy wool *flokati*, *tagari* (brightly woven wool bags), rag rugs, and blankets here. Alas, in recent years, some of these once-local weavings have been imported—sometimes from as far away as China. Still, a number of shops on the main street still sell authentic local crafts, including woodcarvings, copper, and weavings (some still sold by the weight of the wool used). **Anemi** (ℂ **22670/31-701**) often has nice antique reproductions.

When tour buses make a shopping stop here in summer, the tiny village can be seriously overcrowded. Don't despair: Come back in the evening. The shops are still open, and the cafes and restaurants give you a chance to escape from the tourist world of Delphi to the village world of Greece. People often take to the streets in the evening for a *volta* (energetic stroll) on Delphon, the main street. If you climb the steep stairs to the upper town, you'll find yourself on quiet neighborhood streets, where children

Saint George's Day in Arachova

Arachova's main feast day, April 23, honors St. George, the patron saint of shepherds. Locals and visitors celebrate the festival by eating vast amounts of roast lamb washed down with the local red wines and dancing to folk music until the wee hours. (If Apr 23 falls during Lent, the feast day is observed the Tues after Easter.) Make a hotel reservation well ahead if you want to come to the festivities. Also be sure to wish everyone, especially anyone named George, *Chronia polla* (Many more years).

play and families sit in front of their homes. If you come here in ski season, you can enjoy watching the beautiful people (many from Athens) lounging in cafes in their après ski togs. It sometimes seems that the cafe crowd of Kolonaki comes here en masse on winter weekends, so be sure to have a hotel reservation if you come, too. If you want to dance after you lounge, head for **Snow Me** (© 6944/341-317), a popular disco cafe.

For lunch or dinner, try the simple family fare (*Brasto*, boiled goat in broth is often on the menu) at **Taverna Karathanassi,** by the coffee shops in the main square with the lovely freshwater springs. Nearby, the venerable **Taverna Dasaryiris,** which specializes in delicious *kokoretsi* (stuffed entrails), *loukanika* (sausages), and grills, often has an almost entirely local crowd. The homemade *chilopites* (tasty little square noodles) are terrific. If you want a meal with a view, head uphill on the stepped street and ask for directions to the **Kaplanis** restaurant, which has splendid views over the town and countryside and serves a variety of stews, grills, and *mezedes.* Expect to pay from 25€ ($33) for dinner (the tab could easily go well above that, especially if you decide to start your meal with a whiskey and finish off with some cognac). Prices are similar at **Emboriko,** another upscale restaurant very popular with Greeks; reservations at both are almost always necessary. If you're here in winter, try **Fterolakka** or **Agnandi,** both are in the center of the village and are closed in summer. Meals, featuring roasts and grills perked up with excellent *skordalia* (a garlic-potato sauce that the novice may suspect is almost 100% pure garlic) cost from 20€ ($26).

Low season for most Arachova hotels is summer; winter weekends are the most expensive time to stay here. For a room with a view, try the **Anemolia** (© 22670/31-640; fax 22670/31-642; www.anemolia.gr), with 55 rooms a restaurant and a heated pool on a hill above the Delphi road just outside Arachova. Originally a member of the Best Western chain, with American-style bathrooms, it has large, comfortable rooms, many with balcony views down to Delphi and the Gulf of Corinth. Doubles go from 100€ ($130), except on popular winter weekends when prices can be double that. If you want to be in town, both the **Paradisiakos Xenonas Maria** (© 22670/31-803;** www.mariarooms.com) and the **Xenonas Generali** (© 22670/31-529; www.generalis-xenon.com) occupy handsomely restored 19th century *arkontika* (town houses). Doubles at the Maria, with has four rooms and four studios with fridge and hot plate, from 100€ ($130); doubles at the Generali, which has an indoor plunge-pool and sauna, from 200€ ($260). If you want a room (or suite, or villa) with a Jacuzzi, in a "boutique retreat" on the slopes of Parnassus that aims to re-create a "private village," with two pools, a spa, tennis courts, and fitness center, head for the **Santa Marina Arachova Resort and Spa** (© 22670/31-955; www.santa-marina.gr);

doubles from 200€ ($260). Their sister hotel, the **Santa Marina Arachova** (© **22670/31-230;** www.santa-marina.gr) in the village, has doubles from 140€ to 240€ ($182–$312); guests here can use the resort hotel's spa facilities. Both hotels are decorated in lavish country-hotel style, with libraries with fireplaces, dark well-polished wood furniture, and enormous beds heaped with comfy pillows.

PARNASSUS (PARNASSOS) 𝄞𝄞

The good news is that you can drive 23km (14 miles) from Arachova to the **ski resort at Kelaria,** or 27km (17 miles) from Arachova to the **ski resort at Fterolakka,** in about an hour. Each resort is about 2,200m (1½ miles) up the mountain; information available at **www.parnassos-ski.gr.** The bad news is that the road and several incipient hamlets of ski lodges (the Santa Marina Resort is one of the more tasteful developments) have eradicated much of the mountain's isolation and beauty. **Parnassus** is an odd mountain: It's difficult to see its peaks from either Delphi or Arachova, although if you approach from the north, you'll have fine views of its twin summits.

If you come in winter, you can rent ski equipment either in Arachova or at the resorts. Keep in mind that fog and high winds often sweep in suddenly. When this happens, the ski lifts close and the road down the mountain is often also closed, stranding day-trippers until it reopens. In fact, fog can close this road at almost any time, even in summer—something to keep in mind if you decide to drive up for a look around. I was glad to have a bottle of water and cookies in the car when this happened to me one May afternoon.

In summer, don't expect to find the shops, cafes, and restaurants (not to mention the dozen ski runs!) open. If you want to hike Parnassus, there are two possibilities, both with trail markings. The **Hellenic Federation of Mountaineering and Climbing,** 5 Milioni, 10673 Kolonaki (© **210/364-5904;** www.sport.gov.gr) and the **Mountaineering Club** in Athens (© **210/323-4555**) have information on both routes. As always in the mountains, it's not a good idea to make such an excursion alone and it is always wise to check the local weather forecast.

If you begin your climb in Delphi, head uphill past the Sikelianos house and keep going, bearing left above the sanctuary and following the trail markers. Four hours will bring you to the upland meadows known as the **Plateau of Livadi,** where shepherds traditionally pasture their flocks. Want to go farther? Past the meadow is the **Corcyrian Cave** (known locally as Sarantavli, or "Forty Rooms"), where Pan and the Nymphs once were thought to live; beyond are the summits. It's also possible to begin your ascent from Arachova, where it is best to get directions locally. The Road Edition map of Parnassos (no. 42 in the mountain map series) is an excellent investment at 6€ ($7.80), as is Tim Salmon's *The Mountains of Greece* (Cicerone Press). However, nothing substitutes for a companion, especially one who knows the terrain well.

THE MONASTERY OF OSIOS LOUKAS 𝄞𝄞

You'll probably want to see Osios Loukas en route to or from Delphi. You can also do the 96km (60-mile) round-trip via Arachova as a day excursion, although when I last did this in 2006, battling against steady phalanxes of tour buses in both directions, I vowed never to do so again. If you go to Osios Loukas via Levadia, pause at **Schiste (Triodos),** where three roads intersect. This is the spot where the ancients believed that Oedipus unknowingly slew his father. Things got worse: Also unsuspectingly, he married his mother and brought tragedy on himself and his descendants.

The splendid mosaics of **Osios Loukas (Monastery of Saint Luke)** are rivaled only by the mosaics at Daphne outside Athens and in the churches of Thessaloniki. Much of Osios Loukas dates from the 10th and 11th centuries and commemorates not the better-known Saint Luke the Evangelist, but the Blessed Luke, a revered 10th-century hermit, perhaps born in nearby Delphi. Much more than a tourist destination, devout Greek Orthodox visitors consider it a holy spot. This is not the place for sleeveless shirts or shorts: the tomb of Saint Luke in the **Katholikon (main church)** is an important pilgrimage destination.

Osios Loukas perches on a steep slope, with sweeping views over the surrounding countryside. The monastery's buildings are lavishly decorated with brick and a wide variety of jewel-like polychrome marbles. If you are lucky enough to be here when the Katholikon isn't too crowded, enjoy the changing play of light and shadows on the marbles and mosaics. Mosaic scenes from the Bible, including the Nativity and Baptism, glow over head. You may see visitors handing their family icons to a monk, who takes them into the church for a special blessing. Next, head to the smaller **Church of the Theotokos (Mother of God),** with a wall fresco showing Joshua as a warrior and a fine mosaic floor. If you have time, visit the fresco-adorned crypt, and then sit in the courtyard. Imagine what Osios Loukas was like when, rather than today's handful of monks, hundreds of monks lived and worshiped here. The monastery's former refectory (dining room) now houses sculpture and fragments of architectural ornament.

Admission to Osios Loukas costs 3€ ($3.90). Hours are daily, 8am to 2pm and 4 to 7pm from early May to mid-September, 8am to 5pm the rest of the year. (Note that these are the posted times; they are not always observed.) A small cafe on the grounds offers soft drinks, coffee, snacks, and local delicacies. Allow at least an hour for your visit.

2 Two Famous Battlefields: Thermopylae & Chaironeia ⟨★

Both these battlefields lie beside main highways and are easily visited with a brief stop. A seasonal *kantina* (snack shop) is sometimes open at both battlefields.

THERMOPYLAE
194km (120 miles) N of Athens on the Athens-Thessaloniki National Hwy.

One of the most famous battles in history was fought at Thermopylae in 480 B.C. during the Persian king Xerxes's attempt to conquer Greece. To this day, historians speculate on how different the world might have been if Xerxes had succeeded and Greece had become part of the Persian Empire. If you find yourself on the Athens-Thessaloniki Highway, keep an eye out for the larger-than-life **statue of the Spartan king Leonidas,** about halfway through the 6.4km-long (4-mile) Pass of Thermopylae that snakes between the mountains and the sea.

When Xerxes invaded Greece in 480 B.C. with about 100,000 men, soldiers from almost every city-state in south and Central Greece rushed to Thermopylae to try to stop the Persian king. The Greeks might have succeeded in holding the narrow pass of Thermopylae had not a traitor told the Persians of a secret mountain path that allowed them to take control of the pass. As Leonidas and his 300-man royal guard stood and fought at Thermopylae, the main Greek force retreated south to regroup and fight another day. When the fighting at Thermopylae was over, Leonidas and his men lay dead, but the Spartan king had earned immortal fame for his heroism. In 2007 the story was retold in the Hollywood summer hit *300.*

The name Thermopylae (Hot Gates) refers to the warm springs that bubbled here in antiquity, when the pass was considerably narrower than it currently is, now that centuries of silt have built up the seashore. Many of Thermopylae's springs have been partly diverted to spas, such as Kamena Vourla. Unfortunately, overdevelopment has seriously undercut the former charm of the nearby seaside towns. If you want a quick look at some of the springs, look for plumes of smoke after you park near the statue of Leonidas. If you don't see plumes, follow your nose: The smell of sulfur is strong.

CHAIRONEIA

132km (81 miles) NW of Athens on the Athens-Levadhia-Lamia Hwy.

Just north of Levadhia, the Athens-Lamia Highway passes an enormous **stone lion** that marks the site of the common grave of the Theban Sacred Band of warriors, who died here in the Battle of Chaironeia in 338 B.C. It was at Chaironeia that Philip of Macedon, with some 30,000 soldiers, defeated the combined forces of Athens and Thebes and became the most powerful leader in Greece. It was also at Chaironeia that Philip's 18-year-old son Alexander first distinguished himself on the battlefield, when he led the attack against the superbly trained Theban Sacred Band, which fought to the last man. Philip's admiration for the Thebans' courage was such that he allowed them to be buried where they fell on the battlefield.

The stone lion itself, sitting on its haunches with a surprisingly benign expression on its face, was probably erected by Thebes sometime after the battle. With the passing of time, the winds blew soil from the plain almost entirely over the lion. In 1818, two English antiquarians stumbled upon the lion's head; from 1902 to 1904 the Greek Archaeological Service conducted excavations on the battlefield and restored the lion here on the dusty plain of Chaironeia. The small site museum keeps irregular hours.

3 The Vale of Tempe & Ambelakia ★★

326km (202 miles) N of Athens; 27km (16 miles) N of Larissa

The Vale of Tempe, a steep-sided 8km (5-mile) gorge between mounts Olympus and Ossa, has been famous since antiquity as a beauty spot. According to legend, this is where Apollo caught a glimpse of the lovely maiden Daphne bathing in the Peneios River. When Apollo pursued Daphne, she cried out to the gods on nearby Olympus to save her—which they did, by turning her into a laurel tree (*daphne* in Greek). Apollo, who didn't give up easily, plucked a branch from the tree and planted it at his shrine at Delphi. Thereafter, messengers from Delphi came to the Vale of Tempe every 9 years to collect laurel for Apollo's temple.

To this day, laurel, chestnut, and plane trees grow in the Vale of Tempe. Unfortunately, since virtually all north-south traffic in Greece now passes through the Vale, this is no longer the sylvan spot once the haunt of nightingales. The narrow approaches to the Vale have caused many serious road accidents. Still, if you're lucky enough to be here off season, the sound of the gurgling river may be louder than tourists' footsteps on the suspension bridge over the gorge. River rafting is becoming popular here; for information contact Olympos Trekking (oltrek@ote.net.gr). The car toll is 3€ ($3.90). If you park and walk through the Vale, allow at least an hour for your visit.

Keep an eye out for two medieval fortresses here: The remains of **Kastro tis Oreas (Castle of the Beautiful Maiden)** are on the cliffs inside the Vale; and **Platamonas Kastro** is at the northern end of the pass. Unfortunately, you won't have any trouble spotting the souvenir stands throughout the Vale. There is also a small chapel deep in the gorge.

If you want a break from the hustle and bustle of popular tourist destinations such as the Vale of Tempe, take a detour to the mountaintop village of **Ambelakia,** about 6km (4 miles) southeast of the Valem perched amid old oak trees on Mount Kissavos. If you spend an hour or two here—better yet, a night or two—you can experience village Greece, inhale the crisp, clean mountain air, and enjoy the spectacular views of Mount Olympus. Ambelakia, whose name means "vineyards" in Greek, is one of six villages in Greece that formed the **National Network of Tradition, Culture, and Community Life** to preserve their traditions and use local crafts to boost the economy.

Astonishingly, this tiny village was an important center of cotton and silk production in the 17th century, with offices in far-off London. Today, little survives of Ambelakia's earlier wealth, but what does remain is well worth a visit: the handsome late-18th-century **Schwartz House** ✿. (Its somewhat unpredictable hours are usually Tues–Sat 9am–3pm, Sun 9am–2:30pm; admission is 3€/$3.90; no phone.) The Schwartz brothers, two of Ambelakia's wealthiest merchants, lived and worked in Austria, hence the name "Schwartz," a translation of their Greek name "Mavros." Their handsome wooden house, with its overhanging balconies and elaborately frescoed interiors, is an absolute delight—and it is a great satisfaction to see it so carefully restored and cared for. Allow an hour for the guided tour of the house.

It's a good idea to call ahead to the **Nine Muses Hotel** (**Ennea Mousses** on some signs; ✆ **24950/93-405;** h9mouses@hotmail.com), which has 12 rooms from 50€ ($65). The small chalet-style hotel is not always open off season, while in summer all the rooms are often taken by Greek families. Several small restaurants on the main square serve simple grills and salads, including **To Rodi,** run by the Women's Agro-tourism Cooperative, which also has "rent rooms."

4 Mount Olympus ✿✿✿

390km (241 miles) N of Athens; 70km (43 miles) N of Larissa; 100km (62 miles) SW of Thessaloniki

Greece's most famous mountain range, home of the Olympian gods, towers 2,919m (9,751 ft.) above the plains of Thessaly and Macedonia.

The first recorded successful ascent of Olympus's summit Mytikas—nicknamed "the needle"—was in 1913, when two Swiss mountaineers and a local guide made it to the top. Today, for such an imposing mountain, Olympus is surprisingly easy to climb. A number of well-marked paths lead to the summit; climbers can rest or overnight in **shelters** at Stavros (944m/3,096 ft.) and at Spilios Agapitos (2,100m/6,888 ft.). In summer, these paths can be very heavily trafficked. Elegant Greek women make the ascent in high heels (not recommended!).

Still, Olympus is a serious mountain, and no one should attempt it alone—or without water, provisions, and gear. From a distance, it's almost impossible to pick out the summit, although the massive, gnarled, snowcapped range is often visible from Thessaloniki (albeit less and less so, given the area's increasing pollution). Another of its main peaks (it has six), Stafani (2,909m/9,544 ft.), is called the "throne of Zeus."

As always in the mountains, weather conditions can change for the worse without warning. Well into May, severe snowstorms can hit the heights of Olympus—which helps explain why the area has been developed in recent years as a ski resort. The main town on the slopes, and the base camp, as it were, for climbers, is Litochoro.

ESSENTIALS

GETTING THERE   By Bus   Four buses that stop at the Litochoro station (✆ 23520/81-271) run daily from Athens to Katerini. Seven buses a day make the trip from Athens to Larissa; from there you'll find frequent service to Litochoro. All buses leave Athens from the station at 260 Liossion (✆ 210/831-7059). At least eight buses a day leave from Thessaloniki for Litochoro.

By Train   Trains go daily from Athens to Larissa, and from Thessaloniki to Larissa. From Larissa, you can continue to Litochoro by bus. You can also take a train from Athens or Thessaloniki to the Litochoro station (✆ 23520/22-522)—but the station is on the coast 9km (5½ miles) from town, and you'll have to continue on by bus or taxi. Only devoted train lovers will want to come this way.

By Car   Take the Litochoro exit on the Athens-Salonika Highway.

VISITOR INFORMATION   In Litochoro, the **tourist office** (✆ 23520/83-100) faces the bus stop. Information on Olympus is available from the **Hellenic Federation of Mountaineering and Climbing,** 5 Milioni, 10673 Kolonaki, Athens (✆ 210/364-5904; www.sport.gov.gr), and from the **Hellenic Mountaineering Club (EOS; ✆ 210/323-4555** or 210/323-4555 in Athens, 231/278-288 in Thessaloniki, 23520/81-944 in Litochoro; eos@olympus.gr). Olympus is best climbed from June 1 to October 1. The **Spilios Agapitos** refuge can be reached at ✆ 23520/81-800. Rates are flexible but are usually less than 20€ ($26). Make your reservation at the refuge well in advance of your arrival.

FAST FACTS   The **National Bank of Greece,** on Plateia Kentriki, offers currency exchange and has an ATM. The **clinic** (✆ 23520/22-222), 5km (3 miles) outside Litochoro, is signposted; if you need medical care and it is not an emergency, try to get to Thessaloniki. The signposted **police station** (✆ 23520/81-110-1) and the **telephone office (OTE)** are just off the central square, Plateia Kentriki, on the road up Olympus to Priona. The **post office** is on Plateia Kentriki.

CLIMBING MOUNT OLYMPUS

If you plan to climb **Olympus,** check first with the EOS (see "Visitor Information," above) and get the excellent Road Edition map of Olympus (no. 31; 6€/$7.80). If you can, also get a copy of Marc Dubin's *Trekking in Greece.* You should **not** attempt the climb alone; weather here can change in an instant from pleasant to life-threatening: Forest fires are common in summer—when there can also be heavy snows.

Purists will want to begin the ascent at the increasingly developed **ski resort of Litochoro,** while others may prefer to drive from Litochoro as far as **Prionia** (18km/11 miles) and begin the climb there. On foot, the journey from Litochoro to Prionia takes about 4 hours; by car, it's about an hour but seems longer on the twisting road. Reward yourself with a decent meal or even a stiff drink at the small **cafe** in Priona.

From Priona, it's at least a 3-hour climb, much of it over slippery schist slopes and knobby limestone outcroppings, to the **shelter at Spilios Agapitos.** Most climbers begin the final 3-hour ascent at dawn and then do the entire descent, arriving back in Litochoro before dusk. The **Monastery of Ayios Dionysos,** not far from Spilios Agapitos, is a good place to break your downward trek and enjoy the views. In short, your climb will take at least a day and you will probably want to stay overnight at one of the shelters.

WHERE TO STAY & DINE

Most of the restaurant pickings in Litochoro are slim: a number of fast-food joints and so-so small restaurants. If climbers are foodies, they'll be disappointed here, with one notable exception: **En Olympo** (© 23520/21-300; www.gastrodromio.gr) by the large church on the main square has a varied menu including fresh fish and pasta cooked al dente (more than 200 wines and a cheese menu of 22 traditional Greek cheeses!). Mountain-climbing friends who came here in 2007 loved their meal at En Olympo and thought that the **Hotel Xenos Dias,** also on Litochoro's main square, where they paid 50€ ($65) for a double was good value (© **23520/81-234;** fax 23520/81-423; www.hotel-xeniosdias.gr).

Dion Palace Resort Hotel ★ (Kids)   This sprawling beachfront resort, about 6km (4 miles) from Litochoro, includes the main hotel building, its disco, lots of cabanas, and some small "villas." The guest rooms are large and comfortable (renovated in 2004 and 2006), if somewhat bland (as is almost always the case in Greece). In summer, Greek families from Thessaloniki flock here.

Litochoro Beach, Pierias, 60200 Macedonia. © **23520/61-431.** Fax 23520/61-435. www.dionpalace.com. 187 units. 170€–230€ ($221–$299) double. AE, DC, MC, V. Sometimes closed in winter. **Amenities:** 2 restaurants; 4 bars; tennis; 2 pools; spa; children's playground; health club, grocery. In room: A/C, TV, Internet, minibar, hair dryer.

Villa Drossos ★★ (Kids)   The big plus here—which makes reservations in summer a necessity—is the swimming pool in the garden. In a quiet neighborhood, by a church, the Drossos uses bright pastels and floral prints in its furnishings, and all the guest rooms have balconies.

Litochoro, 60200 Macedonia. © **23520/84-561.** Fax 23520/84-563. grigoris@kat.forthnet.gr. 13 units. 90€ ($117) double. MC, V. **Amenities:** Bar/breakfast room; pool. In room: A/C, TV, Internet.

5 The Meteora ★★★

Kalambaka is 356km (220 miles) NW of Athens; the circuit of the Meteora monasteries is approximately 25km (15 miles)

As you drive across the plain of Thessaly, which can seem endless on a hot summer day, you'll suddenly see a cluster of gnarled black peaks outside the town of Kalambaka. Some travelers have compared these crags to the mountains of the moon. The rock formations of the **Meteora** (the word means "in mid-air") are unique. Many geographers speculate that some 30 million years ago, all Thessaly was a vast inland sea; when the sea receded, sweeping the topsoil along, rock formations were left behind. Over the millennia, the Peneios River and the wind carved the rock into the weird, twisted shapes that now rise about 300m (984 ft.) above the plain. The Meteora is especially stunning in winter, when snow caps the Pindos range and when mists swirl around the monasteries.

The monasteries sit atop these sheer, slippery, seemingly unscalable rocks that really do seem to hang "in mid-air." Why did monks settle here, and how did they build anything larger than a hut on the rocks? Small wonder that many monks believe that St. Athanasios (founder of the first monastery here) did not scale the rock, but was carried here by an eagle.

The first monks who climbed the rocks were probably 10th-century ascetics who lived as hermits in caves and spent their days in prayer and meditation. In fact, the word "monk" comes from the Greek for "alone." Over the centuries, more and more hermits and monks seeking to lead the solitary life made their way to the Meteora

> ## Tips   Important Reminders
>
> Although many of the monasteries are officially open from 9am to 6pm, many close from about 1 to 3pm, and others keep abbreviated hours. It's best to start your visit as early in the day as possible, so that you're not left cooling your heels while the monks and nuns have their afternoon siestas. Women should wear skirts, not slacks, and men should wear slacks, not shorts. Try to allow at least a full day here—you don't want to rush your experience of the contemplative life! That said, if you are on a tight schedule, you can visit several monasteries and then do a circuit of the others by car in an hour or so. If you come in winter, dress warmly, as many of the monasteries have little or no heat. Also note that in winter, many small restaurants and hotels in the area may be closed. In compensation, you might get to see the Meteora at its most beautiful: covered with snow and shrouded in mists.

until, by the 14th century St. Athanasios founded the Great Meteoron (Monastery of the Transfiguration). By 1500, there were 24 monasteries here. Six—the Great Meteoron, Varlaam, Roussanou, Ayia Triada, Ayios Nikolaos Anapaphsas, and Ayiou Stefanou—are still inhabited and welcome visitors.

Touring the monasteries is not easy for those who suffer from severe acrophobia and downright impossible for those unable to climb the steep (sometimes slippery) flights of stairs cut into the rock's face. These vertiginous stepped paths are an improvement over what earlier visitors had to endure. When the English traveler Leake visited here in the 19th century, he was ferried up to the Great Meteoron in a net attached by a slender rope to a winch. Leake later wrote, "Visitors' morale was not helped by persistent rumors that the monks only replaced the homemade ropes which held the nets when they broke—usually in midair!"

ESSENTIALS

GETTING THERE   By Train   There are usually about five daily trains from Athens's Larissa station (© 210/821-3882) to Larissa and then on to the Kalambaka station (© 24320/22-451). Allow at least 8 hours for the Athens-Kalambaka trip.

By Bus   Seven buses run daily to Trikkala from the Athens terminal at 260 Liossion (© 210/831-1434). Allow at least 8 hours for the Athens-Kalambaka trip. Buses leave frequently from Trikkala (© 24310/73-130) for Kalambaka (© 24320/22-432). Several buses a day connect Kalambaka and the Meteora monasteries.

By Car   From Athens, take the Athens-Thessaloniki National Highway north to Lamia; from Lamia, take the highway northwest to Kalambaka. From Delphi, take the Lamia-Karditsa-Trikkala-Kalambaka Highway north. Allow at least 6 hours for the Athens-Kalambaka trip.

GETTING AROUND   If you don't have a car, you may want to hire a taxi to visit the Meteora monasteries. Expect to pay between 30€ ($39) and 100€ ($130) to visit the six monasteries usually open to the public. Your fee will vary depending on whether you want a drive-by tour with a stop at one or two monasteries, or a more thorough visit with stops at each. Be sure you are in agreement as to how much time you will have at each monastery. Most drivers are content to wait 30 minutes at each one, while some drivers will accompany you into the monastery and act as guide (and expect a tip).

FAST FACTS   The **tourist office** (© 24320/77-734) on Plateia Riga Fereou, the main square (with the prominent fountain), is usually open Monday to Friday 9am to 1pm and 5 to 8pm in summer, with abbreviated winter hours. Information is also available at the Town Hall (© 24320/22-339). The **National Bank** and the **Ionian Bank,** also on Plateia Riga Fereou, exchange currency and have ATMs. The **clinic** in Kalambaka (© 24320/24-111), the **police** (© 24320/22-109), and the **tourist police** (© 24320/76-100) are about 1km (½ mile) outside town on the road to Ioannina. The **post office** and **telephone office (OTE)** are signposted off Plateia Riga Fereou. **Cafe Hollywood** (© 24320/24-964), on the main drag, Trikalon, and **Arena** (© 24320/77-999) on Plateia Dimoula, function as Internet cafes.

WHAT TO SEE & DO
THE METEORA MONASTERIES

The road from Kalambaka through the Meteora takes you past Ayios Nikolaos, Roussanou, the Great Meteoron, Varlaam, Ayia Triada, and Ayios Stephanos. Perhaps most impressive about the Meteora is the visual from the plain, as one approaches, of the bizarre and stunning visual melding of monasteries and cliffs. If you have time to visit only one monastery, it should be the **Great Meteoron.** You can chat with the monks and enjoy stunning views through the forest of rocks from monastery to monastery. You'll find souvenir stands and places to buy bottled water or soft drinks (but usually no food) outside each monastery.

We've listed the individual phone numbers for each monastery below, but don't be surprised if no one answers: Telephones and the monastic life are not compatible, although an increasing number of monks have cellphones tucked in their monastic robes. There's also a central number for the monasteries (© **24320/22-649**). And don't be surprised if you find one or more of the monasteries closed—usually the one you've just climbed a long series of rock-cut steps to reach.

Ayios Nikolaos Anapaphsas ⭐   This little 14th-century monastery, approached by a relatively gentle path, has splendid **frescoes** by the 16th-century Cretan painter Theophanes the Monk. Don't miss the delightful fresco of the Garden of Eden, with elephants, fantastic beasts, and all manner of fruits and flowers. A good painting of the death of St. Ephraim the Syrian shows scenes from the saint's life, including the pillar atop which he lived for many years in the Syrian desert.

At the time of our visit, no monks were in residence at Ayios Nikolaos, and because tour buses often rush past to get to the Great Meteoron, you may find that you have this spot all to yourself.

© **24320/22-375.** Admission 2€ ($2.60). Daily 9am–6pm. Often closed Fri and in winter.

Ayiou Stefanou ⭐   Founded in the 14th century, Ayiou Stefanou, now a nunnery, is almost on the outskirts of Kalambaka. A bridge from the main road makes it easy to get here. The nuns usually make you feel glad that you've come and sometimes sell very reasonably priced embroideries.

Ayiou Stefanou was badly damaged in both World War II and the Civil War that followed. Many priceless frescoes were defaced and others were totally destroyed, but the monastery's most famous relic was saved: the **head of St. Charalambos,** whose powers include warding off illness. There's also a small **museum** here, with ecclesiastical robes and paraphernalia. Recently, the nuns have been restoring sections of the monastery that had been allowed to decline. Donations are welcome.

© 24320/22-279. Admission 2€ ($2.60). Usually Tues–Sun 9am–2pm and 3:30–6pm.

Ayia Triada ✴✴   It's not easy to say which of the monasteries has the most spectacular position, but Ayia Triada would be near the top of the list. Perched on a slender pinnacle reached only by laboring up 140 steps, Ayia Triada really does seem to belong to another world. The one monk who lives here is usually glad to see visitors and show them around the **church, refectory,** and **courtyard.** Don't miss the **winch,** for years used to bring up supplies and visitors. If this monastery looks more familiar to you than the others, perhaps you remember it from the James Bond movie *For Your Eyes Only,* which was filmed here.

© 24320/22-220. Admission 2€ ($2.60). Daily 8am–1pm and 3–6pm; sometimes 8am–6pm in summer. Often closed Thurs and/or Fri.

The Great Meteoron ✴✴   Although the Great Meteoron was founded in the 14th century, most of what you see here was built in the 16th century by monks from the Holy Mountain of Mount Athos. The **church** here is especially splendid, in the form of a Greek cross inscribed on a square, topped by a **12-sided dome.** Once your eyes get accustomed to the darkness, you'll be able to enjoy the elaborate **frescoes.** If you look up to the dome, you'll see Christ, with the four evangelists, apostles, and prophets ranged below, the church fathers by the altar, and the liturgical feasts of the church year along the walls of the nave. There's also a rather bloodcurdling *Last Judgment* and *Punishment of the Damned* in the narthex. After visiting the church, you may wish to sit awhile in the shady courtyard before visiting the small **museum,** which has a collection of icons and illustrated religious texts. Don't miss the **wine cellar,** whose enormous wooden barrels suggest that monastic life is not all prayer and meditation.

© 24320/22-278. Admission 2€ ($2.60). Wed–Mon 9am–1pm and 3:30–6pm.

Roussanou ✴   Roussanou is relatively accessible, thanks to its new bridge. This 13th-century monastery is now a nunnery, whose inhabitants are usually much more jolly than the monks. If the nuns offer you sweets while you sit in the courtyard between the refectory and the octagonal-domed church, be sure to leave a contribution in the church collection box.

No phone. Admission 2€ ($2.60). Daily 9am–1pm and 3–6pm.

Varlaam ✴✴   A narrow bridge from the main road runs to this 16th-century monastery, which was named for a hermit who lived here in the 14th century and built a tiny chapel on this promontory. The **chapel,** considerably enlarged and decorated with **frescoes,** is now an annex of the main church. Varlaam's founders were two brothers from Ioannina, who considered Ioannina's monastery and gentle lakeside scenery too sybaritic. Presumably the brothers found the Meteora's harsh landscape more to their liking: According to legend, they had to drive away the monster who lived in a cave on the summit before they could settle here. The nicest thing about Varlaam is its **garden;** the monk who sometimes sits here is willing to chat with visitors.

© 24320/22-277. Admission 2€ ($2.60). Sat–Wed 9am–1pm and 3:30–6pm.

THE CATHEDRAL OF THE DORMITION OF THE VIRGIN & THE CENTER OF CONTEMPORARY ART

After visiting the monasteries of the Meteora, you may find it a relief to know that there's only one church to see back in Kalambaka: the 12th-century Cathedral of the Dormition of the Virgin, which is often locked. If it's open, take a look at the frescoes, which date from the 12th to the 16th centuries. Keep an eye out for the ancient marble blocks and column drums pilfered by this church's builders from the earlier Temple of Apollo. An admission fee of 2€ ($2.60) is sometimes charged.

For a complete change of subject and mood, head to the **Center of Contemporary Art,** 38 Patriarchou Dimitriou (© **24320/22-346**), which houses the extensive private collection of Leonidas Beltsios. The museum is officially open daily, 9am to 3pm and 5 to 9pm.

SHOPPING

A lot of tourist shops in Kalambaka (most of which close for the winter) sell the usual carved wooden canes and spoons, rugs, ceramics, and more rugs. One shop worth a look: **Kava Nikos,** on the main drag, 114 Trikalon (©/fax **24320/77-881**). This small liquor shop carries a good selection of wines both in the bottle and from the barrel, and also stocks local Macedonian and Thessalian *tsipouro,* a firewater that makes ouzo seem like a delicate aperitif. If you're lucky enough to be in Kalambaka on a Friday, you can join the crowd at the **farmers' market** that spills onto the streets off Kondyli.

WHERE TO STAY

We suggest that you stay in Kalambaka; Kastraki has some still-charming winding side streets, but it has become very noisy, due to the coaches that rumble to and from the Meteora, the proliferating campgrounds, and the discos. Most of the hotels below have considerably lower prices off season.

Amalia 𝒢𝒢   This rather handsome, large hotel—with two restaurants, a souvenir shop, and a pool—looks almost like a small village from the road. Like most other Amalia hotels, this one is located just too far out of town to make a walk there appealing. The large guest rooms (most with balconies) are tastefully decorated in soft colors, and bathrooms have actual shower stalls. This is a very comfortable place to stay, although you may find yourself feeling like the odd man out if tour groups occupy all the other rooms.

Outside Kalambaka on the Meteora road, 42200 Kalambaka. © **24320/72-216.** Fax 24320/72-457. www.amalia.gr. 173 units. 100€–180€ ($130–$234) double. Rates include breakfast buffet. Often significantly cheaper off season. AE, DC, MC, V. **Amenities:** Restaurant; bar; pool; concierge; shop; room service 7am–midnight. *In room:* A/C, TV, minibar, hair dryer.

Divani Motel 𝒢𝒢   In 2007, the Divani appeared in *Odyssey* magazine's prestigious list of the best hotels in Greece, although we still think that the Amalia's pool and facilities give the Divani stiff competition. You may be swayed toward the Divani, however, by its especially fine views toward the Meteora from the balconied rooms at the back. In addition to its gym, the Divani now boasts its own spa, with Jacuzzis and steam baths. This is also a popular spot for local wedding and baptism receptions, so you may get to spy on Kalambaka society.

Outside Kalambaka on the Meteora road, 42200 Kalambaka. © **24320/23-330.** Fax 24320/23-638. www.divanis.gr. 165 units. 120€–200€ ($156–$260) double. Often significantly cheaper off season. AE, DC, MC, V. **Amenities:** Restaurant; bar; pool; gym; spa. *In room:* A/C, TV, Internet, minibar, hair dryer.

Edelweiss ✦ *Value* Usually open all winter, the Edelweiss is low-key with minimalist decor, freshened by renovations in 2006. Some guest rooms have views of the Meteora. The swimming pool is a real plus; the disco/bar is popular with locals, but might be less popular with weary travelers.

3 El. Venizelou, 42200 Kalambaka. ☎ **24320/23-884.** Fax 24320/24-733. eidelweis@hol.gr. 60 units. 70€ ($91) double. Rates include breakfast. MC, V.

Hotel Meteora ✦✦ *Value* The price is right, some rooms have balconies with Meteora views, and there's Internet access. All that and the very helpful managers, Niko and Kosta Gekas, make this an excellent budget choice.

14 Ploutarchou, 42200 Kalambaka. ☎ **24320/22-367.** Fax 24320/75-550. www.meteorahotels.com. 20 units. 70€ ($91) double. Rates include breakfast. No credit cards.

WHERE TO DINE

We've never had a drop-dead wonderful meal in Meteora—maybe the influence of the monks inhibits exploration of haute cuisine. The places we suggest are perfectly fine but not terribly memorable. We'd welcome readers' comments about **Kipos tou Elia,** on Trikalon, which people seem either to love or hate. It has a garden and a good number of stews, and service that is either praised or criticized!

Gertzos (also known as the **Meteora**) ✦ GREEK This simple taverna has been in Kalambaka for more than 50 years, serving up standard Greek fare but also offering dishes reflecting the owners' Greek heritage in Asia Minor. Unless it's so hot—as it can be in the summer here—that you feel you must order a cold drink, try one of the local wines.

4 Economou. ☎ **24320/22-316.** Main courses 7€–15€ ($9–$20). No credit cards. Usually closed Feb, sometimes longer. In season, daily noon–11pm.

Panellino GREEK When we were here on a chilly but beautiful February visit to the Meteora, Panellino was resolutely open when many other places were closed. The menu consisted of the usual chops and stews, as well as vegetable dishes.

Plateia Riga Fereou. ☎ **24320/24-735.** Main courses 5€–12€ ($6.50–$16). No credit cards. Daily noon–11pm.

Vachos GREEK If you want to eat outdoors, head for Vachos's small garden with views toward Meteora. The food is so well prepared that even standard dishes like zucchini and eggplant stuffed with rice and ground meat taste special. Another plus here: The menu includes several tasty sweets, so you don't have to search out a *zacheroplasteion* (sweet shop) for dessert.

Plateia Riga Fereou. ☎ **24320/24-678.** Main courses 6€–13€ ($7.80–$17). No credit cards. Usually closed Nov–Feb. In season, daily noon–11pm.

13

The Sporades

by John S. Bowman

With their excellent golden sand beaches, fragrant pine trees, and unspoiled villages, you might think that the Sporades ("Scattered") islands have always been major tourist magnets. But because these islands lack major archaeological remains and historical associations, foreigners traditionally headed elsewhere in Greece.

These days, however, the Sporades are no longer the natural retreats they once were. **Skiathos** becomes horrendously crowded in high season—although in spring and fall it can be lovely and relaxing. Even in summer, it's worth a visit by those interested in a beach vacation, good food, and active nightlife. **Skopelos** is nearly as bustling as Skiathos in the high season but isn't quite as sophisticated. Its beaches are fewer and less impressive, but Skopelos town is among the more attractive ports in Greece, and the island offers some pleasant excursions. These two most popular islands also have fine restaurants, fancy hotels, and an international (heavily British) following.

More remote **Skyros** hardly seems a part of the group, especially as its landscape and architecture are more Cycladic. But it has a few excellent beaches, as well as a colorful local culture, and it remains a fine destination for those who want to get away from the crowds. Although space limits do not allow us to describe Alinossos, the fourth of these islands, it might be attractive to those seeking a less popular, more natural island.

STRATEGIES FOR SEEING THE ISLANDS

If you have only 1 to 3 days, plan on seeing just one of the Sporades. If you have a bit more time, you will be able to get a ship directly (from various ports, identified below for each island) to any of them—and a plane in the case of Skiathos and Skyros; if time is a factor, we strongly advise flying to Skiathos or Skyros and staying there. If you have more time, you can continue around the islands via hydrofoils (known as Flying Dolphins) or ferryboats. (*Note:* The frequency of all connections is cut back considerably Sept–May.)

Tips Museum and Site Hours Update

If you visit the Sporades during the summer, check to see when museums and sites are open. They do not always maintain the hours that are officially posted and most will be closed at least 1 day a week.

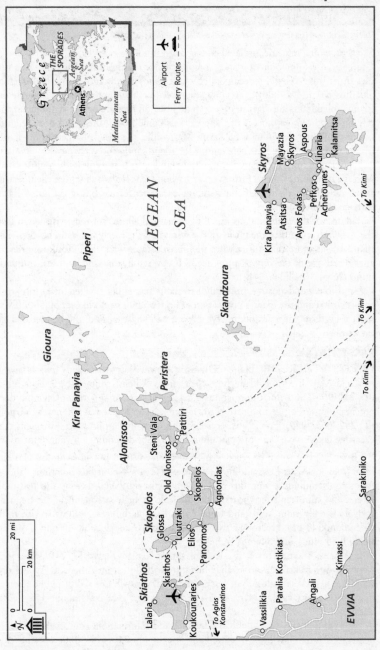

The Sporades

Greece

THE SPORADES

Aegean Sea

Athens

Mediterranean Sea

Airport
Ferry Routes

AEGEAN SEA

Skyros
Mayazia
Skyros
Aspous
Linaria
Kalamitsa
To Kimi
Kira Panayia
Atsitsa
Ayios Fokas
Pefkos
Acherounes

Piperi

Skandzoura

To Kimi

To Kimi

Gioura

Kira Panayia

Peristera
Alonissos
Steni Vala
Patitiri
Old Alonissos

Skopelos
Glossa
Loutraki
Elios
Panormos
Skopelos
Agnondas

Sarakiniko

Skiathos
Lalaria
Skiathos
Koukounaries
To Agios Konstantinos

Vassilikia
Paralia Kostikias
Angali
Kimassi

EVVIA

20 mi
20 km

1 Skiathos

108km (58 nautical miles) from Ayios Konstandinos, which is 166km (103 miles) from Athens

Skiathos, which remained isolated and agrarian until the early 1970s, is today one of Greece's most cosmopolitan islands, a rapid change that has left a few disturbing ripples in its wake. This has become a "package tour" island, and during high season, Skiathos town, also known as Hora, can feel like a shopping mall. Although the island's inhabitants are eager to please, in high season they are often overextended and rely on imported help; many of these workers come from Athens and don't seem to care much about providing local flavor. Meanwhile, the sheer numbers of foreigners means that some show little concern for the island's indigenous character.

Yet Skiathos town does have its attractions, and at its best seems fairly sophisticated, with the handsome Bourtzi fortress on its harbor, some elegant shops, excellent restaurants, and a flashy nightlife. For a memorable experience, take one of the horse-drawn carriages around town.

The rest of the island retains much of its natural allure. For most visitors, in fact, the main attractions are the purity of the water and the lovely fine-sand beaches. The island boasts more than 60 beaches, the most famous of which, **Koukounaries,** is considered one of the very best in Greece. If you relish sun, sand, and sea, and don't mind crowds, you'll love it here.

If possible, avoid Skiathos from July 1 to about September 1, when the tourist crush is at its worst and the island's population of under 5,000 swells to over 50,000. If you must visit during high season, reserve a room well ahead of time and be prepared for the crush.

ESSENTIALS

GETTING THERE   By Plane   Olympic Airways has service daily (twice daily in Apr and May, five times daily June–Sept) from Athens; contact the Athens office (© 210/966-6666) for information and reservations. At this time, Olympic does not maintain an office in Skiathos town, but can be reached at the nearby **airport** (© 24270/22-049). Public bus service to and from the airport is so infrequent that everyone takes a taxi; expect to pay about 6€ ($7.80) depending on your destination.

By Boat   Skiathos can be reached by either ferryboat (3 hr.) or hydrofoil (1½ hr.) from Volos or Ayios Konstandinos. (Volos is at least a 4-hour bus ride from Athens, Ayios Konstandinos a 3-hr. bus ride.) From Kymi on Evvia, there is also hydrofoil service (50 min.) and ferryboat service (4 hr.). In high season, there are frequent hydrofoils daily from Volos and from Ayios Konstandinos, as well as service from Thessaloniki (3 hr.). Hydrofoils also link Skiathos to Skopelos (30–45 min.), Alonissos (60–75 min.), and Skyros (2⅓ hr.).

In Athens, **Alkyon Travel,** 97 Akademias, near Kanigos Square (© **210/383-2545;** www.alkyontravel.com), can arrange bus transportation from Athens to Ayios Konstandinos as well as hydrofoil or ferry tickets. Alkyon will not accept phone reservations—you must appear in person. The 3-hour bus ride costs about 15€ ($20) one-way.

For hydrofoil (Flying Dolphins) schedules and information, contact the **Hellenic Seaways,** Akti Kondyli and 2 Aitolikou, Piraeus (© **210/419-9000;** www.hellenic seaways.gr). For ferryboat information, contact the **G.A. Ferries** line in Piraeus (© **210/ 458-2640;** www.gaferries.com). Ferry tickets can be purchased at travel agencies in

Athens or on the islands. During high season, I recommend that you purchase your boat tickets in advance through the boat lines. While you may purchase tickets at Alkyon in person, they will not reserve ferryboat or hydrofoil tickets for you in advance, and these often sell out.

VISITOR INFORMATION   The town maintains an **information booth** at the western corner of the harbor; in summer, at least, it's open daily from about 9am to 8pm. Meanwhile, private travel agencies abound and can help with most of your requests. We highly recommend **Mare Nostrum Holidays,** 21 Papadiamandis (© **24270/21-463;** marenost@otenet.gr). It books villas, hotels, and rooms; sells tickets to many around-the-island, hydrofoil, and beach caique (skiff) trips; books Olympic Airways flights; exchanges currency; and changes traveler's checks without commission. The staff speak excellent English, are exceedingly well-informed, and have lots of tips on everything from beaches to restaurants. The office is open daily from 8am to 10pm.

GETTING AROUND   By Bus   Skiathos has public bus service along the south coast of the island from the bus station on the harbor to Koukounaries (3€/$3.90), with stops at the beaches in between. A conductor will ask for your destination and assess the fare after the bus starts moving. Buses run at least six times daily April through November; every hour from 9am to 9pm May through October; every half-hour from 8:30am to 10pm June through September; and every 20 minutes from 8:30am to 2:30pm and 3:30pm to midnight July through August.

By Car & Moped   Reliable car and moped agencies, all on the paralia (shore road), include **Avis** (© **24270/21-458;** avisvolos@otenet.gr), run by the friendly Yannis Theofanidis; **Aivalioti's Rent-A-Car** (© **24270/21-246**); and **Creator** (© **24270/ 22-385**). In high season, expect to pay 70€ to 95€ ($91–$124) per day for a small car. Mopeds start at about 25€ ($33) per day.

By Boat   The north-coast beaches, adjacent islands, and historic kastro are most easily reached by caique; these smaller vessels, which post their beach and island tour schedules on signs, sail frequently from the fishing harbor west of the Bourtzi fortress. An around-the-island tour that includes stops at Lalaria Beach and the kastro will cost about 30€ ($39).

The Flying Dolphins agent, **Skiathos Holidays,** on the paralia, is open from 7am to 9:30pm; in high season there are as many as eight high-speed hydrofoils daily to Skopelos and Alonissos. (We feel the extra cost for the hydrofoils is worth it for traveling among the Sporades islands.) There are also daily excursions to Skyros in high season. Call © **24270/22-018** for up-to-date schedules. Note that even if you have a ticket, you must appear at the agent's ticket office at least 30 minutes before the scheduled sailing to get your ticket confirmed and seat assigned. **Vasilis Nikolaou** (© **24270/22-209**), the travel agent at the corner of the paralia and Papadiamandis, sells tickets for the ferryboats to the other islands.

FAST FACTS   The official **American Express** agent is Mare Nostrum Holidays, 21 Papadiamandis (© **24270/21-463;** marenost@otenet.gr); open daily from 8am to 10pm. There are many banks in town, such as the **National Bank of Greece,** Papadiamandis, open Monday through Friday from 8am to 2pm and 7 to 9pm, and Sunday from 9am to noon. The **hospital** (© **24270/22-040**) is on the coast road at the far-west edge of town. For **Internet access,** try Internet Zone Cafe, 28 Evangelistrias (zonecafe@hotmail.com).

A self-service **laundry** is at 14 Georgios Panora (✆ **24270/22-341**), 85m (279 ft.) up Papadiamandis, the street opposite the National Bank; or you can drop off a load at the **Snow White Laundry** (✆ **24270/24-256**) one street up from the paralia, behind the Credit Bank; both are open daily from about 8am to 2pm and 5 to 11pm. The **police station** (✆ **24270/21-111**) is about 250m (820 ft.) from the harbor on Papadiamandis, on the left. The **tourist police** booth is about 15m (49 ft.) farther along on the right. The **post office** (✆ **24270/22-011**) is on Papadiamandis, away from the harbor about 160m (525 ft.) and on the right; it's open Monday through Friday from 7:30am to 2pm. The **telephone office** (OTE; ✆ **24270/22-135**) is on Papadiamandis, on the right, some 30m (98 ft.) beyond the post office. It's open Monday through Friday from 7:30am to 10pm, Saturday and Sunday from 9am to 2pm and 5 to 10pm.

WHAT TO SEE & DO

Skiathos is a relatively modern town, built in 1930 on two low-lying hills, then reconstructed after heavy German bombardment during World War II. The handsome **Bourtzi fortress** (originally from the 13th c., but greatly rebuilt across the centuries) jutting into the middle of the harbor is on an islet connected by a broad causeway. Ferries and hydrofoils stop at the port on the right (east) of the fortress, while fishing boats and excursion caiques dock on the left (west). Whitewashed villas with red-tile roofs line both sides of the harbor. The small church of **Ayios Nikolaos** dominates the hill on the east side as does the larger church of **Trion Ierarchon (Three Archbishops)** on the west side.

The main street leading away from the harbor and up through town is named **Papadiamandis,** after the island's best-known son (see description of the Papadiamandis House, below). Here you'll find numerous restaurants, cafes, and stores, plus services such as Mare Nostrum Holidays, the post office, the telephone office, and the tourist police.

On the west flank of the harbor (the left side as you disembark from the ferry) are numerous outdoor cafes and restaurants, excursion caiques (for the north-coast beaches, adjacent islands, and around-the-island tours) and, at the far corner, the stepped ramp (above the Oasis Café) leading up to the town's next level. Mounting these broad steps will lead you to **Plateia Trion Ierarchon,** a stone-paved square around the town's most important church. The eastern flank, technically the New Paralia, is home to many tourist services as well as a few recommended hotels and many restaurants. At the far end, the harborfront road branches right along the yacht harbor, an important nightlife area in summer, and left toward the airport and points of interest inland.

The Papadiamandis House Alexandros Papadiamandis (1851–1911) was born on Skiathos, and after his adult career as a journalist in Athens, he returned in 1908 and died in this very house. His nearly 200 short stories and novellas, mostly about Greek island life, assured him a major reputation in Greece, but his rather idiosyncratic style and vernacular language make his work difficult to translate into foreign languages. His house is less a museum than a shrine containing personal possessions and tools of his writing trade. (A statue of Papadiamandis stands in front of the Bourtzi fortress on the promontory at the corner of the harbor.)

An alley to right of Papadiamandis (main street), 50m (164 ft.) up from harbor. ✆ 24270/23-843. Admission 2€ ($2.60). Tues–Sun 9:30am–1pm and 5–8pm.

BEACHES

Skiathos is famous for its beaches, and we'll cover the most important ones briefly, proceeding clockwise from the port. The most popular beaches are west of town along 12km (8 miles) of coastal highway. At most of them, you can rent an umbrella and two chairs for about 15€ ($20) per day.

The first, **Megali Ammos,** is the sandy strip below the popular package-tour community of Ftelia. It's so close to town and so packed with groups it probably won't appeal to most. **Vassilias** and **Achladias** are also crowded and developed; **Tzanerias** and **Nostos** are slight improvements. Farther out on the Kalamaki peninsula, south of the highway, **Kanapitsa** is good for fans of watersports; **Kanapitsa Water-Sport Center** (© 24270/21-298) has water and jet skis, windsurfing, air chairs, sailing, and speedboat hire. Scuba divers will want to stop at **Dolphin Diving Center** (© 24270/21-599) at the big Nostos Hotel.

Across the peninsula, **Vromolimnos (Dirty Lake)** is fairly attractive and relatively uncrowded, perhaps because of its unsavory name and the cloudy (but not polluted) water that inspires it. The beach offers water-skiing and windsurfing. **Koulos** and **Ayia Paraskevi** are fairly well regarded. **Platanias,** the next major beach, isn't crowded, perhaps because the big resort hotels here have their own pools and sun decks. Past the next headland, **Troulos** is one of the prettiest beaches, due to its relative isolation, crescent shape, and the islets that guard the small bay. Nearby is **Victoria Leisure Center** (© 24270/49-467), which has rooms to rent, a pool, shops, and two tennis courts.

The last bus stop is at much ballyhooed **Koukounaries** 🎖, 16km (10 miles) from Skiathos town. The bus chugs uphill past the Pallas Hotel luxury resort, then descends and winds alongside the inland waterway, Lake Strofilias, stopping at the edge of a fragrant pine forest. *Koukounaries* means "pine cones" in Greek, and behind this grove of trees is a half-mile-long stretch of fine gold sand in a half-moon-shaped cove. Tucked into the evergreen fold are some changing rooms, a small snack bar, and the concessionaires for beach chairs, umbrellas, and windsurfers. The beach can be extremely crowded but with an easy mix of families, singles, and topless sunbathers. (There are several hotels near the beach, but because of the intense mosquito activity and ticky-tacky construction, we prefer to stay back in town or along the coast road.)

Ayia Eleni, a short but scenic walk from the Koukounaries bus stop (the end of the line) west across the island's tip, is a broad cove popular for windsurfing, as the wind is a bit stronger than at the south-coast beaches but not nearly as gusty as at the north. Across the peninsula, at the far right end of the beach, 15 to 20 minutes of fairly steep grade from the Koukounaries bus stop, is **Banana Beach** (sometimes called Krassa). It's slightly less crowded than Koukounaries, but with the same sand and pine trees. There's a snack bar or two, plus chairs, umbrellas, windsurfers, and jet skis for rent. One stretch of Banana Beach is the island's most fashionable nude beach.

Limonki Xerxes, also called Mandraki, north across the island's tip, a 20-minute walk up the path opposite the Lake Strofilias bus stop, is the cove where Xerxes brought in 10 *triremes* (galleys) to conquer the Hellenic fleet moored at Skiathos during the Persian Wars. It's a pristine and relatively secluded beach for those who crave a quiet spot. **Elia,** east across the little peninsula, is also quite nice. Both beaches have small refreshment kiosks.

Continuing along the northeast coast from Mandraki, you arrive at **Megalos Aselinos,** a windy beach where free camping has taken root. It is linked to the southern coastal highway via the road that leads to the Kounistria monastery (see below). You must continue north when the main road forks off to the right toward the monastery. There's also an official campsite and a fairly good taverna. **Mikros Aselinos,** farther east, is smaller and quieter, and you can reach it via a dirt road that leads off to the left just before the monastery.

Skiathos's north coast is much more rugged and scenic, with steep cliffs, pine forests, rocky hills, and caves. Most of these beaches are accessible only by boat, and of these, one is well worth the effort: **Lalaria** ⊛, on the island's northern tip, is one of Greece's most picturesque beaches (although it is a pebble beach). One of its unique qualities is the **Tripia Petra,** perforated rock cliffs that jut into the sea on both sides of the cove. These have been worn through by the wind and the waves to form perfect archways. You can lie on the gleaming white pebbles and admire the neon-blue Aegean and cloudless sky through their rounded openings. The water at Lalaria is an especially vivid shade of aquamarine because of the highly reflective white pebbles and marble and limestone slabs that coat the sea bottom. The swimming here is excellent, but the undertow can be quite strong; inexperienced swimmers should not venture very far. There are several naturally carved caves in the cliff wall that lines the beach, providing privacy or shade for those who have had too much sun. Lalaria is reached by caique excursions from the port; the fare is about 30€ ($39) for an around-the-island trip, which usually includes a stop for lunch (not included in the fare) at one of the other beaches along the northwest coast.

Three of the island's most spectacular grottoes—**Skotini, Glazia,** and **Halkini**—are just east of Lalaria. Spilia Skotini is particularly impressive, a fantastic 6m-high (20-ft.) sea cave reached through a narrow crevice in the cliff wall just wide enough for caiques to squeeze through. Seagulls drift above you in the cave's cool darkness, while below, fish swim in the 9m (30-ft.) subsurface area. Erosion has created spectacular scenery and many sandy coves along the north and east coasts, though none are as beautiful or well sheltered from the *meltemi* (high winds) as Lalaria beach.

THE KASTRO & THE MONASTERIES

When you want a change from the beach, we recommend an excursion to the **Kastro,** the old fortress-capital on the northernmost point of the island, east of Lalaria beach. The kastro was built in a remote and spectacular site in the 16th century, when the island was overrun by the Turks. It was abandoned shortly after the War of Independence, when such fortifications were no longer necessary. Once joined to firm ground by a drawbridge, it can now be reached by cement stairs. The remains of the more than 300 houses and 22 churches have mostly fallen to the sea, but three of the churches, porcelain plates embedded in their worn stucco facades, still stand, and the original frescoes of one are still visible. From this citadel prospect there are excellent views to the **Kastronisia** islet below and the sparkling Aegean. Kastro can be reached by excursion caique, by mule or donkey tour (available through most travel agencies), or by car via the road that leads northeast out of town, passing the turnoff to the Moni Evangelistrias (see below), and continuing on to the end near the church of Panagia Kardasi. From here it is a mildly demanding 2km (1-mile) walk.

Moni Evangelistrias ⊛ is the more rewarding of the two monasteries that draw many visitors. Public buses travel here sporadically, but with your own vehicle it can be easily visited in not much more than an hour from Skiathos town. (Driving will also allow you to stop and admire the views.) To get here, take the road out of the northeast end and pass by the turnoff to the airport. After less than a kilometer, take the sharp right turnoff (signed) and climb about 3km (2 miles) to the monastery. Dating from the late 18th century, it has been completely (but authentically) restored; its architecture, icons, and woodcarvings are fascinating.

The other monastery, **Panagia Kounistria,** is approached from the coastal highway along the beaches (described above); just before Troulos Beach, take the right branch of the road (signed ASELINOS) and climb about 4km (2½ miles) to the monastery. The pretty 17th-century structure contains some fine icons (although its most important icon is now displayed in the Tris Ierarches Church in Skiathos town). Nothing spectacular, but a satisfying excursion. Horseback enthusiasts should note that **Pinewood Horse Riding Club** is also located on the road to this monastery.

SHOPPING

Skiathos town has no shortage of shops, many offering standard wares but some with distinctive items. The highlight for Greek crafts and folk art is **Archipelago** (✆ 24270/22-163); adjacent to (side of) the Papadiamandis House, it offers a world-class assemblage of exquisite objects of art and folklore, both old and new, including textiles, jewelry, and sculpture. **Galerie Varsakis** (✆ 24270/22-255), on Trion Ierarchon Square above the fishing port, also has a virtually museum-quality collection of folk antiques, embroidered bags and linens, rugs from around the world, and other collectibles. Less stylish but full of curiosities is **Gallery Seraina** (✆ 24270/22-0390), at the first junction of Papadiamandis (opposite the alleyway to the Papadiamandis House); it has a goodly selection of ceramic plates, jewelry, some textiles, and unusual glass lampshades.

WHERE TO STAY

Between July 1 and September 15, it can be very difficult to find accommodations. Try calling ahead from Athens to book a room or, better still, book your accommodations before you leave home. Note that many of the "luxury" hotels were thrown up quickly some years ago, and some have since been managed and maintained poorly— so if you plan an extended stay at a beach resort, we recommend you first check into one of the hotels in town and then look over the possibilities before you commit to an extended rental.

If you crave the restaurant/shopping/nightlife scene, or you've arrived without reservations at one of the resort communities, try setting up base in **Skiathos town.** From here, you can take public buses to the beaches on the south coast or go on caique excursions to the spectacular north coast or other islands.

Families often prefer to stay in two- to four-bedroom villas outside of town or at hotels overlooking a beach, with only an occasional foray into town.

One of the most pleasant parts of Skiathos town is the quiet neighborhood on the hill above the bay at the western end of the port. Numerous **private rooms** to let can be found on and above the winding stairs/street. Take a walk and look for the signs, or ask a passerby or neighborhood merchant. All over the hillside above the eastern harbor are several unlicensed "hotels," basically rooms to rent. You'll be surprised at which buildings turn out to be lodgings.

By the way, the in-town hotels (Alkyon excepted) cannot provide adjacent parking, but there are possibilities at the harbor's far eastern edge of the harbor.

IN & AROUND SKIATHOS TOWN

In addition to the following options, consider moderately priced **Hotel Athos,** on the "ring road" that skirts Skiathos town (✆/fax **24270/22-4777**), which offers ready access to town without the bustle; and **Hotel Meltemi,** on the paralia (© 24270/22-493), a comfortable, modern place on the east side of the harbor (but avoid the front units, which can be noisy). Another choice is 30-unit **Hotel Bourtzi,** 8 Moraitou (© **24270/21-304;** fax 24270/23-243), where doubles go for 150€ ($195). Ask for a unit that faces the back garden.

Hotel Alkyon ⚓ "Location, location, location": that's the motto for all of us who appreciate this hotel. For here you can have the best of both worlds—you can be near the harbor of Skiathos town yet enjoy quiet and seclusion. It's not glitzy or luxurious, but neat and subdued; its rooms are medium-size (and offer taped music), and bathrooms are modern. On-site is a small swimming pool with an adjacent bar. Best of all, the Alkyon is a great place for those who look forward to a shady retreat after time in the sun or exploration of the town.

Far eastern end of paralia, 37002 Skiathos. © 24270/22-981. Fax 24270/21-643. 89 units. 60€–110€ ($78–$143) double. Rates include buffet breakfast. AE, MC, V. Parking in adjacent area. *In room:* A/C, minibar.

Hotel Australia If you've come to Skiathos expecting some style, this plain, yet clean and quiet hotel is not for you—it's definitely for budget travelers. Run by a couple who lived in Australia and speak English quite well, the rooms are sparsely furnished but most have balconies; bathrooms are small but functional. Guests can share a fridge in the hallway.

Parados Evangelistrias, 37002 Skiathos. © 24270/22-488. 18 units. 60€ ($78) double; 75€ ($98) studio with kitchen. No credit cards. Turn right off Papadiamandis at the post office, then take the 1st left. *In room:* No phone.

Hotel Morfo Looking for a slightly "atmospheric" offbeat hotel? Turn right off the main street opposite the National Bank, then left at the plane tree (there's a sign). You'll find this attractive hotel on your left on a quiet back street in the center of town. You enter through a small garden into a festively decorated lobby. The rooms are comfortable and tastefully decorated.

23 Anainiou, 37002 Skiathos. © 24270/21-737. Fax 24270/23-222. 17 units. 90€ ($117) double. No credit cards. *In room:* A/C, fridge.

Hotel Orsa ⚓ One of the most charming small hotels in town is on the western promontory beyond the fishing harbor. To get here, walk down along the west port all the way past the fish stalls, proceed up two flights of steps, and watch for a recessed courtyard on the left, with handsome wrought-iron details. Rooms are standard in size but tastefully decorated; most have windows or balconies overlooking the harbor and the islands beyond. A lovely garden terrace is a perfect place for a tranquil breakfast. For booking, contact **Heliotropio Travel** on the harbor's east end (© **24270/22-430;** fax 24270/21-952; helio@skiathos.gr).

Plakes, 37002 Skiathos. © **24270/22-430.** Fax 24270/21-952. helio@n-skiathos.gr. 17 units. 110€ ($143) double. Rates include breakfast. No credit cards.

ON THE BEACH
Atrium Hotel This is one of the class acts of Skiathos hotels. Its location (on a pine-clad slope overlooking the sea) plus amenities make the Atrium Hotel a most pleasant place to vacation. Admittedly, the shady beach is some 100m (328 ft.) below and across the road but the hotel's beautiful pool sits on a plaza high above the Aegean. The rooms have balconies or terraces that offer views over the sea. The hotel has a popular bar and restaurant; if you like, you can enjoy your meal outdoors on the veranda. We have

always found the desk personnel and staff most courteous and helpful but both the staff and guests here observe a certain level of style in dress and conduct.

Platanias (some 8km/5 miles along the coast road southeast of Skiathos town), 37002 Skiathos. ℂ **24270/49-345.** Fax 24270/49-444. www.atriumhotel.gr. 75 units. 120€–160€ ($155–$208) double; 175€–230€ ($228–$299) for family of 4. Rates include buffet breakfast. MC, V. Parking on grounds. **Amenities:** Restaurant; bar; pool; fitness room; watersports gear; car rentals and tours arranged; gift shop; billiards; Ping-Pong. *In room:* A/C, TV, fridge, hair dryer.

Troulos Bay Hotel *Value*   Though it's not exactly luxurious, this would be my first choice among the island's beach hotels for those looking for an unpretentious and laid-back holiday. It's set on handsomely landscaped grounds on one of the south coast's prettiest little beaches. Like most of Skiathos's hotels, it's used mostly by groups, but individual rooms are often available. The restaurant serves decent food at reasonable prices. The bedrooms are modest but comfortably furnished; most have a balcony over-looking the beach and the lovely wooded islets beyond it. Above all, everyone who stays here reports that they find the staff refreshingly hospitable and helpful.

Troulos (9km/6 miles along the coast road southeast of Skiathos, down from the Alpha Supermarket), 37002 Skiathos. ℂ **24270/49-390.** Fax 24270/49-218. troulosbay@skt.forthnet.gr. 43 units. 120€ ($156) double. Rates include breakfast. MC, V. Parking on grounds.

WHERE TO DINE

As in most of Greece's overdeveloped tourist resorts, cafes, fast-food stands, and over-priced restaurants abound, but there are also plenty of good—even excellent—eater-ies in Skiathos town. Some of the best-regarded restaurants are above the west end of the harbor, around Trion Ierarchon church.

EXPENSIVE

Asprolithos ✿ GREEK/INTERNATIONAL   An elegant ambience, friendly and attentive service, and superb meals of light, updated taverna fare make this one of our favorite places to dine on Skiathos. You can get a classic moussaka here if you want to play it safe, or try specialties like artichokes and prawns smothered in cheese. The excellent snapper baked in wine with wild greens is served with thick french fries that have obviously never seen a freezer. A handsome stone fireplace dominates the main dining room. You can sit at outdoor tables and catch the breeze.

Mavroyiali and Korai (up Papadiamandis a block past the high school, then turn right). ℂ **24270/21-016.** Reservations recommended. Main courses 6€–22€ ($7.80–$29). MC, V. Daily 6pm–midnight. Closed late Oct to mid-Mar.

The Windmill Restaurant ✿✿ INTERNATIONAL   The town's most special dining experience is at an old windmill visible from the paralia. (You can approach it in several ways, but the signed route begins on the street between the back of the Akti and San Remo hotels at the eastern end of the harbor.) It is quite a climb, but well worth it. You couldn't ask for a more romantic setting than on one of the terraces, where you can enjoy the sunset with your meal. The Scottish couple that runs it goes for a fairly imaginative cuisine. Many of the main courses are distinctive, even exotic—roast duck breast, Thai fish cakes, vegetarian specialties. The desserts, too, are unusual, and there are nearly two dozen wines to choose from, including the best from Greece. A three-course meal with house wine will cost a couple some 60€ ($78), but as a one-time treat, it's well worth it.

Located on peak east of Ayios Nikolaos church. ℂ **24270/24-550.** www.skiathosinfo.com. Reservations strongly recommended. Main courses 8€–25€ ($10–$33). MC, V. Daily 7–11pm.

MODERATE

Carnayio Taverna TAVERNA/SEAFOOD   One of the better waterfront tavernas is next to Hotel Alkyon. Favorites over the years have been the fish soup, lamb *you-vetsi,* and grilled fish. The garden setting is still special. If you're here late, you might be lucky enough to see a real round of dancing waiters and diners.

Paralia. ✆ **24270/22-868**. Main courses 5€–16€ ($5.50–$21). AE, V. Daily 8pm–1am.

Taverna Limanakia TAVERNA/SEAFOOD   In the style of its next-door neighbor Carnayio, the Limanakia serves some of the best taverna and seafood dishes on the waterfront. I always vacillate about which of the two neighbors I prefer, but always come away feeling satisfied after a meal at this reliable eatery.

Paralia (at far eastern end, past Hotel Alkyon). ✆ **24270/22-835**. Main courses 5€–16€ ($6.50–$21). MC. Daily 6pm–midnight.

Taverna Mesoyia TAVERNA   You'll have to exert yourself a bit to find some of the best authentic traditional food in town. This little taverna is in the midst of the town's most labyrinthine neighborhood, above the western end of the harbor, but there are signs once you approach it. Try an appetizer such as the fried zucchini balls, enjoy the evening specials, or go for fresh fish in season. (As all Greek restaurants are supposed to, this one reveals when something is frozen—as some fish must be at certain times of the year, when they're illegal to catch.) You'll feel as though you're at an old-fashioned neighborhood bistro, not a large tourist attraction.

Grigoriou (follow the signs behind Trion Ierarchon, high above western end of the harbor). ✆ **24270/21-440**. Main courses 6€–18€ ($7.80–$23). No credit cards. Daily 7pm–midnight.

INEXPENSIVE

Kabourelia Ouzeri GREEK   Although it bills itself as an ouzeri—for drinks and snacks—this is really your standard taverna, and one of the most authentic eateries in town. You can have the ouzo and octopus (which you can see drying on the front line!) combo for 6€ ($7.80); or make a meal of the rich supply of cheese pies, fried feta, olives, and other piquant *mezedes.*

Paralia (on harbor's western stretch). ✆ **24270/21-112**. Main courses 4€–13€ ($5.20–$17). AE, MC, V. Daily 10am–1am.

SKIATHOS AFTER DARK

The **Aegean Festival** takes place from late June to early October, offering occasional performances of ancient Greek tragedies and comedies, traditional music and dance, modern dance and theater, and visiting international troupes. Festival events take place in the outdoor theater at the **Bourtzi Cultural Center,** on the promontory on the harbor. (The center itself, open daily 10am–2pm and 5:30–10pm, hosts art exhibits in its interior.) Performances begin at 9:30pm and usually cost about 15€ ($20); call ✆ **24270/23-717** for information.

Although many may prefer to pass the evening with a **volta** (stroll) along the harbor or around and above the Plateia Trion Ierarchon, there is no denying that Skiathos town has a lively nightlife scene. I'll do my best to single out some of the more recently popular places, but I cannot be responsible for the frequent changes of names.

The main concentration of **nightclubs** is in the warren of streets west of Papadiamandis (left as you come up from the harbor). On Evangelistrias, the street opposite the post office is the **Blue Chips Club;** this street intersects with Polytechniou—also known as "Bar Street": here you'll find **Destiny Bar,** the favorite—and lively—hangout for the gay

Moments **A Local Favorite**

I think the best-kept secret of Skiathos town is the **little outdoor cafe** at the tip of the promontory with the Bourtzi fortress, a 5-minute stroll from the harbor. Removed from the glitter of the town, you can sit and enjoy a (cheap) drink in the cool of the evening and watch the ships come and go: This is the Aegean lifestyle at its best.

crowd; the **Admiral Benbow Club,** which offers something a bit quiet; and the flashier **Spartacus.** At the next intersection south, you'll find **Kirki,** a more intimate bar. Wander back down Papadiamandis to find **Kentavros Bar,** on the left beyond the Papadiamandis House, which plays classic rock and jazz.

On the far west end of the harbor, if you want sports with your drinks, try **Oasis Cafe;** if there's a game of any sort going on, it'll be on the tube. Meanwhile, at the far eastern end of the harbor are a few clubs popular with the younger set—among them, **Remezzo** and **Rock 'n' Roll Bar.**

Movie fans might enjoy the open-air showings at **Attikon** (on Papadiamandis, opposite Mare Nostum Holidays), or at **Cinema Paradiso** (up along the "ring road"). Both have two shows nightly, the first around 8:30pm; tickets are 6€ ($7.80).

2 Skopelos

121km (65 nautical miles) from Ayios Konstandinos, which is 166km (103 miles) from Athens

It was inevitable that handsomely rugged Skopelos would also be developed, but it has happened a bit more wisely and at a slower pace than on Skiathos. Although Skopelos's beaches are neither so numerous nor so pretty, Skopelos town is one of the most attractive ports in Greece, and the island is rich in vegetation, with windswept pines growing down to secluded coves, wide beaches, and terraced cliffs of angled rock slabs. The interior is densely planted with fruit and nut orchards, and Skopelos's unique cuisine makes liberal use of the famous plums and almonds grown here. Like Skiathos, impressive grottoes and bays punctuate the coastline, providing irresistible photo ops. Skopelos is also known for keeping alive *rembetika* music, the Greek version of American "blues," that can be heard in tavernas late in the evening.

ESSENTIALS

GETTING THERE   By Plane   Skopelos cannot be reached directly by plane, but you can fly to nearby Skiathos and take a hydrofoil or ferry to the northern port of Loutraki (below Glossa) or to the more popular Skopelos town.

By Boat   If you're in Athens, take a boat or hydrofoil from Ayios Konstandinos to Skopelos (75 min.). **Alkyon Travel,** 97 Akademias, near Kanigos Square (℗ 210/383-2545), can arrange the 3-hour bus ride from Athens to Ayios Konstandinos (about 15€/$20) and hydrofoil or ferry tickets.

Coming from Central or Northern Greece, depart for Skopelos from Volos (about a 2-hr. trip). For hydrofoil (Flying Dolphins) and ferryboat information, contact **Hellenic Seaways** Akti Kondyli and 2 Aitolikou, Piraeus (℗ 210/419-9000; www.hellenicseaways.gr). For ferryboat information, contact the **G.A. Ferries** line in Piraeus (℗ 210/458-2640; www.gaferries.com). Ferry tickets can be purchased at travel agencies in Athens or on the islands. During high season, I recommend that you purchase your boat tickets in advance through the boat lines. Although you may purchase tickets at Alkyon in person, they will not reserve ferryboat or hydrofoil tickets for you in advance, and these often sell out.

From Skiathos, the ferry to Skopelos takes 90 minutes if you call at Skopelos town, or 45 minutes if you get off at Glossa/Loutraki; the one-way fare to both is about 10€ ($13). Ferry tickets can be purchased at **Vasilis Nikolaou** (© **24270/22-209**), the travel agent at the corner of the Paralia and Papadiamandis. The Flying Dolphin hydrofoil takes 15 minutes to Glossa/Loutraki (four to five times daily; 12€/$16), and 45 minutes to Skopelos (six to eight times daily, 14€/$18). From Skiathos, you can also take one of the many daily excursion boats to Skopelos.

There are infrequent ferryboat connections from Kymi (on Evvia) to Skopelos. Check with **Skopelos Port Authority** (© **24240/22-180**) for current schedules, as they change frequently. As stated previously, I think hydrofoils are worth the extra expense for hopping around the Sporades.

In the port of Skopelos town, hydrofoil tickets can be purchased at the Hellenic Seaways agent, **Madro Travel,** immediately opposite the dock (© **24240/22-300**). It's open all year and also operates as the local Olympic Airways representative, so it can make any arrangements you need.

VISITOR INFORMATION   The **Municipal Tourist Office** of Skopelos is on the waterfront, to the left of the pier as you disembark (© **24240/23-231**); it's open daily from 9:30am to 10pm in high season. It provides information, changes money, and reserves rooms. If you want to call ahead to book a room, the **Association of Owners of Rental Accommodation** maintains a small office on the harbor (© **24240/24-567**).

At the travel agency **Skopelorama Holidays,** about 100m (328 ft.) beyond Hotel Eleni on the left (east) end of the port (© **24240/23-040;** fax 24240/23-243), the friendly staff can help you find a room, exchange money, rent a car, or take an excursion; they know the island inside-out and can provide information on just about anything. It's open daily from 8am to 10pm.

GETTING AROUND   **By Bus**   Skopelos is reasonably well served by public bus; the bus stop in Skopelos town is on the east end of the port. There are four routes. Buses run the main route every half-hour in the high season beginning in Skopelos and making stops at Stafilos, Agnondas, Panormos, the Adrina Beach Hotel, Milia, Elios, Klima, Glossa, and Loutraki. The fare from Skopelos to Glossa is 2€ ($2.60).

By Car & Moped   The most convenient way to see the island is to rent a car or moped at one of the many shops on the port. A four-wheel-drive vehicle at **Motor Tours** (© **24240/22-986;** motortours@skopelos.travel) runs around 65€ ($85), including insurance; expect to pay less for a Fiat Panda. A moped should cost about 20€ ($26) per day.

By Taxi   The taxi stand is at the far end of the waterfront (left off the dock). Taxis will provide service to almost any place on the island. Taxis are not metered—negotiate the fare before accepting a ride. A typical fare, from Skopelos to Glossa, runs 40€ ($52).

By Boat   To visit the more isolated beaches, take one of the large excursion boats; these cost about 65€ ($85) including lunch, and should be booked a day in advance in high season. Excursion boats to Glisteri, Gliphoneri, and Sares beaches operate only in peak season (about 20€/$26). From the port of Agnondas, on the south coast, fishing boats go to Limnonari, one of the island's better beaches.

FAST FACTS   There are several **ATMs** at banks around the harbor. The **health center** is on the road leading out of the east end of town (© **24240/22-222**). Plynthria, a self-service **laundry,** is located (in a basement) just past Adonis Hotel on the upper road at the east end of the harbor (© **24240/22-123**). It's open Monday through Saturday from 9:30am to 1:30pm and 6 to 8pm. The **police station** (© **24240/22-235**) is up the narrow road (Parados 1) to the right of the National Bank, along the harbor. For **Internet access,** try Click & Surf (info@skopelosnetcafe.com), just up from the police station—ask for Platanos Square—then proceed up past the supermarket. The **post office,** on the port's far east end (take the stepped road leading away from the last kiosk, opposite the bus/taxi station), is open Monday through Friday from 8am to 2:30pm. The **telephone office (OTE)** is at the top of a narrow road leading away from the center of the harbor; it's open Monday through Saturday from 8am to 5pm.

WHAT TO SEE & DO

The ferries from Alonissos, Skyros, and Kymi, and most of the hydrofoils and other boats from Skiathos, dock at both Glossa/Loutraki and Skopelos town. Most boats stop first at **Loutraki,** a homely little port near the northern end of the west coast, with the more attractive town of **Glossa** 🖈 high above it. Especially if this is your first visit, we suggest you stay onboard for the trip around the island's northern tip and along the east coast to the island's main harbor, Skopelos town. You'll understand the island's name—"cliff" in Greek—when your boat pulls around the last headland into a huge and nearly perfect C-shaped harbor, and you get your first glimpse of Skopelos town rising like a steep amphitheater around the port.

Skopelos town (also called Hora) is one of Greece's most treasured towns, on par with Hydra and Simi. It scales the steep, low hills around the harbor and has the same winding, narrow paths that characterize the more famous Cycladic islands to the south. Scattered on the slopes of the town are just a few of the island's 123 churches, which must be something of a record for such a small locale. The oldest of these is **Ayios Michali,** past the police station. The waterfront is lined with banks, cafes, travel agencies, and the like. Interspersed among these prosaic offerings are truly regal shade trees. Many of the shops and services are up the main street leading away from the center of the paralia. The back streets are amazingly convoluted (and unnamed); it's best that you wander around and get to know a few familiar landmarks.

The **Venetian Kastro,** which overlooks the town from a rise on the western corner, has been whitewashed. It looks too new to have been built over an archaic Temple of

---

Finds National Marine Park

One of the more unusual attractions of a stay on Skopelos could be a day's excursion to the National Marine Park off the adjacent island of Alonissos. There you are guaranteed to see some of the many dolphins that frequent this protected area. The trip includes a stop at the islet of Psathoura, with a chance to dive into a sunken city, and a visit into the Blue Grotto of Alonissos. Any travel agency in Skopelos will be able to arrange such an excursion on one of several licensed ships.

Athena, and too serene for the Turks to have deemed it impossible to impregnate during the War of Independence in the early 19th century.

At the far eastern end of town is the **Photographic Center of Skopelos** (© **24240/ 24-121**), which during the high season sponsors quite classy photography exhibitions in several locales around town.

SHOPPING

Skopelos has a variety of shops selling Greek and local ceramics, weavings, and jewelry. One of the most stylish is **Armoloi,** in the center of the shops along the harbor (© **24240/22-707**). It sells only Greek jewelry, ceramics, weavings, and silver; some of the objects are old. The owners make the most of the handsome ceramics. Another special store is **Ploumisti,** at a corner of an alley about midway along the paralia (© **24240/22-059**; kalaph-skp@skt.forthnet.gr). It sells beautiful Greek rugs, blankets, jewelry, pottery, and crafts. Its friendly proprietors, Voula and Kostas Kalafatis, are full of helpful information for visitors, especially about the *rembetika* music scene. **Nick Rodios** (© **24240/22-924**), whose gallery is between Hotel Eleni and Skopelorama Holidays agency, is from a Skopelos family who have made ceramics for three generations. His elegant black vessels, at once classical and modern, are a change from the usual pottery found around Greece.

EXPLORING THE ISLAND

The whole island is sprinkled with monasteries and churches, but five **monasteries** south of town can be visited by following a pleasant path that continues south from the beach hotels. The first, **Evangelistria,** was founded by monks from Mount Athos, but it now serves as a nunnery, and the weavings of its present occupants can be bought at a small shop; it's open daily from 8am to 1pm and 4 to 7pm. The fortified monastery of **Ayia Barbara,** now abandoned, contains 15th-century frescoes. **Metamorphosis,** very nearly abandoned, comes alive on August 6, when the feast of the Metamorphosis is celebrated here. **Ayios Prodromos** is a 30-minute hike farther, but it's the handsomest and contains a particularly beautiful iconostasis. **Taxiarchon,** abandoned and overgrown, is at the summit of Mount Polouki to the southeast, a hike recommended only for the hardiest and most dedicated.

There is basically a single highway on the island, with short spurs at each significant settlement. It runs south from Skopelos town, then cuts north and skirts the west coast northwest, eventually arriving at Glossa; it then runs down to Loutraki. The first spur leads off to the left to **Stafilos,** a popular family beach recommended by locals for a good seafood dinner, which you must order in the morning. About half a kilometer across the headland is **Velanio,** where nude bathing is common.

The next settlement west is **Agnondas,** named for a local athlete who brought home the gold from the 569 B.C. Olympic Games. This small fishing village has become a tourist resort thanks to nearby beaches. **Limnonari,** a 15-minute walk farther west and accessible by caique in summer, has a good fine-sand beach in a rather homely and shadeless setting.

The road then turns inland again, through a pine forest, coming out at the coast at **Panormos.** With its sheltered pebble beach, this has become the island's best resort with a number of taverns, hotels, and rooms to let, as well as watersports facilities. The road then climbs again toward **Milia** ⚘, which is considered **the island's best beach.** You will have to walk down about half a kilometer from the bus stop, but you'll find a lovely light-gray beach of sand and pebbles, with the island of Dassia opposite and watersports facilities at **Beach Boys Club** (© **24240/23-995**).

The next town, **Elios (Neo Klima),** was thrown up to shelter the people displaced by the 1965 earthquake. It's become home to many of the locals who operate the resort facilities on the west coast, as well as something of a resort itself.

The main road proceeds on to **Glossa** ⊙, which means "tongue," and that's what the hill on which the town was built looks like from the sea. Most of it was spared during the earthquake, so it remains one of the most Greek and charming towns in the Sporades. Those tempted to stay overnight will find a number of rooms for rent, a good hotel, and a very good taverna. (The hotel is the **Avra;** © **24240/33-550;** fax 24240/33-681.)

Most of the coastline here is craggy and has a few hard-to-reach beaches. Among the best places to catch some rays and do a bit of swimming is the small beach below the picturesque monastery of **Ayios Ioannis,** on the coast east from town, which reminds many of Meteora. (Bring food and water.) As for the port of **Loutraki,** it's a winding 3km (2 miles) down; we don't recommend a stay there.

That ends the road tour of Skopelos, but other sites can be reached from Skopelos town by caique. Along the east coast north of Skopelos is **Glisteri,** a small, pebbled beach with a nearby olive grove offering respite from the sun. It's a good bet when the other beaches are overrun in summer. You can also go by caique to the grotto at **Tripiti,** for the island's best fishing, or to the little island of **Ayios Yioryios,** which has an abandoned monastery.

The whole of Skopelos's 95 sq. km (38 sq. miles) is prime for **hiking** and **biking,** and the interior is still waiting to be explored. There's also **horseback riding, sailing** (ask at the Skopelos travel agencies), and a number of interesting **excursions** to be taken from and around the island. Both Skopelorama Holidays and Madro Travel (see "Visitor Information" and "Getting There," above) operate a fine series of excursions, such as monasteries by coach, a walking tour of the town, and several cruises. Another possibility (May–Oct) is a nature (or town) walk led by a longtime English resident, Heather Parsons (www.skopelos-walks.com). One boat excursion that might appeal to some is to the waters around Skopelos that are part of the **National Marine Park;** lucky visitors may spot Mediterranean monk seals, an endangered species protected within the park.

WHERE TO STAY

In high season, Skopelos is nearly as popular as Skiathos. If you've arrived without reservations and need help, talk to the Skopelorama Holidays agency (see "Visitor Information," above) or to the officials at the town hall. Be sure to look at a room and agree on a price before you accept anything, or you may be unpleasantly surprised. To make matters confusing, there are few street names in the main, older section of Skopelos town, so you'll have to ask for directions in order to find your lodging.

IN SKOPELOS TOWN

Handsome, traditional-style **Hotel Amalia,** along the coast, 500m (1,640 ft.) from the port's center (© **24240/22-688;** fax 24240/23-217), is largely occupied by groups but should have spare rooms in spring and fall.

Hotel Denise   One of the most appealing hotels in Skopelos thanks to its premier location, clean facilities, and its own pool, the Hotel Denise stands atop the hill overlooking the town and commands spectacular vistas of the harbor and Aegean. A wide balcony rings each of the hotel's four stories. The guest rooms have hardwood floors and furniture, and most boast views that are among the best in town. The Denise is popular and open only in high season; before hiking up the steep road, call for a pickup and to check for room availability—or better yet, reserve in advance.

Skopelos town 37003. ☎ **24240/22-678.** Fax 24240/22-769. www.denise.gr. 25 units. 100€ ($130) double. Rates include continental breakfast. Credit cards accepted for deposit only. *In room:* A/C, TV, minibar.

Hotel Drossia *(Value)*   This small hotel next to the Hotel Denise (see above), atop the hill overlooking the town, is a good value. The Drossia is of the same vintage as the Denise, with exceptional views but slightly less expensive and less well-equipped rooms.

Skopelos town 37003. ☎ **24240/22-490.** 10 units. 65€ ($85) double. No credit cards. Closed Oct–May.

Hotel Eleni   Hotel Eleni is a modern hotel that can boast of location and convenience as it is set back from the coast and only 300m (984 ft.) to the left (off the dock) from the harbor's center. After many years spent operating pizzerias in New York, Charlie Hatzidrosos returned from the Bronx to build this establishment. His daughter now operates the hotel and provides gracious service. All guest rooms have balconies.

Skopelos town 37003 ☎ **24240/22-393.** Fax 2424/022-936. 37 units. 70€ ($91) double. AE, MC, V. *In room:* TV, fridge.

Hotel Prince Stafilos   *★*   Although Hotel Prince Stafilos charges considerably more than other Skopelos hotels, it's well worth it—especially since it underwent a major renovation in 2006. The handsomest hotel on the island—made of the stone and wood associated with the island's traditional homes—it's about a half-mile south of town. The friendly owner, Pelopidas Tsitsirgos, is also the architect responsible for the establishment's special charm. The lobby is spacious and attractively decorated with local artifacts. Rooms are larger than those in many Greek hotels and furnished in a more traditional Greek style than standard hotel rooms. The restaurant is quite grand; the swimming pool, large. The hotel provides transportation to and from the town center if you don't feel like walking. Most visitors rave about this place.

About 1.6km (1 mile) from center, Skopelos town 37003. ☎ **24240/22-775.** Fax 24240/22-825. 65 units. 160€ ($208) double. Rates include buffet breakfast. AE, MC, V. **Amenities:** Restaurant; 2 bars; pool. *In room:* A/C.

Skopelos Village   Guests here may want to settle in for a while so they can take advantage of this miniresort's amenities. The buildings are tastefully constructed as "traditional island houses." Each bungalow is equipped with kitchen, private bathroom, and one or two bedrooms, and can sleep from two to six persons. Facilities include a breakfast room and snack bar. In the evening, the restaurant offers Greek meals accompanied by Greek music and dance. The hotel provides free transportation to various beaches.

About a half-mile southeast of town center, Skopelos 37003. ☎ **24240/22-517.** www.skopelosvillage.gr. 36 units. High season bungalow for 2 persons, with a kitchen 175€ ($228), mid-season 125€ ($163). Buffet breakfast extra 10€/$13 per person. MC, V. **Amenities:** 2 restaurants; pool; tennis nearby; children's playground; 24-hr. room service. *In room:* A/C, TV, minibar, hair dryer, safe.

IN PANORMOS

This pleasant little resort is on a horseshoe-shaped cove along the west coast, about halfway between Skopelos town and Glossa. Here you'll find several cafeteria-style snack bars and minimarkets. We recommend it as a base, especially because one of the best hotels on the island—Adrina Beach Hotel (below)—is just above it. As for restaurants, a particularly lively taverna, **Dihta,** is right along the beachfront.

Panormos Travel Office (© **24240/23-380;** fax 24240/23-748) has decent rooms to let; offers phone and fax services; exchanges money; arranges tours (including night squid fishing); and rents cars, motorbikes, and speedboats.

If you can't get a room at the Adrina, try 38-unit **Afroditi Hotel** (© **24240/23-150;** fax 24240/23-152), a more modern choice about 100m (328 ft.) across the road from the beach at Panormos.

Adrina Beach Hotel ⟨ᴋ⟩   This traditional hotel, 500m (1,640 ft.) on the beach beyond Panormos, rates as one of the better ones on the island. The guest rooms are large and tastefully furnished in pastels, each with its own balcony or veranda. In addition to the main building's rooms, eight handsome maisonettes are ranked down the steep slope toward the hotel's private beach. The complex has a big saltwater pool with its own bar, a restaurant, a buffet room, spacious sitting areas indoors and out, a playground, and a minimarket. Conference facilities for 50 to 60 people can be provided.

Panormos, 37003 Skopelos. © 24240/23-371 or 210/682-6886 in Athens. www.adrina.gr. 52 units. 150€ ($195) double. Rates include buffet breakfast. AE, DC, MC, V. **Amenities:** 2 restaurants; bar; pool; children's playground; minimarket. *In room:* A/C, TV, fridge.

IN GLOSSA

There are approximately 100 rooms to rent in the small town of Glossa. Expect to pay about 40€ ($52) for single or double occupancy. The best way to find a room is to visit one of the tavernas or shops and inquire about vacancies. You can ask George Antoniou at **Pythari Souvenir Shop** (© **24240/33-077**) for advice. If you can't find a room in Glossa, you can take a bus or taxi down to Loutraki and check into a pension by the water; or you can head back to Panormos.

WHERE TO DINE
IN SKOPELOS TOWN

Finikas Taverna and Ouzeri ⟨ᴋ⟩ GREEK   Tucked away in the upper back streets of Skopelos is a picturesque garden taverna/ouzeri dominated by a broadleaf palm. The Finikas offers what might be Skopelos's most romantic setting, thanks to its isolated and lovely garden seating. Among the many fine courses are an excellent ratatouille and pork cooked with prunes and apples, a traditional island specialty.

Upper back street of Skopelos town. © 24240/23-247. Main courses 5€–12€ ($6.50–$16). No credit cards. Daily 7pm–2am.

The Garden Restaurant GREEK   Some locals claim this is the best restaurant in town. Two young brothers operate what most people call simply "The Garden," for its setting and casual atmosphere. The food is tasty and often a bit different. We've enjoyed the mushrooms with garlic (an appetizer), and calamari with cheese (a main course).

At harbor's far eastern end, 1st left at corner of Amalia Hotel. © 24240/22-349. www.skopelosweb.gr/kipos. Reservations recommended in high season. Main courses 5€–18€ ($6.50–$23). MC, V. Daily 11am–midnight. Closed Oct to mid-June.

Platanos Jazz Bar SNACK/BAR FOOD   For everything from breakfast to a late-night drink, try this pub. Breakfast in the summer starts as early as 5 or 6am for ferry passengers, who can enjoy coffee, fruit salad with nuts and yogurt, and fresh-squeezed orange juice for about 8€ ($10). Platanos is equally pleasant for evening and late-night drinks. Music from the proprietors' phenomenal collection of jazz records will accompany your meal.

Beneath the enormous plane tree just to the left of the ferry dock. ☏ **24240/23-661**. Main courses 4€–10€ ($5.20–$13). No credit cards. Daily 5am–3am.

IN GLOSSA

Taverna Agnanti ⭐ TRADITIONAL SKOPELITIAN   Highly praised by numerous international travel magazines, this is the place to meet, greet, and eat in Glossa. The food is inexpensive, the staff friendly, and the view spectacular. The menu is standard taverna style, but the proprietors make a point of using the finest fresh products and wines. Specialties include herb fritters, fish stifado with prunes, pork with prunes, and almond pie. Traditional music is occasionally played. The Stamataki family runs this and the nearby souvenir shop Pythari.

Glossa. ☏ **24240/33-076**. agnanti-rest@agnanti-rest.gr. Main courses 5€–20€ ($6.50–$26). No credit cards. Daily 11am–midnight. About 200m (656 ft.) up from the bus stop.

SKOPELOS AFTER DARK

The nightlife scene on Skopelos isn't nearly as active as on neighboring Skiathos, but there are still plenty of bars, late-night cafes, and discos. Most of the coolest bars are on the far (east) side of town, but you can wander the scene around Platanos Square, beyond and along the paralia: **Anemos, Karabia, Barramares, Ionas, Mythos**—one of these places should satisfy. The best place for *bouzouki* music is **Metro** and for *rembetika* try the **Kastro.** For live music with a spectacular view of the town, ask for directions to the **Anatoli Ouzeri.**

3 Skyros (Skiros)

47km (25 nautical miles) from Kymi; 182km (113 miles) from Athens

Skyros is an island with good beaches, attractive whitewashed pillbox architecture, picturesque surroundings, low prices—yet relatively few tourists. Why? Well, it's difficult to get to. In summer, occasional ferries and hydrofoils link Skyros to the other Sporades as well as to ports on the mainland, but these links are either fairly infrequent or involve land transportation to ports that are not on most tourists' itineraries. Aside from that, most visitors to the Sporades seem to prefer the more thickly forested (and thickly touristed) islands. Others of us, however, think Skyros's more meager tourist facilities and the stark contrast between sea, sky, and rugged terrain make it all the more inviting.

Also, many Skyriots have been ambivalent about developing this very traditional island for tourism. Until about 1990, only a handful of hotels existed on the entire island. Since then, Skyros has seen a miniboom in the tourist business, and with the completion of a giant marina, it's set to become yet another tourist hot spot. Don't let this deter you, however; at least for now, Skyros remains an ideal place for a getaway.

ESSENTIALS

GETTING THERE   By Plane   In summer, **Olympic Airways** has about two flights a week between Athens and Skyros. Call the Olympic office in Athens (☏ **210/966-6666**) for information and reservations; the local Olympic representative is **Skyros Travel and Tourism** (☏ **22220/91-123**). A bus meets most flights and goes to Skyros town, Magazia, and sometimes Molos; the fare is 5€ ($6.50). A taxi from the airport is about 15€ ($20), but expect to share a cab.

By Boat   Skyros Shipping Company (www.sne.gr) offers the only ferry service to Skyros; it's operated by a company whose stockholders are all citizens of the island. In summer, it runs twice daily (usually early afternoon and early evening) from Kymi (on the east coast of Evvia) to Skyros, and twice daily (usually early morning and midafternoon) from Skyros to Kymi; the trip takes a little over 2 hours. Off season, there's one ferry each way, leaving Skyros early in the morning and Kymi in late afternoon. The fare is 10€ to 15€ ($13–$20). For information, call the company's office either in Kymi (© **22220/22-020**) or Skyros (© **22220/91-790**). The Skyros Shipping Company's offices also sell connecting bus tickets to Athens; the fare for the 3-hour ride is about 15€ ($20). In Athens, **Alkyon Travel,** 97 Akademia, near Kanigos Square (© **210/383-2545**), arranges bus transportation to Kymi and sells ferry tickets to the Sporades.

If you're trying to "do" the Sporades and want to make connections at Kymi, the tricky part can be the connection with ferries or hydrofoils from the other Sporades islands. When they don't hold to schedule, it's not uncommon to see the Skyros ferry disappearing on the horizon as your ship pulls into Kymi. You might have to make the best of the 24-hour layover and get a room in Paralia Kymi. (We recommend **Hotel Korali,** at © **22220/22-212;** or the older **Hotel Krineion,** at © **22220/22-287**).

From Athens, buses to Kymi and Ayios Konstandinos leave the Terminal B (260 Lission) six times a day, though you should depart no later than 1:30pm; the fare for the 3½-hour trip is about 20€ ($26). From Kymi, you must take a local bus to Paralia Kymi. Ask the bus driver if you're uncertain of the connection.

On Skyros, the ferries and hydrofoils dock at **Linaria,** on the opposite side of the island from Skyros town. The island's only public bus will meet the boat and take you over winding, curving roads to Skyros town for 2€ ($2.60). On request, the bus will also stop at Magazia beach, immediately north below the town, next to Xenia Hotel.

VISITOR INFORMATION   The largest tourist office is **Skyros Travel and Tourism** (© **22220/91-123;** www.skyrostravel.com), next to Skyros Pizza Restaurant in the main market. It's open daily from 8am to 2:30pm and 6:30 to 10:30pm. English-speaking Lefteris Trakos offers assistance with accommodations, currency exchange, Olympic Airways flights (he's the local ticket agent), phone calls, interesting bus and boat tours, and Hellenic Seaways Flying Dolphin tickets.

GETTING AROUND   **By Bus**   The only scheduled service is the Skyros-Linaria shuttle that runs four to five times daily and costs 2€ ($2.60). Skyros Travel (see above) offers a twice-daily beach-excursion bus in high season and daylong island excursions in a small bus with an English-speaking guide (40€/$52); for many, this may be the best way to get an overview of the island.

By Car & Moped   A small car rents for about 70€ ($91) per day, including insurance. Mopeds and motorcycles are available near the police station or the taxi station for about 25€ ($33) per day. The island has a relatively well-developed network of roads.

By Taxi   Taxis can take you just about any place on the island at the standard Greek rates, but discuss the price before setting off; service between Linaria and Skyros costs about 15€ ($20).

On Foot   Skyros is a fine place to hike. The island map, published by Skyros Travel and Tourism, will show you a number of good routes, and it is pretty accurate.

FAST FACTS   The most convenient ATM on Skyros is at the **National Bank of Greece** in the main square of Skyros town. (Because Skyros's tourist services are relatively limited, we recommend bringing cash and/or traveler's checks for emergencies.)

The **clinic** is near the main square (*©* **22220/92-222**). The **police station** (*©* **22220/91-274**) is on the street behind the Skyros Travel Center. The **post office** is near the bus square in Skyros town; it's open Monday through Friday from 8am to 2pm. The **telephone office (OTE)** is opposite the police station. It's open Friday only, from 7:30am to 3pm, but there are card phones in town.

WHAT TO SEE & DO
The Faltaits Historical and Folklore Museum
This is one of the best island folk-art museums in Greece. Located in an old house belonging to the Faltaits family, the private collection of Manos Faltaits contains a large and varied selection of plates, embroidery, weaving, woodworking, and clothing, as well as many rare books and photographs, including some of local men in traditional costumes for Carnival. Attached to the museum is a workshop where young artisans make lovely objects using traditional patterns and materials. The proceeds from the sale of workshop items go to the upkeep of the museum. The museum also has a shop, **Argo,** on the main street of town (*©* **22220/92-158**). It's open daily from 10am to 1pm and 6:30 to 11pm.

Plateia Rupert Brooke. *©* **22220/91-327**. www.faltaits.gr. 2€ ($2.60). Summer Tues–Sun 8:30am–3pm. Off season, ring the bell and someone will probably let you in.

EXPLORING THE ISLAND
All boats dock at **Linaria,** a plain, mostly modern fishing village on the west coast, pleasant enough but not recommended for a stay. Catch the bus waiting on the quay to take you across the narrow middle of the island to the west-coast capital, Skyros town, which is built on a rocky bluff overlooking the sea. (The airport is near the northern tip of the island.) **Skyros town,** which is known on the island as Horio or Hora, looks much like a typical Cycladic hill town, with whitewashed houses built on top of one another. The winding streets and paths are too narrow for cars and mopeds, so most of the traffic is by foot and hoof. After you alight at the bus stop square, continue on up toward the center of town and the main tourist services.

Near the market, signs point to the town's **kastro.** The climb takes 15 minutes, but the view is worth it. On the way you'll pass the church of **Ayia Triada,** which contains interesting frescoes; and the monastery of **Ayios Yioryios Skyrianos.** The monastery was founded in 962 and contains a famous black-faced icon of St. George brought from Constantinople during the Iconoclastic controversy. From one side of the citadel, the view is over the rooftops of the town, and from the other the cliff drops precipitously to the sea. According to one myth, King Lykomides pushed Theseus to his death from here.

The terrace at the far (northern) end of the island is **Plateia Rupert Brooke,** where the English poet, who is buried on the southern tip of the island, is honored by a nude statue, "Immortal Poetry." (Brooke died on a hospital ship off Skyros in 1915 while en route to the Dardanelles as an army officer.) The statue is said to have greatly offended the local people when it was installed, but you're more likely to be amused when you see how pranksters have chosen to deface the hapless bronze figure. (The Faltaits Historical and Folklore Museum, described above, is near this site, as is the not especially distinguished archaeological museum.)

Local customs and dress are currently better preserved on Skyros than in all but a few locales in Greece. Older men can still be seen in baggy blue pants, black caps, and leather sandals with numerous straps, and older women still wear long head scarves. The **embroidery** you will often see women busily working at is famous for its vibrant colors and interesting motifs—such as people dancing hand-in-hand with flowers twining around their limbs and hoopoes with fanciful crests.

Peek into the doorway of any Skyrian home, and you're likely to see what looks like a room from a dollhouse with a miniature table and chairs, as well as **colorful plates**—loads of them—hanging on the wall. These displays are said to date back to the Byzantine era, when the head clerics from Epirus sent 10 families to Skyros to serve as governors. They were given control of all the land not owned by Mount Athos and the Monastery of St. George. For hundreds of years, these 10 families dominated the affairs of Skyros. With Kalamitsa as a safe harbor, the island prospered, and consulates opened from countries near and far. The merchant ships were soon followed by pirates, with whom the ruling families went into business. The families knew what boats were expected and what they were carrying, and the pirates had the ships and bravado to steal the cargo. The pirates, of course, soon took to plundering the islanders as well, but the aristocrats managed to hold onto much of their wealth.

Greek independence reduced the influence of these ruling families, and during the hard times brought by World War I, they were reduced to trading their possessions to the peasant farmers for food. Chief among these bartered items were sets of dinnerware. Plates from China, Italy, Turkey, Egypt, and other exotic places became a sign of wealth, and Skyrian families made elaborate displays of their newly acquired trophies. Whole walls were covered, and by the 1920s local Skyrian craftsmen began making their own plates for the poorer families who couldn't afford the originals. This, at least, is the story they tell.

Moments **The Famous Carnival of Skyros**

The 21-day Carnival celebration is highlighted by a 4-day period leading up to Lent and the day known throughout Greece as *Kathari Deftera* (Clean Monday). On this day, Skyros residents don traditional costumes and perform dances on the town square. Unleavened bread *(lagana)* is served with *taramosalata* and other meatless specialties. (Traditionally, vegetarian food is eaten for 40 days leading up to Easter.) Much of this is traditional throughout Greece, but Skyros adds its own distinctive element. Culminating on midafternoon of the Sunday before Clean Monday is a series of ritual dances and events performed by a group of weirdly costumed men. Some dress as old shepherds in animal skins with belts of sheep bells and masks made of goatskin. Other men dress as women and flirt outrageously. (Skyros seems to have an age-old association with cross-dressing: It was here that Achilles successfully beat the draft during the Trojan war by dressing as a woman, until shrewd Odysseus tricked him into revealing his true gender.) Other celebrants caricature Europeans. All behave outlandishly, reciting ribald poetry and poking fun at bystanders. This ritual is generally thought to be pagan in origin, and what you see has deep roots. Some of the antic elements might seem similar to parts from ancient Greek comedies, and the word tragedy means "goat song," so the goat-costume ceremonies may go way back also.

Skyros is also the home of a unique breed of **wild pygmy ponies,** often compared to the horses depicted on the frieze of the Parthenon and thought to be similar to Shetland ponies. Most of these rare animals have been moved to the nearby island of Skyropoula, though tame ones can still be seen grazing near town. Ask around and you might be able to find a local who will let you ride one.

Every July 15, the ponies of Skyros are assembled and rated as to their characteristics, and then young boys race some of the ponies around a small track.

BEACHES & OUTDOOR PURSUITS

The island is divided almost evenly by its narrow waist; the northern half is fertile and covered with pine forest, while the southern half is barren and quite rugged. Both halves have their attractions, though the most scenic area of the island is probably to the south toward **Tris Boukes,** where Rupert Brooke is buried. The better beaches, however, are in the north.

To get to the beach at **Magazia,** continue down from Plateia Rupert Brooke. (If your load is heavy, take a taxi to Magazia, as it is a hike.) From Magazia, once the site of the town's storehouses (magazines), it's about a half-mile to **Molos,** a fishing village, though the two villages are quickly becoming indistinguishable because of development. There's windsurfing along this beach and, beyond Molos, windsurfing at fairly isolated beaches with nudist sections.

South of town, the beaches are less enticing until you reach **Aspous,** which has a couple of tavernas and rooms to let. **Ahili,** a bit farther south, is where you'll find the big new **marina,** so it's no longer much of a place for swimming. Farther south, the coast gets increasingly rugged and has no roadway.

If you head back across the narrow waist of the island to **Kalamitsa,** the old safe harbor, 3km (2 miles) south of Linaria, you'll find a good clean beach. Buses run here in summer.

North of Linaria, **Acherounes** is a very pretty beach. Beyond it, **Pefkos,** where marble was once quarried, is better sheltered and has a taverna that's open in summer. The next beach north, **Ayios Fokas,** is probably the best on the island, with a lovely white pebble beach and a taverna open in summer. Locals call it paradise, and like all such places it's very difficult to reach. Most Skyrians will suggest walking, but the hike is long and hilly. To get here from Skyros town, take the bus back to Linaria, tell the driver where you're going, get off at the crossroads with Pefkos, and begin your hike west from there.

North of Ayios Fokas is **Atsitsa,** another beach with pine trees, but it's a bit too rocky. It can be reached by road across the Olymbos mountains in the center of the island, and has a few rooms to let. It is also the location of a **holistic health-and-fitness holiday community,** which offers "personal growth" vacations, with courses in fitness, holistic health, creative writing, and handicrafts. For information on its activities, contact the **Skyros Center** in the United Kingdom at 92 Prince of Wales Rd., London NW5 3NE (© **020/7267-4424;** www.skyros.com). This same British outfit runs the **Skyros Centre** at the edge of Skyros town; it differs from the one at Atsitsa in that it offers a somewhat more conventional touristic experience. A 15-minute walk farther north from Atsitsa, **Kira Panagia** is a sandy beach that's a bit better.

The northwest of the island is covered in dense pine forests, spreading down to the Aegean. The rocky shore opens onto gentle bays and coves. This area provides wonderful **hiking** for the fit. Take a taxi (30€/$39) to **Atsitsa,** and arrange for it to return in 5 or 6 hours. Explore the ruins of the ancient mining operation at Atsitsa, then head south for about 7km (4½ miles) to **Ayios Fokas,** a small bay with a tiny taverna perched right on the water. Kali Orfanou, the gracious hostess, will provide you with the meal of your trip: fresh fish caught that morning in the waters before you, vegetables plucked from the garden for your salad, and her own feta cheese and wine. Relax, swim in the bay, and then hike back to your taxi. The ambitious may continue south for 11 or 12km (7–8 miles) to the main road and catch the bus or hail a taxi. Note that this part of the road is mainly uphill. In case you tire or can't pry yourself away from the secluded paradise of Ayios Fokas, Kali offers two extremely primitive rooms with the view of your dreams, but without electricity or toilets.

SHOPPING

Skyros is a good place to buy local crafts, especially embroidery and ceramics. **Ergastiri,** on the main street, sells interesting ceramics, Greek shadow puppets, and a great selection of postcards. **Yiannis Nicholau,** whose studio is next to Xenia Hotel, is known for his handmade plates. You can find good hand-carved wooden chests and chairs made from beech (in the old days it was blackberry wood) from **Lefteris Avgoklouris,** former student of the recently departed master, Baboussis, in Skyros town; his studio (© 22220/91-106) is on Konthili, around the corner from the post office. Another fine carver is **Manolios,** in the main market.

WHERE TO STAY

The island has relatively few hotels, so most visitors to Skyros take private rooms. The best are in the upper part of Skyros town, away from the bus stop, where women in black dresses accost you with cries of "Room! Room!" If you are determined to make arrangements before arriving, you could phone or fax the **Skyros Association of Hotels and Rooms:** © 22220/92-095, fax 22290/92-770. It is better to wait until you are on the scene and contact **Skyros Travel and Tourism** (see "Visitor Information," above). The island of Skyros is somewhat more primitive in its facilities than the other Sporades, so before agreeing to anything, check out the room to ensure that it's what you want.

IN SKYROS TOWN

Hotel Nefeli   One of the best in-town options is furnished in the traditional Skyrian style (and completely upgraded in 2003). The bedrooms and bathrooms are decent in size and well-appointed; many units have fine views. The large downstairs lobby is a welcoming space. Reserve in advance, as the Nefeli is one of the favorite choices on Skyros.

Skyros town center, 34007 Skyros. © **22220/91-964.** Fax 22220/92-061. 16 units. 100€ ($130) double. Breakfast 5€ ($6.50) extra. AE, MC, V. **Amenities:** Restaurant, bar; swimming pool; children's pool; children's play area; room service; Internet access. *In room:* A/C, TV, minibar, dryer.

IN MAGAZIA BEACH & MOLOS

Hotel Angela *(Value*   This is among the most attractive and well-kept abodes in the Molos/Magazia beach area, located near the sprawling Paradise Hotel complex. All rooms are clean and tidy with balconies, but because the hotel is set back about 91m (300 ft.) from the beach, it has only partial sea views. Nevertheless, the facilities and hospitality of the young couple running the Angela make up for its just-off-the-beach location, and it's your best bet for the money.

Molos, 34007 Skyros. © **22220/91-764.** Fax 2222/92-030. anghotel@otenet.gr. 14 units. 90€ ($117) double. No credit cards.

Paradisssos Hotel   This pleasant lodging is at the north end of Magazia beach, in the town of Molos. The older part of the hotel has 40 rooms; these more basic units run about 50% less. We recommend one of the newer section's 20 rooms, which are better kept and have much better light. The hotel is somewhat removed from the main town, but there is a taverna on the premises and another down the street.

Molos, 34007 Skyros. ☎ **22220/91-220.** Fax 22220/91-443. 60 units. 80€ ($104) double in the new building. Breakfast 5€ ($6.50) extra. No credit cards.

Pension Galeni   The small but delightful Pension Galeni offers modest rooms, all with private bathrooms. Ask for one of the front, sea-facing rooms on the top floor for their (currently) unobstructed views. The Galeni overlooks one of the cleanest parts of Magazia beach.

Magazia beach, 34007 Skyros. ☎ **22220/91-379.** 13 units. 65€ ($85) double. No credit cards.

Xenia   With the best location on the beach at Magazia, the Xenia offers some of the nicest (if not cheapest) accommodations on Skyros. The guest rooms have handsome 1950s-style furniture and big bathrooms with tubs, as well as wonderful balconies and sea views. You can get all your meals here if you want. Perhaps the hotel's greatest drawback is the unsightly concrete breakwater that's supposed to protect the beach from erosion.

Magazia Beach, 34007 Skyros. ☎ **22220/92-063.** Fax 22220/92-062. 22 units. 115€ ($150) double. Rates include buffet breakfast. V.

IN ACHEROUNES BEACH
Pegasus Apartments   These fully equipped studios and apartments were built by the resourceful Lefteris Trakos (owner of Skyros Travel). They are at Acherounes, the beach just south of the port of Linaria, on the east coast. One of the pluses of staying here is the chance to see (and ride, if you're under 15) Katerina, a Skyriot pony.

Acherounes Beach, 34007 Skyros. ☎ **22220/91-552.** 8 units. 55€ ($72) studio for 2 persons; 120€ ($156) apt for 3–5 persons. MC, V. *In room:* Minibar.

IN YIRISMATA
Skiros Palace Hotel ✦   If you want to get away from it all and enjoy upscale amenities to boot, this is the place for you. This out-of-the-way resort—about 1.6km (1 mile) north of Molos, and 3km (2 miles) north of Skyros town—has the most luxurious accommodations on the island. The plainly furnished but comfortable guest rooms come with large balconies. The beach across the road is an especially windy, rocky stretch of coastline, with treacherous waters. Facilities include a lovely (saltwater) pool and adjacent bar, some air-conditioned rooms, and a well-planted garden—not to mention a soundproof disco, the island's most sophisticated. A minibus heads into town twice a day.

Yirismata, 34007 Skyros. ☎ **22220/91-994.** www.skiros-palace.gr. 80 units. 110€ ($143) double. Rates include breakfast. AE, DC, MC, V. **Amenities:** 2 restaurants; bar; disco; pool; tennis; basketball court; minibus to town; sailboat for excursions; TV in lobby. *In room:* A/C in some rooms.

WHERE TO DINE
The food in Skyros town is generally pretty good and reasonably priced. **Anemos,** on the main drag (☎ **22220/92-155**), is a nice spot for breakfast, with filtered coffee, omelets, and freshly squeezed juice. Nearby **Skyros Pizza Restaurant** (☎ **22220/91-684**) serves tasty pies as well as other Greek specialties. For dessert, head to **Zaccharoplasteio** (the Greek word for sweet shop/bakery) in the center of town.

Linaria offers three decent tavernas to choose from—**Almyria, Filippeos,** and **Psariotos.**

Kristina's/Pegasus Restaurant ✿ INTERNATIONAL Come here if you need a break from standard Greek fare. Kristina's has been an institution in Skyros town for some years, but in 2000 it moved to the locale of the former Pegasus Restaurant, a neoclassical building (ca. 1890) in the center of town. The Australian proprietor/chef, Kristina, brings a light touch to everything she cooks. Her fricasseed chicken is excellent, her herb bread is tasty, and her desserts, such as cheesecake, are exceptional.

Skyros town. ✆ **2222/91-123.** Reservations recommended in summer. Main courses 6€–18€ ($7.80–$23). No credit cards. Mon–Sat 7am–4pm and 7pm–1am.

Maryetes Grill GRILL One of the oldest and best places in town, the Maryetes is a second-generation-run grill that's equally popular with locals and travelers. Go for the food, not the dining room, which is as simple as can be. We recommend the grilled chicken and meat. A small sampling of salads is also on the menu.

Skyros town. ✆ **22220/91-311.** Main courses 6€–10€ ($7.80–$13). No credit cards. Daily 1–3pm and 6pm–midnight.

Restaurant Kabanero (Value GREEK One of the best dining values in town, this perpetually busy eatery serves the usual Greek menu: moussaka, stuffed peppers and tomatoes, fava, a variety of stewed vegetables, and several kinds of meat. The dishes are tasty and the prices somewhat lower than those at most other places in town.

Skyros town. ✆ **22220/91-240.** Main courses 5€–12€ ($6.50–$16). No credit cards. Daily 1–3pm and 6pm–midnight.

SKYROS AFTER DARK
As usual in such locales, names and atmospheres can change from year to year. But at last checking, the **Kastro Club,** in Linaria, was for dancing. **Stone,** on the road to Magazia, and Linaria's **O Kavos** are other popular hangouts. Aside from these, you'll find few evening diversions other than barhopping on the main street of Skyros town. **Apocalypsis** draws a younger crowd. **Kalypso** attracts a more upscale set of drinkers. **Renaissance** is lively but can be loud. **Rodon** is best for actually listening to music, while **Kata Lathos (By Mistake)** has also gained a following.

14

Highlights of Western Greece: Epirus & Ioannina

by John S. Bowman

Evergreen slopes, deep-set rivers and lush valleys, villages of timbered houses, slate or tile roofs—this can't be Greece. But it is. It's the northwestern corner the Greeks know as **Epirus.** Plentiful rainfall, the rugged Pindos Mountains, and a generally more temperate climate—in places, it seems like Alpine country. And in fact it's one of the few regions in Greece where you'll be enjoying your travels away from the sea.

Epirus and its capital city, **Ioannina,** seem immune to the throngs who crowd the beaches and restaurants, the ferries and ancient sites, of so many parts of Greece these days. It isn't the travel-poster Greece many expect, and it certainly hasn't organized itself around tourism and foreigners.

Although there are plenty of hotels and restaurants, the pace of life in Ioannina

and other Western Greece cities, not to mention in the villages, is still governed by local customs. During the off season, for instance, places such as the post office and information offices may be closed all weekend. Museum hours are cut back, as are the hours of gift shops and many restaurants. And except for some staff in the hotels, better restaurants, and visitor information and car-rental offices, few people speak English, although they may speak Italian, French, or German. You may find yourself sharing a hotel with Greek commercial travelers, and it will probably be harder to find your English-language newspaper or fresh-squeezed orange juice. In other words, this area is for those who enjoy traveling in an authentic foreign land. Try it—you may like it!

A STRATEGY FOR SEEING THE REGION

Visitors to this corner of Greece will come by ship from Italy or Corfu (via Igoumenitsou), by plane from Athens or Thessaloniki, or by car or bus from other parts of Greece. We recommend basing yourself in Ioannina, a city that offers a fine mix of natural attractions, historical associations, and modern amenities. With only 2 or 3 days you can take in the attractions of Ioannina on foot, and you can visit Epirus's other main destination, **Metsovo,** by bus. But you really should rent a car to see most of the other attractions of Epirus, including **Dodona** and the cave at **Perama.** And for the truly adventurous, there are the **Zagori** villages and at least a glimpse of the **Vikos Gorge.** So we recommend a minimum of 4 days for Epirus—2 days for Ioannina, 1 day for Metsovo, and a half-day each for Dodona and the Perama cave.

Tips **Travel Tip**

Visit Epirus between early June and mid-September, unless you don't mind cooler weather. In the winter, you can come up here to ski.

A LOOK AT THE PAST   In their history, Western Greece and Epirus in particular have often gone in different directions from the rest of the country. The early Greek-speaking communities here shared a common culture with the rest of Greece, worshiping many of the same gods. However, many non-Greeks also settled here and influenced day-to-day life. This, coupled with the region's remoteness, meant that the people here did not participate in the grand classical civilization. Social organization remained more tribal, led by small-time kings. The greatest of the Epirote kings, **Pyrrhus** (318–272 B.C.), was constantly waging war. The term "Pyrrhic victory" refers to his victories (over the Romans outside of Rome), which came at great cost. Epirus itself was reduced to a Roman province after 168 B.C. Ioannina, its capital, is said to have been founded by the Emperor Justinian around A.D. 527.

During the **Middle Ages,** Western Greece constantly fell prey to invaders. When the Crusaders conquered Constantinople in 1204, some Greeks decided to set up a new state with Ioannina as the capital, the so-called Despotate of Epirus. It never amounted to much and soon fell under outside control. In 1431 it was taken over by the Turks, who eventually controlled most of Greece (although the Venetians and various other western Europeans gained possession of parts of Western Greece).

Near the end of this 350-year phase, Epirus experienced its most dramatic historic moment. In 1788, **Ali Pasha,** the "Lion of Ioannina," established his own relatively independent domain with Ioannina its capital. Born in Albania, he rose to prominence fighting on behalf of the Ottoman Sultan in Constantinople. An international celebrity in his day, visited by Byron among others, he was a cruel despot who boasted of killing 30,000 people, often in the most brutal fashion. The Ottomans tolerated Ali Pasha as long as they could, but in 1822 they sent a large force to capture him. He hid in a monastery on the islet off Ioannina but was tracked down, killed, and beheaded.

When the Greeks rose up against the Turks in the 1820s, the southern part of Western Greece, centered around Messolonghi, took an active role, but the bulk of Epirus did not join in. Arta, in the southwest, was freed from Turkish rule in 1881, but Epirus did not formally join Greece until after the Second Balkan War of 1913.

Epirus became a battleground twice more, against the invading Italians and Germans in World War II and then in the Greek civil war. Since then, it has enjoyed peace and quiet prosperity.

1 Getting to & around Epirus

GETTING THERE

By Plane   Olympic Airways (© 210/966-6666; www.olympicairlines.gr) offers flights to Ioannina from Athens—usually two a day. Olympic flies at least once a day between Ioannina and Thessaloniki. **Aegean Airlines** (© 210/626-1000; www. aegeanair.com) offers daily flights between Athens and Ioannina. Olympic also flies about once a day from Athens to Aktion, just outside Preveza on the southernmost coast of Epirus; from here you can get a bus to Igoumenitsou and Ioannina or even to the island of Lefkada, which is connected by a viaduct to the mainland.

By Boat **Igoumenitsou,** on the coast opposite Corfu, is the point of entry to northwestern Greece for many people. In summer, ferries connect hourly to Corfu (trip time 1–2 hr., depending on the ship) and less frequently to Kefalonia, Ithaka, and Paxi. A hydrofoil service also runs twice daily during high season, between Corfu and Igoumenitsou (allow about a half-hour). Numerous ferries and ships that put into Igoumenitsou go to and from ports in Italy—Ancona, Bari, Brindisi, Venice; some of these connect with Patras or Piraeus in Greece or with even more distant ports such as Iraklion, Crete, or Cesme, Turkey.

In high season a ferry connects **Astakos**—on the Ionian coast south of Preveza and north of Messolonghi—to the offshore islands of Ithaka and Kefalonia.

The schedules are too complex to list here. For information in advance, contact **Thalassa Travel** in Igoumenitsou, at 20 Ethniki Antistasseos (✆ **26650/22-001**). You can also go to www.ferries.gr.

By Bus The **KTEL** line (✆ **210/512-5954** in Athens, or 26510/26-211 in Ioannina) enters northwestern Greece from points such as Athens (7½ hr.) or Thessaloniki (8 hr.).

By Car **From Athens,** there are two main routes. One takes the inland route north via Livadia, Lamia, Karditsa, Trikkala, Kalambaka, and Ioannina. The second runs via Corinth and then along the southern coast of the Gulf of Corinth to Rio; from there, take the new bridge to Anti-Rio, and then drive north via Messolonghi, Agrinio, and Arta to Ioannina. Alternatively, head to the Ionian coast after Messolonghi, and go up to Igoumenitsou via Astakos, Preveza, and Parga.

The preferred route **from Thessaloniki** goes by Veria west to Kozani and Konitsa and then south to Ioannina. (Sections of a new expressway are now open.) **From western Europe,** you can drive through the former Yugoslavia (now independent nations)—either along the Dalmatian Coast or via the inland expressway—and enter Northern Greece at Florina, from where you head south to Kastoria and Ioannina.

GETTING AROUND

By Bus With enough time, you can see most of Western Greece by bus (add time for side trips); given the many mountainous roads and curves, you might prefer to let others do the driving. **KTEL** provides bus links between most towns in Western Greece. Buses leave for **Athens** and points **north, northwest,** and **northeast** (Igoumenitsou, Metsovo, Konitsa, Kastoria, and Thessaloniki) from Ioannina's **main bus terminal** at 4 Zosimadon (✆ **26510/26-211**). A smaller **bus terminal** in Ioannina (at 19 Vizaniou; ✆ **26510/25-014**) handles travel to the **south** (Parga, Arta, Preveza, Astakos, Messolonghi, and Patras).

By Car Having a car is probably the best way to experience Western Greece at its fullest. Trips take much longer than a map might suggest due to the many mountain roads. (Mopeds and motorcycles are not advised except for the most experienced.) Western Greece doesn't offer the choice in car rentals found in more touristed parts of Greece. We think **Budget** in Ioannina (109 Dodonis; ✆ **26510/43-901**), is the best agency to deal with. This family affair is run by owner Angela Tsamatos, her son Stelios, and genial manager Paul Angelis. Don't expect to haggle during high season—there are a limited number of vehicles for the influx of tourists.

> ### (*Tips*) Museums & Sites Hours Update
>
> If you visit Greece during the summer, check to see when major sites and museums are open. According to the official postings, they should be open from 8am to 7:30pm, but some may close earlier in the day and are often closed 1 day a week.

By Taxi   With all the switchbacks and hairpin roads, you might prefer to take a taxi. Agree on a fee before you set out. Each hour's drive into the countryside should cost about 40€ ($52); each hour's waiting, about 10€ ($13), so that a full day's excursion would run about 140€ ($182). Try to get a driver who speaks some English or a foreign language you understand, and you'll get a guide, too. Reward him in turn with a generous tip.

2 Ioannina

106km (65 miles) E of Igoumenitsou; 452km (277 miles) N of Athens

A sleepy medieval town, Ioannina changed in 1204, when Greeks fleeing Constantinople (after its capture by the Crusaders) arrived and made it the capital of the Despotate of Epirus. The first despot, Michael I, started building the walls that over the next centuries would be enlarged and strengthened by various conquerors—Greeks, Italians, Serbs, and Turks—to become the magnificent walled old town that still exists.

ESSENTIALS

GETTING THERE   By Car   Ioannina is 8 hours from Athens by car.

By Plane   Aegean Airlines, at 11 Pirsinella off Central Square (*©* **280/112-0000** or 26510/65-200; www.aegeanair.com), offers daily flights from and to Athens. **Olympic Airlines** (*©* **26510/26-518** or 26510/23-120) flies to Ioannina from Athens, usually twice a day. At least once a day there are Olympic flights between Ioannina and Thessaloniki. Olympic's office in downtown Ioannina is in a building at the far side of the triangle of greenery at the top of the Central Square. Hours are Monday through Friday from 8am to 3pm; outside those hours, try the airport office at *©* **26510/39-131.** The **airport** is about 4km (2½ miles) from the center of town; public buses (nos. 2 and 7) run frequently from the main square, but you will probably find it more convenient to take a taxi.

VISITOR INFORMATION   Epirus Tourism Directorate, at 39 Leoforos Dodonis (the main street exiting top of square; *©* **26510/41-868;** eotioan@otenet.gr). Summer hours are Monday through Friday from 7:30am to 2:30pm and 5:30 to 8:30pm, Saturday from 9am to 1pm; winter hours are Monday through Friday from 7:30am to 2:30pm.

In summer, the city also maintains an information booth down on the lake, to the left of the fortress and by the quay where you get the boats to the islet Nissi; it's open Monday through Saturday from 10am to 8pm.

Also helpful are the many travel agencies, particularly **Daskalopoulos Yiannis Tour World,** 13 28th Octobriou (*©* **26510/29-667;** www.daskalopoulos-travel.com).

FAST FACTS There are numerous **ATMs** in the center of Ioannina (and also a couple in Metsovo); branches of the big national **banks** can handle all money exchanges. There is an internationally known medical school and **hospital** at Dourouti, some 7km (4 miles) south of Ioannina. There is another hospital at Hatzikosta (2km/1 mile). For **Internet access,** try the **Webcafe** (℗ 26510/83-215), well back on the left in the Sarka Stoa, opposite 16 Pirsinella (leading off the main square); it's open daily from 11am to 3am. **Self Service Laundry,** 3 Tsirigoti (℗ 26510/25-542), around the corner from the KTEL bus station, is open Monday through Saturday from 8am to 2pm, and also Tuesday, Thursday, and Friday from 5 to 8:30pm. The **tourist police** are located at **Police Headquarters,** 11 28th Octobriou 11 (℗ 26510/25-673); it's open daily from 7am to 2am. The main **post office** is on 3 28th Octobriou (℗ 26510/26-437). It's open Monday through Saturday from 7:30am to 8pm; in the off season, it's closed on Saturday. The **telephone office (OTE)** is at the rear (right) on 4 28th Octobriou, open daily from 7am to 10pm.

WHAT TO SEE AND DO

Archaeological Museum ⊀ Housed in a modern building, this fine little provincial museum showcases the small lead tablets found at the **Oracle of Dodona** (see "Side Trips from Ioannina," later in this chapter). Other displays focus on items taken from graves and burial sites in Epirus, ranging from Paleolithic implements (including one of the oldest stone tools in Greece) through the Bronze Age to Roman times. Various bronze works—including a drinking cup, pitcher, vessels, and votive animals—are especially interesting, as is the superb Attic-style sarcophagus dating from the 2nd to 3rd century A.D., with carved scenes from the *Iliad.*

Plateia 25 Martiou (behind clock tower and Greek Army base on Central Sq.). ℗ 26510/25-490. Fax 26510/22-595. Admission 5€ ($5.50) adults, 2€ ($2.60) E.U. seniors over 65. Tues–Sun 8:30am–3pm.

A STROLL AROUND THE *FROURIO:* THE WALLED OLD TOWN & CITADEL ⊀

For many of the centuries that Ioannina fell under the occupation of foreign conquerors, city walls enclosed all the most important structures. There's virtually nothing of historic or architectural importance outside the citadel except on the islet of Nissi. A moat—now filled in—separated the fortress from the mainland. An esplanade now circles the lakeside below the walls, and there are several openings in the wall, but most people enter the walls from **Plateia Giorgio,** which is lined with tavernas and gift shops.

A left turn inside the Plateia Giorgio gate onto Ioustinianou leads (in about 2 blocks) to the **synagogue.** Dating from 1829, this white-walled synagogue remains locked. You must track down someone who can let you in—try asking at the shop of Mrs. Allegra Matsa, 18 Anexartisias (℗ 26510/27-008). Continue around the inside perimeter of the walls until you come to a large clearing. From here, ascend a cobblestoned slope to **Aslan Pasha Cami,** a 17th-century school with cells for Islamic scholars. Its **mosque** now houses the **Municipal Popular Art Museum.** In summer, it's open daily from 8am to 8pm; in winter, Monday through Friday from 8am to 3pm, Saturday and Sunday from 9am to 3pm. Admission is 4€ ($5.20). Aslan Pasha built the mosque in 1618 on the site of an Orthodox church he razed to punish the Christian Greeks for a failed revolt. The exhibits, which include traditional costumes, jewelry, weapons, documents, and household wares, are grouped around the three major religious-ethnic communities of Ioannina: Orthodox Greeks, Muslims, and Jews.

N		
0 — 200 m		
0 — 200 y		

Stratarchu Alexandru Papagu

Plateia Mavili ②③④

⑤

Patriarchu Athenagoru

Elef. Venizelou ①

Karamanlis

⑦ **Citadel** ⑥

Plateia Salongu ●

Main Bus Station ■

⑯

Koran Tsirigoti

⑧

28 Octobriou

Marku Botsari

Papasoglu

⑨

Ethn. Antistaseos

Stadium

⑩

Town Hall

Mitropolis ■

Ch. Trikupi

Archaeological Museum

Lake of Ioannina (Pamvotis)

⑪

Michael Angelou

C

Police Station ■✉

Metsovu

⑫⑬

Plateia Pirrou

⑭

Ay. Marinis

Napoleontos Serva

Ioannu Metaxa

Pamvotidos

Ioannina ●

Greece

Aegean Sea

⊙ **Athens**

Secondary Bus Station ■⑮

Ayia Marini

Dodonis

Bizaniou

Peloponnese

Mediterranean Sea

⑰

ⓘ

ATTRACTIONS ●
Boats to Island **4**
Byzantine Museum **16**
Folk Art Museum **11**
Kastro **14**
Municipal Popular Art
 Museum **5**
Synagogue **7**
Turkish Bazaar **9**

ACCOMMODATIONS ■
Galaxy Hotel **15**
Hotel Kastro **6**
Hotel du Lac **17**
Hotel Olympic **12**
Hotel Palladion **10**

DINING ◆
Gastra **1**
La Fontantina **13**
Pamvotis **3**
The Pharos **2**
To Mantelo **8**

ⓘ Information C OTE ✉ Post Office

When an adjacent minaret and the mosque are illuminated each night, the scene from the lake is captivating.

In the opposite and far corner of the walled town is the innermost citadel, known by its Turkish name, **Itz Kale.** Within it are the **Victory Mosque (Fethiye Cami),** the remains of Ali Pasha's palace, and the alleged **tombs** of Ali Pasha and his wife (see "A Look at the Past," earlier in this chapter, for more info on him). The Greek army occupied this part of the citadel for years; its structures, now restored, include a **Byzantine Museum** located in the rebuilt **palace** and **harem.** The former houses icons and other church-related objects; the latter concentrates on silverwork. Hours are daily from 9am to 3pm; admission is 4€ ($5.20).

Ioannina's Jewish Community

The oldest records of Jews in Ioannina date from the early 1300s but it is believed they had been there for at least a couple centuries—and possibly as long before as the 1st century A.D. Having come directly from the Near East, they like other such Jews in Greece are known as Romaniotes; they spoke a dialect of Greek with some Hebrew and other elements. Over the centuries Ioannina's community grew with infusions of Jews from elsewhere around the Mediterranean, but many then emigrated abroad so that by the mid-20th century there were only about 2,000 Jews in Ioannina. After the Germans occupied Greece in 1941, they eventually rounded up Ioannina's Jews and sent them off to labor and extermination camps, where most of them perished. After the war about 150 returned but today barely 60 Jews live in Ioannina. But they manage to maintain their fine old synagogue. A small **Holocaust Memorial** is located just outside the citadel, on the corner of Karamanlis and Soutsou.

A STROLL AROUND MODERN IOANNINA

Ioannina has become a busy commercial center for all of northwestern Greece (pop. 100,000), and its streets can be crowded and noisy. One interesting retreat is the old **Turkish Bazaar,** down near the walled town and just off the main street, Averoff. In its tiny shops, you may see a few men practicing the old crafts—metalsmiths, jewelry makers, cobblers, tailors, and the like. Averoff will then take you to the edge of the central square with the **clock tower** on the left. Up behind this is the city's **archaeological museum** (see above). When you leave the museum, stroll across the broad, terraced gardens built over the site of what was once the **walled kastro,** where the Christians lived during the Turkish era. Returning to the main street, you are now on the **central square (Plateia Pyrros),** with its full share of cafes and restaurants.

A BOAT TRIP TO THE ISLET OF NISSI (NISSAKI) ☆

If you have only a single day in Ioannina, try to spend at least 2 to 3 hours (including a meal) visiting **Nissi,** the islet in Lake Pamvotis. Small boats leave from the quay below the fortress every half-hour in summer, from 6:30am to 11pm. In the off season, service is every hour—but note that the last boat leaves the island around 10pm. The fare is 1€ ($1.30). The lake has unfortunately become overgrown with algae and is so polluted that local restaurants do not serve the fish taken from it (or so we've been assured).

The boat ride takes barely 10 minutes and, day and night, provides a fine view of Ioannina. You get off near the lobby of three restaurants—each displaying a tank filled with seafood. Resist all until you are truly ready to eat. The specialties of these restaurants include eel, frogs' legs, carp, crayfish, trout, and other imported fish.

The small village here is said to have been founded in the 16th century by refugees from the Mani region of the Peloponnese, but your destination is the five monasteries that predate it. Take the narrow passage between the two restaurants; signs are posted to your left and right. Follow the signs to the left (east), and you will come to the restored **Monastery of Panteleimon.** Little of the original remains.

The monastery houses a **small museum** devoted to the infamous Ali Pasha; its numerous pictures and personal items include his clothing and water pipe. It's open daily, and an attendant will come if it's closed. Admission is 1€ ($1.30). In 1820,

Pasha took refuge here, where he was eventually killed in 1822 by Turks. You may even be shown holes in the floor where it is alleged he was shot from below.

Directly beside this monastery is the **Monastery of the Prodromos (St. John the Baptist),** but most people will want to move on to the western edge of the islet, following the signs to **Moni Filanthropinon** (also known as the **Monastery of Ayios Nikolaos Spanos**). It's sometimes referred to as the "Secret School"; Orthodox priests supposedly maintained a clandestine school here during the Turkish occupation. Founded in the 13th century, it was rebuilt in the 16th century with magnificent frescoes. Seldom does the public get to view such an ensemble of Byzantine frescoes so close up. Although the dim light can be a problem (bring a flashlight), you should be able to recognize such subjects as the life of Christ on the walls of the apse, God and the Apostles in the central dome, and the many saints. Most unexpected, however, are the portrayals of famous ancient Greek sages on the wall of the narthex as you enter—Aristotle, Plato, Plutarch, Solon, and Thucydides. (There's no admission, but it's customary to leave a gratuity with the caretaker.)

About 100m (328 ft.) farther along the trail is **Ayios Nikolaos Dilios** (or **Moni Stratgopoulou**), the oldest monastery (dating from the 11th c.) on Nissi. Its 16th-century frescoes are also of some interest but are in poor condition. (A small tip to the caretaker is called for.) The fifth monastery, **Ayios Eleouses,** is closed to the public.

By now you have earned your meal on Nissi. Choose a restaurant (see "Where to Dine," below).

SHOPPING

It seems as if every third store in old Ioannina sells jewelry, silverware, hammered copper, and embossed brasswork—the traditional crafts. Many of the jewelry stores sell modern work in gold and silver and/or precious and semiprecious jewels. Prices are probably lower than those in more cosmopolitan cities. However, be wary of "antiques" offered in some shops—they may not be all that old, and if they date earlier than 1830, you need an export license!

There's a cluster of jewelry and gift shops opposite the walled citadel. Typical selections of metalwork (and also water pipes) may be found at **Politis Douvflis,** 12 Plateia Yioryio; or at **Nikos Gogonis,** 13 Karamanlis. At 56 and 65 Averoff, **George Minos Moschos** offers a somewhat more unusual selection of silver, jewelry, and older secondhand objects ("antiques"). **Pospotikis Bothers,** 12 Ethnikis Antistaseos, has a fine selection of bronze objects, some antiques jewelry, and reproductions of older metal objects. Here and there you may see embroidered clothing or woven socks, but this region is not especially known for its needlework.

WHERE TO STAY

Although there are no luxury resorts, several hotels here offer a range of accommodations.

EXPENSIVE

Hotel du Lac ✪   This hotel opened in the summer of 1998 and immediately became Ioannina's prime hotel. With its marble and woodwork and its carpets, it exudes luxury; more importantly, its service lives up to its image. The rooms are a bit larger than in many Greek hotels, and many enjoy a view across to the lake; ask for one); bathrooms are state-of-the-art. The buffet breakfast is almost excessive; the regular meals are what you'd expect at a fine hotel. Some might find its distance from the center (a 15-min. walk) a downside, but in return you get a quiet lakeside locale. The only negative: It is often crowded with conference attendees.

Leoforos Andrea Miaouli and Ikkou (along the lake, ½ mile right of the walled citadel), 45221 Ioannina. © 26510/ 59-100. Fax 26510/59-200. 139 units. High season 175€ ($228) double; low season 165€ ($215). Rates include buffet breakfast. AE, DC, MC, V. Parking on grounds. **Amenities:** 2 restaurants; 2 bars; pool; children's pool; children's playground; concierge; tours, taxi rides, and car rentals arranged; conference center; secretarial service; 24-hr. room service; babysitting; same-day laundry and dry cleaning. *In room:* A/C, TV, data and computer lines, minibar, hair dryer, safe.

MODERATE

Hotel Olympic For those who like to be at the center of the action, such as it is in Ioannina, the Olympic is a choice hotel. It has long attracted members of the foreign diplomatic corps, government dignitaries, and such. All that means nothing, of course, if you aren't made to feel welcome and comfortable, and you can be assured of both. The lobby is modest, but the desk service and 24-hour room service are what count. All the corridors, guest rooms, and bathrooms have been renovated since 2004. Ask for an upper-story front room with a view of the distant lake.

2 Melanidi (1 block off Central Sq.), 45220 Ioannina. © 26510/25-888. Fax 26510/22-041. www.hotelolymp.gr. 54 units. High season 130€ ($169) double; low season 110€ ($143) double. No credit cards. Parking close to hotel provided free to guests. **Amenities:** Restaurant; bar; 24-hr. room service; copier; fax. *In room:* A/C, TV, Internet access, ridge, safe.

Hotel Palladion Maybe it's because it's the first hotel in Ioannina I happened to stay in, but I have always liked this place for its combination of features: convenience yet quiet, professional and helpful desk staff, no frills but good value, and the fact that everything works. Rooms of decent size and decor are insulated by windows from most street noise. Bathrooms are standard issue. When I asked to move from one room because of lingering cigarette odor, this happened instantly and with no further questions. Since then, the hotel has set aside floors for nonsmokers. The Palladion often hosts small groups, but this should not interfere with your stay. A final advantage: The hotel has its own parking lot.

1 Botsari (off 28 Octobriou), 45444 Ioannina. © 26510/25-856. Fax 26510/74-034. www.palladionhotel.gr 128 units. High season 130€ ($169) double; low season 120€ ($156) double. Rates include buffet breakfast. AE, DC, MC, V. Private parking lot. **Amenities:** 2 restaurants; bar; airport transfer arranged; tours and car rentals arranged; conference facilities; business center; babysitting; same-day laundry and dry cleaning. *In room:* A/C, TV, hair dryer, safe.

INEXPENSIVE

Hotel Galaxy There's simply not much else to say about this hotel except that the rooms are cheap and clean and the hotel is centrally located. For the budget traveler.

Plateia Pyrros (Central Sq.), 45221 Ioannina. © 26510/25-432. Fax 26510/30-724. 38 units. 60€ ($78). No credit cards.

Hotel Kastro ✦ *Value* As the only hostelry inside the old walled city, this is arguably the most rewarding place to stay in Ioannina—and thus hard to get a room at the last minute. It's a 19th-century house, tastefully restored by the proprietors. Most visitors happily accept its lack of some amenities in return for the unique experience of being here. Basement rooms look out onto street level; showers in the bathrooms are small; breakfast is basic. But for those who enjoy old inns or pensions, this will be a highlight of your visit to Ioannina.

57 Andronikou Paleologou (near the Byzantine Museum, approached from lakeside gateway), 45221 Ioannina. © 26510/22-866. rit-zan@otenet.gr. 7 units. High season 80€–90€ ($104–$117) double. Rates include continental breakfast. No credit cards. Parking outside on street. *In room:* Fan.

WHERE TO DINE
MODERATE

Gastra Restaurant ⚔ GREEK REGIONAL This is a must for those willing to try this regional specialty—food cooked in a *gastra:* A conical cast-iron lid is placed over the iron baking dish (similar to a clay pot) holding the food of choice (lamb, goat, pork, or chicken); it is then placed in an outdoor oven heaped with red-hot embers. The meat then roasts slowly, resulting in an especially succulent, delicious meal. The restaurant has other specialties as well; for an appetizer, try the *skordalia karithia* (walnut-garlic dip), and for dessert, the special crème caramel.

In pleasant weather, sit out front in the shaded garden and watch your meal cook in the open fireplace. On cooler evenings, you can sit inside the handsome restaurant. When the spirit moves you, diners are encouraged to dance to the music. Come here for a leisurely experience, not just for the food. On Sunday, you are advised to leave the restaurant to the citizens of Ioannina. (If it's too crowded and you need your gastra, proceed less than a mile after taking the left turn signed to Igoumenitsou to another, similar restaurant, the **Diogenes.**)

16a Kostaki, Eleousa, along the Airport-Igoumenitsou Hwy. (7km/4 miles outside Ioannina; 3km/2 miles past airport entrance, just before turnoff to Igoumenitsou). ℂ 26510/61-530. www.gastra.gr. Reservations recommended in high season on weekend evenings. Main courses 7€–19€ ($9–$25). No credit cards. Tues–Sun 1–5pm and 8pm–1am. Public bus no.2

Pamvotis GREEK/SEAFOOD If you can have only one meal in Ioannina, head to the islet in the lake. Ask around as to which restaurant is the best, and you'll get a different answer from each person. The choices serve pretty similar dishes, so choose a location that appeals to you. We like this one—near the dock where the little ferries put in. You can pick your lobster, *karavides* (a cross between crayfish and shrimp), trout, or other fish right out of holding tanks. If you're game, try one of the two local specialties: frogs' legs or eel. The white Zitsa Primus, a slightly sparkling white wine from the region, is a perfect accompaniment. For a more natural setting, try **Propodes Restaurant** next to Ayios Panteleimon Monastery. (See "A Boat Trip to the Islet of Nissi," above.)

Nissi Ioannina (the offshore islet). ℂ 26510/81-081. Fax 26510/81-631. Main courses 7€–18€ ($9–$24). MC, V. High season daily 11am–midnight; low season daily 11am–10pm. Ferry from Ioannina's lakefront.

The Plaza GREEK/MEDITERRANEAN This is the house bar/restaurant of the Olympic Hotel and has long been a favorite gathering spot for foreigners and Greeks who like to feel they're at Ioannina's crossroads. Since its total renovation of 2004, the decor is somewhat glitzy but you come here to eat. The menu ranges from Greek to Italian standards. Try a change from the usual Greek dishes; enjoy the risotto, spaghetti carbonara, or a steak filet with one of the fine red wines from Northern Greece—a Naoussa, an Amyntaion, or a Carras. Paris it's not, but The Plaza offers a taste of upscale Ioannina.

2 Melanidi (on ground floor of Olympic Hotel, 1 block off Central Sq.). ℂ 26510/25-147. Fax 26510/22-041. Reservations recommended on holidays and weekends in high season. Main courses 6€–20€ ($7.80–$26). No credit cards. Daily 10am–midnight.

INEXPENSIVE

The Pharos GREEK One of several restaurants set back from the lakefront, the Pharos offers good meals in a pleasant setting. In warm weather, you can sit under the awning in the square opposite. The menu is traditional but offers some variation.

The fried peppers in garlic sauce make a delicious appetizer. For your main course, order whatever's being grilled that day, and get the pilaf instead of potatoes. Feeling flush? Go for the crab or trout. If you're there only for the location, opt for the fresh fruit-salad plate.

13 Plateia Mavili (down along lakefront). ℂ **26510/26-506**. Main courses 6€–17€ ($7.80–$22). No credit cards. Daily 9am–10pm. Closed mid-Oct to Mar. Bus from the central sq. or a 10-min. walk.

To Mantelo *Value* GREEK TAVERNA   Here's a no-frills, traditional Greek taverna that gives you a front-row seat on the square outside the old walled town, where all kinds of characters congregate. For an appetizer, try the marinated, fried peppers, squash, or eggplant. All of the grilled dishes—veal, chicken, lamb, and calves' liver—are good. Be sure to ask for the pilaf. The taverna can feel cramped when it's crowded, but that's what makes it Greek.

Plateia Georgio 15 (opposite the citadel's main entrance). ℂ **26510/25-452**. Main courses 5€–10€ ($5.50–$13). No credit cards. Daily 10am–2am.

3 Side Trips from Ioannina

DODONA (DODONI) ✦

Even if you don't chase after every classical ruin, this one offers a rare reward: a spectacular theater at one of the major oracles of the ancient world. In August, the theater produces classical Greek dramas; ask at a travel agency for specific information.

Dodona is only 22km (14 miles) from Ioannina. With a car, a round-trip visit should take about 3 hours. The bus service is inconvenient—basically only one bus very early in the morning, and then you're stuck at the site for many hours. It's better to spring for a **taxi**—about 50€ ($65) for the round-trip, including an hour's wait. The first 7km (4 miles) are on a main highway due south (signed to Arta); the turn to the right at about 7km (4 miles) is signed Dodona; you proceed about 3km (2 miles) on a relatively flat road before the final 12km (7½ miles) on an ascending and curving road. You'll arrive at a plateau ringed by mountains. The trip becomes part of the experience—you get the sense that you're on a pilgrimage to a remote shrine. Admission to the sacred areas is 3€ ($3.90). In high season, the site is open daily from 8am to 8pm; off season, Monday through Saturday from 10am to 3pm.

The **Oracle of Zeus** at Dodona traces its roots back to the early Hellenistic people who had arrived in northwestern Greece by about 2000 B.C. They probably worshiped Zeus, but at Dodona there was already an earth goddess cult with an oracle that might have based its interpretations on the flights of pigeons. In any case, by about 1400 B.C., it appears that the Zeus-worshiping Greeks had imposed their god on the site and turned the goddess into his consort, Dione.

By this time, too, the priests linked Zeus's presence to the rustling leaves of an oak tree at Dodona and interpreted these sounds as oracular messages. The Greeks set up a shrine around the tree—a simple, protective fence. Over the centuries they built more and more elaborate structures on the site.

Eventually, they established a temple to Zeus here in the 4th century B.C. At that time, the oracle spoke through the bronze statue of a youth with a whip. The wind stirred the whip so it would strike nearby metal cauldrons. Priests then interpreted the reverberations. Many ambitious structures, both religious and secular, were erected at Dodona, but the oracle effectively ceased functioning in the 4th century A.D.—about the time when, it is claimed by some, the original oak died. The oak now on the shrine's site is, of course, a recent planting.

Although the walls are all but destroyed, the magnificent **theater** survives, thanks to its re-assembling in the 19th century. The first theater, built in the 3rd century B.C., is said to have seated 17,000. It was destroyed, but another of the same size replaced it in the 2nd century B.C. Later, the Romans converted the theater into an arena for gladiator contests. The theater, one of the largest on the Greek mainland, has almost the same marvelous acoustics as the famous (but smaller) one at Epidaurus. Just to sit here is an evocative experience.

PERAMA CAVE ⋆ *Kids*

Only about 5km (3 miles) north of Ioannina (the turnoff is past the airport), this cave is actually a series of caverns. It was discovered in 1941, during World War II, when people were seeking hiding places. Now thoroughly developed, with electric lights, steps, and handrails, it features a half-mile walk through a series of vast caverns and narrow passageways. In high season it's open daily from 8am to 8pm; in winter, daily from 9am to 5pm (© **26510/81-521**). Guided tours set out about every 15 minutes from the well-signed entrance in Perama village; the fee is 6€ ($7.80). The guides often don't speak much English; they may only repeat the names assigned to the unusually shaped stalagmites and stalactites. They may also rush everyone through— but you can linger and join the next group! Perama doesn't live up to its boast as one of the most spectacular caves in the world, but it's worth a visit if you haven't been in many caves. *Warning:* At the very end, you must climb what seems like an endless number of steps to come out of the cave. But people of all shapes and ages have made it up and—you emerge into a cafe!

METSOVO ⋆

This traditional mountain village has become so popular that at times its original appeal is in danger of being overwhelmed by tourism at its worst. Still, most visitors find it satisfying—some even find it magical. It's about a 1½-hour bus ride east of Ioannina. A couple of buses go to Metsovo in the morning, but only one returns from Metsovo in the late afternoon that allows for a day in the village. So either pay close attention to the always-changing bus schedule or, better still, rent a car. (Buses also come from Athens and Thessaloniki.)

Metsovo sits at about 1,000m (3,300 ft.) above sea level, nestled among peaks of the Pindos Mountains. In addition to day-trippers, serious nature lovers and hikers are drawn here from all over Greece and Europe. Overnight accommodations are often strained, especially during Greek holidays. And with ski slopes nearby, Metsovo is also a popular winter destination.

The village is renowned for its Alpine-style architecture—stone buildings with wooden balconies and slate roofs. Disneyland it ain't, but don't go to Metsovo thinking you'll discover a quaint native village. There's even a fairly ambitious conference center in town.

Crafts—weaving, embroidery, and woodwork—are on display in many shops along the main street. Some is touristy kitsch, but some is authentically local and handsome. The best can be found at **Metsovo Folk Art Cooperative,** about 50m (164 ft.) from the Egnatia Hotel on the slope above it. To see a traditional Epirote house with furnishings, visit the **Tositsa Mansion** (signposted just above the main street; open daily except Thurs; admission 3€/$3.90).

The **Museum of Folk Art** is in the Arhondiko Tositsa, a 17th-century mansion completely restored by Baron Michalis Tositsa, a wealthy Vlach living in Switzerland. With its paneled rooms, furniture, rugs, clothing, and crafts, it's a superb example of how a prosperous family might once have lived in Epirus. The museum, located on a road above the main street, is open in summer, Monday through Wednesday and Friday through Saturday from 8:30am to 1pm and 4 to 6pm; in winter, it's open the same days but from 3 to 5pm only. Admission is 2€ ($2.60).

Much more typical of Metsovo is the little **church of Ayia Paraskevi** on the main square, with its carved-wood altar screen, silver chandeliers, and copies of Ravenna mosaics.

WHERE TO STAY

If you want to overnight in Metsovo, choosing a hotel is easy: all are relatively inexpensive, all offer acceptable accommodations, and all are to some degree decorated in the regional style. Note that those listed below stay open all year because of the winter sports in the area so all offer central heating. If none of those listed can accommodate you, readers have also recommended the **Bitounis** along the main street (© 26560/41-217; bitounis@met.forthnet.gr)

The Vlachs

One special reason to visit Metsovo is that it's the center (in Greece) of the **Vlach people,** who claim descent from Latin-speaking Wallachians of what is now Romania. The Vlachs were originally shepherds who followed their flocks, and some still do just that; but over the centuries, many other Vlachs settled down in Northern Greece and prospered in crafts, commerce, tourism, and trade. Some wealthier Vlachs made their money dealing in wool and other products from their flocks. Because the Vlachs wrote little of their distinctive Latin-based language down and because it's not taught in the schools, it's in danger of being lost as the new generation marries and moves away. You'll find the Vlachs of Metsovo extremely congenial—and patient—when visitors ask them to "say something in Vlach." (Don't expect your Latin to help much!) A declining number of older people wear traditional Vlach clothing every day, but fancier costumes come out on Sundays and holidays. If you want to see their **dances,** July 26 is the village's feast day but be forewarned—the village will be jammed.

Moments A Special Monastery

Some of the most memorable experiences in Greece come not from visiting major sites but from modest, remote, unexpected encounters. There's just such a thing outside Metsovo—the restored 14th-century **Moni Ayios Nikolaos**—that rewards a little extra effort. It's not just that the church contains some quite spectacular 18th-century frescoes (but lost to sight until the 1950s), a fine iconostasis, and some icons. It's that the resident caretaker is a lovely woman who even if you don't know a word of Greek somehow manages to communicate with you; beyond that, she weaves her own handsome textiles in the Metsovo tradition and will sell them to you—but only if you are interested. Finally there is the monastery's location, high on a slope in a remote setting. There are two ways to get there. One is a half-hour walk down (and hour-long walk back up), a rather steep and rough trail; it's signed from the far corner of the main square; take the second left, head for the clock tower, and then follow the signs. But you can drive closer to it by taking the road out of the town square signed IOANNINA; at about 1km (½ mile), turn left onto the asphalt road signed ANILIO, and wind downward for another 3.5km (2 miles). You will spot the monastery up on the hillside to your left and after parking, you have to scramble through a vineyard. Knock on the monastery door—the caretaker will allow entry during reasonable hours (until 7:30pm in high season).

Galaxias ✸   If you want to be at the center of things, then this should be your choice—but it's for travelers who appreciate the feeling of a country inn. The homey atmosphere emanates from the Barbayanni family, who run this hotel and the restaurant reviewed below. It's by no means a fancy hotel—the rooms are modest in size and decor, the bathrooms just adequate. The decor, lots of wood and stone and textiles, is the traditional style for this region. Ask for a room in the front with a view of the distant mountains.

On a terrace above the main square. ✆ 26560/41-202. Fax 26560/41-124. 10 units, with shower or with tub. High season 95€ ($124) double; low season 70€ ($91) double. Rates include continental breakfast. MC, V. **Amenities:** Restaurant; bar; roof garden; smoking room; pets allowed. *In room:* A/C, TV, fireplace, fridge, dryer, safe.

Hotel Victoria ✸   The Victoria, reminiscent of an Alpine inn, offers a little luxury in a natural setting on the edge of town. Natural materials, large functioning fireplaces, and hearty furnishings make the not especially large guest rooms quite cozy; all have balconies and/or views. And because the Victoria is relatively new (from the late 1980s and completely renovated in 2007), its bathrooms are modern. The hotel maintains its own fine restaurant as well. However, you really come here for the isolation and the views. In winter, the Victoria is frequented mainly by skiers, but it's popular year-round with Greeks and other Europeans. Reservations are advised. By the way—the proprietors are Vlach—here's your chance to learn a few words!

About 1km (½ mile) from the main square. ✆ 26560/41-771. Fax 26560/41-454. 37 units, with shower or with tub. 100€ ($130) double; Christmas and Easter seasons 110€ ($143) double. Rates include continental breakfast. MC, V. **Amenities:** Bar; sauna; swimming pool. *In room:* TV, Jacuzzi, fireplace.

Kassaros Hotel   For a location away from the square (but not as far as the Victoria) and as a favor to your budget, try the Kassaros Hotel. This is the perfect place for an extended or active stay in Metsovo—the proprietor also runs a travel agency, Kassaros Travel, which rents out ski equipment and a snowmobile as well as its own buses for excursions throughout Epirus.

About 90m (300 ft.) along road leading from main square back to Ioannina. (C) 26560/41-800. Fax 26560/41-262. 31 units, with shower or with tub. High season 85€ ($111) double; low season 65€ ($85) double. Rates include continental breakfast. AE, DC, MC, V. **Amenities:** Bar; sauna; Jacuzzi. *In room:* TV.

WHERE TO DINE

Even if you spend only a few hours in Metsovo, you should try a meal at a restaurant that offers traditional Epirote fare. Along the main street, Tositsa, **Taverna Panormiko, Restaurant Toxotis,** and **Cafe Chroni Roof Garden** are all good.

Galaxias ☆ GREEK/REGIONAL   This is far and away my favorite in Metsovo. In warm weather, you can sit outdoors; in cooler weather, sit in the handsome dining room warmed by a cheerful fire. Choose among local specialties: Begin with the *trachana* (bean soup) or a cheese pie with leek. Move on to the spicy sausage or beef patties with leeks and celery baked in a pot. For dessert, try the baklava or yogurt, but be sure to save room for one of the local cheeses, either *metsovonay* (smoked) or *vlachotiri* (mild). To accompany your meal, ask for the local red wine, Katoyi, or if that's in short supply, the house wine.

In the Galaxias Hotel, just above the main square. (C) 26560/41-202. Main courses 5€–17€ ($6.50–$22). MC, V. Daily noon–11pm.

ZAGORI (ZAGORIA/ZAGOROHORIA) & VIKOS GORGE

If you have limited time in northwestern Greece and prefer wilder nature to tourist destinations, you might opt to travel here instead of Metsovo, Dodona, or Perama Cave. The Zagori is the mountainous area just north of Ioannina, a region of about 1,035 sq. km (400 sq. miles) now part of the **Greek National Park System.** About 45 villages here have remained almost unchanged through the centuries. *Note:* The mountainous roads make for slow going.

Trekking into Vikos Gorge

A trek into Vikos Gorge is a serious endeavor. Just to get to the gorge's beginning, you must do a rugged 4½- to 5-hour walk—not including the hike back up. The walk through the entire gorge—approximately 16km (10 miles)—is even more demanding. Do not attempt this without proper gear, supplies, and experience.

If you do decide to go, Monodendri's lower square offers one of the most accessible approaches. The path down into the gorge is signed here. To take part in an organized expedition, join one of the groups put together by **Robinson Travel Agency,** at the edge of Ioannina on the main road to the airport, 10 8th Merarchias ((C) 26510/29-402). More experienced trekkers might prefer to deal with the **Mountain Climbing Association of Ioannina** ((C) 26530/22-138) or the **Mountain Climbing Association of Papingo** ((C) 26530/41-138), based in one of the Zagori villages.

The region's most spectacular sight is **Vikos Gorge.** Do not attempt the hike there without advance preparation and planning. (See the box "Trekking into Vikos Gorge," above.)

Getting around the Zagori without your own vehicle is all but impossible. The buses are too few and far between; on a day trip, you'd have time to visit only one destination before having to return to Ioannina. With a car, you can visit several villages, view Vikos Gorge from above, experience the scenery, and be back in Ioannina within 6 to 8 hours.

Take the main road north out of Ioannina toward Konitsa; turnoffs are clearly marked. Your first destination should be **Monodendri;** after taking the highway north for 19km (13 miles), just past Metamorfosi, take the right turn signed VIKOS GORGE. At about 5km (3 miles), a sign to the right indicates KIPI; the famous high-arched bridges are well worth the brief diversion (8km/5 miles). Regarded as old Turkish structures, they were most likely built in the 19th century for the convenience of pack-horse caravans. The first, single-span bridge is Kokkoros; beyond that is three-arched Plakida Bridge. (If you have the time and inclination, another 11km/7 miles on through Kipi village leads to **Nigades,** with its strikingly handsome **Church of Ayios Yioryios,** built in 1795.) Returning to the main route, proceed about 39km (25 miles), where a sign indicates a turn right onto Monodendri's lower square.

Drive to the small parking lot at the edge of the village square. Proceed on foot from there, following the sign for Vikos Gorge (which directs travelers to Kato Monoden-dri). It's about a 10-minute walk to the lovely little 15th-century **Monastery of Ayia Paraskevi,** perched on the edge of the gorge. The well-protected viewing areas here will be spectacular enough for most people. Only sure-footed and experienced hikers will want to get back on the narrow, unprotected trail above the monastery; the next several hundred meters lead you to even more spectacular views of the gorge—as well as dramatic drops from the path.

Back at the parking lot, continue on the main road for about another half-mile, until you come to **Monodendri's** upper square. (A short cobblestone path leads from the lower to this upper square.) The upper square has several modest hotels and decent restaurants, but unless you seek such amenities, you need not go up there. If you want to have a meal, I recommend either **Katerina's Restaurant** (try her tasty chicken or meat pies!) at the top of the square, or **To Petrino Dasos,** the little taverna on the right as you come up to the square. The **Oxio,** a hotel and restaurant opposite To Petrino Dasos, is another possibility.

To view the gorge from what is known as **Vikos Balcony,** drive up through the upper square and on for another 7km (4½ miles) along the road to Oxia. Leave your car and walk down a stone path to a truly spectacular view. Local signs claim that Vikos Gorge, at 900m (2,950 ft.), is "the world's deepest," but several places around the world might dispute that.

Next stop: **Papingo.** Drivers are usually advised to retrace their entire route back to the main Ioannina-Konitsa highway and then proceed north to the turnoff to Papingo (a 1½-hr. drive). If you're adventurous—and, more importantly, able to ask basic directions in Greek—you can take a perfectly fine asphalt road that cuts that time almost in half because it is a more direct route to the highway. You start down from Monodendri but at about 5km (3 miles), take the (signed) right turn and head across the flatland for Elafatopos; do not go on up to Elafatopos, however, but continue and take the left turn signed KATO PEDINA. You then come to the main highway; turn right and proceed 4km (2½ miles) until a sign to the right indicates Papingo. The drive from this point on offers the kind of scenery best described by a young English traveler, Simon, who said, "It makes you want to stop the car and get out and applaud."

Of the two villages, **Megalo Papingo** and **Micro Papingo**—"Big" and "Little" Papingo, we recommend visiting at least the first. Many regard this as the archetypal Zagori village, with its terrain, streets, homes, roofs, public buildings, and everything else seemingly all made of the same stone. Megalo Papingo has several cafes and restaurants as well as modest hotels. You can always be sure of a meal in Papingo, but rooms may be booked up at various times of the year—such is the reputation of the Zagori in Greece and elsewhere in Europe. Both **Hotel Koulis** (© **26530/41-115;** 50€/$65 double) and the more elegant **Saxonis Houses** (© **26530/41-615;** 80€/$104 double) include private bathroom and breakfast in their rates. If you drive on another mile from Megalo Papingo, you'll come to Micro Papingo, which offers a view of the mountains from another angle. To really get away from it all, stay at the cozy **Dias Guesthouse** here, with its limited but tasty menu (© **26530/41-257;** fax 26530/41-892). A double can be 75€ ($98), but that may be negotiable depending on the tourist traffic.

After all this, you are only about 60km (38 miles) from Ioannina. You can return knowing you've had a taste of the true Epirus.

15

The Ionian Islands

by John S. Bowman

"The isles of Greece, the isles of Greece"—when Lord Byron tossed his bouquet, he was not under the spell of today's popular Cycladic islands but of Western Greece and the Ionian Islands. Located off Greece's northwest coast, the Ionians offer some of the country's loveliest natural settings, including beaches, a fine selection of hotels and restaurants, a distinctive history and lore, and some unusual architectural and archaeological sites.

The Ionian Islands are rainier, greener, and more temperate than other Greek islands, so the high season lasts a little longer, from late June to early September. The roads are generally in fine condition, even if unavoidably steep and twisting. Accommodations range from luxury resorts to quiet little rooms on remote beaches. The local cuisine and wines offer numerous special treats. Among the best are *sofrito,* a spicy veal dish; *bourdetto,* a spicy fish dish; and wines such as Robola, Liapaditiko, and Theotaki (this last preferred by James Bond).

The Ionian Islands (which the Greeks know as the Heptanissi, or "Seven Islands") include **Corfu** (Kerkira), **Paxos** (Paxoi), **Levkas** (Lefkas, Lefkada), **Ithaka** (Ithaki), **Kefalonia** (Kefallinia, Cephalonia), and **Zakinthos** (Zakynthos, Zante); the seventh, **Kithira** (Cythera, Cerigo)— off the south coast of the Peloponnese—is linked only as a government administrative unit. There are many more islands in the archipelago along Greece's northwest coast, including several that are sparsely inhabited.

STRATEGIES FOR SEEING THE ISLANDS

In this chapter, we single out **Corfu** and **Kefalonia,** with a side trip to **Ithaka.** With a couple of weeks to spare, you can take a ship or plane to either Corfu in the north or Zakinthos in the south and then make your way by ship to several of the other Ionians (although outside high season, you will have to do considerable backtracking). If you have only a week, you should get to one of the larger islands the fastest way possible, and then use ships to get to at most a couple of the others. In any case, rent a car to get around the larger islands. If it comes down to visiting only one, Corfu is a prime candidate, but if you want to get off the beaten track, consider Kefalonia or Ithaka. All the Ionians—especially Corfu—are overrun in July and August; aim for June or September, if you can.

A LOOK AT THE PAST   In the fabric of their history, the Ionian Islands can trace certain threads that both tie and distinguish them from the rest of Greece. During the late Bronze Age (1500–1200 B.C.), a Mycenaean culture thrived on at least several of these islands. Although certain names of islands and cities were the same as those used

---

> ⌒ *Tips* **Museums and Sites Hours Update**
>
> If you visit Greece during the summer, check to see when museums and sites are open. According to official notices, they should be open from 8am to 7:30pm, but some may close earlier in the day or even be closed 1 day a week.

---

today—Ithaka, for instance—scholars have never been able to agree on exactly which were the sites described in the *Odyssey.*

People from the city-states on the Greek mainland then recolonized the islands, starting in the 8th century B.C. The Peloponnesian War, in fact, can be traced back to a quarrel between Corinth and its colony at Corcyra (Corfu) that led to Athens's interference and eventually the full-scale war. The islands later fell under the rule of the Romans, then the Byzantine Empire. They remained prey to warring powers and pirates in this part of the Mediterranean for centuries. By the end of the 14th century, Corfu fell under Venice's control, and the Italian language and culture—including Roman Catholicism—became predominant.

When Napoleon's forces overcame Venice in 1797, the French took over here and held sway until 1815. The Ionian Islands then became a protectorate of the British; although the islands experienced peace and prosperity, they were in fact a colony. When parts of Greece gained true independence from the Turks by 1830—due in part to leadership from Ionians such as Ioannis Capodistrias—many Ionians became restless under the British. In 1864, British Prime Minister Gladstone allowed the Ionians to unite with Greece.

During World War II, Italians first occupied these islands, but when the Germans took over, the Ionians, especially Corfu, suffered greatly. Since 1945, the waves of tourists have brought considerable prosperity to the Ionian Islands.

1 Corfu (Kerkira)

32km (20 nautical miles) W of mainland; another 558km (342 miles) NW of Athens

There's Corfu the coast, Corfu the town, and Corfu the island, and they don't necessarily appeal to the same vacationers. Corfu the coast lures travelers who want to escape civilization and head for the water—whether an undeveloped little beach with a simple taverna and rooms to rent, or a spectacular resort. Then there's the more cosmopolitan **Corfu town,** with its distinctive Greek, Italian, French, and British elements. Finally, there's a third and little-known Corfu: the interior, with its lush vegetation and gentle slopes, modest villages and farms, and countless olive and fruit trees. (It should be admitted that there's now a fourth Corfu—rather tacky beach resorts crowded with package tourists from western Europe who can be extremely raucous. You will probably want to avoid this Corfu.)

Whichever Corfu you choose, it should prove pleasing. It was, after all, this island's ancient inhabitants, the Phaeacians, who made Odysseus so comfortable. Visitors today will find Corfu similarly hospitable.

ESSENTIALS

GETTING THERE **By Plane** **Olympic Airways** provides at least three flights daily from and to Athens, and three flights weekly from and to Thessaloniki. Round-trip fare for each route is about 220€ ($286). The Olympic Airways office in Corfu

Western Greece & the Ionian Islands

ALBANIA

ZAGORI

Paleokastritsa

Corfu

Filiates · 6

Ioannina

Perama

Metsovo

Islet of Nissi

Dodona

Lake Pamvotis

Trikkala

Benitses

Igoumenitsou · 5

EPIRUS

Kavos

CORFU (KERKIRA)

Paramythia

Margariti

Parga

PAXOS

Lakka

ANTIPAXOS

E15

Arta

Zalongo

Nikopolis

Ambracian Gulf

To Ancona, Bari & Brindisi

Preveza

Action (Actium)

Lefkas

Vonitsa · 5

Amfilohia

LEFKADA

Nydri

Mitikas

Aetos

Vassiliki

Agrinio

Frikes

Astakos

Fiskardo

E19

KEFALONIA

Vathy

Messolongi

Antirrio

ITHAKA

Rio

Lixouri

Sami

Argostoli

Poros

Gulf of Patras

Patras

Metaxata

Skala

9

Kyllini

PELOPONNESE

74

ZAKINTHOS

Zakinthos

Amalias

Laganas

Vassilikos

Pirgos

IONIAN SEA

N

0   25 mi
0   25 km

Ferry Route - - - -

Greece

Athens *Aegean Sea*

WESTERN GREECE & THE IONIAN ISLANDS

Mediterranean Sea

Tips Kerkira = Corfu

Kerkira is the modern Greek name for Corfu. Look for it on many schedules, maps, brochures, and other publications.

---

town (🕾 **26610/38-694**) is at 11 Polila, down from the Ionian Islands Tourism Office, but agents all over town sell tickets. **Aegean Airlines** also offers occasional flights; in Athens, call 🕾 **210/626-1000;** in Corfu, call 🕾 **26610/27-100.** And now **Airsea Lines** provides hydroplane connections with several points: Brindisi, Italy; Patras on the Greek mainland; and the Ionian islands of Ithaka, Lefkada, Kefalonia, and Paxoi. Fares range from 40€ to 120€ ($52–$156). In Greece, their toll-free number is 🕾 **80111/800-600** or check out their website, www.airsealines.com.

Corfu airport is about 4km (2½ miles) south of the center of Corfu town. Fortunately, the flight patterns of most planes do not bring them over the city. Everyone takes taxis into town; the standard fare should be 8€ ($10) but may fluctuate with destination, amount of luggage, and time of day. Airsea Lines hydroplanes put down at Gouvia, a few miles just north of Corfu town.

By Boat Many lines and ships link Corfu to both Greek and foreign ports. Ferries run almost hourly between Corfu and Igoumenitsou, directly across on the mainland (1–2 hr.), and several go weekly to and from Patras (about 7 hr.). At least during high season, there is now a twice-daily hydrofoil express (about 30 min.) between Corfu and Igoumenitsou. Also in high season are daily ships linking Corfu to ports in Italy— Ancona, Bari, Brindisi, Trieste, Venice—or to Piraeus and/or Patras. The schedules and fares vary so much from year to year that it would be misleading to provide details here; work with a travel agent in your homeland or Greece; or check **www.ferries.gr**. The ship lines are: **Adriatica** (🕾 210/429-0487 in Piraeus), **ANEK Lines** (🕾 210/ 323-3481 in Athens), **Fragline** (🕾 210/821-4171 in Athens), **Hellenic Mediter-ranean Line,** or **HML** (🕾 210/422-5341 in Piraeus), **Minoan Lines** (🕾 210/414-5700 in Piraeus), **Strintzis Lines** (🕾 210/422-5015 in Piraeus), and **Ventouris Line** (🕾 210/988-9280 in Piraeus). In high season, the typical one-way cost from Brindisi to Corfu is about 200€ ($260) to 250€ ($325) for two people in a double cabin with a standard-size vehicle.

Note: If you're coming by yacht from a non-E.U. country, Corfu town is one of Greece's official international entry/exit harbors, with Customs and health authorities as well as passport control.

By Bus KTEL offers service from Athens or Thessaloniki; its ferry carries you between Corfu and Igoumenitsou on the mainland opposite. Buses allow you to get on or off at main points along the way, such as Ioannina. The buses are comfortable enough, but be prepared for many hours of winding roads. The **KTEL office** (🕾 26610/39-627) is located along Leoforos Avramiou, up from the new port.

VISITOR INFORMATION Ionian Islands Tourism Directorate (🕾 26610/37-520) is on the second floor of a modern, unnumbered building at the corner of Rizospaston and Polila in the new town, a block across from the post office. It's open Monday through Friday from 8:30am to 1pm; in July and August, it's also open on Saturday. The office may have brochures with maps of the town and island. Those

Information ⓘ

0 ——— 300 m
0 ——— 300 y
N

NEW PORT

OLD PORT

Arseni

Xenofondos Stratigou

NEW FORTRESS (NEO FROURIO)

Zavitsianou

Donzelot

OLD VENETIAN QUARTER

Byzantine Museum **2**

Museum of Asian Art **3**

Bus Station ■

Solomou

N. Theotoki

Velisariou

Paleologou

Ayios Spyridon Cathedral **4**

Eleftherias

Plateia

Mandraki Harbor

Avrami Hill

Avramiou

Voulgareos

Town Hall **5**

Kapodistriou

Esplanade

OLD FORT (PALEO FROURIO)

I. Theotikos

G. Markora

G. Theotoki

Pandova

Guildford

N. Zambeli

Dessila

Ionian Academy **6**

Garitsa Bay

Polichroni Konstanda

San Rocco Square Local Bus Station ■

Mitropoliti Methodiou

Rizospaston Voulefton ⓘ

Alexandros

Vrala

Archaeological Museum **7**

Demokratias

Corfu Town

Greece

Athens

Aegean Sea

Mediterranean Sea

Archaeological Museum **7**
Ayios Spyridon Cathedral **4**
Byzantine Museum **2**
Ionian Academy **6**
Museum of Asian Art **3**
Palace of St. Michael & St. George **3**
Synagogue **1**
Town Hall **5**

with a particular interest in environmentally responsible tourism can check a most helpful website of a British organization, Friends of Ionia (**www.foi.org.uk**).

GETTING AROUND   By Bus   The dark-blue public buses service Corfu town, its suburbs, and nearby destinations. The semiprivate green-and-cream KTEL buses offer frequent service to points all over the island—Paleokastritsa, Glifada, Sidari, and more. The **KTEL office** (ⓒ **26610/39-627**) is located along Leoforos Avramiou, up from the new port.

By Taxi   In and around Corfu town, a taxi is your best bet—sometimes the only way around, such as to and from the harbor and the airport. Although taxi drivers are supposed to use their meters, many don't, so you should agree on the fare before setting out. You may also decide to use a taxi to visit some of the sites outside Corfu town; again, be sure to agree on the fare beforehand.

By Car   You'll find car-rental agencies all over Corfu. Even so, in high season it can be very difficult to get a vehicle at the spur of the moment. If you're sure of your plans on Corfu, make arrangements with an established international agency before departing home. Otherwise, try **Greek Skies Travel Agency,** in Corfu town at 20A Kapodistriou (ⓒ **26610/33-410;** fax 26610/36-161); or **Avanti Rent A Car,** 12A Ethnikis Antistasseos, along the new port (ⓒ **26610/42-028**).

By Moped   It's easy to rent mopeds, scooters, and motorcycles, but the roads are so curving, narrow, and steep that you should be very experienced before taking on such a vehicle. And insist on a helmet.

FAST FACTS   The official **American Express** agent for Corfu is Greek Skies Travel Agency, 20A Kapodistriou (© **26610/33-410;** fax 26610/36-161). There are numerous **banks** in both the old town and new town; you'll find ATMs at most of them. The **British Consul** is at 1 Menekrates (© **26610/30-055**), at the south end of the town, near the Menekrates monument. There is no U.S. consulate in Corfu. The **hospital** is on Julius Andreatti, and is signed from around town.

There are two convenient **Internet cafes:** Online Cafe, 28 Kapodistriou, along the Esplanade (cafe_online1@yahoo.com); and Netoikos, on 14 Kalochairetou, behind Ayios Spiridon Church. Both are open daily from late morning to late evening. You can count on quick, careful, and fair-priced **laundry** or **dry cleaning** at the Peristeri, 42 Ioannis Theotikos (leading from San Rocco Sq. on the way to the KTEL Bus Terminal). It's open Monday through Saturday from 8am to 2pm, with additional hours on Tuesday, Thursday, and Friday from 6 to 8pm. The **police station** (© **26610/39-575**) is at 19 Leoforos Alexandros (near the post office). The **post office** (© **26610/25-544**) is at 26 Leoforos Alexandros. It's open Monday through Friday from 7:30am to 8pm; in July and August, it's also open for a few hours on Saturday. The main **telephone office (OTE)** is at 9 Mantzarou; it's open Monday through Friday from 7am to midnight, to 10pm on Saturday and holidays.

WHAT TO SEE & DO
THE TOP ATTRACTIONS
Archaeological Museum 🎯   Even if you're not a devotee of ancient history or museums, you should take an hour to visit this small museum. On your way to see its master work, you'll pass a **stone lion** dating from around 575 B.C. (found in the nearby Menekrates tomb, along the waterfront by the museum). Go around and behind it to the large room with arguably the finest example of Archaic temple sculpture extant, the **pediment from the Temple of Artemis.** (The temple itself is just south of Corfu town and dates from about 590 B.C. The remains do not interest most people.) The pediment features the **Gorgon Medusa,** attended by two pantherlike animals. You don't have to be an art historian to note how this predates the great classical works such as the Elgin marbles—not only in the naiveté of its sculpture but also in the emphasis on the monstrous, with the humans so much smaller in scale.

Interesting for comparison is the fragment from another Archaic pediment found at Figare, Corfu. In an adjoining room, it shows Dionysos and a youth reclining on a couch. Only a century younger than the Gorgon pediment, here the humans have reduced the animal in size and placed it under the couch.

1 P. Armeni-Vraila (on the corner of Demokratias, the boulevard along the waterfront). © **26610/30-680.** Admission 4€ ($5.20); free on Sun. Tues–Sun 8:30am–2:30pm. Wheelchair accessible.

Kalypso Star 🄺ids   This glass-bottomed boat takes small groups offshore and provides fascinating views of marine life and undersea formations.

Old port, Corfu town. © **26610/46-525.** www.greeka.com. Admission 15€ ($20) adults, 8€ ($7.80) children. In high season, trips leave daily on the hour 10am–6pm, plus they make a 10pm night trip. Call for the off-season schedule.

Museum of Asian Art   The building itself, an impressive example of neoclassical architecture, was constructed between 1819 and 1824 for several reasons: to serve as the residence of the Lord High Commissioner, the British ruler of the Ionian Islands; to house the headquarters of the Order of St. Michael and St. George; and to provide the assembly room for the Ionian senate. When the British turned the Ionian Islands over to Greece, they gave this building to the king of Greece. As the king seldom spent much time here, it fell into disrepair until after World War II, when it was restored and turned into a museum.

The centerpiece of the museum is the collection of Chinese porcelains, bronzes, and other works from the Shang Dynasty (1500 B.C.) to the Ching Dynasty (19th c.). Go, too, to see the impressive Japanese works: woodblock prints, ceramics, sculpture, watercolors, and *netsuke* (carved sash fasteners). You may not have come to Greece to appreciate Asian art, but this is one of Corfu's several unexpected delights.

The Palace of St. Michael and St. George, north end of Esplanade. (✆ **26610/38-124.** protocol@hepka.culture.gr. Admission 4€ ($5.20). Tues–Sun 8am–2:30pm.

Old Fort (Paleo Frourio)   Originally a promontory attached to the mainland, now separated by a moat, this area is known for its two peaks, *koryphi* in Greek, which gave the town and the island their modern names. A castle crowns each peak; you can get fine views of Albania to the east and Corfu, town and island, to the west. The promontory itself was for a long time the main town, and it appears as such in many old engravings. The Venetians dug the moat in the 16th century; it successfully held off several attempts by the Turks to conquer this outpost of Christianity. What looks like a Greek temple at the south side is in fact a British church (ca. 1830).

In summer, a **Sound-and-Light** show is held several nights a week (in different foreign languages, so be sure to check the schedule).

The Esplanade (opposite the Liston). Admission 4€ ($5.20) adults, 2€ ($2.60) students and seniors over 60. Tues–Fri 8am–8pm; Sat–Sun and holidays 8:30am–3pm.

Petrakis Line   During high season, this is one of several lines that offer several 1-day excursions each week to destinations including Albania, Kefalonia, and Paxoi. On Kefalonia, you visit Melissani Grotto and Drogarati Cave (see later in this chapter) but not Argostoli. The excursion to Albania is becoming popular even though it doesn't go to the capital; the fare for a day trip to Albania now costs about 70€ ($90), which usually includes a midday meal. Most interesting would be to take a brief visit to the major archaeological site of Butrint, a UNESCO World Heritage Site; travel agents in Corfu or at the Albanian port of Saranda where you land will set you up with a guide; prices vary depending on your wants, but in general Albania is still cheap.

9 Venizelou, new port, Corfu town. (✆ **26610/31-649.** Fax 26610/38-787. petrakis@hol.gr.

A STROLL AROUND CORFU TOWN

This is definitely a browser's town, where as you're strolling in search of a snack or souvenir, you may serendipitously discover an old church or monument. To orient yourself, start with the **Esplanade area** bounded by the Old Fort (see above) and the sea on one side. The small haven below and to the north of the Old Fort is known as **Mandraki Harbor,** while the shore to the south is home port to the **Corfu Yacht Club.**

Dousmani bisects the Esplanade; at the far side is the circular monument that honors the union of the Ionian Islands with Greece. You might catch a cricket game at the **Plateia,** the northern part of the field. At the far north side of the Esplanade, the Palace of St. Michael and St. George is the home of the **Museum of Asian Art** (see above). If you proceed along the northwest corner of the palace, you'll come out above

Moments Sitting Still

Probably no one needs to be told that one of the great pleasures of traveling about Greece is just occasionally to sit still—that is, to plunk yourself down on a cafe chair and enjoy a drink a while you observe the passing scene. And arguably no more ideal place to do just that is at one of the cafes that set out their tables and chairs between the Liston and the Esplanade. The Liston, the impressive arcade, is a Greek version of "the List," referring to a list of upper-class and privileged individuals who were the only ones allowed to frequent this site after it was erected in the early 1800s. Gerald Durrell in his 1978 memoir of the family's time on Corfu, *The Garden of the Gods,* says it best: "The Platia [another name for the Liston] . . . was the hub of the island. Here you would sit at a little table under the arches or beneath the shimmering trees and, sooner or later, you would see everyone on the island and hear every facet of every scandal." Well, we may not be that kind of insider, but we can enjoy other pleasures, such as watching a game of cricket being played on the Esplanade (Spianada in Greek), the large greensward. Cricket is a vestige of the island's years under British rule, and another is ginger beer that you might consider sipping while you sit there.

the coast and can make your way around Arseniou above the *mourayia* (medieval sea walls).

On your way you will pass (on the left, up a flight of stairs) the **Byzantine Museum** in the **Church of Antivouniotissa.** Even if you're not a particular fan of Byzantine art, you should enjoy the small but elegant selection of icons from around Corfu; of particular interest are works by Cretan artists who came to Corfu, some of whom went on to Venice. The museum is open Monday from 12:30 to 7pm, Tuesday through Saturday from 8am to 7pm, and Sunday and holidays from 8:30am to 3pm. Admission is 3€ ($3.90).

Proceed along the coast road and descend to the square at the old port. Above its far side rises the **New Fortress,** and beyond this is the new port. Off to the left of the square is a large gateway, what remains of the 16th-century Porta Spilia. Go through it to get to the Plateia Solomou.

If you go left from Plateia Solomou along Velissariou, look on the right for the green doors of the 300-year-old **synagogue,** with its collection of torah crowns. It's open on Saturday from 9am until early evening. To gain entry during the week, call the Jewish Community Center at ℂ **26610/38-802.**

Continue on to the part of Old Corfu known as **Campiello,** with its stepped streets and narrow alleys. You may feel as if you are in a labyrinth—and you will be—but sooner or later you'll emerge onto one or another busy commercial street that will bring you down to the Esplanade.

Heading south on the Esplanade, you'll see a bandstand and at its far end the **Maitland Rotunda,** which honors Sir Thomas Maitland, the first British lord high commissioner of the Ionian Islands. Past this is the statue of Count Ioannis Kapodistrias (1776–1836), the first president of independent Greece.

Head south along the shore road from this end of the Esplanade, and you'll pass the Corfu Palace Hotel (see below) on your right; then the **Archaeological Museum** (see above), up Vraila on the right. After 2 more blocks, off to the right on the corner of Marasli, you'll see the **Tomb of Menekrates,** a circular tomb of a notable who drowned about 600 B.C. Proceeding to the right here onto Leoforos Alexandros will bring you into the heart of new Corfu town.

Back at the Esplanade, the western side of the north half is lined by a wide tree-shaded strip filled with cafe tables and chairs, then a street reserved for pedestrians, and then arcaded buildings patterned after Paris's Rue de Rivoli. Begun by the French and finished by the British, these arcaded buildings, known as the **Liston,** provide a great backdrop for a cup of coffee or a dish of ice cream.

At the back of the Liston is **Kapodistriou,** and perpendicular from this extend several streets that lead into the heart of Old Corfu—a mélange of fine shops, old churches, souvenir stands, and other stores in a maze of streets, alleys, and squares that seem like Venice without the water. The broadest and most stylish is **Nikiforio Theotoki.** At the northern end of Kapodistriou, turn left onto Ayios Spiridon and come to the corner of Filellinon and the **Ayios Spiridon Cathedral,** dedicated to Spiridon, the patron saint of Corfu. Locals credit Spiridon, a 4th-century bishop of Cyprus, with saving Corfu from famine, plagues, and a Turkish siege. Inside the church is the saint's embalmed body in a silver casket, as well as precious gold and silver votive offerings and many fine old icons. Four times a year the faithful parade the remains of St. Spiridon through the streets of old Corfu: Palm Sunday, Holy Saturday, August 1, and the first Sunday in November.

Proceeding up Voulgareos behind the southern end of the Liston, you'll come to the back of the **town hall,** built in 1663 as a Venetian loggia; it later served as a theater. Turn into the square it faces and enter what seems like a Roman piazza, with steps and terraces, the Roman Catholic cathedral on the left and, reigning over the top, the restored Catholic archbishop's residence (now the Bank of Greece).

From here, finish your walk by wandering up and down and in and out the various streets of Old Corfu.

SHOPPING

Corfu town has so many shops selling jewelry, leather goods, olive wood objects, and handmade needlework that it is impossible to single out one or another. If you're looking for needlework, the stores along Filarmonikis (off N. Teotoki) may have something that pleases you; prices are generally fair and uniform.

We would never recommend a trip to Corfu *just* for the kumquat liqueur, but this Chinese fruit has been cultivated on the island since the late 1800s and the liqueur makes a unique treat—or gift if it doesn't appeal to you!

Standing out from the many standard souvenir-gift shops, **Antica,** 25 Ayios Spiridon, leading away from the north end of Liston (© **26610/32-401**), offers unusual older jewelry, plates, textiles, brass, and icons. **Gravures,** 64 Ev. Voulgareos, where the street emerges from the old town to join the new town (© **26610/41-721**), has a fine selection of engravings and prints of scenes from Corfu, all nicely matted. Originals (taken from old books or magazines) can cost 150€ ($195), reproductions as little as 10€ ($13). The elegant **Terracotta,** 2 Filarmonikis, just off N. Theotoki, the main shopping street (©/fax **26610/45-260**), sells only contemporary Greek work: jewelry, one-of-a-kind pieces, ceramics, and small sculptures, some by well-known Greek artists and artisans. Nothing is cheap, but everything is classy.

No dearth of ceramics can be found in Corfu, but we like the **Pottery Workshop,** 15km (10 miles) north of Corfu on the right of the road to Paleokastritsa (© **26610/ 90-704**), where you get to observe Sofoklis Ikonomides and Sissy Moskidou making and decorating all the pottery on sale here. Whether decorative or functional, something will certainly appeal to your taste. Two kilometers (1¼ miles) farther along the road, on the left, is the **Wood's Nest,** offering a large selection of olive wood objects just slightly cheaper than in town.

WHERE TO STAY

The island of Corfu has an apparently inexhaustible choice of accommodations, but in high season (July and Aug), package groups from Europe will book many rooms. Reservations are recommended if you have specific preferences for that time, especially for Corfu town.

IN TOWN
Very Expensive

Corfu Palace Hotel ✦✦   This grand hotel combines the most up-to-date features of a Swiss enterprise (which it is) with Greek hospitality: Every comfort goes hand in hand with modern business and conference conveniences, fine service, and elegant decor. The landscaping feels tropical; the lobby and public areas bespeak luxury. The comfortable guest rooms, while not exceptionally large, are well-appointed; the marbled bathrooms are large. Every balconied room enjoys views of the sea. In addition to its splendid surroundings, superb service, and grand meals, the hotel provides restful isolation above the bay even though it is near the city center. The hotel's two restaurants, the Scheria (a grill room on the poolside terrace) and the Panorama (with a view of the bay), serve Greek and international menus; both vie to claim the finest cuisine on Corfu. Guests can use the facilities of the nearby Corfu Tennis Club and Yacht Club and the Corfu Golf Club, 14km (9 miles) away.

2 Leoforos Demokratias, 49100 Corfu. © **26610/39-485** to -487. Fax 26610/31-749. www.corfupalace.com. 115 units. High season 245€–350€ ($319–$455) double; low season 165€–255€ ($215–$332) double. Children up to age 12 stay free in parent's room (without meals). Rates include buffet breakfast; half-board available. AE, DC, MC, V. Free parking. A 5-min. walk from Esplanade. Along Garitsa Bay, just south of center. **Amenities:** 2 restaurants; 3 bars; 3 pools (1 for children); night-lit tennis courts nearby; bicycle rentals; game room; concierge; tours and car rentals arranged; conference facilities; salon; 24-hr. room service; babysitting; laundry service; dry cleaning; newspaper delivery. *In room:* A/C, TV, minibar, hair dryer, safe.

Moderate

If you prefer old-fashioned period hotels to shiny new accommodations, consider **Astron Hotel,** 15 Donzelot (waterfront road down to old harbor), 49100 Corfu (© **26610/39-505**). It offers up-to-date bathrooms and other facilities while retaining touches of its original charm.

Arcadion Hotel ✦   This hotel's total renovation—in fact, more like a total reconstruction—made it as pleasurable as it is convenient. The rooms have furniture and fabrics in a traditional Corfiot style; bathrooms are up to the highest standards for this class. If you like to be at the center of a city, you can't get much closer than this: When you step out the door, the Esplanade and the Liston are 15m (50 ft.) away and the beach is just a little farther. Admittedly, this also means that on pleasant evenings there will be crowds in front of the hotel, but ask for a room off the front. (All windows are double-glazed for sound control.) It's hard to beat for location and comfort. In the evening, you can sit in the roof garden and enjoy a cool drink with a fabulous view.

44 Kapodistriou, 49100 Corfu. © 26610/30-104. www.arcadionhotel.com. 33 units. All year 95€ ($124) double. Rates include buffet breakfast. AE, MC, V. Public parking lot (fee) nearby. Diagonally across from south end of Liston, facing the Esplanade. **Amenities:** Restaurant; bar; health club; concierge; tours and car rentals arranged; salon; 24-hr. room service; laundry service; dry cleaning. *In room:* A/C, TV, dataport, minibar, hair dryer, safe.

Bella Venezia *Value*   Like the gold-medal winner of the decathlon, this hotel may not win in any single category, but its combined virtues make it the first choice of many. Completely renovated in 2006, the building is a restored neoclassical mansion, with character if not major distinction. The location is just a bit off center and lacks fine views, but it's quiet and close enough to any place you'd want to walk to; a decent beach is 274m (900 ft.) away. The common areas are not especially stylish but they do have atmosphere. Although not luxurious or large, the guest rooms have some old-world touches; the showers, however, are undeniably cramped. There is no restaurant, but there's a colorful patio-garden for breakfast and an enclosed kiosk for light snacks. Finally, the hotel's rates are below those of similar hotels.

4 N. Zambeli (approached from far south end of Esplanade), 49100 Corfu. © 26610/46-500. www.bellavenezia hotel.com. 31 units. High season 125€ ($163) double; low season 105€ ($137) double. Rates include buffet breakfast. AE, DC, MC, V. Parking on adjacent streets. Within walking distance of old and new towns. **Amenities:** Patio for breakfast and snacks; Internet kiosk. *In room:* A/C, TV, Internet.

Cavalieri *★*   If you like your hotels in the discreet old European style, this place is for you. For glitz, look elsewhere. The Cavalieri is in an old building with a small elevator. The main lounge is Italian velvet. Service is low-key, rooms are spare, and bathrooms standard. Ask for one of the front rooms on the upper floors, which boast great views of the Old Fort. Another draw is the rooftop garden, which after 6:30pm offers drinks, sweets, and light meals along with a spectacular view; even if you don't stay here, it's a grand place to pass an hour in the evening. Because of the hotel's appealing location, advance reservations are required much of the year.

4 Kapodistriou, 49100 Corfu. © 26610/39-041. www.cavalieri-hotel.com. 50 units. High season 142€ ($185) double; low season 110€ ($143) double. Rates include buffet breakfast. AE, DC, MC, V. Parking on adjacent streets. Within easy walking distance of old and new towns. At far south end of Esplanade. **Amenities:** Bar; concierge; tours and car rentals arranged; room service 7am–midnight; laundry service; dry cleaning. *In room:* A/C, TV, minibar, hair dryer.

OUTSIDE TOWN
Expensive
Corfu Holiday Palace *★*   Formerly the Hilton, this is a grand hotel in the contemporary manner—more like a resort if you consider the range of its facilities. Its lobby sets the tone—spacious and relaxed. The staff is professional yet friendly. Guest rooms are standard Greek-hotel-size, with comfortable beds and state-of-the art bathrooms. The grounds create a semitropical ambience. In addition to the pools, a lovely private beach below beckons. Kanoni, an island landmark, is nearby. The island's airport is off in the middle distance—not a major problem unless your windows are open, but we suggest you ask for a room facing the sea instead. Patrons get a 50% discount at Corfu Golf Club (18km/12 miles away). Perhaps the biggest surprise of all: One of Greece's major casinos is on the premises—although there has been talk of moving it to the Achilleion, the Kaiser's one-time mansion (see below).

P.O. Box 124, Nausicaa, Kanoni, 49100 Corfu. © 26610/36-540. www.corfuholidaypalace.gr. 266 units. High season 150€–220€ ($195–$286) double; low season 110€–150€ ($143–$195) double. Rates include buffet breakfast. Half board includes a fixed-price menu. Special packages available for extended stays. AE, DC, MC, V. Free parking on grounds. Hotel offers a shuttle bus; public bus no. 2 stops 200m (656 ft.) away; and taxi is easily summoned. About 5km (3 miles) south of Corfu town. **Amenities:** 2 restaurants; 2 bars; 2 pools; lit tennis courts; jogging track; health club; watersports equipment; concierge; tours and car rentals arranged; conference facilities; boutiques; salon; babysitting; laundry service; dry cleaning; bowling, billiards, and table tennis. *In room:* A/C, TV, minibar, hair dryer.

Inexpensive

Fundana Villas ★ *Kids*   This is a new place that will be greatly appreciated by some as a delightful alternative to all the other hostelries listed for Corfu—bungalows off in a completely natural setting. The 12 units vary in size, accommodating from 2 to 7 people, but all have kitchenettes. You are surrounded by fruit trees and the sounds of the Greek countryside and you can imbibe the pure spring water, yet there's a good-size swimming pool and a second smaller one for children. Twice a week the proprietors prepare traditional Corfiot dinners; for other meals you have to drive into Corfu town or Paleokastritsa, but this gives you a chance to sample our several recommendations. (Car rentals can be arranged when you book your room.) You will also have your choice of beaches, none of which is much more than about 15km (9 miles) away; the island's golf course, horseback riding, and a water park are also within a few miles drive. The Spathas is there to help with all your wishes. Some of you may recognize the main house as the residence in the BBC-TV version of Gerald Durrell's "My Family and Other Animals."

1 Odysseos, 49100 Corfu. ℂ 26630/22-532. www.fundanavillas.com. 15 units. High season 75€ ($98) per couple. Self-catering breakfast extra 7€ ($9). MC, V. Parking on grounds. 17km/11miles from Corfu center, about same to Paleokastritsa. **Amenities:** 2 pools; bar; table tennis; Internet; hikes and excursions arranged. *In room:* TV, heating, kitchenette.

WHERE TO DINE
IN TOWN
Expensive

If you're in a celebratory mood, you might consider **Chambor,** 71 Guilford (ℂ **26610/ 39-031**). It's certainly a cut above your average Greek restaurant, but much of what you pay for is the elaborate settings and presentation.

Venetian Well ★ MIDDLE EASTERN/INTERNATIONAL/GREEK   This remains our top pick in Corfu town. Diners sit at a candlelit table in a rather austere little square with a Venetian wellhead (ca. 1699) and a church opposite. When the weather changes, guests sit in a stately room adorned with a mural. The atmosphere is as discreet as the food is inventive. There is no printed menu—you learn what's available from a chalkboard or from your waiter—and there's no predicting what the kitchen will offer on any given evening. Because the chef uses seasonal vegetables, salads vary from month to month. Main courses may range from standard Greek dishes such as beef *giouvetsi* (cooked in a pot) to chicken prepared with exotic ingredients. The wine list is more extensive than in most Greek restaurants.

Plateia Kremasti. ℂ 26610/44-761. Reservations recommended in high season. Main courses 10€–26€ ($13–$34). No credit cards. Mon–Sat noon–midnight. On small square up from old harbor, behind Greek Orthodox cathedral.

Moderate

If you want to dine along the coast, consider **Antranik,** 19 Arseniou (ℂ **26610/22- 301**), located under the awnings on the sea side of the road leading from north of the Esplanade down to the new port. **Faliraki,** at the corner of Kapodistrias and Arseniou, below the wall (ℂ **26610/30-392**), also has a wonderful location right on the water, although the food is standard Greek fare.

Aegli Garden Restaurant GREEK/CONTINENTAL   The tasty and varied menu of this old favorite attracts both residents and travelers to its several dining areas—indoors, in the arcade, under awnings across from the arcade, or along the pedestrian mall of Kapodistriou. Try the selection of *orektika* with the wine or beer on tap. The staff takes special pride in their Corfiote specialties, several of which are traditional Greek foods with rather spicy sauces: filet of fish, octopus, *pastitsada* (baked veal), *baccala* (salted codfish), and *sofrito* (veal). If spiciness isn't your thing, try the swordfish or prawns. Everything is done with great care, including a delicious fresh-fruit salad that you can order by itself—just perfect when you don't fee like a full meal.

23 Kapodistriou. ✆ 26610/31-949. Fax 26610/45-488. Main courses 7€–18€ ($9–$24). AE, DC, MC, V. Daily 9am–1am. In Liston.

Bellissimo GREEK/INTERNATIONAL   This restaurant has lived up to its promise of being a welcome addition to the Corfu scene—unpretentious but serving tasty food. Located on a central and lovely town square, it's run by the hospitable Stergiou family, Corfiots who returned from Canada. They offer a standard Greek menu with some "exotics," including hamburgers and chicken curry. Especially welcome is their modestly priced "Greek sampling plate"—tzatziki, tomatoes-and-cucumber salad, *keftedes* (meatballs), fried potatoes, grilled lamb, and pork souvlaki.

Plateia Lemonia. ✆ 26610/41-112. Main courses 5€–16€ ($6.50–$21). No credit cards. Daily 10:30am–11pm. Just off N. Theotoki.

CORFU TOWN AFTER DARK

Corfu town definitely has a nightlife scene, though many people are content to linger over dinner and then, after a promenade, repair to one of the cafes at the Liston, such as the **Capri, Liston, Europa,** or **Aegli**—all of which have similar selections of light refreshments and drinks. (Treat yourself to the fresh fruit salad at the Aegli!) Others are drawn to the cafes at the north end of the Esplanade, just outside the Liston—**Cafe Bar 92, Magnet,** or **Cool Down.** For a special treat, ascend to the rooftop cafe/bar at **Cavalieri** hotel (see "Where to Stay," above). Another choice is **Lindos Cafe,** overlooking the beach and facilities of the Nautical Club of Corfu. It's approached by steps leading off Leoforos Demokratias, just south and outside the Esplanade. And one of the best-kept secrets of Corfu town is the little **Art Cafe,** to the right and behind the Museum of Asian Art; its garden provides a wonderful, cool, quiet retreat from the hustle and bustle of the rest of the town.

If you enjoy more action—loud music and dancing—several nightspots are along the coast to the north, between Corfu town and the beach resort of Gouvia. They include **Ekati,** a typical Greek nightclub; **Esperides,** featuring Greek music; and **Corfu by Night,** definitely touristy. Be prepared to drop money at these places.

The youngest night crawlers find places that go in and out of favor (and business) from year to year. Among the more enduring up around the Esplanade are the relatively sedate **Aktaion,** just to the right of the Old Fort; and clubs featuring the latest music such as **Hook** and **Base** along Kapodistriou (before the Cavialieri Hotel). Young people seeking more excitement go down past the new port to a strip of flashy discos—**Au Bar, Cristal, Elxis, Privilege.** These clubs charge a cover (about 10€/$13, including one drink).

In summer, frequent **concerts** by orchestras and bands are held on the Esplanade; most of them are free. Corfu town boasts the oldest band in Greece. The **Sound-and-Light** performances are described in the listing for the Old Fort (see "What to See & Do," earlier in this chapter). September brings **Corfu Festival,** with concerts, ballet, opera, and theater performances by a mix of Greek and international companies.

Carnival is celebrated on the last Sunday before Lent with a parade and the burning of an effigy representing the spirit of Carnival.

Still another possibility would be to take one of the boat cruises that go out each night and provide both a refreshing atmosphere and a view of the glittering island. Any travel agency will be able to sign you up for one of these.

For those who like to gamble, the **casino** at the **Corfu Holiday Palace** (see "Where to Stay," above) is a few miles outside of town. Open nightly (8pm–3am) to individuals 23 years or older, it may not have the glamour of Monte Carlo, but it attracts an international set during the high season.

SIDE TRIPS FROM CORFU TOWN
KANONI, PONDIKONISI & ACHILLEION

Although these sites and destinations are not next door to one another and have little in common, they are grouped here because they all lie south of Corfu town and could be visited in less than a full day's outing. Everyone who comes to Corfu town will want to visit these places, even if you go nowhere else on the island. History buffs will revel in the sites' many associations, and even beach people cannot help but be moved by their scenic charms.

Kanoni is approached south of Corfu town via the village Analepsis; it's well signed. Ascending most of the way, you arrive after about 4km (2½ miles) at the circular terrace (on the right). The area is known as Kanoni (after the cannon once sited here). Make your way to the edge and enjoy a wonderful view. Directly below in the inlet are two islets. If you want to visit one or both, you can take a 10-minute walk

---

A Villa with Many Tales to Tell

The Achilleion has enough back stories to support a TV miniseries. To begin with, the personal life of the Empress Elizabeth who built it is one of extravagant eccentricities: all I can say here is to look her up in an encyclopedia or online. But aside from this, it was as the mother of Rudolf that she would acquire legendary fame: He was the young prince who in 1889 was found dead at his hunting lodge at Mayerling, Austria, along with his mistress; although generally assumed to have been a double-suicide, many questions about their deaths were never satisfied. In any case, Elizabeth identified Rudolf with Achilles, and so the villa is really a memorial to him—thus the many statues and motifs associated with Achilles (including the dolphins, for Achilles' mother was the water nymph Thetis). Then in 1898 Elizabeth was assassinated by an anarchist—for no other reason than she was a royal. The villa sat unused until in 1907 Kaiser Wilhelm II of Germany bought it as a summer home. It was appropriated by the Greek government after World War I and used for various government agencies; the Germans used it during their World War II occupation of the island; it then reverted to the Greek National Tourist Organization, which allowed the top floor to be used as a casino (seen in the 1981 James Bond film *For Your Eyes Only*). This closed in 1983, but there has been talk in recent years of reestablishing a casino here. But whatever happens next, the Achilleion has more than it share of tales to tell.

Taking a Dive

All of the bays and coves that make up Paleokastritsa boast clear, sparkling turquoise waters. Both **Korfu Diving** (℃ **26630/41-604;** www.dive-centers.net) and **Achilleion Diving** (℃ **69327/29-011;** www.diving-corfu.com) offer courses for beginners, as well as day excursions for advanced divers.

down a not-that-difficult path from Kanoni; with a vehicle you must retrace the road back from Kanoni a few hundred yards to a signed turnoff (on the left coming back).

One islet is linked to the land by a causeway; here you'll find the **Monastery of Vlakherna.** To get to the other islet, **Pondikonisi (Mouse Island),** you must go by small boat, which is always available (3€/$3.90 round-trip). Legend has it that this rocky islet is a Phaeacian ship that turned to stone after taking Odysseus back to Ithaka. The chapel here dates from the 13th century, and its setting among the cypress trees makes it most picturesque. Many Corfiotes make a pilgrimage here in small boats on August 6. It's also the inspiration for the Swiss painter Arnold Boecklin's well-known work *Isle of the Dead,* which in turn inspired Rachmaninoff's music of the same name.

A causeway across the little inlet to Perama on the main body of the island (the Kanoni road is on a peninsula) is for pedestrians only. So to continue on to your next destination, a villa known as **Achilleion,** you must drive back to the edge of Corfu town and then take another road about 8km (5 miles) to the south, signed to Gastouri and the villa of Achilleion. The villa is open daily from 9am to 4pm. Admission is 6€ ($7.80). Bus no. 10, from Plateia San Rocco, runs directly to the Achilleion several times daily.

Empress Elizabeth of Austria-Hungary built this villa between 1890 and 1891. Approaching the villa from the entrance gate, you will see a slightly Teutonic version of a neoclassical summer palace. Take a walk through at least some of the eclectic rooms. Among the curiosities is the small saddle-seat on which Kaiser Wilhelm II of Germany sat while performing his imperial chores.

The terraced gardens that surround the villa are now lush. Be sure to go all the way around and out to the back terraces. Here you will see the most famous of the statues Elizabeth commissioned, *The Dying Achilles,* by the German sculptor Herter; also, you cannot miss the 4.5m-tall (15-ft.) Achilles that the Kaiser had inscribed, TO THE GREATEST GREEK FROM THE GREATEST GERMAN, a sentiment removed after World War II. But for a truly impressive sight, step to the edge of the terrace and enjoy a spectacular view of Corfu town and much of the eastern coast to the south.

If you have your own car, you can continue on past the Achilleion and descend to the coast between **Benitses** and **Perama;** the first, to the south, has become a popular beach resort. Proceeding north along the coast from Benitses, you come to Perama (another popular beach resort), where a turnoff onto a promontory brings you to the pedestrian causeway opposite Pondikonisi (see above). The main road brings you back to the edge of Corfu town.

PALEOKASTRITSA

If you can make only one excursion on the island, this is certainly a top competitor with Kanoni and the Achilleion. Go to those places for their fascinating histories, to Paleokastritsa for its natural beauty.

The drive here is northwest out of Corfu town via well-marked roads. Follow the coast for about 8km (5½ miles) to Gouvia, then turn inland. (It is on this next stretch that you pass the **Pottery Workshop** and the **Wood's Nest;** see "Shopping," earlier in this chapter.) The road eventually narrows but is asphalt all the way as you gradually descend to the west coast and **Paleokastritsa** (25km/16 miles). There's no missing it: It's been taken over by hotels and restaurants, although some of the bays and coves that make up Paleokastritsa are less developed than others. Tradition claims it as the site of **Scheria,** the capital of the Phaeacians—so one of these beaches should be where Nausicaa found Odysseus, though no remains have been found to substantiate that.

Continue on past the beaches to climb a narrow, winding road to the **Monastery of the Panagia** at the edge of a promontory. (The monastery is about a mile from the beach, and many prefer to go by foot, as parking is next to impossible once you get there.) Although founded in the 13th century, the monastery has no remains that old. It's worth a brief visit, especially at sunset. The monastery's hours are April through October, daily from 7am to 1pm and 3 to 8pm.

More interesting in some ways, and certainly more challenging, is a visit to the **Angelokastro,** the medieval castle that sits high on a pinnacle overlooking all of Pale-okastritsa. Only the most hardy will choose to walk all the way up from the shore, a taxing hour at least. The rest of us will drive back out of Paleokastritsa (2.5km/1½ miles) to a turnoff to the left, signed LAKONES. There commences an endless winding ascent that eventually levels out and provides spectacular views of the coast as the road passes through the villages of Lakones and Krini. (*A word of warning:* Don't attempt to drive this road unless you are comfortable pulling over to the very edge of narrow roads—with sheer drops—to let trucks and buses by, something you will have to do on your way down.) Keep going until the road takes a sharp turn to the right and down, and you'll come to a little parking area. From here, walk up to the castle, only 200m (656 ft.) away but seemingly farther because of the trail's poor condition. What you are rewarded with, though, is one of the most spectacularly sited medieval castles you'll ever visit, some 300m (1,000 ft.) above sea level.

If you've come this far, reward yourself with a meal and the spectacular view at one of the restaurants or cafes on the road outside Lakones: **Bella Vista, Colombo,** or **Casteltron.** At mealtimes in high season, these places are taken over by busloads of tour groups. If you have your own transport, try to eat a bit earlier or later.

On your way back to Corfu town from Paleokastritsa, you can vary your route by heading south through **Ropa Valley,** the agricultural heartland of Corfu. Follow the signs indicating Liapades and Tembloni, but don't bother going into either of these towns. If you have time for a beach stop, consider going over to **Ermones Beach** (the island's only golf club is located above it) or **Glifada Beach.**

WHERE TO STAY & DINE   If you want to spend some time at Paleokastritsa, it's good to get away from the main beach. We like the 70-unit family-run **Hotel Odysseus** (© 26630/41-209; www.odysseushotel.gr), high above the largely undeveloped cove before the main beach. A double in high season goes for 75€ ($98); in low season, the rate is 55€ ($72) double. Rates include buffet breakfast, and the hotel has a pool. The Odysseus is open May to mid-October. Guests have also recommended its restaurant.

On its own peninsula and both fancier and pricier is the 127-unit **Akrotiri Beach Hotel** (© 26630/41-237; www.akrotiri-beach.com), where an air-conditioned double in high season goes for 120€ to 180€ ($156–$234), including buffet breakfast.

Half board can also be arranged. All rooms have balconies and sea views. In addition to the adjacent beaches, it has two pools. It's open May through October.

The restaurants on the main beach in Paleokastritsa are definitely touristy. The **Vrahos** is probably the most stylish. However, if you like to eat where the action is, the best value and most fun at the main beach can be had at the **Apollon Restaurant** in Hotel Apollon-Ermis (© **26630/41-211**). Main courses are 5€ to 16€ ($6.50–$21). I prefer someplace a bit removed, such as **Belvedere Restaurant** (© **26630/41-583**), just below Hotel Odysseus, which serves solid Greek dishes at reasonable prices. Main courses range from 5€ to 16€ ($6.50–$21). The restaurant is open mid-April to late October from 9am to midnight.

2 Kefalonia (Cephalonia)

Here is a Greek island the way they used to be: It pretty much goes its own way while you travel around and through it. That said, Kefalonia does have its natural wonders, a few historical buildings and archaeological sites, and many fine beaches. It also has a full-service tourist industry, with fine hotels, restaurants, travel agencies, car-rental agencies—the whole show. Since Kefalonia was virtually demolished by the earthquake of 1953, most structures on this island are fairly new. And it has long been one of the more prosperous and cosmopolitan parts of Greece, thanks to its islanders' tradition of sailing and trading in the world at large. The filming of the 2001 movie *Captain Corelli's Mandolin* also gave a temporary boost to tourism here. But don't come to Kefalonia for glamour. Come to spend time in a relaxing environment, to enjoy handsome vistas and a lovely countryside.

ESSENTIALS

GETTING THERE   By Plane   From Athens, there are at least three flights daily on **Olympic Airways** (with some flights via Zakinthos). The Argostoli office is at 1 Rokkou Vergoti, the street between the harbor and the square of the Archaeological Museum (© **26710/28-808**). **Kefalonia airport** is 8km (5 miles) outside Argostoli. As there is no public bus, everyone goes to Argostoli by taxi, which costs about 10€ ($13). **Airsea Lines** offers hydroplane connections with Corfu (© **80111/800-600;** www.airsealines.com).

By Boat   As with most Greek islands, it's easier to get to Kefalonia in summer than in the off season, when weather and reduced tourism eliminate the smaller boats. Ferries to Kefalonia are operated by the **Strintzis Line** (© **210/823-6011** in Athens; strintzis-ferries@ferries.gr); if you haven't made arrangements with a travel agent, you can buy tickets dockside. Throughout the year, a car-passenger ferry leaves daily from Patras to Sami (about 2½ hr.) There is also at least one car-passenger ferry daily (1½ hr.) from Killini (on the northwest tip of the Peloponnese) to Argostoli and Poros (on the southeastern coast of Kefalonia).

Beyond these more or less dependable services, during the high-season months of July and August there are alternatives—ships to and from Corfu, Ithaka, Levkas, Brindisi (Italy), or other ports—but they do not necessarily hold to the same schedules every year.

VISITOR INFORMATION   Argostoli Tourism Office in Argostoli is at the Port Authority Building on Ioannis Metaxa along the harbor (© **26710/22-248**). It's open in high season daily from 7:30am to 2:30pm and 5 to 10pm; in low season, Monday through Friday from 8am to 3pm.

GETTING AROUND   By Bus   You can get to almost any point on Kefalonia—even remote beaches, villages, and monasteries—by **KTEL bus** (℗ 26710/22-276 in Argostoli). Schedules, however, are restrictive and may cut deeply into your preferred arrival at any given destination. KTEL also operates special tours to major destinations around the island. The **KTEL station** is on Leoforos A. Tritsi, at the far end of the harbor road, 200m (656 ft.) past Trapano Bridge.

By Taxi   If you don't enjoy driving on twisting mountain roads, taxis are the best alternative. In Argostoli, go to Vallianou (Central) Square and work out an acceptable fare. A trip to Fiskardo, with the driver waiting for 3 to 4 hours, might run to 150€ ($195)—with several passengers splitting the fare, this isn't unreasonable for a day's excursion. Everyone uses taxis on Kefalonia. Although drivers are supposed to use their meters, many don't; agree on the fare before you set off.

By Car   There are literally dozens of car-rental firms, from the well-known international companies to hole-in-the-wall outfits. In Argostoli, we found **Auto Europe,** 3 Lassis (℗ **26710/24-078**); and **Euro Dollar,** 3A R. Vergoti (℗ **26710/23-613**), to be reliable. In high season, rental cars are scarce, so don't expect to haggle. A compact will come to at least 60€ ($78) per day (gas extra); better rates are usually offered for rentals of 3 or more days.

By Moped & Motorcycle   The roads on Kefalonia are asphalt and in decent condition but are often narrow, lack shoulders, and twist around mountain ravines or wind along the edges of sheer drops to the sea. That said, many travelers choose to get around Kefalonia this way. Every city and town has places that will rent two-seater mopeds and motorcycles for about 25€ to 35€ ($33–$46) per day.

FAST FACTS   There are several **banks** with ATMs in the center of Argostoli. The **hospital** (℗ 26710/22-434) is on Souidias (the upper road, above the Trapano Bridge). **Internet access** is available at **Internet Point,** 8 A. Metaxa (℗ **26710/22-227**; www.f2d.gr) or at **Excelixis Computers,** 3 Minoos (℗ **26710/25-530**; xlixis@otenet.gr). **Express Laundry,** 46B Lassi, the upper road that leads to the airport, is open Monday through Saturday from 9:30am to 9pm. A load costs 3€ ($3.90). Argostoli's **tourist police** (℗ 26710/22-200) are on Ioannis Metaxa, on the waterfront across from the port authority. The **post office** is in Argostoli on Lithostrato, opposite no. 18 (℗ 26710/22-124); its hours are Monday through Saturday from 7:30am to 2pm. The main **telephone office (OTE)** is at 8 G. Vergoti. It's open daily, April through September from 7am to midnight, and October through March from 7am to 10pm.

WHAT TO SEE & DO

Staying in Kefalonia's capital and largest city, **Argostoli,** allows you to go off on daily excursions to beaches and mountains yet return to the comforts of a city. It has the island's most diverse offering of hotels and restaurants, and it feels urban. For those who find that Argostoli doesn't offer enough in the way of old-world charm or diversions, we point out some of the other getaway possibilities on Kefalonia.

Argostoli's appeal does not depend on any archaeological, historical, architectural, or artistic particulars. It's a city for observers—travelers who are content strolling or sitting and observing the passing scene: ships coming and going along the waterfront, locals shopping in the market, children playing in the squares. Head to **Vallianou (Central) Square** or the **waterfront** to find a cafe where you can nurse a coffee or ice cream. **Premier Cafe** on the former and **Hotel Olga** on the latter are as nice as any.

Kefalonia & Ithaka

If you do nothing else, walk along the waterfront and check out **Trapano Bridge,** a shortcut from Argostoli (which is actually on its own little peninsula) to the main part of the island.

The best nearby **beaches** are just south of the city in **Lassi,** which now has numerous hotels, pensions, cafes, and restaurants much loved by package groups.

Historical and Folklore Museum of the Corgialenos Library ⊛   I recommend
this museum over the nearby, rather dry archaeological museum. Many so-called folklore museums, little more than typical rooms, have sprung up in Greece in recent years, but this is one of the most authentic and satisfying. Meticulously maintained and well-labeled displays showcase traditional clothing, tools, handicrafts, and objects used in daily life across the centuries. Somewhat unexpected are the displays revealing a stylish upper-middle-class life. Most engaging is a large collection of photographs of pre- and post-1953 earthquake Kefalonia. The gift shop has an especially fine selection of items, including handmade lace.

Ilia Zervou. ℂ **26710/28-835.** Admission 3€ ($3.90). Apr–Oct Mon–Sat 9am–2pm; off season by arrangement. 2 blocks up the hill behind public theater and Archaeological Museum square.

Fun Fact **The Home of Odysseus**

Every schoolchild knows (or at least used to!) that Odysseus, the hero of Homer's epic, came from the island of Ithaka. Over the centuries, a few scholars debated which island this was—some even arguing that in any case it was all a fiction—but in general it came to be accepted that Odysseus's island was the same as the one we know today by that name. In 2005, however, several Englishmen announced that they had established that the true Ithaka of Homer's Odysseus is the **Paliki** peninsula that hangs down along the northwestern coast of Kefalonia. As to the objection that Homer's Ithaka was an island, these men claimed that Paliki had been an island but that seismic forces had since joined it to Kefalonia. As of this writing, there is little archaeological evidence to support this claim—and no remains to visit. But for those who relish Homer, it might be worth the few hours it would take to drive over to Paliki and just check out the land. (There is also a frequent ferry that cuts down the travel time, but when you disembark you would need to get wheels to explore the peninsula.) And in any case, you might consider packing a paperback translation of *The Odyssey*.

SHOPPING

Interesting ceramics are for sale at **Hephaestus,** on the waterfront at 21 May; **Alexander's,** on the corner of Plateia Museio (the square 1 block back from the waterfront); and **The Mistral,** 6 Vironis, up the hill opposite the post office, offering the work of the potter/owner.

For a taste of the local cuisine, consider Kefalonia's prized Golden Honey, tart quince preserve, or almond pralines. Another possibility is a bottle of one of Kefalonia's highly praised wines. You can visit **Calliga Vineyard** (selling white Robola and red Calliga Cava) or **Gentilini Vineyard** (with more expensive wines), both near Argostoli; or **Metaxas Wine Estate,** south of Argostoli. The tourist office (see "Visitor Information," above) on the waterfront will tell you how to arrange a tour.

WHERE TO STAY

Accommodations on Kefalonia range from luxury hotels to basic rooms. During peak times, I strongly recommend reservations. **Filoxenos Travel** (✆ **26710/23-055;** www.filoxenostravel.gr) can help.

EXPENSIVE

White Rocks Hotel & Bungalows 🐾   This low-key place is where travelers catch up on the reading they've meant to do all year. Although not the most elaborate, it is probably the most elegant hotel on Kefalonia. On arriving, you descend a few steps from the main road to enter an almost tropical setting. The lobby is subdued and stylish, a decor that extends to the hotel's guest rooms, which are modest in size but have first-rate bathrooms. Guests have use of their own small beach as well as a larger one which is open to the public. White Rocks is a couple of miles south of Argostoli just above the two beaches. A quiet retreat that may appeal more to the older set.

Platys Yialos, 28100 Argostoli. ✆ **26710/28-332** or 26710/28-335. www.whiterocks.gr. 102 rooms, 60 bungalows. High season 190€ ($247) double; 200€ ($260) bungalow. Rates are for either rooms or bungalows and include breakfast and dinner. AE, DC, V. Closed Nov–Apr. Private parking. Occasional public buses go from the center of town to and from Yialos, but most people take taxis. At the beach at Lassi, outside Argostoli. **Amenities:** Restaurant; bar;

pool; concierge; tours and car rentals arranged; conference facilities; room service 7am–midnight; laundry service; dry cleaning. *In room:* A/C.

MODERATE

In addition to the following options, you might consider the 60-unit **Hotel Miramare,** 2 I. Metaxa, at the far end of the shore road (℃ **26710/25-511;** fax 26710/25-512); it's slightly removed from the town's hustle yet within walking distance of any place you'd want to go.

Cephalonia Star   I don't want to oversell this hotel but it's just the place for those travelers who are never happier than when they are on the waterfront. For such, its location along the bay and balconied front rooms with fine views compensate for its rather undistinguished accommodations. The white-walled rooms are a bit austere—along the lines of American motel rooms—but perfectly adequate. Bathrooms are standard issue, but all are clean and well serviced. There's a cafeteria-restaurant on the premises, but except for breakfast, you'll probably want to patronize Argostoli's many fine eateries, all within a few minutes' walk. In August, a mobile amusement park has been known to set up on the quay just opposite, but then August all over Greece is a carnival.

60 I. Metaxa, 28100 Argostoli. ℃ **26710/23-181.** Fax 26710/23-180. 40 units. Some w/shower or tub. High season 90€ ($117) double; low season 70€ ($91) double. Rates include breakfast. MC, V. Street parking. Along waterfront, across from the port authority. *In room:* A/C, TV.

Hotel Ionian Plaza ✸   Although it doesn't quite qualify as a grand hotel, this is the class act of "downtown" Argostoli, and it's also a fine deal. The lobby, public areas, and guest rooms share a tasteful, comfortable, natural tone. Individual details in the furnishings and decor convey the sense of visiting a fine mansion rather than a commercial hotel. Guest rooms are larger than most, while bathrooms are modern if not mammoth. Breakfast takes place under the awning, and the evening meal could well be at the hotel's own **Il Palazzino** restaurant where the menu has a strong Italian flavor and prices are surprisingly modest. Stay here if you like to be in the heart of a city; the front rooms overlook the Central Square but because no vehicles are allowed there, it's not especially noisy.

Vallianou Sq. (Central Sq.), 28100 Argostoli. ℃ **26710/25-581.** Fax 26710/25-585. 43 units. High season 130€ ($169) double; low season 110€ ($143) double. Rates include buffet breakfast. AE, MC, V. Street parking nearby. **Amenities:** Restaurant; bar; concierge arrangements; room service. *In room:* A/C, TV, fridge, hair dryer.

Mirabel Hotel   This is a fine alternative to the somewhat "classier" Ionian Plaza on the same central square. A pleasant hotel with good-size rooms and modern bathrooms. Many have balconies. A friendly staff is there to arrange for car rentals, excursions, or other needs.

Vallianou Sq. (Central Square) 28100 Argostoli. ℃ **26710/25-381.** www.mirabel.gr. 33 units. High season 95€ ($124) double; low season 60€ ($78) double. Rates include buffet breakfast. AE, MC, V. Street parking nearby. **Amenities:** Bar; lounge; room service. *In room:* A/C, TV, Internet, hair dryer, safe.

INEXPENSIVE

Mouikis Hotel   Completely upgraded, this once bare-bones hotel now offers many of the amenities of other more expensive hotels—air-conditioning and TV in each room, for instance. It's popular with groups but usually has a few rooms available for individual travelers. Bathroom facilities are standard for the class. The desk has safe-deposit boxes. One unusual service: a minibus that takes patrons to a swimming pool that belongs to a nearby resort they also own.

3 Vironis, 28100 Argostoli. © 26710/23-281. Fax 26710/28-010. www.mouikis.com. 39 units. High season 75€ ($98) double; low season 65€ ($85) double. Rates include buffet breakfast. AE, MC, V. Street parking. **Amenities:** Bar; safe. *In room:* A/C, TV, fridge.

WHERE TO DINE

Try the two local specialties: *kreatopita* (meat pie with rice and a tomato sauce under a crust) and *crasato* (pork cooked in wine). The island's prized wines include the Robola, Muscat, and Mavrodaphne.

EXPENSIVE

Captain's Table GREEK/INTERNATIONAL   Generally conceded to be the best restaurant in Argostoli, especially for seafood—but be sure you go to the original just off the central square. Many guests dress up a bit, and there's definitely a touch of celebration to meals at this slightly upscale restaurant. Specialties include the Captain's Soup (fish, lobster, mussels, shrimp, and vegetables), filets of beef, delicate squid, and fried *courgette* (small eggplants). Go early (it can get crowded in high season), order a bottle of wine, and enjoy!

Leoforos Rizopaston. © 26710/23-896. Main courses 6€–20€ ($7.80–$26). MC, V. Daily 6pm–midnight. Just around corner from Central Sq.; identifiable by its boat-model display case.

MODERATE

Consider **Old Plaka Taverna,** 1 I. Metaxa, at the far end of the waterfront (© **26710/ 24-849**), for modest prices and tasty Greek dishes.

La Gondola GREEK/ITALIAN   Everyone should take at least one meal on the main square to experience the "dinner theater," with Argostoli's citizens providing the action. Frankly, all of the restaurants on the square are about the same in quality and menu, but I've enjoyed some special treats at this one. It offers a house wine literally made by the house, and serves a special pizza-dough garlic bread, zesty chicken with lemon sauce, and cannelloni that stands out with its rich texture and distinctive flavor. Staff and diners always seem to enjoy themselves here, so we think you will, too.

Central Sq. © 26710/23-658. Main courses 5€–15€ ($6.50–$20). AE, MC, V. Daily 6pm–2am.

Patsouras 🍴 GREEK   Patsouras continues to live up to its reputation as the favorite of travelers seeking authentic Greek taverna food and ambience. Dine under the awnings on the terrace across from the waterfront, and try either of the local specialties, *kreatopita* (meat pie) or *crasto* (pork in wine). Such standards as the tzatziki and moussaka have a special zest. Greeks love unpretentious tavernas, and you'll see why if you eat at Patsouras.

32 I. Metaxa. © 26710/22-779. Main courses 5€–16€ ($6.50–$21). V. Daily noon–midnight. A 5-min. walk from Central Sq. Along the waterfront.

INEXPENSIVE

Portside Restaurant GREEK   This unpretentious taverna is what the Greeks call a *phisteria*, a restaurant specializing in meats and fish cooked on the grill or spit. Run by a native of Argostoli and his Greek-American wife, it offers hearty breakfasts, regular plates with side portions of salads and potatoes, and a full selection of Greek favorites. On special nights outside the high season, the restaurant roasts a suckling pig. It's popular with Greeks as well as foreigners, and you've got a front-row seat for harborside activities.

58 I. Metaxa. ✆ **26710/24-130.** Main courses 5€–15€ ($6.50–$20). MC, V. Apr–Oct daily 10am–midnight. Along the waterfront, opposite the port authority.

ARGOSTOLI AFTER DARK

Free outdoor concerts are occasionally given in the Central Square. At the end of August, a **Choral Music Festival** hosts choirs from all over Greece and Europe. The grand new **Kefalos Public Theater** stages plays, almost always in Greek and seldom in high season. Young people looking for a bit more action can find a number of cafes, bars, and discos on and around the Central Square; they change names from year to year, but **Cinema Music Club, Rumours, Prive, Stavento, Daccapo,** and **Traffic** have been fairly steady. **Bass,** up by the museum, is a favorite club. If your style runs more to lounging with classic rock, try the **Pub Old House,** off Rizopaston, the palm-tree lined avenue leading away from the main square. At the beach resort of Lassi, **So Simple Bar** is popular.

SIDE TRIPS FROM ARGOSTOLI

FISKARDO, ASSOS & MYRTOS BEACH

We'd choose this excursion if we only had 1 day for a trip outside Argostoli. The end destination is **Fiskardo,** a picturesque port-village that is the only major locale on Kefalonia to have survived the 1953 earthquake. Its charm comes from its many surviving 18th-century structures and its intimate harbor, which attracts an international flotilla of yachts.

You can make a round-trip from Argostoli to Fiskardo in a day on a **KTEL** bus (8€/$10). But with a rental car, you can detour off the main road to the even more picturesque port and village of **Assos** (it adds about 10km/7 miles) and then reward yourself with another short detour down to **Myrtos beach,** one of Greece's great beaches.

Plenty of restaurants dot Fiskardo's harbor. I can recommend **Tassia's, Vassos, Nicholas Taverna** (up on the hillside), and **Panormos** (around the bend). The latter two offer rooms as well. For advance arrangements, contact **Fiskardo Travel** (✆ **26740/41-315;** fax 26710/41-352; ftravel@kef.forthnet.gr). Britons may prefer to deal with the **Greek Islands Club,** which specializes in waterfront apartments and houses (www.greekislandsclub.com).

SAMI, MELISSANI GROTTO & DROGARATI CAVE

When you arrive in Kefalonia, you may come first to Sami, an unexceptional town on the east coast and the island's principal point of entry before tourism put Argostoli in the lead. Sami is still a busy port. Besides the unusual white cliffs seen from the harbor, travelers are drawn by **two caves** to the north of Sami, both of which can be visited on a half-day excursion from Argostoli.

Spili Melissani, about 5km (3 miles) north of Sami, is well signed. Once you're inside, you will be taken by a guide in a small rowboat around a relatively small, partially exposed, partially enclosed lake, whose most spectacular feature is the play of the sun's rays striking the water, which creates a kaleidoscope of colors. It's open daily from 9am to 6pm. Admission is 6€ ($7.80).

On the road that leads west to Argostoli (4km/2 miles from Sami), there's a well-signed turnoff to **Drogarati Cave.** Known for its unusual stalagmites, its large chamber has been used for concerts (once by Maria Callas). You walk through it on your own; the cave is well illuminated but can be slippery. It's open daily from 9am to 6pm, with an admission of 4€ ($5.20).

ITHAKA

Despite the recent claims that Oysseus's Ithaka is now a peninsula off Kefalonia, Ithaka continues to attract those who simply are willing to go along with the traditional linkage of several sites to Homer's epic. (Under this new claim, by the way, present-day Ithaka is said to have been the island of Doulichion, which some ancient authors did in fact claim was Odysseus's home.) Such associations aside, Ithaka appeals to many visitors: It may be small and not easily approached, but its rugged terrain and laid-back villages reward those who enjoy driving through unspoiled Greek countryside.

We strongly recommend that you rent a car in Argostoli first. The boat connecting to Ithaka sails not from Argostoli but from Sami, the port on the east coast of Kefalonia; to make a bus connection with that boat, and then to take a taxi from the tiny isolated port where you disembark on Ithaka, costs far too much time. Rather, in your rented car, drive the 40 minutes from Argostoli to Sami; the boat fare for the car is 10€ ($13), for each individual 2€ ($2.60). Once on Ithaka, you can drive to **Vathy,** the main town, in about 10 minutes, and you'll have wheels with which to explore Ithaka and return to Argostoli, all within a day.

All of the above assumes you are coming to Ithaka on a day trip from Kefalonia. But it is also possible to now to take a hydroplane direct from Corfu: See the **Airsea Lines** website at www.airsealines.com.

Vathy itself is a little port, a miniversion of bigger Greek ports with their bustling tourist-oriented facilities. For help in making any arrangements, try **Polyctor Tours** on the main square (© 26740/33-120; polyctor@ithakiholidays.gr). You might enjoy a cold drink or coffee and admire the bay stretching before you, but otherwise there's not much to do or see here. Instead, drive 16km (10 miles) north to **Moni Katheron;** the 17th-century monastery itself is nothing special, but the bell tower offers a spectacular view over much of Ithaka. For a more ambitious drive, head north via the village of **Anogi,** stopping in its town square to view the little church with centuries-old frescoes and the Venetian bell tower opposite it. Proceed on via Stavros and then down to the northeast coast to **Frikes,** a small fishing village. Finally, take a winding road along the coast to **Kioni,** arranged like an amphitheater around its harbor.

As for the sites associated with the *Odyssey*, what little there is to be seen is questioned by many scholars, but that shouldn't stop you; after all, it's your imagination that makes the Homeric world come alive. From the outskirts of Vathy, you'll see signs for the four principal sites. Three kilometers (1½ miles) northwest of Vathy is the so-called **Cave of the Nymphs,** where Odysseus is said to have hidden the Phaeacians's gifts after he had been brought back (supposedly to the little **Bay of Dexia,** north of the cave). Known locally as Marmarospilia, the small cave is about a half-hour's climb up a slope.

The **Fountain of Arethusa,** where Eumaios is said to have watered his swine, is about 7km (4 miles) south of Vathy; it is known today as the spring of Perapigadi. The **Bay of Ayios Andreas,** below, is claimed to be the spot where Odysseus landed in order to evade Penelope's suitors. To get to the fountain, drive the first 3km (2 miles) by following the signposted road to the south of Vathy as far as it goes; continue on foot another 3km (2 miles) along the path.

About 8km (5 miles) west of Vathy is the site of **Alalkomenai,** claimed by Schliemann among others to be the site of Odysseus's capital; in fact, the remains date from several centuries later than the official dates of the Trojan War. Finally, a road out of Stavros leads down to the **Bay of Polis,** again claimed by some as the port of

Odysseus's capital; in the nearby cave of Louizou, an ancient pottery shard was found with the inscription "my vow to Odysseus," but its age suggests that this was the site of a hero-cult.

For lunch, we recommend **Gregory's Taverna,** on the far northeast corner of Vathy's bay (keep driving, with the bay on your left, even after you think the road may give out). Ideally, you will find a table right on the water, where you can look back at Vathy while you enjoy your fresh fish dinner (not cheap, but then fresh fish never is in Greece).

Most visitors will be able to see what they want of Ithaka in 1 day before setting off to the little ports where the last ferryboat to Kefalonia leaves, usually at 5pm—but ask!

16

Highlights of Northern Greece: Thessaloniki, Mount Athos & the Philip & Alexander Sites

by Sherry Marker

In 1997, Thessaloniki—the capital of Macedonia, the second-largest city in Greece, and the emotional heart of Northern Greece—was the European City of Culture. Thessaloniki had always suffered a bit by being thought of by outsiders as Greece's second city, an also-ran in importance to Athens. Those tourists who did come here usually came to see the city's profusion of Byzantine churches and relics of the Turkish period—and to enjoy the excellent local cuisine. Since 1997, word has gotten out about Thessaloniki's varied charms and a lot more visitors are coming here. Thessaloniki has had a burst of self-confidence and an explosion of renovations, restorations, and innovations. Long-neglected old warehouses in the waterfront Ladadika district have been smartened up and transformed into cafes, restaurants, and galleries. Museums of photography, cinema, and contemporary art have appeared, along with what may be Greece's liveliest avant-garde music scene. Increasingly,

Thessaloniki is a popular destination city for weekending Greeks and jet-setting Europeans who've already "done" Prague and Barcelona. In short, visitors here can still visit the wonderful Byzantine churches for which Thessaloniki has always been famous, but also enjoy the rhythm of today's Thessaloniki, with its varied cuisine, multiplicity of galleries and museums, and virtually all-night-every-night cafe life.

The National Road from Athens to Thessaloniki makes it possible to drive comfortably between Greece's two most important cities in 6 hours—faster, if you drive straight through. Good roads also link the archaeological sites of Vergina, Pella, and Dion—once homes of the mighty warrior Philip II of Macedon and his famous son, Alexander the Great—both to the National Road and to Thessaloniki. Even Mount Athos and its monasteries are linked to Thessaloniki by a good road—although only men are allowed to visit the Holy Mountain.

STRATEGIES FOR SEEING THESSALONIKI AND ENVIRONS

Our suggestions for exploring Thessaloniki are really just that: suggestions. Unlike Athens, with its Acropolis, Thessaloniki has no one "must-see" monument. The main attraction here is the city itself: a city with squares built around churches and Roman palaces, whose markets pulse with life, and whose harborside cafes and promenade refresh the weary.

Some might argue that the splendid **Archaeological Museum** or the **Museum of Byzantine Culture** are the town's "must see" attractions, but others would plead the case for **Ano Poli (Upper City),** the old Turkish Quarter. Still others would simply recommend a leisurely stroll along **Aristotelous Street,** taking in the city's main markets, the ancient agora, several small churches and Turkish baths, the Alatza mosque, and the city's main church, St. Demetrius—and as many sidewalk cafes as possible. Here are some suggestions on how to get to know Thessaloniki (also known as Salonica).

IF YOU HAVE 1 DAY

The city's two major museums—the **Archaeological Museum** and the **Museum of Byzantine Culture**—are handily located side by side near the fairgrounds. Decide whether you'd rather see gold from the tomb of Philip of Macedon, or images of life in Byzantine Thessaloniki, and be the first one through the door at the museum you

---

Macedonian Wine

One of the many pleasures of Macedonia is its wine. Mavromatina retsina and the reds and whites of the Boutsaris winery in Naoussa are famous throughout Greece—and, increasingly, abroad. Check out www.wineroads.gr for information on the vineyards and wineries of Macedonia (click on the British flag for English). The site www.greekwine.gr is also very helpful, as is Miles Lambert-Gocs's paperback, *The Wines of Greece*. You can even plan your visits to the Philip and Alexander sites around your visits to local vineyards!

---

choose. After visiting the museums, stroll back along the harbor past the White Tower to the center of town for lunch. If you feel more energetic, hop a bus or take a taxi to the **Upper City (Ano Poli),** have lunch (perhaps at **Tsinari's Ouzeri**), and stroll downhill. *Reminder:* Most of the churches you want to see here are closed in midafternoon.

After a nap, you might visit some of the Roman monuments and the churches of **Ayia Sofia** and **Ayios Dimitrios** in the city center, keeping in mind that plenty of cafes are nearby, as well as the famous sweet shop **Terkenlis** in Ayia Sofia Square. When you're ready for dinner, head to one of the cheek-by-jowl restaurants in the **Ladadika,** the restored warehouse district which takes its name from the olives and olive oil once stored here. Another not-to-be-missed dinner choice is the justly famous **Thanasis,** in the rambling Modiano Market.

Note: This makes for a very full day, and you'll certainly enjoy Thessaloniki a lot more if you have more than a day here. Byzantine churches take time to find, to see, and to enjoy. Many of the frescoes and mosaics are high up on walls, or faded by time (be sure to bring a strong flashlight).

IF YOU HAVE 2 DAYS

If you have more than a day, abbreviate your first day, so you don't feel obligated to see the city in one fell swoop. You might begin your second day with the **Upper City** and work your way downhill. Start at **Vlatadon Monastery** and then head down, stopping at the enchanting little churches of **Osios David, Nikolaos Orphanos,** and **Profitias Elias.** Even if church architecture, mosaics, and frescoes are not your passion, you'll walk through the narrow streets lined with two-story wood houses dating back to the Turkish period. If you didn't see them on your first day, take in the churches of Ayia Sofia and Ayios Dimitrios when you get back down to the city center and stroll past the Alatza Imaret and Yeni Hamam Baths, relics of the city's Turkish past.

Then, for a change of pace, take in the city's markets that blur one into another: the **Modiano,** the open-air food market on **Athonos Square,** the **Kapani (Vlali),** and **Bezesteni** markets. If you visit all these, you can buy anything from a copper bucket for milking sheep to the sheep itself. Along the way, you can nibble on souvlaki, pastry, or whatever seasonal fruit catches your fancy—and get a bunch of flowers at the **Louloudadika** (flower market) in a 16th-century Turkish bath, the **Yahudi Haman.** If you haven't already seen the **arch of Galerius,** the **Rotunda,** and the **Roman agora,** try to take them in during an evening *volta* (stroll) with frequent breaks along the way at some of Thessaloniki's myriad cafes.

IF YOU HAVE 3 DAYS OR MORE

Thessaloniki is a very lively town: It's fun to spend time here simply wandering and browsing through the shops and galleries along **Tsimiski, Aristotelous, Ayias Sofias,** and pedestrianized **Dimitriou Gounari streets.** Don't miss the enormous neon high heel at the Karidas Shoe Store on the **Via Egnatia** (or the ruined Turkish bath across from the shoe store). In the evening, if you want to see young Thessalonians working at relaxing, take in some of the bars on **Zefxidos Street,** in central **Aristotelous Square,** or at the **Mylos** complex on Andreou Georgou.

When you've had your fill of city pleasures, you may want to head out of Thessaloniki to see some of the sites associated with Philip and Alexander, such as **Vergina, Dion,** or **Pella.** If you'd like to avoid a lot of driving, sign up for one of the efficient day trips that take in these sites. (See "Organized Tours" and "In the Footsteps of Philip of Macedon & Alexander the Great," later in this chapter.) If you plan to see the sites by car, consider exploring them on your way out of town rather than as a day trip, in order to avoid fighting your way in and out of Thessaloniki's fierce traffic.

1 Thessaloniki (Salonika) ★★★

516km (320 miles) N of Athens

When a Greek tells you he's from Athens, he almost always sounds a bit apologetic. Greeks from Thessaloniki, on the other hand, sound, if not smug, very pleased to be from Greece's "Second City." Thessaloniki may be second to Athens in political importance and population, but in popular songs, Thessaloniki is celebrated as "the mother of Macedonia," "the most blessed of cities," "beautiful Thessaloniki," and "the city whose praises are sung."

You, too, may be tempted to sing this city's praises when you take in its wonderful location along the broad expanse of the Thermaic Gulf. You're never far from the sea here; when you least expect it, you can catch a glimpse of waves and boats in the distance. Alas, especially in the summer, you may also notice signs of the harbor's pollution, including a ripe odor. If you're very lucky, you'll see Mount Olympus while you're here: Pollution has increasingly obscured even that imposing landmark.

Greeks are fond of reminding foreigners that when their ancestors were painting themselves blue or living in rude huts, Greeks were sitting in the shade of the Parthenon, reading the plays of Sophocles. Similarly, Thessalonians like to remind Athenians that when Athens languished in the long twilight of its occupation by the Romans and Ottomans, Thessaloniki flourished. It's true: Thessaloniki's strategic location on the main land route from Europe into Asia made it a powerful city during the Roman Empire. Many monuments built here date from the 4th century A.D., from Emperor Galerius's rule.

During the Byzantine Empire (the 4th–15th c. A.D.), Thessaloniki boasted that it was second only to the capital, Constantinople. Thessaloniki's greatest pride—its superb and endearing churches—were built then. After the Turks conquered the Byzantine Empire, Thessaloniki continued to flourish as an important commercial center and port. In the 18th and early 19th centuries, the city's Jewish community was so strong and so prosperous that some called Thessaloniki the "second Jerusalem."

Then, in August 1917, a devastating fire destroyed 80% of the city. Phoenix-like, Thessaloniki rose from the ashes. Unfortunately, only part of the city was rebuilt according to the grand plan of the French architect Ernest Hébrard. More than 130,000 Greek refugees from Asia Minor flooded into Thessaloniki between 1922 and 1923, almost doubling the city's population and leading to enormous unregulated development. Still, Thessaloniki enjoys the broad tree-lined boulevards and parks that Athens so sadly lacks.

Thessaloniki

After World War II, and again in the 1960s, two more growth spurts left much of the city's outskirts crowded and ugly—and all too much of the city center lined with bland apartment buildings. Still, Thessaloniki has none of the horizon-blocking skyscrapers that have proliferated in Athens; earthquake regulations forbid this. The last major earthquake was in 1978. In recent years, the narrow lanes and old-fashioned houses of the upper city (Ano Poli) became sought after for restoration, first into bohemian pads and now into chic urban homes.

Glimpses of the sea, tree-lined streets, magnificent Byzantine churches—all these make visiting Thessaloniki delightful. The food is also noticeably more varied and inventive than in most other parts of Greece. The long traditions of Macedonian cuisine became infused with zesty flavors of the Pontus (the area around the Black Sea where most of the city's refugees had lived). And, there's another reason that the food

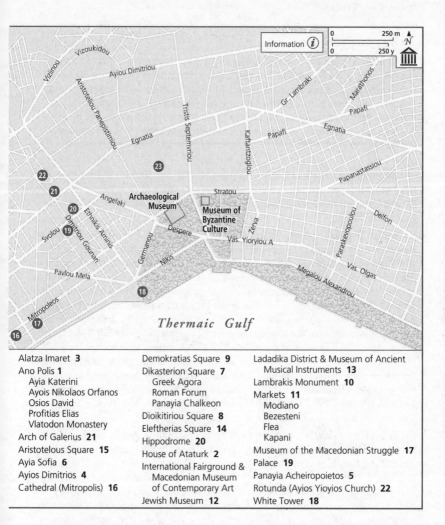

Thermaic Gulf

here is so good: the restaurants cater to local customers; none of them make their living off tourists.

ESSENTIALS

GETTING THERE By Plane Thessaloniki's Macedonia International Airport, 17km/11 miles south of town, is served from Athens International Airport (℘ **210/353-0000;** www.aia.gr) by **Olympic Airways** (℘ **210/966-6666,** or 2310/368-311 in Thessaloniki; www.olympic-airways.gr); **Aegean Air** (℘ **210/998-8300,** or 2310/239-225 in Thessaloniki; www.aegeanair.com) has flights from Athens. EasyJet sometimes serves Thessaloniki; go to www.easyjet.com. From the U.S., there are no direct flights to Thessaloniki. Connections can be made at a number of European cities, including London, Amsterdam, Brussels, Frankfurt, Stuttgart, Munich, Zurich, and Vienna.

> ### ⟨Tips⟩ High Season
>
> The busiest time of the year in Thessaloniki is not summer, but fall, when the
> International Trade Fair and Festival of Greek Songs takes place in September,
> followed by the Demitria celebrations of the city's patron saints in October and
> November. There is also a Film Festival here in November. If you come between
> September and November, be sure to book a hotel in advance—and be pre-
> pared to pay dearly for your room (price hikes of more than 50% are common).

The airport (☎ **2310/411-997** or 2310/473-312) is a 30-minute drive from the
city center. Bus no. 78 runs into the city (usually stopping in Aristotelous Sq. and at
the train station) from about 6am to 11pm and costs 1€ ($1.30). A taxi ride runs
about 12€ ($16).

By Train   Five daily express trains officially make the trip from Athens to Thessaloniki in about 6 hours, but most are extremely crowded, without air-conditioning,
and subject to unexplained delays. If you must take a train, choose the fast **InterCity,**
preferably the overnight sleeper, which has first-class compartments for four to six passengers and sleeper compartments for two to six passengers. Make reservations for
sleeping compartments well in advance at the Larissa train station in Athens (☎ **210/
323-6747;** www.ose.gr). In Thessaloniki, you can purchase tickets at the OSE (train)
station, 28 Monastiriou, the western extension of Egnatia (☎ **2310/599-068**). Coach
tickets Athens to Thessaloniki cost from 35€ ($46), express train service from 50€
($65), sleeper service from 65€ ($85). A taxi ride from the station to Aristotelous
Square takes about 10 minutes and costs about 6€ ($8). Avoid the trek to the train
station to get information and buy tickets, and use the **OSE** (train) office instead, at
18 Aristotelous Sq. (☎ **2310/517-517;** www.ose.gr), 9am to 9pm Tuesday to Friday;
9am to 3pm Monday and Saturday; closed Sunday.

By Bus   Ten air-conditioned buses from Athens make the trip daily to Thessaloniki
in about 7 hours (includes one 20-min. stop at a roadside restaurant with toilet facilities). Buses usually arrive on time. Make reservations in advance at the Athens bus
terminal, 100 Kifissou (☎ **201/512-9233**). A one-way fare costs about 35€ ($46).
Many buses arrive in Thessaloniki at the station at 65 Monastiriou (☎ **2310/510-
834**) opposite the train station, where there are taxis. Some buses stop at the newer
bus station at 194 Iannitsou (☎ **2310/595-408**), west of the train station. For general information on Athens-Macedonia schedules and fares, call ☎ **210/512-4910** or
go to **www.ktel.org**.

By Car   **From Athens,** take the 516km (320-mile) National Road, a four-lane highway that's the best in Greece, although stretches are always being repaired or widened,
which leads to frequent delays. The road, a major truck route, is also often the scene
of serious accidents. Plan on at least 6 hours, if you stop en route. Much of the drive
is extremely scenic. Gas stations are common along the National Road, but you often
must exit to reach them.

If you're driving from other places in **Europe,** you'll probably take the ferry from
the Italian port of Bari, Ancona, or Brindisi to Igoumenitsou on the northwest coast
of Greece, and then drive across the Pindus Mountains to Thessaloniki. The trip is
spectacular; allow at least 5 hours. The southern route (via Ioannina and Kalambaka

to Larissa and the National Rd.) is much less treacherous than the northern alternative (through Kozani)—particularly in winter, although snow can close both routes.
The southern route also passes Kalambaka and the monasteries perched on the awesome pinnacles of the Meteora (see chapter 12). You will almost certainly encounter
the continuing roadwork on the National Highway (called the Via Egnatia, after its
Roman predecessor) designed to link Patras (in the Peloponnese) with Central Greece
and on to Macedonia.

VISITOR INFORMATION   A GNTO (**Greek National Tourist Organization**)
office is in the city center at 136 Tsimiski (© **2310/221-100;** www.saloniki.org).

CITY LAYOUT   Thessaloniki rests on the northern coast of the Thermaic Gulf like
a lopsided turban tilted slightly to the northwest. In its center sits the city's most
famous landmark, the **White Tower,** the best-known remnant of the walls that once
encircled the city. The great walls—begun in antiquity and extended and expanded by
the Byzantines, Venetians, and Turks—came down as the population grew and the city
expanded in the late 19th and early 20th centuries. To the east sprawl the ever-expand-
ing residential districts, while to the west, situated in the area once defined by its
fortresslike Byzantine walls, is the city's **commercial heart.**

In this latter area, bounded on the south by the harbor and on the north by the rising heights of what is called the **Ano Poli (Upper City),** are Thessaloniki's most important shops, banks, hotels, restaurants, archaeological remains, and churches. On its
western edge are the train station, most bus terminals, many shipping docks, the Customs building, and streets lined with warehouses—many now converted into the chic
restaurants and galleries of the **Ladadika district.** Ladadika blurs into **Ksiladika,** the
woodworkers' district, which is beginning to lay claim to its own chic restaurants and
shops, in addition to the carpenter's workshops that originally gave the district its character. On the city center's eastern side, just north of the White Tower and outside what
was once the eastern gate, are the grounds of Aristotle University, the International
Trade Fair, and the **Archaeological and Byzantine museums.** Between the latter and
the White Tower lie the **Municipal Park** and the **State Theater of Northern Greece.**

The commercial area of the city is traversed by four main streets running on an
oblique angle from the southwest to the northeast. The largest, **Egnatia,** runs across
the northern side of the commercial district. On its western end at **Vardari (Dimokratias) Square,** it connects with roads to the west, north, and east. On its eastern end
(under the name of New Egnatia), it connects with highways to the airport and to the
peninsulas of Halkidiki. In the heart of the city, Egnatia is home to discount shops,
cheap hotels, and affordable restaurants. The city's second-most-important commercial route, **Tsimiski,** parallels Egnatia 2 blocks to the south and runs one-way from
east to west. Along its tree-shaded length lie the city's most prestigious shops and
department stores. One block south of Tsimiski and running one-way from west to
east is **Mitropoleos,** so named because the Metropolitan Cathedral sits near its center. Like Tsimiski, it has a number of fine shops and boutiques. Finally, another block
to the south and running along the seaside promenade is **Leoforos Nikis.** Also one-
way from west to east, it begins at the shipping docks and ends at the White Tower.
Along its length is a virtually uninterrupted line of outdoor cafes and bars.

The spacious expanse of **Aristotelous Square,** which borders the sea, is the heart of
downtown Thessaloniki. Ringed with outdoor cafes and restaurants, it is also the
backdrop for the city's major political rallies. Running north and south and connecting Aristotelous with the city's other major square, Dikasterion, is the street named

Aristotelous. A number of book and record stores flank its arcaded sidewalks. **Dikasterion Square** overlooks the partially excavated Roman marketplace and offers welcome trees, the lovely Byzantine church Panagia Chalkeon (Virgin of the Copper Workers), and a restored Turkish bathhouse. You might find an informal market here held by Greek and other refugees from Eastern Europe. Most local buses begin and end their city runs here.

To the south of Dikasterion Square, across Egnatia and on either side of Aristotelous, are the city's main **market areas,** where you can find flowers, fish, sandals, and just about anything else you can think of. The city's second main north-south route, **Ayias Sofias,** lies to the east of Aristotelous Street. In its center, between Egnatia and Tsimiski, stands the church of **St. Sofia.** Look for excellent clothing stores along Ayias Sofias. **Pavlou Mela** runs diagonally southeast from the rear of the church to the White Tower and sports a number of fine bars and cafes; leading directly south to Tsimiski from virtually the same point are the tree-lined pedestrian walkways of **Iktinou** and **Zevksidos,** sites of several outdoor cafes and restaurants. Two blocks east of the rear of Ayias Sofias Square is Thessaloniki's major pedestrian walkway, **Dimitriou Gounari.** Its shop-lined length covers a major Roman thoroughfare leading down from the arch to the Palace of Galerius. The palace area, now partially excavated, opens onto the tree-shaded park of **Navarino Square,** which is crowded with outdoor cafes, bars, and tavernas, and second only to Aristotelous as the city's major gathering place—although many of the artists and intellectuals who gather here would place it first.

Another 2 blocks east lies **Ethnikis Aminis.** While it runs one-way south from Egnatia down to the State Theater and the White Tower, it becomes a two-way street above Egnatia at **Sintrivaniou (Fountain) Square** (the former eastern gate of the city) and leads into winding roadways that run outside the ancient walls to the Upper City.

On the hillside leading down to Thessaloniki proper from the Upper City is the old **Turkish Quarter.** Called, variously, **Ano Poli (Upper City), Eptapirgiou (Seven Gates),** and **To Kastro (Fortress)** it is where some of the finest Byzantine churches—and, increasingly, some elegant restored town houses—are located. This is easily the most pleasant part of Thessaloniki to explore, especially the winding streets around Kalitheas Square, such as Irodotou, as well as pleasant squares such as Romfei Square, in the district known as Koule Kafe, and Tsinari Square, at the juncture of Kleious and Alexandras Papadopoulou. Severe fires in 1997 and 1998 greatly damaged the pine forest of Seih Sou on the upper hills. Although a reforestation project has begun, it will be years before new growth brings back Thessaloniki's "green lungs."

The **Ring Road,** just to the north of the Upper City, goes around Thessaloniki from the southwest to the southeast and connects the National Road from Athens with highways to Thrace and Halkidiki and to the airport at Mikras along the sea to the east.

FINDING AN ADDRESS Because of the orderly east-west, north-south arrangement of streets, finding an address in the **city center** is relatively easy. Numbers begin at the eastern and southern ends of streets and go upward, with even numbers on the right and odd numbers on the left. That said, it's useful to know that most Thessalonians think of addresses in terms of the cross streets or well-known structures near them, and buildings almost never have visible numbers; ask for what you want by name, not by number.

Outside the city center, particularly **north of Egnatia,** finding what you want is difficult, as the streets begin to meander. Even with a good map, you'll probably have

> *Tips* **Driving in Thessaloniki**
>
> The best tip for driving in Thessaloniki is: don't! Driving here is as vexing as in Athens (the system of one-way streets is not indicated accurately on maps). Officially, there is one car for every three Thessalonians—although it often feels closer to one to one! If your hotel does not have parking facilities, your best bet will be to leave your car in the large parking garage in Eleftherias Square, as on-street parking is very difficult. Thessalonians are inventive parkers: When I was last there, the hotel manager said he would show me the hotel parking, stepped outside, and graciously waved me up onto the sidewalk! When Thessaloniki gets its long-promised Metro, congestion here, as in Athens, should be greatly alleviated. Until then, park and lock your car and walk, or take buses or taxis.

trouble, but take it, as the Greeks say, *"Siga, siga"* ("Slowly, slowly"), and you'll find your way.

MAPS   City maps and two excellent guides to the city (*The Thessaloniki Handbook* [with section-by-section maps], by Christos Zafiris; and *Monuments of Thessaloniki* [with an excellent city-center map], by Apostolos Papagiannopoulos) are usually available at bookstores, including **Molho,** 10 Tsimiski, **Ianos,** 7 Aristotelous; and **Malliaris,** 9 Aristotelous.

GETTING AROUND   In the city center, a 20- to 30-minute walk will take you to most attractions, restaurants, and shops. Taxis are usually easy to find, unless you're going to the Upper City. Taxis are reluctant to make this trip because there is little guarantee of a return fare down, and they may—unlawfully—refuse. But if you're in the cab before you state your destination, there's little the driver can do but take you there. Otherwise, it's a steep uphill walk of at least 20 minutes, or you can hop on bus no. 22, which leaves from Eleftherias Square.

By Bus   Buses with double cars are boarded at the rear, where a conductor gives you a ticket and makes change. Single-car buses are boarded at the front; on these, **exact fare** is required. Deposit the fare in the ticket-issuing machine behind the driver's seat. Keep your ticket in case a conductor boards the bus to check them. Fares vary according to the distance traveled; an average journey within Thessaloniki costs about .75€ (95¢).

By Taxi   This is your best bet except, as noted above, when you want to go to the Upper City. Take along a map or have someone write out your destination in Greek, so that you can show the driver where you want to go. Rates are moderate compared to those in the U.S.; tips are not expected, although rounding up the fare is appreciated. Make sure that the driver turns on the taxi meter and that, within the city limits, the rate it uses is no. 1. Rate no. 2 is for outside the city limits. There's an extra 5€ ($6.50) charge for trips from the airport. After midnight, all fares on the meter are doubled.

By Car   There is little reason to use a car within Thessaloniki. Traffic is terrible and legal parking spots are almost impossible to find, even at the large public parking lot in Plateia Eleftherias. But having a car for excursions into Northern Greece will allow you to see and enjoy a lot more than you would either from a bus or on a guided tour. Keep in mind that if you take a day trip, you'll spend at least an hour getting out of and another hour getting back into the city. It makes much better sense to see what you want outside of town on your way in, or out, of Thessaloniki.

Most car-rental agencies, including Avis, Budget, Europcar, and Hertz, have offices at the airport. A car with unlimited mileage costs from 60€ ($78) per day in high season. (*Reminder:* High season is not summer but the time of the Sept–Oct trade and other festivals.) Be sure to ask if the price quoted includes all taxes and insurance—and be sure to take full insurance if your credit card does not provide it. *Tip:* It is invariably cheaper to book a car with an international agency from abroad, not from within Greece.

If you must park within Thessaloniki, and the centrally located pay garage in Plateia Eleftherias is full, you might try the free **Municipal Parking Lot** just south of the Museum of Byzantine Culture at the eastern end of Vas. Olgas. It's about a 20-minute walk from the city center but very near the White Tower and Archaeological Museum. Unfortunately, this is not a very savory spot late at night.

By Boat   It's possible to take ferries and boats from Thessaloniki to a number of Aegean islands (including Crete, Santorini, and Mykonos) and to the Sporades (Skiathos, Skopelos, and Alonissos). Many travel agents around Plateia Eleftherias and Aristotelous Square sell ferry tickets. Centrally located agencies include: **Polaris Travel,** 81 Egnatiou (ⓒ **2310/276-051**); and **Zorpidis Travel,** 4 Salaminos (ⓒ **2310/ 555-955;** www.zorpidis.gr). The harbor police/port authorities can be reached at ⓒ **2310/531-504** to -507. **www.gtp.gr** (Greek Travel Pages) is also useful for boat schedules.

FAST FACTS: Thessaloniki

American Express   The office is at 19 Tsimiski (ⓒ **2310/239-797**); hours are Monday through Thursday from 8am to 2pm and Friday from 8am to 1:30pm.

Currency Exchange & ATMs   All banks exchange currency, as do most hotels and the central post office. The major banks along Tsimiski and Aristoteleos Square have ATMs.

Doctors & Dentists   The **U.S. Consulate** (ⓒ **2310/266-121** or 2310/260-716) has a continually updated list of recommended doctors. In addition, most of the better hotels can reach an English-speaking doctor or dentist.

Drugstores   See "Pharmacies," below.

Embassies & Consulates   The **U.S. Consulate** (ⓒ **2310/242-905** or 2310/260-716) is at 43 Tsimiski. It offers a bare minimum of services. The **UK/Commonwealth Honorary Consul** is at 8 Venizelou (ⓒ **2310/278-006** or 2310/269-984), by appointment only.

Emergencies   The **police hot line** is ⓒ **100**; for non-urgent help, call ⓒ 2310/ 863-393. For **first aid,** call ⓒ **166.** For **car breakdowns,** call ⓒ **104** (the Greek Automobile Touring Club, or ELPA). Also try the **tourist police,** 4 Dodekanisou, near the eastern end of Tsimiski (ⓒ **2310/554-870** or 2310/554-871).

Hospitals & Clinics   The main hospital is the **Ippokration** (ⓒ **2310/892-2000** or 2310/837-921) at 50 Papanastasiou; doctors who speak some English are usually available here. Two private clinics, **Ahepa Hospital,** 1 Kiriaki (ⓒ **2310/993-111**), and **Ayios Loukas** (St. Luke's), on the road to Panorama village northeast of the city (© **2310/342-102** to -104), both have English-speaking doctors.

Internet Access Thessaloniki has many Internet cafes, including centrally located **e-Global**, 117 Egnatia (© **2310/887-711**) and **Meganet**, 5 Plateia Navarino (© **2310/269-591**).

Lost Property Call the **tourist police** at © **2310/554-870** or 2310/554-871.

Newspapers & Magazines English-language publications are available at several kiosks in Aristotelous Square and along Tsimiski.

Pharmacies Pharmacies alternate late-night hours. Lists and addresses of the ones open on a particular night can be found in the local newspapers and the windows of all pharmacies.

Police The 24-hour emergency number is © **100**. The tourist police number is © **2310/554-870** or 2310/554-871.

Post Office The main post office is at 26 Aristotelous (© **2310/278-924**). Hours are Monday through Friday from 7:30am to 8pm, Saturday from 7:30am to 2pm, and Sunday from 9am to 1:30pm.

Restrooms All but the smallest eateries and bars have restrooms that you can request to use without embarrassment. Carrying some tissues with you is a good idea.

Safety Thessaloniki is still an extremely safe city, although the influx of a rough element in recent years means that obvious tourists should exercise the usual big-city caution, especially at night. The only area absolutely to avoid is around Vardaris (Dimokratias) Square, which attracts some shady characters.

Taxis Radio taxis in the city center can be called at © **2310/517-417**. See also "Getting Around," above.

THE TOP ATTRACTIONS: MUSEUMS

Archaeological Museum ★★★   Many of the former stars of the museum—finds from the tombs at Derveni and the Royal Tombs at Vergina—are now on display at Vergina. Don't let the absence of these treasures, however famous and wonderful, keep you from enjoying what's still here, including the spectacular 4th-century-B.C. Derveni krater with its elaborate scenes of the marriage of Dionysios and Ariadne. The combination of sensuality and luxury is memorable. Much of the museum was closed from 2004 to 2006 for extensive renovations. The well-displayed exhibits document the history of Macedonia and Thessaloniki from prehistoric days through the Roman period. It's astonishing that the paper-thin Hellenistic glass vessels and delicate Roman mosaics from private houses have survived in such excellent condition. A portrait bust of 4th-century-A.D. Emperor Galerius shows him as the brawler he was, who entered the army as a recruit and ended up as the emperor who built many of Thessaloniki's surviving monuments.

This severe, low museum was built in 1962, and is considered to be the best example of "architectural modernism" in Thessaloniki—a sad commentary on that genre. The museum shop has postcards, guidebooks, and a number of souvenirs featuring the 16-point star of Macedon. The museum toilet facilities are good. Allow several hours here.

> ⎛ *Fun Fact* **Catching a Local Festival**
>
> If you are in Salonika in September, check with the GNTO for details on the weeklong wine festival usually held in Anhialos, a village 15km (9 miles) northwest of Thessaloniki. Traveling around May 21? The GNTO should also have information on the celebrations in the village of Langadas, 20km (9 miles) northeast of Thessaloniki. It's one of only a few places in Greece and Bulgaria where the devout walk on fire (coals, actually). No one is really sure why the *anastenarides* (firewalkers) do this: Theories include the survival of a pagan custom or the commemoration of an occasion when the devout saved icons from a church conflagration without suffering any burns.

6 Manoli Andronikou (opposite the south side of the International Fairgrounds). ⓒ **2310/830-538.** Fax 2310/861-306. Admission 6€ ($7.80); combined admission to Archaeological and Byzantine museums 9€ ($12). Mon noon–7pm; Tues–Sun 8am–7pm. Hours subject to change. Bus: 58 from Dikasterion Sq., or 11 heading east from anywhere on Egnatia.

Museum of Byzantine Culture ⭐⭐⭐   Along with the Byzantine and Christian Museum in Athens, this is one of Greece's preeminent Byzantine museums. Exhibits cover the development of Byzantine culture from its early beginnings in the Roman world through the fall of Constantinople in 1453; the final exhibits focus on the lasting influence of Byzantine culture in Greece. As at the Archaeological Museum, the exhibits here attempt to tell the story of Thessaloniki and look at its social history through art and artifacts, including such down-to-earth items as drain pipes and cooking pots.

The most impressive exhibits are the 4th- to 6th-century barrel-vaulted tombs found in Thessaloniki, with frescoes showing Old and New Testament scenes as well as scenes in Paradise. You'll see Daniel in the Lions' Den, Christ as the Fisher of Men, and blissful scenes of Paradise, where fruit, fowl, and wine are shown in abundance. The text accompanying the exhibit looks at the transition from the ancient image of the Afterworld as the Elysian Fields to the Christian images of Paradise. Not surprisingly, the museum has a number of important icons, including a 12th-century icon of the Virgin and Christ child. A display of bright mosaics and elaborately carved marble panels salvaged from the church of Ayios Dimitrios after the great fire of 1917 brings home just how splendid that church once was.

The museum shop usually has a range of books on Byzantine culture, as well as museum reproductions and postcards. The toilet facilities are good. Allow several hours here.

2 Leoforos Stratou (just west of the Archaeological Museum). ⓒ **2310/868-570.** Fax 2310/838-597. Admission 6€ ($7.80); combined admission to both the Byzantine and Archaeological museums 9€ ($12). Mon noon–7pm; Tues–Sun 8am–7pm. Hours subject to unannounced changes. Bus: 58 from Dikasterion Sq., or 11 heading east from anywhere on Egnatia.

THE TOP ATTRACTIONS: MONUMENTS

Arch of Galerius ⭐   If you need directions here, try asking for *ee kamara* (the arch), which is what Thessalonians call this hefty monument built by Galerius around A.D. 305 to celebrate a victory over the Persians a few years earlier. Originally, the arch was even larger: Almost half—another entire arch—is missing. Look for the Persians, some in the peaked caps and trousers that the Greeks and Romans found so effeminate and absurd, in the carved panels that tell the story of Galerius's battles. Until 1953, the tram line ran right under this arch. Air pollution from the surrounding traffic steadily erodes many sculptural details. You can take this place in with a glance, or spend a pleasant half-hour admiring the detail.

Just below the Rotunda on Egnatia and Dimitriou Gounari.

Greek Agora & Roman Forum In the 1960s, workmen digging to lay the foundations of new law courts for Thessaloniki came across the remains of the city's ancient Greek agora, which later became the Roman forum. Archaeologists took over and excavated the sprawling complex you see today. As in Athens, this agora/forum was the heart of the ancient city: its commercial, governmental, social, and artistic center—and, as with the Athenian agora, the remains are not easy to identify.

When the Romans came here, they inevitably expanded the Greek agora, creating a two-level forum. You can see the arched remains of the **cryptoporticus,** a retaining wall that supported part of the upper forum. The best-preserved ruin here, the large **Odeum,** or Odeon, is a theater where Romans enjoyed watching both musical performances and fights to the death between gladiators and wild beasts. The Odeum is sometimes still used for summer concerts.

In modern times, the most famous ancient monument here was the stoa with a series of statues facing the Via Egnatia, known as the *Incantadas* (Colonnade of the Enchanted Idols), the name given them by Thessaloniki's then-flourishing community of Sephardic Jews. By the 19th century, much of the colonnade was lost, but a segment remained, incorporated into the courtyard of a Jewish home. When the French scholar Emmanuel Miller saw the colonnade, he knew he had to have it—and got permission to cart the remaining *incantadas* off to the Louvre, where they are to this day. Browse in the few book and print shops in Thessaloniki, and you'll probably see reproductions of a charming engraving of the colonnade by the 18th-century English antiquarians Stuart and Revett. Allow an hour here.

Dikasterion Sq., bounded by Filipou, Agnostou Stratiotou, Olimbou, and Makedonikis Amnis sts.

Hippodrome We know that the ancient hippodrome, where chariot races took place, lies under the square of the same name, because of finds made when modern apartments were built. There are almost no aboveground remains of this ancient racetrack where, in A.D. 390, Emperor Theodosius the Great ordered the slaughter of about 7,000 spectators. The reason: A mob lynched one of Theodosius's favorite charioteers. After that terrible day, people abandoned the Hippodrome, and it became covered by buildings from successive eras.

Tips **An Important Warning**

Strikes that close museums and archaeological sites can occur without warning. Decide what you most want to see in Thessaloniki and go there as soon as possible after your arrival. Something that is open today may be closed the next day, despite what you are told. I speak from painful experience. The official hours in the summer for sites and museums are from 8am to 7:30pm daily; however, this is often not the case in reality. Keep in mind that the opening hours posted at sites and listed at the tourist office often vary considerably.

History 101: The Galerian Monuments

In the 4th century, the Roman Empire was briefly ruled by a complicated system of two primary emperors, each of whom had an assistant—an emperor-in-training, as it were. The hope was that a system of four rulers (known as the tetrarchy) would find it easier to administer the vast Roman Empire than one emperor alone. In the early part of the century, Galerius, one of the tetrarchs, moved his capital from Asia Minor to Thessaloniki. Then he did what any good Roman did in those days—he began to build. He built on a nice, neat, north-south axis flanking the Via Egnatia. The **Rotunda, Arch of Galerius,** the **Palace** at Navarino Square, **Hippodrome,** and parts of the **Roman Forum** are survivors of his ambitious program.

In 1566, the Turks executed St. Cyril here for not converting to Islam. The charming little church of St. Anthony here was, during the Turkish Occupation, a lunatic asylum. In the church, you can still see some of the manacles with which "patients" were imprisoned. Allow half an hour here.
Ippodromou Sq.

Galerius's Palace ✦ The emperor Galerius built himself a palace in Thessaloniki. After all, his co-emperor Diocletian was building himself a perfectly splendid palace at Split, on the Dalmatian coast. Little remains of Galerius's royal home, but even these low ruins give you an idea of the size of the two-story palace with its large central courtyard—fit, in short, for an emperor. The best-preserved part of the complex is the **Octagon,** the mysterious building that some archaeologists think may have been Galerius's throne room. The Octagon, exceptionally opulent and richly decorated with a multicolored marble floor, had two interior recesses. One, a good deal larger than the others, would have been ideal for a throne. That said, it should be noted that a very similar structure built by Diocletian in Spoleto, Italy, was not a throne room but a mausoleum. Allow half an hour here.
Navarino Sq.

Rotunda (aka **Ayios Yioryos**) ✦✦ Some say that Galerius built this massive brick-and-stone structure as his defiantly immodest mausoleum, while others think he intended it to be a temple, perhaps of Zeus. Later in the 4th century, the Byzantine emperor Theodosius the Great converted the rotunda into Ayios Yioryos (Church of St. George), and began the ornamentation of its 6m-thick (20-ft.) walls with mosaics. When the Turks conquered Thessaloniki in the 15th century, they converted the church into a mosque (you'll see the one minaret left from this period) and destroyed many of the exquisite mosaics.

The Rotunda reopened in 1999 after more than a decade spent repairing the damage done by the horrific earthquake of 1978. Artisans and archaeologists worked—and continue to work—with literally millions of tesserae, or tiles, to restore the dazzling mosaics. Now you can see (especially if you bring binoculars) indigo peacocks, garlands of flowers and fruit, and blond curly haired saints and martyrs (and martyred saints) in the mosaics that cover the walls. Try to visit on a Wednesday, when the neighborhood street market stretches for blocks around the Rotunda, and ask about special exhibits or concerts here. Allow an hour to explore.

Ayios Yioryos Sq. at Filipou (1 block north of the juncture of Egnatia and Dimitriou Gounari, just above the Arch of Galerius). (C) 2310/213-627. Free admission except for special events. Daily 8:30am–3pm. Bus: 10 or 11 heading east from anywhere on Egnatia.

White Tower 🐾 What Big Ben is to London, and the Eiffel Tower is to Paris, the 16th-century White Tower is to Thessaloniki. It is the city's most famous landmark, although the tower is no longer white; a 1985 restoration (as part of the celebrations of the 2,300th anniversary of Thessaloniki's founding) removed its whitewash. Due to ongoing restoration, the tower is sometimes closed, but it is well worth seeing up close from outside.

The tower, first built as part of the city's defense walls, then became an Ottoman prison and place of execution (when it was known as the Bloody Tower). Today, several floors house the Museum of the History and Art of Thessaloniki; the artifacts within give an idea of life here through the centuries. That said, artifacts or no artifacts, the most fun here comes from climbing the steep winding staircase that takes you up six floors and leads to terrific views of the city and harbor. Each floor has a round room with alcoves, some of which were once prison cells. At the very top of the staircase, a cafe on the roof rewards you for the climb. If you're here in winter, you'll get an idea of just how dank and forbidding a prison this thick-walled stone tower must have been. Allow an hour here.

Nikis and Pavlou Mela, on the seaside promenade just south of the Archaeological Museum. (C) 2310/267-832. Free admission. Officially, daily 8:30am–3pm. Bus: 58 from Dikasterion Sq., or 11 heading east from anywhere on Egnatia.

CHURCHES 🐾🐾🐾
Thessaloniki's churches are a clear case of the whole being greater than the sum of its parts. Although Ayia Sofia and Ayios Dimitrios are the two best known, the smaller, less well-known churches may give you the greatest pleasure. Notice that some, built in the **basilica** shape, form a rectangle with side aisles; others are in the **cross-in-square** form, which is just what its name says.

Many of these churches keep irregular hours, often closing from about 1 to 5pm. In short, the best way to see them is on one or more morning excursions. You can easily spend a week visiting these churches. Alternatively, you can visit the better-known ones in a rigorous day.

Admission to all churches is free. A small donation in the alms box is appreciated; it is usually found near the door or where votive candles are sold.

IN DOWNTOWN THESSALONIKI
Ayia Sofia 🐾 It's a pity that Thessaloniki's two most important churches—Ayia Sofia (Holy Wisdom) and Ayios Dimitrios (St. Demetrios)—are both heavily restored. Still, each is worth visiting for its importance in the city's history and for its fine mosaics, although both lack the pleasantly dusty ambience and odor of sanctity found in Thessaloniki's less heavily restored churches.

Thessaloniki's 7th-century Ayia Sofia was inspired by the emperor Justinian's famous 6th-century church of Ayia Sofia in Constantinople, although there may have been a modest 4th-century church here. Like the majestic Ayia Sofia in Constantinople (today's Istanbul), Salonika's namesake has an impressively large—in fact, an astonishingly large and astonishingly technical—dome. The ornately carved marble columns supporting the dome were pillaged from earlier monuments (as they were so often in antiquity and throughout the Byzantine era).

Tips   **Dress Appropriately & Keep an Eye on the Time!**

All of these churches, which are places of worship, consider certain casual attire disrespectful (short skirts on women, shorts or sleeveless shirts on men or women). Wear clothing that covers your arms and legs. And remember that most churches close from about 1 to 5pm.

Fortunately, some of Ayia Sofia's original mosaics have survived. The Ascension, with an oddly foreshortened Christ (supported by young angels), and the Virgin Mary with the infant Jesus are especially fine. Look carefully at the mosaics, and you'll notice that some show only crosses and stars and have no human representations. These date from the 8th-century Iconoclastic period, when there was a ban on showing the human figure in religious art. The Iconoclasts destroyed many earlier works of art, including sacred icons, and left us with the word "iconoclast" to describe someone who destroys the past or challenges tradition.

Ayia Sofia Square is one of Thessaloniki's nicest, and most important, squares. A service of thanksgiving was held here when the Allies liberated the city from the Germans on November 2, 1944. Today, much of Thessaloniki heads here for Easter and other important services. Keep an eye out for the "red house" at 31 Ayias Sofias, built in 1925 for a wealthy industrialist; across the way at 33 Ayias Sofias, now with the Terkenlis and Byzantium pastry shop on the ground floor, is another handsome mansion built in the 1920s. Many of the square's finest houses were destroyed in the fire of 1917, which damaged Ayia Sofia church as well. The pastry shop is an excellent spot to rest and refresh yourself after you see the church; until then, you can check out the goodies at www.terkenlis.gr.

Ayia Sofia Sq., between Tsimiski and Egnatia. © **2310/270-253.** Daily 8am–9pm (but often closed 1–5pm).

Ayios Dimitrios (aka Church and Crypt of Ayios Demetrios)   Like Ayia Sofia, Ayios Dimitrios was heavily restored—in fact, almost entirely rebuilt—after the fire of 1917. Consequently, this is a church with an imposing history, some fine mosaics, but very little soul. That's a shame, because the story of Dimitrios is quite stirring: In the 4th century A.D., this site was occupied by a Roman bath, a corner of which was used as a makeshift jail. In A.D. 303, one of the prisoners, young Dimitrios, got into trouble by preaching the Gospel in Salonika. Dimitrios not only refused to renounce his faith but seems to have converted another prisoner, a gladiator who fought and killed Emperor Galerius's favorite gladiator. Galerius was furious and had Dimitrios executed at once. Soon, a shrine here commemorated the martyred Dimitrios; then a small church was built, and in the 7th century A.D., the church was considerably enlarged into its present five-aisled basilica form. After the 1917 fire, the church was rebuilt on and off from 1926 to 1949. You can still see scorch marks from the 1917 conflagration on some of the interior walls.

Almost all the mosaics here are restorations of what was lost in 1917, but a cluster from the 5th to 7th centuries A.D. survives. Look for the lovely, original portrait of the boyish saint with two young children, and the representation of Demetrios with the church founders. (You can see other mosaics salvaged after the fire on display in the Museum of Byzantine Culture.) The mysterious crypt, which you access down a narrow, twisting staircase, reveals several small anterooms and remains of Roman baths;

the crypt sometimes functions as a small gallery. Particularly venerated are the spot where Dimitrios is believed to have been martyred (and where a vial of blood, believed to be the saint's, was found) and the spot with a holy-water font. For centuries, the faithful noted a sweet scent at the font, and believed that myrrh, or perfumed fluid, flowed from the saint himself.

As you leave the church, have a look at the chapel of St. Euthymius, built into the wall of Ayios Dimitrios. The 14th-century frescoes in the little chapel have all the verve lacking in Ayios Dimitrios's heavily restored mosaics.

Corner of Ayiou Dimitriou and Ayiou Nikolaou, 1 block north of the Roman market, at the base of the Upper City. ℭ 032/0213-627. Church and crypt usually Mon 12:30–7pm; Tues–Sat 8am–8pm; Sun 10:30am–8pm. Bus: 22 or 23 leaves about every 10 min. from the stop near the church at the southeast side of Eleftherias Sq.

Ayios Panteleimon   This probably 14th-century church, dedicated to one of the physician saints, is a popular place to light a candle and say a prayer for good health. The church, all that remains of a large monastery on this spot, is usually closed, but its elaborate brick- and stonework makes even a glimpse of it a delight. If you do get inside, note how the central dome is supported by four barrel vaults, a distinctive characteristic of Macedonian churches.

Corner of Egnatia and Iassonidou.

Panagia Acheiropoietos (Church of the Virgin Made Without Hands) ✿   This 5th-century basilica is the only church from Thessaloniki's early Christian days to have survived pretty much intact, without the restorations and renovations that have changed the characters of Ayia Sofia and Ayios Dimitrios. Due to the inexorable rise in street level over the centuries, the church now sits well below the level of today's roads. The marble columns, with their elaborate "perforated" acanthus-leaf decorations, give you a good idea of the Byzantine love of the elaborate—achieved here by vigorous drill work. There are mosaics of floral and vine motifs interspersed with birds and 13th-century frescoes showing some of the 40 Martyrs. The missing martyrs were probably obliterated when the church was converted to a mosque in the 15th century after Salonika fell to the Turks

Ayias Sofia, north of Egnatia. No phone.

Panagia Chalkeon (Virgin of the Copper Workers) ✿   This tiny church with its three domes looks as if it would fit nicely into a miniature village. It has some fine frescoes, but its real glory is its facade, with windows piled above windows, domes above domes. Like the Panagia Acheiropoietos, the 11th-century Panagia Chalkeon now sits considerably below Thessaloniki's modern street level. Some of the copperworkers' shops, from which this church took its name centuries ago, survive nearby. Locals call this the "red church" for its rosy bricks.

Dikasterion Sq. No phone.

IN THE UPPER CITY (ANO POLI) ✿✿✿

Visiting the churches also means exploring the narrow streets of the **Upper City,** with the remains of the massive Byzantine Eptapirigion (Seven-Gated) Walls. *Tsinari,* the old Turkish name of the Upper City, comes from a famous local plane tree. The neighborhood is a maze of cobbled streets, with street-side fountains, corner groceries, and cafes. Many of the wooden houses here have upper floors that project out over the ground floor and overhang the street. This was a clever way of getting as much space into a house as possible on as little land as available. In the 1960s, this area was practically falling down; now, as young Thessalonians reclaim the old quarter, an address here is considered very chic. When you visit, be prepared to get lost at least once. You'll probably discover a wonderful little church, courtyard, or schoolyard while you try to find your way back. *Remember:* The churches close from about 1 to 5pm.

Taking the bus (no. 22 or 23 from Eleftherias Sq.) to the Upper City is an easy ride. You can then walk back downhill. When you get off the bus in the Upper City, have a look at the Byzantine walls around the Acropolis and the Byzantine defense tower called the Tower of Trigoniou.

Ayia Katerini 𝄞 Another of Thessaloniki's fine 14th-century churches, built with a central dome flanked by four cupolas, is now surrounded by new apartment buildings and old homes. With elegant brick and stone work, it is a dignified reminder of one of the city's finest artistic periods. Once inside, look for the wall painting showing the healing of the blind.

Corner of Sachini and Tsamadou, near the Byzantine walls.

Ayios Nikolaos Orfanos 𝄞𝄞 Like Osios David, this seemingly unprepossessing brick-and-stone church holds an astonishing treasure: well-preserved frescoes from the 14th century, the zenith of Thessaloniki's artistic excellence. You can pick out haloed St. Nikolaos himself, standing at the helm of the little boat he's guiding across stormy waters. The other frescoes, as is usual in such cycles, show scenes from the Old and New Testaments, as well as saints and prophets. Next to the church, part of its once-flourishing monastery with an attractive veranda has just been restored, and makes visitors envy those lucky enough to live here. You may acquire a retinue of curious neighborhood children; most drift away in time, but some have hopes of sweets or even money and can be unpleasantly persistent.

Apostolou Pavlou.

Osios David (Latomou Monastery) 𝄞𝄞 I manage to get lost almost every time I come here, but eventually find my way to this absolutely charming 5th- or 6th-century church, with its comfortable, shaded courtyard. Indeed, what a tempting fantasy to think of taking over the caretaker's job, sitting with a book in the little shelter in the courtyard, tending the flowers, and unlocking the church for visitors—who are bound to be impressed, because nothing about Osios David's simple exterior can prepare you for the glorious mosaic of the vision of Ezekiel inside. The vision shows Christ surrounded by the symbols of the four apostles (the angel, eagle, lion, and bull). If there's a finer mosaic in the city, we can't imagine which it could be. According to local lore, the mosaic spent several centuries hidden beneath a calf's skin, which prevented the Turks from finding and destroying it. If you wish, ask the caretaker to turn on the lights—and slip him something for his troubles.

Timotheou, off Ayias Sofia.

Profitias Elias 𝄞 This substantial 14th-century church, whose elaborate brick exterior has recently been restored, is a fine vantage point from which to view the city. Women, who cannot visit Mount Athos, will get an idea from Profitias Elias of the cross-in-square style (with central dome) that is similar to many of the churches on Mount Athos.

Olympiados.

Vlatodon Monastery (aka Vlatades) ✟ As you toil uphill, you'll keep seeing the overhanging walls of the substantial Vlatodon Monastery, founded in the 14th century. In the last few years it has been substantially renovated and expanded, and has lost its "old" feeling. Still, the charming inner courtyard is a cool spot to rest for a moment or two. If the main church is locked, don't be disappointed; the Turks damaged the frescoes badly and they have not been restored. By tradition, the little chapel of Saints Peter and Paul was built on the spot where St. Paul preached when he visited Thessaloniki in A.D. 50.

By the gate to the Acropolis.

MARKETS ✟✟

Thessaloniki's markets are a bit of Levantine exotica that knocks the socks off anything to be found in Athens. And "anything" is precisely what you can find here, whether it's knockoff designer bags, copper pots, piles of black-and-white postcards, and sheep's bells (or sheep's heads for that matter!). It's a great place to stroll, get lost, and have a snack or a meal.

The Bezesteni ✟ It would be wonderful to have a bird's-eye view of the Bezesteni's six domes and four entrances, one on each side. This covered market, built in the late 15th century by Sultan Bayezid II, is one of the best-preserved Turkish monuments in Thessaloniki. Now, it specializes in textiles and jewelry—making it a terrific place to browse and feel transported into an Asian bazaar. While you're in the neighborhood, stroll over to the intersection of Egnatia and Venizelou streets, where restoration work began on Thessaloniki's oldest mosque, the 15th-century **Hazma Bey Mosque,** in the summer of 2007.

Venizelou and Solomou. Usually Mon–Sat 9am–7pm.

Flea Market ✟ Just what its name implies, this market, which sprawls along Tositsa, sells everything from genuine junk to genuine antiques (much more of the former than the latter). Of late, many eastern European sellers have been plying their wares here: usually leather jackets, fake Leica cameras and designer watches, and an odd assortment of alarm clocks, mirrors, and socks.

Tositsa. Usually Mon–Sat 8am–7pm.

Kapani (Vlali) Market ✟ This market sells foods, dry goods, fabrics, and just about everything else you can think of, in a hodgepodge of ramshackle shops crowded one next to the other as far as the eye can see. There's been a market here at least since Turkish times, and probably long before that.

Bounded by Komninon, Egnatia, Aristotelous, and Menexe sts. Mon–Sat about 8am–5pm.

Modiano Market ✟✟ Gypsies with dancing bears once played music in the Modiano Market. The bears are gone, but street musicians still stroll the area. You can easily spend a morning in the glass-roofed market that covers an entire square block, happily wandering from stall to stall and eyeing the fish, meat, fruit, vegetables, flowers, spices, and baked goods on sale. When hunger calls, look for the delicious food at **Thanasis,** or find a seat in one of the other cafes or restaurants.

The roofed market was built in 1922 by the wealthy Jewish merchant Eli Modiano, whose handsome family mansion (at 68 Vas. Sophias) is now the home of the intermittently open **Folklore and Ethnography Museum of Macedonia.** Many of Thessaloniki's surviving 19th-century mansions still stand along Megalou Alexandrou and along Vas. Olgas and Sophias; Vas. Olgas in particular was once known as the "Boulevard of the Châteaux" for its imposing town houses. The **Pinakothiki (Municipal Gallery;** www.thessalonikicity.gr), with an extensive collection of works by Macedonian artists, is in an early-20th-century mansion at 162 Vas. Olgas; its usual hours are Tuesday to Friday, 9am to 1pm and 5 to 9pm; Saturday 5 to 9pm; Sunday 8am to 3pm.

The block bounded by Aristotelous, Ermou, Vasileos Irakleiou, and Komninon sts. Mon–Sat about 7am–5pm.

MORE ATTRACTIONS

Alatza Imaret 𝆺   Along with the Bezesteni, the Alatza Imaret, a former 15th-century mosque with a poorhouse, or almshouse, is one of the best-preserved Turkish buildings in Thessaloniki. *Alatza* (many-colored) refers to the tiles and stones that covered the mosque in its glory days. If you're lucky, it may be open for an exhibition when you visit; in that case, allow half an hour.

Dimitrion Sq., just off Ayiou Nikolaou, half a block north of Kassandrou, 1½ blocks north of the church of Ayios Dimitrios. (℃ **2310/278-587.** Free admission. Open intermittently for exhibitions.

Atatürk's Birthplace   Just behind the consulate, this modest wood-framed house was the 1881 birthplace of Mustafa Kemal (Atatürk), the man who created the modern Turkish state and was its first president. Given to Turkey as a present by the Greek government in 1933, the house has been restored and furnished to reflect the way it must have been at Atatürk's birth. It contains numerous photos of the man, young and old; various letters and papers; and cases containing the clothes and uniforms he wore. An excellent English-language booklet (with photos) explains what's relevant. This is also the Turkish consulate, so you usually get a guided tour by an official. Allow an hour here for the tour.

17 Apostolou Pavlou (8 short blocks east of the church of Ayios Dimitrios). (℃ **2310/248-452.** Free admission. Daily 10am–5pm. Bus: 22 or 23 from Eleftherias Sq.; also stops along El. Venizelou north to Ayiou Dimitriou. Enter through the front gate of the Turkish consulate. Passport or ID card necessary.

International Fairgrounds   If you're in Thessaloniki during the September Trade Fair, you may want to take in some of the exhibits here. Notices of special exhibitions or events are usually posted conspicuously throughout the city. The **Macedonian Museum of Contemporary Art** (℃ **2310/240-002**) makes its home here, so plan to stay for several hours. Open Tuesday through Sunday from 9am to 5pm, June through September, and Tuesday through Sunday from 10am to 2pm and 5 to 9pm, October through May. Admission is 2€ ($2.60).

Entrances at the corners of Angelaki and Tsimiski, and Angelaki and Egnatia. Free admission except during special exhibitions. Irregular hours.

Jewish History Museum (aka Museum of the Jewish Presence in Thessaloniki) 𝆺   This small museum uses photographs and artifacts to portray Jewish life in Thessaloniki. Thessaloniki Jews established the city's first printing press in the early 1500s and founded the city's first newspaper, *El Lunar,* in 1865. The community thrived under the Ottoman Empire, and in 1900, 80,000 of Thessaloniki's 173,000 inhabitants were Jews. Just before World War II, 60,000 Jews lived here; only 2,000 survived the death camps. Today about 1,000 Jewish people reside here.

To visit or attend services at one of Thessaloniki's remaining synagogues, or to see the Holocaust Monument, phone the **Jewish Community Office,** 24 Tsimiski (℃ **2310/272-840**). If you're interested in learning more about the Jewish community in Greece, ask at the GNTO office for the excellent pamphlet *Jewish Heritage in*

Greece, and keep an eye out for the locally published *Jewish Community of Thessaloniki,* as well as Niko Stavroloulakis's books *The Jews of Greece* and *Jewish Sites and Synagogues of Greece.* Allow at least an hour for your visit to the museum.

13 Agios Mina. Ⓒ **2310/250-407.** Fax 2310/275-701. www.jmth.gr. Free admission. Mon–Fri and Sun 11am–2pm; Wed–Thurs usually also 5–8pm.

Lambrakis Monument On May 22, 1963, right-wing forces ran down and killed Grigoris Lambrakis, a leftist member of the parliament, who had been speaking at a peace meeting. Vassilis Vassilikos based his novel *Z* on Lambrakis's death; Costa-Gavras then adapted the novel for his film starring Yves Montand. Lambrakis's assassination and the protests that followed were part of a long series of events culminating in the dictatorship of the colonels in the late 1960s. The bronze monument shows a figure with arms upraised, flanked by a dove of peace.

Intersection of Venizelou, Ermou, and Spandoni.

Museum of Ancient Greek, Byzantine, and Post Byzantine Musical Instruments ✶✶ What is it about music museums? The small one in Athens is one of that city's finest, and Thessaloniki has its own appealing music museum. The three floors of this one house beautifully displayed reproductions of stringed and wind instruments, along with marvelous photographs of instruments from ancient vase paintings or Byzantine manuscripts. Purists may object to the predominance of reproductions here, but the reproductions give viewers a good sense of what the actual instruments looked like. Music sometimes plays softly in the background, the cafe is sometimes open, and if you're lucky, a concert will be scheduled here during your time in Salonika. Allow an hour.

12–14 Katouni, Ladadika. Ⓒ **2310/238-391.** Admission 5€ ($6.50). Tues–Sun 9am–3pm and 5–10pm.

ART GALLERIES

Thessaloniki's best galleries often have exhibitions well worth taking in, although most keep irregular hours. Find out about them from posters in town, from the Greek National Tourism Organization office in Aristotelous Square, and from the listings usually published on Tuesday in *Kathimerini,* the English-language supplement to the *International Herald Tribune.* As you explore the city, feel free to step inside any of the galleries.

Check out **Apothiki,** on Nikis by the waterfront (Ⓒ **2310/240-877**); **Foka,** 17 Foka (Ⓒ **2310/240-362**); **Kalfayan,** 43 Proxenou Koromilia (Ⓒ **2310/231-187**); and **Metamorfosis,** 128 Tsimiski (Ⓒ **2310/285-071**). **Terracotta,** 13 Chrysostomos (aka Chrys.) Smirnis and 76 Mitropoleos (Ⓒ **2310/235-689**),features works by some of Greece's best-known contemporary artists (like Fasianos) as well as works by the up-and-coming.

In addition to these galleries, several museums and other galleries that are open most days during normal business hours, emphasize the art and life of Thessaloniki and Macedonia, with particular reference to the lively pre- and post–World War II art scene. These include the **Municipal Art Gallery,** 162 Vas Olgas (Ⓒ **2310/425-531**), with a collection of 19th to 21st-century works by Greek artists, many from Thessaloniki, the **Gallery of Fine Arts,** 1 Nicephoros; **Germanou,** inside the National Theater Building (Ⓒ **2310/238-601**); the **State Museum of Contemporary Art in Thessaloniki,** 21 Kolokotroni, in the Lazariston Monastery (Ⓒ **2310/589-140;** www.greekstatemuseum.gr), with a collection of 20th- and 21st-century Russian art;

the **Museum of Photography** and the **Center of Contemporary Art** (www.cact.gr), in the waterfront arts complex in Warehouse B1, Port of Salonika, through Gate A off Koundouriotou Street. Galleries are free; museums admission is 3€ ($3.90).

ORGANIZED TOURS

Reputable companies offering tours of Thessaloniki and of the Philip and Alexander sites include **Zorpidis Travel,** 4 Salaminos (© **2310/555-955;** www.zorpidis.gr).and **Kinissi Tours,** 2 Venizelou (© **2310/241-080).**Try the respected British agency **Filoxenia** (© **2310/280-560;** www.filoxenia.co.uk), for "green" ecological tours to the countryside as well as mountaineering excursions.

SPECTATOR SPORTS

Like most Greeks, Thessalonians are keen soccer and basketball fans, rooting for the home teams. (Confusingly, the Aris and PAOK stadiums are home to both basketball *and* soccer teams.) Your best bet if you don't speak or read Greek and want to catch a game is to check with the concierge at your hotel. In general, soccer games are in spring and fall, basketball year-round. **Aris stadium** is in the suburb of Harilaou (© **2310/305-402**), while the much-easier-to-reach **PAOK stadium** is on Ayios Dimitrios, 2 blocks northeast of the International Fairgrounds (© **2310/238-560**).

SHOPPING

Greece's second-largest city offers a wide variety of shops, and since the city center is quite compact, it's easy to explore the major shopping districts. As in Athens—indeed, throughout Greece—most chic boutiques stock imported goods from Europe and the States, usually with a hefty import duty that is passed on to the customer. If you shop the winter (Jan) and summer (late July and Aug) sales, you may find some bargains.

Some Thessaloniki shops still sell crafts by local artists such as coppersmiths and jewelers. You're likely to find something tempting here, sometimes at what constitutes a bargain price for a foreigner. Not surprisingly, most of the shops are near the church of Panagia Chalkeon (Virgin of the Copper Makers) in **Dikasterion Square.**

ANTIQUES

Relics, 3 Yioryio Lassani (© **2310/226-506**), offers high-quality antiques, from silver- and glassware to jewelry, ceramics, prints, Art Nouveau lamps, and Victorian-era dolls. This is a serious shop with serious prices. It's located a block east of the Mitropoleos Cathedral off Mitropoleos; closed on Sunday. You'll also find a number of antiques shops on Mitropoleos and Tositssa streets. *Tip:* Reputable shops will explain that you'll need an export license to take out of Greece any item more than 100 years old.

(Tips) Hitting the Beach

Any beaches within the bay of Thessaloniki are too polluted to be safe, although people do swim at them. Beaches in the communities of Perea and Ayia Triada, 16 to 24km (10–15 miles) along the bay east of the city, are considered reasonably safe. Just past Ayia Triada, on the headland of the bay, is the Greek National Tourism Organization facility of **Akti Thermaikou,** which has a children's playground, changing cabins, snack bars, and tennis courts.

> **Tips Details, Details**
>
> In Thessaloniki, old-style, pre–European Community **shopping hours,** unfathomable to foreigners, still predominate. Stores open at about 9am and close around 1:30 or 2pm for the afternoon siesta. On Tuesday, Thursday, and Friday evenings, some (but not all) reopen from about 5:30 to 8:30pm. In July, however, almost all shops close for the evening. The best time to shop is morning. Note that some of these stores will take major credit cards, but almost all, especially the smaller ones, prefer not to.

ART
See "Art Galleries" above.

BOOKS, NEWSPAPERS & MAGAZINES
Molho, 10 Tsimiski (📞 **2310/277-113**) is the oldest and finest bookstore in Thessaloniki. **Ianos,** 7 Aristotelous (📞 **2310/277-164**), and **Malliaris,** 9 Aristotelous (📞 **2310/276-926**), both have wide selections of Greek and foreign books as well as other publications.

Apostolic Diakonta Bookstore 🔎   Although this handsome bookstore specializes in books on religious matters, it also carries a wide selection on Greece (in English and French, as well as Greek). This is a wonderful place to browse. Even if you can't afford one of the superb photography books of Greece, you can find wonderful cards as well as good reproductions of icons. 9A Ethnikis Aminis, near the Archaeological and Byzantine museums. 📞 **2310/275-126.**

COPPER
At the family-run **Adelphi Kazanzidi,** 12 Klissouras off the western side of Dikasterion Square, a block north of Egnatia (📞 **2310/262-741**), copper-working skills have been passed down from generation to generation. The shop sells numerous finely crafted copper-ware items such as wine carafes, skillets, water heaters, and trays, all handmade on the premises. There are also many copper shops around the Panagia Chalkeon church.

DEPARTMENT STORES
Lambropoulos, 18 Tsimiski (📞 **2310/269-971**), is the best in the city, with five floors of everything and anything you might want, from cosmetics to basketballs. It's a block west of Aristotelous, at the corner of Komninon.

FASHION
For both men's and women's fashions, try the department stores such as Lambropoulos (see above) or the chic—and expensive—boutiques on pedestrian walkway Dimitriou Gounari. One centrally located men's shop (with some English-speaking staff) is the long-established **Oxford Company,** 4 Palaion Patron Germanou (📞 **2310/ 273-087**). On its walls are photos of the family's old cotton mills in Volos.

GIFTS & SOUVENIRS
At **Tanagrea,** on Vogatsikou (a block east of the Metropolitan Cathedral between Mitropoleos and Proxenou Koromila), you'll find a wide selection of handcrafted items by a stable of artisans employed by this well-known chain of stores, which also

---

Tips Pack 'n' Send

Office supplies may sound just like the things you *don't* want to think about on vacation, but if you need stationery, packing tape, scissors, or large envelopes with which to mail purchases home, **Spondilides,** 24 Tsimiski, in the stoa (© **2310/269-825**), is your place. *Tip:* Don't seal your packages until you get to the post office. All parcels are subject to inspection before they are shipped.

---

has outlets in Athens, Crete, and Spetsai. Offerings include ceramics, pewter, silver, leather goods, paintings, glassware, and jewelry.

Pronounced *zeeta mee,* **ZM,** 1 Proxenou Koromila, a block east of Aristotelous Square (© **2310/240-591**), offers three floors of expensive but well-crafted Greek souvenir items such as worry beads, pottery, folk art, rugs, toys, handcrafted caiques, prints, and a few antique silver place settings and jewelry. An extremely tempting gallery-like place to browse.

JEWELRY
Specializing in gold, but not exclusively, the eponymous owner of **Marina,** 62 Mitropoleos, a block east of the Metropolitan Cathedral (© **2310/238-361**), offers her own designs as well as copies of the works of famous Greek jewelers such as LALAoUNIS, with whom she apprenticed. **Haido Deliali,** 1 Vagdamali (© **2310/269-375**), also makes much of the jewelry in her shop.

LEATHER
The best of several leather-goods shops in the area is **Falli,** 11 Askitou (© **2310/229-197**). On the southwest corner of the outdoor market, near Ermou and El. Venizelou, Falli makes and sells shoulder bags, backpacks, attaché cases, and sandals. Try to bargain by looking downcast and disappointed when you hear the price. If you want good-quality leather, resist the eastern European leather vendors who set up stalls on many street corners.

MARKETS
See "Markets" (p. 617) for the Modiano, Kapani, Bezesteni, and flea markets.

MUSIC
Blow Up: The Music Stores, 8 Aristotelous, on the east side of the street a block north of Tsimiski (© **2310/233-255;** www.blowup.gr), **Patsis,** 39 Tsimiski, at the corner of Aristotelous (© **2310/231-805**), **Studio 52,** 46 Dimitrious Gounari (© **2310/271-301**) and the **Virgin Megastore** on Tsimiski (© **2310/243-407**) have excellent selections of Greek music well displayed in their windows and on their shelves. **En Chordes,** 3 Ipodromiou (© **2310/282-248**), sells many kinds of musical instruments and CDs, including Byzantine music.

SHOES
Pak, 3 Ayias Sofias Sq., opposite the north side of the church (© **2310/274-863**), carries a wide selection of high-quality Greek shoes—from hiking boots to high heels—at very acceptable prices. The foreign brands here are much more expensive.

SWEETS

In a city where sweetness is next to godliness, the venerable **Agapitos,** 53 Tsimiski (© **2310/279-107**), gets rave reviews. All are made with great, mouthwatering, high-caloric care. One of the branches of the excellent sweet shop, **Terkenlis,** is nearby at 30 Tsimiski, so you can easily compare and contrast. Both are closed on Sunday. Don't panic: **Averof,** 11 Vas. Georgiou (© **2310/814-284**), Thessaloniki's famous Kosher bakery, is usually open 365 days a year.

WHERE TO STAY

Because of Thessaloniki's long history as a center for national and international trade, its large hotels have traditionally focused on serving the needs of commercial rather than leisure travelers. Recommendations below avoid large, expensive hotels that have amenities more appealing to business travelers (large conference rooms) than to independent travelers (good location and pleasant accommodations). One welcome exception: the Mediterranean Palace Hotel. In recent years, Thessaloniki has gained several "boutique" hotels, notably the Capsis Bristol Hotel; in addition, some old standbys, such as the Tourist, Le Palace, the Olympia, and the Plaza Art Hotel have undergone extensive renovations.

It makes sense to reserve in advance year-round to avoid difficulties during Thessaloniki's many trade fairs, festivals, and associated cultural events. Bookings peak in September and October, when the International Trade Fair is quickly followed by the month-long Demetria cultural festival (not to mention the Festival of Greek Songs and the Film Festival!). Expect a hefty surcharge (sometimes 50% or more) on the regular rates during the fairs and festivals. Hotel prices here can be especially confusing, with online booking often advertising, but not always producing, prices much lower than those quoted by the hotels.

VERY EXPENSIVE

Capsis Bristol Hotel 𝒜𝒜   This very small, very elegant boutique hotel in a late-19th-century building in the Ladadika district is the place to stay if the Mediterranean Palace hotel is too big and impersonal for your taste. Guest rooms are individually and lovingly decorated with antiques and paintings—and named after famous Macedonian heroes. (You might choose the Alexander Room.) *Tip:* Be sure not to confuse this hotel with the massive 415-unit Capsis Hotel, also in the Capsis group, located out of the center near the train station.

2 Olimpiou and Katouni, 54626 Thessaloniki. © **2310/506-500.** www.capsisbristol.gr. 20 units. 280€–415€ ($364–$540) double. AE, DC, MC, V. **Amenities:** Restaurant; bar; concierge; business center; 24-hr. room service; babysitting; laundry. *In room:* A/C, TV, dataport, minibar.

Makedonia Palace 𝒜 *Kids*   The Makedonia Palace, now managed by the Grecotel Group as a five-star luxury resort hotel, draws both business travelers and Greek families on holiday—not to mention high-stepping gamblers. (Europe's largest casino is next door; see "Thessaloniki After Dark," later in this chapter.) In the usual manner of Greek hotel decor, the serious glitz is concentrated in the lobby and the guest rooms are rather bland. All units have balconies and picture windows, but if you stay here, insist on a seaside room. (Why pay all that money and not have the view?) If you don't want to head back into town, the hotel's restaurants include a sushi bar and the rooftop **Porfyra** restaurant, serving up international cuisine with splendid views over the city and Gulf.

2 Leoforos Megalou Alexandrou (on the seafront promenade a half-mile east of the White Tower), 54640 Thessaloniki. ℰ **231/089-7197.** Fax 231/089-7211. www.grecotel.gr. 284 units. 300€–500€ ($390–$650) double. Discounts sometimes available off season. AE, DC, MC, V. **Amenities:** 3 restaurants; 2 bars; 2 outdoor pools (saltwater and freshwater); tennis courts; children's playground; health club and spa; concierge; airport pickup arranged; business center; shopping arcade; 24-hr. room service. *In room:* A/C, TV, dataport (most units), minibar, safe (most units).

Mediterranean Palace Hotel 🏵🏵🏵 In 1997 the Mediterranean Palace opened in the Ladadika district, with its tempting restaurants and cafes, and its location, comforts, and service continue to make it Thessaloniki's best hotel. Balconied front rooms overlook the harbor, and almost every unit in the house is large and furnished with comfortable beds, spiffy wall-to-wall carpeting, and cozy chairs, including some relaxing leather recliners. Many of the guest rooms have especially nice touches, such as decorative moldings and large walk-in closets—and if you want to make a phone call from your bathroom, this is the place to do it. As for the suites, with their large living rooms, kitchenettes, and bedrooms, we could happily live in one for months. It's no small wonder that the hotel consistently appears in *Odyssey* magazine's list of the best hotels in Greece. Everyone we know who has stayed here agrees that this is *the* place to stay in Thessaloniki. Be sure to check for special packages, when the rates have been known to drop as low as 100€ ($130).

3 Salaminos and Karatassou, 54626 Thessaloniki. ℰ **2310/552-554.** Fax 2310/552-622. www.mediterranean-palace. gr. 120 units. 180€–350€ ($234–$455) double. American-style buffet breakfast 12€ ($16). AE, DC, MC, V. **Amenities:** 2 restaurants; 2 bars; concierge; business center; shopping arcade; 24-hr. room service; same-day laundry/dry-cleaning services; nonsmoking rooms. *In room:* A/C, TV, dataport, kitchenette (suites), minibar, safe.

EXPENSIVE

Electra Palace Hotel 🏵🏵 Overlooking Thessaloniki's main square, the Electra Palace, with its handsome, curved, arcaded facade, has the nicest location in town—except when there are noisy demonstrations in Aristotle Square. The Electra added a welcome rooftop pool and restaurant in 2004. If you stay here, insist on one of the fourth- or fifth-floor rooms with a balcony overlooking the square; some of the interior rooms are astonishingly small—I speak from experience!

9A Aristotelous Sq., 54624 Thessaloniki. ℰ **2310/232-221.** Fax 2310/235-947. electrapalace@the.forthnet.gr. 70 units. 180€–300€ ($235–$390) double. Rates include American-style buffet breakfast. AE, DC, MC, V. **Amenities:** 2 restaurants; 2 bars; outdoor rooftop pool; health club and spa; concierge; business center; 24-hr. room service; nonsmoking rooms. *In room:* A/C, TV, minibar.

MODERATE/INEXPENSIVE

Hotel Olympia 🏵 Well-traveled Greek friends who stayed here in 2007 loved their room and praised the restaurant. That's probably because much-needed renovations have smartened the hotel greatly; some of the bathrooms are positively elegant. Rooms

---

A Note About Rates & Hair Dryers

The rates given in this section are for high season in summer—they should be lower in winter, and **higher** during trade fairs and the Demetria festival. As always, ask about discounts if you plan a long-term or off-season visit. Note that many hotels require that you pay for an expensive breakfast (a "compulsory" meal). As for hair dryers, they are now standard in Thessaloniki hotels; that said, I always travel with my own miniature dual-current dryer for the inevitable exception to the rule.

are more bland, but good-size, with good beds and—still a pleasant surprise in a Greek hotel—decent reading lights. The Olympia's location, at the northern end of the Roman market, is central (St. Demetrios Church and the flea market are also nearby) and quieter than some of the nearby main drags.

65 Olympou, 54631 Thessaloniki. © 2310/235-421. Fax 2310/276-133. www.olympia.com.gr. 111 units. 125€–145€ ($163–$189) double. Compulsory breakfast 10€ ($13). AE, DC, MC, V. **Amenities:** Restaurant; bar; business center. *In room:* A/C, TV, Internet, minibar.

Hotel Orestias Castorias ★★ *Value*   This formerly modest little hotel has undergone a considerable face-lift in the last few years and is now one of the best buys in town. The location, near the Roman Forum, is quiet; the rooms have balconies (no. 27 overlooks a quiet garden; front rooms overlook the Forum). The staff is welcoming. Many guests are budget-conscious Europeans. One drawback: There is no elevator.

14 Agnostou Stratiotou, 54631 Thessaloniki. © 2310/536-280. Fax 2310/276-572. www.okhotel.gr. 28 units. 50€–65€ ($65–$85) double. No credit cards. **Amenities:** Lounge; Internet access. *In room:* A/C, TV.

Hotel Tourist ★ *Value*   Renovations in 2005 transformed the Hotel Tourist from dingy to spiffy. The gold-gilt borders of the high ceilings gleam, the crystal chandeliers sparkle, the breakfast room is a welcome addition. That said, the rooms are still on the small side and some of the bathrooms are small enough to make me resolve (again) to take up yoga. Still, an excellent value in a great location.

21 Mitropoleos, 54624 Thessaloniki. © 2310/270-501. Fax 2310/226-865. www.touristhotel.gr. 37 units. 85€ ($110) double. Discounts usually offered for booking through the hotel's website. Inquire about reduced rates. No credit cards. *In room:* A/C, TV, fridge.

Le Palace (Pallas) Hotel ★★   This small hotel with a central location has high ceilings, gilt "palatial" style public rooms, and Art Deco touches. Many Thessaloniki fans make a point of returning here year after year, drawn by the Palace's elegant but cozy ambience; most bathrooms have a tub as well as a shower, not standard in Greek hotels. The in-house restaurant is good, and the breakfast buffet is lavish.

12 Tsimiski, 54624 Thessaloniki. © 2310/257-400. Fax 2310/256-589. www.lepalace.gr. 58 units. 130€ ($169) double. AE, DC, MC, V. **Amenities:** Bar. *In room:* A/C, TV, dataport.

Mandrino Hotel ★ *Value*   A complete renovation turned this centrally located hotel into a good choice at a good price. Egnatia Street is a main thoroughfare and shopping street, so don't expect tranquillity; rear rooms are usually less noisy than those facing Egnatia. The Mandrino does have nonsmoking rooms, which is unusual in Greece.

29 Egnatia, 54624 Thessaloniki. © 2310/526-321 to -325. Fax 2310/526-321. www.mandrino.gr. 72 units. 100€ double. Discounts usually offered for booking through the hotel's website. AE, MC, V. **Amenities:** Bar; lounge; business center w/Internet access. *In room:* A/C, TV, minibar.

Plaza Art Hotel ★ *Value*   With a great location in Ladadikia, close to scads of restaurants and cafes, the Plaza offers excellent value. The rooms are not my idea of restful: red curtains and bedspreads, red and white walls, and lively prints on some of the furniture.

5 Paggeou, 54631 Thessaloniki. © 2310/520-120. www.hotelplaza.gr. 35 units. 80€–120€ ($104–$156) double. No credit cards. **Amenities:** Breakfast room; Internet access. *In room:* A/C, TV, minibar.

JUST OUTSIDE THESSALONIKI

We assume that you want to spend your time in Thessaloniki, rather than stay outside the city and go back and forth. But, just in case, here are some suggestions.

For those who cannot abide staying in any city in the summer, but still want to spend time in this city, the sprawling four-story **Philippion,** in the forest of Sheih-Sou to the north of the Upper City (© 2310/203-321; www.philippion.gr), is a good choice. Unfortunately, a series of recent summer fires has badly scarred the lovely surrounding forests. The Philippion overlooks Thessaloniki and is a 25-minute drive from the city center (hotel shuttle buses go into town frequently). The guest rooms are large and sunny, the best being on the third floor to the rear, with a view of the city.

Facilities include a pool, children's playground, and good restaurant, with local specialties such as mussels in hot-pepper sauce; live entertainment is sometimes offered in the evening. The clientele is mostly vacationing Greek families, who can be rather boisterous. The hotel's proximity to the Ring Road makes it extremely easy to reach the airport (15 min. away) and the main highways to Athens, Halkidiki, and Thrace.

If the Philippion is full, and you want a place out of town, try **Panorama** (© 2310/341-266; www.hotelpanorama.gr), 26 Analipsos, Panorama, a lovely, wooded suburb of Thessaloniki. This hotel does not have the facilities for children that the Philippion has and is usually very quiet, with fine views toward Thessaloniki and Mount Olympus. The restaurant is well respected.

Finally, if you are just passing through and changing planes at the Thessaloniki airport, try the **Hyatt Regency Casino Thessaloniki** (© 2310/401-234). It's near the airport, about 13km (8 miles) from Thessaloniki itself, and has a large casino, pools, tennis courts, spas, restaurants—everything, in short, to pass the time between flights.

The Philippion's doubles begin at 160€ ($208); the Panorama's double rooms begin at 135€ ($176); the Hyatt Regency's doubles begin at 200€ ($260).

WHERE TO DINE

Most restaurants and tavernas offer cuisine of a distinctly Thessalonian character (see "The Food of Thessaloniki," below), including game, while ouzeries specialize almost exclusively in *mezedes.* The restaurants and tavernas usually have an excellent selection of *mezedes* as well (you may be tempted to make a meal of starters alone), while some ouzeries might offer more substantial main courses. Sadly, the increased pollution in the bay has reached a point that makes us no longer recommend the fish tavernas on the outskirts of town. If you insist on fish, try the **Miami** (© 2310/447-996) or **Porto Marina** (© 2310/451-333); both serve fresh fish that is not from the bay, both are quite expensive, and both are in the suburb of Nea Krini, a 20-minute taxi ride from the center of town.

Even in the most expensive establishments, the dress code is casual for men; ties and jackets are rare. Women, on the other hand, are resolutely chic, in (very) little black dresses or more conservative trouser suits, but always with elegant handbags and shoes. Make reservations, but the only way to guarantee a table is to arrive before most Greeks come out to dine. If you don't want to risk waiting, try to arrive for lunch before 1pm and for dinner no later than 8:30pm.

Note: Most Thessaloniki restaurants do not accept credit cards.

RESTAURANTS & TAVERNAS
Expensive/Moderate
Draft GREEK/INTERNATIONAL ⊛ Draft is yet another Ladadika spot capitalizing on the seemingly endless local love of beer and *mezedes.* After all, what could be more pleasant than to sit in the garden nibbling on salmon rolls with caviar, vegetable dips and fritters, and shrimp in hot sauce? Come to think of it, I've never ordered an

The Food of Thessaloniki

It's a vexing question: To what extent has Thessaloniki's cuisine been influenced by Turkish cuisine? Observe that the use of spices, the delicate hand with fish, the wide variety of vegetable dishes, and the extravagantly rich pastries so popular in Thessaloniki are not unknown in Turkey. As any Greek will tell you, this is because the Turks, during their long occupation of Greece, absorbed—stole, actually—the secrets of Greek cuisine. Some might argue that when the Turks withdrew from Greece, they took many of those secrets with them. Others would simply say that in some parts of Greece—such as Thessaloniki—a love of cuisine and a devotion to spices lives on.

In fact, it's the spices that set Thessaloniki's cuisine apart from that of the rest of Greece. Take the peppers. The most famous Macedonian peppers are the red *florines*, originally grown in the town of Florina, but now raised throughout Macedonia. These can be sweet or so hot that they lift off the top of your head. We like both varieties, but we'd be a lot more relaxed when taking that first bite if we knew whether any individual *florina* were going to be sweet or pyrotechnic.

In addition to the *florines*, there are some *really* hot peppers traditionally grown in the Macedonian town of Piperia (the Greek word for "pepper"). These peppers are dried, then flaked, and the result, called *boukovo*, is sprinkled liberally into just about everything. *Tip:* In some Thessaloniki restaurants, in addition to the salt and black pepper on your table, you'll find another shaker, of red pepper. Treat it with respect.

entree here, but choose instead to make very tasty meals of *mezedes*. A wide variety of ouzo and wine is available.

3 Lycourgous, Ladadika. ✆ **2310/555-518.** www.draft.gr. Main courses 10€–18€ ($13–$23). DC, V. Mon–Sat 9pm–1am.

Kioupia ⟡ GREEK   This taverna with brick walls and wood floor in the old warehouse district has excellent *stifada* (stews), *keftadakia* (meatballs), and spicy *gardoubitsa* (liver and garlic). Crisp layers of filo (pastry) wrap a number of ingredients that include eggplant, zucchini, lamb with cheese, and minced beef with cheese. Dessert brings a range of Greek and Turkish sweets; the house retsina is excellent; and the wine list is extensive. The same management runs the nearby **Amorgos,** 4 Panaiou and Doxis, Ladadika (✆ **2310/557-161**), which specializes in fresh fish.

3–5 Morihovou Sq., Ladadika. ✆ **2310/553-239.** Fax 2310/553-579. www.kioupia.gr. Reservations recommended after 9pm. Main courses 12€–15€ ($16–$20). AE, MC, V. Mon–Sat 1pm–1am.

Krikelas ⟡⟡ GREEK   In 1999, Krikelas, a Thessaloniki institution since the 1940s, opened a branch in the Ladadika district, just across from the Mediterranean Palace Hotel. For visitors, the new Krikelas is conveniently located, and the food is as good as ever. The specialties: a mouthwatering variety of *mezedes* and whatever game is in season (including quail, pheasant, rabbit, boar, and partridge). A regional specialty, *spetzofai*, combines seasonal vegetables with a pungent country sausage. For dessert, try the homemade halva with almonds. The wine list at both branches is serious, although you can get a perfectly fine bottle for around 12€ ($16).

6 Salaminos, Ladadika. ℡/fax **2310/501-600**. Also 32 Eth. Antistaseos. ℡ **2310/451-289**. Fax 2310/451-690. Reservations usually not accepted. Main courses 15€–20€ ($20–$26). No credit cards. Mon–Sat 11:30am–2am. Usually closed July–Aug (but the Ladadika branch may be open then).

Le Café ⭐ *Value* GREEK/CONTINENTAL   You can get a salad, spaghetti, a sandwich, or just a coffee at this cafe, which has a curved balcony and large windows on the ground floor. Some people show up to read their morning papers and are still here by midafternoon. This is a nice spot to sit, read, and people-watch.

12 Tsimiski (corner of Tsimiski and Venizelou). ℡ **2310/275-625**. Fax 2310/221-270. Main courses 8€–12€ ($10–$16). No credit cards. Mon–Sat about 9am–1am.

Tiffany's ⭐ GREEK/CONTINENTAL   This popular place, with wood paneling and pictures of Old Salonika on the walls, seats about 100 and attracts an interesting mix of people; regulars who drop in every night for a quick bite, and then the gaggles of 20-somethings who sit at the window tables and wait to be seen. We're in the distinct minority in that we find the two house specialties—*bifsteki* Tiffany's (steak stuffed with cheese and tomatoes) and *hanoym borek* (casserole of roasted chicken, ham, veal, and cheese)—both rather bland. On the other hand, we've had fun trying to figure out the principle behind the music here, which can alternate between Harry Belafonte and Greek golden oldies.

3 Iktinou (on the walkway between Tsimiski and the church of Ayia Sofia). ℡ **2310/274-022**. Reservations recommended after 10pm. Main courses 8€–20€ ($10–$26). No credit cards. Daily 11:30am–2am.

Wolves ⭐ GREEK   This warm, dark-wood, old-fashioned restaurant, established in 1977, has a cook reputed among locals to be one of the best in Thessaloniki when it comes to making delicacies out of such basic Greek fare as pastitsio and moussaka. Try the roasted red peppers from Florina as one of your starters. For the main course, sample the house moussaka, the oregano-flavored stewed pork or lamb, or the batter-fried codfish in garlic sauce—or take a look at the day's special on the kitchen's display counter.

6 Vas. Olgas (1 block in and 2 blocks east of the Makedonia Palace Hotel). ℡ **2310/812-855**. Main courses 8€–15€ ($10–$20). No credit cards. Mon–Sat 12:30pm–1am; Sun 12:30–5pm. Usually closed Dec 12–Mar 1 and Aug 5–15.

Zythos ⭐⭐ GREEK/CONTINENTAL   This was one of the first restaurants to open in the restored warehouse district, and it's still very popular with ladies who lunch, young lovers, harried businesspeople, and groups of golden youths. The decor is wood and brick, as you'd expect in a former warehouse, although the slim young waiters in their chic black slacks or skirts hardly suggest warehouse workers. We can vouch for the croquettes of vegetables, *saganaki* (fried cheese), and veggie pasta. Usually one of the two daily specials is a vegetarian choice. Reservations are a good idea on weekends. If you like Zythos, try its branch, **Dore Zythos**, 7 Tsirogianni (℡ **2310-279-010**), by the White Tower, which sometimes has live music.

5 Katouni, Ladadika. ℡ **2310/540-284**. Main courses 8€–18€ ($10–$23). No credit cards. Daily 11am–1am.

Inexpensive

Two local places for your consideration: **Tsarouhas,** 78 Olymbou, near Dikasterion Square, seems to be open at all hours (although it closes in July and Aug), and serves *patsatzidhika,* the tripe soup that's supposed to cure all that ails you. In the Upper City, head to **To Yedi,** 13 Ioannis Papareska (℡ **2310/246-495**), outside the gates of the Eptapirgiou prison, to sit under the trees, relax, and try the *keftedes* and other *mezedes*.

Kentrike Stoa ⭐ GREEK/CONTINENTAL   This snacks-and-drinks place in the Central Market is up a winding metal staircase from the market itself. The ceiling is covered with parachute cloth, jazz contends with shouts from the market below, and the languid 20-something crowd tolerates outsiders gracefully—and can be fun to watch as they vie to impress one another.

32 Vas. Hrakleiou. ⓒ **2310/278-242**. Snacks 3€–12€ ($3.90–$16). No credit cards. Mon–Sat noon–1am.

Loutros ⭐⭐ GREEK   For years, Loutros occupied part of an old Turkish bath; now it's in new quarters and still serves fried minnows (which you eat whole) and delicious mussels, as well as tasty *horta* (greens) and *florines* (spicy red peppers). The music here is usually very Levantine-sounding—which, in Greece, is a polite way of saying that it sounds absolutely Turkish.

5 M. Kountoura (opposite the Bezesten). ⓒ **2310/228-895**. Main courses 7€–12€ ($9.10–$16). MC, V. Mon–Sat 11am–midnight.

Thanasis (Myrobolos Smyrnis) ⭐⭐⭐ GREEK   For 47 years, Thessalonians have been beating a path to this small taverna that serves zesty home-style cooking—including stuffed squid and mussels (both fried or steamed). In fact, the first customer through the door in the new millennium was Greek Prime Minister Simitis. The sign over the door reads H MYPOBOLOS SMYRNH (Miraculous Smyrna), but everyone knows it equally well by the name of its marvelously genial owner, Thanasis. This place is always packed, with a seemingly endless number of workers, businesspeople, artists, prostitutes, actors, and other characters from the high and low walks of Thessaloniki. The potato salad, cheese croquettes, spicy peppers with cheese, squid stuffed with cheese and rice, grilled fish and meats, and excellent *bakaliaro* (batter-fried cod) are all wonderful, as is the mood in this tiny restaurant with photos and old prints on the walls. The music is usually very loud, but if I had to eat every meal at one place in Thessaloniki, this would be it.

Ermou and 32 Komninon (just inside Modiano Market). ⓒ **2310/274-170**. Fax 2310/347-062. Reservations necessary after 10pm. Main courses 8€–12€ ($10–$16). No credit cards. Mon–Sat about 8am–3am.

OUZERIES

Although ouzeries specialize in ouzo and the *mezedes* that go with them, you need not drink ouzo, or any kind of alcoholic beverage, to enjoy the marvelous variety of foods they offer: octopus, meatballs, shrimp, squid, taramosalata (fish roe puréed with oil and bread), tzatziki (cucumber, yogurt, and garlic), *melitzanosalata* (eggplant purée), cheeses, and salads of potatoes, beets, or beans. Go with your waiter to look at the offerings and point to what you want. The price we give is for a selection of three or more *mezedes;* you can eat cheaply at these places, or run up an impressive tab, depending on how many snacks and ouzos you want to try.

Aproopto Light ⭐ GREEK   Highly popular with professionals of the nearby State Theatre and other artistic types, this place serves excellent *mezedes* as well as mussels with spinach, leeks a la Parisienne, and *saganaki* (fried cheese). Its relatively small, convivial, well-decorated sidewalk and interior dining areas are usually packed.

6 Zevksidos (a pedestrian walkway off the eastern end of the church of Ayia Sofia). ⓒ **2310/241-141**. 10€–15€ ($13–$20) for a variety of *mezedes*. No credit cards. Daily noon–1:30am.

Aristotelous ★★★ GREEK   After all these years, Aristotelous is still packed during the peak lunch and dinner hours, and remains popular with writers, artists, and everyone else in the know, so you should come either early or late, or you'll end up waiting at least 20 minutes. Indoor and outdoor seating areas between high-rise office buildings contribute to the crush and, somehow, the charm. You can and should linger for hours, which is why it's often so hard to get a table. The variety of *mezedes* is sumptuous. Try the fried zucchini and eggplant, the *ktipiti* (feta cheese mashed with hot peppers and olive oil) and, for something more substantial, the *soupia* (stuffed cuttlefish). Also delicious is homemade halva for dessert.

8 Aristotelous (in a cul-de-sac between office buildings on the east side of Aristotelous, just north of Tsimiski). ⓒ **2310/230-762**. Reservations not accepted. 15€–30€ ($20–$39) for a variety of *mezedes*. No credit cards. Mon–Sat 10am–2am; Sun 11am–6pm.

Ouzerie Melathron ★ GREEK   This is one of a chain of ouzo and *mezedes* places, most of which are in northern Greece. You'll find a wide choice of ouzos and *mezedes*, including the popular *saganaki* (fried cheese), *keftedes* (meatballs), grilled hot or cold octopus, sprats, and local olives.

23 Eleftherious Venizelou and Ermou. ⓒ **2310/220-043**. 15€–30€ ($20–$39) for a variety of *mezedes*. No credit cards. Usually closed July–Aug.

Tsinari's ★ GREEK   A very welcome place to plop down for a rest from sightseeing in the Upper City (Ano Polis), this ouzeri started life as a Turkish coffeehouse, and may be the only such spot to have survived the great fire of 1917. There's a wide variety of *mezedes* and, in my experience, somewhat capricious hours.

72 Papadopoulou. ⓒ **2310/284-028**. 10€–20€ ($13–$26) for a variety of *mezedes*. No credit cards.

THESSALONIKI AFTER DARK

Thessaloniki does not really awaken until after dark, and when it does, it seems at times as if the entire populace has come out to amuse itself. In addition to the cultural festivals held in the fall, there are lots of theater and pop and classical concerts year-round. Though many publications list events, and posters splattered everywhere announce them, they will all be Greek to you. Ask for information at your hotel, or stop by the office of the **Greek National Tourism Organization (EOT),** 8 Aristotelous Sq. (ⓒ **2310/271-888** or 2310/222-935).

Meanwhile, the city seems festooned with enough bars and clubs to serve a population twice its size, yet all of them are crowded to the bursting point—and more open every year. For some of the liveliest nightlife in town, try one of the cafes in the waterfront Ladidika district, or along the harbor on Nikis Street, or head inland to sample the cafes on pedestrianized Zefxidos and Iktinos streets. In the heat of summer, many cafes move to beach locations in the eastern suburbs, but you'll still find plenty of action in town including the Regency Casino Thessaloniki (www.thessaloniki.recency. hyatt.com), by Thessaloniki International Airport.

The casino is popular year-round, mostly with foreigners, and often draws charter flights filled with eastern European tourists. It may be harsh to say, but this casino will appeal most to sociologists interested in the gambling customs and costumes of tour groups, but this is certainly not the place to go for the kind of gambling glitz and glamour of Vegas or Reno. It's open 24 hours, and the 20€ ($26) entrance fee is often waived between 8am and 6pm.

Only in Thessaloniki

Taking what the Greeks call a *volta* (stroll) along the seaside promenade, particularly at sunset or under a full moon, is one of the greatest pleasures of being in Thessaloniki. At the **White Tower,** look for the occasional peanut vendors and the city's only horse-drawn carriage, which you can rent for a ride.

You might also decide to take an hour (or longer) to **cruise** the harbor on one of the small boats that dock just east of the tower. Posted signs advertise cruises of different lengths and prices.

THE PERFORMING ARTS

Kratiko Theatro (State Theatre of Northern Greece) has two venues. In winter, it stages plays in the **Royal State Theatre,** next to the White Tower (✆ **2310/860-966**); in summer, it stages plays at **Theatro Dasous (Forest Theatre),** an open-air amphitheater in the forested hilltop area east of the Upper City (✆ **2310/245-307**). The company presents ancient and modern Greek plays, as well as Greek translations of foreign plays by a range of authors as varied as Christopher Marlowe and Arthur Miller.

In summer, the Forest Theatre, which has a marvelous view of the city, also hosts lively, well-attended concerts by popular Greek singers and composers, as well as performances by visiting ballet companies.

Thessaloniki's splendid **Megaron Mousikis (Concert Hall),** 25 Martiou and Paralia (✆ **2310/895-800**), opened in 2000. Check with your hotel concierge or at the hall for a concert schedule. **Aristotle University Concert Hall** also hosts concerts (it's on Nea Egnatia, opposite the northern entrance of the International Trade Fairgrounds) September through May (✆ **2310/283-343**).

FESTIVALS

DEMETRIA FESTIVAL   In honor of the patron saint of Thessaloniki, St. Dimitrios, whose name day is October 26, this prestigious cultural festival runs every October and includes the Greek Film Festival as well as many theatrical and musical events, all of them performed by major and minor artists from around the country.

THE FEAST OF SAINTS CONSTANTINE & ELENI (MAY 21)   On or around the feast of the first Christian emperor and his mother, villagers in **Ayia Eleni** (80km/50 miles northeast of Thessaloniki) and at **Langadas** (12km/7 miles northeast of Thessaloniki) engage in *pirovassia* (fire dancing). Crowds come from all over Macedonia to see the faithful dance over a bed of hot coals. When they're done, they feast on the roasted black bull sacrificed earlier in the day. In case you're wondering—yes, much of what's done here preserves pre-Christian rites.

INTERNATIONAL TRADE FAIR FESTIVAL   This takes place every year during the first 2 weeks in September and draws businesspeople from around the world. The international fairgrounds have lots of exhibits, so hotel rooms are very hard to find.

THE BAR, CLUB & MUSIC SCENE

In July and August, many of Thessaloniki's best bars and clubs shut down. Some immediately reopen branches along a section of the road leading east along the coast, about a mile before the airport. This, plus the fact that new or newly decorated and renamed venues are constantly opening while others go out of fashion and close, makes it virtually impossible to recommend any with certainty. In town, in the summer of 2007, Greek friends of mine were heading to bars like **Urban** and the improbably named **Pasta Flora Darling!** on Zefxidos Street, but they were pretty sure they'll be looking for new spots next summer. On Kolokotroni Street, by the State Museum of Contemporary Art, the **Kitchen Bar** in yet another restored warehouse is one place where you can begin, or end, your revels with breakfast.

One place, however, we can recommend without hesitation. Not only is it a permanent fixture of Thessaloniki nightlife year-round, but it incorporates by far the best of the bar, music, and club scenes in the city.

Milos 🏛🏛🏛 Within the grounds of an old, wonderfully restored flour-mill complex, the Milos (*mee*-los) complex contains a club for blues, folk, jazz, and pop groups; a nightclub featuring Greek singers and comedians; a bar/disco; an outdoor concert stage and movie theater; several exhibition rooms and art galleries; a cafe; and an ouzeri that serves more than 30 kinds of *mezedes*. Almost as soon as it opened in 1990, Milos became one of the top musical venues in the country. Each summer, performers from around the world (and from throughout Greece) appear here and perform everything from golden oldies to neo-grunge. If you want to be sure of a seat, it's a good idea to arrive before the clubs open at 10pm. The ouzeri, cafe, and galleries open from about 11am on. Go west on Tsimiski to its end and turn left onto 28 Octobriou. At the first traffic light, turn right onto Andreadou Yioryiou and continue to the end of the street. This is quite a hike from the center, and you may want to take a cab. 56 Andreadou Yioryiou. © **2310/551-838** or 2310/525-968. www.mylos.gr. Cover varies: usually no more than 30€ ($39); drinks around 10€ ($13).

2 In the Footsteps of Philip of Macedon & Alexander the Great 🏛🏛

Every year, more and more people head north to Macedonia to see the cluster of ancient sites associated with **Philip II of Macedon** and his famous son, **Alexander the Great;** these include **Pella, Vergina,** and **Dion.** Many of these visitors are Greeks whose interest in things Macedonian intensified in 1991 when, just across the border, the former Yugoslavian district of Macedonia proclaimed itself a republic. How dare these non-Greeks take the name of Macedonia, Greeks asked—forgetting that their own ancestors had not considered Philip of Macedon a Greek! Most of all, Greeks were furious that Philip's best-known royal symbol—a star with 16 rays—appeared on the new Macedonia's flag. Throughout Greece, debates raged over whether this new self-styled Macedonia had imperialistic aims. For once, Greece's long-standing enmity with Turkey was ignored, as Greeks painted MACEDONIA IS GREECE on almost every road and wall in the country. Things calmed down after the new Republic of Macedonia changed its flag, but many Greeks are still rediscovering their ancestral links with Philip, the northern king who conquered Greece in 338 B.C.

The renewed interest in Philip (382–336 B.C.), Alexander (356–323 B.C.), and Macedonia itself has led the Greek Archaeological Service to redouble its efforts to excavate the Macedonian royal sites and build site museums. And that, of course, means that there's much more to see aboveground than there was even a few years ago.

ESSENTIALS

GETTING THERE   The only enjoyable and efficient ways to see the places where Philip of Macedon and Alexander the Great lived and reigned are by car or with a tour. (*Tip:* Prices on rental cars from international agencies are lower when the car is booked in advance from outside Greece.) **Budget Rent-A-Car** has offices at the airport (℗ **2310/471-491**) and in the city at 15 Angelaki (℗ **2310/274-272** or 2310/229-519), opposite the International Fairgrounds. Other rental offices are **Avis,** 3 Leoforos Nikis (℗ **2310/227-126** or 2310/683-300), at the western end of the harbor, opposite the docks; **Europcar,** 5 Papandreou (℗ **2310/836-333**); and **Hertz,** 4 El. Venizelou (℗ **2310/224-906**), on Eleftherias Square.

Several Athens-based companies, such as **CHAT** and **American Express,** offer tours of Central and Northern Greece that take in the most important Macedonian sites. **Zorpidis Travel**, 4 Salaminios (℗ **2310/244-400**) is a reputable Thessaloniki company offering tours of the Philip and Alexander sites. A day trip to Pella, Edessa, Veria, and Vergina, or to Philippa, Kavala, and Amphipolis, costs from 100€ ($130). It is vital to make an advance reservation. Avoid visiting on a summer weekend, when crowds of Greeks flock to these sites.

By Bus   If you try to visit these sites by local bus, you may feel that it takes you longer to see them than it took Alexander to conquer the world. Still, if you have lots of time and love buses, you can visit the following sites by bus from Thessaloniki. For **Pella,** there are sometimes direct buses; failing that, take a bus to Edessa and ask to be let off at Pella. For **Vergina**, take a bus to Veria, and then a local bus to the site of Vergina. To travel from Pella to Vergina, take the Thessaloniki bus from Pella to Halkidona, where you can get a bus to Veria. This may involve a substantial wait. For **Dion,** take a bus to Katerini and then a local bus to Dion. For up-to-date information on bus schedules and departure points, check with the **Greek National Tourism Organization** in Thessaloniki (℗ **2310/2721-100**); the bus information line (℗ **2310/512-122**) is unlikely to have English-speaking staff. If you read Greek, the Thessaloniki daily newspaper *Macedonia* also lists bus schedules.

VISITOR INFORMATION   If you stop in Athens or Thessaloniki before visiting these sites, drop by the **Greek National Tourism Organization (EOT)** in Athens at 7 Tsohas (℗ **210/870-7000;** www.gnto.gr), or in Thessaloniki at 133 Tsimiski (℗ **2310/271-888**), and get a copy of the brochure *Greece/Macedonia* as well as any other brochures for individual sites. At each site, ask whether a free Culture Ministry brochure is available.

PELLA 🅖

Pella, once the capital of the Macedonian kingdom and the birthplace of Philip II of Macedon in 382 B.C. and his famous son, Alexander the Great, in 356 B.C., is easy to spot. The **archaeological site** and **museum** are right beside the highway (a 40km/24-mile drive west of Thessaloniki on the E86 Hwy. to Edessa).

In antiquity, a navigable inlet connected Pella to the broad Thermaic Gulf that borders Thessaloniki. Over the centuries, the inlet silted up, leaving Pella landlocked, but in Philip and Alexander's day, ships would have sailed here and docked in what is now a dusty plain. The city itself is thought to have covered at least 13 sq. km (5 sq. miles), of which only a fraction has been excavated.

There's more than enough of Pella aboveground to give you an idea of this stylish city, with its large, square agora (market and civic center) bordered by colonnaded stoas and flanked by streets lined with shrines, sanctuaries, temples, and private homes. The lovely frescoes that once adorned house walls are gone, but a number of handsome **pebble mosaic floors** remain, both on the site and in the museum. These gaily painted houses with sheltered inner courtyards must have been exceptionally pleasant. Long ago, families might have passed an evening discussing the Athenian playwright Euripides's *The Bacchae,* which had its premiere here around 408 B.C. in the as-yet-undiscovered theater.

Unfortunately, the dwelling you'd probably most like to see—the **palace** where both Philip and his son Alexander were born—is not open to the public. Not to worry: You can drive or walk to the hilltop north of the site and peer over the wire fence to get an idea of how large this royal home was. In fact, the palace covered 60,000 sq. m (645,835 sq. ft.). Somewhere in this vast complex, Aristotle tutored the young Alexander. The view from the hill is still tremendous, but it must have been truly breathtaking in antiquity, when the palace overlooked both the plain and the channel down which ships sailed, bringing supplies from around the Mediterranean.

Pella's small **museum** is superb, especially the glorious pebble mosaics found in the excavated 4th-century-B.C. homes. The two best-known mosaics show a lion hunt and the god of wine, Dionysos, riding a leopard. The lion hunt is especially tantalizing. It's a powerful depiction of a lion and two youths—one of whom may be Alexander. Some scholars suggest that the mosaic records an incident when the young Alexander was saved by a friend from a lunging lion. Others suspect that this is merely a genre scene of a hunt. You can compare the marble bust of Alexander in the museum with the youth under attack in the lion hunt and decide for yourself. Be sure to see whether the gold and jewelry from 25 6th-century-B.C. tombs discovered here in 2005 is on view yet. Allow at least 2 hours to visit the site and museum.

ⓒ 23820/31-160 or 23820/31-278. Combined museum and site admission 6€ ($7.80). Mon noon–7pm; Tues–Sun 8am–7pm; winter until 3pm.

WHERE TO STAY & DINE

After you visit the site, you may want to take in **Edessa,** 45km (27 miles) west of Pella, a scenic cliff-top town with bubbling waterfalls and pleasant, small cafes and restaurants. We like **Paeti** on 18 Oktobriou, which serves hearty meals that include game in season. The real point of a meal in Edessa is to enjoy the rushing waterfall. Note that it will be crowded on summer weekends, when many Thessalonians come here to escape the summer heat.

If it's the weekend or if you're rushed after visiting Pella, you can grab a bite at one of the small roadside restaurants by the fountain beside the (signposted) remains of BATHS OF ALEXANDER, a Hellenistic fountain incorporated into a Roman bath about a kilometer from Pella on the Edessa road.

As far as overnighting here, keep in mind that Edessa is a popular year-round destination for Thessalonians. It has only about 125 hotel rooms, and on weekends you will have trouble finding a vacancy. The nicest place in town is the eight-unit **Varosi** (*ⓒ* **23810/21-865;** www.varosi.gr), in a carefully restored family-operated 18th-century stone town house (ask for directions locally); doubles are 60€ to 75€ ($78–$98). The 44-unit **Katarraktes,** 18 Karanou, Edessa (*ⓒ* **23810/22-300**), with rooms from 55€ to 75€ ($72–$98) is perfectly fine.

History 101: Philip & Alexander

When Philip was born in 382 B.C., most Greeks thought of Macedonians—if they thought of them at all—as one of the rude northern tribes of barbarians who lived in the back of beyond. Macedonians, after all, were not even allowed to participate in the Panhellenic Games at Delphi. Clearly, this irritated Philip. By 346 B.C., after conquering a number of Athenian colonies and allied cities, Philip had won a place on Delphi's governing board. A few years later, in 338 B.C., despite Demosthenes's best oratorical efforts to alert the Athenians to Philip's intentions, the Macedonian king had conquered all of Greece. Two years later, Philip was dead, cut down as he strolled to see a performance in the theater at his capital city of Vergina. Some said that his young son Alexander was behind the assassination, while others wondered how the unproven youth could rule Macedonia, let alone Greece.

No one, except perhaps Alexander himself, could have imagined that by the time he died at 33, he would have conquered much of the known world as far east as India. Alexander's early death makes it impossible to know what he would have done with the rest of his life, once he had no new worlds to conquer. Some scholars think that Alexander was a visionary bent not only on conquering but also on uniting the world into a "brotherhood of man." This, they suggest, is why Alexander contracted so many foreign marriages and accepted conquered princes into his retinue. Other scholars, more cynical, think that Alexander's marriages and his use of former enemies were simply shrewd political moves. The truth probably lies between the two theories.

In any event, after Alexander's death, his former comrades turned on one another and destroyed his empire. Within a few generations, Macedon was once more a northern kingdom in the back of beyond, living on memories of its brief period of international importance.

VERGINA & ENVIRONS: THE TOMBS AT LEUKADIA, THE TOWN OF VERIA & NEARBY VINEYARDS ✸✸✸

Vergina is 20km (12 miles) south of Pella and 62km (38 miles) west of Thessaloniki, just outside the hamlet of Palatitsa. It's well signposted off the main road and poorly signposted from Thessaloniki. If you're short on time, head for the museum. If not, explore the **Vergina site (Palace of Palatitsia)** and the **Royal Tombs Museum** (✆ **23310/92-347**). Combined museum and site admission is 8€ ($10). Summer hours for both are Monday from noon to 7pm and Tuesday through Sunday from 8:30am to 7pm; in the off season, the site and museum close at 5pm. Allow at least 3 hours to visit both.

Vergina (known as Aigai in ancient times) is the most important of the royal Macedonian sites. Philip lived here when not at Pella and in 336 B.C. died here. Preliminary excavations suggest that the palace was enormous, with an inner courtyard about 14 sq. m (147 sq. ft.). Around the courtyard ran a Doric colonnade; the bases of some of its 60 columns are still in place and give you a sense of the courtyard's size. The

History 101: Philip's Tomb

Vergina's first excavator, the French archaeologist Leon Heuzey, prophesied in 1876 that when Vergina was fully excavated, "the importance of its ruins for Macedonia will be comparable to Pompeii." The Greek Archaeological Service began to work here in the 1930s and uncovered several tombs that looked like small temples. For years, the excavators nibbled away at the largest burial mound of all, the **Great Tumulus,** measuring 110m (361 ft.) across and 12m (39 ft.) high, containing a number of burials. One tomb they found was almost totally destroyed, another well-preserved but robbed. Still, head excavator Manolis Andronikos remained convinced that he was excavating ancient Aigai, Philip's capital city, and might yet find Philip's own tomb.

Finally, in 1977—on the last day of the excavation season—Andronikos and his workers opened the massive marble gates of the final remaining tomb. As Andronikos later wrote in *Vergina: The Royal Tombs:*

> *We saw a sight which it was not possible for me to have imagined, because until then such an ossuary (a container for bones) had never been found—all-gold—with an impressive relief star on its lid. We lifted it from the sarcophagus, placed it on the floor, and opened it. Our eyes nearly popped out of our sockets and our breathing stopped; there unmistakably were charred bones placed in a carefully formed pile and still retaining the color of the purple cloth in which they had once been wrapped. If those were royal remains, then, had I held the bones of Philip in my hands?*

Andronikos—and virtually all of Greece—answered his question with a resounding "Yes," in large part because of the other objects found in the tomb. The gold wreaths, Andronikos felt, were too fine to belong to anyone but a king. And surely the little ivory portrait heads were the spitting images of Philip and Alexander themselves. And, most persuasive of all, what about the unequally sized bronze greaves (shin guards) found in the tomb? Philip was known to have legs of different length, due to an early injury.

It is difficult to overestimate the Philip-fever that swept through Greece when Andronikos announced that he had found Philip's tomb and identified Vergina as Ancient Aigai, Philip's capital city. Although some spoilsport scholars have questioned whether this is, in fact, Philip's tomb, those scholars are not Greek. Greeks regard with horror any suggestion that this splendid tomb may have belonged to Arrhidaeos, the son of Philip known only for his lack of distinction.

palace also had a long, airy, colonnaded veranda running the length of its north side, overlooking the theater. It's quite possible that the royal family watched spectacles in the theater from the comfort of the palace veranda.

Unfortunately for Philip, that's not what he did on the fatal day in 336 B.C. when he was assassinated en route from the palace to take in a performance at the theater. Some scholars surmise that Alexander was behind the assassination. Others said that the young prince was not noticeably grief-stricken by his father's death, and left it at that. You can sit in the **theater**, the only really impressive remains, and contemplate the moment when Philip realized that he was about to be struck down.

As you drive from the site to the Royal Tombs Museum, notice the hundreds of low mounds on the gentle hills of the Macedonian plain. Some of the more than 300 **burial mounds** found here date from as long ago as the Iron Age, although many are from the time of Philip himself. Robbers looted most of these graves in antiquity. Fortunately—and almost miraculously—the tomb identified as Philip's lay undisturbed for almost 2,000 years. How it was found is one of the great stories of archaeology, deserving a place beside accounts of how Schliemann found Troy and excavated the "Tomb of Agamemnon" at Mycenae.

The arched roof of the **Royal Tombs Museum** re-creates a sense of the Great Tumulus itself, as does the passageway leading into the tomb area. A helpful video (Greek and English) is usually shown throughout the day. Each of the tombs is protected by a glass wall, but seeing the tombs this way is the next-best thing to standing inside them. Give your eyes time to get accustomed to the darkness, then enjoy the vibrant decorative paintings on the sculptured facades of the templelike tombs and the spectacular gold objects found in the frescoed chambers. The monumental paintings here are among only a handful to have survived from antiquity.

Most Greek (and fewer non-Greek) archaeologists think that the gold *larnax* (box) with the 16-pointed star held the bones of Philip II of Macedon, that the small ivory head is his portrait, and that the bronze greaves were part of his armor. The 4th-century bronze crater from Derveni, with wild scenes of a Dionysiac revel, is less controversial, and absolutely superb. The Hellenistic Greeks did not go in for understatement!

VERIA (VEROIA) & ITS BYZANTINE, JEWISH & TURKISH REMAINS 𝄞

The hill town of Veria (Veroia), rich in medieval remains, is 15km (9 miles) northwest of Vergina. The **Municipal Culture Office** (𝄯 23110/27-914), at the corner of Pavlou Mela and Bizantiou in the center of town, has helpful maps and brochures. Veria, in the throes of development, still has a number of old streets, wood houses with overhanging bay windows, more than 50 small Byzantine churches (usually locked), a 15th-century cathedral, and a good number of buildings from the Ottoman period, including a former mosque and *hamam* (bath). You can stop here for a quick coffee and get a sense of the town, or spend a pleasant day here. If you're here in winter, you'll encounter skiers who come to the Veria Ski Center on Mt. Vermion at Souli (𝄯 **23310/49-226;** www.seli-ski.gr).

At the corner of Anixeos and Pasteur, the handsome 1930s Vlachoyiannis town house displays the collection of the restored Museum of Modern History and Art; it also has a cafe. If you combine visits to the museum exhibits with visits to a cluster of nearby 20th-century houses, "eclectic" in style, you'll get a sense of how people in Veria lived in the first half of the 20th century. Nearby, the new **Byzantine Museum** is in the restored Markos mill (© 23310/25-847). Admission is 2€ ($2.60); hours are Tuesday to Sunday 8:30am to 3pm (closed Mon). Only the truly devoted will wish to visit the small **Archaeological Museum,** 47 Anoixeos (© 23310/24-972), which features finds from local sites. Admission is 2€ ($2.60); hours are Tuesday through Sunday from 8:30am to 3pm. Don't feel bad if it's closed; you'll have much more fun wandering the streets of this old town, with its considerable Turkish remains and old Jewish quarter; the synagogue, not easy to find, is in the Barbouta district.

THE NAOUSSA VINEYARDS

About halfway between Veria and Edessa, on the slopes of Mount Vermion, you'll see roadside signs for several vineyards open to the public. At Naoussa, a region famous for its wine, **Stenimachos Winery,** run by the well-known Boutari vintners, offers tours (sometimes in English) of the winery most work days. For information, call © 23320/41-666 or go to www.boutari.gr. You can also check with the **GNTO** in Thessaloniki (© 2310/271-888).

WHERE TO STAY & DINE FOR VERGINA AND VERIA

The 10-unit **Dimitra** (© 23310/92-900) and the 10-unit **Vergina Pension** (© 23310/92-510), both near the Vergina site, are both reasonably priced small family-run hotels; the Dimitra has studios with full kitchenettes. Neither takes credit cards; doubles from 50€ ($65) at the Vergina, from 65€ ($85) at the Dimitra. Of the local restaurants, the **Filippion** (also spelled **Philippion**), with cafeteria-style lunch service, is reliable.

In Veria, the 37-unit **Hotel Makedonia,** 50 Kontogeorgaki (©/fax **23310/66-902** or 23310/66-946), is the best hotel in town, with a quiet location. It has the bland ambience of a businessperson's, rather than a traveler's, hotel. Rooms come with air-conditioning and TVs. The new **Veria,** km 6.5 on the Veria-Naousa Highway (© **23310/93-112**), gets a fair amount of tour business. Although staying here makes exploring Veria itself a mini-excursion, you may find the pool so welcoming that you never leave. The rooms are standard Greek-hotel quality, but most have pleasant balconies as well as air-conditioning and TVs. Also, the hotel is set back from the highway just enough to make traffic noise manageable. Both the Makedonia and the Veria usually offer doubles from 60€ to 100€ ($78–$130). Two tavernas, **Nikos** and **Kostalar,** are usually excellent; ask for directions in Veria, as the streets are not signposted.

DION 🏛🏛

The **Dion Archaeological Site and Museum** (© 23510/53-206) has an idyllic site just beyond the Vale of Tempe, in the foothills of Mount Olympus. The site is outside the village of Dio, about 8km (5 miles) west of the DION sign on the E75, the main Athens-Thessaloniki highway (and 78km/48 miles south of Thessaloniki). **Warning:** This is a dangerous turn off the highway; reentry is also difficult. Combined admission to the site and museum is 6€ ($7.80). Hours are Monday from 10:30am to 7pm and Tuesday through Sunday from 8:30am to 7pm; both close at 3pm in the off season. Allow at least 2 hours for your visit.

This is an unusually green spot, with pine groves and farm fields watered by springs fed by the melting snow that clings to Olympus's peaks year-round. If you can, bring a picnic; after you visit the excavations and museum, linger a while at the picnic tables at the site.

Excavation here continues, unearthing more and more of ancient Dion. New pathways have been constructed to help visitors tour the site, and helpful signs have gone up. In mid-August, the **Olympos Festival** (© **23510/76-401**) presents concerts at the ancient site.

According to legend, Dion was founded as a religious sanctuary back in the mists of time, but its constant water supply led both Philip and Alexander to change the character of the sacred site and establish military training camps here. Philip bivouacked at Dion before he marched south to conquer Greece, while Alexander drilled his men here before heading east to conquer Asia.

According to a story preserved by the 2nd-century-A.D. biographer Plutarch, it was at Dion that Alexander, then only 8 years old, first saw Bucephalos, the handsome black stallion soon to be his favorite mount. Philip bought the horse but found that neither he nor any of his men could ride it. Alexander asked his father if he could have a go at taming the creature. Muttering that if *he* could not tame the horse, an 8-year-old hardly could, Philip nonetheless agreed to give Alexander a chance. Immediately, Alexander turned Bucephalos so that he could not see his shadow, leapt up, and galloped away. When the young prince returned from his ride, Philip said, "My son, look for a kingdom equal to you. Macedonia is too small."

Although Dion—which sits by a narrow pass between Thessaly and Macedonia—was an important military camp first for the Macedonians and then for the Romans, it is much more than the Fort Bragg of antiquity. The Romans adorned Dion with a **theater** (bigger and better than the Hellenistic one, as was the Roman habit) and built **sanctuaries** to the healing god Asclepius, the nurturing goddess Demeter, and the popular Egyptian goddess Isis. In addition, of course, the Romans built **baths**—and baths being large structures, a good deal remains for you to explore. Copies of statues found in the sanctuaries have been erected at the site, while the originals are tucked away safely in the museum.

There's a great deal to see at Dion, but I have to confess that some of my happiest visits have been spent picnicking under the shade trees—especially in spring, when the Greek wildflowers more than live up to their reputation. From here, you can make excursions onto the site, following the course of a stoa, admiring the statue of Isis seemingly admiring her reflection in a pool, and imagining the day that Alexander, all of 22 years old, mounted Bucephalos and set off to conquer the world.

The Dion **museum** is a heartening example of a well-funded and well-cared-for provincial museum. An English-language video and the English-language museum labels help foreign visitors understand the importance of what they are seeing, while models of the ancient site make the Dion of Philip and Alexander easy to visualize. Exhibits include statues of the children of Asclepius (lined up as though posing for a family photo), grave monuments, votive offerings, mosaics and, best of all, a wonderful copper water organ probably made in the 2nd century A.D.; today it would be the hit of any music hall.

WHERE TO STAY & DINE

Choose from several cafes and restaurants in the village near the Hotel Dion and also along the road that bisects the site and museum. An archaeologist friend reports eating well at the **Dionysos,** which serves good roast goat, *loukanika* (sausages), and the usual chops and salads. Expect to pay about 12€ ($16) for lunch or dinner unless you go overboard on the roast goat, which is priced by the kilo and will raise your tab a few more euros. It's signposted on the main road that bisects the site.

Dion Palace Resort Hotel (★ *(Kids* This enormous beachfront resort occupies "44 acres next by the wave," as its website proclaims. The entire complex offers rooms in the hotel itself and in cabana/villas. The villas (eight with private pool) are more expensive than the in-hotel accommodations. With tennis, riding, sailing, and more, the Dion Palace is very popular with Greek and German families. Others may prefer the little Hotel Dion near the site, described below.

Litochoro Beach, Gritsa, 60200 Macedonia. ℂ 03520/61-431. www.dionpalace.com. 182 units. 120€–200€ ($156–$260) double. Compulsory breakfast 10€ ($13). AE, MC, V. Sometimes closed in winter. **Amenities:** Restaurant; 2 bars; 2 pools (fresh- and saltwater); tennis; riding; sailing; concierge. *In room:* A/C, TV, minibar, hair dryer.

Hotel Dion (★ The rooms here are good-size, economically furnished, and pleasant; most have balconies. When I stayed here, the town was deliciously quiet all night—except for a few late-night motorcycles and some early-morning roosters. One problem: The owners are not always around, so if you stop here without a reservation, it may take a bit of time to find them.

Dion, 60200 Macedonia. ℂ 23510/53-682. 20 units. 70€ ($91) double. Rates include breakfast. MC, V. Considerable reductions possible off season. **Amenities:** Breakfast room/bar. *In room:* TV.

3 Mount Athos (The Holy Mountain) (★(★(★

130km (80 miles) SE of Thessaloniki

The most important thing to know about Mount Athos is that you can't just come here. And if you're a woman, you can't come here at all. In 1926, Athos was declared a Theocratic Republic. Although part of Greece, it is self-governing—hence, the need for an entry permit. Up-to-date information on permits should be available at two websites (www.macedonian-heritage.gr/Athos and www.ouranoupoli.com) and at the **Holy Executive of the Holy Mt. Athos Pilgrim's Bureau,** 14 Karamanli, Thessaloniki (ℂ **2310/861-611**). Recently, there have been mutterings that antidiscrimination regulations of the European Common Market may force Athos to open its doors to women; to avoid potential complications, However, Mount Athos has refused any Common Market funds for restoration of its monasteries and it is highly unlikely that the bureaucrats of the Common Market will prove a match for the monks of Athos and their centuries of tradition.

Ouranopolis is the jumping-off point for Mount Athos, but unfortunately, it is an increasingly unappealing little town filled with souvenir shops. However, the handsome tower immortalized in Joyce Nankivell Loch's *A Fringe of Blue* still stands. Joyce Loch and her husband, Sydney, both Quakers, lived in Ouranopolis on and off from the 1920s to the 1960s and worked with villagers and refugees from Asia Minor. For some years, the tower was both the Lochs' home and a weaving school; today it houses exhibits.

There is almost always at least one boat a day at 9:45am from Ouranopolis to Mount Athos. In summer, additional departures are often scheduled.

If you can't go to Athos itself from Ouranopolis, take one of the **excursion boats** that cruise around the peninsula (tickets cost about 20€/$26). The **Ouranopolis Port Authority** (ℂ **23770/71-248**) usually has information on the excursion boats. (When Prince Charles visited Athos in 2004, Camilla Parker-Bowles circled the Holy Mount on the Royal Yacht.) The views of the rugged, pine-clad mountain promontory are superb, and you'll be able to see a number of the monasteries, most of which

> **Tips Visiting Athos**
>
> If you visit Mount Athos, you will walk almost everywhere, and stay and eat at the monasteries you have come to visit, which certainly simplifies things. "Simple" is a key word here—both your accommodations and food (Athos is a vegetarian's paradise) will be very basic. Taste some of the wine made on Athos and sold throughout Greece; the Tsantali white (not all of which is made here, despite its labels) is particularly refreshing, while the Metochi Mylopotamou made at the Great Lavra Monastery is also well regarded. Keep in mind that although most monasteries will not accept direct payment in cash for food and lodgings, you can make a donation in the church.
>
> As always, when walking in Greece, keep in mind the danger of fires, and be sure to dispose of any matches or cigarettes with care.
>
> Also, do not show up at the monasteries in the afternoon, when the monks are taking their siestas.

were built between the 9th and 19th centuries. Most look like little villages from the outside, perched on astonishingly high and sturdy stone foundations and surrounded by massive walls. There are presently 20 functioning monasteries on Mount Athos, many visible from the sea.

The first, and still the most important, monastery, the **Great Lavra** or **Meyistis Lavras** ("Lavra" means a community of monks), was founded around 960, and others quickly followed. In 1060, an imperial decree barred "every woman, every child, eunuch, smooth faced person, and female animal" from Athos, which suggests that there had been incidents of inventive nonchastity over the years. In recent years, hens have been allowed onto Athos to produce eggs, and cats to catch vermin.

Today, there are 20 active monasteries, with at least that many again closed over the centuries. Solitary hermits still live on Athos, but most monks follow a communal rather than an isolated life. In fact, monastic life has had something of a revival; Father Gabriel, gardener at the Iviron Monastery, was quoted in the July 28, 1998, Athenian newspaper *Kathimerini* as saying, "More are interested in becoming monks than we are ready to accept." According to the same story, Father Gabriel has added to his gardening duties the preparation of a computer catalog of manuscripts and icons. When asked if this would take a very long time, he replied, "We've got all eternity."

THE MOST IMPORTANT MONASTERIES ON MOUNT ATHOS

THE GREAT LAVRA   The first (about A.D. 960) monastery founded on Athos and hence the foremost, the Great Lavra has the red-painted katholikon characteristic of Athos's monasteries. Its 15th-century frescoes, especially those showing exuberant singers and dancers in the Chapel of Koukouzelissa, are delightful. Try ⓒ **23370/23-758** to make a reservation to spend the night.

THE MONASTERY OF CHELANDARIOU   This monastery was founded in the 12th century by St. Sabbas of Serbia. Fortunately, Sabbas's father was the king of Serbia, which guaranteed a handsome endowment. Some scholars think that the lovely frescoes in the church here were done by the same painter who decorated the walls of Ayios Nikolaos Orfanos in Thessaloniki (p. 616). You can try to make a reservation here by calling ⓒ **23370/23-797.**

THE MONASTERY OF DIONISSIOU   This 14th-century monastery seems to grow right out of a rock above the sea. Its dizzily overhanging balconies are braced by precarious-looking wood supports. Favored by the emperor Alexios III Komnenos, Dionissiou has a superb collection of manuscripts, as well as an icon said to be the oldest on Athos. You can try to make a reservation by calling ℂ **23370/23-687** or by faxing 23370/23-686.

THE MONASTERY OF IVERON   Iveron, founded in the 10th century, looks from the sea like a medieval hill town—only the hill is actually the monastery's solid foundation. Try ℂ **23370/23-643** for overnight reservations.

THE MONASTERY OF VATOPEDI   Founded only a decade after the Great Lavra, Vatopedi's long outline of red-and-white tile-roofed buildings is clearly visible from the sea. Try ℂ **23370/23-219** for overnight reservations.

WHERE TO STAY IN OURANOPOLIS

Xenia ★★   This sprawling beachside resort hotel with two-story stone-and-concrete bungalow-like units in a wooded setting by the sea is less than 5 minutes outside Ouranopolis. The large, tile-floored guest rooms have balconies (ask for a room facing the sea), most have desks and good reading lamps, and all have excellent bathroom facilities. The Xenia offers all the creature comforts you may have missed while visiting Athos, including several restaurants, fresh- and saltwater pools, riding, tennis, and its own beach. The Xenia has been here since the 1960s—and some of its summer guests are Thessalonians who have come back with their families year after year.

Ouranopolis, 63075 Macedonia. ℂ **23770/71-412.** Fax 23770/71-362. www.papcorp.gr. 120 units. 160€ ($208) double. Compulsory breakfast 10€ ($13). AE, DC, MC, V. **Amenities:** Restaurant; bar; 2 pools; tennis. *In room:* A/C, TV, minibar, hair dryer.

17

The Northeastern Aegean Islands

by John S. Bowman

Looking for a new or different experience with Greek islands, some that still give a sense that this is how Greeks live? The three covered in this chapter—**Samos, Hios** (Chios), and **Lesvos** (Mitilini)—might be the destination for you. Far removed from the Greek mainland and dispersed along the coast of Turkey, these islands are still relatively untouched by tourism. Vacationers here tend to be concentrated in a few resorts, leaving the interiors and much of the coast open to exploration. Along their coasts, you'll find some of the finest beaches in the Aegean, and within the interiors richly forested valleys, precipitous mountain slopes, and exquisite mountain villages. These agricultural islands produce olives, grapes, and honey in abundance, providing the basis for excellent local cuisine.

The influence of Asia Minor is not as evident as you might expect, given the proximity of the Turkish coast. What you may notice is the sizable Greek military presence—certain areas of each island are occupied by the military and are strictly off-limits, which shouldn't bother you unless you're hiking or biking in the area. Even though this military presence is a sore point with the Turks, travel between Greece and Turkey remains unrestricted,

and relations between the two countries on a personal level seem amicable. Many travelers use the Northeastern Aegean islands as jumping-off points for Turkey: In particular, Samos (only 3km/2 miles away at the closest point) offers easy access to **Ephesus.**

STRATEGIES FOR SEEING THE ISLANDS

Since the distances between islands are substantial, island-hopping by boat can be costly and time-consuming. Add the fact that each island is quite large, and it becomes clear that you're best off choosing one or two islands to explore in-depth rather than attempting a grand tour. Both **Olympic Airlines** and **Aegean Airlines** offer some inter-island flights that are relatively inexpensive, frequent, and fast. If you travel by ferry, you'll find that departure times are more reasonable for travel from north to south, whereas traveling in the opposite direction usually involves departures in the middle of the night. The islands are too large and the roads often too rough for mopeds to be a safe option; because the bus routes and schedules are highly restricting, you'll find that if you want to get around it's necessary to rent a car.

> **(Tips) Museums and Sites Hours Update**
>
> If you visit these islands during the summer, check to see when sites and museums are open before setting out. The officially posted hours are not always maintained and most are closed 1 day a week.

---

1 Samos

322km (174 nautical miles) NE of Piraeus

The most mountainous and densely forested of the Northeastern Aegean isles, Samos appears wild and mysterious as you approach its north coast by ferry. The hills plunging to the sea are jagged with cypresses, and craggy peaks hide among the clouds. Samos experienced a series of wildfires during the summer of 2000, which briefly brought the island to the attention of the international press, but effects of that event have faded.

In recent years, Samos has played host to that highly impersonal form of mass tourism involving "package" groups from Europe. This is mostly confined to the eastern coastal resorts—Vathi, Pithagorio, and Kokkari—all of which have developed a generic waterfront of hotels, cafes, and souvenir shops. The rugged splendor of the island's interior hides the most interesting and beautiful villages. Difficult terrain and a remote location made these villages an apt refuge from pirates in medieval times; in this age, the same qualities have spared them from tourism's worst excesses.

Although Samos has several fine archaeological sites, the island is most noted for its excellent beaches and abundant opportunities for hiking, cycling, and windsurfing. Those who remember nothing from studying geometry except the Pythagorean Theorem may be pleased to know that Pythagoas was born on Samos about 580 B.C. Also, Samos is the best crossover point for those who want to visit **Ephesus,** one of the most important archaeological sites in Asia Minor.

GETTING THERE Although ferries connect Piraeus to Samos, the trip is long. The best way to get here is to fly.

By Plane Both **Olympic Airways** and **Aegean Airlines** offer several flights daily between Athens and Samos. Contact Olympic Airways in Athens at (C) **210/966-6666,** or check out www.olympicairlines.gr. Contact **Aegean Airlines** ((C) **801/112-0000** or check www.aegeanair.com). The Samos airport is 3km (2 miles) from Pithagorio, on the road to Ireon; from the airport you can take a taxi to Vathi (25€/$33) or Pithagorio (20€/$26).

By Boat The principal port of Samos is **Vathi,** also called Samos; the other two ports are **Karlovassi** and **Pithagorio.** Ferries from the Cyclades usually stop at both Vathi and Karlovassi: Take care not to get off at the wrong port! There are daily boats (sometimes two) from Piraeus to Karlovassi (11–14 hr.) and Vathi (8–14 hr.); in the opposite direction, ferries travel daily or nearly daily from Samos to Mykonos (5½ hr.). Boats to Hios from Vathi via Karlovassi (5 hr.) travel three times per week; there is also a once-weekly Rhodes-Vathi-Lesvos-Alexandroupoli run. Boats (mostly hydrofoils) to the Dodecanese islands depart regularly from Vathi and Pithagorio. If you want to travel one-way to Turkey, Turkish ferries depart daily (Apr 1–Oct 31; less regular off season); a visa is required for all American, Canadian, British, and Irish citizens who intend to stay for more than 1 day. Be sure to inquire in advance about current visa regulations with a local travel agency. For more information on visas, see "A Side Trip to Turkey: Kusadasi & Ephesus," below.

VATHI, KARLOVASSI & THE NORTHERN COAST

Vathi (aka Samos town) on the northeast coast and Karlovassi to the northwest are the two principal ports of Samos and the island's largest towns. Neither is particularly exciting, and we recommend both as convenient bases rather than as destinations in themselves.

Vathi becomes a slightly overextended resort town in high season but is beautifully situated in a fine natural harbor. An extensive development project in Pithagora Square and along the paralia (beachfront road) allows visitors to walk on a widened pedestrian pathway along the water and take in open-air concerts at the large bandstand. The old town, **Ano Vathi,** rises to the hilltops in steep, narrow streets that hide a few small tavernas and cafes. Karlovassi is somewhat less interesting as a town—although it's adjacent to several of the best beaches on the island, the town is spread out and offers fewer amenities than Vathi. Most tourist facilities are clustered along the water at the west end of town, forming a tiny beach resort with several hotels, restaurants, grocery stores, and souvenir shops. The old town hovers above the lower town on the slopes of a near-vertical pillar of rock; the lovely small chapel of **Ayia Triada** is at the rock's summit.

The **north coast** of the island is wild and steep, with mountains rising abruptly from the water's edge. One of the most interesting areas to explore is the **Platanakia** region, known for its rushing streams, lush valleys, and picturesque mountain villages. A sequence of excellent **beaches** between Kokkari and Karlovassi includes the two finest beaches on the island: **Micro Seitani** and **Megalo Seitani;** you can reach them via a short boat ride or a somewhat long hike to the west of Karlovassi.

ESSENTIALS

VISITOR INFORMATION   There is an official **tourist office** at 107 Themistioklis Sofouli (© **22730/28-582**), but it is easier to go directly to private travel agencies for information. Try one of the three major travel agencies in Samos: **Ellinas Tours,** 263 Themistoklis Sofouli (© **22730/89-110;** ellinastours@acn.gr); **Rhenia Tours,** 15 Themistoklis Sofouli (© **22730/88-800;** info@rhenia.gr); and **Samina Tours,** 67 Themistoklis Sofouli (© **22730/87-000;** www.samina.gr). Here you can make arrangements for accommodations and excursions (including excursions to Turkey, Patmos, and Fourni, as well as tours of Samos), rent cars, and so on. The Diavlos website (www.diavlos.gr) has information on ferries, attractions, and accommodations. Another website with useful information is www.samos-travel.com.

GETTING AROUND   By Bus   There's good public bus service on Samos throughout the year, with significantly expanded summer schedules. The **Vathi bus terminal** (© **22730/27-262**) is a block inland from the south end of the port on Kanari. The bus makes the 20-minute trip between Vathi and Pithagorio frequently. Buses also travel to Kokkari, the inland village of Mitilini, Pirgos, Marathokambos, Votsalakia beach, and Karlovassi. Schedules are posted in English at the bus terminal.

By Boat   From Karlovassi there are daily excursion boats to **Megalo Seitani,** the best fine-sand beach on the island. A once-weekly around-the-island tour aboard the *Samos Star* is a great way to see the island's remarkable coastline, much of it inaccessible by car. The excursion boat departs from Pithagorio at 8:30am (a bus from Vathi departs at 7:30am), currently on Tuesday, and returns to Pithagorio at 5:30pm; the fare is 70€ ($91). Book with one of the travel agencies listed above. Most excursions depart from

Pithagorio, although many offer bus service from Vathi an hour prior to departure; for descriptions, see "Pithagorio & the Southern Coast," later in this chapter.

By Car & Moped **Autoplan** (17 Themistoklis Sofouli; ⓒ **22730/23-555;** autoplan@ internet.gr) and **Aramis Rent a Car** (at the pier in Vathi; ⓒ **22730/23-253;** www. rentacaringreece.com) offer good prices and selections. The least expensive car in high season is about 70€ ($91), including insurance and 100 free kilometers (62 miles). Mopeds go for 20€ to 30€ ($26–$39) per day. But there are other agencies, so shop around.

By Taxi The principal taxi stand in Vathi is on Plateia Pithagora, facing the paralia. The fare from Vathi to Pithagorio is about 16€ ($21). To book by phone, call ⓒ **22730/23-777** in Vathi, or 22730/33-300 in Karlovassi.

Bicycling For renting a bicycle, go online to www.samos-travel.com, where you will find that InterHermes in Vathi (ⓒ **22730/28-833**) and AutoLand in Kokkari (the beach resort just west of Vathi; ⓒ **22730/92-825**) offer this service. Stark Tours in Kirkland, Washington (ⓒ **800/381-3315;** www.starktours.com), has occasionally conducted more ambitious bike tours for groups on Samos.

FAST FACTS The **banks** in Vathi are on the paralia in the vicinity of Plateia Pithagora and are open Monday through Thursday from 8am to 2pm, Friday from 8am to 1:30pm; most have ATMs. Most travel agents change money, sometimes at bank rates, and they're open later. The island's **hospital** (ⓒ **22730/83-100**) is in Vathi. **Internet access** is available at Diavlos Internet Cafe (www.diavlos.gr) on the paralia next to the police station; Diavlos is open daily from 9:30am to 11pm, May through October; morning only, November through April. A **self-service laundry** (ⓒ **22730/28-833**), behind Aeolis Hotel on the town's market street, is open daily from 8am to 11pm. The **post office** (ⓒ **22730/27-304**) is on the same street as the Olympic Airways office, 1 block farther in from the paralia and 2 blocks from the bus station. The **telephone office** (OTE, ⓒ **22730/28-499**) is down the street from the Olympic Airways office in the direction of the archaeological museum. The **tourist police** (ⓒ **22730/81-000**) are on the paralia, by the turn into the bus station.

ATTRACTIONS

Archaeological Museum ⭐
This fine museum is actually two buildings at the south end of the harbor, near the post office. The newest building houses sculpture—the island's best sculptors traveled all over the Hellenistic world to create their art. The most remarkable work is a massive *kouros* (statue of a boy), which stands 5m (16 ft.) tall. The large and varied collection of bronze votives found at the Heraion is also impressive.

Kapetan Yimnasiarhou Kateveni (near park and behind town hall). ⓒ **22730/27-469**. Admission 3€ ($3.90), seniors 2€ ($2.60). Tues–Sun 8:30am–3pm.

Moni Vronta
The 15th-century fortified monastery of Moni Vronta is on a high mountain overlooking the sea and the lovely hilltop village of Vourliotes. Few if any monks live there these days but a caretaker is usually about; if the gate is locked when you arrive, try knocking—one of the soldiers from a nearby surveillance post may be around to let you in. Ask to see the *spileo* (cave), an old chapel in the thickness of the outer wall that holds a collection of ancient objects, some from the time of the monastery's founding. To get there, continue driving uphill about 2km (1 mile) past the village of Vourliotes (see below).

Vourliotes. No phone. Free admission. Daily 8am–5pm. 23km (15 miles) west of Vathi.

Vathi

ACCOMMODATIONS ■
Hotel Paradissos **6**
Pension Avli **3**
Pythagoras Hotel **1**
Samos Hotel **2**

DINING ◆
Christos Taverna **4**
Ta Kotopoula **5**

THREE HILL TOWNS ON THE RUGGED NORTH COAST

Amid the densely wooded valleys, cascading streams, and terraced slopes of Samos's *Platanakia* region, hide many villages that sought to evade the pirates who repeatedly ravaged all settlements visible from the sea. Three of the most picturesque of the surviving hill villages in this region are Manolates, Vourliotes, and Stavrinides.

Manolates is a 4km (2½-mile) drive uphill from the coast road. The village was until recently inaccessible by car, but once the paved road was built, many more visitors have come here to explore the steep, narrow cobblestone streets. There are several tavernas, numerous shops, and two kafenions (where the locals go).

Vourliotes, about 20km (13 miles) west of Vathi, was settled largely by repatriated Greeks from the town of Vourla in Turkey. It's the largest producer of wine in the region, and the local wine is among the best on the island. Walk from the parking lot at the Moni Vronta turnoff to the charming central square. Try **Manolis Taverna** (✆ **22730/93-290**), on the left as you enter the square, which has good *revidokefi-edes,* a delicious local dish made with chickpea flour and cheese. Also on the square, across from Manolis, is a small market whose displays seem not to have changed in the past 50 years. Be sure to visit the monastery of **Moni Vronta** (aka Vrontiani), 2km (1 mile) above the town (see "Attractions," above).

A Side Trip to Turkey: Kusadasi & Ephesus

In high season, two boats a day make the run between Vathi and Kusadasi, Turkey, itself a popular, well-developed resort but of interest to us as the gateway to the magnificent archaeological site at Ephesus. Although located in Turkey, Ephesus was a Greek city, famous among other things for its Temple of Artemis, one of the Seven Wonders of the Ancient World. A major commercial city in the Eastern Mediterranean, it fell to the Romans, and it was under their rule that an important Christian community and church were established here. Excursion boats depart daily from Vathi and on certain days an excursion also departs from Pithagorio. A round-trip ticket to Kusadasi that includes the boat fare, port fees, and the guided tour with the entrance fee costs about 100€ ($130). If you're not returning the same day, you'll need to investigate visa requirements. These are granted without difficulty at time of sailing and cost $20 for Americans, C$50 for Canadians, £15 for U.K. citizens, €10 for Irish citizens, and A$25 for Australians; New Zealanders don't need a visa. The travel agencies recommended above will help you with arrangements.

Stavrinides, perched on the mountainside high above Ayios Konstandinos, is the least touristic of the Platanakia villages. Here the tavernas and the few shops cater primarily to the villagers. **Taverna Irida** in the first square of the village offers good, simple food. A walking path between Stavrinides and Manolates makes an exceptional outing; the route out from Stavrinides is signposted.

The easiest way to visit these towns is by car. The island buses are an option if you don't mind the steep 4-to-6km (2½–3¾-mile) walk from the coastal road to the villages. An abundance of footpaths connect these villages—ask locally for routes. **Ambelos Tours** (© 22730/94-442; folas@otenet.gr) in Ayios Konstandinos, operated by the friendly and extremely knowledgeable Manolis Folas, is a useful resource. Manolis is also a good source for renting traditional houses in the hilltop village of Ano Ayios Konstandinos. Each unit sleeps three, and costs about 45€ ($59) per night.

BEACHES

The closest decent beach to Vathi is **Gagou,** 2km (1 mile) north of the pier. But the best beaches on Samos are found along the north coast, the most beautiful and rugged part of the island. The busy seaside resort of **Kokkari,** 10km (6 miles) west of Vathi, has several beaches in rock coves as well as the crowded stretch of sand running parallel to the town's main road. To find the smaller cove beaches, head seaward from the main square. Just west of Kokkari is **Tsamadou,** a short walk down from the coast road, which offers sufficient seclusion for nude sunbathing. Continue west past Karlovassi to find **Potami,** an excellent long pebble-and-sand beach with road access.

The two best beaches on the island, **Micro Seitani** (★) and **Megalo Seitani** (★), are accessible only by boat or on foot. Boat excursions depart daily from the pier in Karlovassi. To get here on foot, continue past the parking lot for the beach at Potami on a dirt road; walking time to the first beach is 45 minutes. After about 5 minutes of uphill walking, the road splits—turn right, continuing to follow the coast. After another 5 minutes of walking, three obvious paths turn off to the right in close succession. Take the third, marked by a cairn, and follow the well-worn path another half-hour to Micro

Seitani, a glorious pebble-and-cobble beach in a rocky cove. On the beach's far side, a ladder scales the cliff to the trail which will take you after an additional 30 minutes of walking to Megalo Seitani, as incredible a stretch of sea sand as any in the Aegean. At the far end of Megalo Seitani are a few houses and a taverna; the near end, at the outlet of a magnificent cliff-walled gorge, is completely undeveloped.

OUTDOOR PURSUITS

BICYCLING   Samos has many dirt roads and trails perfect for mountain biking. The only obstacles are the size of the island, which limits the number of routes available for day trips, and the fact that much of the backcountry is off-limits due to Greek military operations. Bike rentals, information about trails, and guided mountain-bike tours are available in Vathi at **Bike** (*©* **22730/24-404**). The shop is open daily from 8:30am to 2pm and 5 to 9pm; it's behind the old church opposite the port, on the market street. The bikes are high quality and the rental includes helmet, pump, and repair kit; clipless pedals and shoes are also available for an extra charge. The basic aluminum-frame bike is 20€ ($26) per day; the full-suspension bike is 30€ ($39).

WALKING   Some of the best walking on the island is in and around the Platanakia region of Samos's north coast, where well-marked trails connect several lovely hilltop villages. Manolates and Vourliotes (see above) are among the villages on this network of trails. A trail goes from Manolates to the summit of Mount Ambelos, the second-highest peak on Samos at 1,153m (3,780 ft.); the demanding round-trip takes about 5 hours. Those seeking a more "professional" exploration of the truly natural Samos might try one of outfits listed at "Special-Interest Trips" in chapter 2, "Planning Your Trip to Greece," p. 53.

WHERE TO STAY
Vathi
Hotel Paradissos   Despite a central location just off the paralia and a block away from the bus station, the walled garden and pool terrace here seem a world away from the traffic and dust of Vathi. Drinks and simple Greek food are served all day at the poolside bar. The pool invites lingering, with lounge chairs and umbrellas for sunning, and shaded tables for meals or drinks. All guest rooms have balconies, although the views aren't great. Bathrooms are small, but they do have full tubs. Note that although there is air-conditioning in every room, it isn't turned on until sometime in July (unlike the majority of hotels, which will turn on the air-conditioning in June if it's needed—and it usually is).

21 Kanari, Vathi, 83100 Samos. *©* **22730/23-911.** Fax 22730/28-754. 51 units. 90€ ($117) double. Rates include continental breakfast. MC, V. Closed Nov–Mar. **Amenities:** Restaurant; bar; pool; tours and car rentals arranged; 24-hr. room service. *In room:* A/C, TV, minibar, hair dryer.

Pension Avli *(Value)*   Although you won't find any luxuries here, you will discover the most charming and romantic pension on the island. Abundant bougainvillea fill the arcaded courtyard of this former 18th-century convent. Most rooms have been renovated within the last few years, but there is no denying they are spartan, with minimal furnishings. Each tiny bathroom is encased entirely in a plastic shell, making a shower a surreal experience. This is definitely a place for those with big imaginations and small budgets.

2 Areos, Vathi, 83100 Samos. *©* **22730/22-939.** 20 units. 45€ ($59) double. No credit cards. Turn in from the paralia at Agrotiki Trapeza (down from Aeolis Hotel), turn left on town's market street, and you'll see the Avli's unassuming sign directly ahead. *In room:* No phone.

Pythagoras Hotel This plain but comfortable family hotel on a hill overlooking Vathi Bay offers the best views in town from its nine seaside units and from the restaurant terrace. Guest rooms facing the road can be noisy—book ahead to ensure a unit on the water. Guest rooms and bathrooms are small, clean, and minimally furnished. The neighborhood cafe/restaurant downstairs serves a good, inexpensive breakfast, light meals, and snacks from 6:45am to midnight. Hotel staff will meet you at the port or airport at any time, a generous offer given the frequency of early-morning ferry arrivals.

12 Kallistratou, Kalami, Vathi, 83100 Samos. ℂ **22730/28-422.** Fax 22730/28-893. 19 units. From 48€ ($63) double. MC, V. On the coast road, 600m (1,968 ft.) north of the pier. **Amenities:** Restaurant; bar. *In room:* Satellite TV and Internet access can be arranged.

Samos Hotel For travelers who simply want a modern hotel on the harbor with all (well, most of) the amenities, this is *the* place in Vathi. Located right along the paralia, the hotel is subject to a certain amount of harbor noise. But the hotel is air-conditioned, making it somewhat insulated. Rooms—which have ceiling fans in place of air-conditioning units—are nothing special in size or decor, but beds and bathrooms are comfortable; most have balconies overlooking the harbor. Only about a 20-minute walk from Gagou Beach, this functional hotel is not for those seeking atmosphere.

11 Themistoklis Sofouli, 83100 Vathi. ℂ **22730/28-377.** Fax 22730/28-842. 105 units. High season 85€ ($111) double; low season 65€ ($85) double. Rates include continental breakfast. MC, V. **Amenities:** 2 restaurants; 2 bars; pool; Jacuzzi; game room; concierge; tours and car rentals arranged; conference facilities; 24-hr. room service; roof garden. *In room:* TV, fridge, hair dryer, safe, ceiling fan.

Ayios Konstandinos

This coastal town in the heart of the Platanakia region is a great base for touring the north coast of Samos. Ask Manolis Folas of **Ambelos Tours** (ℂ **22730/94-442;** folas@otenet.gr) about traditional houses for rent: Each unit sleeps three and costs about 45€ ($59) per night.

Daphne Hotel 🛱 The Daphne is the finest small hotel on the island. Artfully incised into the steep hillside in a series of terraces, the hotel commands a fine view of the stream valley leading to Manolates and a wide sweep of sea. The dining room has a large picture window and a terrace that steps down to the pool and an exquisite view. All rooms are moderate in size and have balconies with the same great view; bathrooms have both shower and tub. This is a good location for walkers, with many trails nearby to Manolates and other hill towns. Make your reservations well in advance, as this hotel is filled through much of the summer by European tour groups. There is free transportation to and from the airport or the port; due to the somewhat remote location, you'll probably want a car during your stay here.

Ayios Konstandinos, 83200 Samos. ℂ **22730/94-003** or 22730/94-493. Fax 22730/94-594. www.daphne-hotel.gr. 35 units. 75€ ($98) double. Rates include breakfast. V. Take the 1st right after turning onto the Manolates road, 19km (12 miles) from Vathi. Closed Nov–Apr. **Amenities:** Restaurant; swimming pool; pool bar; TV lounge. *In room:* A/C, music.

WHERE TO DINE
Vathi

The food along the paralia in Vathi is mostly tourist-quality and mediocre; you'll find the best restaurants in the small towns away from the harbor. The local wines on Samos have for a long time been known for their excellence. (As Byron exclaimed, "Fill high the bowl with Samian wine!") Samaina is a good, dry white; Selana, a relatively dry rosé. The Greeks here also like sweet wines, with names like Nectar, Doux, and Anthemis. Almost any restaurant on the island will serve one or all of these choices.

Christos Taverna GREEK   This simple little taverna, under a covered alleyway decorated with odd antiques, is to the left off Plateia Pithagora as you come up from the port. The food is simply prepared and presented; it comes in generous portions and is remarkably good. Try the *revidokeftedes,* a Samian specialty made with cheese fried in chickpea batter.

Plateia Ayiou Nikolaou. ✆ 22730/24-792. Main courses 6€–14€ ($7.80–$18). No credit cards. Daily 11am–11pm.

Ta Kotopoula GREEK   Ta Kotopoula is located on the outskirts of Vathi, somewhat hard to find but worth the trouble. From the harbor's south end, walk inland past the Olympic Airways office and the post office, bearing right with the road as it climbs toward Ano Vathi. Where the road splits around a large tree, about 700m (2,296 ft.) from the harbor, you'll see the vine-sheltered terrace of this taverna on the left. The food is basic Greek fare, but the ingredients are exceptionally fresh—chicken being the specialty as the name suggests. Local wine is available by the carafe.

Vathi. ✆ 22730/28-415. Main courses 6€–15€ ($7.80–$20). No credit cards. Daily 11am–11pm.

Ayios Konstandinos

Platanakia Paradisos GREEK   Paradisos is a large garden taverna located at the Manolates turnoff from the coast highway; it has been in the Folas family for nearly 30 years and has been operating as a taverna for more than 100. Mr. Folas, the owner, makes his own wine from the excellent Samian grapes. Mrs. Folas's *tiropita*—freshly baked after 7pm—is made from local goat cheese wrapped in a flaky pastry. Live traditional music is performed Wednesday and Saturday nights in summer.

Ayios Konstandinos. ✆ 22730/94-208. Main courses 5€–15€ ($6.50–$20). No credit cards. Daily 3–11pm.

VATHI AFTER DARK

"In" places change from year to year but one of the hottest discos in Vathi has been **Metropolis,** behind the Paradise Hotel. For *bouzouki,* there's **Zorba's,** out of town on the road to Mitilini. Various kinds of bars line the lanes just off the port. **Number Nine,** at 9 Kephalopoulou, beyond the jetty on the right, is one of the oldest and best known.

PITHAGORIO & THE SOUTHERN COAST

Pithagorio, south across the island from Vathi, is a charming but overcrowded seaside resort built on the site of an ancient village and harbor. Although this is a convenient base for touring the southern half of Samos, the town exists primarily for the tour groups that pack its streets in the summer. We recommend staying here for a day or two to explore the nearby historic sites, then moving on to the more interesting and authentic villages of the north coast.

ESSENTIALS

GETTING THERE   By Plane   The Samos airport is 3km (2 miles) from Pithagorio; from the airport, you can take a taxi into town for 10€ ($13).

By Boat   Ferries from the Cyclades typically don't stop at Pithagorio, so you'll need to take a taxi or bus from Vathi. Near-daily hydrofoil service links Pithagorio and Patmos (60–90 min.), Lipsi (1½–3 hr.), Leros (1½–3 hr.), Kalymnos (3–6 hr.), and Kos (3–4 hr.); there are also excursion boats to Patmos four times weekly. Check the most current ferry schedules at the **Pithagorio Municipal Tourist Office** (✆ 22730/ 61-389 or 22730/61-022; www.gtp.gr), or at **Pithagorio Port Authority** (✆ 22730/ 61-225).

By Bus Buses depart frequently for the 20-minute trip between Vathi and Pithagorio. Contact the **Vathi bus terminal** (✆ 22730/27-262) for current schedules.

VISITOR INFORMATION The **Pithagorio Municipal Tourist Office** (✆ 22730/61-389 or 22730/61-022) is on the main street, Likourgou Logotheti, 1 block up from the paralia; its hours are daily from 8am to 10pm. Here you can get information on ferries, buses, island excursions, accommodations, car rental, and just about anything else. Pick up the handy *Map of Pithagorion,* which lists accommodations, attractions, and other helpful information.

GETTING AROUND   By Bus The Pithagorio **bus terminal** is in the center of town, at the corner of Polykrates (the road to Vathi) and Likourgou Logotheti. The bus makes the 20-minute trip between Vathi and Pithagorio frequently. There are also four buses daily from Pithagorio to Ireon (near the Heraion archaeological site).

By Boat Summertime **excursion boats** from the Pithagorio harbor go to **Psili Ammos beach** (on the east end of the island) daily, and to the island of **Ikaria** three times weekly. A popular day cruise goes to **Samiopoula,** a small island with a single taverna and a long sandy beach. Boats leave daily at 9:15am and return to Pithagorio at 5pm; the fare of 25€ ($33) includes lunch. Four times each week, the *Samos Star* sails to **Patmos,** departing from Pithagorio at 8am and returning the same day at 4pm; travel time to Patmos is 2 hours, and the fare is 40€ ($52). A Sunday excursion to the tiny isle of **Fourni,** also aboard the *Samos Star,* gives you 6 hours to check out the beaches and sample the island's renowned fish tavernas; the boat leaves Pithagorio at 8:30am and the cost is 30€ ($39) per person. A once-weekly **around-the-island tour** aboard the *Samos Star* offers a great way to see this island's remarkable coastline, much of it inaccessible by road. The excursion boat departs from Pithagorio at 8:30am (a bus from Vathi departs at 7:30am) on Tuesday and returns to Pithagorio at 5:30pm; the fare is 50€ ($65).

By Car & Moped   Aramis Rent a Car has a branch near the bus station in Pithagorio (✆ 22730/62-267). It often has the best prices, but shop around.

By Taxi The taxi stand is on the main street, Likourgou Logotheti, where it meets the harbor. The fare from Vathi to Pithagorio is 16€ ($21). To book by phone, call ✆ 22730/61-450.

FAST FACTS   National Bank (✆ 22730/61-234), opposite the bus stop, has an ATM. A small **clinic** (✆ 22730/61-111) on Plateia Irinis, next to the town hall, is located 1 block in from the beach near the port police. Access the **Internet** at Nefeli (✆ 22730/61-719), a cafe on the paralia's north side (left if you're facing the harbor), open from 11am to 2am daily. The rate is 5€ ($6.50) per hour for use of one of the two computers. Alex Stavrides runs a self-service **laundry** off the main street on the road to the old basilica; Metamorphosis Sotiros is open daily from 9am to 9pm, in summer until 11pm. The **post office** is several blocks up from the paralia on the main street, past the bus stop. The **telephone office (OTE)** is on the paralia near the pier (✆ 22730/61-399). The **police** (✆ 22730/61-100) are a short distance up Polikrates, the main road to Vathi.

ATTRACTIONS

Efpalinion Tunnel ✦ One of the most impressive engineering accomplishments of the ancient world, this 1,000m (3,280-ft.) tunnel through the mountain above Pithagorio was excavated to transport water from mountain streams to ancient Vathi. The great architect Efpalinos directed two teams of workers digging from each side, and after nearly 15 years they met within a few meters of each other. If you can muster the courage to squeeze through the first 20m (66 ft.)—the tunnel is a mere sliver in the rock for this distance—you'll see that it soon widens considerably, and you can comfortably walk another 100m (328 ft.) into the mountain. Even though a generator supposedly starts up in the event of a power outage, you might be more comfortable carrying a flashlight.

Pithagorio. ℂ **22730/61-400.** Admission 3€ ($3.90) adults, 1.50€ ($1.95) students and seniors, free for youths under 18. Tues–Sun 8:45am–2:45pm. 3km (2 miles) northwest of Pithagorio; sign posted off the main road to Vathi.

Heraion   All that survives of the largest of all Greek temples is its massive foundation, a lone reconstructed column, and some copies of the original statuary. A forest of columns once surrounded this temple, so many that rival Ionian cities were so impressed that they rebuilt many of their ancient temples in similar style. The Temple of Artemis in nearby Ephesus is a direct imitation of the great Samian structure. The Heraion was rebuilt and greatly expanded under Polycrates. It was damaged during numerous invasions and finally destroyed by a series of earthquakes.

Ireon. ℂ **22730/95-277** or 22730/27-469 (the Archaeological Museum in Vathi). Admission 3€ ($3.90) adults, 1.50€ ($1.95) students and seniors, free for youths under 18. Tues–Sun 8am–2:30pm. 9km (5½ miles) southwest of Pithagorio, signposted off the road to Ireon.

BEACHES
In Pithagorio, the local beach stretches from Logotheti Castle at the west side of town several kilometers to Potokaki and the airport. Expect this beach to be packed throughout the summer. Excursion boats depart daily in the summer for **Psili Ammos,** 5km (3 miles) to the east. The daily boats also leave Pithagorio for **Samiopoula,** an island off the south coast with two good beaches.

On the south coast of the island, the most popular beaches are on Marathokambos Bay. The once-tiny village of **Ormos Marathokambos** has several tavernas and a growing number of hotels and pensions. Its rock-and-pebble beach is long and narrow, with windsurfing an option. A couple of kilometers farther west of Ormos Marathokambos is **Votsalakia,** a somewhat nicer beach.

WHERE TO STAY
Rooms in Pithagorio are quickly filled by tour groups, so don't count on finding a place here if you haven't booked well in advance.

Georgios Sandalis Hotel   Above Pithagorio, this homey establishment has a front garden bursting with colorful blossoms. The tastefully decorated rooms all have balconies with French doors. Back rooms face quiet hills and another flower garden, while the front units face a busy street and can be noisy. All rooms have kitchenettes with fridge; only some rooms have air-conditioning (extra charge if used). No meals are served on the premises, but breakfast can be had at reduced rates at family-owned Enplo Café nearby on harbor. The friendly Sandalises are gracious hosts; they spent many years in Chicago and speak perfect English.

Pithagorio, 83103 Samos. ℂ **22730/61-691.** http://samos-hotels.com/en/index.htm. 12 units. 40€ ($52) double. No credit cards. Head north on Polykrates (the road to Vathi); hotel is on your left, about 100m (328 ft.) from the bus station. *In room:* TV, fridge, safe.

Hotel Zorbas *Value*   This place is more pension than hotel, but the rooms are comfortable. Seven units have great views of Pithagorio Harbor. The atmosphere is decidedly casual and friendly—the hotel lobby doubles as the Mathios family's living room.

The hotel is on a steep hill on the north side of town, a healthy climb from the paralia at the port police station. Rooms facing the sea have spacious balconies with views over the rooftops to fishing boats docked in the harbor, while street-side rooms are a bit noisier and have no views. Breakfast is served on a terrace facing the sea.

Damos, Pithagorio, 83103 Samos. ℂ **22730/61-009.** Fax 22730/61-012. 12 units. 55€ ($72) double. Breakfast 5€ ($6.50). No credit cards.

WHERE TO DINE

Esperides Tavern INTERNATIONAL   This pleasant restaurant with a walled garden is a few blocks inland from the port, and west of the main street. You'll find uniformed waiters and a dressier crowd here. The Continental and Greek dishes are well presented and will appeal to a wide variety of palates—try the baked chicken with any vegetables in season.

Pithagorio. ℂ **22730/61-767.** Reservations recommended in summer. Main courses 6€–18€ ($7.80–$24). No credit cards. Daily 6pm–midnight.

Varka ✹ GREEK/SEAFOOD   This ouzeri/taverna is in a stand of salt pines at the south end of the port. Delicious fresh fish, grilled meats, and a surprising variety of *mezedes* (appetizers) are produced in the small kitchen. The grilled octopus, strung up on a line to dry, and the pink *barbounia* (clear gray mullet), cooked to perfection over a charcoal grill, are the true standouts of a meal here. The cafe pavilion by the water is a cool, breezy location for a drink or dessert.

Paralia, Pithagorio. ℂ **22730/61-088.** www.varka.gr. Main courses 7€–20€ ($9.10–$26). MC, V. Daily noon–midnight. Closed Nov–Apr.

2 Hios (Chios)

283km (153 nautical miles) NE of Piraeus

"Craggy Hios," as Homer dubbed it—and he should know, since this is said to be his native home—remains relatively unspoiled, and that's why I continue to recommend it. Those seeking just to relax will find the black-pebble beaches on the southeast coast of the island well attended, but white-sand beaches on the west coast see far fewer people. The majestic mountain setting of **Nea Moni**—an 11th-century Byzantine monastery in the center of the island—and the extraordinary mosaics of its chapel make for an unforgettable visit. The mastic villages on the island's south side are among the most unusual medieval towns in Greece; the towns get their name from a tree resin used in chewing gum, paints, and perfumes that grows nowhere else in the world.

The paralia of **Hios town** is likely to be your first glimpse of the island, and admittedly it isn't an especially appealing sight—unappealing modern buildings and generic cafes have taken over what must once have been a fine harbor. Thankfully, a few pockets of the original town farther inland have survived earthquakes, wars, and neglect. The kastro, the mosque on the main square, the mansions of Kampos, and the occasional grand gateway (often leading nowhere) are among the signs of a more prosperous and architecturally harmonious past.

ESSENTIALS

GETTING THERE   By Plane   Both **Olympic Airways** and **Aegean Airlines** offer several flights daily between Athens and Chios. Contact Olympic Airways in Athens at ℂ **210/966-6666,** or check out www.olympicairlines.gr. Contact **Aegean Airlines** (ℂ **801/112-0000** or check www.aegeanair.com). Olympic also offers flights

---

Tips An Important Warning on Car Rentals on Hios

Currently, anyone who is not carrying a driver's license from a country in the European Union must have an International Driver's License to rent a car on Hios. If you expect to rent a car during your stay on Hios, get an International Driver's License before leaving your home country—for whatever reason, the police here enforce this regulation. Relatively easy and cheap to obtain, it can be issued through national automobile associations.

---

once or twice a week with Lesvos (Mitilini) and Thessaloniki. If you arrive by plane, count on taking a cab into town at about 15€ ($20) for the 7km (4¼-mile) ride.

By Boat   From Piraeus, one daily car ferry leaves bound for Hios (8–9 hr.); there's also a daily connection with Lesvos (3 hr.). Three ferries weekly serve Limnos (9 hr.) and Thessaloniki (16–19 hr.), two ferries weekly to Samos (5 hr.), and one weekly to Siros (5 hr.). Check with **Hios Port Authority** (© 22710/44-434; www.gtp.gr) for current schedules.

VISITOR INFORMATION   The **Tourist Information Office** on 18 Kanari (© 22710/44-389) stocks free brochures, including maps; it's located on the second street from the north end of the harbor, between the harbor and the Central (Plastira) Square. In summer it's open Monday to Friday from 7am to 2:30pm and 6:30 to 9:30pm, Saturday and Sunday from 10am to 1pm; reduced hours off season. Ask here (or at any travel agency) about free guided tours to some of Chios's major sites, sponsored by the island's government.

Another mine of information is **Chios Tours** (© 22710/29-444; www.chios tours.gr), 4 Kokkali. The office is open Monday through Saturday from 8:30am to 1:30pm and 5:30 to 8:30pm. The staff will assist you with a room search, often at a discount. The free *Hios Summertime* magazine has a lot of useful information, as well as maps. The sites **www.chios.com** and **www.chiosnet.gr** are also helpful.

GETTING AROUND   By Bus   All buses depart from one of the two bus stations in Hios town. The **blue buses** (© 22710/23-086), which leave from the blue bus station on the north side of the public garden by Plateia Plastira, serve local destinations like Karfas to the south and Daskalopetra to the north. The **green long-distance KTEL buses** (© 22710/27-507) leave from the green bus station, a block south of the park near the main taxi stand. Six buses a day depart to Mesta, eight a day to Piryi, five to Kardamila, and four to Emborio, but only two buses a week to Volissos and to Nea Moni. Fares are 1€ to 5€ ($1.30–$6.50).

By Car   Hios is a large, fun island to explore, so we recommend a car. **Vassilakis Rent-A-Car** (© 22710/29-300; www.chios.gr/vassilakis) is at 3 Evangelos Chandrs, or try **Pangosmio Rent a Car** (© 2810/811-750; www.pangosmio.gr).

By Taxi   Taxis are easily found at the port, though the taxi station is beyond the OTE, on the northeast corner of the central square. You can call © **22710/41-111** or 22710/43-312 for a cab. Fares from Hios town run about 20€ ($26) to Piryi, 25€ ($33) to Mesta, and 30€ ($39) round-trip to Nea Moni.

Bicycling/Moped   Hios is too large, and the hills too big, for most bicyclists; rent a motorbike, and if you're experienced with these, you're better off with a car.

FAST FACTS **Commercial Bank (Emboriki Trapeza)** and **Ergo Bank** are located at the harbor's north end near the corner of Kanari. Both have ATMs and are open Monday through Thursday from 8am to 2pm, Friday from 8am to 1:30pm. The **hospital** is 7km (4¼ miles) from the center of Hios town (© **22710/44-301**). **Internet access** is available daily from 9am to midnight at Enter Internet Cafe (© **22710/ 41-058**), 98 Aegeou, at the paralia's south end. One hour online costs 4€ ($5.20). There's a full-service **laundry** around the corner from the post office on Psichari (© **22710/44-801**); one load costs 15€ ($20), and the turnaround time is about 24 hours. The **post office** is at the corner of Omirou and Rodokanaki (© **22710/ 44-350**). The **telephone office (OTE)** is across the street from the tourist office on Kanari (© **131**). The **tourist police** are headquartered at the harbor's northernmost tip, at Neorion 35 (© **22710/44-427**).

ATTRACTIONS

Argenti Museum and Koraï Library ⊛   Philip Argenti was the great historian of Hios, a local aristocrat who devoted his life and savings to the recording of island history, costumes, customs, and architecture. The museum consists largely of his personal collection of folk art, costumes, and implements, supplemented with a gallery of family portraits and copies of Eugene Delacroix's *Massacre of Hios*, a masterpiece depicting the Turkish massacre of the local population in 1822. On display in the lobby are numerous old maps of the island. The library is excellent, with much of its collection in English and French. If you're interested in local architecture and village life, ask to see the collection of drawings by Dimitris Pikionis (a renowned 20th-c. Greek architect). The drawings of the Kampos mansions and village houses are beautiful, and have yet to be published.

Koraï, Hios town. © **22710/44-246.** Museum admission 3€ ($3.90); free admission to library. Both Mon–Thurs 8am–2pm; Fri 8am–2pm and 5–7:30pm; Sat 8am–12:30pm.

Nea Moni ⊛⊛   The 11th-century monastery of Nea Moni is one of the great architectural and artistic treasures of Greece. The monastery is in a spectacular setting high in the mountains overlooking Hios town. Its grounds are extensive—the monastery was once home to 1,000 monks—but the resident population has dwindled to several elderly nuns. The focus of the rambling complex is the katholikon, or principal church, whose square nave has eight niches supporting the dome. Within these niches are a sequence of extraordinary mosaics, among the finest examples of Byzantine art. Sadly, a seemingly interminable process of restoration often conceals the most beautiful of these behind scaffolding. You can still see the portrayals of the saints in the narthex, and a representation of Christ washing the disciples' feet. The museum contains a collection of gifts to the monastery, including several fine 17th-century icons. Also of interest is the cistern, a cavernous vaulted room with columns (bring a flashlight); and the small Chapel of the Holy Cross at the entrance to the monastery, dedicated to the martyrs of the 1822 massacre by the Turks (the skulls and bones displayed are those of the victims themselves). The long barrel-vaulted refectory is a beautiful space, its curved apse dating from the 11th century.

The bus to Nea Moni is part of an island excursion operated by KTEL, departing from the Hios town bus station Tuesday and Friday at 9am and returning at 4:30pm. The route: Nea Moni to Anavatos to Lithi beach to Armolia and back to Hios town; it costs 20€ ($26) per person. A taxi will cost about 30€ ($39) round-trip from Hios town, including a half-hour at the monastery.

Nea Moni. No phone. Free admission to monastery grounds and katholikon; museum admission 3€ ($3.90) adults, 1€ ($1.30) students and seniors. Monastery grounds and katholikon daily 8am–1pm and 4–8pm; museum Tues–Sun 8am–1pm. 17km (11 miles) west of Hios town.

A DAY TRIP TO THE MASTIC VILLAGES: PIRYI, MESTA & OLIMBI *

The most interesting day trip on Hios is the excursion to the mastic villages in the southern part of the island, which offer one of the best examples of medieval town architecture in all of Greece. Mastic is a gum derived from the resin of the mastic tree, used in candies, paints, perfumes, and medicines. It was a source of great wealth for these towns in the Middle Ages, and it is still produced in small quantities. All the towns were originally fortified, with an outer wall formed by an unbroken line of houses with no doors and few windows facing out. You can see this distinctive plan at all three towns, although in Piryi and Olimbi, the original medieval village has been engulfed by more recent construction.

Piryi is known for a rare technique of geometric decoration, known as *Ksisti*. In the main square, this technique reaches a level of extraordinary virtuosity. The beautiful **Ayioi Apostoli** church and every available surface of every building are banded with horizontal decorations in a remarkable variety of motifs. At the town center is the tower for which the village was named, now mostly in ruins. It was originally the heart of the city's defenses, and a final place of refuge during sieges.

Mesta is the best-preserved medieval village on Hios, a maze of narrow streets and dark covered passages. The town has two fine churches, each unique on the island. **Megas Taxiarchis,** built in the 19th century, is one of the largest churches in Greece, and it was clearly built to impress. The arcaded porch with its fine pebble terrace and bell tower create a solemn and harmonious transition to the cathedral precinct. The other church in town, **Paleos Taxiarchis,** is located a few blocks below the main square. As the name suggests, this is the older of the two, built in the 14th century. The most notable feature here is the carved wooden iconostasis, whose surface is incised with miniature designs of unbelievable intricacy. If either church is closed, you can ask for the gatekeeper in the central square.

Olimbi is the least well known of the three. Though not as spectacular as Piryi nor as intact as Mesta, it contains many medieval buildings. It has a central tower similar to that of Piryi, and stone vaults connect the houses.

Piryi is the closest of the three villages to Hios town, at 26km (16 miles); Olimbi and Mesta are within 10km (6 miles) of Piryi. The easiest way to see all three villages is by car. Taxis from Hios to Piryi cost about 20€ ($26). KTEL buses travel from Hios to Piryi eight times a day, and to Mesta five times a day. The bus to Piryi is 4€ ($5.20), to Mesta 5€ ($6.50).

BEACHES

There's no question that Hios has the best beaches in the Northeastern Aegean. They're cleaner, less crowded, and more plentiful than those of Samos or Lesvos, and would be the envy of any Cycladic isle.

The fine-sand beach of **Karfas,** 7km (4¼ miles) south of Hios town, is the closest decent beach to the town center; it can be reached by a local (blue) bus. The rapid development of tourism in this town ensures, however, that the beach will be crowded.

The most popular beach on the south coast is **Mavra Volia** ("black pebbles") in the town of Emborio. Continue over the rocks to the right from the man-made town beach to find the main beach. Walking on the smooth black rocks feels and sounds

Moments **An Epic Experience**

Little has been made so far of one of Chios's greatest claims to fame: the birth-place and home of Homer, but knowing he is associated with this island adds a special buzz to your visit. In fact, it is one of many islands or cities around the Eastern Mediterranean that lay claim to this honor, but Chios's is probably the oldest and strongest. In any case, Chios has been adopted as the home by a group of modern scholars in Homeric studies and each year this Academia Homerica holds a weeklong session on Chios where students and scholars gather to lecture, study, and learn more about Homer. (Best is simply to search online for "academia homerica.") But because most visitors will not be able to spend a week with Homer, I have a better suggestion: bring a paperback copy of the *Iliad* or the *Odyssey* to read in your downtime here—on a beach or in a cafe. If you like the classics, it's an experience you will treasure.

like marching through a room filled with marbles. The panorama of the beach, slightly curving coastline, and distant headland is a memorable sight. Buses from Hios town or from Piryi (8km/5 miles away) run regularly to Emborio. A short distance south is the south coast's best beach, **Vroulidia** ⋇, a 5km (3-mile) drive in from the Emborio road. This white-pebble-and-sand beach in a rocky cove offers great views of the craggy coastline.

The west coast of the island has a number of stunning beaches. **Elinda Cove** shel-ters a long cobble beach, a 600m (1,968-ft.) drive in from the main road between Lithi and Volissos. Another excellent beach on this road is **Tigani-Makria Ammos,** about 4km (2½ miles) north of Elinda; turn at a sign for the beach and drive in 1.5km (1 mile) to this long white-pebble beach. (There's also a small cove-sheltered cobble beach about 300m/984 ft. before the main beach.) There are three beaches below Volissos, the best of which is Lefkathia, just north of the harbor of Volissos (Limnia).

South of Elinda, the long safe beach at **Lithi Bay** is popular with families. Of the several tavernas there, we recommend **Ta Tria Adelphia (The Three Brothers;** ☏ **22710/73-208**). It's the last taverna you come to as you're walking along the beach.

The beaches of the north coast are less remarkable. **Nagos** (4km/2½ miles north of Kardamila) is a charming town in a small, spring-fed oasis, with a cobble beach and two tavernas on the water. This beach can get very crowded—the secret is to hike to the two small beaches a little to the east. To find them, take the small road behind the white house near the windmill.

WHERE TO STAY
HIOS TOWN
Chios Chandris Hotel   For those who prefer a modern hotel with resort-type facil-ities within walking distance of the town's attractions, this is the place to be. Rooms are of standard size and decor, but there are suites and studios for those who want something a bit roomier; almost all units have views overlooking the port of Chios Town. During the summer you can take your meals or drinks at the poolside cafe. There's no need to oversell this hotel—what recommends it is the fact that after a day of enjoying other places in town or around the island, you can stroll back in about 10 minutes and be in the pool.

2 Euyenias Handri (in the port), 82100 Hios. ✆ **22710/44-401.** Fax 22710/25-768. www.chandris.gr. 139 units. 160€ ($208) double; 175€–235€ ($228–$306) suite or studio. DC, MC, V. Rates include breakfast. Parking adjacent to hotel. **Amenities:** Restaurant; 2 bars; pool; tennis courts nearby; concierge; business center; Wi-Fi in public areas; tours and car rentals arranged; salon; 24-hr. room service; laundry service; dry cleaning. *In room:* A/C, TV, dataport, minibar, hair dryer.

Hotel Kyma ✿   Our favorite in-town lodging was built in 1917 as a private villa for shipping magnate John Livanos. (You'll notice the portraits of the lovely Mrs. Livanos on the ceiling in the ground-floor breakfast room.) Though the hotel is of historic interest—the treaty with Turkey was signed here in 1922—most of the original architectural details are gone, and the rooms have been renovated in a modern style. Many units have views of the sea, and a few have big whirlpool baths.

1 Evyenias Handri (on the port), 82100 Hios. ✆ **22710/44-500.** Fax 22710/44-600. kyma@chi.forthnet.gr. 59 units. 90€ ($117) double. Rates include breakfast. No credit cards. *In room:* A/C, TV.

KARFAS

Karfas, 7km (4½ miles) south of Hios town around Cape Ayia Eleni, is a resort area exploding with tourist groups in summer. It has a fine-sand beach lined with resort hotels.

Hotel Erytha   Built in 1990, the Erytha currently offers the most luxurious accommodations in the vicinity of Hios town. The spacious double rooms of this sprawling resort are distributed among five beachfront buildings connected by plant-filled terraces. The outdoor breakfast area steps down to the pool terrace, which is just above a tiny cove and private beach. Guest rooms are simply furnished. All have balconies and most face the sea, although a few open onto the terraces between buildings. Bathrooms are moderate in size, and include a tub/shower combo. The 21 studios and apartments in a separate building aren't as well maintained as units in the main hotel. The kitchen facilities in the studios and apartments are minimal: You're better off avoiding them entirely. The air-conditioning operates only in July and August.

Karfas, 82100 Hios. ✆ **22710/32-311.** Fax 22710/32-182. erytha@compulink.gr. 102 units. 140€–160€ ($182–$208) double. Rates include breakfast. AE, DC, MC, V. Closed Nov–Apr. *In room:* A/C, TV, minibar.

KARDAMILA

Kardamila, on the northeastern coast, is our choice among the resort towns because it's prosperous, self-sufficient, and not at all touristy.

Hotel Kardamila ✿   This modern resort hotel was built for the guests and business associates of the town's ship owners and officers, and it has its own small cobble beach. The guest rooms are large and plain, with modern bathrooms and balconies overlooking the beach. The gracious Theo Spordilis, formerly with Hotel Kyma, has taken over its management, so you can be sure the service will be good.

Kardamila, 82300 Hios. ✆ **22710/23-353.** Fax 22710/23-354. (Contact Hotel Kyma for reservations.) 32 units. 115€ ($150) double. Rates include breakfast. No credit cards. Closed Nov–Apr. *In room:* A/C.

VOLISSOS

This small hilltop village is one of the most beautiful on the island. A fine Byzantine castle overlooks the steep streets of the town, which contains numerous cafes and tavernas. Volissos is too far north to be a convenient base for touring the whole island, but if you want to get to know part of it, you couldn't choose a better focus for your explorations.

Volissos Traditional Houses (★ The care with which these village houses have been restored is unique on this island, if not in the whole northeastern Aegean. The beamed ceilings, often supported by forked tree limbs—a method of construction described in the *Odyssey*—are finely crafted and quite beautiful. Built into the stone walls are niches, fireplaces, cupboards, and couches. This spirit of inventiveness is also seen in imaginative recycling: A cattle yoke serves as a beam, while salvaged doors and shutters from the village have become mirrors or furniture. The houses and apartments are distributed throughout the village of Volissos, so your neighbors are likely to be locals rather than fellow tourists. Each apartment and house has a small kitchen, a spacious bathroom, and one or two bedrooms. The largest units (on two floors of a house) have two bedrooms, sitting rooms, kitchens, and large terraces. There are shops in the village that can satisfy most basic needs.

Volissos, Hios. (℃ **22740/21-421** or 22740/21-413. Fax 22740/21-521. volissos@otenet.gr. 16 units. 50€–90€ ($65–$117) double. Closed Nov–Apr. No credit cards. *In room:* A/C, no phone.

MESTA
The best-preserved medieval fortified village on Hios, Mesta is a good base for touring the mastic villages (see above) and the island's south coast.

Pipidis Traditional Houses (★ These four homes, built more than 500 years ago, have been restored and opened by the Greek National Tourism Organization as part of its Traditional Settlements program. The houses have a medieval character, with vaulted ceilings and irregularly sculpted stone walls (covered in plaster and whitewash). One unfortunate aspect of these authentic dwellings is the dearth of natural light: If a room has any windows at all, they're small and placed high in the wall. Each house comes equipped with a kitchen, a bathroom, and enough sleeping space for two to six people.

Mesta, Hios. (℃ **22710/76-029.** 4 units. 60€ ($78) double; 80€ ($104) 4 persons. No credit cards. Closed Nov–Apr. *In room:* No phone.

WHERE TO DINE
HIOS TOWN
Hios Marine Club GREEK This simple taverna serves the standard Greek dishes, pasta, grilled meats, and fish—but it's good! Don't be put off by the ugly yellow-and-white concrete facade. It's on the bay at the edge of town, just south of the port, 50m (164 ft.) beyond Hotel Chandris.

1 Nenitousi. (℃ **22710/23-184.** Main courses 5€–17€ ($6.50–$22). MC, V. Daily noon–2am.

Hotzas Taverna GREEK Hotzas is a small taverna that offers a basic but well-prepared selection. It's the best option in a town not known for its restaurants. The summer dining area is a luxuriant garden with lemon trees and abundant flowers. There's no menu; you choose from a few unsurprising but delicious offerings each night. Many of the dishes are meat-based but some are fish-based—and squid is always available. This place isn't easy to find: Take Kountouriotou in from the harbor, and look for the first right turn after a major road merges at an oblique angle from the right; after this it's another 50m (164 ft.) before the taverna appears on your left.

3 Yioryiou Kondili. (℃ **22710/42-787.** Main courses 5€–18€ ($6.50–$24). No credit cards. Mon–Sat 6–11pm.

LANGADA

Yiorgo Passa's Taverna 🍴 GREEK/SEAFOOD   Langada is a fishing village with a strip of five or six outdoor fish tavernas lining the harbor. Our favorite of these is Yiorgo Passa's Taverna, the first on the left as you approach the waterfront. Prices are relatively low—fish is traditionally priced per kilo—portions are generous, and the ambience is warm and friendly. *Note:* There are evening dinner cruises to Langada from Hios; check with Chios Tours (see "Visitor Information," earlier) for details.

Langada. 🕐 **22710/74-218.** Fish from 50€ ($65) per kilo. No credit cards. Daily 11am–2am. 20km (12 miles) north of Hios town on the Kardamila road.

MESTA

Messaionas Taverna GREEK   You will almost certainly have come to Mesta if only to visit the 14th-century Paleos Taxiarchis church with its remarkable carved wooden iconostasis, so while you're here, take a meal at this homey taverna on the main square. The menu features a great variety of *mezedes,* many with interesting variations on traditional dishes. The stuffed tomatoes with pine nuts and raisins are delicious, as are the fried dishes like *domatokeftedes* (tomatoes with herbs) or *tiropitakia* (cheese balls).

Mesta. 🕐 **22710/76-050.** Main courses 5€–15€ ($6.50–$20). No credit cards. Daily 11am–midnight.

3 Lesvos (Mitilini)

348km (188 nautical miles) NE of Piraeus

Roughly triangular Lesvos—now called Mitilini in many Greek publications—is the third-largest island in Greece, with a population of some 120,000. As a large, bustling island, it long failed to bother itself with attracting tourists but in recent years it has been developing itself as a destination. In particular, it has been promoting itself as the birthplace of Sappho, the ancient poet.

The three principal towns—**Mitilini, Molivos,** and **Eressos**—are near the corners of the triangle. Mitilini and Molivos are about as different as two towns on the same island could possibly be. Mitilini is a working port town low on sophistication or pretension, with little organized tourism and lots of local character. Molivos is a picture-postcard seaside village, a truly beautiful place, but in the summer it exists only for tourism. Due to its remote location, Eressos is a good destination for a day trip, but not a recommended base for touring the island.

Not to be missed are the Archaeological and Theophilos museums in Mitilini; the town of **Mandamados** and its celebrated icon (the east-coast road, between Mandamados and Mitilini, is the most scenic on the island); the remarkable, mile-long beach of **Eressos;** and the labyrinthine streets of Molivos's castle-crowned hill.

Getting around on Lesvos is somewhat complicated by the presence of two huge tear-shaped bays in the south coast, which splits the island at its center. Because bus schedules are not designed for day-trippers, this is one island where you'll definitely want a car to get around.

GETTING THERE   By Plane   Both **Olympic Airways** and **Aegean Airlines** offer several flights daily between Athens and Lesvos (Mitilini); both also offer occasional flights to Thessaloniki. Contact Olympic Airways in Athens at 🕐 **210/966-6666,** or check out www.olympicairlines.gr. Contact **Aegean Airlines** (🕐 **801/112-0000** or check www.aegeanair.com). The **airport** (🕐 **22510/61-490** or

Sappho and Lesvos

In recent years, Lesvos—because of its associations with the poet Sappho (ca. 612 B.C.–?)—has become a favorite destination of lesbians from many parts of the world. Although very little is known about Sappho's life, it is accepted that she was born here (see Eressos, later in this chapter). It is also accepted that she was the leader of some sort of circle of young women; certainly some of her finest verses express warm feelings toward females. But it is not really clear that she was herself a lesbian—she married and had a daughter. Little of her poetry survives but what there is has retained the admiration of readers and critics across the ages. So by all means, come to Lesvos in tribute to Sappho, but don't forget that the tribute that authors really want is that their works be read.

22510/61-590) is 7km (4 miles) south of Mitilini. There's no bus to the town; a taxi will cost about 10€ ($13).

By Boat   The principal port of Lesvos is Mitilini, from which almost all the ferries arrive and depart, although there is some ferry traffic through the west-coast port of Sigri. There's one ferry daily to Mitilini from Piraeus, stopping at Hios (10–12 hr.); there are also several ferries weekly from Rafina to Sigri (9 hr.). There are daily boats in both directions between Mitilini and Hios (3 hr.). Two boats call weekly at Mitilini from Kavala (10 hr.) and Thessaloniki (10–13 hr.), stopping at Limnos on the way. There's also one ferry a week from Siros (9 hr.). Check schedules with a local travel agent, **www.gtp.gr**, the **Mitilini Port Authority** (© **22510/28-827**), or **Sigri Port Authority** (© **22530/54-433**).

Once you get to Lesvos, double-check the boat schedule for your departure, as the harbor is extremely busy in the summer and service is often inexplicably irregular.

MITILINI & SOUTHEAST LESVOS

With an ambience more like that of a big mainland city than a Greek island port, Mitilini isn't to everyone's taste. Your first impression is likely to be one of noise, and traffic. Commercial development has resulted in a modern generic beachfront; the only signs of a more auspicious past are the cathedral dome and the considerable remains of a hilltop castle. Still, once you leave the paralia, there's little or nothing in the way of amenities for tourists, which can be refreshing for those who enjoy seeing how others actually live. In the vicinity of Ermou (the market street), Mitilini's crumbling ocher alleys contain a mix of traditional coffeehouses, artisans' studios, ouzeries, stylish jewelry shops, and stores selling antiques and clothing. Although good restaurants are notably absent in the town center, a few authentic tavernas lie on the outskirts of town.

ESSENTIALS

VISITOR INFORMATION   The Greek National Tourism Organization (EOT) has turned its functions over to the **North Aegean Islands Tourism Directorate.** Its office is at 6 James Aristarchou, 81100 Mitilini (© **22510/42-511;** fax 22510/27-601). Primarily an administrative center, the office is not especially set up to provide hands-on help for tourists. It's open daily from 8am to 2:30pm, with extended hours in the high season. The **tourist police** (© **22510/22-276**) may also be helpful, but private travel agencies are your best bet for information.

GETTING AROUND   By Bus   There are two bus stations in Mitilini, one for local and the other for round-the-island routes. The **local bus station** (© 22510/ 28-725) is near the harbor's north end, by the (closed) Folklife Museum and across from the Commercial Bank (Emporiki Trapeza). Local buses on Lesvos are frequent, running every hour from 6am to 9pm most of the year. The destinations covered are all within 12km (7½ miles) of Mitilini, and include Thermi, Moria, and Pamfilla to the north; and Varia, Ayia Marina, and Loutra to the south. The most expensive local fare is 4€ ($5.20). The posted schedule is hard to read, but ticket-sellers can decipher it. You can catch the **round-the-island KTEL buses** (© 22510/28-873) in Mitilini at the port's south end behind Argo Hotel. There's daily service in summer to Kaloni and Molivos (four times), Mandamados (once), Plomari (four times), and Eressos and Sigri (once).

By Car   Rental prices in Mitilini tend to be high, so be sure to shop around. A good place to start is **Payless Car Rental** (automoto@otenet.gr), with offices at the airport (© **22510/61-665**) and on the port in Mitilini (© **22510/43-555**), near the local (north) bus station. Summer daily rates start at around 70€ ($91) with 100 free kilometers; each kilometer over 100 is an additional 1€ ($1.30). Assuming an average day's drive is 150km (94 miles), count on paying about 100€ ($136) a day.

By Taxi   Lesvos is a big island. The one-way taxi fare from Mitilini to Molivos is about 40€ ($52); from Mitilini to Eressos or Sigri, about 60€ ($78). The main taxi stand in Mitilini is on Plateia Kyprion Patrioton, a long block inland from the port's southern end; there's a smaller taxi stand at the port's north end, near the local bus station.

FAST FACTS   The **area code** for Mitilini is 22510, for Molivos (Mithimna) and Eressos 22530, and for Plomari 22520. There are **ATMs** at several banks on the port, including the Ioniki Trapeza and Agrotiki Trapeza (both south of the local bus station). **Vostani Hospital** (© **22510/43-777**) on P. Vostani, southeast of town, will take care of emergencies. **Glaros Laundry** (© **22510/27-065**), opposite the tourist police near the ferry pier, is open from 9am to 2pm and 6 to 8pm; the turnaround time is usually 24 hours. The **post office** and the **telephone office (OTE)** are on Plateia Kyprion Patrioton, 1 block inland from the town hall at the south end of the port. The principal **taxi stand** is also on Plateia Kyprion Patrioton. The **tourist police** (© **22510/22-776**) are located just east of the ferry quay.

ATTRACTIONS
Archaeological Museums of Mitilini   The excellent Mitilini Archaeological Museum was augmented recently by the construction of a large new museum a short distance up the hill toward the kastro. The museums have the same hours, and the price of admission includes both locations. The new museum presents extensive Roman antiquities of Lesvos and some finds from the early Christian basilica of Ayios Andreas in Eressos. The highlight of its collection is a reconstructed Roman house from the 3rd century B.C., whose elaborate mosaic floors depict scenes from comedies of the poet Menander and from classical mythology. All the exhibits are thoughtfully presented, with plenty of explanatory notes in English. Entering the yard of the original archaeological museum, you're greeted by massive marble lions rearing menacingly on their hind legs, perhaps representing the bronze lion sculpted by Hephaestus, which is said to roam the island of Lesvos and serve as its guardian. A rear building houses more marble sculpture and inscribed tablets, while the main museum contains

---

Moments Excursion to a Mountain Village

An enjoyable destination for a day trip is the rural hamlet of **Ayiassos,** 23km (14 miles) west of Mitilini. The town, built on the foothills of Mount Olymbos, consists of traditional gray-stone houses (with wooden "Turkish" balconies, often covered in flowering vines), narrow cobblestone lanes, and fine small churches. Here local craftspeople still turn out their ceramic wares by hand. Excursion buses can bring you from Mitilini, or you can share a taxi (about 50€/$65 for the ride and a reasonably brief wait).

---

figurines, pottery, gold jewelry, and other finds from Thermi, the Mitilini kastro, and other ancient Lesvos sites.

7 Eftaliou, Myrina. © **22510/28-032.** Admission 3€ ($3.90) adults, 1€ ($1.30) students and seniors. Tues–Sun 8:30am–3pm. A block north of the tourist police station, just inland from the ferry pier.

Kastro   Perched on a steep hill north of the city, the extensive ruins of Mitilini's castle are fun to explore and offer fine views of city and sea from the ramparts. The kastro was founded by Justinian in the 6th century A.D., and was restored and enlarged in 1737 by the Genoese. The Turks also renovated and built extensive additions to the castle during their occupation. In several places you can see fragments of marble columns embedded in the castle walls—these are blocks taken from a 7th-century-B.C. Temple of Apollo by the Genoese. Look for the underground cistern at the north end of the castle precinct: This echoing chamber is a beautiful place, with domed vaults reflected in the pool below. In summer, the castle is sometimes used as a performing-arts center.

8th Noemvriou, Mitilini. © **22510/27-297.** Admission 3€ ($3.90) adults, 1€ ($1.30) students and seniors. Tues–Sun 8am–2:30pm. Just past the new Archaeological Museum, turn right on the path to the kastro.

Theophilos Museum ☆   One of the most interesting sights near Mitilini is this small museum in the former house of folk artist Hatzimichalis Theophilos (1868–1934). Most of Theophilos's works adorned the walls of tavernas and ouzeries, often painted in exchange for food. Theophilos died in poverty, and none of his work would have survived if it weren't for the efforts of art critic Theriade (see below), who commissioned the paintings on display here during the last years of the painter's life. These primitive watercolors depicting ordinary people, daily life, and local landscapes are now widely celebrated, and are also exhibited at the Museum of Folk Art in Athens. Be sure to take in the curious photographs showing the artist dressed as Alexander the Great.

Varia. © **22510/41-644.** Admission 3€ ($3.90). Tues–Sun 9am–1pm and 4:30–8pm. 3km (2 miles) south of Mitilini, on airport road next to Theriade Museum.

Theriade Library and Museum of Modern Art   The Theriade Library and Museum of Modern Art is in the home of Stratis Eleftheriadis, a native of Lesvos who emigrated to Paris and became a prominent art critic and publisher. (Theriade is the Gallicized version of his surname.) On display are copies of his published works, including *Minotaure* and *Verve* magazines, as well as his personal collection of works by Picasso, Matisse, Miró, Chagall, and other modern artists.

Varia. © **22510/23-372.** Admission 3€ ($3.90). Tues–Sun 9am–1pm and 5–8pm. 3km (2 miles) south of Mitilini, on airport road next to Theophilos Museum.

WHERE TO STAY

Hotel Erato   On a busy street just south of the port, this hotel offers convenience, cleanliness, a friendly and helpful staff, and a noise level marginally below that in many portside hotels. Most of the small bright rooms have balconies facing the street, with a view over the traffic to Mitilini Bay. The four-story hotel was converted from a medical clinic and retains an atmosphere of institutional anonymity; on the positive side, it's very well maintained, and the high-pressure showers and fluffy towels are a bonus. *Note:* If you intend to pay by credit card, do so well in advance of your planned departure.

P. Vostani, Mitilini, 81000 Lesvos. ✆ **22510/41-160.** Fax 22510/47-656. 20 units. 75€ ($98) double. MC, V. Open year-round. *In room:* A/C, TV.

Hotel Sappho   The Sappho is a no-nonsense but conveniently located hotel, offering simple accommodations at moderate rates. Nine rooms have balconies facing the port (and can be a bit noisy in the morning); the rest have no balconies and face a sunny rear courtyard. All units have wall-to-wall carpets, white walls, minimal furnishings, and tiny bathrooms with showers. A breakfast room on the second floor has an outdoor terrace with a fine port view.

31 Palou Kountourioti, Mitilini, 81000 Lesvos. ✆ **22510/22-888.** Fax 22510/24-522. 29 units. 60€ ($78) double. Continental breakfast 6€ ($7.80). AE, V. *In room:* A/C, TV

Villa 1900   The Villa 1900 is a somewhat upscale pension in a fine old house on the edge of town, about 700m (2,296 ft.) south of the Mitilini port. The best rooms (nos. 3 and 7) are quite spacious, with ornate painted ceilings. However, the smaller ones (nos. 6, 8, and 9) are claustrophobic and overpriced. The remaining two units are plain but adequate, and offer reasonable value for your money. The house is buffered from street noise by a small front garden; a larger garden with abundant fruit trees begins at the back terrace and offers a pleasant shaded retreat. The amiable owners speak no English, but someone is usually on hand to translate.

A Side Trip to Pergamum in Turkey

From Mitilini, there's a direct connection to Turkey via its port of Ayvalik, a densely wooded fishing village that makes a refreshing base camp from which to tour the ancient Greek site of Pergamum. The acropolis of Pergamum is sited on a dramatic hilltop, with substantial remains of the town on the surrounding slopes. The complex dates back to at least the 4th century B.C., and there are significant remains from this period through Roman and Byzantine times. It is one of Turkey's most important archaeological sites. All-inclusive 1-day tours to Pergamum—including round-trip boat fare, bus ride to the site, and guided tour—cost about 60€ ($78); inquire at Mitilini travel agencies such as **Dimakis Tours** (✆ **22510/27-865**), 73 Koundouriotou; or **Aeolic Cruises Travel Agency** (✆ **22510/46-601**), 47A Koutouriotou. Ships to Turkey usually sail three times a week, more often in high season if the demand is there. Passport is required but no visa is required for a 1-day visit. U.S., British, Irish, Canadians, and Australians need a visa for even an overnight; it costs between 45€ and 55€ ($60–$75) but is good for 90 days in Turkey. Your visa is issued at the Customs House upon your arrival in Ayvalik.

24 P. Vostani, Mitilini, 81000 Lesvos. ℂ 22510/23-448. Fax 22510/28-034. 7 units. 80€ ($104) double. No credit cards. 150m (492 ft.) south of the Olympic Airways office, opposite the stadium. *In room:* A/C, fridge, no phone.

WHERE TO DINE

Mitilini has more portside cafes than your average bustling harbor town. A cluster of chairs around the small lighthouse at the point heralds the most scenic (as well as the windiest) of the many small ouzeries that specialize in grilled octopus, squid, shrimp, and local fish. We found that some of the best restaurants were a short taxi ride outside the city.

Averof 1841 Grill GREEK   This taverna, located midport near the Sappho Hotel, is one of the better grills around, and one of the only restaurants in Mitilini center worth trying. Its beef dishes are particularly good. Try any of the tender souvlaki dishes or the lamb with potatoes.

Port, Mitilini. ℂ 22510/22-180. Main courses 5€–17€ ($6.50–$22). No credit cards. Daily 7am–5pm and 7–11pm.

O Rembetis GREEK   Kato Halikas is a hilltop village on the outskirts of Mitilini, and although this simple taverna might be hard to find, it's well worth the effort. At the south end of the terrace you can sit beneath the branches of a high sycamore and enjoy a panoramic view of the port. The food isn't sophisticated or surprising, but it's very Greek, and the clientele is primarily local. There's no menu, so listen to the waiter's descriptions or take a look in the kitchen—there's usually fresh fish in addition to the taverna standards. The wind can be brisk on this hilly site, so bring a jacket if the night is cool. The best way to get here is by taxi; the fare is about 3€ ($3.90) each way.

Kato Halikas, Mitilini. ℂ 22510/27-150. Main courses 5€–16€ ($6.50–$21). No credit cards. Daily 8pm–midnight.

Salavos GREEK   Despite its location on the busy airport road, this small taverna is one of the best in Mitilini. A garden terrace in back offers partial shelter from road noise. The seafood is fresh and delicious; try the calamari stuffed with feta, vegetables, and herbs. The restaurant is very popular with locals, who fill the place on summer nights. As you travel south from Mitilini toward the airport, it's about 3km (2 miles) from town, on the right. Taxi fare is about 3€ ($3.90) each way.

Mitilini. ℂ 22510/22-237. Main courses 4€–17€ ($5.20–$22). No credit cards. Daily noon–1am.

MITILINI AFTER DARK

In Mitilini, there's plenty of nightlife action at both ends of the harbor. The east side tends to be younger, cheaper, and more informal—**Hott Spott** (63 Koundouriotou) being one such. The more sophisticated places are off the harbor's south end. Outdoor **Park Cinema,** on the road immediately below the stadium, and **Pallas,** on Vournazo (by the post office), are both open May through September. Summer occasionally brings professional entertainment to the Kastro.

MOLIVOS & NORTHEAST LESVOS

Molivos (aka Mithimna) is at the northern tip of the island's triangle. It's a highly picturesque, castle-crowned village where mansions of stone and pink-pastel stucco are capped by red-tile roofs. Balconies and windowsills are decorated with geraniums and roses.

The town has long been popular with package-tour groups, especially during the summer months. Souvenir shops, car-rental agencies, and travel agents outnumber local merchants, and the restaurants are geared toward tourists. Despite this, it is a beautiful place to visit and a convenient base for touring the island.

ESSENTIALS

GETTING THERE   By Bus   KTEL buses (ⓒ 22510/28-873) connect Molivos with Mitilini four times daily in the high season. The Molivos bus stop is just past the Municipal Tourist Office on the road to Mitilini.

By Taxi   The one-way taxi fare from Mitilini to Molivos is about 40€ ($52).

VISITOR INFORMATION   The **Municipal Tourist Office,** 6 J. Aristarchou on the road heading down to the sea (ⓒ 22530/71-347), is housed in a tiny building next to the National Bank. It's open Monday through Friday. **Tsalis Tours,** 2 J. Aristarchou (ⓒ 22530/41-729; tsalis@otenet.gr), can book car rentals, accommodations, and excursions. Both the tourist office and Tsalis are open daily in summer from 8:30am to 9:30pm.

GETTING AROUND   By Car   There are numerous rental agencies in Molivos, and rates are comparable to those in Mitilini.

By Boat   Boat taxis to neighboring beaches can be arranged at the port or in a travel agency (see Tsalis Tours, above).

By Bus   Tickets for day excursions by bus can be bought in any of the local travel agencies. The destinations include Thermi/Ayiassos (45€/$59), Mitilini town (25€/$33), Sigri/Eressos (45€/$59), and Plomari (50€/$65); the excursions are offered once or twice each week in the summer.

FAST FACTS   An ATM can be found at the **National Bank,** next to the Municipal Tourist Office on the Mitilini road. The **Internet** can be accessed at Communication and Travel (ⓒ 22530/71-900) on the main road to the port. The **police** (ⓒ 22530/71-222) are up from the port, on the road to the town cemetery; the **port police** (ⓒ 22530/71-307) are, predictably, on the port. The **post office** (ⓒ 22530/71-246) is on the path circling up to the castle—turn right (up) past the National Bank.

ATTRACTIONS

Kastro   The hilltop Genoese castle is better preserved than Mitilini town, but it's much less extensive and not as interesting to explore. There is, however, a great view from the walls, worth the price of admission in itself. There's a stage in the southwest corner of the courtyard, often used for theatrical performances in the summer. To get here by car, turn uphill at the bus stop and follow signs to the castle parking lot. On foot, the castle is most easily approached from the town, a steep climb no matter which of the many labyrinthine streets you choose.

Molivos. No phone. Admission 3€ ($3.90) adults, 1€ ($1.30) students and seniors. Tues–Sun 8:30am–3pm.

Mandamados Monastery ⓐ   Mandamados is a lovely village on a high inland plateau, renowned primarily for the remarkable icon of the Archangel Michael housed in the local monastery. A powerful story is associated with the creation of the icon: It is said that during a certain pirate raid, all but one of the monks were slaughtered. This one survivor, emerging from hiding to find the bloody corpses of his dead companions, responded to the horror of the moment with an extraordinary act. Gathering the blood-soaked earth, he fashioned in it the face of man, an icon in relief of the Archangel Michael. This simple icon, its lips worn away by the kisses of pilgrims, can be found at the center of the iconostasis at the back of the main chapel.

Mandamados. Free admission. Daily 6am–10pm. 24km (15 miles) east of Molivos, 36km (23 miles) northwest of Mitilini.

BEACHES

The long, narrow town beach in Molivos is rocky and crowded near the town, but becomes sandier and less populous as you continue south. The beach in **Petra,** 6km (3¾ miles) south of Molivos, is considerably more pleasant. The beach at **Tsonia,** 30km (19 miles) east of Molivos, is only accessible via a difficult rutted road, and isn't particularly attractive. The best beach on the island is 70km (44 miles) southwest of Molivos in **Skala Eressos** (see "An Excursion to Western Lesvos," below).

SHOPPING

Molivos is unfortunately dominated by tacky souvenir shops. To find more authentic local wares, you'll have to explore neighboring towns. **Mandamados,** known as a center for pottery, has numerous ceramics studios. **Eleni Lioliou** (✆ 22530/61-170), on the road to the monastery, sells brightly painted bowls, plates, and mugs. **Anna Fonti** (✆ 22530/61-433), on a pedestrian street in the village, produces plates with intricate designs in brilliant turquoise and blue. Also in Mandamados is the diminutive studio of icon painter **Dimitris Hatzanagnostou** (✆ 22530/61-318), who produces large-scale icons for churches and portable icons for purchase.

WHERE TO STAY
MODERATE

Hotel-Bungalows Delphinia ✿ Often rated the best hotel on Lesvos, one of the major attractions of this white-stucco and gray-stone resort is its panoramic setting above the Aegean. A path leads 200m (656 ft.) from the hotel to a fine-sand beach and a recreation complex with saltwater swimming pool, snack bar, and tennis courts (the latter illuminated for night games). The hotel rooms are simple, with small, shower-only bathrooms. The 57 bungalows are more spacious: The living room has a couch that pulls out to provide an extra bed, most bathrooms include a bathtub, and each unit has either a large terrace or a balcony. Breakfast at the hotel is served on a terrace, while the bungalows include free room service for breakfast only. The second-floor rooms in the bungalows are the most spacious, have the best views (as well as air-conditioning and TV), and cost a bit more.

Molivos, 81108 Lesvos. ✆ **22530/71-315** or 22530/71-580. Fax 22530/71-524. 122 units. 85€–105€ ($111–$137) double; 120€–140€ ($156–$182) 2-person bungalow. Rates include buffet breakfast. AE, DC, V. Parking adjacent. 1 mile from town center. **Amenities:** Restaurant; bar; pool; 3 night-lit tennis courts; basketball; volleyball; table tennis; children's playground; tours and car rentals arranged; fax and photocopying arranged; 24-hr. room service; babysitting; laundry service; dry cleaning. *In room:* A/C, TV, minibar.

Hotel Olive Press This charming hotel in town is—you guessed it—an old converted olive press. Part of its attraction is its location right on the beach. The rooms are on the small side, but are comfortable, with terrazzo floors, handsome furnishings, and bathtubs. Some of the units have windows opening onto great sea views, with waves lapping just beneath. The nice inner courtyard has several gardens. Staff is gracious and friendly. On the downside is that the rear rooms can be noisy in July and August when young people gather at a popular bar nearby.

Molivos, 81108 Lesvos. ✆ **22530/71-205** or 22530/71-646. Fax 22530/71-647. 50 units. 95€ ($124) double (includes breakfast); 140€ ($182) studio. Closed Nov–May. AE, DC, V. **Amenities:** Bar; small pool; tennis court. *In room:* A/C, TV.

INEXPENSIVE

Sea Horse Pension (Thalassio Alogo)   Set among a cluster of relatively new Class
C hotels below the old town, near the port, is this smaller, homier pension. The
friendly manager, Stergios, keeps the rooms tidy. All units come with a balcony facing
the sea; four also have minimal kitchen facilities. On-site are a restaurant and an in-
house travel agency.

Molivos, 81108 Lesvos. ⓒ 22530/71-630 or 22530/71-320. Fax 22530/71-374. 16 units. 65€ ($85) double. Conti-
nental breakfast 7€ ($9.10). No credit cards. **Amenities:** Restaurant; tour desk. *In room:* A/C, TV, fridge, hair dryer.

WHERE TO DINE

Captain's Table ☆ SEAFOOD/VEGETARIAN   Overlooking the harbor at
Molivos, this is many visitors' favorite restaurant in the area. It's run by Melinda, an
Australian, and her Greek husband, Theo. Although the emphasis is now on fresh fish,
the menu still offers some of Melinda's excellent trademark vegetable dishes. Try *imam
bayeldi,* a dish made with eggplant, onions, tomato, and garlic. Then there's the
smoked and grilled mackerel—or the fresh mussels with the house white, if that's to
your taste. Live *bouzouki* music is played 3 nights a week. Needless to say, the restaurant is crowded in high season.

The Harbor, Molivos. ⓒ 22530/71-241. Main courses 6€–20€ ($7.80–$26). V. Daily 11am–1am.

Octopus SEAFOOD   One of the oldest restaurants on the harbor of Molivos, the
Octopus has had to serve tasty food in order to survive the tides of fashion. It specializes in grilled fish and meats but offers a selection of other dishes—peppers stuffed
with spicy cheese, for instance. And your waiter can not only help you assemble your
meal, but he can also advise you about the island's attractions.

The Harbor, Molivos. ⓒ 22530/71-317. Main courses 5€–18€ ($6.50–$23). No credit cards. Daily 11am–1am.

Tropicana ☆ CAFE   Stroll up into the old town to sip a cappuccino or have a dish of
ice cream at this outdoor cafe, which offers soothing classical music and a relaxed ambience. The owner, Hari Procoplou, learned the secrets of ice creamery in Los Angeles.

Molivos. ⓒ 22510/71-869. Snacks/desserts 3€–14€ ($3.90–$18). No credit cards. Daily 8am–1am.

MOLIVOS AFTER DARK

Vangelis Bouzouki (no phone) is Molivos's top acoustic *bouzouki* club. It's located
west from Molivos on the road to Efthalou, past the Sappho Tours office. After about
a 10-minute walk outside of town, you'll see a sign that points to an olive grove. Follow it for another 500m (1,640 ft.) through the orchard until you reach a clearing
with gnarled olive trees and a few stray sheep. When you see the circular cement dance
floor, surrounded by clumps of cafe tables, you've found the club. Have some ouzo
and late-night *mezedes,* and sit back to enjoy the show. Inquire at the tourist offices
about summer theatrical performances in the kastro.

Appendix:
The Greek Language

1 Making Your Way in Greek

There are many different kinds of Greek—the Greek of conversation in the street, the Greek used at a fashionable dinner party, the Greek used in newspapers, the Greek of a government notice, the Greek used by a novelist or a poet, and more—and they can differ from one another in grammar and in vocabulary much more than the English of, for example, a conversation at the water cooler and that of an editorial in the New York Times. Why this is so is a long—and we mean long—story. Greek, like English, has a long written history molded by influential works that continue to be read and studied for centuries—in Greek even for millennia—so that, as in English, older words and styles of expression remain available for use even while the spoken language happily evolves on its own.

Also like English, Greek has kept the spelling of its words largely unchanged even though their pronunciation has changed in fundamental ways. In English this spelling lag has extended for some 5 centuries, but in Greek it is 25 centuries old. This makes it easier for us to read Shakespeare and for Greeks to read Herodotus than it might otherwise be, but it also means that Greek children, like English-speaking children, have to learn to spell words that they already know to use in conversation.

Our dilemma is further complicated by the fact that many Greek words and names have entered our language not directly but by way of Latin or French, and so have become familiar to English speakers in forms that owe something to those languages. When these words are directly transliterated from modern Greek (and that means from Greek in its modern pronunciation, not the ancient one that Romans heard), they almost always appear in a form other than the one you may have read about in school. "Perikles" for Pericles or "Delfi" for Delphi are relatively innocent examples; "Thivi" for Thebes or "Omiros" for Homer can give you an idea of the traps often in store for the innocent traveler. The bottom line is that the names of towns, streets, hotels, items on menus, historical figures, archaeological sites—you name it—are likely to have more than one spelling as you come across them in books, on maps, or before your very eyes.

Sometimes the name of a place has simply changed over the centuries. If you think you've just arrived in Santorini but you see a sign welcoming you to Thira, smile, remember you're in Greece, and take heart. (Santorini is the name the Venetians used, and it became common in Europe for that reason. Thira is the original Greek name.) You're where you want to be. This appendix offers a few aids to help you make your way in Greek. First: Remember that literacy is virtually universal in Greece. The table below will help you move from Greek signs or directions to a sense of how they should sound. This transliteration of modern Greek is used throughout this book, except in reference to names that have become household words in English, like Athens, Socrates, Olympus, and so on. The good news here is that you won't be confused as long as you have your nose in your book; the bad news is that confusion is probably inevitable as soon as your eyes leave the page. All you have to say is what you are looking for, raising your voice at the end of the word to let your listener know it's a question, and bingo!—someone will help.

Do remember that *óhi*, although it can sound a bit like "okay," in fact means "no," and that *ne*, which can sound like a twangy "nay," means "yes." To complicate matters, some everyday gestures will be different from those you are used to: Greeks nod their heads upward to express an unspoken *óhi* and downward (or downward and to one side) for an unspoken *ne*. When a Greek turns his or her head from side to side at you—and you will see this despite your best efforts—it is a polite way of signaling, "I can't make out what you're saying." And remember: Almost any 40-year-old Greek can read Greek, and most people under 30 can also make out some English. If you find that your attempts at speaking fall on deaf ears, show someone the word for what you want and if you stumble over *efharisto* (thank you) you can place your hand over your heart and bow your head slightly.

ALPHABET		TRANSLITERATED AS	PRONOUNCED AS IN
A α	álfa	a	*f*ather
B β	víta	v	*v*iper
Γ γ	gámma	g before α, ο, ω, and consonants	*g*et
		y before αι, ε, ει, η, ι, οι, υ	*y*es
		ng before κ, γ, χ, or ξ	si*ng*er
Δ δ	thélta	th	*th*e (not as the *th-* in "thin")
E ε	épsilon	e	s*e*t
Z ζ	zíta	z	la*z*y
H η	íta	i	magaz*i*ne
Θ θ	thíta	th	*th*in (not as the *th-* in "the")
I ι	ióta	i	magaz*i*ne
		y before a, o	*y*ard, *y*ore
K κ	káppa	k	*k*eep
Λ λ	lámtha	l	*l*eap
M μ	mi	m	*m*arry
N ν	ni	n	*n*ever
Ξ ξ	ksi	ks	ta*x*i
O o	ómicron	o	b*ou*ght
Π π	pi	p	*p*et
P ρ	ro	r	*r*ound
Σ σ/ς	sígma	s before vowels or θ, κ, π, τ, φ, χ, ψ	*s*ay
		z before β, γ, δ, ζ	
		y before λ, μ, ν, ρ	la*z*
T τ	taf	t	*t*ake
Y υ	ípsilon	i	magaz*i*ne

ALPHABET	TRANSLITERATED AS	PRONOUNCED AS IN
Φ φ fi	f	*fee*
Χ χ chi	h	*h*ero (before e and i sounds; like the *ch-* in Scottish "loch" otherwise
Ψ ψ psi	ps	colla*ps*e
Ω ω ómega	o	b*o*ught

COMBINATIONS	TRANSLITERATED AS	PRONOUNCED AS IN
αι	e	g*e*t
αϊ	ai	*ai*sle
αυ before vowels or β, γ, δ, ζ, λ, μ, ν, ρ	av	*Av*e Maria
αυ before θ, κ, ξ, π, σ, τ, φ, χ, ψ	af	pil*af*
ει i		magaz*i*ne
ευ before vowels or β, γ, δ, ζ, λ, μ, ν, ρ	ev	*ev*er
ευ before θ, κ, ξ, π, σ, τ, φ, χ, ψ	ef	l*ef*t
μπ at beginning of word	b	*b*ane
μπ in middle of word	mb	lu*mb*er
ντ at beginning of word	d	*d*umb
ντ in middle of word	nd	sle*nd*er
Οι	i	magaz*i*ne
Οϊ	oi	*oi*l
Ου	ou	s*ou*p
τζ	dz	roa*ds*
τσ	ts	ge*ts*
υι	i	magaz*i*ne

2 Useful Words & Phrases

When you're asking for or about something and have to rely on single words or short phrases, it's an excellent idea to use "sas parakaló" to introduce or conclude almost anything you say.

Airport   Aerothrómio
Automobile   Aftokínito
Avenue   Leofóros

Bad	Kakós, -kí, -kó*
Bank	Trápeza
Breakfast	Proinó
Bus	Leoforío
Can you tell me?	Boríte ná moú píte?
Cheap	Ft(h)inó
Church	Ekklissía
Closed	Klistós, stí, stó*
Coffeehouse	Kafenío
Cold	Kríos, -a, -o*
Dinner	Vrathinó
Do you speak English?	Miláte Angliká?
Excuse me.	Signómi(n).
Expensive	Akrivós, -í, -ó*
Farewell!	Stó ka-ló! *(to person leaving)*
Glad to meet you.	Chéro polí.**
Good	Kalós, lí, ló*
Goodbye.	Adío *or* chérete.**
Good health (cheers)!	Stín (i)yá sas *or* Yá-mas!
Good morning *or* Good day.	Kaliméra.
Good evening.	Kalispéra.
Good night.	Kaliníchta.**
Hello!	Yássas *or* chérete!**
Here	Ethó
Hot	Zestós, -stí, -stó*
Hotel	Xenothochío**
How are you?	Tí kánete *or* Pós íst(h)e?
How far?	Pósso makriá?
How long?	Póssi óra *or* Pósso(n) keró?
How much does it cost?	Póso káni?
I am a vegetarian.	Íme hortophágos.
I am from New York.	Íme apó tí(n) Néa(n) Iórki.
I am lost *or* I have lost the way.	Écho chathí *or* Écho chási tón drómo(n).**
I'm sorry.	Singnómi.
I'm sorry, but I don't speak Greek (well).	Lipoúme, allá thén miláo elliniká (kalá).
I don't understand.	Thén katalavéno.
I don't understand, please repeat it.	Thén katalavéno, péste to páli, sás parakaló.

I want to go to the airport.	Thélo ná páo stó aerothrómio.
I want a glass of beer.	Thélo éna potíri bíra.
I would like a room.	Tha íthela ena thomátio.
It's (not) all right.	(Dén) íne en dáxi.
Left (direction)	Aristerá
Lunch	Messimerianó
Map	Chártis**
Market (place)	Agorá
Mr.	Kírios
Mrs.	Kiría
My name is . . .	Onomázome . . .
New	Kenoúryos, -ya, -yo*
No	Óchi**
Old	Paleós, -leá, -leó* (*pronounce* palyós, -lyá, -lyó)
Open	Anichtós, -chtí, -chtó*
Patisserie	Zacharoplastío**
Pharmacy	Pharmakío
Please *or* You're welcome.	Parakaló.
Please call a taxi (for me).	Parakaló, fonáxte éna taxi (yá ména).
Point out to me, please . . .	Thíkste mou, sas parakaló . . .
Post office	Tachidromío**
Restaurant	Estiatório
Restroom	Tó méros *or* I toualétta
Right (direction)	Dexiá
Saint	Áyios, ayía, *(plural)* áyi-i (*abbreviated* ay)
Square	Plateia
Street	Odós
Show me on the map.	Díxte mou stó(n) chárti.**
Station (bus, train)	Stathmos (leoforíou, trénou)
Stop (bus)	Stási(s) (leoforíou)
Thank you (very much).	Efcharistó (polí).**
Today	Símera
Tomorrow	Ávrio
Very nice	Polí oréos, -a, -o*
Very well	Polí kalá *or* En dáxi
What?	Tí?
What time is it?	Tí ôra íne?
What's your name?	Pós onomázest(h)e?

Where is . . . ?	Poú íne . . . ?
Where am I?	Pou íme?
Why?	Yatí?

* Masculine ending -os, feminine ending -a or -i, neuter ending -o.

** Remember, *ch* should be pronounced as in Scottish *loch* or German *ich,* not as in the word *church.*

NUMBERS

0	Midén	18	Dekaoktó	151	Ekatón
1	Éna	19	Dekaenyá		penínda éna
2	Dío	20	Íkossi	152	Ekatón
3	Tría	21	Íkossi éna		penínda dío
4	Téssera	22	Íkossi dío	200	Diakóssya
5	Pénde	30	Triánda	300	Triakóssya
6	Éxi	40	Saránda	400	Tetrakóssya
7	Eftá	50	Penínda	500	Pendakóssya
8	Októ	60	Exínda	600	Exakóssya
9	Enyá	70	Evdomínda	700	Eftakóssya
10	Déka	80	Ogdónda	800	Oktakóssya
11	Éndeka	90	Enenínda	900	Enyakóssya
12	Dódeka	100	Ekató(n)	1,000	Chílya*
13	Dekatría	101	Ekatón éna	2,000	Dío chilyádes*
14	Dekatéssera	102	Ekatón dío	3,000	Trís chilyádes*
15	Dekapénde	150	Ekatón	4,000	Tésseris
16	Dekaéxi		penínda		chilyádes*
17	Dekaeftá			5,000	Pénde chilyádes*

DAYS OF THE WEEK

Monday	Deftéra	Friday	Paraskeví
Tuesday	Tríti	Saturday	Sávvato
Wednesday	Tetárti	Sunday	Kiriakí
Thursday	Pémpti		

MENU TERMS

arní avgolémono   lamb with lemon sauce
arní soúvlas   spit-roasted lamb
arní yiouvétsi   baked lamb with orzo
bakaliáro (skordaliá)   cod (with garlic)
barboúnia (skáras)   red mullet (grilled)
briám   vegetable stew
brizóla chiriní   pork steak or chop
brizóla moscharísia   beef or veal steak

choriátiki saláta   "village" salad ("Greek" salad to Americans)

dolmades   stuffed vine leaves

domátes yemistés mé rízi   tomatoes stuffed with rice

eksóhiko   lamb and vegetables wrapped in filo

garídes   shrimp

glóssa (tiganití)   sole (fried)

kalamarákia (tiganitá)   squid (fried)

kalamarákia (yemistá)   squid (stuffed)

kaparosaláta   salad of minced caper leaves and onion

karavídes   crayfish

keftedes   fried meatballs

kotópoulo soúvlas   spit-roasted chicken

kotópoulo yemistó   stuffed chicken

kouloúri   pretzel-like roll covered with sesame seeds

loukánika   spiced sausages

loukoumades   round doughnut center–like pastries deep-fried, then drenched with honey and topped with powdered sugar and cinnamon

melitzanosaláta   eggplant salad

moussaká   meat-and-eggplant casserole

oktapódi   octopus

païdákia   lamb chops

paradisiako   traditional Greek cooking

pastítsio   baked pasta with meat

piláfi rízi   rice pilaf

piperiá yemistá   stuffed green peppers

revídia   chickpeas

saganáki   grilled cheese

skordaliá   hot garlic-and-beet dip

soupiés yemistés   stuffed cuttlefish

souvlaki   lamb (sometimes veal) on the skewer

spanokópita   spinach pie

stifádo   stew, often of rabbit or veal

taramosaláta   fish roe with mayonnaise

tirópita   cheese pie

tsípoura   dorado

tzatzíki   yogurt-cucumber-garlic dip

youvarlákia   boiled meatballs with rice

* Remember, ch should be pronounced as in Scottish *loch* or German *ich,* not as in the word *church.*

Index

CLOSED
due to
accidental demolition

WEGEN BISSIGEN
EICHHÖRNCHEN GESCHLOSSEN

CERRADO
CABRAS

Κλειστό
Μετεωρίτες

POOL CLOSED
プールも
ELECTRIC EELS
閉鎖中

Hotel
closed for
facelifting

FERMÉ POUR
RAISON
DE GRÈVE
DES BONNES

FECHADO!
POR CAUSA DE
ATAQUES DOS CROCODILOS

I don't speak
sign language.

A hotel can close for all kinds of reasons.
Our Guarantee ensures that if your hotel's undergoing construction, we'll
let you know in advance. In fact, we cover your entire travel experience.
See www.travelocity.com/guarantee for details.

travelocity®
You'll never roam alone.